THE CAMBRIDGE HISTORY OF
RELIGIONS IN LATIN AMERICA

The *Cambridge History of Religions in Latin America* covers religious history in Latin America from pre-Conquest times until the present. This publication is significant because of the historical and contemporary centrality of religion in the life of Latin America, a region that has been growing in global importance. It is also timely because of the rapid process of religious change that the region is undergoing. And lastly, it is significant because of the region's religious distinctiveness in global comparative terms, which contributes to its importance for debates over religion, globalization, and modernity. This volume incorporates new currents in scholarship to address the breadth of Latin American religion, including religions of the African diaspora, indigenous spiritual expressions, new religious movements, alternative spiritualities, and secularizing tendencies.

VIRGINIA GARRARD-BURNETT is a professor of history at the University of Texas, Austin. She has authored numerous articles and chapters; edited three collected volumes (of which this is the fourth); and written two monographs, the most recent of which is entitled *Terror in the Land of the Holy Spirit: Guatemala Under General Efraín Ríos Montt, 1982–1983* (2010). Her forthcoming monograph is on new Christian movements in Latin America, and she is currently co-authoring the *Oxford History of Modern Latin America*.

PAUL FRESTON is the CIGI Chair in Religion and Politics in Global Context at the Balsillie School of International Affairs and Wilfrid Laurier University, Canada. He is also professor colaborador on the post-graduate programme in sociology at the Universidade Federal de São Carlos, Brazil. He has worked mainly on religion and politics, the growth of popular forms of Protestantism in Latin America, and questions of religion and globalization. His books include *Evangelicals and Politics in Asia, Africa and Latin America* (Cambridge University Press, 2001); *Protestant Political Parties: a Global Survey* (2004); (ed.) *Evangelical Christianity and Democracy in Latin America* (2008); and (coauthored) *Nem Anjos Nem Demônios: Interpretações Sociológicas do Pentecostalismo* (1994).

STEPHEN C. DOVE is an assistant professor of history and Latin American studies at Centre College. He earned his PhD at the University of Texas, Austin and has published several articles about Protestantism and Pentecostalism in Latin America. His current book manuscript is a study of the transition from missionary to local Protestantism in early-twentieth-century Guatemala.

THE CAMBRIDGE HISTORY OF RELIGIONS IN LATIN AMERICA

★

EDITED BY

VIRGINIA GARRARD-BURNETT
University of Texas, Austin

PAUL FRESTON
Balsillie School of International Affairs

STEPHEN C. DOVE
Centre College

CAMBRIDGE
UNIVERSITY PRESS

32 Avenue of the Americas, New York, NY 10013-2473, USA

Cambridge University Press is part of the University of Cambridge.

It furthers the University's mission by disseminating knowledge in the pursuit of education, learning, and research at the highest international levels of excellence.

www.cambridge.org
Information on this title: www.cambridge.org/9780521767330

© Cambridge University Press 2016

This publication is in copyright. Subject to statutory exception and to the provisions of relevant collective licensing agreements, no reproduction of any part may take place without the written permission of Cambridge University Press.

First published 2016

Printed in the United States of America

A catalog record for this publication is available from the British Library.

Library of Congress Cataloging in Publication Data
Names: Garrard-Burnett, Virginia, 1957– editor. | Freston, Paul, editor. | Dove, Stephen C., editor.
Title: The Cambridge history of religions in Latin America / [edited by] Virginia Garrard-Burnett, University of Texas, Austin; Paul Freston, Balsillie School of International Affairs; Stephen C. Dove, Centre College.
Description: New York : Cambridge University Press, 2016. | Includes bibliographical references and index.
Identifiers: LCCN 2015043645 | ISBN 9780521767330 (hardback)
Subjects: LCSH: Latin America – Religion – History. | Religion and sociology – Latin America – History. | BISAC: HISTORY / Latin America / General.
Classification: LCC BL2540.C365 2016 | DDC 200.98–dc23
LC record available at http://lccn.loc.gov/2015043645

ISBN 978-0-521-76733-0 Hardback

Cambridge University Press has no responsibility for the persistence or accuracy of URLs for external or third-party Internet Web sites referred to in this publication and does not guarantee that any content on such Web sites is, or will remain, accurate or appropriate.

This volume is dedicated to

My mother, Mary Ida Barnds Garrard
–V. G.-B.

My wife, Yolanda Maria Braga Freston
–P. F.

My wife, Megan Dove
–S. C. D.

Contents

List of Tables and Figure   page xii
List of Contributors   xiii
Acknowledgments   xxiii

1 · Introduction to the Cambridge History of
Religions in Latin America   1
VIRGINIA GARRARD-BURNETT, PAUL FRESTON,
AND STEPHEN C. DOVE

2 · Religion in the Pre-Contact New World:
Mesoamerica and the Andes   22
DAVID TAVÁREZ

3 · Religion in the Pre-Contact Old World:
Europe   34
CARLOS M. N. EIRE

4 · Religion in the Pre-Contact Old World:
Africa   47
ASONZEH UKAH

5 · Extending Christendom:
Religious Understanding of the Other   62
MIGUEL LEÓN-PORTILLA

6 · New World "Savages," Anthropophagy, and
the European Religious Imagination   77
AMOS MEGGED

Contents

7 · Evangelization and Indigenous Religious
Reactions to Conquest and Colonization   87
MANUEL AGUILAR-MORENO

8 · Tridentine Catholicism in the New World   107
BRIAN LARKIN

9 · The Inquisition in the New World   133
BRUNO FEITLER
TRANSLATED BY RODRIGO FRESTON

10 · Saint, Shrines, and Festival Days in
Colonial Spanish America   143
FRANCES L. RAMOS

11 · The Baroque Church   160
PAMELA VOEKEL

12 · The Spanish Missions of North and South America   173
RAMÓN A. GUTIÉRREZ

13 · The Church, Africans, and Slave Religion in
Latin America   198
JOAN BRISTOL

14 · Messianic and Revitalization Movements   207
MIGUEL C. LEATHAM

15 · The Expulsion of the Jesuits and the Late
Colonial Period   220
JOHN LYNCH

16 · The Church and Latin American Independence   231
JEFFREY L. KLAIBER

17 · Liberalism, Anticlericalism, and Antireligious
Currents in the Nineteenth Century   251
MATTHEW BUTLER

18 · Religious Devotion, Rebellion, and Messianic Movements:
Popular Catholicism in the Nineteenth Century   269
DOUGLASS SULLIVAN-GONZÁLEZ

Contents

19 · Historical Protestantism in Latin America   286
STEPHEN C. DOVE

20 · Immigrant Protestantism:
The Lutheran Church in Latin America   304
MARTIN N. DREHER

21 · Marianism in Latin America   319
TIMOTHY MATOVINA

22 · Secularism and Secularization   331
TRANSLATED BY JOSÉ ADRIAN BARRAGÁN
ROBERTO J. BLANCARTE

23 · The Revival of Latin American Catholicism, 1900–1960   346
BONAR L. HERNÁNDEZ SANDOVAL

24 · The Intellectual Roots of Liberation Theology   359
IVAN PETRELLA

25 · Progressive Catholicism in Latin America:
Sources and Its Evolution from Vatican II to Pope Francis   372
MANUEL A. VÁSQUEZ AND ANNA L. PETERSON

26 · The Catholic Church and Dictatorship   398
SUSAN FITZPATRICK-BEHRENS

27 · Latin American Pentecostalism as a New Form of
Popular Religion   414
ANDRÉ CORTEN
TRANSLATED BY ASHELY M. VOEKS

28 · History, Current Reality, and Prospects of
Pentecostalism in Latin America   430
PAUL FRESTON

29 · The Religious Media and Visual
Culture in Latin America   451
KARINA KOSICKI BELLOTTI

30 · The Catholic Charismatic Renewal and the Incipient
Pentecostalization of Latin American Catholicism   462
JAKOB EGERIS THORSEN

Contents

31 · Contemporary Popular Catholicism in Latin America 480
JENNIFER SCHEPER HUGHES

32 · Catholicism and Political Parties in
Modern Latin America 491
MICHAEL FLEET

33 · Human Rights:
An Ongoing Concern 505
CHRISTINE KOVIC

34 · Religion and Gender in Latin America 525
KEVIN LEWIS O'NEILL

35 · Christian Churches, Reproduction, and
Sexuality in Latin America 547
MARIA DAS DORES CAMPOS MACHADO
TRANSLATED BY RODRIGO FRESTON

36 · Indigenous Peoples:
Religious Change and Political Awakening 559
TIMOTHY J. STEIGENGA AND SANDRA LAZO DE LA VEGA

37 · Inculturation Theology and the "New Evangelization" 591
ANDREW ORTA

38 · African Diaspora Religions in Latin America Today 603
STEPHEN SELKA

39 · Afro-Caribbean Religious Expressions 633
MIGUEL A. DE LA TORRE

40 · Spiritism in Latin America 648
SIDNEY M. GREENFIELD

41 · Transnationalism, Globalization, and
Latin American Religions 666
TODD HARTCH

42 · Religious Identity and Emigration from Latin America 680
THOMAS A. TWEED

Contents

43 · Neither Catholics nor Protestants:
Mormons, Jehovah's Witnesses, Adventists, and
La Luz del Mundo   690
PATRICIA FORTUNY AND HENRI GOOREN

44 · Jews and Judaism in Latin America   709
JEFFREY LESSER

45 · Islam in Latin America   714
CECÍLIA L. MARIZ
TRANSLATED BY RODRIGO FRESTON

46 · Asian Religions in Latin America   723
JEFFREY LESSER

47 · Ecumenism in Latin America:
Between the Marketplace and the Desert   729
EDIN SUED ABUMANSSUR
TRANSLATED BY RODRIGO FRESTON

48 · The Religious Field in Latin America:
Autonomy and Fragmentation   739
DAVID LEHMANN

49 · Pathways to the Future   764
DANIEL H. LEVINE

Index   775

Tables and Figure

Tables

42.1	US foreign born by region of birth and date of arrival	page 681
42.2	US immigration by country from major Latin American sending nations, 1901–2000	682

Figure

49.1	Street preacher in Sololá, Guatemala, 1968	765

Contributors

EDIN SUED ABUMANSSUR is a professor of social science and an Associate in the Department of Religious Sciences at Pontifical Catholic University of São Paulo, Brazil (PUC-SP). He is an instructor of graduate studies in religious sciences, a researcher on Pentecostalism and organized crime in the outskirts of São Paulo, and a peer reviewer for several academic journals in the field of social science and religion.

MANUEL AGUILAR-MORENO is a professor of art history at California State University in Los Angeles. He is a renowned expert on pre-Columbian civilizations, the colonial history of Mexico, and the Mexican Muralism. Dr. Aguilar-Moreno has published on a wide range of subjects, including Mesoamerican art and history, colonial art and history of Mexico with emphasis in the Indian-Christian art of the transculturation process, funerary art, and the pre-Columbian ballgame.

ROBERTO J. BLANCARTE is a research professor at El Colegio de México. He is also an associate researcher with the Grupo de Sociología de Religiones y de la Laicidad (GSRL). He is the author of several books and articles including *Laicidad en México: La construcción de la República Laica en México* (2013), and *Sexo, religión y democracia* (Editorial Planeta, 2008). He has also edited several volumes including *Laicidad, estudios introductorios* (El Colegio Mexiquense, 2012), *Las leyes de reforma y el Estado Laico: Importancia histórica y validez contemporánea* (El Colegio de México, 2013), *Culturas e identidades de la colección los grandes problemas de México* (El Colegio de México, 2010), and *Los Retos de la Laicidad y la Secularización en el mundo contemporáneo* (El Colegio de México, 2008).

JOAN BRISTOL is an associate professor of history at George Mason University. She is the author of *Christians, Blasphemers, and Witches: Afro-Mexican Ritual Practice in the Seventeenth Century* (University of New Mexico Press, Diálogos series, 2007). Bristol's publications appear in the *Boletín del Archivo General de la Nación* (Mexico), *Journal of Colonialism and Colonial History*, *Journal of Africana Religions*, *History Compass*, and several edited volumes and encyclopedias.

MATTHEW BUTLER is an associate professor of the history of modern Mexico at the University of Texas at Austin. He is the author of *Popular Piety and Political Identity in Mexico's Cristero Rebellion: Michoacan, 1927–1929* (Oxford University Press/British Academy, 2004) and editor of *Faith and Impiety in Revolutionary Mexico* (Palgrave Macmillan, 2007). He is also co-editor of *Mexico in Transition: New Perspectives on Mexican Agrarian History, Nineteenth and Twentieth Centuries* (CIESAS, 2013) and co-editor of a forthcoming volume on regional Catholicisms in Mexico. His current book project focuses on the history of liberal Catholicism in revolutionary Mexico.

ANDRÉ CORTEN is a professor in the Department of Political Science at the University of Quebec at Montreal. He is a founding member of the Groupe de Recherche sur les Imaginaires Politiques en Amérique Latine (GRIPAL) and author or editor of a number of works about Latin America including *L'interpellation plébéienne en Amérique latine:Violence, actions directes et virage à gauche* (with Catherine Huart and Ricardo Peñafiel; Karthala / Presses de l'Université du Québec, 2012), *Between Babel and Pentecost: Transnational Pentecostalism in Africa and Latin America* (with Ruth Marshall; Indiana University Press, 2001), *L'alchimie politique du miracle: Discours de la guérison divine et langue politique en Amérique latine*, and *Pentecostalism in Brazil* (Éditions Balzac, 1999)

MARIA DAS DORES CAMPOS MACHADO is a researcher of Conselho Nacional de Desenvolvimento Científico e Tecnológico (Brazil) and a lecturer at the Federal University of Rio de Janeiro, where she coordinates the Centre of Research of Religion, Social Action and Politics. She is the author of various articles about the Christian groups in Brazil and has published the books *Política e Religião* (Editora FGV, 2006) and *Carismáticos e Pentecostais: Adesão religiosa e seus efeitos na esfera familiar* (Editora Autores Associados, 1996). She is also one of the organizers of the books *Religiões e Homossexualidades* (Editora FGV, 2010) and *Os votos de Deus* (Fundação Joaquim Nabuco, Editora Massangana, 2005).

MIGUEL A. DE LA TORRE is a professor of social ethics and Latino/a studies at the Iliff School of Theology in Denver, Colorado. In 2012, he served as president of the Society of Christian Ethics. He is the author of several books including *Reading the Bible from the Margins* (Orbis Books, 2002) and *Introducing Latino/a Theologies* (coauthored; Orbis Books, 2001).

STEPHEN C. DOVE is an assistant professor of history and Latin American studies at Centre College. He earned his PhD at the University of Texas at Austin and has published several articles about Protestantism and Pentecostalism in Latin America. His current book manuscript is a study of the transition from missionary to local Protestantism in early-twentieth century Guatemala.

MARTIN N. DREHER is a faculty member in history at the Universidade do Vale do Rio dos Sinos (UNISINOS) in Brazil. His teaching and research focus on the history of the Reformation and German immigration to Latin America.

CARLOS M. N. EIRE was born in Havana in 1950 and fled to the United States without his parents at the age of eleven. He is now the T. L. Riggs Professor of History and Religious Studies at Yale, where he has served as chair of the Department of Religious Studies and the Renaissance Studies Program. He has taught at St. John's University in Minnesota and the University of Virginia and has been a Fulbright scholar in Spain, a Fellow of the Institute for Advanced Study in Princeton, and a member of the Lilly Foundation's Seminar in Lived Theology. He is the author of several scholarly books, including *War Against the Idols* (Cambridge University Press, 1986), *From Madrid to Purgatory* (Cambridge University Press, 1995), and *A Very Brief History of Eternity* (Princeton University Press, 2010). A past president of the American Society for Reformation Research, he is best known outside scholarly circles as the author of the memoir *Waiting for Snow in Havana* (Free Press, 2003), which won the nonfiction National Book Award, and his second memoir, *Learning to Die in Miami* (Free Press, 2010). All of his books are banned in Cuba, where he has been proclaimed an enemy of the state – a distinction he regards as the highest of all honors.

BRUNO FEITLER teaches modern history in the School of Philosophy, Letters and Human Sciences at the Universidade Federal do São Paulo (UNIFESP) in Brazil. He is the author of *Nas malhas da consciência: Igreja e Inquisição no Brasil. Nordeste 1640–1750* (Alameda / Phoebus, 2007) and *Inquisition, juifs et nouveaux-chrétiens au Brésil: le Nordeste – XVIIème et XVIIIème siècles* (Universitaire Pers Leuven, 2003).

SUSAN FITZPATRICK-BEHRENS is a professor of Latin American history at California State University, Northridge. Her book, *The Maryknoll Catholic Mission in Peru: Transnational Faith and Transformation, 1943–1989*, was published in 2012 by University of Notre Dame Press. She is currently preparing a manuscript tentatively titled *Strange Bedfellows: Catholic-Civil Alliances and their Unintended Outcomes in Revolutionary Guatemala, 1943–1996*, which examines the intersections of transnational religious and secular aid and the ways it facilitated Maya activism. She is co-editor with Manuel Vásquez and David Orique of the forthcoming *Oxford Handbook of Christianity in Latin America*. Fitzpatrick-Behrens received research support from the American Council of Learned Societies and the David Rockefeller Center for Latin American Studies at Harvard University.

MICHAEL FLEET is a professor emeritus of political science at Marquette University. He is the co-author of *The Catholic Church and Democracy in Chile and Peru* (University of Notre Dame Press, 1997) and the author of *The Rise of Fall of Chilean Christian Democracy* (Princeton University Press, 1985).

PATRICIA FORTUNY received a PhD in social anthropology from University College London in 1995. She has been a full-time researcher at the Center of Research and Advanced Studies in Social Anthropology (CIESAS) since 1988, first in Occidente, Guadalajara, Jalisco, and since 2002, in CIESAS Peninsular in Mérida, Yucatán. Her line of research centered in the 1980s on religious minorities and from 1999 onward she engaged in the study of religion and Mexican migration to the United States. She published two books on religious minorities from Mexico and coordinated one on religious affiliation and modern values in Guadalajara, Jalisco. She has written numerous articles and chapters in Spanish and English, on religion conversion, migration and churches, gender, power and space, and other related topics. Her research interests include Catholic, Protestant, and New Age Mexican emigrants to the United States, as well as migrant civic organization with special attention to Yucatec Mayas, and interdisciplinary work on visual anthropology on returnee Mayas in Yucatan.

PAUL FRESTON is the CIGI Chair in Religion and Politics in Global Context at the Balsillie School of International Affairs and Wilfrid Laurier University, Canada. He is also professor colaborador on the postgraduate programme in sociology at the Universidade Federal de São Carlos, Brazil. He has worked mainly on religion and politics, the growth of popular forms of Protestantism in Latin America, and questions of religion and globalization. His books include *Evangelicals and Politics in Asia, Africa and Latin America* (Cambridge University Press, 2001); *Protestant Political Parties: a Global Survey* (Ashgate, 2004); (ed.) *Evangelical Christianity and Democracy in Latin America* (Oxford University Press, 2008);

and (coauthored) *Nem Anjos Nem Demônios: Interpretações Sociológicas do Pentecostalismo* (Vozes, 1994).

VIRGINIA GARRARD-BURNETT earned her PhD in history from Tulane University. She is a professor of history at the University of Texas, Austin. She has authored numerous articles and chapters, edited three collected volumes (of which this is the fourth), and written two monographs, the most recent of which is *Terror in the Land of the Holy Spirit: Guatemala Under General Efraín Ríos Montt, 1982–1983* (Oxford University Press, 2010). Her forthcoming monograph is on new Christian movements in Latin America.

HENRI GOOREN is a Dutch cultural anthropologist who has published especially on conversion and on Pentecostalism, Protestantism, Mormonism, and Roman Catholicism in Latin America. After working at the Netherlands Organization for Scientific Research (NWO), he joined the Inter-university Institute for Missiological and Ecumenical Research at Utrecht University in the research program Conversions Careers and Culture Politics in Pentecostalism: A Comparative Study in Four Continents (2003–2007). In August 2007, Gooren became an assistant professor of anthropology at Oakland University in Rochester, Michigan, where he received tenure in 2011. Palgrave-Macmillan published his book *Religious Disaffiliation and Conversion: Tracing Patterns of Change in Faith Practices* in 2010. He conducted fieldwork research on the Pentecostalization of religion and society in Paraguay and Chile in 2010–2012, sponsored by the John Templeton Foundation. He is currently working on a monograph elaborating this topic.

SIDNEY M. GREENFIELD is a professor of anthropology emeritus at the University of Wisconsin–Milwaukee and currently co-chair of the Columbia University Seminars on Brazil, Studies in Religion and Knowledge, Technology and Social Systems. He has conducted ethnographic research mostly in Brazil but also in Barbados and New Bedford, Massachusetts on a wide range of problems, including family and kinship, patronage and politics, entrepreneurship, Spiritist surgery and healing, syncretized religions and Evangelical Protestants in Brazilian politics. He has conducted ethnohistorical and historical research in Portugal and the Atlantic Islands on the history of slavery and plantations. He is the author or editor of eight books; producer, director, and author of five video documentaries; and has published some 140 articles and reviews in books and professional journals. At present he is completing a book in Portuguese with a Brazilian colleague on Evangelicals in Brazilian politics.

RAMÓN A. GUTIÉRREZ is the Preston & Sterling Morton Distinguished Service Professor of United States History and the College at the University of Chicago. He is the author of *When Jesus Came the Corn Mothers Went Away: Marriage, Sexuality, and Power in New Mexico, 1500–1846* (Stanford University Press, 1991) and the co-editor of *Mexicans in California: Transformations and Challenges* (University of Illinois Press, 2009).

TODD HARTCH is the author of *The Prophet of Cuernavaca: Ivan Illich and the Crisis of the West* (Oxford University Press, 2015) and *The Rebirth of Latin American Christianity* (Oxford University Press, 2014). He teaches Latin American history at Eastern Kentucky University.

BONAR L. HERNÁNDEZ SANDOVAL earned his PhD at the University of Texas at Austin. He is an assistant professor of Latin American history at Iowa State University. His research explores the intersection between religious identity and social change during the Cold

Contributors

War in Guatemala. He is the author of "Reforming Catholicism: Vatican Diplomacy in Guatemala during the 1920s and 1930s," *The Americas* 71:2 (October 2014) and "'Restoring All Things in Christ': Social Catholicism, Urban Workers, and the Cold War in Guatemala" in *Beyond the Shadow of the Eagle: New Histories of Latin America's Cold War*, edited by Virginia Garrard-Burnett, Mark Lawrence, and Julio Moreno (University of New Mexico Press, 2013).

KARINA KOSICKI BELLOTTI has PhD in cultural history from the State University of Campinas (Brazil) and is a professor in the Department of History at the Federal University of Paraná (Brazil). She conducts research on Brazilian and American Protestantism/ Pentecostalism and their relation with the media and the market in the nineteenth and twentieth centuries. She is the author of various articles and chapters of books published in Brazil and the United States, among which are the books *Mídia Presbiteriana no Brasil – Luz para o Caminho e Editora Cultura Cristã, 1976–2001* (Anablume, 2005), *Delas é o reino dos déus: a mídia evangélica na cultura pós-moderna do Brasil: 1950–2000* (Annablume, 2010), and the article "The History of a Little Brazilian Ant: Material Culture in Evangelical Children's Media in Brazil, 1980s Present."

JEFFREY L. KLAIBER, SJ, earned his PhD in history from Catholic University. A native of Indiana, he spent most of his life and ministry in Peru. A well-regarded scholar and teacher of Peruvian political history and church history, Fr. Klaiber served as professor of history at the Catholic University in Lima for nearly four decades, beginning in 1976. He was also a professor of theology and a counselor at the University of El Pacífico in Lima (1977–1982). In addition to teaching at the Catholic University, he was a professor of history at Antonio Ruiz de Montoya University in Lima, Peru, from 2004–2014. Fr. Klaiber served as a visiting professor at Georgetown University (1990–1991); St. Joseph's University, Philadelphia (2000–2001); and Boston College (2006–2008). For many years he also did pastoral work in the Jesuit parish Virgen de Nazareth in Lima. Fr. Klaiber passed away on March 4, 2014.

CHRISTINE KOVIC, an associate professor of anthropology at the University of Houston-Clear Lake, has conducted research in the areas of human rights for the past twenty years. She is the author of *Mayan Voices for Human Rights: Displaced Catholics in Highland Chiapas* (University of Texas Press, 2005), *Women of Chiapas: Making History in Times of Struggle and Hope* (co-editor with Christine Eber, Routledge, 2003), and a series of articles and book chapters. Her current research addresses the intersection of human rights and immigration, with emphasis on Central American migrants crossing Mexico in the journey north and on the organizing efforts of Latina/os in the United States.

BRIAN LARKIN is a professor of history at the College of St. Benedict/St. John's University (Minnesota). He is the author of *The Very Nature of God: Baroque Catholicism and Religious Reform in Bourbon Mexico City* (University of New Mexico Press, 2010) and various articles on the religious history of colonial Mexico. He is currently researching Eucharistic piety in the colonial Archdiocese of Mexico.

SANDRA LAZO DE LA VEGA has served as a research associate for the Program for Immigration, Religion, and Social Change at the University of Florida and a scholar intern at the Woodrow Wilson International Center for Scholars. She co-authored *Against the Tide: Immigrants, Day Laborers, and Community in Jupiter, Florida* (University of Wisconsin

Press, 2013) with Timothy Steigenga and has published several articles and chapters on immigration, transnationalism, gender, and religion including recent publications in the *Journal of Migration and Human Security* and *Migraciones Internacionales*. She received her BA from the Wilkes Honors College of Florida Atlantic University and her MA in Latin American Studies from Florida International University.

MIGUEL C. LEATHAM is a sociocultural anthropologist (PhD 1993, University of New Mexico) and director of the Anthropology Program at Texas Christian University, in Fort Worth, Texas. He specializes in the study of Latin American and Mexican-American cultures, with a research focus on religious change. He has carried out extensive ethnological fieldwork in Michoacán State, Mexico on the recruitment of peasants to a large millenarian colony, and has conducted a study of schism and reunification in a temple of the Caodaist Vietnamese millenarian sect in Dallas, Texas. His articles have appeared in the *Journal of Contemporary Religion*, *Religion and the Social Order*, the *Journal for the Scientific Study of Religion*, and the *Encyclopedia of Religion*. He has published on millenarianism, new religious movement schism, recruitment processes, Pentecostal expansion, the nature of ethnography in the millenarian setting, and religious movement types in Latin America. Currently, he has an ethnographic book manuscript in progress surveying the developmental history, recruitment and conversion processes, and culture of the Nueva Jerusalén millenarian colony.

DAVID LEHMANN is a social scientist who has worked all his life on and in Latin America. Among the subjects he has written about are agricultural development, religion, and multiculturalism. His main works on Latin America are *Democracy and Development in Latin America: Economics, Politics and Religion in the Postwar Period* (Temple University Press, 1992), and *Struggle for the Spirit: Popular Culture and Religious Transformation in Brazil and Latin America* (Polity, 1996). With Batia Siebzehner he has also written a book on religion and ethnicity in Israel *The Remaking of Israeli Judaism: The Challenge of Shas* (Oxford University Press, 2006). In 2007 he began to work on multiculturalism and affirmative action policies in Brazil and Mexico. His edited book *The Crisis of Multiculturalism in Latin America* will appear in 2016. He is currently emeritus professor at Cambridge University and his latest project is about Messianic Jews worldwide.

MIGUEL LEÓN-PORTILLA is a professor at the National Autonomous University of Mexico. He is an anthropologist and historian of Náhuatl philology and philosophy. He is the author of numerous books including *La filosofía náhuatl estudiada en sus fuentes* (Universidad Nacional Autónoma de Mexico, 1956). *Visión de los vencidos: crónicas indígenas* (Universidad Nacional Autónoma de Mexico, 1959), and *Tonantzin Guadalupe: pensamiento náhuatl y mensaje Cristiano en el "Nican Mopohua"* (El Colegio Nacional, 2000).

JEFFREY LESSER is the Samuel Candler Dobbs Professor and chair of the Department of History at Emory University. His newest book is *Immigration, Ethnicity and National Identity in Brazil* (Cambridge University Press, 2013). He is also the author of three other prize-winning books (all published in English and Portuguese), *A Discontented Diaspora: Japanese-Brazilians and the Meanings of Ethnic Militancy* (Duke University Press, 2007), *Negotiating National Identity: Immigrants, Minorities and the Struggle for Ethnicity in Brazil* (Duke University Press, 1999), and *Welcoming the Undesirables: Brazil and the Jewish Question* (University of California Press, 1994).

Contributors

DANIEL H. LEVINE is a professor of political science, emeritus at the University of Michigan, and Profesor Honorario at the Pontificia Universidad Católica del Perú. He has published widely on issues of religion and politics, democracy, democratization, and civil society and social movements in Latin America. He is the author of nine books – *Conflict and Political Change in Venezuela* (Princeton University Press, 2015), *Religion and Politics in Latin America*, *Religion and Political Conflict in Latin America* (University of North Carolina Press, 1986), *Popular Voices in Latin American Catholicism* (Princeton University Press, 2014), *Constructing Culture and Power in Latin America* (University of Michigan Press, 1993), *Voces Populares en el Catolicismo Latinoamericano* (Centro de Estudios y Publicaciones [CEP], 1996), *The Quality of Democracy in Latin America* (Lynne Rienner, 2011), and *Politics, Religion, and Society in Latin America* (Lynne Rienner, 2011) – along with numerous articles and chapters in books in English, Spanish, French, and German.

JOHN LYNCH is an emeritus professor of Latin American history and former director of the Institute of Latin American Studies, University of London. He is the author of more than a dozen books on Latin America including *New Worlds: A Religious History of Latin America* (Yale University Press, 2012) and *Simón Bolívar: A Life* (Yale University Press, 2006).

CECÍLIA L. MARIZ received her PhD in sociology at Boston University (UNI, 1989). She is currently a professor of sociology at Universidade do Estado do Rio de Janeiro (UERJ) and researcher at the Brazilian National Council for Scientific Research (CNPq). For the last thirty years her research projects have focused on religions in Brazil, and she has published on Pentecostalism, Catholicism, and Islam in that country. She is the author of *Coping with Poverty: Pentecostal and Base Communities in Brazil* (Temple University Press, 1994) and has published several articles in Brazilian and International academic journals.

TIMOTHY MATOVINA is a professor of theology and co-director of the Institute for Latino Studies at the University of Notre Dame. He works in the area of theology and culture, with specialization in US Catholic and US Latino theology and religion. His most recent book, *Latino Catholicism: Transformation in America's Largest Church* (Princeton University Press, 2011), has won five book awards, including selection as a CHOICE "Outstanding Academic Title" for 2012. His current book project is tentatively titled *Engaging a New World: Theologies of Guadalupe in the Americas*.

AMOS MEGGED is an associate professor in the Department of General History at the University of Haifa, Israel. He is author of *Social Memory in Ancient and Colonial Mesoamerica* (Cambridge University Press, 2010) and *Cambio y persistencia: la religión indígena en Chiapas, 1521–1680* (CIESAS, 2008). He is also the co-editor of *Mesoamerican Memory: Enduring Systems of Remembrance* (University of Oklahoma Press, 2012) and a member of the editorial board for the *Oxford Bibliographies in Latin American Studies* and *Colonial Latin American Historical Review*.

KEVIN LEWIS O'NEILL is an associate professor in the Department for the Study of Religion and the Centre for Diaspora and Transnational Studies at the University of Toronto. He is the author of *City of God: Christian Citizenship in Postwar Guatemala* (University of California Press, 2010) and *Secure the Soul: Christian Piety and Gang Prevention in Guatemala* (University of California Press, 2015).

ANDREW ORTA is a professor of anthropology at the University of Illinois. He is a sociocultural anthropologist with research specializations in Bolivia, where he has conducted ethnographic research with Aymara communities since 1989. His book, *Catechizing Culture: Missionaries, Aymara and the "New Evangelization"* (Columbia University Press, 2004), presents an ethnography of the "theology of inculturation," examining missionary–Aymara interactions, the complex politics of revalorized indigenous religious practices, and the integral role of Catholicism and its representatives in the production of local indigenous communities. His more recent work in the region focuses on the impact of processes of neoliberal political decentralization on the reproduction of local community institutions and identities. Another current project examines the anthropology of capitalism, international business, and business education in the United States.

ANNA L. PETERSON received her AB from the University of California at Berkeley and her PhD from the University of Chicago. She teaches in the Religion Department at the University of Florida, where she is affiliated with Center for Latin American Studies. Her main areas of research and teaching interest include religion and politics in Latin America and also social, environmental, and animal ethics. Her recent books include *Being Animal: Beasts and Boundaries in Nature Ethics* (Columbia University Press, 2013), *Everyday Ethics and Social Change* (Columbia University Press, 2009), and *Seeds of the Kingdom* (Oxford University Press, 2005).

IVAN PETRELLA holds a PhD in religious studies and law from Harvard University. He is the author of *The Future of Liberation Theology: An Argument and Manifesto* (Ashgate, 2004) and *Beyond Liberation Theology: A Polemic* (SCM Press, 2013) and editor of *Latin American Liberation Theology: The Next Generation* (Orbis Books, 2005). He is currently a professor at Universidad Torcuato Di Tell and Universidad de San Andres in Buenos Aires, Argentina. He was also elected to the City of Buenos Aires State legislature in 2013 and holds office until 2017.

FRANCES L. RAMOS received her PhD from the University of Texas at Austin in 2005 and is currently associate professor of Latin American history at the University of South Florida, Tampa. Her major work, *Identity, Ritual, and Power in Colonial Puebla* (University of Arizona Press, 2012), is a study of the political culture of late seventeenth- and eighteenth-century Puebla de los Ángeles and received the Rocky Mountain Council of Latin American Studies' Michael C. Meyer Award for Best Book on Mexico published between 2008 and 2012. She has published in the *Americas*, *Relaciones*, and *Historia Mexicana*, as well as several compilations in both Spanish and English, and her research has been funded by the Social Science Research Council, the Fulbright-Hays Program, and, most recently, the National Endowment for the Humanities. Her current project focuses on networks of communication, gossip, and political discourse during the War of the Spanish Succession (1701–1714) in New Spain.

JENNIFER SCHEPER HUGHES is an associate professor in the Department of History at the University of California, Riverside and is the founding co-director of UC Riverside's Institute for the Study of Immigration and Religion. Her research and teaching focus on the history of lived religion in Latin America, especially religious conversion and indigenous Christianity in Mexico. Material religion, the religious image, and religion and affect are also primary subjects of her research. Hughes' first book, *Biography of a Mexican Crucifix: Lived Religion and Local Faith from the Conquest to the Present* (Oxford University

Press, 2010), is a history of popular devotion to devotional images of the suffering Christ in Mexico. She is currently working on a project that explores Latino religious practice in California. She served for five years as the co-chair of the Religion in Latin America and Caribbean Group of the American Academy of Religion.

STEPHEN SELKA is a cultural anthropologist who earned his PhD from the University at Albany, SUNY in 2003. His research focuses on religion, politics, and tourism in northeastern Brazil, where he has conducted ethnographic research since 1999. His first book, *Religion and the Politics of Ethnic Identity in Bahia, Brazil* (University Press of Florida, 2007), explores the various ways that Afro-Brazilians in both Christian and African-derived religious communities construct their ethnic identities and struggle against racism. He is currently working on a second book, *Branding Brazil: Religion and the Uses of Heritage in Bahia*, which looks at the construction of Brazilian national identity through in the context of global tourism. Dr. Selka is currently an associate professor of religious studies at Indiana University.

TIMOTHY J. STEIGENGA is a professor of political science and chair of the social sciences and humanities at the Wilkes Honors College of Florida Atlantic University. He is the author/editor of six books and numerous other publications on religion, politics, and migration. His most recent books include *Living Illegal: The Human Face of Unauthorized Immigration* (New Press, 2011) coauthored with Marie Friedman Marquardt, Philip Williams, and Manuel Vásquez and *Against the Tide: Immigrants, Day Laborers, and Community in Jupiter, Florida* (University of Wisconsin Press: 2013) coauthored with Sandra Lazo de la Vega.

DOUGLASS SULLIVAN-GONZÁLEZ is an associate professor of history and dean of the Sally McDonnell Barksdale Honors College at the University of Mississippi. He is the author of *Piety, Power and Politics: Religion and National Formation in Guatemala, 1821–1871* (University of Pittsburgh Press, 1998). He also coedited, with Charles Reagan Wilson, *The South and the Caribbean* (University Press of Mississippi, 2001).

DAVID TAVÁREZ is an associate professor of anthropology at Vassar College. He is the author of *The Invisible War: Indigenous Devotions, Discipline, and Dissent in Colonial Mexico* (Stanford University Press, 2011; paperback, 2013; Spanish-language edition, 2012), a co-editor (with Susan Schroeder, Anne Cruz, and Cristián Roa) of *Chimalpahin's Conquest: A Nahua Historian's Rewriting of Francisco López de Gómara's* La conquista de México (Stanford University Press, 2010; Spanish-language edition, 2012), and a coauthor (with Louise Burkhart and Elizabeth Boone) of *Painted Words: Nahua Catholicism, Politics, and Memory in the Atzaqualco Pictorial Catechism* (Dumbarton Oaks, 2016).

JAKOB EGERIS THORSEN received his PhD from Aarhus University in Denmark. He is currently a postdoctoral research fellow at the Section for Theology at Aarhus University. Thorsen is the author of *Charismatic Practice and Catholic Parish Life – the Incipient Pentecostalization of the Church in Guatemala and Latin America* (Brill, 2015) and has published various articles and anthology chapters on religion in Latin America, Catholicism, and systematic theology.

THOMAS A. TWEED is the Harold and Martha Welch Professor of American Studies and a professor of history at the University of Notre Dame. He is also Faculty Fellow in the Institute of Latino Studies. He previously taught at the University of Texas, the

University of Miami, and the University of North Carolina. Dr. Tweed's research includes six books and a six-volume series of historical documents. In 1997 he published *Our Lady of the Exile: Diasporic Religion at a Cuban Catholic Shrine in Miami* (Oxford University Press, 2002), which won the American Academy of Religion's book award. Tweed's *Crossing and Dwelling: A Theory of Religion* was published by Harvard University Press in 2006, and his historical study of the Basilica of the National Shrine of the Immaculate Conception in Washington appeared in 2011 as *America's Church: The National Shrine and Catholic Presence in the Nation's Capital, 1917–1997* (Oxford University Press, 2011). *America's Church* also received the annual book award by the American Academy of Religion. Tweed has served as the president of the American Society for the Study of Religion (ASSR), and in 2015 he was president of the American Academy of Religion (AAR).

ASONZEH UKAH is a sociologist/historian of religion. He joined the University of Cape Town, South Africa, in 2013. Before then, he taught at the University of Bayreuth, Germany, from 2005 to 2013. He studied at the University of Ibadan, Nigeria, and the University of Bayreuth, Germany. In addition to numerous publications in peer-reviewed journals and contributions of book chapters, he is the author of *A New Paradigm of Pentecostal Power: A Study of the Redeemed Christian Church of God in Nigeria* (Africa World Press 2008). He is the Director of Research Institute on Christianity and Society in Africa (RICSA), University of Cape Town, South Africa.

MANUEL A. VÁSQUEZ is a professor of religion at the University of Florida. He is the author of *More than Belief: A Materialist Theory of Religion* (Oxford University Press, 2011) and *The Brazilian Popular Church and the Crisis of Modernity* (Cambridge University Press, 1998). He also coauthored *Living 'Illegal': The Human Face of Unauthorized Immigration* (New Press, 2011; updated and expanded 2nd edition 2013) and *Globalizing the Sacred: Religion across the Americas* (Rutgers University Press, 2003). His coedited volumes, including *The Diaspora of Brazilian Religion* (Brill, 2013), *A Place to Be: Brazilian, Guatemalan, and Mexican Immigrants in Florida's New Destinations* (Rutgers University Press, 2009), *Latin American Religions: Histories and Documents in Context* (NYU Press, 2008), and *Immigrant Faiths: Transforming Religious Life in America* (AltaMira, 2005).

PAMELA VOEKEL is the author of *Alone Before God: The Religious Origins of Modernity in Mexico* (Duke University Press, 2002). She is the co-founder of the Tepoztlán Institute for the Transnational History of the Americas, a week-long seminar held annually in Mexico, and a co-founder of Freedom University Georgia, which provides rigorous college-level courses for the undocumented students banned from Georgia's top research universities (www.freedomuniversitygeorgia.com). She has published on a range of topics, including the intersections of religion and politics in Mexico, popular religion in Latin America, and theory and methods in transnational history. She is currently finishing a second book, tentatively titled *For God and Liberty: Catholicism and Democracy in the Atlantic World in the Age of Revolution*.

Acknowledgments

We would like to thank all those who have made this volume, long in realization, possible, including the editors at Cambridge and, especially, the contributors, whose efforts and patience are very much appreciated. Special thanks to those who undertook the challenge of translating of a few of the articles into English: Rodrigo Freston, José Adrian Barragán, and Ashely M. Voeks. We are also grateful to the Department of History at the University of Texas at Austin for providing graduate assistants to help with the nuts-and-bolts of this project. Special thanks go to Juandrea Marie Bates, whose careful eye, meticulous reading, and boundless good cheer have helped to make volume this possible.

Last but not least, we wish to remember three of our colleagues who did not live to see this book come to fruition: Jeffrey Klaiber, S.J., Edward L. Cleary, O.P., and Ogbu Kalu. We stand on the shoulders of giants.

I

Introduction to the Cambridge History of Religions in Latin America

VIRGINIA GARRARD-BURNETT, PAUL FRESTON, AND STEPHEN C. DOVE

The *Cambridge History of Religions in Latin America* is a timely publication, for at least three reasons. The first is the historical and contemporary centrality of religion in the life of Latin America, a region that has itself been growing in global importance. A second is that the Latin American religious field is undergoing an extremely rapid process of change. Third, Latin America is important because of its religious distinctiveness in global comparative terms. In this Introduction, we expand briefly on each of these factors.

Historical Centrality of Religion in Latin America

We suggest that it is possible, even useful, to view the entire history of Latin America as religious history. The Spanish and Portuguese conquest of the New World was, both legally and ideologically, a "religious" endeavor, the conversion of its native peoples being the sine qua non of conquest and colonization. As we shall see, despite pockets of resistance, the "spiritual conquest" of northern Latin America was more or less complete by the end of the sixteenth century.

Much of South America, at least those areas touched by European conquest and colonization, however, had been evangelized by the end of the seventeenth. Robert Ricard's notion of a "spiritual conquest" (a phrase he coined in the early 1930s that refers to both the spiritual and institutional expansion of Roman Catholicism in the New World) does not begin to convey the complexity and ambiguities of faith and practice among native people in the conquest zones. It does, however, provide a sense of the pervasive Catholic hegemony – social and ideological, as well as spiritual – that would define Latin America for most of its history. Indeed, during the colonial period, the region was not even known as "Latin America," but simply as part of the realm of Christendom located in the overseas colonies of the Iberian Catholic kings. So dominant was the hegemony of the colonial Church, not only in terms of its institutions but also in its sway over hearts, minds, and fealty, that the reduction and marginalization of the Church became a chief preoccupation of nation-building statesmen in the nineteenth century.

The colonial religious history of Latin America, marked by conquest, colonization, resistance, accommodation, and adaptation, closely parallels the region's secular history and shares many of the same themes. Although we find it important to sketch out the institutional history of the Iberian Catholic Church in the New World – this being the "bones" that give structure to our historical understanding – this work also engages the more recent historiographical studies that examine the intersection of religion with race, ethnicity, gender, and secular culture. We also recognize that Christianity posed, and to some extent, continues to offer, important epistemological problems for non-Western peoples and their established belief systems. Thus, this volume explores the spiritual dimensions of what Hans Sieber called the "creolized religions" that emerge from the collision and conjunction of European, indigenous, and African cosmovisions.

That said, there is no question that Catholicism was at the center of Spain and Portugal's conquests of the Americas. The stereotype of conquest in the name of "God, Gold, and Glory" is based in fact, but the role played by Catholicism and Catholic identity (as opposed to an individual Iberian's personal beliefs and pious practice) is much more complex than this basic equation suggests. Certainly, the Roman Catholic Church was as powerful a political player as existed anywhere in Europe in the fifteenth and sixteenth centuries, and this accounts in part for why the rationale for conquest and the rules for its conduct were cast in terms that melded religious and imperial motives quite seamlessly.

To cynical modern eyes, it is difficult to reconcile the zealous Christian rhetoric of the conquistadors with the more peaceable sensibilities that we now associate with an ideal ethic of "Christian behavior." But for many Iberians in the sixteenth century, Christianity and, specifically, Catholicism was a militant faith, and Catholicism was so fully interwoven with what we now consider to be secular issues such as identity and citizenship that it was impossible to untangle the different strands. Columbus left Spain on his first voyage in 1492 just five months after the North African Moors abandoned their last Iberian outpost in the southern city of Granada. The Spanish liberation of Granada signaled the end of the 700-year occupation of the peninsula by Muslim North Africans. The struggle to evict the Moors, known as the *Reconquista*, lasted several centuries, during which time the Spaniards identified themselves first

Introduction

as Christians fighting the infidels, and only secondarily as allegiants of the various Iberian kingdoms.

As many of the first Spaniards in the New World were themselves veterans of the *Reconquista*, it is not surprising that they would bring with them the crusaders' mentality and methods. The *Reconquista* gave Spaniards a perspective on civil hierarchy in which religion was a deciding factor. Like all Europeans at the time, Iberian people in the early sixteenth century identified the known world of the West not so much by secular geopolitical definitions, but rather in terms of "Christendom." For Iberians, the world was divided into the dichotomy that the Argentinean scholar and statesman Domingo Faustino Sarmiento would much later designate as "civilization and barbarism." The definition of who comprised the category of "civilized," the *"gente decente"* (decent people), invoked a much wider range of criteria than we might suspect from our vantage: it measured the "civility" of a people by the color of their skin, their class, general conduct, material achievements, art, eating habits, mode of dress, and, above all, religion. Loyalty to the holy Catholic faith might have little to do in a practical sense with personal morality and ethics, but it clearly defined political fealty and social identity. Thus, although the Aztec cities might be quite "civilized" in Spanish eyes, the Aztec people's religious beliefs and bloody rituals relegated them to the category of barbarians, deserving of conquest and in need of redemption. In turn, the religion of the Europeans seemed equally confounding to the indigenous people.

The process of the conversion of the Americas was both ambitious and ultimately ambivalent. Through some coercion and a significant amount of innovation on the part of the friars – methods to attract natives to the faith sometimes included plays and dances, ballads and songs, translated into the language of the listeners – indigenous people under Spanish control, with some notable exceptions, converted readily, if only nominally, to Christianity. Although Catholic orthodoxy deeply permeated the spiritual lives of many converts as time went on, for others the "conversion" was entirely superficial. Some clung tenaciously to their own beliefs, occulting them behind a Catholic veneer. Others superimposed Christian doctrine onto a traditional context, producing a body of belief that they considered to be Catholic but that bore little resemblance to orthodox European faith or ritual. This meant that, from the beginning, Catholicism was molded by local preferences and conditions into a wide variety of forms and mutations that belied the ideal of a single, dogmatic, orthodox, and unitary universal Church.

The fusion of religious ideas and imagery also became common in Latin America among slaves, whom Europeans brought to the New World from

Africa in ever increasing numbers from the second half of the sixteenth century until well into the nineteenth century. For Africans, the process of conversion, mirroring their circumstances, was even less voluntary than it was for the New World natives. All the same, Portuguese slave holders in Brazil and Spaniards in the Caribbean and coastal zones where slavery was practiced on a large scale generally did not feel an obligation to go much beyond a perfunctory conversion of their charges. Under these circumstances, slaves managed to covertly maintain much of their own religions, hiding them from their masters by lending the Catholic saints the qualities of their own spiritual entities, and obscuring the meaning of certain religious practices, such as drumming, into what appeared to be harmless entertainment. With the passage of time, African beliefs began to coexist more comfortably with Christian ones, producing systems of religious bricolage such as Brazil's Candomblé or Cuba's Santería that are neither fully African nor fully Christian and are unique to the regions and peoples from which they originated.

However, the reach of the Church in colonial Spanish America and, to a somewhat lesser extent, in Portuguese America (where the Church was neither as rich nor as powerful) stretched beyond the conquest of hearts and spirits. As an institution, the Catholic Church was the single most influential political and economic player in the colonial world, with a presence and authority that often exceeded that of the Crown. At one level, Church and Crown shared a power in both practice and parity, as evidenced by the arrangement known as the *patronato real* (in Portuguese, *padroado*), that allowed the Crown (rather than Rome) to maintain the Church and propagate the faith, including the establishment and construction of all churches and monasteries and to administer collection of the tithe. By a more ordinary measure, however, the Church was more of an actual presence in the remote regions of the New World than the colonial government, located in the distant regional capitals of Mexico City, Lima, Buenos Aires, or Quito (or Salvador and later Rio de Janeiro in the Portuguese possessions), could ever hope to be. Even in areas so isolated that a priest might pass through only once every few years to perform basic sacramental services such as marriages, baptisms, and masses for the dead, a community would typically maintain a chapel and organize itself according to the spatial schema imposed by the colonial Church, the *parroquia*. Local inhabitants would also observe the major celebrations, obligations, and rhythms of the liturgical calendar, thus investing community members with a sense of belonging in their view toward the Church (if not always toward the clergy, whom they often thought to be rapacious) that they did not necessarily feel toward the Crown or, later, the state.

The Church was also the most pervasive economic institution in colonial Spanish America and Brazil, at a time when few other international financial organizations existed to serve the region. The Church acquired vast funds through bequests; tithes; fees paid for sacraments; dowries of young women who entered convents; rentals on Church-owned properties; and ownership of real estate outright, which it possessed, theoretically at least, in perpetuity. By the end of the eighteenth century, the Church was the largest landowner in all of Latin America and also the primary financial institution from which most *criollos* (New World–born Spaniards) borrowed money to buy land or to invest in other ventures. The Catholic Church was also a key benefactor of honor and status, the coveted social currency of Iberian life. A vocation in the Church was avidly sought out by pious, wealthy families who might have second sons who could not inherit their fathers' lands, or daughters who wanted to become nuns out of a real sense of religious vocation or to avoid the only alternative open to them, that of wife and mother.

The Church put much of its money into education and the intellectual life of the colonies, over which it had virtually sole control until the late eighteenth century. With the exception of a few Crown colleges, the Church (most often the Jesuits) founded and operated all the schools in Spanish and Portuguese America; as a result, every educated person during the colonial period was the product of an ecclesiastical education. The Church, moreover, was the keeper of public morals and intellectual hegemony. The Spanish Inquisition, established by Queen Isabella in 1478, monitored the influx of dangerous or subversive thought into Spanish America (such as Lutheran tracts or books written by the Enlightenment philosophers) and guarded religious and political conformity.

By the end of the colonial period in Latin America, the Christendom model (that is to say, the hegemony of Christian symbols, iconography, calendrical methods, social mores, hierarchical values – in short, the vast epistemology of Christianity, far beyond the basic issues of belief and practice) had left a deep imprint on Spanish America, if somewhat less so in the Portuguese colony. It is hardly surprising, then, that when independence came to Latin America in the first decades of the nineteenth century, the Catholic Church found itself caught between the two elite polarities of the state-formation project. These were the Liberals (modernists who viewed the Church as backward and also as the state's only real competitor for new citizens' hearts and minds) and the Conservatives (who saw the Church as the holy bastion of the status quo). The Church was also the source of a ready-made catalog of potent symbols and images, already heavy with valence for the general population, which new political actors could either combat or incorporate into the trappings of nationhood. Such was the case, most famously, with the Virgin of Guadalupe in Mexico, who was co-opted from strictly Catholic significance into the symbol of Mexican nationalism; or the less well-known Sacred Heart of Jesus in Ecuador, which became the focus of Ecuadorian national identity under Conservatives in the nineteenth century.

When modernizing Liberals gained control of most areas of Latin America in the second half of the nineteenth century, their agendas carried a powerful anti-Catholic subtext. Under Liberal rule, Protestant missionaries, mostly from the United States, undertook work in much of Latin America, offering a new variety of Christianity that Liberals valued as much – or more – for its emphasis on literacy, education, and opposition to Catholic hegemony as for its religious teachings. As Liberal anticlerical measures brought more and more stress to the institutional Roman Catholic Church, it slowly began to recede in the social and religious landscape of the region. The official Church's decline was particularly evident in two zones located far from state and ecclesiastical authorities, where its institutional resources had always been stretched thin even in more favorable times. These were the densely populated but nearly inaccessible indigenous areas and the frontier regions far from the metropolises of the emerging nation-states.

While the institutional Church began to vanish from the nineteenth-century countryside, Catholicism as a lived religion emphatically did not. To the contrary, a type of popular Catholicism as practiced and interpreted by an enthusiastic local laity quickly emerged to supplement and eventually replace orthodox Catholicism in many indigenous regions and on the far geographic frontier, where it blossomed without benefit of clergy. The manifestations of popular religion in these areas were not merely reactions to the reduced presence of the Church, but also represented local adaptations of vital elements of the faith. In many areas, this unlicensed "folk Catholicism" typically grafted elements of local spirituality, legend, and shamanism onto orthodox Catholic dogma, resulting in a fusion of indigenous and Catholic beliefs that were specific and resonant to a given locality and community. In many indigenous regions of northern Latin America, Mesoamerica in particular, it would be the *cofradías* – the religious sodalities introduced by the Spaniards during the colonial period – that assumed religious authority over local practices and beliefs, building up a body of *costumbre*, or local custom and practice, that became the unique religious marker of identity in indigenous communities. Elsewhere, traditional beliefs that centuries of Christian contact had never effectively snuffed out reemerged into the public forum.

Introduction

In the early twentieth century, the now more autonomous and therefore "Romanized" Catholic Church sent missionaries to Latin America to weed out syncretic practices and reintroduce Catholic orthodoxy into communities where "folk Catholicism" (i.e., Catholicism filtered through the lens of local beliefs, imagery, and parochial tastes) prevailed. But the weeding-out was far from successful. Rural folk Catholicism survived, alongside the multitude of sanctioned and unsanctioned popular devotions found across the continent – the candles, novenas, prayers to uncanonized saints, images, holy powders, charms, and pilgrimages – around which everyday people built their religious lives, whether the official Church approved of them or not. People's religious imaginations, then as now, were rich and voracious, and they eagerly embraced spiritual innovations – Spiritism, or African practices, for example – without feeling any particular sense of disloyalty or contradiction with the teaching of the Holy Mother Church. This devout but often ad hoc religious life both inside and outside the official Church continued to define the lives of many "ordinary" Catholics across the Americas.

The formal institutional Church did not, of course, disappear with the Liberal reforms of the late nineteenth century. During the decades prior to World War II, despite some new initiatives to address the increasingly injurious effects on Catholicism of modern capitalism, secularism, and totalitarian political movements, the institutional Roman Church continued to take for granted that Latin America was an unassailable Catholic bastion, despite the hostility of its many secular and anticlerical governments. This was true inasmuch as people almost universally considered themselves to be Catholic, if only nominally so. In the Brazilian census of 1940, for example, Catholics still comprised more than 95 percent of the population. But by mid-century, new kinds of ideologies – mostly political – had, for many, begun to flame the passions that active Catholic religiosity had once kindled.

The global Church had begun much earlier to address the threat to its spiritual hegemony in a papal encyclical issued by Pope Leo XIII, popularly known as the "working man's pope." In 1891, the pivotal encyclical *Rerum Novarum* advanced the position that social morality and the principles of justice and charity should regulate the relationship between capital and labor. Although this encyclical resulted in important new currents in Catholic social thought and praxis, *Rerum Novarum* had a much greater effect in Europe than in Latin America, at least in the first half of the twentieth century. In 1931, Pope Pius XI furthered this thinking with his encyclical *Quadragesimo Anno*, which spoke to the ethical implications of these issues; but the Church nonetheless failed to regain the political and economic viability that it had lost in Latin

America over the course of the long nineteenth century, even as the people themselves remained staunchly Catholic throughout most of the region.

This changed dramatically, however, in the postwar period, when the spread of communism through Eastern Europe and then to Cuba served notice that no land could be considered inexorably Catholic, not even in Latin America. It was in the immediate wake of the Cuban Revolution of 1959 that the Church began to take stock of the fact that it needed to establish a broad new paradigm to combat a variety of forces that threatened its ancient base of influence over the faithful across the Catholic world. First among these were the "isms," such as communism, Protestantism, and secularism that combined with urbanization and other demographic changes to pull people away from traditional lifestyles and worldviews. But at its root, the most serious danger was modernity itself; by the mid-twentieth century its emphasis on extreme individuality, materialism, and reification of capitalism offered a grave challenge not just to the Church, but also to religion in general. And the Catholic Church knew it.

With this in mind, in October 1962 Pope John XXIII convened the Second Vatican Council. The objective was to "open the Church to the world" and, essentially, to reclaim Catholicism's moral and temporal authority by reasserting its relevance to people living in modern times. In particular, Vatican II offered a renewed emphasis on the Church's role in the problems of the secular world. It is this last element that caught the interest and enthusiasm of many clergy in Latin America, who believed that Vatican II signaled a new commitment in the Church's obligation to the poor. In 1968, the Bishops' Conference of Latin America (Consejo Episcopal Latinoamericano – CELAM) convened its second General Conference in Medellín, Colombia, at which the bishops called for a specific application of Vatican II to the region. The conference articulated the Church's "preferential option for the poor" and called for biblically based consciousness raising (*"conscientização"* in Portuguese or *"concientización"* in Spanish) to help the poor take control of their lives in the secular world. This action-based faith became known as Liberation Theology, and it had a galvanizing effect throughout Latin America, bringing thousands of the faithful to an informed understanding of their beliefs and to social action for the very first time.

Within a decade, however, the official Church had begun to move in a different direction. In 1979, the Latin American bishops met again, this time in Puebla, Mexico, where they issued documents that suggested a subtle but definitive official distancing from Liberation Theology. One factor behind this retreat was the Church's sense of responsibility for the literally thousands of clergy and lay Catholics who had become politicized through consciousness raising, and who had died or "disappeared" because of their work for social justice through the Church. (The assassination of El Salvador's Archbishop Oscar Romero in March 1980 would only underscore this preoccupation.) Second, a year earlier, in 1978, Karol Józef Wojtyła had been elected pope and taken the name of John Paul II. He turned out to be a charismatic but conservative pope whose experience in communist Poland had made him wary of Church association with revolutionary popular movements. Undergirding these concerns was the bishops' not altogether incorrect perception that Liberation Theology had become a divisive issue within the Catholic Church structure, pitting radical against conservative and rich against poor, and threatening to wrench apart the *corpus christi*, the very body of the Church itself.

As time went on, the Vatican continued to encourage the Latin American bishops to distance themselves from Liberation Theology, as many of them in fact always had. It bears noting that in Argentina – home to then-Jesuit provincial Jorge Mario Bergoglio, now Pope Francis – the official Church and the military enjoyed a close symbiotic relationship during the Dirty War against the political left, which unfolded during the heyday of Liberation Theology. The Argentine case points to the fact that Liberation Theology, even at its apex in the late 1970s, and despite its fame and high moral purpose, was actually a minority movement in worldwide Catholicism, even within Latin America. In 1992, CELAM convened once again, this time in Santo Domingo, where it issued yet another series of pastoral letters that further distanced the formal Church from the precepts of Liberation Theology. The fifth CELAM, which met at Aparecida, Brazil in 2007, seemed to indicate clearly that the Church's focus in the new century would be on ecclesial and family-focused social matters, such as prioritizing opposition to abortion and same-sex marriage over other types of pastoral concerns.

Yet history is not without its surprises. The election in 2013 of Pope Francis, the first Latin American pope, did not mark a return to Liberation Theology by any means. But it did signal a turn toward what might be called a Latin American ecclesial sensibility for the poor and disenfranchised, and a movement away from the emphasis on sexual strictures for the faithful and on institutional protection that had preoccupied his predecessors and provoked the alienation of many Catholics worldwide. It is too early to tell if Pope Francis' pastoral directives will refocus and invigorate global Catholicism in the twenty-first century, and whether his papacy will help to staunch the flow of Catholics out of the Church, especially in Latin America. But at this writing, the winds of change appear to be gently shifting once again in the Catholic Church's direction.

Looking Forward

We conclude this section with a word on the contemporary importance of religion in Latin America. If the historical importance of religion in the region is generally recognized, its contemporary role is often overlooked. In part, this is due to the fact that in global comparative terms, the region can be characterized as *tranquilly religious*,[1] rather than either *secularized* or *defensively religious*. That is, it is at the same time among the most highly religious regions of the world, but its religiousness is not as socially and politically contentious (much less, violent) as in some other parts of the world.

The religious tranquility of Latin America comes out in Inglehart's analysis of the World Values Survey. The region is characterized by strong emphasis on traditional values such as religion, but also on the free choice and self-expression that are more common in wealthy countries. Thus, says Inglehart, Latin America rivals the Islamic world in the importance given to religion (even if the level of practice is only moderate in global terms). But in subjective well-being and sense of being in control of one's life, the region rivals the Nordic countries.

Similarly, the Pew Forum's 2014 survey of religion in Latin America shows that belief in God characterizes more than 99 percent of the population of Guatemala and Nicaragua, and more than 90 percent everywhere in the region with the exception of Latin America's persistent outlier in questions of religion, Uruguay (and even there belief in God is as high as 81 percent). Those who say religion is very important in their lives range from 90 percent in Honduras down to 41 percent in Chile and only 28 percent in Uruguay; but answers in fourteen of the nineteen Latin American countries surveyed are (often far) higher than the 56 percent response in the supposedly very religious United States.[2]

Rapid Change in the Latin American Religious Field

Latin America was born under the sign of Christendom, the territorial and monopolistic conception of a Christian world. It was an export of a particular incarnation of the European Christendom model, characterized by the

---

[1] Paul Freston, "As duas transições futuras: Católicos, Protestantes e sociedade na América Latina," *Ciencias Sociales y Religión/Ciências Sociais e Religião*, 12, no. 12 (October 2010): 13–30.

[2] Pew Forum on Religion and Public Life, *Religion in Latin America: Widespread Change in a Historically Catholic Region* (Washington, DC: 2014). pewforum.org//files/2014/11/Religion-in-Latin-America-11-12-PM-full-PDF.pdf.

triumphalism of the Iberian *reconquista* and by the caesaropapist rule of the Church by the Spanish and Portuguese Crowns. The religious motifs in colonization (however sincerely held), allied to the fact that the colonizers either dominated numerically or at least retained political control after independence, meant that the Christendom model left a huge imprint.

Royal patronage, of course, often kept the Catholic Church on a shoestring and impeded the development of an indigenous clergy. With few priests, formal practice was always low, and "popular" Catholicism was lay-run and often heterodox. Yet it put down such deep roots that for long after the formal "deregulation of the religious market" (in the late nineteenth or early twentieth centuries) there was little overt abandonment of the Church. Ironically, in the last few decades, Latin America has become the heartland of global Catholicism (numerically, and in occupancy of the throne of St. Peter) at the very time its hegemony there has been eroded. This traditionally Catholic world is now fast changing, resulting mainly in a growing pluralism within Christianity (growth of Pentecostalism; new initiatives within Catholicism) but also in a growing pluralism beyond it, marked among other things by a rise in the number of people who claim "no religion."

The novelty of Latin America as compared to religious change in other parts of the world is that a previous Catholic near-monopoly is being eroded by Protestantism *from within* (not significantly stimulated by missionaries or immigrants) and *from the bottom up* (not by top-down "national Reformations"). Latin America's Catholic Christendom is being penetrated directly by voluntarist evangelicalism without going through a "Protestant Reformation" first. This is different from the northern European model, which went from Catholic Christendom to national reformation, followed by the growth of voluntarist evangelicalism in free churches and in pietistic movements within the state church. It is also different from the southern European model in which Catholicism remains hegemonic in the religious field (though creating a substantial antireligious sector) and all forms of Protestantism essentially fail. It also differs from the US model of plural colonization and denominationalism as the deliberate solution to Church–state relations.

Latin America's internally driven change increasingly affects even those who remain Catholic. What was previously a culturally determined identity ('if you are Latin American you are Catholic') has become an identity to be chosen and affirmed in the face of well-known and broadly available alternatives. In any case, the traditional Catholic claim to be an essential part of Latin American identity had lost plausibility as pluralism has increased and Protestantism (especially in its Pentecostal forms) has become deep rooted.

This inherently unstable and bottom-up transformation is already resulting in diverse patterns across the region, and thus in growing religious diversity *between countries* within Latin America. The 2014 Pew survey *Religion in Latin America*, which covered the whole of the region except for Cuba, illustrates what is happening. Although the 425 million Latin American Catholics constitute some 40 percent of Catholics across the globe, they now represent only 69 percent of Latin Americans. Some countries are still considerably above that regional average: Paraguay is 89 percent Catholic; Mexico, 81 percent; Colombia and Ecuador, 79 percent. But others are far below it: Nicaragua, Guatemala and El Salvador only 50 percent; Honduras on 46 percent; and Uruguay at just 42 percent.

Meanwhile, Protestants now constitute 19 percent of the Latin American population. Much of this growth is extremely recent, as more than half of Latin American Protestants are converts (the figure for Colombia reaches 74 percent). But Protestant expansion, though region-wide, is far from uniform. At the top end, we find four neighboring Central American republics: Honduras and Guatemala on 41 percent, Nicaragua on 40 percent, and El Salvador on 36 percent. Next come Puerto Rico (33 percent) and Brazil (26 percent). At the other end of the scale, Paraguay is only 7 percent Protestant and Mexico 9 percent. Although Protestants have not overtaken Catholics in any Latin American country, they come closest in Honduras (41 to 46 percent).

The Pew survey employs two other categories: "unaffiliated" and "other religions." The "unaffiliated" are 8 percent regionally, varying from a low of 1 percent in Paraguay and 4 percent in Bolivia and Peru, to a high of 18 percent in the Dominican Republic and an extraordinary 37 percent in Uruguay. Few of those, however, are atheists: 10 percent in Uruguay, but no other country passes 4 percent. Meanwhile, the category of "other religions" is only 4 percent regionally, and never above 6 percent in any country.

If religious change in Latin America is going to produce internal diversification, what does the Pew snapshot tell us? One of us (Freston) feels that we can start to see some distinct "zones" emerging. The first zone is that of *Christian near-parity*, comprising Central America and the Caribbean lands of Puerto Rico and the Dominican Republic. At the core of this zone are the four northern Central American countries that are approaching parity of Catholics and Protestants, both being highly practicing. Then there is a fringe, in the southern part of the Central American isthmus and in the Caribbean, that represents a weaker version of the same trend.

The second zone, which can be called *Christian pluralism*, is constituted by Brazil, where there is still a substantial Catholic "lead," but with a larger-than-regional-average Protestantism that continues to grow quickly and a Catholicism that is still not highly practicing.

The third zone is that of *eroding Catholic dominance*. It comprises a swath of South America from Venezuela, through Colombia, Ecuador, and Peru, to Bolivia. This zone still enjoys relatively strong Catholic percentages (all close to or above three-quarters of the population), with Protestant communities that are below the regional average but sometimes quite fast-growing in recent times. Fourth, there are two geographically distinct zones of *resistant Catholic dominance*, represented by Paraguay and Mexico, the only two countries whose Catholicism remains above 80 percent and whose Protestantism is still in single digits.

Lastly, there is a zone of *religious and nonreligious pluralism*, comprising the Southern Cone countries of Argentina, Chile, and Uruguay. The last of these, of course, stands out for its very unique percentage of "unaffiliated" (37 percent), which almost rivals its percentage of Catholics (42 percent) and makes it the only country where Protestants (15 percent) are not the second force. But there is also something of a larger Southern Cone pattern developing (even spilling over somewhat into the two southernmost states of Brazil). Thus, Uruguay, Chile, and Argentina constitute the three Latin American countries that give least importance to religion in life. They are the only countries that have double-digit indices of low commitment on Pew's "Religious Commitment Index." And they are also the countries with the lowest percentages of Catholics who describe themselves as "charismatic."

A recent volume on the notion of "Latin America" talks of its double origin. One source was in a network of Iberian-American intellectuals in France, such as the Colombian poet José María Torres Caicedo, whose 1857 poem *Las Dos Américas* exalted "the race of Latin America," which "has before it the Saxon race, its mortal enemy." Caicedo regarded the Catholic religion as a key part of the common cultural heritage of the *"raza de la América latina."* The other source of the concept was among French politicians and intellectuals close to the emperor Napoleon III, with their notion of a Latin racial union under the leadership of France, the only nation capable of resisting the rise of the Protestant countries and the Anglo-Saxon race.

"Latin America" is thus born as a defensive concept, a child of the nineteenth century and its essentialist racial and religious thought, whose originators would presumably find disturbing the degree to which the region has since been de-Catholicized. There was, it is true, another sector of the *criollo* elite that expressed admiration for the pragmatism and efficiency of the United States, the emerging power of the time. But that elite sector sought support for its pro-Americanism in the work of the racial theorists of the period. The current de-Catholicization of Latin America is quite different; it has emerged from grassroots sectors, disproportionately nonwhite. In any case, Protestant growth is only one way in which the supposed common heritage of Latin America is under fire. The similarities created by Iberian conquest, Catholic religion, and largely *criollo* post-independence governance are being challenged by increasing economic diversity, indigenous "awakening," and broader religious pluralism.

A second comment about the current religious transformations is that it is possible to see them not so much as a betrayal of "Latin America," but rather as the belated outworking of alternative projects that were aborted in the early years of the European presence in the region. In the 1530s, Bartolomé de las Casas wrote about *The Only Method of Attracting All People to the True Faith*. "The means to effect this end are not to rob, to scandalize, to capture or destroy them, or to lay waste their lands." Instead "the one and only method of teaching men the true religion was established by Divine Providence for the whole world, and for all times: that is, by persuading the understanding through reasons, and by gently attracting or exhorting the will." In justification of this method, Las Casas cited reason, the Church Fathers, Christ, the Apostles, and the "most ancient tradition of the Church."[3] In addition, Carlos Garma, mentions the early attempts to use indigenous languages in evangelization and to produce a native clergy, projects that were later abandoned by the colonial Catholic Church and reintroduced centuries afterwards by Protestant missionaries. It can be argued that the Lascasian project of peaceful persuasion, and its corollaries of communication in the language of the people by a clergy that has emerged from the people, is reintroduced by historical Protestantism, popularized by Pentecostalism, and brought full circle as it is taken up by various forms of contemporary Catholicism, from the Base Communities to the Charismatic Renewal. Of course, the ambiguities of Las Casas himself are not absent from these contemporary implementations, whether under Catholic or Protestant guise.

Be that as it may, authors such as Grace Davie and David Martin have stressed how Latin America used to mirror Latin Europe in its religious field, but has now shifted somewhat in the direction of the United States, driven by Pentecostals' rejection of syncretism in favor of a pluralistic model of the

---

3 Lewis Hanke, *The Spanish Struggle for Justice in the Conquest of America* (Boston: Little, Brown & Co., 1949), 7; George Sanderlin (ed.), *Bartolomé de las Casas: A Selection of His Writings* (New York: Alfred Knopf, 1971), 158.

religious field. We would phrase it somewhat differently: from being similar to southern Europe, Latin America has moved somewhat in the direction of the United States (in the sense of greater Christian pluralism), but also in the direction of sub-Saharan Africa (with its multitude of thriving Pentecostal and charismatic forms of Christianity).

The final comment on the religious transformations in the region is that they are probably approaching some important tipping points. Catholic decline and Protestant growth will both have their limits. In the case of Brazil, the Protestant ceiling will probably be reached within two or three decades, as a result of two main factors. First, Catholic decline (currently at about 1 percent per year) will not go on indefinitely; there is a solid nucleus of practicing Catholics that will not disappear. Second, Protestantism currently receives only just over one of every two people who abandon Catholicism. And besides, the Catholic Church is slowly learning to compete better.

This perspective on Brazil has been challenged by Alves, Cavenaghi, and Barros, who characterize the state of Rio de Janeiro (45.8 percent Catholics; 29.4 percent Protestants; 15.6 percent "nonreligious"; 9.2 percent "other religions") as the most religiously diverse in the country. This diversity is accentuated in the poor urban periphery of Greater Rio: 37.4 percent Catholic and 34.5 percent Protestant. Many *municípios* already have more Protestants than Catholics. This region, they point out, seems to be two decades ahead of the rest of the country; the current indices for Brazil as a whole are strikingly similar to those of Metropolitan Greater Rio twenty years ago. And, they stress, there does not yet seem to be any "floor" to Catholic decline.

Whatever the case, the changes in Latin America, which have been dramatic enough, appear set to be even greater in coming decades. We are not far from a tipping point in which old patterns of relationships among religion, state, and society not only will be questioned but also may be entirely changed. Multidimensional pluralism, numerical decline, relative institutional weakness, and the effects of democracy and the fragmenting of civil society may lead to Catholic loss of "churchly" status, in which the old sociopolitical roles will have become unsustainable. We can call this critical moment the "Catholic transition."[4]

However, there will also be a "Protestant transition," a ceiling on Protestant growth and therefore on its political aspirations. This ceiling will not be

---

4 Paul Freston, "As duas transições futuras: Católicos, Protestantes e sociedade na América Latina." *Ciencias Sociales y Religión/Ciências Sociais e Religião*, 12(12), October (2010): 13–30, at 28.

uniform throughout the region. But everywhere, it will radically change the nature of Latin American Protestantism and its relationship to society, politics, and other religions.

Several factors might favor stronger Catholic resistance to Protestant advance than in the past. One is demography. Catholic clericalism and "heavy" territorial structure struggled in eras characterized by demographic mobility. But now, population growth is slowing, internal migrations are diminishing, and urban growth is going more to medium-sized cities, all of which should favor Catholicism's capacity to react. A second factor is Catholic adaptation. It was almost inevitable that Catholicism would suffer heavy losses once real religious competition began. But that is only a first moment. As Froehle and Gautier say, "In countries [outside Latin America] where the Church has long existed side by side with evangelical Protestants in an open, pluralist setting, Catholics have developed particularly strong forms of local parish life, commitment to practice and participation, and a sense of stewardship and relatively high church giving. In other words, the Church has learned from the strengths characteristic of these other Christian traditions."[5] It is probably not coincidental that the most vibrant Catholic movement in much of Latin America today, the Charismatic Renewal, began in the United States and fits well with the Latin American Church's need to reinvent itself in a more "denominational" context. Significantly, the 2014 Pew survey found that, across the region, 40 percent of Catholics now identify (at least when asked in a survey) as "charismatic." The Catholic Charismatic Renewal is, par excellence, a Catholicism for a religious field based more on a "denominational" model; it promotes a reaffiliation to the religion of one's birth, helping it to survive in a model of competitive pluralism in which religion is more and more a conscious individual choice. (Interestingly, the Pew survey also found that in the Central American countries that have near-parity of Catholics and Protestants, the Catholics are highly practicing.)

We can thus foresee a religious future comprising a Catholicism that is slimmer but revitalized, more practicing, and committed; together with a large but stable (and highly fragmented) Protestantism; and finally a considerable sector of non-Christian religions and of "non-religious." In this pluralist future, Catholicism would maintain its position as the largest single religious confession, with residual social and political privileges, especially as the divided Protestants would struggle to create solid representative institutions.

---

5 Bryan Froehle and Mary Gautier, *Global Catholicism* (Maryknoll, NY: Orbis, 2003), 132.

What else can we foresee? For instance, will Latin America simply be the last part of the old Christendom to secularize? Of course, if secularization is structurally determined by modernity, that is obviously the case, and the current explosion of Pentecostal churches and of the Catholic Charismatic Renewal must be a temporary effervescence. If, however, secularization is culturally contingent, one of several possible "modernities," then factors such as the differential impact of the Enlightenment on Latin American society (largely confined to elites), the current reassertion of indigenous peoples (especially in the Andean and Mayan regions), and the deep grassroots penetration by Pentecostal and Catholic charismatic spirituality might pull Latin America in a different direction.

The Importance of Latin America in Debates about Religion and Globalization

In debates on religion in a globalizing world, Latin America is often the "Cinderella region," overlooked in comparison to Europe and North America, and even to Africa and Asia because of their more recent de-colonization and massive presence of the other world religions. But Latin America deserves more global comparative attention, for several reasons.

One reason is that it illustrates possible futures for religion in globalizing times, in which the dichotomous "relativism versus fundamentalism" model posited by various scholars is nuanced by attention to "hybridity" and "peaceful conversionism," both of which are flourishing in Latin America. The former is, of course, a classic Latin American response, building on a tradition of synthetic heterodoxies at the popular level. But overlapping with this, while also introducing significant modification, is the conversionist response best exemplified by Pentecostalism. Latin American Pentecostalism is a major example of a religious globalization that is conversionist rather than diasporic; and in terms of cultural and political implications, there is a fundamental difference between diasporic globalization and conversionist globalization. The fact that Latin American religious change is due largely to conversion points to an important contrast with Europe, where the new religious pluralism results more from immigration and secularization.

José Casanova emphasizes how globalization undermines territorially based national religion, with its monopolistic claims that parallel those of the nation-state. Under globalization new forms emerge or are strengthened in all world religions, at individual, group, and societal levels. Individual mysticism, always an option for elites and religious virtuosi, becomes more generally available (reaching at least the middle classes in Latin America); at the group level, there are expanded possibilities for voluntary associations on the 'denominational' model; and transnational churches, freed from territorial constraints, reappear as globalized imagined communities. Thus Catholicism reemerges as a transnational religious regime, progressively gaining control over national churches. In 1999, Pope John Paul II consecrated Guadalupe as Virgin of all the Americas and urged bishops to cease viewing themselves as national hierarchies. And although Catholicism attempts to maximize the spaces offered by globalization to a transnational religion with a centralized structure, its upstart rival in Latin America, Pentecostalism, exemplifies the response of a decentralized religion with no territorial roots.

A second reason for greater attention to Latin America is that the debate about religion and modernity needs to be more global. Both history and recent changes contribute to the importance of Latin America for discussing these large questions of religion and modernity. The three most globalized religions (in numbers, geographical spread, and social influence) are currently Islam, Catholicism, and Pentecostalism, and Latin America is now a major site for the latter two. Catholicism and Protestantism (especially in Pentecostal form) now constitute (along with Islam) the major grassroots religious actors in poor and volatile regions of the world. Latin America exemplifies the new global reality of Christianity as a major religion of the world's poor and powerless. As such, the region must be included more in attempts to make the debate about religion and modernity global in scope. This debate has been dominated by a discussion of Europe (the secularization model) and North America (the market model); any attempts to go beyond are usually limited to a discussion of Islam. But the idea of "multiple modernities" challenges the assumption that modernizing societies are convergent and that either Europe or North America are "lead societies." A third reason for recommending greater global awareness of Latin American religion is that it increasingly matters not only to the region itself but also to other parts of the world, whether through transnational migration of Latin Americans, missionary exporting in various forms of religious transnationalism, or through the growing geopolitical and economic importance of key actors such as Brazil and Mexico.

Lastly, Latin America is important for current global debates on religion and human rights. The region has (courtesy of Pentecostalism) become a major site of controversies surrounding proselytization. It also at times illustrates the tension between the Catholic Church's support for religious freedom and its desire to hold on to its privileged position in traditionally Catholic areas of the world. The current moment, in fact, may be the worst of both worlds for religious contribution to the defense of human rights in the region.

Introduction

On the one hand, the Catholic Church no longer enjoys unchallenged hegemony but has not yet adjusted to the new situation; if it had to combat a new round of repressive regimes, the old methods of resistance would be less effective. At the same time, Pentecostalism is still largely alienated by the culture of the human rights movement, which has difficulty incorporating a lower class religious movement that is successful at proselytizing under a competitive pluralist conception of the religious field, and struggles to relate to Pentecostalism's discourse of individual empowerment through the discovery of personal agency.

Contents

The Cambridge History of Religions in Latin America covers Latin American religious history from pre-Conquest times until the present. (Our definition of Latin America includes the Spanish-speaking Caribbean.) We begin with an analysis of religion before the Conquest, both in the "New World" as well as in both the relevant parts of the "Old World," Europe, and Africa. We proceed with an examination of the religious dimensions of, and reactions to, conquest and colonization. We then look at the institutionalized colonial Church and at various dimensions of the *criollo* Catholicism that resulted from it.

One of the overtly religious novelties of the post-independence period is the possibility for Protestant Christianity to establish itself. Another significant religious transformation stemming from the nineteenth century is Catholic reform, responding not merely to the arrival of religious rivals but also to the strengthened contact with global Catholicism by the late nineteenth century and the dramatic transformations of global Catholicism after the mid-twentieth century. Transformations within Catholicism are matched in the second half of the twentieth century by changes in the non-Catholic religious field, as religious pluralism comes to Latin America.

We then look at aspects of the relationship between religions and the State in the late twentieth and early twenty-first centuries, whether that should be understood as a "deprivatization" of Latin American Catholicism or as merely a transformation of what had always been a public religion. Deprivatization seems to be more clearly the case with Protestantism in the region, above all in the case of the Pentecostals. The Pentecostals are also the main (but not the only) reason for asking whether Catholicism at the end of the millennium is undergoing erosion or renewal. Whether it is being eroded or renewed (or both), its nature has certainly changed as it seeks to find its way as one religious option among others, while still replete with many of the advantages and disadvantages of its former status.

One of the greatest forces behind the transformations in the religious field has been gender, especially the changes in women's rights and roles that are the theme of subsequent chapters. And, as shown next, indigenous peoples are another highly significant factor in religious change, especially in some parts of the region, involving the two main branches of Christianity as well as the revival of indigenous traditions. The African diaspora in Latin America is the theme of the following chapters, both in its religious pluralism and in the strengthening and transformation of the Afro-Brazilian and Afro-Caribbean religions.

We then cast an eye over an increasingly important phenomenon, that of Latin American religious transnationalism, both within the region and far beyond. Latin American religious phenomena have become global players, not merely in accompanying the diaspora of Latin Americans but also in relation to the religious lives of some North Americans, Europeans, Africans, and Asians.

We further explore the religious pluralism of contemporary Latin America in the following chapters, which examine not only the other "world religions" but also smaller new groups (such as the Mormons), as well as some phenomena that are peculiarly strong in the region (such as Spiritism) or that represent original syntheses (such as Luz del Mundo). But pluralism goes beyond religion (while also representing its "other face"), as various forms of secularization increasingly occur within Latin America. Finally, in a concluding chapter by one of the most experienced scholars of Latin American religion, Daniel Levine, puts much of this history and contemporary transformation in broader perspective.

A note on sourcing in this volume. Because this project is encyclopedic in scope, we have opted to omit much of the scholarly apparatus of footnoting, except in the case of direct quotations. However, please note that all references are readily provided in the bibliography that follows each chapter.

Bibliography and Suggested Readings

Alves, J. E. D., S. M. Cavenaghi, and L. F. W. Barros. "A transição religiosa Brasileira e o processo de difusão das filiações evangélicas no Rio de Janeiro." *Horizonte*, 12(36), Oct–Dec (2014): 1055–1085.

Brandalise, Carla. "A ideia e concepcao de 'Latinidade' nas Americas: A disputa entre as nacoes." In Ari Pedro Oro (ed.), *Latinidade da América Latina: Enfoques sócio-antropológicos*, 21–59. São Paulo: Aderaldo& Rothschild, 2008.

Casanova, José. "Religion, the New Millenium and Globalization." *Sociology of Religion*, 62(4), Winter (2001): 415–442.

"Rethinking Secularization: A Global Comparative Perspective." *The Hedgehog Review*, 8(1–2), Spring–Summer (2006): 7–23.

Davie, Grace. *Europe: The Exceptional Case*. London: Darton, Longman & Todd, 2002.

Freston, Paul. "As duas transições futuras: Católicos, Protestantes e sociedade na América Latina." *Ciencias Sociales y Religión/Ciências Sociais e Religião*, 12(12), October (2010): 13–30.

"Religious Pluralism, Democracy and Human Rights in Latin America." In T. Banchoff and R. Wuthnow (eds.), *Religion and the Global Politics of Human Rights*, 101–127. New York: Oxford University Press, 2011.

Froehle, Bryan, and Mary Gautier. *Global Catholicism*. Maryknoll, NY: Orbis, 2003.

Garma, Carlos. "Misión, sincretismo y evangelización: Catolicismo y Protestantismo comparados." In Ari Pedro Oro (ed.), *Latinidade da América Latina: Enfoques sócio-antropológicos*, 129–148. São Paulo: Aderaldo & Rothschild, 2008.

Hanke, Lewis. *The Spanish Struggle for Justice in the Conquest of America*. Boston: Little, Brown & Co., 1949.

Inglehart, Ronald. "Cultural Change, Religion, Subjective Well-Being, and Democracy in Latin America." In Frances Hagopian (ed.), *Religious Pluralism, Democracy, and the Catholic Church in Latin America*, 67–95. Notre Dame, IN: University of Notre Dame Press, 2009.

Martin, David. *Tongues of Fire*. Oxford: Blackwell, 1990.

Pew Forum on Religion and Public Life. *Religion in Latin America: Widespread Change in a Historically Catholic Region*. Washington, DC. 2014. pewforum.org/ /files/2014/11/Religion-in-Latin-America-11-12-PM-full-PDF.pdf.

Sanderlin, George, ed. *Bartolomé de las Casas: A Selection of His Writings*. New York: Alfred Knopf, 1971.

2
Religion in the Pre-Contact New World: Mesoamerica and the Andes

DAVID TAVÁREZ

This chapter summarizes archaeological, ethnohistorical, and linguistic data regarding religious practices in two important cultural areas in Latin America, Mesoamerica and the Andes. It begins with an analysis of the development of Mesoamerican religion from the Formative to the Postclassic periods, continues with an appraisal of Inca state religion and an ancient regional cosmology in central Peru, and closes with a brief comparison of Mesoamerican and Andean cosmological beliefs and practices.

Religion in Mesoamerica from the Formative to the Postclassic

Four major periods in the archaeology and ethnohistory of Mesoamerica correlate with important shifts in religious practices: hunter-gatherer Archaic societies (8000–1600 BCE); Formative socially stratified communities with ceremonial centers (1600 BCE–200 CE); the Classic (200–800 CE), characterized by major ceremonial centers; and the Postclassic (800–1519 CE), which begins with the collapse of Classic sites and ends with the emergence of militarized states.

The key structuring principle for the organization of Mesoamerican devotions from ca. 600–500 BCE until late colonial times was the systematic use of two separate but interlocking calendars: a 260-day divinatory cycle and a 365-day vague solar year. The 260-day count designated each day by combining the numbers 1 to 13 with one of twenty day signs named after animals, natural forces, or objects ($13 \times 20 = 260$), and was subdivided into twenty periods of thirteen days. Each day was associated with a deity. The 260-day count contained within a multitude of smaller cycles, including multiples of 4, 7, and 9. The 365-day calendar was divided into eighteen groups of twenty days, and were often commemorated through public ceremonies orchestrated by elites for the purpose of propitiating divine entities. The last five days in the count were regarded as infelicitous days. As this count does not coincide with the duration of the solar year, 365.25 days, the rapport between this count and equinox and solstice events was probably a variable one.

The use of the 365-day and the 260-day counts as parallel cycles allowed calendrical specialists to name each 365-day period after a day in the 260-day calendar. The structural relationship between these counts ensured that the names for these years would fall on a particular sequence of four day signs, or "year bearers." Hence, the use of the 260-day and the 365-day counts side by side allowed calendrical specialists to give a specific designation to each of the 18,980 days in a cycle of 52 vague solar years of 365 days (as opposed to 365.25 days), as in the formula 1-Earthquake, the first of 52 Zapotec vague solar years, and 1-Cayman, the first day of the 260-day count. The management of these two counts was a constant preoccupation for both commoners and elites. Both groups viewed the link between the two interlocking calendars and agriculture, the primary mode of subsistence, as a naturalized relationship between a body of sacred knowledge and the structure and history of the cosmos.

Besides these two counts, the Maya had a "Long Count" of 13 *baktuns* (each comprising 400 periods of 360 days), which began on a mythohistorical date equivalent to September 8, 3114 BCE in the Gregorian calendar, and restarted again 5125.25 solar years later, most recently on December 23, 2012. This lengthy cycle, which did not spell doom but had important cosmological meanings, allowed Maya priests to specify dates in three systems: Long Count, divinatory calendar, and 365-day year, along with their interactions with lunar cycles and the cycle of Venus. These counts provided the temporal structure for collective religious observances that took place in large ceremonial centers overseen by rulers and ritual specialists associated with the state.

Mesoamerican religious practice rested on the belief that there existed a permanent need for an exchange of offerings between humans and divine entities, a cosmological contract that may be summarized through Émile Durkheim's influential formula, *do ut des*, "I give so you may give." The Mesoamerican semantics of sacrificial offerings were staggeringly complex, as the power of such gifts hinged on the sacrificer's goals, felicitous times in the ritual count, the correct appraisal of the wishes of divine entities, oral and bodily performance, and the precise arraying of offerings. Caves and mountains were often associated with founding ancestors, as shown in the *Historia Tolteca-Chichimeca*. Leading ceremonial complexes developed as layers of new architectural features built above earlier structures, sponsored by succeeding local rulers, and punctuated by elaborate arrays of inaugural human and animal sacrifices, as exemplified by the various building stages of the Mexica Templo Mayor. In both public and private realms, ritual specialists consumed mushrooms, peyote, and other hallucinogens to communicate with divine entities. Human blood was regarded as a particularly powerful offering, while animal sacrifice was used as a viable proxy. The former was taken from sacrificial victims or in acts of self-sacrifice during which earlobes, fingers, arms, legs, or genitalia were cut with blades, spines, and thorns. Prized animal sacrifices included eagles, turkeys, dogs, and small birds. Besides blood, several items were appropriate sacred gifts: copal, paper, cacao, maize, and other important cultigens. During individual consultations, specialists instructed petitioners on the proper presentation of offerings; asked them to fast and abstain from sex; healed them with herbal remedies; and performed divination by means of a broad array of techniques that included casting grains, measuring limbs with their hands, looking at water, reading ashes, and interpreting dreams.

Classic and Postclassic Mesoamerican ceremonial centers, which served as models of the cosmos, shared two important features: temple complexes built in layers by succeeding generations of rulers and a court for ball games whose outcomes had cosmological and political significance, with architectural plans influenced by astronomical observations. The Maya and the Zapotec are two Classic-period societies notable for their development of a complex iconographic tradition that merged humans, animals, and natural forces with a calendrical and writing system. A main purpose of Classic Maya architectural programs was to celebrate the exploits of a *k'uhul ajaw* (divine ruler). For this purpose, Maya artists erected stelae and carved lintels depicting these rulers as they assumed office, performed public rituals, propitiated deities, communicated with their ancestors, conducted warfare, and commemorated the ending of a *k'atun* (20 periods of 360 days). Each successive ruler attempted to expand on his predecessor's architectural and iconographic plan.

The epitome of Classic Zapotec religion is found in Monte Albán, a site with monumental architecture; elite tombs and living quarters; and a large assembly of stone carvings, some of which were recycled from other sites in Mexico's Valley of Oaxaca. The most striking depiction of individuals tied to religious practice in this site are the so-called "Danzantes," a group of individual slabs, each containing a full-body portrait, accompanied by a name glyph. Even if these engravings may represent sacrificial victims, a recent reconstruction of their primary context suggests they were depictions of individuals ordered by age and social rank in an idealized public depiction of collective ceremonies. Zapotec tombs located throughout

Oaxaca often contained large ceramic effigy vessels, which depict specialists who impersonated a number of supernaturals and deity complexes, including deities associated with rain and thunder (Cocijo), maize (Cozobi), and water and fertility (Huichana or Nohuichana), among other entities. Although Zapotec hieroglyphic writing is not yet fully understood, public monuments may contain information comparable to that of Maya stelae, such as names of rulers, actions performed, and dates of ceremonies. There are multiple lines of evidence for the worship of sacred being regarded as ancestors, from scenes that may depict deified ancestors to the reuse of royal tombs and the cult of sacred bundles in Postclassic and colonial times that contained bones and hair from ancestors.

Unlike its Maya and Zapotec neighbors, the influential central Mexican site of Teotihuacan was governed by rulers and priests who did not emphasize the trajectory of individual lords over time. At its height ca. 500 CE, Teotihuacan was the most densely populated urban center in Mesoamerica (120,000–200,000 inhabitants), and a unique setting for neighborhoods established by peoples from the Gulf Coast, Oaxaca, and the Maya region. This city was the most important locus in Mesoamerica for craft production and trade. Teotihuacan's representation of a rain deity, featuring fangs and circular eye ornaments and later known in Nahuatl as Tlaloc, and a plumed serpent deity, called Quetzalcoatl in Nahuatl and K'ukulcan in Yucatec Maya, was diffused widely throughout Mesoamerica. Various locations in this city featured fresco paintings depicting water-giving deities, aquatic motifs, and scenes of human sacrifice featuring jaguars and dancing warriors with hearts atop spears. Moreover, Teotihuacan's architectural plan was developed as a representation of the Mesoamerican cosmos, divided into three different layers: Underworld, Earth, and Sky.

A major transition in Mesoamerican religious practice and social organization began in the early Postclassic period. Some sites, such as the Classic Maya-influenced murals of Cacaxtla, Puebla, and the Mexican-style regalia of Maya nobles depicted in Terminal Classic stelae at Seibal, attest to cross-regional influences. The site of Chichén Itzá, which began as a Classic period center, was expanded in the Postclassic by the construction of a new district featuring a temple; a columned hall; and stone sculptures depicting eagle warriors, jaguar warriors, and skull racks that seem closely influenced by similar structures in the Postclassic central Mexican site of Tula. Although earlier scholarship interpreted these similarities as evidence of a military conquest of Maya sites by central Mexican armies, more recent work suggests a more complex set of religious, diplomatic, and/or political interaction among elites. In this period, Cholula emerged as the most important pilgrimage site in the region, with a focus on the cult of Quetzalcoatl; in this site, a hill shaped by human action stood as the largest temple structure in Mesoamerica.

Postclassic and early colonial codices – texts painted on tree-bark paper or leather featuring semasiographic (language-neutral) writing in Central Mexico and syllabic writing among the Maya – contain a wealth of information about Mesoamerican cosmology, religious practice, and sociopolitical history. Although very few pre-Conquest codices have survived, those produced shortly after contact share many elements with their pre-Columbian counterparts. There exist four pre-Columbian Maya texts, which contain calendrical calculations and cosmological events associated with specific dates, and data on lunar phases, eclipses, and the Venus cycle. Central Mexican codices may be divided into three groups. The Mixtec tradition is represented by four pre-Columbian texts – Bodley, Colombino-Becker, Zouche-Nuttall, and Vienna – and four early colonial works – Becker II, Egerton/Sánchez Solís, Muro, and Selden. These works provide a narrative about the emergence of the Mixtec people from a mythical tree at Apoala, the creation of the world, and recount the deeds of Postclassic Mixtec rulers such as Lady 6-Monkey and Lord 8-Deer. The Mexica tradition is represented by the texts now known as Borbonicus, Tonalamatl Aubin, Telleriano-Remensis, Vaticanus A / Ríos, and Tudela. Finally, the Borgia Group consists of texts known as Aubin 20, Borgia, Cospi, Fejérváry-Mayer, Laud, Porfirio Díaz Reverse, and Vaticanus B. The Borgia and Mexica texts contain about 102 pictorial almanacs. The first image in the Fejérváry-Mayer summarizes the Mesoamerican Postclassic cosmos as a powerful chronotope (a spatiotemporal continuum). A central figure – Xiuhteuctli, who presided over the calendar – is surrounded by four cosmological trees, each representing a cardinal point, and each associated with a deity pair, a color, and a type of bird. Four locations in between each cardinal point are associated with year bearers. This map of cosmological space is intertwined with two separate iterations of the 260-day count.

During the Late Postclassic, the Mexica erected a sacred landscape in their capital, Mexico–Tenochtitlán. The most important structure in it was the Templo Mayor, a representation of a sacred mountain, which was composed of seven succeeding building stages tied with specific rulers, had two temples on its summit, and contained multiple iconographic references to the Mexica tutelary deity, Huitzilopochtli. The militaristic orientation of Mexica society called for a constant stream of captives who were taken during mock combats known as Flowery Wars or surrendered in quotas by neighboring states under Mexica rule. The public and massive sacrifice of these captives was believed to maintain the solar cycle. Mexica priests proclaimed that Tlalocan, a watery afterlife realm, was reserved for warriors who died in combat, women who died in childbirth, or those who died by drowning; all others went to Mictlan, the realm of the Lord of the Underworld. Mexica beliefs were depicted in a rich array of stone sculptures. Some of them, such as the Teocalli of the Holy War, refer to both former Mexica rulers and to Mexica deities; others, such as Tizocic's Stone, depict military victories over other Mesoamerican communities. An influential proposal groups Mexica deities into three broad domains – deities of creation; of war and sacrifice; and of fertility, agriculture, and water.

There were two important distinctions between the Mexica notion of *teotl* and that of a Greco-Roman deity: the former was embodied in public rituals linked to calendrical cycles by designated representatives; moreover, some Nahua foundational ancestors underwent a transformation from human to *teotl*. A *teotl* was closely linked to his or her *teixiptla*, a term etymologically related to corporeal representation: it may derive from *ix-*, "face, surface" and *xip-*, "peel, skin." In Mexica state rituals, a *teixiptla* designated both humans and objects that stood in for a sacred entity, particularly for deities in rituals performed at the end of 20-day periods in the 365-day count, such as Centeotl, Tezcatlipoca, Ilamateuctli, and Xipe Totec. The most celebrated deity substitute was Tezcatlipoca's *teixiptla*, who was worshipped as the embodiment of a sacred being associated with creative destruction, divination, and warfare for an entire 365-day period; at the end of this cycle, this *teixiptla* was sacrificed in public during the feast of Toxcatl. In colonial times, Nahua ritual specialists continued to embody deities through a sacred language known as *nahualtocaitl*.

Inca State Religion and the Regional Cosmology of Huarochirí

Among all the various religious traditions in the Andes, the best documented one before European contact is Inca religion, which was closely tied to state organization. Indeed, the very foundation of the Inca capital in Cuzco is presented as a mythohistorical narrative that explains both the birth of the state and the close relationship between history and sacred landscapes. According to the chronicler Garcilaso de la Vega (1943), the first Inca couple, Manco Capac and Mama Ocllo, left Lake Titicaca in a northward journey that brought them to the hill of Huanacauri, where Manco's staff penetrates the earth, signaling the place where a new state would be established. Another narrative recounts the emergence of the Ayar siblings from Pacariqtambo, "Inn of Dawn/Hiding," who travel the Andes and perform foundational feats. For instance, the female ancestor Mama Huaco slaughters one of the inhabitants of the Cuzco region, who leave so that the Inca may settle; and the male ancestor Ayar Uchu becomes a sacred rock, henceforth known as the *huaca* – or sacred physical manifestation – of Huanacauri.

Andean society was based on a social and kinship unit called *ayllu*, associated with a specific territory and a sacred landscape, which was further subdivided into *hanan* (upper) and *hurin* (lower) halves. Cuzco itself existed as a macro-ayllu of sorts, with six separate *panaca* (royal lineage groups) in Hanan Cuzco, and five in Hurin Cuzco. The epicenter of state religion in Cuzco was the Inti Cancha (Sun Temple). Pachacutic Inca Yupanqui, an Inca ruler who expanded the empire and reorganized state religion, renamed this enclosure as Cori Cancha (Gold Temple) and also rebuilt it. This temple contained a representation of Inti, with the creator deity Viracocha on his right and the lightning deity Chuqui Ylla on his left. From the Cori Cancha, forty-one imaginary lines, or *ceques*, radiated outward like the spokes of a wheel. These lines were associated with a total of about 340 important *huacas* located in and around the Cuzco Valley.

Inca religion overlay a broad array of regional cosmologies, some of which were centered on sacred pre-Incaic sites, such as those of Apurímac, Chinchaycamac, Catequil, or Mullipampa. Chief among these sites was the complex at Pachacamac, dedicated to the cult of the eponymous deity. This center, reputed for its oracular capacities, featured an elaborate series of dwellings and temples reserved exclusively for *aclla*, young women who were devoted to the cult of the Sun; some of them produced textiles that were later redistributed by the Inca ruler. Throughout the Andes, local cosmologies were anchored in the worship of *apos*, sacred beings whose earthly manifestations, such as objects or landscape features, were called *huacas*. As the Inca empire expanded its territory between the mid-fifteenth and the early sixteenth centuries, the Cuzco elites managed a state cult that focused on manifestations of the Sun and Lightning. In an attempt to manage local religion and to avoid potential rebellions, the principal *huacas* of conquered states were brought to Cuzco, where the Inca awarded them property and servants. The close relationship between religious and state authority was also emphasized by the public worship of mummified ancestors, which included former Inca rulers who continued to own property and to communicate and grant favors to the living through their representatives. Principal *huacas* were also consulted by Inca rulers, so they would assist them with political, military, and diplomatic matters.

In the Andes, various types of ritual specialists conducted propitiatory and divination practices. An important priest known as *huacapvillac* communicated with huacas; the *malquipvillac* spoke with mummified ancestors, while the *punchaopvillac* paid homage to the Sun and the *libiaopavillac* to lightning. During festivals, celebrants fasted and abstained from sexual intercourse, and also revealed their transgression to an *aucachic*. Priests in Cuzco provided auguries to city elites by performing a *callpa*, or the interpretation of signs found on the hearts of recently sacrificed camelids, and *hamurpa* specialists read the entrails of other animals. Just as the *socyac* divined by using maize grains, the *pacharicuc* made auguries based on how certain spiders, which were kept in human bones, fell onto the ground.

A colonial source written in a coastal variant of standardized Quechua, or *lengua general*, provides us with an unparalleled opportunity to learn about a regional Andean cosmology. This text, known as the Huarochirí manuscript, is a compilation of accounts about Andean deities, cosmological forces, and social groups. The manuscript is associated with the namesake valley region near the central Peruvian Andes of Central Peru. The work was composed in the early seventeenth century under the supervision of Francisco de Avila, a Jesuit who managed a long campaign to extirpate traditional Andean religious practices. The main author and scribe for these texts was Cristóbal Choque Casa, the son of an Andean chief local who collaborated with Avila in the uprooting of traditional religious practices.

This manuscript draws a distinction between two broad eras: the *ñaupa pacha*, or "ancient times," a period that includes most events recounted in the texts, and the Christian era. There are three periods marked by extraordinary events during the *ñaupa pacha*. The first one is presided over by Yana Ñamca and Tuta Ñamca, two *huacas* that are later defeated at the beginning of the second period by Huallallo Caruincho, an anthropophagous *huaca* who then claimed hegemony over the people of the region, ordering each household to bear two children, one for the family to keep and another for his nourishment. The second period ends with the appearance of Paria Caca, a powerful *huaca* composed of five brothers, who defeats Huallallo Caruincho and becomes the dominant *huaca* in the Huarochirí region. The birth of Paria Caca is a crucial event: it is said that he and his four brothers were born as five falcons from five eggs. Paria Caca has its female counterpart in Chaupi Ñamca, a similarly fivefold *huaca* integrated by Chaupi Ñamca and her four sisters. The third period begins with the arrival of the Spanish in Cajamarca and the subsequent demise of Paria Caca's cult. This demise is alluded to in a narrative in which Huayna Capac, the last Inca to complete his reign before the Spanish conquest, agrees to marry a Spanish woman through the intervention of the mischievous *huaca* Cuni Raya.

The Huarochirí manuscript at times records somewhat contradictory accounts regarding powerful Andean deities. For instance, it states that an ancient *huaca* called Cuni Raya existed before the creation of the world, and that Cuni Raya "gave shape to mountains, forests, rivers, animals, and agricultural fields." However, Cuni Raya is also portrayed in this work as a trickster figure who wears humble clothing. Among his deeds, he impregnates a female huaca without her knowledge and causes her to descend to the coast by the Pachacamac sanctuary, where she turns to stone. In some sections, this work designates this deity as Cuni Raya Viracocha. Salomon and Urioste suggest that this identification mirrored Ávila's interests, as he was intent on finding a supreme deity similar to the Christian god in the figure of Viracocha, a powerful deity worshipped throughout the Andes associated with the creation of the world and humankind.

Conclusion

Perhaps there are three viable generalizations regarding Amerindian religions in Mesoamerica and the Andes when European colonizers first confronted them in the sixteenth century. First, in contrast with Christianity and other world religions, there may not have been a strong demarcation between a realm associated exclusively with religion and the sacred and a realm associated with civic practice, sociopolitical organization, and non-sacred history and social memory. Second, an individual's identity as a believer or practitioner was not based on the acceptance or rejection of a core set of beliefs about the cosmos. Therefore, two defining features of Christianity – the punishment of heresy and proselytization activities directed toward recruiting new believers – were epistemological impossibilities.

Third, and perhaps most importantly, local and state cosmologies were deeply rooted in the history and organization of autonomous territorial and social units. In the two or three centuries prior to the Spanish conquest, Mesoamerican and Andean polities were defined as entities by one or more traditional lineages, land-holding rights, and the public worship of local deities and the celebration of holidays tied to one or more calendars. Each community had one or more hereditary rulers, and most were part of a highly structured and often modular political unit that possessed a clearly demarcated territory and a shared set of ancestors. The Nahua version of this unit, called *altepetl*, may be regarded as a unit comparable to the Andean *ayllu*, even if the latter had a stronger tendency to privilege modular subunits. In both cases, a set of relations linked a historically constituted community with an often exclusive set of deities and ancestors. Hence, individuals were born into a set of naturalized relations with deities and local landscape features, were regarded as members of a particular *ayllu* or *altepetl* since birth, and held numerous responsibilities and rights in their polity of residence. As mediators, ritual specialists played a crucial role in the economy of ritual exchange. Rulers and priests provided for the well-being of the community through the performance of collective or state ritual practices, and specialists performed ceremonies marking transitions in the socialization of individuals and addressed illnesses, misfortunes, and interpersonal conflict.

Bibliography and Suggested Readings

Arriaga, Pablo José de. *Extirpación de la idolatría del Perú*. Madrid: Biblioteca de Autores Españoles, 1968 [1621].

Aveni, Anthony. *Skywatchers of Ancient Mexico*. Austin: University of Texas Press, 1980.

Bauer, Brian. *The Sacred Landscape of the Inca: The Cusco Ceque System*. Austin: University of Texas Press, 2010.

Berdan, Frances F., Richard E. Blanton, Elizabeth Hill Boone, Mary G. Hodge, Michael E. Smith, and Emily Umberger. *Aztec Imperial Strategies*. Washington, DC: Dumbarton Oaks Research Library and Collection, 1996.

Boone, Elizabeth. *Cycles of Time and Meaning in the Mexican Books of Fate*. Austin: University of Texas Press, 2007.

Cabello de Valboa, Miguel. *Miscelánea antártica*. Lima: Universidad Nacional Mayor de San Marcos, 1951 [1586].

Carrasco, Davíd. *City of Sacrifice: The Aztec Empire and the Role of Violence in Civilization*. Boston: The Beacon Press, 2000.

Caso, Alfonso. "La correlación de los años azteca y cristiano." *Revista Mexicana de Estudios Antropológicos* 3 (1939): 11–45.

Cobo, Bernabé. *History of the Inca Empire*. Austin: University of Texas Press, 1979.

Duviols, Pierre. *Proceso y visitas de idolatrías. Cajatambo, siglo XVII*. Lima: Pontificia Universidad Católica del Perú, 2003.

Garcilaso de la Vega, Inca. *Comentarios reales de los Incas*. Buenos Aires: Emecé, 1943 [1609].

Hendon, Julia, and Rosemary Joyce, eds. *Mesoamerican Archaeology*. New York: Wiley-Blackwell, 2004.

Houston, Stephen, and Takeshi Inomata. *The Classic Maya*. New York: Cambridge University Press, 2009.

Hvidtfeldt, Arild. *Teotl and Ixiptlatli: Central Conceptions in Ancient Mexican Religion*. Copenhagen: Munksgaard, 1958.

Joyce, Arthur. "Sacred Space and Social Relations in the Valley of Oaxaca." In Julia Hendon and Rosemary Joyce (eds.),*Mesoamerican Archaeology*, 192–216. New York: Wiley-Blackwell, 2004.

Justeson, John, and David Tavárez. "The Correlation of the Colonial Northern Zapotec Calendar with European Chronology." In Clive Ruggles and Gary Urton (eds.), *Cultural Astronomy in New World Cosmologies: Essays in Honor of Anthony Aveni*, 19–96. Niwot: University of Colorado Press, 2007.

Kirchhoff, Paul, Lina Odena Güemes, and Luis Reyes García. *Historia tolteca-chichimeca*. México: Centro de Investigaciones y Estudios en Antropología Social, Fondo de Cultura Económica, 1989.

Kowalski, Jeff, and Cynthia Kristan-Graham, eds. *Twin Tollans: Chichén Itzá, Tula, and the Epiclassic to Early Postclassic Mesoamerican World*. Washington, DC: Dumbarton Oaks Research Library & Collection, 2007.

López Austin, Alfredo, and Leonardo López Luján. *Monte Sagrado-Templo Mayor: El cerro y la pirámide en la tradición religiosa mesoamericana*. México: Universidad Nacional Autónoma de México, 2009.

MacCormack, Sabine. *Religion in the Andes: Vision and Imagination in Early Colonial Peru*. Princeton, NJ: Princeton University Press, 1991.

Manzanilla, Linda. "Corporate Groups and Domestic Activities at Teotihuacan." *Latin American Antiquity* 7, no. 3 (1996): 228–246.

——— "Houses and Ancestors, Altars and Relics: Mortuary Patterns at Teotihuacan, Central Mexico." *Archeological Papers of the American Anthropological Association* 11, no. 1 (2002): 55–65.

Marcus, Joyce, and Kent V. Flannery. *Zapotec Civilization*. London: Thames and Hudson, 1996.

Milbrath, Susan. *Star Gods of the Maya: Astronomy in Art, Folklore, and Calendars*. Austin: University of Texas Press, 1999.

Miller, Mary Ellen. *The Art of Mesoamerica*. New York: Thames and Hudson, 2006.

Nicholson, Henry B. "Religion in Pre-Hispanic Central Mexico." *Handbook of Middle American Indians*, 10 (1971): 395–446.

Oudijk, Michel. *Historiography of the Be`niza`a: The Postclassic and Early Colonial Periods (1000–1600 A.D.)*. Leiden, Germany: CNWS Publications, 2000.

Pasztory, Esther. *Teotihuacan: An Experiment in Living*. Norman: University of Oklahoma Press, 1997.

Paxton, Merideth. *The Cosmos of the Yucatec Maya: Cycles and Steps from the Madrid Codex*. Albuquerque: University of New Mexico Press, 2001.

Rice, Prudence M. *Maya Political Science: Time, Astronomy, and the Cosmos*. Austin: University of Texas Press, 2004.

Rostworowski de Diez Canseco, María. *History of the Inca Realm*. Cambridge: Cambridge University Press, 1999.

Ruiz de Alarcón, Hernando. *Treatise on the Heathen Institutions that Today Live Among the Indians Native to this New Spain*. Trans. and ed. J. Richard Andrews and Ross Hassig. Norman: University of Oklahoma Press, 1984.

Sahagún, Bernardino de. *The Florentine Codex: General History of the Things of New Spain*. Books 1–12, 13 vols. Trans. and ed. Arthur J. O. Anderson and Charles E. Dibble. Salt Lake City: University of Utah Press, 1950–1982.

Breve compendio de los ritos idolátricos que los indios de esta Nueva España usaban en tiempo de su infidelidad. México: Lince Editores, 1990.

Salomon, Frank and George Urioste. *The Huarochirí Manuscript: A Testament of Ancient and Colonial Andean Religion*. Austin: University of Texas Press, 1991.

Serna, Jacinto de la. *Manual de Ministros de Indios para el conocimiento de sus idolatrías y extirpación de ellas*. Anales del Museo Nacional de México (Primera época) 6: 261–475, 1892.

Silverblatt, Irene. *Moon, Sun, and Witches: Gender Ideologies and Class in Inca and Colonial Peru*. Princeton, NJ: Princeton University Press, 1987.

Smith-Stark, Thomas. "Dioses, sacerdotes, y sacrificio—una mirada a la religion zapoteca a través del Vocabulario en lengua Çapoteca (1578) de Juan de Cordova." In *La religión de los Binnigula'sa'*, ed. Víctor de la Cruz and Marcus Winter, 89–195. Oaxaca: Instituto Estatal de Educación Pública de Oaxaca, 1999.

Sugiyama, Saburo. "Governance and Polity at Classic Teotihuacan." In Julia Hendon and Rosemary Joyce (eds.), *Mesoamerican Archaeology*, 97–123. New York: Wiley-Blackwell, 2004.

Taube, Karl. "Aztec Religion: Creation, Sacrifice, and Renewal." In Felipe Solís (ed.), *The Aztec Empire*, 169–177. New York: The Solomon Guggenheim Museum, 2004.

Taylor, Gerald. *Ritos y tradiciones de Huarochirí*. Lima: Instituto de Estudios Peruanos – Instituto Francés de Estudios Andinos, 1987.

Tavárez, David. *The Invisible War: Indigenous Devotions, Discipline, and Dissent in Colonial Mexico*. Stanford: Stanford University Press, 2011.

Tena, Rafael. *El calendario mexica y la cronografía*. México: Instituto Nacional de Antropología e Historia, 1987.

Urcid, Javier. *Zapotec Hieroglyphic Writing*. Studies in Pre-Columbian Art & Archaeology, Washington, DC: Dumbarton Oaks Research Library and Collection, 2001.

Urton, Gary. *The History of a Myth: Pacariqtambo and the Origin of the Inkas*. Austin: University of Texas Press, 1990.

Zuidema, R. Thomas. *The Ceque System of Cuzco*. Leyden: E. J. Brill, 1964.

3

Religion in the Pre-Contact Old World: Europe

CARLOS M. N. EIRE

Late Medieval Europe: An Age of Faith?

In 1492, European civilization was deeply religious. To say this or to assert that this was "an age of faith" – a generalization made by many a history textbook – is not to say that Europeans were necessarily pious, or that they lived up to their ideals, or that they understood or believed the doctrines professed by their Church. Religion was simply there. It was as unavoidable as the air everyone breathed or the words they spoke. In many ways, religion functioned as a language of sorts in premodern Europe: it was a means of making all human interaction intelligible according to a certain set values, a means of making sense of life and of imposing a certain sense of order on the world.

Experts on European religion agree on one issue: religious devotion increased during the fifteenth century. Definitely the evidence is overwhelming. But this is where agreement ends. Some historians tend to see this increased fervor as hollow and anxious and ripe for reform[1]; others see it as robust and satisfying.[2] Some perceive the clergy and their flocks as sharing a common piety[3]; others detect a great gulf between them.[4] Where some discern genuine Christian fervor, others find far too many surviving pre-Christian elements. Some have gone as far as to argue that much of late Medieval religion was "magical,"[5] while

---

1 Johan Huizinga, *The Autumn of the Middle Ages* (Chicago: University of Chicago Press, 1980); Bernd Moeller, *Imperial Cities and the Reformation* (Philadelphia: Fortress Press, 1972); Steven Ozment, *The Reformation in the Cities* (New Haven, CT: Yale University Press, 1975).
2 Eamon Duffy, *The Stripping of the Altars* (New Haven, CT: Yale University Press, 1992); John Bossy, *Christianity in the West, 1400–1700* (New York: Oxford University Press, 1985).
3 William Christian, *Local Religion in Sixteenth Century Spain* (Princeton, NJ: Princeton University Press, 1981).
4 Carlo Ginzburg, *The Cheese and the Worms* (Baltimore: Johns Hopkins University Press, 1980); Philippe Ariès, *The Hour of Our Death* (New York: Knopf, 1981).
5 Keith Thomas, *Religion and the Decline of Magic* (London: Widenfeld and Nicolson, 1971).

others propose that Europe was not truly "Christianized" until the sixteenth century.[6] Whether religious life at that time was sincere or hollow, vibrant or anxious, nearly pagan or truly Christian is beside the point, however. All experts seem to agree: religion was an integral part of life at the turn of the fifteenth century, and Western Europeans were investing much of their time, energy, and resources into it.

But what was this religion like?

The religion shared officially by all Western European Christians was one that sought to establish links between heaven and earth, sacred and profane, soul and body, the divine and the human, and also between neighbors. Religion was more practical than theoretical: though informed by the theology of the Church, it was not focused as much on thinking about beliefs, or on myth, as on rituals, symbols, and ethics. Behavior was the stuff of religion, and the body and its five senses were strongly involved in the central Christian promise of redemption. The world was continually in the process of being sacralized, that is, of being brought into contact with the divine. This sacralization of the world took place in multiple interlocking spheres of behavior, all of which were seamlessly woven into the fabric of daily life, reflecting a broad spectrum of attitudes, from the most reverent to the most disrespectful. In other words, it was a sacralization ever in the making, ever fleeting and furtive, never complete, never totally pure.

Social Structures

Though there were many local variants, all of late Medieval Western Christendom shared some fundamental traits in regard to basic social structures. One way of understanding Medieval society is to see it as divided into three classes: those who fought (the nobility), those who labored (farmers, artisans, and merchants), and those who prayed (the clergy).[7] An even more basic division, as far as religion is concerned, reduces Medieval society to just two classes: the clergy and the laity.[8]

---

6 Jean Delumeau, *Catholicism between Luther and Voltaire* (London: Burns and Oates, 1971).
7 Georges Duby, *The Three Orders: Feudal Society Imagined* (Chicago: University of Chicago Press, 1980).
8 The Latin *clericus* is derived from the Greek, *klerikos*, meaning 'of or pertaining to an inheritance' In the case of Christians, an obvious reference to the authority that their leaders claimed to have directly from Christ and his twelve apostles. Any Christian who was not a cleric came to be known as a lay person, or collectively, as the laity, a term that reveals its utter simplicity in its Greek origin, *laos*, or *laikos*, "the people."

The distinction between clerical and lay, though somewhat blurry and controversial at times, dominated much of religious life, in theory as well as in practice. Those with spiritual authority were known as *the clergy*. In the practice of religion, the clergy were the professionals – a truism confirmed by the fact that clerics were known as *religiosi*, that is, the religious. They were the interpreters of its beliefs, the ministers of its rituals, the guardians of its symbols, the custodians of its ethics. In theory, they were *in* the world, but not *of* the world. They were the gatekeepers of the afterlife, shepherding most souls to their ultimate destiny in heaven via a stint in purgatory, that antechamber to heaven where sins were gradually cleansed. Those who went straight to hell, of course, could blame only themselves for their gross moral failure, not the clergy. Since the twelfth century the terms "temporal" or "secular" had come to denote anything that was mired in earthly time, anything not Churchly, or beneath the ostensible dignity of the clergy: that is, anything not spiritual, or sacred, or concerned with eternity.

Nonetheless, as much as the clergy tried to distinguish between sacred and secular, or to lay claim to power or privilege in the name of God, the line between the two realms could not ever be drawn very clearly – given the way that religion suffused all aspects of life – and it often led to conflicts between "the Church" and "the world," that is, between the clergy and lay rulers. Though it is certainly appropriate to speak of "the Church" as a single entity within Medieval Christendom, and also to speak of "the clergy," the fact remains that this Church was no monolithic institution, but rather a dizzying assemblage of units managed by clerics with overlapping and sometimes conflicting authority – clerics who were sometimes very "worldly" or even corrupt. In the long run, given the somewhat bewildering organization of the Church, which was the result of fifteen centuries of tradition and haphazard development, it could be argued that Christendom was bound together more effectively through the piety of the Church than through its authority structure.

Late Medieval Piety

Sacred Rites

The rites of the Church known as "sacraments," which were administered by its priests, were the basic structure of piety and the framework for devotion. Sacraments were those rituals considered to be most important: literally, according to the ancient Latin meaning, a *sacramentum* was a seal on a contract. In this case, the contract affirmed through ritual was nothing less than

God's saving covenant with the human race. Simply put, sacraments were the most essential rituals: no sacraments, no salvation. Though early Medieval theologians did not always agree on what rites should be considered sacraments, by the thirteenth century, the Roman Catholic Church had defined the sacraments clearly and set their number at seven. In 1439, these seven sacraments were proclaimed as official dogma: baptism, confirmation, penance, the Eucharist, marriage, ordination as a cleric, and extreme unction administered to the dying. These rites served specific functions for each individual and the community as a whole: initiation (baptism), purification and sanctification (penance), transitions in life (confirmation, marriage, ordination, extreme unction), and communion with the divine (the Eucharist).

The Eucharist was the most densely encoded Catholic ritual and the centerpiece of all piety. The celebration of this sacrament took place within the ritual commonly called "the mass," during which, according to the teaching of the Church, bread and wine were miraculously transformed into the body and blood of Christ, and offered for consumption by the faithful. Though the laity attended mass regularly, especially on Sundays and feast days, to pray and witness the consecration of the bread and wine, very few people actually partook of the physical communion with God offered to them in this sacrament.

Though lay communion was rare, the mass still played a pivotal role in piety: it brought communities together for prayer, instruction, and celebration more often than any other ritual. As the ultimate ritual in which the divine was addressed and made present, the mass also acquired a therapeutic value. So-called "votive" masses could be offered to ward off or correct as many ills as can befall the human race: to protect crops from hail, to be spared from plagues, to prevent evil thoughts or lust, and even to help find lost objects. The mass also loomed large for yet another reason. Because every mass was believed to transcend time and space, and to link all Christians, past and present, to Christ's sacrifice on the cross, this ritual also assumed specific spiritual and social functions connecting the living and the dead. In the spiritual realm, masses for the dead ostensibly shortened the time spent in purgatory by the souls of the deceased. In practical terms, these masses functioned on various levels to cement relations among kin and neighbors. An immensely appealing balm to troubled consciences, masses for the dead became a key element of European piety by the end of the fifteenth century.

Within and beyond the ritual of the mass, the consecrated bread also became a focus of devotion. Because the Church taught that Christ was made physically present in the Eucharistic bread and wine, the mass itself, and the consecrated bread especially, became the supreme *locus divinitatis*, the ultimate materialization of the divine. If each consecrated bread wafer was indeed God, then devotion to this object, called a "host" (Latin: *hostia* = sacrificial victim), seemed right and just. Consecrated hosts were displayed for adoration in special vessels known as *monstrances*, which could be set up inside the churches or taken out for processions. In the fifteenth century the yearly feast devoted to the Eucharist, *Corpus Christi*, or *Domini*, which had been established in 1264, assumed an especially privileged place on the Christian calendar. This summer feast was observed in towns and cities with pageants, mystery plays, and grand processions that involved the whole community, especially its elites.

Piety was significantly affected by the fact that all of this sacramental ritual was conducted in Latin throughout Western Europe, from Portugal to Poland and from Sicily to Iceland. This uniformity in the language of ritual made the Church more universal and bound together a vast array of disparate cultures. The Latin language assumed a sacred and mystical quality – an attribute that constantly made manifest the different identities of the clergy and the laity.

Sacred Space

Though the sacred and profane were deeply intertwined in late Medieval religion, one of the most salient traits of Medieval piety was its keen fixation on specific earthly points that were considered closer to heaven. Consequently, much of religious life revolved around the processes of identifying, confirming, approaching, and venerating those special links between heaven and earth, and of seeking to tap their supernatural power. In brief, piety was strongly inclined to localize the divine, make it tangible, and harness its power.

The most basic spatial distinction was that between sacred and mundane space. Churches were the most obvious and most numerous sacred sites. Every church was the house of God, and a nexus between heaven and earth, principally because God made Himself present in all his houses through the celebration of the Eucharist. But not all churches were equally prominent. Divine power was believed to reside more strongly in churches where certain saints and martyrs were buried, or where divine apparitions and visions had taken place, or in churches that enshrined certain relics or sacred objects. These shrines, revered for their miraculous powers, could draw worshipers from near and far. The promise of healings – most often physical rather than spiritual – made the map of Europe bristle with urban and rural shrines.

Saints' graves and their relics were also singularly sacred and powerful. Relics were the physical traces of human beings who had died and gone to heaven; as such, they localized the heavenly and divine. By the fifteenth century, the cult of relics was deeply woven into the fabric of piety and thriving. But for every genuine relic, there seemed to be many of doubtful origin. Remnants of the true cross of Christ could be found nearly everywhere; the head of John the Baptist was revered in at least seven different shrines; fragments and entire bodies of the apostles were claimed simultaneously in unlikely places.

In addition to relics, churches also contained sacred paintings and statues, and piety was intensely focused on these objects. Sacred images were visual representations of the holy: like relics, they localized and made present the divine. Images were not just the *libri pauperum*, or books of the poor and illiterate, as some of the clergy taught, they were also the focus of veneration. Though the official theology of the Church distinguished between the worship offered to God alone (*latria*) and the reverence (*dulia*) shown to images, this distinction was ambiguously understood and observed in piety. People knelt and bowed as they prayed before images, burned candles and incense, or offered flowers to them, for they were approached as points of contact with heaven.

Ritual had a place outdoors too, as did symbols. Pilgrimages were a way of sanctifying space: the very process of traveling to a holy site was both a means of devotion and a sacralizing gesture. Pilgrimages could cover short distances, to a local shrine, or incredibly long ones to a more distant holy place, such as the Holy Land. These trips were undertaken for all sorts of reasons, and especially as a means of fulfilling vows or atoning for sins, but as anyone who has read *The Canterbury Tales* knows, pilgrims were not necessarily devout and pilgrimages could be anything but an act of genuine penance.

The other most common type of outdoor ritual was the procession, especially in those parts of Christendom where the climate was more favorable. Processions usually took place during feast days, or on special occasions, and were believed to sanctify mundane space temporarily. On a social level, pilgrimages and processions were a means of forging group identity, as well as of confirming or establishing the rank and status of the participants.

Sacred Time

If space was a grid upon which sacred spaces could be plotted, so, too, was time itself, for heaven and earth were believed to intersect differently at specific times. Medieval piety had a rhythmic quality – an endlessly cyclical oscillation between feasting and fasting that was determined by the calendar.

The shortest cycle was the week, which marked off Sunday as a sacred day, a holy time when attendance at mass was required and all work should cease. Feasts that marked certain events in salvation history were observed universally by all the faithful. Among these were Epiphany, Good Friday, Easter,

Pentecost, and Christmas. Other major feasts such as Corpus Christi and All Saints' Day were also universally observed. Saints were honored on the anniversary of their deaths, according to the Church calendar, and the observance of these feast days varied from place to place. Feasts were marked by the celebration of special masses, processions, and public celebrations. Evidence suggests that religious feasts could often turn into riotous self-indulgent occasions in which lines dissolved between the sacred and profane.

In addition to Sundays and feast days, the liturgical calendar also marked off certain seasons. The Christmas season, which celebrated the birth of Jesus, and the Easter season, which celebrated his resurrection, were both marked by joyous celebrations. But each of these two major feasts came at the end of long periods in which fasting was required: the four weeks of Advent in December and the forty days of Lent in late winter/early spring. Fasting was considered a penitential exercise that helped tame carnal instincts. It was also a penitential act that helped atone for sins and that helped soften God's wrath in times of plague, war, and famine.

Feasting and fasting were a perpetual rhythm of piety, often well-balanced, but sometimes discordant and prone to extreme swings in mood and behavior. Throughout much of Europe, for instance, the penitential season of Lent was preceded by days or weeks of feasting, a time known as Carnival, which was not officially on the Church calendar. Carnival was a celebration of indulgence in food, drink, and sex: it was the mirror inversion of Lent and a paradoxical constant in piety.

Sacred Bonds

Social relations, too, were sacralized to a considerable extent, and in myriad ways. Nearly every aspect of communal life involved some sort of ritual; nearly every relation, bond, and association required sanctification. Dealings with one's king, magistrate, and neighbor were formally framed in religious terms. For instance, monarchs and other civil rulers were installed in their offices and granted authority through religious ceremonies. Some monarchs, such as the kings of France and England, claimed that their consecration imbued them with sacrality and even gave them healing powers; before the thirteenth century, some theologians even thought of the consecration of rulers as a sacrament.[9] Initiating craftsmen into guilds, closing contracts, signing pacts and treaties, writing last wills and testaments, or testifying in court were

---

9 Ernst Kantorowicz, *The King's Two Bodies* (Princeton, NJ: Princeton University Press, 1957).

all routine social interactions that required some ritual act, though not necessarily the presence of the clergy.

Reified through ritual, the religious bonds of community could also transcend time and space, for the sacred rites that linked Christians over vast distances and across frontiers also linked them across the ages to the dead. Consequently, a distinctive feature of late Medieval piety was the commerce between those on earth and those in the afterlife. The saints in heaven were sought out as patrons and intercessors; and the souls in purgatory were showered with attention.

Communities and individuals established patron/client relationships with the saints, and their association could take on a distinctively transactional quality. The laity routinely sought favors from patrons by means of pledges, or vows, which usually involved the performing of some act of reverence if the favor was granted. Many local celebrations of saints' feasts were, in fact, established through vows that had been made in times of distress, such as droughts and plagues.

As the cult of the saints expanded, so did the patronage system whereby each saint was assigned special spheres of influence over particular social groups and specific needs. The most popular saint of all was the Virgin Mary, Mother of God and Queen of Heaven, who was considered the most effective advocate. Paradoxically, Mary was the most universal saint, revered everywhere, but also the most local, for she was often assigned a regional persona, especially at shrines where miraculous images were venerated, where she was known as "Our Lady *of* ... (place name)," such as at Montserrat in Catalonia, or Chartres in France, or Walsingham in England, or, eventually, Guadalupe in Mexico.

Among the living, the bonds of Christian fellowship were further enhanced through baptism, which required that every infant have godparents, who were not necessarily blood relations. Bonds were also strengthened by the formation of associations known as confraternities (also called brotherhoods, guilds, or sodalities). Confraternities could include both men and women, and sometimes children. Membership was voluntary, and each confraternity usually devoted itself to a narrow range of devotional activities. Their objectives varied widely, but always involved the fulfillment of both spiritual and physical needs.

On the spiritual side, fellowship and communal prayer were a large part of confraternity life, as were processions and the establishment of chapels and shrines. On the physical side, most confraternities were involved in charitable work. Confraternities could specialize in caring for the sick, meeting the needs of the poor and homeless, or burying the dead. Confraternities were not only the living conscience of Christian Europe, but also its sturdiest social safety net. Until the sixteenth century, in much of Europe, the poor, ill, and needy were often assisted by confraternities rather than the clergy or civil authorities. Membership in a confraternity ensured one of fellowship and assistance, as well as of the spiritual merits earned by acts of charity and devotion. In a clerically dominated society, it may have also offered the laity an opportunity to take the initiative and to express a relative degree spiritual independence. At the same time, confraternities also met mundane social needs related to identity and status.

Sacred Behavior

Religion meant much more than attendance at public rituals or the profession of certain beliefs: it involved *doing* certain things and *avoiding* others in two spheres of behavior: private devotion and ethics. Private devotion consisted primarily of the recitation of prayers and of reading. The prayer life of the laity consisted mainly of the repetition of short orations, which were memorized in childhood, especially the *Pater Noster* (Our Father, or Lord's Prayer), the *Ave Maria* (Hail Mary), the *Gloria* (Glory Be), and the *Credo* (I Believe, or Creed), and a few others. On the whole, then, prayers tended to be fixed formulae, repeatedly recited over an entire lifetime. Number and repetition were key. One of the more popular devotions among the laity was the rosary: a ring of beads arranged as numerical sets that marked a specific number of "Ave Marias," "Pater Nosters," and "Glorias." Extemporaneous prayer was possible, but uncommon among the laity. The literate laity had access to a wider range of prayers in books known as primers or books of hours, which contained biblical readings, psalms, hymns, and prayers. These books did not encourage improvisation in prayer; on the contrary, the fixed texts of the prayers themselves were held to have a power of their own, and their efficacy depended on a literal recitation and on frequent repetition.

The invention of the printing press and the expansion of literacy increased devotional reading among the laity considerably after 1455, as devotional treatises and lives of the saints were reproduced in the thousands, instantly. Devotional texts could be practical manuals, such as the *Ars Moriendi*, or *Art of Dying* (fifteenth century), which helped the laity prepare for a good death, and *Imitatio Christi*, *The Imitation of Christ*, by Thomas à Kempis (fifteenth century), an immensely popular text, which introduced self-denying models of behavior and meditation to the laity.

Ethics, or morality, was another essential component of piety: in fact, much of religion had a legalistic focus and involved actions rather than thoughts. Avoiding sin and practicing virtue were crucial, for sins made one deserve punishment, both in this life and the next; virtue, of course, was the key to eternal bliss. Much of life was carefully codified, and much of religion revolved around what one should or should not do, what was permissible or forbidden. Sermons and devotional literature tended to promote the imitation of self-denying role models as the surest road to salvation. Asceticism, or self-denial, was not reserved for monks and nuns alone: fasting, sexual abstinence, and self-control were required of the laity too, though on a lesser scale.

Sacred Contention: Distinguishing Truth from Error

Though lay piety was symbiotically related to the theology, worship, and ethics of the Church, and even shaped them to some extent, it also often tested or crossed the boundaries of what was deemed proper by the clergy. As a rule, the further that lay piety sought to distance itself from the clergy, the more likely it was that it would be condemned. One area of constant tension between the clergy and the laity was the interpretation of ritual and its adaptation to purposes that could be deemed "magical" or "superstitious," such as scattering consecrated hosts on the ground to ensure a good harvest, or insisting that certain votive masses be celebrated with a specific number of candles. Contention over such issues was not inevitable in all cases, however, for the clergy themselves could also share the same attitudes and behavior, and even promote them, as in the cases of priests who performed the rites of exorcism on swarms of locusts, seeking to drive away the demons that supposedly possessed them.

Exorcisms and other rites aimed against the devil were an integral part of piety because both the clergy and the laity believed that evil was personified in spiritual entities who had some degree of control over the material world, and who could wreak havoc on the human race. Demons lurked everywhere, causing harm and constantly tempting humans to sin; even worse, demons attracted veneration in exchange for magical or miraculous favors. Such beliefs had become so closely intertwined in the Middle Ages as to make the boundaries with the demonic one of the most troublesome in Medieval piety, especially when it came to many ancestral folk customs, which could easily be labeled as "demonic" by the clergy.

The spiritual world was not just full of demons in Medieval piety, but also with good spirits who sometimes communicated with the human race. Apparitions of Christ, Mary, the angels, and saints were frequently reported, not just by monks and nuns, but also by lay people. These extraordinary religious experiences on the part of the laity helped give shape to piety, but also sometimes gave rise to friction with the clergy. Lay visionaries who claimed to see Christ, Mary, or some saint or angel could give rise to cults and shrines, but not without the clergy's endorsement. The same was true of clerics who reported visions too. Winning approval could be a difficult and divisive process, principally because distinguishing between the demonic and the divine was not always easy, as proven by the case of the peasant visionary Joan of Arc. Though she was burnt as a heretic and a witch in 1431, with the backing of the bishop of Beauvais and the University of Paris, Joan was declared innocent by Pope Callistus III in 1456, and eventually canonized as a saint in 1920.

Beyond the confines of Christian ritual, lay people and even clerics could also engage in many practices that could be considered of pre-Christian origin, and which the higher clergy judged as heathenish or demonic. Magic, necromancy, and witchcraft abounded in Europe well into the early modern period, always impinging upon and even becoming the focus of piety at all levels of society. Medieval piety could be so fluid, and so prone to admixture with elements that could be deemed non-Christian, that scholars such as Erasmus of Rotterdam (1469–1536) could openly criticize much of the piety of his day as a continuation of paganism – an accusation that would be echoed by every Protestant reformer.

Conclusion

When the Spanish began to conquer and settle the New World they brought with them an immensely complex religious life, and they could not help but interpret the religion of the natives they encountered according to a mentality shaped by their own Catholicism, and especially by distinctions between "true" and "false" symbols and rituals or between genuine religion and "superstition," or "idolatry." Ironically, at the very same time that the Spanish were judging the religions of Native Americans as false and idolatrous, Protestant Christians were rejecting Catholicism itself on exactly the same terms back in Europe. Take, for instance, what the Protestant reformer John Calvin had to say about the religion of his childhood, which he rejected and fought against. Calvin was born in 1509, in northern France, when Western Europe was still wholly Catholic: "I remember what I saw them do to images in our parish when I was a small boy," he testified, shaking a rhetorical finger in disgust. What he saw was this: on feast days, the ignorant folk of his native Noyon would decorate all of the images, bedecking them with flowers and lighting candles beneath them. Their devotion was so blind, and so wrong, said Calvin, that they even did this to figures of the devil.[10] As he summed it up, Medieval Catholicism was nothing but an "abominable sacrilege and Babylonish pollution."[11] He went as far as to argue that his fellow Frenchmen should flee from their native land and shake the dust from their feet, for, as he put it, "any country where the worship of God is abolished and his religion is annihilated well deserves to be regarded as foreign and profane."[12]

If one compares what Calvin has to say about Medieval Catholic piety with what the Spanish *conquistadores* said at just about the same time about Aztec religiosity, it is impossible *not* to spot many similarities.[13] In both cases, the religion of "the Other" was viewed with revulsion, as demonic and dehumanizing. In and of itself, this similarity may not seem very remarkable, as it is common enough for one culture to demonize another. But one must pause and consider that in Calvin's case "the Other" were his own people, his kin, his parents, his own past self, and that the sacrifice that made him recoil in horror was that of the mass, not that in which blood-stained priests tore out the beating hearts of their victims.

How could this happen? How was it that a European baptized into the Catholic Church as an infant and reared in a totally Catholic culture could come to see his own religion as that of "the Other," and as an absolute evil? This is a question that has no easy answer, but, in and of itself, speaks volumes about the complexities of religious life in Europe at the time of the encounter with the New World.

Bibliography and Suggested Readings

Ariès, Philippe. *The Hour of Our Death*. New York: Knopf, 1981.
Bossy, John. *Christianity in the West, 1400–1700*. New York: Oxford University Press, 1985.
Brown, Peter. *The Cult of the Saints*. Chicago: University of Chicago Press, 1981.
Calvin, John. *Inventory of Relics*. In *Ioannis Calvini opera quae supersunt omnia*, 59 vols. Braunschweig: Schwetschke, 1863–1900.

---

10 John Calvin, *Advertissement tresutile* (Inventory of Relics), *Ioannis Calvini opera quae supersunt omnia*, 59 vols. (Braunschweig: C.A. Schwetschke, 1863–1900), vol. 6, 452 (Hereafter cited as OC.)
11 John Calvin, *De fugiendis impiorum illicitis sacris* (On Shunning the Rites of the Ungodly), OC vol. 5, 239.
12 John Calvin, *Quatre sermons de M. Iehan Calvin traictans des matières fort utiles pour nostre temps: Quatrieme Sermon* (Fourth Sermon), OC vol. 8, 437.
13 Bernal Diaz del Castillo, *The Discovery and Conquest of Mexico, 1517–1521* (Oxford: Routledge Cruzon, 2005), 50, 161–163, 225, 256, 309, 467.

Cameron, Euan. *Enchanted Europe: Superstition, Reason, and Religion, 1250–1750*, New York: Oxford University Press, 2011.

Chatellier, Louis. *The Europe of the Devout*. New York: Cambridge University Press, 1989.

Christian, William. *Local Religion in Sixteenth Century Spain*. Princeton, NJ: Princeton University Press, 1981.

Clark, Stuart. *Thinking with Demons*. Oxford: Clarendon Press, 1997.

Delumeau, Jean. *Catholicism between Luther and Voltaire*. London: Burns and Oates, 1971.

Duby, Georges. *The Three Orders: Feudal Society Imagined*. Chicago: University of Chicago Press, 1980.

Duffy, Eamon. *The Stripping of the Altars*. New Haven, CT: Yale University Press, 1992.

Ginzburg, Carlo. *The Cheese and the Worms*. Baltimore: Johns Hopkins University Press, 1980.

Huizinga, Johan. *The Autumn of the Middle Ages*, Chicago: University of Chicago Press, 1996.

Kantorowicz, Ernst. *The King's Two Bodies: A Study in Mediaeval Political Theology*. Princeton, NJ: Princeton University Press, 1957.

Keitt, Andrew. *Inventing the Sacred*. Leiden: Brill, 2005.

Moeller, Bernd. *Imperial Cities and the Reformation*. Philadelphia: Fortress Press, 1972.

Ozment, Steven. *The Reformation in the Cities*. New Haven, CT: Yale University Press, 1975.

Strocchia, Sharon. *Death and ritual in Renaissance Florence*. Baltimore: Johns Hopkins University Press, 1992.

Thomas, Keith. *Religion and the Decline of Magic*. London: Widenfeld and Nicolson, 1971.

4
Religion in the Pre-Contact Old World: Africa

ASONZEH UKAH

John Mbiti begins his now classic textbook *African Religions and Philosophy* by stating what many would consider a truism: "Africans are notoriously religious, and each people have its own religious system with a set of beliefs and practices. Religion permeates into all departments of life so fully that it is not easy or possible always to isolate it."[1] Sub-Saharan Africa before European intrusion was made up of well-established, vibrant societies and cultures, different kingdoms of varying sizes and sophistication, rich in civilization, the arts, law, and religious traditions. For example, the Benin Kingdom in the seventeenth century was characterized by a highly stable and effective administrative structure headed by the *Oba* (King); extensive and complex commercial network; legal codes; and a highly evolved civilization that generated unparalleled works of art, many of which had ritual significance. Many of the religiously and ritually inspired artistic productions were taken away by the first Europeans who made contact with the Kingdom and can be seen in museums all over the Western world today.

A defining feature of this pre-contact Africa was the interconnectivity of the different spheres of life, generally believed to be saturated with vital power; between the spiritual and the material, where there was no separation between the religious and the secular as it has been understood since European Enlightenment period. Similarly, as is the case today, pre-contact Africa was characterized by variety and diversity in all spheres of life: ethnicities, cultures, and above all, religions, even as these religions are part of the indigenous cosmovisions of the people. The crux of African cosmovisions is deeply and irresistibly animated; J. D. Y. Peel aptly describes it as "unsecular," signifying by this the pivotal role and inescapable presence of religion in

---

[1] John S. Mbiti, *African Religions and Philosophy* (London: Heinemann Educational Books, 1969), 1.

the formation and organization of social, cultural, political, and economic structures and lifestyles.[2] The reconstruction of African pre-contact religion by Western scholars and Western-trained African – often Christian – scholars has been fraught with difficulties for many reasons such as misinterpretations, eurocentricism, and outright denigration. However, this present attempt makes no claims to comprehensiveness either in depth or scope of coverage, but endeavors to avoid the pitfalls in previous efforts. A reconstruction of such cosmovisions demonstrates ordered systems and harmonious wholes in and through which the peoples of Africa generate sense, values, meaning, and belongings and have their being. The African spiritual world is the locus of inexorable power that the peoples believe can be harnessed for diverse purposes.

African indigenous religions are not by nature proselytizing: membership is by ascription; one is born into it and participates in the spiritual activities of the group to which he or she belongs by birth or by blood. As one must be born into a group to be part of its spiritual universe and system of metaphysical order, the land, a physical part of the earth to which the group lays claim to, is an important entity in many African societies' religious and spiritual existences. Because there is no separation between the world of humans and the undergirding spiritual universe of the gods and spirits, many African languages lack specific words for "religion." For the Yorùbá, for instance, what could loosely translate to the Euro-American notion of "religion" is "country fashion"; similarly, *"ofufere chi,"* which roughly translates into the modern notion of religion, among the Igbo strictly means "the worship of gods." For Africans, religion connotes all the interactive and transactive relations between different constellations of power that are perceived to exist in nature, the worlds of the spirits and gods, and the human world.

Spiritual or religious practices and behavior such as prayers, sacrifices, invocations, and moral conduct, which suffuse the practical activities and experiences of daily life, are ordered to bring out the three principal goals of life. These are the blessings of wealth, the blessings of children, and the blessings of long life with its corollary of health. In the understanding of the people, this is the core of the divine plan for humans; hence the entire creation encompassing the physical environment with its flora and fauna, as well as the spiritual universe of unseen forces and entities, are designed to foster the realization of these triple objectives.

---

2 J.D.Y. Peel, *Religious Encounter and the Making of the Yoruba*, (Bloomington: Indiana University Press, 2000), p. 317.

This chapter articulates African religious ideas and practices uncontaminated by external influences or foreign religions. It is organized under five sections: an introduction; the African worlds; the universe of the gods; religion as healing; and finally, a conclusion. Examples are drawn mainly from West Africa, where the resilience of indigenous religious formations is most strongly felt; furthermore, the discussion is in the present tense because the ideas and practices discussed here are still alive and practiced by a large number of Africans irrespective of education, socioeconomic status, or even conversion to proselytizing world religions such as Islam and Christianity. If Islam and Christianity have any foothold in Africa today, one may argue that it is as a result of the spiritual infrastructure furnished by the irrepressible African indigenous cosmovisions.

The African Worlds

In the construction of African cosmovisions, it is important to recognize and underscore the existence of three conceptually distinct but inseparably intimate worlds: the human order with its social formations; the physical or natural, nonhuman world; and the spiritual universe. These three orders of existence are interrelated and constitute an ordered, holistic sphere of interactions and powers or vital forces, each informing and sustaining the other in complex ways. In the African ordering of things, it is inconceivable to think of one order without the others. Their interactions generate a hierarchy of entities or beings and a plethora of rituals, patterns, symbolisms, sacred objects, and persons and religious practices that inform the ways of life and thought patterns of Africans. The understanding of the linkages between these worlds also informs how problems are solved, diseases cured, and resources managed and structured. Traditional conceptions of peace and harmony, for example, emphasize a proper coordination of all three worlds. The human, the physical, and the spiritual are interlinked to provide harmonious environments for the realization of human potentials and goals as well as sustained development.

The human world is made up of humans and their social environments: social organizations, community life, family, and socioeconomic and political formations. Although Africans understand that they form an integral part of the physical, natural world, they make a distinction between the human and the natural world, recognizing the latter to be made up of nonhuman but material aspects of the physical world such as forest, the land, groves, animals and fishes, rocks, vegetation, rivers, hills, and mountains. The created order is recognized as a realm of forces that can be harnessed for the good of humans. These forces can also be harnessed for antisocial ends. Human beings depend on the physical world for their survival and material sustenance; the natural world also constitutes a sphere of mediation between the human and the spiritual worlds. Certain creatures, for example, or natural phenomena, are believed to be messengers of specific deities relaying information from one realm of existence to the other.

The spiritual world belongs to the Supreme Being, the divinities, the ancestors (and the unborn, who are reincarnates of ancestral spirits), and other spirit entities, some of which are benevolent while others are malevolent. The Igbo of southeast Nigeria, for example, conceive of five principal categories of spiritual beings inhabiting the spiritual universe: the Supreme Being (*Chukwu/ Chukwu abiama/Chineke*), deities (*mmuo*), spirit-forces (*arusi*), the ancestors (*ndichie*), and agwu (*medicine*). Although spiritual entities are invisible, they are – with the probable exception of the Supreme Deity – believed to inhabit physical, often natural objects such as huge trees, caves, hills, water bodies, and even the physical earth. Among the different peoples of West Africa, the real owners of the land are the ancestors who inhabit it and sacrelize it with their presence and spiritual force. Hence, among the Igbo, "it is indignity to the dead to be buried in a piece of land to which the deceased has no right as a member" of the clan.[3] In African worldviews the three worlds interact creatively to produce a harmonious existence. Although it may appear that humans are at the center of these worlds, each plays significant roles in the generation of meaning and survival. The next section adumbrates on the world of the gods and other spiritual entities such as the ancestors and divinities that strongly impinge on the human and natural orders of existence.

The Universe of the Gods

The Great Creator-Spirit

The world of the gods, deities, and spirits is a sphere of hierarchized spiritual entities such as God or the Supreme Being, deities or divinities, ancestral spirits and human spirits, or ghosts and other nonhuman spirits. The Supreme Being is the creator of all that exists except Her-/Himself. The Supreme Being administers the natural and human realms through the mediatory functions of arch-deities and deities and other spiritual agents who interact with humans

---

3 Osmund A. C. Anigbo, *Igbo Elite and Western Europe* (Onitsha: Africana-FEP Publishers Limited, 1992), 29.

through a wide array of instruments and structures such as rituals, sacrifices, songs, dances, prayers, and invocations.

The conceptualization of this spiritual universe is deeply rooted in the construction of another dimension of African experience: time. Time is nonlinear and understood as "periods of action;" it encapsulates the past, the present, and the future. The past belongs to a cohort of spiritual entities, particularly the ancestral spirits or the living dead; the present is the context of action for living humans, whereas the future belongs to the yet-to-be-born. Similar to the three orders of existence of human, spiritual, and natural world, all three spheres of experience of time interact at different levels of complexity. For Africans, therefore, time is not so much chronometric or a continuum of movement from the past to the future through the present as it is a series of events and interactions involving humans and nonhuman, spiritual entities in a densely animated universe. Events or reality at the material, human, level are perceived to be manifestations or influenced by the spiritual, unseen, nonmaterial level – both past and future.

At the apex of the ontological order is the spiritual world of the gods, which is the hub around which spiritual behavior revolves, although the anticipated benefits are material and this-worldly. At the center of this order is a Supreme Being or deity recognized by a diversity of names and praise-names among different African peoples. The existence of God among Africans is not a question of philosophical articulation or refinement, but of a fundamental experience of spiritual, moral, and mystical existence. As Bolaji Idowu succinctly describes, "In Africa, each people has a local name for God," which in some cases may be a generic name for deity in general or a unique one specially reserved for the Supreme Being that distinguishes Him/Her from lesser divinities or deities.[4] A few examples from West African societies will suffice here: among the *Akan* of Ghana, God is called *Onyame* (God of fullness/satisfaction) or *onyankopon*; among the Yorùbá, *Olodumare* (the immutable, absolute Lord of excellence); and among the Igbo, *Chukwu* (Great God) or *Chineke* (God who creates). The names of God among different African societies demonstrate the reality of the Supreme Being in their everyday existence as creator and sustainer or providence. As creator of all things – including the divinities – Chukwu is also "the organizer of the world" who introduced night (hence weekdays) and day as well as commerce into human experience.

Although the people perceive the Supreme Being as ever-present in their existence and experience, there are few shrines dedicated to Him/Her partly

---

4 Bolaji E. Idowu, *African Traditional Religion: A Definition* (London: SCM Press, 1973), 149.

because the entire world and the sky belong to Him/Her and partly because S/he is believed to be the Great One, it is inconceivable to localize or confine Her/Him to an altar, shrine, or temple. Even though there is no public, direct worship of Olodumare among the Yorùbá of Nigeria, among the Akan, Onyame is approached by votaries who have altars and shrines dedicated to Her/Him for worship. The same is the case among the Igbo of Nigeria where Chukwu has public cults.

Deities

Bolaji Idowu characterizes West Africa as "the home of divinities" with "a very crowded pantheon."[5] African religions are populated by a large array of deities or divinities, who, in terms of daily propitiation and rituals, receive much more attention than God. They are conceived as children of God – "brought into being" but not created – His/Her agents or aspects of His/Her character, nature, or metaphysical attributes; they are vested with power and authority accordingly. As agents of the Supreme Being, these spirit beings are messengers or ministers who carry out commands and orders of the creator. They are generically called *Orishas* (divine beings) among the Yorùbá. Each divinity is ascribed a local name among a given society that is also descriptive of its functions and duties within the divine ordering of the created realm. Each has its own cult community, shrine, or temple, and priesthood and cult emblem(s). Frequently among certain societies, divinities are ordered around a principal archdivinity: among the Yorùbá *Orisha-nlá* – entrusted with the task of assisting in creating the physical universe as well as humans – while among the Igbo *Ala (or Ani/Ana* according to dialectical variation), the Earth deity, fulfills this role.

Prominent orishas among the Yorùbá include *Ogun*, the divinity of iron who with his machete carved out the limbs of humans in the creation process; *Eshu*, the orisha of crossroads, entrances, and markets, a great communicator and errand deity who ferries messages between the orishas and Olodumare or between votaries and the orishas. Similarly, *Shango* is the deity of thunder and lightning who epitomizes the wrath and justice of the Supreme Deity; *Orunmila* or *Ifa* is the deity of wisdom, hence divination. Other orishas functioning as the terrestrial manifestation of Olodumare include *Yemoja*, the mother of many river deities and by far the most popular river deity. Known as the "mother of fishes," she is also the ruler of Ogun River; another prominent river deity is *Oshun*, ruler of Oshun River and the deity of fertility, wealth, and

---

5 Ibid., 165, 169.

beauty. Described by Bolaji Idowu as "the Poseidon of Yorùbá conception," *Olukun* is the orisha of oceans or seas.[6] As part of human experiences of illness and disease, there is among the Yorùbá *Shopona* or *Obaluaya*, the orisha of epidemics or specifically smallpox; *Osanyin* is the deity of herbal medicine – as a description of his duties and responsibilities, his name is derived from the Yorùbá verb, *"sunwon,"* meaning "to be well."

In Igbo religious thought, spiritual beings are organized into two principal categories: the sky-deities and the earth-deities. The former revolve around the Supreme Deity who inhabits the sky or heaven; these deities include the thunder deity, the sky deity (*Igwe*), and the sun deity (*Anyanwu*). The latter (earth deities) rotate and function according to the order of *Ala*, Great Earth-Mother, who superintends the affairs of the earth and the underworld (*okuru-uwa/ala-mmuo*) and is associated with such deities as *Ahajioku* or *Njoku* (the Yam-deity), *Agwu* (medicine), *Afa* (the divination-deity), the fertility deity (*Ala*), *Ikenga* (deity of achievement/enterprise/fortune), and *Iyi* (river deity). In Igbo cosmology, Ala "is the spirit of the land and the source of all life within it. She is not the creator of life [as that is the prerogative of Chineke – the Creator-God], only the direction of its flow."[7] Ala is the closest and dearest of all the deities, the most commanding deities in private and public affairs, the "Great mother" and symbol of life revered for her focus on social life, the fountainhead of social morality, unity, and source of legal sanctions.

Among different African societies there are different numbers of divinities. The Yorùbá are believed to have the most, although even here the figures vary from source to source: 201, 401, 600, or 1,700. Because traditional religions are dynamic, borrowing and fusing different aspects of religious practices from neighboring communities, these figures change even within a single community. Also, the process of deification of ancestors and cult-heroes adds to the existing numbers of divinities. What is of practical importance to votaries is their scope of functions rather than numbers; they are conceived to cover the different aspects of human experience and needs.

Ancestors

Broadly, spirits of deceased humans constitute one important category of spiritual beings in the African worldview. These spirits could be conceived of as good or bad according to the fulfillment of certain criteria to be discussed later. In many African cultures, animals and plants are believed to be endowed

---

6 Ibid., 95.
7 Anigbo, *Igbo Elite and Western Europe*, 33.

with spirits or forces, some of which are powerful enough to impact on human activities; however, spirits of deceased humans are accorded more regard because of the many roles – ritual, ethical, social, environmental – that they fulfill. Humans who, at death, satisfy the prescribed conditions are inducted into ancestorhood, receive ritual offerings, and are capable of reincarnating into the family. Ancestors are so important in the African religious worldview that some scholars have – obviously mistakenly – claimed that Africans worship not God but ancestors. As Geoffrey Parrinder correctly notes, it is impossible to grasp the religious foundations of African worldview without understanding the role and place of ancestors: they constitute a principal strand in the daily organization and administration of families and communities. Although, as Laurenti Magesa asserts, in the African worldview "God stands as the ultimate guardian of the moral order of the universe for the sole, ultimate purpose of benefiting humanity," the practical moral guidance of individual families and communities devolves to ancestors, who, by virtue of their experience, ritual worthiness, and closeness to the ultimate truth of the Supreme Deity, understand how best to conduct one's daily affairs. Ancestors exercise their powers over ritual and moral conduct of their families and communities "by right of their primogeniture and proximity to God by death."[8]

Aside from ancestor veneration being an irrefutable indicator of African belief in life-after-death, it is also a strong pillar of ethical conception of existential life. In many societies, it is not the spirit of every dead human who becomes an ancestor; there are stringent conditions – social, ritual, and moral – to be met before ancestorhood is attained. Among the Igbo of Nigeria, ancestors are known as *Ndichie*; these are those whose disincarnate spirits have been elevated to such a status as to receive special ritual veneration and cult attention. The spirits of the dead who failed to attain ancestorhood are called *Ogeli* (wandering spirits); they do not receive ritual veneration and may be considered troublesome and malignant, in which case they may become subjects of ritual exorcism to keep them from harming living family members. These include spirits of children who died without initiation, of those who died without children of their own, or of those buried without appropriate funeral rites.

Although conditions to be attained before becoming an ancestor may vary from society to society, there are common elements such as living a morally upright, exemplary life worthy of emulation by the living, particularly the

---

8 Laurenti Magesa, *African Religion: The Moral Traditions of Abundant Life* (Maryknoll, NY: Orbis Books, 1997), 47.

youth and dying what some societies consider as "God's death," that is, at a relatively advanced age and of no illness considered an abomination such as leprosy, suicide, smallpox, epilepsy, accident, and so forth. Death by any of these means is considered untimely and may be viewed as a consequence of divine wrath or ritual infraction. A further condition for attaining the status of an ancestor is full burial rituals – rites of passage from one state of life to another; victims of untimely death are excluded from these. Because a person's offspring are those who are entitled to carry out the necessary funeral rites, having a child – and in some societies such as the Igbo, a male child – is a necessary condition to be met for the rank of ancestor. Offspring are also those with the prerogative of offering sacrifices and pouring libations to the ancestors at the family shrine.

Ancestors are ascribed superhuman qualities because of their closeness to the source of supernatural power, God. They provide moral guidance and instruction as well as benefaction or punishment to humans. Further, they are protectors of their descendants and the society at large: "they are the direct watchdogs of the moral behaviour of the individual, the family, the clan and the entire society with which they are associated."[9] By their functions, ancestors maintain social sanction and social cohesion; they are loved for their closeness and powers to reward good behavior and ward off evil and dreaded for their justified anger and punishment. Although descendants usually obey the moral directions of ancestors, any perceived capriciousness on their part is viewed with strong resentment by humans, who may rebuke or reprimand them in strong ritualistic words and gestures.

Religion as Healing

In African cosmology, a principal function of religion is to actualize a person's destiny in an environment populated with baleful, menacing spirits, to bring about healing. Achieving one's destiny entails living the good life, which is summed up in the Yorùbá concept of *Alafia*. Frequently used as a form of greeting among friends and neighbors, *alafia* ordinarily translates as "peace"; however, it consistently carries the more nuanced meaning of health, success, and prosperity. It embraces the totality of a person's anatomical, social, economic, psychological, and spiritual well-being. Significantly, it is rooted in the dynamic, holistic worldview of the African that encompasses a person's well-being and harmony between humans and their kind, between humans

---

9 Ibid, 48.

and the physical environment or nature, and between humans and the spiritual entities that impinge on their concrete circumstances.

Healing is the restoration of a disharmonious relationship between an aspect or aspects of life to a harmonious balance. It is not simply the elimination of disease or physical "inability to function in normal activity" but the restoration of a disturbed cosmic/spiritual/metaphysical order either as it relates to an individual or to a family or a whole clan. Because for Africans illness afflicts a person as a total entity rather than only a part of the person's anatomy, likewise, to be healthy is a holistic concept that entails an individual's total harmony with all the forces that she or he interacts with, material well-being, and the fulfillment of existential goals as well as ultimate destiny. Although the human body is important in the African system of thought because it is the "surface" where deities inscribe their authority and sometimes inhabit through possession and revelatory and divinatory processes, healing transcends this "surface" to reconcile and harmonize the inhabiting human spirit with other spheres of spiritual or metaphysical influences.

The intensely religious character of the African worldview informs the perception, definition, and interpretation of health and ill health, and consequently, the pathways to healing and health. Ill health does not simply afflict the body but the total person; thus healing is directed to the whole person as well, dealing with not just the "how" but also with the "why" of the illness. Religious behavior is designed to manage the physical and metaphysical well-being of a person from *before* birth to *after* death; there are fecundity rites to protect pregnant women and initiate their prenatal babies into the religious world of the group; there are also rites that follow the death of a person to usher his or her spirit honorably into the world of the ancestors. Among many African communities, the art and practice of medicine and healing are "anchored in the world of the gods." The Igbo deity of medicine and healing is Agwu, revered for his wisdom as well as recklessness and confusion, who both blesses and harasses his votaries. It is a most versatile deity with a two-edged face and ambivalent nature. This conception of the deity points to the ambivalence of suprahuman forces for good and ill, the power of the healer to restore order and health but also to inflict disorder and violent actions.

The body and its well-being is a central concern in the African indigenous system of thought and action. In this respect, religion functions as a primary, and by no means exclusive, technique of maintaining and restoring the body to its principal functions and duties. The relationship between religion and healing evokes cultural understanding that transcends the physical body to embrace a holistic perspective of life, nature, and the supernatural. Medicine and healing are inextricably related to divination and sacrifice. According to Emefie Ikenga-Metuh, for Africans medicine conveys the ideas of forces or powers contained in nature such as properties of certain roots, herbs, and animal parts that can be extracted; mixed in appropriate proportions; and activated through ritual invocations, libations, sacrifices, and other similar rituals and applied to the solution of a variety of human problems.[10]

Sacrifices (*aja* in Igbo or *ebo* in Yorùbá) are usually of animal, liquid, and cereal offerings to the Supreme Deity, the divinities, or ancestors, although human sacrifices were sometimes deemed necessary for the safety of the community or the burial of titled personalities. Animal blood is believed to contain *ase*, force or power, to satisfy the deities and bring about that which supplicants request or desire, in this case the restoration of health and harmony in an individual or in the community. Because it is the gods who determine which herbs, roots, and animal parts should heal what type of illness, the rituals and invocations acknowledge the power of the deities over the forces of nature and solicit their support in bringing about positive outcomes for the good of the human community.

Godwin Sogolo captures the core conceptualization of ill health among Africans when he asserts that

> [I]n Africa a person is said to be ill when he is afflicted by forces such as hunger, unemployment, laziness, strained human relationship, lack of money, infertility, domestic problems, etc. He is considered ill in so far as these factors impair his productive abilities and, therefore, his overall capacity to fulfill his aspirations in life.[11]

As broad as this conceptualization is, it encompasses both the symptom and the cause of illness: whatever impairs the productive abilities of an individual in the realization of his or her aspirations and destiny. In this regard, lack of peace of mind, crop failure, poverty, and infertility all count as circumstances that demand healing intervention. Material troubles and misfortunes are frequently but not always conceived as the outworking of the malicious intentions of baleful spirits and evil individuals that require intense religious intention. Ill-being is not, therefore, the presence of disease or absence of health but may connote a fourfold situation of physical ailment (such as a pain

---

10 Emefie Ikenga-Metuh, *Comparative Studies of African Religions* (Onitsha: Imico Publishers, 1987), pp. 221–222.
11 Godwin Sogolo, *Foundations of African Philosophy: A Definitive Analysis of Conceptual Issues in African Thought* (Ibadan: Ibadan University Press, 1993), 109.

in the leg or fever); present misfortune (which may include failure of crops or livestock or death of a family member); possible future misfortune; and lastly, deviation from socially accepted patterns of behavior.

Africans seek explanations of ill health and other misfortunes through two broad means: primary and secondary causes. Primary causes of illness are those predisposing factors generally not explicable in physical or material terms; some are supernatural while others are psychological. The guilt resulting from the contravention of communal norms or morality or strained relationship with other persons in the community may predispose an individual to ill health, as the balance existing in the cosmic order has been broken or disturbed. The connection between the gods and illness is often reinforced by appealing to breached kinship morality because the gods and ancestors are keepers of the moral order and harmony in the community.

Secondary causes of illness establish a direct causal relationship, such as could be discerned in the understanding that eating a rotten fruit would result in stomach upset. The Yorùbá concept of *kokoro* is one such example; kokoro are small organisms, some of which are visible to the eye whereas others are not. They are believed to infiltrate fruits and grains and other improperly kept edible items. When humans consume food corrupted by the presence and activities of kokoro, they are liable to become ill as a result. Other secondary causes of illness recognized in African theory of illness include natural causes (e.g., certain animals' and insects' activities such as those of mosquitoes and snakes could be harmful to humans); spiritual causes (the anger of gods/spirits/ancestors as a result of moral or ritual infraction results in illness); the activities of evil spirits or persons (such as witches and sorcerers); inherited illness such as insanity, psychosis, and other psychiatric disorders; and finally, stress or guilt resulting from a strained relationship (unpaid debt, for example) or breached ritual or moral norms of a community.

From the preceding examples and as David Westerlund has detailed in his seminal work, it is not the case, as some scholars have posited,[12] that Africans attribute *all* illnesses and diseases to the activities of supernatural beings.[13] Because of the holistic, dynamic conception of life, health, and ill health, the healing processes are directed to the whole person (body, spirit,

---

12 S. Kirson Weinberg, "Mental Healing and Social change in West Africa", *Social Problems*, vol. 11, no. 3 (1964): 257–269.
13 David Westerlund, *African Indigenous Religions and Disease Causation: From Spiritual Beings to Living Humans* (Leiden: Brill, 2006), pp. 165f.

and mind) by focusing on both the primary and secondary causes of illness. The pathways to health are diverse: some are plainly secular while others are more ritualistic. A mixture of herbs and leaves could be prepared for a case of fever or dysentery while a diviner (called *dibia-afa* by the Igbo and *babalawo* by the Yorùbá) may be consulted if the first line of treatment fails to bring about a positive outcome. The diviner reads the minds of the gods and discerns the possible, often underlying, cause(s) of the illness and recommends present action such as ritual sacrifice as well as consultation of a healer (*dibia-ogwu* [Igbo] or *osegun* [Yorùbá]), who would deal with the primary and secondary causes of illness and restore the disturbed harmony brought about by the illness.

Conclusion

The African cosmovision is a deeply spiritual construct that informs practical and existential quests and lifestyles. In this construct, religion and culture are so inextricably intertwined that it is impossible to discuss one without the other. Consequently, the religious ideas that structured this worldview issues in a rich variety of rituals (rites of passage, sacrifices, prayers, libation, etc.), festivals, sacred songs, music, dance, myths and traditions, cultural identities, symbolisms, and artistic practices, which through contact with Europeans and the ensuing slave trade, were transmitted to the so-called New World, resulting in new, creative formations of religious cultures, first among the African slaves but now also among wide and varied sections of the world. The resilience of African religious cultures and values sustained many in the past in both Africa and the New World; it still sustains many more today even in the presence of aggressively proselytizing foreign religions such as Islam and Christianity, often designed to "[extinguish] traditional cultures and forms of existence."[14]

Bibliography and Suggested Readings

Aguwa, Jude C. U. *The Agwu Deity in Igbo Religion: A Study of the Patron Spirit of Divination and Medicine in an African Society*. Enugu: Fourth Dimension Publishing Company Limited, 2002.

Ajibade, George Olusola. "Hearthstones: Religion, Ethics and Medicine in the Healing Process in the Traditional Yorùbá Society." In Beatrice Nicolini (ed.), *Studies in*

---

[14] Douglas E. Thomas, *African Traditional Religion in the Modern World* (Jefferson, NC: McFarland & Company, 2005), 179.

Witchcraft, Magic, War and Peace in Africa: Nineteenth and Twentieth Centuries, 193–213. Lewiston, NY: The Edwin Mellen Press, 2006.

Anigbo, Osmund A. C. *Commensality and Human Relationship among the Igbo.* Nsukka: University of Nigeria Press 1987.

Igbo Elite and Western Europe. Onitsha: Africana-FEP Publishers Limited, 1992.

Cox, James. *From Primitive to Indigenous: The Academic Study of Indigenous Religions.* Hampshire: Ashgate, 2007.

Falola, Toyin, and Demola Babalola. "Religion and Economy in Pre-Colonial Nigeria." In Jacob K. Olupona and Toyin Falola (eds), *Religion and Society in Nigeria: Historical and Sociological Perspectives*, 151–169. Ibadan: Spectrum Books Limited, 1991.

Hallgren, Roland. "Religion and Health among the Yoruba." *Orita: Ibadan Journal of Religious Studies*, XXIV / 1–2 (1992), 67–75.

Idowu, Bolaji E. *Olumare: God in Yoruba Belief.* London: Longman Press, 1962.

African Traditional Religion: A Definition. London: SCM Press, 1973.

Ikenga-Metuh, Emefie. "The Religious Dimension of African Cosmologies: A Case Study of the Igbo of Nigeria," *West African Religion*, 17, no. 2 (1978): 9–20.

Comparative Studies of African Traditional Religions. Onitsha: Imico Publishers, 1987.

African Religions in Western Conceptual Schemes: The Problem of Interpretation, 2nd ed. Jos: Emico Press, 1991.

Ityavyar, Dennis A. "African Traditional Medicine with Reference to a Wholistic View of Sickness and Health Care." In E. Ikenga-Metuh and Olowo Ojoade (eds.), *Nigerian Cultural Heritage*. Onitsha: Imico Publishing Company, 1990.

Kalu, Ogbu U. *The Embattled Gods: Christianization of Igboland 1841–1991.* Lagos: Minaj Publishers, 1996.

Lugira, Aloysius Muzzanganda. *African Religions: A Prolegomenal Essay on the Emergence and Meaning of African Autochthonous Religions.* Nyangwe, Zaire: Omenana Publishers, 1981.

Magesa, Laurenti. *African Religion: The Moral Traditions of Abundant Life.* Maryknoll, NY: Orbis Books, 1997.

Mbiti, John S. *African Religions and Philosophy.* London: Heinemann Educational Books, 1969.

Olupona, Jacob K., and Terry Rey (eds.), *Òrìsà Devotion as World Religion: The Globalization of Yorùbá Religious Culture.* Madison: University of Wisconsin Press, 2008.

Parrinder, Geoffrey. *African Traditional Religion*. London: Hutchinson University Library, 1954.

P'Bitek, Okot. *African Religions in Western Scholarship.* Nairobi: Kenya Literature Bureau, 1971.

Religion of the Central Luo. Nairobi: Kenya Literature Bureau, 1971.

Peel, J. D. Y. "An Africanist Revisits Magic and the Millennium." In Eileen Barker, James A. Beckford, and Karel Dobbelaere (eds.), *Secularization, Rationalism and Sectarianism: Essays in Honour of Bryan R. Wilson.* Oxford: Oxford University Press, 1993.

Religious Encounter and the Making of the Yoruba. Bloomington: Indiana University Press, 2000.

Sogolo, Godwin. *Foundations of African Philosophy: A Definitive Analysis of Conceptual Issues in African Thought.* Ibadan: Ibadan University Press, 1993.

Thomas, Douglas E. *African Traditional Religion in the Modern World.* Jefferson, NC: McFarland & Company, 2005.

Ukah, Asonzeh. "African Christianities: Features, Prospects and Problems." www.ifeas.uni-mainz.de/workingpapers/AP79.pdf. 2007.

Weinberg, S. Kirson. "Mental Healing and Social Change in West Africa." *Social Problems*, 11, no. 3 (1964): 257–269.

Westerlund, David. *African Religions in Western Scholarship: A Preliminary Study of the Religious and Political Background*, Stockholm: Almqvist & Wiksell, 1985.

African Indigenous Religions and Disease Causation: From Spiritual Beings to Living Humans, Leiden: Brill, 2006.

5

Extending Christendom:
Religious Understanding of the Other

MIGUEL LEÓN-PORTILLA

Friars sent to the New World in the sixteenth century were from Spain and were the product of early modern Europe. Their cultural baggage was still in large part Medieval, although in some cases it was colored by Renaissance humanism. They followed in the footsteps of discoverers and conquerors, those in search of gold and fame. However, the aim of the friars was different. Whereas the conquistadors imposed the king's authority, as well as demands for tribute and labor, the missionaries set out to make Christians of the people who for millennia had been practicing what the Europeans regarded as idolatry. They sought to undertake another kind of conquest: to expand Christendom. In such an ambitious endeavor, understanding the Other was an inescapable prerequisite.

Although they shared similar purposes, the Franciscans, Dominicans, Augustinians, and later the Jesuits went on to interact with the Indians in distinct ways in their efforts to comprehend those whom they desired to draw into the fold of Christendom. The process was slow and arduous, and the friars' results varied from the moment they first encountered native peoples in the Caribbean islands and later on terra firma. The heterogeneity and diversity of the indigenous peoples of the New World would only complicate their task.

In the early days, two major challenges concerned the friars. The first was to clarify the origin and nature of the Indians, who had heretofore been entirely unknown to the people of the Old World. The other, no less serious, was the need for the missionaries to develop a successful strategy for inducing the native population to abandon their idolatrous beliefs and practices and embrace Christianity.

On the first of these matters, there arose sharp differences among the friars, which at times even led to contradictions. The subject of the ethnic origins of the inhabitants of the newly found continent led to considerable speculation. Even the name of "Indian" resulted from a confusion of identity, that

Spaniards initially hoped that the American natives were in fact from the South Asian continent. Did the so-called Indians descend from the children of Noah after the Flood? Did they come from the Ten Lost Tribes of Israel described by the prophet Hosea? Or could their origin be found elsewhere?

Another dimension of this concern had to do with the intellectual capacity of the Indians. Were they really rational beings? And as a consequence, were they apt or not to receive the faith and sacraments of Christianity? At the beginning, this issue hounded many a friar and provoked controversies that even spurred the intervention of the Pope himself. The issues of the Indians' origin and nature led to a series of other questions, including, for example, whether they should be treated as children or as vassals. Were the Indians incapable of governing themselves? Could they enter the priesthood – and if so, should they be ruled with an iron fist? Such questions arose from the friars' perceptions of the Indians as lazy, with an inclination to lie, steal, and carry out vices as horrendous as anthropophagy and sodomy. The answers to these sorts of questions had a direct bearing not only on the friars' interpretations of the very nature of the Indians, but also on the strategies devised to convert them.

A related concern was that of idolatry. It was visible in practices as execrable as human sacrifice and cannibalism, and in many representations of gods that were interpreted as monstrous and that had to be destroyed. The Christian friars viewed the idolatrous practices and beliefs of the diverse groups – including human sacrifice and what has been called ritual cannibalism – as signs of barbarity, demonic influence, and as indications of a deficiency in rationality. This, in some cases, led the missionaries to conclude that it would be extremely difficult for the Indians to be able to understand the dogmas of Christianity and to genuinely convert to it.

The pursuit and persecution of idolatry became an obsession. It resulted in a head-on clash with the devil, as the enemy of the human race. The friars regarded their undertaking – ranging from learning indigenous languages, investigating the ways of life and thought of the natives, to strategies to do away with idolatry and expel the devil – as an essential part of their mission to the lands of the New World. However, that obsession with idolatry fueled campaigns of destruction that led to razing temples, tearing down sculptures, and burning paintings and codices. At the same time, these same friars wrote works describing the idolatry of different groups so other friars and crown authorities could identify idolatry when they saw it. Ironically, some of these very books provide the most detailed extant accounts we have today of indigenous life and religious practice prior to the time of the Conquest.

The Origin and Nature of the Indians

The origin of the Indians provided fodder for much theological and philosophical debate: Where had the Indians been since the time of Creation, at the time of the Flood, for example? It was impossible, however, to formulate an answer universally accepted by all. Dominican Fray Gregorio García, in his work *Origen de los indios del Nuevo Mundo*, presented and discussed a number of views, including several that attributed a location in the region of the Mediterranean Sea as the place of origin of the people who populated the New World. Perhaps the most frequent claim was that the Indians descended from the Tribes of Israel who were lost in the time of Shalmanesar. The main argument in ecclesiastical circles supporting this claim was that the Indians had descended from the Jews, based on their "perversity" and many of their customs.

Although a recurrent theme, the matter of origin did not have the same importance and repercussions as that concerning the nature of the Indians, particularly when it came to their rational capacity and ways of life. Writings by churchmen and explorers typically described the Indians as tending to vices, laziness, lechery, lies, and witchcraft, lacking good upbringing and virtue. All of these factors placed obstacles in the path of the friars' purpose: the true conversion of the Indians to Christianity.

These negative and castigating descriptions of the Indians appear with the first arrival of the Spaniards in the Caribbean islands, particularly in Santo Domingo, so numerous accounts have come down to us on the Spanish perception of the Native people. Of considerable interest are the testimonies from enquiries made in 1517, at the time that friars from the Hieronymite order served as governors there. The prior of La Mejorada, Fray Luis de Figueroa, in the company of three other Hieronymites, questioned Spanish residents regarded as "people of awareness, fearful of God, well mannered ... and who have experience with those Indians." Their purpose was to find the ways to proceed for their "conversion to Christianity, as well as their preservation and good treatment," and to profit from them in the case of the *encomenderos*, the Spaniards who had received grants of land and Indians, who served to pay tribute, in the form of goods and labor, and to whom the Indians could be entrusted to live in a Christian atmosphere.

The enquiry covered the following points: How much time had they been in contact with the Indians and did they know of their life and customs? What was the intellectual capacity of the Indians? Did the Spaniards believe the Indians could remain free, or would it be better to have them in *encomiendas*? Finally, the Hieronymites inquired as to whether the Indians could be Christianized in this way, even remaining as *encomendados*, tribute-payers, for perpetuity.

Although responses to these questions differed somewhat, in general the witnesses were in agreement with one another. Declaring that they knew and had dealt with the Indians, they insisted "they have many vices and that their behavior was not in the service of Our Lord, and their inclination is to be idle." They also claimed that "[the Indians] have no capacity to be able to govern themselves as any Spaniard no matter how uncouth he may be ... and they lack full or even half reason to be able to do anything;" because this, "they are not people to be placed in liberty." Concerning the situation of the Indians on *encomiendas*, they agreed that this would be not only convenient, but also necessary for their protection and to accomplish their preservation and conversion to Christianity.[1]

As we can see, the responses of these Spaniards, including not a few *encomenderos*, paint an extremely negative image of the Indians. It is worth recalling in this context that a few years earlier, in 1511, Dominican Fray Antón de Montesinos had offered a very different perspective, delivered in two sermons in the main church of Santo Domingo in which he harshly condemned the *encomenderos* and other Spaniards for their ill treatment of the Indians. Among other points, he said to those present at the mass:

> All of you are in mortal sin ... With what right and with what justice do you have to be so cruel and to hold restless Indians in terrible servitude? With what authority have you made such detestable wars against these people who were gentle and pacific on their lands, where you have inflicted death and unheard harm on so many of them? How can you have them so oppressed and fatigued, without giving them food and curing them of the illnesses that befall them from the excessive work that you give them and of which they die, or in other words, that kill them, to extract and acquire gold each day? And what care do you have of he who teaches them so they may know their God and creator, so they may be baptized, so they may hear mass, so they may keep their religious celebrations and Sundays? These people, are they not men? Don't they have rational souls? Are you not obliged to love them as you love yourselves? Don't you understand this? Don't you feel this?[2]

---

1 "Interrogatorio jeronimiano, 1517," Archivo General de Indias [AGI], legajo 1624 in Emilio Rodríguez Demorizi, *Los dominicos y las encomiendas de indios de la Isla Española* (Santo Domingo: Academia Dominicana de la Historia, 1971), 273–354.
2 Cited in Fray Bartolomé de las Casas in *Historia de las Indias*, 3 vols., ed. by Agustín Millares Carlo (Mexico City: Fondo de Cultura Económica, 1965), II, 441–442.

It would seem that this sermon fell on deaf ears, because the *encomenderos* continued to regard the Indians as inferior beings, virtually lacking rational capacity.

Opposing Images of the Nature of the Indians

What took place on the Caribbean islands, particularly in Santo Domingo, foretold in several ways what later occurred in New Spain (or Mexico), Peru, and in other parts of the *terra firma* in the New World. Beginning in 1515, Bartolomé de las Casas, a former *encomendero*, joined the Dominican order and participated in the debates concerning the nature of the Indians and the defense of the Indians themselves. He was responsible for, among other things, expelling the Hieronymites, with whom he was not in agreement for their utter lack of interest in the rights of the Natives.

The subject of the intellectual capacity of the Indians, considered on its own and in relation to the ways of achieving their conversion to Christianity, continued to be a topic of ardent debate. Bartolomé de las Casas, in the company of Antonio de Montesinos, traveled to Spain to explain to Charles V the injustices that were committed against the Indians and to find remedies for them. Although ultimately unable to meet with the Emperor, he was able to speak with several jurists and theologians. As a result, he succeeded in at least securing the removal of the aforementioned Hieronymite friars from the New World.

An event that fanned the fires of the dispute over the nature of the Indians took place around 1520. The Dominicans had sent two members of their religious order to convert the Indians of Chiribí, in what is today Venezuela, in 1519. In response to the Spanish incursions, the Chiribí rose up in retaliation and killed the missionaries in 1520. As a result of this event, Dominican Fray Tomás Ortiz denounced the indigenous population to the Council of the Indies.

> These are the attributes of the Indians for which they do not deserve liberties. They eat human flesh in their land; they are sodomites more than any other generation ... there is no justice amongst them; they go about naked, they have neither love nor shame; they are fools, crazy, they do not tell the truth ... they are fickle ... they are bestial and they value being abominable in vices ... They are not capable of doctrine nor punishment; they are cruel and vindictive traitors who never forgive, they are enemies of religion ... They are filthy, they eat lice and spiders and raw worms wherever they find them; they have neither the art or cunning of men.[3]

---

3 Cited in Pedro Mártir de Anglería, *Décadas del Nuevo Mundo*, 2 vols. (Mexico City: José Porrúa e Hijos, 1965 [1524]), II, 609.

Such a description of the Indians – one of the most negative opinions expressed by a friar – must have made an impression on the members of the Council of the Indies. Shortly thereafter, the same Fray Tomás Ortiz, accompanied by Fray Domingo de Betanzos and three other Dominicans, traveled to Mexico in 1526 to establish a religious Vicariate, which later became the province of Santiago de México. A year later, Ortiz returned to Spain and Betanzos stayed on to head the Dominicans. The latter continued to speak of the incapacity and vices of the Indians.

Apparently influenced by Fray Tomás Ortiz, Betanzos set out on a campaign to fully discredit the Natives. Two documents addressed to the Council of the Indies in this vein in 1532 and 1534 reveal the image that he had developed of them. A supporter of the notion that the *encomienda* granting of Indians be for perpetuity, he alleged that, "The Indians are of such vile condition that they do nothing out of virtue, instead out of pure fear ... the capacity of the Indians is commonly no more than that of seven- or eight-year-old children." In the same text, he expresses what became a sort of obsession in his work:

> The judgment and sentence of God who has been given to them, so that all of them shall die and no memory of them remain because their sins are so horrible and against all nature as has ever been found ... I am very certain that all of the Indians shall come to an end and die out very soon.[4]

When several Franciscans found out about Betanzos's denunciations, they also sought to convey to the Council of the Indies their staunch refutation of such an assessment. They began by attributing everything to the devil, no longer citing the idolatrous acts committed by the Natives, but rather the ideas expressed by Betanzos "giving to understand that the Indians of New Spain are incapable." To reinforce their claims, they asked the members of the Council to ask themselves "if he had learned the language of the Indians and what were the sermons that he had written ... and since he did not cut his teeth in pronouncing the language of the Indians, he should close and cover his mouth with stone and mud."

In this account, signed by French Fray Jacobo de Tastera and the celebrated Fray Martín de Valencia, as well as by Fray Antonio de Ciudad Rodrigo, all well-known Franciscans, they pondered the virtues and capacity of the Indians. "The children of the natives of this land write well, sing Gregorian and organun and counterpoint chants, and they make choir books, they teach

---

4 Fray Domingo de Betanzos, *Memoria* to the Consejo de Indias, 1536, AGI, Indiferente general, 1524.

others music," they wrote. "They preach what we teach them to the people and they say it with very good spirit."[5]

In the meantime, New Spain was in turmoil. Nuño Beltrán de Guzmán, president of the first Audiencia of New Spain, was committing all sorts of abusive acts that wronged the Indians. To a large extent as a result of the denunciations made by the first bishop of Mexico, the Franciscan Juan de Zumárraga, Nuño Beltrán, was finally deposed and sent back to Spain as a penalty for his abuse. The second Audiencia, however, established in 1533, was presided over by the former bishop of Santo Domingo, Sebastián Ramírez de Fuenleal. Ramirez de Fuenleal was a prudent man who was favorably interested in the condition of the Indians. Most Franciscans sympathized with him and shared a similar understanding of the native population, as evinced in the chronicles that several of them wrote at the time.

Minaya, Garcés, and the Papal Bull Sublimis Deus

At some time after the arrival of Ramírez de Fuenleal, Fray Bernardino de Minaya and Fray Bartolomé de las Casas, both members of the Domincan order, also arrived in New Spain. They were both friends and of like mind when it came to the Indians. Minaya, on the one hand, was convinced by Fray Julián Garcés, the bishop of Tlaxcala, who was also a Dominican, to write to Pope Paul III with a different plea: he requested an end to the disputes on the intellectual capacity of the Indians on the grounds that questioning it had already been an obstacle for their conversion to Christianity.

Paul III reacted favorably, and in June 1537 he issued the bull *Sublimis Deus*, closely following the ideas of Bishop Garcés. The bull expressly opposed those who

> ...dare to say in all parts that the western and southern Indians, just as other people who had come to our attention in these times, should be regarded as brutish animals ... And they reduce them to slavery, burdening them with work that they would never impose even on the beasts that serve them.

After denouncing these forms of thought and action, Paul III stated that these people

> ...are not only capable of the Christian faith as true men, but also that according to what we have been told, are extremely eager to turn to this faith. [So that it is decreed and declared] they must not be deprived of liberty nor of the

---

5 *Diversos*, May 3, 1533, Archivo Histórico Nacional, Madrid.

control of their possessions ... and they must not be reduced to slavery ... and they must be drawn to the Christian faith through the preaching of the word of God and through the example set by good customs.[6]

This was a triumph for Bishop Fray Julián Garcés and Fray Bernardino de Minaya. The thought and action of Fray Bartolomé de las Casas and other friars now rested on solid foundations. Although some clerics, such as Betanzos, continued to insist on their opinions concerning the intellectual incapacity of the Indians, the debate took different paths.

The Indians According to Bartolomé de las Casas

Once established on the continent and living in Guatemala in 1537, Las Casas wrote *Tratado sobre la única forma de atraer a los indios al cristianismo* (Treatise on the Only Way to Attract the Indians to Christianity). In essence it advocated a pacific approach in search of free persuasion. His work was a complement to the bull *Sublimis Deus* in that it spelled out in detail the path that should be followed to attract the Indians to Christianity through peaceful means until they could be convinced to convert.

In addition to what was expressed in his treatise, in 1542 he wrote his well-known *Brevísima relación de la destrucción de las Indias* (Very Brief Relation of the Destruction of the Indies). In this work, Las Casa offered a denunciation of the Spanish subjugation of the natives, eloquently e describing how the Spaniards mistreated and killed the Indians. Las Casas insisted that the natives were free by nature and there was no valid argument to enslave them.

On his return to Spain, he participated in 1542 in the Junta de Valladolid, the so-called "rationality debates" in which Las Casas and theologian Juan Sepúlveda contested and ultimately settled the issue of indigenous rationality and capacity for full Christian understanding once and for all. This event also resulted in "The New Laws" that recognized the dignity of the Indians and established the nonperpetuity of the *encomiendas*. Soon after he was appointed Bishop of Chiapas and in line with his principles, Las Casas excommunicated the *encomenderos* for their abuses against the Indians. He believed the Indians could be converted to Christianity without the use of force.

Las Casas then wrote two works that had enormous repercussions. One was his *Historia de las Indias* in which he related what had occurred since Christopher Columbus's first voyage and in which he repeatedly denounced the actions carried out against the Indians. The other work was his *Apologética*

---

6 Bull *Sublimis Deus*, facsimile of Latin text and translation into Spanish in Mariano Cuevas, *Documentos inéditos del siglo XV* (Mexico City: Editorial Porrúa, 1975), 88–94.

Historia. In this, he set out to amply show, through comparisons with other peoples, how the Indians not only possessed intellectual capacity, but also an extremely elevated degree of it. In Las Casas' very positive rendering, the natives are goodhearted; they are moderate; they build cities; they are extremely religious; and they appreciate proper forms of government.

The Image of the Indians According to Other Friars

Works by other missionaries repeated the idea that the native people had been idolatrous and that their beliefs and practices were inspired by the devil. No longer attributed to a deficiency in rational capacity, the devil became the reason why it was extremely difficult to convert them to Christianity. In the beginning, this is what one of the first Franciscans who arrived in Mexico in 1524, Fray Toribio de Benavente Motolinía, believed. According to his words in *Memoriales o Historia de las cosas de Nueva España y de los naturales de ella*, "as long as [the cult to the demons] is not removed, preaching would be of little use and the work of the friars would be in vain." As a result of this perspective, Fray Toribio undertook several campaigns to destroy ancient temples, images of gods, and other objects. The persecution of idolatry continued and shows that on this matter the friars were intransigent. It was not enough to preach against the pre-Hispanic religion; instead, they felt the need to destroy all vestiges of it.

However, as this same friar wrote, the Indians "although blinded by their idolatry, often took darkness for light ... they had some commendable laws and customs ... and in that manner, they governed themselves and punished transgressors."[7] Unlike what was oft repeated by his contemporary Fray Domingo de Betanzos, Fray Toribio thought that the Indians would come to an end not by reason of God's punishment, but rather because of the way they were treated: "We saw the carnage that [the Spaniards] wreaked upon them and the oppression used with them so we had thought that there would be no Indians among all the people in four years and this was what they said amongst themselves and among the Spaniards as well."[8]

Fray Toribio's assessment coincided with that of other Franciscans, such as Jacobo de Tastera, who wrote to the Council of the Indies on the rational capacity of the natives and their receptivity to embrace Christianity. To support this idea, he declared that several millions had already accepted the faith. The Friars used any means possible, even resorting to royal authority. It

---

7 Fray Toribio de Benavente Motolinía, *Memoriales o Historia de las cosas de Nueva España y de los naturales de ella* (Mexico City: Universidad Nacional Autónoma de México, 1971), 352.
8 Ibid.

cannot be presupposed that "any means" were invariably voluntary or peaceful: if an Indian who was already converted should fall back on his former beliefs, he must be punished, and, if deemed necessary, given the death penalty. Such was the case of the Lord of Tezcoco, Carlos Ometochtzin, grandson of Nezahualcoyotl, who was tried by the Inquisition and burned at the stake in 1539.

Another Franciscan, Fray Bernardino de Sahagún, had a different, more enlightened way of thinking. He believed that before undertaking the task of conversion, it was necessary to know in depth the language and culture of the Indians. Based on the conviction that idolatry dwelt among them, he carried out extensive research to become familiar with their nature and religious beliefs to gain an understanding of how to eradicate it. Aided by natives who had been his students at the Colegio de Santa Cruz de Tlatelolco, he conducted his investigations over a number of years. The fruit of his prolonged investigation was his comprehensive *Historia general de las cosas de Nueva España*. In it, he transcribed the numerous testimonies in Nahuatl that he was able to collect from wise elders with whom he conversed. Parallel to this, he prepared a somewhat free translation into Spanish of these testimonies. In his bilingual work, known today as the *Florentine Codex*, we have the most valuable information that has been gathered on the culture and language of the ancient Mexicans.

Sahagún has been regarded by many as the father of anthropology in the New World for the method that he devised and applied to collect information. In the course of his enquiries, he came to profoundly admire indigenous culture. In more than a few instances in his *Historia*, he praised the abilities, wisdom, and virtues of the Indians. In his prologue to book I, he wrote:

> All this work will be very useful to learn the degree of perfection of this Mexican people, which has not yet been known, because there came over them that curse which Jeremiah, in the name of God, thundered upon Judea and Jerusalem ... This has literally happened to these Indians by way of the Spaniards. They and all their possessions were so trampled underfoot and destroyed that no vestige remained of what they were before. Thus they are considered as barbarians, as a people at the lowest level of perfection, when in reality (excluding some injustices their mode of governance contained) in matters of good conduct they surpass many other nations which have great confidence in their administrations.[9]

---

9 Bernardino de Sahagún, *Historia general de las cosas de Nueva España*, ed. by Alfredo López Austin and Josefina García Quintana, 3 vols. (Mexico City: Editorial Porrúa, 2000), 62–63. English from Bernardino de Sahagún, *Florentine Codex, General History of the Things of New Spain, Introductions and Indices*, transl. by Arthur J. O. Anderson and

Sahagún's magnum opus covered information on ancient gods, religious celebrations, the calendar, auguries and predictions, moral philosophy and theology, trade, vices and virtues of the Mexicans, nature (minerals, plants, and animals), as well as an indigenous version of the Spanish conquest. Sahagún held a firm conviction that knowing all of these subjects in depth would allow him and others who shared the same concern to know what the ancient culture of the Indians had once been and could bring them closer to the Native people. By acknowledging their outstanding intellectual capacity, he presented them as worthy of respect and admiration.

The case of Augustinian Fray Alonso de la Vera Cruz was in some ways similar. He came to Mexico in 1537 and taught at the Colegio de Tiripetío in Michoacán, and later, with the foundation of the University of Mexico in 1553, he became a professor. An erudite man, he brought sixty-six boxes of books with him for the friars and their students to use. In his writings on the Indians, he described their attributes and defended them from the injustices to which they were subjected.

In *Tratado acerca del dominio de los infieles y de la guerra justa* (Treatise on the Subjugation of the Infidels and Just War), he posited a series of doubts and expressed what he thought about the Indians and their situation after having been conquered. In the tenth doubt as to whether the king of Castile could make war on the Indians, among many other things, he declared:

> Nor does it avail ought to allege the passage of Aristotle, *Politics*, book I, to the effect that some are by nature slave and others free. He calls those slaves by nature who are either children or simple-minded who must be directed and led rather than take the lead ... the inhabitants of the New World are not only not children or simple minded but in their own way are outstanding, and at least some of them in their own way are most eminent... From all this it follows that they are alleging an unjust title whoever they be who imagine that these natives are unworthy of dominion or of their kingdom or anything else of which they are legitimate owners.[10]

In the doubts that Fray Alonso de la Vera Cruz raised in his treatise, he recognized the Indian people's primordial dominion to rule themselves. This contrasted sharply with the pretensions that others had claimed to legitimize the Conquest.

Charles E. Dibble (Santa Fe: The School of American Research and The University of Utah, 1982), 47.

10 Fray Alonso de la Vera Cruz, "Relectio de dominio infidelium et iusto bello," included in *The Writings of Alonso de la Vera Cruz*, ed. and transl. into English by Ernest J. Burrus, S. J., "Defense of the Indians" (Saint Louis: Saint Louis University, 1968), II, 371–373.

In addition to the images that these friars conceived and expressed concerning the Indians, others also merit consideration. Among them is the Dominican Fray Diego Durán, who in *Historia de las Indias de la Nueva España* explained the development of the history of ancient Mexico in detail, although he harped repeatedly on the subject of idolatry. For him, the Indians descended from the Israelites. He cited the following as evidence of this claim: all of them regarded themselves as chosen by their god, some by Jehovah, others by Huitzilopochtli; both groups embarked on a pilgrimage in search of a promised land; on their march, the Jews carried the Ark of the Covenant, while the Indians carried on their backs an ark made of reeds with the effigy of their god; the Jews, according to Psalm 106, had offered human sacrifice, including their own sons, and the Indians also practiced sacrifice; the Jews built the Tower of Babel, the Indians an extremely tall pyramid at Cholula; both peoples had rules of a religious nature concerning food; both sacrificed animals.

In different parts of his work, when speaking of the character and religious practices of the Indians, citing various books of the Old Testament, he stated, "It seems to me that even without other explanations we have sufficient proof that these Indians descend from the Hebrews." As for the sincerity of the Indians in their conversion to Christianity, Durán expressed his doubts and offered facts in proof of it: in their religious celebrations and songs they mixed their ancient beliefs with those of Christianity. However, beyond any hypocrisies and defects, he had to acknowledge that the Indians had outstanding virtues: they were generous, they governed with order, they preserved their history.

Franciscan Diego de Landa, who worked among the Maya in Yucatán, also merits attention. Although it is true that in an *auto-da-fé* he burned ancient indigenous codices and thus destroyed most of the written legacy of Classic Mayan culture, it is also true that in *Relación de las cosas de Yucatán* he offered valuable information on the cultural creations of the Maya, their cities, monuments, and writing system. Landa's work, more than others, is interwoven with favorable and adverse assessments of the Maya world. He recognized that they had a social and political organization worthy of esteem and he presented them as a cultivated people admirable in many respects: wise men and astronomers were among them and they had books and writing. As for their abilities to compute time, he stated that "they have their year as perfect as ours." They were deeply religious, but their beliefs and rites were idolatrous, including several forms of human sacrifice and even of their own children. In addition to heart extraction, they practiced arrow sacrifice on their victims.

Landa recognized that the Spaniards were extremely cruel to the Maya. He declared that, "some of the principal lords of the province of Cupul were burned alive and they hanged others ... they seized the principal people, and they put them in irons [sic a pillory] in a house, and they set fire to the house and they were burned alive with the greatest inhumanity in the world."[11] Landa's *Relación* includes a large body of testimonies that allow us to know about the Maya before and after the Spanish conquest.

Another member of the same religious order was Fray Jerónimo de Mendieta. He worked for several decades in Mexico and, at an advanced age, he wrote *Historia eclesiástica indiana*, a lengthy work that he completed around 1597. In it, in addition to dealing with the ancient beliefs and cultural creations of the Indians, he dealt extensively with what took place starting with the arrival of the friars, particularly the Franciscans. He praised the ability of the indigenous people for the arts and the skill that they demonstrated when they were taught by the missionaries. Also, he noted that they were docile and generous; he even said that they were almost like angels. As for the relationship of the Indians with the Spaniards, he condemned the abuses that the latter perpetrated and he pointed out that by setting a bad example, they made the name Christian abhorrent. From his perspective, the Indians preferred the Franciscans of all the friars, but he did not think they should enter religious orders. With sadness he confirmed the dramatic decrease in the Indian population as a result of epidemics and the mistreatment they were subjected to. The *Historia eclesiástica indiana* is a work in which, from many points of view, the virtues and defects of the Indians are presented and discussed.

And in Peru...

As in Mexico, when the friars first came in contact with the Quechua, Aymara, and other indigenous groups in the Andean region, they assumed that their objective was to convert them and eradicate native beliefs and rites, which they believed to be of demonic. And within Peru, like in Mexico, two distinct visions emerged concerning the Indians. Although he never traveled as far south as Peru (his travels to South America extending only as far as an evangelistic foray into modern-day Venezuela), the teachings and writings of Fray Bartolomé de las Casas influenced Christian humanistic thinking among some

---

11 Fray Diego de Landa, *Relación de las cosas de Yucatán* (Mexico City: Editorial Pedro Robredo, 1938), 142. English from: Alfred M. Tozzer, edited and translated, "Landa's Relación de las Cosas de Yucatán, A Translation," *Papers of the Peabody Museum of American Archaeology and Ethnology, Harvard University*, Vol. XVIII (Cambridge: Harvard University, 1941), 59–60.

friars in Peru, particularly the Dominicans. Among these was Fray Domingo de Santo Tomás, the author of the first dictionary of the Quechua language and the first Quechua grammar, who modestly stated that the Indians who helped him to prepare his work were its authors. Another influential Dominican who also saw the Indians from Father De las Casas's view of Christian humanism was Fray Tomás de San Martín.

On the other hand, many Franciscans and Augustinians believed that the Indians deserved God's punishment for their idolatry, and extirpation of idolatry became a major preoccupation. This was the attitude of Franciscans Fray Juan de Chávez and Fray Gaspar de Vera. Among the Augustinians, according to the words of Fray Antonio de la Calancha in his chronicle on his religious order, there were friars in his congregation who with great zeal destroyed a large number of their idols, because they believed that the Indians were in the thrall of the devil.

Jesuit José de Acosta in *Historia natural y moral de las Indias*, published in 1590, was responsible for a well-documented, penetrating vision, based on his experience in the New World, in the viceroyalties of both Peru and Mexico, where he had spent several years. Although he devoted some chapters to idolatry and the acts of the devil, when writing about the indigenous peoples from the two viceroyalties and from other regions, he stated "that the opinion of those who hold that the Indians are men lacking in understanding is false." Furthermore, he suggested the Indians "in that to which they apply have great advantages over us," in other words, over the Spaniards.[12]

Written with a sense of modernity, Acosta's work surveys the history of Inca and Aztec rulers, as well as their cultural creations, describing their achievements and their deficiencies. By establishing comparisons between the Natives of Peru and those of Mexico, he proceeded with objectivity and knowledge of cause. Father Acosta's contribution is, in sum, a balanced work in which the images of the Indians appear in the holistic vision of their idolatrous beliefs and practices with which he contrasts their cultural achievements, many of which strike him as worthy of admiration.

Final Remarks

This overview reveals that the minds of Spanish friars in the New World were framed by Medieval conceptions of humanity, colored on occasion by

---

12 José de Acosta, *Historia natural y moral de las Indias* (Mexico City: Fondo de Cultura Económica, 1962), 280.

Renaissance humanism. Although the friars initially embraced grim and even contradictory images of the native people, they ultimately came to recognize, at least on some level, the intellectual capacity of the Indians. This is what made both their conversion to Christianity and the cultural mixing that would characterize the New World encounter possible.

Bibliography and Suggested Readings

Acosta, José de. *Historia natural y moral de las Indias*. Mexico City, Fondo de Cultura Económica. 1962.

Benavente Motolinía, Toribio de. *Memoriales o Historia de las cosas de Nueva España y de los naturales de ella*. Mexico City, Universidad Nacional Autónoma de México, 1971.

Burrus, Ernest J. *The Writings of Alonso de la Vera Cruz*. Saint Louis, Saint Louis University, 1968.

Durán, Diego. *The History of the Indies of New Spain*, trans. by Doris Heyden. Norman, University of Oklahoma Press, 1994.

García, Gregorio. *Origen de los indios del Nuevo Mundo* [1607]. Mexico City, Fondo de Cultura Económica, 1986.

Landa, Diego de. *Relación de las cosas de Yucatán*. Mexico City, Editorial Pedro Robredo, 1938.

Millares, Agustín. *Historia de las Indias*, 3 vols. Mexico City, Fondo de Cultura Económica, 1965.

Mills, Kenneth. *Idolatry and Its Enemies: Colonial Andean Religion and Extirpation, 1640–1750*. Princeton, NJ: Princeton University Press, 2012.

Rodríguez Demorizi, Emilio. *Los dominicos y las encomiendas de indios de la Isla Española*. Santo Domingo, Academia Dominicana de la Historia, 1971.

Sahagún, Bernardino de. *Florentine Codex, General History of the Things of New Spain*. Santa Fe: The School of American Research and The University of Utah, 1982.

6

New World "Savages," Anthropophagy, and the European Religious Imagination

AMOS MEGGED

During the first half of the sixteenth century, the European Medieval idea of "the world turned upside down" became the mental framework of contact and conquest in the Americas. This framework produced a dichotomous European understanding of the indigenous American population as either the Indian-of-Paradise or the barbarous savage. During their first encounters with the native peoples of the New World, these European imaginations of the Other drew freely and promiscuously from religious conceptions, "scientific" conjecture, and folklore that were, on occasion, burnished by native practices that the Europeans found novel and shocking. In Columbus's mental constructs of the time, as Anthony Pagden has commented, "the 'otherness' of their world, although not eliminated (they still remain 'bestial,' a mark by which Columbus's men can measure their own 'errors') has been made accountable."[1] On the one hand, Europeans recognized a common humanity with New World natives, as evinced in their immediate desires to convert, as well as mate, with them. On the other, exotic and terrifying customs such as cannibalism, a practice that Spaniards claimed to observe in the Caribbean and that they understood as not merely revolting but also as an abomination against God, allowed the Europeans to categorize the natives as beings who dwelled well outside the limits of civilization and of Christendom.

Yet even the debate over cannibalism remained two-sided. From one perspective, it allowed the "domestication" of the "Other" by transforming the indigenous into distinct, familiar categories that emptied and denied any novelty in them. For example, in Bartolomé de Las Casas's *Apologética historia*, readers are presented with numerous parallels between Amerindian cultural traits and those of the ancient world. From another, European minds continued to define the "Other" as being in an unchangeable and extreme state of

---

[1] Anthony Pagden, "Ius et Factum: Text and Experience in the Writing of Bartolomé de Las Casas," *Representations* 33 (Winter 1991), 147–162.

esoteric diversity and perversity. The existence of a *mundus preversus et inversus* of the cannibals on the close limits of Europe opened the road for a complex interplay of inverted roles assigned to these peoples by European observers. The assimilation of some recognizable parts of the marvelous "Other" in both theological and philosophical debates – for example, as a mirror for the neglected and isolated facets of human nature or as a model for an alternative way of subsistence – did not reduce the barriers between civilized Europe and the supposedly savage communities of the barbarians across the seas. To the contrary, it cemented those barriers. Throughout the process of "discovery" of new peoples and new lands, Europeans routinely adjusted and reinforced the cognitive categories of defining their customs, their bodies, their styles, and their natural environment. Nevertheless, the most influential element within this process was that the innate dichotomy between reason and misrule remained entrenched.

We see this most clearly in the work of early missionaries and explorers to the region, whose ethnographic descriptions are deeply, and understandably, encoded in European conceptions of culture and identity that were built firmly around the twin pillars of "true religion and virtue." Early representations of natives often came from documents produced by religious orders or other adventurers and included books, chronicles, paintings, and sculptures. For example, Hans Staden published his *True History* in 1557. In this work, the first published about Brazil, Staden described his nine months in captivity among the "wild, naked, fierce, man-eating folk of the New World, America." His observations include typologies such as "country of savages" and "savage people Toppinikin" (his name for Brazil's native peoples).

Staden's work was the first in a long line of travel narratives about Brazil. In 1585, Father Fernão Cardim wrote the *Epistolary Narrative of a Voyage and Jesuit Mission* and the treatise *On the Origin of the Indians of Brazil*. His work is of interest because it offers a contemporary view of the country and its people, but there is a large element of fantasy in his account of the indigenous peoples. Other travel narratives of this period include the *Diário de navegação da armada que foi á terra do Brasil em 1530* (Log of the Fleet That Visited Brazil in 1530) by Pero Lopes de Souza. There is also an extended reference to Brazil in the book written by the Italian navigator Francesco Antonio Pigafeta about the expedition of Ferdinand Magellan, *Viaggio intorno del Mondo* (Journey around the World). Additional early works include Richard Hakluyt's *The Principal Navigations, Voyages, Traffiques and Discoveries of the English Nation, 1552–1616* and the "Neue German Gazette" (New Zeutung ausz persillandt), a manuscript dating from 1515. Collectively, these works represent some of the very earliest "ethnographies" of the New World rendered through European, Christian eyes.

Following the initial accounts of native customs and practices of the West Indies and Brazil, the conquest of New Spain brought into play yet another category – human sacrifices, which were practiced to varying degrees by both the Mayas of Yucatan and the Mexica of Central Mexico. The world of the Mexica was, as Bernal Díaz del Castillo noted in his accounts, a profoundly civilized one if measured by the magnificent city of Tenochtitlán, the Aztec capital, but the key elements of Mesoamerican religion – most notably the prevalence of blood sacrifice – cast them beyond the pale. This category reinforced the already prevailing process of the European "cannibalization" of the New World and its inhabitants. Europeans conceived such repellent customs as cannibalism and idolatry to be the products of the Original Sin, not biology or cultural relativism.

During most of the sixteenth and seventeenth centuries, the allegation of cannibalism extended to the greater part of the inhabitants of the New World at the same time as the figure of the cannibal was being developed and disseminated in European folklore. Parallel to this development, yet another vision of cannibalism impacted the European mind. Ritual cannibalism, as a means of vengeance, had become the new element supplemented into European travelers' accounts of the New World to the already absorbed image of anthropophagy as originating out of sheer bestial nutritional needs among distinct human groups. In this manner, anthropophagy was transferred from the realm of nature into the terrain of culture.

The theological debates of the sixteenth century between Catholics and Protestants also reformulated the meaning of idolatry on the continent itself, as well as overseas. During the 1520s, Protestant reformers such as Huldrych Zwingli and Andreas Karlstadt spoke vehemently against the veneration of images and the false reverence of Catholic "idols." They compared Catholic veneration to heathen idolatry and utterly rejected their toleration. During their sermons, they openly encouraged organized and spontaneous acts of iconoclasm and consequently kindled the fire of "the war on idols" that spread across Europe. In the 1550s and 1560s, during the Council of Trent, Catholic reformers mildly transformed the significance and role formerly attached to the saints' images but did not do away with the practice of their adoration entirely.

In Protestant pamphlets and woodcuts of the period, the Papal State in Rome was envisaged as the Land of All Evil where idolatry was openly practiced. When observed in the New World, Europeans interpreted idolatry as an unreformed religion, caught up in superstition. Across the Atlantic, in the lands of Peru, for example, the debate among men of the Church and the mendicants over what was idolatry was based on earlier Christian observations about the Roman world and idolatry there. Inca religious practices were largely made comparable with Roman practices, and the actions taken against them, as similar to the ones initiated by the first Christians in the Roman Empire. Nevertheless, the debate over idols also stirred up a novel evaluation of what the definition of civilization was. European chroniclers of the sixteenth century who observed Inca religion "found idolatrous religion to be perfectly compatible with good government,"[2] and authors such as Bartolomé de Las Casas emphasized the continuum from classical antiquity to Christian Europe, to the Americas, in terms of what made up a civilization.

As the theological debates between Protestants and Catholics developed, the meaning of idolatry in the New World became increasingly entangled within the European theological polemic over the Eucharist and its association by the Protestants as an act of a human sacrifice and theophagy. Accordingly, the idolaters of the New World were portrayed as "God-eaters" (*teofagos*), whose goal was to devour the flesh of Christ not only physically but also spiritually. It was in these lands that the imperative of Lent, that is, fasting and sexual abstinence, was "openly ridiculed."[3] In Protestant eyes, Catholic practices were paralleled to those observed by the New World idolaters, and both were ruled by "a carnal monarchy" and by "God-eating" priests. The "drugs" induced during their abominable rites were no different than the mass, the barbarous rite that conjured cannibalism with its theophagy. In the text that accompanies the *Histoire de la mappe-monde papistiqve* (The New Papal *mapamundi*, published in 1567) Jean-Batiste Trento compares Catholics to the indigenous idolaters of the New World but then says that "there are more cannibals [among the papists] here and now and they are more cruel and barbarous than those who are born in Brazil."[4]

Sixteenth-century observers such as Bartolomé de Las Casas of the Dominican order and José de Acosta of the Jesuits radically deviated from this impression and interpretation by sanctifying those who were sacrificed by the Aztecs. In his *Apologética Historia Sumaria*, Las Casas compares those sacrificed with Christian martyrs, and Acosta goes further to compare them

---

2 Sabine MacCormack, "Gods, Demons, and Idols in the Andes," *Journal of the History of Ideas* 67 (October 2006), 623–647 at 631.
3 André Thevet, "Les Singularités des la France Antarctique (1557)," in Frank Lestringant ed., *Le Brésil d'André Thevet* (Paris: Chadeigne, 1997), 29.
4 Ibid., 299.

to the actual Host of Catholic communion. Under the influence of Las Casas's observations, the French thinker Michel de Montaigne compared European atrocities committed against enemies, such as employing dogs against living persons or burning them alive on the stake, with human sacrifices among the Aztecs. He concluded that eating the flesh of men after their death was less savage than those European atrocities.

This ambivalent reaction to indigenous Americans was also present among the conquistadors. In 1519, Hernán Cortés and his fellow Spanish conquistadors embodied what Tzvetan Todorov illustrated as the superior European capacity for communication. Cortés took an interest in the Amerindians by learning about their language, their forms of political organization, and their methods of transmitting messages. Nevertheless, Cortés, like the rest of his men, was a product of the ideology of the post-Reconquista era of the Catholic Monarchs, and his intolerance of native Mexican religion had its roots in the hostile environment of the persecution of *conversos* (Jewish converts) and *moriscos* (Muslim converts) in Spain following the Reconquest in 1492. In October of 1519, when the conquistadors first landed on the shores of Campeche, Mexico and encountered the first Totonac idols there, Bernal Díaz del Castillo observed how they approached indigenous religion:

> Cortés asked Melchorejo, who understood the language well, what the old Indian was saying, for he was informed that he was preaching evil things, and he sent for the Cacique and all the principal chiefs and the priest himself and, as well as he could through the aid of our interpreter, he told them that if we were to be brothers they must cast those most evil Idols out of their temple, for they were not gods at all but very evil things, which led them astray and could lead their souls to hell. Then he spoke to them about good and holy things, and told them to set up in the place of their Idols an image of Our Lady which he gave them, and a cross, which would always aid them and bring good harvests and would save their souls, and he told them in a very excellent way other things about our holy faith.[5]

Conversion to Christianity in Mesoamerica was not always a simple model of replacement. During the mid-1520s and 1530s, both Franciscan and Dominican friars fully applied Nahua ideograms to their catechism classes conducted in the newly erected convents to simplify the learning and understanding of the rudiments of Christian faith for the recently baptized indigenous lords. The four prayers were thus translated into traditional pictography,

---

[5] David Carrasco, Ed., *The History of the Conquest of New Spain by Bernal Díaz del Castillo* (Albuquerque: University of New Mexico Press, 2008), 31.

and native ideograms were used to convey the verbal component as near as possible to the original Latin words. However, such attempts to bring things closer to Nahua forms of recording and comprehension had been abandoned once the Franciscans and the Dominicans realized that such methods could mistakenly lead these neophytes astray, back to idolatry. As already noted, Spanish Church officials viewed parts of these visual expressions as harmful and idolatrous. However, they considered others efficient tools for evangelization, as highlighted at the time in the Franciscan Codex written by Friar Toribio de Benavente.

One of the best examples for European treatment of idolatry and the practice of human sacrifice during this initial phase appears in the *Annals of Cuauhtinchan*, which tells of the hanging in 1528 of don Tomás Uillacapitz in the market-place in Tepeyacac by order of the Franciscan friar Cristóbal de Santiago. The hanging took place in the presence of dignitaries from the neighboring communities of Tecamachalco, Quecholac, Acatzinco, Tecalco, and Cuauhtinchan. The subtext concerns the cannibalistic ritual consumption of a sacrificial victim on top of the mountains Chiquilichtepetl and Tziuhquemecan. The victim, Tochayotl (a pre-Columbian title for a rabbit-hunter), was allegedly quartered on a wooden scaffolding, his heart was pulled out, and the rest of his parts were left hanging in different locations. With Tomás Uillacapitz's consent and participation, another local dignitary, Chipeua, conducted a sacrificial meal at the site, together with his mother and brother-in-law.

The word applied in the *Cuauhtinchan Annal* to describe the acts performed by the participants is the Nahuatl *tlatzotzonaliztli*. This word can mean "the act of stringing or plucking a musical instrument," and it is followed by the sentence referring to a song of the "devil" (*tlacatecolotl*).[6] *Tlatzotzonaliztli* can also refer metaphorically to the harmony in the binding together a group of people in a sacred act of sacrifice. So, what is recorded in the subtext here is that the participants, together with other women, are described as metaphorically "tuning" their instruments of a ritual sacrifice at the site of a bath (*tlaattilli*), probably for the sake of a preliminary act of purification. There, they are also subsequently described as having cast lots to choose the prospective sacrificial victim, and eventually they chose a child. The *Códice Vaticanus A*, composed around the same period as the *Cuauhtinchan Annal*, contains a vivid pictorial account of such an act in which five male figures hold a sacrificial victim by

---

6 Frances Karttunen, *An Analytical Dictionary of Nahuatl* (Norman: University of Oklahoma Press, 1992).

his arms and legs, as one of them cuts open his chest and pulls out his bleeding heart with the stone blade. On the lower part, three additional bleeding victims await their fate.

European interpretation and misinterpretation of indigenous spiritual practices also extended beyond human bloodletting and cannibalism. One example of these other practices is the sacred bundles that contained the animated substances and spirits (*teotl*) of the godly effigies (*ixiptla*). A vivid description of these bundles comes from the famous 1536 Zumárraga idolatry trial of the Tenochca overseers of the sacred Mexica bundles (*tlaquimilolli*). From June until November 1539, the Holy Office under New Spain's first bishop, Juan de Zumárraga, conducted the trial of the indigenous lord of Texcoco, don Carlos Chichimecatecotl. Don Carlos was burned alive at the end of the trial, after conviction on accusations of idolatry, sacrifices, concubinage, and heresy against the Spanish Church and State. Many of the declarations against don Carlos were made by his half-brother, don Lorenzo de Luna, governor of the province of Texcoco, whom the Viceroy Antonio de Mendoza had placed in charge of investigating idolatry in this province and its environs. On that same occasion, Bishop Zumarrága also paid a visit to a local hill that was a holy site, after having heard of an idolatrous sculpture there, which he ordered eradicated "so that no memory of those should survive."[7]

The Spanish clergy's obvious misinterpretation of what they saw and extinguished in Texcoco is significant and needs clarifications. In pre-Columbian Mesoamerican thinking, bundles (*tlaquimilolli*), held two types of objects: effigies of gods and instruments of bloodletting. The objects were shrouded in a textile and tied with a narrow strip of white cloth, *Sak h'un* ("white paper"), in Maya, symbolizing the wrapping of the young maize leaves in which godly effigies had been kept for protection in the Mayan stelae. Bundles were opened for public display during ceremonies of accession. The two major representations of sacred bundles in the Mixtec pictographic manuscripts and in the Nahua "historic" codices were the Bundle of the Magic Stick and the sacred bundle of the godly relics. The latter were wrapped in cloth and carried on the backs of the founding leaders on their route of migration or during ceremonies of accession to the throne.

In both Mixtec and Nahua iconography, the palm tree and feather bundles also appear as an integral part of major offerings made in times of primordial foundations, during the inauguration of rulers, and during matrimony

---

[7] The entire process is described in the Proceso Inquisitorial del cacique de Texcoco, don Carlos Ometochtzin, the grandson of Nezahualcoyotl. Publication No. 1 of the AGN (1910), 29.

between ruling lineages. The bundles were represented in the Texcocan hideaway in the form of mummified bodies wrapped in shrouds and fastened with cords. Therefore, their wrapping clearly simulated an act of veiling and protection, a defense against supernatural threats, similar to the wrapping of the human body before the final death and departure of the soul.

A clearer interpretation of the significance of wrapping appears in Ferndando Ruiz de Alarcón's *Treatise on Heathen Superstitions*. He cites two elderly inhabitants of Atenanco, don Baltasar de Aquino and don Diego de San Matheo, who described to him the types of sacrificial offerings that local men and women would carry to the sites of worship at the top of mounds and hills. These included "some skeins of thick cotton thread poorly spun, or some small piece of cloth woven of that kind of thread ... and they used to accompany the offering with that which they call *quauhamatl*, which is a kind of a white paper like linen that is made in Tepozotlan from the soft bark of a tree. The offering used to be wrapped in this paper, [possibly simulating the wrapping or bundling of the dead body], and it served together with the cotton as something for the god or idol who had been educated among the friars, to whom it was being offered to wear."[8] In this account, the paper serves both for wrapping the incense offerings and for covering the godly effigy.

Yet another Inquisitorial process of 1545 exemplifies both how the Spanish clergy gradually identified the pre-Columbian gods with the Catholic saints and also their attitude toward lingering idolatrous practices among the indigenous nobility. Such was the case of Tomás Tonal, of Izucar, Mexico. Tomás, who had been educated among the friars at the local convent and was believed to be a true Christian, was denounced by don Antonio, a local noble of Izucar. The denunciation included an account of how Tomás had left behind a chest full of cloths and feathers at the chapel of San Miguel [St. Michael the Archangel]. After he underwent torture, Tomás Tonal denounced many others from the surrounding communities and declared that his offering was not dedicated to San Miguel but rather to Titlacahuan Moyocoyotzin, "god of Whole," also named "Telpochtli, the devil" "who becomes, both young and old." The offerings were thus directed toward the major Aztec deity, Tezcatlipoca, who, according to one of the local priests in charge of incensing the idols, "was equal to San Miguel."[9]

---

8 Ruiz de Alarcón, Hernando, Andrews and Hassig, *Treatise on the Heathen Superstitions*, Ch. 4.
9 "Proceso contra Tomás Tunail, indio de Izucar, por haber ofrecido una petaca," 1545, AGN, Inquisicíon Vol. 52, exp. 20.

The image of the young angel with his sword appeared to the locals as similar to their young god of war, and a dedication to this god, Tezcatlipoca, was believed to cause discord and war between communities, which was the source for prisoners caught in the battle field for the sake of a human sacrifice, out of whom the heart and blood were drawn out to feed the gods. In this manner, Tezcatlipoca supplied the necessary nourishment, for so the natural elements would comply with all their obligations and functions so that no cataclysm of the earth should occur. As the trial records describe, the offerings to this god of war came from different persons from diverse towns in the area. Among them was an Indian whose daughter was ill, and for the sake of curing her he dedicated an offering of feathers to Tepetitlan, the "young person next to the Mountain," who was Telpochtli, of the San Miguel chapel. The chapel had been erected on the exact site where formerly there was a sanctuary dedicated to Tezcatlipoca, and the effigy of that god was buried at the foot of that mountain. In 1605, the local priest encountered near the mountain of Xuchiapan a medium-size stone idol, and many other idols made of mud, that were placed in a certain order, within a circle of stones. An Indian woman married to a Spaniard told him that the idols "were images of the kings, their ancestors."[10]

Missionary accounts of the Nahua and Purépecha cultures of Mexico published between 1533 and 1581 unanimously interpreted the Indians as Gentiles corrupted by the devil and given over to devil worship. The optimism of earlier writers such as Andrés de Olmos (1533) and Martin de La Coruña (1541) gave way to the more objective accounts of Francisco de La Navas (1553–54) and Bernardino de Sahagún (1558) and, by the 1570s, to the pessimism of Diego Durán and Juan de Tovar, who condemned the survival of idolatry among the evangelized natives. But the most pressing challenge for the missionaries, by the mid-sixteenth century, became the need for a far more concise identification and of epitomizing what was the all-encompassing meaning of idolatry, and what were its limits.

Bibliography and Suggested Readings

Carrasco, David, Ed. *The History of the Conquest of New Spain by Bernal Díaz del Castillo*. Albuquerque: University of New Mexico Press, 2008.

Greenleaf, Richard E. *Zumárraga and the Mexican Inquisition, 1536–1543*. Washington, DC: Academy of American Franciscan History, 1961.

10 "Carta de Fray Alonso de Montero sobre ciertos ídolos en Izúcar, 1605," AGN, Inquisicíon Vol. 281, fol. 625.

Inquisición y sociedad en el México Colonial. Madrid: J. Porrúa Turanzas, 1985.

Johnson, Carina L. "Idolatrous Cultures and the Practice of Religion." *Journal of the History of Ideas* 67(4) (2006): 597–621.

Karttunen, Frances. *An Analytical Dictionary of Nahuatl.* Norman: University of Oklahoma Press, 1992.

Lestringant, Frank. *Le Brésil d'André Thevet.* Paris: Chadeigne, 1997.

MacCormack, Sabine. "Gods, Demons, and Idols in the Andes," *Journal of the History of Ideas* 67 (October 2006): 623–647.

Pagden, Anthony. "Ius et Factum: Text and Experience in the Writing of Bartolomé de Las Casas." *Representations,* 33 (Winter 1991): 147–162.

Ragon, Pierre. "Demonolatrie" et demonologie dans les recherches sur la civilisation mexicaine au XVIe siècle." *Revue d'Histoire Moderne et Contemporaine,* 35 (April–June 1988): 163–182.

Ruiz de Alarcón, Hernando, J. Richard Andrews, and Ross Hassig Eds. *Treatise on the Heathen Superstitions that Today Live among the Indians Native to this New Spain, 1629.* Norman: University of Oklahoma Press, 1984.

Schaefer, Stacy B. "The Cosmos Contained, the Temple Where Sun and Moon Meet" In Stacy B. Schaefer and Peter T. Furst (eds.), *People of the Peyote Huichol Indian History, Religion, & Survival,* 332–372. Albuquerque: University of New Mexico, 1996.

Todorov, Tzvetan. *The Conquest of America: The Question of the Other,* trans. Richard Howard. New York: Harper Perennial, 1992.

Vignolo, Paulo. "Hic Sunt Canibales, El Canibalismo Del Nuevo Mundo en el imaginario europeo (1492–1729)." *Anuario Colombiano de Historia Social y de la Cultura,* 32 (2005): 151–188.

7

Evangelization and Indigenous Religious Reactions to Conquest and Colonization

MANUEL AGUILAR-MORENO

The Spanish conquest and colonization of the American continent involved the destruction of diverse indigenous cultures and the imposition of a new culture on the defeated. The exploitation of indigenous people was so intensive in the Caribbean that the Dominican priest Fray Antonio de Montesinos denounced the mistreatment of the Indians allowed by Governor Diego Colón (Christopher Columbus's son) in a 1511 Lenten sermon. In his celebrated speech, he said, "Tell me, by what right or justice do you hold these Indians in such cruel and horrible slavery?... Are they not men? Do they not have rational souls? Are you not bound to love them as you love yourselves?"[1] It is important to ponder the tragic wounds left by the conquest and evangelization in the minds of the Indians, and how these slowly healed in the process of transculturation.

One of the approaches to understand the complex mentality of modern Latin American people is to address the spiritual conflict created by Spanish evangelization in the sixteenth century. There is no question of the success of the Spaniards in establishing a visible church. The constructed buildings, instituted ceremonies, founded sodalities (*cofradías*), and the catechism echoed through most of the land. The problem lies in measuring the authenticity of the conversion that in many cases was superficial, so that the level of assimilation and understanding of Christian doctrine presents many doubts. The pre-Columbian peoples both in Mesoamerica and the Andean region had a deep ancestral religion that the Spanish suddenly questioned and eventually destroyed. There were different reactions to the imposition of Christianity among indigenous peoples, ranging from incomplete and distorted conversions to *nepantlismo*, a condition of confusion in which one loses a past identity without assimilating a new one. There were also situations of passive or

---

[1] Fray Bartolomé de las Casas in *Historia de las Indias*, 3 vols., edited by Agustín Millares Carlo (Mexico City: Fondo de Cultura Económica, 1965), II, 441–442.

active resistance. The final result of the process of conversion was a syncretism in which most natives accepted the new faith with a rudimentary understanding of its premises while maintaining some of the internal and external symbols of their older, native religious customs.

In modern Mexico, the syncretism of the old and new religions remains apparent and clearly reflects the outcome of ideological evolution during colonial times. Two examples illustrate the point. First, several sanctuaries in Mexico emphasize different manifestations of the Virgin Mary, but the most important images form a tetralogy: the Virgin of Guadalupe, the Virgin of Zapopan, the Virgin of San Juan de los Lagos, and the Virgin of Talpa. They are connected with pilgrimages to seek favors. People consider these manifestations of Mary as "sisters or cousins" (an undercurrent of polytheism) and believe that one in particular (according to their choice) is more powerful than the others.

Second, in Atotonilco, Guanajuato, the Sanctuary of Jesus the Nazarene is located next door to a house for "spiritual exercises." Many peasants go to Atotonilco on pilgrimage and to participate in the exercises, and they still use rope crosses on their necks and rope whips (*disciplinas*) with the intention of punishing the sinful flesh. This is a very old practice of southern Spanish Catholicism that in the sixteenth century appealed to the Indians because it was an expiation practice that reminded them symbolically of human sacrifice. Startlingly, the Catholic diocese continues to allow this type of worship that intertwines superstition and magical prayers with Christian orthodoxy in a very heterodox way, to the extent that street vendors sell a prayer to the *Santísima Muerte* (Holy Death) that embodies an incantation to cause grief or death to an enemy.

These examples are only two of many that illustrate the legacies of the difficulties faced by the Catholic missionaries in the sixteenth century in converting the indigenous people. Some of the coincidental similarities between the rival religious systems helped them in their work, but such parallelisms proved to be two-edged swords, as both religious systems offered an array of divine persons, whether Aztec deities or Catholic saints, who specialized in particular human needs. This resulted in an interwoven, syncretic worldview that raises questions about what the identities of Christ and Christianity actually were in the minds of the conquered indigenous people.

Despite their very deep concerns with idolatry, the friars made many intentional linkages between Christian and indigenous liturgical practices. The friars implemented processions and festivals with dancing and singing dedicated to God, the Virgin Mary, and the saints. Such *fiestas patronales* (patron saint festivals) successfully mirrored familiar practices such as singing and dancing that the indigenous had taken part of within the rituals of their old beliefs, but such similar practices also instilled a sense among the natives that the Catholic saints were nothing more than secondary and tutelary deities. The friars also devised conversion plays around Christian themes such as creation, the passion of Christ, and *pastorelas* (theatrical representations of the nativity of Jesus and the struggle between good and evil) in which the Indians had the chance to dress and express themselves in their own way. They also began the practice of decorating church altars with offerings and the custom of *altares de muertos* on the Day of the Dead.

Although the Spanish friars abhorred native religion, some – the Franciscans in particular – believed that native peoples played a central role in God's unfolding plan of salvation. The *Rethorica Christiana* of Diego de Valadés (1579) illustrates the utopia about which the missionaries dreamed. It consisted in the creation of a "Paradise" in which the Indians played the roles of perpetual children, trying to live up to the principles of perfect Christianity. The Franciscans, deeply influenced by the Medieval millenarian ideas of Joachim de Fiore, embraced an apocalyptic view of the future: for them, the New World offered a historic opportunity to fulfill centuries of religious speculation through the completion of biblical prophecies that predicted that all the people of the world would be converted to Christianity.

The friars also saw an opportunity to realize Thomas More's utopian vision of an earthly Christian paradise by creating a theocracy that only friars and Indians could share. The objective was to realize the apocalyptic vision of the City of God (Revelation 21) on earth. In other words, the Celestial Jerusalem would be adapted to the American reality and become the *Jerusalén Indiana* (Indian Jerusalem). This is evinced in much of the religious art of early sixteenth century New Spain, including the image of the *Tota Pulchra* painted on the walls of the Franciscan monastery in Huejotzingo, Martin de Voss's *Saint John Writing the Apocalypse* depicting the celestial Jerusalem, and a representation in stone of the Last Judgment in one of the *posa* chapels of the Franciscan atrium at Calpan. In short, from a religious standpoint, the sixteenth century was both the Age of Exploration and the Age of the Apocalypse.

To give sense and form to that desire, the friars erected a multitude of fortress-monasteries throughout Latin America. Their merlons and thick walls quickly transformed them into symbols of the spiritual militancy of a kingdom under construction. That architecture, the work of friars and Indians, produced impressive monastic compounds as tangible evidence of their faith. Meanwhile, within their interiors they devised pictorial programs that still show the aspirations of half a millennium ago. Images and scenes from Genesis to the Apocalypse again revive the eternal pilgrimage in search of Paradise. The universe itself was reinterpreted in those Mexican convents, but if the indigenous were integral to the celestial world, they were not protected in the temporal one. The contradiction and paradox of the role and work of the religious orders lies in the fact that the missionaries were part of the system of colonization and although some – if not all – of the friars objected to the many abuses against the indigenous conducted by their countrymen, they nonetheless supported the institution of the colony with all its implications. Evangelization and conquest would go hand in hand.

Religious Orders in Mexico

It took more than two decades after Columbus's landing in 1492 for Spanish military and geographic explorations to begin in the region later known as New Spain (Mexico). In 1517, Francisco Hernández de Córdoba discovered the peninsula of Yucatán, and in 1518, a new expedition led by Juan de Grijalva explored Yucatán, Campeche, and Tabasco. During this journey, Father Juan Díaz celebrated the first Catholic mass on the American mainland.

A year later, in 1519, Hernán Cortés led the third and most important expedition. After reconnoitering Yucatán, Campeche, and Tabasco anew, Cortés landed in Veracruz, where in addition to founding the first European city on the mainland, he conceived the conquest of these lands. The Mercedarian Fray Bartolomé de Olmedo and the secular priest Juan Díaz, the first clerics in the continental New World, also accompanied the Cortés expedition. Conquistador and chronicler Bernal Díaz del Castillo relates that Olmedo was Cortés's confessor and moderated his actions, that he preached to the Indians with the help of the interpreter Jerónimo de Aguilar, and that he baptized the lords of Tlaxcala. It was Olmedo who wrote a catechism for the Indians, one of the first of its kind in the New World.

The colonization and conversion of the Indians of Mexico started after the fall of Tenochtitlán in 1521. Thanks to a decree by Pope Alexander VI in 1501, the Spanish kings obtained the *Patronato Real* that allowed the Roman Catholic Church in Spain to enjoy exclusive right to the conversion of the Indians of the New World. Evangelization also functioned as a justification for the conquest. Specifically, the Spanish Crown obtained the right to manage church tithes; to nominate bishops; and to send clerics to establish missions, churches, monasteries, and hospitals. The Crown, in turn, promised to provide permanent economic support of all official evangelistic enterprises, such as the costs of holy sculptures, buildings, and clerical salaries. The pope officially recognized Spain's claims to newly conquered lands only after the conversion of the Indians living in the territories. Pope Paul III issued another bull, the 1537 *Sublimis Deus*, in which he affirmed that, contrary to many contemporary European opinions, the Indians of the New World must be rational beings, deserving of liberty, education, and happiness.

The first members of a religious order to arrive in New Spain were three Franciscan friars sent by Charles V in 1523. Like the emperor himself, the three were Flemish. Pedro de Gante, Juan de Tecto, and Juan de Aora were accomplished intellectuals. Tecto was a professor of theology at the Sorbonne, prior of the order for the city of Ghent, and confessor to Charles V. Aora was also a person of great erudition, a distinguished theologian and speaker, and was said to be the brother of the king of Scotland.

Pedro de Gante was a close relative of Charles V and perhaps the most well-known of the evangelist friars. He dedicated himself to teaching the Indians to read and speak Spanish, to singing and playing musical instruments, and to preaching Christian doctrine. He founded a school where Indian children learned many kinds of professions and crafts. He learned Nahuatl and wrote a Nahuatl catechism. He commissioned the first open chapel, called San José de los Naturales, to teach doctrine and preach the mass to the crowds of gathered Indians. Pedro de Gante so dedicated himself to evangelization and so loved the Indians that his death in 1572 reportedly caused the natives great grief.

The first group of missionaries authorized by the pope arrived in 1524. Known as the "Twelve Apostles," this extraordinary group of Franciscans had great successes in terms of actually affecting conversions, and the twelve were also writers, linguists, teachers, able organizers, and men of peace. Well-known in Spain, their leader was Fray Martín de Valencia, provincial of San Gabriel de Extremadura. On arriving Fray Martín is said to have asked Fray Juan de Tecto what he and his Flemish companions had been able to accomplish in their first year. Fray Juan answered that they had mastered "a theology Saint Augustine never knew," explaining that for Mexico, the Nahuatl language was as vital as conventional theology.[2]

The selection of twelve friars to form the group had significance as a conscious reference not only to the twelve apostles of Christ but also to the twelve clerics who with Saint Francis founded the order. Church tradition also

---

2 John McAndrew *The Open-Air Churches of Sixteenth-Century Mexico* (Cambridge, MA: Harvard University Press, 1965), 69.

dictated that twelve was the ideal number for a monastic community. The twelve missionaries of New Spain equated their task with Christ's apostles, who set out to preach the word all over the world after they received the gift of languages at Pentecost.

When the twelve arrived at Tenochtitlán in 1524, Cortés met them followed by a procession of other conquistadors and Indian caciques, all carrying wooden crosses. Cortés advanced 500 feet on his knees, removed his hat, and threw his cape on the ground so that fray Martín de Valencia could walk upon it, thus symbolically re-creating the entrance of Jesus into Jerusalem on Palm Sunday. Still kneeling, Cortés kissed the friar's hands and the hem of his habit. The other Spanish and Indian caciques repeated Cortés's gesture with the other friars. This symbolic and dramatic action impressed the Indians. They expressed surprise at seeing the powerful conquistadors showing respect and deference for humble friars. Paintings in the convents of Ozumba and Tlalmanalco depict this event.

The year 1524 also saw the establishment of the first four convents in New Spain, each with four friars: México-Tenochtitlan, Texcoco, Tlaxcala, and Huejotzingo. The latter convent features a famous mural portrait of the twelve friars. In 1530, more missionaries founded convents at Tepeaca, Cuauhtitlan, Toluca, and Tlalmanalco. Beginning in 1535 with the first Viceroy, Antonio de Mendoza, and his successor Luis de Velasco, colonial support for the Franciscan order steadily increased. By 1559, there were 380 friars in New Spain.

The missionary work of the Franciscans was the most important work of that kind during the sixteenth century. These friars were the most effective among the diverse orders in their conversion of the Indians, pacification, and social stabilization. Although in the early years the friars did not speak Nahuatl, they won the respect of the Indians with their honesty, sincerity, and loving attention. They ate the same food as the Indians: *tortillas* of maize, *capulines* (a kind of cherry), *tunas* (prickly pears), and *nopales*. The friars, for the most part, protected the Indians from the abuses of the conquistadors and *encomenderos* (owners of *encomiendas*, the assignment to a colonist of land and a group of Indians who were to serve him with tribute and labor), thus often earning their trust. In Cuauhtinchan, for example, the Indians refused to accept the replacement of the Franciscans by the Augustinians. They closed the church and refused to feed the new missionaries. In another case, San Juan Teotihuacan, the Indians protested a change in personnel, stating, "We love the Franciscans and we consider them to be our own fathers, because they walk barefoot just like us. They eat the same [things] as we do. They sit on the ground, they are humble like us, and above all they love us as if we were their own children."[3]

The Franciscan chroniclers recorded many important events of the Spiritual Conquest of New Spain. For example, Toribio de Benavente (Motolinía), one of the original twelve, wrote the *Memoriales*, and Bernardino de Sahagún wrote his *Historia General de las Cosas de la Nueva España* (Florentine Codex). The impressive missionizing work of the Franciscans extended to much of Mexico: the center (states of México, Querétaro, Morelos, Puebla, and Tlaxcala), the west (Jalisco, Colima, Michoacán, and Guanajuato), the peninsula of Yucatán and the north (Zacatecas, Durango and San Luis Potosí), and included even Guatemala, California, and Texas.

The Order of Preachers, or Dominicans, arrived in New Spain in 1526. Their efforts there, led by Fray Tomás Ortiz, got off to a rocky start. Of the original twelve friars, five died in the first year and an additional four became so ill they returned to Spain. The Dominicans were observant monks like the Franciscans, but they adopted a less paternalistic attitude toward the Indians. The most famous of these was Fray Bartolomé de las Casas, the bishop of Chiapas, who received the title Protector of the Indians. Las Casas raised energetic protests and denounced the exploitation of the Indians by their Spanish masters throughout his career in the Caribbean and Central America.

Although the Augustinians began in the thirteenth century with a focus on the contemplative ascetic life, by the sixteenth century the order reoriented itself to a program of evangelization. Like the Franciscans, the Augustinians considered the New World an earthly paradise free from sin, a Garden of Eden where they hoped to create a City of God, which was the utopia of Saint Augustine. They were both the most liberal order in administering the sacraments and the most apocalyptic, as they viewed the work of conversion as a cosmic battle between Christ and Satan for the souls of the Indians. Seven Augustinians directed by Fray Francisco de la Cruz arrived in Mexico in 1533. They limited their activities to sections of Mexico not already under the control of the Franciscans or Dominicans. Doña Isabel, daughter of the Aztec emperor Moctezuma II, contributed the land for the first Augustinian convent in Mexico City.

By 1559, Augustinians in Mexico counted some 200 friars and forty convents. Fray Alonso de la Veracruz was among the more notable Augustinians in Mexico. He wrote important works on philosophy and theology, subjects

---

3 Fray Geronimo de Mendieta, Historia Eclesiástica Indiana (1547–96). Estudio analítico de Joaquín García Icazbalceta (México: Editorial Porrúa. 1971), 12.

he also taught at the recently founded University of Mexico. He was also a professor of arts and philosophy at the Augustinian college in Michoacán, founded in 1540, which could be considered the first university in the Americas except for its lack of a royal *cédula* (warrant).

In addition to the convent in Mexico City, the Augustinians founded their principal convent at Acolman in 1550. From there, they established a network of missions that extended from Yecapixtla in northern Morelos to Actopan, Ixmiquilpan, Metztitlan, and Molango in Hidalgo, to Cuitzeo and Yuriria in Michoacan and Guanajuato, respectively. By the end of the sixteenth century the chronicler Gerónimo de Mendieta wrote that the three mendicant orders controlled about 350 convents and about 1,500 friars combined.

In 1555, don Vasco de Quiroga, Bishop of Michoacán, was in negotiations with Ignacio de Loyola, who in 1540 received papal approval for the recently founded Company of Jesus (i.e., the Jesuits) to send priests to the New World, but several events delayed the Jesuit project in the New World. Among these were the death of Loyola in 1556, the illness of four Jesuits who planned to travel with Quiroga, and finally the death of Quiroga himself in 1565. Thus, the Jesuits arrived in Mexico in 1572, and their arrival marked the beginning of a new epoch. Rather than focusing on the conversion of the Indians, the Jesuits concentrated their efforts on fostering education and on channeling the talents and abilities of the youth of New Spain.

Because the Jesuits arrived in Mexico at the end of the sixteenth century, most of their evangelical activities took place in the seventeenth and eighteenth centuries. They played an important role in the development of education in both Mexico and Peru and helped create the idea of an American consciousness, which led eventually to a national identity. It is very clear that when the Jesuits arrived, the "Spiritual Conquest" of the mendicant friars was almost complete. Thus, they worked above the foundations of the newly Christianized civilization, focusing their efforts on the education of the creoles and mestizos, motivating them to think broadly and critically.

Barely a year after arriving in New Spain, the Jesuits opened their first college, dedicated to Saints Peter and Paul, followed soon by the colleges of San Miguel, San Bernardo, and San Gregorio in Mexico City. Some years later, the last three joined to form the College de San Ildefonso. Especially important among the Jesuit colleges were San Francisco Javier in Tepotzotlán and San Gregorio in Mexico City. The Tepotzotlan town *cacique*, Martín Maldonado, donated the land for the founding of San Francisco Javier College, which trained Jesuit novices until the expulsion of the order in 1767. Among other things, Jesuit novices at the colleges were all required to learn indigenous languages. The Jesuits also adopted the failed Franciscan project of training indigenous priests, although the Crown later killed this initiative with an order prohibiting native clergy.

In terms of the locations of missions, the Jesuits arrived in New Spain at a time when the mendicant orders had already evangelized most of the explored regions. So the Jesuits took their missionary efforts to the limits of the explored lands in the north. They worked among tribes such as the Tepehuanes and Tarahumaras, who, it appeared to the clergy, seemed to forget from one day to the next the lessons of the missionaries and who killed the priests and their work. Colonial policies of establishing *presidios* (forts) on the frontiers and of leaving evangelization efforts completely in the hands of the missionaries contributed to the large number of religious martyrs.

Jesuit martyrs far exceeded those of the mendicant orders. However, every time a missionary was martyred in the line of duty, two more wanted to take his place regardless of the risk. Not only did the missionaries follow colonial troops, but they also set out on their own to pacify territories where military forces were defeated. Thus, the Jesuits Juan Manuel Salvatierra, Juan Ugarte, and Francisco Eusebio Kino were responsible in part for the Spanish acquisition of Baja California. As Vicente Riva Palacios wrote in *México a través de los siglos*, "the seventeenth-century Jesuits were the representatives of the burning apostolic spirit of the previous century."[4]

Religious Orders in Peru

The evangelization in the Andes officially started with the early attempts of conversion made by Fray Vicente Valverde and several other Dominican friars in 1532. However, this activity was limited to the administration of baptisms and some occasional marriages and confirmations. The real and effective evangelization of Peru started in 1570, when Viceroy Francisco de Toledo established political stability by executing the last rebel Inca Tupac Amaru and punishing the principal leaders of an Andean religious movement known as the Taki Onqoy (dancing sickness). Its adherents were itinerant dancers and teachers who claimed to be possessed by Andean gods, whose cosmology showed a creative blending of indigenous traditions of cataclysm and rebirth with the Christian symbolism of destruction and resurrection, and who foretold the imminent triumph of Andean gods and the end of Spanish rule.

---

4 Vicente Riva Palacios, *México a través de los siglos* México (México: T.I. Ballescá y Cía., 1887), vii.

Viceroy Toledo promoted the resettlement of Andeans into towns and villages (*reducciones*) that were conceived as crucial not only to the exploitation of Indian labor but also for the Christianization and Hispanicization of the Indian people. The arrival of the Jesuits in 1568 reinforced the challenging missionary task. Archbishop Toribio Alfonso de Mogrovejo, who served from 1581 to 1605, believed that Andeans needed reform that would be advanced only through better instruction and more careful pastoral surveillance by adequately trained clergy. He was a moderate supporter of the peaceful evangelization, but there were some more radical Catholic leaders who believed in a forceful evangelization to fight the signs of idolatry. Under the advice of these radical churchmen, the systematic extirpation of idolatry began with the next two archbishops, Bartolomé Lobo Guerrero (1609–1622), who had been an official of the Inquisition, and Gonzalo de Campo (1625–1626).

In 1609 a very theatrical *auto de fe* took place in Lima with the participation of the parish priest of the town of Huarochirí. The priests had Hernando Pauccar, the minister of the worship of important regional gods like Chaupi Ñamca and Paria Caca, tied to a pole and lit a fire in front of him in which they burned several idols and mummified bodies of ancestors (*malquism* and other ritual objects). The purpose was to serve as a public lesson that the civil and religious authorities would repress and extirpate by all means any sign of superstition or religious error.

Strategies of Evangelization

In both New Spain and Peru, evangelization created a spiritual conflict for the Indians. In a way, this conflict helps explain the complexities of modern-day societies. The friars in their conversion efforts took advantage of coincidental similarities between Christianity and native religions. However, these similarities were a double-edged sword, as both religious systems featured structures of classifying divine beings, whether indigenous deities or Catholic saints, with special attributes and qualities. This led to religious syncretism, or the blending, of indigenous and Christian symbols, rituals, and beliefs.

In New Spain, the ancestral cult of the rain and agricultural fertility god Tlaloc offers a typical example of syncretism. For Tlaloc, the friars substituted the image of San Isidro Labrador, the protector of the fields and the harvest. Interestingly, some images of San Isidro actually feature the stylized face of the god Tlaloc. This indicates that for the natives of certain parts of Mexico, San Isidro and Tlaloc, although dressed differently, represented the same personage. Thus, when the Indians prayed to San Isidro for a good rainy season, they were in fact praying to Tlaloc.

The friars also taught the Indians that the devil was a figure opposed to both God and to all that was good. As there was no exact equivalent of the devil in native religion, the friars substituted the term *Tlacatecolotl*, meaning "owl," or "human-owl." The *Tlacatecolotl* was a creature associated with the night, witchcraft, apparitions, human sickness, and death. Although the Aztecs conceived of *Tlacatecolotl* as possessed of superhuman powers, they also believed he was essentially human. In merging the two, the friars played on convenient Aztec conceptions of a dualistic world.

Both the *conquistadors* and the missionaries tried to stamp out pagan religion by destroying idols and sanctuaries. The friars often substituted images of Christ or the Virgin Mary in the place of pagan deities at important pre-conquest pilgrimage sites. This is the case at the sanctuary of Chalma, where even today one cannot tell if visitors are worshipping the Christian image of the Señor de Chalma or the ancient Oztoteotl, the ancestral cave god of the local Otomí Indians. Another, more important, example is the shrine of the Virgin de Guadalupe, which was an important Aztec shrine to Tonantzin, "our revered Mother," long before the miraculous apparition most Mexicans believe in. Tonantzin was a title related to Coatlicue, the Aztec Mother Earth goddess. In the Andean world there was an identification between Pachamama, the Inca Earth Goddess, and the Virgin Mary, called the Virgin of the Andes, which became in the indigenous imaginary a colonial Andean goddess.

To facilitate the conversion process and education, the missionaries often collected the Indians into newly planned towns. Even today, one can still see the urban layout of these communities, called mission towns or Indian towns. The convent or church was at the heart of each of these villages. The Indians built their new homes around the churchyard. This urban plan helped foster a sense of community and also helped the evangelization efforts of the friars, wherein, according to colonial chroniclers, clerics sometimes performed thousands of baptisms per day.

In addition to convents and churches, the friars in some cases built hospitals in these communities. The clerics also opened schools where they taught boys and girls skills such as ironwork, carpentry, masonry, tailoring, shoemaking, painting, sculpture, ceramics, furniture making, and metallurgy. To teach Christian doctrine, friars produced written several catechisms in Spanish and indigenous languages. Fray Luis Caldera even created a catechism with images, carrying paintings from town to town that represented heaven, hell, purgatory, and the sacraments. Caldera even went to the extreme of providing a theatrical representation of hell by throwing dogs and cats into a flaming oven so the Indians could get an idea of its torments.

Art and Architecture of Conversion

The dialogue established between the Spanish friars as European voices and the Indians as native interlocutors produced a variety of physical manifestations. One of the most important results of this cultural dialogue was the *tequitqui*, or so-called *Indian-Christian* art that shows the creative, conceptual, and material expression of the Indians in that process of transculturation. *Tequitqui* is an art in evolution that manifests the Indian ideological interpretation of a complex reality. In Nahuatl, *tequitqui* means one who pays tribute. *Tequitqui* has a parallel in the Islamic art of Spain, called *mudéjar*, which has approximately the same meaning. Each term refers to the art that the conquered made for their conquerors or the conquerors' assumption of the style of the conquered.

Tequitqui art is the interpretation of European architectural and decorative features according to the techniques and cosmovision of the Indians, while derived from the religious images that they drew from the friars' books. The *tequitqui* style appears in almost all of the approximately 350 convents founded in New Spain during the sixteenth century, covering a range of surfaces including facades, portals, cloisters, chapels, baptismal and holy water fonts, atrium crosses, and mural paintings. In time, *Indian-Christian* art defined its own canon and was no longer either Spanish or Indian but rather uniquely Mexican.

However, not all of the friars' artistic choices were a transcultural mixing like *tequitqui*. They also intentionally incorporated conquest and replacement into their motifs. In most cases the friars built their churches and monasteries on top of pre-Columbian platforms using the very stones removed from those destroyed structures. Like European cathedrals, they were also built to be admired from a distance for their imposing and awe-inspiring size. The monasteries of New Spain included some architectural features not found in their European antecedents. The most prominent of these features was the *atrio* (patio), which usually included a large, open chapel for preaching to large crowds and a series of smaller *posa* chapels for processions or instructions to smaller groups or individuals.

The Spanish friars understood that the Indians performed most religious rituals, from dances to human sacrifices, in the plazas around their *Teocallis*, or temples. Priests standing in the temple sanctuary high above the plazas directed the rituals below, where all the people were gathered. Given this precursor, the Spanish friars devised the *"iglesia al aire libre,"* the open-air church, to facilitate conversion. In this case, the open-air *atrio* of the church became a kind of nave and substituted for the pre-Columbian plaza ritual space, while the open chapel was the presbyterium. Practical considerations also guided this decision. The large open-air spaces of church and convent *atrios* could hold many people, far more than the small-roofed interiors of typical European churches.

The *atrio* was a space of great dimensions, usually square in shape and bounded by strong walls topped with merlons or other battlements. Access to the typical *atrio* was through one or more open porticos placed halfway along each side. The friars oriented the *atrio* to the cardinal directions, which for the Indians were the four directions of the universe. In the *atrio*, the clerics conducted the mass, gave the sacraments, and presented theatrical adaptations of Christian stories, which were the first contact with the new faith for many Indians.

In 1579, Fray Diego de Valadés, resident of the convent of San Francisco de Tlaxcala, published an idealized view of the sixteenth-century convent *atrio* in his *Rethorica Christiana*. The plan features a great rectangular space with openings on three sides. *Posa* chapels dedicated to teaching boys, girls, men, and women mark each of the four corners. Believers carry the sick through two of the entrances. A funeral procession with the cross at the head enters the third portal. Acolytes and singers follow. Valadés depicted the activities common in convent *atrios*: Fray Pedro de Gante instructing students with painted images; a group of Indian cantores; teaching the creation of the world with paintings; preparations for a marriage; writing names in the parish registry; the sacrament of marriage; the sacrament of baptism; teaching how to confess sins; teaching how to do penance; and teaching the catechism.

Two arcades run along the lower edge of the image. The left is dedicated to confession and the right to the Eucharist, the mass, and extreme unction. Seated in the center of the arcades, a friar dispenses justice in a dispute. Just above is the signature of Diego de Valadés. An allegory of the universal Church occupies center of the image. The twelve first friars carry the allegory on their shoulders. St. Francis and fray Martín de Valencia lead the group. The inscription below reads: "The first to bring the Holy Church of Rome to the New World of the Indies." God the Father, Christ, the Virgin Mary, and an angel appear amid heavenly clouds above the cupola of the allegorical temple. Thus, Valadés represented the ideal of the evangelistic activities of the

Franciscans: the utopia of an earthly Paradise where the Indians of the New World would live the principles of a perfect Christianity. In this representation, Valadés is presenting the Church of Rome as the substitution of the World Tree in the Indian sacred space.[5]

Convent *atrios* usually featured the so-called atrial crosses that marked the center of the universe and that for the friars was Christ symbolized by the cross and for the Indians represented the Tree of Life. There were also small enclosures, called *posa* chapels, at the corners that served as places to pause and pray. These were also important during processions or the performance of the *Via Crucis*, which featured candles, song, clouds of incense, and speeches. The priest exited the sanctuary with the sacred Host and made a circuit of the four chapels in the *atrio* followed by parishioners.

Unfortunately, the completion of so many permanent convents and the full mobilization of the evangelistic program coincided with the massive collapse of the Indian population. Terrible epidemics of smallpox, measles, typhus, and plague decimated native populations by as much as 90 percent. The friars also had to contend with the constant envy and criticism of a secular clergy who resented the power and privileges accorded the regular orders. The Franciscans, for example, were accused of trying to build a Franciscan empire. By the first decade of the seventeenth century, the Spanish Crown and secular Church hierarchy had come to fear that the friars represented a threat to the monarchy itself; so the king decided to place the conversion of the Indians under the control of the secular Church.

Thus, the Spiritual Conquest and the utopian vision of the Indian Jerusalem came to an end. Without a doubt, the missionaries were integral to the conquest of the Americas, as conversion often preceded colonization. Today, the impressive monuments of the churches' convents stand in mute testimonial to their efforts.

Indigenous Reactions to Christianity

The indigenous reactions to these evangelization processes in both New Spain and Peru were diverse and complex. Resistance was one response, and 1539 marked one of the most famous examples of indigenous religious resistance, the dramatic trial of Don Carlos Ometochtli-Chichimecatecuhtli, the *cacique* of Tetzcoco and the grandson of the great king Netzahualcoyotl. Don Carlos was baptized by the Franciscans and was an alumnus of the School of Santa

---

5 McAndrew, 294–295.

Cruz de Tlatelolco. In 1539, he was accused of idolatry and concubinage by the Inquisition under the direction of Bishop Juan de Zumárraga.

In Don Carlos's house, the Spaniards found altars and a profusion of idols, and his ten-year-old son declared that he had not learned Christian doctrine because his father discouraged him from going to church. Other witnesses declared that Don Carlos recommended that his subjects not learn the Catholic teachings because they should follow "the ideas they had and were believed by their ancestors, and to live in the way they lived."[6] He admitted that his niece was his lover, but he denied having spoken against or opposing the Catholic Church. His wife, in spite of his infidelities, affirmed that she never saw him worshipping idols. Despite a lack of solid evidence against him, Don Carlos was sentenced to death.

It is strange that Zumárraga was so severe with the sentence, especially because he was not a cruel man and in general he had shown benevolence to other "heretical" Indians. It is possible that he thought that as an important Indian leader, Don Carlos could have been the head of an anti-Catholic movement of large proportions, and so he wanted to set a harsh example to instill fear in the Indians and to suppress idolatrous practices. Whatever the case, Don Carlos was burned at the stake with the charge of being a "proselytizing heretic."[7] As a result of the harsh punishment of this notorious case and a similar case in the Yucatán a few years later, the Inquisition moved away from prosecuting indigenous converts for heresy.

In the Andean religion, what Spanish Christians often called the Indians' idolatry was both a form of both resistance and an adaptation to the imposition of Christianity. Mainly during the seventeenth century, the Catholic Church in the Archdiocese of Lima set up a vigorous investigatory and penal process known as the extirpation of idolatry with the objective to eliminate ancient religious practices and to establish a more orthodox assimilation of the Christian doctrine. Thus, we can see Andean history through the lens of a struggle between idolatry (colonial Andean religion) and its enemies (Christianity and Christian extirpators). Andean beliefs and practices survived because they changed and adapted to colonial realities where people assimilated Christian terms, ideas, rituals, and explanations into an expanding religious framework. The pre-Hispanic landscape was replete with sacred and historical meanings organized in *ayllus*, which were basic kin groups or families claiming ties to a common ancestor. The Spaniards founded their

---

[6] Robert Ricard, *La Conquista Espiritual de México* (México: Editorial JUS, 1947), 470–473.
[7] Ibid., 473.

grid-patterned *pueblos* on the already existing *ayllus* similarly to the way they did on the *altepetls* in Central Mexico. The Archdiocese of Lima counted more than 131,000 Andean parishioners around 1644 and extended over a very complicated geography.

In 1583, the third Provincial Council of Lima decreed, following the pastoral concerns expressed at the Council of Trent (1545–1563), that one priest should serve no more than 200 to 300 families in Peru. In spite of the efforts made in the early seventeenth century, there were only 175 priests to take care of the 162 parishes that constituted the Archdiocese of Lima. These numbers show that the Church was behind its objective and could not effectively cover and monitor all the regions assigned. This situation and the complex geographical and social conditions in the Andes made it impossible for the Catholic Church to develop a spiritual conquest similar to the one in New Spain.

The clearest manifestation of the idolatry was the worship to *huacas*, a term used to refer to a wide variety of holy things and places including peaks of mountains with special shapes, temples, ancestral mummy bundles (*malquis*), burial places, and the gods themselves. Worship to *huacas* of stone was an embodiment and reinterpretation of a long cultural past. According to this concept, the *ayllus* usually traced their lineage back to a divine forefather, a progenitor from a distant past who, on making some contribution to the world, was transformed into part of the landscape, living on as an eternal force and a protector of the *pueblo*. *Huacas* had once lived on the earth, where they had carried out their various feats, and the landscape displayed what amounted to living proof of this. When the *huacas'* exploits on earth were completed, it was common for them to turn to stone, either in their own shapes or in those of animals or appropriate symbols. This divine lithomorphosis – turning to stone – hardly spelled the end of their power over the lives of their descendants; on the contrary, it made their power everlasting. The *huaca* ancestors represented an otherworldly stability and permanence, but they were simultaneously active forces that remained integrated in the world of their people.

The transformation into stone usually occurred at some conspicuous site in a god's mythical wanderings, at the point where the *huaca* had made a most lasting contribution or where he or she had been overcome by a better. Such sites became sacred, inseparable from the memory of the *huacas* themselves. *Huacas* became places of religious pilgrimage where the peoples who believed themselves descended from these divine progenitors would bring offerings, give regular worship, and look for continuing support and guidance. The

Andean landscape with its mountain peaks, outcroppings of rock, peculiar boulders, and life-giving springs was thus full of religious meaning.

The *Huarochirí Manuscript* tells of a very famous and widely worshipped *huaca* called Pariacaca who had terrific power and wisdom and made an irrigation channel for the towns of Cupara and Quinti. According to a legend recollected by Jesuit priests, the giant *huaca* Viracocha, after emerging from Lake Titicaca, created there the world and the first human beings.

The *huacas* were familial gods and agricultural deities, concerned with crops and their seeding, irrigation, soil fertility, and harvest and with access to pasture, streams, and springs. In this manner, the *huacas* had an intrinsic relationship with the land. The religious belief in *huacas* was a means of comprehending and coping with human defenselessness in the face of drought, crop failure, disease, death, and the threat of all kinds of natural catastrophes. After the arrival of Christianity, the process of syncretism of the Catholic and Andean religions disguised *huacas* as Christian saints that are the patrons of the *pueblos*, ensuring their survival.

There were also lesser divinities associated with kinship called *chancas* (lineage gods) and *conopas* (personal gods of fecundity). The *chancas* were usually figures of stone, occasionally adorned with wax, coins, and other objects. They were small and moveable and were considered powerful familial gods. The *conopas* were small portable stones, sometimes natural but often sculpted to represent certain animals (commonly llamas and alpacas) or produce (usually maize or potatoes), normally having a direct connection with fertility rituals and prayers. *Chancas* and *conopas* were usually addressed by the extirpators as "fetishes" or "idols."

After decades of anti-idolatry campaigns, Archbishop Hernando Arias de Ugarte (1630–1638) ceased sponsoring them directly from Lima. However, Arias's skepticism about extirpation was only a brief halt because the next Archbishop Pedro de Villagómez (1641–1671) initiated the most frenetic activity of extirpation in the history of Peru. Villagómez organized a very solemn religious ceremony in the Cathedral of Lima for the send-off of the *visitadores de idolatría*, well-educated priests charged with rooting out idols, an action that showed the great institutional support for the renewal of the battle against idolatry. However, the Villagómez campaign, despite its apparent success in repressing the idolatry, had problems of lack of funding, corruption of some of the officials, conflicts with the Jesuits, and criticisms by opponents of the method of extirpation.

The case of Pedro Gamboy provides an example of the extreme operation of the extirpation campaign of Villagómez. Gamboy was condemned for his involvement in love rituals along with a host of other charges. His punishment was to wear a wooden cross around his neck for the rest of his life, to endure 100 lashes in public, and to participate in a procession of shame. In that procession, he wore a *coroza* (pointed headgear worn by a religious offender), was naked to the waist, and rode astride a beast while a crier broadcast his crimes for all to hear. Finally, he was to be banished for four years to the Casa de Santa Cruz, the sorcerers' prison, in the Cercado de Lima. The purpose of all of these actions was to discipline, humiliate, and ridicule the offenders before their own people and also to destroy physically the so-called instruments of idolatry.

In the eyes of most Spaniards in Peru, idolatry was more than another society's mistaken religion; it was the result of the interventions of the devil. For Church leaders, Satan was a formidable adversary who faced few limitations, and his powers of metamorphosis and capacity for spirit-like flight made it easy for him to deceive indigenous people. This was the ecclesiastic mentality that promoted arbitrary and excessive efforts at extirpation. In anti-idolatry investigations, we find accusations of Andean beliefs via manifestations of the phenomena of human flight, metamorphosis, and participation in witches' Sabbaths – a free fusion of European notions of demonology and native beliefs.

The colonial introduction of the concept of the devil confused matters further. One account portrays Satan as a deity opposed to Christ or, in some cases, as a sibling of Jesus who claims to be the rightful god of the Indians. In other words, the indigenous imaginary transformed the Judeo-Christian devil into another *huaca* of threatening and evil powers. It was against this backdrop that the extirpators took the fight against idolatry as a cosmic battle between the forces of good and evil.

In the post-Villagómez era (1642–1750), extirpation was not promoted directly by the Archbishops of Lima, but the Church continued to conduct idolatry investigations. The Catholic Church in Peru, little by little, assumed the fact that the indigenous people needed a religious reformation through a better Christian instruction based in more moderate methodologies, such as the teaching of the catechism, doctrine classes, and preaching sermons against idolatry.

Even so, the systematic campaigns of the extirpation were stern, temporary measures and shows of force that represent perhaps the most sustained religious persecution of indigenous peoples in the history of colonial Spanish America. The fact that in general, the *huacas*, *malquis*, *chancas*, and *conopas* did not disappear, even for Indian people who professed to be Christian, is a reflection of the failure of the process of the extirpation. Moreover, the extirpation encouraged an aversion to what was being presented in that time as official Christianity. As Kenneth Mills argued, with the religious repression the Indian wise men learned a valuable lesson: they instructed people to keep their true beliefs to themselves.

Conclusion

The legacies of these religious and cultural survivals are still evident in Mexico and the Andes today. *Nahuatlized* and *quechuanized* Spanish are clear external markers, and many people also practice a syncretic Catholic religion that retains some of the magic of the past. *Cofradías* and patron saint festivals, the celebration of the Cult of the Dead, and many other traditions are clearly mestizo. This raises the question, Who conquered whom? If we see the conquest as a military and material fact, the victors, without a doubt, were the Spaniards. However, from the spiritual and cultural point of view, the picture is far more ambiguous. The transculturation of three centuries produced new ethnic identities that are evident through the history, art, and religion of Latin American people. *"Lo latinoamericano"* began with the first encounter between the two cultures, when the transplanted Spaniards began to eat corn, manioc, chocolate, and chiles, and the Indians began to imprint their artistic and cultural canons on Spanish art and architecture. The *tequitqui* art and the Catholic religion were an integral part of the historical process of transculturation that led to the formation of Latin American identities. The process of creating the cultures of Mexico, Peru, and other countries of Latin America began in the sixteenth century, at the moment of contact between cultures and religions. The rest of their history has been, in part, a consequence of that seminal period. The mentality of the Latin American people is the product of the contradictions of the coexistence of magic, culture, and religion, a process in which the ancient pre-Columbian deities merged with the Christian sacred images rather than simply being replaced by them.

Bibliography and Suggested Readings

Aguilar-Moreno, Manuel. *Utopía De Piedra: El Arte Tequitqui De México*. Guadalajara: Conexión Gráfica, 2005.

Andrien, Kenneth. *Andean Worlds: Indigenous History, Culture and Consciousness Under Spanish Rule, 1532–1825*. Albuquerque: University Of New Mexico Press, 2001.

Andrien, Kenneth, and Rolena Adorno (eds.). *Transatlantic Encounters: Europeans and Andeans in the Sixteenth Century*. Berkeley: University Of California Press, 1991.

Burkhart, Louise M. *The Slippery Earth: Nahua-Christian Moral Dialogue In Sixteenth-Century Mexico*. Tucson: University Of Arizona Press, 1989.

Cervantes, Fernando. *The Devil in the New World. The Impact of Diabolism in New Spain*. New Haven, CT: Yale University Press, 1994.

Clendinnen, Inga. *Ambivalent Conquests. Maya and Spaniard in Yucatan, 1517–1570*. Cambridge: Cambridge University Press, 1987.

Damian, Carol. *The Virgin of the Andes: Art and Ritual in Colonial Cuzco*. Miami: Grassfield Press, 1995.

Diaz, Marco. *La Arquitectura de los Jesuitas en Nueva España: Las Instituciones de Apoyo, Colegios y Templos*. México: Universidad Nacional Autónoma de México, 1982.

Farriss, Nancy M. *Maya Society under Colonial Rule: The Collective Enterprise Of Survival*. Princeton, NJ: Princeton University Press, 1984.

Gibson, Charles. *The Aztecs under Spanish Rule: A History of the Indians of the Valley of Mexico, 1519–1810*. Stanford, CA: Stanford University Press, 1964.

Gruzinski, Serge. *The Conquest of Mexico: The Incorporation of Indian Societies into the Western World, 16th-18th Centuries*. Cambridge and Oxford: Polity Press, 1993.

Lockhart, James. *The Nahuas after the Conquest: A Social and Cultural History of the Indians of Central Mexico, Sixteenth Through Eighteenth Centuries*. Stanford, CA: Stanford University Press, 1992.

MacCormick, Sabine. *Religion in the Andes: Vision and Imagination in Early Colonial Peru*. Princeton, NJ: Princeton University Press, 1991.

McAndrew, John. *The Open-Air Churches of Sixteenth-Century Mexico*. Cambridge, MA: Harvard University Press, 1965.

Mendieta, Geronimo, *Historia Eclesiástica Indiana (1547–96)*. Estudio analítico de Joaquín García Icazbalceta. México: Editorial Porrúa, 1971.

Mills, Kenneth. *Idolatry and Its Enemies: Colonial Andean Religion and Extirpation, 1640–1750*. Princeton, NJ: Princeton University Press, 1997.

Perry, Richard. *Mexico's Fortress Monasteries*. Santa Barbara: Espadaña Press, 1992.

Ricard, Robert. *La Conquista Espiritual de México*. México: Editorial JUS, 1947.

Wachtel, Nathan. *Los Vencidos: Los Indios de Perú Frente a la Conquista Española (1530–1570)*. Madrid: Alianza, 1976.

8

Tridentine Catholicism in the New World

BRIAN LARKIN

In August 1617 Isabel Flores de Oliva, later known as St. Rose of Lima, died at the age of thirty-one. During her short life she was renowned in Peru for her holiness. She had gained her reputation by following a time-honored model of female sanctity. It was a strict model that called for renunciation of the world, the scourging of the flesh, and total devotion to God. According to testimony after her death, St. Rose fulfilled these prescriptions fully. At age twenty-six, she began to wear the Dominican habit as a member of its Third Order and, though not a nun, withdrew from the world to live in seclusion. She refrained from speaking and, when she engaged in conversation, kept her eyes downcast. She fasted regularly, so much so that she endangered her health. Doctors admonished her to eat more, but she replied that simply taking the Eucharist filled her stomach. She prayed endlessly. To prevent herself from nodding off during prayer, she tied her hair to a nail in the wall. She also mortified her flesh frequently. She poured cold water over her body to drain it of color and wore hairshirts, a crown of thorns, and a heavy chain wrapped around her waist. She wore the chain for so long that it stuck to her flesh and when she fell ill its removal caused her great pain.

Because of her heroic asceticism, Isabel Flores de Oliva was considered a saint by the people of Lima during her life. On her death, the city's faithful flocked to her home to seek relics from her body and clothing, and after her burial, many people, often ill or crippled, visited her tomb. It was reported that many were cured by touching either remnants of her clothing or the earth near her grave. Despite this outpouring of local devotion and her popular canonization by the devout of Lima, the institutional Catholic Church did not recognize St. Rose's holy status until 1671, when it officially canonized her after a thorough investigation.

St. Rose of Lima's life and death reveal many aspects of Tridentine Catholicism in the Americas. Tridentine Catholicism refers to the devotions of the faithful, the religiosity promoted by the clergy, and the institutional practices of the Catholic Church from the mid-sixteenth to the late eighteenth centuries. In the Americas, the era of Tridentine Catholicism is roughly contemporaneous with the colonial period. By the mid-sixteenth century in Europe, calls for reform from within the Church and the bourgeoning challenge of Protestantism prompted the Catholic Church to convoke a general council of bishops and theologians. They met at the Council of Trent (1545–1563), and its decrees guided Church policy and shaped Catholic piety for the next three centuries. By the end of the eighteenth century in Europe and the Americas, elements within the Church attempted to redirect piety and institutional practice. These late-eighteenth-century attempts to reform Catholicism were influenced by the Enlightenment and sought to remake the Church for a new age. These reforms, however, were never endorsed by a new general council of the Church and did not wholly displace the practices of Tridentine Catholicism.

At the Council of Trent, Catholic thinkers confronted calls for reform. Protestants had criticized late Medieval piety as superstitious and even idolatrous. Protestant reformers impugned what they considered an overreliance on the saints and recourse to their relics and images in times of danger. They derided the magical practices of the faithful, such as performing the sign of the cross or wearing blessed medals or rosaries to ward off evil. They criticized the overly ritualized nature of Catholic practice and even rejected some of the Church's sacraments. Most recognized only baptism and the Eucharist and discarded the rest. Even in terms of the Eucharist, Protestants challenged Catholic tradition. Although Protestants did not share a single Eucharistic theology, they generally discounted the Catholic doctrine of transubstantiation, the belief that, after the consecration by the priest during the mass, Christ resides bodily in a disc of bread and a cup of wine. Most Protestants also challenged the necessity of good works for salvation, declaring either that faith in Christ alone was sufficient or that salvation was a free gift from God that humans could do nothing to merit. In place of these late Medieval devotions that privileged the miraculous and the easy commingling of the sacred and profane, Protestants offered the faithful a simplified faith grounded in scripture. They advocated a personal relationship with God based on an understanding of his eminence and goodness. For Protestants, the lone Christian should contemplate God and offer directly to Him an inner tribute from the heart and mind. For them, the age of miracles had come to a close.

At the Council of Trent, Catholic leaders largely defended traditional piety. They upheld the veneration of saints, defended the corporeal presence of Christ in the Eucharist, and supported the ritual nature of religious engagement. In short, they endorsed the sense of the miraculous and the presence of the sacred within the world. In fact, the Church after Trent defiantly advocated traditional devotions and sought to increase their scale and splendor to counter Protestantism. The Tridentine Church, however, did not entirely disregard reformers' critiques. It sought to curb "excesses" in popular piety, moderate the credulity of the faithful, and more firmly establish clerical oversight of religious activity. Nonetheless, Tridentine Catholicism largely consisted of a reinvigoration of traditional forms of piety in the face of Protestant critique.

Although the prelates of the Church gathered at Trent paid little attention to the newly colonized Americas, the decrees they promulgated impacted the fledgling colonial Church and structured its subsequent growth. Tridentine Catholicism was brought to the local level by provincial Church councils in Lima (1582–1583) and Mexico City (1585). These meetings encouraged the florescence of the vibrant, lavish, and dramatic piety of the colonial period. We can see its results in the life and death of St. Rose of Lima. Although she lived in seclusion, she practiced a highly flamboyant piety. Her dramatic asceticism and withdrawal from the world established her reputation for sanctity. She was devoted to the Eucharist and believed in its miraculous power (conquering her hunger despite her rigorous fasts). More revealing, after her death, the faithful of Lima treated her according to the principles of traditional piety. Like other saints, she bridged the gap between this world and the next. Limeños flocked to her grave and her home in search of relics and miraculous cures, for they knew that the sacred resided in the world and could be touched and held. They also knew that saints, as friends of God and humans, were likely to aid them in troubled times. These beliefs were entirely orthodox and, in them, we see that the traditional endured in Tridentine Catholicism. But the lengthy investigation into St. Rose's life and miracles before her official canonization reveals the growing wariness of the institutional Church and its desire to more closely regulate the dramatic piety of Tridentine Catholicism.

Tridentine Piety in the Americas

Although the local practices of Tridentine piety varied from place to place and changed over time, they rested on five basic elements, most of which had a long history within Christianity: (1) sacred immanence, or the ability of the sacred to inhere within physical objects; (2) ritual and performative piety; (3) the ornate decoration of sacred space; (4) the collective nature of Catholic devotion; and (5) mysticism. The pious practices of the majority of Catholics revolved around the first four elements. Only a select few, like St. Rose of Lima, practiced the more solitary and inwardly focused path of mysticism.

Sacred immanence – divine presence – was the most important feature of Tridentine piety, and it has a long history. Almost from the beginning of Christianity, relics of saints served as loci for the manifestation of the sacred in the world. Early Christians venerated the earthly remains of the new faith's martyrs and built shrines upon their graves. They resorted to these relics to cure illness and cast out demons, for the bones of martyrs maintained a link with their spirits in heaven and thus manifested sacred power within the world. Eventually, by the tenth century, images of saints would function in much the same way. Although not the physical remains of saints, the likeness they shared with their heavenly prototypes created a bridge between this world and the next. The Medieval faithful appealed to images for aid in this world and succor at the time of death as their souls awaited judgment before the divine throne.

The Eucharist served as the other great site of sacred immanence for Christians. Given its centrality in Catholic belief, it is somewhat surprising that the doctrine of Christ's corporeal presence in the Eucharistic species, the bread and wine, was not codified until the thirteenth century. At the Fourth Lateran Council (1215), the Church declared the doctrine that would eventually become known as transubstantiation: that the priest at the altar truly invoked the bodily presence of Christ into bread and wine. The faithful would soon come to worship the Eucharist much as they had venerated relics and images.

Protestants generally critiqued the notion of sacred immanence. Martin Luther viewed saintly images as solely didactic, conveying the stories of salvation history to unlettered Christians. He never rejected the concept of Christ's corporeal presence in the Eucharist, but was uncomfortable with the doctrine of transubstantiation. John Calvin proved far more decisive in his repudiation of sacred immanence. He held a radically spiritual conception of divinity and declared that the sacred could not be confined within physical objects. For him, relics were simply bone, and images wood and canvas. To venerate them was to idolatrize. For him, the idea that Christ bodily resided in the Eucharist was abhorrent. He argued that God dwelt spiritually within the bread and wine, but as spirit, could not be confined within objects of the world.

At Trent, Catholic prelates defended sacred immanence, but at the same time attempted to curb its excesses. They restated the doctrine of transubstantiation, decreeing that the Eucharist truly is the body and blood of Christ. They also endorsed the sacred nature of saintly images, though more cautiously than in their statements concerning the Eucharist. They declared that images do not contain the essences of the saints they represent: painting and statues were only canvas and wood. But because these images shared a likeness of form with the saints they depicted, they "referred" devotions practiced before them to the appropriate saint. In other words, saintly images did not physically manifest the sacred within the world; rather, they opened special channels of communication between this world and the next. (In practice, however, this fine distinction was often ignored.) Because the world was still open to the sacred, Trent endorsed physical devotions to sites of immanence. It approved traditional practices like pilgrimages, processions, and gift giving to images and the adoration of the consecrated host. But it did not endorse sacred immanence without some reservation. It called on bishops to approve all relics in their dioceses and to remove all unseemly representations of saints from churches and other public places. For Catholics, the sacred could still erupt within the world, but now ideally only in clerically approved and decorous places.

Catholics in the colonial Americas fully participated in this religion of sacred immanence. As seen in the example of St. Rose, the population of Lima converged on her home and tomb in hopes of obtaining a relic. Limeños did so because they understood that the remnants of her body, clothing, and other objects with which she had had intimate contact were imbued with sacred power. They were literally pieces of the sacred that they could touch, caress, and even kiss. They could resort to them in times of need to plead for aid. Or on a more general level, they could keep the relics in their homes as talismans to ward off evil and live under the protection of St. Rose.

Relics constituted one locus of sacred immanence in the Americas, but probably the least common. In the first decades of colonization, the Americas contained few relics, for it produced no local saints until the seventeenth century. Nonetheless, trade from Europe soon brought numerous saintly remains to the new colonies. Of course individuals sought relics for their own purposes, but the trade in relics was necessitated by the foundation of the Church in the New World. According to Catholic theology, each church building must be consecrated with a relic. Soon so many relics circulated in the Americas that they could not be properly verified. In the mid-eighteenth century, Francisco Antonio de Lorenzana (1722–1804), the Archbishop of Mexico, defended the authenticity of relics of anonymous saints housed in the Metropolitan Cathedral of Mexico City despite Tridentine proscriptions against such practices. He claimed that countless unnamed martyrs had perished for their faith, and so it was not unreasonable to store their bones in churches and venerate them.

In the colonial Americas, images were much more common sites of sacred immanence than relics. Europeans brought many with them as they conquered and settled. More important, however, images began to be produced locally in the Americas even in the early stages of colonization. The Church attempted to regulate their production as early as 1555, when the First Mexican Provincial Council ordered bishops to examine the religious knowledge and orthodoxy of image makers. Whatever the effects of these attempts, images of Christ, the Virgin Mary, and other saints soon abounded in the Americas. Painted on canvas, sculpted of wood, or printed on paper, they filled churches and shrines and resided in the homes of the devout, both rich and poor. Some of these images earned reputations for being miraculous and became the focuses of local and regional devotions. During the colonial period, few if any miraculous images in the Americas drew devotees from farther away.

Many of these miraculous images were of Christ. For example, in Mexico the Cristos of Chalma and Santa Teresa (Ixmiquilpán) both served as loci of sacred power and attracted pilgrims. According to tradition, Augustinian friars evangelizing in the Ocuiltec village of Chalma southwest of Mexico City discovered a cave in 1537 that had served as a pre-Columbian pilgrimage site. When they returned to destroy the indigenous "idol" and replace it with a crucifix, they found to their astonishment that the Indian image had already been cast down and broken and in its place stood a crucifix. Whatever the veracity of the story, it is clear that the Lord of Chalma manifested sacred power, and those who lived in the region made pilgrimages to him over the colonial period to seek his aid. The Christ of Santa Teresa earned its miraculous reputation later. According to legend, this crucifix originally resided in the Otomí village of Mapathé (in the modern state of Hidalgo). It was not well cared for and in a state of disrepair. It was an image of little importance until, in the early seventeenth century, it miraculously renovated itself. News of this tremendous event reached Mexico City, and the archbishop ordered it removed from the village and housed in the Carmelite convent of Santa Teresa la Antigua. Because of its miraculous reputation, the Indian village of Mapathé fought to reclaim the crucifix but failed. It remained in the convent of Mexico City, where urban residents could easily approach it to access its divine power.

Although images of any saint could manifest sacred power, images of Mary the mother of Christ were the most common sources of saintly sacred immanence in the Americas. The popularity of the Virgin was due in part to the advocacy of the institutional Tridentine Church. Concerned about the abundance of local cults to saints of little renown and suspect heritage in Medieval Europe, the Tridentine Church sought to replace these figures of devotion with the Virgin. The Church's program coincided with long-term lay trends of increasing devotion to Mary. Both of these help account for the remarkable profusion of Marian images in the colonial Americas. The *Zodiaco mariano* (Marian Zodiac) is but one example that attests to the Virgin's popularity. Begun in the late seventeenth century by the Mexican Jesuit Francisco de Florencia, the *Zodiaco* catalogues numerous miraculous images of Mary in New Spain. The work records the legends and miracle stories of more than 100 such images. It was a celebration of the great favor that the Virgin had bestowed upon the colony and a patriotic statement by a creole (person of European heritage born in the New World) about Mexico's special status as a recipient of tremendous heavenly grace. Almost all of the Marian images described by Florencia had only local reputations and drew devotions from relatively small areas. Only a few images of the Virgin gained regional reputations during the colonial period and attracted devotees from greater distances.

The most renowned Marian image in South America was the Virgin of Copacabana, located on the shores of Lake Titicaca in modern Bolivia. It was sculpted by Francisco Tito Yupanqui, an indigenous artist, in 1582 and was modeled on the Virgin of Candlemas. In the 1580s the indigenous community near Copacabana suffered a famine and decided to create and honor an image of Mary to curry her favor. Tito Yupanqui, who had not been fully trained in European styles, crafted an initial image that Church officials rejected. Two years later, determined to create an acceptable image, he began work on what subsequently became the Virgin of Copacabana. At first, local priests were not enthusiastic about this image either. But one priest, Francisco Navarrete, under whose care Tito Yupanqui had left the statue, had a vision of rays of fire emerging from it. This experience began the miraculous reputation of the Virgin of Copacabana, and her fame spread as she performed other miracles, such as curing Indians from the region. Because of her growing fame, the Church decided to turn over the parish of Copacabana from the secular clergy to the Augustinian order. It was thought that the Augustinians, who arrived in 1589, could better promote the cult. To honor the image more appropriately and accommodate pilgrims, the Augustinians began to build a large basilica in 1631 and placed the image in a sumptuous altarscreen. The grand church continues to house the miraculous image and shelter devotees who visit this site of sacred immanence.

Certainly, the most famous miraculous image of the Virgin in the Americas is Our Lady of Guadalupe. According to tradition, the Virgin appeared to Juan Diego in 1531 on the hill at Tepeyac, a pre-Columbian indigenous site just north of Mexico City. She asked him to convey a message to the bishop to build a shrine for her on the site of the apparition. After two failed attempts to gain an audience with the prelate, the Virgin gave Juan Diego a sign to convince him. He was to gather roses growing out of season on the hill and present them to the bishop as evidence of the apparition. Juan Diego collected the flowers and wrapped them in his *tilma* (indigenous cloak). When he gained admission to the bishop's chamber, he unrolled his cloak to show him the roses. But on the inside, an image of the Virgin appeared. The divine sign overwhelmed the bishop, who then ordered a church constructed at Tepeyac for the veneration of Our Lady of Guadalupe. The first written account of this legend did not appear until 1648 and was written by the creole priest Miguel Sánchez. Although certainly a fiction modeled on European apparition accounts, it is clear that a shrine dedicated to the Virgin of Guadalupe was functioning by the mid-1550s at Tepeyac. Early testimonies agree that the image of the dark-skinned Virgin of Guadalupe located there was painted by a human hand. Although the identity of the artist may never be known for certain, it is possible that Marcos de Aquino, an indigenous painter, created it. Whatever the origins of the image, it is evident that the shrine at Tepeyac was a center for local devotions in the sixteenth century. The Virgin of Guadalupe's fame began to increase in the mid-seventeenth century when Mexican priests, inspired by Miguel Sánchez's account, proclaimed her apparition and miracles in numerous sermons. Her growing reputation led Church officials to build a larger church at Tepeyac beginning in 1695. Her fame grew exponentially in 1737, when her image was brought to Mexico City and paraded through the streets to halt a plague that ravaged the city. Thankful for her aid, the populace of Mexico City expanded devotions to her, and the Church proclaimed her patroness of New Spain in 1757. The Virgin of Guadalupe, however, did not become a truly national symbol representing all Mexicans until after the wars of independence in the early nineteenth century when she became associated with the Mexican insurgency.

In addition to relics and images, the last site of sacred immanence in Tridentine Catholicism was the Eucharist. The Eucharist was the most perfect locus of sacred power because, according to Catholic theology, it truly was the body and blood of Christ, his "real presence." Whereas relics and images opened channels to the sacred, the Eucharist was in itself divine. It was also the most common site of sacred immanence. For every day, in almost every church in the colonial Americas, priests consecrated bread and wine during the mass and thus made Christ physically present within the world. Although most of the faithful did not receive communion (ingest the host) more than a few times a year, they encountered and reverenced it frequently. It was obligatory for Catholics to attend mass every Sunday and holy day. Those who followed this precept must have witnessed at least ninety masses over the course of a year. Of course, the devout often attended mass more frequently, even daily.

During the mass, the congregants witnessed the elevation of the bread and wine at the moment of consecration and were encouraged to gaze upon them adoringly, communing with the Eucharist through the eye. It was not unusual for the faithful to enter churches throughout the day just to witness the elevation as numerous priests celebrated many private masses at collateral altars in the great urban churches of the Americas. Stealing quick glances at the Eucharist during the elevation was not the only means for Catholics to encounter the physical presence of Christ. Often, the host was displayed in splendid monstrances, ornate display stands for the host usually in the form of a sunburst, on the high altars of churches. On these occasions, Catholics could linger as they worshipped Christ's physical presence.

The ubiquitous manifestations of the sacred within the world in large measure account for the second element of Tridentine Catholicism: the performative and ritual nature of piety. Because God and the saints manifested themselves physically in the world, they required the attention of the faithful. Moreover, because they resided within physical objects, the devout could literally touch and ingest them. The physicality of the sacred thus privileged a corporeal and performative piety. Although Tridentine Catholics could worship God and venerate the saints with their hearts and minds, much of their religious practice was bodily and ritualistic. This does not mean that their piety was mechanical or empty. Rather, their bodies were vehicles for experiencing the sacred. The divine, because of its physicality, could be felt and incorporated into the body through the senses. Performative and ritual forms of piety, then, were not lesser ways of connecting with the sacred, but rather logical and privileged forms of worship in a religion of sacred immanence.

Because relics and images manifested the essences of saints, the faithful honored them in corporeal ways. As we have seen, Catholics made pilgrimages to their shrines. There, they sought to make physical contact with them. As mentioned previously, the devout of Lima desired to possess and hold remnants of St. Rose's clothes and they touched the earth next to her tomb. Some, who could not make pilgrimages on their own, often contented themselves by drinking water that had been placed in contact with a relic or image. This proximity imbued the water with the miraculous powers of the holy object and thus made it spiritually efficacious.

Catholics likewise paraded images through villages and cities in times of danger to plead for saintly aid or in times of celebration to honor and thank saints. As we have seen, the populace of Mexico City processed the Virgin of Guadalupe through the city in 1737 to seek her aid during a deadly epidemic. The faithful resorted to her only after the traditional means of curbing plagues, processing Our Lady of Remedies through the city, had failed. The people of Mexico City also frequently paraded images of St. Joseph through the streets to stop earthquakes. Processions, however, were not only for times of danger. More often, they were features of holy day celebrations. On a saint's feast day, churches that possessed images of the saint would organize joyous processions that usually included food, drink, and fireworks. More somber processions were held during Holy Week to commemorate the passion and death of Christ. In these processions, images of the crucified Christ, Christ in the tomb, and the Virgin of Sorrows dominated. Whether pleading for aid, celebrating the glories of saints, or recalling passages from salvation history, processions honored images and, through them, the holy figures they represented. Catholics in procession demonstrated their faith as they physically manipulated sites of sacred immanence.

The faithful honored the Eucharist in much the same way as they did images. They cast adoring gazes upon and processed with it in during Corpus Christi celebrations. Corpus Christi was the grandest of Tridentine religious festivals. It was the summer celebration of Christ's corporeal presence in the Eucharist. Cities throughout the Americas held great processions that included all social ranks. In Mexico City, Corpus was celebrated since the early sixteenth century. The city council spent lavishly on the festival, draping the city's buildings with banners, constructing portable altars for images of saints, and paying for dances, religious dramas, fireworks, jousts, and a post-processional feast. The procession itself was led by the poor, with festive giants representing all the world's people, and a dragon symbolizing sin defeated by the Eucharist. Next came the city's confraternities (pious lay brotherhoods), religious orders and other ecclesiastical corporations, and secular dignitaries. At the end of the procession was the Eucharist displayed in a magnificent monstrance. The entire action was designed to symbolically unite all social orders in a hierarchical arrangement determined by proximity to the Eucharist.

Corpus processions were similarly spectacular in Cuzco, the indigenous heart of the viceroyalty of Peru. The indigenous populations of the area participated prominently in the festivities. Although Spaniards there designed the processions to symbolize Indians defeated by the Eucharist, indigenous participants inscribed their own meanings of them. Indians *curacas* (nobles), dressed in traditional elite garb, processed at the head of their indigenous parishes and the images the indigenous participants carried. In these processions and artistic representations curacas commissioned to record their patronage of the festival, they represented themselves as powerful mediators between Spanish authorities and indigenous communities. Although they infused indigenous meanings into Corpus, it is clear that they engaged in a performative celebration of Christ's corporeal manifestation in the Eucharist.

Performative piety to honor sites of sacred immanence could be much less dramatic than pilgrimages and processions. In fact, the most common way of venerating images and relics and worshipping the Eucharist was to bestow gifts upon them. A gift to a site of sacred immanence demonstrated the giver's piety and was a means to curry favor with the holy person thus honored. Some gave gifts to images and the Eucharist to seek cures for illness, to thank the holy figure for favors rendered, to obtain grace for their souls, or simply to glorify God and His saints. Of course, a gift could perform many or all of these functions at once. The most common gift was light, in the form of wax for candles or oil for lamps. Light honored relics, images, and the Eucharist equally well and was inexpensive enough for even the poor to purchase. It marked the presence of the sacred and represented the lights of glory. The faithful also bestowed clothing and jewelry, but these gifts were restricted to images. Statues of saints were often clothed as they stood in churches and were magnificently attired during processions. Gifts of clothing and jewelry increased their splendor and symbolically called upon the honored saints to protect their devotees. Other common gifts included flowers, incense, and other minor adornments.

Performative piety, however, included more than devotions to sites of sacred immanence. Tridentine Catholicism, following Medieval practice, was highly liturgical, focused on the performance of the sacraments, especially the mass. Ritual action possessed great power, for it forged links with the sacred and assured the proper relationship between humans and God. The intellectual rationale for the efficacy of ritual piety was encapsulated in the performance of the mass. During this rite, the priest symbolically reenacted the passion and death of Christ. This symbolic performance collapsed time and created a mimetic link with Christ's historic sacrifice. This symbolic resonance, much as the shared likeness between saintly image and heavenly prototype, allowed the sacred to imbue the world. According to Catholic theology, the mass did not simply recall Christ's suffering and crucifixion; it literally re-created them and thus shared in their salvific effect. This understanding of ritual action spilled beyond the priestly order and the mass and imbued much of Tridentine piety. Hence, Catholics mortified their flesh in imitation of Christ's passion and acted in other symbolic ways to forge intimate connections with salvation history and earn grace for their souls. In a broader sense, they understood the great importance of properly performed ritual and expended much energy in ritual observance.

Protestants and Catholics bickered over the efficacy of ritual piety. Reformers attacked traditional understandings of the importance and effect of ritual. Their critique in part stemmed from their repudiation of sacred immanence. If the divine could not be located within physical objects, it followed that ritual action could not invoke the sacred into the world. It also came from their rejection of the theology of good works. Because salvation was either earned merely by faith or was entirely a gift from God, ritual action lost all power to attain grace. Protestant theology stripped religious ritual of its sacred efficacy and rendered it merely a means of commemoration. For this reason, they radically simplified ritual practice and cast aside many traditional sacraments. Catholics in turn rejected Protestant understandings of ritual piety, and at the Council of Trent, reaffirmed the sacred power of ritual and the full range of traditional sacraments. This Catholic defense of ritual piety in large part explains its enduring appeal in the colonial Americas. The Tridentine Church, however, did attempt to regulate ritual piety more closely than before. This greater oversight consisted largely of trying to standardize the performance of the sacraments, which local traditions had diversified over the Medieval period. To this end, the Church published the Tridentine Missal, a detailed guide for the proper celebration of the sacraments, in 1570. Because the academic study of the liturgy in the colonial Americas is virtually nonexistent, it is unclear what impact this had on religious practice.

Although the mass was the central focus of Tridentine ritual, the faithful engaged in many other forms of ritual piety. They orchestrated symbolic actions that, like the mass, were intended to resonate with aspects of salvation history and gain grace for their souls. These symbolic gestures did not invoke the physical presence of the sacred in the world. Only the priest at the altar could do that. But they did forge mystical unions with the sacred that showered celestial grace upon the performer. The most dramatic form of this type of ritual piety was self-mortification. As we saw in the example of St. Rose of

Lima, Catholics beat and deprived their flesh to imitate Christ's passion and death and thus participate in their salvific effect. In fact, one witness recorded that Rose had told him that "Our Lord had rewarded her with so much pain, of a kind she had not believed a human body could withstand. [It was] nothing like the kind [of pain] He Himself had suffered, [she had said], yet she was bewildered at having enjoyed so much forgiveness from God's hand."[1] In this statement is exemplified the Tridentine understanding of ritual piety: symbolic reenactments of events from sacred history bestow grace on the actor. Self-mortification was not limited to the hyperascetic like Rose of Lima.

Much of the faithful practiced mortifications, though on a milder scale. Self-flagellation was a common practice, encouraged by popular devotional treatises published in the colonial Americas. Although we will never know just how often people whipped themselves in imitation of Christ's passion in the privacy of their own homes, it is clear that self-flagellation was publicly practiced during Holy Week processions. In fact, the Third Mexican Provincial Council (1585) recorded that processions of the *penitentes* drew great crowds, and the Fourth Mexican Provincial Council (1771) stated that such processions continued into the late colonial period. Given the popularity of penitential confraternities, pious brotherhoods established precisely for public self-flagellation, in the colonial Americas, it is likely that dramatic mortification of the body to ritually re-create Christ's suffering was widespread among the populace.

Lay ritual piety took other, less flamboyant, forms as well. For instance, the sign of the cross, the common action of tracing a cross on the forehead and chest with the hand, functioned in much the same way as self-flagellation to bestow grace on the performer. One highly popular catechism written by Gerónimo de Ripalda (1536?–1618) and published repeatedly over the colonial period in the Americas encouraged believers to perform the sign of the cross frequently because it was an efficacious action that liberated the performer from evil. It worked because the fleeting action of human hands symbolically represented the true cross upon which Christ was crucified and so made mystically present its divine power. Perhaps just as common, the faithful used numeric and temporal symbolism in their devotions to create symbolic resonances with salvation history. For example, Catholics often had masses celebrated for the benefit of their souls or those of their departed loved ones. Oftentimes, they would order symbolic numbers of masses or have them

---

[1] Kenneth Mills, William B. Taylor, and Sandra Lauderdale Graham, eds., *Colonial Latin America: A Documentary History* (Wilmington, DE: Scholarly Resources, 2002), 204.

celebrated on symbolic days to increase their celestial efficacy. It was common, for instance, to order three masses in honor of the Trinity, five in memory of the five wounds of Christ, or seven in remembrance of the seven sorrows of the Virgin Mary. Such symbolic performances could form part of almost any religious action. One could recite nine Hail Maries to the nine choirs of angels, distribute alms to twelve poor people in honor of the twelve apostles, or commission thirty-three poor people to accompany one's corpse in a funeral procession in representation of the thirty-three years that, according to Christian tradition, Christ lived as man. Or masses could be performed on Thursdays in remembrance of the Last Supper or donations given to a hospital on a saint's feast day in special reverence of that holy person. In all of these cases, the symbolic performances resonated with aspects of salvation history and thus mystically showered their grace upon the performer (or commissioner) of the acts. Just as in the mass, ritual performance worked wonders.

Although these lay ritual performances were widespread in the colonial Americas, the institutional Tridentine Church was uneasy about them. The Council of Trent instructed Catholics that the mass was the central mystery of the faith and a unique ritual performance. As the true reiteration of Christ's passion and crucifixion, it conferred grace. Other ritual accoutrements, such as special numbers of masses or certain arrangements or colors of candles, did nothing to enhance its efficacy. Provincial councils in the Americas restated this understanding. Nonetheless, lay ritual piety remained a central feature of Tridentine Catholicism, and the Church, though uneasy about it, never seriously attempted to discourage it.

Sacred immanence and ritual piety help account for a third pillar of Tridentine Catholic practice, the lavish adornment of sacred space. During the Middle Ages Christians tended to ornament churches richly. They did so for many reasons: to exhibit their social status and wealth to the community, to demonstrate their devotion to God and the saints, and to obtain grace for their souls by performing good works in favor of the Church. More important, however, was the desire to honor sites of sacred immanence and embellish the performance of the mass.

Because the sacred was located in the Eucharist and saintly images contained within church buildings, Catholics treated these edifices with honor. The worldly manifestations of God, the heavenly king, and the saints – the heavenly courtiers – demanded material care and refinement. So the faithful spent lavishly to adorn their mundane houses and offer them a tribute befitting their exalted status. This rich ornamentation rendered churches microcosms of the heavenly kingdom and allowed the faithful to envision the splendors of the next world. These ornate spaces were designed to fill Christians with awe and induce within them a felt, corporeal experience of the might and glory of God. Not only did ornate church buildings house sites of sacred immanence; they also served in their entirety to situate the devout within heaven on earth and to overwhelm their senses with the felt presence of the divine. Churches also served as the setting for the mass and the consecration of the Eucharist. Engaged in a religion of ritual observance, Christians carefully and elaborately set the stage for the performance of the mass to heighten its drama. To ignore the staging of the mass and equip churches poorly would have undermined the ritual performance so central to Medieval Catholicism.

The Medieval tendency toward the ornate became a universal compulsion of the Tridentine Church as it countered Protestant practice. Because they generally denied the possibility of sacred immanence and the effectiveness of ritual piety, Protestants as a rule stripped church buildings of their ornamentation. The denuded Protestant church encouraged believers, free from ornamental distraction, to concentrate on the word of God as read during the service and on the exhortations of the minister. The Tridentine Church deliberately endorsed the proliferation of sacred ornamentation in defense of traditional piety. The artistic and architectural movement associated with this Catholic defense became known as the Baroque. The papacy sponsored the construction of the first Baroque churches in Italy in the 1580s, and from there, the movement spread to the rest of Catholic Europe and the Americas. It arrived in the New World in the first half of the seventeenth century, and the faithful enthusiastically supported it. They donated vast sums to construct numerous parish churches, convents, and monasteries and to adorn them richly.

Baroque church interiors were magnificent sites designed to overwhelm the senses, induce a corporeal experience of God's power, and raise consciousness toward the sacred. Altarscreens dominated church interiors in the colonial Americas. Urban churches often contained many of them, for they soared behind a church's main and numerous collateral altars. Constructed of wood, they were most often gilded or covered in silver. They housed in their many niches multiple paintings and statues of saints. They were illuminated by numerous candles and lamps, and the flickering light of their flames danced on images and gilded surfaces. The towering, golden altarscreen served as a repository for sacred images and the backdrop for the celebration of the mass. But altarscreens were only one component of Baroque ornamentation. Church walls were often painted with vivid frescos or covered with paintings that depicted sacred stories. In many churches, the eye could find no place to rest as it moved from glittering altarscreens to paintings and back again. But sight was only one of the senses engaged by the Baroque church interior. Music or chanting resounded in the ear and incense filled the nostril.

The Chapel of Our Lady of the Rosary in the church of Santo Domingo in Lima exemplifies the sumptuousness of the Baroque. The altar of Our Lady, which stood to the right of the main altar, was covered entirely with silver. A statue of Our Lady resided in a niche in the center of the altarscreen. According to one early nineteenth-century witness, the image was richly dressed and wore a crown of diamonds and other gems. It held a rosary of fine, large pearls and possessed such a profusion of clothing that its caretakers changed its outfit every day. In front of the altarscreen's niche burned fifteen large candles and before the altar fourteen large, silver lamps were lighted. Next to the lamps, eight silver bird cages hung, and the signing of the birds accompanied the music of the organ and signing of the divine office. Many more silver candlesticks held numerous other candles, all casting a dancing light on the altar. Furthermore, before the altar stood four urns emitting perfumes. The witness recounts that on feast days more than a thousand candles at a time burned before the altar and the choir sang without pause. Although the ornamentation of this chapel was exceptionally rich, it was not unique. Many chapels and churches in the colonial Americas, especially in urban centers and wealthy mining towns, possessed such lavish adornment.

In these sumptuous sacred spaces, Catholics experienced God's presence in and through their bodies. The dramatic sights, sounds, and smells of church interiors struck the senses and induced felt experience of the sacred. For Tridentine Catholics the body was not an obstacle to piety, but rather a vehicle for devotion. The faithful used their senses to feel God and their bodies to invoke the sacred through ritual performance and to literally touch the divine in its many earthly manifestations. Tridentine Catholicism was a corporeal affair more than a cerebral one.

The fourth component of Tridentine Catholicism was its collective nature. Tridentine Catholics never stood entirely alone before God. They were united in the mystical body of Christ and the community of saints. As part of these communities, they shared in the merits of Christ, the saints, and their fellow Christians. Although each Catholic must accumulate the grace necessary by the time of death and judgment to earn salvation, or at least an entrance into purgatory that promised eventual admission into glory, he or she could rely on the aid of his or her fellows. Through participation in the sacraments, especially the mass, Catholics could partake in the salvific grace of Christ. For, in the organic unity of the mystical body of Christ, all members shared in his merits. Just as important, as part of the community of saints, each lone Catholic was linked to all others living and dead. Thus, Christians could pray and perform good works for their fellows both living and dead and help them accrue the grace necessary for a positive divine judgment or for a speedy passage through purgatory. Likewise, once they had died, their living brethren could aid them. In short, the Tridentine Catholic community was an ongoing, spiritual mutual aid society. This in large part explains the collective nature of much Catholic worship. Catholics prayed and performed sacred rites together because they were all united in a collective enterprise for salvation.

The clearest expression of Catholic collective devotion was the confraternity. Confraternities were pious organizations of predominantly lay people that arose in Europe in the High Middle Ages as cities grew. They structured microcommunities of the faithful in these growing, anonymous urban environments and linked the devout together in mutual bonds of spiritual obligation. Confraternities were generally open to all social ranks, but some restricted membership to only men or women; to members of particular professions; or especially in the Americas, to members of certain racial groups. Each confraternity was dedicated to a particular saint or advocation of Christ or the Virgin. Confreres, or confraternity members, pledged to honor their saintly patrons and as a group to celebrate their feast days with a procession, mass, and meal. Confraternities also performed other pious activities. Some administered hospitals, granted dowries to poor girls so that they could marry honorably, visited the sick, or accompanied the holy sacrament as it was brought to the dying.

Some confraternities were dedicated to particular types of devotions, like self-flagellation or literally singing God's praises. Whatever their particular pious activities, most confraternities required members to aid each other in illness or need and to attend the funerals of and pray for deceased members. In these ways, confraternities extended Catholic community and united diverse members into a pious collective. No single confrere need rely on him- or herself to gain the grace necessary for salvation. One prayed and performed good works on the behalf of all confraternity members, both living and dead, in the knowledge that once deceased, one would likewise benefit from the prayer and work of the confraternity.

Confraternities were widespread in the colonial Americas. The conquistadors founded the first ones in the early years after the conquest. For example, Hernán Cortés established the Knights of the Cross in Mexico in 1526, only five years after the fall of the Aztec Empire. The zeal of the faithful soon led to the proliferation of confraternal foundations. Cities had multiple confraternities.

Mexico City had more than 140 by the end of the eighteenth century, and almost all towns and villages had at least one. The popularity of particular confraternities waxed and waned, and sometimes a confraternity would fade out of existence as its membership declined or its finances floundered. But in general confraternities flourished for the majority of the Tridentine era in the Americas.

Despite the ritualistic and collective nature of Tridentine Catholicism, it allowed another path to God – mysticism – that only a few pursued. The mystic sought union with God largely in seclusion and through mental exercises. For much of the history of Christianity, the mystic attempted to obliterate the ego through meditation and thus empty the soul. Cleansed of individual will, the solitary mystic lay open to receive the spirit of God and to be subsumed under His will.

By the time of the Council of Trent, the institutional Church began to suspect the orthodoxy of this type of mystical practice. Mysticism, however, did not cease. During the latter half of the sixteenth century, orthodox Catholic mystics pursued a new path. Inspired by the spiritual exercises promoted by Ignatius Loyola (1491–1556) and the new Jesuit order he founded, they meditated intensely on scenes from salvation history, such as the passion. They attempted to visualize in concrete detail, for instance, the agonies of Christ and they used these exercises as springboards to communicate directly with God. Whatever the method of meditation, the mystic typically accompanied these mental exercises with forms of bodily deprivation – fasts, solitary confinement, and self-mortification – to still the flesh and thus aid the soul as it sought God. The practice of mysticism, despite its venerable history in Christianity, was the purview of the few. Only the intensely devout could withdraw from the world and devout themselves entirely to the inward quest for God. Although these few religious specialists practiced a religiosity in some ways at odds with the ritualistic and collective piety of the many, they were often regarded as holy by the Christian faithful, who sought their aid and advice. In fact, many mystics, such as St. Rose of Lima, after death were recognized by the Church and faithful as saints who enjoyed the company of God.

The vast majority of mystics in the New World were women, and many of these were either nuns or connected to religious orders. As we have seen, St. Rose, though not a nun, was a member of the Dominican Third Order. Francisca de los Ángeles, a mystic from the Mexican provincial city of Querétaro, provides another example of a mystic with intimate ties to a religious order. In 1685, at the age of nine Francisca was deeply moved by a Franciscan urban missionary campaign. As the Franciscans preached fiery sermons and performed public acts of self-mortification, Francisca felt a religious calling. She joined the Third Order of St. Francis as a young girl and withdrew from the world to contemplate God. The Franciscans early recognized her religious vocation and supported her through many trials, not the least of which was an accusation of false mysticism and a subsequent investigation by the Holy Office of the Inquisition in 1690s.

Francisca maintained close ties with the Franciscans and submitted to the discipline of Franciscan confessors. Complying with their admonitions, she kept a journal of her visions. During her mystical experiences, she entered purgatory and plucked souls from the purifying flames so that they could ascend to heaven. The intercessory role of mystics – particularly female mystics – with the blessed souls of purgatory had a long history within Catholicism, and Francisca's visionary experiences were entirely orthodox.

More unusual, however, were Francisca's visions of aiding the Franciscan missionaries as they evangelized Indians on the Texas frontier. In these visions, Francisca assumed a masculine role of active missionary life and public preaching. In some ways, she performed these roles in reality. Although by 1701 she had begun to administer a *beaterio*, a religious house for women who took simple vows (as opposed to the solemn, binding vows of a nun) and sought to enforce enclosure upon it, Francisca maintained contacts with the people of Querétaro. For instance, she received crucifixes, religious medals, and rosaries from them so that she could deliver them to God during her visions and have Him bless them. These items circulated among the faithful and were deemed special relics. In 1713 the Inquisition confiscated the items and declared that they had no special celestial status. The institutional Church was still willing to accept mysticism as a privileged path to God, but the Tridentine wariness of superstition prompted it to curb its "excesses."

Tridentine regulation of mysticism is equally clear in the numerous cases of false mysticism tried by the Inquisition in the Americas. The Inquisition in New Spain opened proceedings against more than a hundred suspected false mystics from the late sixteenth to the early nineteenth century. Most of the accused practiced forms of mysticism quite similar or identical to those practiced by orthodox mystics. Their visions often imitated the Baroque religious art that hung in churches and private homes and centered on Christ and the Virgin. On occasion, however, their visions shaded into the unorthodox. These "false" mystics were more likely to incorporate aspects of daily life into visions and sometimes they diverged radically from orthodoxy.

For instance, in the late-eighteenth century the mestiza visionary María Lucía Celis described visions of Christ and the Virgin. She reported that both had appeared to her before she was to receive communion. They asked her if she would nurse upon them, which she did. This imagery of nursing from the breast of the Virgin or the wounds of Christ was not uncommon within Catholicism, for it expressed Christ's divine nourishing of the faithful through the Eucharist. But it became less common during the Tridentine era. Celis more clearly passed into unorthodoxy when, after she had suckled, she offered her breast to both Christ and Mary – an offer that they accepted. This reciprocity of nourishment in her vision sealed Celis' fate before the Inquisition.

In many cases, however, the visions of the "false" mystics were orthodox. But the Inquisition prosecuted them because of the visionaries' lowly social status. Many "false" mystics were of mixed race, poor, and unaffiliated with powerful ecclesiastical patrons. Again we see that, although the Tridentine Church promoted the relatively easy coexistence of the sacred and profane, it distrusted "excesses" and sought to regulate lay piety so that it did not spill beyond acceptable bounds established by learned clerics.

Social Characteristics of Tridentine Catholicism

The Council of Trent issued its decrees with its eyes trained on Europe. But unlike Europe, the new colonies in the Americas did not face a serious Protestant threat and were racially diverse. How did Tridentine prescriptions, designed to shape the piety of a relatively homogeneous Europe, fare among the heterogeneous populations of the New World? Not surprisingly, orthodox Tridentine piety was confined largely to the cities and towns of the Americas, urban areas dominated by Spanish authority.

Tridentine Catholicism, however, was not restricted to the Spanish populations of these towns and cities. As we have already seen, urban indigenous groups and *castas* (people of mixed race) engaged in many forms of Tridentine piety. The indigenous parishes of Cuzco marched in Corpus Christi processions and castas engaged in mystical piety. Just like Spaniards, urban Indians, castas, and blacks reverenced images and the Eucharist, attended mass, mortified their flesh, and joined confraternities. In fact, these populations often established their own confraternities in which members joined together in collective worship.

In Mexico, for instance, confraternities of blacks and mulattoes were known for their humility and often performed public acts of self-flagellation. Of course, it would be erroneous to think that members of these racial groups understood their religious practices in the same ways as Spanish Catholics in the Americas. It is likely that their religious activities held multiple meanings for them, some of which were certainly unorthodox from a European perspective. For instance, indigenous participation in Cuzco's Corpus processions may have been as much about establishing Indian identity and native elite claims to authority as honoring the Eucharist. But it is also likely that Indian participants understood at some level the Christian meaning of Corpus – that it celebrated the bodily presence of Christian divinity within the world.

The impact of Tridentine Catholicism on Indian villages was more tenuous. The complex religious identity of the indigenous population of the colonial Americas is beyond the scope of this chapter, but suffice it to say that many sedentary indigenous groups that lived close to Spanish seats of power early adopted many forms of Tridentine Catholicism. Missionaries introduced images and the Eucharist, the liturgical calendar and its celebrations, and confraternities to the populations they evangelized.

By the mid-sixteenth century, native-language documents reveal that the Nahua residents of central Mexico incorporated Christian images into their households and honored them with gifts. Also, by the beginning of the seventeenth century, most Indian villages supported confraternities that financed the village church and its religious celebrations. Many rural Indians considered themselves good Christians and bestowed bequests upon the Church in their wills. On the other hand, many rural Indians, despite their identities as Christians, maintained indigenous conceptions of the divine. Indians in central and southern Mexico, for instance, continued to seek connection with the sacred through use of alcohol and hallucinogenic substances. Many rural Indians in Peru and Bolivia continued to perceive divinity within the landscape, especially mountains and outcroppings of rock. Some even continued to honor indigenous images that Spaniards considered idols.

Tridentine Catholicism in many ways facilitated this complicated religious mixing. The promotion of multiple sites of sacred immanence coincided with pre-Columbian religious traditions and allowed Indians more easily to transfer traditional devotions to Christian ones. For instance, local Indians honored the Christ of Chalma as early as the mid-sixteenth century. It may have been easier to do so because this image resided in a pre-Columbian sacred site. What they understood their devotions to the Christ of Chalma to mean, however, is unclear. Nonetheless, this early substitution probably took on greater shades of Christian meaning as the colonial period wore on. Tridentine collective piety likewise aided religious conversion. As European disease and forced labor decimated the indigenous population, Indians often regrouped in new (and much reduced) settlements. In these indigenous villages, the Catholic confraternity served as a means of community formation. Linked together in devotions, the community forged an identity that allowed for cohesion in the face colonial pressures.

The Tridentine Church was generally content to accept externals as signs of conversion. Idolatry campaigns aimed at the extirpation of indigenous religious items and rituals broke out in Peru and Mexico in the first half of the seventeenth century, and the Church continued to suspect the orthodoxy of Indian Christianity. But the Church by and large viewed Indians as permanent children, incapable of fully mastering the subtleties of Catholic mysteries. Especially by the late-seventeenth century, ecclesiastics considered Indians to be Christians, but they also simply expected them to be "superstitious."

Late-Eighteenth-Century Religious Reform

Influenced by Enlightenment rationality, some ecclesiastics and lay people attempted to reform religious culture in the Americas (and Europe) in the second half of the eighteenth century. In many ways, their program resembled late Medieval calls for reform within the Catholic Church and rested on a more spiritual and less immanential conception of divinity. These "enlightened" thinkers promoted a more interior religious practice focused on the individual believer's relationship with God. They called on Catholics to trust in a loving God, to offer a spiritual tribute directly to Him, and to contemplate Him by reading scripture and the early Church fathers.

Although reformers offered Catholics a positive image of a new faith, much of their campaign consisted in undermining Tridentine piety. Because they conceived of the divine as spirit, they tended to reject sacred immanence that underlay Tridentine Catholicism and were suspicious of excessive devotion to images and relics. In fact, they wanted Catholics to stop viewing saints as miracle workers, and instead to see them as paragons of Christian virtue worthy of imitation. Likewise, they distrusted lay ritual piety. Because God was spirit, He demanded a spiritual worship – one centered on the heart and mind rather than the body. Mental prayer and religious reading became the hallmarks of reformed piety as performative religiosity was denigrated.

Reformers also desired to simplify church interiors. For them, ornate churches did not move the soul toward the sacred; rather, they distracted the mind during the mass. The simplicity of neoclassical art and architecture was more to their taste than the exuberance of the Baroque. Furthermore, they tended to privilege the individual's direct relationship with God and so tended to shun collective forms of piety. Last, they distrusted the mystical path to God, for it did not conform to their rationalized religiosity.

The reformers, however, were still Catholic and confined by the decrees of Trent. Although they sought to modernize religion, they did not overturn Tridentine orthodoxy. Rather, they sought to reinterpret Catholicism and shift the balance toward the cognitive and spiritual and away from the ritual and corporeal. For instance, they never denied the doctrine of transubstantiation or the ritual efficacy of the mass. Nor did they attack venerable images and relics. But they did attempt to limit manifestations of sacred immanence and substantially simplify Catholic practice.

Religious reform certainly had an impact on late-colonial religious practice, the most dramatic example being the population's changing attitude toward funerals. For much of the colonial period, funerals of the elite were splendorous affairs. It was common for numerous members of multiple religious orders and of the secular clergy, as well as confraternities and the poor, to march in the cortege that accompanied the corpse from the home of the deceased to the church. In the church, orchestras and choirs provided music and countless candles burned on catafalques, decorated wooden structures on which the coffin rested during the requiem mass. Elite families customarily printed invitation cards and distributed them among the populace to increase the number of faithful who attended the funeral and prayed for the final repose of the deceased's soul.

After the funeral, those gathered feasted at a meal provided by the family and the corpse was laid to rest in a crypt or grave under the church floor, with locations closer to the main altar costing more than distant ones. Thus, even in death, hierarchy was maintained, for the church floor marked social status by proximity to the altar. By the end of the eighteenth century, funerals for the elite began to change as many elected for simplicity. They reduced the size of their corteges and forbade music, invitations, and the post-funeral feast. They also selected burial sites outside the church, either in the parish or new suburban cemeteries.

Many factors influenced the rising desire for simplicity in funeral arrangements, not least of which was the Bourbon monarchy's attempt to ban church burials and move cemeteries outside of cities for the sake of sanitation. Also important, however, was a growing reaction against Tridentine exuberance. Many members of the elite now believed that virtue and thus social status derived not from profligate spending on pomp, but rather from moderation. This new practice of elite moderation critiqued Tridentine splendor and at the same time undermined the collective nature of Tridentine piety. Now, the deceased faced judgment with a reduced accompaniment of prayers from their Christian fellows as funeral attendance declined. Furthermore, the simple funeral helped undermine the hierarchal nature of colonial society, for much of the elite, by opting to rest in less stratified cemeteries, no longer marked their status in death.

The decline in confraternities at the end of the colonial period also reveals the decline of collective Tridentine piety. The faithful began to abandon these organizations that had once served as sacred brotherhoods dedicated to the spiritual aid of fellows both living and dead. Membership in confraternities began to decline and, more telling, how the faithful spoke about them changed. At the beginning of the eighteenth century, the faithful who wrote last wills and testaments generally referred to the sacred obligations of confraternal membership in these documents. They called on their fellow confreres to attend their funerals and to pray for them as they had done for others during their lives.

By the end of the century, however, confreres who wrote wills most often spoke of confraternities as sources of money to help defray funeral expenses. In the discourse of testators, the confraternity no longer served as a sacred congregation of the faithful linked together in the communal quest for salvation. Rather, it had become a financial aid society that allowed families to finance funerals and burials. By the end of the colonial period, Catholics certainly faced God's judgment more solitarily than before.

Reformed Catholicism, however, never displaced Tridentine piety during the colonial period. Reformed piety was largely restricted to the elite and middling social sectors. The majority of the population continued to practice Tridentine rites well after independence. Furthermore, even among the elite, reformed piety was a minority religious practice. Although simple funerals grew in popularity, they never were a universal fashion. In fact, only a minority of the elite ever requested a humble funeral or burial. Also, the simple funeral could mean different things to different people. Some certainly requested a simple funeral to mark their adherence to reformed Catholicism, but others who asked for such a funeral did not. Many who arranged simple funerals saw them rather as a statement of personal humility and never sought to undermine Tridentine religious practice. Although they desired simplicity in the personalized rite of the funeral, they continued to support exuberance in other religious ceremonies.

Conclusion

Tridentine Catholicism represented both tradition and innovation. The Tridentine Church promoted Medieval forms of piety to defy Protestant critiques of traditional theology, but at the same time responding to both Catholic and Protestant reformers, more closely supervised religious practice and sought to curb "excesses" in lay devotions. Tridentine Catholicism was suffused with the miraculous and privileged ritual action and the corporeal experience of the sacred. It was also a collective religion and linked Catholics into a communal quest for salvation. By the end of the colonial period in the Americas, elements within the Church sought to redefine Catholicism and promote a more sedate and individual religiosity in keeping with their Enlightenment rationality. This reforming project, however, proved at best a moderate success. The faithful maintained many aspects of Tridentine piety as new, independent nations emerged in nineteenth-century Latin America.

Bibliography and Suggested Readings

Brading, David A. *Mexican Phoenix: Our Lady of Guadalupe: Image and Tradition Across Five Centuries*. Cambridge: Cambridge University Press, 2001.

Brown, Peter. *The Cult of the Saints: Its Rise and Function in Latin Christianity*. Chicago: University of Chicago Press, 1981.

Calvo, Thomas. "El Zodiaco de la nueva Eva: el culto mariano en la América septentrional hacia 1700." In Clara García Ayluardo and Manuel Ramos Medina (eds.), *Manifestaciones religiosas en el mundo colonial Americano*, Vol. 2 *Mujeres, instituciones y culto a María*. México: UIA, Departamento de Historia; INAH, Dirección de Estudios Históricos; CONDUMEX, Centro de Estudios de Historia de México, 1994.

Curcio-Nagy, Linda A. "Giants and Gypsies: Corpus Christi in Colonial Mexico City." In William H. Beezley, Cheryl English Martin, and William E. French (eds.), *Rituals of Rule, Rituals of Resistance: Public Celebrations and Popular Culture in Mexico*. Wilmington, DE: Scholarly Resources, 1994.

Dean, Carolyn. *Inka Bodies and the Body of Christ: Corpus Christi in Colonial Cuzco, Peru*. Durham, NC: Duke University Press, 1999.

Donahue-Wallace, Kelly. *Art and Architecture of Viceregal Latin America, 1521–1821*. Albuquerque: University of New Mexico Press, 2008.

Eire, Carlos. *War Against the Idols: The Reformation of Worship from Erasmus to Calvin*. Cambridge: Cambridge University Press, 1986.

Goodpasture, H. McKennie. *Cross and Sword: An Eyewitness History of Christianity in Latin America*. New York: Orbis, 1989.

Gunnarsdóttir, Ellen. *Mexican Karismata: The Baroque vocation of Francisca de los Ángeles, 1674–1744*. Lincoln: University of Nebraska Press, 2004.

Jaffary, Nora E. *False Mystics: Deviant Orthodoxy in Colonial Mexico*. Lincoln: University of Nebraska Press, 2004.

Larkin, Brian R. *The Very Nature of God: Baroque Catholicism and Religious Reform in Bourbon Mexico City*. Albuquerque: University of New Mexico Press, 2010.

Lockhart, James. *The Nahuas After the Conquest: A Social and Cultural History of the Indians of Central Mexico, Sixteenth through Eighteenth Centuries*. Stanford, CA: Stanford University Press, 1992.

Mills, Kenneth. *Idolatry and Its Enemies: Colonial Andean Religion and Extirpation, 1640–1750*. Princeton, NJ: Princeton University Press, 1997.

Mills, Kenneth, William B. Taylor, and Sandra Lauderdale Graham, eds., *Colonial Latin America: A Documentary History*. Wilmington, DE: Scholarly Resources, 2002.

Rubial García, Antonio. "Icons of Devotion: The Appropriation and Use of Saints in New Spain." In Martin Austin Nesvig (ed.), *Local Religion in Colonial Mexico*. Albuquerque: University of New Mexico Press, 2006.

Salles-Reese, Verónica. *From Viracocha to the Virgin of Copacabana: Representation of the Sacred at Lake Titicaca*. Austin: University of Texas Press, 1997.

Taylor, William B. *Magistrates of the Sacred: Priests and Parishioners in Eighteenth-Century Mexico*. Stanford, CA: Stanford University Press, 1996.

Turner, Victor, and Edith L. B. Turner. *Image and Pilgrimage in Christian Culture: Anthropological Perspectives*. New York: Columbia University Press, 1978.

Van Deusen, Nancy E. *Between the Sacred and the Worldly: The Institutional and Cultural Practice of Recogimiento in Colonial Lima*. Stanford, CA: Stanford University Press, 2001.

Voekel, Pamela. *Alone Before God: The Religious Origins of Modernity in Mexico*. Durham, NC: Duke University Press, 2002.

von Germeten, Nicole. *Black Blood Brothers: Confraternities and Social Mobility for Afro-Mexicans*. Gainesville: University of Florida Press, 2006.

9

The Inquisition in the New World

BRUNO FEITLER
TRANSLATED BY RODRIGO FRESTON

The Inquisition in the New World traces its origins to the establishment of the Tribunal of the Holy Office of the Inquisition in Spain in 1476. This Spanish Inquisition was established by Pope Sixtus IV at King Ferdinand and Queen Isabelle's request and had the objective of fighting heresy, especially *Judaizing*, which was the belief and respect for ancestral rituals practiced by Jews converted to Catholicism (often under duress) and their descendants. In the particular case of Spain, the Inquisition was also a strong element of royal centralization in a state only recently integrated and in which different kingdoms and duchies maintained their institutions practically intact.

The foundation of the Portuguese inquisitorial tribunal in 1536 took a very similar shape to the Spanish Holy Office and also focused primarily on the Judaizing heresy that persisted more than a quarter of a century after the forced conversions of Jews in 1497. In the end, both in Portugal and in Spain (even before the expulsion of the Moors in 1604), the Inquisition was one of the main pillars of exclusivist Catholicism, an element that was at the core of Portuguese and Spanish identity in the early modern age. In the New World, the Inquisition followed patterns established in Europe, but it also changed in relation to the unique contexts of the colonies. In these contexts, it is especially important to note that although the jurisdiction of the Holy Office in the Americas initially involved charges of heresy (disagreement from baptized people of the Church's dogmas), other moral offenses gradually full under its purview as well.

The Inquisition before "the Inquisition"

Almost immediately after the Spanish discovery of the New World, both the Church and the Crown deemed it necessary to implement an inquisitorial tribunal in the newly conquered territories. One of the first Spaniards to ask for its introduction was Friar Bartolomé de las Casas in 1516, who requested the establishment of the Holy Office as a means of standardizing procedures of religious trials for newly converted natives. In 1519 general inquisitor Adriano of Utrecht was the one to name the first apostolic inquisitors with jurisdiction over all of the Indies (which at the time was an area no larger than the Greater Antilles and a few territories in current Panama and Venezuela). They also named Alonso Manso, bishop of San Juan of Puerto Rico, and the Dominican Pedro of Cordoba, who actually did not seem to act as an inquisitor. Manso conducted only a few proceedings of little impact.

The rapid geographic expansion of Spanish domain with the conquest of New Spain from 1519 to 1521 and the need for religious control among the diverse populations of the growing empire led to a diversification of inquisitorial methods. Religious orders had a central role in this process of constructing a colonial society. In this context, in 1522, Pope Adrian VI (ex-Spanish general inquisitor), granted to the regular orders the exercise of practically all episcopal powers in places where a prelate spent more than one day on his trip. This delegation included powers to judicially investigate and try offenses relating to faith. What became known as the "Monastic Inquisition" began to occur in the main areas of the colony and its vicinity. This happened even despite resistance from some of the episcopal authorities. Significantly, however, there was support from Hernán Cortés, New Spain's conqueror and political leader.

The first inquisitor in Mexico was a Franciscan, and the next two were Dominicans. They conducted around fifty proceedings, most of which involved cases of native idolatry, blasphemy, and Judaism – above all from *conversos*, converts from Judaism – which both Church and Crown feared as a threat to emerging colonial society. It was no accident that the first two people burnt at the stake in a Mexican *auto-da-fé* were convicted of practicing Judaism.

Outside of Mexico City, Franciscans and Dominicans continued to exercise inquisitorial powers in places far removed from the episcopal see. They judged the indigenous people in their missions while the new bishop, and later archbishop, of Mexico, Franciscan friar Juan de Zumárraga (1534–1548) exercised the same powers in the capital and surrounding areas from 1536 onwards with the title of Apostolic Inquisitor. Both Zumárraga and the missionaries used inquisitorial powers. The archbishop opened more than 200 procedures – chiefly against blasphemers, Judaizers, and recalcitrant Indians – and missionaries wielded the power of the Inquisition over the natives in the territories they worked in. Many villages suffered from the provincial

Franciscans' conduct in Yucatán in 1562, where Diego de Landa destroyed the Maya sacred texts and compelled indigenous religious leaders to adhere to the standards of orthodoxy established by the Holy Office.

In the meantime, in Teitipac, in the diocese of Oaxaca, a Dominican friar performed a similar role, leading at least two Indians accused of idolatry to the stake. Among the most notorious cases was one judged by Mexico's Bishop Zumárraga against Don Carlos Chichimecatecuhtli, an elder of Texcoco, who was burned at the stake in November of 1539. He was executed for preaching heresy, that is, not only for believing in heresies (following indigenous rituals and customs despite being baptized) but also for luring members of his community to follow in his footsteps.

Many Church officials considered the conduct of Zumárraga and the friars to be excessive, which amplified the debate about the activities of the Inquisition in the New World. The core question under consideration was whether indigenous people, who were usually not very well catechized and were newly converted, should be treated like the European Christians and held to the same standards of orthodoxy, thus deserving the same sanctions under the Inquisition, or whether their newness to the faith justified a separate religious judicial system. The difficult assimilation of the Moors and of the Jews in Spain also influenced these debates.

Bishops Zumárraga's successor as apostolic inquisitor in *tierra firme* was the visitor Francisco Tello de Sandoval (1544–1547), who received jurisdiction over the whole viceroyalty, which now included all the territory and peoples of the former Aztec empire and beyond, to include vast northern and southern frontiers. Sandoval admonished his chief inquisitor to direct the Tribunal's work with more moderation, especially regarding the question of native "heresy," and he went so far as to review the proceeding against the elder of Texcoco. After the death of Zumárraga, his successor in the archbishopric, Alonso de Montúfar (1554–1572), echoing the fear of the spread of Protestantism after the Council of Trent, directed inquisitorial repression away from the indigenous population and aimed it instead toward European heretics. Montúfar also condemned the excessive zeal of members of the regular orders in disciplining the recently baptized.

The Foundation of the Tribunals

This was the complex context that led the Crown to overhaul its policy regarding the Inquisition in the New World. King Philip II (1556–1581) faced both the threat of the Protestant enemies to the Spanish empire and the strong pressure from the pope because of the failures of missions in the Americas, which were under the responsibility of the king under the *Patronato* (*Padroado* in Portuguese; patronage, or the power of the Crown to, among other things, appoint Church officials). The king also had to deal with a turbulent social environment both in Mexico and in Peru (where the bishops did not get to exercise a relevant inquisitorial power), as well as the constant complaints about the Spaniards' bad moral and religious behavior. In 1568, Philip II gathered a junta in Madrid that made a series of important decisions in relation to the government in the Indies. These included the creation of two new inquisitorial tribunals, one in Lima, Peru, and the other in Mexico City. In Lima the edict was published in November of 1569 in the presence of the recently arrived inquisitor, granting him jurisdiction over all Spanish territories south of the Panama isthmus. The Mexican tribunal, solemnly set up in November of 1571, had jurisdiction over all the viceroyalty of New Spain, which included the distant Philippines.

In 1610, a third American inquisitorial tribunal was created in Cartagena de Indias. This was a response to complaints of the inquisitors of Lima, who resented that their juridical territory included such distant and inaccessible territories. More importantly, the creation of a third tribunal was also an attempt to more effectively contain the suspected spread of Judaizing heresy in the New World, which saw its population of *conversos* ostensibly increase with the union of Portugal with the rest of the Iberian kingdoms in 1580. The new tribunal was tasked with judging cases occurring in the Caribbean and in the viceroyalty of New Granada, roughly the territories of the current republics of Colombia, Panama, and Venezuela. This was the definitive configuration of the Inquisition in the Americas.

In the Portuguese dominions, Philip III and Philip IV, during the period of the Iberian Union (1580–1640) and more specifically in the context of the external threats from 1620 to 1640, tried to create a tribunal first in Salvador of Bahia and then in Rio de Janeiro. Whether because of the resistance of the Portuguese Holy Office or because of the end of Castilian domination in 1640, however, these tribunals were never established. This did not mean that "heretics" in the Portuguese New World went unnoticed, however. Rather, Portuguese territories in the Americas, as well as in their other Atlantic possessions, remained under the jurisdiction of the inquisitorial tribunal of Lisbon, where all defendants proceeding from these regions were taken and tried.

In Spanish territories, the distance from American tribunals to the Supreme Council and the general inquisitor in Madrid and the subsequent difficulties of communication, meant that ever since the tribunals were set up the inquisitors had greater autonomy in relation to the center than their counterparts in Europe in terms of the proceedings. The inquisitors could hand out verdicts without consulting the Supreme Council, except in cases that necessitated being handed over to the secular arm (capital cases that meant the person would be burned at the stake).

In addition, the possibility of appeal to a higher instance was restricted. The inquisitors could act autonomously regarding the control of printing and circulation of books and were free to visit districts, leaving local work to *comisarios* (deputies). These *comisarios* were usually learned clergymen and holders of ecclesiastical benefits who were settled in the main colonial cities. They were the privileged correspondents of the inquisitors and charged with making local inquiries and arrests. The network of *comisarios* in Spanish territories was created at the same time as the tribunals, even though there were difficulties in finding skilled people, while in Brazil it began to be formed only toward the end of the seventeenth century.

Furthermore, *comisarios* linked to the tribunals in Mexico, Lima, and Cartagena had more autonomy than those in Portuguese America, where any judicial act needed to be preapproved by the inquisitorial board. Inquisitors also relied on *familiares*, lay officials of the Inquisition, who acted only when solicited by superior instances, above all during arrests and the sending of prisoners to the tribunals. They also participated in the *auto-da-fé* ceremonies. *Familiares* usually were not supposed to investigate or receive accusations. However, a primary role of the lay inquisitorial post was social legitimation since the qualification procedure – which distinguished them as legitimate old Christians – and the privileges that they benefited from led to many applying for the post with the hope of social ascension.

The *Instrucciones* written down by the Spanish general inquisitor in the context of the Junta of 1568 also concluded in a definitive manner the issue of inquisitorial jurisdiction over Christianized Indians. After the excesses of the first years of conquest, the Inquisition was granted jurisdiction only over baptized people. Therefore, the tribunal was forbidden to try nonbaptized Indians under any circumstances. The *Instrucciones* also decreed that the inquisitors should not try any Indians at all until further notice, focusing their energies only on Europeans. Instead, natives who committed any heresies or offenses related to them were to be tried by civil or episcopal tribunals. These alternative juridical bodies would hardly have been more benign than the Holy Office, but they were, in any case, more skilled at adapting the repressive instruments to the slow procedure of Christianization of the natives.

In Brazil, although there was no encompassing legislation as in the case of Spanish America, the Indians were also exempt from inquisitorial jurisdiction in practice. But Africans and *mestizos* could be tried by the Holy Office, including for acts that were considered heathenish by the Church. These were typically acts mistaken for witchcraft. From a social perspective, this exemption for natives had unforeseen consequences. Solange Alberro describes a case in which two *mestizos* pretended to be Indians, talking like them and speaking Mayan, therefore escaping inquisitorial jurisdiction. The vastness of the indigenous world, especially in Spanish America, impervious to the inquisitorial message, even if only by the tongue, was a refuge for all types of heretics.

Inquisitorial Action

Although often associated with punishment, the main objective of the Holy Office was to obtain a confession and, therefore, the reconciliation of the penitent to the Church's bosom. However, spontaneous confessions were few in number and, at the end, it was accusations that led people to the Inquisition. Without these confessions and without the witnesses that legally confirmed those offenses, the inquisitors could not convict the defendant. To instigate confessions and, above all, accusations, the Inquisition in the New World published edicts of faith, just as in Europe, that described the offenses of inquisitorial jurisdiction.

These included any type of heresy, especially Judaizing or Muslim ("Moorish") practices and beliefs, Protestantism, witchcraft, *alumbradismo* (an Iberian Christian heresy), divination, and pacts with the devil. Additional offenses included attempts to hinder the actions of the Holy Office and moral offenses such as bigamy and *solicitatio ad turpia* (i.e., confessors who solicited their penitents, in the act of confession, to perform sexual acts). In the case of Portuguese America, this also included sodomy, which did not fall under inquisitorial jurisdiction in Spanish America.

Over the course of the colonial period, the types of offenses that the inquisitorial tribunal most frequently entertained began to change. By the eighteenth century, cases of free thinkers, suspected Protestants, and masons attracted most attention, while cases of bigamy, for example, were curtailed. The edicts of faith described these offenses and exhorted people to accuse those they thought guilty. In Spanish America, according to the *Instrucciones* of 1569, the edicts were to be read out every three years during Lent in the cities where there was a tribunal and in all settlements with more than 300 residents; this was under the responsibility of the *comisarios*.

In Brazil, the first news of an edict being dispatched, besides the one published during the inquisitorial visit from 1592 to 1595, appears in 1598. The inquisitors of Lisbon sent them to the bishops and later to the *comisarios* so that they would be distributed among vicars and priests, who in turn should publish them every year during Lent.

Besides the general edicts already mentioned, the tribunals produced specific edicts of far-reaching scope, such as edicts of forbidden books and others related to specific offenses. This is where one can notice some colonial originality. In Brazil, for example, the Holy Office issued edicts against *bolsa de mandinga* (an amulet of Afro-Brazilian syncretic origin), while in Mexico, the Inquisition published edicts against those that consumed or used procedures of indigenous origin, such as the *peyote*, the *puyomate*, and the *ololiuhqui*, or against black ventriloquists ("who speak through their chest"). The Church looked upon such substances as evidence of a pact with the devil.

Once the supposed heretics and sinners were sent to the inquisitorial prisons, the trial itself started, during which the defendant was required to recognize and confess his sins before the inquisitors, even though he did not have access to the accusations or to the names of his accusers. Trials could last for years, during which the prisoner theoretically had to remain completely isolated from the rest of the world. This psychological pressure would often work to force the penitent toward confession, but there are also reports of dramatic suicides. There is also evidence of communication between defendants and their servants and slaves, who easily circulated between both worlds, not to mention the fact that *alcaides* and prison guards accepted bribes. Inquisitors had, at times, personal relationships with the defendants, which allowed for all sorts of negotiations. All of these personal interactions helped to mediate the Holy Office's administration of justice.

Once the judicial proceeding was over, the sentences were read out. Most of them were of abjuration of mistakes committed, which meant the reintegration of the defendant into the Church's bosom. These "reconciled people" would then receive various punishments that were dependent on the offense, which could include seizure of their assets; corporal punishments (whippings and prison); banishments and forced labor; spiritual punishments; and use of the *sambenito*, a penitential garment that served as a mark of great infamy that thenceforth would burden the penitent and his family.

Those who denied having committed offenses, when the witnesses were legally sufficient, were "delivered" to the secular arm, which typically ordered them burned at the stake, the legal punishment in civil jurisdiction for the cases of heresy, with lesser penalties meted out for lesser crimes. The few people who maintained faith in their "errors" in the presence of the inquisitors were sentenced to capital punishment. Most people burned at the stake fit into the first category; many were victims of discrimination and of the arbitrary judicial proceedings in practice during the Inquisition.

Those who agreed to die as Catholics were garroted before their bodies were sent to the flames. Few died like Judaizer Francisco Maldonado de Silva, who was burnt alive in Lima in 1634 as a martyr of his faith. In the Lima tribunal, 1,700 people in all were convicted, of which around fifty were burned, thirty-five in person and the rest in effigy, with proceedings that happened in default or that continued after the death or the flight of the defendant. The Cartagena tribunal tried around 800 proceedings, with five people handed over to the secular arm.

The most virulent tribunal was, without a doubt, the Mexican Holy Office. Between 1571 and 1700, its period of greater activity, 2,000 proceedings were opened, with around thirty-five people handed over to the secular arm. The legal proceedings of people in Brazil tried by the Portuguese Inquisition reached around 1,100. Of this total, twenty-nine were handed over to the secular arm, twenty were burned in person, and nine were tried and sentenced in effigy. Most defendants in Brazil (more than 50 percent) were tried for Judaism. This pattern was similar to that of Portugal, but with a different chronology. In Brazil, most cases were concentrated in the first half of the eighteenth century.

In Spanish America, the prosecution of Judaism was also the most striking, and were the cases tried with the most rigor, although such cases are relatively few in number in proportion to the large number of cases that came before the Spanish-American Inquisitions. "Judaizante" cases made up fewer than 20 percent of the accusations that came before the Mexican and Peruvian tribunals, and only 10 percent of the cases heard in Cartagena. In Spanish America, most cases were related to smaller offenses such as blasphemy, witchcraft, and superstitious practices. Cases of bigamy were also a typical offense in the colonies.

This said, the chronology of the Spanish American Inquisitions followed relatively clear patterns. For example, in the godly battle against heresy, where an important number of English, French, and Dutch pirates and sailors were tried for "Lutheranism" around 1570, the first two American tribunals were set up, in large part to combat the Protestant threat. The persecution of the Judaizers initially became intense in the 1590s and especially in the 1640s and 1650s, in the context of the end of the Iberian Union and of the fear of a revolt from the many Portuguese residents in Spanish land. During this period, the three American tribunals worked almost jointly. They were able to definitively defeat the network of solidarity of the Portuguese New Christians, while also destroying the Crypto-Judaism of the region.

The sentences given out by the inquisitors were usually read during the public *autos-da-fé*, which were ceremonies that occurred inside of important churches or in especially adorned squares for the occasion. The objective of these ceremonies was to make the population observe, simultaneously, both the mercy with which the Inquisition treated those who made penance and the rigor with which the unrepentant were punished. They were pedagogic ceremonies, but they also served an additional purpose from an institutional point of view, as this was the place where the inquisitor showed his power before other local authorities, such as bishops and viceroys, with whom misunderstandings over issues of jurisdiction, finance, or precedence were common. However, such ceremonies were expensive and made sense only when there were an important number of sentences to be read and when the offenses being tried caused a stir, such as the cases of heresy.

Because of the costs involved, public *autos-da-fé* were relatively rare in the Americas, although a few *autos-da-fé* were celebrated in Brazil during the inquisitorial visits of the end of the sixteenth and beginning of the seventeenth centuries. Thus, the *autos-da-fé* did not have the same impact in the Americas as they did in Europe (where, depending on the tribunal, such public displays could end up being an annual event), be it because they were practically irrelevant or because of the relatively small number of people (considering the continent's total population) that effectively watched the *autos* in Mexico or Lima. The actual conduct of the Holy Office in the New World can therefore be relativized, especially because most of the population – the Indians – was not under its jurisdiction.

Nevertheless, throughout the colonial period, the Holy Office continued to make itself feared and respected, even in the immense New World. But this did not stop the Holy Office from declining and losing the prestige it had for a while among local institutions by the turn of the nineteenth century. This decline happened for many reasons including a general reduction in the number of legal proceedings, especially those of formal heresy, the system of corruption and the slack behavior of the inquisitorial ministers, and the deterioration of the tribunals' revenue.

Finally, the influx of new ideas from the Enlightenment challenged the judicial and, to some extent, even the moral authority of Catholicism. These came to Spanish America first via the Bourbon reforms, to Brazil through the innovations of Marquis de Pombal in Portugal. Later, these ideas would take the form of the independence movements that would topple the old regimes in the Americas. It is no wonder that the end of the Inquisition coincides with the decline of the colonial order. The Spanish inquisitorial tribunals were abolished at first by the constitutions of Cadiz, promulgated by the *Cortes Generales* of Spain in 1812, but restored with the return to the throne of Ferdinand VII in 1814. The Inquisition was definitively abolished in the Spanish Americas by royal decree in 1820. In Portugal, the Inquisition continued to work in theory during the French occupation and was officially abolished only in 1821.

Bibliography and Suggested Readings

Alberro, Solange. *Inquisición y sociedad em México 1571–1700*. México: Fondo de Cultura Econômica, 1996 [1988].

Escobar, Ricardo. Quevedo. *Inquisición y judaizantes em América Española (siglos XVI-XVII)*. Bogotá: Editorial Universidad Del Rosario, 2008.

Feitler, Bruno. *Nas malhas da consciência. Igreja e Inquisição no Brasil: Nordeste 1640–1750*. São Paulo: Alameda / Phoebus, 2008.

Greenleaf, Richard. *The Mexican Inquisition in Sixteenth Century*. Albuquerque: University of New Mexico Press, 1969.

Medina, José Toribio. *Historia del Tribunal del Santo Oficio de la Inquisición de Lima*. Santiago: Fondo Histórico Bibliográfico J. T. Medina, 1956 [1887].

Historia del Tribunal del Santo Oficio de la Inquisición de México. México: Ediciones Fuente Cultural, 1952 [1903].

Millar Carvacho, René. Carvacho, *Inquisición y Sociedad en el Virreinato Peruano. Estudios sobre el Tribunal de la Inquisición de Lima*. Santiago: Instituto Riva-Agüero / Ediciones Universidad Católica de Chile, 1998.

Nesvig, Martin Austin. *Ideology and Inquisition. The World of the Censor in Early Mexico*. New Haven / London: Yale University Press, 2009.

Perez Villanueva Joaquin, and Bartolomé Escandell Bonet (dir.). *Historia de La Inquisicion em España y America*. Madrid: Biblioteca de Autores Cristianos / Centro de Estudios Inquisitoriales, 1984 vol. I ("El conocimiento científico y el proceso histórico de la Institución [1478–1834]").

Prosperi, Adriano (dir.), with de Vincenzo Lavenia e de John Tedeschi. *Dizionario storico dell'Inquisizione*, direção. Pisa: Edizioni della Normale, 2010 (in print). Verbetes: "Brasile" (Bruno Feitler); "Cartagena de Índias" (Ricardo Escobar Quevedo); "Lima" (René Millar Carvacho) e "Messico" (Rosalba Piazza).

Vainfas, Ronaldo, Bruno Feitler, and Lana Lage (eds.). *A Inquisição em xeque. Temas, controvérsias, estudos de caso*. Rio de Janeiro: EdUERJ, 2003.

10

Saint, Shrines, and Festival Days in Colonial Spanish America

FRANCES L. RAMOS

By the mid-eighteenth century, cities throughout colonial Spanish America enjoyed the protection of a multitude of divine intercessors; Mexico City, Santiago de Chile, and Santiago de Guatemala had a reported fourteen, fifteen, and thirty patron saints respectively. Like the Spanish monarch who received advice from a retinue of legal advisors, God also counted on His saintly advisors to promote causes and to advocate on behalf of specific constituencies. Embracing a central tenet of the *Pater Noster* ("On earth as it is in Heaven"), individuals, guilds, confraternities, and even polities often established a council of saints to act as their *abogados*, or lawyers, in God's "celestial court."

In the sixteenth century, Protestant reformers challenged Catholicism's reliance on divine intermediaries, arguing that not only did saints represent needless obstacles between man and God, but also that devotion to saints smacked of idolatry. During the Catholic Counter Reformation (ca. 1560–1648) the Church responded to criticism by underscoring the importance of the very aspects of the religion that Protestants abhorred. So, while Protestants labeled most Catholic priests corrupt and ignorant intermediaries, the Church responded by highlighting the importance of priests, while also creating a structure through which to educate and supervise them more effectively.

The cult of the saints underwent a similar transformation. The Council of Trent (1545–1563) characterized saints as essential agents in the heavenly kingdom. According to the second decree of Session Twenty-Five, those "who deny that saints, who enjoy eternal happiness in heaven, are to be invoked; or who assert either that they do not pray for men; or, that our invocation of them to pray for each of us individually is idolatry ... are to be utterly condemned."[1] However, the Church also made it significantly more difficult for

---

1 Session XXV, "On the Invocation, Veneration, and Relics of Saints, and on Sacred Images," in *Canons and Decrees of the Council of Trent*, trans. H. J. Schroeder (Rockford, IL: TAN Books, 1978 [1941]), 215.

local holy people to rise to the status of saint and eventually created a standing committee of cardinals to approve contenders for sanctity. Between 1625 and 1634, Pope Urban VIII formalized the status of *beati*, an intermediate category between locally revered holy person and canonized saint, and now supporters of a local holy person would have to wait fifty years after the death of their candidate to initiate a canonization process.

Despite the papacy's new stringent rules, the Church continued to support the cult of the saints, which found avid followers in colonial Spanish America. After Trent, priests started emphasizing saints primarily as models of Christian virtue, but individuals, families, and communities continued to appeal to saints during periods of economic uncertainty, natural catastrophe, and the seemingly relentless cycle of disease and epidemic. By appealing to saints, people eased feelings of powerlessness, and arguably, given the particularly tough challenges of life on the periphery, they came to depend more on saints in the New World than they did in the Old. In the midst of the demographic catastrophe of the sixteenth and early seventeenth centuries, indigenous subjects throughout the Andes and Mesoamerica embraced the cult of the saints.

This chapter examines the process by which saints' cults grew and developed in Spain's colonial cities. As we will see, the cult of the saints often worked to strengthen disparate identities while holding the larger figurative body (municipality, diocese, colony, empire) together. Highly fragmented in nature, the social and political body of the Spanish Empire mirrored the mystical body of the Christ, with guilds, confraternities, and other corporations acting as "limbs" within the organism. Yet, Spanish America, as a body politic and community of royal Catholic subjects, also resembled a *matryoshka*, or Russian nesting doll, in that it contained a multitude of smaller communities – or "bodies" – nested inside it. Saints moved within this complex world and enjoyed followings at every level; an individual, for example, may have sought succor at a local shrine, but then asked for protection from the patron saint of his confraternity; meanwhile, he would have benefitted from the patron saint of his municipality, of his colony, and even of the empire. Sometimes, cities took advantage of the popularity of a particular saint by transforming him or her into a patron of the municipality. Devotees, moreover, took this patronage seriously. Saints, after all, could be called on to address family-, work-, and health-related problems, but they also represented the first line of defense against dramatic catastrophe. Individuals, organizations, and even polities appropriated saints and regarded them both as advocates and willing participants in the process of identity creation.

Saints, moreover, played a fundamental role in the evangelization of non-Christian people. In both Mesoamerica and the Andes, saints reminded native people of their traditional gods and the broad similarities between natives systems of belief and Catholicism invited confusion. In the Andes, Catholic novitiates likely understood saints as resembling *huacas* (parts of the natural landscape like hills or mountains that embodied ancestor spirits or other supernatural entities). A myriad of characteristics distinguished *huacas* from saints, but like saints, *huacas* usually affiliated themselves with a particular group and/or locality. *Huacas* "responded" to the needs of their supplicants, and just as the cult of the saints provided a variety of specialists who people could appeal to, each *huaca* had an individual strength and track record of success. During the infamous extirpation campaign of the early seventeenth century (1609–1622) priests came to see saints as "effective antidotes to idolatry," and some even pushed for the canonization of Martín de Porras (1570–1647), a mulatto barber who cured using chants and prayers, to, in a way, balance the religious "playing field."[2]

As scholars have long recognized, native people largely embraced the outward symbols and rituals of Christianity, but evangelizers had a harder time changing peoples' hearts and minds. When promoting Christianity in post-Conquest Mexico, Hernán Cortés and his supporters touted the practical benefits of replacing idols with Christian images and, as historian Serge Gruzinski explained, "Christianization was thus laid down in terms of images and idols that were perceived as competitive, and in a certain sense equivalent, entities, one dispensing – supposedly – the same advantages to the natives as the other."[3] In both viceroyalties, indigenous people came to confuse saints with gods, but even after differences had been largely clarified, new converts did not always distinguish between an image of a saint and the actual saint. In fact, to the dismay of many missionaries in central Mexico, some Indians came to regard images of saints as *ixiptla*, or receptacles of the saint's supernatural essence or power. Eventually, however, many indigenous people came to share the same idiom of devotion as Creoles, *penininsulares*, and *castas*, especially in the larger cities of Mexico and Peru where constant contact and an effusive religious culture helped to create a semblance of homogeneity.

Scholars have long demonstrated an interest in the unifying potential of saints, most notably through the Virgin of Guadalupe, the so-called "master

---

2 Celia Cussen, "The Search for Idols and Saints in Colonial Peru: Linking Extirpation and Beatification," *Hispanic American Historical Review* 85:3 (2005), 420.

3 Serge Gruzinski, *Images at War: Mexico from Columbus to Blade Runner (1492–2019)* (Durham, NC: Duke University Press, 2001), 37.

symbol" of Mexico. By the late nineteenth century, she helped to define the still-divided Mexican citizenry as *"guadalupanos,"* but in the mid-eighteenth century she largely functioned as a symbol of proto-nationalism for frustrated Creoles who found themselves increasingly subject to charges of inferiority by Old World people. Historians have examined the extent of the Virgin of Guadalupe's popularity among Mexico's Creoles (who elected her patroness in 1746) and her role as a tool of recruitment during the wars of independence.

Several scholars have also examined the cult of Saint Rose (Santa Rosa) of Lima, the first Creole saint and one of only three people from Spanish America to attain canonization during the colonial period. Luis Miguel Glave Testino and Teodoro Hampe Martínez, for example, have argued that her canonization in 1671 would not have been possible without the support of influential and wealthy *limeños* who regarded Rosa as an extension of their privileged class and as a symbol, of course, of the capital city of Lima.[4] Creoles in New Spain also used Santa Rosa to contest their supposed inferiority, and in the viceroyalty of Peru, she eventually came to represent competing movements in favor and against independence. Scholarship, therefore, has focused largely on colonial saints who represented overarching meta-identities, partially as a way of understanding the tenuous ties that bound postcolonial people together.

Yet, as William Taylor has recently noted, historians of Spanish America have also tended to focus on Marian devotion to the exclusion not only of other saints' cults, but particularly the history of miraculous images of Christ. Of 480 shrines compiled by Taylor that attracted followings in the viceroyalty of New Spain since the sixteenth century, 261 are dedicated to Christ while the remaining 219 are devoted to representations of the Virgin Mary.[5] Clearly, much research is left to be done, not only in regard to the importance of the cult of Christ versus the Virgin Mary in colonial Mexico, but also to the implications of the broader cult of the saints to the development of New World societies.

Within the past decade, historians have increasingly turned to the role of saints as symbols of more localized urban identities, or as embodiments of a

---

[4] Luis Miguel Glave Testino, *De Rosa y espinas: economía, sociedad y mentalidades andinas, siglo XVIII* (Lima: Instituto de Estudios Peruanos, 1998); Teodoro Hampe Martínez, *Santidad e identidad criolla: estudio del proceso de canonización de Santa Rosa* (Cuzco, Peru: Centro de Estudios Regionales Andinos "Bartolomé de las Casas, 1998). On Saint Rose's role in New Spain and Peru's Independence movements, see Ramón Mujica Pinilla, *Rosa limensis: Mística, política e iconografía en torno a la patrona de América* (Lima: IFEA, 2001).

[5] William B. Taylor, "Two Shrines of the Cristo Renovado: Religion and Peasant Politics in Late Colonial Mexico," *American Historical Review* 110: 4 (October 2005), 946.

person's love for their *"patria chica,"* or "little homeland." Studies by Antonio Rubial and Ronald Morgan emphasize the role of hagiographies in inspiring local patriotism; Rubial, moreover, has also analyzed the process by which the Crown sometimes appropriated the cause of a local holy person, as it did with famed *poblano* bishop Juan de Palafox y Mendoza (1600–1659), whose image it reshaped to promote Bourbon absolutism.[6] When appropriating a cult of a local holy person, the Crown built on a preexisting base of support, and Spanish-American cities proved fertile ground for the development of not only local "saints," but also cults centered on miraculous images.

This work speaks to the implications of the cult of the saints to urban religious life and to the ways by which those in power sometimes appropriated cults with established followings. As we will see, specific cults acted as centripetal forces, drawing followers from across Spanish America's complex social and racial hierarchy. When a cult attracted an avid following, municipal leaders, institutions, and even the Crown sometimes sought to appropriate it. What is more, most cults required the support of secular and ecclesiastical elites to thrive. Elites, however, did not try to force people to believe in a saint, but rather aimed to channel and regulate peoples' devotion; while doing so, they enhanced the prestige of their particular institutions.

Promoting Shrines and Images

Saints enjoyed pockets of intense devotion in distinct regions, but the reasons for why and how a cult initially took root and gained followers varied considerably. Friars on the front lines of evangelization promoted saints in some way associated with their orders, as well as popular intermediaries such as Saint Michael, Saint James, and the Virgin Mary, but the secular Church also involved itself actively in cult promotion. For example, prior to the sixteenth century, Saint Joseph did not enjoy a large following in Spain, but in 1555, the Second Mexican Provincial Council elected him patron of the conquest and conversion of the viceroyalty. By then, the regular and secular church had cemented the view of indigenous people as perpetual children and the episcopate likely chose Saint Joseph to represent the patriarchy of both church and state.

---

6 Ronald J. Morgan, *Spanish American Saints and the Rhetoric of Identity, 1600–1810* (Tucson: University of Arizona Press, 2002); Antonio Rubial García, *La santidad controvertida: Hagiografía y conciencia criolla alrededor de los venerables no canonizados de Nueva España* (Mexico City: Fondo de Cultura Económica, 1999).

In the sixteenth century, religious leaders turned to images and relics to Christianize and, in a sense, "Europeanize" the American landscape. In 1578, Jesuits in Mexico City organized elaborate festivities in honor of the arrival of 214 relics of European saints, donated by none other than Pope Gregory VIII to be placed in churches throughout Mexico City. Many Spanish-American cities enshrined European relics, which local histories then singled out as sources of civic pride. Convents, hospitals, and parishes actively promoted specific cults, not only to enhance devotion, but also to collect alms that would benefit their organizations. Through relics, statues, paintings, and the printing of engravings of a saint, promoters of cults sought to inspire and "Hispanicize" Spanish America's overwhelmingly illiterate population.

Engravings served as both a practical and portable tool of religious diffusion; after a visit to a shrine or a feast-day celebration, people could return home with a tangible reminder of the experience to place on their home altars. In 1743, Franciscan friar Francisco Antonio de la Rosa Figueroa had an image of the Virgin Mary from his parish of Nativitas, Mexico, made over by a native artisan from Tlatelolco. To promote this "new" cult, the friar had 4,000 commemorative engravings printed for distribution during a procession. Illustrating the importance of engravings, he would later recount that out of the thirty-five miracles attributed to the Virgin, most were associated not with the effigy, but with the engravings. Vendors, moreover, sold engravings of holy people in markets throughout the New World, and sometimes got into trouble for doing so. Mexican Inquisition records reveal numerous investigations into engravings of "unofficial" local saints such as Puebla's Juan de Palafox y Mendoza and the mystic Catharina de San Juan (ca. 1600–1688).

Some shrines benefitted from a supportive institution that could pay for the printing of engravings and for elaborate processions, while others did not. Nevertheless, shrines developed throughout the centuries on the outskirts of large cities. Some of these became popular pilgrimage sites while others devolved into ruins, but most started in similar ways. When in imminent danger, early modern Catholics typically appealed to a saint, vowing to somehow promote his or her cult if spared. If the saint had a shrine nearby, individuals would sometimes make a special pilgrimage to the site and leave an *ex voto*, or small painting, testifying to the miracle. Spanish immigrants, however, often felt more attached to shrines back home. For example, a sixteenth-century *encomendero* from the Trujillo valley prayed to the original Our Lady of Guadalupe from Extremadura while imprisoned in Peru. He vowed that if released, he would make a pilgrimage to the site, which he later did. He returned with a sculpted copy of the Virgin around 1560, and by 1599 the image had developed a large cult following.

Variations of this pattern repeated throughout the New World. Sometimes the receiver of a miracle could not return to Spain, but this did not stop him or her from acting as an agent of religious diffusion. A tempest struck during Captain Gaspar de Jimena Villanueva's return voyage to Spain in the sixteenth century. Fearing for his life, he prayed to Our Lady of Grace, vowing to build a temple in her honor if spared. The storm stopped within view of San Juan de Ulúa, Veracruz and everyone survived, along with their property. In 1598, the municipal council of Puebla de los Ángeles granted the captain a piece of land to build his temple on the outskirts of the indigenous parish of Saint Sebastian. Puebla, widely considered the most orthodox city in the colonies, had at least forty shrines surrounding it, most founded by grateful beneficiaries of miracles.

Cults, then, acted as cultural bridges between America and Europe. Philip III understood the unifying potential of saints and asked the viceregal governments, dioceses, and municipal councils of Mexico and Peru to support the cause of Saint Isidore, the eleventh- and twelfth-century farmer who appeared to King Alfonso of Castile in 1212 and helped him defeat the Moors in a pivotal battle. Cities throughout the empire responded with donations, but Quito went farther, and even started a confraternity in his honor. In addition to Saint Isidore, in 1622 Spain had three other native sons who were promoted to sainthood: Saint Ignatius of Loyola, Saint Francis Javier, and Saint Teresa of Ávila. All four became immensely popular in America. In 1673, upon the orders of Charles II and his advisors, cities throughout the empire celebrated the canonization of Saint Ferdinand III, the thirteenth-century king of Castile, who, among other important achievements, reconquered Seville from the Moors in 1248. He served as a symbol of pride for the ailing Seville in the seventeenth century, and during the reign of Ferdinand VI, dioceses in Mexico began celebrating his feast day partially as a way to promote Bourbon absolutism. The city of Puebla began celebrating his feast day in 1753 on the orders of the viceroy, and councilmen agreed to honor San Fernando perpetually as the "titular saint of our king."

Saints, therefore, helped to bridge the cultural distance between Spain and America, but New World communities also took pride in those holy people who, if not born in America, demonstrated saintly qualities while laboring in the region. True, only three Spanish Americans achieved official canonization during the colonial period, but New World people also adored "martyrs" from the immediate post-Conquest period, in addition to local holy people who later became candidates for sanctity. The municipal council, or *cabildo*, of Lima, for example, inaugurated the canonization campaign of Francisco Solano, a Franciscan born in Spain, but who died while evangelizing in Peru. Similarly, the *cabildo* of Santiago de Guatemala helped inaugurate the campaign of the Bethlehemite missionary Pedro de San José Betancur, known as Hermano Pedro, who died at the age of forty-one exhausted by his service to the poor.

With the development of some of these "native" cults, religious officials clearly sought to complement the sacralization of the American landscape with elements of regional history. With the support of the religious orders or secular church, rural shrines also developed in honor of homegrown martyrs. For example, in the sixteenth century, Franciscans enshrined the remains of a small boy from Tlaxcala named Cristobál who was killed by his father in 1527 for, presumably, delivering hidden idols to missionaries. European saints, moreover, reportedly appeared to humble Catholics throughout Spanish America during the sixteenth, seventeenth, and eighteenth centuries, and the places where many of these miracles took place developed shrines.

Apparition stories from the Old and New Worlds usually conformed to an established script. Possibly, those who claimed to see a holy image either had heard enough of these stories to mold their account into an acceptable narrative or by the time the stories were finally written down years later, popular memory had reshaped them. Although some accounts veered away from the standard plot line, most had a saint revealing him- or herself to a humble boy or man in an isolated location; the saint would then demand that a shrine be built in his or her honor. Stories of this kind abound, with the most well-known probably being that of the Virgin of Guadalupe, who appeared to the Indian Juan Diego on a hillside outside Mexico City in 1531.

Yet, tales of apparitions span the centuries and regions of Spanish America. In the early seventeenth century, a statue of the Virgin Mary purportedly revealed herself to an austere hermit named Juan Bautista de Jesús in the diocese of Puebla. He lived in the countryside with the image for eighteen months and witnessed her perform numerous miracles. Eventually, Bishop Juan de Palafox y Mendoza encouraged the hermit to hand it over for safekeeping in Puebla de los Ángeles. After approximately eight months in the bishop's private oratory, the statue travelled with an explorer and friend of Palafox to the "conquest" of California and later to Peru, where she helped put down a rebellion in Chile.

When the statue was returned to Puebla thirty years later, the city received her with an elaborate ceremony and eventually named her "*Nuestra Señora de la*

Defensa" (Our Lady of the Defense) and enshrined her in the cathedral's Altar of the Kings. She came to represent the city as a whole, leading eighteenth-century chronicler Miguel de Alcalá y Mendiola to note that "Mexico City is glorious for having both the Virgin of the Remedies and the Virgin of Guadalupe looking out for it, but this angelic city has *la Defensa*."[7] On several occasions, *poblanos* appealed to her to defend the Crown. In 1707, for example, on learning that the queen was expecting Spain's first Bourbon prince or princess, Puebla de los Ángeles chose to give thanks to God with a novena, a mass, and litanies devoted to Our Lady of the Defense. As an authentic product of Puebla's religious culture and as a symbol of *poblano* identity, Our Lady of the Defense proved a perfect vehicle through which to express the city's loyalty.

Many saints "appeared" in the dioceses of Mexico and served as the foundation of successful cults. In 1631, Saint Michael reportedly appeared to an Indian atop the mountain Tzopiloatl near the city of Tlaxcala in the diocese of Puebla, and directed him to a nearby miraculous fountain of water that had been frequented by idolaters. Learning of the miracle, Bishop Palafox built a permanent shrine at the site, leading to an increase in its popularity. Many shrines contained fountains with "healing waters," and this one attracted a steady stream of pilgrims. Because Saint Michael served as the nearby city of Puebla's primary patron, *poblanos* reportedly grew very fond of this particular invocation, which became known as Saint Michael of the Miracles.

As the last two examples illustrate, saints often developed into symbols of civic pride. Bishop Palafox's decision to appropriate the shrine of Saint Michael stands to reason, given that the archangel already served as Puebla's patron saint, but metropolises throughout Spanish America took pride in the shrines that graced their hinterland. Many chroniclers pointed to New Spain's Marian shrines as markers of divine favor, and in the eighteenth century, Mariano Fernández de Echeverría wrote a history of the four principal shrines of the Virgin Mary that surrounded Mexico City: Our Lady of Guadalupe to the north, Our Lady of Piety to the south, Our Lady of the Bullet to the east, and the Virgin of the Remedies to the west, referring to the sacred images as the bulwarks of Mexico. Similarly, Guadalajara also had four Marian shrines located on its outskirts, which, according to chronicler Matías de la Mota Padilla, served as "strong towers" that protected it.[8] Clearly,

---

7 Miguel de Alcalá y Mendiola, *Descripción en bosquejo de la imperial cesárea muy noble y muy leal ciudad de Puebla de los Ángeles* (Puebla: Benemérita Universidad Autónoma de Puebla, 1992), 96.

8 Thomas Calvo, "El zodiaco de la Nueva Eva: El culto mariano en la América Septentrional hacía 1700," in *Manifestaciones en el mundo colonial urbano*, ed. Clara García Ayluardo and Manuel Ramos Medina (Mexico City: INAH, 1997), 269.

city dwellers saw miraculous shrines as sources of pride, but also as practical defensive barriers. This may partially explain why urbanites often took pains to maintain a connection between their cities and rural shrines.

Frequently, annual pilgrimages started within the boundaries of a city and as devotees approached a shrine (often on a hill), they would stop at smaller shrines along the way, almost like moving through the Stations of the Cross. Historian William Christian has noted that a saint's insistence on residing outside the confines of an urban center "may be an echo or a metaphor for what was in some sense a liberation of devotion from parish control – or, put another way, the resistance of local religion to the growing claims of the church."[9] But although perhaps true on the foundation of a shrine, these could not have continued to function without the support of religious or secular authorities within the neighboring city. Many shrines fell into ruin precisely because they lacked the backing of an *obra pía*, or pious works fund, to support a full-time chaplain.

Shrines flourished with financial support, such as Bishop Palafox's funding of the shrine of Saint Michael of the Miracles, or through the sponsoring of annual *fiestas* and processions that linked the town spatially to the outlying shrine. By the eighteenth century, pious residents of Mexico City would make the annual pilgrimage to the hillside of Tepeyac not only to celebrate the Virgin of Guadalupe's feast day, but also to break from their workaday routines. Similarly, on Saint John the Baptist's feast day, Lima's viceroy, archbishop, and an entourage of devotees travelled to a parish in the neighboring *pampa de las Amancaes* to pray before a famous miraculous effigy and play games, dance, and bet on cockfights. Pilgrimages, therefore, integrated city and countryside spatially and, in a sense, psychologically, through pious devotion and festive play.

Electing and Appropriating Patron Saints

Convents, hospitals, and parishes all nurtured the cults of particular images, as did cathedral chapters and municipal councils on an even wider scale. Yet, even in a diocesan see, the municipal council, or *cabildo*, elected the city's patron saints. Small populations often had only one patron but, as noted, large cities usually had many. When the date of a city's foundation coincided with a feast day, municipal leaders often named the settlement after the saint, who then became its first patron; this occurred in Santiago de los Caballeros,

---

9 William A. Christian, *Local Religion in Sixteenth-Century Spain* (Princeton, NJ: Princeton University Press, 1981), 91.

Guatemala, San Francisco de Quito, and Nuestra Señora de la Paz, as well as in numerous other settlements throughout the region. Councilmen could then add to the pantheon by electing advocates to negotiate with God regarding an immediate threat to the community. Often, *cabildos* sought the aid of tried and true specialists, as when Caracas elected Saint George to combat the worms that had been destroying the city's wheat fields, and Vera Cruz placed itself under the patronage of Saint Sebastian to protect itself from a virulent yellow fever epidemic, but sometimes they sought the help of generalists for particular problems, as when Santiago de Costa Rica elected Saint Ann to free itself from rabid dogs or when Quito elected Our Lady of Mercy as an advocate against earthquakes. When confronting grave situations, *cabildos* often made their selection through a drawing, thereby allowing a saint to choose to be an advocate for him- or herself.

The religious culture of the Spanish Empire tended to fragment along corporate lines with organizations, ranging from merchant guilds to confraternities, enjoying the patronage of at least one patron saint or personification of Christ. To complicate matters, New Spain had more than 200 guilds and most of these had an affiliated confraternity under the patronage of a divine figure. Most large cities had numerous confraternities, but all communities had at least one, and people who practiced the same profession tended to congregate in the same barrio and join the same confraternity, so urban religiosity tended to be barrio-focused. Some confraternities were reserved for members of the same ethnic group or social class; in 1639, for example, Lima had twenty-six confraternities for Spaniards, nineteen for indigenous people and forty for blacks or mulattos. But however much they reinforced distinct group identities, confraternities also worked to bring people together.

Confraternity membership helped to mitigate the "anonymity of the parish," compelling people to become more directly and intimately involved in community life.[10] A confraternity always had its own chapel either in a church, convent, hospital, or school, and this reinforced membership in interlocked communities; people, in a sense, developed loyalties to distinct communities within their broader *patria chica*. Yet, carrying the statue of their patron saint aloft, confraternity members always participated in city-wide devotions such as annual Holy Week and Corpus Christi processions. Typically, these events showcased difference, with native people processing in their traditional dress and elites in European finery. While doing so, participants also

---

10 D. A. Brading, "La devoción católica y la heterodoxia en el México Borbónico," in *Manifestaciones religiosas en el mundo colonial urbano*, ed. Clara García Ayluardo and Manuel Ramos Medina (Mexico City: INAH, 1997), 37.

celebrated their membership in the collective body politic and body of Christ. Furthermore, many confraternities also welcomed people from outside their ethnic group or social class, and feast-day celebrations generally encouraged interconfraternity cooperation.

Saints, then, could serve as symbols of distinct identities, while at the same time enforcing other types of group or intergroup affiliation, and patron saints of cities played a key role in creating and reinforcing interrelated identities. Religious orders often pushed to have their own saints named patrons of a city and significantly, sometimes fortified their petitions with claims that their candidate served as the patron of other European cities, thereby promoting a broader trans-Atlantic Catholic identity. While providing a cultural link to Europe, patron saints also provided a *cabildo* or cathedral chapter vehicles through which to strengthen ties to convents and parishes throughout the city. Feast days of patron saints involved a procession of councilmen, religious leaders, and other so-called "republican gentlemen" to the parish or convent that would perpetually host the event. In the seventeenth century, feast days of patron saints often involved fireworks, mock jousts, and even bullfights, whereas in the eighteenth century they became significantly pared down.

Nevertheless, primary patrons such as Puebla's Saint Michael continued to have elaborate feast-day celebrations through the eighteenth century. In the seventeenth century, the *cabildos* of Mexico City and Puebla held a *paseo del pendón*, or "parading of the royal standard," on their primary patron's day, which mimicked the act of taking possession in the name of the king. By the eighteenth century, the councilmen of Puebla could no longer afford this costly event, but the *cabildo* continued to hold bullfights to commemorate the archangel's feast day through 1721 and continued to sponsor an elaborate mass and procession, replete with fireworks, through independence. By honoring the cult of Saint Michael with an elaborate celebration, councilmen acknowledged the origin myth of the city, or the claim that the first bishop of Tlaxcala, Julián Garcés, saw the site for the future Puebla in a dream on the eve of the archangel's feast day. Yet, elements of the festivity also highlighted the authority of councilmen. In 1736, for example, the council ordered a half dozen *cámaras*, or single explosions, to be set off at midnight just as the *cabildo* entered the church on the eve of the feast day, and for another half dozen that exploded as the *cabildo* departed the cathedral following vespers. As councilmen entered the church the next morning, an artisan set off another half dozen, and as councilmen departed, he treated attendees to yet another round of explosions. Through the feast day of Saint Michael, councilmen celebrated their privileged role as the heads of the body politic and invited the city to commemorate its unique history.

Profane elements of feast-day celebrations encouraged widespread enthusiasm for a cult while also allowing organizers and participants to benefit politically. The mystery of the Immaculate Conception, for example, became dogma in sixteenth- and seventeenth-century Spain and by expressing devotion to the Virgin of the Immaculate Conception, devotees articulated several identities at once. In 1616, the *cabildo* of Puebla agreed to celebrate the feast day of the Immaculate Conception "in imitation of other cities, of Spain and of Christendom."[11] The council, moreover, acknowledged that the cathedral already celebrated the feast day, as it had long placed itself under her advocacy. Councilmen, however, wished to celebrate not only their devotion to the Immaculate Conception and their city, but also their class and family alliances. Puebla's councilmen planned on placing daughters in Puebla's Convent of the Immaculate Conception, which would be inaugurated in 1617.

In 1619, the *cabildo* finally held an elaborate celebration for the Virgin, spending approximately 600 pesos on the event. Councilmen, moreover, made a solemn oath to defend the mystery and when the Crown asked cities throughout its empire to swear the same oath nearly three decades later, Puebla's council could boast that it already had. Nevertheless, in a show of devotion to the Virgin and the king, the council made another solemn oath during a ceremony inside Puebla's Cathedral. Other groups continued to express their devotion to the Immaculate Conception publicly. In 1675, for example, the city's wealthy merchants sponsored a sermon in her honor.

Feast days, therefore, allowed organizations to express distinct but interlocked identities. Furthermore, *cabildos* and cathedral chapters also used their influence to "rein in" specific barrio-based devotions. When natural disaster struck a diocesan see, the *cabildo* and cathedral chapter often co-sponsored processions, novenas, or litanies in honor of a city's most miraculous images and transported the image, in procession, to the cathedral, where it would remain temporarily. In 1747, for example, during a serious drought and epidemic, the *cabildo* of Puebla sent two emissaries to the bishop to ask for permission to take Jesus the Nazarene, housed in the parish of Saint Joseph, on procession. When the saint's confraternity explained that it could not afford the candles to illuminate the image, the *cabildo* agreed to cover the expense. Both organizations, therefore, attempted to create a cohesive religious culture out of

---

11 Antonio de Peralta Castañeda, *Sermon de la Purissima Concepcion de la Virgen Maria Nuestra Señora. Predicado en la fiesta, que celebró para la repetición del juramento [...]* (Puebla de los Angeles: Juan de Borja Infante, 1654).

barrio-based devotions, but this is not to say that they were the sole promoters of intergroup cooperation. Nevertheless, for a particular cult to transform into a city-wide devotion, it required nurturing on the part of the "heads" of the body politic. In fact, when a particular organization (such as a convent or school) invited a cathedral chapter or the *cabildo* to a feast-day mass, they often asked its members to "authorize" the event with their presence.

Cabildos and cathedral chapters often associated themselves with cults that already had strong followings and, in a way, sought to benefit by establishing ties of dependency. As illustrated by the case of the Immaculate Conception, the Spanish monarch also shared in, and encouraged, the faith of his subjects. In 1611, the *cabildo* of Puebla reaffirmed a long-standing oath to honor Saint Joseph as one of its patron saints. Unlike with other feast days for which the *cabildo* donated twenty-five pesos annually, those of Saint Joseph (and Saint Michael) received considerably more support. When the *cabildo* reaffirmed its oath to Joseph, the Patriarch already served as the patron of the carpenters' guild and of the city's second largest parish. So, instead of marking the feast day on March 9th with a simple procession and mass, the *cabildo* agreed to participate in the parish's feast-day celebrations and to take over its octave, adding bullfights, mock battles, a sung mass, and musicians on the eve of the event. In 1638, the cathedral began celebrating an annual novena for Saint Joseph in September, and the *cabildo* assumed responsibility for hosting the events on the last day. In 1680, the city received a royal decree naming Joseph patron of the Spanish Empire and the *cabildo* vowed to celebrate and partially subsidize a special celebration for Joseph, distinguished from the two other commemorations as the *"patrocinio,"* or patronage, of Joseph over Spanish America.

Conclusion

As illustrated through the examples of the Virgin of the Immaculate Conception and Saint Joseph, the Crown also promoted saints who had strong regional followings. This is not to suggest, however, that the Spanish monarch cynically took advantage of his subjects' piety to strengthen royal authority. The monarch shared the same faith as his subjects and responded to the growing popularity of particular cults. Nevertheless, when those in positions of authority endorsed a saint or, in the case of apparitions or miraculous images, a local devotion, a cult naturally grew in size.

In the second half of the eighteenth century, Bourbon administrators would challenge what it perceived as the ostentation of baroque religion and would order *cabildos* to reduce their number of patron saints. In this way, reformers sought to trim municipal expenditure while also limiting the profane elements of religious celebrations. But, despite its reforms, the Crown still encouraged cults of those saints that seemed to embody its new centralizing directives. Not only did the Crown encourage cities to celebrate the feast day of Saint Ferdinand III, but it also encouraged other cults that broadcast its legitimacy. In Mexico City, for example, the Crown limited substantially the amount that the municipal council could spend on ceremony, but increased spending for the feast day of Saint Hippolytus – the occasion that marked the conquest of Tenóchtitlan. Although desirous of limiting expenditure, the Crown clearly prioritized exalting its own supremacy, celebrating its conquest of the New World, as well as the "reconquest" of the colonial bureaucracy.

Throughout the colonial period, people – from the humblest of backgrounds to the heights of the Spanish bureaucracy – utilized saints as symbols of identity. Early modern people regarded saints as spiritual intercessors, but they also regarded saints as symbolic extensions of themselves, their families, and the organizations in which they claimed membership. Throughout the colonial period, individuals sought the patronage of specific saints for a variety of reasons, but largely because they perceived evidence of miracle working. Saints functioned as "specialists" or "generalists" who could be appealed to for a variety of reasons, but once a cult – whether centered on a local apparition or a miraculous image – gained a sizeable following, an order, diocese, or municipal council could choose to absorb it, promote it, and institutionalize it. Saints, then, often transitioned from having a small following to having a larger more institutionalized cult through the support of ecclesiastical and/or secular institutions.

At all levels, saints acted as symbolic bridges that provided immigrants with a link to the Old World or helped to tie ethnic groups and organizations together. In towns or cities, saints served as cornerstones of communities, and helped to integrate members into the broader *patria chica*. Through the cult of the saints, people would celebrate their place in the imperial body politic, their town, parish, barrio, or confraternity. Saints, therefore, allowed people to seek divine aid while articulating various identities at once.

Bibliography and Suggested Readings

Alcalá y Mendiola, Miguel de. *Descripción en bosquejo de la imperial cesárea muy noble y muy leal ciudad de Puebla de los Ángeles*. Puebla: Benemérita Universidad Autónoma de Puebla, 1992.

Bayle, Constantino. *Los cabildo seculares en la América Española*. Madrid: Sapienta, 1952.

Bazarte Martínez, Alicia. *Las cofradías de españoles en la ciudad de México (1526–1869)*. Mexico City: Universidad Autónoma Metropolitana, 1989.

Brading, D. A. "La devoción católica y la heterodoxia en el México Borbónico." In *Manifestaciones en el mundo colonial urbano*, edited by Clara García Ayluardo and Manuel Ramos Medina, 25–49. Mexico City: INAH, 1997.

Mexican Phoenix: Our Lady of Guadalupe: Image and Tradition Across Five Centuries. Cambridge: Cambridge University Press, 2001.

Burke, Peter. "How to be a Counter-Reformation Saint." In *Religion and Society in Early Modern Europe*, edited by Kaspar Greyerz, 45–55. London: George Allen & Unwin, 1984.

Calvo, Thomas. "El zodiaco de la Nueva Eva: El culto mariano en la América Septentrional hacía 1700." In *Manifestaciones en el mundo colonial urbano*, edited by Clara García Ayluardo and Manuel Ramos Medina, 267–282. Mexico City: INAH, 1997.

Carrera Stampa, Manuel. *Los gremios mexicanos.* Mexico City: Edición y Distribución IberoAmericana de Publicaciones, 1954.

Christian, William A. *Local Religion in Sixteenth-Century Spain.* Princeton, NJ: Princeton University Press, 1989.

Cussen, Celia. "The Search for Idols and Saints in Colonial Peru: Linking Extirpation and Beatification." *Hispanic American Historical Review*, 85, no.3 (2005): 417–448.

Dias Chamorro, Joseph. *Sermon, que predico [...] en la solemne fiesta de la Purissima Concepcion de la santissima Virgen Maria Nuestra Señora; que celebraron los mercaderes de esta ciudad [...]* Puebla: Imprenta de la Viuda de Juan de Borja, 1675.

Fernández de Echeverría y Veytia, Mariano. *Baluartes de México: Relación Histórica de las cuatro sagradas, y milagrosas imágenes de Nuestra Señora la Virgen María que se veneran en la muy noble, leal, e imperial ciudad de México [...]* Mexico City: Imprenta de A. Valdés, 1820.

Historia de la fundación de la ciudad de la Puebla de los Ángeles en la Nueva España, Vol. 2. Puebla: Ediciones Altiplano, 1963.

Florencia, Francisco de. *Narracion de la marabillosa aparicion, que hizo el Archangel San Miguel a Diego Lazaro de San Francisco [...].* Sevilla: Imprenta de las Siete Revueltas, n.d.

Garrido Aspero, María José. *Las fiestas cívicas históricas en la ciudad de México, 1765–1823.* Mexico City: Instituto Mora 2006.

Glave Testino, Luis Miguel. *De Rosa y espinas: economía, sociedad y mentalidades andinas, siglo XVIII.* Lima: Instituto de Estudios Peruanos, 1998.

Gruzinski, Serge. *Images at War: Mexico from Columbus to Blade Runner (1492–2019).* Durham, NC: Duke University Press, 2001.

Hampe Martínez, Teodoro. *Santidad e identidad criolla: Estudio del proceso de canonización de Santa Rosa.* Cuzco: Centro de Estudios Regionales Andinos "Bartolomé de las Casas, 1998.

Lafaye, Jacques. *Quetzalcoatl and Guadalupe: The Formation of the National Consciousness in Mexico.* Trans. Benjamin Keen. Chicago: University of Chicago Press, 1976.

Lévano Medina, Diego Edgar. "El mundo imaginado: La cofradía de Nuestra Señora de Copacabana y la religiosidad andina manifestada." In *Angeli Novi: prácitcas evangelizadoras, representaciones artísticas y construcciones del catolicismo en América (Siglos XVII–XX)*, edited by Fernando Armas Asin, 113–144. Lima: Pontificia Universidad Católica del Perú, 2004.

Loreto López, RosaRosalva, "La fiesta de la Concepción y las identidades colectivas, Puebla (1619–1636)." In *Manifestaciones religiosas en el mundo colonial americano*, Vol. 2, edited by Clara García Ayluardo and Manuel Ramos Medina, 87–104. Mexico City: Universidad Iberoamericana, 1993–1994.

Mills, Kenneth. "Diego de Ocaña's Hagiography of New and Renewed Devotion in Colonial Peru." In *Colonial Saints: Discovering the Holy in the Americas*, edited by Allan Greer and Jodi Bilinkoff, 51–75. New York: Routledge, 2003.

———. "The Naturalization of Andean Christianities." In *Cambridge History of Christianity*, Vol. 6: *Reform and Expansion*, edited by R. Po-chia Hsia, 504–535. Cambridge: Cambridge University Press, 2007.

Morgan, Ronald J. *Spanish American Saints and the Rhetoric of Identity, 1600–1810*. Tucson: University of Arizona Press, 2002.

Mujica Pinilla, Ramón. *Rosa limensis: Mística, política e iconografía en torno a la patrona de América*. Lima: IFEA, 2001.

Peralta Castañeda, Antonio de. *Sermon de la Purissima Concepcion de la Virgen Maria Nuestra Señora. Predicado en la fiesta, que celebró para la repetición del juramento [...]*. Puebla de los Angeles: Juan de Borja Infante, 1654.

Ragon, Pierre. "Los santos patronos de las ciudades del México Central (Siglos XVI y XVII)," *Historia Mexicana*, 52, no. 2 (2002): 361–389.

Reverter-Pezet, Guillermo. *Las cofradías en el virreynato del Peru*. Lima: n.p., 1985.

Rubial García, Antonio. "Icons of Devotion: The Appropriation and Use of Saints in New Spain." In *Local Religion in Colonial Mexico*, edited by Martin Austin Nesvig, 37–61. Albuquerque: University of New Mexico Press, 2006.

———. *La santidad controvertida: Hagiografía y conciencia criolla alrededor de los venerables no canonizados de Nueva España*. Mexico City: Universidad Nacional Autonóma de México, Fondo de Cultura Económica, 1999.

Salgado de Somoza, Pedro. *Breve noticia de la devotisima imagen de Nuestra Señora de la Defensa [...]*. Mexico City: Imprenta de Luis Abadiano y Valdes, 1845; first published in 1686.

Schroeder, H.J., trans., *Canons and Decrees of the Council of Trent*. Rockford, IL: TAN Books, 1978 (1941).

Taylor, William B. "Between Nativitas and Mexico City: An Eighteenth-Century Pastor's Local Religion." In *Local Religion in Colonial Mexico*, edited by Martin Austin Nesvig, 91–117. Albuquerque: University of New Mexico Press, 2003.

———. "Two Shrines of the Cristo Renovado: Religion and Peasant Politics in Late Colonial Mexico." *The American Historical Review* 110, no. 4 (October 2005): 945–974.

Villaseñor Black, Charlene. *Creating the Cult of Saint Joseph: Art and Gender in the Spanish Empire*. Princeton, NJ: Princeton University Press, 2006.

Wunder, Amanda Jaye. *The Search for Sanctity in Baroque Seville: The Canonization of San Fernando and the Making of Golden-Age Culture, 1624–1729*. PhD diss., Princeton University, 2002.

11

The Baroque Church

PAMELA VOEKEL

The Baroque was a style of sacred art expressing the orthodoxy that characterized the Catholic Church from the late sixteenth to the late eighteenth centuries. Its visible features are quite distinct from theological emphases and expressive styles that preceded and followed it. In contrast to both the Erasmian devotion of early Franciscans or the proto-Jansenist Catholicism of the Enlightenment, Baroque Catholicism promoted priestly and saintly mediation, a sensual path to salvation, a highly communal notion of the relationship to the Divine, and the expectation that any element of the mundane world could be punctured by the miraculous at any time – all with the tacit or explicit approval of both Church and state.

While the Baroque style of art and piety was not fully coterminous with the Catholic Reformation itself, the historical events of Catholic renewal frame it. The Council of Trent – the official meetings of Church dignitaries and delegates spanning the years 1545 to 1563 – inaugurated this long period of codification and creativity that responded most urgently to the challenge of Protestantism (hence the meeting site in the obscure German town of Trent). As well, Baroque magnificence constituted the Church's reaction to the new scientific epistemologies coming from thinkers such as Descartes and Newton.

More broadly, however, Catholic Reform was also the Church's answer to the internal critics charging abuses and heterodoxy. Trent representatives contended with a rising tide of censure against the "Roman Babylon," a strain of criticism that the Council itself never fully put to rest. Throughout the era, these critics refused to mince words about the evils within the Church. There reigned art, not the Word of God; there patronage, not religious merit, determined ecclesiastical appointments; there arbitrary laws guided decisions about where God's truth should reign. The Council represented a circling of the wagons in the face of these attacks. Some Tridentine solutions sought to correct aberrations; others boldly clarified the distance between the orthodox

Church and emerging Protestantism by reaffirming the truth of its distinct doctrines and practices. For the Baroque period, the most salient of these included mediation through Church officials and saints, sensual display, communalism, and enthusiastic embrace of miracles in the midst of everyday life. The first and second Mexican Provincial Councils (1555 and 1565) shared Trent's warm embrace of these trends. In 1585, the third Mexican Provincial Council formally embraced the Council of Trent's teachings. The Baroque was thus formally validated in the New World, and indeed would reach its peak on American shores.

But if the Baroque was a response to the Protestant disenchantment of the world (that is, the replacement of a faith centered on the miraculous and on the teachings and traditions of the magisterium to one more focused on the primacy of written scripture and individual experience), to scientific rationality, and to internal discord, it was also a technique of rule. The system of Baroque spectacle was intended to awe the senses of the new urban crowds of the long seventeenth century into an appreciation of their elite seducers, as many historians have argued. It was, however, an imperfect system of domination. By offering multiple nodes of access to the sacred, this spectacular religious formation provided subalterns opportunities to control them for their own purposes and vie for power and sanctification.

Miraculous Saintly Mediation

The Baroque turn in the seventeenth-century Catholic Church marked an about-face from the poverty and simplicity of the early Franciscans who had first evangelized in the New World. Most of these friars hailed from the provincial house of San Gabriel in Extremadura, a place pledged to the "living gospel" of extreme poverty. Intellectually enthralled to the millenarian vision of Joaquim de Fiore, many of these earlier friars had believed a new Christ would usher in a world of perfect charity peopled by the meekest and most humble. Others had cleaved to the teachings of Spain's reformed Cardinal Francisco Jímenez, famed for shutting down opulent monasteries. Still others had embraced the simple, almost-unmediated piety of Erasmus of Rotterdam, with its skepticism about miracles and its call to return to the simplicity of the early Church shorn of the centuries' accretions of saints' cults and holy relics. Spanish settlers in the New World, the friars had feared, brought with them a decadent and corrupt Church unbefitting the new millennium, a tainted Catholicism centered on dubious saints and false miracles. Franciscan churches thus eschewed elaborate ornamentation and other sins of the corrupt world. All this would begin to change in the late sixteenth century.

The Council of Trent, again, provided a major historical impetus for the proliferation of miraculous saints' images and relics during the Baroque. In particular, the concluding twenty-fifth session of the Council was adamant that images of Christ, Mary, and the saints be displayed in churches as testimony to the miracles God had performed through them, as well as for their salutary ethical examples. As in any status-based society, of course, the circle of saints demanded exclusivity to maintain its lofty position. Trent proved instrumental in regulating admission to this most exclusive of confraternities, condemning apocryphal saints, and in 1587 the embattled Church moved against saints' cults that lacked official approval. From this time forward, a rigorous legal investigation, featuring advocates for the cult of the saints, as well as a "devil's advocate" who represented the opposition, judged the candidates on their performance of miracles, doctrinal purity, and heroic virtue. Only when a candidate had passed this initial beatification process was he or she elevated for canonization by the pope. Holy woman Rose of Lima (Santa Rosa de Lima) originally came before the Vatican's Sacred Congregation of Holy Rites in 1634, but Pope Urban VIII's reforms summarily shut down consideration of her case. Angling to shore up the saints' respectability in light of a rising tide of skepticism, Urban expanded the Council of Trent's criteria for sanctity, demanding extensive historical documentation and a waiting period of fifty years between a candidate's death and sanctification. In 1668 Rose was finally beatified. In 1669 Clement IX declared her patron of Lima and Peru; in 1670 Clement X made her patron of America and the Philippines; and in 1671 she became America's first official saint.

Not all holy figures won official approval, of course, and during the Baroque era the laity energetically sought succor from holy people who held only the imprimatur of popularity, particularly women outside the Church's official male hierarchy. Originally from India, Catarina de San Juan, the famous "China Poblana," was ferried to New Spain by Portuguese slave traders. Under the Jesuits' tutelage, she did what female religious did best: prayed incessantly for the entire Church community, experienced visions, and prophesied about the souls of important religious and political figures in Puebla and the larger colony. Her Jesuit mentors promoted her canonization through official channels – to no avail. But official approval of her miraculous interventions mattered little to Puebla's devout; her house became a popular pilgrimage site and shrine and her image appeared on home altars even before her 1688 death. Beatification proceedings, inquisition hearings, and idolatry records from the

Archdiocese of Lima tell a similar story: the general populace, including influential authorities, sought the mediation of nuns and *beatas* for matters as various and sundry as auspicious travel dates, lost objects, minor health problems, and the exact whereabouts of dead relatives in purgatory and beyond.

Saints' relics came in for scrutiny in their turn, and the Church formalized the process for obtaining approval through a bishop, although, as with holy people, popularity and efficaciousness often mattered more than official approval. Additional routes for legitimation of relics were provided by the Congregation of Rites and later through the Congregation of Relics and Indulgences. Although the Church often tussled with the laity over whose imprimatur conferred authenticity on holy relics, it actively encouraged the faithful to seek their powerful aid for worldly afflictions. Tridentine and later reformers tightened their control over the sorting out process, and attempted to curb the worst cases of idolatry, but the influential council issued no explicit condemnation of ordinary Catholics' practices concerning the saints. Pilgrimages, the cult of favor-dispensing images, appending *ex voto* offerings to images, the cult of relics – all of these practices continued unchecked, and private devotions were as prevalent as public ones. Almost all wealthy and some impoverished households owned one or two of statues proudly housed in a *retablo*, a brightly decorated wooden cabinet with doors, and wealthy silver magnates and merchants even built their own chapels and collected printed hagiographies of the saints they kept in adjacent libraries. By regulating sainthood, indeed, the Church endorsed it with renewed confidence; this was no Erasmian purge of superfluous saints but the Church's attempt to bring its cults under its own control. Reverence for saints' tombs grew after Trent's endorsement of the cult of relics and subsequent pontifical edicts in the 1620s and 1630s.

Wracked by periodic plagues and the constant threat of sudden death through illness, accident, and childbirth, the faithful of the Baroque Catholic World sought God's mercy through direct physical contact with the surfeit of the sacred contained in holy relics – both those officially blessed and those with only the imprimatur of popularity. The soil surrounding the Lima tomb of Franciscan missionary Francisco Solano, his body parts, and even droplets of the oil from the lamps at the holy site calmed tempestuous waters, smothered fire, stanched bleeding, and put the flight to gout and malign fever. Not surprisingly, he was beatified in 1679 and canonized in 1726 with little resistance. At his death in roughly 1599, another Franciscan, Sebastián de Aparicio, sweated the familiar aromatic liquid that signaled his miraculous defeat of death and bodily putrefaction with its attendant stench. Aparicio specialized in bringing dead children back to life and bereft parents naturally mobbed his Mexico City tomb to entreat miracles, which he delivered. When one man placed a cloth with a drop of the holy man's sweat on his dead child's forehead he immediately came back to life; another child two hours drowned revived after contact with Aparicio's remains. In stark contrast to the later Enlightenment or to sixteenth-century friars' penchant for the bleak Augustinianism of Erasmus (emphasizing the depravity of man redeemed by God's grace), these miracles knew no boundaries of status or gender; elite Spaniards as well as humble Indians thronged tombs and sought succor from holy relics. One of the most famous court painters of the early seventeenth century cured his wife's dropsy by placing a scrap of a holy man's blood-stained habit on her racing heart; royalty swept chapels or performed other mundane tasks to complete promises to favor-granting saints.

Images, like relics, offered the faithful direct, tangible conduits to God's mercy, and their caretakers often whisked them through the streets to homes of those stricken with disease so the afflicted could touch them. When Mexico City faced a devastating typhus epidemic in 1737, hundreds of images were borne through the streets in supplication, forming a "shield of arms" widely believed to have saved the city. Stories of miraculous images abounded in the Americas. One of the most prodigious of these icons in late-eighteenth-century Mexico City was of the child Jesus bequeathed by an Indian artisan to the convent of San Juan de la Peniténcia. During a particularly jarring earthquake, the arch above the image creaked and threatened to collapse, but the diminutive baby Jesus propped it up with two of his small fingers. In 1768, chronicler Juan Manuel de San Vicente, an administrator of the city's comedy coliseum, noted that the feat impressed the faithful, who frequently requested he be brought from his altar to their sick beds. By regulating sainthood, indeed, the Church endorsed it with renewed confidence.

The Sensual Path to Salvation

The Council of Trent affirmed that given man's weak nature, visible reminders of God's majesty enhanced rather than occluded the understanding of the Divine. During the mid-seventeenth century three successive popes confronted the Protestants' austere God by funding an architectural extravaganza in the Catholic world that rejected frozen, logical Renaissance designs in favor of soaring columns, swirling movement, and dazzling light. Pope Urban VIII spared no expense, spending a tenth of the papal states' annual income on famed sculptor Bernini's most dazzling commission: the immense ornamental canopy over St. Peter's tomb that features the monstrously enlarged Barberini bees crawling up the supporting columns.

In silver-rich New Spain and in the Andes, art and the interiors of Baroque churches radiated God's majesty, and a hybrid Baroque featuring local designs and images dazzled congregants and abetted the Christian sacralization of the Americas. In the little church in Tonantzinintla, Puebla, Mexico cherubs and saints had decidedly Indian faces and local flora and fauna adorn the columns and walls. Andean artist Diego Quispe Tito and the Cuzco School of indigenous painters broke with the artists guilds after the devastating 1650 earthquake spurred demand to replace the city's lost art. These overwhelmingly indigenous painters created new versions of Christian iconography: angels with harquebuses; new saints from America, including first-to-be-canonized Saint Rose of Lima; and mountain-shaped virgins modeled after the Pachamama (Earth Mother) – all appear in these highly original canvases. In 1633, Bogotá's Church of San Francisco acquired a retable composed of square-framed biblical scenes featuring protagonists set in the lush tropical surrounding typical of Colombia's lower altitudes. Serpentine monsters with massive mouths that disgorged tobacco leaves, cactus flowers, and pomegranates enlivened the façade of Arequipa Peru's Jesuit church in the late seventeenth century.

Indeed, the theology of external magnificence as a road to the eternal seems to have resonated with particular force in the New World, where Indian conversion was of primary importance. Faced with the daunting task of converting the Pueblo Indians in the early seventeenth century, for example, Franciscan friar Alonso de Molina paraphrased Trent's theology almost word for word, noting that incense, candles, vestments, and music were essential to bring Indians to God because they were forgetful of internal matters and needed to be helped along the path by means of external displays that aroused their senses. Likewise, Augustinian chronicler Antonio de la Calancha noted in a 1638 eulogy to Our Lady of Grace, an avocation of Mary venerated in a Lima priory, that the image's beauty attracted its many devotees. Her beauty was not incidental to her success as a heavenly mediator, he explained, because in spiritual matters our nature rests in delightful images, which purchase hearts through the eyes. More dynamically, theatrical representations of God's majesty provided a bridge of communication across the language and cultural chasm between the neophytes and the proselytizers. Paraliturgies such as dances and theater often proved more effective pedagogical tools than the catechism, or so many priests believed.

To combat the Protestant disenchantment of the world, Catholic images of God and Christ and the saints awoke from their Renaissance slumber, becoming more physically accessible, more human, more roiled with worldly emotions. Bernini's Saint Teresa swoons in an almost sexual-looking ecstasy; Pedro de Lugo Albarracin's 1656 Lord of Great Power, housed in a pilgrimage chapel overlooking Bogotá, depicts a bleeding Christ tethered to a stake and imploring the viewer with his anguished face. In the gold-rich Minais Gerais region of Brazil, slave descendant Antonio Francisco Lisboa's life-sized soapstone statues of the twelve Old Testament prophets beckoned to the faithful from the sanctuary perched atop a dramatic hilltop. Lisboa's statues seem to sway, to reach out, almost to move, and even stone columns swirled with motion.

European Baroque-era oil painting featured Christ figures that lean forward from their crucifixes to embrace or drape their arms around saints. The Cristo Aparecido showed frequent signs of life in Mexico City, and his neighbor the Cristo Renovado trembled on his cross, bled, and opened his eyes for the faithful of all social statuses, who found these miracles immanently plausible. Protestants had attempted to erase God's eruptions from the physical world. As if in self-defense, images and relics throughout the Catholic world awoke from their Renaissance slumber in the long seventeenth century, sweating, weeping, swaying, and proffering miraculous cures.

In the New World context, however, the necessity of mediation was always a fraught concept. There is ample evidence that during the Baroque era some natives and Africans who embraced the outward forms of saintly mediation were not as Christian as they perhaps appeared at first blush. Many groups stayed faithful to decidedly indigenous or African paths to God, under color of Baroque Catholicism. Priests and friars often turned a blind eye to the dance and fasting that led to the trance state that opened one to the sacred. These activities, however, were not incidental to union with God but rather constitutive of it, and therefore actually contradicted the official emphasis on priests and saints as middlemen. Pre-contact Indian culture and African religions had distinctive kinetic experiences of the sacred, such as trances and possession, and these sensory and emotional experiences endured well into the colonial period, despite the outward focus on Christian saints or avocations of Mary. In early eighteenth-century Jalapa, an African slave led a series of rituals centered on Saint Anthony in which native people participated by performing traditional dances. Considered to be the group's shaman, the slave entered into a trance, consulted with the spirits, and relayed the advice received from the supernatural world – the Church as mediator with the divine could not have been more superfluous. Peyote or a small handful of mushrooms had a similar effect: it made it possible to join the Virgin and saints without recourse to a Spanish priest. "Man-gods," native spiritual and political leaders, were commonplace during the period in New Spain, their political authority justified by their possession by order, their condition as containers for the divinity – a decidedly pre-Hispanic and unpriestly mode of communion with the supernatural.

Communal Piety

Like their saints, lay believers themselves were anything but passive during the Baroque period. The laity vigorously organized confraternities and third orders dedicated to mutual aid and to the care and tending of saints' images, pilgrimage sites, and charities. These brotherhoods worshipped their patron saints at side altars in churches and participated in civil and religious ceremonies. In exchange for small membership fees, members received succor when sick and the guarantee of collective attention to their soul's plight on death, including well-attended funerals. In a not atypical example, in the middle of the eighteenth century, each deceased member of the Third Order of São Francisco in Bahia received 178 masses for his soul; a total of 5,000 masses were celebrated annually for the departed. A single church typically housed several confraternities and the majority of the laity belonged to at least one, while some elites held membership in as many as five or six. Some confraternities welcomed members from within a given profession, such as slave merchants or tailors. These mutual spiritual and secular aid societies were not without their critics, of course, and ecclesiastical authorities attempted to maintain a semblance of control over their activities. A 1604 papal bull required that new brotherhoods receive the prior approval of diocesan authorities; and hierarchs encouraged the establishment of archconfraternities (a type of "super" confraternity granted the authority by the Church to aggregate other confraternities of the same nature), whose bylaws and norms set the standard for confraternities.

Membership tended to break down on the basis of social rank and geographic, racial, and ethnic origin. In Bahia, membership in the Santa Casa de Misercórdia was restricted to those of "clean blood," old Christians without the taint of Jewish or Moorish ancestry. This category included most of the city's aristocratic residents, whose high-status membership allowed them to direct hospitals, sanctuaries, orphanages, and cemeteries. But high rank was not a prerequisite for confraternity participation more generally. According to probate records, the vast majority of blacks and mulattoes in Bahia belonged to a confraternity. These brotherhoods divided along ethnic lines with *crioulos* – blacks born in Brazil – mulattos, and Africans all grouped into their own organizations; African confraternities were further divided by ethnic distinctions such as Angolan or *Jeje*, although these identities faded as the eighteenth century wore on.

In New Spain, black and Indian women – barred from becoming nuns – played more active roles in Baroque-era confraternities than did Spanish women, and African women passed confraternity membership downward to their children through the maternal line, as they would have done with possessions in their matrilineal African societies of origin. Although ecclesiastical authorities repeatedly denied Afro-Bahians permission to celebrate with African dances and drums, these brotherhoods feted their patron saints in fine raiment with colorful banners, crosses, and statues of the saints on portable wooden platforms. Even the neophyte Christians of Baroque Catholicism never faced the terrible absolutes of spiritual life unaccompanied. Religious orders, and, for the laity, confraternities and third orders (laypeople affiliated with a given religious order) offered solidarity entirely in keeping with the corporate self-conception of the *ancien regime*, with its juridically fixed ethnic and occupational identities.

In keeping with this communal approach to the sacred, in many Andean parishes, catechetical instruction centered on orchestrated group performances rather than direct dialogue between a single priest and an individual catechumen. A performance might take place three mornings a week in the church atrium with a priest or his Indian assistant reciting or singing the basic prayers for the group to repeat. The assembly then sang the common prayers together while processing into the church from the atrium. The Jesuits in particular were wont to lead these processions through the town's streets, with carefully ordered groups from each *ayllu* parish singing the basic prayers together.

The Maya of the Yucatán demonstrated a similar corporate bond with the sacred, although priests were often entirely peripheral to the goings-on. Early on, Spanish conquistadors had displaced native elites from regional trade, warfare, and diplomacy and then retreated back into the cities; formerly cosmopolitan indigenous rulers became the masters of small worlds, their influence shrinking to control of the individual villages dotting the countryside. Their religious imagination followed suit, as transcendent, all-encompassing divinities such as Itzamma or Hunabku or later the Christian God lost adherents to the local patron deities, the new Catholic saints, who reflected the Mayans' new social ken. The deity at the top level died off among the newly provincial Maya, not to be replaced. Through their patron saints, however, Mayans maintained a corporate bond with the sacred; little evidence suggests that individuals approached the saints or God on their own. Moreover, gentle Mary and the blessed saints were less mediators or moral exemplars than morally neutral beings and thus decidedly Mayan. In a continuance of pre-Conquest understandings of man's relationship to the sacred, the towns fed these demigods at elaborate festivals so they would in turn feed the citizens. What made these patron saint cults syncretic was not their form – which was entirely Christian – but their meaning, which remained almost entirely Mayan.

Logic of Rule

Though austere Protestantism provoked the Church into a Baroque frenzy during the long seventeenth century, the Baroque was more than a religious style concept, a sensual, mediated, miraculous, and communal path to the sacred. It was also a monarchical-seignorial form of mass culture, the very cultural logic of late feudalism. Ceremony, opulence, and theatricality are not reflections of class power during this period, but the very means of its creation. Aristocrats and monarchs associated themselves with the majesty of heaven and orchestrated a mass culture that shocked and awed new urban crowds. Its sublime beauty eluded the masses' comprehension even as it rendered them dumbstruck – or so the scholarly consensus would have it.

Likewise, historians have noted that the lavish street theatrics of monarchs, nobles, and ecclesiastical dignitaries in the burgeoning cities revealed particular assumptions about man's internal nature. The task of those who wished to rule new urban crowds was not to suppress the passions nor even stoically to silence them. Rather, they tried to make use of their force. The goal was to enthrall, to channel the passions to an appreciation of the legitimacy of the powers that flattered them.

In the prevalent scholarly analysis, Baroque culture radiates downward from elites to the masses and from city to countryside – an elite-controlled Church sanctifies rigid social hierarchies through myriad means and monarchy, aristocracy, and Church control access to the sacred through their ownership of miraculous conduits of divine mercy such as paintings, saints' images, and holy relics. That monarchical power worked by dazzling its subjects with the sumptuousness of heaven brought to earth during this period is unassailable.

Archbishop-Viceroy Fray García Guerra's 1608 entry into Mexico City included an honor guard of twenty-two liveried magistrates carrying a massive purple and gold canopy with brocade trimming that billowed above the archbishop. Dressed in glittering vestments, the new viceroy and his retinue wended their way through streets lined with the awed populace. Rich tapestries and bright-hued fabrics spilled from windows and balconies along the parade route. During the oath to the Bourbon king in 1760, the prosperous silversmith guild of Mexico City cordoned off an entire street and placed sixty-foot triumphal arches on either end. A connecting balustrade sported fifty-four emblems, mirrors, fountains, and elaborate tapestries. On a central platform sat a statue of the king in regal garments. Silver panels lined the balustrade and 7,600 candles illuminated the two arches, creating the appearance of daytime at night. Sixteen young men danced before the creation in fine clothes, spelling out "Viva Carlos Quarto" with letters on their hats. Enthralled crowds were jostled out of their trance only by soldiers asking them to leave so that waiting visitors could enter the space.

That the Church became more urban during this period is also beyond dispute. The austere and far-flung monastery complexes so characteristic of the early Franciscans, those exemplars of apostolic poverty, ceded to glittering urban parish churches and richly adorned cathedrals beginning in the late sixteenth century. In New Spain, as the native population cratered in 1620, cultivated lands shrank and fallow expanded; cities and towns hollowed out; and many rural Indian communities disappeared entirely. Retreating from the ravaged countryside to the warm embrace of Mexico City and its wealthy silver magnates and lavish court, missionary friars brought their miraculous images, relics, and paintings with them.

The diminutive Christ of Totolapan awoke in 1583 to find firm hands wresting him from his cross – hands that then secreted him through a high window into the night and a journey to the capital. The Augustinians act of *furta sacra*, holy theft, was not an anomaly: a raucous protest of both Spaniards and Indians rocked Ixmiquilpán in 1621 when the archbishop transferred their Cristo Renovado to a convent of Carmelite nuns in Mexico City. If the friars and the archbishop responded to demographic collapse in the countryside by ferrying miraculous statues and paintings to the capital, at the same time New World elites clustered in cities willed generous pious bequests that allowed the Church to collect valuable works of art and miraculous *sacra* (holy items).

At first blush, the festival of Corpus Christi in colonial Cuzco, highland capital of the former Inca Empire, perfectly illustrates the awesomeness of the growing urban theaters of baroque Spanish power. Dating from the thirteenth century, Corpus Christi received a boost from a Council of Trent (session 13, October 11, 1551) anxious to affirm the Church's doctrine of Christ's Real Presence in the Eucharist, a rallying point for critics sidling toward Protestantism. Corpus Christi heralds a victor, Christ himself, embodied in the consecrated host, and celebrates God's victory over sin and mortality and the Church's triumph over heretics. In the fraught religious environment of mid-sixteenth century Europe, the Council had summarily condemned anyone who refused to celebrate the procession of the Blessed Sacrament. As it did throughout the Catholic world, in colonial Cuzco the host processed through the city's street through triumphal arches of roman origin accompanied by fireworks and short plays or dialogues; every corporate group in the city wended its way through the boisterous crowds, illustrating the sanctification of worldly precedence through literal proximity to Christ's body and through their sponsorship of elaborately wrought processional carts with religious themes. High-ranking and opulently dressed secular and religious officials and the Spanish nobility jostled for pride of place near the sacred object, with natives and artisan and merchant guilds and lesser officials arrayed behind them – a moving map of divinely sanctioned colonial hierarchies. In European Corpus festivals Sampson vanquished the Philistines, Christians quelled Moors, and angels prevailed over Satan. The obvious loser, the heretic to be vanquished in Cuzco, was the Andeans themselves.

But if Andeans were cast in the role of the vanquished Moors and Philistines, that is not the role they played in Cuzco's Baroque Corpus festivities. Cuzco's native rulers (*caciques*) were indeed positioned in the procession subservient to the conquering Spanish. However, they donned lavish ceremonial garb, including elaborate jewel-encrusted headdresses that rivaled the towering wigs worn by French aristocratic women. In pre-Hispanic times, a retinue of vassals bearing symbols of the Sapa Inca's lofty rank accompanied him on ceremonial occasions. In the post-Conquest period, shorn of the retinues, the *caciques* moved these symbols to their headdresses. The flowers indicative of Incan authority, the miniature pennants with classic geometric designs, a menagerie of images of Andean animals associated with Incan power – all of these symbols formerly borne through the streets by the ruler's minions found their way into the headdresses, along with post-Conquest accretions such as miniature castles identical to the one in Cuzco's official coat of arms.

Caciques shimmered in the colorful fabrics with golden accouterments formerly reserved for Incan rulers. Billowing lace sleeves and tunics with embroidered with flowers, insects, and butterflies inspired by European brocade; solar pectorals worn on the chest – if anything, these native rulers' clothes rivaled their elaborate headdresses and declared them masters of Baroque spectacle. *Caciques* in the Corpus Christi festivities, in other words, certainly performed their subservience to the Spanish and Christianity, but they also theatrically proclaimed their right to mediate between Indian communities and the Spanish based on their direct relationship to the pre-Hispanic Inca nobility. Their place in this genealogy translated into status in post-Conquest society.

Mediators between things or people have profound significance in an Andean cosmology that continually strives to balance opposites. The *caciques* in the Corpus procession stressed their role as mediators rather than playing the no-win game of colonial mimesis, of striving to be like the Spanish or passively representing alterity and defeat; as well, other Indian ethnic groups vied to authorize their competing visions of the past during the Corpus Christi procession. The Baroque was a theater of sanctified power to be sure, but that power did not radiate from a lofty pinnacle downward toward a passive audience. In the late eighteenth century a new form of devotion challenged the fundamental tenets of Baroque Catholicism. The resulting conflict consumed influential portions of urban society and prompted a reevaluation of the Baroque Church's essential components – and of the justifications and techniques of social rule.

Bibliography and Suggested Readings

Dean, Carolyn J. *Inka Bodies and the Body of Christ: Corpus Christi in Colonial Cuzco, Peru*. Durham: Duke University Press, 1999.

Hughes, Jennifer Scheper. *Biography of a Mexican Crucifix: Lived Religion and Local Faith from the Conquest to the Present*. New York and London: Oxford University Press, 2010.

Kraup, Monika, and Parkinson Zamora, Lois, eds. *Baroque New Worlds: Representation, Transculturation, Counterconquest*. Durham, NC: Duke University Press, 2010.

Levy, Evonne, and Mills, Kenneth, eds. *Lexikon of the Hispanic Baroque: Transatlantic Exchange and Transformation*. Austin: University of Texas Press, 2014.

Maravall, José Antonio. *Culture of the Baroque: Analysis of a Historical Structure*. Minneapolis: University of Minnesota Press, 1986.

Paz, Octavio. *Sor Juana: Or, the Traps of Faith*. New York: Belknap, 1990.

Voekel, Pamela. *Alone Before God. The Religious Origins of Modernity in Mexico*. Durham: Duke University Press, 2002.

12

The Spanish Missions of North and South America

RAMÓN A. GUTIÉRREZ

This chapter traces the establishment of Christian missions on the sparsely populated peripheries of Spain's colonial empire in North and South America between 1492 and 1800. To understand why and where these missions developed, to better appreciate how these centers of Christianization were organized by the Mendicant Orders and the Jesuits, let us begin by examining the patterns of Spanish colonization in the dense urban centers of New Spain and Peru. Only by comparison with central places can we better appreciate the modified patterns and processes that unfolded on the peripheries, thus making the missions the distinctive places they became.

Christopher Columbus's 1492 voyage westward to find a new passage to India spotted land on October 12 at the Bahamian island of Guanaharí, which he renamed San Salvador, after the Holy Savior, Jesus Christ. In three subsequent Columbian voyages, and in many others that his compatriots undertook, the Spanish learned that they had not reached India but instead discovered two vast new continents with incredible natural and human resources, populated by native peoples of varying residential density and enormous organizational complexity.

The major centers of civilization inhabited by the Aztecs and the Incas were of greatest interest to the Spanish. They were easy to conquer for a host of reasons. The empire of the Aztecs centered in Tenochtitlán had been created and expanded through warfare and violence, and maintained through intermarriage, the forced resettlement of elites, and the regular extraction of tribute from new subjects through long-established processes that supported elites and the construction of major civil works such as temples and pyramids. Tribute demands apparently had bred deep resentments toward the Aztecs, which Hernán Cortés learned about and exploited to his advantage in 1519, seeking native allies to hasten his advance and conquest of the empire in 1521.

Francisco Pizarro and his soldiers found the Inca Empire, its hub in Cuzco, Peru, ravaged by a civil war in 1532, a conflict rooted in a sibling rivalry over lineal succession to the throne. Both of these imperial centers were quickly conquered despite the military odds in their favor. The spread of European pathogens, of smallpox and various influenzas, was but one of the crucial factors in weakening indigenous resistance to conquest. To this we must add the speed and dexterity of the horses the conquistadors used in battle, their superior guns and firepower, and of course, their lust for gold and wealth, which was complexly enmeshed in a zealous, crusading spirit against infidels.

From the first moments of contact with the native peoples the Spanish mistakenly called Indians, the emissaries of the Christian monarchs of Castile and Aragon gathered the natives to make their intentions well known. Ceremoniously the conquering Spaniards declared that their sovereignty over the Indians was in the name of their savior, Jesus Christ, through an authority that had been passed directly to them by the pontiffs of Rome. If they willingly accepted the superiority of Christians and embraced their religion, there would be peace. If they did not, noted the *requerimiento*, the required pronouncement that established Spanish political authority over the Indies through the threat of war, then "I will enter forcefully against you, and I will make war everywhere and however I can, and I will subject you to the yoke and obedience of the Church and His Majesty, and I will take your wives and children, and I will make them slaves . . . and I will take your goods, and I will do to you all the evil and damages that a lord may do to vassals who do not obey or receive him."[1] Once the Requirement had been pronounced and the natives had indicated their acceptance of the Word of God, or whatever they might have understood of what was uttered in a totally incomprehensible tongue, the conquerors marked their sovereignty by constructing crosses, fashioning altars for the celebration of mass, and staging grand theatrical acts meant to convey the import of their new religious and secular masters, the priests and soldiers.

For Christopher Columbus, for Hernán Cortés, and for a number of the Spanish conquistadors who ventured to the Americas, their forays into these new lands were motivated by a complicated mix of both religious and much more vainglorious goals. Cortés, for example, was a deeply religious man. Particularly devoted to the Blessed Virgin Mary, he carried an image of her everywhere he went, prayed and attended mass daily, and had emblazoned on the standard he took into battle the words: "Friends, let us follow the cross, and if we have faith, then truly we will be victorious under this banner."

---

[1] Patricia Seed, *Ceremonies of Possession in Europe's Conquest of the New World, 1492–1640* (Cambridge: Cambridge University Press, 1995), 69.

Bernal Díaz del Castillo, on whose account of the conquest of New Spain we now most rely, described the enthusiasm and vigor with which Cortés set about constructing crosses, destroying idols, humiliating native priests, ordering masses celebrated and sermons preached, demanding even that baptisms be performed in rapid fire without instruction. Fray Bartolomé de Olmedo, the Mercedarian friar who accompanied Cortés's expedition to Mexico in 1519, was much more cautious, advocating much more patience, and certainly more instruction before such sacred symbols as the cross and statues of the Virgin Mary were left in the hands of heathens, sitting atop altars on which previously the devil had been worshiped.[2]

Once the military conquest of the Aztecs was complete Cortés was particularly concerned for their spiritual welfare, finding his rule over pagans particularly immoral. He requested and soon received a contingent of twelve Franciscans to serve as the twelve apostles for this new land. When they arrived in Mexico City in 1524, under the leadership of Fray Martín de Valencia, Cortés gathered all the lords and populace of Tenochtitlán to behold how he greeted them. When the moment arrived, Cortés approached the friars on horseback, dismounted before them, fell to his knees, and then kissed their hands and hems. Cortés then ordered the native nobility to do likewise, teaching by example the respect the Indians should show the Franciscans.

Although no equally dramatic acts were staged by Francisco Pizarro to hasten the Christianization of the Incas, Fray Vicente Valverde and four Dominican friars who had accompanied the conquering party quickly began their work in Peru in 1534. Valverde, as the Bishop of Cuzco, by 1538 had laid the foundations for a cathedral. An ambitious ecclesiastical building project followed, rapidly dotting the landscape with churches, monasteries, hospitals, and schools.

Every conquering expedition to the Americas had among its members priests and lay brothers charged with the Christianization of whatever pagans they might encounter. The Franciscans and the Dominicans were by far the two religious orders with the largest number of personnel toiling in the Americas. But Mercedarians, Augustinians, and much later Jesuits, were also present. The Society of Jesus, which Ignatius Loyola founded in 1540, initially focused its energy on India, Japan, and China, and only later, in the 1580s, began to proselytize in Mexico, Central America, the Andean highlands, and the Chaco of southern South America.

2 Robert Ricard, *The Spiritual Conquest of Mexico: An Essay on the Apostolate and the Evangelizing Methods of the Mendicant Orders in New Spain, 1523–1572* (Berkeley: University of California Press, 1966), 16–18.

By the 1550s, the Spanish and the Portuguese had gained a fundamental knowledge of the geography and social organization of the native populations on both continents. There were sprawling imperial hubs such as those of the Aztecs in Tenochtitlán and the Incas in Cuzco; there were major urban centers such as those of the Maya in the Yucatán; there were small village clusters, which the Spaniards called *rancherías*, which were agrarian-based settlements of dispersed, loosely aggregated mud houses or brush huts; and there were nomads who seasonally foraged over immense but clearly demarcated terrains that often encompassed a host of ecological zones. The imperial centers and well-established towns, with their hierarchical social organization, religious structures, craft specialization, and prolific and diverse sedentary agricultural base, naturally made them the primary sites of intensive Spanish colonization. For as one of New Spain's viceroys, don Luis Velasco so cogently noted, "no one comes to the Indies to plow and to sow, but only to eat and loaf."[3]

To eat and loaf with minimal effort, the Spanish needed dense indigenous populations whose state or city-state formations had a prolific agrarian base and were already well-organized and accustomed to the production and routine payment of tribute in the form of food and labor to their aristocracy or conquering states. In central Mexico and the highlands of Peru they found this in close proximity to mineral wealth. In these places much of the indigenous social organization and productive capacity was left intact after the Spanish conquest. Indeed, many of these urban centers had historically undergone similar cycles of conquest by previous ascendant states and were thus used to paying tribute and having their local gods subordinated to those of their victors.

The indigenous populations living in *rancherías*, not generally subject to states or accustomed to the payment of tribute to anyone, semisedentary and organized around households and clans, were of secondary interest to the colonial state and its settlers. The nomadic hunters and gathers, who foraged over vast expanses, whose aggregates rarely numbered in the hundreds, and who were considered nuisances to the tranquility of urban life, even by indigenous sedentary agriculturalists, were even of lesser interest to the Spanish. Deemed too troublesome, too unruly, and too resource intensive to dominate, the Spanish Crown only used them strategically when European imperial rivals threatened American frontier boundaries or approaches to their mineral wealth. Then, projects to settle them took place, alternatively arming them

---

3 Don Luis Velasco to King Philip III, December 17, 1608, in *Don Juan de Oñate: Colonizer of New Mexico, 1595–1628*, eds. and trans., George P. Hammond and Agapito Rey (Albuquerque: University of New Mexico Press, 1953), 1068.

to disrupt English, French, and Russian forays into marginally settled lands claimed by Spain.

The *encomienda* was the main instrument the conquistadors used to establish their lordship over the Indians throughout the Americas both at their centers and at their margins. *Encomienda*, a noun derived from the verb *encomendar*, which means "to entrust," was a grant, euphemistically referred to as an entrustment of Indians who were obliged to pay tribute to their *encomendero*, the person to whom they had been entrusted. *Encomederos* in turn were obligated to protect their *encomienda*'s residents from enemy attack and to Christianize them. The largest and most prolific *encomiendas* were quickly handed out by the conquering leaders to their relatives, allies, and friends, and to wealthy, influential, and senior men. The basic native units of social organization in any particular place, be it a village, town, or province, were given out as personal *encomiendas*. Natives retained ownership of their own lands, with the *encomenderos* usually given adjacent *estancias*, or land grants. These estancias were the source of great friction in Indian–white relations, and clerical-secular disputes during the colonial period.

By the time the mendicant orders (Holy Orders dating from the Middle Ages that took vows of poverty) arrived in central Mexico and Peru, all the major Indian towns had already been distributed as *encomiendas*. The task of the friars was to construct a church and begin the conversion of the natives. Christianization was often at odds with the tribute demands of the *encomenderos*. *Encomenderos* and friars bitterly fought over the treatment of the Indians and shrilly contested how they each used native labor. Every church was granted a plot of land at its start for the development of its own provision. Without Indian labor church compounds could not be built nor its lands made productive. Here was the rub.

Fray Bartolomé de las Casas emerged as one of the best known champions of the Indians in the Americas, noting how the ravages of warfare, disease, depression and hyperexploitation on *encomiendas* was quickly leading to their annihilation. Largely because of the debates that las Casas and others provoked in Spain, the Crown's conscience was stirred and the most exploitative features of the *encomienda* were curtailed by the promulgation of the New Law in 1542. In 1573 the Crown further outlawed grand expeditions of conquest such as those Pizarro and Cortés had staged. "Discoveries are not to be called conquests," the Ordinances of Discovery stated. "Since we wish them to be carried out peacefully and charitably, we do not want the use of the term 'conquest' to offer an excuse for the employment of force or the causing of injury to the Indians."[4] Henceforth, only peaceful settlement directed by missionaries would be allowed into remote, as of then unsettled areas.

The arrival of large numbers of Spanish and European immigrants in Mexico and Peru, prompted by the 1546 almost simultaneous discovery of rich silver deposits in Potosí, Bolivia, and in Mexico's near north, around Zacatecas, precipitated the settlement of the peripheries of both of these regions. The silver mines had to be provisioned with equipment and manpower, and the population that was gathering in these places needed the basic necessities of life. Expeditions in the 1560s, now nominally led by missionaries, but accompanied by well-fortified military contingents, began expanding into New Spain's far north, into what are today the Mexican states of Chihuahua, Sonora, Coahuila, and Baja California Norte and Sur and the American states of California, Arizona, New Mexico, and Texas. By 1562 the Indian communities of Nueva Vizcaya had been parceled out as *encomiendas*, as were those of Nuevo León by 1579, and New Mexico's by 1598.

The Missions of New Mexico

The desire to carry the Gospel to New Spain's far north was the logical outcome of the Franciscan missionary enterprise that had begun in the Valley of Mexico in 1524. As the Indian *doctrinas* (parishes) they had established to convert the natives were increasingly secularized and placed under Episcopal control, the friars had two choices. They could retreat to monastic life or push into new missionary fields. Fueled by millennial dreams and the desire to die as martyrs, the most zealous friars ventured north. Geographically the Franciscans primarily went into what are now the Mexican north central states of Durango, Chihuahua, and the American states of New Mexico and Arizona, while the Jesuits ministered in what is now the Mexican state of the Baja California and the Pacific coast states of Sinaloa and Sonora. Only in New Mexico were dense population centers based on sedentary agriculture found among the city-dwelling Pueblo Indians of the Upper Rio Grande drainage. It was naturally here that the most impressive evangelizing activities transpired between 1598 and 1821.

In New Mexico three mission types were employed to respond to the various level of indigenous social organization; this was a pattern that would be repeated throughout the Americas various ways. Christianity was primarily an

---

4 "Ordenanzas de su magestad hechas para los nuevos discubrimientos, conquistas y pacificaciones, July de 1573," in *History of Latin American Civilization*, ed. Lewis Hanke (Boston: Little, Brown and Company, 1967), Vol. 1, 149–152.

urban religion and thus the dominant type, the missions of occupation, were simply superimposed atop the boundaries of well-established towns, at those very places where the Spaniards had already distributed the Indian towns as *encomiendas*. Once the Christianization was well under way and the friars felt secure in their work, they explored the surrounding *rancherías*, preaching and offering gifts to the Indians in the hopes of creating missions of penetration into which they could gather a host of widely dispersed villages into a much smaller number of towns.

The missions of the Jémez area – San José Guisewa and San Diego de la Congregación – were formed in this way, gathering twelve hamlets into two mission centers, which were known as *congregaciones* or *reducciones*. From these *congregaciones* the friars ventured out even further, into lands in which nomadic hunters and gathers raided and traded. If the friars' words and works proved particularly successful with these peripatetic people, the goal was to gather them into *reducciones*, and as their stability increased and their population grew, to finally make them into formal *doctrinas*. This basic pattern of concentrating widely dispersed nucleated populations into mission centers also was employed throughout the peripheries of Spanish America, in the missions of Paraguay and northern Argentina in the early 1600s, in those of Texas starting in 1715, and in those formed in California starting in 1769.

By the 1560s the Franciscans and other mendicant orders had mastered a fundamental understanding of indigenous beliefs and thus tried to present themselves to the Indians in categories the natives understood. Indigenous religious life was organized around chieftaincies devoted to planting and hunting, warfare and peacemaking, curing and rainmaking. It was as *caciques*, or as native chiefs and shamans capable of satisfying material and spiritual needs, that the missionaries approached the neophytes. Entering most areas with military escorts, the missionaries tried to make the Indians understand that they too were mighty lords capable of unleashing the power of the Spanish state, intervening to moderate or forestall its force, leading herds of domesticated animals, and carrying with them a range of seeds and plants to make native lands blossom in quantitatively significant ways. Wheat and barley, apples, pears, plums and grapes, pigs, cows, and chickens were but a few of the inducements to mission life the *padres* offered. To these must be added the basic medicine chests they carried and the ritual objects – their crosses and chalices, their vestments and altars, their religious statuary and rosaries – that became the focus of instruction and Christian life.

The basic method the missionaries used to convert the Indians was based on the model they themselves had undergone in their own spiritual formation as religious men. To transform the "outer man" (behavior) and the "inner man" (the soul), one had to begin by purging oneself of all that was flesh and blood, all that one had or could have in the world, particularly those enemies of the soul, lust and pride. Once the purgation was complete, the body and soul were ready to be illuminated by the way, by the truth, and by the light of Jesus Christ. Finally, as one reached spiritual perfection, one yearned for a mystical marriage with Christ, which could be manifested in various ways. Martyrdom, either literal or figurative, was the most common of these, leading the soul to a mystical marriage with Christ.

The Christianization of the Indians proceeded in similar fashion, first by purging them of the devil's control and leading them "out from the darkness of paganism and the soberness of death [and into the] Father of Light," by preaching and coaxing, by gifting and hosting, and when necessary, with the sting of the lash. The Indians had to renounce Satan, banish his earthly assistant (native chiefs), and forsake their superstitious idols and beliefs. To ensure this the padres profaned native ceremonial chambers, incinerated the idols they found there, and created a new sacral topography by superimposing a church and altars, where once the Indians had worshipped their demons. Purging the Indians of their major sin of lust was next in importance, demanding monogamous marriages of them, chastity before the sacramental state, and lifelong fidelity afterward. Violators of these new rules of sexual morality were publicly whipped, placed in stocks, and sheared of their locks. Indeed, it was the imposition of chastity, marital monogamy, and fidelity that was to prove one of the greatest sources of friction during the initial years of Christianization and cause for rebellion. In 1680, for example, Popé, the leader of the Great Pueblo Revolt, enlisted people in his movement by promising that "Who shall kill a Spaniard will get an Indian woman for a wife, and he who kills four will get four women, and he who kills ten or more will have a like number of women."[5]

Once purified of their sinful ways, the Indians were ready to receive the illuminating light of the gospel. But many years of proselytizing among the Indians had taught the missionaries that the Indian adults were a very weak foundation for the New Jerusalem. If Christianity were to be firmly planted, it would only be through the young. Their goal thus became to snatch the young boys from the devil through baptism, while their sexual purity was still intact, and to use them as a cadre to extirpate idolatry and propagate the

---

5 Declaration of Pedro García, a Tagno Indian, August 25, 1680, in Charles W. Hackett, ed., *Revolt of the Pueblo Indians of New Mexico and Otermín's Attempted Reconquest, 1680–1682* (Albuquerque: University of New Mexico Press, 1942), Vol. I, 24–25.

faith. Fray Gerónimo de Mendieta stated the strategy very succinctly when he explained that the children became "the preachers, and the children were the ministers for the destruction of idolatry."[6]

So that the Indians boys would give their complete obedience to the Catholic priests, they first frequently witnessed the humiliation of their biological fathers as a sign of the impotence of their native gods. This the friars did by staging such things as didactic religious dramas in which the young boys played angels vanquishing devils and infidels, personified by Indian adults. The friars also used abundant carrots for this task, offering the boys land, seeds, manufactured goods, livestock, meat, and education in animal husbandry in return for baptism and obedience to God's law. They gave them access to marriage and sanctioned sexual activity, all with the goal of making them faithful Christians.

The illumination of the Indian was also accomplished through intensive education at the *doctrinas*, utilizing the various catechisms that had been prepared by the mendicant orders in Mexico and Peru for the edification of Indian souls. The pedagogy elaborated in these relied extensively on the rote memorization of standard prayers and an inventory of law and sins. The neophytes were taught the "Credo," the "Pater Noster," the "Ave Regina," and "Salve Regina," along with the Ten Commandments, the moral and venial sins, the cardinal virtues and works of mercy, as well as the enemies of the soul – the world, the devil, and the flesh. As fidelity to the mission's rules was not always followed, or at least not as faithfully as the padres wanted, they relied on the *policía espiritual*, on native assistants who served as the "spiritual police." Each parish also counted on several *fiscales* (church wardens) for this task. These were disciplinarians who maintained order during services, punished the morally lax, mobilized production on church lands, and supervised the construction of ecclesiastical buildings. Equally important were the *temastianos* (Indian catechists) who led converts in prayer and the memorization of the catechism.

How the missionaries approached an explication and understanding of the sacraments in the conversion of the Indians depended highly on their own mastery of the Indian languages. In general terms, the Jesuits seem to have expended more effort in the learning of Indian languages than did the Franciscans. Mastering native languages was also highly dependent on how long their assignments in particular places lasted. The Franciscans and Jesuits both toiled in areas of immense linguistic diversity. If they were moved

---

6 Gerónimo de Mendieta, *Historia eclesiástica Indiana*, Lib. 3, chapter 28, 91 as quoted in Pius J. Barth, *Franciscan Education and the Social Order in Spanish North America, 1502–1821* (Chicago: University of Chicago Press, 1950), 198.

every three years to a new mission where a different language was spoken, it was unlikely that the missionary would ever gain more than a rudimentary understanding of it.

To overcome their linguistic limitations, the Franciscans placed a great deal of emphasis on the use of paraliturgies and teaching through example, fearing that they might inadvertently nurture heretical understandings of the sacraments. The Jesuits, perhaps because they were founded as a religious society to extirpate heresy, more readily translated concepts into the Indian languages that appeared to closely resemble Spanish ones. The end result was the more extensive translation of their sermons, their catechisms, and their confession manuals into the vernacular, and their use in the labor of conversion.

By choosing to evangelize through the use of paraliturgies the Franciscans controlled the timing and staging of native dances and rites of passage, regardless of their deeper meanings to the Indians. They attempted, for example, to conflate the Pueblo *katsina* cult, or the worship of the ancestral dead, with the cult of the saints. They maintained the indigenous sacral geography and superimposed chapels and altars atop native shrines to gods of fertility. The Pueblo Indians employed a lunar calendar for their rituals of planting and harvest, and so Christmas and Corpus Christi, which centuries earlier in Europe had replaced the pagan winter and the summer solstices, were used to fuse Christian and indigenous calendric rhythms. The Franciscan devotion to the crucified Christ naturally led to spectacular use of the crosses in ritual and to penitential rites associated with bloodletting, purification, authority, and renewal in the native cosmology.

We have only the Franciscans' own records to tell us how successful the labor of conversion really was. This was always measured in the number of Indians living in *doctrinas*. At the point of contact in 1540 there were perhaps as many as 280,000 Pueblo Indians residing in several hundred dispersed villages, or so the logs of Francisco Vásquez de Coronado's expedition report. When don Juan de Oñate reconnoitered roughly the same terrain in 1598, only about 80,000 natives remained, living in 134 villages. By 1640 this population had declined to some 60,000 individuals residing in 43 towns; by 1769 only 20 pueblos still existed, housing 17,000 souls. The friars always counted the total indigenous population residing in towns as equivalent with the number of Indian converts.

What did conversion mean in this context? How genuine was it? Conversion is a fundamental change in beliefs whereby a person accepted the reality and omnipotence of the Spanish God and vowed to obey Him and His ministers. By this standard the number of true Christian souls was vastly inflated by census counts, an inflation born of exuberant clerical misinterpretation. There can be no doubt that some of these were true conversions. There were the Christianized boys painstakingly educated by the friars who, on their instruction, ransacked pueblos extirpating idolatry. The friars tell us in their letters and reports that pre-Conquest fissures in the organization of town were further exacerbated by newborn distinctions between Christianized Indians and "pagans," between Hispanicized converts and traditionalists who clung tenaciously, if clandestinely, to ancestral ways.

The problem remains to assess how deeply or shallowly, how warmly or lukewarmly baptized Indians understood the beliefs they had embraced. And this is fundamentally a problem of translation. Leaving aside the fact that few of the friars spoke or understood the Indians languages, we must ask whether Catholicism, with it monotheistic emphasis on one God and its moral vision of good and evil, heaven and hell, could have been translated into terms the Pueblo Indians fully understood, given their animistic beliefs and monistic cosmological mental universe lacking either sin or hell. I think it could not have been done too effectively, no matter how great the effort. The simple reason is that the clerical model of re-formation and evangelism, with its pronounced emphasis on externality – transforming the "outer person" (behavior) to change the "inner person" (the soul) – predisposed the friars to believe that indigenous dissimulations, performed under the threat of violence and force, were true conversions. An evangelization strategy of eradicating native rites and substituting Christian ones that mimicked indigenous gestures and paraphernalia, no matter how divergent their respective meanings, also led the friars to misinterpret the apparent piety with which the Indians worshipped God.

Those Pueblo Indians who nominally pledged allegiance to Christianity and at least superficially forsook their native ways did so, in part out of fear and in part to reap the technological and cultural innovations offered by the mission friars. For Indian residents of small villages constantly under attack by nomads, despoiled of their food, and forced to abandon well-watered spots, the mission padres offered the semblance of protection. In numbers there was strength, and behind the massive walls of mission compounds there was security. Christianization to these persons meant a reliable meat supply and iron implements of various sorts. It thus does not strain the imagination too much to envision why such persons, having undoubtedly heard of the conquest of the Aztecs, were understandably nervous and ambivalent about the arrival of the Christians and allied themselves with the new order.

From 1598 to the early 1660s the Franciscans, provincial governors, and colonists of New Mexico fiercely contested each other's use and control of native land and labor. The violent suppression of indigenous religious practices, drought, famine, and pestilence took their toll until Spanish control over *encomiendas* started to unravel in the mid-1660s, with Indians fleeing as apostates. As apostates these Indians joined the Apaches, Navajos, Kiowa, Ute, and Comanche nomads who encircled the villages of the Upper Rio Grande drainage, and when faced with the same food shortages, started raiding the missions with particular force. Unable to withstand the attacks, exhausted by the tribute they were forced to pay, and convinced that only by reverting to their ancient religion would their gods favor them with abundance and peace, the Indians bolted on August 10, 1680.

The Pueblo Revolt put an end to the Spanish presence in New Mexico for thirteen years and became the first successful indigenous revolt against Spanish colonialism in the Americas. The Spanish Crown eventually reestablished its authority over New Mexico's Pueblo Indians in 1693, but gone was the hated *encomienda* and gone too were the zealous friars who were determined to impose Christianity at any cost. The friars who returned to the Kingdom of New Mexico in the early 1700s were more timid and much more accepting of indigenous religiosity, gradually shifting their attention away from the Indian Pueblos and onto the Spanish and mestizo towns that became the centers of eighteenth-century civilian settlement. The Pueblo Indian missions in 1700 had a population of roughly 5,000 persons and were self-governed, with institutions and officers akin to those in independent towns.

After the 1680 Pueblo Revolt, the Spanish Crown continued to support the Franciscans' work and additionally recruited Jesuits to establish missions in New Spain's north. What was basically different in *doctrinas* that the Jesuits established in the *Pimería Alta* (roughly the northern Mexican states of Sonora and Sinaloa and the southern part of Arizona) in 1687, in Baja California in 1697, and that the Franciscans built in Texas in 1715, and in Alta California in 1769, was that these were sparsely populated places where some of the indigenous populations were organized into *rancherías* but where the majority lived as nomads. By 1680 too these hunters and gatherers had become mounted equestrians and were particularly fierce as warriors and raiders. The technological and agrarian innovations the missions offered sedentary agriculturalists were virtually meaningless to these nomads.

Fearing revolts in Mexico's north akin to that of the Pueblo Indians in 1680, concerned about Russian, English, and French interlopers coveting the land routes into the silver mines of Zacatecas where by then one-third of all the world's silver was being extracted, and seeking to nominally colonize the north at minimal cost, the Crown dispatched missionaries to the north. We will return to the missions of California shortly, but let us first turn to Paraguay, where the *doctrinas* founded there by the Jesuits were contemporary with those of New Mexico.

The Missions of Paraguay

To understand where, how, and why the Jesuit missions developed in what is now Paraguay, let us begin by first reviewing some geography. If one looks at a map of southern South America today, the space is dominated by Brazil on the east, with Uruguay and Argentina at its southern border. Argentina is immense, geographically divided into three physical zones. The first zone, the *pampas* or grassy alluvial plains that start at the mouth of the Rio de la Plata estuary where Buenos Aires was established, extends in a northwestern direction and is fed by three major rivers: the Paraná, Paraguay, and Uruguay Rivers. The source of these rivers is roughly what became Paraguay. It is a hilly area interspersed by well-watered forests, savannas, and grassy fields, all of which were well suited to agricultural production, and thus the area of most indigenous and Spanish colonial settlement. It was here that the Jesuits formed their thirty famous missions among the semisedentary Guaraní Indians.

The Jesuits of course founded more than a hundred missions in southern South America, but these thirty were the ones that became the most contentious because of their productivity and control over large numbers of converts. The third geographic zone, the Gran Chaco, sits west of Paraguay, in what is now the northeastern part of Argentina. This is an area of flat alluvial plains that drain the eastern side of the Andes, which are often flooded and not particularly useful for agricultural production. The indigenous populations here were nomadic raiders who often attacked the Guaraní farmers east of them.

The impulse that led to the formation of missions in this part of southern South America originated in the search for mineral wealth. Shortly after the conquest of Peru was complete, in 1535 the Spanish Crown sponsored a massive expedition led by Pedro de Mendoza with some 1,300 soldiers, larger than had been used in either the conquests of Mexico or Peru, to establish settlements along the Atlantic coast of southern South America. The expedition had been prompted by Sebastian Cabot's encounter in 1526 with survivors of Díaz de Solís's expedition into southern Brazil a decade earlier. Cabot was presented with silver ornaments, which had probably been obtained from the

Incas, and told of rich empires to the west. Pedro de Mendoza and his party landed in the Rio de la Plata, so-called the "River of Silver" because of the wealth they expected to find, and founded Buenos Aires in 1536.

There was neither fame nor fortune here, only fierce nomadic Indians who were impossible to conquer and were unwilling to provide the expedition's members with even the most minimal amounts of food. Sustaining themselves on rats and the decaying bodies of their compatriots, several members of the expedition abandoned their position to explore the headlands of the Paraguay River looking for a better port, one not swept by such forceful winds and located in close proximity to agrarian peoples. On August 15, 1537, the feast day of Our Lady of the Assumption, they laid the foundation for the fort they named Asunción, with the expectation that it would be from here that they would explore the lands further west.

The Guaraní Indians living in the vast territory east and southeast of Asunción quickly embraced the Spanish as allies, hoping to stave off the nomadic enemies that surrounded them. The Spanish were equally eager to have such friends, given how disastrous their expedition had been and how desperate they were for food. The Spanish never intended to settle here permanently, only to use it as a base from which to search for Indian civilizations with massive mineral wealth, which they believed lay to the west. Eventually silver was discovered at Potosí, Bolivia in 1546, and this quickened communication between Buenos Aires, Asunción, and Potosí.

The Guaraní, who numbered roughly 200,000 in 1537, were a group who practiced slash-and-burn agriculture, supplementing their diet with hunting and fishing. In their sexual division of labor men were responsible for clearing fields of trees and stumps. The women did all the planting and harvesting. These were not particularly fertile lands, which were quickly leached of their nutrients, rarely producing more than a few crop cycles before it was time to move on. Socially organized into patrilineages, Guaraní encampments were small in number and expanse, and were led by headmen (*caciques*) and shamans. Social hierarchy was minimal. They lived from hand to mouth, producing little surplus, and devoid of any tributary structures based on class. Other than inequalities based on age, the unequal appropriation of labor was based on gender, with women performing the work of planting and domestic reproduction for their husbands and their tribal leaders who availed themselves of these according to the number of wives and female kin they each had.

The Guaraní were particularly disappointing for the young soldiers, but they accommodated to the reality that they were being treated as native caciques, with all that meant locally. By consorting with Guaraní women and availing themselves of the labor customarily provided their husbands, Spaniards saw their circumstances radically improve, particularly if they gathered multiple concubines, as native headmen did. Eating food produced by Guaraní women, bedding them and thus producing mixed-blood children who were considered "Spanish," Asunción quickly became a thoroughly mestizo Spanish-Guaraní outpost in which European technology and ideas thoroughly suffused indigenous ways and vice versa. Many things deemed and denominated as "Spanish" were so only in name. By 1557 Asunción had a total population of about 1,200 persons.

The Guaraní had no organizational unit that easily loaned itself to division as *encomiendas*. Only gradually, by gathering indigenous women, the children of their multiple "wives, and the female relatives of these women and servants,"[7] were the soldiers able to forge an institution that would be called an *encomienda* with which they mobilized enough labor to sustain themselves and to produce a few exports. This way of obtaining indigenous female labor for purposes of reproduction and trade was recognized by the Crown in 1556 with the title *encomienda originaria*.

"Original" here meant that it was unique to Paraguay, differentiating it from the classic *encomienda* of central Mexico and Peru, and from a third form that was also born of necessity as the *encomienda mitaya*. Indigenous rotational labor drafts, first under Inca, and then under Spanish rule, had been known as the *mita*. When the New Laws of 1542 abolished the distribution of new *encomiendas* and curtailed the inheritance of existing ones, the *mita* became its replacement. To the Spaniards living around Asunción who had not managed to penetrate Guaraní society through seduction and/or through force, small indigenous settlements were given to them as *encomiendas mitayas*. Obviously, what was missing from such grants was the tribute; they could only avail themselves of whatever labor they could extract from Indians who did not hesitate to move on when they felt wronged.

The first Jesuits to minister in Paraguay arrived in 1587, having been invited by the Asunción bishop. They quickly focused their energy first on ministering to the Indians concentrated in *encomiendas*, and then on sending priests to congregate the unsettled nomadic Indians into missions. From the very start of their endeavors the Jesuits came into sharp conflict with the Spanish settlers. According to the members of the Society of Jesus, these men were living in scandalous and shameful ways, exploiting women, living with

---

7 Frederick Reiter, *They Built Utopia: The Jesuit Missions in Paraguay, 1610–1768* (Potomac, MD: Scripta Hunanistica, 1995), 78.

them in concubinage, procreating with abandon, and seriously inhibiting Christianization.

While the Jesuits were eager to spread the word of God among the hostile nomads that inhabited the Gran Chaco and the grasslands northwest of Buenos Aires, the nomads saw no benefit to Christianization, only its pain in the form of disease, labor exploitation, and subjection to enslavement and death. The Jesuits had virtually no success in permanently congregating these Indians despite decades of efforts and a host of martyrs. Finally the Jesuits shifted their evangelization strategy, abandoning both the Indians living in *encomiendas* near Asunción and nomads, and instead founding missions among the Guaraní at places far removed from the corrupting influence of civilians, which would become havens for Indians wanting to become good Christians. Like the Franciscans of seventeenth-century New Mexico who were determined to create a theocracy, a New Jerusalem on earth, so the Jesuits marched forward the same goal.

The Jesuit province of Paraguay was founded in 1606 by Father Diego de Torres Bollo and seven priests to advance this specific goal. Invoking the language of the 1573 Ordinances of Discovery, their objective was to wage a spiritual conquest for Indian minds and bodies, winning them over to Christianity gently, through sermons and gifts, by persuasion and example, free from the taxation and the labor exploitation of *encomenderos*. The first *reducción* or *doctrina* among semisedentary Indians occurred in 1609, at San Ignacio Guazú, on the northeastern portion of what was then Spanish/Portuguese contested territory, which ultimately became the Brazilian province of Paraná. In 1611, a reduction was likewise established at San Ignacio Miri. Jesuit personnel grew rapidly in the years that followed, as did the number of Indians living in missions. By 1613, 113 members of the Society of Jesus were working in Paraguay. The number of missions quickly grew to more than 100, with the number of souls gathered at these sites rising from 30,548 souls in 1648 to 141,182 in 1732, before declining to 73,910 by 1740. By 1750 the number of Guaraní living in doctrinas was back up to 104,483, which seems to indicate that as the population declined due to disease, the Jesuits redoubled their efforts to congregate new converts. In 1767, when the Jesuits were expelled from Paraguay, there were seventy-seven of them working in thirty-three missions.

Despite the missionaries' efforts to build church compounds, the reductions were never stable places, shifting constantly, some quickly disappearing almost as rapidly as they were constructed for the complex reasons noted previously. Concentration made nomadic and semisedentary populations more susceptible to disease. They were also easy targets for attack both from

Brazilian slave raiders and mounted nomads who sought food surplus and livestock gathered at missions.

The Spanish colonists were an equal threat. As their own *encomienda* Indians died off from disease and overwork, the neophytes gathered at missions became a constantly coveted source of labor. The settlers were particularly resentful of the Jesuits not only because of this monopoly on Indian labor but also because the missions had established productive farms with export products such as the native tea, *yerba maté*, which rivaled the settlers' own production of this crop. Further complicating the political geography were the slave raiders of southern Brazil, who also wanted access to the same labor that the Spanish wanted. Had the Spanish settlers of Asunción not armed the Guaraní as allies against enemy nomads, the superior force of arms the Spanish and Portuguese wielded would have settled these disputes rapidly. But the Jesuits followed suit, armed the Guaraní to protect their missions, and gave them all the rudimentary structures of civic organization to function as independent towns.

What developed at the thirty Jesuit missions of Paraguay that endured over time were centers for the Christianization of the Indians that were not unlike those the Franciscans had created in northern New Spain. These were intensive sites for instruction in the Gospel, the inculcation of a new body ethics, and the creation of a new mode of existence based on imported European technologies around livestock and agricultural production. At the *doctrinas*, the Jesuits instructed the Indians using catechisms translated into Guaraní, gathering their neophytes several times daily for pray and song, didactic theatrical stunts, and the performance of indigenous dances, which were now timed to the Christian calendar, under clerical supervision, and closely monitored by the spiritual police who did not hesitate to punish apostates and back-sliders.

Much as the Franciscans in northern Mexico opted for the extensive use of paraliturgies over sacramentalism in their evangelization strategies, so too did the Jesuits. Presenting themselves as powerful *caciques*, the Jesuits distributed gifts for which they took nothing in return, and offered esoteric knowledge and rituals they said would connect humans to a powerful, all-loving God. They held the power to distribute women to men as wives, to dole out land, to cure the sick with their potent medicines, and to squash dissent by force of arms.

As occurred throughout much of Mexico and Peru, the Jesuits in Paraguay also focused their energy on the native boys, seeing in their virginal purity, their lack of knowledge about the ancient gods, and their indebtedness to the Jesuits for material rewards the best hope for deeply implanting the Word of God among the heathens. Whenever the Jesuits ventured to new areas to preach and to persuade the Indians to gather willingly into a mission, they were always accompanied by Guaraní-speaking boys who could preach, speak eloquently with elders about the Christian God, and assist in the construction of crosses and altars.

The Jesuit missions of Paraguay were enormously successful in isolating the Indians from the sinful corruption of civilians who, according to the priests, were the source of the debauchery, exploitation, and depression one found among those Indians gathered in *encomiendas*. The Jesuit farms were prolific, cloaking and feeding the Indians gathered, militarily protecting them from all but the most forceful local contestants. But the assaults came, and they came at a quickening pace. There were influential native shamans who convinced their former kin to abandon their mission, martyr their priests, and live happily again with as many wives as they chose. The descendants of the first colonists who wanted the lands the missions occupied and the laborers who worked them constantly petitioned the king for these, railing about the arrogance and competition they faced from the missionaries. At the level of competing empires, both Portugal and Spain claimed the territory on which the Jesuit missions stood.

Finally the expulsion of the Order from Spain's empire all around the globe in 1767, driven by these imperial politics and local rivalries, finally led to the declension of the Jesuit missions in Paraguay. Their assets were quickly divided among Spanish and Portuguese colonists. The Indians were just as rapidly dispersed, pressed into slavery and debt peonage in Spanish towns, or driven to the resumption of peripatetic lives.

The Missions of Alta California

What is now the state of California was known as Alta California during the colonial period and it was here, hugging the coast from south to north, that a chain of missions was established by Fray Junípero Serra and a small group of Franciscans. Beginning with the foundation of a garrison and Mission San Diego de Alcalá in 1769, twenty more mission communities were created, ending with the establishment of Mission San Francisco de Solano in 1823. Located at what is today Sonoma, California, San Francisco de Solano was built just a few miles south of the Russian settlement at Fort Ross, which itself had been constructed in 1812.

The impulse to begin the settlement of Alta California was born of imperial goals. Increasing Russian and English exploration of Alta California, the belief that a splendid port could be built at Monterey for the Manila galleon, along with Enlightenment ideas about the necessity of bringing manufacturing, agriculture, and trade to New Spain's far north, were the reasons for sending a colonizing party. To provision the copper and silver mining towns and to safeguard this region from rivals, in 1768 the Crown dispatched Fray Junípero Serra and fourteen Franciscans to Alta California even though they had just arrived to replace the exiled Jesuits at the struggling and almost failed missions of Baja California. Serra's party did as it was ordered, handing over the administration of Baja's missions to the Dominicans and marching north.

From the perspective of the Franciscans their goal in Alta California was to bring Christianity to the Indians living on the "rim of Christendom." This sparsely settled terrain was populated mostly by hunters and gatherers living in constantly shifting encampments that were organized around clans, and that ranged in size from fifty to one hundred individuals. The work of the missions progressed very slowly because of the difficulty of congregating such small and widely dispersed groups. By 1773, after only five years in the province, the Franciscans, who now numbered nineteen and were divided over five missions, admitted that they had been able to congregate and baptize only 500 individuals.

Though the civilian military population of sixty had been parceled among the missions and the garrisons or *presidios* at San Diego and Monterey, the friars already had a long litany of complaints against them. These largely young and single men were abusing Indian labor and were sinfully consorting with the native women. Given that Alta California had to be provisioned by sea, there being yet no land route from Sinaloa or Sonora over which food and the colony's basic needs could travel, the planting of fields and the development of herds were of paramount import. Indian labor was necessary for the reproduction of the colony and so the friars and soldiers naturally competed for it. The former claimed that Indian exploitation was slowing conversions and baptisms; the latter countered that they too had to survive if they were to offer protection to the friars against Indian rebellions, which had already occurred at a number of places, most brutally at San Diego in 1775.

In the years that followed the first civilian settlements in Alta California were established. San José was begun with fourteen families in 1777, as was Nuestra Señora la Reina de Los Angeles de Porciúncula, with eleven families in 1781. Three additional grand mission compounds were constructed – San Buenaventura (1782), Santa Barbara (1786), and Purísima Concepción (1787) – but the pace of conversions did not hasten. Rather, the rate of declension only increased.

Of all the mission fields established in Spanish America, those in Alta California are undoubtedly the best studied, most discussed, and probably most handsomely preserved to this day. Since the 1890s the image of the State of California and its public relations around the world has been deeply shaped by the missions as icons and by the work of the work of the heroic Franciscans who built them. Many of the missions stood abandoned and crumbling in 1850. They were subsequently restored, given small museums and curio stores, and made into popular tour destinations such as state parks in the 1940s and 1950s.

The romance of the Spanish bygone days, of the placid missions and their indefatigable personnel, and of a native population that putatively had mysteriously disappeared, certainly had its charm as an Anglo-Protestant morality tale at a time the state of California was becoming the sixth largest economy in the world. The descendants and defenders of the native populations steadily contested such a romanticization of the past, arguing that the missions were concentration camps and unacknowledged sites of genocide. A slew of studies chronicling the massive decline of the indigenous populations caused by their aggregation and the Christian program of acculturation began appearing after World War II, in the wake of global decolonization movements. The beatification of Fray Junípero Serra by Pope John Paul II in 1988 and his elevation to sainthood by Pope Francis in 2015 only added grist to this mill.

But the reality is a good bit more stark. As a result of the atrocities that occurred during World War I, in the years that followed medical science turned its attention to the study of biological responses to physical deprivation. Armed with the conclusions of such work, two professors at the University of California, Berkeley, set out to document what had transpired at the missions of Alta California. Sherburne F. Cook, a professor of physiology, and Woodrow Borah, a historian and demographer, started publishing their conclusions about the native populations that had been aggregated into missions in 1937 and continued to do so for the next forty years.

One of Cook's first and most shocking conclusions was that "From the available date we find that from 1779 to 1833 there were 29,100 births and 62,600 deaths. The excess of deaths over births was then 33,500, indicating an extremely rapid population decline."[8] There were a variety of reasons for this that could mostly be attributed to diseases, confinement, the sexual regime of the missions, and poor diet. The Indians had no resistance to smallpox, measles, and flu epidemics. The soldiers had infected Indian women with

---

8 Sherburne Cook, *The Conflict between the California Indian and White Civilization* (Berkeley: University of California Press, 1976), 16.

syphilis, and in turn the women had infected their husbands and their infants. Aggregation in mission compounds and close confinement in dormitories at night had hastened the spread of disease, which was only compounded by inadequate food supplies and the intensity of the labor regime. The friars closely regulated the sexual activity of their neophytes and sanctioned it only in monogamous marriage, thus quickly leading to a precipitous drop in native birth rates. Those Indians physically able to flee did, at a rate of about 10 to 16 percent per year. Soldiers were usually dispatched to recapture apostates, and once back at the missions were made public examples with the sting of the lash.

From 1769 to roughly 1790 the missionaries of Alta California used invitations, gifts, and sermonic persuasion to gather the Indians on missions. But when this failed, the military was used to stage campaigns to congregate the Indians forcefully at the missions, where their coerced labor was necessary to sustain the colony. Flogging became the principal way of enforcing discipline.

At most of the Christian missions that dotted the Americas, the whip became the uncontested symbol of authority, which neither the mendicant orders nor the Jesuits hesitated to swing to make a point. From the perspective of the padres and the dictates of law, they stood in relationship to their Indian converts as parents stood in relationship to their children; the Indians were wards who had to be corrected for insubordination, for backsliding, even for fleeing the missions as apostates. Corporal punishment in the form of lashes, shackles, and placement in stocks was common. Fray Junípero Serra acknowledged that this was the way he and his brothers dealt with the Indians. Writing Alta California's Governor, don Felipe de Neve on January 7, 1780, he stated:

> That spiritual fathers should punish their sons, the Indians with blows appears to be as old as the conquest of these kingdoms: so general in fact that the saints do not seem to be any exception to the rule ... In the life of Saint Francis Solano ... we read that while he had a special gift from God to soften the ferocity of the most barbarous by the sweetness of his presence and his words, nevertheless, in the running of his mission in the province of Tucumán in Peru ... when they failed to carry out his orders, he gave direction for his Indians to be whipped.[9]

Serra was quite aware that at several missions the friars had been excessive in whipping their wards, considerably surpassing the twenty-five lashes that

---

9 Antonine Tibesar, ed., *Writings of Junipero Serra*, 4 vols. (Washington, DC: Academy of American Franciscan History, 1955–560), 3: 408–418.

were considered the maximum an adult could endure. Writing his superior in 1776, Serra affirmed that he had counseled his brothers to curb the extent and zeal with which this punishment was doled. "I feel confident that where there may have been too much severity, things will be put right," he said. Serra understood that the Franciscans needed military protection because many Indian apostates were intent on retaliating for the floggings they had received.

Cook's conclusions about the decimation of California's Indians, the mission's coerced labor, its regime of sexual abstinence, and its "severe and unwarranted punitive discipline" were quickly amplified by Carey McWilliams, a popular writer, eventual editor of *The Nation*, and a champion of America's minorities. In his 1947 book, *Southern California Country*, McWilliams told "the story of the Missions not in the conventional manner, that is, from the point of view of the Franciscans, but from the point of view of the real parties in interest, namely the Indians." He went on to criticize the Franciscans, writing: "With the best theological intentions in the world, the Franciscan padres eliminated the Indians with the effectiveness of Nazis operating concentration camps." While Sherburne Cook had concluded that the mission diet was "suboptimal," McWilliams intensified the critiques, writing that the neophytes "were kept in a state of chronic undernourishment in order to retard the tendency to fugitivism."[10]

In 1948, just a year after McWilliams's book appeared, a Historical Commission for the Serra Cause, was formed in Fresno, California to propose the canonization of Fray Junípero Serra as a saint in the Roman Catholic Church. Testimony and historical materials were gathered by the Franciscan Order for presentation to the Church's Congregation of Sacred Rites, charged with recommending to the pope whether Serra should be declared a saint, which it finally did in 1988, with the beatification of Father Serra by Pope John Paul II, beatification being the first formal step toward the declaration of his sainthood. The California Indians, who had theoretically disappeared, started to talk back, expressing their revulsion over the pope's act. They had not been consulted, nor had testimony been taken from them about the impact of the missions on their lives. Citing oral histories that had been recorded in the 1870s with individuals who had actually lived on missions, Indian activists such as Rupert Costo, Jeannette Henry Costo, and CheeQweesh Auh-Ho-Oh lampooned the process and Serra himself, as a slave-driving sadist who had brutalized the Indians and systematically practiced genocide on them.

---

10 Carey McWilliams, *Southern California Country: An Island on the Land* (New York: Duell, Sloan & Pearce, 1946), vii.

The Costos edited and published a mission counter-narrative, which belatedly appeared in 1987, entitled *The Missions of California: A Legacy of Genocide*, its title setting the terms of the debate. Thaddeus Shubsda, the bishop of Monterey, replied with his own set of hired historical guns (six academic historians and two museum curators), issuing *The Serra Report* on November 24, 1986, the 273rd anniversary of Junípero Serra's birth. Attesting that Serra had not been sadistic, had not exploited the Indians, the words of historian Doyce Nunis, Jr. cogently summarized the volume's tone and its failure to engage the historical and anthropological evidence about indigenous life, which by then was quite well known: "For the first time it [Roman Catholicism] dignified the individual. Up until that time the Indians had no sense of fidelity to each other, there was no spirit of loyalty. There was no spirit of commitment ... they had no idea of a social compact, in the strongest sense of the word. They had no sense of morality."[11]

In September of 1987, Pope John Paul II visited the United States and met with Indian activists about the Serra case. The pope acknowledged the "mistake and wrongs" that had been perpetrated by the Church on native peoples, but in the next breath praised Serra's missionary work. Unmoved by the protest, on September 25, 1988, the Pope beatified Fray Junípero Serra, moving him within one step of official canonization as a saint, a process that Pope Francis completed in 2015.

Conclusions

The Spanish missions of North and South America were state-sponsored institutions that were charged with settling the frontiers of the empire with religious personnel at minimal cost. The pious men who ventured to New Mexico, to Paraguay, and to Texas and California did so with the best intentions of bringing both the physical and the psychological benefits of Christianity to individuals that they deemed lazy and ignorant as children, living promiscuously in polygamous marriages, some practicing cannibalism, clearly ensnared by Satan and destined to eternal damnation. Christianity functioned best in urban contexts where one could gather larger numbers for the administration of rituals and rites of passage by a small number of personnel. Those indigenous sedentary, semisedentary, and nomadic people who accepted Christianity did so because of force or its threat, or presuming it a palliative to more brutal forms of exploitation at the hands of colonists. The

---

[11] James A. Sandos, "Junípero Serra's Canonization and the Historical Record," *American Historical Review*, Vol. 93 (December 1988), 1253–1269, at 1265.

missions taught those neophytes gathered in them how to construct churches, schools, dormitories, infirmaries, and craft shops, as well as the basics of agricultural production and animal husbandry. These radically transformed their material lives and social organization native groups, particularly along gendered lines in relationship to marriage, landholding, and the nature of work.

Converting the Indians to a new religion was less successful for a number of reasons. Death due to disease, to overwork, and to attack by enemies intensified because of concentration into villages. Many of the men of the cloth who labored converting Indians were forced to "baptize the devil," superimposing Christian symbols and practices atop indigenous ones, thereby creating a thoroughly syncretic religious culture, much as the biological mixing of Spaniards and Indians created mestizo societies. The Spanish Crown always envisioned the missions as temporary institutions that would intensively transform the Indians into Christians, Hispanicize them, and prepare their incorporation into Spanish colonial society. But nowhere did the missions last the decade they were given for their work and instead clung paternalistically to the neophytes for labor, as pawns in political rivalries, and as ways to aggrandize the power of the Church. During the years of the independence movement in Spanish America from 1807 to 1821, most of the missions were secularized and placed under the control of the secular clergy. Only the Indian towns that had deep pre-Columbian origins and had not been decimated by disease and exploitation managed to survive intact. The rest of the mission Indians were dispersed, left landless, and ultimately incorporated into Hispanic society through peonage relationships.

Bibliography and Suggested Readings

Arturo Zavala, Silvio. *La encomienda Indiana*. México: Editorial Porrúa, 1992.

Bannon, John Francis. *The Spanish Borderlands Frontier 1513–1821*. Albuquerque: University of New Mexico Press, 1974.

Cook, Sherburne. *The Conflict between the California Indian and White Civilization*. Berkeley: University of California Press, 1976.

Costo, Rupert, and Jeannette Henry Costo, eds. *The Missions of California: A Legacy of Genocide*. San Francisco: The Indian Historian Press, 1987.

de las Casas, Bartolomé. *A Short Account of the Destruction of the Indies*. New York: Penguin Books, 1992.

Ferández Méndez, Eugenio. *Las encomiendas y esclavitud de los indios de Puero Rico, 1508–1550*. Río Piedras: Editorial Universitaria de la Universidad de Puerto Rico, 1976.

Ganson, Barbara. *The Guaraní under Spanish Rule in the Río de la Plata*. Stanford, CA: Stanford University Press, 2003.

Gerhard, Peter. *The Northern Frontier of New Spain*. Princeton, NJ: Princeton University Press, 1982.

Guest, Francis F. "Junípero Serra and His Approach to the Indians," *Southern California Quarterly*, 67 (Fall 1985): 223–261.

Gutiérrez, Ramón A. *When Jesus Came, the Corn Mothers Went Away: Marriage, Sexuality and Power in New Mexico, 1500–1846*. Stanford, CA: Stanford University Press, 1991.

Hackett, Charles W. *Revolt of the Pueblo Indians of New Mexico and Otermín's Attempted Reconquest, 1680–1682*. Albuquerque: University of New Mexico Press, 1942.

Hammond, George P., and Agapito Rey. *Don Juan de Oñate: Colonizer of New Mexico, 1595–1628*. Albuquerque: University of New Mexico Press, 1953.

Hanke, Lewis. *History of Latin American Civilization*. Boston: Little, Brown and Company, 1967.

Hodge, Fredrick W., George P. Hammond, and Agapito Rey. *Fray Alonso de Benavides' Revised Memorial of 1634*. Albuquerque: University of New Mexico Press, 1945.

Lockhart, James, and Stuart B. Schwartz. *Early Latin America: A History of Colonial Spanish America and Brazil*. Cambridge: Cambridge University Press, 1983.

McWilliams, Carey. *Southern California Country: An Island on the Land*. New York: Duell, Sloan & Pearce, 1946.

Reiter, Frederick J. *They Built Utopia: The Jesuit Missions in Paraguay, 1610–1768*. Potomac, MD: Scripta Humanistica, 1995.

Reyes, Bárbara O. *Private Women, Public Lives: Gender and the Missions of the Californias*. Austin: University of Texas Press, 2009.

Ricard, Robert. *The Spiritual Conquest of Mexico: An Essay on the Apostolate and the Evangelizing Methods of the Mendicant Orders in New Spain, 1523–1572*. Berkeley: University of California Press, 1966.

Sanchez, Rosaura. *Telling Identities: The Californio Testimonios*. Minneapolis: University of Minnesota Press, 1995.

Sandos, James A. "Junípero Serra's Canonization and the Historical Record," *American Historical Review*, 93 (December 1988): 1253–1269.

Service, Elman R. *Spanish-Guaraní Relations in Early Colonial Paraguay*. Westport, CT: Greenwood Press, 1971.

Steward, Julian H. *Handbook of South American Indians*. Washington, DC: US Government Printing Office, 1946–1959.

Trexler, Richard. "We Think, They Act: Clerical Readings of Missionary Theatre in 16th Century New Spain." In Steven Kaplan (ed.), *Understanding Popular Culture*, 189–228. Ithaca, NY: Cornell University Press, 1984.

Weber, David J. *Bárbaros: Spaniards and their Savages in the Age of Enlightenment*. New Haven, CT: Yale University Press, 2005.

Weckmann, Luis. *The Medieval Heritage of Mexico*. Trans. Frances M. López-Morillas. New York: Fordham University Press, 1992.

13

The Church, Africans, and Slave Religion in Latin America

JOAN BRISTOL

African and African-American slaves had a variety of interactions and relationships with the Catholic Church in Latin America between 1500, when enslaved Africans first arrived in the Americas, and 1888, when slavery was abolished in Brazil, the last slaveholding region in the Americas. The relationship between slavery and the Church was especially strong in Spanish and Portuguese America, where the institutional Catholic Church as well as religious orders played an important role in establishing colonial rule and where the Catholic Church was closely tied to state power. As in other areas of the Americas, the Church played a role in slave religion as well.

The Catholic Church influenced slavery and slave religion in different ways depending on location, time period, the particular colonial power in question, and the kind of access to Church resources that enslaved people had. Individual preferences and motivations on the part of representatives of the Church and enslaved people may have played the most important role in determining the shape of slave religion in particular regions. This chapter addresses Spanish and Portuguese America, but includes relevant examples from the French Caribbean as well. Although this chapter focuses on enslaved people it is important to remember that not all Afro-Latin Americans were enslaved in the colonial period and that the religious experiences of enslaved and free people of all ethnic and social groups frequently overlapped.

Catholicism and the Theory of Slavery

Religion shaped Atlantic slavery in important ways from the very beginning of the trade. The spread of Christianity was a central motivation, at least theoretically, for European exploration into the Atlantic. When Portuguese-sponsored mariners began sailing down the west coast of Africa in the fifteenth century papal bulls gave them the right to trade with Africans in exchange for evangelizing them. Pope Alexander VI arranged the 1494 Treaty of Tordesillas, giving Spain jurisdiction over territories to be discovered west of the Cape Verde Islands and Portugal jurisdiction over the lands to the east, precisely because the Iberian monarchs agreed to convert any inhabitants they encountered. Portuguese merchants were more interested in commerce than in spreading Christianity, however, and soon added enslaved people to the list of commodities they traded for in forts along the African coast. Although Catholic missionaries attempted to evangelize and baptize enslaved people in trading forts, their efforts were often thwarted by the desires of slave traders to move people through the sale process quickly. Missionaries had more luck evangelizing among African nobles, particularly in the Kingdom of Kongo, where the king adopted Catholicism as the state religion in the 1490s. Thus, enslaved people from certain parts of Africa already practiced some form of Christianity before they became involved in the trade, while enslaved Africans whose first contact with Catholicism was through hasty baptism ceremonies in slave trading forts were usually Christian in name only.

However, although Portuguese slave traders often ignored their supposed evangelizing missions, Portuguese and Spanish clerics and jurists considered the very question of labor to be a religious issue in both Africa and the Americas. Shortly after Columbus's arrival in the Caribbean, Spanish settlers began to mine gold using forced indigenous labor. Spanish friars, including the famous Dominican Bartolomé de Las Casas, who became known as the "Protector of the Indians" for his vociferous defense of the indigenous, sent letters to the king and preached sermons protesting against native enslavement.

These clerics argued that indigenous Americans were innocents who should be treated gently and taught about Christianity. In the early sixteenth century, the Spanish and Portuguese Crowns responded to these clerical protests by declaring that the indigenous inhabitants of the Americas were free and could be enslaved only in a just war. "Just war doctrine" held that Christians could enslave non-Christians only if they refused to accept Catholicism, and it was used as a way to legitimize slavery in Africa as well as the Americas. In 1537, Pope Paul III sent a brief to the Archbishop of Toledo declaring that anyone who enslaved indigenous workers would be excommunicated, and a papal bull issued the same year proclaimed an end to slavery and retroactively canceled all contracts for trading slaves, although this was not widely applied and certainly was not applied to enslaved Africans.

The Spanish and Portuguese Crowns issued frequent proclamations during the sixteenth century prohibiting indigenous slavery except in cases of just war when indigenous people were actively resisting European advances.

Despite these royal interventions, Native Americans were bound up in a variety of unfree labor arrangements throughout the colonial period, some of which the Spaniards directly justified through religious ideology. Under the *encomienda* system, for example, the Crown entrusted individual Spaniards with the spiritual education of natives in specific villages, in return for which they received tribute and labor from their subjects. Although in most cases the *encomienda* system was nothing more than forced labor, the practice was justified through the idea that Spanish *encomenderos* were evangelizing their charges. Thus we see how intimately forced labor and religion were bound up in colonial Latin America.

In the early sixteenth century, as the indigenous populations of the Caribbean and mainland declined and in some cases disappeared in the wake of devastating epidemics of European diseases, Spanish and Portuguese settlers began importing enslaved West and West-Central Africans to work in their American colonies. The theologians who protested against indigenous slavery did not complain about African slavery. Bartolomé de Las Casas even suggested that Spanish and African slaves be substituted for indigenous workers in the commercial enterprises of the New World, although toward the end of his life he condemned African slavery. Few Europeans challenged the justice of enslaving Africans in any sustained way, however, and most Spanish and Portuguese ecclesiastics accepted the logic that supported the enslavement of Africans.

Yet some criticized the legality of the methods of enslavement. Some clerics argued that, because it was impossible to ascertain if enslaved people had been acquired legally, the entire trade was illegal. Others argued that enslaved Africans did not fit the Aristotelian criteria of natural slaves, uncivilized sinners who were meant to serve others, as they had cultures and social structures. Ecclesiastical scholars also argued that forced conversion of enslaved people was illegal, as one had to accept Christianity willingly for conversion to be legitimate. These writers and a handful of others deplored the terrible ways that enslaved people were treated during the trade, and they acknowledged that unjust slavery occurred frequently. Yet most stopped short of questioning the idea that Africans could be enslaved. Even Alonso de Sandoval, a seventeenth-century Jesuit who ministered to newly arrived slaves at the South American port of Cartagena and advocated on their behalf for better treatment, accepted that Africans were meant to be enslaved. Sandoval did criticize the way that traders and owners treated slaves and was particularly worried about the ways that this mistreatment could impede slaves' opportunities to practice Christianity.

Although individual clergy and the Spanish Crown wanted Africans and their descendants to be Christians, there was no doubt in their minds that they were also meant to be slaves. Although religious concerns precluded indigenous slavery, they justified African slavery. If these clerical protests against slavery were rare, it is almost impossible to find examples of enslaved people commenting explicitly on the Church's stance on slavery in this formative early colonial period. On the other hand, one may interpret implicit or explicit resistance to Christianity and slavery in the religion that slaves practiced, as we shall discuss in the text that follows.

Slave Christianity or Church-Sanctioned Religious Practice

To understand Afro-Latin American religious practices, Catholic and non-Catholic, it is important to first look at how enslaved Africans became Christian. The Crown and Church defined enslaved Africans as Christians. In fact, Iberian powers, anxious to keep their dominions free of Judaism, Islam, and later in the sixteenth century Protestantism, required that all immigrants to their colonies, whether free or unfree, be Catholic. Yet evangelization and education efforts aimed at Africans and Afro-Creoles (New World–born people) were sporadic and their effects uneven. Enslaved Africans (those not born into Christianity) became Christians in three general ways. First, as mentioned previously, some enslaved Africans were Christians or at least had come into contact with Catholic missionaries in Africa prior to their enslavement. This was particularly true for West-Central Africans, where the Kingdom of Kongo adopted Christianity in the sixteenth century and Christian missionaries made inroads in neighboring regions. French Capuchins and others also worked on the Gold Coast and elsewhere in West Africa beginning in the seventeenth century as well.

A second group of Africans converted to Christianity after they were enslaved. By the mid-sixteenth century, Portuguese missionaries were baptizing slaves in trading posts in Africa. Such conversions, however, did not produce Catholics who were well versed in doctrine and practice; sixteenth-, seventeenth-, and eighteenth-century Spanish American clergy complained that African slaves arrived in the New World unbaptized and ignorant about matters of faith. A third group of enslaved Africans became educated in Catholicism after arriving in the Americas. In some cases owners undertook the religious education of their slaves. Jesuits, Dominicans, and members of other religious orders also ministered to slaves in Spanish and Portuguese

America. In addition, Africans and Afro-Latin Americans learned about Christian practice by attending church services and the public religious events (such as festivals, religious plays, processions, and inquisitorial *autos-de-fé*) that were common to everyday life in Latin America.

Enslaved Africans and their descendants practiced orthodox Christianity in much the same ways that other people did in colonial Latin America. They attended church with their masters and on their own, owned religious objects, and observed the sacraments. Although non-Europeans were not allowed to become priests, free people of African descent and indigenous men took minor orders, were tonsured, became lay brothers, and occasionally professed as friars. Enslaved women worked in convents as servants to the nuns. Some seem to have followed the customs of the nuns they lived with, including the seventeenth-century black slave Ursula de Jesus who became a *donada*, or lay sister, in Lima and wrote about her experiences. In an unusual example from seventeenth-century Puebla, Discalced Carmelite nuns and male clerics even urged an enslaved West African woman named Juana Esperanza de San Alberto to take orders as a nun because of her reputation for extreme piety. She did this only on her deathbed, however. Yet the fact that Juana Esperanza was held up as a model of religious virtue for other women of her time reminds us that Catholic practice was a significant part of Afro-Latin American slave religion.

A more common way that enslaved Afro-Latin Americans participated in Catholic life was through membership in confraternities, lay organizations usually based in parish churches and organized around devotion to particular saints. Confraternities served all members of the population in Latin America and they functioned as mutual aid societies, supporting members when they were ill or otherwise in need and paying for members' funerals. Africans and their descendants belonged to mixed confraternities and also formed their own groups restricted to those of African descent. In some cases, members of slave confraternities bought the freedom of enslaved members in addition to their more standard mutual aid functions.

These organizations also gave enslaved and free Afro-Latin Americans opportunities to attain some social status by serving as officers. In many areas these groups encouraged the maintenance or formation of identities based on African origin – in Mexico, Peru, Argentina, and Brazil confraternities formed around people from specific African ethnic groups. In other cases, confraternities were developed around racial identities – creole blacks and mulattos formed their own confraternities in Spanish and Portuguese America, for example. In some cases elites and government officials suspected confraternities of being the site of subversion – in Mexico City, for example, rumors circulated that black confraternities were conspiring to overthrow Spanish rule and put their own rulers in power. Officials responded by executing the heads of prominent black confraternities in 1612. In general, however, enslaved Afro-Latin Americans practiced Catholicism in much the same way as non-slaves.

Slave Religion Outside of the Catholic Church

In addition to Catholic practice, enslaved Afro-Latin Americans developed their own rituals, often derived from African practiced and directed toward dealing with the hardships and disruptions inherent in slave life. It is important to note that slaves often practiced these non-Catholic practices alongside Catholicism. Although authorities were very interested in ensuring that colonial residents practiced Catholicism in an orthodox form, slaves and others do not seem to have drawn such a distinct line among different religious practices.

One large set of slave practices involved healing, which outside observers also labeled "magic" or "witchcraft." Healing practices varied across time, space, and individual practitioner and situation. In this context, the term "healing" should be understood broadly – Afro-Latin Americans used these practices for both physical healing, such as curing illnesses, as well as psychic healing. For example, "love magic" was designed to make people fall in love or to control wayward romantic partners. Enslaved people also used these rituals on their owners, hoping to make masters treat them better. Mexican slaves bought powders from Native American sellers and put them in their owners' chocolate and clothing.

Enslaved peoples' religious technologies were African based and also drew on indigenous and European healing traditions. For example, slaves in Mexico developed healing rites involving peyote (an indigenous American plant long used by natives of Mexico) as well as amulets containing objects including written prayers, hair, feathers, and seeds. These amulets may have had connections to West and West-Central African customs of wearing pouches containing herbs, beads, and shells to protect wearers from evil and to prevent specific illnesses. Muslims in Senegal wore *grigri* (talismans) containing Koranic verses. Kongo ritual specialists in West-Central Africa sold protective charms or amulets (*minkisi*) that protected wearers from the ill will and witchcraft of people or spirits. Enslaved Africans did not just use these practices in their own lives – in many cases from Latin America enslaved people acted as practitioners and religious specialists, dispensing medicines and enacting the rituals surrounding them. Europeans often consulted these Afro-Latin American practitioners in time of need. Thus enslaved Africans were able to attain a measure of status and make some money through knowledge of healing rituals and they contributed important elements to Latin American cultural and religious traditions.

In Brazil and the Caribbean slaves' ritual practices grew into recognizable African-based religions, including Santería or Lucumí in Cuba, Candomblé in Brazil (especially associated with Salvador de Bahia), and Vodou in Haiti. These African-based religious practices have strong connections to West Africa, most explicitly the Yorùbá and Fon areas (present-day Nigeria and Benin), as well as West-Central Africa (particularly the Congo-Angola region). Enslaved people from these regions arrived in large numbers in Brazil and the Caribbean in the eighteenth and nineteenth centuries and these African-based religions developed in this period. *Orishas*, deities or manifestations of a creator god, were central to Yorùbá ritual practice. Fon people referred to similar deities as *loa*. Enslaved West Africans brought these deities to the Americas and they became central to the religious practices that slaves developed in Brazil and the Caribbean.

These West and West-Central African practices were not transplanted to the Americas wholesale, however. First, enslaved Africans from different areas contributed practices to these African-American religions, so that Kongo as well as Fon and Yorùbá elements are strong in Haitian Vodou and Brazilian Candomblé. Second, slaves combined elements of Catholic practices with African practices. In Brazil, slaves did this within the Catholic religious organizations that clerics and colonial authorities encouraged, notably the confraternities mentioned previously.

In Cuba, slaves venerated their deities in *cabildos*, mutual aid societies based around specific African ethnic identities. In these organizations members began to identify African deities with particular Catholic saints. In Brazil, for example, the *orisha Shango* became identified with the Catholic Saint Barbara. Both were associated with thunder and lightning in their own traditions. Different ideas exist about how this identification functioned; some scholars argue that the saint was just a figurehead and that the real object of veneration was the *orisha*, while others argue that the saint and *orisha* became fused in the minds of slaves. The relationships between *orishas* and saints changed over time as well.

These African-based practices survive in Brazil and the Caribbean among large sectors of the population. The form of their practice has continued since the time of slavery, although practitioners are now more open than they were under slavery, when African-based activities had to be concealed from European authorities. Deities and adherents relate to each other in these African-based religions through possession. Devotees of particular deities gather together and initiates become possessed by the deity. While the initiates are in this state devotees can approach them as if they are the deity and be healed or communicate in other ways. African elements such as Yorùbá chants and drums are also part of the ceremonies.

Control is a very important theme in the discussion of slave religion and the relationship between the Catholic Church and slavery. Colonial authorities were constantly worried about slave rebellions, particularly in areas such as the Caribbean where the enslaved population vastly outnumbered the European and European-descent population. Although authorities may have hoped that religious organizations would play a pacifying role in slaves' lives by integrating them into European culture, they also worried that slave religious practices could incite rebellion.

The healing practices and African-based religions discussed earlier were illegal under colonial rule and authorities worried that even the orthodox practice of Christianity could be subversive. We see this in the 1612 example in which Spanish authorities in Mexico were worried that black confraternities could be the sites of rebellion. Religious affiliation and organizations did in fact allow enslaved people to form communities and at times conspire against authorities. For example, in 1835 Muslim Hausa and Yorùbá slaves from West Africa led a revolt in Salvador de Bahia. The revolutionary potential of slave religion was most fully realized in the French colony of Saint-Domingue, now Haiti, where in 1791 a revolt led by a slave named Boukman began with a Vodou ceremony and, after a long and bloody war, ended with Haitian independence.

Conclusion

The Catholic Church, the institution of slavery, and African and Creole slaves had multiple and intersecting relationships over the 400 years of Latin American slavery. Church leaders supported slavery and theologians provided a religious justification for the institution. At the same time, the Church hierarchy and individual clerics supported slave confraternities, within which Afro-Latin Americans created communities and even maintained important aspects of African religious and other cultural traditions. Enslaved Latin Americans practiced Catholicism in orthodox ways, while at the same time developing and maintaining other religious traditions that authorities prohibited. Religious practice brought enslaved Afro-Latin Americans into contact with many other groups, including members of other African ethnic groups (both slave and free), Native Americans, and Europeans, and members of these different groups shared ritual knowledge to develop new religious forms. Religion was both an important means though which enslaved Afro-Latin Americans survived slavery as well as a significant contribution to the religious tapestry of Latin American societies.

Bibliography and Suggested Readings

Andrews, George Reid. *Afro-Argentines of Buenos Aires, 1800–1900*. Madison: University of Wisconsin Press, 1980.
Bristol, Joan Cameron. *Christians, Blasphemers, and Witches: Afro-Mexican Ritual Practice in the Seventeenth Century*. Albuquerque: University of New Mexico Press, 2007.
de Jesús, Ursula. *The Souls of Purgatory: The Spiritual Diary of a Seventeenth-Century Afro-Peruvian Mystic, Ursula de Jesús*, edited by Nancy E. van Deusen. Albuquerque: University of New Mexico Press, 2004.
Miller, Joseph C. *Way of Death: Merchant Capitalism and the Angolan Slave Trade 1730–1830*. Madison: University of Wisconsin Press, 1988.
Reis, Joaõ Jose. *Slave Rebellion in Brazil: The Muslim Uprising of 1835 in Bahia*. Baltimore: Johns Hopkins University Press, 1985.
Russell-Wood, A. J. R. *The Black Man in Slavery and Freedom in Colonial Brazil*. New York: Macmillan, 1982.
Sandoval, Alonso de. *Un tratado sobre la esclavitud*. Transc. Enriqueta Vila Vilar. Madrid: Alianza Editorial, 1987.
Thornton, John K. *Africa and Africans in the Making of the Atlantic World, 1400–1800*. New York: Cambridge University Press, 1998.
    "Religious and Ceremonial Life in the Kongo and Mbundu Areas." In Linda M. Heywood (ed.), *Central Africans and Cultural Transformations in the American Diaspora*. Cambridge: Cambridge University Press, 2002.
von Germeten, Nicole. *Black Blood Brothers: Confraternities and Social Mobility for Afro-Mexicans*. Gainesville: University of Florida Press, 2006.

14
Messianic and Revitalization Movements

MIGUEL C. LEATHAM

Latin American peoples have a rich history of religious revitalization movements beginning with the early colonial period and continuing to the present day. Movements of change in the region are rooted in the central roles that religion plays throughout Latin American indigenous and national cultures, especially that of social and political critique, and as a primary means of seeking material help under adverse conditions. Examples of Latin American revitalization movements of the millenarian (eschatological-transformational) type, including those often labeled as messianic, have been abundant. They are the focus of this chapter. Wright offers the following characterization of millenarianism ("world-transforming movements"):

> In terms of ideology, world-transforming movements predict total and imminent change while placing themselves within an interpretation of history that affirms the necessity and inevitability of that change. The source of current social ills is typically located in some intractable human dilemma that has persisted throughout history and culminated in the present world. World-transforming movements believe that the unprecedented opportunity for resolution of the problem must be seized because sudden and cataclysmic change is virtually around the corner. The ideology also identifies and outlines the unique historical role of the movement in facilitating this transformation.[1]

For this discussion, messianism is considered a subtype of millenarianism, referring to the belief in a prophetic deliverer, usually associated with an end-time eschatology.

---

[1] Stuart Wright, *Leaving Cults: The Dynamics of Defection* (Monograph Series No. 7, Washington, DC: Society for the Scientific Study of Religion, 1987), 12.

Brazilian Millenarianism

Millenarian movements and ideas have had a greater impact on regional and national life in Brazil than in any other Latin American country. Pessar observes that Brazilian millenarianism is an "ongoing social production," a "traveling cultural formation" that has continually spawned revitalization movements since the early colonial era. Indigenous and mixed-heritage peoples of the rural sector have generated numerous movements, yet millenarianism is hardly documented for the Afro-Brazilian population. The difference may be due to an absence of millenarian sources in the African religious traditions that background the Creole Candomblé, whereas both indigenous and *mestiço* religious traditions contain extensive millenarian thought derived from both indigenous and Portuguese sources.

Indigenous Movements

The *terra-sem-mal* (land without evil) movements among sixteenth-century Amazonian and Paraguayan indigenous societies possessed elements that resemble millenarian premises. They drew substantial attention from Portuguese authorities during the sixteenth century. The prophets of land-without-evil movements were visionary, charismatic chiefs or shaman-prophets who typically exhorted their followers to set off in search of the resting place of ancestors and culture heroes. The migrants would find eternal rest and immortality in a distant land, often imagined in myth as lying across the sea. The visions followed a common Native American mythological pattern in which cyclical cataclysms are followed by the restoration of social order and human populations by a remnant few. There are cases of some coastal Tupí-Guaraní whose migration appears to have been motivated only by prophetic pronouncements of impending cyclical destructions, rather than by subsistence or conflict-related motives. Thus, some scholars are of the opinion that land-without-evil movements likely preexisted Portuguese contact and should not be interpreted simply as representing attempts to escape colonial control.

Jesuit priests documented land-without-evil movements with definite millenarian characteristics. Coastal indigenous prophets proclaimed in their villages that they were reincarnations of mythical heroes and exhorted villagers to give up all work, to dance, and to expect gardening implements and hunting arrows to work magically by themselves. All subsistence would be provided miraculously. Prophecies emanating from gourds promised immortality and the reversal of aging in an ideal era.

The numerous syncretic *santidade* movements – which emphasized Christian perfectionism – of the late sixteenth century occurring among indigenous societies impacted by missions were decidedly messianic in character. They combined mythological and mass migration themes found in the land-without-evil movements with selected features derived from contact with Catholicism. In the Reconçavo movement of Bahia in the 1590s, a Jesuit-educated Indian – known as António by the Inquisition and as "Great God" by his followers – blended Catholic and indigenous religious elements in his prophecies and rituals. Followers held that dancing before a sacred figurine would free Indians from slavery under the whites, while white settlers who did not set Indian slaves free would change into trees and rocks. The movement enjoyed strong appeal among escaped indigenous slaves from the *sertão* plantations. The governor of Bahia wiped out the Reconçavo with military force. Messianic indigenous movements tended to shift toward the Guaraní and Chiriguano areas of Paraguay after 1600, with uprisings accompanying some of them. Generally, santidade movements constituted pan-tribal efforts to resist Indian resettlement for missionization (reduction) and forced acculturation. In important ways, they resemble later nativistic indigenous movements in the upper Amazon, as well as in other Latin American regions and the United States.

Societies in the northwest Amazon region have generated millenarian movements, such as that of the messiah Venancio Christu of the 1850s. Such movements constituted efforts to combat the effects of colonization by using selected indigenous myth and ritual having overlaps with Catholicism. Brown argues that millenarian movements in the upper Amazon that involved acculturation and changes in hierarchical organization also point to an internal cultural critique.[2] Movement participants hoped that the selective adoption of Euro-Brazilian cultural features would allow them access to mystical power believed to be more efficacious for achieving prosperity than that accessible through indigenous ritual means, as occurred in the Melanesian cargo cults.

Another scholar documents a messianic prophet, believed to be a reincarnation of Christ prophesying imminent destruction by flood, among the Cocama in the Peruvian Amazon during the years 1969–1972. Scholars view the associated movement as a response to Brazilian oil exploration, massive abandonment of cultivation among the Cocama in favor of salaried labor in

---

[2] Michael F. Brown, "Beyond Resistance: A Comparative Study of Utopian Renewal in Amazonia." *Ethnohistory*, 38, no. 4 (Fall, 1999): 388–413.

the oil fields, economic exploitation, and the progressive loss of ethnic identity due to sustained contact with mestizos and urbanization.

Portuguese Millenarianist Influences in Brazil

The millenarian movements of Brazilian peasants since the early colonial period have drawn on a variety of eschatological sources dating to sixteenth-century Portugal, backgrounded by folk-Catholic traditions. Among these sources, the most significant are the mythological current known as *Sebastianismo*, or *Quinto Império* (Fifth Empire), and the preaching of Father António Vieira, a renowned seventeenth-century Jesuit orator and missionary.

Millenarian conceptualizations of Portugal's national destiny were forged during the sixteenth century as a response to Spanish expansionism, crypto-Jewish interest in messianic scriptural interpretations stemming from persecution by the Inquisition, and the threat of the decline of the young Portuguese empire. Central to this millenarian ideology were traditions about a messianic figure, King Sebastião, who would bring greatness and wealth to Portugal in a new era. Sebastianist myth was introduced into Brazil via the influence of Portuguese Jesuits during the colonial period and became more deeply entrenched in the rural interior of the northeast, or *sertão* region, than on the coast.

The suppression of the Jesuits and other religious orders in the missions of the rural northeast during the latter half of the 1700s intensified a laicization process that transferred Catholic leadership increasingly to brotherhoods (*irmandades*) and third-order folk-Catholic lay groups that later provided models for building religious movement organization. In addition, the lay thaumaturgical (miracle-working) folk saint, or *beato*, and the ascetic itinerant preacher (*ermitão*) types, aspects of which in many cases have characterized the same individual, frequently have filled the role of the millenarian prophet in the northeast. The folk saint represents an outgrowth of the cult of the saints, wherein the folk saint acts as a powerful patron for the needy. Folk Catholic–based millenarian movements sprang into existence continually during the nineteenth century as peasant forms of protest and self-defense.

Northeast Peasant Millenarianism

Large-scale millenarian movements under the direction of messianic figures occurred among the Brazilian peasantry from about 1815 until the 1940s. The most noteworthy among these are O Paraíso Terrestre (1817), O Reino Encantado (whose prophet ordered human sacrifices for the return of King

Sebastião in 1836), Império do Belo Monte (1873–1897), Joaseiro do Norte (1889–1934), and the Contestado Rebellion of 1912–1916. Generally, Sebastianist expectations were key to the belief structures of these movements. Some early nineteenth-century movements focused on the restoration of Portuguese rule and Sebastianist longings for wealth, but the movements of the turn of the century clearly emerged as responses to rapid changes in the political economy of Brazil and in the policies of the Catholic Church at the end of the nineteenth and beginning of the twentieth centuries.

The movements of Império do Belo Monte (sometimes called "Canudos") and Joaseiro in the northeast centered on two folk-saint prophets, António Mendes Maciel – known as "Conselheiro," the Counselor – and Father Cícero Romão Batista. Conselheiro was an ascetic, itinerant preacher who proclaimed the evils of the new Brazilian Republic because of its ungodly separation of church and state and capitalistic economic shifts, involving increasing abandonment of traditional patron–client ties between peasants and landholders. A series of devastating droughts (to which the northeast has always been prone) struck the impoverished region, causing mass migrations and horrific loss of life, exacerbating the effects of the political-economic transformations on the region's peasantry. Aided by his twelve apostles, Conselheiro preached that the loss of the monarchical state of Emperor Dom Pedro II was to blame for the misfortunes of the peasantry and that Judgment Day and Christ's Second Coming would occur before the year 1900. At least four military attacks on the movement claimed thousands of lives, culminating in the lengthy siege of 1897 that resulted in the death of the prophet and the razing of the colony. Peasant traditions in the area maintained afterward that the Counselor would return with King Sebastião to rule Brazil.

The holy city of Joaseiro do Norte was the largest religious movement colony ever formed in the Americas. Father Cícero Romão Batista developed the colony around an existing hamlet of the same name in the northeastern state of Pará. During Lent of 1883, a Eucharistic miracle occurred in which, while Father Cícero distributed communion, blood issued from the host on the tongue of a young laundress, Maria de Araújo. Father Cícero interpreted this sign as meaning that Christ had shed his blood anew for the salvation of the world at the hamlet and that the Last Judgment was at hand. Therefore, Joaseiro was marked to become a "new Jerusalem." News of the miracle, combined with the priest's reputation as a holy man and *thaumaturge* (miracle maker), sparked mass pilgrimages and the building of a chapel. In a short time, a city sprang up around Father Cícero, now known as holy patriarch and patron. Joaseiro, today one of the largest cities in the Northeast, grew from 2,000 to more than 15,000 between the time of the miracle and 1900.

Millenarian communities continue today to generate interest in Brazilian society and spring up in various regions of the country. Examples are the Valley of the Dawn, near Brasília and the Santa Brígida movement of Bahia state. This was founded in the 1930s by the folk-saint *thaumaturge*, Pedro Velho.

Interpreting Brazilian Peasant Millenarianism

The great movements of late nineteenth-century Brazil provided comfort to rural masses by providing work, security, and structure to peasants in a time of rapid political and economic transitions, rampant rural violence, and drought. Queiroz argues that Brazilian peasant messianisms attempted to defend and restore a kin-based model of economic relationships threatened by the introduction of capitalist contractual relationships in the Republican era. She observes that the movements represent the "insertion of the messianic group into the existing political structure," and thus did not tend to be revolutionary ideologically. Hierarchy and social class were to be preserved, while a messianic figure would make people return to customs that the peasantry traditionally valued under the monarchy. Millenarian prophets acted as "substitute patrons" who condemned the new arrangements and who could redistribute the necessities of life to the poor when landowners would no longer do so. In addition, prophets reacted to the Catholic hierarchy's attempts to Romanize Brazilian Catholic teaching and practice through the introduction of foreign clergy. The changes led to attacks on churches in northeastern cities during the 1870s, inspired by the popular conviction that "evildoers" were taking over the Church.[3]

Andean Religious Movements

The Indigenous Cosmological Background

Andean millenarianism blends elements of ancient indigenous cosmology and apocalyptic thinking promulgated by the colonial Spanish clergy. Indigenous Andean cosmology provides an enabling symbolic framework for millenarian activity, especially messianism. Kechwa (Inca) cosmology before and since Spanish colonization has represented time in terms of successive eras

---

3 Maria Isaura Pereira de Queiroz, *O Mesianismo: No Brasil e no mundo* (São Paulo: Editora Alfa-Omega, 1977).

or worlds. Each era emerges from a *pachakuti*, translated as "world reversal," or, more literally, "transformation of the earth." Cataclysmic upheavals of this sort are believed to involve symmetrical inversions of social and political order, as well as the departure and return of creator or founding gods. The Spanish invasion and the fall of the Inca Empire, viewed by the Kechwa as a *pachakuti*, enhanced the symbolic importance of the concept in indigenous consciousness.

Spanish Millenarianist Influences

Much of Spanish millenarianist thought in the Americas traces back to the early Franciscan missionaries of colonial Mexico and Peru, many of whom followed the prophecies and the commentary on the Apocalypse by the twelfth-century mystic Joachim de Fiore. Inspired by Fiorite prophecy, friars envisioned building a Catholic utopia of monastic clergy and Indians, removed from the corrupting influences of Spanish secular society. Native Andean conceptions of *pachakuti* were reinterpreted to varying degrees in light of missionaries' millenarianist preaching, providing a symbolic framework underpinning millenarian movements from the late sixteenth century onward.

Indigenous Andean Millenarian Movements

The earliest well-documented Andean religious movement, a nativistic expression among the Peruvian Kechwa in the 1560s, is that of Taki Onqoy (Sickness of the Dance). Various prophets predicted a coming destruction by deluge, a common mythical theme in the ancient Andes, in a *pachakuti*, after which all native Andean *wakas* – earth shrines and sacred beings – would have their turn at re-creating the world by triumphing over the Christian God and expelling the Spanish overlords. Followers consumed large amounts of corn beer (*chicha*) and coca leaves, danced, and chanted. The movement rejected forms of forced acculturation, such as Spanish-imposed dress; practiced purification rites including fasting and sexual abstinence; and refused to enter Catholic churches. Kechwa persons who received Catholic baptism and did not make offerings to the ancestral *wakas* would be changed into upside-down llamas. Taki Onqoy was violently suppressed by the Spanish.

Indigenous Andean peoples interpreted the conquest as a cosmic inversion whereby Christ had subjugated the indigenous deities and *wakas* until the time when a new *pachakuti* would occur. In the case of Taki Onqoy, popular tradition held that the year 1565 marked the one-thousandth anniversary of the founding of the Inca empire and that each creative era would last a thousand years. A world reversal sought by the Taki Onqoy followers promised to restore Incan order and to dispel the cosmic disorder and desacralization of the Earth's surface brought about by Spanish rule. Thus, the cyclical nature of *pachakuti*-related cosmology became conjoined to Catholic millennialist and messianic symbolism in colonial-period movements.

A messianic feature of Andean millenarian thought, the *Inkarrí* myth cycle, gained prominence during the eighteenth century and remains embedded in cultural memory today in parts of highland Peru and Bolivia. Inkarrí myth diversified considerably during the twentieth century. The name Inkarrí reflects colonial-era syncretic processes, deriving as it does from the Kechwa term (*sapa inka*) for the ruler of the Tawantinsuyu state (the Inca empire) and the Spanish word *rey*, king. During the eighteenth century, movements tended to develop around the Inkarrí tradition, a new critique of the Spanish invasion that anticipates the return of an Inca ruler to restore an Andean sense of cosmic order. Some versions of the myth contain Catholic-derived eschatological references to a final judgment, possibly owing to Fiorite missionary influences.

Inkarrí mythology, based on the memory of the last Inca, Atahuallpa, generally holds that Inkarrí was beheaded by the Spaniards and his head buried or stolen. Graziano maintains that the figure of Inkarrí represents a fusion of details about the deaths of the emperor Atahuallpa and of the last claimant of the Inca throne, Tupac Amaru, whose severed head was buried in Cuzco.[4] Jesus Christ, who is from Heaven, came and replaced Inkarrí, who is of the earth. The head of Inkarrí since then has been regenerating a body downward into the earth, while his head will eventually emerge to victoriously restore the order of the pre-Hispanic Incan state of Tawantinsuyu. Thus, Inkarrí myths highlight the central theme of the Taki Onqoy movement, proclaiming a suppression and eventual victorious return of the *wakas* to defeat Christ, the collective representation of the Spanish colonial regime.

The Peruvian Asociación Evangélica de la Misión Israelita del Nuevo Pacto Universal (AEMINPU), founded in 1958, employs several motifs found in Inkarrí milllenarian thought. Its prophet, Ezequiel Ataucusi Gamonal (1918–2000), known to his followers as Ezequiel, was an indigenous Peruvian who joined the Seventh-Day Adventists in the 1950s. Claiming to inaugurate the millennium of Christ in "privileged Peru," Ataucusi referred to himself as the "New

---

4 Frank Graziano, *The Millennial New World* (New York and Oxford: Oxford University Press, 1999), 188.

Inca," "Son of Man," and the "Christ of the West." The prophet blended elements of Inkarrí and pachakuti-related cosmology with Old Testament symbolism to form a kind of "neo-Inca nationalism." Anthropologist Juan Ossio, who knew the prophet personally, has suggested that Ezequiel's interest in the year 2000 as the year of the millenarian judgment sprang from the notion of 500-year intervals between *pachakutis*.[5] The prophet placed himself in the line of the Inca kings, dubbing the mythical Incan founder, Manco Capac, the first Peruvian prophet.

The sect has grown substantially in Peru and Bolivia, with an estimated membership of between 60,000 and 200,000 at the turn of the twenty-first century. Temples in coastal cities provide contact points for the recruitment of highland migrants who constitute the majority of recruits. Over the past thirty years, thousands of followers have settled in the sect's "Promised Land" agricultural colonies in the eastern jungle region (*la selva*) of Peru, where redistributive practices are allegedly modeled on those supposed to have been implemented in the Inca empire. AEMINPU members practice an Adventist-derived asceticism, wear tunics (perhaps partly referencing Inca custom), hold a strong work ethic, and employ Old Testament–inspired rituals. Members also engage in glossolalia and liturgical dancing.

AEMINPU's recruitment motifs include issues related to personal reform, as also found in studies of Latin American Pentecostal recruitment and conversion. However, the sect may also provide a potentially appealing compromise for indigenous Peruvians seeking a path between native Andean identity and an exploitative national society. As Graziano suggests, "[AEMINPU] offers a measure of continuity because it adapts traditional Andean messianism to the new knowledge, experiences, and problems of migrants redefining themselves in urban settlements."[6] Indeed, as in the case of Latin American Pentecostal recruitment, AEMINPU membership may provide relief from such problems of urban *barriada* (slum) living as domestic abuse, men's alcoholism, and an attenuation of kinship and ethnic ties with the mountain communities of origin. In addition, Thompson notes that perhaps the success of the colonies' economic and recruitment efforts – particularly in the *selva* (lowland jungle) – has reduced the prominence of millenarian ideology for the sect as a whole since the 1990s.[7] A routinization process may be

---

5 Damien Thompson, "A Peruvian Messiah and the Retreat from Apocalypse," in *Christian Millenarianism: From the Early Church to Waco*, ed. Stephen Hunt (Bloomington IN: Indiana University Press, 2001), 190.
6 Graziano, 244.
7 Thompson, 187–195.

underway, boosted by the involvement of Ezequiel in secular politics as his Israelite Party's candidate for president. However, few published studies of AEMINPU are available and much fieldwork on this group is still needed to clarify its associated recruitment motifs. The case of AEMINPU clearly indicates that a deeply rooted Andean millenarianism continues to thrive in the twenty-first century.

Mexican Millenarian Movements

Indigenous religious movements in Mexico since the Spanish conquest have largely taken nativistic and messianic forms. A constant theme throughout these movements has been the search for a millenarian Indian utopia that is both nativistic (and thus, restorationist) and innovative. European cultural features frequently have been selectively blended with indigenous symbols and reinterpreted in terms of indigenous peoples' quest for autonomy.

Mesoamerican shamanic prophets prophesied such portents as the return of ancestors, eternal youth, and the destruction of the world by earthquake. Gruzinski documents the cases of a number of colonial-era Indian prophets whose messianic claims, based on pre-Columbian Mesoamerican ideas, brought them condemnation by Spanish authorities.[8] Bricker's notable study of movements among the Highland Maya of Mexico and Guatemala show that millenarian activities, usually strongly motivated by mistreatment at the hands of national society, proliferated in these cultures up to the twentieth century.[9] The spectacular nativistic movement among the Chiapanec Maya, sometimes known as Cuscat's War (1867–1869), featured a succession of two messianic leaders, an indigenous uprising, and an attempt to create an Indian Christ by crucifying a Mayan boy. An Oaxacan Chinantec prophet received messages from the Great God Engineer, threatening catastrophe in response to the Mexican government's plans to build a dam in their area.

A widely publicized case of Mexican millenarianism occurring in recent decades is that of the sectarian colony of Nueva Jerusalén, founded in 1973 in the *tierra caliente* region of Michoacán State. The sect was founded by *mestizos*, but includes a significant indigenous membership from throughout southern Mexico. The colony reached a population of nearly 5,000 within its

---

8 Serge Gruzinski, *Man-Gods in the Mexican Highlands: Indian Power and Colonial Society, 1520–1800* (Stanford, CA: Stanford University Press, 1989).
9 Victoria R. Bricker, *The Indian Christ, the Indian King: The Historical Substrate of Mayan Myth and Ritual* (Austin: University of Texas Press, 1981).

first decade. Nueva Jerusalén derives its charter from a founding myth about Marian apparitions to a peasant woman and the prophetic activities of Father Nabor Cárdenas (who died in 2008), a local parish priest.

The Virgin of the Rosary requested that Father Nabor establish a colony to preserve a sinful world from apocalyptic destruction in the year 2000. The sect holds that God will not tolerate much longer what are seen as heretical reforms of the Second Vatican council, an alleged massive Catholic apostasy, and rampant immorality, especially among youth. Father Nabor rejected the Novus Ordo Mass and other changes brought about by Vatican II, following Catholic Traditionalist thought, and assumed the role of the Virgin Mary's chosen son who would lead her children into the millennium. Nueva Jerusalén enjoins on its residents a world-rejecting, penitential lifestyle so as to stay divine punishment of the world and to win time for recruiting new members.

The most prominent recruitment motifs found among the sect's members focus on the quest for men's self-reform from alcoholism, marital infidelity, and for an escape from violence – themes also known to have been important in the growth of the Brazilian holy cities, as well as for Latin American Pentecostalism. Millenarian ideology appears to have played a reduced role in most of the rural recruits' decisions to move to the colony, although the urgency of millenarianism certainly undergirds the ascetic discipline instituted by the prophet. Nueva Jerusalén represents one of but a few cases in which life history research has been applied to the analysis of a Latin American movement colony to identify the effects of social, religious, and economic forces on peasant recruitment decisions.

Conclusion

Latin American societies have generated an impressive variety of revitalization movements over the past 500 years. Most notably, millenarian movements that have blended indigenous, national, and transnational religious influences have provided the region's marginalized populations with vehicles for protest and self-defense; a means of resisting, as well as accommodating, acculturation; and a path toward the restoration of health.

Bibliography and Suggested Readings

Allen, Catherine J. *The Hold Life Has: Coca and Cultural Identity in an Andean Community*, 2nd ed. Washington, DC and New York: Smithsonian Institution Press, 2002.

Barabas, Alicia M. "Chinantec Messianism: The Mediator of the Divine." In Elías Sevilla-Casas (ed.), *Western Expansion and Indigenous Peoples: The Heritage of Las Casas*, 221–254. The Hague and Paris: Mouton, 1977.
Utopías indias: Movimientos socioreligiosos en México. México: Grijalbo, 1989.
Bricker, Victoria R. *The Indian Christ, the Indian King: The Historical Substrate of Mayan Myth and Ritual*. Austin: University of Texas Press, 1981.
Brown, Michael F. "Beyond Resistance: A Comparative Study of Utopian Renewal in Amazonia." *Ethnohistory*, 38, no. 4 (Fall, 1999): 388–413.
Chesnut, R. Andrew. *Born Again in Brazil: The Pentecostal Boom and the Pathogens of Poverty*. New Brunswick, NJ: Rutgers University Press, 1997.
Della Cava, Ralph. *Miracle at Joaseiro*. New York: Columbia University Press, 1970.
Diacon, Todd A. *Millenarian Vision, Capitalist Reality: Brazil's Contestado Rebellion, 1912–1916*. Durham, NC and London: Duke University Press, 1991.
Graziano, Frank. *The Millennial New World*. New York and Oxford: Oxford University Press, 1999.
Gruzinski, Serge. *Man-Gods in the Mexican Highlands: Indian Power and Colonial Society, 1520–1800*. Stanford, CA: Stanford University Press, 1989.
Holston, James. "Alternative Modernities: Statecraft and Religious Imagination in the Valley of the Dawn." *American Ethnologist*, 26, no. 3 (August, 1999): 605–631.
Leatham, Miguel C. "Practical Religion and Peasant Recruitment to Non-Catholic Groups in Latin America." *Religion and the Social Order*, 6 (1996): 175–190.
"Rethinking Religious Decision Making in Peasant Millenarianism: The Case of Nueva Jerusalén." *Journal of Contemporary Religion*, 12, no. 3 (October, 1997): 295–309.
Levine, Robert M. *Vale of Tears: Revisiting the Canudos Massacre in Northeastern Brazil, 1893–1897*. Berkeley, Los Angeles and Oxford: University of California Press, 1992.
Lima Vasconcellos, Pedro. "Apocalypses in the History of Brazil." *Journal for the Study of the New Testament*, 25, no. 2 (December, 2002): 235–254.
López-Baralt, Mercedes. *El retorno del Inca rey: mito y profecía en el mundo andino*. Madrid: Playor, 1987.
MacCormack, Sabine. "Pachacuti: Miracles, Punishments, and Last Judgment: Visionary Past and Prophetic Future in Early Colonial Peru." *American Historical Review*, 93, no. 4 (1988): 960–1006.
Myscofski, Carol A. *When Men Walk Dry: Portuguese Messianism in Brazil*. Atlanta, Georgia: Scholars Press, 1988.
Pease G. Y., Franklin. "El mito de Inkarrí y la visión de los vencidos." In Juan M. Ossio A. (ed.), *Ideología mesiánica del mundo andino*, 439–458. Lima: Ignacio Prado Pastor, 1973.
Pessar, Patricia R. *From Fanatics to Folk: Brazilian Millenarianism and Popular Culture*. Durham, NC: Duke University Press, 2004.
"Revolution, Salvation, Extermination: The Future of Millenarianism in Brazil." In Susan Abbott and John Van Willingen (eds.), *Predicting Sociocultural Change*, 95–114. Athens, GA: University of Georgia Press, 1980.
"Unmasking the Politics of Religion: The Case of Brazilian Millenarianism." *Journal of Latin American Lore*, 7 (Winter, 1981): 255–277.
Phelan, John Leddy. *The Millennial Kingdom of the Franciscans in the New World*. 2nd ed., revised. Berkeley and Los Angeles: University of California Press, 1970.

Queiroz, Maria Isaura Pereira de. *O Mesianismo: No Brazil e no mundo*. Sao Paulo: Editora Alfa-Omega, 1977.

Rappaport, Joanne. "El mesianismo y las transformaciones de símbolos mesiánicos en Tierradentro." *Revista Colombiana de Antropología*, 23(1980–1981): 365–413.

Regan, Jaime. "Mesianismo cocama: Un movimiento de resistencia en la Amazonia peruana." *América Indígena*, 48, no. 1 (enero-marzo, 1988), 127–138.

Ribeiro, René. "Brazilian Messianic Movements." In Sylvia Thrupp (ed.), *Millennial Dreams in Action: Essays in Comparative Study*, 55–69. Comparative Studies in Society and History, Supplement II. The Hague: Mouton, 1962.

Thompson, Damien. "A Peruvian Messiah and the Retreat from Apocalypse." In Stephen Hunt (ed.), *Christian Millenarianism: From the Early Church to Waco*, 187–195. Bloomington and Indianapolis: Indiana University Press, 2001.

Wachtel, Nathan. "Rebeliones y milenarismo." In Juan M. Ossio A. (ed.), *Ideología mesiánica del mundo andino*, 103–142. Lima: Ignacio Prado Pastor, 1973.

Wallace, Anthony F. C. "Revitalization Movements: Some Theoretical Considerations for their Comparative Study." *American Anthropologist*, 58, no. 2(1956): 264–281.

Wright, Robin, and Jonathan D. Hill. "History, Ritual, and Myth: Nineteenth Century Millenarian Movements in the Northwest Amazon." *Ethnohistory*, 33, no. 1 (Winter, 1986): 31–54.

Wright, Stuart. *Leaving Cults: The Dynamics of Defection*. Monograph Series No. 7. Washington, DC: Society for the Scientific Study of Religion, 1987.

15

The Expulsion of the Jesuits and the Late Colonial Period

JOHN LYNCH

In 1766 there were some 2,630 Jesuits in Spanish America, living and working in missions, colleges, and plantations. The order had resources in property as well as personnel, and was one of the largest land and slave owners on the continent. In Mexico it owned forty-one rural estates, twenty-seven colleges, and numerous churches. In Chile, Jesuit property including funds, goods, slaves, cattle, and real estate amounted to 1,961,148 pesos, a sum greater than the annual budget of the colony.

Suddenly, in July and August 1767, all Jesuits, *peninsulares*, Creoles, and foreigners were expelled from America and their properties confiscated. The expulsion was conducted as a military operation and repeated in all the major Jesuit houses. A detachment of troops would appear without warning late at night and order the residents to prepare themselves for a long journey. They were taken under escort to the nearest port, where they embarked for Europe, most of them to Italy. A reluctant pope was persuaded to admit them to his states, more than 5,000 Jesuits in all from Spain and America, to live there on a state pension of 100 pesos a year, paid in effect from their own confiscated property.

Religion was not the only, or even the prime motive for the expulsion. The Jesuits were nothing if not Catholics. The Jesuit historian Juan de Mariana, writing in the sixteenth century, observed that religion and ecclesiastical power were "often a cloak used by princes to cover their actions and even to disguise great deceits."[1] Religious habits had not changed. The Spanish Bourbon monarchy strove to control the Church, to cut its jurisdiction and tap its resources. There was little opposition from the Church itself. The secular

---

1 Juan de Mariana, *Historia General de España* (2 vols., Madrid: Gaspar y Roig, [1855] 1950), I, 156, 159.

An earlier version of this entry appears in John Lynch, *New Worlds: A Religious History of Latin America* (New Haven, CT: Yale University Press, 2012).

bishops and clergy were already too dependent on the state for their careers and their livelihoods to offer serious resistance. They accepted the principle, if not all the details, of state control in matters of religion and collaborated wholeheartedly in Bourbon rule in America. The monarch in Madrid, the bishop in his diocese – both occupied the imperial palace.

The religious orders were less affected by patronage and policy and had a history of freedom from episcopal and therefore from state control; but this did not give them immunity from the attentions of Bourbon government, which had other means of tackling clerical independence. First, they transformed the missions and *doctrinas* of the orders into ordinary parishes in a process of "secularization," which served to marginalize the regulars and reduce their numbers. Second, on April 2, 1767, the Bourbon rulers took even more drastic action against the Jesuits: a royal Pragmatic ordered their expulsion from the king's dominions, thus beginning a war of attrition against the order that culminated in its dissolution in 1773.

Official obsession with secrecy and security was superfluous. There was no Jesuit resistance, but there was popular outrage. In Mexico the expulsion merged with tax and mining grievances to produce popular riots and revolts. In Guanajuato, there were attacks on government buildings. In San Luis Potosí, a mob seized the Jesuit fathers and refused to permit them to be escorted into exile. The *visitador*, José de Gálvez, and the viceroy, the Marquis of Croix, sanctioned repressive measures against the rebels, including eighty-five hangings, and the Inquisition too had its say. Gálvez alleged that the Jesuits themselves incited the riots to prevent their expulsion, encouraging the mob to hurl "sacrilegious blasphemies against the king's religion."[2] There was no evidence for any of these charges, as the voice of dissent made clear. A flood of anonymous pamphlets and fly-sheets accused the government of planning to destroy the Catholic religion, while Francisco Antonio Lorenzana, archbishop of Mexico, and Francisco Fabián y Fuero, bishop of Puebla, were attacked for their sycophantic pastoral letters in which they applauded the expulsion as a divine judgement against "impious and fanatical Jesuits."

A different scenario played out in the Río de la Plata. At 3 o'clock in the morning of July 12, 1767 Fernando Fabro, a military officer dispatched from Buenos Aires with eighty soldiers, rang the doorbell at the Jesuit College in Córdoba, their principal base in the region. The porter who opened the door found two pistols at his chest. The 133 Jesuits of the College, priests

---

[2] José de Gálvez, *Informe sobre las rebeliones populares de 1767*, ed. Felipe Castro Gutiérrez (Mexico: Universidad Nacional Autónoma de México 1990), 23–24.

and novices, were herded into one room at bayonet point to hear the royal decree ordering expulsion and the expropriation of their property. They then spent ten days imprisoned in the refectory, while Fabro made an inventory of their possessions. On July 23 all the Córdoba Jesuits were put in transports and taken to Buenos Aires where, on August 19, 1767, they were embarked for Spain, arriving at Puerto de Santa María on January 6, 1768. Meanwhile Governor Francisco de Bucareli, fearing Indian opposition of the kind experienced in the Guaraní war, backed the expulsion of the Jesuits from their missions in Paraguay with a veritable army of troops. These precautions, plus the need to find replacements for the Jesuits, prolonged the operation in Paraguay, but eventually it too was carried out peacefully and without opposition.

In Chile, on receiving his secret orders in August 1767, the governor had all the Andean passes closed, shipping stopped, auxiliaries recruited, and at 3 a.m. on August 26 his troops surrounded Jesuit houses throughout the colony, arrested the astonished clergy, and sent them under escort to the port of Valparaiso. The inventory of Jesuit property was begun immediately.

Rejected by the state, the Jesuits received no lifeline from the Church. Bourbon bishops resented any claim to exemption from their jurisdiction, and their solidarity with the Crown was notorious. On both counts they distrusted Jesuits. In Mexico Bishop Fabián y Fuero, encouraged by Lorenzana, justified the expulsion as a "legitimate use of the rights which God gave the king along with his Crown."[3] Lorenzana himself enumerated his own charges against the Jesuits in a series of pastoral letters. They were guilty of the pernicious doctrine of probabilism with its attendant lax moral principles, and they promoted the doctrine of tyrannicide. They spread false doctrines and fanaticism in convents of nuns. They were greedy for wealth and power, claimed precedence over other orders and independence of the bishops, and sought to influence students in their favor. In Mexico they accumulated riches, business, and property, and their well-stocked haciendas even produced fighting bulls. Lorenzana exhorted the faithful "to obey and be silent," and to give unqualified assent to the king, who had been "commissioned by God to guard his subjects from influences dangerous to their faith."[4] Lorenzana went further: he persuaded the Mexican Provincial Council to demand the extinction of the

---

3 Pastoral letter, October 28, 1767, quoted by N. M. Farriss, *Crown and Clergy in Colonial Mexico, 1759–1821: The Crisis of Ecclesiastical Privilege* (London: The Altheon Press, 1968), 52, 131–132.

4 Luis Sierra Nava-Lasa, *El Cardenal Lorenzana y la Ilustración, I* (Madrid: Fundacion Universitaria Espanola, Seminario Cisneros 1975), 121–123.

Society of Jesus, a statement cited by Spanish officials in their successful lobbying of the papacy for such a decision in 1773. In Mexico, therefore, the faithful observed two current manifestations of state religion: an arbitrary exercise of power and forceful repression of resistance.

In the Río de la Plata the situation was more complex. On the one hand the Jesuits were alleged to be the commanders behind the War of Paraguay (1754–1756) and the king was convinced that members of the Society were solely responsible for the resistance of the Indians. On the other hand, they appeared to be indispensable to the missions in a country chronically short of clergy. Manuel Antonio de la Torre, bishop of Paraguay from 1756, a Spaniard from the secular clergy, began his ministry in cordial relations with the Jesuits and his diocesan visitation yielded a favorable report not only on their pastoral work but also on their temporal care of the Indians, whose standard of living was superior to that of many Spaniards in Paraguay. Later, as bishop of Buenos Aires at the time of the expulsion, De la Torre was less sympathetic to the Jesuits and, surrounded by officials, followed the official line.

Charles III treated the expulsion of the Jesuits from all his kingdoms as a secret between himself and God. In the Pragmatic of April 2, 1767 he claimed that he acted from the "supreme executive power which the Almighty has placed in my hands" but gave only the vaguest of reasons: "the obligation by which I am bound to maintain my peoples in subordination, tranquility and justice, and further urgent, just and necessary reasons which I keep in my royal soul." But this was not a lofty argument between the Enlightenment and religion, between a progressive government and a burnt-out order. It was a question of power. Charles III had an ingrained prejudice against Jesuits.[5] He saw an insidious and wealthy organization that had once defended regicide. They still retained their special vow of obedience to the pope and their reputation of papal agents.

An order with an international organization whose headquarters were outside of Spain was regarded as inherently incompatible with absolutism and an obstacle to a number of government policies. The Jesuits existed outside the regalist system; they were not servants of the state, beholden to state patronage, obedient to state objectives. Their opposition to one of the favorite "causes" of the Bourbons, the canonization of the anti-Jesuit bishop of Puebla, Juan de Palafox, and their general ubiquity in Church and state confirmed Charles III in his view that Jesuits were troublemakers and a challenge to royal power. He had the resolute support of his ministers, some of whom

---

5 John Lynch, *Bourbon Spain 1700–1808* (Oxford: Blackwell, 1989), 281–283.

came from a class that resented the influence of the Jesuits in university education and their affiliation with the higher aristocracy.

The Jesuits also had enemies among a wider clerical and lay public. Their defense of good works as well as faith in the process of salvation and their more relaxed interpretation of Catholic moral theology brought them into conflict not only with Jansenists but also with other orders, and they had few friends among Augustinians and Dominicans. Memories of the time when they virtually monopolized the royal confessional and controlled ecclesiastical patronage and policy were still fresh and there were many clerics who bore personal grudges against the Society of Jesus. Religious conflict became a code for political positions. To be a "Jesuit" meant to belong to a group of elitist graduates and to disapprove of reforms introduced by plebeian ministers; to be a "Jansenist" was to be a supporter of regalism, an opponent of Rome, and a friend of heterodoxy. Crisis came in 1766 when food and tax riots in Madrid directly challenged the government. Although there were obvious social and economic reasons for the discontent, the government preferred to believe that they had been instigated by the Jesuits and their allies who wished to change the government and block further reform. This version of events was assiduously promoted by the Count of Campomanes, fiscal of the Council of Castile, whose inquiry into the riots produced a long and detailed indictment of the Jesuits and provided the theoretical justification for the expulsion.

Campomanes focused on Spain and it was in the metropolis that the Jesuits came under the direct scrutiny of the Crown. But America added its own fuel to the charges against the Jesuits, especially the existence of what ministers called "the Jesuit kingdom of Paraguay." The allegations condemned the missionary methods of the Jesuits based on inculturation and for their imperious attitudes. They were "missionaries only in name, but in fact they behaved as sovereigns." The Spanish government published the data supplied by an ex-Jesuit, Bernardo Ibañez de Echavarri. Twice expelled from the order in the Río de la Plata for policy disagreements, Ibañez was present in Buenos Aires and Paraguay during the crucial years 1755–1761, and compiled a flawed and mendacious work of propaganda. This was then used by the government, especially by Campomanes, to justify first the expulsion and then the desired extinction of the order.

The main thesis of Ibañez was that the Guaraní mission was established and ruled as a sovereign state, a veritable kingdom, with the general its king, the provincials his viceroys; and this king exercised all the legislative, fiscal, and military powers of a sovereign. The fact of its independence and absolute sovereignty was proved by the existence of an Indian army, created, armed, and trained by the Jesuits. He cited a letter from the Paraguayan provincial, Ignacio de Arteaga (August 6, 1727): "if the Indians are not well trained in arms, then these missions are not well defended against the heathen, the Spaniards, and the Portuguese." And to keep the Indians under control the Jesuits "allowed them only enough education to be useful to the Jesuits themselves." A further criticism was provided by the presence of more foreign priests than Spanish, and a closed-door policy toward Spanish settlers. From all this the Crown concluded: "Their own documents prove that in their Paraguayan missions they have established an absolute monarchy; or to speak more precisely, an incredible despotism contrary to all divine and human laws."[6]

Ibañez alleged that the Jesuits appropriated an "enormous surplus" from Paraguay (in fact by no means the richest of their American provinces) for use by the general of the Society toward its common expenses. Campomanes too referred to the Jesuits' accumulation of wealth in the Indies: they refused to pay tithes on their own agricultural production, while they took all the produce from the labor of the Indians for the profit of the Society. The Jesuits owned vast properties in America – estates, ranches, and plantations – which they themselves managed as commercial enterprises to fund their various activities. This wealth was a sore point with royal officials.

The Jesuits stubbornly resisted payment of tithes and opposed all attempts by the authorities to force them to do so, thus depriving Crown and bishops of substantial revenue. The dispute dragged on throughout the seventeenth and early eighteenth centuries. In 1750 the Crown accepted a compromise, according to which the Jesuits had to pay a tithe of one-thirtieth of production. But the argument continued, until a royal order of December 4, 1766, shortly before the expulsion, obliged the Jesuits in America to pay the whole tithe.

Paraguay was the most dramatic scene of Jesuit enterprise and focus of greatest controversy. The Jesuits had not always been opponents of the Crown. Indeed, the two had a mutual interest in confronting Portuguese invaders and regional Creole rebels. At a time of Jesuit influence in Madrid they obtained from the Council of the Indies a royal *cedula* confirming the various privileges and immunities of their Guaraní missions. The Indians had to pay only a low rate of tribute, in exchange for constituting a permanent militia at the orders of the royal authorities. The Jesuits were allowed to retain the particular

---

6 Bernardo Ibáñez de Echavarri, *El reyno jesuitico del Paraguay* (Madrid, 1770), 20–36, 45–46, 58, 72.

economic and social system characteristic of their Guaraní communities. And the moderate form of the *Patronato Real* (royal patronage and supervision of the Church) prevailing in their mission was confirmed. The *"Cédula Grande"* of 1743, which gave the Jesuits controls over tens of thousands of Guaraní, was not easily obtained: it cost the Jesuits large sums of money in bribes to the officials who prepared the *cédula*, and payment was made from funds illegally transferred from the Río de la Plata via Lisbon and London.

The victories gained in 1743 and their apparently invincible positions in Spain and in Rome misled the Jesuits. In 1750 the Treaty of Madrid between Spain and Portugal rearranged the boundaries of the Río de la Plata: in exchange for the Portuguese *Colônia* Spain ceded territory that contained seven of the thirty Guaraní missions of the Jesuits. The missionaries were ordered to leave immediately and resettle their Indians in Spanish territory; in an instant 30,000 Indians found themselves ruined and homeless. Amidst a storm of protests from Jesuits and other critics in America, the Jesuit General ordered obedience and the order took steps to comply. The Paraguayan province, however, was outraged and in a series of compelling arguments pressed Madrid for a change of the boundary line. What was the moral authority of the treaty? Was it right to displace 30,000 innocent people, deprive them of their property, and banish them hundreds of miles to a wilderness, their only compensation one peso each? Which had primary claim to obedience, Spanish law or moral law?

There were many answers from the missionaries, some passionately critical of the treaty, others openly hostile to Spanish orders and their general's advice. In the end they had to comply, partly to avoid the scandal of rebellion, partly to preserve their charges from worse harm. But they could not prevent resistance by the Indians, already alienated from the Portuguese through their long experience of slave hunters from Brazil, aggravated in the eighteenth century by the labor demands of the Mato Grosso gold fields. Hundreds of Indian lives were lost and great suffering was inflicted upon the mission communities before the colonial authorities crushed the rebellion. The Jesuits too were victims. The Guaraní war gave the Spanish authorities the opportunity to distort or fabricate evidence against the missionaries and eventually to incriminate the whole Jesuit order.

When Spanish and Portuguese forces occupied the seven rebel missions in 1756 they found a number of foreigners among the Jesuits, a consequence of previous concessions allowing them to recruit up to one-third of their American personnel outside Spain. This was a privilege granted to no other order and was an exception to one of Spain's strictest colonial laws. In 1760, the Crown revoked the concession and Campomanes subsequently explained why: "National loyalty does not exist in such missionaries; the interest of the order is their only motivation."[7] The expulsion was a means to exert total control over the Church in America, removing the one possibility of dissent; and to control the Church was to control society.

The reaction in America to the expulsion of the Jesuits, a large proportion of whom were Americans by birth, was apathetic, except in Mexico. When push came to shove, the order was isolated. True, there were expressions of regret and resentment among former pupils and other friends, and the despotic nature of the expulsion left a memory that would later be invoked against Bourbon rule. But there was no action in their support at the time. The bishops were in favor of expulsion, indifferent, or complacent. The Jesuits had always fought for their exemptions from episcopal control and had few friends among bishops. From the secular clergy they could expect little solidarity, even less from other religious orders.

Their disputes with Dominicans and Augustinians over theology, education, and missionary methods were notorious. Franciscans, who had a number of American bishops in their ranks, harbored historic resentments. The attitude of lay people was ambiguous. Merchants, perhaps, saw Jesuits as rivals in trade, landowners as competitors for land. Creoles valued them as educators of their children, but this was not enough to produce a movement in their favor. Mission Indians, especially in Paraguay, had the means of causing trouble, if they had been given a lead, but in fact the Jesuits acted to calm their neophytes, conscious of their ultimate weakness.

The departure of the Jesuits was not the last gasp of a dying institution. The order was at its peak, vocations were numerous, priests models of their kind. Although the Spanish government would never admit it, the expulsion of the Jesuits from America left a gap that was not easily filled. The Church suffered from loss of dynamic pastors and teachers, and the missions never recovered their former prosperity; these facts were frankly admitted by viceroys in New Granada and elsewhere. Jesuit schools, colleges, and estates were taken over by other institutions or sold in public auction to interested buyers.

The expulsion was a particular blow to secondary education, which the state and ecclesiastical authorities failed to make good, in spite of some success in expanding primary schools. The colonial government sought to ensure that the property of the Jesuits was used for establishing new teaching centers. But in Mexico the colony's leading colleges were closed; Michoacán alone

---

[7] Pedro Rodríguez de Campomanes, *Dictamen fiscal de expulsión de los jesuitas de España* (1766-1767), ed. Jorge Cejudo and Teófanes Egido (Madrid, 1977), 130.

lost seven. In Bogotá, hopes of establishing a public university to replace that left by the Jesuits were not fulfilled. In Buenos Aires, an attempt was made to use Jesuit property to establish a university, but this failed for lack of teachers, books, equipment, and will; Buenos Aires had to be satisfied with the Colegio de San Carlos, established in 1783, whose curriculum and teaching made few concessions to modernity or the Enlightenment. Royal decrees, here and throughout Spanish America, prohibited the continuation of Jesuit teaching, or alleged Jesuit teaching. This did not signify the advent of new learning, but a reversion to older orthodoxies, to Aquinas instead of Suárez, to moral certainty instead of probabilism, and to the proscription of any ultramontane doctrines (that is, a strong emphasis on the perogatives and power of the pope) as opposed to the regalian rights of the Crown. The expulsion was not an example of applied enlightenment. Juan Pablo Viscardo, Peruvian victim of the expulsion, poured his resentment of Bourbon absolutism into his *Lettre aux Espagnols-Américains*, published from exile in 1799 and quickly recognized as a classic statement of colonial grievance and national independence: "The interests of our country are precisely our interests ... and we alone have the right to exercise the functions of government, to the benefit of the *patria* and ourselves."[8]

As missionaries the Jesuits left a large number of neophytes, some 478,000 in Spanish America and the Philippines; of these 26 percent were in New Spain, 24 percent in the Río de la Plata. Other orders, including the Dominicans and Franciscans, were still active and continued to educate and evangelize. In California, where the missions were wrongly reputed to be wealthy and to contain silver mines but in fact were underfunded, the Franciscans pursued the work of evangelization with some success. In other regions alternatives were sometimes found, but often a vacuum was left. In Mexico Viceroy Revillagigedo did not doubt that the missions deteriorated after the expulsion: "When the Jesuits were expelled they were not promptly replaced by other religious, and their property was committed to incompetent and greedy individuals who totally squandered it."[9]

In the Guaraní reductions, home of some 300,000 Indians and almost 500 missionaries, the Jesuits had successfully solved the problem of the material subsistence of the Indians. And these, far from being passive wards of

---

8 Merle E. Simmons, *Los escritos de Juan Pablo Viscardo y Guzmán* (Caracas: Universidad Catolica Andres Bello, 1983), 366.
9 Revillagigedo quoted by Luis Nava Sierra, *El Cardenal Lorenzana* (Madrid: Fundación Universitaria Española, Seminario Cisneros, 1975), 193.

the priests, were active participants in all aspects of mission life – mediators between European ideas and local reality. Now, however, there were those in anti-Jesuit circles who argued that this had all taken place at the expense of the Guaranís' freedom.

The reaction of the Spanish authorities against the community system established by the Jesuits thus had a theoretical as well as a practical side. The Jesuits' detractors in Bourbon government employed arguments in favor of individual liberty and private property, which were ironically out of tune with the leaders of the Enlightenment. But the secular thinkers of the Enlightenment, in even greater irony, expressed enthusiasm for the Jesuit missions; even the customary opponents of the Jesuit order such as Voltaire, Montesquieu, and the ex-Jesuit Raynal commended the "Jesuit state" as a rational sociological experiment. Yet despite this unusual contestation, the decision to secularize moved forward.

In default of any alternative plan the Jesuit system of government had to be left in place and the community system maintained, substituting secular priests and administrators for the Jesuits. The new officials were not only less efficient than the Jesuits but also less honest and regarded their task as a means of personal profit, while the Indians were robbed of their property by gangs of Spanish and Portuguese rustlers. They began to desert the missions and many made their way to neighboring regions and also to Buenos Aires and Montevideo, where in spite of the alleged demoralizing effects of the Jesuit regime they had initiative enough to earn a living and to work for wages as laborers and artisans.

In the years after 1750 the Church had taken or invited measures that weakened its own structure and demoralized its clergy. The expulsion of the Jesuits, the marginalization of the remaining orders, and the attack on clerical immunity all served to alienate some of the clergy and alert many more. Policies designed to increase the power of the monarchy over the Church and restrict the place of priesthood and religion in public life were part of the centralizing project characteristic of the Bourbons, who emphasized law over custom, the secular over the sacred, power over piety. Priests were told in effect that officials knew best. Only the bishops and higher clergy were comfortable with Bourbon rule. But the commanding position gained by secular officials, the retreat of churchmen from many areas of jurisdiction, and the close association of the altar and the throne brought the Church dangerously close to the colonial state. When this collapsed the Church would find that it did not have an independent support.

Bibliography and Suggested Readings

Block, David. *Mission Culture on the Upper Amazon: Native Tradition, Jesuit Enterprise, and Secular Policy in Moxos, 1660–1880.* Lincoln: University of Nebraska Press, 1994.

Egido, Teófanes. "La expulsión de los jesuítas de España." In Ricardo García-Villoslada (ed.), *Historia de la Iglesia en España.* Madrid: Editorial Biblioteca Autores Cristianos, 1979.

Farriss, N. M. *Crown and Clergy in Colonial Mexico, 1759–1821: The Crisis of Ecclesiastical Privilege.* London: Athlone Press, 1968.

Gálvez, José de. *Informe sobre las rebeliones populares de 1767*, edited By Felipe Castro Gutiérrez. Mexico: Serie de Historia Novohispana, 1990.

Hernández, Pablo. *El extrañamiento de los jesuítas del Río de la Plata y de las misiones del Paraguay por decreto de Carlos III.* Madrid: V. Suárez, 1908.

Ibáñez de Echavarri, Bernardo. *El reyno jesuitico del Paraguay por siglo y medio negado y oculto, hoy demostrado y descubierto.* Madrid: Colección de documents, 1768–1770, 1770.

Lynch, John. *Bourbon Spain 1700–1808.* Oxford: Blackwell, 1989.

Mariana, Juan de. *Historia General de España.* Madrid: Gaspar y Roig, 1950.

Mörner, Magnus. "La expulsión de la Compañía de Jesús." In Pedro Borges (ed.), *Historia de la Iglesia en Hispanoamérica y Filipinas (siglos XV-XIX)* 2 vols., Madrid: Editorial Biblioteca Autores Cristianos, 1992.

The Political and Economic Activities of the Jesuits in the Plata Region. The Hapsburg Era. Stockholm: Victor Pettersons Bokindustri Aktiebolag. 1953.

Sierra Nava-Lasa, Luis. *El Cardenal Lorenzana y la ilustración, I.* Madrid: Fundación Universitaria Española, Seminario Cisneros, 1975.

Simmons, Merle E. *Los escritos de Juan Pablo Viscardo y Guzmán.* Caracas: Universidad Catolica Andres Bello, 1983.

16

The Church and Latin American Independence

JEFFREY L. KLAIBER

The rumblings of independence of Latin America were first heard in the cloisters of convents and monasteries more than a century before the actual wars broke out. The Crown and local authorities placed reform of the Roman Catholic Church at the top of their priorities for renovating and regenerating the entire empire. Beyond question, the Church needed reforming: the monasteries and convents were crowded with friars and nuns with no real vocation; the Church had become the largest landowner; and there were too many priests of the secular clergy, many of whom were poorly paid or educated, especially those living in the countryside. In short, the Latin American Church in the eighteenth century looked very much like the Church in Europe on the eve of the Reformation.

But in its attempts to reform the Church in the seventeenth and eighteenth centuries, the Crown was frequently heavy-handed and instead of reform, it produced widespread resentment, especially among the Creole (New World–born European) clergy. One example was the *alternativa*. In the face of rising creole numbers and influence in the ranks of the religious orders the Crown imposed the *alternativa* by which every other provincial or major superior had to be a *peninsular* (Iberian-born Spaniard). That particular "reform" provoked outcries of protest and even led to a violent confrontation in 1680 in the streets of Lima between Franciscans, most of whom were Creoles, and the soldiers who escorted a newly appointed Spanish superior to his residence in the Franciscan monastery in the center of the city. In the following century the Spanish Bourbons, in power since 1700, introduced many other restrictions on the religious: the Crown placed a limit on the number who could enter the orders; it curbed the power to acquire property and established the right of individual religious to have recourse to secular courts. The Crown implemented these measures in response to the growing impression in a changing political milieu that the religious orders needed to be reformed and that their sphere of influence should be limited to the missions or specific tasks such as education. In 1749, all Indian doctrines administered by the religious in Lima and Mexico City were turned over to the secular clergy. But what the Bourbons understood by "reform," people living in the New World often perceived as abuses. The expulsion of the Jesuits in 1767 was received with shock, incredulity, and in some cases, provoked riots in protest.

The secular clergy also felt the impact of Bourbon reformism. In New Spain, the Crown turned control over the tithes to local juntas, and in 1795 eliminated clerical immunity from secular courts. What most rankled the Creole clergy, however, was the fact that even after 300 years the top positions in the Church, bishoprics and wealthy parishes, were still awarded to Spaniards, many of whom were newcomers to the New World. As Servando Teresa de Mier, a leading conspirator in the independence of Mexico, stated in 1813: "For the past thirty years the wealthiest parishes have been given over with preference to European clergymen fresh from Spain, or formed in Tridentine seminaries; by the nature of things these posts should have been reserved for native-born clergy."[1] Mier also noted that of the 703 bishops in the entire history of Spanish America, only 279 had been Creoles. In this sense, the resentment of the Creole clergy, both secular and religious, mirrored the same growing resentment among Creoles in general over Spanish predominance in the political and religious structure of the New World.

During the wars of independence the clergy played a significant, and in some cases, a decisive role, in influencing Creoles or indigenous people to support or to oppose the movement. As a general rule, the majority of the upper clergy, all of whom had been named by the king under the system of patronage, opposed the cause of independence, and this included a few Creole bishops. But a significant number of the lower secular clergy, most of whom were Creoles, supported the cause. Mariano Cuevas, the Jesuit historian, claimed that around 6,000 of the 8,000 priests in Mexico sympathized with the independence movement, although those numbers are probably exaggerated. According to another more contemporary Jesuit historian, Agustín Churruca, the actual number of priests who openly instigated rebellion and took up arms (a position more militant than mere support of independence) was only around 1.7 percent. In Peru, out of a total of around 3,000 religious and secular

---

[1] Fray Servando Teresa de Mier [José Guerra], *Historia de la revolución de Nueva España, antiguamente Anahuac o verdadero origen y causa de ella con la relación de sus progresos hasta el presente* [1813]. Facsimile edition with preliminary study by Manuel Calvillo, 3rd ed. (Mexico, D.F.: Instituto Mexicano del Seguro Social, 1980), I: 337.

priests at the time of independence, some 390 participated as insurgents, collaborators, or propagandists.

Just as there were priests for and against independence, both sides cited Church teachings to legitimize their cause. For the royalists the case was clear: God himself sanctioned the monarchy that governed Spain and the New World. To rebel against the king was tantamount to disobedience to God. A rebel became not only a political criminal but also a religious apostate. But the insurgents, both priests and lay, cited the works of Francisco Suárez and other scholastic thinkers who held that God had deposited all political power in the people, who, in turn, had the right to delegate that power to the king or to whomever they pleased.

In 1808, Napoleon placed Charles IV and his son Fernando in captivity. In that situation, the different *juntas* in the New World refused to recognize the provisional government in Spain on the grounds that their loyalty was to the king, not to Spain the nation. In the absence of the king, the Americans believed that they had the right to form their own governments. Initially the New World juntas were *fidelistas*, that is, they swore to remain faithful and rule in the king's name in his absence. But when Ferdinand returned to power in 1814, he refused to recognize the juntas. In the face of this intransigence New World leaders, priests, lawyers, and military all reasserted even more categorically that their claim to rule their own land was a God-given right, not a prerogative of the king. Although the prevalent historiography points to the secular, francophone, and Enlightenment-influenced roots of Latin American independence movements, the evidence indicates that the influence of the French Revolution on the Spanish-American independence movements has been overstated. In fact, even though independence leaders read the works of the French philosophers, they eschewed the antireligious facets of the revolution. As Morelos in Mexico asserted, "We are more religious than the Europeans."[2]

Jesuit Precursors

The Jesuits were not in Latin America at the time of independence, having been expelled from Brazil in 1759 and Spanish America in 1767 and 1768. But their writings in Europe influenced the intellectuals, politicians, and military who led the independence movement. Technically, they were no longer

---

2 Agustín Churruca Paláez, *El pensamiento insurgente de Morelos* (Mexico, D.F.: Editorial Porrúa, 1983), 106.

Jesuits at all, because in 1773 Pope Clement XIV suppressed the Jesuit order. Nevertheless, the 2,000 Latin American ex-Jesuits who were confined to the papal states continued to see themselves as Jesuits. To their detriment, so did the Spanish government, because it would not allow them, even as ex-Jesuits, to return to their homelands. Francisco Clavijero, one of the exiled Mexican Jesuits, wrote with pride on the greatness of his country's indigenous heritage. His work was widely read in Mexico and even found a place in Thomas Jefferson's library. In the same vein, the Chilean Jesuit Juan Ignacio de Molina extolled Chile's natural resources and expressed his admiration for the Araucanians' valor and love of freedom. The Araucanians (today called Mapuches) befriended the Jesuit missionaries but resisted all encroachments by Spanish soldiers. In the words of Miquel Batllori, these and other Jesuit authors fostered a "pre-national regionalism."

The majority of the exiled Jesuits accepted their fate and did not criticize Spain, much less entertain revolutionary thoughts. But two in particular did: Juan José Godoy, a Chilean, and Juan Pablo Viscardo y Guzmán, a Peruvian, were frequent visitors to London, where they attempted to persuade the British government to help liberate Latin America from the Spanish. As early as 1781, Viscardo had urged the British to come to the aid of Tupac Amaru II and his rebellion in Peru. Later, he wrote lengthy essays in which he described the people, the customs, and the potential wealth of Latin America in the hopes of arousing England's interest in the region. In one of his essays, he called upon the British to send an expeditionary force to support a general uprising among the Latin Americans. His most famous writing was a forty-page pamphlet, *Carta a los españoles americanos* (Letter Addressed to the Spanish Americans), possibly modeled on Thomas Paine's *Common Sense*, in which he challenged his fellow Creoles to "be a different people" and break their bonds with the mother country.[3]

Viscardo's *Letter* stands as one of the first open declarations in favor of outright independence, twenty years before it became a reality. On his deathbed in 1798 he turned his papers over to Rufus King, the American ambassador in London. King, in turn, showed the *Letter* to Francisco Miranda, a Venezuelan conspirator, who had the revolutionary document translated from the French (the original in Spanish was lost) to Spanish and disseminated it throughout Venezuela and the Caribbean. The *Letter* was translated into English in 1808. Copies of it showed up in Buenos Aires in 1816 and in Lima in 1822.

---

3 Juan Pablo Viscardo y Guzmán, *Letter to the Spanish Americans*, with a foreword by David A. Brading (Providence, RI: The John Carter Brown Library, 2002), 81.

Enlightened Bishops and Clergy

The eighteenth-century Catholic Church was the object of a reform movement, both from above and below. The Bourbons appointed bishops who reflected the mentality of the enlightened despots: they aimed to modernize society, to carry out some social and economic reforms, but political change was not part of their agenda. A notable example of the latter was Manuel Abad y Queipo, bishop-elect (he was never officially consecrated a bishop) of Michoacán, 1810–1815. Born in Spain, he arrived in Mexico as a young priest. In his writing, he called for economic and social reforms to alleviate the plight of the Indians. He also called attention to the need for clerical reform. He noted that there were too many priests, too poorly paid, with little hope of advancement in their careers. At the same time he called for more *mestizos* and Indians in the seminaries. For all his enlightened ideas, however, he opposed the independence movement when it broke out.

In Peru there were similar reform-minded bishops. In Trujillo, on the northern coast, Baltasar Jaime Martínez de Compañón conducted a three-year (1782–1785) visit of his diocese during which he ordered new roads built, founded new Indian towns and schools, and had drawings made of all the fauna and flora of northern Peru. In Arequipa in the south, Bishop Pedro José Chávez de la Rosa (1788–1805) also implemented many reform projects that included updating the curricula in the local seminary. He failed in one area, however: the convent of Santa Catalina. When he passed over an upper-class nun to be prioress by appointing another nun of a lower social status, he provoked the wrath of the displaced nuns and their upper-class families. This particular case, as well as the *alternativa*, illustrates what was typical of Bourbon administrators and their bishops: they proposed reforms that, though well-meaning, were carried out in such an authoritarian fashion that in the end they produced resentment and, in some cases, outright rejection.

The Creole clergy, at least those who managed to become pastors in urban areas, generally came from the middle and lower middle classes, with a few from the local aristocracy. They were well educated and almost all had university degrees. In his study of the Mexican clergy, William Taylor noted that the pastors of the wealthiest parishes came from established families, but the majority of pastors in Mexico City and Guadalajara came from the middle and lower middle classes. Many were sons of merchants, carpenters, military, or ranchers. In a similar study on Peru, Antonine Tibesar reviewed the curricula vitae of 100 pastors in Lima between 1750 and 1820. The results are strikingly similar to those of Taylor for Mexico. Of the 100 pastors, ten came from the nobility; twelve from wealthy families; and fifty-four from poorer families belonging to the state bureaucracy, the military, or the merchant class. Another eight simply stated that their families had fallen on hard economic times. Whatever their economic status, however, their level of education was on par with that of members of any of the professions. Twenty-nine had at least one doctorate, nineteen had a licentiate, and nine were lawyers as well as priests.

What is most striking, at least for the modern eye, is their motivation, which they state quite clearly in their autobiographies. Twenty-six write that their parents wanted them to be priests. Another thirty-one state that they needed the salary of a pastor to support their parents and other relatives. Only ten claim that they became priests to serve the people. Of course, in the eighteenth century, the priesthood was perceived more as a profession than a vocation, or a spiritual calling. It is no surprise that the two largest groups at the first constituent congresses in Latin America belonged to the two most prestigious professions: priests and lawyers.

The Creole clergy who were trained in the reformed seminaries, like Creoles everywhere, adhered to the dictum: *Obedezco pero no cumplo*: I obey but I do not comply. They read all of the books, especially Rousseau, which the Inquisition forbade. In one notable case, the rector of San Carlos Convictorio (boarding school) in Lima, Toribio Rodríguez de Mendoza, a Creole secular priest, was reprimanded when the Inquisition discovered while conducting an official visit that he had all the forbidden books in his own office. A few years later, Rodríguez was elected to Peru's first constitutional assembly (1822–1823). He was delighted to see that the majority of his fellow delegates were graduates of San Carlos.

Hidalgo and Morelos

Miguel Hidalgo would be a fairly typical example of the Creole clergy who supported the independence movement. The son of an overseer on a hacienda, he studied at the Jesuit college of Valladolid, where the curriculum had been reformed to acquaint students with the latest ideas in mathematics, physics, geography, and history. Later, he enrolled in San Nicolás, a college run by the diocese of Valladolid. There he deepened his classical formation, and he also studied Tarascan and Nahuatl, two of Mexico's many Indian languages. He was also widely known for his erudition and, in addition, he was a model entrepreneur. In the small town of Dolores where he served as parish priest, he founded a pottery plant, an apiary to produce beeswax, and workshops for carpentry, and also cultivated wine and olive oil.

The independence movement began abruptly and in an unexpected manner. Hidalgo was involved in a pro-independence conspiracy with other Creoles, notably Ignacio Allende and Juan de Aldama, both militia officers, but an informer betrayed the plot. In desperation Hidalgo fled to Dolores, and on September 16, 1810 he rang the church bells and summoned the Indians to rise up. To the cry of "Long live the Virgin of Guadalupe and death to the *Gachupines* (peninsular Spaniards)!" Hidalgo left Dolores with a small band of Indians, but within the next several weeks the ranks of the revolutionary army swelled to around 80,000.

The summons to fight under the banner of the Virgin of Guadalupe inspired the Indians and mestizos with messianic fervor. Hidalgo's ragtag "soldiers," armed with lances, sticks, and stones, looted several towns and massacred many Spaniards. But as the mob neared Mexico City it faced organized resistance from disciplined regular soldiers. Either out of fear or prudence, Hidalgo decided not to march on the city. He then moved north, but during the march many of his followers melted away, and finally, in April, 1811, Hidalgo himself was captured. He was tried by a military court and again by the Inquisition, which found him guilty of heresy. On July 30 in Chihuahua he was executed by a firing squad, along with Allende, Aldama, and other followers.

Hidalgo's movement failed in large part because he was taken by surprise and unprepared. Furthermore, he had never planned to begin the revolution with the Indians. As a consequence, he had no clear goals, neither immediate nor strategic. Along the way, he decreed several social reforms (abolition of slavery, the end of taxation, and the redistribution of land to the Indians), but he never explicitly stated what his movement was about, and, in fact, never called for independence. Furthermore, the absence of Creoles was also a decisive factor. The vast majority of Creoles looked askance at a movement that threatened to bring about a social revolution. The first phase of the independence movement ended in utter failure; nevertheless, the cause was soon taken up again in the south by José María Morelos, also a priest, who was even more messianic and socially radical than Hidalgo. He was also a better commander.

Between 1810 and 1815, Morelos kept the insurgency alive in the hills of southern Mexico. He turned his army of 9,000 Indians into very effective guerrilla units, which attacked royalist forces while successfully eluding them until the end. Unlike Hidalgo, his former teacher, Morales was a mestizo and belonged to the mass of the unemployed lower clergy. He placed his movement under the protection of the Virgin of Guadalupe, whom he hailed as the "Patroness of Freedom" and the "Protector of Mexico's Independence." In 1813, Morelos convened a congress that promulgated a constitution the following year in the small town of Apatzingán. The new constitution formally proclaimed the independence of Mexico and declared the equality of all Mexicans under the law. Black slavery and indigenous tribute were abolished. On one point the document was not so tolerant: only the Catholic religion would be permitted in the new Republic of Mexico. In 1815, his guerrilla force nearly wiped out, Morelos was finally captured, tried, and executed.

The first phase of the Mexican independence movement, then, was dominated by priests and most of the followers were indigenous or mestizos. According to Mariano Cuevas, between 1810 and 1815, royalists executed some 125 priests. A member of the *audiencia*, or ruling board, declared in 1812: "No one can deny that the ecclesiastics were the principal authors of this rebellion."[4] There were, of course, some Creole officers, such as Ignacio Allende and Guadalupe Victoria (later to become president of the country), who lent their expertise to the movement. In South America, Simón Bolívar, a rational strategist with no messianic pretensions, alluded to what he termed the "fanaticism" of the Mexican insurgents. But, he noted with approval, "political enthusiasm has been mixed with religion to produce a vehement fervor in favor of the sacred cause of liberty."[5]

The independence of Mexico was finally achieved by the very persons and social groups that had opposed Hidalgo and Morelos. In 1821 Agustín de Iturbide, a Creole officer who had fought against the insurgent priests, seized power and ended Spanish rule. Under his 1821 Plan of Iguala, Iturbide summoned all Mexicans to stand for the three principles of religion, union, and liberty.

To understand why the conservatives now wanted independence, it is necessary to take into account changing circumstances in Spain. In 1812, while Ferdinand was still held in captivity by Napoleon, delegates from America and Spain had gathered together in Cádiz and wrote a liberal constitution that proclaimed Spain a constitutional monarchy. But in 1814 Ferdinand returned to power and rejected the constitution. In 1820, however, the military commander, Rafael de Riego, rebelled and imposed the 1812 constitution on the king, who was forced to accept it. The liberals who seized power decreed a

---

4 Nancy Farriss, *Crown and Clergy in Colonial Mexico, 1759–1821. The Crisis of Ecclesiastical Privilege* (London: Athlone Press, 1968), 200.
5 Leopoldo Zea (ed.), *Fuentes de la cultura latinoamericana* (Mexico: Fondo de Cultura Económica, 1993), 1: 31.

series of anticlerical measures: elimination of ecclesiastical immunity, suppression of the Jesuits (for the second time), and the confiscation of several monasteries.

At that point the Creoles in Mexico and in almost all the rest of Latin America decided that they preferred independence and the preservation of their traditional values rather than life under an anticlerical government in Spain. When Iturbide proclaimed the Plan of Iguala, he was supported by the bishops and the vast majority of the clergy. The constitutional assembly which met between 1823 and 1824 established the Catholic religion as the only one permitted. Of the 144 elected deputies, one half were lawyers and one quarter were clerics.

An important representative figure among the clergy was Fray Servando Teresa de Mier, cited earlier. Mier, a Dominican priest, was exiled to Spain in 1794 after delivering a sermon in which he declared that thanks to the Virgin of Guadalupe, Mexico no longer needed Spain for spiritual guidance. He escaped and went to France, at which point he became a perpetual conspirator for the cause. He left the Dominicans in 1802 and became a secular priest. He later fought with the Spanish against Napoleon's invasion, visited London and Philadelphia, and finally ended up a member of Mexico's first constituent congress. He was conservative in religion, yet liberal in politics. He rejected the antireligious excesses of the French revolution, but he admired the political system of the United States. As a member of congress, he opposed religious toleration, but he also opposed Iturbide, who had himself crowned emperor of Mexico. Under pressure Iturbide finally abandoned Mexico, returning in 1824 only to be executed as a traitor.

Moving from north to south, we will now examine the Church in the independence movements of the rest of Latin America.

The Viceroyalty of New Granada

Independence movements broke out early on everywhere in New Grenada (Venezuela, Colombia, and Ecuador): Quito in 1809, and Caracas, Cartagena, and Bogotá in 1810. In August, 1809, a small group of notables, among them several clergymen, signed the act of independence of Ecuador in the church of San Agustín. But in 1810 the conspirators were all rounded up and executed by an army sent from Lima. In the next phase of the independence movement, José Cuero y Caicedo, a native of Cali, Colombia, became one of the few bishops who openly supported independence. In 1811, he was elected a member of a new junta that convened a constituent congress, and he himself was elected its president. In his support of Ecuadoran independence he was opposed by the bishops of Cuenca and Guayaquil. In 1813 when a royalist army seized Quito, Cuero y Caicedo was exiled to Lima, where he died in 1815.

In July 1810 the Creoles of Bogotá deposed the viceroy and installed a junta, which convoked an electoral college to prepare the way for a constituent assembly. Among the forty-three members of the electoral college, ten were ecclesiastics elected from both the secular and religious clergy. The clerical presence was so noticeable that the first president of Cundinamarca (one of the several regional states that proclaimed its independence), Jorge Tadeo Lozano, qualified Colombia's emancipation as a "clerical revolution."

In Venezuela, as everywhere, there were clergy for and against the cause. In April, 1810, a group of notables in Caracas overthrew the Spanish authorities and convened a congress that declared independence in July, 1811. Seven of the thirty-seven deputies in the first congress were priests. The newly arrived archbishop, Narciso Coll y Prat, a Spaniard, played a most ambiguous role. He initially accepted independence and swore fidelity to the new government, and later celebrated a mass to inaugurate the new congress. But in March, 1812, a devastating earthquake struck Caracas and the surrounding areas. He attributed the earthquake to God's anger over the patriots' rebellion. When royalist forces retook Venezuela in July of that year he openly welcomed them. But his accommodating stances placed him under a cloud, and won him no friends on either side. In 1816 the Spanish authorities sent him back to Spain, where he was named bishop of Palencia in 1822, the year he died.

The Viceroyalty of Peru

Lima, like Mexico City, was a center of royal power and wealth. As such it was a stronghold of resistance to the independence movement. Independence finally came to the viceregal capital when José de San Martín entered in July 1821. But there were independence movements in the interior provinces long before that date, especially in Cuzco. The rebellion of Tupac Amaru II in 1780 was the most serious pre-independence movement in Peru. Although most of Tupac Amaru's followers were indigenous and mestizos, some Creole priests were sympathetic toward the new Inca, although none actively participated in it. Spanish authorities captured and executed Túpac Amaru in 1781 and his movement was bloodily repressed.

As a result, there were no other notable uprisings until 1812 in Huánuco, in the southern Andes, when the indigenous populace rose up in protest over the abuses of local authorities and Spanish merchants. But the uprising was supported by local Creoles and mestizos. Several religious stood out as ringleaders: Friar Marcos Durán Martel, an Agustinian and a native of Huánuco; Ignacio Villavicencio, originally from Cuzco; and Mariano Aspiazu, a Mercedarian who had participated in the Creole conspiracy in Quito. Some of the priests were pastors of Indian *doctrinas* (similar to parishes) and therefore sympathetic to the Indians' complaints. Later, during the trials, Durán was accused of being the "captain of the Indians and mestizos in rebellion."[6] He was sentenced to serve in a hospital in Ceuta for ten years and forbidden to ever return to Peru. One Spanish priest, who reported to the archbishop of Lima, had less than kindly thoughts about the clergy in Huánuco: "Of all the clergy, friars and principal citizens in Huánuco, there are not even four who do not deserve to be hanged."[7]

The most important independence movement in Peru broke out in Cuzco in 1814. The previous year several Creoles, notably the Angulo brothers, who were landowners, attempted to seize power in the name of the 1812 Cádiz constitution. In 1814 they tried again and succeeded. They also placed at the front of the conspiracy Mateo Pumachua, an Indian leader who had fought against Túpac Amaru. Pumacahua appealed to the indigenous people, who promptly followed him. The bishop, José de Pérez Armendáriz, a Creole, was known to be sympathetic to the movement. Pumacahua led a force of 5,000 Indians and mestizos toward Arequipa, while two other armies headed for Ayacucho and Upper Peru. In Arequipa, Pumacahua summoned a public assembly and argued in favor of the constitution of Cádiz. But in the midst of cries of fidelity to Ferdinand VII, Mariano José de Arce, a local priest, termed Ferdinand a "despot" and called for absolute separation from Spain. Years later, Arce was elected to Peru's constituent congress. But most *Arequipeños* were not so radical and voted in favor of fidelity to the king, and welcomed the royalist army when it finally arrived. The army then set out in pursuit of Pumacahua, captured him, and had him and the Angulo brothers tried and executed.

In the meantime, Ildefonso de las Muñecas, a priest originally from Argentina and one of the conspirators in Cuzco, led an army to Upper Peru, where he was captured and killed in 1816. He is commemorated today as a forerunner of the independence of Bolivia. The army that headed for Huamanga was commanded by Manuel Hurtado and Mariano Angulo and accompanied by the chaplain, José Gabriel Béjar. They, too, were captured, tried, and executed.

---

6 Ella Dunbar Temple (ed.), *Conspiraciones y rebeliones en el siglo XIX*, tome III, vol. 1 of *Colección documental de la independencia del Perú* (Lima: Comisión Nacional del Sesquicentenario de la Independencia, 1971), xli.
7 Ibid., tome III, vol. 4, p. 219.

Another priest involved in the Cuzco conspiracy, Francisco Carrascón, was one of the few Spanish-born clergy who fought for the cause. He was captured and sent to Spain, where he was imprisoned. The bishop, Armendáriz, who died in 1818 at the age of ninety, was not touched because of his advanced years. After the rebellion had been thoroughly put down, the royal audience of Cuzco imposed a drastic reform of the clergy and closed the local seminary. From that moment until the arrival of San Martín and Bolivar in 1821 there were no other notable pro-independence movements in Peru.

When San Martín entered Lima in 1821 he was unopposed, as the royalist army had already abandoned the viceregal capital. In an open *cabildo* held on July 15, the leading citizens signed the act of independence. Among the first signatures was that of the archbishop, Bartolomé Las Heras, who had cautiously condemned the movement until it became a fait accompli. In spite of his gesture of acceptance, he was forced to return to Spain. But the Creole clergymen who supported the cause, although a minority, were hailed as heroes. In the constitutional congress of 1822–1823, of the seventy-nine deputies and substitutes who were elected, twenty-eight were lawyers and twenty-six were priests. Luna Pizarro, a priest from Arequipa and later archbishop of Lima, was elected president of the congress. Most of the clergy voted with the majority in favor of religious tolerance, but under pressure from many leading citizens of Lima, the delegates backed down and proscribed the practice of non-Catholic religions.

The Church in Upper Peru fit the general pattern. The three bishops (La Paz, Chuquisaca, and Santa Cruz) all opposed independence. The bishop of La Paz, Remigio La Santa, even organized the defense of the city. The Franciscans in the missionary college of Tarija all vehemently supported the royalist cause. The clergy who did support independence were a minority. Perhaps more typical of the rest was Matías Terrazas, a leading Creole clergyman in Chuquisaca (today Sucre) who managed to straddle both sides of the fence. Among his many important positions, he was vice rector of the seminary, a professor at the university, and a lawyer for the *Audiencia*; at one time he had been proposed as a candidate for coadjutor bishop. During the entire independence period he was a faithful servant of the royalist bishop, Benet María Moixó, a Catalan. But when the insurgent armies arrived in 1825, he immediately embraced the cause and seconded General José Antonio de Sucre's suggestion that a campaign be organized to win over the local pastors to the cause. At the same time, he was a staunch defender of the Church's privileges. He opposed a decree of Bolívar that aimed to confiscate Church wealth and suppress monasteries and convents.

Río de la Plata

The clergy also played important roles in all the political events leading up to Argentina's independence. In 1806 and 1807 the British, anticipating the collapse of the Spanish empire, invaded Buenos Aires. The local citizens threw the invaders out, a feat that emboldened them to take even more radical steps. In May 1810, a town assembly of 251 notables, including twenty-seven ecclesiastics, voted to depose the viceroy and establish a junta to rule in the name of the king. The bishop of Buenos Aires, Benito de Lué, who was present, opposed the move, and later the bishop of Tucumán, also a Spaniard, strongly opposed independence. But the bishop of Salta, Nicolás Videla del Pino, a Creole, later to become the auxiliary bishop of Buenos Aires, gave his blessing to the cause. The nine-man junta included one secular priest, Manuel Alberti, who had strongly supported the move to depose the viceroy in the general council. Later, in December, the junta was expanded to include new members from the interior provinces, among them, Gregorio Funes, one of the most important protagonists of Argentina's independence and early republican history. Funes, the dean of the Cathedral of Córdoba and rector of the University, was subsequently elected president of the junta.

After a period of anarchy, in 1816 a constituent congress was convened in Tucumán. Of the thirty representatives, twelve were ecclesiastics: two religious, three canons, and seven secular priests. In July the congress declared the independence of the "United Provinces of South America." The following year the congress moved to Buenos Aires and Funes was elected its president. The new constitution was finally promulgated in 1819.

Chile

In Chile, a relatively autonomous captaincy general belonging to the viceroyalty of Peru, the majority of the clergy was pro-royalist. According to the Chilean historian José Toribio Medina, of the 190 secular priests in Santiago, only twenty-two were pro-independence, and of the 500 religious clergy, only seventy supported the cause. The bishops of Santiago and Concepción were also staunch defenders of the king. But the supporters of independence were not lacking in stature. They included the auxiliary bishop of Santiago, Rafael Andreas, and the vicar general of the diocese, José Ignacio Cienfuegos, later named the bishop of Concepción. In fact, the pro-independence faction among the clergy seized control of the process from the beginning.

Two brothers, Vicente Larraín, a canon, and Joaquín Larraín, a Mercedarian, planned the town assembly and drew up the list of the members to make up the junta that assumed power in September, 1811. Another religious, the prior of the Dominican monastery, Marcos Vásquez, was credited with persuading the governor, Mateo de Toro y Zambrano, to attend the town council, thus lending it legitimacy.

The priests who conspired to control the process, unlike the Mexican insurgents, belonged to families that made up the commercial and landowning elite of Chile. Of the 200 or so members invited to the town assembly, thirty-eight were clergymen, most of whom favored self-government. The assembly elected a junta, to rule in the name of the king. The junta in turn convened a constituent congress that met in July 1811, but in September José María Carrera, a Creole leader, backed by Joaquín Larraín, now an ex-Mercedarian, but still a priest, seized control of the congress. However, the congress did not last long because in December Carrera, not pleased with the results, dissolved it. During this period, known as the "Patria Vieja" (1811–1814), other clergymen played prominent roles. Among them, Camilo Henríquez, a religious, published a pro-independence newspaper, *La Aurora de Chile*. By 1814 royalist forces had regained control of Santiago and the first phase of independence ended.

But in 1817 José de San Martín and Bernardo O'Higgins marched into Santiago together and proclaimed the independence of Chile. O'Higgins expelled the pro-royalist bishop, José Santiago Rodríguez, to Mendoza, then a part of Chile, and installed José Ignacio Cienfuegos as the ecclesiastical governor. O'Higgins summoned the people to sign the book acknowledging their acceptance of independence. Surprising enough, even though independence was a fait accompli, only sixty-eight of the 200 members of the secular clergy, and 175 of the 600 members of the religious clergy, signed the book.

In spite of their minority position, the pro-independence clergy continued to play prominent roles in the next several constituent congresses. For a while Cienfuegos, the head of the diocese of Santiago, was also named president of the senate under O'Higgins. In the constitutional congress convened by O'Higgins in 1822, eight deputies out of thirty were priests. But the 1822 constitution was never put into effect, and under pressure from local citizens, unhappy with his authoritarian tendencies, O'Higgins himself resigned that year and went into exile. A new constitution was written in 1823 and another one in 1828. In all of these constitutions Catholicism was proclaimed the religion of the state to the exclusion of all others. After Chile made its peace with Rome toward the end of the decade, Cienfuegos was named bishop of

Concepción and Manuel Vicuña Larraín, a neutral figure who curried favor with all sides, was named bishop of Santiago.

The Papacy

Two popes, Pius VII in 1816 and Leo XII in 1824, exhorted the Latin Americans to remain faithful to their legitimate sovereign, Ferdinand VII. But these popes were prompted to write their exhortations by Ferdinand himself via his ambassador to the Vatican, Antonio Vargas Laguna, a layman. As a consequence of royal patronage, the pope had little say about the Latin American Church, and most of his information about Latin America came from the Spanish ambassador. Even the Jesuits, who did have direct contact with their general in Rome, were now gone. On several occasions the Mexican insurgents attempted to communicate with Bishop John Carroll in Baltimore, and through him inform the pope of their intentions. But these letters apparently never made it past the Spanish authorities. Vargas Laguna himself prepared part of the papal texts, which included high praises of "our beloved son Ferdinand," but that also put Latin American independence in the worst possible light: "it is to be observed how ... books and pamphlets are disseminated which disdain, despise and make the ecclesiastical and civil powers hateful."[8]

The comparison that loomed in the background was, of course, the highly anticlerical and antireligious French Revolution. Yet Vargas failed in what he most wanted: neither papal document contains an outright condemnation of the independence movement, much less the threat of excommunication. In fact, the king later expressed his dissatisfaction with that failure in a letter to the pope. Nevertheless, once the letters were in the hands of the king, the pope had no control over their publication. The king had the 1824 letter published in 1825, months after the last battles of independence in Peru. When he learned of that condemnation, a Chilean liberal, Vial del Río, commented somewhat bitterly: "What have we Americans done for the universal pastor to despise us and hold us in contempt?"[9]

In fact, however, the pope did attempt to contact Latin America before independence was finally secured. In 1824 Leo XII sent a mission headed by Giovanni Muzi, with the title of "apostolic vicar," to Argentina and Chile. The purpose of the mission was to establish direct contact between Latin America and the papacy and name new bishops for vacant dioceses, but

---

8 Pedro de Leturia, *Relaciones entre la Santa Sede e Hispanoamérica, II: Época de Bolivar (1800–1835)* (Caracas: Sociedad Bolivariana de Venezuela, 1959), 266–269.
9 Ibid., p. 278.

without necessarily recognizing the independence of the new republics. Muzi was coldly received in Buenos Aires by Bernardo Rivadavia, the leading liberal minister and a staunch regalist who resented papal interference in internal Church affairs. When Muzi reached Santiago he discovered that the problem was not so much the government, but the Church. The ecclesiastical governor, José Ignacio Cienfuegos, who had been named by O'Higgins, entertained hopes of being named auxiliary bishop, but Muzi mistrusted him and resented government pressure to have him promoted. Finally, he returned to Rome without having accomplished anything. He did, however, exchange courteous letters with Bolívar, who invited Muzi to Lima to name bishops to fill in several vacancies. But Muzi was already leaving America behind when the invitation arrived.

In the end, the new republics established relations with the Vatican through concordats – agreements between the Vatican and secular governments – by which each government proposed candidates for vacant dioceses, but Rome made the final selection. Within fifteen to twenty years after independence the Church was nearly fully restored, with new bishops, all Latin Americans, and the seminaries, closed during the wars, reopened. As a result, the Latin American Church, which in colonial times was in reality a Spanish Church, now officially came under the direct control of Rome. The Church in Brazil did not come under the direct jurisdiction of the papacy until after the fall of the monarchy in 1889.

But this process of Romanization was fraught with ambiguities. On the one hand, Latin American Catholics could look to Rome for inspiration in their struggles with anticlerical liberals. On the other hand, the priests and bishops, trained in the new Romanized seminaries, imposed a Church model that was often divorced from the realities of Latin America. At the same time the liberal priests who supported independence were marginalized within the Church. By mid-century, the bonds of solidarity that had drawn liberals and priests together in a common cause during the wars of independence no longer existed.

Cuba

The independence of Latin America ended where it had begun: in the Caribbean. Haiti, which then included Santo Domingo, won its independence from France in 1804, but because the majority of the clergy was either French- or Spanish-born, it had little sympathy for the cause. But in Cuba, the last important colony to achieve independence, Cuban-born priests participated in the numerous conspiracies and uprisings that broke out during the nineteenth century. In particular, Felix Varela, a secular priest, is considered one of the most important precursors of that island's independence. Born in Havana in 1788, Varela taught philosophy at San Carlos Seminary and in 1822 was elected a representative to the Cortes in Spain. He proposed abolishing slavery and recognizing the independence of the rest of Latin America. He also voted to take away the king's power. But in 1823 France invaded Spain to reimpose absolutism, and Varela and other liberals were condemned to death. But Varela managed to flee to New York, where he published *El Habanero*, a subversive newspaper that called for the independence of Cuba. He later served as vicar general of the diocese of New York, and retired to St. Augustine, Florida, where he died in 1853.

During the Ten Years War (1868–1878) many Cuban-born priests, who made up the majority of the rural clergy, fought for the cause. Some were executed; others were imprisoned or exiled. Again, in the 1895 uprising led by José Martí, a few priests also participated, although in lesser numbers. Noteworthy among them was Guillermo González Arocha, who served as a captain in the revolutionary army and later as a representative to the Cuban congress. Naturally, the Spanish clergy, who predominated in parishes and religious schools in the cities, opposed the movement. Nevertheless, the American occupying force, especially under General Leonard Wood, treated the Church benignly, and even helped resolve the Church's property claims against the colonial government. At the same time, the American occupiers, fully in harmony with the sentiments of Cuban liberals, separated church and state in 1899.

Remaining Questions

That the Catholic Church played a key role in the independence of Latin America is beyond doubt. But there are some remaining unanswered questions. Did the Creole clergy fight as priests or as Creoles? Was there a substantial difference between a Creole lawyer and a Creole priest, both of whom fought and served together in the constituent congresses? Most likely, the insurgent Creole priests made no such distinctions in their own minds. In one important area the difference was crucial: the priests alone had the means and the ability to influence the indigenous population, for or against the cause.

But this raises another question: Were the priests social reformers? Certainly, both Hidalgo and Morelos proclaimed social and pro-Indian reforms. But most of the liberal priests in the constituent assemblies were rather ideological liberals (democracy, the rule of law, separation of powers), but not social reformers. Of course, they believed that the Indian could be uplifted through education, but not through immediate social change. Finally, with the exception of Peru, very few of the priests who fought for independence believed in religious tolerance. On the positive side, one can safely argue that the pro-independence priests and religious, Viscardo y Guzmán with his *Letter*, or Hidalgo and Morelos in Mexico under the banner of Our Lady of Guadalupe, lent a religious legitimacy to the cause of Latin American independence that it would not have had without them.

Bibliography and Suggested Readings

Aparicio, Manuel Jesús. *El clero patriota en la revolución de 1814*. Cuzco, 1974.
Araneda, Fidel. *Historia de la Iglesia de Chile*. Santiago: Ediciones Paulinas, 1986.
Barnadas, Josep. "La Iglesia ante la emancipación en Bolivia." *Perú, Bolivia, Ecuador*. Vol. VIII of *Historia general de la Iglesia en América Latina*, 183–192. CEHILA (Comisión de Estudios de Historia de la Iglesia en América Latina). Salamanca: Sígueme, 1987.
Basadre, Jorge. *Historia de la República del Perú, 1822–1933*. 18 vols. 9th ed. Lima: el Comercio, 2005.
Batllori, Miguel. *La cultura hispano-italiana de los jesuitas expulsos*. Madrid: Biblioteca Románica-Hispánica; Editorial Gredos, 1966.
Brading, David A. *Church and State in Bourbon Mexico. The Diocese of Michoacán, 1749–1810*. Cambridge: Cambridge University Press, 1994.
    The First America. The Spanish Monarchy, Creole Patriots, and the Liberal State, 1492–1867. New York: Cambridge University Press, 1991.
Connaughton, Brian F. *Clerical Ideology in a Revolutionary Age. The Guadalajara Church and the Idea of the Mexican Nation, 1788–1853*. Trans. Mark Alan Healey Calgary, Canada: University of Calgary Press; Boulder: University Press of Colorado, 2003.
Cuevas, Mariano. *Historia de la Iglesia en Mexico*. 5 vols. 5th ed. Mexico, D.F.: Editorial Patria, 1947.
Churruca Paláez, Agustín. *El pensamiento insurgente de Morelos*. Mexico, D.F.: Editorial Porrúa, 1983.
Dunbar Temple, Ella, ed. *Conspiraciones y rebeliones en el siglo XIX*. tome 4, vol. 1 of *Colección documental de la Independencia del Perú*. Lima: Comisión Nacional del Sesquicentenario de la Independencia del Perú, 1971.
Eguiguren, Luis Antonio. *La revolución de 1814*. Lima: Oficina Tipográfica de "La Opnión Nacional," 1914.
Farriss, Nancy. *Crown and Clergy in Colonial Mexico, 1759–1821. The Crisis of Ecclesiastical Privilege*. London: Athlone Press, 1968.
Fisher, John. *Bourbon Peru, 1750–1824*. Liverpool: Liverpool University Press, 2003.
Fisher, Lilian Estelle. *Champion of Reform. Manuel Abad y Queipo*. New York: Library Publishers, 1955.
Gallagher, Mary A. Y. *Imperial Reform and the Struggle for Regional Self-Determination: Bishops, Intendants and Creole Elites in Arequipa, Peru (1748–1816)*. PhD diss., The City University of New York, 1978.

González, Fernán. "La Iglesia ante la emancipación en Colombia." *Colombia y Venezuela.* Vol. II of *HIstoria general de la Iglesia en América Latina.* 249–275. CEHILA (Comisión de Estudios de Historia de la Iglesia en América Latina). Salamanca: Ediciones Sígueme, 1981.

Hamil, Jr., Hugh M. *The Hidalgo Revolt. Prelude to the Mexican Independence.* Gainesville: University of Florida Press, 1966; reprint, Westport, CT: Greenwood Press, 1981.

Klaiber, Jeffrey. *The Jesuits in Latin America, 1549–2000.* St. Louis: The Institute of Jesuit Sources, 2009.

Larrúa Guedes, Salvador. *Grandes figures y sucesos de la Iglesia cubana.* Santo Domingo: Publicaciones del Centro de Estudios Sociales P. Juan Montalvo, S.J., 1996.

Leturia, Pedro de. *Relaciones entre la Santa Sede e Hispanomérica.* 3 vols. Caracas: Sociedad Boliviariana de Venezuela, 1959.

Maza, Manuel. *El clero cubano y la independencia. Las investigaciones de Francisco González del Valle (1881–1942).* Santo Domingo: Centro de Estudios Sociales P. Juan Montalvo, S.J., 1993.

Mecham, J. Lloyd. *Church and State in Latin America.* Rev. ed. Chapel Hill: The University of North Carolina Press, 1966.

Mier, Servando Teresa de. *Historia de la revolución de Nueva España, antiguamente Anahuac o verdadero origen y causa de ella con la relación de sus progresos hasta el presente.* Fascimile ed. With premilinary study by Manuel Calvillo. 2 vols. 3rd ed. Mexico, D.F.: Instituto Mexicano de Seguro Social, 1980.

O'Gorman, Edmundo. *Fray Servando Teresa de Mier: Ideario politico.* Caracas: Biblioteca Ayacucho, 1978.

Rieu-Millan, Marie Laure. *Los diputados americanos en las cortes de Cádiz.* Madrid: Consejo Superior de Investigaciones Científicas, 1990.

Rodríguez O., Jaime E. *Mexico in the Age of Democratic Revolutions, 1750–1850.* Boulder, CO: Lynne Rienner, 1994.

Romero Carranza, Ambrosio, Alberto Rodríguez Varela, and Eduardo Ventura Flores Pirán. *Historia política de la Argentina.* 3 vols. Buenos Aires: Ediciones Pannedille, 1970.

Ronan, Charles E. *Francisco Javier Clavijero, S.J. (1731–1787), Figure of the Mexican Enlightenment: His Life and Works.* Rome: Institutum Historicum S.I.; Chicago: Loyola University Press, 1977.

Juan Ignacio Molina. The World's Window on Chile. New York: Peter Lang, 2002.

Salinas, Maximiliano. "La Iglesia ante la emancipación de Chile." *Cono Sur.* Vol. IX of *Historia general de la Iglesia en América Latina.* 255–270. CEHILA (Comisión de Estudios de Historia de la Iglesia en América Latina). Salamanca: Sígueme, 1994.

Schwaller, Robert. "The Episcopal Succession in Spanish America, 1800–1850." *The Americas.* vol. 24, no. 3 (January, 1968): 207–271.

Sparks Miró-Quesada, Consuelo. *The Role of the Clergy during the Struggle of Independence in Peru.* PhD diss., The University of Pittsburgh, 1972.

St. Clair Segurado, Eva María. *Expulsión y exilio de la Provincia jesuítica Mexicana (1767–1820).* Alicante: Publicaciones de la Universidad de Alicante, 2005.

Stoetzer, O. Carlos. *The Scholastic Roots of the Spanish American Revolution.* New York: Fordham University Press, 1978.

Taylor, William. *Ministros de lo sagrado*. Trans. Oscar Mazín Gómez and Paul Kersey. 2 vols. Zamora, Michoacán: El Colegio de Michoacán; Mexico, D.F.: Secretaría de Gobernación; El Colegio de México, 1999.

Tibesar, Antonine. "The Alternativa: A Study in Spanish-Creole Relations in Seventeenth-Century Peru." *The Americas*. 11, no. 3 (January, 1955): 229–283.

——— "The Lima Pastors, 1750–1820: Their Origins and Studies as Taken from their Autobiographies." *The Americas*. 20, no. 1 (July, 1971): 39–56.

——— "The Peruvian Church at the Time of Independence in the Light of Vatican II." *The Americas*. 26, no. 4 (April, 1970): 349–375.

Vargas Ugarte, Rubén. *El episcopado en los tiempos de la emancipación sudamericana*. 3rd ed. Lima, 1962.

Viscardo y Guzmán, Juan Pablo. *Carta a los españoles americanos*. With a foreword by David A. Brading. Providence, RI: The John Carter Brown Library, 2002.

Zea, Leopoldo, ed. *Fuentes de la cultura latinoamericana*. 3 vols. Mexico, D.F.: Fondo de Cultura Económica, 1993.

Zevallos, Noe, ed. *Toribio de Mendoza*. Tome I, vol. 2 of *Colección documental de la Independencia del Perú*. Lima: Comisión Nacional del Sesquicentenario de la Independencia del Perú, 1972.

17
Liberalism, Anticlericalism, and Antireligious Currents in the Nineteenth Century

MATTHEW BUTLER

"I ate monks for breakfast; I had monks for lunch; I breathed monks; they dominated everything." Thus Peruvian Positivist and anarchist Manuel González Prada – like other anticlericals, a seminary truant prone to fist-shaking at God – remembered his nineteenth-century childhood. In a general sense, González Prada's sarcasm reminds us that exponents of nineteenth-century radicalism or irreligion were, almost invariably, also anticlerical because of the clergy's historic weight as a corps. It is true, conversely, that not all anticlericals were liberal: as we shall see, there was a conservative anticlericalism espoused by mid-century *caudillos* such as Juan Manuel Rosas in Argentina or Rafael Carrera in Guatemala. Anticlericalism was the common denominator, however; hence for this chapter it is perhaps simplest to explore all three parts of the problem using that protean concept, and to treat liberalism and scientific unbelief – insofar as they embodied an approach to Churches – as subsets of a larger anticlerical family.

Anticlericalism, it is often stated, is a nineteenth-century neologism that describes a phenomenon as old as Christianity. By the same token, we should evaluate the spread of anticlerical ideas over the *longue durée*, or at least from the perspective of Latin America's "long" nineteenth century, which conventionally spanned the mid-eighteenth century to the early twentieth. It is the eighteenth century, in fact, that saw the development of Latin America's most venerable anticlerical ideology in the form of regalism: that is, Gallican churchmanship alloyed to Bourbon absolutism and Americanized, initially, within the legal device of royal patronage of the colonial Church.

This Catholic Enlightenment tradition, it should be noted, overrode the more cooperative spirit that had imbued patronage prior to 1700, when the Habsburgs permitted the Church vast corporate privileges in recognition of its role as co-partner in administering the Americas. Yet it was the statist tradition that was inherited by, and accounts for much that was paradoxical about, later generations of anticlericals, starting with nineteenth-century liberals. For all that these reformers talked of separating Church and state, the temptation to impose invasive controls over religion was too great to resist. Regalism – royal authority, especially in Church affairs – not liberalism, thus provides our basic continuity.

Adjusting the periodization is necessary for reasons other than disentangling anticlericalism's ideological taproots. First, it makes it possible to avoid giving too much causal weight to independence, which was achieved in the 1820s but often took the form of conservative wars against the anticlericalism emanating from the Cádiz Cortes (Spain's first "national" assembly, held during the Napoleonic occupation in 1810). Independence *was* vital in that it widened cracks in the Church–state compact and upset the legal scaffold of patronage that had contained them; yet the underlying problems, and anticlerical proposals, were older. Second, one must not imbue political conservatism with a spirit of sacral monarchism, which is the next pitfall if we do not disaggregate anticlericalism and liberalism.

This association, admittedly, is a staple of reactionary Catholic historiography, which lionizes strongmen such as Rosas as restorers of throne-and-altar harmony. Again, appearances are deceptive: *rosismo* (Rosas' political project) may not have been so overtly anticlerical as Argentine liberalism, but in practice *el restaurador* was as destructive of the ecclesiastical writ as Rivadavia or Sarmiento, two later Argentine leaders who were patently anticlerical in both outlook and deed. The Church was his, yet Rosas used this instrument to propagate a messianic political religion, not to restore the plenitude of clerical privileges.

Until the 1880s, in fact, when the anticlerical paradigm fell under the influence of Positivism, it is simplest to say that liberals and conservatives were anticlerical in different ways. They applied the regalist credo differentially and in line with specific, if not contradictory, ideas about religion and the Church. Despite its war cry of *religión y fueros* (religion and special Church privilege) it was not the case that conservatism was perforce "clericalist," let alone beneficial to the Church; or that liberalism, if often anticlerical, was necessarily irreligious or secularizing.

With a view to describing this plurality of anticlericalisms, it may be useful to define the term in the abstract. One venerable theory views it as bourgeois mystification, a way of sublimating class antagonisms in symbolic violence. In a similar vein, others see anticlericalism as a feature of new democracies with Catholic parties and peasant electorates: "in these conditions,"

Chadwick writes, "God was a political slogan, anti-God another slogan."[1] These definitions are unworkably Eurocentric, and also collapse anticlericalism's ideological dimension, reducing it to a function of mass democracy. Others define anticlericalism as opposition to the power of the clergy, which makes the concept dynamic and allows anticlericalism to evolve in response to diversifying clericalisms (hence "political," "social," and "educational" variants exist). This, though, presents us with an excessively determined constant, anticlericalism as eternal riposte. That is correct in that the word's prefix carries a negative charge, but ideological in that it echoes the Manichean tropes of anticlericals themselves: hence, clergy are ominous black birds, cassocks flapping like vulture's wings, or sinister papists plotting in the sacristy gloom; anticlericals, by contrast, are the permanent guardians of a nation under siege, like torch-carrying sentinels minted on silver coins.

Yet, as we have stressed, anticlericalism is not objectively a bringer of light, the sun moving across a dial. It can precede clericalism empirically, if not semantically, as at independence. Both Church and state, in addition, thought their association would continue beyond 1820: the discovery that it could not was painful and slow and gave rise to a dialectical hardening of positions on both sides. Yet it still took many anticlericals forty years to abandon the principle of an established Church.

We can solve these apparent contradictions, perhaps, by following René Rémond and seeing anticlericalism as a "positive political ideology," rather than a mere critique, even a kind of faith.[2] As such, lines constricting sacred jurisdiction – making lay what is deemed clerical – can be drawn with infinite looseness or tightness, depending on the positive religious state that is imagined as clericalism's other. Historically, we should note, the division is often made selectively, such that battles occur on specific fronts rather than between total spheres: the critical question at any time may be Church *mortmain* (inalienable land ownership), religious education, the religious orders, or a combination. Nor is there an objective frontier between the sacred and profane orders, given that both are intrinsic to Christianity as a religious system. As a relative concept, finally, anticlericalism bonds easily with other ideologies: Protestantism, deism, liberalism, anarchism, even liberal Catholicism. Often, in fact, these adjuncts will define *what* is clerical, *where* appropriate lines should be drawn. The anticlerical desire to render unto God and Caesar

---

[1] Owen Chadwick, *The Secularization of the European Mind in the Nineteenth Century* (Cambridge: Cambridge University Press, 1975), 124.
[2] René Rémond, *L'anticléricalisme en France de 1815 à nos jours* (Paris: Fayard, 1976), 3–16.

is constant, therefore, but is recalibrated according to changing contexts and the more precise ideological syntheses that occur over time.

With these caveats made, it becomes possible to develop a historical typology that distinguishes among anticlericalisms. Thus Jeffrey Klaiber identifies post-independence liberalism, mid-century constitutionalism, and "radical" (scientific) anticlericalism as key types, which is suggestive but downplays the eighteenth-century origins of later clerophobia and the radicalism (even theological angst) of some nonscientific anticlericalism.[3] Jean Meyer, meanwhile, sees a 170-year offensive against the Church occurring in three "movements": the first, from 1750 to 1850, saw Bourbon and republican elites lead the charge against Rome and accentuate patronal rights over reformed (proto-) national Churches; the second, from roughly 1840 to 1880, saw liberals seek to separate Church–state prerogatives but in a way that still suggested a reformist concept of religion, now puritanical and deistic, rather than metaphysical neutrality; while the third movement corresponds roughly to the period 1870–1930, and was marked by the advance of scientific politics.[4]

Meyer's orchestral metaphor is appropriate in that it captures anticlericalism's complex phrasing, given that early refrains – plans for national Churches, patronage decrees, deportations of Jesuits – were often reprised in subsequent phases. If no crude teleology is possible, it is still apparent that a major shift occurred from the 1870s. Previously the emphasis was on *reforming* the Church and purifying religion in line with some sort of Christian millennium.

That myth was often primitive, sometimes colonial; but the idea of return – retying a thread to Christianity's golden age in search of a nonclerical, suitably *republican* Church – was common. It emerges in popular novellas as late as Altamirano's *La navidad en las montañas* (Mexico, 1871). Henceforth, religion itself, not just its rotting ecclesial props, was dismissed. Christianity was not an antique treasure in need of excavation, or a Franciscan codex in need of fresh color, but an intellectual fossil symbolizing an immature phase in human evolution. For Positivists, religion belonged *in* the past, not just to it; they possessed a Darwinian confidence in its extinction and desired to hasten its demise as a philosophical proposition through education. With God dead, Churches would eventually wither on the vine; hence this was still anticlericalism, albeit by a subtler, more materialistic road.

---

3 Jeffrey Klaiber, "Anticlericalism in the Nineteenth and Early Twentieth Centuries," in *Religion and Society in Latin America: Interpretive Essays from Conquest to Present*, eds. Lee Penyak and Walter Petry (Maryknoll NY: Orbis Press, 2009), 157–174.
4 Jean Meyer, *Historia de los cristianos en América Latina, siglos XIX y XX* (Mexico: Editorial Vuelta, 1989), 18.

In what follows, I attempt to distinguish three phases using the aforementioned periodization, setting each within a broader vision of Church–state relations in accordance with our definition of anticlericalism. Thus I will call the first period that of "Church-nations," in which political elites – priests among them – asserted regalist-style rights of national patronage over the Church and called for a reform of the clergy in a context of emerging republicanism. Rarely, if ever, did these anticlericals abandon the assumption that confessional identities should gird civic ones, or question the view that an official, state-run Church was desirable.

A second, "nations-with-Churches" period saw a series of constitutional reorderings in which this older anticlericalism was alloyed to political and economic liberalism. Now anticlericals sought to separate Church and state, instead of deploying the clergy as a government department. As a rule, controversy centered on the problems of ecclesiastical wealth and the Church's social function. Still, liberals retained a benign vision of religion, implicitly Catholicism, as a source of social ethics and cohesion; moreover, they acted on an impulse to "spiritualize" the Church, and for this reason were reluctant to surrender controls over religion. Even an independent Church must preach a cult to the state's liking, which was contradictory; and, because they resisted, uncooperative Churches were cast into a kind of civic limbo by anticlericals like Mosquera in Colombia, not just disestablished but disenfranchised.

In a final, "nations-beyond-Churches" phase, the anticlericals' emphasis was on material progress; this, in the language of the time, would leave Churches behind as relics of a "metaphysical" age preceding a new, Positivist dawn. The Positivists were "Jacobins of the Third Age," as Ramón López Velarde versified in Mexico: instead of mocking clerical feet of clay, the attack switched to the Church's basis in divinity, its last and greatest untruth.

Church-Nations, ca. 1750–1850

In this period the Church was generally conceived as an exclusive (proto-)national community, bonded to a plurality of viceroyalties and latterly nation-states whose authority in matters of ecclesiastical government trumped Rome's. The regalism of the high colony was reasserted after independence, when it was recast, first in republican guise and then, gradually, in union with the principles of liberalism. At this time, however, thoroughly *liberal* reforms – in Morazán's Central America or Gómez Farías's Mexico – tended to be short lived. Mainstream anticlericalism until the 1840s instead involved patriotic wrangling over jurisdiction because the

Church, thinking itself free of colonial patronage, was unwilling to accept new chains simply by decree; and because Latin American elites, conscious of their republics' fragility, refused to accept a position over the Church inferior to the Crown's. At independence, sovereignty over the Church was reinvested in the people, the new regalists claimed; henceforth, the anticlerical noose was drawn tight in jurisdictional matters, especially concerning Rome, but elsewhere loosely.

Anticlericalism in this period tended to be *cismontane*, opposed to the reversion of authority over the American Churches to Rome as a corollary of Spain's defeat. In practical terms, it focused on colonial privileges that thwarted national ecclesiastical sovereignty or created unnatural distinctions between citizens: hence the abolition of *fueros* (the Church's legal forum) and tithes (often replaced with a state salary for priests); the secularization of religious orders and their assimilation into episcopal structures; the mooting of schismatic Churches; and the imposition of ecclesiastical loyalty oaths. This period saw the aggressive assumption of patronage rights; further erasing of the Church's colonial template as an ecclesiastical state-within-the-state; and the priesthood's utilization as forgers of moral citizens in new polities.

In sum, Bourbon anticlericalism abounded, albeit with a new republican purpose. The objective was a streamlined state Catholicism, which was neither strictly liberal nor irreligious. Indeed, this anticlericalism was premised on the rational religion of the Catholic Enlightenment, in which reason meant subjecting Church history to criticism and separating "true" Christianity from falsehood. In Peru, for example, lawyer Manuel Lorenzo de Vidaurre argued in his *Proyecto del Código Eclesiástico* (1830) that the state should deny claims of Roman jurisdictional made later than 300 A.D. as fraudulent, and appoint its own bishops as in early Christianity. Francisco de Paula González Vigil, *cura* of Tacna (also Peru), argued in his *Defensa de la autoridad de los gobiernos y de los obispos contra las pretensiones de la curia romana* (1848–1849) that the Church should be placed under civic-episcopal protectorates. González Vigil's call for "Peter to be Peter" – Christendom's spiritual head, not its bogus emperor – typified this encyclopedic anticlericalism and was unique only in that it placed the blame at the feet of cardinals in the curia, not popes. True religion was a good, González Vigil insisted, "a powerful element of order and tranquility, [and] ineffable stimulus to love and justice," which it was the state's duty to protect.[5]

---

5 Jeffrey Klaiber, *Religion and Revolution in Peru, 1824–1976* (Notre Dame: University of Notre Dame Press, 1977).

Vidaurre's critique was thus made from within Catholicism, and with a presumption that a reformed state Church was a vital agent of national integration. This was not surprising, perhaps, given that Catholicism represented one of few inclusive communities on which a plausible sense of national belonging could be superimposed, at least once the Church was externally reconfigured. As in France, Catholicism was infused with a republican spirit and prescribed as a civil religion. The Church was the citizenry at prayer, and the clergy must assist in preaching the nation into existence. "A bishop is a useful person," as Bolívar observed to Santander when the Spanish prelate of Popoyán swore a constitutional oath in Gran Colombia.[6] Or, as one of Doctor Francia's cronies menacingly put it to the Asunción congress (1814), "the ecclesiastical community will be ... modified in all its parts to the system of liberty of the *Patria*, such that no cleric who is not an adherent of the liberty of the *Patria* or who is not useful to the public cause will confess, practice his ministry, or be given a living."

A spirit of confessional republicanism animated the laws across South America. Gran Colombia's Patronage Law (1824) was modeled on France's *constitution civile* and empowered the executive to present to ecclesiastical posts, deal with Rome, approve Church councils, and regulate clerical discipline. On the Río de la Plata, Rivadavia's *Ley de reforma del clero* (1822) imposed a unitary model based on the *constitution civile* on the Argentine Church. The law placed ecclesiastical authority in the hands of the *cabildo*, which was baptized the "Senate of the Clergy" and subjected to state control. The law also dissolved regular orders, on grounds that only secularized priests could assimilate to republican norms. *Fueros* and tithes also went. In sum, Rivadavia linked devotional life to a republican imaginary by creating a Church whose modes of religious expression and organization were reduced to the minimum. The Church as a single community must reflect, even achieve, the republic; hence national flags festooned the altars and priests were constantly reminded of their dual aspect as citizen-ministers. An aloof, "Tridentine" clergy must become patriotic.

In Paraguay, Doctor José de Gaspar Francia – the doctorate was in theology – carried this tendency to dictatorial extremes. Francia required an oath of clerical loyalty to the nation in 1814; the following year he broke with Rome and governed the Church through a vicar general, Céspedes, whom he invested with episcopal powers. Subsequently Francia racialized the

---

6 Mary Watters, *A History of the Church in Venezuela, 1810–1930* (New York: Ams Press, 1971), 72.

marriage sacrament by preventing unions of Creoles and Europeans, convened a Church council (1819), and secularized the religious (1824). Céspedes surrendered to Francia's posturings, as he put it, because "the Vicar General of the Republic was born a citizen before he became a priest." The fact that *El Supremo* shipped clerical opponents off to insalubrious frontier parishes must have cemented this sense of loyalty.[7]

Mexican statebuilders had similar assumptions, the Dominican friar Servando Teresa de Mier among them. But there was a radical democratic twist. Mier in particular – a correspondent of the *abbé* Grégoire and a notorious anti-*guadalupanista* – admired the constitutional *curés* and called for a self-governing Mexican Church modeled on ancient and revolutionary precedent. Those who denied *the people's* right to govern through elected bishops Mier denounced as "false decretalists, scholastics, ultramontanists, or Molinists," which again showed that the debate was anything but secular.

The arrival in Mexico in 1825 of *Etsi Iam Diu* – a disastrous papal bull urging Spain's ex-colonies to resubmit – pushed Mier to the brink of schism. According to Mier, the pope was Christendom's spiritual chief but any national Church could manage its own succession if it had bishops to consecrate others. If Rome would not yield over independence, Mier wrote, "let us return to the ancient and sacred discipline of the Church; to rule ourselves by those true and legitimate canons."[8] Again, the approach was to marry regalism and a primitive Church ethos in a republican system, whether this led to *El Supremo*'s tyranny, Rivadavia's aristocratic Church senate, or Fray Servando's sovereignty of the faithful. The main emphasis was on the elision of Church and *patria*, but not on liberty of the Church from the state or of society from religion.

This can be seen in cases where conservative rulers followed anticlerical trajectories, in the sense of rolling back the Church's perimeter as an independent sphere, yet did so from a different religious perspective. In Argentina, for example, Juan Manuel de Rosas (1829–1852) was not the clericalist often described but, paradoxically, a religious conservative operating within a regalist framework. Thus, where liberals asserted national rights over the Church to implement a vision of Christian primitivism, Rosas was enamored of the missionary fervor of the sixteenth century. He was obsessed with the notion that a spiritual reconquest could pacify the countryside; thus he sent priests

---

7 John Hoyt Williams, "Dictatorship and the Church: Doctor Francia in Paraguay," *A Journal of Church and State* 15, no. 3 (1973): 419–436.
8 Michael Costeloe, *Church and State in Independent Mexico: A Study of the Patronage Debate, 1821–1857* (London: Royal Historical Society, 1978), 60.

to war-torn parishes and managed their activities through pastoral rides in which he called for the moralization of the *pueblo* through customary prayers and feasts. From 1835, Rosas amplified this approach by inviting Dominicans, Franciscans, and Jesuits to Argentina to undertake springtime missions.

Though the historical underpinnings were different, Rosas's "Federal" Church was no less clerophobic than Rivadavia's. Certainly it did not seek the equilibrium of the early colony, in which an aggregated, corporate Church was the state's partner: rather, a "Habsburg" model was simply applied with "Bourbon" severity. For Rosas shared Rivadavia's conception of the Church as pliant inculcator of state virtues, as was seen in his requirement of an ecclesiastical loyalty oath (1835) and the reading of federalist panegyrics from the pulpit. His extreme violations of the Church's canonical authority extended to placing his own portrait on the altar for veneration, a Supreme Being in *épaulettes*: preachers "must talk about Him, as the savior of the Fatherland," the nuncio in Río complained.

The regulars' opposition to being used as the regime's "vile instruments," as one priest put it, also grew, and in 1841, Rosas expelled the Jesuits.[9] When he died, the Church's decay was exposed: no priests had been ordained for years, which left a decrepit pastorate struggling in sees of staggering size. In sum, Rosas asserted state power to enact a sixteenth-century religious fantasy made dangerous by a cult of *caudillismo*. The endless parish *Te Deums*, in which the faithful donned the restorer's favored red sashes, revealed the "barbaric" character of religious *rosismo* that Sarmiento mocked in his seminal semi-fictional novel about the Rosas regime, *Facundo*: churches were stone corrals, and friars the branding irons with which a lord of the pampas marked his cattle before dispatching them for slaughter.

Rafael Carrera, Guatemala's unlettered, rural *caudillo* (1839–1865), was another conservative believer in pulpit power. The Church he confronted was truly fragile: dotted with interim curacies and so heterodox, a priest wrote in 1838, that boy messiahs performed miracles and mass in candle-lit forest clearings. Under Carrera, the clergy was used to preach a nationalistic, covenanter theology: Guatemalans were bronze Israelites and Carrera a Mosaic redeemer, come to recover the religious traditions wounded by the liberals. Some preferments followed: like Rosas, Carrera permitted the return of the regulars, but not of their property or *fueros*; pastoral visits were also resumed by Bishop García Peláez, with the result that Carrera was

---

9 Roberto di Stefano, "El laberinto religioso de Juan Manuel de Rosas," *Anuario de Estudios Americanos* 63, no. 1 (2006): 19–50.

rewarded with a Concordat (1852) confirming Guatemala's rights of patronage. Despite this agreement, Carrera siphoned off a religious tax known as *la fábrica*, strong-armed the Church to fund his wars against El Salvador, and refused the Jesuits entry in 1845 when García Peláez was slow to pay up. García Peláez also sat ashen-faced as Carrera rebuked him for neglecting Indian parishes or suppressing popular devotions. On occasion – as when crossed by the *cura* of Mazatenango in 1855 – Carrera denounced priests as traitorous scoundrels in need of whipping.

Once again, a conservative patron leeched off the Church, made it a supine accomplice, and forced the clergy to seek terms with popular religion; theology was twisted into a sacral nationalism and pastoral activity farmed out to the regulars. But all was in the interests of republican consolidation. If liberals tended to be hermeneutical scolds, therefore, nagging for biblical reforms, conservatives were neocolonial brutes, protesting love for the Church but raising fists and scrounging money when it suited them. Arguably the prevailing mode of religion varied more than the underlying, instrumental ethos. One-sided patronage – in a word, religious Bourbonism – was the hallmark of anticlericalism in this period for liberal and conservative alike.

Nations with Churches, ca. 1850–1880

Some of these assumptions went forward but generally the emphasis shifted at mid-century as anticlericalism became alloyed more with political and economic liberalism. Physiocratic arguments against Church wealth were not new, but circumstances had prevented their previous application: recall the failed reform of Gómez Farías in Mexico, which ended civil coercion of the tithe (1833) and proposed the expropriation of monastic property. Recall, too, Father Mora's *Disertación sobre la naturaleza y aplicación de las rentas y bienes eclesiásticos*, published in Mexico that year, which argued that natural property rights were vested in individuals, as the building blocks of society, but not associations like churches. Mora did not dispute the Church's social right to property, but as such this could be regulated by the state. The untouchably "spiritual" quality of ecclesiastical wealth was a clerical myth. Such arguments, which questioned the Church's socioeconomic point, were precursory. The liberal onslaught against the Church did not occur for a generation and in a context of political polarization. Even Benito Juárez – icon of Mexico's *Reforma* (1855–1860) – was "illiberal" as governor of Oaxaca (1847–1852) in that he scrutinized providence for guidance, attended Holy Week celebrations, and befriended the clergy.

Civil wars between conservatives and liberals exercised a radicalizing function, however, and not just in Mexico. As the political impossibility of enjoying patronage over a Church that had repositioned itself as a "perfect" – meaning institutionally complete – society sank in, liberals reconceptualized the Church as a separate entity, in the state's purview but not organically linked. If this period was also marked by the celebration of some Roman concordats, principally in Central and Andean America, the more seismic development was Church–state separation in the biggest countries or in those with the biggest Churches, for instance, Mexico and Colombia. As a corollary, religious toleration was introduced; there was a systematic application of liberalism to Church property, such that full-scale nationalizations or dissolutions were effected; and there was a separating-out of religious/secular functions, as Church control over the life-cycle, hence over citizens' institutional allegiances, was ended through the creation of civil registries, liturgies, and cemeteries. Public religious processionals were also banned. In sum, the state strove to become *the* institutional reality through its ritual embrace of the citizen and by secularizing God's acre. Anticlericalism now stressed the clergy's reduction to an inner forum of conscience, leaving the public sphere purged of religion. Although not completely departing from a religious matrix, anticlericalism was becoming *laico* (*laicized*), committed to secular states and the cloistering of religious impulses.

The distinction between privatizing and eradicating religion is key. Few liberals agreed with Ignacio Ramírez, Juárez's justice minister, who proclaimed, "There is no God." On the contrary, most concurred that religion had a moralizing role in national life, and that the Church must work for the flock in this world as in the next. Yet the Church's refusal to accept state patronage after independence revealed how it had forgotten its own injunction to obey the powers that be. As they saw it, liberals did not seek the Church's destruction, just its reduction: they would make the Church go back to spiritual basics by stripping away its accumulated wealth and ending its disastrous political incursions. The assumption was that a Church with few interests would be less self-interested, more mindful of its primordial mission. The congress that produced Mexico's 1857 constitution assembled a choir of pious anticlericals: Juan Díaz Covarrubias contrasted "the true spirit of religion" taught by village *curas* and the cultic pomp of "noble clergy." The Church owned huge estates and lived idly off rent, Guillermo Prieto charged. Melchor Ocampo argued that sacramental fees encouraged evasion, hence bastardy, concubinage, and the throwing away of unshriven corpses; villages squandered money gilding plaster saints, but did not know the Word.

As these complaints suggest, mid-century liberals were not disinterested in a religious sense, content merely to decouple Church and state; nor was their criticism simply economistic. Rather, liberals nurtured a vision of an unmediated religion in which priestly interventions and material props were cut to the bone. Hence the emphasis on rational religion remained, but now took a deistic form stressing natural religion and the illumination of conscience. González Vigil urged Peruvians to follow conscience and natural law in an 1860 essay, "Natural Religion"; another Peruvian, Mariano Amezaga, argued in the 1870s for a cult based on natural law, as religion was a great verity but "religions" – meaning Catholicism – "a solemn lie." A natural disposition to adore God and practice simple morality had been vitiated by religious castes. In 1860s Mexico, too, the Catholic schism endorsed by Ocampo enjoined the faithful to follow the soul's inner light. Liberalism, in sum, was now inspired not just by scripture and patriotism, but by the spirituality of Rousseau's Savoyard vicar. As a bonus, it was thought, the responsible exercise of individual conscience would create a tolerant, mature citizenry able to exercise its political and economic freedoms.

There was a problem in that a prescriptive view of religion contravened the idea of Church–state separation and full freedom of worship, basic rights that many liberals were reluctant to grant. In Mexico's constituent congress, for example, many argued against freedom of worship for fear, as one delegate put it, that Indians would soon be found prostrate at Cuatimotzin's throne. True liberals were outraged: Christ did not ask his followers what their Church was, said Ramírez, so why should states? Castillo Velasco advanced another argument: established Churches were not answerable to society, so were haughty. At bottom, however, many liberals still believed that the only bond in a divided society was religious: they hoped that a minimalist Catholicism would support the liberal order and enshrined this notion implicitly in the 1857 constitution. The discovery, in wartime, that this equivocation would not work partly explains the harsh anticlericalisms that came later. Mexico's Reform Wars (1858–1860), in which liberal armies confronted conservatives promising Catholic restoration, saw religious toleration introduced punitively by fiat.

Anticlericalism became an increasingly spiteful genre, as the Church extricated itself from the liberal nation: sacred images went on the bonfire, church bells were melted into cannon barrels, and matadors strode across the sand to kill bulls called Pío Nono, a burlesque of the current pope. In the Restored Republic that followed Maximilian's Empire (1862–1867), Anglican solutions in the form of national schisms were abandoned, Protestant competitors invited in, and the Reform laws elevated to constitutional status (1873).

The same sense of initial hesitation can be seen in the liberals' efforts to expropriate Church wealth. Liberals held that clerical mortmain – the permanent alienation of property to the Church – caused economic stagnation, as such property tended to leave circulation permanently. Theory thus dictated that national wealth be diverted from unproductive corporations to dynamic individuals. For all this, the famous Lerdo Law (1856), which disamortized Church wealth not used for cultic purposes, was a half-measure, as it forced the Church to sell off assets but allowed it to keep the cash in the form of mortgages. The real aims were to create a yeoman middle class and turn a *rentier* Church into a rational economic actor, the nation's realtor. Hopes of a Church-sponsored agrarian reform also died in battle, and the liberal response was nationalization of Church wealth by force, without recompense, in 1859.

Mexico was not unique. In Colombia, José Hilario López's reforms (1849–1853) included an attempt to force the Church to realize its assets, the state taking half, in exchange for a salary. The following decade, after a defeated conservative revolt, Tomás Cipriano de Mosquera (1861–1864) magnified state powers over the Church in the infamous *tuición de cultos* decree, which imposed state licenses on clergy. The 1863 Constitution declared freedom of worship, prohibited clergy from politicking, and outlawed clerical property. This followed an 1861 decree that disallowed mortmain as one of "the greatest obstacles" (so said Mosquera's preamble) to liberty. As in Mexico, however, dissolution's economic goals were not reached. Instead, properties were auctioned cheaply (rent was deemed equivalent to 6 percent worth), favoring cash-rich speculators and officialdom over peasant proprietors.

Again as in Mexico, Colombia's Church faced schism and an increasingly sectarian anticlericalism. Mosquera, excommunicated by Pius IX, proclaimed his Catholicism and threatened to break his stick over the Bishop of Antioquia's head if he would not swear on the constitution. In rural Antioquia, Colombia's Vendée, the clergy divided into a schismatic faction of *padres sometidos* (subjugated clergy) and a refractory majority that preached illegally in forest clearings. In the civil wars of 1876–1877, this situation was reprised. The bishops fled to the hills: mass went on in barns and caves, and church valuables went into the ground. By the 1870s, therefore, disenchanted liberals were driving wedges between civic and confessional identities, but even these radicals evidenced a vestigial regalism. If clergy would not act as ideal citizens, even under duress, then the state would treat them not just as ordinary citizens, but as *less* than citizens, a group debarred from owning property, expressing political opinions, or wearing cassocks in the streets without permission from the public power.

Guzmán Blanco's Venezuelan dictatorship was by now an anachronism in its pursuit of the patronage. A slight at the hands of the archbishop of Caracas, Silvestre Guevara – who refused to solemnize Guzmán Blanco's coup with a Te Deum in 1870 – saw the prelate banished. In 1873–1874, Guzmán Blanco extinguished convents for nuns, destroyed the seminaries, abolished clerical celibacy, established a civil registry, and placed the Patronage Law on constitutional footing. Since Rome still refused to remove Guevara, Guzmán Blanco declared Caracas a *sede vacante* (1873) and threatened to assume headship of the Church. In 1875, he conceived a schism and pressed Congress for a law that would make the Church "exclusively Venezuelan, regulated in accordance with the principles and practices of the primitive religion of Jesus." Probably Guzmán Blanco was less concerned with apostolic purity than with pressing Rome for Guevara's resignation: with this secured, in 1876, the Venezuelan schism was shelved.

Nations beyond Churches, ca. 1880–1900s

Late-nineteenth-century anticlericalism was also committed to keeping the state religion-free, but differed in that it was also secularizing, philosophically ill-disposed to religion. Such a stance was ultimately more threatening, even though physical attacks on the Church decreased after 1880. Yet this was only because first principles constituted the battleground, now that elites had become interested in scientific solutions to national problems. Various strands of Positivist thought conspired against religion. Comte's division of human history into epochs of metaphysical, philosophical, and scientific knowledge presupposed a materialistic notion of progress and condemned religion as backward. Social Darwinism, which considered Anglo-Saxon countries to be ahead in the struggle for national survival, characterized Catholic peoples as less advanced than Protestant ones. The fact that constitutional liberalism had failed to bring progress lent itself to a social Darwinistic reading: that Latin American elites should administer their societies expeditiously and undemocratically, accelerating their intellectual and economic evolution. Religious mores, and with them clerical authority, were conceived as being outside the trajectory of socioeconomic modernization.

Intellectually, this shift is clearly seen in González Prada's writings, which encapsulated feelings of national despair after Peru's defeat in the War of the Pacific (1879–1884). González Prada – a student of Bakunin and Proudhon as well as Nietzsche, Darwin, and Comte – demanded society's complete emancipation from religion, which he denounced as superstition. His jest that he had an "anti-Catholic knee," preventing genuflection, contains the essential idea that anticlericals now opposed revelation as an absurdity. It was mystery, not just priests, that shrouded Peruvians in ignorance and stunted the faculty of reason. Nature provided ethics and science a futuristic "God," a fact that should be reflected in an education system "cured of any religious virus." Note that the archaeological metaphor of religion as tarnished metal, pure but for surface grime, had shifted to the scientific trope of religion as infection, inherently harmful.

González Prada was nonetheless unusual in that his belief in science bespoke a curiosity that absorbed, but was not satisfied by, Positivism. On the contrary, by the 1890s his readings were taking him beyond the idea that secular dictatorship was a solution for Latin America. Economic liberalism and political authoritarianism, González Prada now argued, were adjuncts of Catholicism, in that priest, politico, and empresario formed part of one "brutalizing trinity." From 1900, González Prada assumed an anarchist posture, arguing that anticlericalism was sterile unless it targeted the great props of religion, property and the state, freeing the individual in three dimensions. A few other militant anticlericals – Mexico's Flores Magón, for instance, or Mariátegui in Peru –reached similar conclusions at this same time.

Generally, political anticlericalism moved at a slower pace. Guatemala's liberal revolutionaries of the 1870s, while reprising some anticlerical reforms, moved in a Positivistic direction under plantocrat presidents García Granados and Rufino Barrios. The opening broadsides were those of an earlier period: the expulsion of the Jesuits, in 1871, and of Archbishop Piñol y Aycinena, for protesting the expulsion in a pastoral letter. Barrios's arrival as interim president (1872) saw the expropriation of the Oratorians' *fincas*, and the dissolution of male orders on grounds that they were unproductive bodies. As president, Barrios nationalized ecclesiastical property, including real estate, confraternity funds, and convents, and invested it in a rural credit bank (1873). In 1874, came the exclaustration of nuns and an educational reform that required the teaching of scientific knowledge and a secularized ethics called "morality and urbanity." The 1879 constitution enshrined separation, as well as religious toleration, and outlawed religious processions and the use of clerical vestments outside church; additional laws secularized the cemeteries and secularized marriage vows, as well as legalizing the practice of Protestantism. This was a transitional anticlericalism, in sum, that revived old features alongside the image of a nation reoriented toward scientific, export-style development. Satirical propaganda propagated this idea in its depiction of trains crashing into churches, technology scattering the incomprehending monks.

Argentine anticlericals also championed a Positivistic approach to education in the 1880s. As in Guatemala, this was linked to economic changes, given that export-led developments in both cases provided the rationale and wealth for a national school system. Likewise, the 1880s saw a scientific revolution in government, above all in the ranks of the Partido Autonomista Nacional (PAN). This body endorsed Positivistic notions of scientific progress and the idea that Catholicism should be refuted as a doctrine by education. An expanding Church and its political proxies, spearheaded by the likes of Juan Manuel de Estrada, denounced "Positivist fanaticism" and prepared for battle. The clash, in 1883, surrounded a seemingly innocuous bill that prescribed the teaching of ethics in schools from a Catholic perspective but promised an opt-out for non-Catholic parents. This nod to religious pluralism caused a furor in the chamber of deputies, which struck the bill down; liberals saw their chance and voted in Law 1420, which excluded religious teaching altogether and introduced classes on "morals and manners" instead.

As political tension rose, anticlerical measures – the apostolic delegate's expulsion, the suspension of bishops – intensified, leading to the formation of a powerful Catholic Union in 1884. Here Catholics were accused of opposing religious pluralism, liberals of violating constitutional rights to religious education. Yet the conflict involved deeper conceptions of Argentine history, each of which existed within a republican framework. Opponents of Law 1420 stressed the indissociability of morals and religion, and argued that the accomplishment of independence reaffirmed an implicitly Catholic vision of the state. Thus, corporations such as the Church must be protected as guarantors of the nation's conscience. Advocates of Law 1420 argued that democracy required unitary, not dual solidarities, and that Catholicism encouraged disunity except as a private value. In a word, Catholic deputies saw the state as reflective of society; Positivistic liberals viewed it as constitutive of a society in which religion's role was to vanish.

In Mexico, the Porfiriato (1876–1911) is usually considered a period of anticlerical retreat, which descriptively it was: iconoclasm was gone, at least until the 1910 revolution. For reasons previously outlined, however, a clear (and to Catholics, insidious) line of anticlericalism ran through the 1880s to 1900s in the form of Positivist education, even though political tension was largely contained by the regime's pragmatism. Gabino Barreda was Positivism's leading advocate, arguing that the state should exercise jurisdiction solely in the material order and have no truck with religion in its schools. Yet Barreda went beyond classical liberalism in his assertion that religious beliefs were outmoded, simply a source of political discord: metaphysics, he said, had given rise to "sterile social disturbances." Other Positivists, such as Porfirio Parra, critiqued *juarista* liberals' deism as unscientific, an affront to the laicist principle. Francisco Bulnes, Positivism's historian, was overtly critical of Díaz's conciliation of organized Catholicism and liberalism, which he viewed as an oxymoron, given that science demonstrated evolutionary change while religion clung to the immutable. Catholic social doctrine, which criticized Porfirian inequalities, merely provided a sentimental rationale for turning society into a "poorhouse."

Conclusion

Anticlericalism proceeded by stages, delineating the function of priests and religion in varied brushstrokes using lighter or darker colors. Anticlericals, at different times, viewed Catholicism as an altar of nationhood in need of de-Romanizing, a temple for morals and manners requiring less priestcraft, or an obsolete intellectual system worthy of disdain. The Church was the nave of the republic, an ethical school, or, finally, a shrunken museum piece. For all their certainties, some Positivists found this last vision hard to live with, or left a glimmer of space for religion. Justo Sierra, at Mexico's education ministry, held the Spencerian belief that human liberty should increase with order, so late in life conceded a new role for metaphysics at some more advanced point in evolution. Even González Prada, at the time of his death in 1918, was modestly skeptical about his own skepticism, in verse at least. God was still a possibility, albeit an imperfectly human one, a late ode suggested: *"Si hay un Sér omnipotente, Rey de hormigas y de soles/ Es acaso tan injusto/ Como nosotros los hombres."*[10] Perhaps these were just classic deathbed dilemmas. As anticlericalism came full circle, however, becoming emphatically secular in the present and even having lost sight of God in the past, it is perhaps revealing that some of its leading disciples projected a myth of return into the future.

Bibliography and Suggested Readings

Bazant, Jan. *Los bienes de la Iglesia en México, 1856–1875: Aspectos económicos y sociales de la revolución liberal.* Mexico City: El Colegio de México, 1971.

Chadwick, Owen. *The Secularization of the European Mind in the Nineteenth Century.* Cambridge: Cambridge University Press, 1975.

Costeloe, Michael. *Church and State in Independent Mexico: A Study of the Patronage Debate, 1821–1857.* London: The Royal History Society, 1978.

---

10 Cited in Klaiber, *Religion and Revolution*, 33.

Covo, Jacqueline. *Las ideas de la reforma en México (1855–1861)*. Mexico City: Universidad Nacional Autónoma de México, Coordinación de Humanidades, 1983.

Klaiber, Jeffrey "Anticlericalism in the Nineteenth and Early Twentieth Centuries." In Lee Penyak and Walter Petry (eds.), *Religion and Society in Latin America: Interpretive Essays from Conquest to Present*, 157–174. Maryknoll, NY: Orbis Books, 2009.

Religion and Revolution in Peru, 1824–1976. Norte Dame, University of Notre Dame Press, 1977.

Londoño-Vega, Patrícia. *Religion, Society, and Culture in Colombia: Antioquia and Medellín, 1850–1930*. Oxford: Oxford University Press, 2002.

Lynch, John. "The Catholic Church in Latin America, 1830–1930." In Leslie Bethell (ed.), *Cambridge History of Latin America*, Vol. IV (Cambridge: Cambridge University Press, 1986), 527–595.

Mecham, John Lloyd. *Church and State in Latin America: A History of Politico-Ecclesiastical Relations*. Chapel Hill: University of North Carolina Press, 1966.

Meyer, Jean. *Historia de los cristianos en América Latina, siglos XIX y XX*. Mexico City: Vuelta, 1988.

Rémond, René. *L'anticléricalisme en France de 1815 à nos jours*. Paris: Fayard, 1976.

Sánchez, José. *Anticlericalism: A Brief History*. Notre Dame: University of Notre Dame, 1972.

Stefano, Roberto di. "El laberinto religioso de Juan Manuel de Rosas," *Anuario de Estudios Americanos* 63, no. 1 (2006): 19–50.

El púlpito y la plaza: Clero, sociedad, y política de la monarquía católica a la república rosista. Buenos Aires: Siglo XXI Ediciones, 2004.

Sullivan-González, Douglass. *Piety, Power, and Politics: Religion and Nation Formation in Guatemala, 1821–1871*. Pittsburgh: University of Pittsburgh Press, 1998.

Watters, Mary. *A History of the Church in Venezuela, 1810–1930*. Chapel Hill: University of North Carolina Press, 1933.

Williams, John Hoyt. "Dictatorship and the Church: Doctor Francia in Paraguay," *A Journal of Church and State* 15, no. 3 (1973): 419–436.

18

Religious Devotion, Rebellion, and Messianic Movements: Popular Catholicism in the Nineteenth Century

DOUGLASS SULLIVAN-GONZÁLEZ

The nineteenth-century religious landscape in Latin America emerged forcefully with the clarion call of the Vodou priest Dutty Boukman. His religiously inspired and African-inherited convictions in 1791 initiated the decade-long rebellion that ended French dominance of the colonial territory and concluded with the liberty of tens of thousands of African slaves on that island in 1804. Just a bit more than 100 years later, in the northern state of Pernambuco, Brazil, the final chapter of religious history in nineteenth century Latin America finished with a similar vision inspired by deeply held religious convictions, the messianic movement of Antônio Conselheiro in the Brazilian backlands of Canudos. His utopic dream of a multiclass and multiethnic Brazil fell to the secularizing forces of the coastal elites bent on controlling the fanatical and dark-skinned peoples of Brazil's *sertões* (backlands) and ensuring an ordered development that did not hearken to a religiously imbued faith in the monarchy of times past. These two events form the historical and symbolic parameters of the power of religious faith within slave-based societies during the nineteenth century.

The Spanish colonial world bequeathed similar convulsions within its territories, but the large number of indigenous peoples in the Mexica valley and in the Andean world created a different dynamic compared to the historical slave societies of the Caribbean and Brazil. A curious intermingling of pre-Conquest devotions with Spanish Catholicism produced its own regionally based, autochthonous faith expressions emphasizing different degrees of Spanish and indigenous features. At the height of this creative moment of faith production in the mid-eighteenth century, the Bourbon throne attempted to minimize the Catholic Church's role in the political economy while Enlightenment ideals challenged the Baroque – read "image laden" – nature of Latin American Catholicism.

Given the Independence movements in the first two decades of the nineteenth century, the newly founded secularizing state inspired by these Enlightenment ideals attempted to purge Catholicism's privileged position in society and liberate its peoples to pursue rational, economic policies devoid of such superstition. The shock of such policies produced multiple responses in the classically studied church–state conflict: many resigned to accept the new realities while others staunchly rejected the new political arrangements of the nineteenth century. A battered Catholic clergy, looking to reassert the Catholic faith within the new political world, ultimately depended on the appeal of miraculous images to protect coveted social space in this new world as fierce competitors moved into the religious market. Religious rebellion, messianic movements, and renewed devotion to the particular Marian and Christ shrines throughout the region marked the religious landscape of Catholicism during the nineteenth century.

The historiography of religion and religiosity in Latin America's nineteenth century followed the lead of J. Lloyd Mecham's 1934 *Church and State in Latin America*, a classic tome written in the aftermath of the Cristero Rebellion in Mexico, 1926–1929. Mecham attempted to come to grips with the horrific showdown between the secularizing revolutionary state led by Plutarco Elías Calles, who had hoped to extirpate all atavistic faith from Mexico's *campesinos* and the devout followers of the Catholic Church who took up arms with the battle cry, *Qué viva Cristo Rey!* What historic context had produced such a travesty of a showdown between people of faith and state officials? Mecham saw in the turmoil of the nineteenth century the seeds of contempt and mistrust sown by both Catholic and state officials who labored to arrange new understandings of power and public standing with the demise of the colonial state and the emergence of the fledgling nations.

Mecham provided a well-worked analysis of the legal and political questions that haunted state and religious officials in Venezuela, Colombia, Ecuador, Peru, Bolivia, Paraguay, Argentina, Brazil, Uruguay, the Caribbean, and Central America, with the majority of his focus on three stages of church and state conflict in Mexico from 1821 through 1933.[1] He traced the difficult questions that plagued officials regardless of their convictions. Would the nascent state assume the colonial privilege of patronage over Church leadership and its appointments? To what degree would the national governments

---

1 John Lloyd Mecham, *Church and State in Latin America; a History of Politicoecclesiastical Relations* (Chapel Hill: The University of North Carolina Press, 1934); Fredrick B. Pike, *The Conflict Between Church and State in Latin America*, Borzoi Books on Latin America (New York: Knopf, 1964).

continue to protect Catholicism's religious hegemony from competing pre-Conquest faiths and from external threats now posed by a strengthened Protestant Church and from Masonic commitments to rational governance emanating from Europe and the United States? Would the new governments protect the economic foundation of the Catholic Church by ensuring the collection of the dreaded tithe or first fruits? Would the new countries, void of a coveted bishopric, fall to the temptation of creating their own to enhance the sustainability of their nascent political project? Mecham's deft answers created the conceptual framework to understand Catholicism in nineteenth century Latin America. The methodological shift away from Mecham's top-down history made possible one that emphasized a history told through the eyes of the participants at the bottom of the political and social pyramid.

Jean Meyer's three-volume analysis of the Cristero rebellion in 1974 (French edition) forced Latin American historians to look beyond the machinations of elite power plays among church and state officials and to focus on the motivations of the people involved in the rank and file of the Cristero rebellion. Meyer spent hours on horseback riding the hills and valleys of the Mexican countryside collecting interviews with the Cristero soldiers and offered historians an electric understanding of deeply felt convictions of those who took arms to defend their faith from the onslaught of the Mexican revolutionary state.[2] Meyer's work, combined with the earlier historic opening of the Latin American Catholic Church following Vatican II in 1963 and the Episcopal Conference of Latin American Bishops in Medellín, Colombia in 1968, encouraged both professional and lay historians and theologians to look at the concrete expressions of the faith. Thus, many dedicated themselves to understand "popular religion" and "popular Catholicism," emphasizing the plebeian expressions of faith in contradistinction to those of the professional clergy and even elite manifestations of faith.[3] Historians struggled to understand the conceptual parameters of the term "popular religion" and to refine the questions surrounding its usage to capture the linkages among the various actors that comprise the faith fact.

Natalie Z. Davis's *Society and Culture in Early Modern France* and Peter Brown's *The Cult of Saints* enabled many of us to transcend the simplistic elite-popular dynamic and explore the multifaceted relations among the

---

[2] Jean A. Meyer, *The Cristero Rebellion: The Mexican People Between Church and State, 1926–1929*, trans. Richard Southern, Cambridge Latin American Studies (Cambridge: Cambridge University Press, 1976).

[3] Norbert Greinacher and Norbert Mette, eds., *Popular Religion*, Concilium. Religion in the Eighties (Edinburgh: T. & T. Clark, 1986).

clergy and the believer that shaped the contours and actions of the faithful. A study of popular Catholicism in nineteenth-century Latin America attempts to look at the rebellious and accommodating expressions of the faith from Christian and non-Christian sources that transformed acts of piety and devotion among all peoples, both lay and the clergy. The Catholic Church in Latin America, though hierarchical in nature among the diocesan priests and bishops, included the mendicant orders that cultivated loyalty to its expressions of the faith that supported and diverged from leading bishops and priests.

The Latin American colonial experience is strewn with the carnage of clashes between the regular orders and the diocesan priests, and the nineteenth century proved no different where the regular orders survived the forced secularization by state forces. If the Catholic Church failed to keep the clerical troops marching in order, certainly the faithful did not always respond to orders from the top. The study of popular religion, and in this particular case, popular Catholicism, encompasses the dynamic interplay among and within the Church hierarchy, among and within the faithful, and the creative interplay between both groups and fragmented groups who allied with others along this spectrum of faith. How one methodologically teases out the shared and multiple interests in these ever-changing coalitions depends on the evidence and the imaginative eye of the historian!

Mecham's work did provide the historical context for understanding popular Catholicism. The demanding questions situate themselves in an extraordinary tug-of-war between the forces of secular rationality and the religious convictions of Catholic Church officials during the entirety of the nineteenth century. Austen Ivereigh's clever analysis *The Politics of Religion in an Age of Revival* discussed the lines drawn in eighteenth-century Europe that spilled over into Latin America in the nineteenth century, "the high noon of this battle." The "forces of rationality, modernity and progress" pitched battles with the Catholic Church and its allies, "defenders of eternal principles and ancestral rights and the most formidable obstacle to the pretensions of the modern State."[4] Ivereigh rightly posits that the "modernising, secularising, democratising liberal project reached maturity" between the 1820s and the First World War.

That success story collided with another, the Catholic revival. The lengthy and ferocious battle over public space between these two groups "colored" and "defined" the boundaries of politics in the Southern Hemisphere. Notice,

---

4 Austen Ivereigh, ed., "Introduction. The Politics of Religion in an Age of Revival," in *The Politics of Religion in an Age of Revival*. Studies in Nineteenth-Century Europe and Latin America, Nineteenth-Century Latin American Series (London: Institute of Latin American Studies, 2000), 1.

he surmised, how liberal and secularizing forces claimed a popular mandate in their bid to win this battle. Liberal historians pointed to a decreasing religiosity in the nineteenth century and claimed that clerical forces defended privilege in their antimodern crusade. Anticlericalism, then, represented a popular fury against a superstitious institution that utilized religion to advance economically. The evidence from recent historical investigations points to a resurgence of the Catholic Church and not a decline, "an ecclesiastical restoration." Rome asserted itself during the tenure of Pope Pius IX (1846–1878) and Pope Leo XIII (1878–1903), and the Church grew institutionally, particularly among women in the regular orders dedicated to the active life. Orphanages, hospitals, and schools appeared to meet the needs of growing primate cities and Catholics employed the ranks to make it happen.[5] What then do we make of popular Catholicism during this century of conflict?

Given this elaborate battle for the hearts and minds of ordinary people among secular and religious groups, we can first capture a glimpse of popular Catholicism in the early nineteenth century by examining the religious expressions tolerated, condoned, or condemned by ecclesiastical authorities during the initial rebellions and actual revolutions that led to the collapse of the Spanish colonial world. Many a soldier crafted battle standards and shouted war cries to implore the local saints to intervene on their behalf, to protect them from harm, and to lead their forces to victory. The Virgin of Guadalupe assumes an extraordinary role in the historiographical renderings of the independence movement in Mexico, and it has cornered the proverbial market for many historians to portray the substance and the longevity of the people's religious devotion. We know that José María Morelos ordered the Virgin of Guadalupe to adorn the hats of his soldiers, his soldiers carried a banner with the Virgin adorning it that can be seen today in Mexico's National Museum of History, and he wished in his *Sentimientos de la Nación* that all Mexicans honor December 12th as the day of the Virgin of Guadalupe.

Eric Van Young recently argued, though, that he could not find evidence to sustain the claim of the shrine's transcendent appeal among those in arms. "But there is precious little evidence of a Pavlovian response by Mexican country people, Indians in particular, to the brandishing of the Virgin of Guadalupe as at once a banner of popular rebellion and an umbrella for a cross-class, cross-ethnic alliance between Creole and indigenous insurgents."[6] Van Young's

---

5 Ivereigh, "The Politics of Religion," 5–6.
6 Eric Van Young, "Popular Religion and the Politics of Insurgency in Mexico, 1810–1821," in *The Politics of Religion in an Age of Revival. Studies in Nineteenth-Century Latin America*, ed. Austen Ivereigh, Nineteenth-Century Latin American Series (London: Institute of Latin American Studies, 2000), 82–83.

assertions seemed to confirm in part what William Taylor had discovered two decades earlier in a sampling of parish baptismal records among eight parishes ranging from Guadalajara and Jalisco to Oaxaca. Acknowledging the methodological difficulty to measure the religious devotion of peoples, Taylor looked at more than 18,000 baptismal records to gauge the popularity of the name "Guadalupe." Fifty-seven percent of those records examined pertained to those classified as "Indians" and the rest as "Spanish, mestizos, and mulattos." Taylor discovered that a very high percentage of women were named María and Guadalupe compared to men, and that the name María outnumbered Guadalupe irrespective of one's ethnicity, "suggesting a powerful cult of Mary generally." Non-Indians carried the name Guadalupe more often than Indians (3.3 to 1) and Indians carried the name Guadalupe more often than non-Indians when their birth coincided with the month honoring the patron saint (December). The popularity of the name Guadalupe for non-Indians did not depend on one's birth month. Thus, the name Guadalupe had taken root more fashionably among Spanish, mestizos, and mulattos than Indians, an affirmation in line with Van Young's conclusions.

Much of our historiography dealing with the independence movements and the early national governments depend on those first works of reflections by the participants themselves, and we are tempted to take the actions and words of those in power as signs of intense devotion. We do know, as demonstrated in the case of Guadalupe in Mexico, that soldiers and devotees in other independence movements looked to the shrines for sustenance and protection and victory. Generals and new governments sanctioned their modern experiments by crowning a particular shrine as the patron saint of the movement and ultimately, the country.

The Argentine General Manuel Belgrano encouraged San Martín to maintain *Nuestra Señora de los Mercedes* as the *generala* of the armies whereas the *Congreso General de Tucumán* of 1816 proclaimed the beatified and canonized nun Santa Rosa de Lima as the patron saint of independence. Cuba's revolutionaries, much later in the nineteenth century, were to have paid homage to *La Virgin de la Caridad de Cobre* (or also, *la Virgen Mambisa*), and Bolivians in 1852 declared *Nuestra Señora del Carmen* as the patron saint of the Republic. These shrines, rooted within a general devotion of the Catholic faith and particularized in the expression of nineteenth-century Latin America, became the bedrock of the faithful during the tempest years of the rule of the caudillo, especially during the first half of the century.

David A. Brading argued that these images represented their heavenly originals and possessed a sacred presence that cultivated devotion among the faithful.[7] Though challenged by Protestants and warned by Catholic councils not to perceive any power in the shrines other than to honor what they represent, the colonial faithful in Latin America more than venerated the shrines: they praised their miraculous origins and curative powers. Post-independence politics in Latin America strengthened the local nature of many shrines given the intense fighting and upheaval. Caudillos and various elite interest groups fought to impose personal agendas or different visions on their region that led to a fragmentation of the early political arrangements, from Mexico to Gran Colombia to the United Provinces of La Plata. Roads were blocked by soldiers with weapons and passports demanded for travel within and without the new states.

The chaos of the early national period, then, impeded the colonial, transregional devotion of many shrines and diminished the monitoring role of the clergy. Local *cofradías* (religious brotherhoods and sisterhoods), whether organized or not, assumed control of the community's religious shrines and important fiestas. Not until the consolidation of political regimes in the latter part of the nineteenth century and the introduction of rail and better roads did the appeal of the shrines once again supersede the native province and enhance clerical control over local faith production.

The Crucified Christ of Esquipulas, Guatemala, exemplified this ebb and flow of popularity from the eighteenth century to the beginning of the twentieth. Sculpted by a local resident of the colonial capital of Antigua in 1595, the Crucified Christ of Esquipulas, also known today more by its twentieth century name, the Black Christ, reached prominence when Guatemala's first bishop testified to its curative powers in the early eighteenth century. An imperial sanctuary was constructed and completed in 1758, and the local cleric wrote many accounts of its healing abilities. Travelers and other bishops marveled that as many as 100,000 pilgrims visited the shrine in eastern Guatemala during its titular fair and fiesta of January 15th. Others in Central America and in New Spain created replicas of the Crucified Christ of Esquipulas to honor its spiritual gifts.

Independence, first from Spain in 1821 and then from Mexico in 1823, brought a decade of civil war to the former captaincy of Guatemala, and the liberal vision of the Honduran Francisco Morazán quelled the war with

---

7   D. A. Brading, "Divine Idea and 'Our Mother': Elite and Popular Understanding in the Cult of Our Lady of Guadalupe of Mexico," in *Elite and Popular Religion*, ed. Kate Cooper and Jeremy Gregory (Rochester, NY: Boydell and Brewer, 2006), 241; Hans Belting, *Likeness and Presence: A History of the Image Before the Era of Art*, trans. Edmund Japhcott (Chicago: University of Chicago Press, 1994). Brading cites Belting's insights in this powerful analysis of the retrenchment of the devotion of images in colonial Latin America.

military triumph and instituted classic liberal repression of the regular orders and curtailed the Catholic Church's control over many essential public rituals. The wars devastated the free travel of the region, and the cleric of Esquipulas wrote in 1830 that the Crucified Christ had lost its appeal among the many whites who used to travel to great distances to petition for its intervention.[8]

A cholera epidemic, most likely introduced through Esquipulas by a wayfarer from Honduras in 1837, unleashed a series of popular revolts and challenges to the liberal government. Rafael Carrera organized the disaffected and seized control of Guatemala definitively in 1840 with the final defeat of Morazán, aided in part by clergy and parishioners from eastern Guatemala who had felt the brunt of liberal policies for more than a decade. Carrera's hold on power, tenuous at first but solidified in the 1850s, enabled Church officials to begin to rebuild the weakened institution. Carrera, of mulatto or mestizo origins, represented the first nonwhite to seize power of a Latin American country outside of the Caribbean in the nineteenth century. His assent to the highest political position scandalized whites, who would comment decades later on the backwardness and atavistic, pro-Church policies of the Conservative interlude that had impeded development.

Carrera's victory created an extraordinary opening for nonwhites to exercise control over their religious space. Though the clergy remained wary of Carrera's ultimate intentions, those who had followed the caudillo into battle with shouts of "Long live religion" and "Death to foreign heretics" soon restored lost worship practices with or without the priest! A pastoral visit to western Guatemala, in Sololá and Totonicapán, in 1846, brought substantial reports of widespread religious practices among the Indians of Santa Catarina Ixtahuacán, and clerics blamed "native superstitions and popular European errors transmitted by the conquerors." In the adjoining canton of San Miguel, one Indian leader took the priestly vestments, robed himself, and danced in the church.[9] Liberals (and even conservative clerics!) never forgot such narratives of religious autonomy during the Carrera years.

The Esquipulas shrine of the Crucified Christ provoked debate among whites in this same period given its blackening condition due to the accumulation of soot and dirt. The color of the shrine, its darkened tones mentioned in the 1758 praises of the dedication of the temple, did not provoke much

---

8 Miguel Muñoz, *Doctrina cristiana sobre el culto de las imágenes, y noticia verdadera de la imágen milagrosa que se venera en el santuario del pueblo de Esquipulas, con una novena al fin dedicada al dulcísimo nobre de Jesus*, reprint, 1830 (Guatemala: N.p., 1889).

9 Douglass Sullivan-González, *Piety, Power, and Politics. Religion and Nation Formation in Guatemala, 1821–1871* (Pittsburgh: University of Pittsburgh Press, 1998), 47.

consternation, but created the possibilities of a greater narrative for the Creole clerics to discuss its transcendent powers among all peoples – indigenous, African, and mestizo. By 1844, with the gradual emergence of a conceptual framework for biological racism in the postcolonial world, the darkness of the shrine provoked consternation among the clergy. One cleric protested the darkened colors in correspondence with Church authorities. Muñoz, the former parish priest of Esquipulas, defended the multivalent character of the shrine's color, noting that while blackness represented sin and evil for those with a whiter disposition, whiteness denoted leprous evil among people of color. His skilled defense of the evolving incarnation of the Crucified Christ settled the debate for the moment but did not resolve the growing unease with the shrine's color, nor did it generate renewed devotion.[10] Chaos caused by war, rebellion, and banditry had diminished the concurrence of the faithful during the first half of the century even though eastern Guatemalans maintained faithful vigilance.

Liberals from western Guatemala triumphed definitively over Guatemala's conservative forces, now sustained by Carrera's followers in 1871, and unleashed a series of measures, including expulsions and exile for high-ranking clergy and for the members of the regular orders. Seizure of Church assets and property, coupled with severe limitation of the existing clergy, initiated a half-century decline in the number of priests. By the turn of the century, Guatemala's Catholic Church was but a minor fraction of its prime at the beginning of the nineteenth. Clergy fled the war-torn area of Esquipulas and shied away from appointment to what had been a very lucrative post during the first two decades of liberal rule.

First, a religiously inspired revolt inflamed the eastern mountains until it was crushed, and Esquipulas, known for its wealth, became the source of constant incursions by both rebels and pro-government forces. Then, as state officials cracked down on the Catholic Church, the leadership in distant Esquipulas suffered repeated verbal and physical assaults until an unspoken peace settled relations in the final decade of the nineteenth century. Juan Paz Solórzano became the parish priest of Esquipulas in 1901 and discovered the shrine to be in disarray, even covered with a wig. He immediately reorganized the parish, cleaned the shrine, and looked to discover its history and power. He included and updated the number of miraculous acts attributed to the shrine from both

---

10 Miguel Muñoz, "En que VSY se digna," letter, Cartas, 1845.37, AHAG (Guatemala, 1845) The Archivo Histórico Arquidiocesano de Guatemala (AHAG), the Guatemalan Catholic Church's archive contains a rich source of colonial and national correspondence between parish priests and their governing bishops in Guatemala City.

the colonial and early national periods. The successful tract prepared the foundation for the cleric to push for a greater recognition of the shrine.

Solórzano, encouraged by his Mexican counterparts, published his 1904 rendering of the history and importance of the Crucified Christ of Esquipulas. Indirect evidence suggests that the savvy Esquipulas priest imitated the successful coronation of Mexico's Virgin of Guadalupe in 1895, called the "most important and transcendental event in the history" of Mexico. Prelates from Canada, the United States, the Caribbean, and Mexico joined in the praise and adulation of the Virgin of Guadalupe. D. A. Brading attributed the successful coronation to the Mexican attentiveness to a similar regal affair in Lourdes. As in France, so in Mexico. As in Mexico, so in Guatemala.

Juan Paz Solórzano's publication of a rustic pamphlet caught the attention of the Guatemalan archbishop, and a decade later, and with similar fanfare, the archbishop, with blessings from Rome, crowned the Crucified Christ of Esquipulas as the titular saint of Guatemala. Solórzano published two well-manicured treatises that incorporated a popular novena from the 1758 dedication of the sanctuary; Miguel Muñoz's original thoughts on the history of the shrine; a series of up-to-date reflections on the power of holy images for Catholic believers; and a synopsis of recent attacks launched by the decidedly un-Christian Protestants missionaries who lampooned the Black Beelzebub's iconic nature. The image of Esquipulas had returned to center stage, not only for the nonwhites of eastern Guatemala, but also for the whites of the capital and for the Central American region.

The nineteenth-century drama around the Crucified Christ of Esquipulas followed a pattern endemic to popular shrines in Spanish Latin America. War and rebellions disrupted the colonial pattern of festive and transregional celebrations of religious shrines; State measures limited and diminished clerical presence and control during the initial struggles with the Church; the shrines became, by default, localized with limited appeal; the Catholic revival and renewed clerical presence in the second half of the century prompted a rediscovery of the power of the religious shrine; and the faithful attempted to link the shrine's destiny to the new political configuration of the nation, usually with focused publications, and sometimes with national celebrations. Where the church and state remained closely linked, as in the case of Peru, the evidence still indicates a diminished clerical presence in the first decades of independence and a revived interest in the shrines during the latter part of the nineteenth century.

The Gothic basilica that contains the colonial shrine, Our Lady of Lujan (*Nuestra Señora de Lujan*), located about 70 kilometers west of Buenos Aires, was planned and built in the latter part of the nineteenth century. An extraordinary push to recognize the miraculous nature of its selection near the Lujan River and to publicize its miraculous powers coincided with the 1885 publication of *Historia de Nuestra Señora de Lujan: Su origen, su santuario, su villa, sus milagros y su culto, por un sacerdote de la congregación de la misión*. During the initial years of independence, the liberal government of Rivadavia hardened its position against the Catholic Church and ordered the visiting Papal delegates to abandon Buenos Aires, censoring them from officiating at any mass. The humiliated apostolic delegates departed and traveled to the village of Lujan in January 1824 and paid homage to Our Lady of Lujan without any interference from the local administrators. One of the delegates happened to be the Canon Mastai Ferreti, who would become the one of the two longest reigning popes, Pious IX, the pope who initiated the Catholic revival in the latter half of the nineteenth century, emphasizing in particular the *Syllabus of Errors* to confront liberalism, the confirmation of Mary's Immaculate Conception, and papal infallibility. The story, retold now in 1885, proved to be divine proof of the popularity and election of Our Lady of Lujan.

What happened between independence and this time of renewal? We can only speculate given the paucity of sources combined with the dearth of ecclesiastical presence in Argentina compared to other former Spanish colonies. The Rosas dictatorship maintained a tight fist over all public gatherings, and Church officials and the religious institution withered under his domain. By the end of his rule, wrote Ivereigh, the Church "was stagnant" while seminaries remained idle and the religious orders emptied.[11] Most likely, the rule of the caudillo fragmented the institution and local expressions of faith, far from the gaze of the dictator, flourished quietly.

The remarkable colonial story of America's first saint, Rosa de Santa María (1586–1617), known popularly as Rosa de Lima, who observed a life of penitence and mortification, became an extraordinary model of discipline and devotion for the faithful within the first century of Conquest. Her lifestyle of fasting and self-flagellation took its toll on her young body. Her death attracted immediate international attention, and many became devotees of her life and habits.

Given the political timidity of the Church officials and Peruvian Creoles to work toward independence from Spain (and thanks to the generosity of their northern and southern neighbors who encouraged them), one must wonder

---

11 Austen Ivereigh, "The Shape of the State: Liberals and Catholics in the Dispute Over Law 1420 of 1884 in Argentina," in *The Politics of Religion in an Age of Revival*, ed. Austen Ivereigh (London: Institute of Latin American Studies, 2000), 170–171.

how local officials and the faithful understood her inspiring example in light of the political changes of the day. Of the more than 400 publications surrounding Rosa de Lima, with the majority in the seventeenth and twentieth centuries, very few were published in the first half of the nineteenth century.

Notably, José Manuel took the first step to incorporate her memory into the new political project that evolved post-independence. His 1827 *Vida de la glorisa vírgen Dominicana Santa Rosa de Sta. María, natural de Lima y patrón principal de las Américas* held Rosa de Lima as a model given her postmortem difficulties with the Holy Inquisition. The story of her resoluteness both during and after her life created a cultural bridge for all good Catholics to celebrate her as the patron saint of the Americas. Remarkably, very few writings about her emerged in the nineteenth century until the 1880s, when a plethora of monographs appeared to celebrate three centuries of the birth of Rosa de Lima. The saint once again became a crucial moment of Catholic identity, not only for Peru and the rest of South America, but also for the Church worldwide as it confronted revolutionary projects that threatened it.

The faithful in Brazil and its borderlands exercised their faith with much more autonomy during the late eighteenth and nineteenth centuries. Emilio Noya wrote of a Marian shrine along the Paraná River that resembled "the figure of aboriginal body" in contrast to the predictable Marian shrines. He also noted that the Africans who participated in the War of the Triple Alliance from 1865 to 1869 remained in the area after the hostilities and revered a shrine dedicated to one of the magi who visited the infant Jesus, San Baltasar. The particular image reflected many Ethiopian traits and the Africans celebrated festivities in its honor with the dance typical of Candomblé and the sound of tamborines.[12]

Travelers to Brazil noted the residual Catholicism among slaves and commented on the longstanding Muslim faith that transcended the ritual of the Catholic Church. "You can scarcely look into a basket in which the *quitandeiras* carry fruit without seeing a *fetisch*," a piece of charcoal to ward off the evil eye.[13] Police visited frequently, in the district of São Paulo, to break up temples or houses called "Zangus" or "batuques" that encouraged African frivolity and gambling.[14] Portuguese whites and their descendants had good cause to suspect the power of religious faith in the lives of their slaves.

---

12 Emilio Noya, *Imaginería religiosa y santoral profano de corrientes* (Argentina: Artes Offset, 1994), 45–46, 78–79.
13 Rev. James C. Fletcher and Rev. D. P. Kidder, *Brazil and the Brazilians Portrayed in Historical and Descriptive Sketches* (London: Sampson Low, Son, and Marston, 1866), 136.
14 Roger Batide, *As religiões africanas no Brasil*, Maria Eloisa Capellato and Olívia Krähenbühl, reprint, 1960 (São Paulo, Brasil: Livraria Pioneira Editora, 1973), 195–196.

Stuart Schwartz demonstrated the power of religion within the lives of a liberated group of Brazilian slaves who proposed a treaty after they killed the sugar mill's overseer and broke free from their master for three years, inspired by their counterparts in Haiti. In return for their cooperation, the marooned slaves demanded a liberal enjoyment of saints' days to savor their political and economic gains. João José Reis wrote convincingly of the Muslim uprising of 1835 in Bahia that slaves had planned to revolt on the day of Our Lady of Guidance while worshipers prayed and celebrated. Religion mattered from the center to the periphery of Brazil's political economy.

The autonomy experienced by many on the periphery of ecclesiastical control also produced well-known messianic movements in Brazil, where charismatic leaders demanded spiritual cleansing and sacrificial living among their followers to deal with the fallen nature of the world. Given the significant transition from slavery to freedom for thousands of Brazilians, from monarchy to republic, in the latter half of the nineteenth century, multiple social movements challenged authorities and led to tragic showdowns in some cases. In the classic, comparative study of messianic movements worldwide and in Brazil, in particular, Maria Queiroz analyzed the restorationist impulse behind such social movements and concluded that the committed pushed to incarnate their ideals in the practical day-to-day world of their existence.[15]

In the case of Antônio Conselheiro, Ralph Della Cava argued that the explosive movement led by the counselor grew out of the Catholic revival of the late nineteenth century. That stunning surge among clerical and lay produced a conflict when one renegade Catholic cleric created charity houses, *Casas de Caridade*, to care for orphaned girls. He recruited lay women (*beatas*) and men (*beatos*) outside the bounds of formal diocesan control. "Conselheiro was a *beato*, a wondering servant of the Church eagerly encouraged by local priests for whom his activities were undertaken and on whom his status in the backlands depended."[16] That local bishops issued circulars to prohibit laymen from speaking from the pulpits spoke highly of the counselor's speaking abilities and the freedom he exercised traveling from pulpit to pulpit in the abandoned backlands of Brazil. His criticism of the Republic may not have been a restorationist impulse in favor of the monarchy as reported robustly by da Cunha, but might have reflected a partisan act in favor of a Bahian colonel.[17] The opposing Baron of Geremoabo

---

15 Maria Isaura Pereira de Queiroz, *O Messianismo no Brasil e no Mundo*, 3 (São Paulo: Editora Alfa Omega, 2003), 157.
16 Ralph Della Cava. "Brazilian Messianism and National Institutions: A Reappraisal of Canudos and Joaseiro." *The Hispanic American Historical Review* 48, no. 3 (August 1968): 407.
17 Cava, "Brazilian Messianism," 412.

utilized Conselheiro's words and actions to paint the lay preacher as a retrograde monarchist who rallied departmental and coastal elites to confront the ex-slaves who now threatened their way of life:

> Today things aren't what they used to be ... [We have to contend with] that damned "Conselheiro Antônio," who is exercising more power now than the first Napoleon. I no longer feel Brazilian: the worst offense a man can commit is to call me a Brazilian subject. I am thinking about naturalizing myself African. We will soon see this *sertão* confiscated by [Conselheiro] and his people, who now number more than 16,000, all miserable ex-slaves and criminals form every province, without a single one who is a human being; [Conselheiro is] imposing his own laws, raising an army of soldiers, and doing anything he wishes.[18]

Federal forces brutally repressed the Canudos settlement in 1897 and silenced its preacher permanently; the state's actions, however, did not stymie the words and actions of other prophetic leaders who would arise later to challenge both religious and secular authorities. The deepest religious convictions within humanity always generate the possibility of a different tomorrow, where lion and lamb can sleep together without fear, hunger, and pain.

Popular Catholicism rooted itself within the colonial worlds of Portuguese and Spanish America, and given independence in the beginning of the nineteenth century, emerged forcefully during military engagements and then found expression in localized, miracle-producing shrines. The church–state conflicts that captivated much of the local politics hampered institutional control over local faith production and enabled devotees to protect their community's implicit covenant with the divine and to ward off threats from the extraordinary changes that would come their way. Believers and participants depended on those agreements to see them through the insurrections and rebellions that ultimately wrested control of the political economy from their Iberian dons, and when the nascent state governments threatened their religious pact, they joined local military strongmen to push back and even overpower those who had sought to curtail worship and religiosity. Roaming preachers took up the prophetic call to restore some notion of what had been lost in the tumultuous changes of the nineteenth century, and state leadership reacted with a fury to challenge the alternative political models suggested in the religious critique.

---

18 Robert M Levine, *Vale of Tears: Revisiting the Canudos Massacre in Northeastern Brazil, 1893–1897* (Berkeley: University of California Press, 1992), 140.

These homegrown movements converged with the Catholic Church's world commitment to revive its institution and to challenge liberal notions of democracy and the market. Spirited clerics and lay leaders combined their efforts through modern, liberal methods of printing and publishing to combat the perceived evils of the very liberalism that had threatened their religious project. By the end of the nineteenth century, with Pope Leo XIII's spiritual detente with modern liberal democracy, the faithful discovered sufficient social space to revel in worship with a strengthened Catholic institution. Though the twentieth century brought revolutionary change through the global market and through world war, the pious, in concert with clergy and bishop, continued to explore how to live out the ideals and goals of their faith within the confines of the nation.

Bibliography and Suggested Readings

Batide, Roger. *As religiões africanas no Brasil*. Maria Eloisa Capellato and Olívia Krähenbühl. 1960. São Paulo, Brasil: Livraria Pioneira Editora, 1973.

Belting, Hans. *Likeness and Presence: A History of the Image before the Era of Art*. Translated by Edmund Japhcott. Chicago: University of Chicago Press, 1994.

Bermúdez, José Manuel. *Vida de la gloriosa vírgen Dominicana Santa Rosa de Sta. María, natural de Lima y patrón principal de las Américas*. Lima: Imprenta de los Huérfanos, 1827.

Brading, D. A. "Divine Idea and 'Our Mother': Elite and Popular Understanding in the Cult of Our Lady of Guadalupe of Mexico." In Kate Cooper and Jeremy Gregory (eds.), *Elite and Popular Religion*, 240–260. Rochester, NY: Boydell and Brewer, 2006.

The First America: The Spanish Monarchy, Creole Patriots, and the Liberal State 1492–1867. Cambridge: Cambridge University Press, 1991.

Mexican Phoenix: Our Lady of Guadalupe: Image and Tradition Across Five Centuries. Cambridge: Cambridge University Press, 2001.

Brown, Peter. *The Cult of the Saints: Its Rise and Function in Latin Christianity*. Haskell Lectures on History of Religions, no. 2. Chicago: University of Chicago Press, 1981.

Cava, Ralph Della. "Brazilian Messianism and National Institutions: A Reappraisal of Canudos and Joaseiro." *The Hispanic American Historical Review*, 48, no. 3 (August 1968): 402–420.

Concurso Literario en Honor de Santa Rosa de Lima Celebrado en Esta Ciudad en el Tercer Centenario de su Nacimiento: 30 de Abril de 1886. Lima: Imp. de Torres Aguirre, 1886.

Cunha, Euclides da. *Rebellion in the Backlands*. Translated by Samuel Putnam. 1944. Chicago: University of Chicago Press, 1984.

Davis, Natalie Z. *Society and Culture in Early Modern France: Eight Essays*. Stanford, CA: Stanford University Press, 1975.

"Some Tasks and Themes in the Study of Popular Religion." In Charles Trinkaus and Heiko O. Oberman (eds.), *The Pursuit of Holiness in Late Medieval and Renaissance Religion*, 307–336. Leiden: Brill, 1974.

Fick, Carolyn E. *The Making of Haiti: The Saint Domingue Revolution from Below*. Knoxville: University of Tennessee Press, 1990.

Fletcher, Rev. James C., and Rev. D. P. Kidder. *Brazil and the Brazilians Portrayed in Historical and Descriptive Sketches*. London: Sampson Low, Son, and Marston, 1866.

Greer, Allan, and Jodi Bilinkoff, eds. *Colonial Saints: Discovering the Holy in the Americas, 1500–1800*. New York: Routledge, 2003.

Greinacher, Norbert, and Norbert Mette, eds. *Popular Religion*. Concilium. Religion in the Eighties. Edinburgh: T. & T. Clark, 1986.

Heimann, Mary. "Catholic Revivalism in Worship and Devotion." In Sheridan Gilley and Brian Stanley (eds.), *The Cambridge History of Christianity. World Christianities, c.1815-c.1914*, 70–83. Cambridge: Cambridge University Press, 2006.

Horst, Oscar H., Robert N. Thomas, and John M. Hunter. "Difusión del Culto al Cristo Negro Crucificado de Esquipulas." *Mesoamérica*, 52 (Enero-Diciembre 2010): 143–158.

Ivereigh, Austen, ed. "Introduction. The Politics of Religion in an Age of Revival." In *The Politics of Religion in an Age of Revival. Studies in Nineteenth-Century Europe and Latin America*. Nineteenth-Century Latin American Series, 1–21. London: Institute of Latin American Studies, 2000.

"The Shape of the State: Liberals and Catholics in the Dispute Over Law 1420 of 1884 in Argentina." In Austen Ivereigh (ed.), *The Politics of Religion in an Age of Revival*, 166–187. London: Institute of Latin American Studies, 2000.

Levine, Robert M. *Vale of Tears: Revisiting the Canudos Massacre in Northeastern Brazil, 1893–1897*. Berkeley: University of California Press, 1992.

Martínez, Teodoro Hampe. "Santa Rosa de Lima y la identidad criolla en el Perú colonial." *Revista de Historia de América*, no. 121 (January–December 1996): 7–26.

Matovelle, José Julio María. *Imágenes y santuarios celebres de la Vírgen Santísima*. Vol. 5:2 of *Obras completas*. Cuenca, Ecuador: Imprenta L.N.S. de Editorial "Don Bosco," 1981.

Mecham, J. Lloyd. *Church and State in Latin America; a History of Politicoecclesiastical Relations*. Chapel Hill: The University of North Carolina press, 1934.

Meyer, Jean A. *The Cristero Rebellion: The Mexican People between Church and State, 1926–1929*. Trans. Richard Southern. Cambridge: Cambridge University Press, 1976.

Montúfar, Lorenzo. *Reseña Histórica de Centro-América*, Vol. II. Guatemala: Tip. de "El Progreso", 1878.

Muñoz, Miguel. *Doctrina cristiana sobre el culto de las imágenes, y noticia verdadera de la imágen milagrosa que se venera en el santuario del pueblo de Esquipulas, con una novena al fin dedicada al dulcísimo nobre de Jesus*. 1830. Guatemala: N.p., 1889.

"En que VSY se digna." Letter. Cartas, 1845.37. AHAG. Guatemala, 1845.

Navarrete Cáceres, Carlos. *Las rimas del peregrino. Poesía popular en oraciones, alabados y novenas al Cristo de Esquipulas*. Mexico: Universidad Nacional Autónoma de México, 2007.

Noya, Emilio. *Imaginería religiosa y santoral profano de corrientes*. Argentina: Artes Offset, 1994.

Paz Solórzano, Juan. *Contra los protestantes*. Guatemala City: Tipografía Sánchez & de Guise, 1909.

Documentos históricos referentes a la sagrada imagen del Señor Crucificado de Esquipulas y de su santuario. Guatemala City: Tipografía Sánchez & de Guise, 1904.

Historia del Señor Crucificado de Esquipulas, de su santuario; romerías; antigua provincia eclesiástica de Chiquimula de la Sierra y actual vicaría foránea; como tambien de otras muchas cosas dignas de saberse. Guatemala: Imp. Arenales Hijos, 1914.

Segunda parte de la historia del Señor Crucificado del Santuario de Esquipulas. Guatemala City: Tip. Arenales Hijos, 1916.

Pike, Fredrick B. *The Conflict between Church and State in Latin America.* Borzoi Books on Latin America. New York: Knopf, 1964.

Pompejano, Daniele. "El dios negro de los hombres blancos." *Mesoamérica,* no. 51 (enero–diciembre 2009): 123–149.

Prien, Hans-Jürgen. *La historia del cristianismo en América Latina.* Salamanca: Ediciones Sígueme, 1985.

Prince, Carlos. *Vida Edificante de la Gloriosa Santa Rosa de Lima, Patrona Universal de América, Filipinas é Indias.* Lima: Carlos Prince, Impresor, 1886.

Queiroz, Maria Isaura Pereira de. *O Messianismo no Brasil e no Mundo.* 3. São Paulo: Editora Alfa Omega, 2003.

Reis, João José. *Slave Rebellion in Brazil: The Muslim Uprising of 1835 in Bahia.* Trans. Arthur Brakel. Johns Hopkins Studies in Atlantic History and Culture. Baltimore: Johns Hopkins University Press, 1993.

Un Sacerdote. *Historia de Nrta Sra de Lujan. Su origen, su santuario, su villa, sus milagros y su culto.* Vol. I of *Historia de Ntra Sra de Lujan.* Buenos Aires: Pablo E. Coni, 1885.

Historia de Nrta Sra de Lujan. Su origen, su santuario, su villa, sus milagros y su culto. Vol. II of *Historia de Ntra Sra de Lujan.* Buenos Aires: Pablo E. Coni, 1885.

Schwartz, Stuart B. "Resistance and Accommodation in Eighteenth-Century Brazil: The Slaves' View of Slavery." *Hispanic American Historical Review* 57, no. 1 (February 1977): 69–81.

Sullivan-González, Douglass. *Piety, Power, and Politics. Religion and Nation Formation in Guatemala, 1821–1871.* Pittsburgh: University of Pittsburgh Press, 1998.

Taylor, William B. "The Virgin of Guadalupe in New Spain: An Inquiry into the Social History of Marian Devotion." *American Ethnologist* 14, no. 1 (February 1987): 9–33.

Van Oss, Adriaan C. *Catholic Colonialism: A Parish History of Guatemala 1524–1821.* Cambridge: Cambridge University Press, 1986.

Van Young, Eric. "Popular Religion and the Politics of Insurgency in Mexico, 1810–1821." In Austen Ivereigh (ed.), *The Politics of Religion in an Age of Revival. Studies in the Nineteenth-Century Europe and Latin America,* 74–114. Nineteenth-Century Latin American Series. London: Institute of Latin American Studies, 2000.

Vargas Ugarte, Ruben. *Historia del culto de Maria en Iberoamérica y de sus imágenes y santuarios más celebrados.* Tercera edición. Madrid: Talleres Gráficos Jura, 1956.

Voekel, Pamela. *Alone Before God: The Religious Origins of Modernity in Mexico.* Durham, NC: Duke University Press, 2002.

Woodward, Jr., Ralph Lee. *Rafael Carrera and the Emergence of the Republic of Guatemala, 1821–1873.* Athens: The University of Georgia Press, 1993.

Young, Eric Van. *The Other Rebellion: Popular Violence, Ideology, and the Mexican Struggle for Independence, 1810–1821.* Stanford, CA: Stanford University Press, 2001.

Zúñiga, Olga Portuondo. *La Virgen de la Caridad del Cobre Simbolo de Cubanía.* Madrid: Agualarga Editores, S.L., 2002.

19

Historical Protestantism in Latin America

STEPHEN C. DOVE

Although Protestantism has been a visible presence in Latin America since the late nineteenth century, it was only in the last two decades of the twentieth century that it emerged as a popular topic of scholarly study. This shift in awareness was largely a product of public events such as the 1982 coup d'état in Guatemala led by Pentecostal Efraín Ríos Montt and of statistical revelations that Protestant growth rates were mushrooming in countries ranging from Brazil to Chile to El Salvador. In light of these new data, scholars and journalists in the late twentieth century began to analyze the "emergence" of this seemingly foreign religion in a historically Catholic region, and their conclusions usually focused on topics such as Pentecostalization, political engagement, and shifts in religious demographics.

While these late-twentieth-century developments were important, scholarly and media focus on those issues often overlooked the reality that Protestantism was not actually new to Latin America, but rather had a long, complex history there. Foreign missionaries introduced Protestantism to the region in the early 1800s, and by the mid-1900s the religion had experienced the influence of local converts in areas of both theology and practice. In both its missionary origins and its local adaptation, what has been central to the history of Protestantism in Latin America is not its otherness but rather how intertwined this minority movement has been with broader political and social changes in the region. Historical Protestantism has been both a recipient of and a participant in these changes, and as such stands as an integrated part of modern Latin American history rather than as a novel appendix introduced only recently.

The Early Nineteenth Century: Protestantism's Slow Entrance

Despite its proximity to the United States (the largest exporter of missionary Protestantism in the world), Latin America was the last of the major world regions targeted by Protestant missionaries. In Asia and Africa, foreign missionary work began in earnest in the late eighteenth century, but except for a few isolated and inward-looking European settlements, Latin America remained virtually devoid of Protestant influences until nearly a century later. The reasons for this delayed entrance of Protestantism into Latin America were both political and theological. Prior to the 1820s, Protestantism in the Spanish empire was illegal, and suspected converts were subject to the Inquisition. Even if a missionary-minded Protestant had an inclination to cross into Spanish territory from the United States or British Honduras (modern Belize), the long-standing imperial rivalry between Britain and Spain assured English-speaking foreigners of extra scrutiny and, in turn, extra difficulty in making any headway in efforts to proselytize.

Following independence, the political impediments to Protestantism slowly disappeared as many young republics adopted liberal constitutions that abolished the religious monopoly of the Catholic Church and endorsed, at least officially, free choice in matters of religion. However, the first Protestants to take advantage of these openings were not missionaries but rather diplomats, businessmen, and colonization groups – Lutherans and Anglicans, for example – who considered themselves more as expatriates than as evangelizers. Only rarely did these groups attempt to establish missionary programs in the nineteenth century, even among their closest neighbors; and so the development of expatriate Protestantism did not produce any large-scale groups of local converts. Thus, with a few notable exceptions examined in the text that follows, before the 1850s there was little to no native Latin American Protestantism even though there were foreign Protestants in Latin America.

On theological grounds, the late entry of Protestantism into Latin America rested on ambivalent responses to Catholicism within missionary sending agencies. Protestant churches in the nineteenth century did not lack for anti-Catholic rhetoric, but at the same time they recognized a distinction between Catholicism and other religions. Protestant mission atlases of the late nineteenth and early twentieth centuries often divided their maps into two sections: one labeled "Christian" that included Protestant, Catholic, and Orthodox (Greek and Russian) subheadings and the second labeled "non-Christian" that included Mohammedan (Muslim), Buddhist, Brahman (Hindu), and Heathen subheadings. In general, British mission societies gravitated toward their imperial territories, which included areas dominated by Buddhism, Hinduism, and Islam. Throughout the 1800s, Protestant denominations in the United States also expressed a preference for the "heathen" regions that had not been exposed to any form of Christianity, especially China and

Southeast Asia. Even as late as 1910, when more than 1,000 Protestant mission representatives met at the World Missionary Conference in Edinburgh, the official proceedings made no mention of Latin America because of disagreements about whether the region was already Christianized as a result of its Roman Catholic heritage.

With these political and theological impediments, Protestant growth was indeed slow at first. In 1856, an encyclopedia of global missionary work reported only two permanent Protestant missionary enterprises anywhere in the former American colonies of the Spanish and Portuguese empires. One was a group of chapels belonging to the American Seaman's Friend Society in southern Brazil, which targeted transitory sailors rather than native Brazilians. The other was a mission station of the Methodist Episcopal Church in Buenos Aires, established in 1836. However, that mission operated primarily in English and did not attempt to form a Spanish-speaking congregation until 1867. By contrast, the same encyclopedia reported that in 1856, sixty-nine missionaries from fifteen mission groups operated in China and 120 missionaries from eleven groups worked in West Africa.

This general comparison of missionary activity across world regions is instructive for understanding the relatively late arrival of Protestantism in Latin American and for assessing the priorities of US and British missionaries. However, the actual details reported are not entirely accurate. It is true that by the mid-nineteenth century, there were few enduring Protestant communities composed of native Latin Americans. Likewise, it is true that most denominational and cooperative agencies clearly preferred to focus their energy and expenditures on the "heathen" lands of Asia and Africa. However, several individuals and at least one organization had made inroads into Latin America by the middle of the century, decades before most denominational mission boards invested money or personnel to establish native churches in the region. The overlooked nature of this early history partially results from the fact that the pioneering missionaries in Latin America were primarily from Britain and continental Europe. By contrast, US agents dominated Protestant missionary activity in Latin America from the late nineteenth century onwards. Since the early European missionary endeavors seldom contributed directly to the history of the later developing and longer lasting US projects, the internal histories of these later groups often elide the earlier European contributions.

Among early Protestant activities in Latin America, the most common agent used by Europeans was the *colporteur*, a traveling salesman who specialized in religious literature such as New Testaments. Colportage began in eighteenth-century Europe as a way to distribute both secular and religious literature in rural areas, but the profession quickly became dominated by religious publishers. By the nineteenth century, Bible societies had invested so much into colportage that they had developed a near-global distribution network that supplied single, young men with bibles and tracts to sell in areas beyond the reach of traditional missionaries.

More than a dozen colporteurs operated in Latin America during and immediately following the political openings created by independence movements. The earliest and most widely traveled of these was James Thomson, an agent of the British and Foreign Bible Society who made two tours of the region, first from 1818 to 1825 in South America and then from 1827 to 1838 in Mexico, Central America, and the Caribbean. Thomson's first appointment in South America included not only selling bibles but also promoting the Lancasterian educational system, which advocated training students as fellow teachers. This was particularly important to new national governments on the continent that welcomed advice on setting up public education systems to replace the Catholic-dominated educational models of the colonial period. Although Thomson was a dedicated Bible seller, early-twentieth-century Argentine historian Juan Ramos reported, "he did more for the schools than for the diffusion of the Bible."[1] Thomson's second tour was more focused on the evangelism and less on spreading the Lancasterian model. He left London in 1827 with 1,000 copies of Scripture and a mandate to bring back any native translations of the Bible that he might encounter. Even though his task was more singular than his first tour, his results regarding the Bible proved similar. An 1833 report of the British and Foreign Bible Society commented on Thomson's trip to Mexico and the Caribbean, "In the course of this journey, the successes he met with were comparatively small, while the evidences continually presented to him of the Scriptures being needed were many and painful."[2]

It is difficult to assess the long-term impact of early colporteurs like Thomson. None of these pioneers organized Protestant communities that survived beyond his departure, and other less tangible results varied widely. Some colporteurs self-reported that their efforts were failures. Henry Dunn, an Anglican priest who visited Guatemala from 1827 to 1828, wrote in his

---

[1] Quoted in Webster E. Browning, "Joseph Lancaster, James Thomson, and the Lancasterian System of Mutual Instruction, with Special Reference to Hispanic America," *HAHR* 4:1 (April 1921), 67.
[2] *The Twenty-ninth Report of the British and Foreign Bible Society* (London: J. Moyes, 1933), lxxvi.

travelogue, "From what I was able to observe, as well as from the number (of religious tracts) disposed of, there existed no demand for such books."[3]

Other colporteurs did leave a lasting mark even if their legacies did not match their high expectations. In 1843, British Baptist layman Frederick Crowe took it upon himself to distribute Protestant literature in Guatemala even though the conservative government that had come to power since Dunn's tour forbade such activity. Eventually, Crowe received some meager funding from the British and Foreign Bible Society, but he received less favor from the secular and Catholic authorities in Guatemala. After three years of legal wrangling and two rounds of book confiscations, the Guatemalan government expelled Crowe in 1846. However, by the time Crowe left Guatemala, his makeshift school had educated dozens of students including the sons of Liberal politicians.

Only one of these students became Protestant, but several others participated in the Liberal revolution of 1871 that would, among other things, permit the practice of Protestantism in Guatemala. The most notable of these students was Lorenzo Montúfar, a future minister of foreign relations in both Costa Rica and Guatemala and the lead author of Guatemala's 1879 Constitution. Although Montúfar never became a Protestant, Crowe's effect on the Central American statesman was clear. In his memoirs, Montúfar characterized both Crowe and Protestantism as important forces in the battle against the Conservative Party and entrenched political interests. This equation of Protestantism with Liberal Party principles and politics paved the way for the later opening of Central America to Protestant missionaries and foreshadowed a religious-political alliance that would be important for Protestants throughout Latin America later in the century.

Even before colporteurs, there was another Protestant intervention in Latin America that, although more localized, produced the oldest continuously functioning native Protestant community in the region. In the mid-eighteenth century, the Spanish and British empires engaged in a series of trade wars to gain the upper hand in the Caribbean. As part of this conflict, Britain established diplomatic relations with the autonomous indigenous communities along the Miskito Coast of modern Nicaragua. One element of this offensive was the deployment of missionaries from the Society for the Propagation of the Gospel beginning in 1743. Over the next four decades, Anglican missionaries baptized hundreds of Miskito indigenous people, including members of

---

3 Henry Dunn, *Guatimala: Or the United Provinces of Central America in 1827-8, Being Sketches and Memorandums Made During a Twelve Months' Residence in That Republic, by Henry Dunn* (New York: G. and C. Carvill, 1828), 125.

the ruling families. By 1785, however, the effects of tropical diseases on missionaries and conflicts with nearby traders led the British to abandon their missionary work on the coast. Nonetheless, an autochthonous church continued to operate in the missionaries' absence, and the Miskito indigenous elite continued to send their children to British schools in Jamaica.

For the next seven decades, Protestantism among the Miskito existed with limited outside influence. However, in 1849, Moravian missionaries from Saxony established a mission on the Miskito Coast at the behest of a Prussian prince who considered the area a potential colonization site. Germanic settlers never followed, but the missionaries were successful nonetheless. In the 1850s, the leading Miskito family joined the Moravian church, and by the end of the century virtually the entire indigenous population identified itself as Moravian. European influence declined as the century waned, and the Miskito kingdom officially became part of Nicaragua in 1894. However, the Miskito continued to hold fast to their Protestant religion. In fact, Protestant identity among the Miskito was so strong that the Sandinista government expressed concerns in the 1980s that the eastern coast of the country might secede because of their religious difference from the rest of the country.

Beyond the efforts of British colporteurs and Prussian Moravians, there were a handful of small, isolated, and mostly unsuccessful Protestant missionary endeavors elsewhere in the region. For example, during the Mexican-American War (1846–1848), chaplains in the US military distributed bibles as their units marched through Mexico, and a few years later at the southern extreme of the continent, an ill-fated attempt by England's Patagonia Missionary Society to convert the indigenous people of Tierra del Fuego ended when all seven missionaries died of starvation. Many small episodes like these indicate isolated attempts at Protestant evangelization in Latin America prior to the mid-1800s, but few beyond colportage and the Moravian mission proved to have a lasting impact.

The Advent of Denominationalism

After these meager beginnings, there was little reason to believe that Protestantism would gain a foothold in Latin America. However, in the latter half of the nineteenth century, US denominations began directing at least a portion of their missionary budgets toward coordinated and institutionalized efforts in Latin America. This shift, which marked a departure from the ad hoc style of colportage, arose from a number of diverse factors including opportunities provided by personal networks, the development of US expansionist ideologies, and new theologies of missions. However, one nonreligious catalyst proved especially integral to the expansion of denominational missions throughout Latin America in the late nineteenth century, and that was the rise of political regimes that mixed traditional liberalism with scientific positivism.

Ironically, at the same time that ideas such as modernism and scientific theory began to challenge Protestantism for ideological supremacy in the United States, those same ideas created an open door for the importation of historical Protestantism into Latin America. In the North Atlantic, science and modernism paved the way for secularization. Further south, liberal leaders used those ideas for a similar but much more specific project of anticlericalism that sought to weaken the influence of the Catholic hierarchy.

Because of this narrow focus on the political power of the Catholic Church, the various anticlerical movements of the late nineteenth and early twentieth centuries did not demand a complete shift to secularization, and for liberal leaders in Latin America, Protestantism provided an ideal counterweight to Catholic hegemony. This was particularly true in matters of education, where liberal governments eagerly recruited Protestant educators – paid for and staffed by foreign denominations – to replace Catholic parochial schools. Protestantism also offered liberals a ready-made ally in campaigns against vices such as alcoholism and gambling that were the centerpieces of efforts to reform poor, and especially indigenous, populations.

Some of the earliest examples of these ideological alliances come from Chile and Brazil. The first missionary to establish a permanent station in Chile was David Trumbull, who arrived in 1845 as a Congregationalist and later affiliated with the Presbyterians. Trumbull's first mission at Valparaiso offered only English services for expatriates, but he soon switched his focus to the local population and even became a naturalized citizen of Chile. In addition to forming the first Protestant church in the country, Trumbull was known for using his printing press and his pulpit to advocate for liberal secular initiatives including religious tolerance laws, secular cemeteries, civil marriage, and educational reform. On his death in 1889, his eulogists included not only Protestant converts but also the Chilean senate, which saluted "one of (Chile's) most distinguished citizens" by standing in silence to honor him.

In Brazil, US Methodists sent missionaries to work with Portuguese-speaking populations as early as 1836, but strong opposition from the Catholic hierarchy forced them from the country a few years later. In 1855, however, Scottish Congregationalists Robert and Sarah Kalley initiated a second attempt at evangelizing Brazil by focusing directly on the elite ruling class in the court of the Brazilian monarchy. The Kalleys' evangelism centered on the imperial city of Petrópolis near Rio de Janeiro, where they founded the first lasting Protestant church in Brazil, the Igreja Evangélica Fluminense, and baptized several members of the aristocracy. Their strategy of allying with the elite earned them not only protection against Catholic opponents but also the personal friendship of Brazilian Emperor Pedro II who, despite being a monarch, was a proponent of modernization and liberalization.

The connections between liberal politics and Protestant beginnings in Chile and Brazil were direct, but in later cases the links were even closer, so close in fact that in some countries like Guatemala they were even causal. The first permanent missionary to Guatemala, Presbyterian John Hill, arrived in 1882 at the behest of President Justo Rufino Barrios and even entered the country for the first time as part of the president's retinue. Barrios, like many other positivist leaders in Latin America, believed Protestantism would be a civilizing force among the large indigenous population of the country. His support of the Presbyterians included mandating that cabinet ministers send their children to Hill's school and granting the denomination confiscated Catholic property just one block from the capital city's main plaza, a downtown lot that is still home to a Presbyterian congregation.

In Mexico, the connection between political positivism and Protestantism was also strong but not so direct. US mission boards did not send official agents to Mexico until 1870 because potential conflicts with Catholic political interests blocked earlier plans. In 1836, the American Baptists – not yet split into northern and southern branches – reported that the republics of Texas and Mexico still remained "inaccessible to the Christian missionary," but the Baptists held out hope that circumstances would soon change so that "the banner of the true cross may yet be planted in the city of Montezuma." The political change these Baptists desired was slower in coming than they expected. Not until 1864 did the Baptist mission board – then representing the northern half of the country – report that liberal triumph over the "Church Party" created conditions suitable for the opening of what they believed to be the first Protestant church in Mexico, located in the border city of Matamoros.

US Presbyterians also looked south to Mexico in the 1830s and actually made some unofficial progress as early as 1852 when Melinda Rankin, a Presbyterian laywoman, traveled without the blessing of either her church or the Mexican government to Matamoros to distribute bibles and open a Protestant girls' school. Rankin's missionary endeavors were both solitary and illegal until the passing of Mexico's 1857 Constitution and the subsequent Reform Laws of the 1860s.

Even with these laws, it still took another decade for the effects of the US Civil War to abate and for Porfirio Díaz to pursue the US-friendly policies that allowed for a true flourishing of Protestant churches in Mexico. Although Díaz was not as hands-on in religious matters as other Latin American leaders, his encouragement was integral to the Protestants' success. Díaz personally befriended several missionaries, and he encouraged them to teach the working class and peasants in hopes of instilling an ideal that Max Weber would later call the Protestant work ethic. It was also during Díaz's dictatorship that anticlerical politicians in local and state governments began viewing Protestants as ideological allies and encouraging these religious dissidents to move into their regions.

Protestant Challengers to Denominationalism

With friendly, or at least less antagonistic, governments throughout much of Latin America and with more resources dedicated to Latin America by US denominations, historical Protestantism had firmly entrenched itself in the region by the beginning of the twentieth century. Entrenchment, however, should not be confused with numerical success. At the turn of the century, foreign missionary organizations from the United States and Europe reported a combined 140,000 native constituents in the region (including British Honduras and Dutch Guiana). At the same time, they estimated the population of Latin America to be 54.5 million, meaning that less than one-quarter of 1 percent of the population showed a sustained interest in Protestantism in 1900.

As denominational Protestantism began to gain this small but lasting foothold in Catholic Latin America, it encountered a new religious challenger, not from within Latin America but from the United States. Beginning in the 1890s and accelerating in the early twentieth century, so-called "faith missions" became increasingly dominant in the Protestant universe and especially in Latin America. By definition, these faith missions were an uncoordinated collection of individuals and groups, but they did hold in common a few distinctive features that differentiated them from the denominations that pioneered Protestant work in Latin America.

First, missionaries representing these groups did not receive regular funding through established denominational mission boards but raised money through their own piecemeal networks of churches. This meant that faith missionaries' funding was less certain (hence, their name), but it also meant that missionaries had an incentive to be more efficient in their proselytism because donors were free to shift their funds to more effective missionaries elsewhere. This efficiency led to a second, practical trait shared by faith missions. They tended to shift their focus away from elites and toward the conversion of groups on the margins of society such as indigenous Latin Americans and migrants to urban areas. Although less connected to money and power, these people often had more social motivations to switch religions, and so they often proved to be a more fruitful field. This difference was especially important in the early twentieth century as many Latin American countries experienced the social stresses associated with modernizing economies and industrialization.

Finally, faith missions usually – though not always – espoused a more conservative and more end-times-oriented theology than their denominational counterparts. Even though faith missions originated before the fundamentalist-modernist controversies, those debates about issues such as biblical literalism, higher criticism, and the nature of sin crystallized the identity of many of the extra-denominational groups that shaped Protestantism in twentieth-century Latin America.

As many US denominations moved toward progressive ideas like the Social Gospel movement, disenchanted conservatives broke away from old institutions and gathered around evangelistic personalities such as Dwight L. Moody and C. I. Scofield, who served as the godfathers of various faith missions, including some of the largest of these in Latin America. Motivated by their belief that Christ's return was imminent, faith missions quickly spun a web of missionaries around the globe. In Latin America, organizations such as Wycliffe Bible Translators, the Central American Mission (CAM), and the Latin American Mission began to wield just as much influence as traditional denominations such as Presbyterians, Baptists, and Methodists because of their appeal to marginalized populations.

Although denominations and faith missions eventually became partners, their early relationships were filled with tension. The first of the faith missions to arrive in Latin America was the Texas-based Central American Mission in 1890. The potential friction between this new group and established denominations such as the Presbyterians was clear when the CAM announced its purpose was to spread the Gospel to the "unevangelized" region of Central America that other mission groups were "passing over." If indirect criticisms were not strong enough, CAM missionaries obliged with more biting critiques such as Albert Bishop's 1899 assessment that in Guatemala, where Presbyterians had been working for seventeen years, he doubted that more than twenty-five people in the country were really Christian. Clearly, the Presbyterian form of the Gospel was not strong enough for more conservative faith missionaries such as Bishop.

The impact of faith missions was not just that they challenged established denominational missions. They also increased the likelihood that individual missionaries would engage in spiritual entrepreneurship and stray outside the boundaries set by US institutions, even faith missions. This was made possible by the fact that faith missionaries were free to seek funding and support without the approval of their mission board. The most significant case of this entrepreneurship in Latin America, and perhaps worldwide, was that of Cameron Townsend. Townsend arrived in Guatemala in 1917 as a colporteur and joined the CAM two years later. Although not the first missionary to win converts among the country's indigenous population, he quickly became the most successful. Along with his wife Elvira, a former member of the Presbyterian mission, Townsend moved to a Kakchiquel Maya community where he completed the first translation of the New Testament into that language.

However, Townsend's vision was bigger than a single translation into a relatively isolated indigenous language. In 1929, with his Kakchiquel translation nearing completion, Townsend proposed a large-scale shift of the CAM's energies away from Spanish-language ministry in Central America and toward a hemispheric evangelization of indigenous groups that would employ airplanes, radio signals, and professional linguists.

The CAM's financial supporters dismissed this idea as too audacious and resource-intensive, but his plan did capture the imagination of Moisés Sáenz, who was the intellectual leader of the Mexican government's education department (Secretaría de Educación Pública – SEP) in the 1930s and also a product of missionary schools in Monterrey and Mexico City. In 1931, Saenz invited Townsend to pursue his large-scale translation projects in partnership with the Mexican government, and in 1932, Townsend resigned from the CAM. In Mexico, with the support of president Lázaro Cárdenas and a new set of financial backers from his native California, Townsend established his own faith mission – or more precisely, two faith missions. The first was the evangelistic group Wycliffe Bible Translators, and the second was the academic and officially secular Summer Institute of Linguistics. In reality, however, these two organizations operated seamlessly and became the largest faith mission in the world by the end of the twentieth century, spreading both Bible translations and anthropological controversy from Mexico to the Amazon and beyond as they placed missionaries among even the remotest indigenous groups of Latin America, Africa, and Asia.

Although faith missions significantly altered the landscape of Protestantism in Latin America, they by no means replaced denominational missions. Denominational missionaries continued their evangelizing, but winning converts and organizing churches remained a slow and arduous process. Over time, denominations lost ground to faith missions, and later Pentecostalism, in terms of evangelism. However, an area of ministry where denominations excelled was creating service institutions. By 1910, Protestant schools and hospitals operated by denominational missionaries had sprung up in every corner of Latin America. Across the region, more than 500 schools served 30,000 students from the elementary to the college level. In the medical field, missionaries operated twenty hospitals and six nursing schools by the turn of the century and served more than 100,000 patients annually. Even though faith missions were diversifying the job of proselytism, education and medicine remained a decidedly denominational task, with Methodists and Presbyterians running two-thirds of all mission schools and one-half of all mission hospitals in Latin America.

The most prominent product of Protestant educational institutions was the aforementioned Sáenz, who not only provided intellectual leadership for the Mexican government's education department in the 1930s but also coordinated hemispheric indigenous education and acculturation projects in the first half of the twentieth century. Sáenz and hundreds of other Latin Americans including Peru's Victor Raúl Haya de la Torre, the founder of the American Popular Revolutionary Alliance political party, were products of a Protestant education, but examples of specific pupils do not represent the entirety of Protestant educational influence. For example, in Peru, where early conversion rates were mediocre at best, Methodist schools had an outsized influence on national education policy under the modernizing regimes of the early twentieth century. By 1927, Protestants represented only 0.2 percent of the Peruvian population but operated 8 percent of the country's private and religious schools.

Because missionaries employed modern pedagogical theories like John Dewey's pragmatism, leading Peruvian educators used these campuses as laboratories to test ideas about incorporating sports, language study, hygiene, civics, and other activities into the national curriculum. Missionaries did use school campuses as preaching points, but they downplayed the role of evangelism inside of these educational institutions. In fact, the stated goal of Methodists in Peru was not to convert students but rather "to build better citizens for Peru – better world citizens."[4] They did this by emphasizing the same modernizing ideals that their allies in the liberal government did, including business courses, English instruction, and toleration. Thus,

---

4 Juan Fonseca Ariza, *Misioneros y civilizadores: protestantismo y modernización en el Perú (1915–1930)* (Lima: Pontificia Universidad Católica del Perú, 2002), 197.

although Protestants by no means spiritually conquered Peru or the rest of Latin America in the early twentieth century, they did exert significant influence on the future of many countries through education policy.

Shifts to Local Leadership

Through the early twentieth century, the story of historical Protestantism in Latin America was largely an account of foreign individuals and institutions more so than the story of local converts or leaders. This emphasis is somewhat unfair, as even at the earliest stages of Protestant development in Latin America, so-called "native helpers" – local translators, workers, and evangelists – played significant roles in shaping and expanding congregations. However, it is often difficult to assess the contributions of these Latin American Protestants in the earliest decades of the movement because foreign missionaries dominated the task of writing – and therefore interpreting – the historical record. For instance, in Guatemala at the turn of the twentieth century, CAM missionaries reported discovering multiple congregations of fifty to sixty worshippers in the country's western highlands that had been started by native colporteurs, most of whom remained unnamed in missionary reports. Elision of their identity was not the only slight paid to these early Protestant leaders either. Despite the fact that each of these locally led congregations was twice the size of the largest missionary-led church in the capital city, CAM missionaries still informed their US supporters, "Missionaries from the home land are needed to instruct and direct the native workers and pastor the flock. Rarely do the natives make good pastors."[5]

Even taking into account the under-recorded native contributions of this early period, the character of Protestantism in Latin American at this point remained more missionary than local. Local preachers and colporteurs may have been more effective in this period than foreign missionaries, but the movement's center of gravity continued to rest in the institutions and individuals imported from North America and Europe. As the twentieth century approached its midpoint, however, the balance between foreign and domestic forces began to tip dramatically in favor of local influence, and this shift initiated a trend of explosive Protestant growth in practically every corner of Latin America.

Even though the balance of influence shifted from foreign to local throughout Latin America, it seldom – if ever – occurred the same way in two different

---

5 *Central American Bulletin*, 15 July, 1905, 15–16.

places. Two examples, one from Cuba and the other from Chile, illustrate the extent of this variation and also provide some basic principles for understanding other nationalization movements. Although no two national contexts were exactly the same, these examples highlight the two most common factors in church nationalization movements – politics and Pentecostalism. Throughout the region, these two issues would be the most common motivations for local congregations to separate from missionary oversight.

Cuba represents both the earliest and probably the most exceptional case of national Protestantism in Latin America. While the rest of the region experienced a roughly linear move from missionary to local Protestantism beginning in the first half of the twentieth century, Cubans organized national churches as early as the 1870s only to see those institutions fall under foreign control as a result of dramatic political changes at the turn of the century and then return to local control again after the revolution of 1959. The first Protestant congregation *in* Cuba was an 1871 Anglican mission to sailors and immigrants. However, the first Protestant congregation *composed of Cubans* actually formed five years earlier in New York City, when a group of exiled dissidents organized the first Spanish-speaking Anglican congregation in the world. Highlighting the intersection of religious and political ideology in the congregation was the fact that its priest, Joaquín de Palma, was an active member of the revolutionary junta during the Ten Years' War. Similar congregations also formed in the 1870s in Key West, Philadelphia, and New Orleans, where exiles' anti-Spanish sentiment often manifested itself as anti-Catholicism.

At the end of the Ten Years' War in 1878, Protestant Cubans began moving back to the island, and they brought their religion with them. By 1883, there were a sufficient number of Spanish-speaking Anglicans in the province of Matanzas to request an official mission from the Episcopal Church. However, when the US denomination declined to send a missionary, a Cuban priest living in Key West named Juan Batista Báez took charge of Protestant work on the island that included more than 1,500 communicants in six locations. Historian Luis Martínez-Fernández characterizes these churches not only as "national" but also as "nationalist" because adherents stood in religious and cultural opposition to the Roman Catholic Church of the Spanish metropole. However, after the US intervention of 1898 and the consequent rise in foreign missionary activity, it was Catholicism that became the religion of independence-minded nationalists and Protestantism that became the religion of imperialism. This was underlined rhetorically by the fact that US denominations such as the Southern Baptists organized Cuban mission work under their Home Mission Boards rather than their Foreign Mission Boards.

Thus, from 1898 until the revolution of 1959, Protestantism in Cuba took on the missionary character that most other areas of Latin America were beginning to shed at the same time. Although some individual pastors separated from missionary-aligned national bodies during the first half of the twentieth century, most churches remained firmly tethered to US mission boards until 1959. Only when the United States and Cuba severed diplomatic relations in 1961 did most churches began acting autonomously, and even after that break a few still remained dependent on US funds funneled through backdoor channels.

In Chile, unlike in Cuba, it was Pentecostalization rather than politics that drove one of the most dramatic nationalization movements in Latin American Protestantism. Also unlike in Cuba, it was a US missionary, Willis C. Hoover, who initiated the nationalization process. Hoover arrived in Chile in 1889 and in 1902 began working as pastor of the country's largest Methodist congregation in Valparaiso. Frustrated with his lack of success evangelizing poor migrants coming from rural areas to one of Chile's largest cities, Hoover searched for new tactics, and by 1909 he found his answer in the charismatic worship of Pentecostalism, in this case inspired not by the 1906 Azusa Street Revival in California but by the 1905 Mukti Revival in India.

Although Hoover's innovative approach successfully attracted new worshippers, the Methodist Chile Conference resoundingly denounced his methods as "anti-Methodist, contrary to Scriptures, and irrational." As a result, three congregations that participated in the revival – composed largely of working-class Chileans – split from the missionary-approved denomination and formed the National Methodist Church in 1910. Soon after, this group invited Hoover to take the reins of leadership, but having a foreigner, even one not on the payroll of a foreign mission board, at the helm of a national Protestant church organization did not sit well with all members of the new group. Hoover continued in his position for two decades, but in 1933 the national church split into two denominations, one led by Hoover and the other strictly national. Interestingly, members of both of these organizations began referring to themselves as *criollos pentecostales* later in the century to differentiate themselves from newer Pentecostals won over by later arriving US missionaries.

Historical Protestantism at the End of the Twentieth Century

To say that Latin American Protestantism shifted from foreign to local control by the mid-twentieth century does not mean that US denominations or faith missions disappeared from the region. In fact, just the opposite occurred; as the century progressed, the number of missionaries in Latin America continued to grow. However, their roles changed dramatically. Increasingly, missionaries focused on task-specific projects, most notably the Wycliffe Bible Translators' efforts to produce the New Testament in indigenous languages. Meanwhile, the job of leading local churches increasingly fell to natives of Latin American countries. With the mantle of leadership now on the shoulders of Latin Americans, Protestants in the region began to occupy themselves with theological and practical questions different than – though not completely separate from – their sister churches in the North Atlantic. As was foreshadowed in the rise of Chilean national churches, one of the most dramatic changes in Latin American Protestantism – even historical Protestantism – in the late twentieth century was Pentecostalism.

The rise of Pentecostalism is a complex topic whose scope extends beyond this discussion of historical Protestantism, but it is important to note that the two movements are not disconnected. Beginning in the late twentieth century, most new converts to Evangelicalism in Latin America joined Pentecostal rather than historical Protestant congregations or denominations. In several cases, large groups of historical Protestant congregations themselves adopted Pentecostalism en masse without giving up their denominational heritage, as the Igreja Presbiteriana Renovada of Brazil did in 1975 when it separated from other Presbyterians in the country. However, this shift toward Pentecostalism did not represent the creation of a totally new type of Christianity. Often, though not always, Pentecostals and historical Protestants viewed themselves as one group. Significantly, the primary self-referents for both groups were, and remain, terms like *evangélico*, *creyente/crente*, or *cristiano/cristão* rather than *protestante* or *pentecostal*. These preferred names self-consciously include both Pentecostalism and historical Protestantism. Also, during public events, notably the five hundredth anniversary of Martin Luther's birth in 1983, Pentecostals and historical Protestants often joined together in celebration.

A second area of particular concern to Protestants in late-twentieth-century Latin America was the relationship of faith to politics. As with the rise of Pentecostalism, there was no single Protestant response to the question of how believers should engage politically, especially in times of increasing state violence. For example, during Nicaragua's Sandinista conflict, Protestants found themselves facing off across political battle lines, with the Baptist-led group CEPAD sympathizing with the leftist Sandinista political program, while more theologically conservative Protestants joined the Pentecostal Assembly of God to condemn the revolution.

Throughout Latin America, the common ground shared by Latin American Protestants in politics has not been their ideology but rather an uneasiness with the quiescent position commonly espoused by missionaries. Members of historic Protestant churches have staked out definite political positions across the political spectrum, from supporting authoritarian regimes to advocating for revolution. This trend toward political engagement, usually frowned upon by foreign missionaries, was even evident as early as the Mexican Revolution when many Protestant pastors and lay people – both men and women – participated first in anti-reelectionist clubs and later in the northern armies of Obregon and Carranza while US missionaries sat on the sidelines. Even as they claimed active roles in politics, historical Protestants in the twentieth century almost always assumed the minority role in political coalitions, in large part because the movement reached a statistical plateau late in the twentieth century. Historical Protestants remain a sizable minority in most Latin American countries, but declining growth rates, especially relative to Pentecostalism, have limited their influence.

Conclusion

In the twenty-first century, historical Protestantism remains a minority religion in Latin America, and it now competes for adherents not only with traditional Catholicism but also with Pentecostalism, Catholic renewal movements, revived folk religions, and secularism. In the face of this religious pluralism, the earlier growth of historical Protestantism has subsided in most areas and given way to numerical stability or even decline. It is important to note, however, that historical Protestantism is not only a recipient of the effects of this growing pluralism; it also played a significant role in forming this same trend through its historical participation in broader social and political changes in the region.

Far from being an anomalous external addendum to Latin American religious history, historical Protestantism has been an integral minority religion in the region and has been part of – if not always at the center of – many of the most important trends in modern Latin America history. In the early nineteenth century, Protestant colporteurs and missionaries worked with new nationalists to help design some of the first state institutions, especially in the field of education. Later in the nineteenth century, the arrival and first successes of Protestant missionaries were intertwined with the rise of liberal regimes and the development of various toleration laws. In the twentieth century, Protestantism was one of many institutions in the region that offered an alternative social option in the face of changes wrought by modernization, and later historical Protestants actively engaged with ideologies from across the political spectrum. In the twenty-first century, although foreign missionaries still operate in the region, historical Protestantism has become a local religion, with theologies and priorities set from within national contexts. In the future, it will be these national churches more than foreign missionaries that make decisions about how historical Protestantism will navigate the cultural and social realities of life in Latin America.

Bibliography and Suggested Readings

Baldwin, Deborah. *Protestants in the Mexican Revolution: Missionaries, Ministers, and Social Change*. Chicago: University of Illinois, 1990.
Bastian, Jean-Pierre. *Los disidentes: Sociedades protestantes y revolución en México, 1872–1911*. México: Fondo de Cultura Económica, 1989.
　Protestantismos y modernidad latino-americana: Historia de unas minorías religiosas activas en América Latina. México: Fondo de Cultura Económica, 1994.
Brusco, Elizabeth E. *The Reformation of Machismo: Evangelical Conversion and Gender in Colombia*. Austin: University of Texas Press, 1995.
Corse, Theron Edward. *Protestants, Revolution, and the Cuba-U.S. Bond*. Gainesville: University Press of Florida, 2007.
Fonseca Ariza, Juan. *Misioneros y civilizadores: Protestantismo y modernización en el Perú (1915–1930)*. Lima: Pontificia Universidad Católica del Perú, 2002.
Garrard-Burnett, Virginia. *Protestantism in Guatemala: Living in the New Jerusalem*. Austin: University of Texas Press, 1998.
Garrard-Burnett, Virginia, and David Stoll, eds. *Rethinking Protestantism in Latin America*. Philadelphia: Temple University Press, 1993.
Hartch, Todd. *Missionaries of the State: The Summer Institute of Linguistics, State Formation, and Indigenous Mexico, 1935–1985*. Tuscaloosa: University of Alabama Press, 2006.
Martin, David. *Tongues of Fire: The Explosion of Protestantism in Latin America*. Cambridge, MA: Blackwell, 1990.
Martínez Fernández, Luis. *Protestantism and Political Conflict in the Nineteenth-Century Hispanic Caribbean*. New Brunswick, NJ: Rutgers University Press, 2002.
Mondragón, Carlos. *Like Leaven in the Dough: Protestant Social Thought in Latin America, 1920–1950*. Madison, NJ: Fairleigh Dickinson University Press, 2010.
Smith, Calvin L. *Revolution, Revival, and Religious Conflict in Sandinista Nicaragua*. Boston: Brill, 2007.
Stoll, David. *Is Latin America Turning Protestant? The Politics of Evangelical Growth*. Berkeley: University of California, 1990.
Svelmoe, William Lawrence. *A New Vision for Missions: William Cameron Townsend, the Wycliffe Bible Translators, and the Culture of Early Evangelical Faith Missions, 1896–1945*. Tuscaloosa: University of Alabama Press, 2008.

20

Immigrant Protestantism: The Lutheran Church in Latin America

MARTIN N. DREHER

Historical Development and Legal Status

At the outset of the sixteenth-century European expansion to the Americas, the Portuguese and Spanish possessions remained off-limits for Lutheranism and for the other major religion that was strongly associated with northern European expansion, Anglicanism. There were, to be sure, a few isolated episodes during the colonial period in which Lutheran Christians took part. Thus, for instance, in 1528, in the period when the Spanish Kingdom and the Holy Roman Empire were ruled by the same monarch, under the titles of Charles I and Charles V, respectively, Welser came to Venezuela and a handful of Lutherans participated in the exploration of that territory. Whether they bore witness to their faith is unknown. The same might be said of Ulrich Schmiedl from Straubing and Hans Staden from Hessen. The former took part in the foundation of Buenos Aires; the latter stayed on after being stranded on Brazilian shores. Although the first Lutheran congregation in the region was founded in 1666 on the Danish Virgin Island of St. Thomas, and the second followed in 1743 in present-day Suriname, at the time a Dutch colony, we can speak of a Lutheran history in Latin America and the Caribbean only from the nineteenth century onward. Only after the independence movements of that period did a significant Lutheran influx into Latin America take place. Whatever their origins, whether immigrants, merchants, craftsmen, refugees, or missionaries, the different strands of Lutheran influx also explain the variety of influences found within Latin America Lutheranism.

Immigrant Lutheranism

In 1824, only a few weeks apart, the first Lutheran congregations were founded in Brazil, one in Nova Friburgo, near Rio de Janeiro, and the other in São Leopoldo, in southern Brazil. Further South, German immigrants likewise founded congregations in Buenos Aires (1843), Montevideo (1857), and Asunción (1893). After 1870 a number of congregations were formed in the provinces of Misiones and Entre Rios, in Argentina. In 1890 the Evangelical Synod of the River Plate was established. Finally, around Lake Llanquihue in southern Chile, Lutheran congregations were set up in Osorno (1863) and Puerto Montt, again by German immigrants. The Evangelical Synod of Chile was established in 1903.

Merchant and Craftsmen Congregations

In northern Latin America merchants and craftsmen founded congregations in Mexico (1861), Caracas (1894), Lima (1899), La Paz (1923), and Guatemala (1929), though the congregations of Rio de Janeiro and São Paulo in Brazil were originally merchant and craftsmen congregations as well.

Lutheran Missions

The evangelical missionary societies established primarily during the nineteenth century never really viewed Latin America as a missionary field. Strange as it may seem, this observation expresses a characteristic attitude of Lutheranism vis-à-vis the Roman Catholic Church. Lutherans always viewed Roman Catholics as Christians, and therefore not objects of mission work, let alone of rebaptism. This attitude did not change even when it became clear that the Roman Catholic Church was not in a position to evangelize even half the population to which it was entitled under the old rights of patronage. Such was also the conduct of Lutheran immigrant congregations and synods. This posture is often wrongly claimed to have had racial or ethnic origins. Instead, it was grounded in theological principles. Quite a different stance was taken by most churches from Reformed and Anglo-Saxon backgrounds that actively carried out mission work among Catholics from the mid-nineteenth century onward, and adopted rebaptism as a rule, on the grounds that Roman Catholics were not Christian.

North American Lutherans only later came to favor mission work in Latin America, owing to influence from the North American Evangelical movement and the Monroe Doctrine. The United Lutheran Church started work in Puerto Rico in 1898. In 1908 the same church also became involved in mission work in Argentina. This eventually led to the formation of the United Evangelical Lutheran Church of Argentina. The membership of this church was originally only Spanish speaking, although today it comprises mostly descendants of European immigrants. In 1901 the Lutheran Church – Missouri Synod started sending out missionaries to Brazil, followed in 1905 by missionaries to Argentina, whose activity was limited, a few exceptions notwithstanding, to descendants of German immigrants. Thus, all Lutheran churches in the Southern Cone of Latin America share the same ethnic background.

In the Anglophone and Danish-speaking Caribbean, Lutheran missions had existed since the seventeenth century. In 1951 this missionary field was joined with the mission on Puerto Rico to form the Caribbean Synod of the American Lutheran Church. The mission in Puerto Rico had been initiated by theology student Gustav Sigfrid Swenson, who arrived on the island only two months after the armistice in the Spanish-American War. Deeply influenced by the revival movement, Swenson believed that the American protectorate over Puerto Rico had great missionary significance. His activity could be compared to what today would be called a "faith mission." Swenson's work was taken over by the General Council, later the Lutheran Church in America, in 1899.

A further Lutheran activity in the Caribbean region that merits mention is the mission work initiated in Cuba in 1912 by the Lutheran Church – Missouri Synod. These congregations were left to their own devices after the North American pastors pulled out of Cuba in 1959. In 1987, however, the Lutheran World Federation began sending pastors to Cuba again.

All Lutheran congregations in Central America basically hail from the activity of the Lutheran Church – Missouri Synod. German immigration to Guatemala goes back to the mid-nineteenth century and Germans made up a small but economically significant portion of the population by the early twentieth century. Initially, German pastors were active in that country, but all German institutions in the country, including German-language schools and churches, were repressed during World War II and many pastors left the country. After World War II the work was taken up by Missouri Synod pastors. Guatemala became a base for further work in El Salvador (1952) and Costa Rica (1962). In Panama the Lutheran presence started with the activity of a military chaplain (1942). When European refugees started coming to Central America, the Lutheran World Federation (LWF) sent out itinerant ministers to the region, beginning in 1953. This led to the creation of congregations in San José (Costa Rica), Managua, Tegucigalpa, and San Salvador. A characteristic trait of present-day Lutheran churches in Central America is the cooperation among congregations, in remarkable contrast to the past, when they often operated apart from, or even against, one another.

Bolivia holds a peculiar position in South America. This is where the highest proportion of Lutherans among the indigenous population is found. A German-speaking congregation was founded in La Paz as early as 1923. Native language work began a decade later, when a Lutheran Bible School in Minneapolis, Minnesota formed the South American Mission Prayer League (later renamed World Mission Prayer League) in 1937 and sent the first two missionaries to Bolivia the following year. Without any kind of institutional ties, the missionaries lived on donations from individual North American Lutherans as a "Faith Mission." Mission stations were set up, and in 1944 the Hacienda Coaba was purchased to serve as a home for orphaned children. A school and a Bible study program to promote the development of native workers soon followed, and the first home-grown missionaries were ordained in 1954. The Bolivian Evangelical Lutheran Church was established in 1957. However, following a ground swell of nationalism, local leaders assumed overall control of the church in 1967, at which point North American missionaries left the country.

The Lutheran church in Venezuela goes back to nineteenth-century German craftsmen. After World War II the church was given a boost with the arrival of Latvian and Hungarian refugees. The gradual consolidation of these traditions resulted in the present-day Evangelical Lutheran Church in Venezuela. Also active in the country since 1951, the Lutheran Church – Missouri Synod gave rise to the Lutheran Church of Venezuela.

In Colombia we have a Lutheran church that looks back at a tale of woe. As was the case with other evangelical denominations, the Lutheran church faced persecution between the years 1948 and 1957. Historically, the church originated from immigration, Wisconsin Synod missionary efforts, and a "faith mission" initiative. The beginnings in Ecuador were similar. Primarily at work there were immigrants, the World Mission Prayer League, and the Santal Mission. The small number of Lutherans in Peru hail from German immigration, as well as the Sower Bible Mission and the Norwegian Mission.

Immigrant Churches

In the Southern Cone of South America we find a Lutheran church made up almost exclusively of immigrant descendants. One exception would be the United Evangelical Lutheran Church in Argentina and a small group of Lutheran congregations in Uruguay. However, even in those churches there is a mix of immigration and mission backgrounds. This is also the area with the largest group of Lutherans in Latin America and the Caribbean.

In Argentina one must start with the United Evangelical Lutheran Church, which originated from a 1908 United Evangelical Lutheran Church in Argentina mission initiative among Spanish-speaking Argentines. The picture changed after World War II and the heavy influx of European refugees. Besides Spanish, sermons now were held in Latvian, Estonian, Hungarian, Slovak, and German. Church membership in 2005 is 7,000. The 30,000 member, Lutheran Church – Missouri Synod associated Evangelical Lutheran Church of Argentina is the second largest Lutheran church in that country. Its history goes back to 1905, when Missouri Synod pastors arrived to take care of German immigrants and their descendants. Most of the members have a Russian-German background. The largest Lutheran World Federation member church in Argentina is the Evangelical Church of the River Plate, with 45,000 members, a "United" church, characterized by the fact that about half its members come from a Lutheran background, while the other half comes from the Reformed Confession. The church was originally established in 1843. In 1899 the Evangelical Synod of the River Plate was founded, encompassing congregations in Argentina, Uruguay, and Paraguay. Almost all members descend from German immigrants.

The history of the Lutheran Church in Chile started in 1849, when Germans and Swiss settled in the southern part of the country. The first congregation was founded in 1853, the Evangelical Synod in 1903. Having changed its name to German Evangelical Church in Chile in 1937, it was renamed Evangelical Lutheran Church in Chile in 1959. After the US-supported September 11, 1973 military coup d'état deposed President Salvador Allende and Augusto Pinochet seized power there was a great deal of tension within the church, which eventually led to a split. The Lutheran Church in Chile was then established, which now has a membership of 11,800, while the Evangelical Lutheran Church in Chile numbers 3,000 members. At present both church bodies are entering into dialogue with a view to reunification. Some isolated congregations remain independent; one is linked to the Lutheran Church – Missouri Synod.

Lutheranism was introduced in Brazil in 1824, though accounts of sporadic previous Lutheran visitors to the country exist, as was mentioned earlier. Five synods were established that eventually formed the Evangelical Church of the Lutheran Confession in Brazil (2005 membership: 710,000), as well as the Evangelical Lutheran Church of Brazil (223,588 members), formerly the Brazilian District of the Missouri Synod. An Association of Free Lutheran Congregations counts 1,050 members. Some additional free congregations also exist, most of which are of Pomeranian background, but their precise membership has not been clearly determined.

A case study of Lutheran congregational and church life in Latin America is presented in the text that follows through the example of the Evangelical Church of the Lutheran Confession in Brazil. However, some overall characteristics of Lutheranism in this part of the world could be summarized at this point. Lutheranism did not come to the area in the wake of the sixteenth-century European expansion. To begin with, it had traits of isolated European colonies, as in the Virgin Islands, Puerto Rico, and Suriname, but Lutheranism also came as a diaconal ministry to these islands, siding with suffering African slaves. In contrast, Lutheranism as an immigrant church arrived in Brazil and Argentina as part of an official attempt to "whiten" countries with a high proportion of African slaves in their populations. The multiplicity of theological tendencies nowadays has given rise to some division within the churches. Some congregations have been heavily influenced by Pentecostal movements, in some cases leading to the practice of rebaptism of Catholic converts. On the other hand, there are remarkable signs of ecumenical cooperation as well. Although Lutheran churches on the whole have maintained a strong ethnic profile, there has been a concerted effort to break through ethnic barriers, especially in larger cities. Lutheran churches have on the whole taken a strong stand on political and social issues. The main contributing factor in this sociopolitical awareness has been the independent theological reflection taking place throughout Latin America. The case study of Brazil will illustrate many of these region-wide features.

The Example of the Evangelical Church of the Lutheran Confession in Brazil (Igreja Evangélica de Confissão Luterana no Brasil – IECLB)

The history of the IECLB cannot be dissociated from the wretched living conditions that a broad spectrum of the European population was exposed to during the nineteenth century. Rural exodus, industrialization, failed agrarian reforms, unbridled urban growth, and agricultural collapse due to cheaper imports from Argentina, Australia, and the United States all contributed to a massive emigration from Europe. Hordes of laborers, peasants, and indentured servants took every opportunity to leave the torn social fabric and widespread economic crises of their homelands.

Germans, Swiss, Dutch, Danes, Norwegians, Swedes, Austrians, Italians, Poles, Russians, Spaniards, Portuguese, and members of many other nationalities immigrated to Brazil. Among them were many Protestants: Lutherans, United, Reformed, Waldensians, and Baptists. The congregations and synods of these immigrants would later form the IECLB, which explains one of the main characteristics of this church: a great diversity of piety. This distinguishing trait grew out of concessions and discussions, as well as the ability on the part of its congregations to live and grow together.

The arrival of the different groups of immigrants that later formed the IECLB, as well as other mainstream Protestant denominations, was made possible by world events that gave rise to huge transformations in the former Portuguese colony. At the time of Brazilian independence (1822), the Portuguese patronage system was preserved, but a special arrangement was reached between the British and the Portuguese Crowns in 1808 whereby people of other beliefs were allowed entry into Brazil, provided that their religious gatherings be held in houses that did not look like churches, and that the official religion be respected. This meant that there was no specific legislation concerning Protestant marriages and burials; these and other restrictions meant that it was impossible to raise the children of mixed marriages in the Lutheran faith.

Such areas of ambiguity would later become a source of mounting tension, but in the meantime, economic and political motives spoke louder than religious considerations. Newly independent, Brazil needed an army. For security purposes the settlement of unpopulated areas was called for, especially in southern Brazil, threatened as it was by encroachment from the River Plate region. Roads had to be built, and the military outposts to protect these roads needed provisions.

Two further aspects, perhaps not overtly manifested but nevertheless evident, justified the interest in Brazil for European immigrants. One was based on race, the other on economics. Ever since the 1804 rebellion in Haiti and the slaughter of its white minority, slaveholding oligarchies in Brazil had felt a growing sense of unease. The Brazilian population pyramid presented an overwhelming proportion of slaves and slave descendants. Slave rebellions in the state of Bahia in 1806, and the Portuguese royal family's transfer to Brazil in 1808, led to the conclusion that a "whitening" of the population was urgently needed. Such a "whitening" process, however, could be reached only by granting permission for large-scale intake of European immigrants, including Protestants, and by the substitution of slave workers by white salaried workers. This led to the rise, on the one hand, of small rural properties, tilled by a peasant and his own family. On the other hand, it led to the gradual replacement of slaves by immigrants on large rural properties. In fact, when slavery was finally abolished in 1888, the black population, which had been responsible for the wealth of the nation up to that point, was pushed to the margins of the Brazilian production system and confined to the growing slums in the major cities.

On a larger economic scale, the influx of white immigrants and the establishment of small agricultural properties made it easier for the Brazilian economy to adapt to the international market. An intermediary social class was formed between large landowners and slaves, a Brazilian middle class, as it were, a consuming class for the products available on the world market.

These aspects of demographics, economics, and political history are highly significant for understanding the history of the IECLB. First of all, despite having come to the country as "substitutes" for slaves, the descendants of Brazilian Lutherans have never showed any particular solidarity for the fate of the black population. For many years, in fact, belonging to the IECLB was synonymous with belonging to the middle class. Later, however, owing to long-standing economic difficulties in the country as a whole, this social group has dwindled sharply, which has undeniably had dramatic consequences on church membership. Second, for historical reasons, most church members to this day come from a rural background. In very large urban centers, by contrast, Lutherans belong to a minority. Congregations there have different characteristics: businessmen or employees of foreign companies who stay in the country only for a limited number of years. This explains why assimilation into the Brazilian context has been easier for rural congregations than for urban ones, where an openness to discuss national issues has only recently become commonly accepted.

Summing up, Lutheranism did not come to Brazil as a result of the activity of mission societies, but as a consequence of immigration. Lutherans in Brazil descend mainly from the 300,000 German immigrants who came to the country, 60 percent of whom were Protestant.

The Beginnings

The beginnings were anything but easy. The immigrants were sent to the three southernmost provinces of the country, Rio Grande do Sul, Santa Catarina and Paraná, though there were some smaller groups that settled in the southeastern provinces of São Paulo, Rio de Janeiro, Minas Gerais, and Espírito Santo. As the first immigrant groups brought their own pastors along, the first congregations were established shortly after their arrival in the new country: in Nova Friburgo (1824), São Leopoldo (1824), and Três Forquilhas (1826). In the imperial capital Rio de Janeiro the first congregation was founded in 1827. Santa Catarina started receiving immigrants only at a later date, so the first congregations in that state were Blumenau (1850) and Dona Francisca (now Joinville) (1851).

Lutheran congregations were basically on their own and could express their faith only within certain bounds. Suffice it to say that Protestant marriages were neither recognized nor legally valid until the early 1860s, when the issue was finally given some attention. Mixed marriages could be celebrated only in the Roman Catholic churches, and the children of such marriages could be raised only in the Catholic faith. This situation changed only with the proclamation of the Republic in 1889 and the subsequent separation of church and state.

The immigrants had to organize their church lives themselves. The first worship services were held in palm-covered huts. Sometime later the first congregational building would appear, typically a dual-purpose school and church. Beside this building would be the Lutheran cemetery, for Protestants could not be buried with Catholics. A building serving exclusively as a church would not be allowed until much later.

As the number of pastors was limited, the immigrants had to improvise and choose ministers among the members. The theological principle of the "priesthood of all the saints" was turned into a practical reality within Brazilian congregations in the figure of the "colonist-pastor." This individual would work in his fields and perform pastoral duties whenever needed. When, in later years, pastors with seminary education or academic studies were sent to Brazil, these colonist-pastors would be derided as "pseudo-pastors." As they often carried out the duties of school teacher and pastor, and as the school building often served as the place of worship, this gave rise to the dyad church–school, pastor–teacher, which became a distinguishing trait of IECLB history.

Through this intense collaboration on the part of teachers in congregational life the clericalization of the church could be averted for an extended period of time. In recent years most teachers who perform catechetical duties in the church have been ordained, and the church is finding it difficult to clearly define the position and the role of the catechists, which has unfortunately led to growing clericalization within the church. However, we can to this day observe the strong collective sense revealed in the language used by members of the congregation when referring to "our" cemetery, "our" school, "our" parsonage, "our" pastor. The ecclesiological shortcoming of such a communal church was that the concept rarely went beyond the congregational or parish boundaries. On the other hand, the ecclesiological shortcoming of the present day is that the concept "church" becomes more and more centralized on the pastor alone.

Initial Church Structures

The dominance of Prussia and the emergence of Pan-Germanism led to the "rediscovery" of the immigrants who had left for Brazil after the failure of the liberal revolution (1848). The Oberkirchenrat in Berlin, the Basel Mission Society, and the Evangelical Society for Protestant Germans in America (Barmen) started sending out pastors with university educations or graduates from mission houses to congregations in Brazil in 1837, 1861, and 1865, respectively. In 1897, the Lutheran organization Gotteskasten (*"God's Chest"*) started sending out pastors educated in Hermannsburg, Kropp, and Neuendettelsau. The same institutions also sent out a number of teachers. This important aid was supplemented with the foundation of the *Diasporaseminar* in 1911, originally set up by the Oberkirchenrat Berlin in Soest/Westphalia, then in Ilsenburg/Harz. In this seminary pastors were educated exclusively for the South American diaspora. Although undeniably important for the church at the time, it also seems clear that this initiative from the Prussian *Landeskirche* had the effect of delaying considerably the implementation of pastoral education in Brazil.

The arrival of large numbers of pastors, especially after 1864, marks the beginning of a second stage in the history of the Evangelical Church of the Lutheran Confession in Brazil: the first attempt undertaken to unite the different congregations into one body dates from 1868. Although that particular attempt failed, others followed and led to the formation of four regional churches: the Rio Grande Synod (1886), the Evangelical-Lutheran Synod of Santa Catarina, Paraná and other States of South America (1905), the Association of Evangelical Congregations of Santa Catarina and Paraná (1911), and the Central Brazil Synod (1912).

The activity of the pastors sent out from the United States by the Lutheran Church – Missouri Synod led to the foundation in 1900 of a fifth church organization, which, however, went its own way and eventually became the Evangelical Lutheran Church of Brazil (Igreja Evangélica Luterana do Brasil – IELB). In spite of differences in teaching, the members of both churches have the same immigration background, which often allows for a certain amount of flexibility in the allegiance of church members.

In the beginning, the main task of the synods was to advance and defend the interests of the different congregations and their members in the face of state authorities. The distinctive presence of the laity in their governing bodies preserved the unity of the congregations. On the other hand, the emergence of synods also allowed for cooperation over the years in the field of church publications, pastoral care of internal migrants and new immigrants, youth groups, and women's groups. Yet, very rarely did the synods take the opportunity to take a stand regarding issues of Brazilian life. Most importantly, the synods were a heterogeneous gathering place for religious, economic, political, and ethnic groups that lived on the fringes of Brazilian society. This marginalized existence was encouraged by the legislation during the Empire and by the predominance of Augusto Comte's Positivism during the first four decades of the Republic (after 1889). All this notwithstanding, the synods did make an important contribution to the community at large through their teachers: until World War II there was practically no illiteracy among Lutherans in Brazil.

Between the Gospel and Ideology

At the time of the Second Reich's expansionism, especially following the fall of Bismarck, the hardships faced by descendants of German immigrants in Brazil – and also Swiss, Scandinavian, and Dutch – were relentlessly exposed by German diplomacy. By providing substantial aid for local German publications and schools, and by intensifying visits by German naval vessels to countries with a significant German population, an outright attempt was made to secure markets for German industry. Among the theorists of German colonialism were some who went a step further and worked out a plan that would create a "New Germany" in southern Brazil. Chief among them was Friedrich Fabri, the mission inspector of the Rheinische Mission Society. German diplomacy aimed to attain its objective mainly by preserving the German character of German immigrants overseas. This explains why, in 1900, a church law was passed that allowed the inclusion of German congregations within the Berlin Oberkirchenrat, which would provide them with personnel and material support. Undoubtedly, this assistance from church entities must also be understood as Christian charity. Nevertheless, it contributed little to the autonomy of the Brazilian Lutheran church, which to this day still struggles with an identity that owes more to *Deutschtum* than to Lutheranism.

When the Deutsche Evangelische Kirchenbund allowed the inclusion of Lutheran synods in Brazil in 1924, the life of the Lutheran church in Brazil became even more dependent on Germany. Furthermore, all internal discussions within the German church were thereby transposed to Brazil as well, with the establishment of organizations such as the "German Christians in Brazil," the "National Socialist Ministry in Brazil," and the "Working Group of the Confessing Church in Brazil."

The congregations suffered the most during the two world wars. Financial difficulties intensified; pastors were interned in prisoner camps; the German language was outlawed in school and church. Despite such tribulations, the war years did have a salutary effect, for they allowed the strengthening of the synods, which had lost sight of their self-reliance because of their dependence on German church institutions. They were suddenly forced to lead the life of the Lutheran church in Brazil themselves. The education of teachers already had a long tradition, the first teachers' training institution having been founded in 1899. In terms of pastoral education, however, little had been done. The noticeable shortage of pastors led to the opening of the Evangelical Pre-Seminary in Cachoeira do Sul in 1921. The *Proseminar* was later moved to São Leopoldo and served as the foundation for the *Spiegelberg* educational complex, where in 1946 the Theological School was established, which now, as the Higher School of Theology, is responsible for the whole theological training program of the IECLB.

A diaconal mother house has also existed on the *Spiegelberg* since 1939. Collaboration among women was a feature of immigrant life ever since the first settlements were founded. Used to helping each other in daily life, women in congregations soon started working together, using the proceeds from their handicraft to provide for their needs, be it the care of newborns and their mothers, or new church towers and bells. This later gave rise to the Evangelical Women's Association, the Frauenhilfe, which was initially supported by deaconesses from Wittenberg or Kaiserswerth. Evangelical women promoted the education of local deaconesses and the establishment of a Brazilian Diaconal Mother House and were in fact able to fulfill this dream even before the church leaders could carry out the plan of educating local pastors. Female diaconal work has been a hallmark of autonomous local church work in the Lutheran church in Brazil ever since.

A New Beginning

The end of World War II marks the beginning of a third stage in the history of the IECLB. While some foresaw the end of the Lutheran church in Brazil along with the decline of its ethnic foundation, others viewed the moment as a sign that reorientation was possible. Seeking collaboration among the sister synods, they founded the Sinodal Federation in 1949. At its first General Council in 1950 in São Leopoldo, the Federation, shortly thereafter renamed the Evangelical Church of the Lutheran Confession in Brazil, gave expression to its identity and program by declaring itself a Church of Jesus Christ in Brazil, bound by the Augsburg Confession and Luther's Small Catechism, and open to the worldwide church as a member of the World Council of Churches and of the Lutheran World Federation.

This programmatic statement has since guided the service of the IECLB in Brazil and within the ecumenical community. Whereas in the past the synods were oriented more toward Europe than Brazil, it is now emphasized that the future of this church lies in Latin America. Commitment to the Gospel has consequences for political, cultural, and economic life for Brazil and for Brazilians. In addition, confessional commitment has been highlighted. In the past, only one of the synods had a clearly confessional foundation, acknowledging the Book of Concord as its Confession of Faith. Over the years, however, the other three synods adopted the Small Catechism and the Augsburg Confession as their bases.

The years between 1949 and 1968 were devoted to structural issues and adjustments, and to the quest to implement responsible stewardship of property, time, and gifts.

In the Eye of the Storm

During the years that followed World War II, Brazil had to deal with all of the problems associated with the quick transition from an agrarian to an industrial society. The political, social, and economic turmoil that rocked the country did not leave the church unaffected. After a military coup in 1964 the country lived under a dictatorship for more than twenty years. Growing political unrest, both in the countryside and in the large cities, led to increased repression on the part of the government. At the same time the IECLB was preparing to host the Fifth General Assembly of the Lutheran World Federation, to be held in Porto Alegre in 1970. However, the assembly was transferred to France at short notice due to protests over the abuse of human rights in Brazil, and in hindsight, because of the lack of missionary vision on the part of global Lutheranism. This was a hard blow to the IECLB, for at the same time as the decision was taken to move the Assembly, the document that would later be called the "Curitiba Document," made public in October 1970 at the General Council of the Church, was ready for publication. In it, the IECLB announced the abandonment of its inward-looking perspective in favor of an attitude of responsibility for the country as a whole. By stressing that the church "must turn itself to human beings as a whole, not just to their souls," the document maintained that this view had "consequences for all aspects of life, including physical, cultural, social, economic and political (...), for all issues connected to public welfare." The document made it clear that the IECLB had been given a prophetic task toward church and society. Citing Ezekiel 33:7 it asserted that the church had "to carry out a critical function – not a controlling function, but that of watchman (...) and conscience to the nation. In certain situations the church, in an unbiased manner and always with the intention of finding a just and appropriate solution, will seek to call the attention of authorities and remind them of their responsibilities."

The objection to the demands placed by the state on its citizens in the name of the doctrine of national security is clear from the following quote: "The fatherland will be honored and loved, its symbols will be respected and displayed with civic dignity. However, a Christian may not speak of the fatherland in deifying categories."

What caused such a change of course? The guidelines from the 1950s? No doubt. The shock of the relocation of the Fifth General Assembly? Perhaps. The main reason, however, might be found in everyday life in Brazil, which became unbearable for small landowners and rural workers in the 1970s. This affected the IECLB in a number of ways. While historically its members had been concentrated primarily in the southern states of Brazil, this church of immigrants started undergoing a demographic transition: pushed out of their land, a growing proportion of church members were gradually joining the shantytown populations on the outskirts of large cities. Others sought new frontiers to settle, with the consequence that more and more Lutherans settled in areas of remote colonization deep in the tropical forests of Mato Grosso, Rondônia, and Goiás.

The following years saw wave upon wave of change. The political and social situation in the country led one wing of the church to engage in intense collaboration with the theological current known as Liberation Theology. Here the rediscovery of Luther's *Theologia Crucis* was particularly important. Church declarations were regularly made on a number of issues: appeals for amnesty, protests against the suffering of small landowners displaced by dam constructions, disputes with the National Foundation for the Indians (FUNAI), demands for land rights, and agrarian reform. These activities were also responsible for continuous growth in the ecumenical collaboration of the IECLB.

In a parallel development, another wing of the church became strongly involved in the evangelical pietistic movement introduced in the IECLB by pastors from the World Mission Prayer League. To begin with, there was a sharp cleavage between these seemingly irreconcilable camps. Lately, however, mutual appreciation has gained the upper hand, giving rise to a new awareness of the richness of diversity, which has resulted in broad efforts to renew the worship services, hymns, and liturgy to include and reconcile these previously opposing views.

Bibliography and Suggested Readings

Bachmann, Theodor. "Lutherische Kirchen in der Welt 1977." In *Lutherische Rundschau. Zeitschrift des Lutherischen Weltbundes*. 27 Jg. Heft 2/3. 1977.

Lutheran Churches in the World: A Handbook. Minneapolis: Augsburg Publishing House, 1977.

Bastian, Jean-Pierre. *Historia Del Protestantismo en América Latina*. México: Casa Unidad de Publicaciones, 1990.

Dreher, Martin N. *Igreja e Germanidade. Estudo crítico da História da Igreja Evangélica de Confissão Luterana no Brasil*, 2ªed. São Leopoldo: Sinodal, 2003.

A Igreja Latino-Americana no Contexto Mundial, 2ªed. São Leopoldo: Sinodal. 2005.

Hennig, Martin. *Sie gingen übers Meer. Die evangelischen Kirchen deutscher Herkunft in Übersee, ihre Eigenart, ihre Probleme und ihre Arbeit*. Hamburg: Agentur des Rauhen Hauses, o.J. 1960.

Hermann, Stewart. "Die Reformation in Latein-Amerika." In Heinz Brunott, and Ruppel, Erich (eds.), *Gott ist am Werk. Festschrift für Landesbischof D. Hanns Lilje zum sechzigsten Geburtstag am 10. August 1959*, 126–134.Hamburg: Furche-Verlag, 1959.

Leskö, Béla. "Die Entdeckung der Identität in einer neuen Kultur und Gesellschaft in Südamerika." In Vajta, Vilmos (ed.), *Die Evangelisch-Lutherische Kirche. Vergangenheit und Gegenwart*, 341–357. Stuttgart: Evangelisches Verlagswerk, 1977.

Pfeiffer, Johannes. *Auf Luthers Spuren in Lateinamerika*. Erlangen: Verlag der Ev.-Luth. Mission, 1969.

Prien, Hans-Jürgen. *Die Geschichte des Christentums in Lateinamerika*. Göttingen: Vandenhoeck & Ruprecht, 1978.

21

Marianism in Latin America

TIMOTHY MATOVINA

Every country in Latin America and the Caribbean has a national Marian patroness. Our Lady of Altagracia (Highest Grace) is acclaimed in the Dominican Republic as the first evangelizer of the Americas, since she is associated with the first place where Spanish Catholics sought to spread their faith in the New World. Our Lady of Copacabana is esteemed as patroness of Bolivia, as well as the Queen of the Incas among Quechua and Aymara indigenous peoples. Reflecting Spanish colonizers' devotional proclivities, various national images are associated with the Immaculate Conception, the Catholic belief that Mary was conceived without original sin.

Among these images are Our Lady of the Miracles of Caacupé of Paraguay, Our Lady of Aparecida of Brazil, and Nicaragua's Our Lady of the Immaculate Conception of El Viejo. The numerous invocations of Mary in Latin America include Our Lady of Sorrows, Our Lady of Remedies, and Our Lady of Mercy. Such titles underscore that Mary is much more than just a national symbol or religious icon. For millions of Latin American devotees she is, as historian Linda Hall so aptly put it, "a palpable presence, an understanding and giving being to whom access is proximate and immediate."[1] While many of her faithful have called her the Virgin Mary and understood the Catholic belief that she is not God but an intercessor before God, in practice a number of them turn to her as a mother who herself wields divine power.

Marian devotion originated in Latin America with the arrival of Iberian Catholics, who persuaded and often compelled native peoples and African slaves to participate in their religious traditions. Attributes such as Mary's beauty, maternal affection, and power to affect miracles attracted the devotion of many. At the same time, as scholars such as theologian Orlando Espín have observed, in the context of conquest and enslavement "it was only a matter

---

[1] Linda B. Hall, *Mary, Mother and Warrior: The Virgin in Spain and the Americas* (Austin: University of Texas Press, 2004), 1.

of time before the vanquished projected their family and social experiences onto God." Consequently, their understanding of "God all too often resembled their [overbearing] earthly fathers and lords. In this context the mother of Jesus became a necessary religious symbol of compassion and care in an otherwise cruel system."[2]

Thus, from the beginning veneration of Mary in Latin America was multivalent. Iberians tended to perceive her as blessing their colonial project while numerous natives and Africans turned to her for protection in the face of dire hardships and the imposition of a new religious system. The adaptability of Marian traditions has enabled devotees to tailor their engagement of Mary to their specific needs and circumstances ever since. For five centuries, Latin Americans of all backgrounds have sought her intercession and protection for a host of concerns: epidemics, drought, floods, failed crops, fire, earthquakes, enemy attacks, illness of every kind, financial hardships, success in personal ventures, safety during migration, family well-being, and independence and social movements, as well as the counterefforts to repress those struggles. Consciously or not, Mary's faithful have also engaged her both to justify and to contest cultural mores dictating women's domesticity, as well as class hierarchies in Latin American communities and societies.

To this day, preachers, activists, writers, artists, and devotees note the varied understandings and even ambiguities of Latin American devotion to Mary, such as the incongruity between celebratory claims about her power to uplift and unite diverse peoples even amidst the ongoing social marginalization of devotees like African-descended, indigenous, and mixed-race populations. The veneration of Cuba's Nuestra Señora de la Caridad del Cobre (Our Lady of Charity of El Cobre) illustrates this ambiguity. This devotion emerged during the early-seventeenth century in the mining settlement of El Cobre near the southeast coast of Cuba. The Spanish Crown confiscated the mines and the administration of the slaves who worked them in 1670, changes the now "royal slaves" supported because they afforded them greater autonomy in local affairs and in their everyday lives. Subsequently, royal slave Juan Moreno gave the first documented testimony on the origins of the devotion. His 1687 account stated that around 1612 he and two Indian brothers, Rodrigo and Juan Joyos (spelled "Hoyos" in contemporary accounts), found the image with the inscription "I am the Virgin of Charity" in the Bay of Nipe. Devotees deemed the image to be miraculous because it was found floating in the water but

---

2 Orlando O. Espín, *The Faith of the People: Theological Reflections on Popular Catholicism* (Maryknoll, NY: Orbis, 1997), 59.

not wet. Mysterious lights led authorities to understand Our Lady of Charity wanted to be enshrined near the mines where the slaves worked, and soon her faithful attributed many wonders to her intercession.

Various factors led to the expansion of the devotion to Our Lady of Charity. These included reports of miracles and shrine supporters' promotion of their occurrence, a consequent increase in donations that helped expand facilities and ritual celebrations in her honor, the fervor of El Cobre royal slaves who grounded their claims to dignity and self-determination in their patroness, the efforts of chaplains assigned to the sanctuary, and the codification of the cult in priests' writings that enhanced its official sanction. In 1756, Cuban bishop Pedro Agustín Morell de Santa Cruz observed that "the sanctuary of El Cobre is the richest, most frequented, and most devout on the Island, and the Lady of Charity the most miraculous of all those venerated [in Cuba]."[3]

Her fame now solidified and still growing, it is not surprising that when Cuban soldiers fought for independence from Spain in the Ten Years' War of 1868–1878 and the victorious conflict of 1895–1898, they sought her protection, deeming her "la Virgen Mambisa" (the Revolutionary Virgin). Veterans of the latter struggle gathered at a 1915 reunion in El Cobre to celebrate Our Lady of Charity's September 8 feast day and to offer thanksgiving for her protection. They petitioned Pope Benedict XV to officially name her the patroness of Cuba, which he did the following year.

As Our Lady of Charity's link to the Cuban nation eclipsed her earlier local patronage, various observers highlighted the African influence on the devotion through their association of la Caridad del Cobre with the Yorùbá goddess Oshún and with the practice of Santería, which draws on African as well as Catholic religious traditions. Devotees also altered details in the narrative of la Caridad's origins. Today, most Cubans recount that the three devotees who discovered the image in the Bay of Nipe were respectively African, indigenous, and Spanish, a multiracial claim buttressing national pride in the racial harmony that allegedly marked the formation of the Cuban nation. Some state the first devotees all had the same first name and call them "los tres Juanes" (the three Johns). Yet, analysts such as Olga Portuondo Zúñiga contend such representations of Our Lady of Charity often hyperbolically "project a utopia of ethno-cultural unity onto the Cuban people."[4]

---

[3] María Elena Díaz, *The Virgin, the King, and the Royal Slaves of El Cobre: Negotiating Freedom in Colonial Cuba, 1670–1780* (Stanford, CA: Stanford University Press, 2000), 116.

[4] Olga Portuondo Zúñiga, *La Virgen de la Caridad del Cobre: Símbolo de cubanía* (Madrid: Agualarga, 2001), 22.

The most widespread of Marian devotions in the Americas is that to Mexico's Our Lady of Guadalupe. After Jesus of Nazareth, her image is the most reproduced religious icon in the Western Hemisphere. She appears on home altars, t-shirts, tattoos, murals, parish churches, medals, refrigerator magnets, wall hangings, and in countless conversations and daily prayers. The Guadalupe basilica on the hill of Tepeyac in Mexico City is the most visited pilgrimage site on the American continent. Basilicas and shrines dedicated to her are found as far south as Santa Fe, Argentina and as far north as Johnstown, Cape Breton, Nova Scotia.

Although each Marian tradition in Latin America developed within distinct local circumstances and devotional trajectories, Guadalupe illustrates commonalties among a number of these traditions. One common feature is Mary's close association with the lowly and the downtrodden, in this case Guadalupe's apparitions to the indigenous neophyte Juan Diego, whom Pope John Paul II canonized a saint in 2002. Proponents of the Guadalupe tradition view the Nahuatl-language *Nican mopohua* (a title derived from the document's first words, "here is recounted") as the foundational text for the apparitions. In intricate and poetic detail, the text narrates the well-known tale of Juan Diego's tender encounters with Guadalupe, who sent him to request that Juan de Zumárraga, the first bishop of Mexico, build a temple in her honor at Tepeyac. At first, the bishop doubted the celestial origins of this request, but he came to believe when Juan Diego presented him exquisite flowers that were out of season and the image of Guadalupe miraculously appeared on the humble indigenous man's *tilma* (cloak). As with other Marian traditions, numerous devotees resonate with Juan Diego's lowly status, experiences of rejection, encounter with a loving mother, and final vindication.

Another common feature is that the genesis of particular Marian images is often shrouded in mystery. In the instance of the Guadalupe tradition, the search for origins has been a source of vigorous debate. The first uncontested primary sources that illuminate the practice of Guadalupan devotion are a controversial 1556 oration and the depositions gathered in response to it. Fray Francisco de Bustamante's sermon on the feast of the Nativity of the Virgin Mary sharply criticized Mexico City archbishop Alonso de Montúfar's promotion of Guadalupan devotion. Bustamante reportedly called for a prohibition of this devotion and accused the archbishop of being deceived in his enthusiastic support of it. He claimed many indigenous believed Guadalupe was a goddess and that her image itself worked miracles, a number of them abandoning or wavering in the Christian faith when their pleas for miracles went unanswered. Montúfar immediately ordered an investigation of Bustamante's oration. However, though the nine witnesses selected for the inquiry took a deferential stance toward the archbishop, no punitive action was taken. A note on the official documentation for the inquiry declared without explanation that the proceedings were "suspended" and "dead."[5]

No one doubts that a chapel dedicated to Guadalupe at Tepeyac has been active since at least the mid-sixteenth century sermon of Bustamante. However, there is longstanding disagreement about whether the chapel or belief in Guadalupe's reported apparitions to Juan Diego came first. The core question of the ongoing debate is whether reports of Juan Diego's miraculous encounter with Guadalupe initiated the chapel and its devotion or, on the contrary, whether the apparition narrative is a later invention that provided a mythical origin for an already existing image and pious tradition. Those who hold the latter position point to evidence such as the lapse of more than a century between the 1531 date given for the apparitions and the first published apparition accounts, as well as the lack of documentation about the apparitions among prominent sixteenth-century Catholic leaders in New Spain, including the complete absence of Guadalupe references in the known writings of Juan de Zumárraga. Conversely, those who uphold the foundational status of the apparition tradition argue that the Spaniards' disdain for the allegedly inferior native people accounts for the delay of more than a century before an official inquiry recorded indigenous testimony about Guadalupe and Juan Diego. They also contend that written documentation on the apparitions such as the *Nican mopohua* was extant much earlier than its first formal publication. Thus, the heart of the debate is disagreement about the validity of oral testimony; the viability of historical arguments from silence; and the authenticity, authorship, proper dating, and significance of critical primary sources, especially the *Nican mopohua* itself.

"Scientific" studies of the *tilma* are another important component of this debate. Those who uphold the apparition tradition have claimed for centuries that the *tilma* has miraculous origins. Artist Miguel Cabrera stated famously in a 1756 treatise after examining the image with the most prestigious painters in Mexico City, "this canvas, and its celestial painting, appears to be exempt from the common laws of nature."[6] Detractors contend that such conclusions are based on piety rather than scientific evidence. They also cite primary

---

5 "Información por el sermón de 1556," in Ernesto De la Torre Villar and Ramiro Navarro de Anda, eds., *Testimonios históricos Guadalupanos* (Mexico City: Fondo de Cultura Económica, 1982), 36–72, at 44, 72.
6 Miguel Cabrera, *Maravilla Americana...* (1756), in *Testimonios históricos Guadalupanos*, De la Torre Villar and Navarro de Anda, eds., 494–528, at 507.

sources such as the depositions from the inquiry into the Bustamante sermon, in which witnesses related Bustamante's claim that an indigenous artist named Marcos painted the Guadalupe image.

Despite ongoing controversies, millions of devotees have no doubt about the authenticity of the apparition narrative and the miraculous origins of the Guadalupe image. The inordinate attention given in Guadalupan studies to historical origins – an issue repeatedly addressed since the eighteenth century but never resolved – overshadows an equally vital historical question that is rarely engaged: Given the plentiful miraculous images of Christ, Mary, and the saints that dotted the sacred landscape of colonial Mexico, how did the Guadalupe cult rise above all others and emerge from a local devotion to become a regional, national, and then international phenomenon?

This is a fundamental question for the history of national Marian images throughout Latin America, and the various factors contributing to Guadalupe's rise to prominence have parallels in other locales. Like many Marian and other holy figures, the primary reason that Guadalupe's fame spread was the testimonies of miracles and trust in her aid that her devotees recounted about her. The Spanish Catholic imagination tended to view God as stern and distant, intensifying appeals to Guadalupe and other manifestations of Mary as compassionate mother and intercessor. British traveler Miles Philips observed in 1573 that devotees "say that our Lady of Guadalupe doeth worke a number of miracles."[7] Samuel Stradanus, a Flemish artist and New Spain resident who ran a lithography business, made an engraving (ca. 1615) that depicts the Guadalupe image surrounded by eight scenes of the more renowned miracles Spanish devotees attributed to her, apparently drawn from *ex votos* these supplicants had enshrined at the Guadalupe chapel. The eight scenes and six other miracles are also described in the *Nican motecpana* ("here is an ordered account"), which begins with three miracles Guadalupe reportedly granted indigenous devotees. Collectively, these accounts range from petitioners being saved from a misfired arrow, horse accident, falling lamp, or an unspecified epidemic to healings of headaches, dropsy, and severe swelling of the feet and neck.

Increasing claims of healings and other miraculous interventions on behalf of individual supplicants led devotees to petition Guadalupe's intercession for communal needs, such as during the devastating Mexico City flood of 1629. Archbishop Francisco Manso y Zúñiga mandated that the Guadalupe image

---

[7] David A. Brading, *Mexican Phoenix: Our Lady of Guadalupe, Image and Tradition across Five Centuries* (Cambridge: Cambridge University Press, 2001), 2.

be moved from the basilica to the cathedral in the center of the city (the only time the Guadalupe image has ever been publicly processed from Tepeyac), where it remained until 1634 when the flood subsided. Many devotees credited Guadalupe with tempering the effects of the floodwaters after the initial torrents of 1629 and with the final relief from the inundation. A similar attribution occurred after the disastrous *matlazahuatl* (typhus or typhoid fever) epidemic of 1736–1737, which claimed more than 40,000 lives in Mexico City alone. The widespread acclamation of Our Lady of Guadalupe's miraculous protection in that instance played a significant role in Pope Benedict XIV declaring her the patroness of New Spain in 1754.

Theological and pastoral treatises have helped expand, refashion, and codify Marian devotion for centuries. Two Mexico City diocesan priests authored the first of these works on Guadalupe: Miguel Sánchez's *Imagen de la Virgen María* (1648) and Luis Laso de la Vega's *Huei tlamahuiçoltica* ("By a Great Miracle," 1649). Sánchez was a pastor and theologian who specialized in patristic or early Christian writings. The primary focus of his book was to examine Guadalupe and the evangelization of Mexico vis-à-vis the wider Christian tradition, particularly the writings of Augustine and the image of the "woman clothed with the sun" in Revelation 12. His erudite volume had five major sections that successively treated Guadalupe's providential role in the conquest of Mexico, the Guadalupe apparition narrative (the first published account of the apparitions), a theological reflection on the Guadalupe image, a summary of post-apparition developments in the Guadalupe site and tradition, and a narration and analysis of seven miracles attributed to Guadalupe.

Laso de la Vega, who was appointed vicar of the Guadalupe basilica in 1647, penned a glowing commendation for inclusion in Sánchez's volume and published his own book just a few months later. Though the precise relationship between the two works remains a debated topic, the contents of the *Huei tlamahuiçoltica* reveal their close correlation. It is a composite text that encompasses the first formal publication of both the *Nican mopohua* version of the apparition narrative and the *Nican motecpana* miracle accounts, as well as a description of the Guadalupe image and a summary of Mary's influence in New Spain. Nonetheless, the absence throughout the *Huei tlamahuiçoltica* of the theological elaboration and the numerous scriptural and patristic references found in *Imagen de la Virgen María* reveal Laso de la Vega's purpose of providing a pastoral manual to promote Guadalupan devotion and Christian faith among Nahuatl-speaking residents.

Preaching has also influenced the spread of devotion to Guadalupe and other Marian images. Collectively, the approximately 100 extant published

Guadalupe sermons from 1661–1802 elaborate various themes that echo Sánchez's analysis of Guadalupe, such as God's providential guidance in Mexican history, Guadalupe's appearance as a foundational event for the Church in Mexico, and the blessings and miracles that await those who appeal to Guadalupe and contemplate her countenance in the sacred *tilma*. A number of sermons even repeat directly Sánchez's biblical analogies such as his association of Moses, Mount Sinai, and the Ark of the Covenant with Juan Diego, Tepeyac, and the Guadalupe image. As historian David Brading has observed with regard to these sermons, "Nowhere was [Sánchez's] influence more obvious than in the application of Augustinian typology to the interpretation of the Mexican Virgin."[8] Priests sent to rural parishes after receiving their seminary training in Mexico City, the epicenter of the devotion, expanded the geographic range and density of Guadalupe's influence.

As with other Marian traditions that arose to national prominence, increasingly elaborate celebrations, churches dedicated to Guadalupe, and Guadalupan art further enhanced Guadalupe's acclaim. Like the original chapel, donations from the devout helped finance subsequent building projects such as the first two Guadalupe basilicas, dedicated in 1622 and 1709 respectively. From 1675 to 1676, the viceroy of New Spain constructed a grand highway that linked the Guadalupe basilica with the main plaza in Mexico City. It was lined with fifteen chapels dedicated to the fifteen mysteries of the most widespread Catholic devotion to Mary, the rosary. Concurrently, liturgical and devotional celebrations expanded. For example, on the memorable occasion of Guadalupe's triumphant return to Tepeyac after the floods of 1629–1634 abated, Guadalupe was celebrated with a procession enhanced with numerous candles, bonfires, choral hymns, musical accompaniment, tapestries, decorative arches, pious confraternities marching with their banners, and the participation of the general populace. In the wake of Sánchez's influential publication, Guadalupan devotion spread through the construction of the first church edifices dedicated to her beyond the vicinity of Tepeyac, beginning in 1654 with the efforts of leaders in San Luis Potosí (approximately 250 miles north of Mexico City) to secure a "real portrait" of Guadalupe and "build a house for she who housed our God and Lord ... the true effigy of the queen of angels."[9] The flourishing of artistic renderings of Guadalupe and

---

8 Francisco Raymond Schulte, *Mexican Spirituality: Its Sources and Mission in the Earliest Guadalupan Sermons* (Lanham, MD: Rowman and Littlefield, 2002); Brading, *Mexican Phoenix*, 96–101, 146–168. Quote from page 165.

9 Jorge E. Traslosheros H., "The Construction of the First Shrine and Sanctuary of Our Lady of Guadalupe in San Luis Potosí, 1654–1664," *Journal of Hispanic/Latino Theology* 5 (August 1997): 7–19.

devotional copies of her image accompanied and promoted the widening circle of her influence.

Tepeyac's location at a principal crossroads also abetted Guadalupe's growing popularity. Situated on the outskirts of New Spain's capital of Mexico City, it marked the point where the road to the northern interior and its silver mines branched off, as well as the main road from the east and Veracruz, the primary port for transatlantic travel. From the 1560s onward, archbishops, viceroys, and other prominent Mexico City residents met arriving Spanish dignitaries at Tepeyac and ceremoniously ushered them into the city. Some viceroys made the three-mile trek from Mexico City's main plaza to visit the Guadalupe chapel as often as once a week, providing an example of piety for other residents. The links among the Tepeyac shrine, the capital city, and the leading figures of New Spain enhanced Guadalupe's status among Marian and other holy images in the viceroyalty.

Mexico's struggle for independence from Spain and its aftermath marked the culmination of Guadalupe's rise to national prominence and illuminated another key factor in the evolution of Marian devotion in Latin America – her strong link to national pride and identity. Father Miguel Hidalgo, the father of Mexican independence, raised the banner of Guadalupe in his famous cry for independence on September 16, 1810. Over the following decade, numerous insurgents fought under her banner until they gained independence in 1821. During the course of the war, the geographic mobility of the population brought residents from isolated areas into more sustained contact with Guadalupan devotion. The eventual winning of independence and the public homage that Mexico's first leaders offered Guadalupe sealed her status as the national emblem. Nineteenth-century writings on Guadalupe such as the influential work of novelist and journalist Ignacio Manuel Altamirano focused intently on Guadalupe's role within the Mexican nation. An ardent, youthful supporter of anticlerical measures, Altamirano subsequently dedicated himself to literary pursuits in which he portrayed Mexican Catholic traditions like Guadalupe with great respect and admiration. He forcefully articulated the sentiment that not only had Guadalupe liberated Mexico from Spain, but also that her December 12 feast day was the sole occasion when the Mexican nation was free from social and class divisiveness. Altamirano marveled at the way Mexicans of all castes and political persuasions gathered in "equality before the Virgin," though he did not explore how such reported harmony in ritual and devotion could be extended to other arenas of Mexican life. Still, his concluding statement about Guadalupe's centrality in Mexico was frequently quoted among preachers, journalists, and other commentators well into the twentieth century: "The day that the cult of the Indian Virgin [of Guadalupe] disappears, the Mexican nationality will also disappear."[10]

Church officials have endeavored to bolster Latin Americans' Marian piety as a means to strengthen their adherence to Catholic faith and teachings. A number have highlighted Mary as a model for evangelization in the Americas, as John Paul II's various proclamations about Our Lady of Guadalupe illustrate. John Paul II acclaimed Guadalupe as the mother of God who proclaims Christ to the Americas, an announcement of the Christian Gospel in a manner that from her first appearance respected native symbols and cultures. In his words, she is the "star of the first and the new evangelization," and her image and message present "an impressive example of a perfectly inculturated evangelization."[11] Thus, Guadalupe teaches that evangelization – the mission of proclaiming Christ in word and deed to which all the baptized are called – is most effectively served not when Christians impose their cultural ways as if they were intrinsic to the Gospel but rather when they creatively announce the Gospel in a manner that deeply embeds it within a local cultural context. Although by no means have these high ideals been practiced in all evangelization efforts in the Americas, John Paul II and other Church leaders point to Mary as the exemplar her devotees are to imitate.

An impetus for Mary's renown in Latin America during recent decades is the strong links her faithful make between her and struggles for human rights. Indigenous peoples in Chiapas, Mexico and farm workers in the United States, for example, have invoked Guadalupe to strengthen and support them in their demands for justice. Women such as Brazilian theologians Ivone Gebara and Maria Clara Bingemer and Chicana writer Sandra Cisneros have presented Guadalupe as an advocate for counteracting the "traditional" gender roles and expectations that Guadalupe purportedly buttresses. During her childhood and young adult years, Cisneros learned to perceive Guadalupe as a source of divine sanction for a familial and cultural code of silence about women's bodies and sexuality, as well as a double standard of feminine purity and masculine promiscuity. But subsequent experiences and her association of Guadalupe with the pre-Columbian antecedent Tonantzin enabled her to reinterpret and embrace Guadalupe as a brown-skinned, feminine manifestation of divine power who can enable women to see the totality of their corporeal existence as created in the divine image.

---

10 Ignacio Manuel Altamirano, "La Fiesta de Guadalupe" (1884), in De la Torre Villar and Navarro de Anda, eds., *Testimonios históricos* 1127–1210, at 1129, 1210.
11 John Paul II, *Ecclesia in America* (1999), no. 11. http://w2.vatican.va/content/john-paul-ii/en/apost_exhortations/documents/hf_jp-ii_exh_22011999_ecclesia-in-america.html

The rise of theological analyses focused on liberation in Latin America has further shaped contemporary devotion and understandings of Mary. In contrast with the colonial and nationalistic interpretations of previous centuries, these analyses accentuate Mary's love and compassion for the conquered indigenous peoples and for the downtrodden in other times and places. Thus various recent theological works on Guadalupe examine the *Nican mopohua* from an indigenous perspective, such as those of Clodomiro Siller Acuña, Richard Nebel, and Virgilio Elizondo.[12]

These writers see the Guadalupe event as a counter-narrative to the complete defeat of the native peoples. They note that Guadalupe's words of comfort to Juan Diego are given effect in the narrative's dramatic reversals. At the beginning of the story, only Guadalupe has trust in Juan Diego; by the end, the bishop and his assistants believe he is truly her messenger. At the outset of the account, Juan Diego stands meekly before the bishop; in the end, the stooped *indio* stands erect while the bishop and his household kneel before him and venerate the image on his *tilma*. Throughout the account, Juan Diego must journey to the center of the city from Tepeyac some three miles to the north; at the end of the narration, the bishop and his entourage accompany Juan Diego to Tepeyac, where they will build the temple that Guadalupe requested. Symbolically, the presence of the ecclesial leadership and the church they are constructing are thus moved from the center of their capital city out to the margins among the indigenous people.

Those who propose this interpretation of the *Nican mopohua* avow that it urgently demands that Christians hear the voice of the forgotten and marginalized, help them to sense their dignity as God's sons and daughters, and preferentially choose them as the recipients of the Church's proclamation of the Gospel, service, and struggle for a more just social order.

The growth of Pentecostal and evangelical religious movements in Latin America has heightened the significance of Mary for ecumenical relations. A number of Protestant pastors vehemently discourage Marian devotion, even labeling it antibiblical or idolatrous. But others have sought ways to incorporate Mary into their faith traditions. Some Protestant congregations even celebrate Marian feasts such as that of Our Lady of Guadalupe. Lutheran theologian and priest Maxwell Johnson has acclaimed Guadalupe as a source

---

12 Clodomiro L. Siller Acuña, *Flor y canto del Tepeyac: Historia de las apariciones de Santa María de Guadalupe; Texto y comentario* (Xalapa, Veracruz: Servir, 1981); Richard Nebel, *Santa María Tonantzin, Virgen de Guadalupe: Continuidad y transformación religiosa en México* (Mexico City: Fondo de Cultura Económica, 1995); Virgilio Elizondo, *Guadalupe: Mother of the New Creation* (Maryknoll, NY: Orbis, 1997).

of "hope and strength to a people wandering in despair." He also notes that "Guadalupe permeates Hispanic-Latino culture in the Americas" and thus "*not* to pay wider and close theological attention to the image, narrative, and cult of the Virgin of Guadalupe would be a serious error" for those who minister among Latino peoples.[13] Indeed, it is not unusual for evangélico converts to return to the Catholic Church because they miss their relationship with the Virgin. Protestant responses illustrate that, even among those who criticize her and her faithful, Mary's influence in Latin America continues to evolve in pervasive and often unexpected ways.

Bibliography and Suggested Readings

Brading, D. A. *Mexican Phoenix: Our Lady of Guadalupe, Image and Tradition across Five Centuries*. Cambridge: Cambridge University Press, 2001.

Díaz, María Elena. *The Virgin, the King, and the Royal Slaves of El Cobre: Negotiating Freedom in Colonial Cuba, 1670–1780*. Stanford, CA: Stanford University Press, 2000.

Espín, Orlando O. *The Faith of the People: Theological Reflections on Popular Catholicism*. Maryknoll, NY: Orbis, 1997.

Hall, Linda B. *Mary, Mother and Warrior: The Virgin in Spain and the Americas*. Austin: University of Texas Press, 2004.

John Paul II. *Ecclesia in America* (1999), no. 11. http://w2.vatican.va/content/john-paul-ii/en/apost_exhortations/documents/hf_jp-ii_exh_22011999_ecclesia-in-america.html

Johnson, Maxwell. *The Virgin of Guadalupe: Theological Reflections of an Anglo-Lutheran Liturgist*. Lanham, MD: Rowman and Littlefield. 2002.

Matovina, Timothy. "Theologies of Guadalupe: From the Spanish Colonial Era to Pope John Paul II." *Theological Studies* 70 (March 2009): 61–91.

Peterson, Jeanette Favrot. *Visualizing Guadalupe: From Black Madonna to Queen of the Americas*. Austin: University of Texas Press, 2014.

Poole, Stafford. *Our Lady of Guadalupe: The Origins and Sources of a Mexican National Symbol, 1531–1797*. Tucson: University of Arizona Press, 1995.

Portuondo Zúñiga, Olga. *La Virgen de la Caridad del Cobre: Símbolo de cubanía*. Madrid: Agualarga, 2001.

Schmidt, Jalane D. *Cachita's Streets: The Virgin of Charity, Race, and Revolution in Cuba*. Durham, NC: Duke University Press, 2015.

Taylor, William B. *Shrines and Miraculous Images: Religious Life in Mexico before the Reforma*. Albuquerque: University of New Mexico Press, 2010.

---

13 Maxwell Johnson, *The Virgin of Guadalupe: Theological Reflections of an Anglo-Lutheran Liturgist* (Lanham, MD: Rowman and Littlefield, 2002), 8, 9.

22

Secularism and Secularization

TRANSLATED BY JOSÉ ADRIAN BARRAGÁN

ROBERTO J. BLANCARTE

One of the greatest changes to present-day Latin America, relative to its colonial period, is the modern liberal political regime embodied in republicanism. As they gained independence in the early-nineteenth century, the vast majority of the new nations in the region experienced a transformation not only in their style of governance but also the very sources of legitimacy for political institutions. The transition from monarchy to republicanism implied that a divinity or a religious institution no longer legitimated political power, as had been the case under the Spanish and Portuguese monarchs. Instead, popular sovereignty became the source of legitimating authority, and at least theoretically, God or the Church were no longer the ultimate sources of power. Instead, the people were the source of power, and so the locus of political authority shifted from a Catholic regime to secular ones. The history of this process of laicization, or the secularization of political institutions (not always accompanied simultaneously by a process of secularization of society), generated spaces for certain political and social freedoms, either by their imposition by secularist forces or by their gradual social transformation from within. Although the term laicization is practically unknown in the English language, it is commonly used in Latin languages to refer to the separation of religion from public affairs within the state, whereas secularization refers to this process of separation in society as a whole. These distinctions are critical as we explore the development of the secular in nineteenth- and twentieth-century Latin America.

In the context of the ideological struggle between conservatives and liberals in the nineteenth century, the twin ideas of laicization and secularization refer us to another equally important observation in the history of Latin America, namely the resistance of the Catholic hierarchy to the changes propelled by liberalism, which the Church perceived as a direct assault on its temporal and spiritual interests. Hence secularism, understood as a combative, anticlerical attitude aimed to debilitate ecclesiastical power, always accompanied political secularization, defined as the process of the creation of public institutions autonomous from any church or religion. On more than one occasion, this led to diverse means of ideological and political polarization, although the struggles did not always revolve around the conservative–liberal dichotomy. Toward the end of the nineteenth century, in fact, the distinction between these polar positions thinned, and more populist and radical ideological viewpoints emerged. As time went by, the real dilemma in this matter became more evident: on one hand a regime that, lacking a better definition could be called "confessional" and on the other hand another kind of regime that we could call "lay" (laico) or "secular." This dilution of the difference between conservatives and liberals resulted from *caudillo* (strong-man) or populist positions, which made regime types more difficult to define. Also other types of "traditions," such as "jurisdictionalism" inherited form regalism – in which the state or the Crown regulates Church affairs – often brought tension to old alliances. Even ideologically conservative governments ultimately came into conflict with the Catholic hierarchy as they imposed jurisdictionalist measures that appropriated the wealth of the church, diminished its power, or utilized it as a political means.

Two centuries after Latin American independence, however, new trends have emerged. The tendency toward confrontation between church and state has given way to forms of regulating the religious that are more inclined to the recognition of a plurality of beliefs. These new regulations focus on a range of issues including human rights, freedom of conscience, and the priority of democratic politics. However, this transition is not a simple erasure of past movements such as confessionalism or nineteenth-century liberalism in favor of newer political approaches such as laicity. Instead, old trends allied to new dynamics are at a crossroads between laicity or pluri-confessionalism. It is not yet clear which of these contradictory regime proposals will prevail.

The New Republics: Between Regalism and Patronage

The first independent Spanish-American nations were born as Catholic republics, with states linked to an exclusive religion and intolerant toward the exercise of any other. Meanwhile, the rulers of all the new countries born out of the breakdown of the Spanish Empire in America claimed inheritance to the *patronato real* (royal patronage), the papal grant giving Spanish monarchs rights over ecclesiastic regulation. They produced constitutions that protected the Catholic religion, privileged the Roman Church, and were intolerant of other faiths, all within the reasoning of a special relationship with the Holy See. Nevertheless, the fact that the new governments pretended to offer privileges to the Catholic religion did not necessarily translate into their subjugation to the dictates of the Church. On the contrary, it meant that the state always claimed the implicit rights of the *patronato*, and as such, a control over clerical activities and the ecclesiastic institution. Thus, there exists a direct link among the regalism of the Spanish Crown, the regulation of the *patronato*, and the formation of a secularist thought. The issue of the *patronato*, which evolved into a jurisdictional claim over the Catholic Church, became the poisoned inheritance of the first independent Catholic republics of Spanish America.

In the decades following independence, the power of the Catholic Church in Spanish America was seriously challenged. At its core, this challenge was a mixture of political liberalism, jurisdictionalism inherited from regalism and the practice of the *patronato*, and the enormous material necessities of the new governments. In those countries, a growing conviction emerged that viewed the dominant position of the Church as an obstacle to the economic opportunities of the people and the country as a whole, as well as a challenge to the establishment of individual political liberties. The establishment of republics under the principle of popular sovereignty also led to the inevitable clash regarding the source of legitimacy of political institutions. The *patronato* existed because it imparted regalist jurisdictionalism, but it did not constitute a lay regime, other than incipiently, as it continued to rely on ecclesiastic authority.

The fact that the new independent states in Spanish America were born as Catholic republics with liberal ideologies generated irreconcilable contradictions that set the tone of philosophical debates and political conflicts in the following two centuries. Latin American liberals from the first half of the nineteenth century decided to establish republics that built egalitarian societies in opposition to the *ancien régime*, represented by the Spanish monarchy. Nevertheless, preoccupied by the lack of elements of national integration, they conceived the Republic as Catholic, granting it privileges and being intolerant toward the exercise of any other. Of course, this way of understanding the Republic collided directly with the principles of liberty and equality, thereby establishing a source of contradictions and conflicts.

On the other hand, the emergence of political liberalism led to open conflicts between liberals and conservatives, the latter supported by the Catholic hierarchy. When the liberals emerged triumphant in the mid- to late-nineteenth century, they sought to subdue the Church instead of secularizing society. In some cases, they made use of the Church as a political instrument, rather than laicizing public institutions. Therefore, before us is a conflict that, in some instances, resulted in political measures of separation or laicization of the state, but only as a consequence of the impossibility to convert the Catholic Church into an allied, yet subdued, institution.

In Latin America, the triumph of liberalism led to an incipient religious plurality. The laicization process of public institutions, however, would be more complex as many states kept relying on the authority (and therefore the legitimacy) of the Catholic Church. Some countries carried out a formal separation between church and state, especially where the concern over public educational instruction became an important part of the laicization process. Nevertheless, because of the absence of economic means, the extension of lay schooling was limited during the nineteenth century. Other countries, particularly in Central and South America, unilaterally maintained the *patronato* and imposed liberal reforms from that position. Finally, in many of the nations where liberalism had difficulties prevailing, or conservative governments returned, long-lasting concordats were established with the Holy See.

Regardless, between 1880 and 1930, in the vast majority of the Latin American countries where liberalism had not triumphed earlier, liberal regimes were created that imposed lay measures such as the abolishment of the forced tithe, the nationalization of ecclesiastic property, the establishment of a civil registrar for births, the civil contract of marriage, the secularization of cemeteries, and a formal separation between church and state. For the most part, these were oligarchical regimes based on agro-export economic models that sought the reduction of ecclesiastic properties to put lands and properties on the market, which also implied control of the Church's power, more so for economic than for political reasons. In no few cases, bellicose conflicts or civil wars between conservatives and liberals preceded these measures. The ideals of liberty, then, were tied to the need to promote the circulation of wealth, to the conviction that political power could not be shared, and to militant anticlericalism.

As the nineteenth century came to a close, it was evident that the oligarchies of both factions were inclined to impose an order for progress based on authoritarian enlightened regimes, influenced by positivism and the scientific ideal of modernity. In this context, the church simultaneously appeared as a necessary institution for the preservation of the moral order and as an obstacle for social progress. Thus, save in isolated cases, the Catholic hierarchy remained in the political spheres of power in Latin American countries. This incomplete transition from sacred authority to popular sovereignty led to spirited laicist efforts that became nothing more than half-measures toward a laicity of the state. The regimes did not stop depending on support from the Catholic Church, nor did they become truly democratic governments supported by popular will. During the rule of the oligarchic regimes, authoritarianism, political manipulation, *caudillismo*, and repression became a constant in Latin America. Laicism prevailed, but laicity had yet to be built.

Populism and the Moral Concordats

At the dawn of the twentieth century, Latin America's oligarchical regimes began to show signs of fragmentation. Mexico was the first to fall at the hands of other members of the oligarchy who, with the support of a growing middle class, reclaimed the cause for democracy. The subsequent popular outbreak transformed the movement into a true social revolution with enormous repercussions on the politico-religious level. In Mexico, the support from the ecclesiastical hierarchy and the National Catholic Party for the coup leader and military dictator Victoriano Huerta sealed the destiny of church–state relations and led to nearly a century of continuous anticlerical laws, repression, open wars, and uncomfortable arrangements under the guise of official laicism. In this sense Mexico, along with Uruguay and subsequently Cuba, was an exception in twentieth-century Latin America.

The economic crisis of 1929, military coups d'état, growing pressure from the nascent middle class, and growing popular demands led to the fall of most oligarchic, agro-export regimes. Their failure revealed the extent of the weaknesses of the laicist measures put into practice in Latin America. In most cases, liberal oligarchies were unable to build a solid, institutional secular base. They focused their efforts on reducing the material wealth of the Church and established nongovernmental institutions for rites of passage. But except for very rare cases, the oligarchies could not do without the source of religious authority. Instead, they relied on it when they could and failed to build a solid democracy that consolidated a sovereign regime with the support of the people. As a result, after the overthrow of the oligarchies, the symbolic power of the Church remained intact and ready to rebuild itself.

Between approximately 1930 and 1980, a relationship between the Church and the state developed that could well be defined as a period of Catholic nationalism or that of the "moral concordats."[1] This was the case for Brazil and Argentina, where populist-style military governments were installed with

---

[1] This term, derived from a Brazilian bishop, was retaken in Kenneth Serbin, *Secret Dialogues: Church-State Relations, Torture, and Social Justice in Authoritarian Brazil* (Pittsburgh, PA: University of Pittsburgh Press, 2000), 4.

the backing of the Church. In Brazil, an uprising of young lieutenants brought to power Getúlio Vargas, who established a formal pact, or "moral concordat," that remained in place through various populist governments until the early 1960s. Afterwards, in Brazil as in other Latin American countries, the common fear of radical, socialist, or communist social movements contributed to an informal agreement between the military and the Church. In 1931, Brazil allowed for the return of religious education in public schools. In 1934, its Constitution incorporated the measure, and proclaimed the indissolubility of marriage and religious assistance at military installations, hospitals, and penitentiaries. The 1946 Constitution reiterated these measures, likened religious marriage to a civil one, and granted legal status to religious associations. In Argentina, the Church saw itself as a representative of the nation before a state that had violated Natural Law and imposed liberalism onto the population. When the oligarchic regime fell apart, at the same time that the stock market crashed, the church insisted in its identity between Church and nation. According to the religious institution, since Argentina was a Catholic nation, it became necessary that the country abandon its laicist orientation, foreign to its "true" tradition, and return to its origins. The state, as a result, needed to support the Catholic Church, considered the central institution for the culture and identity of the nation, and so a regalist spirit returned under the ideal of a Catholic nation. In turn, the Catholic hierarchy supported the various military governments – though not without many ambiguities, complexities, and contradictions – in exchange for a new status for the ecclesiastical institution and, above all, for a new definition of the national identity and culture no longer identified with progress and secular modernity, but with national "traditions" and Catholicism. Thus, during this period, even without considering the Catholic Church as the official one, the Argentine state kept its Catholic faith, determined that its president should belong to said communion; established that the government must support the conversion of the Indians; and favored the formulation of a concordat with the Holy See. On the other hand, the rationale of the *patronato* was maintained through the sanction of the passage of papal bulls and other documents, as well as the formulation of senatorial shortlists for the appointment of bishops and their selection by the president of the republic for their presentation and approval by the Holy See.

 The arrival of corporatism and populisms after liberal predominance had a diverse effect in Latin America, but in general terms, it allowed for the readjusting of the Catholic Church. Colombia is a curious case, for it went against the tide of the general processes in Latin America. During the period of liberal oligarchies, Colombia secured its regime's conservatism through the signing of a concordat that remained in effect until 1930. The arrival of the liberal governments, which ruled from that year until 1946, made possible the establishment of some laicization policies of public institutions. In the postwar period, the Colombian political system aligned itself again with the general tendencies of the Latin American region. In the case of Mexico, marked by the effects of anticlerical persecutions during the Cristero War (1926–1929), the Catholic Church and the state came to a so-called modus vivendi after 1938. Unlike in other Latin American countries, this was not a case of building a Catholic nationalism because the state maintained its lay or secular character, particularly through public education and a strict separation of spheres. Neither did the Mexican revolutionary regime want to share power with the ecclesiastic institution; it preferred to adhere to a political authoritarianism with a democratic façade. The 1917 Constitution replaced the liberal constitution of 1857 but also introduced a series of anticlerical articles that prohibited the establishment of monastic orders; denied the church any special legal status, thus prohibiting the ownership of property; and prevented the participation of the clergy in national politics. In spite of this, in some places, the reconciliation led to the slow recovery of some of the episcopate's power.

The other element central to understanding the relative restraint to the secularization processes of public institutions in Latin America is the particular positioning of the region in the context of the Cold War. The Holy See aligned itself fully with the "Truman Doctrine" and the anticommunist discourse of the postwar period. This was not a new position; the Holy See had, since the mid-nineteenth century, published various encyclicals condemning liberalism, socialism, and communism equally. However, in the new context, communism presented itself as a global threat against the faith. In the Latin American case, these fears linked to anticommunism intensified after the triumph of the Cuban Revolution in 1959, which, among other things, stood out due to its anticlerical tone. The Catholic hierarchy linked up with the doctrine of national security in the decades of the 1960s and 70s. This doctrine maintained the notion of a Western Christian civilization that needed to defend itself from atheist communism. In this sense, the alliance among the economic, political, and religious elites was seen as natural, against any movement or association that claimed to fight for social justice or any changes in the regime's structure. Some authors have argued that this alliance was based more on temporal-ideological, rather than religious, coincidences. For example, Kenneth Serbin argues, "Church influence on the military was based on mutual admiration for hierarchy, discipline and tradition – not on a profound teaching of Christian values. The church was likewise unprepared to comprehend security matters beyond a reflex action against Communism."[2] Nonetheless, the "moral concordat" was something more than a simple, circumstantial, ideological alliance; it was based on the repudiation of secular modernity with all of its social implications, including the development of an egalitarian, democratic, and pluralistic society. "Catholic nationalism" was not a superficial ideological construction or a circumstantial political alliance; rather, it represented a nation based on the hegemony of one religion and of certain traditional (that is, antimodern) values that permeated social, military and political institutions, and unions. This alliance fell apart when certain sectors of the Church abandoned this traditional model and sought to combine their religious values with other secular, socialist, Marxist, or simply liberal and democratic models.

In effect, just as the Catholic Church produced a reaction against liberalism, socialism, and communism, it also generated an internal reaction against its own Christian social doctrine. Paradoxically, it would be the Catholic militants themselves, often educated by the social organizations of the Church, who criticized the Church's position and radicalized politically. The extent to which these positions were fed by or contributed to a growing secularized society and to the bylaws of the more secular public institutions remains unclear. However, it is known that they contributed to form an internal criticism of the more clericalist, antimodern, and antisecular vision of the ecclesiastic establishment. Many Catholic movements passed from developmentalism to liberationism, giving way to more radical expressions that would later gather under the "Liberation Theology" label, or would be expressed even in political or guerrilla movements. The Church was divided and there were plenty of cases in which one ultraconservative sector within it supported government repression of the more progressive groups who fought for social justice and human rights. Nothing from the preceding signified that Catholic progressivism, whether it was called Christian democracy, Liberation Theology, or Christian-influenced guerrillas, constituted a thorough secular and modern political proposal. It answered, still, to an integral vision of the world that rejected the separation of spheres that the secularization process had generated and that leads to a distinction between the political and the religious.

In the Southern Cone, the moral concordat and Catholic nationalism suffered a severe setback with the increased repression toward Church sectors involved in social movements during military rule. Although high-level

---

2 Serbin, *Secret*, 46.

negotiations eased tensions in many occasions, the distancing between Church and state led to the end of the moral concordat and a larger, more effective separation of the political and religious spheres. After the fall of the military dictatorship in Argentina, the prior support of the Catholic hierarchy for the pro-coup military junta would also affect the church–state relationship, although not convincingly, as the web of conservative cooperation between the militaries, oligarchy, and bishops remained nearly intact for many years. In Chile, on the other hand, the role of the Church in the defense of human rights and against the repression from Pinochet's coup-leading regime allowed for an extension of the central role of the Chilean Catholic Church in the political life of the country. In other latitudes, such as in Andean, Central American, and Caribbean countries, Catholic nationalism was not as evident. Nonetheless, the alliance among the oligarchy, military, and ecclesiastic hierarchs always functioned at the expense of social transformations and of the few possibilities of the establishment of lay or secular measures. In places where the progressive sectors of the Church dared to dissent and question such an alliance, such as in El Salvador, they were harshly repressed, many times with the blessing of extreme right Catholic groups.

In the aforementioned social and political context, another consequence of the growing distance between military regimes and the Catholic Church was the rise of Evangelical churches as political actors. In Brazil, as in Chile, Peru, and Guatemala, governments sought in other religious leaders the legitimacy that the Catholic hierarchy denied them. This would have long-term effects because in many of these countries, religious minorities, especially Pentecostal Evangelicals, demanded a place in the public sphere of the democracies that arose out of the rubble of military or authoritarian regimes. The effect was not a secularization of public institutions due to an acknowledgment of the growing pluralization of faiths, following the European experience, but a colonization of the public space by religions, now plural, beyond the continuous and hegemonic presence of Catholicism.

Laicity and Secularization at the Dawn of the Third Millennium

During the last two decades of the twentieth century the world witnessed what could only be interpreted as a return of religion to the public sphere. In reality, it was a new verification of facts that questioned the secularization paradigm of modern societies. Nonetheless, as the Latin American case demonstrates, religion never left the public sphere. The participation of lay

Catholics and priests in political struggles, or that of the hierarchs, who generally sided with the oligarchs, or the multiple expressions of Liberal Theology, or the Christian-influenced guerrillas, were nothing more than different manifestations of the permanence of religion in political, and therefore public, life in these countries. In spite of this, since the end of the twentieth century and the beginning of the new millennium, four factors have permitted the reactivation of laicity of public institutions: (1) the growing secularization of Latin American society; (2) the gestation of an effective and significant religious plurality; (3) a greater consciousness of the need to protect human rights, especially those of minorities, in the increasingly recognized diversity; and (4) the gradual, but real, democratization of Latin American societies.

Latin Americans remain an especially religious people. Either through an institutional affiliation or under various manifestations of popular religiosity, between 90 and 95 percent of the population in the region declare themselves as followers of a particular faith. This does not, however, prevent the simultaneous development of a secularization process spurred by a growing social differentiation, the privatization of the religious, the self-"mundanization" of churches, and the reconfiguration of beliefs. Secularization, in this sense, means that the believers no longer adopt traditional forms of religiosity, they are no longer regular participants, they no longer believe in the dogmas of the hegemonic church, they no longer follow its moral dictates, nor do they assume that political and public positions must derive from these.

Multiple polls show that, independently of the level of economic development, Latin American societies are moving away from institutional religious practices. In Argentina, for example, only around 12 percent of Catholic parishioners view their relationship with God through the mediation of the ecclesiastic institution, consulting with the priest, and worshipping frequently. In fact, the majority of Argentine Catholics (more than 40 percent) fall in the category of the faithful who maintain an "on their own" relationship with God and attend religious worship sporadically or only on special occasions.[3] In Brazil the weekly attendance at religious ceremonies also does not exceed 20 percent. In Mexico, up to 35 percent of Catholics say that they attend mass at least once a week, but only 18 percent of the general population stated that they had attended their church, synagogue, or religious temple more than thirty times in the previous year. Even more symptomatic, some 67 percent of Catholics polled stated that they had not practiced the sacrament of penance

---

3 Fortunato Mallimaci, comp. *Atlas de las creencias religiosas en Argentina* (Buenos Aires: Editorial Biblios, 2003).

and reconciliation (confession) in more than a year. In Uruguay, in 2001, only 2.8 percent of Catholics identified themselves as highly practicing, and only 11.6 percent as practicing. It is important to clarify that, in all of Latin America, this profile varies among Evangelicals and members of other religions, where participation tends to be higher, which could impact the general tendency as the numbers of minority faiths grow.

Beyond declining institutional religious practice, which speaks of a religiosity in transformation, other figures account for the distancing of believers from the doctrinal and moral norms of their religious institutions. In a 2003 survey, Catholics from Mexico, Colombia, and Bolivia were asked which areas they believed the Catholic Church should devote its attention to. It appeared that Catholics of those countries prefer a church more devoted to social than to political issues. Counseling Catholics in their moral formation, promoting the defense of human rights, and helping the poor were preferred over informing the public on political issues or working for public policies to reflect Catholic beliefs. The survey found amazing similarities in the answers concerning certain gender issues such as approval for teaching all contraceptive methods and not only abstinence (Mexico, 89 percent; Colombia, 88 percent; Bolivia, 86 percent), the use of contraception methods and still be considered good Catholics (Mexico, 84 percent; Colombia, 87 percent; Bolivia, 81 percent), the acceptance of open homosexuality (Mexico, 65 percent; Colombia, 60 percent; Bolivia, 53 percent), the need for the Church to accept the use of contraception (Mexico, 72 percent; Colombia, 83 percent; Bolivia, 71 percent), of condoms (Mexico, 85 percent; Colombia, 93 percent; Bolivia, 81 percent) and the denunciation of domestic violence (Mexico, 92 percent; Colombia, 96 percent; Bolivia, 96 percent).

Therefore, if we think of secularization more in terms of social differentiation and people's (in this case Catholics') distance from their official religious doctrine, although still belonging to their church, we would have to agree that a process of secularization appears in the three countries surveyed and that differences among them are minimal in many of these matters, even though their economic, social, and political developments are quite different. Regardless, a parallel process of laicization or secularization of public institutions does not always follow.

Meanwhile, plurality has begun to take its effect on the region, even if late. In Latin America, where laicity is more of a condition than a product of the religious plurality of the Church and religious denominations different from Catholicism, they could be introduced only after freedom of religion laws were enacted in the decades following independence. It was not, however, until well into the twentieth century that the religious monopoly of the Catholic Church was seriously put to the test. Whereas until 1950 the percentage of non-Catholics was minimal (between 2 and 5 percent), at the dawn of the twenty-first century that number rises to roughly between 20 and 30 percent of all Latin Americans. There are some countries, such as Brazil, where the number of Catholics falls under 60 percent. Paradoxically, though symptomatically, Mexico, one of the most secular and laic states in the region, is the second-most Catholic country in Latin American (82.7 percent), although in constant decline; it falls just under Paraguay (88 percent). Other countries have descending percentages of Catholics by population, such as Colombia (80.2 percent), Peru (81.3 percent), Argentina (76.5 percent), and Chile (67.3 percent). In Central America, that figure is at about 50 percent and in Uruguay the number of "indifferents" (34.5 percent) and professed atheists (11.5 percent) is practically the same (46 percent when added) as that of the "religious" (47.3 percent). Protestants, Pentecostal Evangelicals, Jehovah Witnesses, and Mormons add to the non-Catholics in great numbers and constitute an important sector of the population that must be taken into account when enacting public laws and policies. A real impulse, then, has pushed for the establishment of a state that is independent of the particular religious norms and the formulation of lay policies to guarantee, among other things, the equality of churches before the law and the protection from religious-based discrimination.

Furthermore, the end of military dictatorships and the break-up of authoritarian regimes have been accompanied by a greater understanding of human rights in Latin American societies. This has had an effect on a growing defense of the freedom of conscience and of numerous other freedoms attached to it. It allows for the raising of awareness in regard to the enormous diversity in society and that this recognition must turn into guarantees and rights for ethnic, religious, sexual, and other minorities, independently of the will of the majorities. In fact, the respect toward those rights has become the principal indicator of the level of secularization of public institutions. Some countries have put forth legislation on the matter, even if political practice does not follow the norm to the letter and cultural inertias continue to influence society. Finally, the arrival of truly democratic regimes in Latin America, especially since the 1980s, has meant the strengthening of the primary element of laicity of public institutions: that is, the transfer of forms of legitimacy based on the sacred to those of political authority based on popular sovereignty. This has resulted in the configuration of increasingly lay or secular states, whether or not they identify themselves as such, that respond in great measure to the plural necessities and exigencies of the diverse social sectors and their visions of life, more so than to one specific religious doctrine.

Despite the aforementioned advances, however, as the need for a laic state becomes more visible, in countries where religious minorities are increasingly more powerful and influential the tendency is not toward the laicization of the state but rather to a pluriconfessionalism of it. In countries such as Brazil, Chile, and Peru, the pressure from minorities and the electoral courtship from many politicians has led to an understanding of distribution of favors and clientelistic privileges. In this manner, instead of eliminating ancestral privileges and the political influence of the predominant church, what can now be seen is the granting of privileges to other denominations with the capacity to represent and mobilize politically, always leaving other churches and religions outside of the scheme and perpetuating their unequal and unfair treatment. In Brazil, this has led to the formation of the "evangelical bench" and in Chile the "Te Deum." In places like Peru and Central America, the confessionality of the state alone is pluralized but public institutions are not laicized.

The greatest obstacle to the laicization of public institutions comes from the churches that are not accustomed to carrying out their mission outside of the state or without its help, as well as from the political institutions that, in the presence of the lack of credibility and authority, continue to turn to churches and religions to strengthen their legitimacy. The latter means that despite the evident process of social secularization, the political elite do not always see the need to laicize public institutions further. As such, even in places where it is assumed that the state is laic, such as in Brazil, Cuba, Guatemala, or Mexico, the negotiations between the political and religious spheres occasionally allow for the introduction of religious considerations and components in public legislation and policies. Otherwise, political culture in many countries, such as in Argentina or Peru, remain essentially Catholic or Christian, which means that even when secularizing changes are brought about, such as the decriminalization of abortion under certain circumstances or same-sex marriage, a particularly religious reasoning prevails.

The preceding notwithstanding, the social and political transformations in Latin America continue. Despite traditions and politico-ecclesiastical negotiations, this has resulted in the forced laicization of the Latin American state. The tendency toward secularization and the need to laicize public institutions appear, nonetheless, to be fighting against the ancient regalist and jurisdictionalist understanding, which used religion as part of its politics of cohesion and social control, making way in the present for a pluriconfessional scheme of privileges for the more important churches and those more capable of mobilizing political support. In this way, the laicization of public institutions that democratization and religious plurality pose and demand is confronted by the option of pluriconfessionality, which in turn is tied, to the clientelistic and populist tendencies of some regimes. The result is a growing tension between two models of society: one that perpetuates the ancient regalist, jurisdictionalist, and even laicist traditions, and another that aspires to a real democratization and desacralization of public space.

The present dilemma in Latin America in regard to beliefs and freedoms is not, then, between Christianity and laicism, but between two types of regimes. The first, which we could call "pluriconfessional," perpetuates inequality, privileges, and the collusion between political and religious power, in a scheme of greater participation of some minorities under the Catholic cultural and social hegemony. The second, which we can call "laicity," claims to generate conditions of equality through the elimination of privileges, and against the discrimination of minorities of any type, not only religious, in the context of a secular and democratic culture where the management of power and legitimacy of public institutions depend on the sovereign will of the people and not on the religious or the sacred. It is not clear if in the future the laicizing tendency backed by social secularization will prevail or if the inertia of the complicity between political and religious powers will predominate.

Bibliography and Suggested Readings

Arias, Ricardo. *El episcopado colombiano: Intransigencia y laicidad (1850–2000.)* Bogotá: CIESO, Uniades, ICANH, 2003.

Beozzo, José Oscar. "A Igreja entre a Revolução de 1930, o Estado Novo e a redemocratização." In Boris Fausto (ed.), *História geral da civilização brasileira*, t. 3, Vol. 4. São Paolo: Difusão Européia do Livro, 1986.

de Roux, Rodolfo Ramón. *Una iglesia en estado de alerta: Funciones sociales y funcionamiento del catolicismo colombiano, 1930–1980.* Bogotá: Servicio Colombiano de Comunicación Social, 1983.

di Stefano, Roberto, and Loris Zanatta, *Historia de la Iglesia Argentina: Desde la Conquista hasta fines del siglo XX.* Buenos Aires: Grijalbo-Mondadori, 2000.

Instituto Mexicano de Doctrina Social Cristiana, Encuesta Nacional de Cultura y Práctica Religiosa en México, Ipsos Public Affairs, abril 2014. Realizada del 24 de agosto al 23 de septiembre de 2013. http://www.encuestacreerenmexico.mx/docs/encuesta_creer_2014.pdf

Mallimaci, Fortunato, comp. *Atlas de las creencias religiosas en Argentina.* Buenos Aires: Editorial Biblios, 2003.

"Nacionalismo católico y cultura laica en Argentina." In Roberto Blancarte (ed.), *Los retos de la laicidad y la secularización en el mundo contemporáneo*, 239–261. México: El Colegio de México, 2007.

Mecham, John Lloyd. *Church and State in Latin America: A History of Politico-Ecclesiastical Relations*. Chapel Hill: The University of North Carolina Press, 1934.

Morales, Francisco and Oscar Mazín, "La iglesia en la Nueva España: Los años de consolidación." In Josefina Zoraida Vázquez, Lorenzo Ochoa, Bernardo García Martínez, et al. (ed.), *Gran Historia de México Ilustrada*, vol. 2: *Nueva España de 1521 a 1750*, 121–140. México: CONACULTA-INAH, 2002.

Pattee, Richard. *El catolicismo contemporáneo en Hispanoamérica*. Buenos Aires: Editorial Fides, 1951.

Poulat, Émile. *Liberté, laïcité: La guerre de deux France et le principe de la modernité*. Paris: Cerf/Cujas, 1987.

Serbin, Kenneth. *Secret Dialogues: Church-State Relations, Torture, and Social Justice in Authoritarian Brazil*. Pittsburgh, PA: University of Pittsburgh Press, 2000.

23

The Revival of Latin American Catholicism, 1900–1960

BONAR L. HERNÁNDEZ SANDOVAL

In 1925, a papal diplomat stationed in Central America portrayed the state of Guatemalan Catholicism as "truly deplorable." It was plagued, he concluded, by the "paganism" of the Maya population. For the diplomat, this bleak religious landscape stemmed from a severe shortage of Catholic priests.[1] In 1941, the Jesuit priest Alberto Hurtado echoed this conclusion when he noted that there were 15,000 priests for a total population of 130,000,000 in Latin America, or one priest for every 9,000 inhabitants. Given this scenario, during the first half of the twentieth century the Church found itself disconnected from the Latin American population. This was particularly the case among rural parishioners, who often believed in and practiced a variety of "folk Catholicism" that was often far removed from the religious orthodoxy of the institutional Roman Church. A similar situation existed in the cities, where Catholic priests faced the advance of secularism, the proliferation of philosophies of the left, especially socialism and communism, and an increasing Protestant presence.

Such context provides an entrée into the history of Catholicism in Latin America between 1900 and 1960. This chapter delves into this history by emphasizing the social and institutional dimension of Catholicism. It begins by providing an overview of the history of the Catholic Church at the beginning of the twentieth century, giving particular attention to the expansion of folk beliefs and practices – or what clerics labeled as "paganism" – among the population. It then examines the reemergence of the official or institutional Church (constituting the leadership of the national Churches) among the Latin American masses. In some countries, such resurgence began with the emergence of a Church–state rapprochement, which not infrequently was the byproduct of the liberal dictatorships and populist regimes of the first half of the twentieth century. With some notable exceptions, political conciliation

---

[1] Archivio della Sacra Congregazioni degli Affari Ecclesiastici Straordinari (A.E.S.), Vatican City, Guatemala, 1924–1925, pos. 62, fasc. 5: Resumen de lo explicado en estas notas.

paved the ground for the institutional expansion of the Church. The discussion that follows, therefore, chronicles the Church's institutional and political renaissance and, more broadly, the revival of Latin American Catholicism during the first half of the twentieth century.

The Church on the Eve of the Twentieth Century

Latin American independence and its aftermath fundamentally altered the history of the Catholic Church. It served to weaken the institutional Church by causing the departure of large numbers of the Spanish clergy from the Americas. The Church also became invariably involved in and tied to the conflict between Liberalism and Conservatism. While Liberals viewed the Church's wealth and political influence as an impediment to the material and intellectual progress of Latin America, Conservatives conceived the Church as an integral component to the sociopolitical stability of postcolonial societies. During the 1820s and 1830s, Liberals in countries such as Mexico, Guatemala, and Brazil enforced policies that strictly limited the Church's role in society to a narrowly defined religious one. The Church was removed from its public social role with the seizure and secularization of its schools, hospitals, and cemeteries and its financial base was destroyed with the expropriation of Church properties.

Anticlericalism reached its high point when Liberals came to power during the "age of liberalism" in the second half of the nineteenth century. The intensity of anticlerical reforms varied from country to country, but they nonetheless had an unquestionable impact on Catholicism. Liberal governments across Latin America implemented anticlerical laws that curtailed, if not destroyed, the temporal power of the Latin American Church. Mexico became the epicenter of this anticlerical campaign. By the time a liberal constitution had gone into effect in 1857, the Church had already lost much of its properties, its monopoly over education, and the *fuero eclesiástico*, which had given Catholic priests immunity from civil jurisdiction. Anticlerical legislation also resulted in the expulsion of foreign-born Catholic priests and nuns (especially those in religious orders). Soon thereafter other Latin American governments – including in Guatemala, Venezuela, Colombia, Uruguay, Argentina, and Brazil – enacted comparable anticlerical laws.

These reforms crippled the Church's ability to control the religious life of Latin America. The Catholic priests and nuns who remained after the implementation of anticlerical laws were often disproportionally concentrated in urban centers. Unable to exercise the monopoly over education it had enjoyed during the colonial period and hamstrung by the lack of religious personnel, the official Church became an ever more distant institution in the countryside, with the consequence that rural Catholics lost substantial touch with the sacramental life, doctrine, and hierarchical structure of the Church. This distance in turn further strengthened Latin America's long-standing heterodox religious expressions.

Expressions of Popular Religiosity

Anticlerical reform gave birth to a demoralized institution with little influence over the religiosity of the population. Some Catholics, including urban elites, responded by distancing themselves from the Church and all formal religion. Others, mainly women, continued with a very traditional approach to spirituality, while the members of the rural masses, in the absence of priests and functioning churches, often turned to their own versions of religion. As during colonial times, "popular religion" thrived in parallel – and often combined – with the religious beliefs and practices supported by the official Church. Parishioners learned to mold religion to suit their own spiritual and material needs.

One prominent manifestation of the centrality of popular religion and the institutional weakness of the Church was the proliferation of "faith healers." These popular religious figures illustrate the Church's inability to control the contours of popular religiosity. In Mexico during the early 1920s, hundreds of rural Catholics in the state of Guanajuato sought to benefit from the curative powers of José Fidencio Sintora Constantino, or "El Niño Fidencio." Sintora performed the functions of a physician and, in claiming to have received his healing abilities from an otherworldly source, usurped a role reserved for priests. The mass devotion that developed around El Niño Fidencio and other faith healers, including the Cuban Hilario Mustelier Garzón, or "San Hilarón," exposed the rift between rural Catholics and the official Church, as well as the tenuous nature of clerical power. Their popularity was symptomatic of the Church's weakness but also revealed the various mediums through which Latin Americans put forward their own, "non-official" religious expressions.[2]

The absence of Catholic priests also offered opportunities for women to shape local religious practices. Like male "faith healers," women sometimes assumed functions that Catholic priests had traditionally fulfilled. The Puerto

---

2 Other mediums included processions, which Matthew Butler examines in his "Trouble Afoot? Pilgrimage in Cristero Mexico City," in *Faith and Impiety in Revolutionary Mexico*, ed. Matthew Butler (New York: Palgrave Macmillan, 2007), 149–157.

Rican countryside permitted women such as Julia Vázquez to become both spiritual and physical healers. Beginning in the early 1920s, Vásquez found a substantial following among the illiterate Catholic peasantry in eastern Puerto Rico. Known as "La Samaritana," Vázquez gained fame for her supposed ability to communicate with spirits, including with the spirit of a defunct parish priest. Vázquez's popularity can be explained by her ability to appeal to the religious sensibilities of Catholics and non-Catholics alike: she succeeded in presenting herself as the intermediary between the official Church and Puerto Rican parishioners in the countryside.

These religious changes cannot be disassociated from broader social transformations. To a large extent, the shortage of priests explains why many Latin Americans decided to follow El Niño Fidencio and La Santamarina, but the advance of capitalist economic relations also shaped the religious landscape. One need only recall the importance of new migratory movements in explaining why, in the aftermath of his death in 1938, Juan Castillo Morales, better known as "Juan Soldado," became a "miracle worker" among the residents of Tijuana in northern Mexico. *Tijuanenses*, many of whom were migrant laborers, found in Juan Soldado a religious figure that could help alleviate their spiritual and economic burdens. An equally revealing figure was Olivorio Mateo, or "Dios Oliverio," who surfaced as a faith healer among illiterate peasant communities in the Dominican Republic. Like the leaders of various millenarian movements of the early twentieth century, he gained a following in part because of social and political disruptions caused by the introduction of market-oriented agriculture.

Popular religious expressions often extended to a blending of religious beliefs and practices. Societies in the Caribbean and Brazil frequently combined African and Catholic beliefs and practices, while communities in much of the rest of Latin America often merged together Catholic and Indian religious traditions. During the early twentieth century, *Umbanda* emerged as one of many Afro-Catholic religious mixtures in Brazil. Such amalgams became most evident in the *Umbandista* pantheon of gods, which included both Catholic saints and the *orishas*, the deities of *Umbanda*.

In Mesoamerica, anticlericalism gave way to the strengthening of "syncretic" practices that were already a staple of rural religious life. In the Guatemalan highlands, for instance, the shortage of Catholic clergymen beginning in the colonial period permitted Maya communities to develop a form of "folk Catholicism," or *costumbre*. *Costumbristas* (the practitioners of *costumbre*) developed a parallel devotion to Catholic saints and veneration of Mayan gods and spirits. They incorporated aspects of indigenous religion into a variant of Catholicism that, in the eyes of Catholic priests, looked a great deal like "paganism." In so doing, Mayan communities, like the practitioners of *Umbanda*, responded to the Church's weakness by formulating their "non-official" versions of Catholicism.

One should be careful not to exaggerate the division between popular religious expressions and the official Church (or elite forms of religiosity). The apparition of the Virgin of Ixpantepec in Oaxaca, Mexico, during the 1920s provides a case in point. Women and indigenous groups became the most fervent believers of the Marian apparition. Rural parish priests, who harbored doubts about the event, often tolerated veneration of the Virgin of Ixpantepec because they concluded that, in the context of a weakened Church, accommodation rather than rejection would allow the Church to maintain a degree of influence among Oaxacans. As in many parts of Latin America, parishioners and the few priests who could be found in urban and rural parishes remained "engaged" with each other, even as they often clashed over their own definitions of Catholic orthodoxy.

A Church–State Rapprochement

During the first half of the twentieth century, the official Church looked for ways to regain its presence in society by adjusting to Latin America's political context. In the twentieth century, as Liberalism gradually became less dynamic and doctrinaire (and in many cases dictatorial and corrupt) and as populist regimes began to influence political life, new political arrangements permitted the consolidation of a modus vivendi between the state and the Catholic Church. Such easing in tensions eventually paved the ground for the institutional resurgence of Latin American Catholicism. This development occurred gradually at different times in different places, having its origins in the changing nature of the Latin American states, as well as in the growing influence of the Vatican over the affairs of the national Catholic Churches in Latin America.

In some countries, Church–state rapprochement went hand in hand with the rise of liberal dictatorships. Liberal dictators wanted the support of the Church for their regimes and viewed Church–state conciliation as conducive to the creation of national unity. They recognized that the Church could act as an agent of social and political stability. In Mexico, for example, a Church–state *entente* began to emerge during the regime of Porfirio Díaz (1876–1911). The *Porfiriato* gave way to a Liberal–Conservative accommodation that emphasized political stability and material progress over the dogmatic and divisive anticlericalism of the earlier nineteenth century. The Mexican government began to shift from a policy of confrontation and repression to one of controlled accommodation toward the Church.

This nascent period of Church–state conciliation permitted Church leaders to establish seminaries, Catholic schools, Catholic newspapers, and a Catholic party (Partido Católico Nacional) – all changes that gave the official Church a presence in Mexican society. One of the most revealing cases of Church–state conciliation took place in Oaxaca under Eulogio Gillow, the Mexican archbishop who headed the Oaxacan Church between 1887 and 1922. This rapprochement materialized, not through the dismantling of the anticlerical system, but through the good rapport that Gillow maintained with Díaz and liberal politicians at the state level. Such a relationship required for these politicians to soften or even ignore the application of anticlerical laws and for the Church to avoid involvement in political matters. It was often the case that Oaxacan civil authorities allowed teachers to teach Catholic doctrine at the state's public schools and, in contradiction to the country's anticlerical tradition, government officials participated in public religious festivals and other events.

Moreover, national and Vatican Church leaders understood that, if the Church was to play a role in postcolonial society, it had to adjust to the new political climate and, if necessary, enter into political alliances with governments. This was the case in some countries in Central and South America. In Peru, for instance, Archbishop Emilio Lisson (1918–1931) spearheaded a political rapprochement with the regime of Augusto Leguía. Similarly, by the early decades of the twentieth century Church leaders in Guatemala had learned to cooperate with Liberal dictators.

Church–state cooperation was an important aspect of the dictatorship of Manuel Estrada Cabrera (1898–1920). Estrada Cabrera, like Díaz, recognized the importance of the Church's political support. Eager to extend the Church's doctrinal authority, Guatemalan Archbishop Ricardo Casanova Estrada (1886–1913), who, having been sent into exile in 1887, returned to the country in 1897 and established a period of more or less amicable relations with the Guatemalan dictator. An aspect of this new era was that, in siding with Liberal dictators, Casanova, Lisson, and other Church leaders generally avoided issuing public statements that touched upon social and political matters. Most of their pastoral letters centered on ecclesiastical reforms and religious instruction and thus avoided upsetting the status quo.

In other countries, a Church–state *entente* evolved together with the rise of populist regimes beginning in the 1920s and 1930s. Developments in Europe provided the model for Church–state conciliation. During this period, the Vatican, determined to ensure the protection of the Church's rights, negotiated a series of agreements with fascist Italy and Germany. In Latin America, the years that followed the First World War gave rise to "populist" regimes – invariably controlled by the military and often supported by urban workers – that maintained friendly relations with the Catholic Church.

During the 1930s and 1940s, the Argentine Church adapted to the emerging era of mass populist politics. It came to sympathize with populist and military regimes because it perceived them as a bulwark against liberalism, communism, and secularism. Influential figures such as Monsignor Gustavo Franceschi articulated a type of "national Catholicism" that closely mirrored the ideology and policies of European fascist regimes and the *hispanidad* movement of the early twentieth century, but that also originated in a homegrown right-wing ideological posture that equated Argentine national identity with Catholicism. A period of cordial Church–state relations began to coalesce during the populist regime of Juan Domingo Perón (1946–1955). Determined to consolidate his power, Perón adopted a favorable policy toward the Catholic Church. He permitted the Church to play a role in society by requiring public schools to provide religious education. Although the Argentine state did not relinquish its monopoly over the provision of education, Perón's policy did go against the country's long-standing tradition of secular education.

Meanwhile, Church leaders viewed Perón's populist policies as consistent with the Church's posture vis-à-vis the "social problem" espoused in the social doctrine of the Church, as represented by the contents of papal encyclicals such as *Rerum Novarum* (1891) and *Quadragesimo Anno* (1931). They found much congruence between the Church's position in regard to the social condition of workers and Perón's pro-labor policies. With few exceptions, thus, the Church supported Perón during the 1946 presidential campaign and the early years of his administration.

As the case of Brazil demonstrates, the Church's stress on hierarchy and social harmony created a building block for ideological and political convergence with the state. In particular, Cardinal Sebastião Leme, the archbishop of Rio de Janeiro (1930–1942), helped bring about a new period of Church–state collaboration. He viewed the populist leader Getúlio Vargas and his corporatist *Estado Novo* (New State) as congruent with the Church's hierarchical vision of society. Vargas, who ruled Brazil on two different occasions between 1930 and 1954, valued the support of the Brazilian Church and its flock, including the working class. His government responded favorably to the Church by outlawing divorce, giving clerics the right to vote and putting religious marriage on an equal standing with civil marriage. Political exigencies dictated the course of Church–state relations: populist leaders wanted the support of Catholics, while the Church sought to become a social and (in some instances) a political force.

It is important to keep in mind that Church–state conciliation progressed but not without conflict. Anticlerical politicians often argued that they were merely following the law of the land, which in many instances still restricted the role of the Church to purely spiritual matters. The informal arrangements struck often felt apart once these politicians either left office or were removed from power, as occurred in Mexico during the Mexican Revolution and the Cristero rebellion (1926–1929). Even in countries where there apparently existed a seamless Church collaboration, conflict was not completely absent from the relations between politicians and clerics. Ricardo Pittini, the archbishop of Santo Domingo (1935–1961), for example, established amicable relations with Rafael Trujillo but this Church–state modus vivendi was finally put to the test when during the 1940s Pittini publicly criticized Trujillo's brutal regime.

In other countries, in contrast, there was no significant Church–state tension. Since the colonial period, the Chilean Church had not been a major property holder, which meant that Liberals were not as prone to attack its interests as in other countries. In addition, middle-class, often populist, political parties recognized the need to avoid conflict with the Church as a way to push forward social reform. Church leaders, for their part, generally accepted legislation that fit the anticlerical model, as was the case in 1925 when a new constitution led to the separation of Church and state. They viewed disestablishment as a way to put an end to its dependence on the state. The course of Church–state relations rested both on conflict and collaboration.

The Institutional Resurgence of Catholicism

Regardless of the frequent contentiousness of Church–state relations, the political changes described in the preceding text gave national and Vatican Church leaders the space to rebuild the weakened Church. They allowed for the institutional resurgence of Latin American Catholicism. The Vatican spearheaded this revival. During the first half of the twentieth century, Popes Pius XI and Pius XII – eager to extend their doctrinal and moral authority in a part of the world that they viewed as a battleground in the Church's fight against liberalism, communism, and Protestantism – expanded their power throughout Latin America through papal representatives, or nuncios, and diplomatic missions, or apostolic nunciatures.

Papal power also became reality in the form of new political arrangements and the growing Romanization of Latin American Catholicism. In the 1930s, the good rapport between papal representatives and the administration of Jorge Ubico permitted the Church to gradually reassert its influence among Guatemalans. A less evident aspect of Rome's power was the fact that, beginning in the closing years of the nineteenth century, numerous Latin American clerics received their education at Rome's Colegio Pío Latinoamericano. Furthermore, Vatican emissaries sometimes pushed the national Catholic Churches to establish new seminaries, create new dioceses, and organize national and international congresses.

As part of the Vatican's campaign to revive Latin American Catholicism, an unprecedented number of foreign religious personnel from Europe and the United States were recruited for Latin America after the 1930s. The growth of the Church, owing to the very weak seminaries in most countries, to a large extent depended on the influx of foreign priests and nuns. These newly arrived priests and nuns sought to combat the existence of heterodox religious expressions and the perceived influence of leftist political doctrines among workers and peasants. They also saw themselves as a bulwark against the growing presence of Protestant missionaries. By the early 1940s, priests and nuns associated with the Catholic Foreign Mission Society of America, better known as Maryknoll, had begun to establish rural mission territories in countries such as Peru, Chile, Bolivia, Ecuador, Panama, and Guatemala. The Italian Franciscans, the Salesians, the Marists, the Sacred Heart missionaries of Spain, and others, as well as various congregations of nuns, also began to arrive to rebuild the Catholic educational system and serve in the countryside.

A related phenomenon was the proliferation of lay Catholic organizations, mostly based on models imported from abroad. Organized and directed by Catholic clergymen, these associations and their members generally sought to deepen the involvement of Catholics in the structures of the official Church. Many of these organizations were purely devotional and spiritual in nature and attracted mainly women. In Argentina, for instance, the *Señoras de San Vicente de Paúl* focused their activities on charity work and religious instruction. In other countries, these organizations came in the form of religious confraternities mainly geared toward the veneration of Catholic saints. Other associations existed primarily to create ties between the official Church and urban workers. They focused on social matters by encouraging workers to follow the Church's social doctrine and providing them with important social services.

The most significant of these Catholic organizations was Catholic Action. Part of the Church's response to secularism, communism, and Protestantism, it sought, in the words of Pope Pius X in 1903, to bring about a "restoration of all things in Christ" and to usher a "re-Christianization" of society. Catholic Action differed from past Catholic movements because its influence extended to diverse sectors of the population. Its "specialized" groups included university students, workers, and peasant communities, originally organized along gender lines.

Catholic Action often developed as a middle-class and urban movement. In Peru, Chile, and Argentina, the middle class viewed the social doctrine of the Church as the best alternative to secularism, communism, and the control of politics by the upper sectors of society. In other places, Catholic Action took a more "populist" trajectory. For example, when Cold War politics began to permeate political and religious discourses, the *Juventud Obrera Católica* worked in tandem with Church leaders to combat left-wing doctrines among organized labor.

A rural Catholic Action movement appeared in other countries. In Guatemala, for instance, rural Catholic Action groups emerged among the Maya population to counter folk religious practices. Similar rural programs flourished elsewhere in Central and South America. Both urban and rural Catholic Action groups produced a generation of Catholic social activists who later became advocates of sociopolitical reform by joining Catholic-inspired organizations such as the Christian Democratic Party, as well as non-Catholic social and political movements. Through Catholic lay organizations, Catholic communities (including Catholic intellectuals) began to grapple with issues of political and socioeconomic reform.

Conclusion

By the 1950s, therefore, important political and institutional changes meant to revitalize the Church in Latin America were in place. For one, a truly Latin American Church was beginning to emerge. This became evident in 1955, when the Holy See pushed the national Churches of Latin America to form a continent-wide institution, the Consejo Episcopal Latinoamericano (CELAM). Based in Bogotá, Colombia, CELAM first met in Rio de Janeiro, Brazil, where the Latin American bishops addressed such regional issues as the shortage of religious personnel, the lack of religious instruction, and the "threats" posed by Protestantism and communism. Likewise, the members of the religious orders began to institute their own transnational organizations, including the Confederación Latinoamericana y Caribeña de Religiosos in 1959. Moreover, Latin American bishops and Catholic priests and nuns began to form their own national-level structures. Through these and Catholic lay organizations, the Latin American clergy and the laity began to see the problems in their respective dioceses as part of broader concerns affecting the Latin American Church and Latin American society. In this respect, a rapidly changing and much healthier Church greeted the initiatives the Second Vatican Council encountered in the early 1960s.

Bibliography and Suggested Readings

Bazant, Jan. *Los bienes de la Iglesia en México (1856–1875): aspectos económicos y sociales de la Revolución liberal*. Mexico City: Colegio de México, 1977.

Betances, Emelio. *The Catholic Church and Power Politics in Latin America: The Dominican Case in Comparative Perspective*. Plymouth, UK: Rowman & Littlefield, 2007.

Brown, Diana D. *Umbanda: Religion and Politics in Urban Brazil*. New York: Columbia University Press, 1986.

Bruneau, Thomas C. *The Political Transformation of the Brazilian Catholic Church*. Cambridge: Cambridge University Press, 1974.

Butler, Mathew *Popular Piety and Political Identity in Mexico's Cristero Rebellion*. Oxford: Oxford University Press, 2004.

"Trouble Afoot? Pilgrimage in Cristero Mexico City." In Matthew Butler (ed.), *Faith and Impiety in Revolutionary Mexico*, 149–157. New York: Palgrave Macmillan, 2007.

Caimari, Lila M. *Perón y la Iglesia Católica: Religión, Estado y sociedad en la Argentina (1943–1955)*. Buenos Aires: Ariel Historia, 1995.

Costeloe, Michael P. *Church Wealth in Mexico: A Study of the "Juzgado de Capellanías" in the Archbishopric of Mexico, 1800–1856*. Cambridge: Cambridge University Press, 1967.

Deutsch, Sandra McGee. *Las Derechas: The Extreme Right in Argentina, Brazil, and Chile, 1890–1939*. Stanford, CA: Stanford University Press, 1999.

Diacon, Todd A. *Millenarian Vision, Capitalist Reality: Brazil's Contestado Rebellion, 1912–1916*. Durham, NC: Duke University Press, 1991.

Fitzpatrick-Behrens, Susan. *The Maryknoll Catholic Mission in Peru, 1943–1989: Transnational Faith and Transformations*. Notre Dame, IN: University of Notre Dame Press, 2011.

Gill, Anthony James. *Rendering Unto Caesar: The Catholic Church and the State in Latin America*. Chicago: University of Chicago Press, 1998.

Hale, Lindsay. "*Pretos Velhos* in Brazil: The Old Black Slaves of the Umbanda Religion." In Virginia Garrard-Burnett (ed.), *On Earth as It Is in Heaven: Religion in Latin America*, 107–132. Wilmington, DE: Rowman & Littlefield, 2000.

Hernández, Bonar. "Reforming Catholicism: Papal Power in Guatemala during the 1920s and 1930s." *The Americas* 71, no. 2 (October 2014): 255–280.

"Re-Conquering the Working Youth: The Guatemalan Young Christian Workers." In Mark Atwood Lawrence, Virginia Garrard-Burnett, and Julio E. Moreno (eds.), *Beyond the Shadow of the Eagle: New Histories of Latin America's Cold War*. Albuquerque: University of New Mexico Press, 2013.

Holleran, Mary P. *Church and State in Guatemala*. New York: Columbia University Press, 1947.

Klaiber, Jeffrey. *The Church, Dictatorships, and Democracy in Latin America*. New York: Orbis Books, 1999.

Langer, Erick D. *Franciscan Missions of the Chiriguano Frontier in the Heart of South America, 1830–1949*. Durham, NC: Duke University Press, 2009.

Levine, Robert M. *Vale of Tears: Revisiting the Canudos Massacre in Northeastern Brazil, 1893–1897*. Berkeley: University of California Press, 1992.

Londoño-Vega, Patricia. *Religion, Culture, and Society in Colombia: Medellín and Antioquia, 1850–1930*. Oxford: Oxford University Press, 2002.

Lundius, Jan, and Matts Lundahl. *Peasants and Religion: A Socioeconomic Study of Dios Olivorio and the Palma Sola Movement in the Dominican Republic*. London: Routledge, 1999.

Macklin, Barbara June, and N. Ross Crumrine. "Three North Mexican Folk Saint Movements." *Comparative Studies in Society and History*, 15 (1973): 89–105.

Mainwaring, Scott. *The Catholic Church and Politics in Brazil, 1916–1985*. Stanford, CA: Stanford University Press, 1986.

Mead, Karen. "Welfare and the Catholic Church in Argentina: Conferencias de Señoras de San Vicente de Paúl." *The Americas*, 58, no. 1 (July 2001): 91–119.

Mecham, John Lloyd. *Church and State in Latin America: A History of Politico-ecclesiastical Relations*, revised ed. Chapel Hill: University of North Carolina Press, 1966.

Meyer, Jean A. *La cristiada*, trans. Aurelio Garzón del Camino. 3 vols. Mexico City: Siglo XIX Editores, 1973.

Historia de los cristianos en América Latina, siglo XIX y XX. Mexico City: Vuelta, 1989.

Miller, Hubert J. *La Iglesia y el estado en tiempo de Justo Rufino Barrios*, trans. Jorge Luján Muñoz. Guatemala City: Editorial Universitaria, 1976.

Mills, Kenneth R. *Idolatry and Its Enemies: Colonial Andean Religion and Extirpation, 1640–1750*. Princeton, NJ: Princeton University Press, 1997.

Purnell, Jennie. *Popular Movements and State Formation in Revolutionary Mexico: The Agraristas and Cristeros of Michoacán*. Durham, NC: Duke University Press, 1999.

Reis, Joao Jose. *Death Is a Festival: Funeral Rites and Rebellion in Nineteenth-Century Brazil*. trans. H. Sabrina Gledhill. Chapel Hill: University of North Carolina Press, 2003.

Rhodes, Anthony. *The Vatican in the Age of the Dictators, 1922–1945*. London: Holt, Rinehart and Winston, 1974.

Román, Reinaldo L. *Governing Spirits: Religion, Miracles, Spectacles in Cuba and Puerto Rico, 1898–1956*. Chapel Hill: University of North Carolina Press, 2007.

Schmitt, Karl M. "Catholic Adjustment to the Secular State: the Case of Mexico, 1867–1911," *Catholic Historical Review*, 48 (1962): 513–532.

Smith, Brian H. *The Church and Politics in Chile: Challenges to Modern Catholicism*. Princeton, NJ: Princeton University Press, 1982.

Sullivan-Gonzáles, Douglass. *Piety, Power, and Politics. Religion and Nation Formation in Guatemala, 1821–1871*. Pittsburgh: University of Pittsburgh Press, 1998.

Todaro Williams, Margaret. "Integralism and the Brazilian Catholic Church." *The Hispanic American Historical Review*, 54, no. 3 (August 1974): 431–452.

Vanderwood, Paul J. "Religion: Official, Popular, and Otherwise." In *Estudios Mexicanos*, 16, no. 2 (Summer 2000): 411–442.

Walker, Charles. *Smoldering Ashes: Cuzco and the Creation of Republican Peru, 1780–1840*. Durham, NC: Duke University Press, 1999.

Wright-Rios, Edward. *Revolutions in Mexican Catholicism: Reform and Revelation in Oaxaca, 1887–1934*. Durham, NC: Duke University Press, 2009.

Zanatta, Loris. *Perón y el mito de la nación católica: Iglesia y ejército en los orígenes del peronismo (1943–1946)*, trans. Luciana Daelli. Buenos Aires: Editorial Sudamericana, 1999.

Zanca, José A. *Los intelectuales católicos y el fin de la cristiandad, 1955–1966*. Mexico City: Fondo de Cultura Económica, 2006.

24

The Intellectual Roots of Liberation Theology

IVAN PETRELLA

Latin American Liberation Theology begins with a cry of despair (I'm hungry, I'm thirsty, I'm in pain) that awakens in others the awareness of suffering and injustice and demands a response. It is a theology born out of oppression and slavery. To be more precise, Liberation Theology emerges as a reaction to human suffering and the modes of thinking, theological or otherwise, that justify that suffering. That reaction, moreover, traditionally has two parts, analytically separate yet inseparable in terms of the actual practice: one part directed toward reforming Christianity, the other directed toward reforming society. The first part seeks to undermine and revise the ideas that cause and justify oppression, and the second seeks to delegitimize and change the institutions that support it.

The Stirring of the Liberationist Impulse

According to Enrique Dussel, one of Liberation Theology's founding figures and its preeminent historian, Liberation Theology was not born at the famous meeting of the Latin American Episcopal Conference at Medellin in 1968, nor at the Second Vatican Council held between 1962 and 1965. It was born much earlier, with the reaction to the 1492 "discovery," conquest, and enslavement of the Americas and indigenous American peoples by the Spanish and Portuguese explorers. For Dussel, the first recorded "critical-prophetic cry" or reaction that marks the beginning of Latin American Liberation Theology comes in the voice of the Dominican friar Antonio de Montesinos, who in 1511 on the Island of Hispaniola, delivered a scathing sermon approved by all his brethren denouncing the oppression of indigenous peoples.[1]

---

[1] Enrique Dussel, *Teología de la Liberación: Un Panorama de su Desarrollo* (Mexico City: Potrerillos Editores, 1995), 11.

Montesinos's sermons worked on both the theological and political fronts. Theologically, he denounced an understanding of Christianity that deprived indigenous American people of any and all rights. Politically, in reaction to Montesino's preaching and Dominican pressure, King Ferdinand of Spain enacted the 1512 Laws of Burgos, the first attempt to codify a set of laws governing Spanish conduct in the new territories that forbade mistreatment of native people and endorsed their conversion to Catholicism.

Another central early figure in the liberationist stirring was Bartolomé de las Casas, also a Dominican friar, who heard Montesino's sermons first hand and subsequently converted from being a slaveholder to being the primary advocate for Indian rights. Most famously, Las Casas debated Juan Ginés de Sepúlveda in the Valladolid debate of 1550–1551, where he argued that the Bible did not justify the oppression of Indians and that peaceful missionary activity was the only route toward their conversion. His theological stance was supported and reinforced by political activism. He advocated the end of the *encomienda* land owning system that subjugated Indians; defended their intrinsic humanity; argued that they had a right to self-defense, even to wage just war against the Spanish Crown; and wrote *A Short Account of the Destruction of the Indies* that described abuses committed by Spaniards against Native Americans during the process of colonization and sent it to the attention to then-prince Philip II of Spain. His account is largely responsible for the passage of the new Spanish colonial laws known as the New Laws of 1542, which abolished native slavery for the first time in European colonial history and led to the Valladolid debate.

While Montesinos provided the first recorded cry against injustice, Dussel claims that Las Casas developed the first theology of liberation by embracing the rights of the oppressed, identifying structural injustice and power imbalances between different parts of the world, and granting the oppressed the right to rebel, even violently if necessary. Gustavo Gutiérrez, contemporary Liberation Theology's most prominent figure and the Peruvian priest who coined the phrase "theology of liberation" in his 1971 book of the same name, dedicates a whole book to Las Casas' life and thought. In both Montesinos and Las Casas, therefore, we see the two parts that have since characterized Liberation Theology: on the one hand, the denunciation and revision of theological ideas; and on the other, the attempt to rethink and revise the institutions (thus the Laws of Burgos and the New Laws of 1542) that undergird structural oppression.

The Gestation of Liberation Theology

These historical legacies notwithstanding, the twentieth-century movement known as Liberation Theology was born at the crossroads of a changing

Catholic Church and the revolutionary political and economic ferment of the late 1950s and 1960s. In the first case, Papal social encyclicals such as *Mater et Magistra*, *Pacem in Terris*, and *Popularum Progressio* focused on worker's economic rights and the rights of poor nations in relation to rich nations. Most importantly, the Second Vatican Council (1962–65) opened the door for a fundamental rethinking of the relation between the Christian faith and the world. In particular, the Council asserted that the relationship between the Church and the world was no longer a one-way street or monologue where the former lectured and taught while the latter listened and learned. Now the Council asserted that the Church could also learn from the world, and the monologue became a dialogue. In practice, this meant that national episcopates were granted greater leeway and initiative in adapting Vatican teaching to local circumstances. In addition to this shift, the Council also asserted the value of secular historical progress as part of God's work. In practice, this meant that, for example, social movements could be granted theological significance and become the focus of theological reflection. In a nutshell, the Second Vatican Council brought the Catholic closer to the secular world by, to some degree, blurring or making less clear-cut the boundaries between them.

In the second case, the Cuban Revolution of 1959, the failure of the decade of development, and John F. Kennedy's "Alliance for Progress," as well as the exhaustion of import substitution models of development led to the rejection of reformist measures to ease the massive poverty that plagued Latin America. Political and economic views became increasingly radicalized as groups of priests, workers, students, and intellectuals organized into militant revolutionary groups that espoused socialism. Camilo Torres, a priest who joined the Colombian National Liberation Army and died as a guerrilla fighter in 1966, is the most famous example of this trend. Concurrently, starting in Brazil in 1964, a succession of military coups imposed national security states. For many, neither democracy nor capitalism could solve the continent's ills. Democracy, moreover, criticized as purely formal rather than substantive, was seen as a sham, the velvet glove covering capitalism's iron fist.

These two trends, religious and political, came to a head at the Second General Conference of Latin American Bishops at Medellín, Colombia, in 1968. The conference, following the reforms enacted by the Second Vatican Council that called for taking into account particular social contexts, began by analyzing Latin America's situation. The bishops concluded that the continent suffered from both internal and external colonialism caused by a foreign exploitation that created structures of institutionalized violence. Mere development, the concluding documents asserted, would not be able to overcome this condition of dependency. The notion of liberation emerged as the alternative.

Liberation theology's foundational texts, those of its inception and expansion, were written from within this worldview. They share the following presuppositions: a sharp dichotomy between revolution and political reform, the first deemed as the only real alternative while the second was seen as useless or as an ideological smokescreen that supports the status quo; a perception of the poor as the primary and at times even the exclusive agents of social change; a sharp dichotomy between socialism and capitalism, socialism as the only social system that could overcome and remedy the injustice of the latter; and, finally, priority was given to politics in the narrow sense of struggle for the takeover of state power, with scant attention to issues of gender, race, sexual orientation, and popular religion and culture.

The Growth of Liberation Theology

All of Liberation Theology's foundational figures pursued advanced study outside of Latin America. José Míguez Bonino, perhaps the most important Protestant liberation theologian, studied at Union Theological Seminary in New York City. Juan Luis Segundo studied at Louvain in Belgium, Gutiérrez at Louvain and Lyon, Hugo Assmann at Münster in Germany, Dussel in Paris and Münster as well, and Leonardo Boff in Munich. These are the figures who wrote the books that revolutionized theology. They include Gustavo Gutiérrez's *A Theology of Liberation* (1971), Leonardo Boff's *Jesus Christ, Liberator* (1972), Hugo Assmann's *Theology for a Nomad Church* (which is an incomplete translation of his 1973 book *Teología desde la praxis de la liberación*), Juan Luis Segundo's *The Liberation of Theology* (1975) and José Míguez Bonino's *Doing Theology in a Revolutionary Situation* (1975). What did they define as new about their understanding of theology? What elements did they say made Latin American Liberation Theology different from other theological strands being produced in the North Atlantic world, in Europe and the United States? There are two main elements that these foundational works have in common.

The first element was Liberation Theology's "epistemological revolution," that is, the attempt to do theology from the standpoint of the oppressed. Assmann put it bluntly: "Any kind of Christian theology today, even in the rich and dominant countries, which does not have as its starting point the historic situation of dependence and domination of 2/3 of humankind, with its 30 million dead of hunger and malnutrition will not be able to position itself... Its questions will not be the real questions. It will not touch the real person."[2] Liberation theologians, therefore, must ground their thinking in the issues that concern the poor. Theology is relevant only insofar as it can address the plight of the vast majority of humankind that lives in poverty. The stance, moreover, is not just theoretical. Liberation theologians, such as Clodovis Boff, Leonardo's brother, argues, "must share in some way in the liberative process, be committed to the oppressed." First comes liberative practice, only after does theology emerge: "Before we do theology, we have to do liberation."[3] Active involvement in the actual lives and struggles of the poor is seen as a necessary precondition for doing Liberation Theology. In fact, those lives, those struggles, are supposed to be the raw material with which theology is made.

Liberation theologians saw this epistemological shift as marking a break with the theology of their teachers. Gutiérrez, for example, argued that traditionally theology has been motivated by the problem of the skeptic or the unbeliever. Take one of the classic texts of modern philosophy of religion, Schleiermacher's *On Religion: Speeches to Its Cultured Despisers*. The title itself points to the theologian's main interlocutor, the despiser of religion, the skeptic, the person who thinks that the Christian faith is at best anachronistic and perhaps even dangerous. Take also Karl Rahner's audience in the *Foundations of the Christian Faith*, which he himself describes as a person who "is living in an intellectual and spiritual situation today ... which does not allow Christianity to appear as something indisputable and to be taken for granted" or Gordon Kaufman's realization at the starting point of *In Face of Mystery* that "many in our time have become especially insensitive to how implausible, indeed unacceptable or even intolerable, is the understanding of God which we have inherited."[4] In all these cases the theologian confronts the skeptic and searches for a vocabulary that would allow for thinking and talking about God in a world where God's existence is in doubt. Modern theology, from the perspective of our liberation theologians, has as its starting point the skeptic or unbeliever and as its agenda offering reasons and arguments for the rationality

---

[2] Hugo Assmann, *Teología Desde la Praxis de la Liberación* (Salamanca: Ediciones Sigueme, 1973), 40.

[3] Clodovis Boff, "Epistemology and Method of the Theology of Liberation," in *Mysterium Liberationis: Fundamental Concepts of Liberation Theology*, ed. Ignacio Ellacuria and Jon Sobrino (Maryknoll, NY: Orbis Books, 1993), 73. This essay remains the best outline of the method followed by the early canonical group of liberation theologians.

[4] Karl Rahner, *Foundations of Christian Faith: An Introduction to the Idea of Christianity*, trans. William V. Dych (New York: Seabury Press, Crossroads, 1978), 5; Gordon Kaufman, *In Face of Mystery: A Constructive Theology* (Cambridge: Harvard University Press, 1993), 3.

of belief in God. The goal is to show why religion is not mere superstition. It is the person who doubts that sets the agenda.

Liberation theologians believed that their surroundings required a radically different type of theology. They did not live in Europe; they lived in Latin America. They were not surrounded by wealth and prosperity but were surrounded by poverty. Their interlocutors were not skeptical Europeans, but poor Christian Latin Americans. The key issue was not lack of faith: it was poverty. The problem was not to convince people that God was real, for the Latin American poor believed in God. The problem was figuring out what God had to say in the context of massive poverty and oppression. Liberation Theology's challenge, therefore, came not from the skeptic but from those whom Gutiérrez famously described as the nonperson or the nonhuman, the human being who is not recognized as such by the prevailing social order. Remember that Dussel argued that Liberation Theology begins with a cry of despair: for liberationist theologians the main challenge comes from the fact that a vast majority of Latin America's population lacks the basic services required for a decent existence. These people are quite literally nonhuman or lacking full personhood in the sense that they do not seem to count for the way the continent uses its resources. The goal, then, is liberation, understood as the overcoming of oppression and its causes.

The epistemological break in which theology is to be done from the standpoint of the poor was also tied to a social scientific break. Liberation theologians abandoned development theory and embraced dependency theory, especially the version developed by Andre Gunder Frank. Development theory, in a nutshell, argued that Latin America and other underdeveloped parts of the world just needed to catch up with Europe and the United States. In this conception, these countries needed to copy the political and economic institutions of the affluent West – capitalism and liberal democracy – and they would eventually prosper. For development theory, the obstacles to catching up were internal to poor regions and countries. They were traditional societies that had yet to embark on the path of modernization. Once they did, they would become wealthy. There were no global constraints. Frank argued precisely the contrary. For him, Latin American underdevelopment is the product of capitalist development in other parts of the world. Latin American poverty, therefore, is the flip side of Western affluence. Capitalism in this scenario is a game that is rigged to benefit one part of the world while damaging another. It necessarily produces underdevelopment. Modernization theory, therefore, is a sham. Latin America needs to decide between two poles: capitalist underdevelopment or socialist revolution. There are no other options.

This brings us to the second element Liberation Theology's foundational works have in common. While the first is the epistemological break just described, the second is what I call the practical/moral imperative – Liberation Theology's commitment to thinking about ideas by thinking about institutions. The social sciences played a central role. With the epistemological shift, this is the other element that liberation theologians understood as unique to Liberation Theology. Basically, the idea is that theological concepts need to be developed politically and economically if they are to be given content and escape the grasp of the status quo. The way to do so was to think in terms of historical projects, "a midway term between a utopia, a vision which makes no attempt to connect itself historically to the present, and a program, a technically developed model for the organization of society. A historical project is defined enough to force options in terms of the basic structures of society."[5]

Although all liberation theologies at least implicitly recognize this need, it was most fully developed by the first generation of Latin American liberation theologians. So José Míguez Bonino points out that "expressions and symbols such as 'justice', 'peace', 'redemption' ... cannot be operative except in terms of historical projects which must incorporate, and indeed, always do incorporate, an analytical and ideological human, secular, verifiable dimension."[6] They realized that theological categories lack detailed content and remain empty, unless they are developed in terms of their political and economic consequences. These ideas need to be given real-world content; they need to be imagined as historical projects or societal models, concretely realized in an approximate fashion.

Here Liberation Theology defined itself over and against the other main progressive theology of the time, the German political theology as developed by Jürgen Moltmann and Johan Baptist Metz. Liberation Theology's disagreement with political theology revolved around the relationship between God's reign and politics. At the center of the dispute lay the notion of a historical project. Bonino asks: "Do historical happenings, i.e., historical human action in its diverse dimensions – political, cultural, economic – have any value in terms of the Kingdom which God prepares and will gloriously establish in the Parousia of the Lord?"[7] He notes that Moltmann and Metz explicate the relationship

---

[5] José Míguez Bonino, *Doing Theology in a Revolutionary Situation*, ed. William H. Lazareth, Confrontation Books (Philadelphia: Fortress Press, 1975), 38.

[6] On the importance of historical projects for Liberation Theology see Ivan Petrella, *The Future of Liberation Theology: An Argument and Manifesto* (London, England: SCM Press, 2006).

[7] Bonino, *Doing Theology in a Revolutionary Situation*, 139.

between politics and God's reign with terms like "anticipation," "sketch," and "analogy." The result is that there is no causal connection between the two. Bonino concludes: "In other words, historical action is not really significant for the Kingdom; at most, it may succeed to project provisory images which remind us of it. These images must not be taken too seriously in order to avoid absolutizing them. The historical significance of the expectation of the Kingdom is preeminently to protect us from any too strong commitment to a present *historical project!*"[8]

For Moltmann, God's reign serves a critical function that keeps us from turning any earthly project into an idol. There is thus an absolute distinction between God's reign and a historical project. For Bonino and Liberation Theology, however, such an absolute distinction pushes theology into the hands of the status quo: "we believe that European theologians must de-sacralize their conception of 'critical freedom' and recognize the human, ideological contents it carries. When they conceive critical freedom as the form in which God's eschatological Kingdom impinges on the political realm, they are simply opting for *one* particular ideology, that of liberalism."[9] Liberation Theology's point against political theology and theology generally, therefore, is that there is no standpoint that escapes thinking in terms of historical projects. For the simple reason that theological concepts have political import, every theology is tied to a historical project whether that project is explicitly stated or not. The very attempt to stand above and relativize all human politics ends by supporting one particular historical project, that of the status quo.

The Consolidation of Liberation Theology

Liberation Theology shook the global theological landscape. Liberation theologian's books were translated and taught all over the world. They became theological celebrities. Dissertations, essays, and books were written about Liberation Theology. Concepts such as "liberation" and "the preferential option for the poor" made their way into mainstream theology as well. The movement influenced academic theology and practical politics, with the Sandinista Revolution in 1979 and the 1980 assassination by a right-wing death squad of Oscar Arnulfo Romero, archbishop of San Salvador, while saying mass the two primary examples of the latter. On the other hand, the Vatican with Pope John Paul II and Cardinal Joseph Ratzinger (later Pope Benedict

---

8 Ibid., 140.
9 Ibid, 149.

XVI) as head of the Congregation for the Doctrine of the Faith worked to limit Liberation Theology's influence. Essentially, they silenced theologians, replaced progressive with conservative bishops, and condemned aspects of the theology and co-opted others.

Between 1983 and 1986 the Vatican issued three documents concerning Liberation Theology. In the first, Cardinal Ratzinger made ten observations about Gutiérrez's theology in which he asserted that a political interpretation of the Bible came dangerously close to temporal messianism and that the focus on practice over orthodoxy was essentially Marxist. In the second and most famous document, the 1984 "Instructions on Certain Aspects of the Theology of Liberation" the Congregation for the Doctrine of the Faith condemned the use of Marxism as a social scientific tool for analyzing reality, accused Liberation Theology of reducing "liberation" to a purely political motif, and claimed that liberation theologians drew an equivalency between their understanding of the poor and the Marxist notion of the proletariat, among other points: "One needs to be on guard against the politicization of existence which, misunderstanding the entire meaning of the Kingdom of God and the transcendence of the person, begins to sacralize politics and betray the religion of the people in favor of the projects of the revolution."[10]

In 1986 the Congregation for the Doctrine of the Faith issued a final document titled "Instruction on Christian Freedom and Liberation," which, although still critical of calls for revolution and the focus on social structures as the preferred venue for change, proceeded to incorporate central liberationist themes such as liberation, the preferential option for the poor, and even the Base Communities. Gutiérrez saw this fact as a triumph on the part of Liberation Theology. It succeeded in incorporating some of its themes into Vatican teaching. Other liberation theologians remained skeptical. Joseph Comblin, for example, stated "The words are there, but always in a context that avoids all possibility of conflict: no one feels denounced. In this way Liberation Theology's themes acquire a level of generality, abstraction and also of insignificance so that they become valid for all peoples, for all continents." For Comblin, the Vatican sought to co-opt and castrate Liberation Theology's radical intentions.[11]

---

10 The Instruction can be found at www.vatican.va/roman_curia/congregations/cfaith/documents/rc_con_cfaith_doc_19840806_theology-liberation_en.html

11 José Comblin, "La Iglesia Latinoamericana Desde Puebla a Santo Domingo," in *Cambio Social y Pensamiento Cristiano en América Latina*, ed. Jose Comblin, Jose I. Gonzalez Faus, and Jon Sobrino (Madrid: Editorial Trotta, 1993), 51.

It is important to note that practically all of Liberation Theology's foundational figures were members of the Catholic priesthood. They were thus not indifferent to Vatican critique and pressure. In 1985, the Vatican silenced the Brazilian Franciscan priest and theologian Leonardo Boff for a year for his book *Church, Charism and Power*. He was almost silenced again in 1992, but he responded by leaving the Franciscan Order and the priesthood. Later, in 2007, the then-seventy-year-old Jesuit Jon Sobrino was censored for "propositions that might cause harm to the faithful."[12] Essentially, liberation theologians were confronted with a choice. They could either continue to develop the more politically radical implications of their theology, or they could continue to work as priests at the grassroots level. Not surprisingly, most chose to continue serving their communities.

The year 1989 marked changes in the intellectual and political context within which liberation theologians worked. The first change lies in the collapse of socialism. The fall of the Berlin Wall on November 9th represented the loss of a practical alternative to capitalism. Even the prospect of an alternative seemed to have disappeared from view. A second change lay in the seeming decline in the nation-state's ability to control economic activity within its own boundaries. The third change lied in the upsurge of culture, gender, and sexuality as politically contested sites and the subsequent downgrading of the traditional political sphere, the struggle for state power. The year 1989 was significant for Liberation Theology for another reason as well. Despite the fact that a large portion of the world saw the end of socialism as the surge of freedom, just a week after the wall fell in Europe, in El Salvador six prominent Jesuits including Ignacio Ellacuría, liberation theologian and rector of the University of San Salvador, were brutally murdered in their university home. Jon Sobrino happened to be abroad at the time; otherwise he too would have been murdered. The wall may well have fallen, but being a liberation theologian in war-torn Central America was still a great risk.

The Dissemination of Liberation Theology

Analysts and liberation theologians themselves read the fall of socialism and Vatican pressure as a moment of reckoning for Liberation Theology. After a period of soul searching, Liberation Theology emerged from the reckoning renewed. The renewal has three main parts.

12 Congregation for the Doctrine of Faith. Explanatory Note on the Notification on the works Father Jon SOBRINO, SJ. Available at: www.vatican.va/roman_curia/congregations/cfaith/documents/rc_con_cfaith_doc_20061126_nota-sobrino_en.html

In the first place the priests and (occasionally) the bishops who were once Liberation Theology's most avid proponents are no longer actively generating theology. As we have seen, Vatican pressure compelled most liberationist theologians to cease writing the kind of books that got them in trouble. Instead, they toned down their rhetoric, abandoned Marxism as a social-scientific framework, and went back in more conventionally pastoral ways in their parishes and communities That role, instead, has been taken over by lay people.

Today the most acute and provocative Liberation Theology is no longer produced by priests but by lay people of a wide variety of life experience – Catholic, Protestant, even agnostic, lesbian, homosexual, bisexual, indigenous – who are mostly immune to Vatican pressure. The Ecumenical Department of Investigations (Departamento Ecuménico de Investigaciones – DEI) in Costa Rica was an early key player in this development. DEI was founded by Hugo Assmann in 1974 and since then has focused on work that brings together theology and economics. In particular, the institute seeks to show that economics hides an implicit theology that demands human sacrifices – the well-being of the market is more important than the well-being of the person. But they also deal with issues of gender, indigenous rights, and popular movements. Franz Hinkelammert, Jung Mo Sung, and Elsa Tamez, three of its main exponents, are laypeople. In addition, the most radical developments within Liberation Theology are now also being produced within universities by Latin American intellectuals, often working abroad.

Second, the emergence of the layperson as the main theoretical exponent brought with it new disciplinary tools, approaches, and topics. The late Marcella Althaus-Reid provided the most important example. Althaus-Reid, a professor at the University of Edinburgh in Scotland, studied in Buenos Aires under José Míguez Bonino in ISEDET, an ecumenical Protestant seminary. Her work integrates Liberation Theology, queer and bisexual studies, feminist theory, and economics in a combination that would have been unthinkable in the priestly origins and consolidation of Liberation Theology. But she is not the only one. Nancy Bedford, once a professor at Instituto Superior Evangélico de Estudios Teológicos (ISEDET), replaced Rosemary Radford Ruether at Garret Evangelical Seminary and brings together Latin American, Latina and feminist analysis in her work. In my particular case, I have tried to incorporate critical legal studies and comparative political economy into Liberation Theology's framework as well as move beyond thinking about Latin American, black, womanist, Latino/a, feminist, queer, and other liberation theologies as if they were closed compartments. While making the argument is beyond the scope of this chapter, I believe there are reasons to see them as all part of the same movement.

Finally, one of the most interesting developments in recent years has been the expansion or dissemination of Liberation Theology into other disciplines. This is different from liberation theologians integrating new disciplines into their theology. In this case, central liberationist insights make their way into other fields of knowledge. We might be witnessing what I have described, and encouraged, as a new type of liberation theologian: the emergence of "undercover theologians" who essentially do Liberation Theology beyond the scope and confines of theology.[13] Paul Farmer, a medical anthropologist and ethicist at Harvard Medical School and founder of Partners in Health, provides a prominent example as he rethinks his discipline in light of Liberation Theology's epistemological shift. Farmer notes, for example, that "diseases themselves make a preferential option for the poor." But medical research does not focus on the communities that are most threatened by illness. Tuberculosis, for instance, is barely a threat for the affluent. Yet "tuberculosis deaths *now* – which each year number in the millions – occur almost exclusively among the poor, whether they reside in the inner cities of the United States or in the poor countries of the Southern hemisphere."[14] Farmer's work as a doctor and medical anthropologist parallels the works of a liberation theologian within theology. Both try to reshape their disciplines around the concerns of the poor. This going "undercover," this dissemination into other disciplines is, as of today, Liberation Theology's most promising and far-reaching transformation.[15]

Bibliography and Suggested Readings

Assmann, Hugo. *Teología Desde la Praxis de la Liberación*. Salamanca: Ediciones Sigueme, 1973.
Boff, Clodovis. "Epistemology and Method of the Theology of Liberation." In Ignacio Ellacuria and Jon Sobrino (eds.), *Mysterium Liberationis: Fundamental Concepts of Liberation Theology*, 57–84. Maryknoll, NY: Orbis Books, 1993.
Boff, Clodovis, and Leonardo Boff, *Introducing Liberation Theology*. Maryknoll, NY: Orbis Books, 1987.

---

[13] Ivan Petrella, *Beyond Liberation Theology: A Polemic* (London, England: SCM Press, 2008), 148–150
[14] Paul Farmer, *Pathologies of Power: Health, Human Rights, and the New War on the Poor* (Berkeley: University of California Press, 2003), 140 and 147 respectively.
[15] See Daniel G. Groody and Gustavo Gutiérrez (eds.), *The Preferential Option for the Poor beyond Theology* (Notre Dame, Indiana: University of Notre Dame Press, 2014)

Bonino, José Míguez. *Doing Theology in a Revolutionary Situation*, ed. William H. Lazareth, Confrontation Books. Philadelphia: Fortress Press, 1975.

Comblin, José. "La Iglesia Latinoamericana Desde Puebla a Santo Domingo." In (eds.), *Cambio Social y Pensamiento Cristiano en América Latina*, 29–56. Madrid: Editorial Trotta, 1993.

Dussel, Enrique. *Teología de la Liberación: Un Panorama de su Desarrollo*. Ciudad de México: Potrerillos Editores, 1995.

Farmer, Paul. *Pathologies of Power: Health, Human Rights, and the New War on the Poor*. Berkeley: University of California Press, 2003.

Gremillion, Joseph ed., *The Gospel of Peace and Justice: Catholic Social Teaching Since Pope John*. Maryknoll, NY: Orbis Books, 1976.

Groody, Daniel and Gutiérrez, Gustavo (eds.), *The Preferential Option for the Poor beyond Theology*. Notre Dame, Indiana: University of Notre Dame Press, 2014.

Gutiérrez, Gustavo. *Las Casas: In Search of the Poor of Jesus Christ*. Maryknoll, NY: Orbis Books, 1993.

Teología Desde el Reverso de la Historia. Lima, Peru: CEP, 1977.

Kaufman, Gordon. *In Face of Mystery: A Constructive Theology*. Cambridge, MA: Harvard University Press, 1993.

Kay, Cristobal *Latin American Theories of Development and Underdevelopment*. New York: Routledge, 1989.

Las Casas, Bartolome. *Historia de las Indias III*. Madrid: Imprenta de Ginesta, 1994.

Libanio, Joao Batista. "Panorama de la Teología de América Latina en los Últimos Veinte Años." In Jose Comblin, Jose Gonzalez Faus, and Jon Sobrino (eds.), *Cambio Social y Pensamiento Cristiano en América Latina*, 57–78. Madrid: Editorial Trotta, 1993.

McGovern, Arthur. *Liberation Theology and Its Critics: Toward an Assessment*. Maryknoll, NY: Orbis Books, 1989.

Petrella, Ivan. *Beyond Liberation Theology: A Polemic*. London: SCM Press, 2008.

The Future of Liberation Theology: An Argument and Manifesto. London: SCM Press, 2006.

Rahner, Karl. *Foundations of Christian Faith: An Introduction to the Idea of Christianity*, trans. William V. Dych. New York: Crossroads-Seabury Press, 1978.

Ratzinger, Joseph. "Ten Observations on the Theology of Gustavo Gutierrez." In Alfred T. Hennelly (ed.), *Liberation Theology: A Documentary History*, 348–350. Maryknoll, NY: Orbis Books, 1990.

Sanderlin, George ed., *Witness: Writing of Bartolome de las Casas*. Maryknoll, NY: Orbis Books, 1993.

Smith, Christian. *The Emergence of Liberation Theology: Radical Religion and Social Movement Theory*. Chicago: The University of Chicago Press, 1991.

25

Progressive Catholicism in Latin America: Sources and Its Evolution from Vatican II to Pope Francis

MANUEL A. VÁSQUEZ AND ANNA L. PETERSON

Reporting on the 2014 visit to the Vatican by Gustavo Gutiérrez, one of the founders of Liberation Theology, *U.S. Catholic* commented that "it is starting to look like liberation theology is on its way 'in.'" In fact, Gutiérrez "received a hero's welcome."[1] This welcome is all the more remarkable given the deep suspicions that previous popes Benedict XVI and John Paul II harbored about Liberation Theology. Gutierrez's positive reception in Rome reflects a broader change in official attitudes toward Liberation Theology and progressive Catholicism in general. One factor behind this shift is undoubtedly the election of Argentinian Jesuit Jorge Bergoglio, the first Latin American pope, who came of age as a pastor during the heyday of Latin American Catholicism in the late 1960s and 1970s.

Bergoglio's papacy – as Pope Francis – is still too young to evaluate. However, his call to take the "faith into the streets" and "bring the Church closer to the people" demonstrates the enduring vitality of Latin American progressive Catholicism. This continued relevance, reflected in the rapprochement between the Vatican and Liberation Theology, has roots in complex ecclesial, social, and political factors. This chapter examines these roots to understand the historical development and contemporary standing of progressive Catholicism in Latin America. It complements Chapter 24 on Liberation Theology, focusing not so much on progressive Catholicism's theological and ethical underpinnings as on the intra-ecclesial dynamics and the interplay among Church, state, and society that have shaped both its origins and its contemporary status.

---

1 Kira Dault, "Gutierrez Visits the Vatican," www.uscatholic.org/blog/201402/gutierrez-visits-vatican-28525 (Accessed June 17, 2014).

Pre-origins

Although the immediate sources of contemporary Latin American progressive Catholicism are the Second Vatican Council (1962–1965) and the subsequent meeting of the Latin American bishops in Medellín in 1968 to discuss the implications of the council's call for *aggiornamento*, its roots can be traced back to Dominican priest Antonio de Montesinos, who in 1511 delivered a fiery sermon condemning the abuse of Taíno Indians on the island of Hispaniola. Presenting himself in prophetic terms as "the voice of Christ crying in the wilderness," Montesinos is reported to have challenged the colonists that the destruction, enslavement, and exploitation of innocent people constituted a "mortal sin" that threatened Spain's salvation. "Be sure that in your present state you can no more be saved than the Moors or Turks who do not have and do not want the faith of Jesus Christ."[2] Present at the service was Bartolomé de las Casas, who would eventually become the first priest ordained in the Americas and the bishop of Chiapas. Montesinos's sermon marked a turning point for Las Casas, spurring his transformation from an *encomendero* to an articulate and tireless advocate of the right of the native populations. The core element of Las Casas's advocacy was his claim that the natives were persons, in many cases "endowed with excellent conduct," even "gentleness," in contrast to frequent cruelty and savagery of the Spaniards. Las Casas advanced his claim in a famous debate with Spanish theologian Juan Ginés de Sepúlveda at the Council of Valladolid in 1550.

> From this it is clear that the basis for Sepúlveda's teaching that these [indigenous] people are uncivilized and ignorant is worse than false. Yet even if we were to grant that this race has no keenness of mind and artistic ability, certainly they are not, in consequence, obliged to submit themselves to those who are more intelligent and to adopt their ways, so that, if they refuse, they may be subdued by having war waged against them and be enslaved, as happens today.[3]

If indigenous people were persons with souls, it followed that they could be converted through peaceful means and that accorded a measure of dignity. Although in defending indigenous peoples, Las Casas reproduced the colonial stereotype of the "noble savage," his advocacy for those at the margins of

---

2 www.digitalhistory.uh.edu/learning_history/spain/spain_montesinos.cfm (Accessed January 7, 2014). The sermon was reported by Bartolomé de las Casas.
3 Bartolomé de las Casas, *In Defense of the Indians*, trans. Stafford Poole (DeKalb: Northern Illinois University Press, 1974),

society and his stress on the link between Christianity and social justice will be key themes in Latin American progressive Catholicism.

There were other defenders of the indigenous peoples, such as Antonio de Valdivieso, bishop of Nicaragua and a disciple of Las Casas. Valdivieso was assassinated by *encomenderos* upset at his denunciations of the mistreatment of the Indians. Another precursor of liberationist themes was the mulatto Jesuit António Vieira, who worked in Maranhão and Bahia, Brazil. Although Vieira did not oppose the institution of slavery, he condemned the enslavement of indigenous peoples and the brutal treatment of African slaves. The Jesuit reductions in Brazil and Paraguay in the seventeenth and eighteenth centuries were also prototypes of contemporary progressive Catholicism in some ways – at least insofar as they offered a measure of autonomy to the Tupi-Guaraní people by providing an alternative to the exploitative plantation system.

Catholic support for indigenous and African people, however, was the exception during the colonial period. Progressivism was held in check by the Royal Patronage (*patronato real*), which allowed the Christianization of the New World at the cost of linking the fate of the Church to that of hierarchical colonial order. During the independence period, the entwinement of Church and Crown came under fire and some members of the clergy supported the insurrectional movements. Most notable was the parish priest Miguel Hidalgo y Costilla, whose *Grito de Dolores* in 1810 marked the beginning of the Mexican war of independence. However, despite the militancy of some individual priests, the Church consistently sided with the royalists, leading to periodic tensions with the emerging secular nation-states, many of which promulgated strongly anticlerical constitutions. Following independence, clerical elites reestablished close alliances with the new national governments, once again limiting spaces for the development of progressive forms of Catholicism.

In Europe, there were also dynamics that militated against progressive Catholicism. In response to the Reformation, the Roman Church largely adopted an antimodernist approach, opposed to freedom of conscience and the priesthood of all believers as threats to its monopoly over religious truth. Catholic antimodernism was exacerbated by the anticlericalism of many emerging secular governments. This strong antimodernist undercurrent culminated in the promulgation of *The Syllabus of Errors* by Pope Pius IX in 1864, which condemned not only secularism and Protestantism but also socialism, democracy, civil society, and rationalism. In addition, the Church reacted to the loss of the papal states by affirming the dogma of the infallibility of the pope (when speaking *ex cathedra*) in the First Vatican Council (1869–1870).

Despite these powerful conservative winds, the late nineteenth century also saw global political, economic, and ideological changes, including urbanization and industrialization, which compelled Catholic leaders to rethink some of Vatican I's conservative positions to come closer to the plight of the growing working classes and urban poor. The important encyclical *Rerum Novarum*, issued in 1891 by Pope Leo XIII, addressed the proper relationship between capital and labor, condemning "the misery and wretchedness pressing so unjustly on the majority of the working class" and affirming the right of workers to form unions. Leo XIII even appears to lay the groundwork for the preferential option for the poor that will later be the hallmark of Latin American progressive Catholicism: "God Himself seems to incline rather to those who suffer misfortune; for Jesus Christ calls the poor 'blessed'; He lovingly invites those in labor and grief to come to Him for solace; and He displays the tenderest charity toward the lowly and the oppressed. These reflections cannot fail to keep down the pride of the well-to-do, and to give heart to the unfortunate; to move the former to be generous and the latter to be moderate in their desires."[4] In that sense, *Rerum Novarum* inaugurates contemporary Catholic social teaching, charting a third way, one that rejects socialism and affirms private property, but stresses the need for capital to serve the common good and for the state and the Church to protect the most vulnerable members of society. *Rerum Novarum* was echoed in *Quadragesimo Anno* (1931). Both served as the bases for *Mater et Magistra* (1961) and *Pacem in Terris* (1963), written by John XXIII in the wake of Vatican II. The Second Vatican Council, in turn, foreshadowed some of the social and internal concerns central to global and perhaps especially Latin American Catholic thinking.

In Europe and beyond, modernist currents within the Church gained support after World War I, particularly through the work of Catholic Action. This movement began as a set of informal programs, starting in Europe and later spreading to the Americas, which aimed to increase lay participation and to address "this-worldly" events from a Catholic perspective and also to reduce the influence of secular ideologies on working-class Catholics. Catholic Action became an official Church program, with branches specifically for youth as well, in 1930. As pastoral agents began to accompany the lives of workers and students, Catholic Action shed some of its conservative tenor. One of the movement's early leaders, the Belgian priest Joseph Cardijn, developed an innovative pastoral method, called "see–judge–act," as a tool for lay

---

4 Pope Leo XIII, *Rerum Novarum: Encyclical on Capital and Labor*, no. 24. www.vatican.va/holy_father/leo_xiii/encyclicals/documents/hf_l-xiii_enc_15051891_rerum-novarum_en.html, accessed on July 10, 2014.

Catholics to reflect on, evaluate, and act in the secular world. Cardijn's deductive pedagogy began with the everyday reality of laypeople and drew from Catholic social teaching to generate actions that would transform this reality. This program played an enormous influence on Latin American progressive Catholicism, nurturing the *"pé no chão"* (foot-on-the ground, or grassroots) approach of Liberation Theology and the lay-focused methodology of Base Christian Communities.

Another important Catholic lay movement of the pre-Vatican II era was the *Cursillos de Cristiandad*, or short courses in Christianity. The *cursillos* were initiated in Spain in the late 1940s and spread throughout the 1950s and early 1960s in North and Latin America, as part of an effort to increase lay participation in the Church. The courses usually brought together groups of thirty to forty men (or on occasion women), often for a three-day retreat.

Catholic Action and the *cursillos* were reformist movements, presenting the Church as the "third way," a moderate alternative to both communism and capitalism. Certainly, early advocates of these programs did not anticipate their influence on later progressive, even radical, Catholic streams such as Liberation Theology. Programs such as Catholic Action relied on moral and material support from Church leaders, including parishes and religious orders, and most crucially, bishops and diocesan officials. Catholic Action also gave rise to groups such as the Catholic youth and student movements and a host of Catholic peasant federations, many of which became more radical in the late 1960s and 1970s in the face of violent repression by a wave of military dictatorships.

Vatican II and Latin America

Beginning in the early 1960s, a combination of intra- and extra-ecclesial pressures pushed the Catholic Church to question its role as a pillar of the status quo. The Second Vatican Council, held from 1962 to 1965, provided the most important impetus for change within the Church. Building on reformist undercurrents, bishops gathered at Vatican II engaged in a process of *aggorniamento*, the "updating" or "bring-it-up-to-date" of the Church. In general terms, this meant that the Church could no longer see itself in sharp opposition to modernity, nor could it speak to the laity from a distant and often authoritarian stance. Instead, the post-conciliar Church redefined itself as the "pilgrim People of God" and sought new forms of engagement with the world.

The Second Vatican Council's final document, *Gaudium et Spes* (*Pastoral Constitution on the Church in the Modern World*), literally "Joy and Hope," expressed an altogether different spirit than the defensive and condemnatory tone of Vatican I. *Gaudium et Spes* voiced optimism about humanity's capacity to transform the world and the Church's desire to share in this process of change. "With the help of the Holy Spirit, it is the task of the entire People of God, especially pastors and theologians, to hear, distinguish and interpret the many voices of our age, and to judge them in the light of the divine word, so that revealed truth can always be more deeply penetrated, better understood and set forth to greater advantage."[5] Learning to read the signs of the times would help the Church to understand Jesus Christ's message "more penetratingly, express it better, and adjust it more successfully to our times." It would also help advance his salvific work through the daily actions of Catholics, as a foretaste of the coming Reign of God.

In terms of social justice, *Gaudium et Spes* affirmed that the Church has a responsibility to act in the world on behalf of the poor and weak; that the right "to have a share of earthly goods sufficient for oneself and one's family" takes precedence over the right of the wealthy to accumulate private property; and that poor individuals and poor nations have the right to political equality. The document also addressed itself in particular to the Church in the developing world, spurring laypeople and clergy to seek ecclesial forms that could embody the Church's concern for social justice. Beyond repositioning the Church in the contemporary world, Vatican II ushered in the important changes in liturgy, such as the use of the vernacular, and collegiality within the Church, empowering regional episcopal bodies such as the Consejo Episcopal Latinoamericano (CELAM – the Latin American Episcopal Council), which had been created in Rio de Janeiro in 1955, not only to advance the Council's message but also to undertake reforms that would bring local churches closer to the reality of everyday Catholics. While the Latin American bishops did not play a central role in the elaboration of Vatican II's documents, they were deeply influenced by the Council's call for a greater engagement with the burning issues of the time.

Medellín: Latin America in the Light of the Council

Following Rome's lead, the Latin American Bishops' Conference (CELAM) met in 1968 in Medellín, Colombia to examine Latin American reality in the light of the Council. Using the see–judge–act method of Catholic Action,

---

[5] *Gaudium et Spes*, in *Documents of Vatican II*, ed. Walter Abbott (New York: American Press, 1966), no. 69.

the bishops reflected on the challenges facing the region. The main problem they saw was widespread poverty, which was exacerbated by developmentalist models advanced by the United States. They also addressed the impact of the Cuban Revolution, which since 1959 had offered an alternative to this model that many Latin Americans found attractive, especially in contrast to the wave of military dictatorships that swept the region. The overthrow of the reforming president of João Goulart in 1964 added Brazil to the lengthening list of military-ruled nations in the hemisphere, including El Salvador, Guatemala, Nicaragua, Paraguay, and the Dominican Republic. Coups followed in Peru (1968), Chile and Uruguay (1973), and Argentina (1976). Many dictators and military juntas received covert, and sometimes open, support from the US government.

CELAM's meeting at Medellín proved a watershed for the Latin American Church, opening a new era in both ecclesial structure and the Church's social role. In the face of the "misery that besets large masses of human beings in all of our countries,"

> The Latin American Church has a message for all people on this continent who "hunger and thirst after justice." The very God who creates us in his image and likeness, creates the "earth and all that is in it for the use of all people and all nations, in such a way that created goods can reach all in a more just manner," and gives them power to transform and perfect the world in solidarity. It is the same God who, in the fullness of time, sends his Son in the flesh, so that he might come to liberate everyone from the slavery to which sin has subjected them: hunger, misery, all oppression and ignorance, in a word, that injustice and hatred which have their origin in human selfishness. Thus, for our authentic liberation, all of us need a profound conversion so that "the kingdom of justice, love and peace," might come to us.[6]

Concretely, the conference called for the "the formation of national communities that reflect a global organization, where all of the peoples but more especially the lower classes have, by means of territorial and functional structures, an active and receptive, creative and decisive participation in the construction of a new society." Pastorally, the most prominent of these grassroots organizations were the comunidades eclesiales de base (CEBs – Ecclesial Base or Christian Communities), which the Latin American bishops described as "the first and fundamental ecclesiastical nucleus."

---

6 CELAM (Conference of Latin American Bishops), *The Medellín Document: Justice*, www.shc.edu/theolibrary/resources/medjust.htm (Accessed July 10, 2014).

The origins of CEBs are varied and somewhat unclear. Some Catholic Action projects in the 1950s used methods that were later to characterize Base Communities, including group discussions of the Bible and Church documents. By the early 1960s, new lay-focused, locally based groups – proto Base Communities of a sort – had emerged in a number of places. Among the most influential projects was one in the San Miguelito neighborhood in Panama City, where Leo Mahon, a North American priest, began working in 1963. Mahon developed a series of courses called "the family of God," which included such topics as "the Christian ideal," "sin," "the prodigal son," "sex and marriage," and "the community." The "family of God" embodied Mahon's goal of a new kind of Christian community, composed of laypeople who met regularly to discuss everyday issues in the light of faith. Mahon's experiment in Panama City drew attention and visitors, including founders of some of the first CEBs in Nicaragua and El Salvador.

Similar pastoral and grassroots projects emerged in the late 1950s and early 1960s in Barra do Piraí in the State of Rio de Janeiro and in Nísia Floresta in the archdiocese of Natal, the latter under the leadership of bishop Eugenio Sales, who later on, during tenure as archbishop of Rio de Janeiro, became openly hostile to CEBs. In Brazil, the development of CEBs was deeply influenced by the Brazilian educator and philosopher Paulo Freire's popular pedagogy. Through his literacy campaign in the Brazilian northeast, which relied on *escolas radiofônicas* [radio schools], Freire developed a dialogical model of popular education that strongly resonated with Catholic Action's see–judge–act. The goal of Freire's popular pedagogy was not simply to teach poor people to read by rote, but to engage in an open-ended process of *conscientização* [consciousness-raising] that would enable them to "name their own reality," that is, to build from their own cultural resources tools that would empower them to transform the world according to their designs.

CEBs adapted many of the tools of Freire's popular education programs. Typically, CEBs began at the initiative of priests or nuns, often with moral and material support from superiors in their diocese or religious order. The pastoral workers most often started by visiting and getting to know local residents. After this acquaintance period, members (usually from twelve to thirty per community) undertook a series of courses (*cursillos*), which usually lasted several months. In rural areas, where many parishes lacked permanent priests, *cursillos* were often offered not by local pastoral agents but by centers serving regions as large as an entire diocese. Laypeople trained in these courses would then return to their own villages, to serve as catechists or as lay preachers (known in some areas as "delegates of the word of God," *delegados de la palabra*) to help form communities. In the courses, members related the Bible to current events or local concerns, thus developing a critical understanding of their faith and their social reality. After the *cursillos*, leaders and participants would often come together in a retreat, or *encuentro*, where participants would reflect on the *cursillos*, solidify their bonds with each other, and reaffirm their commitment to energetic involvement in Church programs.

The backbone of CEB work, however, was made up of the weekly meetings at which the members would select a particular event or problem in the life of their neighborhood and draw from a biblical passage to reflect on its causes and consequences. In some case, these reflections led to collective actions to address the issue. However, CEBs were a very diverse movement. Most often, they focused on local issues such as the creation soup kitchens, food pantries, or childcare centers, or the undertaking of literacy campaigns or neighborhood improvement efforts. In some cases, Church-based activists addressed larger-scale issues such as human rights, land reform, and democratic governance.

In a few cases, particularly in the context of widespread repression and civil war in Nicaragua and El Salvador in the 1970s and 1980s, CEBs built strong connections to full-fledged revolutionary movements. Although most Catholic activists, both clergy and lay, participated nonviolently, a number of lay activists did join armed groups, especially in Nicaragua and El Salvador. Many members of the community in Solentiname, for example, eventually joined the Sandinista Front for National Liberation (Frente Sandinista de Liberación Nacional [FSLN]), the guerrilla organization that fought and, in 1979, defeated the dictator Anastasio Somoza. A number of Nicaraguan priests actively supported the FSLN, and a number became members of the post-1979 revolutionary government, including Ernesto Cardenal, who became minister of culture, and his brother Fernando, a Jesuit, who became minister of education.

As Daniel Levine rightly notes, even in cases of explicit political involvement, we should not forget the CEBs' "original and enduring religious nature." He further observes that "the clash of popular desires for liturgy with activist stress on 'useful' collective action is a permanent feature of much base community life."[7] This is not surprising because CEBs are an attempt to embody eschatology in the midst of the contradictions of history.

Even recognizing this diversity, it is clear that by making the Bible more accessible, especially in rural areas, and approaching it through individual

---

7 Daniel Levine, *Popular Voices in Latin American Catholicism* (Princeton, NJ: Princeton University Press, 1992), 46–47.

reflection and group discussion, Base Communities played a key role in the development of local voice and grassroots leadership during a period of Latin American history characterized by the severe repression of other civic organizations. CEBs contributed to political mobilization in at least three ways. First, democratization in the local religious community called into question institutional structures and existing systems of authority, often leading to demands for greater democracy and accountability in larger religious and political institutions. The fact that efforts to democratize the Church itself often failed, due to opposition from the hierarchy, probably encouraged Catholic activists to turn their attention to secular politics. Second, CEBs often helped people develop leadership and organizing skills that later provided the foundation for political organizing, especially in rural areas.

Participation in CEBs taught many people to speak in public, to reach consensus, to act as a group, to share responsibilities, and to practice democratic methods of organization and decision-making – skills that proved invaluable in the formation of peasant and neighborhood associations. Third, Base Communities strengthened collective identity by bringing together people who might have hesitated to gather for explicitly political purposes. Based on biblical calls to unity and on a post-conciliar view of the Church as the "people of God," CEBs encouraged group cohesion on a familial and local level, sometimes providing a foundation for more political forms of solidarity later on.

In addition to the pastoral and ecclesial innovations of the CEBs, the Medellín conference underlined a new ideological and moral conviction. Especially important was the bishops' condemnation of the "institutionalized violence" of poverty.

> As the Christian believes in the productiveness of peace in order to achieve justice, he [sic] also believes that justice is a prerequisite for peace. He recognizes that in many instances Latin America finds itself faced with a situation of injustice that can be called institutionalized violence, when, because of a structural deficiency of industry and agriculture, of national and international economy, of cultural and political life, "whole towns lack necessities, live in such dependence as hinders all initiative and responsibility as well as every possibility for cultural promotion and participation in social and political life," thus violating fundamental rights. This situation demands all-embracing, courageous, urgent and profoundly renovating transformations.[8]

---

8 Anna Lisa Peterson, Manuel A. Vásquez, ed. *Latin American Religions: Histories and Documents in Context* (New York: New York University Press, 2008), 217.

Going beyond traditional views of sin as a personal transgression or as the mark of inherited human corruption, the Latin American bishops expanded the definition of sin to include political and economic structures that violated the value of the person as creatures made in God's image. Moreover, they concluded that only a transformation of these structures could achieve the peace and social justice demanded by the Bible and the Catholic tradition. The bishops also acknowledged the Catholic Church's culpability in supporting unjust social structures in the past and affirmed the Church's present responsibility to work for socioeconomic justice.

Liberation Theology: Key Themes

The Medellín discussions and documents were influenced by a number of experts, such as Peruvian theologian Gustavo Gutiérrez, who drew from their experiences with Catholic Action and the work of theologians such as Henri de Lubac, Yves Congar, Karl Rahner, Hans Küng, and Edward Schillebeeckx, all of whom played key roles in Vatican II. Gutiérrez developed some of the themes that he had first proposed at Medellin in a 1970 article entitled "Notes for a Theology of Liberation," which is widely considered a founding document of Liberation Theology. In this article, Gutiérrez affirmed that "the term 'development' does not seem to express well the yearning of contemporary men [sic] for more human living conditions." He goes on to write that "the word 'liberation' ... conveys better the human side of the problem. Once we call the poor countries oppressed and dominated, the word 'liberation' is appropriate ... Man begins to see himself as a creative subject: he seizes more and more the reins of his own destiny, directing it toward a society where he will be free from every kind of slavery." He then concludes that "[t]o speak of liberation ... is to hint at the biblical sources that illuminate man's presence and actions in history: the liberation from sin by Christ our Redeemer and the bringing of new life."[9]

In his critique of development and his call to shift the analytical and theological focus to liberation, Gutiérrez was also influenced by dependency theory, which has shown that the development of core countries in the capitalist world system meant the underdevelopment of peripheral countries in Latin America, as well as by post-colonial movements that had given voice "the people without history," as anthropologist Eric Wolf put it. However, it

---

9 Gustavo Gutierrez, "Notes for a Theology of Liberation." *Theological Studies* 31, no. 2 (June 1970): 243–261.

would be wrong to think of Gutiérrez's theology as simply a religious expression of Marxist and post-colonial currents in Latin American social sciences. Gutiérrez is doing nothing short of upending traditional scholastic theology that starts from universal concepts and doctrines, working out their implication for history and practice. As he puts it, "[t]heology is reflection, a critical attitude. Theology follows; it is a second step. What Hegel used to say about philosophy can likewise be applied to theology: it rises only at sundown. The pastoral activity of the Church does not flow as a conclusion from theological premises. Theology does not produce pastoral activity; rather it reflects upon it."[10] Theology does not depart from orthodoxy but from "orthopraxy," as a critical reflection on the life and action of a community that is seeking to live its commitment to Jesus Christ in history. Through its praxis-centered approach, Liberation Theology has inspired a variety of contextual theologies such as *mujerista*, womanist, *minjung*, Latino, migrant, indigenous, inculturated, and intercultural theologies that go far beyond Latin America.

Gutiérrez bases his overturning of traditional theology on biblical passages that show a God of love who intervenes in history on behalf of His people. "Biblical faith means knowing history and believing in the God who reveals himself in it. God makes himself known through his works."[11] These works have to do with liberation. "The Lord frees the Jewish people from slavery and oppression. And he makes sure he does it through signs that will make his activity visible. But this breach with a situation of exploitation will be real only thanks to the fulfillment of a promise: that the people would be settled in 'a land where milk and honey flow' – the Promised Land..."[12] Here Gutiérrez points to one of the paradigmatic prophetic events in Liberation Theology: the story of the Exodus, which narrates the liberation of people of Israel from bondage in Egypt.

For Gutiérrez and other liberation theologians, the Exodus points to a "God who not only governs history, but who orientates it in the direction of the establishment of justice and right. He is more than a provident God. He is a God who takes sides with the poor and liberates them from slavery and oppression."[13] These themes provide the biblical and theological bases for "the preferential option for the poor," which becomes the hallmark of Latin

---

10 Gustavo Gutiérrez, *A Theology of Liberation: History, Politics, and Salvation* (Maryknoll, NY: Orbis, 1973), 11.
11 Gustavo Gutiérrez, *The Power of the Poor in History: Selected Writings* (Maryknoll, NY: Orbis, 1983), 3.
12 Ibid., 6.
13 Ibid., 7.

American Catholicism, ratified at the third meeting of CELAM in Puebla in 1979.

Other Latin American liberation theologians elaborate on Gutiérrez's themes and add their own significant contributions. Salvadoran Jon Sobrino, for example, develops a compelling Christology that starts with the historical Jesus born among the poor and choosing to proclaim his Gospel among them. Sobrino portrays an embodied, suffering Jesus Christ who takes upon himself the condition of humanity at its most vulnerable. "Sin is that which brought death to the Son of God. Today too, then, sin is that which brings death to the children of God, to human beings; it may be sudden, violent death, or it may be the slow, unremitting death caused by unjust structures."[14] In that sense, Jesus Christ's resurrection is the ultimate "paradigm of liberation," his and humanity's triumph over the "idols of death."

Anna Peterson has shown that this Christology was central to how progressive Salvadoran Catholics made sense of persecution that they suffered at the hands of the military government from the early 1970s on. They read the martyrdom of fellow grassroots Catholic activist as *imitatio Christi*, with the blood of the martyrs serving as the seeds for the coming reign of God. Certainly, this is how progressive Salvadoran Catholics understood Archbishop Óscar Romero, who was assassinated by a para-military group for his denunciation of widespread civil rights violations by the military regime.

Brazilian theologian Leonardo Boff, for his part, addressed the issue of ecclesiology, seeking to draw the implication of Liberation Theology of the institutional Church. According to him,

> The categories of People of God and Church-communion call for a better distribution of *potestas sacra* (sacred power) within the Church and so demand a redefinition of the roles of the bishop and priest while allowing for new ministries and a new style of religious life incarnated in the life of the people. The hierarchy is functional and is not an ontological establishment of classes of Christians.[15]

For Boff, Liberation Theology demands dealing with "the violation of human rights in the Church," that is, the centralization of decision making within the Church, the election of bishops and priests without "grassroots consultation with the People of God," the discrimination of women and their

---

[14] Jon Sobrino, *Christology at the Crossroads: A Latin American Approach* (Maryknoll, NY: Orbis, 1978), xvii.

[15] Leonardo Boff, *Church: Charism and Power: Liberation Theology and the Institutional Church* (New York: Crossroads, 1985), 10.

exclusion from positions of power, and the censorship of dissent. He attributes these violations to "the structure that to a great degree is independent of persons." "From a sociological perspective, the Church operates out of an authoritarian system ... that is indebted to centuries-old patterns, and two patterns are worth noting in particular: the experience of Roman power and the feudal structure."[16] The question for Boff is whether "this assuming of societal characteristics [which] was necessary for its continuation in the world" responds to the signs of the times. "The Roman and feudal style of power in the Church today ... constitutes one of the principal sources of conflict with the rising consciousness of human rights." As an alternative, Boff suggests the CEBs as a more participatory and reciprocal way of being Church, in which "the hierarchy does not exist to subordinate but rather to nourish the spirit of fraternity and unity."[17]

Boff's challenge to hierarchy, presenting it as a historical reality rather than an ontological or divinely prescribed order, earned him censure by the Congregation for the Doctrine of the Faith in the wake of John Paul II's papacy.

Puebla and the Papacy of John Paul II

El Salvador's martyred Monseñor Romero might have been unique in his unwavering defense of human rights and advocacy of social justice. Official support for progressive initiatives was uneven across the region. Brazilian progressives generally enjoyed the widest support, with the National Conference of Brazilian Bishops (CNBB) establishing a dense network of offices and programs for women, indigenous people, landless peasants, youth, urban workers, and other disadvantaged social groups. In other countries and dioceses, however, episcopal support was lukewarm or nonexistent, which often meant that progressive innovations faltered, as in Colombia and Argentina.

Yet in other countries, hostility developed between Church authorities and advocates of progressive reforms, such as in Nicaragua. Variation existed not just between but also within countries, as in Mexico, where bishops in the dioceses of Cuernavaca and Chiapas spearheaded significant reforms. Even in Romero's El Salvador, reforms were largely limited to the Archdiocese of San Salvador, where he presided, and were openly opposed by the bishops of San Vicente and San Miguel. Cultural and historical factors also shaped the emergence of new Catholic forms. In areas with large indigenous populations, such

---

16 Ibid., 40.
17 Ibid., 164.

as the Andes, Guatemala, and southern Mexico, pastoral agents and laypeople often drew on native practices, just as Church activists in parts of Brazil integrated African-based traditions.

Many progressive bishops played an indispensable role in the implementation of the conclusions of Vatican II and Medellín. These bishops nurtured initiatives such as CEBs, *Círculos Bíblicos* [biblical circles], *centros de formación* [formation centers], legal aid offices, archives documenting human rights abuses, and *pastorales de acompañamiento* [ministries among activists in various peasant, student, and worker movements], often providing institutional protection against the repressive power of the national security state. Although there are too many to mention, some deserve special recognition. In Brazil, Hélder Câmara, the archbishop of Olinda and Recife, not only played a key role in the formation of CELAM in 1955 and the organization of conference in Medellín, but also founded the Seminário Regional do Nordeste II (SERENE II) and the Theological Institute of Recife, who trained priests and lay pastoral agents in liberationist thought. Paulo Evaristo Arns, Cardinal of São Paulo, not only denounced the military dictatorship vocally, but also collaborated with Presbyterian minister Jaime Wright in photocopying and smuggling the military government's records on torture, which eventually became the basis for *Brazil Never Again*, a book that played a key role in the transition to democracy and civilian rule. Pedro Casáldaliga, bishop of São Félix do Araguaia, advocated strongly for indigenous peoples and small farmers through the Conselho Indigenista Missionário (CIMI) and the Comissão Pastoral da Terra (CPT), as well as against US policy in Central America.

In Chile, Cardinal Raúl Silva Enríquez created the Vicaría de la Solidaridad to document and denounce human rights abuses during the regime of Augusto Pinochet and Committee of Cooperation for Peace in Chile (Comité por la Paz Chilena – COPACHI), which aided in the transition to civilian rule. In Peru, Archbishop Juan Landázuri of Lima, who served as vice president at conference in Medellín, founded the National Office for Social Information (Oficina Nacional de Información Social – ONIS), at which Gustavo Gutiérrez presented the first outline of his theology of liberation at a meeting in July 1968. In México, Samuel Ruiz, bishop of San Cristóbal de las Casas advanced an inculturated Liberation Theology as way to make the Gospel relevant in the context of local cultural traditions and in the daily lives of the indigenous people.

Beyond the bishops, it is also important to emphasize the vital role of grassroots activists and religious orders that made the promotion of social justice central to their pastoral work. Priests and nuns from religious orders did not depend on supportive bishops, and in many areas they initiated some of the most dynamic and influential pastoral projects. The Jesuits were especially active in Central America and elsewhere, with many killed by the military regime in El Salvador. Members of other religious orders, such as Franciscans and the Sisters of St. Clare, also undertook pastoral innovations throughout the region, often working in areas where diocesan priests were unable to launch significant reforms.

Diocesan support for progressive projects and leaders dwindled after the election of John Paul II as pope in 1978. Following a tumultuous trip to Central America, during which John Paul II chastised Ernesto Cardenal for not resigning from his post in the Sandinista government and was heckled by the crowd during his sermon for not condemning more strongly the Contra war, the Vatican's priorities shifted toward a restoration drive that sought to rein in the more radical implications of the Second Vatican Council. John Paul II appointed Cardinal Joseph Ratzinger as head of the Congregation for the Doctrine of the Faith to lead this drive. It prioritized a "new evangelization," which placed the focus on individual spiritual renewal and conversion as a strategy to counter the forces of secularization, particularly in Europe, and the rapid growth of evangelical Protestantism, especially Pentecostalism, in the Global South.

The change of priorities translated into the appointment of conservative bishops to replace bishops who had been supportive of progressive Catholicism. Sensing the shift at the Vatican, conservative bishops led by Cardinal Alfonso López Trujillo mounted a challenge at CELAM's 1979 meeting in Puebla, Mexico, which threatened to undo reforms and initiatives advanced by progressive bishops. In opening the meeting at Puebla, John Paul II already hinted at the change in emphasis: he called the Latin American bishops to take "Medellin's conclusions as [the] point of departure, with all the positive elements contained therein, but without disregarding the incorrect interpretations that have sometimes resulted and that call for calm discernment, opportune criticism, and clear-cut stances."[18] He went on to declare that "[c]arefully watching over purity of doctrine, basic in building up the Christian community, is therefore the primary and irreplaceable duty of the pastor, of the teacher of faith – in conjunction with the proclamation of the Gospel ... Besides oneness in charity, oneness in truth ever remains an urgent

---

18 John Paul II, "Opening Address at the Third General Conference of the Latin American Episcopate," www.vatican.va/holy_father/john_paul_ii/speeches/1979/january/documents/hf_jp-ii_spe_19790128_messico-puebla-episc-latam_en.html (Accessed July 10, 2014).

demand upon us." John Paul also explicitly rejected readings that "purport to depict Jesus as a political activist, as a fighter against Roman domination and the authorities, and even as someone involved in the class struggle. This conception of Christ as a political figure, a revolutionary, as the subversive of Nazareth, does not tally with the Church's catechesis," he maintained. Instead, Jesus Christ "unequivocally rejects recourse to violence. He opens his message of conversion to all, and he does not exclude even the publicans. The perspective of his mission goes much deeper. It has to do with complete and integral salvation through a love that brings transformation, peace, pardon, and reconciliation."

Still, progressive bishops and their theological and pastoral advisors rallied and were able to make the preferential option for the poor the hallmark of the Puebla meeting. The final document called for

> ...the need for conversion on the part of the whole Church to a preferential option for the poor, an option aimed at their integral liberation ... Committed to the poor, we condemn as anti-evangelical the extreme poverty that affects an extremely large part of the population on our continent. We will make every effort to understand and denounce the mechanisms that generate this poverty.[19]

The new bishops appointed by John Paul II not only began to tip the balance at Puebla toward the more conservative forces in the Latin American episcopacy, but also resulted in the dismantling of many progressive pastoral initiatives. An illustrative example was the naming of José Cardoso Sobrinho as replacement of the retiring Hélder Câmara. Archbishop Sobrinho promptly closed down SENERE II and ITER. John Paul II's focus on defending the purity of the doctrine would also inform the actions of the Congregation for the Doctrine of the Faith as it sought to investigate deviations from orthodoxy among liberation theologians such as Leonardo Boff, Gustavo Gutiérrez, and Jon Sobrino. This investigation culminated with the publication of *Instructions on Certain Aspects of the "Theology of Liberation"* (1984).[20] The document seeks "to draw the attention of pastors, theologians, and all the faithful to the deviations, and risks of deviation, damaging to the faith and to Christian living, that are brought about by certain forms of liberation theology which use, in an insufficiently critical manner, concepts borrowed from various currents

---

19 Documento de Puebla, Tercera Conferencia del Episcopado Latinoamericano (1979), no. 1134, www.celam.org/doc_conferencias/Documento_Conclusivo_Puebla.pdf (Accessed July 10, 2014).
20 www.vatican.va/roman_curia/congregations/cfaith/documents/rc_con_cfaith_doc_19840806_theology-liberation_en.html (Accessed July 10, 2014).

of Marxist thought." These currents of thought mistakenly lead some "to emphasize, unilaterally, the liberation from servitude of an earthly and temporal kind. They do so in such a way that they seem to put liberation from sin in second place, and so fail to give it the primary importance it is due."

The document also points to the "fact that atheism and the denial of the human person, his liberty and rights, are at the core of the Marxist theory. This theory, then, contains errors which directly threaten the truths of the faith regarding the eternal destiny of individual persons." Furthermore, the use of Marxism by some liberation theologians leads to an emphasis on class struggle that flies in the face of the universality of Christian love and salvation. "The conclusion is drawn that the class struggle thus understood divides the Church herself, and that in light of this struggle even ecclesial realities must be judged. The claim is even made that it would be maintaining an illusion with bad faith to propose that love in its universality can conquer what is the primary structural law of capitalism."

The Vatican's critique of Liberation Theology is softened somewhat and placed in the context of a larger critique of modernity in the follow-up *Instruction on Christian Freedom* (1986). Nevertheless, Cardinal Joseph Ratzinger (who became Pope Benedict XVI) still insisted that "Truth is the precondition of freedom," not the "partisan truth" offered by Marxism's notion of class consciousness, but the truth of the Gospel as proclaimed by the Church. He also stressed the need for union with the hierarchy and fidelity with the Church's teaching.

> The new basic communities or other groups of Christians which have arisen ... are a source of great hope for the Church. If they really live in unity with the local Church and the universal Church, they will be a real expression of communion ... Their fidelity to their mission will depend on how careful they are to educate their members in the fullness of the Christian faith through listening to the Word of God, fidelity to the teaching of the Magisterium, to the hierarchical order of the Church and to the sacramental Life. If this condition is fulfilled, their experience, rooted in a commitment to the complete liberation of man, becomes a treasure for the whole Church.[21]

A similar drive for institutional unity and doctrinal purity would characterize the papacy of Benedict XVI, often at the cost of the progressive emphasis on social justice.

---

21 Cited in Henry Bettenson, Chris Maunder, ed., *Documents of the Christian Church*, 4th ed. (New York: Oxford University Press, 2011), 371.

The Repositioning of Progressive Catholicism

Changes in the institutional Church dovetailed with the disintegration of the Soviet Union, the fall of the Berlin Wall, and the rise of neoliberal capitalism to produce a rethinking of the nature and place of Latin American progressive Catholicism. It had never been numerically the largest sector of the Latin American Catholic Church, a distinction that still belongs to traditional popular Catholicism with its cult of the saints, Marian devotions, pilgrimages, festivals, rituals of penance, and miraculous apparitions. Nonetheless, in the political and economic turmoil of the 1960s, 1970s, and early 1980s, progressive Catholicism had gained great public visibility for its valiant stand against dictatorial regimes often supported by the United States as part of its Cold War struggle with the Soviet bloc. The collapse of this bipolar world and the gradual transitions to democracy and civilian rule from the mid-1980s in many ways undermined Latin American progressive Catholicism's vision of its mission. Grassroots leaders who had found protection and support in the Church as the only viable space in civil society now found the opening on multiple spaces to express their voice and exercise their political agency. In turn, this migration of grassroots to expanding and multiplying secular civic spaces depleted progressive Catholicism of some of its most dynamic grassroots leadership.

In that sense, although we cannot ignore the weight of the Church's restoration, Latin American Catholicism became a victim of its own success. Movements such as the *Movimento dos Sem Terra* [The Landless Movement] in Brazil, which was deeply inspired activist of the Church's *Comissão Pastoral da Terra*, now stood on their own, as social actors on their own accord. Luiz Inácio Lula da Silva, who had founded the Workers Party in collaboration with the progressive Catholic sectors in the Greater São Paulo region, would eventually become president of Brazil. And Mauricio Funes, president of El Salvador from 2009 to 2014, was educated by the Jesuits, whose progressive initiatives and statements made them a target of military repression throughout the country's civil war.

The legacy of progressive Catholicism is, thus, more long term and structural than the dwindling number of Base Communities might suggest. Still, from the 1990s, the Latin American Catholic Church turned its attention to John Paul II's new evangelization crusade in an attempt to reconnect lapsed Catholics with the faith and stem the explosive growth of Evangelical Protestantism, particularly Pentecostalism, throughout the region. The New Evangelization relied heavily on piety-oriented groups such as the Catholic Charismatic

Renewal Movement, Opus Dei, the Neo-Catechumenate Movement, and the Legionaries of Christ, which tended to focus more on personal spiritual transformation. This focus did not mean that these groups did not have a public presence. Quite the contrary, targeting the growing urban middle classes, they projected their message through the expert use of electronic media and their interventions in the political fields around issues connected to family and sexuality. In the case of Opus Dei, the Neo-Catechumenate Movement, and the Legionaries of Christ, the effort to shape the public sphere came through living out conservative moral values not only within the family but also in the workplace, and more generally, in everyday life in the midst of secularizing societies.

With its emphasis on a personal, intense, and immediate experience of the sacred, the Catholic Charismatic Renewal (CCR) appeared to succeed where the CEBs had failed in mobilizing large masses of Catholics. It did so by lifting a page from Pentecostalism's strategic combination of powerful collective events beamed nationally and globally through TV and the Internet and old-fashioned intimate prayer groups and door-to-door evangelization. In fact, Andrew Chesnut suggests that for many Catholics, the CCR represents a more attractive option than Pentecostalism, because it allows a break from the past afforded by the powerful experience of the Holy Spirit without breaking connections with tradition. In particular, the Charismatic renewal stresses the centrality of Marian devotions and of the sacraments, thereby reaffirming the authority of the clergy. The CCR, however, has not always been embraced at the parish level, where many pastoral agents see it as a movement interested primarily in promoting its way of being Catholic at the cost of the multiple activities and organizations that are part of parish life.

Marjo de Theije cautions against overdrawing the distinction between the Catholic Catholic Renewal and CEBs. She argues that on the ground, "[b]oth groups have the reading and interpretation of the Scriptures as an important element in their practice," connecting the word of God with everyday life.[22] Moreover, they both create opportunities for ordinary men and women for voice and leadership in the process of giving "meaning and form to their own religious lives" at the local level. So that, from "the perspective of the parishioners ... the differences between CEBs and CCR groups are more a matter of style than content. The idea that the two movements are fundamentally opposed to each other finds little support at the local level."

---

22 Marjo de Theije, "CEBs and Catholic Charismatics in Brazil," in *Latin American Religion in Motion*, eds. Christian Smith and Joshua Prokopy (New York: Routledge, 1999), 120.

In de Theije's view, the two movements express "the continuity of 'being Catholic,' but with widespread cross-fertilization and cross-participation." Her conclusion reflects the fact that progressive Catholicism in Latin America is not static, that it is capable of cross-fertilization with emerging trends in the Church and of adaptations to the changing environment, being able to rearticulate the meaning of the preferential option for the poor for present-day Latin America, which is no longer marked by military dictatorship and civil wars, but that continues to be characterized by deep social inequalities as well as by new forms of insecurity arising from the drug trade and transnational gangs and criminal syndicates. While Francis's papacy is still too incipient to draw any firm conclusions, this rearticulation may be what is happening.

Pope Francis and Beyond

Since his election as Pope Francis in 2013, Cardinal Jorge Bergoglio has generated great expectations. Highlighting his simplicity, down-to-earth nature, and work among the poor in Buenos Aires, the media almost immediately presented him as pragmatic man of the people, in stark contrast to the cerebral aloofness of his predecessor, Benedict XVI, whose rigid defense of Catholic orthodoxy and penchant for order and hierarchy aided and abetted the Vatican's culture of secrecy, which, in turn, allowed corruption, infighting, and sexual abuse scandals to flourish within the Church. Bergoglio himself offered support to this reading: he adopted the name Francis in honor of St. Francis of Assisi, whose vows of poverty challenged the Church in the Middle Ages; he refused to wear the specially tailored red loafers that were sartorial trademarks of Benedict and many of his predecessors; he chose not to move to the traditional papal accommodations, electing instead the more modest Domus Santa Marta, the Vatican guesthouse for cardinals and priests; he took care of his hotel bill without exerting the prerogatives of his office; and he rode together with his fellow cardinals after being elected. A 2013 article in *The New York Times* goes even further, pointing to Francis's denunciation of "the 'cult of money' and the greed he sees driving the world financial system, as signs of his 'affinity for liberation theology'."[23] The article goes on to cite a speech by the new pope on the ethics of financing: "The financial crisis which we are experiencing makes us forget that its ultimate origin is to be found in

---

23 Rachel Donadio, "Francis' Humility and Emphasis on the Poor Strike a New Tone at the Vatican," May 25, 2013. www.nytimes.com/2013/05/26/world/europe/pope-francis-changes-tone-at-the-vatican.html?pagewanted=all&_r=0 (Accessed July 10, 2013).

a profound human crisis ... We have created new idols. The worship of the golden calf of old has found a new and heartless image in the cult of money and the dictatorship of an economy which is faceless and lacking any truly humane goal." The article concludes that Francis's speeches clearly draw on the themes of Liberation Theology, a movement that seeks to use the teachings of the Gospel to help free people from poverty and that has been particularly strong in his native Latin America. In the 1980s, Benedict XVI, as Cardinal Joseph Ratzinger, the head of the Vatican's doctrinal office, led a campaign to rein in the movement, which he saw as too closely tied to some Marxist political elements. Francis studied with an Argentine Jesuit priest who was a proponent of Liberation Theology, and Father Federico Lombardi, a Vatican spokesman, acknowledged the echoes. "But what is clear is that he was always against the strains of liberation theology that had an ideological Marxist element," he said.

The evidence of a shift at the Vatican under Francis has also gone beyond symbols. He formed a consultative panel of eight cardinals that will help him confront the tough challenges faced by the Church. The panel reflects the geographic distribution of Catholicism far better than the College of Cardinals, which remains heavily European. The permanent advisory council named by Francis contains cardinals from the Americas, Asia, and Africa, including Sean Patrick O'Malley, a Franciscan who has been credited with cleaning up the Archdiocese of Boston, which witnessed some of the most egregious cases of sexual abuse and cover up under Cardinal Bernard Law. Oscar Rodríguez Maradiaga, the Archbishop of Tegucigalpa, Honduras and head of Caritas International, will serve as the panel's coordinator. One of the proposals that the council will consider is term limits for positions within the Vatican bureaucracy to avoid entrenched careerism. These changes seem to be rekindling Vatican II's spirit of collegiality after the conservative restoration and may have a wide-ranging impact on the Church's governance.

Although there have been persistent concerns about Bergoglio's failure to take a more vocal stance vis-à-vis the military dictatorship in Argentina during the 1970s, progressive Catholics in Latin America have welcomed his election. Although it may not represent a complete vindication of the preferential option for the poor as read by Liberation Theology, at the least Francis's election marks an end to the Vatican's single-minded quest for discipline and orthodoxy. Theologian Leonardo Boff, for instance, pointed not only to Gustavo Gutiérrez's visit to the Vatican, but also to the fact that the new Prefect of the Congregation for the Doctrine of the Faith, Cardinal Gerhard Müller, declared that "[t]he Latin American ecclesial and theological movement known as

'Liberation Theology', which spread to other parts of the world after the Second Vatican Council, should in my opinion be included among the most important currents in twentieth century Catholic theology."[24] In fact, Müller has even coauthored a book with Gustavo Gutiérrez entitle on *"On the Side of the Poor: The Theology of Liberation."* In Boff's eyes, this collaboration indicates the possibility of a "truce" that may allow for a recognition that "some vehement mobilizations of ecclesial sectors against Liberation Theology were more motivated by some preferences in political orientation than by the desire to safeguard [*guardar*] and affirm the Apostles' faith."[25]

It is undeniable that Francis has placed the preferential option for the poor front and center in ways that have changed the ways in which bishops engage the faithful. For instance, the US bishops "are rethinking what kinds of houses they live in, and what kinds of cars they drive. They are wondering whether, in anticipation of the 2016 presidential election, they need to rewrite their advice to parishioners to make sure that poverty, and not just abortion, is discussed as a high-priority issue. And they are trying to get better about returning phone calls, reaching out to the disenchanted and the disenfranchised, and showing up at events."[26]

Nevertheless, Francis has rearticulated this option in ways that do not always correspond with liberationist readings of the term. Although Latin American Liberation Theology is very diverse, most versions call for a rigorous sociological and economic analysis of the conditions that lead to the production and persistence of poverty. This analysis may or may not borrow from the Marxism, as the goal is to come up with the most robust examination of the signs of the times. This analysis is a necessary, feet-on-the-ground precondition for deep reflection in the light of Christian resources in a see–judge–act spiral that led to faith-informed actions to address injustices, even if through small grassroots practices.

Francis seems, instead, to think of poverty primarily as a virtue, as a marker of service, frugality, honesty, purifying suffering, and loyalty at time of general

---

24 Gianni Valente, "The War between the Liberation Theology Movement and Rome Is Over," *La Stampa*, June 21, 2013. http://vaticaninsider.lastampa.it/en/the-vatican/detail/articolo/teologia-della-liberazione-freedom-theology-teologia-de-la-libertad-vaticano-vatican-25842/ (Accessed June 17, 2014).
25 Leonardo Boff, "Roma e a Teologia da Libertação: fim da Guerra," http://leonardoboff.wordpress.com/2013/07/04/roma-e-a-teologia-da-libertacao-fim-da-guerra (Accessed July 10, 2013).
26 Michael Paulson, "U.S. Bishops Seek to Match Vatican Shift in Tone," *The New York Times*, June 12, 2014. www.nytimes.com/2014/06/13/us/us-bishops-seek-to-match-vatican-in-shifting-tone.html?_r=0

indignation toward the excesses and wastefulness of contemporary capitalism. Poverty above all implies a call for moral and spiritual conversion in the midst of a Church that has lost a great deal of its moral standing. This view is clear in his first encyclical *Lumen Fidei*, which he coauthored with Benedict XVI. Francis cites Francis of Assisi and Mother Teresa of Calcutta as models for work among the poor. "They understood the mystery at work in them. In drawing near to the suffering, they were certainly not able to eliminate all their pain or to eliminate every evil. To those who suffer, God does not provide arguments which explain everything; rather his response is that of an accompanying presence ... Suffering reminds us that faith's service to the common good is always one of hope – a hope which looks ever ahead in the knowledge that only from God, from the future which comes from the risen Jesus, can our society find solid and lasting foundations."[27] In other words, the primary pastoral task is to mitigate the effects of poverty and to offer the poor hope of a better life, not to accompany them in their struggles to build societies that reflect Catholic social teaching.

Francis's trip to Brazil to attend World Youth Day offered further evidence of his rearticulation of progressive Catholic themes. He called to the masses of young people to "stir things up," "to make a mess, to disturb complacency." Francis also stated that "[n]o one can remain insensitive to the inequalities that persist in the world!" and he also critiqued the forcible "pacification" program advanced by the Brazilian government in preparation for the World Cup and Olympics, affirming that "no amount of pacification will be able to last, nor will harmony and happiness be attained in a society that ignores, pushes to the margins or excludes a part of it."

Nevertheless, Francis's call to "revolution" is different from the streets protests that gripped Brazil just a few days before his visit. While the pope acknowledges the right of the people to protest in "an orderly, peaceful, and responsible fashion," he refers, rather, to a revolution of the heart, one that can bring more faith, love, and solidarity to a world in which "young people who have lost faith in the Church or even in God because of the counter-witness of Christians and ministers of the gospel ... So many young people who have lost faith in political institutions, because they see in them only selfishness and corruption." In other words, the call to revolution is primarily and fundamentally a call to evangelization. In this sense, there are clear continuities

---

27 Francis, "Encyclical Letter Lumen Fidei" www.vatican.va/holy_father/francesco/encyclicals/documents/papa-francesco_20130629_enciclica-lumen-fidei_en.html, number 52.

between Francis's critique of the "culture of selfishness and individualism" and Benedict XVI's and John Paul II's denunciations of the "dictatorship of relativism" and the "culture of death."

If the visit to Brazil is an indication, the genius of Francis might be his ability to bridge between liberationist and charismatic pastoral approaches. He has taken the preferential option for the poor, minus its more political implications and in-depth analysis of the social roots of injustice, and blended it with the embodied intimacy and cathartic affectivity of the Catholic Charismatic Renewal movement, but without the showiness that often accompanies this movement. It is a charismatic stance read through "the grammar of simplicity," following the Jesuit tradition.

The long-term pastoral impact of this synthesis is an open question, but at the very minimum, it shows the enduring vitality of Latin American progressive Catholicism. Rather than being dead, as some scholars had avowed in light of the rapid growth of Pentecostalism and the concomitant Catholic response through the CCR movement, progressive Catholicism in the region continues to demonstrate creativity, flexibility, and relevance.

Bibliography and Suggested Readings

Berryman, Phillip. *Liberation Theology: Essential Facts about the Revolutionary Movement in Latin America – and Beyond*. Philadelphia, PA: Temple University Press, 1987.

Bettenson, Henry, and Chris Maunder, ed. *Documents of the Christian Church*, 4th ed. New York: Oxford University Press, 2011.

Boff, Leonardo. *Church: Charism and Power: Liberation Theology and the Institutional Church*. New York: Crossroads, 1985.

Bruneau, Thomas. *The Church in Brazil: The Politics of Religion*. Austin: University of Texas Press, 1982.

Carranza, Brenda. *Renovação carismática católica: Origens, mudanças e tendências*. Aparecida, SP: Editora Santuário, 2000.

CELAM (Conference of Latin American Bishops). *The Church in the Present-Day Transformation of Latin America in the Light of the Council: Medellín Conclusions*. Washington, DC: National Conference of Catholic Bishops, 1979.

Chesnut, Andrew. *Competitive Spirits: Latin America's New Religious Economy*. New York: Oxford University Press, 2003.

de las Casas, Bartolomé. *In Defense of the Indians*, trans. Stafford Poole. DeKalb: Northern Illinois University Press, 1974.

Dodson, Michael, and Laura O'Shaughnessy. *Nicaragua's Other Revolution: Religious Faith and Political Struggle*. Chapel Hill: University of North Carolina Press, 1990.

Gaudium et Spes. In *Documents of Vatican II*. New York: American Press, 1966.

Gutierrez, Gustavo. "Notes for a Theology of Liberation." *Theological Studies*, 31, no. 2 (June 1970): 243–261.

Levine, Daniel. *Popular Voices in Latin American Catholicism*. Princeton, NJ: Princeton University Press, 1992.

Mainwaring, Scott. *The Catholic Church and Politics in Brazil 1916–1985*. Stanford, CA: Stanford University Press, 1986.

Peterson, Anna. *Martyrdom and the Politics of Religion*. Albany: State University of New York Press, 1997.

Peterson, Anna L., and Manuel A. Vásquez, ed. *Latin American Religions: Histories and Documents in Context*, 217. New York: New York University Press, 2008.

Pope Leo XIII, *Rerum Novarum: Encyclical on Capital and Labor*, no. 24. www.vatican.va/holy_father/leo_xiii/encyclicals/documents/hf_l-xiii_enc_15051891_novarum_en.html (Accessed July 10, 2014).

Randall, Margaret. *Christians in the Nicaraguan Revolution*. Vancouver: New Star Books, 1983.

Sobrino, Jon. *Christology at the Crossroads: A Latin American Approach*. Maryknoll, NY: Orbis, 1978.

Theije, Marjo de. "CEBs and Catholic Charismatics in Brazil." Christian Smith and Joshua Prokopy (eds.), *Latin American Religion in Motion*, 108–120. New York: Routledge, 1999.

Vásquez, Manuel A. *The Brazilian Popular Church and the Crisis of Modernity*. Cambridge: Cambridge University Press, 1998.

26

The Catholic Church and Dictatorship

SUSAN FITZPATRICK-BEHRENS

The Catholic Church historically appeared allied with authoritarian governments in Latin America. As a result, it surprised many when, in the latter third of the twentieth century, the Church became a vocal critic of dictatorships and an outspoken supporter of human rights in the region. To some the change appeared pragmatic. The Catholic Church embraced human rights because it feared losing power to secularizing states and alternative Christianities. Others traced the changes to new theological currents and an encounter with the poor following the Second Vatican Council (1962–1965). This chapter seeks to place changes in the Catholic Church's relations with dictators in Latin America in historical context and to illustrate how the particularities of individual countries influenced these relations.

Colonial Era

Roman Catholic popes helped to define the Iberian project in the Americas. The Holy See granted the Spanish Crown the *real patronato de las Indias*, mandating that it Christianize natives and granting it rights to tithes and first fruits of the Churches of the Indies, as well as universal patronage over the Catholic Church in the Indies. The confluence of Church and Crown power in colonial Latin America ensured that Catholicism sanctioned the legitimacy of everything from children to laws. Practices of faith imposed on colonial subjects and legal authority vested in Church agents established the clergy as crucial intermediaries among indigenous, African-descendent, mestizo, and Iberian peoples. The Church imbued daily rituals, weekly celebrations, annual processions, and public expressions of power with a religious character. These factors made the Catholic Church an ally of the Crown, but also a potential competitor for power.

Independence

The Catholic Church became a powerful political force during the independence era. Iberian officials' efforts to rein in Church power with the Bourbon reforms contributed to movements for independence. In Alto Peru (modern Peru and Bolivia) the Tupác Amarú rebellion, identified by some historians as a precursor to independence, depended on clerical support. Andean leaders initially allied with Cuzco's Bishop Moscoso y Peralta, who later excommunicated them. Large-scale indigenous rebellion spread most rapidly in communities where priests supported it and Andean leaders conjured indigenous-Catholic visions of reform to motivate followers. In New Spain, clergy provided the impetus for what became the wars for independence. Creole Jesuits expelled from New Spain became articulate agents of a nascent Mexican nationalism that helped solidify opposition to the Crown. The provincial priests Miguel Hidalgo and José María Morelos initiated the independence movement, using the image of Our Lady of Guadalupe to unify the population. In Argentina, the Dominican friar Ignacio Grela was among the independence leaders and clergy encouraged indigenous support for independence.

Clerics' roles in these rebellions reveal divisions within the colonial Church linked to the status of parishioners and to the clergy's position within the hierarchy. Creole clergy engaged in rebellions often ministered to the poor and marginal. Most clergy who supported the nascent independence movements appeared from modest or middle-class backgrounds. Higher Church dignitaries usually supported the Crown. Rebellion resulted from a confluence of Crown efforts to extract economic resources, to impose authority, and to control clergy. This confluence negatively affected the Catholic Church, but also colonial subjects. The Catholic Church's role in independence suggested that clerical support for authoritarian rule was contingent on local conditions, status of clergy, and their relationship to parishioners.

Nineteenth Century

Many governments of newly independent Latin American countries maintained Catholicism as the official state religion, and few tolerated religious freedom in the early nineteenth century. Yet conflict arose between Church and state as countries embraced Liberal precepts and raided Church coffers to support government projects. Catholic clergy maintained a powerful presence in rural areas and among popular classes, allowing them to buttress or to undermine state power. In Guatemala, after Liberals sought to assert control over the Church by expelling Jesuits and Capuchins and introducing anticlerical legislation in the mid-1820s, they confronted violent opposition by indigenous communities led by priests. In Mexico, the Catholic Church remained a defining influence in rural communities even as it sought to introduce changes. In Peru, independent governments retained the *patronato real* and created a "state-Church" unified as it had been during the colonial period.

Military dictatorship characterized many post-independence governments in Latin America, but the Catholic Church only critiqued authoritarian power, when its own position seemed threatened. In Paraguay, clergy played a central role in maintaining what would become the longest surviving dictatorship in the region. In Guatemala, the *patronato real* was restored for the military dictator Rafael Carrera. In Mexico, Porfirio Diaz smoothed relations with the Church following Liberal attacks on it instituted by the Constitution of 1857.

Twentieth Century

Even as the Catholic Church in Latin America fought to maintain its place, the groundwork was laid for change. From the mid-nineteenth to early twentieth century Liberalism and the emergence of the "social question" pushed the Catholic Church toward reform. Pope Leo XIII's social encyclical *Rerum Novarum* (1891: Rights and Duties of Capital and Labor) promoted awareness of social justice and legitimized social action, while Pope Pius X's *Lacrimabili Statu* (1912: On the Indians of South America) condemned the "crimes and outrages" committed against indigenous peoples. Although paternalistic and conservative in nature, Catholic Action, introduced by Pope Pius XI in the early twentieth century to promote lay participation, marked a slow shift from exclusive clerical power.

By the 1950s, the Latin American Church had changed. The Conference of Latin American Bishops (CELAM) formed in 1955 allowed the hierarchy to speak with a unified voice. Roman seminary training of Latin American clerics created a cadre of men with shared experience and theological formation. An influx of foreign clergy during and after World War II, combined with an increase in international Catholic aid brought by agencies such as the German *Miserior*, Belgian Aid to the Church in Need, and United

States Catholic Relief Services reduced Latin America's Catholic Church's dependence on states and facilitated expansion of networks. Catholic networks played an especially important role in marginalized urban and rural communities, where clergy participated in the lives of the poor. These religious changes occurred in the context of the 1959 Cuban Revolution and the wave of reform, revolution, and counterrevolution it helped spark in the region. The reforms introduced by the Second Vatican Council became integrated into this Latin American context, contributing to the development of Liberation Theology.

Daniel H. Levine argues that new religious ideas, combined with Catholic grassroots organizing, facilitated activism and the development of nets of solidarity in Latin America in the late 1960s and early 1970s. In his view, the rise of dictatorship in the region at this time simultaneously reinforced and undermined these networks and activism. Dictatorial attacks against all reformist sectors of civil society sometimes made the Catholic Church a safe space for organizing. Yet, this conjuncture marked a radical change. In some cases, repressive agents of state murdered bishops and priests, raped and murdered nuns and laity, and expelled clergy. The drama of this violence and its incongruity in a region defined historically as Catholic pointed to direct confrontation between the Church and state. Yet, this broad picture obscures complexities.

With the exception of Argentina, all repressive regimes that came to power in the latter third of the twentieth century identified the Catholic Church as an oppositional force. But the reasons for and degree of opposition differed dramatically. Although progressive sectors composed of clergy serving parishes in marginal areas came to support popular and occasionally even revolutionary movements, most members of the Latin American hierarchy eschewed radicalization and often even reform. Many times, what came to be defined as "Catholic radicalism" was little more than vocal, institutionalized support for basic human rights in the face of dictatorial repression. In a few cases, Catholic clergy and members of the hierarchy supported reformist dictators. In all cases, the Vatican played a determining and increasingly conservative role in Latin America, sanctioning priests, nuns, and theologians and replacing reformers in the Catholic hierarchy with advocates of radical orthodoxy. Foreign clergy and their economic resources also played a crucial, though understated, role. The challenge of understanding the Catholic Church and dictatorship in contemporary Latin America may be seen through differences in illustrative cases of distinct countries.

The Catholic Church, Reform, and Dictators: Peru's Juan Velasco Alvarado and Panama's Omar Torrijos

The relationship between the Catholic Church and reformist dictators in contemporary Latin America has not been the focus of extensive research. Juan Velasco Alvarado and Omar Torrijos both came to power through military coups in 1968. Each president exhibited dictatorial authority, while promoting populist change. Both engaged the Catholic Church.

In 1963, Leo Mahon, pastor of a successful parish among Puerto Ricans in inner city Chicago, received permission to start an experimental parish in Panama. With a team of two US priests later joined by five women religious, and local lay leaders Mahon facilitated the development of a highly successful experimental parish in San Miguelito, an impoverished urban community. His efforts preceded the conclusion of the Second Vatican Council and Liberation Theology and drew national and international attention. They also attracted resentment from Panamanian clergy, who saw the foreigners as "arrogant" outsiders. In 1965, Cardinal Albert Meyer of Chicago, who authorized the Panama experiment, died, leaving Mahon with limited support from the hierarchy in the United States or Panama.

San Miguelito remained an isolated project, almost an enclave, yet the community's unity, organization, and progressivism made it a potentially important political force. Mahon and his parish presented the first organized opposition to the Torrijos' coup. Subsequently, Torrijos (a non-Catholic and notorious womanizer) turned to Mahon to establish San Miguelito as a "model community," offering government aid for public works channeled through the organizational structure and leadership of the parish. In the short term, this effort benefitted the community, but it also led to co-optation of Church leaders.

The situation changed in 1970, when the military engineered the disappearance of Hector Gallegos, a progressive Colombian priest serving in Panama. San Miguelito organized a protest, but no one paid attention. As Mahon observed, "We were ignored, because we were no longer a threat to the government."[1] Lacking support from Panamanian clergy and representatives of the hierarchy, San Miguelito could neither pressure Torrijos nor provide him

---

[1] Leo Mahon with Nancy Davis, *Fire Under My Feet: A Memoir of God's Power in Panama* (Maryknoll: Orbis Books, 2007), 131.

with sufficient popular support to merit co-optation. San Miguelito suffered demise through disregard. Mahon's contract was not renewed.

Peru's General Juan Velasco Alvarado, who also appealed for Catholic support, acted aggressively to transform conditions for his country's impoverished rural and urban citizens. He declared the "Day of the Indian," supported bilingual education, recognized urban "slums" as *pueblos jóvenes* (young towns), nationalized industries, and introduced a radical program of agrarian reform. In Peru, the Church had a vast sector of foreign clergy, but an equally important core of national clergy and members of the hierarchy entrenched in a progressive Latin American Catholic network. Velasco was a product of the progressive Peruvian Church. In the 1960s, Jesuit Peruvian Father Romeo Luna Victoria developed courses at the Center for Advanced Military Studies (CAEM), where he taught members of Velasco's coalition.

The confluence of a presence of wealthy foreign clergy with dynamic networks in impoverished rural and urban communities and access to international Catholic Church aid, articulate Peruvian Catholic leaders, and a powerful progressive hierarchy made the Catholic Church an important ally for the Velasco regime, facilitating its reforms. When General Francisco Morales Bermúdez took control of Peru's military regime in 1975, terminating Velasco's reformist experiment by instituting devastating austerity measures, the Catholic Church distanced itself from the government.

In 1980, Peru returned to democracy at the same time that the Shining Path (Partido Comunista del Perú-Sendero Luminoso – PCP-SL) initiated an armed conflict that devastated the country. The Catholic Church appeared caught between Peru's repressive military forces, later declared responsible for 30 percent of the deaths, and the brutal PCP-SL, responsible for 54 percent of the deaths. In this context, the Catholic Church supported human rights, engaging its networks in rural and urban communities and ties to international aid to create *vicarías de solidaridad*. This effort placed the Church in a stance oppositional to both the government and the Shining Path, helping it to gain legitimacy as an independent force. As the armed conflict drew to a close, the Vatican replaced progressive members of the Peruvian hierarchy with conservative clergy, effectively silencing the Church's progressive sector.

The Catholic Church, South America, Repression, and Dictators – Brazil and Chile

While reformist military dictators came to power in Peru and Panama, much of South America fell to the control of violently repressive military dictators.

In rapid succession, the military took power in Brazil (1964), Bolivia (1964), Uruguay (1973), Chile (1973), and Argentina (1976). The Brazilian dictatorship appeared closest in form to that of Peru in its relationship to the Catholic Church. In Brazil, after an initial period from 1964 to 1970, when Catholic officials viewed the military coup favorably, the Church and the military appeared to be in direct confrontation. The Catholic hierarchy organized into the National Conference of Bishops of Brazil (CNBB), laity engaged in Christian Base Communities, and clergy vocally criticized the Brazilian military. Some clergy and laity also allied with radical movements. Between 1968 and 1978, 122 members of the Church were imprisoned, including nine bishops, eighty-four priests, thirteen seminarians, and six women religious. An additional 274 pastoral agents were detained.

Yet, historian Ken Serbin's research demonstrated that even in the face of confrontation, dialogue occurred between high Church and military officials.[2] Serbin argues that a historic relationship in which the Church and military worked together to promote development and reform in the country made it possible for leaders of these institutions to maintain "secret dialogues" even at the height of their public conflict from 1970 to 1974. As was true of Peru, the military in Brazil included devoutly Catholic high-level officials. By the 1970s, Brazil had 250 bishops, supporting Christian Base Communities, and, though they ranged from conservative to progressive, through the CNBB bishops spoke with a unified voice. Brazil's clergy included a large number of foreigners with access to international aid. Although only a small percentage of Brazil's population were considered active, practicing Catholics, some four million were organized into Christian Base Communities, forming a powerful progressive laity in the country. These conditions made dialogue between the Church and military possible and desirable for leaders of both institutions.

While the relationship between the Church and dictatorship in Brazil was characterized by both confrontation and negotiation, that in Chile, where there was no radical armed movement, became directly confrontational. In 1973, General Augusto Pinochet violently overthrew the democratically elected socialist president, Salvador Allende. In the first weeks after the coup, some 1,500 people were killed and as many as 100,000 detained often in sports stadiums or arenas where they were tortured. At first, Catholic Cardinal Raúl Silva Henríquez, along with Protestant, Greek Orthodox, and Jewish religious leaders maintained cordial relations with the new military government, while

---

2 Kenneth P. Serbin, *Secret Dialogues: Church-State Relations, Torture, and Social Justice in Authoritarian Brazil* (Pittsburgh: University of Pittsburgh Press, 2000), 2.

condemning violence. Other Chilean bishops directly supported the coup, thanking the military for saving the country from Marxism. Nonetheless, support and cooperation turned to assistance for victims of military repression. Protestant and Catholic leaders together formed "the Committee of Cooperation for Peace," to aid victims of violence. It was dismantled in 1975 as a result of military pressure. Ecumenical groups, with support from the World Council of Churches in Geneva, also created the Committee of Cooperation for Peace (Comité por la Paz Chilena – COPACHI) co-directed by Lutheran bishop Helmut Frenz and Catholic auxiliary bishop Santiago Fernando Ariztía.

In 1976, Chile's Cardinal Silva Henríquez founded the Vicariate of Solidarity. The Vicariate documented and defended against state-directed violence and communicated news of human rights abuses to the international community. The Vicariate also organized meetings, seminars, roundtables, and discussions, giving opponents of the Pinochet regime a nominally protected space to meet and organize. Indeed, after the coup, churches became the only institutions that could function openly with any degree of freedom. As a result, although the Catholic Church lost adherents during the Allende years, it attracted large-scale popular support during the dictatorship.

Although Chile's hierarchy was not uniformly progressive, its members presented a unified front to protect human rights. Moreover, the Vicariate received support from Pope John Paul II, who, when he visited Chile in 1987, publicly shunned Pinochet. Thus, the Chilean Church confronting the Pinochet regime enjoyed popular support from laity, a unified hierarchy, and support from the pope. These conditions, combined with the presence of foreign clergy and resources, and ecumenical work with Protestants, allowed it to oppose directly the dictatorship. As was true in other countries, Pope John Paul II gradually replaced progressive members of the hierarchy with conservatives and discouraged lay engagement, thereby weakening the reformist segment of the Church.

The Catholic Church, Central America, Revolution – Nicaragua, El Salvador, Guatemala

Nicaragua, El Salvador, and Guatemala arguably created the image of the contemporary Catholic Church as an ally or even instigator of armed revolutionary movements seeking to overthrow military dictatorships. The countries all developed powerful grassroots Catholic movements (sometimes allied with revolutionary organizations) that traced their origins to the early 1960s, relied on foreign clergy with access to international resources and articulate national clergy, and experienced divided hierarchies with bishops and archbishops supporting reform, opposing it, and changing their stance in response to political exigencies. The Vatican played a public role in each country.

In 1979, the Sandinista National Liberation Front (Frente Sandinista de Liberación Nacional – FSLN) overthrew Anastacio Somoza Debayle, terminating the fifty-six-year Somoza family dictatorship in Nicaragua. Ernesto Cardenal, a Catholic priest and poet, established an experimental Christian community in 1966. Cardenal's community, along with Christian Base Communities formed by Spanish Father José de la Jara and others, vocally criticized the Somoza dictatorship. Even as segments of the Nicaraguan Church affiliated with grassroots groups opposed Somoza, the institutional Church retained close ties with the government. Some clergy even served as paid public employees and ambassadors.

In 1970, Monsignor Obando y Bravo, a supporter of human rights and critic of the Somoza regime, became Archbishop of Nicaragua. In 1974 he condemned electoral fraud and defended the Church in its political activism, but three years later in 1977 he condemned revolutionary movements and called for "active non-violence." Obando y Bravo supported a peaceful General Strike declared in response to the assassination of journalist Pedro Joaquín Chamorro in 1978. Somoza responded by shutting down Radio Católica, forcing the Catholic hierarchy to respond by calling for Somoza's resignation. Once the Sandinistas came to power, Obando y Bravo became an ardent critic, but clergy, including Fathers Ernesto Cardenal and Maryknoll mission Father Miguel D'Escoto, accepted positions working with the government.

In 1980, after visiting Pope John Paul II, Archbishop Obando y Bravo condemned the leaders of the FSLN as Marxist, proclaiming that "Christian faith and Marxism could not coexist."[3] In 1981, conservative Nicaraguan bishops demanded that priests occupying public offices return to their priestly duties or be sanctioned. The conservative hierarchy also attacked comunidades eclesiales de base (CEBs) allied with the Sandinistas – identifying them as representatives of a parallel Church – a position Pope John Paul II supported in 1982 when he referred to the CEBs as a "people's Church" without "lawful pastors." This opposition by the conservative hierarchy to progressive clergy and the mass-based Sandinista movement culminated with Obando y Bravo's

---

[3] Manzar Foroohar, *The Catholic Church and Social Change in Nicaragua* (Albany: State University of New York Press, 1989), 202.

support for the US-supported Contra force's efforts to overthrow violently the Sandinista government.[4]

If Nicaragua signaled the role the Catholic Church might play in revolutionary change as advocate and opponent, El Salvador illustrated the consequences for the Catholic Church and laity of opposing a US-supported military force. One of the most defining events of this period occurred on March 24, 1980, when the military directed the assassination of Archbishop Oscar Romero, the most vocal and articulate advocate for social justice and opponent of violent repression in the country, while he said mass. In December of the same year, the Salvadoran military brutally raped and murdered three women religious and a female lay missionary. These murders simultaneously signaled that the historic sanctity of the Catholic Church no longer guaranteed the safety of bishops, priests, or nuns and far less that of laity and enhanced an image of the Catholic Church as a source of subversion. It could be argued that the final symbolic salvo of the Salvadoran armed forces' violent repression came in 1989 with the murder of six Jesuit priests, Elba Ramos, who cooked for them, and her daughter, Celina on the campus of the Jesuit Universidad Centroamericana "José Simeón Canas."

These acts of violence and the powerful imagery associated with them reveal the central role the Catholic Church played in revolutionary El Salvador even as they conceal the complexity of that role. It is noteworthy that the women religious and the lay missionary were from the United States, while five of the Jesuits were Spanish-born priests who in 1949 settled in the country, where they spent their adult lives. The murdered clergy and Archbishop Romero had been involved directly and indirectly with Christian Base Communities that grew and developed in the late 1960s, becoming increasingly radicalized by the repression they suffered from security forces and linked to the Farabundo Martí National Liberation Front (Frente Farabundo Martí para la Liberación Nacional – FMLN) in the 1970s.

In the context of devastating military violence against grassroots groups, which caused the deaths of 75,000 people, Archbishop Romero approved "violence of legitimate defense" and "legitimate insurrectional violence" when "the changes in the structures of oppressive violence are delayed, and when it is believed that the structures can be kept in being through repressive violence."[5] The day before his murder, Archbishop Romero appealed directly to soldiers,

---

4 Ibid., 211.
5 Anna L. Peterson, *Martyrdom and the Politics of Religion: Progressive Catholicism in El Salvador's Civil War* (Albany: State University of New York Press, 1997) p. 112.

police, and civil guardsmen. "Brothers, you come from our own people. You are killing your own brother peasants when any human order to kill must be subordinate to the law of God which says, 'Thou shalt not kill.'"[6] A confluence of grassroots community, foreign clergy, national clergy, and the archbishop with minimal support from conservative bishops in the context of a country mobilized by the Nicaraguan revolution, local revolutionary forces of the FMLN, and repression by the Salvadoran armed forces promoted a directly oppositional stance between the Catholic Church and military dictatorship.

Following the murder of Archbishop Romero, the Vatican provided cautious, equivocal support for El Salvador's progressive Catholic sector. Pope John Paul II named Oscar Romero's ally and confidante, Jesuit Arturo Rivera Damas, as apostolic administrator of San Salvador, but refused to confirm him as Archbishop until 1983. Although he had allied with CEBs and Liberation Theology before Romero's murder, Rivera Damas acted with caution and moderation. He lacked Vatican sanction granted to archbishops and support from conservative fellow bishops. Moreover, he confronted a reality in which the sacred aura that historically protected members of the Catholic hierarchy in El Salvador had been shattered. Rivera Damas became a key figure in peace negotiations.

Guatemala represents a case of extreme military-directed violence against a largely unarmed civilian population in response to the presence of revolutionary movements that, in some cases, became allied with grassroots Catholic movements. The United Nations Historical Clarification Commission declared the armed conflict to be genocide, with state-directed forces and paramilitaries responsible for 93 percent of the violence that killed 200,000 people, 83 percent of whom were indigenous. As was true in El Salvador, Guatemala's Catholic hierarchy remained divided in its response to the violence. By contrast, however, Guatemala's Archbishop, Mario Casariego, allied with the military. Guatemala's military blamed the Catholic Church and foreign clergy for "subversion" in the country.

Arguably the most dramatic and tragically ineffectual act by a member of the Guatemalan hierarchy came in 1980 (the year of the Church murders in El Salvador). Juan Gerardi, bishop of the K'iche' indigenous Santa Cruz del Quiché, closed his diocese in response to the massacre of hundreds of grassroots Catholics, the murder of thirteen priests and catechists, and threats to his own

---

6 Oscar Romero, "Archbishop Oscar Romero: The Last Sermon (March 1980) [The Church and Human Liberation]," in *The Central American Crisis Reader*, edited by Robert S. Leiken and Barry Rubin (New York: Summit Books, 1987), 377–380, at 380.

life. Gerardi spoke directly to Pope John Paul II about the situation of his diocese. The pope responded with a letter of support for the Guatemalan Bishops' Conference denouncing the violence. In 1984, Gerardi returned to Guatemala and with support from Archbishop Próspero Penados del Barrio helped create and coordinate the Archbishop's Human Rights Office, where he participated in peace talks and initiated the Catholic Church's truth commission investigation, the Recovery of Historical Memory Project (Recuperación de la Memoria Histórica – REMHI). It could be argued that the ultimate symbolic salvo of the conflict between segments of the Catholic Church and the Guatemalan military came in 1998, when the security forces effected the murder of Juan Gerardi just two days after the publication of REMHI's *Guatemala: Nunca Más*.

In each of these cases, the military responded to Catholic grassroots organizing with violent repression of communities and clergy, forcing local hierarchies to respond directly and by appealing to the Vatican for support. The Vatican acted pragmatically, seeking to protect Church power when clergy were attacked directly by providing occasional support to local hierarchies, while condemning clergy and theologians affiliated with Liberation Theology. Members of local hierarchies in countries where clergy and grassroots Catholics suffered direct military violence sometimes took vocal stances by condemning military violation of human rights. Other members of the hierarchy and clergy maintained a conservative stance either passively accepting the status quo or, as in the case of Obando y Bravo, promoting counterrevolution.

The Catholic Church Allied with Military Dictatorship: Argentina

Frequently described as "silent" about military violations of human rights, the Catholic Church might better be characterized as actively allied with the military in Argentina. Following a 1976 coup, Argentina's military was responsible for the murder and disappearance of some 15,000 to 30,000 people. Emilio F. Mignone, president and founder of the Center for Legal and Social Studies (Centro de Estudios Legales y Sociales – CELS) and author of *Witness to the Truth*, recounts that only four bishops out of some eighty prelates took an open stance against military violations of human rights. One of the four, Bishop Enrique Angelelli of La Rioja, was murdered in a car crash made to appear accidental. Angelelli was among nineteen ordained men Argentine security forces physically eliminated.

The Catholic hierarchy aided the military by offering ideological support, providing military vicars, mediating with victims' families, and actively participating in torture. Members of the Church hierarchy met with high military officials prior to the 1976 coup offering support for their actions. Clergy also ministered to military officials, soldiers, and their families offering mass and sacraments including confession and absolution. Individual clergy, including Christian von Wernich, former chaplain of the police department convicted in 2007, participated in torture sessions and offered confession to political prisoners. Parents and relatives of the disappeared who appealed to Archbishop Adolfo Servando Tortolo and Monsignor Emilio Teodoro Grasselli for assistance received virtually no support. These Catholic authorities maintained detailed records of reported disappearances and assured families of assistance, but rarely delivered, thereby mitigating direct confrontation and perhaps acting as a source of information to the military.

In *El Silencio*, Argentine journalist Horacio Verbitsky detailed Church agency in shielding the military from investigation into human rights violations. The book recounted the Church's role in hiding political prisoners during a 1979 Inter-American Commission on Human Rights visit to Argentina. Prior to the visit, the navy transferred sixty prisoners held in the naval Escuela de Mecánica de la Armada (ESMA), a prison and torture center, to Argentine Cardinal Aramburu's villa on the outskirts of Buenos Aires. As a result, the Commission failed to locate political prisoners. Verbitsky also asserted that in 1976 Bishop Jorge Bergoglio (later to become Pope Francis I), provincial superior for the Argentine Jesuits, called on Fathers Orlando Yorio and Francisco Jalics to cease their ministry in an impoverished urban community. When they refused, he withdrew Jesuit support for the priests. Verbitsky alleged that Bergoglio notified the military that the priests no longer enjoyed Jesuit protection. As a result, the military kidnapped and tortured Yorio and Jalics for six months. Bergoglio, Vatican spokesman Jesuit Father Federico Lombardi, and Argentine human rights activist Adolfo Perez Esquivel have denied strongly this allegation.

Although details differ, it is clear that the Argentine Catholic hierarchy supported the military dictatorship and directly and indirectly facilitated human rights violations. The incongruity with the reaction of the Catholic Church to dictatorship in other countries of Central and South America at this time may be attributed to structural differences in Argentina. The Argentine Catholic Church embraced a position of dependence on the state and military. Laws enacted from the nineteenth century through the years of military dictatorship allowed the Argentine government to maintain the *patronato real*; guaranteed Catholicism as the official state religion; established military vicariates with status equal to dioceses; and provided for state-funded salaries and pensions for bishops, clergy, and seminarians. Moreover, whereas in other Central and South American countries the presence of foreign clergy and resources helped to mitigate Catholic Church dependence on states and facilitated the development of popular networks and Christian Base Communities, Argentina received a strikingly small number of foreign clergy during the period of mission expansion from the 1950s through the 1970s. In 1968, only eighty-one United States clergy were active in Argentina. By contrast, Brazil had 699, Chile 322, and Peru 693.

Conclusion

The conditions that made the Catholic Church an important voice during the era of dictatorship and revolution diminished or disappeared following the transition to democracy in the region. Beginning in the 1960s and accelerating in the 1980s, Protestant churches grew rapidly in Latin America, attracting thousands of converts and eliminating Catholicism's status as the dominant religion. The number of Catholic clergy declined precipitously in the post-Vatican II era as hundreds of priests and religious became laicized and few people entered seminaries and convents. The number of US and European clergy, who formed a core of missionaries to Latin America in the 1960s and 1970s, diminished dramatically. International Catholic and ecumenical aid that poured into Latin America during the era of dictatorship shifted to other regions with greater immediate needs. Finally, the Vatican took an increasingly hardline stance against Liberation Theology and progressive Catholics, naming conservatives to the hierarchy, silencing clergy and theologians, and withdrawing support for grassroots groups.

Bibliography and Suggested Readings

Berryman, Phillip, *The Religious Roots of Rebellion: Christians in Central American Revolutions*. Maryknoll: Orbis Books, 1984.

Bidegain, Ana María. "From Catholic Action to Liberation Theology: The Historical Process of the Laity in Latin America in the Twentieth Century." Helen Kellogg Institute for International Studies, Working Paper #48, 1985.

Blancarte, Roberto. *Historia de la Iglesia católica en México*. Mexico City: Fondo Cultura Económica, 1992.

Brading, David A. *First America: Spanish Monarchy, Creole Patriots and the Liberal State, 1492–1866*. Cambridge: Cambridge University Press, 1993.

Brett, Edward T. "Archbishop Arturo Rivera Damas and the Struggle for Social Justice in El Salvador." *The Catholic Historical Review*, 94, no. 4 (October: 2008): 717–739.

Campbell, Leon G. "Church and State in Colonial Peru: The Bishop of Cuzco and the Túpac Amaru Rebellion of 1780." *Journal of Church and State*, 22, no. 2 (1980): 251–270.

Chesnut, Andrew, "A Preferential Option for the Spirit: The Catholic Charismatic Renewal in Latin America's New Religious Economy." *Latin American Politics and Society*, 45, no. 1 (Spring, 2003): 55–85.

Cleary, Edward L. *The Struggle for Human Rights in Latin America*. Westport, CT: Praeger, 1997.

Edwards, Lisa M. *Roman Virtues: The Education of Latin American Clergy in Rome, 1858–1962*. New York: Peter Lang, 2011.

Fitzpatrick-Behrens, Susan. *The Maryknoll Catholic Mission in Peru: Transnational Faith and Transformation, 1943–1989*. Notre Dame, IN: University of Notre Dame Press, 2012.

Foroohar, Manzar. *The Catholic Church and Social Change in Nicaragua*. Albany: State University of New York Press, 1989.

Gill, Anthony. *Rendering unto Caesar: The Catholic Church and the State in Latin America*. Chicago and London: University of Chicago Press, 1998.

Goldman, Francisco. *The Art of Political Murder: Who Killed the Bishop?* New York: Grove Press, 2007.

Holleran, Mary P. *Church and State in Guatemala*. New York: Columbia University Press, 1949.

Klaiber, Jeffrey. *The Church, Dictatorships, and Democracy in Latin America*. Maryknoll, NY: Orbis Books, 1998.

Kovic, Christine, *Mayan Voices for Human Rights: Displaced Catholics in Highland Chiapas*. Austin: University of Texas Press, 2005.

LeGrand, Catherine. "Canadian Catholic Priests and the Trujillo Dictatorship in the Dominican Republic, 1930–1961 ... and After." Paper presented to the Canadian Council of Area Studies Learned Societies (CCASLS), Montreal, April 27–May 1, 2005.

Levine, Daniel H. "From Church and State to Religion and Politics and Back Again." *World Affairs*, 150, no. 2 (Fall 1987): 93–108.

Lowden, Pamela. *Moral Opposition to Authoritarian Rule in Chile, 1973–1990*. Oxford: St. Anthony Press, 1996.

Lynch, John. *New Worlds: A Religious History of Latin America*. New Haven and London: Yale University Press, 2012.

Mahon, Leo with Nancy Davis, *Fire Under My Feet: A Memoir of God's Power in Panama*. Maryknoll, NY: Orbis Books, 2007.

Manz, Beatriz. *Paradise in Ashes: A Guatemalan Journey of Courage, Terror, and Hope*. Berkeley and Los Angeles: University of California Press, 2004.

Mecham, J. Lloyd, *Church and State in Latin America: A History of Politico-Ecclesiastical Relations*. Chapel Hill: The University of North Carolina Press, 1934, 1966.

Mignone, Emilio F. *Witness to the Truth: The Complicity of the Church and Dictatorship in Argentina, 1976–1983*. Trans. Phillip Berryman. Maryknoll, NY: Orbis Books, 1988.

Montgomery, Tommie Sue. *Revolution in El Salvador: From Civil Strife to Civil Peace*. Boulder: Westview Press, 1995.

Otera, Santiago, and Judith Escribano. "The Cook, the Dog, the Priest, and His Lover: Who Killed Bishop Gerardi and Why?" In Michael A. Hayes and David Tombs (eds.), *Truth and Memory: The Church and Human Rights in El Salvador and Guatemala*, 59–81. Gloucester: Gracewing, 2001.

Peterson, Anna L. *Martyrdom and the Politics of Religion: Progressive Catholicism in El Salvador's Civil War*. Albany: State University of New York Press, 1997.

Serbin, Kenneth P. *Secret Dialogues: Church-State Relations, Torture, and Social Justice in Authoritarian Brazil.* Pittsburgh: University of Pittsburgh Press, 2000.

Smith, Brian H. "Chile: Deepening the Allegiance of Working-Class Sectors to the Church in the 1970s." In Daniel H. Levine (ed.), *Religion and Political Conflict in Latin America,* 156–186. Chapel Hill: University of North Carolina Press, 1986.

  The Church and Politics in Chile: Challenges to Modern Catholicism. Princeton, NJ: Princeton University Press, 1982.

Sullivan-González, Douglas. *Piety, Power, and Politics: Religion and Nation Formation in Guatemala, 1821–1871.* Pittsburgh: University of Pittsburgh Press, 1998.

Szeminski, Jan. "'Why Kill the Spaniard?' New Perspectives on Andean Insurrectionary Ideology in the 18th Century." In Steve Stern (ed.), *Resistance, Rebellion and Consciousness in the Andean Peasant World 18th to 20th Centuries,* 166–192. Madison: University of Wisconsin Press, 1987.

Verbitsky, Horacio. *El Silencio: De Paulo VI a Bergoglio. Las relaciones secretas de la Iglesia con la ESMA.* Sudamericana: Buenos Aires, 2005.

Whitfield, Teresa. *Paying the Price: Ignacio Ellacuría and the Murdered Jesuits of El Salvador.* Philadelphia: Temple University Press, 2012.

Winn, Peter, ed. *Victims of the Chilean Miracle: Workers and Neoliberalism in the Pinochet Era, 1973–2002.* Durham and London: Duke University Press, 2004.

Wright-Rios, Edward. *Revolutions in Mexican Catholicism: Reform and Revelation in Oaxaca, 1887–1934.* Durham and London: Duke University Press, 2009.

27

Latin American Pentecostalism as a New Form of Popular Religion

ANDRÉ CORTEN

TRANSLATED BY ASHELY M. VOEKS

Over the past thirty years, daily religious life in Latin America has undergone a dramatic transformation. Once exceptional expressions and uses of religion have become commonplace among large segments of the population who practice Pentecostalism. In the street, it is normal to see an individual walking with a Bible in hand, proudly defending his or her personal religious beliefs. In the home, many working-class women have used spirituality to reassert control over their familial life. On television, pastors exorcise demons. In poorer neighborhoods, many people tie their experiences in exuberant services involving divine healing practices to deliverance from poverty itself. This transformation is what led urban specialist Mike Davis to comment, "Pentecostalism is the largest self-organized movement of urban poor in the world."[1] And this transformation is especially noteworthy for its bottom-up rather than top-down trajectory.

Pentecostalism at the Heart of a Catholic Subcontinent

The miracle has long been part of the Latin American world. However, the miracle that many Latin Americans believe in no longer pertains to the magical realism envisioned by the famous Latin American literary movement associated with Alejo Carpentier and Gabriel García Márquez. Instead, the miracles are found in Pentecostalism. Today, what sets popular Pentecostalism apart from traditional beliefs is not only the presence of spirits or ghosts, but also that at the same time both become a part of a reality attributed to and in alliance with Satan. Along these same lines, then, Satan has control over the

---

[1] Raul Zibechi, "Pentecostalism in South America's Social Movements," *Upside Down World*, October 15, 2008, http://upsidedownworld.org/main/international-archives-60/1529-pentecostalism-and-south-americas-social-movements (Accessed November 2, 2015).

wrath of sickness, disease, and hardships that families must endure and the oppressiveness caused by failure or dismissal from work. Deliverance becomes a necessity. To achieve it, an individual must convert himself or "open his heart to Jesus" through the miracles of Pentecostalism.

Latin America is not the only region where, in the 1980s, Pentecostalism took hold as the new form of popular religion, though the phenomenon did assume a sense of originality there, as Latin America was fundamentally Catholic because of its colonial history. When small churches began to flourish and spread to urban neighborhoods and rural villages, the Catholic Church generally attributed this growth to the intrusion of American Protestant sects. Most notably, Catholics pointed to documents from the US government portraying the expansion of evangelical churches as a means of resisting the influence of Liberation Theology, which they considered to be crypto-communist.

At first, the militant proselytism and the often scrupulous viewpoints advocated by these churches (notably in regard to alcohol consumption) shocked the residents of working-class neighborhoods just as much as they did intellectuals, who interpreted these religious practices as unusual responses to Latin American customs or culture. It was not until after the 1990s, however, that ordinary people (outside of Pentecostals themselves) began to view the phenomenon from a lens outside of the Catholic Church. However, the Church must deal not only with the wave of Pentecostal "cults" that emerged in the late-twentieth century but also with the spirit-filled denominations that were established more than a century ago in Latin America (and likewise in Africa). This is the case, for example, with Assembléia de Deus, which was founded in Brazil in 1911 – although the Assemblies of God would not be introduced in the United States until 1914.

A Common Speech

One of the first features that distinguished this new twentieth-century form of Protestantism – even from its purported origins at the 1906 Azusa Revival in Los Angeles, California – was speaking in tongues (or glossolalia). At the same time, speaking in tongues became a trait that would force all Christian churches – both Protestant and Catholic – to acknowledge, often against their will, the notion of a "gift" from the Holy Spirit. When considering the 1960s, then, we will talk about "Catholic Pentecostalism," better known today as the Charismatic Renewal, which was affected by this movement.

As the characteristic trait of Pentecostalism, speaking in tongues derives from the experience of the apostles on the day of Pentecost as described in

Acts 2:4, "All of them were filled with the Holy Spirit and began to speak in other languages, as the Spirit gave them ability." Thereafter, speaking in tongues faded as a common Church practice except in certain major heretical movements, such as Donatism in the third century, which adopted the practice as a distinguishing feature of direct contact with God. This was in spite of the fact that Paul, in his First Letter to the Corinthians, established validity of glossolalia, writing, "For those who speak in a tongue do not speak to other people but to God; for nobody understands them, since they are speaking the mysteries in the Spirit."

Outside of these theological considerations, speaking in tongues is of primary importance when looking to understand the popular nature of Pentecostalism's spread in Latin America. Here it is a question of disparate spheres of knowledge, where people with a low level of formal education generally find themselves much more at ease with the practice than their better-educated counterparts, who are more likely to focus their devotion on *logos*, usually the written word. Individuals who undergo "baptism in the Spririt" will carry on in languages that seem incoherent to others, as they undergo a somatic, or bodily, experience of the divine that lies outside of language and words.

Above all, speaking in tongues is a characteristic feature of the first wave of Pentecostal expansion. Occasionally, this practice fades from the foreground in favor of other equally widespread practices, such as divine healing or exorcism of demons. Be that as it may, speaking in tongues remains a very common practice within syncretic cults, or even in Churches that address a culture where poverty is rampant. For example, in Haiti, a Pentecostal offshoot that directly interacts with Vodou practices has developed in the slums and semi-urban areas. The Celestial Church of Christ, as it is called, can also be found in certain areas of Montreal and New York.

Pastors, assistant pastors, and even followers break out in unintelligible speech, mixing Spanish, English, Creole, and French – as much patois, perhaps, as glossolalia. Occasionally, certain Church members, or those who possess the gift of interpretation, will provide a much more comprehensible translation of what was originally spoken in tongues. They typically do so in a grand or exalted manner. To provide another example, there are also international churches that teach glossolalia, such as the Pentecostal Deus é amor, which, according to Paul Freston, recruits from the poorest social classes. Founded by Brazilian David Miranda in 1962, this church consists of nearly 11,000 temples across 136 countries and invites its members to practice speaking in tongues.

Aside from these particular instances, as well as those involving small churches in which the pastor will speak in tongues as a sort of solo performance, glossolalia is also practiced during vigils at large church congregations under an alternate form called powerful prayer, a raucous and almost fanatic prayer in which each attendee repeats a portion of the improvised sequence. Although this trance-like practice is no longer the distinctive feature of Pentecostal churches, as was the case from about 1920 to 1940, it still has a profound effect on Pentecostal culture.

Divine Healing or a Popular Means of Healthcare

Over time, the idea of divine healing has also developed within Pentecostalism, expanding our conception of this new form of popular religion. Pentecostal healing aims to address two tensions exacerbated by underdevelopment: the need for physical healing and the struggle against evil forces. These two tensions have affected late-twentieth-century Pentecostal expansion, which can be divided into two periods: 1950 to 1980 and 1980 to the present day.

Since 1950, life expectancy worldwide has risen by about twenty years, and as a result, the gap between an individual's projected lifespan in developed countries and those in Latin America has diminished. Today, the average life expectancy in Latin America is seventy years, whereas in developed countries, this number has reached eighty. In South America, even though inhabitants live to be much older than in previous decades, many continue to live poorly. Malnutrition affects nearly half of the population, and consequently serves as an indicator of a general shortcoming in terms of overall healthcare. Moreover, owing to inadequate measures taken at both the medical and pharmaceutical levels, many people have little hope of this shortcoming being corrected. In their everyday lives, many of those from the poor and working class came to terms with sickness and misfortune by taking misery out of its biomedical context and making it a part of common speech.

Divine healing is a direct response to these social inequities. Through their expressions, individuals are able to convey social suffering. Via a belief in the power of faith to heal, Pentecostals manage to live with misfortune and view their plight from a standpoint not of victim, but of having overcome hardship. Thus, Pentecostalism's circle of influence effectively inverts misfortune from social suffering to empowerment.

This is a kind of political expression, although it is not a protest or a call for reform. The notion of "making," that is, the idea of implementing change through action, is not what is at stake. Rather than looking to "make," healing is concerned with self-reform. To provide a more rational explanation, an individual is healed because of a shift in attitude toward personal miseries, choosing to see them as relative and thus giving life a new meaning. In this way, Pentecostals move away from action, or "making," without proposing a material alternative. In this instance, however, there is a divide that we may very well qualify as a political expression of misery, but even if there are political aspects to the expression of suffering, in no way does it concern institutional politics.

Divine healing does not replace, nor does it supplement, an organized system of healthcare. Although many Pentecostals do find relief from their physical maladies through faith healing, Pentecostal healing does not assume a measure of significance in national health systems, contrary to the Catholic Church's traditional practices. Pentecostal healing is not systemic, but rather, it is presented in terms of what it does for individual believers. It provides them with a new stance vis-à-vis all that comprises the misfortune and suffering felt by the poor and working classes.

A Radiophonic Culture

From 1950 to 1980, Pentecostal churches – in particular the International Church of the Foursquare Gospel, founded in the United States in 1922 by Aimee Simple McPherson – spread their message about healing throughout Latin America and the United States by telling and repeating miraculous stories through radio programming. In effect, since the 1950s, Pentecostalism has been an avant-garde movement in the world of media, combining the growth of radio (and soon television) as new technologies of evangelization. With radio broadcasting, Pentecostalism broke away from the written word, but such a break did not exclude the practice of reading scripture directly, a cornerstone of Protestant religious authority (*sola scriptura*). Rather, the physical form of the Bible became even more fundamentally important and even treated as a sort of fetish object.

Through radio broadcasts, preachers would often reference a particular passage or verse, which was learned by heart and could be recited from memory. They would then offer stories of healing, underscored by specific Bible passages that took on new valences of meaning and significance. Often, the audience also received these messages without mediation by local clergy, and so the media broke not only from the written word but also from the pastor's authority – or at least his traditional authority in the context of the local church.

The rise and expansive use of radio in certain Pentecostal churches corresponded to a major social transformation in Latin America as a whole, the demographic inversion from rural to urban living. Over the course of thirty years from 1950 to 1980, the majority of the region underwent urbanization. In 1950, 30 percent of the population resided in cities with more than 20,000 inhabitants, while in 1980, this same figure exceeded 50 percent.

Likewise, this shift toward urbanization characterized the first body of literature focusing on Pentecostalism and its growth as scholars disputed whether Pentecostalism was a response to modernization or part of modernization. According to Christian Lalive d'Epinay, a pioneer in research on Pentecostalism in Latin America, during the anomic phase of a transitional period of modernization, Pentecostalism provided an idealized reconstruction of traditional society. For Lalive, in seeking a substitute community, a Pentecostal remained more oriented toward his or her traditional past than toward the development of modernity, seeking out churches in the new urban migrant slums to "reproduce the authoritarianism of the hacienda." With this orientation toward the past, the pastor replaced the paternalist figure of the *hacendero*.

Contrarily, according to Emilio Willems, Pentecostalism itself was a factor affecting adaptation to an urban environment. The break from the value system and religious practices of a popular Catholicism, as well as from its authority over traditional local power structures, he suggested, implies an adherence to this new religious movement. Willems posited that Pentecostalism was a product of modernization rather than a response to it.

Nationalization as Part of Transnationalization

Various forms of Pentecostalism that are of foreign origin – particularly in Central America and the Caribbean – were "nationalized" in the twentieth century, as missionary-founded churches transferred to local pastorates and financing, and new churches sprang up without any missionary sponsorship whatsoever. Such was the case with churches such as Chile para Cristo, or Brasil para Cristo, whose name evokes the nationalist spirit of its founders. When these changes took place, places of worship changed as well. New, national Pentecostal groups often left traditional church buildings to renovate secular and urban constructions to suit their needs, renting spaces such as cinemas, gymnasiums, or stadiums in which to conduct their services. In other cases, a denomination is transnational, but local pastors at the national level hold power and authority. Some of Latin America's largest and most evangelically aggressive Pentecostal churches are entirely "homegrown," having been conceived of and founded by Latin American pastors in the 1960s or the 1970s. The Brazilian mega-church, the Igreja Universal do Reino de Deus (IURD), founded in the mid-1970s, today is one of the largest and richest denominations in the world, with congregations spread throughout Latin America, Africa, Europe, and North America.

Like the IURD, several large Latin American denominations have committed to a process of internationalization, a "reverse missionary movement" from South to North. Some of these include Mexico's Luz del Mundo, the Brazilian Deus e Amor, and the Puerto Rican Iglesia de Dios Pentecostal. This process of internationalization follows from migratory movements that are partly intraregional, but also oriented toward the United States. The expansion of internationalized Latin American churches follows growth lines of immigration from the region. From the 1970s on, these movements have gained considerable momentum. Migration within and between Latin American countries doubled from 1970 to 1980, whereas the number of Latin American immigrants established in the United States by 2006 reveals a remarkable curve, reaching an estimated 43 million (with 28 million and 8 million of Mexican and Caribbean origin, respectively). To a large extent, such churches cater mainly to Latin American immigrants living in the United States, rather than to English-speaking Anglo or African Americans. For undocumented immigrants in particular, such churches are seen to provide safe havens and venues for self-help and improvement that are available to all, regardless of legal status.

Much of the movement toward transnational Pentecostalism was not intentional but rather began with rural pastors crossing borders because of motives that were as much personal as pastoral. These pastors accompanied their immigrant compatriots who ended up in Mexico (as refugees from the wars in Central America), Venezuela (fleeing Columbia), and the United States (coming from Haiti or the Dominican Republic where some authoritarian regimes employ severe forms of punishment). In these movements, they developed networks of hospitality and personal acquaintance that transcended national boundaries. This movement created a transnational vision that was inspired not only by religion but also by the struggle for economic and social survival in which their followers are so deeply entrenched.

In the Global North – Europe and the United States – connections have also been established between pastors and followers of Latin American and African churches. Among the latter, certain groups are also internationalized, as is the case with the Ghanaian Church of Pentecost, or the Nigerian super-church, the Redeemmed Christian Church of God. Whereas these churches all becomes nodes in what Karla Poewe has called a "global charismatic network," they also remain deeply embedded in parochial religious worldviews and habitus.[2] For example, in response to expenditures surrounding fruitless attempts at calming Vodou or Candomblé spirits perceived as evil, pastors suggest a conversion to Jesus. For many, when faced with "evil curses" and "evil spirits," they believe they are in battle against something real, and that these forces of evil are in fact the manifestation of Satan that can be countered only by the direct intervention of the Holy Spirit. This Spiritual Warfare provides a venue for the complex interaction of culture anxieties and Pentecostal remediation.

There are two principal elements that characterize early twenty-first century neopentecostalism: the dramatized struggle of churches against the evil forces of Satan and the use of television. As far as both of these characteristics are concerned, neopententecostalism embodies a form of popular religion. With its own terms for identifying demonic possession, neopententecostalism addresses many aspects of hardship in daily life. The IURD has established a list of the most common symptoms of these demonic possessions including nervousness, constant migraines, insomnia, dismay, fainting, suicidal thoughts, hallucinations, vice, and depression. According to anthropologist Rondaldo de Almeida, "It (the IURD) identifies the origin of demons in other practices, specifically those of Afro-Brazilian religions."[3]

In the IURD, dramatization of the struggle against evil is particularly prominent in working-class congregations, and the drama itself creates its own informal lexical register of expressions. This register draws, in part, on Afro-Brazilian religions' concept of trance, but the trance is reworked according to Christian symbolism, especially the laying on of hands. The various intervention strategies of pastors, who may challenge a member directly by asking, "What is your name?" and expecting a response from a demon, are devised so that a spirit may manifest itself and eventually be chased away. Such instances could be likened to a kind of relentless verbal war, with the address directed at Satan serving as justification for any and all harsh or abusive language. This theatricality creates a scene that is informal in nature and extremely vibrant in terms of language. In addition to language, this display of violence also manifests through the body. Bodies "tremble, cry, scream,

---

2 Karla Poewe, ed., *Charismatic Christianity as a Global Culture* (Columbia: University of South Carolina Press, 1994).

3 Ari Pedro Oro, André Corten, André, and Jean-Pierre Dozon, eds., *Igreja Universal do Reino de Deus. Os novos conquistadores da fé* (São Paulo: Paulinas, 2003), 323.

twist and collapse to the floor, until they are chased away by the injunctions and firm imposition of the pastor's hands, who works 'in the name of Jesus.'"[4]

When viewed from the room where it is taking place, one could even make the connection between this scene and images of physical violence prevalent in Latin America. Nevertheless, dramatization is quite different than what one might witness during an exorcism session in Recife, Caracas, Buenos Aires, Abidjan, Maputo, or even in London or New York. Even though the Universal Church, which comprises 9,600 pastors and 22,000 direct-hire posts in 4,700 temples across 172 countries, is very centralized and almost always directed by Brazilian pastors or bishops, it still manages to adapt to each country's beliefs. Semán notes the following for Argentina in particular:

> It is in effect impossible to develop anti-Afro-Brazilian demonology in this new territory with the same force, and in a manner that would require the IURD to give Argentinians, at the very least, an overview of these demons. Nevertheless, there are practices common to some parishes within the Argentinian public that stem from cosmological principles and that break from modern culture's biomedical and dualist visions. While these concepts are of little concern among the erudite, they are relevant to the working class, and in a way that allows room for the IURD to practice their antagonistic sacred rites. So, if a struggle against the *exus* (beloved demons in Afro-Brazilian rituals) is within the realm of possibility, the IURD will nevertheless, in Argentina, make a formidable enemy out of *curanderos* (healers), the *mal de ojo* (evil eye), *envidia* (longing/desire) and the *gaulichos* (devils unleashed by nearby enemies, from the surrounding area or the family).[5]

If the Universal Church and Deus é Amor are compatible with societies far removed from the network of Brazilian intermediaries and reclaim elements of North American demonology, these churches pride themselves on the strong foundation they have established in Africa. Why? What do these Churches have to offer in a place where sorcery is the preeminent matrix for shaping evil? By showing these convulsing bodies and giving a voice to spirits, who are merely secondary to Satan, pastors confer a quasi-ontological status on occult forces, which are often associated with mental illness in urban or working-class areas; and yet they continue to threaten the psychological stability of people with precarious status. These churches instill confidence in a proletarian multitude by making them believe that their agony is not caused

---

4 André Mary, "Le pentecôtisme brésilien en terre africaine. L'Universel abstrait du Royaume de Dieu," *Cahiers d'Études Africaines*, 167 (2002–2003), 470.
5 Ari Pedro Oro, André Corten, and Jean-Pierre Dozon (eds.), *Igreja Universal do Reino de Deus: Os novos conquistadores da fé* (São Paulo: Paulinas, 2003), 73–74.

by mental illness, but rather by an attack from a force that is perfectly real. When faced with such might, only the Holy Spirit or Jesus is capable of taking the upper hand, and it is through the Church that this opposing force may be summoned.

Success stories stemming from African churches, as recounted by Pentecostal journals and television broadcasts, improve the chances of instilling a fear of demons in the Latin American mentality. In a way, these stories give a renewed vitality to exorcism and liberation sessions in Brazilian, Venezuelan, and Colombian churches. Furthermore, aside from Friday worship devoted to deliverance and liberation in the IURD, on Tuesdays several churches have introduced, whether or not it is in conjunction with the healing service, the ritual of *descarrego* (release). This expression, which comes from Spiritism, refers to the moment of relief when the exorcised no longer feels the weight of evils oppressing him or her. Here, a call for deliverance from doubt and malevolent forces meets the common people's responsiveness and inclination toward the intervention of hidden forces. In a globalized world, where the working class is systematically disadvantaged in the so-called transparent market struggles, this inclination does nothing but grow. Demons are becoming increasingly urbanized and correspond to the evils of global cities, where we are also starting to see both urban legends and every form of neurosis more or less treated by psychotherapy.

A New Discourse on Poverty

Pentecostal transnationalism also opened up a new mode of interpretation in the late twentieth century. Coming from largely impoverished countries, many Pentecostals became mindful of a different type of discourse circulating throughout Pentecostalism in the United States that attributed poverty to Satan and "the abundant life" – measured in material terms – to God's grace and goodness. The secret to liberation from poverty in this system was placing one's trust in Jesus and claiming God's blessing. Better known as "prosperity gospel," this teaching spread across the United States through prominent figures such as Kenneth Hagin, Kenneth Copeland, Oral Roberts, and T. L. Osborn, but it quickly spread worldwide. In South Korea, David Yonggi Cho founded and continues to conduct services at the Yoido Full Gospel Central Church, which has become a global model in terms of this doctrine's expansion. According to Cho, poverty, sickness, and hardship have their origins in sin or Satan. Inversely, to be rich and in good health is proof of divine blessing.

While the prosperity gospel was growing, another religious trend developed in Latin America that addressed the issue of poverty in an entirely different manner – Liberation Theology. This theology also dealt with the question of sin, but social rather than personal sin. Christians following a liberationist approach feel confronted by both social sin and structural sin as a result of oppression and injustices inflicted on the poor. Overcoming social sin means coming together and working to effectuate structural change in a way that promotes more participation and justice. The poor, then, are essential to the Gospel, and being evangelical within Liberation Theology means siding with the poor and their struggles.

In the 1980s, the rivalry between prosperity theology and Liberation Theology seemed to give the upper hand to Liberation Theology. Ecclesiastical Base Communities, the principal advocates and building blocks of Liberation Theology, reached thousands of people while Liberation Theology was systematically linked to popular progressive regimes like the Sandinistas in Nicaragua. Conversely, the concept of the prosperity gospel was treated in a pejorative fashion, with the media interpreting it as a distinctly consumerist model. However, in the 1990s so-called "neo-Pentecostal" churches such as the Universal Church of the Kingdom of God (Igreja Universal do Reino de Deus, or IURD) began to make names for themselves by monopolizing media to spread their version of the prosperity gospel, and the dynamics between these two movements shifted. By the end of the twentieth century, prosperity theology – though still derided by outsiders – claimed an outsized following in Latin America relative to Liberation Theology.

Televangelism

If certain churches seem very reluctant toward television and its reputation as a network perpetuating deprivation, other churches – and not only the so-called "neo-Pentecostal" – are resorting to increasingly sophisticated and modern means of communication. Even though the heavy reliance on television looks more and more to means of communication available at a national level, one particular model that continues to be influential is North American televangelism.

Traditionally speaking, televangelism disrupts the relationship between the sacred and profane according to two different models. The famous televangelist Billy Graham introduced the first such model in the post–World War II period, when new media and opportunities opened up expanding evangelization beyond tent revivals and church buildings. By preaching in stadiums or auditoriums, Graham created a new place of worship, with a potential congregation of millions, not hundreds. His model would serve many televangelists to follow, whether German, Korean, African, Puerto Rican, or Brazilian.

The television screen brings followers, and even curious onlookers come together for trans-denominational gatherings. During communion, amidst the familiar feeling of exhilaration typically associated with a sporting event or musical performance, individuals actively reshape how the place of worship is perceived, thus demonstrating a capacity to modify the significance given to a particular place or venue, even for people who are not physically present in that place. The sacred space becomes intimately linked to popular culture. Here, we see the transformation of a secular space – a stadium, or even a viewer's living room – into one suited for ecclesiastical gatherings.

A second quality associated with televangelism is that of a figure – a preacher or other religious celebrity – whose principal quality is his or her charisma, a key quality that sociologist Max Weber long ago associated with dynamic religious actors. Such charismatic figures are able to establish a powerful plausible link between the profane and the sacred. A leading figure is the US televangelist Pat Robertson, whose the television program *The 700 Club* and all-Christian television station, PTL, was the first to intentionally fuse secular content such as news and information within an evangelical Christian perspective, in the early 1970s. Because Robertson is also political and his charismatic rhetoric is sometimes incendiary – he had called for the assassination of Venezuelan president Hugo Chávez and blamed Haiti's catastrophic 2011 earthquake on a "pact with the devil" – his show is controversial but remains popular after more than forty years on the air. Robertson broadcasts from the same studio where he conducts his interviews, typically speaking in an informal and moderate tone. The layout of this studio is made to resemble a living room like that in any family's home. However, it is precisely in this homely environment where the sacred may emerge, through testimonies of miracles recounted by average people over airwaves and to the televangelist. This transition from the ordinary to the extraordinary is essential to the idea of the sacred being within the reach of ordinary people. Likewise, as the tele-spectator is situated in a setting that acts as a living room, his immediate environment is also one of daily life.

The golden era of televangelism in the United States, according to Jacques Gutwirth, spans from 1975 and 1987. Today, North American televangelism has lost its appeal, although we should not discount its numbers as negligible. The relative decline is often attributed to a transition from the terrestrial platform to cable television and other social media. Corruption and sex scandals that have swirled around several televangelists certainly played a role as well.

On the other hand, Robertson and other televangelists, namely Billy Graham, remain national figures: one a pre-presidential candidate and the other a spiritual advisor to presidents including Richard Nixon, Jimmy Carter, Bill Clinton, George W. Bush, and Barack Obama.

The golden era of televangelism in Latin America, however, did not even take off until the 1990s. This rise corresponded to a rather surprising growth in the number of television sets owned by individuals across every strata of society, including the poor, which is in sharp contrast with Africa and Asia. Thus, in Mexico, for example, from 1975 to 1995, the number of television sets per 100 people increased from three to fifteen. In large Latin American cities, the proportion would be about 20 percent (or nearly one television set per family), whereas in Africa and Asia, despite the increase in family size and a much slower urbanization rate, this same number does not exceed 5 percent. Televangelism has been especially important in Brazil, where in 1989 the Universal Church bought the commercial television network TV Record, which quickly became the third largest station in the country. Operating from dozens of different over-the-air broadcast centers spread across Brazil's vast territory, TV Record was able to reach the living rooms of homes with neither satellite nor cable television. TV Record, which airs religious programs nightly, also has a broadcast audience of Latin American immigrants in the United States and some countries in Africa. Within the Universal Church, the television itself has become its own ritual object. In this context, television reconfigures the sacred, but unlike the living room set of North American televangelists, TV Record and similar platforms across the region typically lead back to the premises of the temples. This is what distinguishes televangelism within the Universal Church from North American televangelists. It is in the material space of the Church, not through television, that followers not only offer money through their tithes but also where money takes on a supposed sanctity.

Conclusion

In the late-twentieth and early twenty-first centuries, Pentecostalism created a number of new, popular religious expressions in Latin America. French sociologist Pierre Bourdieu said that popular culture is often "a purely verbal and inconsequential (and therefore pseudo-revolutionary) inversion of the class racism which reduces working-class practices to barbarism or vulgarity."[6]

---

6 Pierre Bourdieu, *Méditations pascaliennes* (Paris: Seuil, 1997), 92–93.

Is this not how one deals with the "emotional insurgency" appearing in "grotesque gesticulations" that is Pentecostalism?[7] Add another mark of condescension. Pentecostalism with its "prosperity gospel" would be the supreme expression of the estrangement of neoliberalism.

Indeed, as highlighted by Gramsci, Pentecostalism may be seen as an expression of common sense with its dual consciousness: "one which is implicit in his activity and which in reality unites him with all his fellow workers in the practical transformation of the real world; and one, superficially explicit or verbal, which he has inherited from the past and uncritically absorbed."[8] The paradox of Pentecostalism is that it is oriented toward the future, and the conscience, which is contained in its action and appears as an adaption/resistance of the masses to the extreme threat posed by neoliberalism and verbal consciousness, is inherited from popular postmodern psychology gurus through the power of words and social capacity.

Bibliography and Suggested Readings

Anderson, Allan H., and Walter J. Hollenweger, eds. *Pentecostals after a Century: Global Perspectives on a Movement in Transition.* Sheffield, UK: Sheffield Academic Press, 1999.

Aubrée, Marion. "Religião e violência numa perspectiva transcultural e transnacional – As violências multiples do religioso." In Mabel Salgado Pereira and Lyndon de A Santos (eds.), *Religião e Violência em tempos de globalização*, 173–195.São Paulo: Paulinas, 2004.

Badie, Bertand, and Sandrine Tolotti, eds. *L'état du monde: annuaire économique, géopolitique mondiale.* Paris: La Découverte, 2008.

Bastian, Jean-Pierre. *Protestantismos y modernidad latino-americana: Historia de unas minorías religiosas activas en América Latina.* México: Fondo de Culra Económica, 1994.

Bastian, Jean-Pierre, François Guichard, and Christine Messiant, eds. *Des protestantismes en "lusophonie catholique," Lusotopie: Enjeux contemporains dans les espaces lusophones.* Paris: Karthala, 1998.

Beyer, Peter. *Religion and Globalisation.* London: SAGE, 1994.

Blancarte, Roberto. *Historia de la Iglesia Católica en México.* México: Fondo de Cultura Económica, 1990,

Boudewijnse, Barbara, André Droogers, and Frans Kamsteeg, Frans, eds. *More than Opium: An Anthropological Approach to Latin American and Caribbean Pentecostal Praxis.* Lanham, MD: Scarecrow Press, 1998.

Bourdieu, Pierre. *Méditations pascaliennes.* Paris: Seuil, 1997.

Brusco, Elizabeth. *The Reformation of Machismo: Evangelical Conversion and Gender in Colombia.* Austin: University of Texas Press, 1995.

---

7 David Martin, *Tongues of Fire: The Explosion of Protestantism in Latin America* (Oxford: Blackwell, 1990), 30.
8 Antonio Gramsci and André Tosel, *Textes Antonio Gramsci* (Paris: Éditions Sociales), 1983, 30.

Campos, Leonildo Silveira. *Teatro, Templo e Mercado: Organinização e Marketing de um Empreendimento Neopentecostal*. Petrópolis: Editora Vozes, 1997.

Chesnut Andrew R. *Born Again in Brazil: The Pentecostal Boom and the Pathogens of Poverty*. New Brunswick, NJ: Rutgers University Press, 1997.

Corten, André. *Alchimie politique du miracle. Discours de la guérison divine et langue politique en Amérique latine*. Montréal: Éditions Balzac, 1999.

Pentecostalism in Brazil: Emotion of the Poor and Theological Romanticism. Basingstoke, UK: Macmillan Press, 1999.

Corten, André, and Ruth Marshall-Fratani, eds. *Between Babel and Pentecost. Transnational Pentecostalism in Africa and Latin America*. Bloomington: Indiana University Press, 2001.

Cox, Harvey. *Fire From Heaven: The Rise of Pentecostal Spirituality and the Reshaping of Religion in the Twenty-first Century*. Reading: Addison-Wesley, 1994.

Davis, Mike. *Planet of Slums*. London: Verso, 2006.

De la Torre, Renée. *Los hijos de la luz: Discurso, identidad y poder en la Luz del Mundo*. México: ITESO, 2000.

Fancello, Sandra. *Les aventuriers du pentecôtisme ghanéen: Nation, conversion et délivrance en Afrique de l'Ouest*. Paris: Karthala, 2006.

Frank, André Gunder. *The Development of Underdevelopment*. New York: Monthly Review Press. 1966.

Freston, Paul. *Evangelicals and Politics in Asia, Africa, and Latin America*. New York: Cambridge University Press, 2001.

Protestantes e Política no Brasil: de Constituinte ao Impeachment. Campinas: UNICAMP, Tese de doutorado, 1993.

Garrard-Burnett, Virginia and David Stoll, eds. *Rethinking Protestantism in Latin America*. Philadelphia: Temple University, 1993.

Gramsci, Antonio, and André Tosel. *Textes Antonio Gramsci*. Paris: Éditions sociales, 1983.

Gurwirth, Jacques. *L'Église électronique. La saga des télévangélistes*. Paris: Bayard, 1998.

Lalive d'Epinay, Christian. *Haven of the Masses: A Study of the Pentecostal Movement in Chile*. London: Lutterworth Press, 1969.

Leca, Nathalie, "Pentecôtismes en Corée," *Archives des Sciences Sociales des Religions*, 105 (1999): 99–123.

Lehmann, David. *Struggle for the Spirit: Religious Transformation and Popular Culture in Brazil and Latin America*. Cambridge, UK: Polity Press, 1996.

Mariano, Ricardo. *Neo-pentecostais: Sociologia do Novo Pentecostalismo no Brasil*, São Paulo: Edições Loyola, 1999.

Martin, David. *Tongues of Fire: The Explosion of Protestantism in Latin America*. Oxford: Blackwell, 1990.

Mary, André. "Le pentecôtisme brésilien en terre africaine. L'Universel abstrait du Royaume de Dieu." *Cahiers d'Études Africaines*, 167 (2002): 463–478.

Morton, Kelsey T. *Tongue Speaking: An Experiment in Spiritual Experience*. Garden City, NY: Doubleday, 1964.

Oro, Ari Pedro, André Corten, and Jean-Pierre Dozon, eds. *Igreja Universal do Reino de Deus: Os novos conquistadores da fé*. São Paulo: Paulinas, 2003.

Poewe, Karla, ed. *Charismatic Christianity as a Global Culture*. Columbia: University of South Carolina Press, 1994.

Rolim, Francisco Cartaxo. "Pentecôtisme et Société au Brésil." *Social Compass*, 26, no. 2–3 (1979): 345–372.

Smith, Christian. *The Emergence of Liberation Theology: Radical Religion and the Social Movement Theory*. Chicago: University of Chicago Press, 1991.

Stoll, David. *Is Latin America Turning Protestant? The Politics of Evangelical Growth* Berkeley: University of California Press, 1990.

Vonarx, Nicolas. "Les Églises de l'Armée Céleste comme Églises de guérison en Haïti: Un développement qui repose sur une double légitimité." *Social Compass*, 54, no. 1 (2007): 113–127.

Willems, Emilio. *Followers of the New Faith: Culture Change and Rise of Protestantism in Brazil and Chile*, Nashville: Vanderbilt University Press, 1967.

28

History, Current Reality, and Prospects of Pentecostalism in Latin America

PAUL FRESTON

Academic interest in Latin American Pentecostalism grew markedly only from the 1990s, once its size and importance were impossible to ignore. This belated interest probably reflected Pentecostalism's presumed "backwardness" and "inauthenticity" vis-à-vis some of its religious rivals at the "popular" level, as well as a secularization theory based supposition that its shelf-life would be short. Since then, the study of Latin American Pentecostalism has become the main site for tracing the religious change that has swept the region, and a laboratory for studying the mass Protestantism of the "Global South" and the "southward shift" of Christianity.

In Latin America, Pentecostalism has outstripped "historical Protestantism" (as non-Pentecostal Protestants are known), far more so than in other regions of massive Protestant growth such as sub-Saharan Africa, South Korea, and the Chinese world. Brazil's heavily Pentecostalized Protestantism is now the second largest in the world (in numbers of practicing members), and Pentecostalism has changed significantly the way Protestantism as a whole is perceived by society. Latin America illustrates both of the main lines of global expansion of evangelical Christianity detected by David Martin: the attraction of voluntaristic popular Christianity that emphasizes the Spirit, "spreading in partial alignment with ... Anglo-American influence" and ethnic-minority evangelicalism, involving "the emergence of minority self-consciousness which leaps over the ... local majority and links itself to evangelicalism as an expression of transnational modernity."[1] While the latter is found mainly in Asia, a similar process of "leaping over" the local majority to express a transnational modernity may now be accelerating in heavily Amerindian regions of Latin America. However, work on the historical development of Latin American Pentecostalism has lagged behind. There has been little study of the

---

[1] David Martin, "Evangelical Expansion in Global Society." In D. Lewis (ed.) *Christianity Reborn* (Grand Rapids: Eerdmans 2004), 277.

evolution of churches and their relationship to society. We lack information on the large churches as dynamically evolving institutions.

It is true that historical research on Pentecostalism is not easy. Some groups have few written sources; others produce in-house accounts that are very distant from academic canons. In addition, Pentecostalism has a tense relationship with history. Named after the descent of the Holy Spirit at Pentecost, it sees itself as a return to origins. Domestic histories thus concentrate on the (epic) origins of the denomination, seen as a recovery of Pentecost; later events are reduced virtually to geographical expansion. There is little idea of development, as all is contained in the original event. And most (though not all) Pentecostals do not accept that their religious phenomena are rooted in actions analyzable by the historical and social sciences.

Pentecostalism arrived early in Latin America; "early," that is, in relation to its putative origin in the United States. That origin is itself the object of historiographical debates. Three main versions predominate: the "white" American origin around events in Kansas in 1900–1901; the "black" American origin centered on the Azusa Street revival in Los Angeles from 1906; and the "global" multiorigins account which nods politely toward Azusa but insists that "Pentecostalism did not arise in a single event, place or phenomenon, but in a plethora of different types of revivalist Christianity" in places as far apart as Wales, Korea, and India.[2] The Indian revival of 1905, which Allan Anderson describes as at least as "full-grown" a Pentecostal revival as Azusa, actually provided the first contact with Pentecostalism for the person who introduced it to Chile. But others point out that both the intra-American debate ("white" versus "black" origins) and the America-versus-global debate are often prisoners of contemporary identity politics.

In any case, as a movement of blacks, immigrants, and the poor in general, there were Mexicans and Mexican-Americans present at the meetings in Azusa Street. Key factors in the rapid international expansion were the many American missionaries in contact with events at home, and the many immigrants in the United States in contact with their homelands and with countrymen elsewhere. Chile, Mexico, and Brazil respectively are examples of these three routes. From being the "neglected continent" of Protestant missions, Latin America became the focus of a type of missionary effort that differed notably from its "historical" counterparts. When not introduced by returning Latin Americans, it was brought by a new breed of North American

---

2 Allan Anderson, *To the Ends of the Earth: Pentecostalism and the Transformation of World Christianity* (New York: Oxford University Press, 2013).

or European missionaries, fiercely independent, strongly supernaturalistic, and convinced that all the preparation they needed was their experience of the Holy Spirit. Mostly working class, they valued divine calling over education, and most would never have been accepted by historical mission boards. The result was that Pentecostalism was in its infancy when it reached Latin America, and this favored its autochthonous development. Without large resources or established denominations, and more interested in an urgent evangelistic thrust than in institutional creation, it did not copy the relations of foreign dependence that characterized the historical missions.

Nevertheless, the Pentecostal pioneers were not operating in a vacuum. There had been national forerunners of a more enthusiastic Protestantism in Brazil, such as José Manoel da Conceição, the ex-Catholic priest turned Presbyterian pastor, as well as Miguel Vieira Ferreira, who founded the Brazilian Evangelical Church in 1879, preaching direct communication with God unmediated by the Scriptures. But it was a church for the rich; Vieira was from a leading political family. At the time, popular Pentecostalism would scarcely have been possible.

The Brazilian tradition also included messianic movements, proto-Pentecostal in their autonomous popular clientele and, at times, charismas such as prophecy and glossolalia. The last major movements coincided with Pentecostalism's first timid steps. Later, continued economic growth, individual social mobility and bureaucratic and military centralization impeded large messianic movements. Pentecostalism may have represented a realignment of religiously expressed nonconformity within a framework that was nonviolent, institutionalized, and integrated into the productive process.

Historical Protestantism in Latin America, despite conversionist efforts from the mid-nineteenth century, remained distant from the masses and achieved modest success only in Brazil. Protestantism became numerically successful among the lower classes only with Pentecostalism. In 1907, the Methodist missionary Willis Hoover in Chile, informed of the novelty by friends in India and the United States, began to teach Pentecostal doctrine. After a revival in Valparaíso in 1909, his followers were expelled from the Methodist Church and founded a denomination that later became the Pentecostal Methodist Church, now Chile's largest Protestant grouping. The same year saw the first Pentecostal conversions in Argentina through Luigi Francescon, an Italian artisan living in Chicago and evangelist of the Italian diaspora. No church resulted immediately from his work in Argentina; however, in 1910 Francescon inaugurated the Christian Congregation among Italians in São Paulo. The early 1910s also saw beginnings in Central America (through independent

North American missionaries) and in Mexico (partly by returning emigrants). A start was made in Peru in 1919 by the American Assemblies of God and in Venezuela by an independent missionary, but the remaining South American republics were slow off the mark. The last country to witness the effective start of a Pentecostal church was Ecuador in 1956.

Everywhere, initial fortunes were modest. It was only in the 1950s that significant growth appeared in Chile and Brazil. But by the 1980s, Pentecostalism was attracting attention in most countries of the region.

Generally speaking, most Pentecostal churches (unlike historical ones) were founded either by Latin Americans who broke with an existing Protestant denomination, or by returning emigrants, or by independent foreign missionaries (often from the underside of American society, and often themselves European immigrants to the United States), and only rarely by a foreign Pentecostal denomination. In some countries, independent groups would subsequently seek North American links; in other countries, this was unknown, and groups founded from abroad tended quickly to achieve autonomy. The result is that Latin American Pentecostalism now consists of a huge number of denominations, a few of which originated abroad (such as the Assemblies of God, AG), while the majority are homegrown (such as Brazil for Christ and the Universal Church of the Kingdom of God, in Brazil; or the Methodist Pentecostal Church and the Evangelical Pentecostal Church, in Chile). In Brazil, of the six denominations that have had the most historical and contemporary importance, the Assemblies of God were founded by Swedes; the Christian Congregation was founded by an Italian; the Four-Square, by Americans; and the other three (Brazil for Christ, God Is Love, and the Universal Church of the Kingdom of God) were founded by Brazilians.

The social composition of the founders of Latin America's major Pentecostal groups includes proletarians such as the foundryman Daniel Berg (AG-Brazil), the construction worker Manoel de Mello (Brazil for Christ), and the coalminer Victor Mora (National Wesleyan Church – Chile); independent artisans such as Luigi Francescon (Christian Congregation – Brazil) and the barbers and shoemakers of the Apostolic Church – Mexico; and lower middle class white-collar such as Edir Macedo (Universal Church – Brazil) and many American and Scandinavian missionaries. Rare are the founders of elite or even upper middle class origin, such as Willis Hoover, a nonpracticing doctor.

Latin American Pentecostalism shows considerable diversity in denominational composition and processes of nationalization. Brazil's historical churches bred some movements for autonomy in the late nineteenth century, so the subsequent historical/Pentecostal divide does not correspond to a missionary/nationalist one. In Chile, however, the historicals (mainline Protestants) made little impact. The peasants were very dependent and the upper class was firmly allied to the Catholic Church, making Chilean society far less permeable to religious dissent. Thus, the Methodist schism of 1909 marked the break between missionaries and nationals, between a foreign mentality and local sensitivity to the extraordinary, between middle class cultural forms and the popular classes. Chilean Pentecostalism is thus accentuatedly national in origin, a fact of which its leaders are proud.

Neighbouring Peru is different in several respects. There, Pentecostalism has been less important within Protestantism, really taking off only in the 1970s. The Pentecostal field has been dominated by the Assemblies of God (AG), which resulted from American missionaries and whose history is punctuated by nationalist conflicts. The first AG missionaries (1919) occupied the region assigned to them by an interdenominational Committee of Cooperation, the northern Sierra, where linguistic difficulties and religious intolerance limited expansion. In 1937, the American headquarters sent a representative with "'the express intention of organizing and centralizing authority' along the lines of the AG-USA."[3] The first Board of Directors was exclusively foreign; Peruvians only effectively took over leadership after a nationalist military regime came to power in the country in 1968. Conflicts between missionaries and nationals were endemic, leading to numerous nationalist schisms – a contrast with the absence of such schisms in the Swedish-influenced Brazilian AG.

El Salvador differs once again. Its now very large Protestantism has a Pentecostal field traditionally divided between two large churches (AG and Church of God) and a plethora of neo-Pentecostal groups of American or Guatemalan origin. It was for long overwhelmingly rural, a possible factor in its far weaker political presence than in Guatemala. US missionaries were important in its urbanization. The AG's origins go back to an independent Canadian missionary in the 1910s; the American church took over in 1930. The Church of God began in 1940 by a similar process. This pattern, of groups started by independent missionaries or breakaway nationals later seeking affiliation to a US denomination, is typical of areas where historical Protestantism was weak.

Argentine Pentecostalism began with the Christian Assembly among Italian immigrants, whose roots go back to Francescon's visit in 1909 but whose ecclesiastical organization dates from 1916. However, for many

---

[3] Rubén Zavala, *Historia de las Asambleas de Dios del Perú* (Lima: Ediciones Dios es Amor, 1989), 82.

decades, Pentecostalism was more readily accepted by indigenous peoples or central or northern European immigrants. The greatest resistance was from descendants of Italian or Spanish immigrants, who did not want to risk foregoing identification with this new Catholic country. Compared to Chile, slow growth in Argentina had much to do with Protestantism's identification with immigrants; compared to Brazil, Italian immigrants to Argentina did not regard local Catholicism as weak and foreign and did not supply many converts. Only in the 1950s did Pentecostalism find an expression among the urban poor following the failure of Peronist populism, and reached new heights after redemocratization in the early 1980s had left the Catholic Church shaken by its association with militarism. Ecclesiastical history until then had been marked by the establishment of churches either by independent missionaries in the early days or by breakaway nationals from the 1950s, and subsequent links with US churches, subordinating freedom to security.

In Guatemala, elite charismatic churches have an unusually high profile, but historical Protestantism is weak. The first Protestant missionaries arrived from the United States invited and personally escorted by a liberal president. His anticlerical policies were enforced rigorously for decades. Protestant missions were showered with privileges, but growth was slow. Beginnings of work in indigenous languages after 1919 and the reformist antimissionary regime of Arbenz (1950–1954) laid the basis for the meteoric trajectory of autonomous Protestantism from the 1960s. In the process, lower class Pentecostal churches and middle and upper class charismatic churches became the overwhelming majority.

Protestant penetration of the Guatemalan elite originated in rejection of Vatican II reforms. The Charismatic Catholic alternative was blocked by the hierarchy. In addition, the 1976 earthquake had stimulated the arrival of independent charismatic groups from the United States, among them the Church of the Word (Verbo), which soon recruited future president General Efraín Ríos Montt. The model was copied by members of the elite, such as Harold Caballeros, a former lawyer from a prominent family who founded El Shaddai, the church of future president Jorge Serrano. These churches, often called "neo-Pentecostal," usually have strong charismatic leaders, often with contacts with US evangelicals, and emphasize prosperity teaching and "spiritual warfare."

Brazil's huge Pentecostalism comprises hundreds of small denominations but is dominated by a handful of large ones. These major churches result from three 'waves' of institutional creation. The first wave was in the 1910s, with the arrival of the Christian Congregation (1910) and the Assemblies of God

(1911), who virtually had the field to themselves for forty years. The second wave occurred in the 1950s and early 1960s; the relationship to society became more dynamic and three large groups began: the Church of the Four-Square Gospel (1951), Brazil for Christ (1955) and God Is Love (1962). All began in São Paulo. The third wave started in the late 1970s and gained strength in the 1980s. Its main representatives are the Universal Church of the Kingdom of God (1977) and the International Church of the Grace of God (1980). By the end of the century, the Universal Church had become immensely powerful and controversial, owning a major television network (TV Record) and electing a large caucus to congress. With its prosperity gospel and strong hierarchical leadership, it had become very wealthy and was building major cathedrals. These groups, which started life in Rio de Janeiro, once again updated Pentecostalism's relationship to society, increasing its theological, liturgical, ethical, and aesthetical diversity.

Why these three moments of institutional creation? The first wave corresponds to Pentecostalism's origin and early international expansion. Initial reception in Brazil is limited. The second wave begins when urbanization and mass society, especially in São Paulo, make possible a Pentecostalism that breaks with existing models, sparked by the arrival of the Four-Square, with its methods forged in the birthplace of modern mass media, interwar California. But the best initial use of the model is not made by the foreign Four-Square but by its creative nationalist adaptation, Brazil for Christ. The third wave occurs after authoritarian modernization of the country, especially in communications, when more than two-thirds of the population are urbanized and the "lost decade" of the 1980s is beginning. The wave starts in Rio de Janeiro, economically decadent and beset by violence, gambling mafias, and populist politics. In contrast to the second wave of São Paulo churches founded by migrants of low cultural level, the third wave has more urbanized leaders of a slightly higher cultural level and whiter skin. It adapts to urban culture influenced by television and the yuppie ethic.

The concept of waves emphasizes Pentecostalism's versatility, but also the way each church carries the marks of the era in which it was born. "Sects tend to be more influenced than they know ... by the prevailing secular facilities of the period of their emergence."[4] New groups have freedom to adapt because they do not carry decades of tradition. Difficulty in updating causes waves of intra-Pentecostal institutional creation that renew the relationship to culture,

---

4 Bryan Wilson, *Religion in Sociological Perspective* (New York: Oxford University Press, 1982), 106.

society, and even the state, as well as innovating in theology, organization, and ethics. (It should be stressed that this history refers to the predominantly lower class churches in Brazil. The middle class has been increasingly reached from the 1960s by charismatic breakaways from the historical churches, and from the 1980s by independent communities with innovative and sometimes controversial methods, such as Reborn in Christ and Heal Our Land, whose founders are often upper middle class people with entrepreneurial experience.) The major Brazilian Pentecostal denominations, then, illustrate the "wave thesis" of sects carrying their birthmarks, notwithstanding internal evolution and attempts to adjust to changes in society, culture, and the religious field.

The Assemblies of God (AG) are today by far the largest Protestant grouping, partly because they were the only major Protestant church whose initial expansion was outside the Rio-São Paulo axis. It thus established a presence at the North and North-East *starting points* of the future migratory flows. The AG was started in the northern city of Belém in 1911 by two Swedes who had emigrated to the United States. They were Baptists who had encountered Pentecostalism in Chicago. From 1914, more Swedish missionaries arrived. The links were primarily with Sweden and secondarily with the Swedish community in the United States.

The Swedish missionaries who influenced the early AG came from a religiously, socially, and culturally homogeneous country in which they were marginalized. They despised the Swedish state church, with its social and political status and its educated and theologically liberal clergy. They were bearers of a lay and countercultural religion, modest in its social aspirations. The Swedes' posture of suffering and cultural marginalization gave the Brazilian AG greater freedom to develop. They did not create powerful institutions that could retard the handing over of leadership. Their personal lives were simple, setting an example that helped the first generation of Brazilian leaders to be relatively indifferent to upward social mobility. The Swedes also rejected an emphasis on formal education that would have reinforced the missionary's status over the national.

In 1930 the Swedes gave complete autonomy to the Brazilian church. The main impulse behind the handover seems to have come from Sweden. Reacting against the experience of a Protestant state church, Swedish Pentecostals zealously defended the complete autonomy of the local congregation, and accused their missionaries in Brazil of building a nationwide organization. This handover occurred when the church was still very Northern and North-Eastern. The AG mentality for long bore the marks of this double origin: the early twentieth-century Swedish Pentecostal experience of cultural marginalization; and the patriarchal and preindustrial society of the Brazilian North and North-East from the 1930s to 1960s.

The Brazilian AG is oligarchical, grouped in lineages around *caudilho*-type *pastores-presidentes*. The AG is a complex web of (geographically intertwined) networks of mother-churches and dependent churches. The General Convention, comprising state conventions and affiliated ministries, is a relatively weak center.

As one would expect with this model, the AG has suffered many schisms, the largest being that between the Madureira Convention and the General Convention in 1989. Madureira is one of the oligarchical lineages, founded by an especially successful *caudilho*, whose growth threatened the survival of the others, leading to its exclusion from the General Convention. There have also been many smaller schisms of upwardly mobile groups who wished to modify the behavioral taboos. The AG is riven by tensions between the desire for respectability and the "populist" religious tradition that values the socially "humble" person as more receptive to the Gospel.

The other large church of the first wave, the Christian Congregation (CC), was founded among Italian immigrants in São Paulo in 1910. The founder was an Italian layman living in Chicago, and he was the only foreigner ever to work with the church. He never lived in Brazil, but his frequent visits (until the late 1940s) were fundamental for sedimenting a church based on oral and familial tradition.

The CC spread rapidly into immigrant regions of the interior. But it soon felt the need to guarantee survival by a transition to Portuguese, by means of a "revelation" to the elders in 1935. Today, the CC is still heavily concentrated in São Paulo and neighboring states. It is largely a rural and small town church, mainly because of its rejection of all mass methods such as radio, television, open-air preaching, or literature. Dissemination is only in churches and through personal contacts. A strong belief in predestination (probably acquired by the founder in his passage through American Presbyterianism) maintains this pattern, and has important effects on the CC's relationship to modernity. Predestinationism frees its members from the pressure to adapt methods constantly, in the name of evangelistic efficacy, to social change and technological advance. Another factor is the absence of a paid clergy (the church is run by unpaid elders), thus reducing operating costs and avoiding the careerist tendencies of professional clergy. The CC is far from the current mercantilist public image of Pentecostals in Brazil.

The Church of the Four-Square Gospel sparked the second Pentecostal wave. The Four-Square started in 1920s Los Angeles, the Mecca of exotic religious groups and the growing entertainment industry, where its Canadian female founder presented Pentecostalism in a new dress. It arrived in Brazil when its cultural style began to make sense in the center-south of the country. Appropriately, the first missionary had been an actor in Hollywood westerns. He conducted successful circus-tent divine healing campaigns in São Paulo, before founding a church in 1954.

At first, progress was modest. Brazil for Christ, the breakaway nationalist group, stole the crowds and headlines. Initially, the Four-Square's importance in Brazil was restricted to its role as importer of religious techniques for the new mass society, which were then adapted by Brazilians in a process of import substitution. With the Four-Square, sin and hell are displaced by physical and psychological healing (an adaptation to consumer society sensitivities and demands of the religious market); some behavioral taboos are relaxed as dysfunctional for broad urban sectors; and a bolder methodology using new styles of communication and venues other than churches is introduced. Divine healing as such was not new, but its massification and practice in public places was. In the 1980s, the Four-Square began to grow rapidly, with a membership somewhat socially superior to that of other large Pentecostal denominations.

The first large church started by a Brazilian was Brazil for Christ (Brasil para Cristo – BPC). While the country advanced "fifty years in five" (the slogan of President Kubitschek, elected in 1955, the year of the BPC's founding), a North-Eastern working-class migrant in São Paulo epitomized the nationalist and populist spirit of the times, building an autonomous religious empire unprecedented in Brazil. Manoel de Mello, the son of a poor tenant-farmer, became a construction worker and an AG deacon. He later joined the Four-Square, soon leaving to start a church with, as he said, "exclusively Brazilian roots." The nationalist vein reflected the desire for greater social visibility, overcoming Pentecostalism's cramped mentality. His attitude was far more positive than the traditional one of besieged fortress. If Brazil could win the battle for "development," it could be "for Christ" as well. The rejection of foreign domination was spreading, and BPC was the Pentecostal equivalent.

The BPC rented secular spaces such as cinemas and stadiums, invested heavily in radio programs, and even experimented briefly with television. In the early years, it was essentially a São Paulo phenomenon. In the vibrant populist political culture of the period, Mello broke with Pentecostal taboo against political involvement in 1962 and elected his own candidates. In the same year, he began the construction of the main temple, holding some 8,000 people. Political resources were obtained for the building, via the BPC's politicians, through presenting it as for social projects.

In the 1960s, Mello became famous for criticizing the military regime, and defending social justice and an ecumenical vision. But his strongest political statements were for external consumption only. His entry into the World Council of Churches (WCC) in 1969 was a marriage of convenience, motivated mainly by the WCC's desire to attract Third World Pentecostals, and Mello's hope of material help for projects. Mello's personalism, however, soon gave way to a more faceless institutionalized structure. He lacked the administrative qualities to create a lasting empire, and his leadership was replaced by a bureaucratic hierarchy. When he was sidelined from the church, the new leadership immediately left the WCC.

The third major initiative of the "second wave" was God Is Love (Igreja Pentecostal Deus é Amor – IPDA). The founder, David Miranda, is a Southerner of culturally limited but not poor rural origin. In São Paulo, he converted to a small Pentecostal church, and in 1962 started the IPDA, soon moving to a city-center square; downtown passers-by would be the church's base, and not a working class suburb. Extensive use of radio has been central to church life. Television, however, is not used at all, and members are forbidden to watch it: an example of the influence of conditions pertaining at the time of foundation on the life of a sect. The IPDA's strong sectarianism is also shown in rigid formulas of "separation from the world," a hair-splitting legalistic recipe of sanctified life. Among the prohibitions are ball games for children older than seven; red clothes for men; and heels of more than three centimeters when the heel is narrow or four centimeters when broad.

The IPDA's attraction is mainly to the very poor and those who want a "heavy doctrine" to keep them on track. Visible poverty is greater in its services than in those of other major churches. Several elements were anticipations of the third wave: uniformed lay helpers, exorcisms at the front, interviews with demons. But it is an amateur version, poor and culturally outdated. The IPDA also innovated in its frontal attack on Umbanda and in adaptation of Catholic elements such as anointing objects and periods of special prayer analogous to novenas. But the IPDA belongs, chronologically and sociologically, to the second wave. Miranda himself has so far braked any *aggiornamento* of the church through his desire to maintain a strictly family business.

The main church of the third wave is the Universal Church of the Kingdom of God (Igreja Universal do Reino de Deus - IURD). Founded in 1977, it took off in the following decade. The name points to a different context from the nationalism of the 1950s that had influenced Brazil for Christ. The third wave adapts to the changes of the military period (1964–1985): industrial deepening; rapid urbanization; the modern mass media that reach virtually the whole population; the crisis of Catholicism and the growth of Umbanda; and the economic stagnation of the 1980s. The new Pentecostalism adapts easily to urban culture influenced by television and a consumerist ethic.

The founder, Edir Macedo, was from a lower middle-class family from the state of Rio. Of Catholic origin, he had entered the New Life church after a short time in Umbanda. New Life, founded in 1960 by a Canadian ex-AG missionary, was also the origin of the founders of two other third-wave churches. It was less legalistic, and attracted lower middle class men who elaborated innovative recipes for mass Pentecostalism.

The IURD is a religion of large cities, and emphasizes healings, exorcisms, and prosperity. The third wave's emphasis on exorcism in part reflects a perception that the real competitor at the popular level is Umbanda and not Catholicism. In traditional Pentecostalism, the demons are kept at a distance. In the IURD, they are sought out and confronted. The pastors call the demons, under the names of Umbanda entities, to manifest themselves in people present. The Umbanda worldview is retained, but its signs are inverted.

The IURD breaks with traditional Protestant dependence on the Word, making ample use of the other senses: the Consecrated Rose, the Anointed Soap-Powder, the Jonah's Cry Vigil ("inside a symbolic representation of a whale"). However, we still see Pietist emphases. Its ethical teaching diverges from Pentecostal tradition in only two basic aspects: it is more liberal on feminine clothing and beauty, and in no areas are there disciplinary controls. The IURD attracts some social types who are very rarely seen in, for example, an AG meeting. The initial approximation is easy and uncommitted. The IURD intersects two bridges: with Brazilian religious tradition and with the urban culture of modern Brazil. The cultural styles of the Universal pastor and his AG counterpart are striking contrasts, paralleling that between the late twentieth-century entrepreneur (conspicuous consumption, exhibitionist style) and the old sober business class.

The IURD's message is characterized by prosperity theology. In Brazil's "savage capitalism," it proclaims the survival of the most faithful. However, the recipe is not limited to religious actions, but includes a realistic assessment of economic opportunities. As one sermon said: "It's not enough just to give the 'sacrifice' [a special offering to the church] and cross your arms. You have to leave your job and open a business, even if it's only selling popcorn on the street." Its publications contain hints on opening various branches of business. It may, therefore, reinforce the work ethic and petty entrepreneurial initiative.

The IURD has developed a bold strategy of penetration of social spaces, unparalleled by previous Protestant groups in Brazil. All its economic empire (and political force) is functional for its religious mission. In 1989, it bought TV Record, now the second largest television network in the country. The need for political support to obtain government approval of the transfer launched its political involvement, leading eventually to a sizeable congressional caucus elected by church members, besides other allies in Congress and government.

Current Reality

Some already speak of a crisis of Pentecostalism in Latin America. The symptoms are flattening growth curves, lack of regular attendance, and considerable apostasy. Evidence is adduced from Guatemala and Chile, Mexico, and Costa Rica. The conclusion is that, whereas Catholicism has difficulty keeping a high percentage of nominal untutored adherents once changing religion has become socially acceptable, Pentecostalism has difficulties for the opposite reason: it is too demanding morally and socially.

This is a plausible prediction, to which one can add a loss of prestige once Pentecostalism's limited ability to effect societal (as distinct from personal) transformation is realized. Nevertheless, while curves have flattened somewhat in some countries, in others they are still upward. While Chilean Pentecostals do seem less practicing, other countries show very high rates of weekly practice (86 percent in Brazil). Finally, "apostasy" can be merely a stage (usually in early adulthood) before a later return.

Nevertheless, there may be good reasons for thinking that overall Protestant leveling off is not very distant. My concept of leveling off is not based on previous predictions, such as Christian Lalive D'Epinay's idea of a social class limitation (which may apply to Chile but not to most countries), or Edward Cleary's notion of the incapacity of Pentecostalism to become a mass religion because it is too demanding (every day in Brazil morally and socially more flexible churches are created!).[5] Even so, the Protestant ceiling in Brazil will probably be reached within two or three decades. There are two factors in this prediction. First, Catholic decline (currently 1 percent per year) will reach a limit; there is a solid nucleus of about 25 to 30 percent of the population that will not disappear. Second, Protestantism currently receives only just over one of every two people who abandon Catholicism. And the Catholic Church is learning (albeit slowly) to compete better and diversify its appeal, which

---

5 Christain Lalive D'Epinay *O Refúgio das Massas* (Rio de Janeiro" Paz e Terra, 1970), 76.

will put a ceiling on Protestant aspirations. But another possibility is that the Protestant ceiling will be determined even earlier, by damage to its image caused by scandals, authoritarian leadership, unfulfilled promises, negative political reputation, and limited ability to produce social transformation. We can foresee a Brazilian future comprising a Catholicism that is slimmer (perhaps just above or below half the population) but revitalized and more practicing, followed by a large but stable (and highly fragmented) Protestantism, and a considerable sector of non-Christian religions and of "nonreligious."

Pentecostalism has been the engine of this religious change, for a number of reasons. The first is its very numerical success: throughout Latin America, Pentecostalism is now the second religious force (except in Uruguay, where it loses to the "nonreligious"). The second is its "Pentecostalizing" of other sectors (through imitation as in the Catholic Charismatic Renewal, or through hostile reactions that lead to changes in competing religions). And finally, Pentecostalism effectively introduces a new model of the religious field. In relation to Brazil, Otávio Velho talks of Pentecostalism's denaturalizing of the hegemonic national ideology (both popular and erudite), which considers "mixture" as typically Brazilian. I have called this model *hierarchical syncretism* (combining nonexclusiveness with acceptance of Catholic institutional hegemony); but Pentecostalism is the first major grassroots religion to reject this hegemony and propose an alternative that we can call *competitive pluralism*.[6]

How is this reflected in statistical data? The best data are presumably from national censuses (although these never take into account the Latin American tradition of double affiliation). But only six countries have recent census data on religion.

Brazil's census of 2010 showed a Protestant population of 22.2 percent. On the evidence of past censuses, the Protestant growth rate as a percentage of the population was between 20 percent and 33 percent per decade, from 1890 to 1990. This constant rate was shattered in the 1990–2000 period, when Protestantism grew by 75 percent. It then fell to 43 percent between 2000 and 2010. This slowing in the 2000s was largely due to weaker growth among Pentecostal churches of the third wave. Pentecostal expansion in Brazil has been greatest in the most economically and demographically dynamic spaces, that is, metropolitan areas of the South-East and agricultural frontiers of the North and Center-West. In metropolitan regions, Pentecostals are located

---

6 Otávio Velho, "An Assessment of the Interreligious Situation in Brazil," in *World Council of Churches*, 2000. www.wcc-coe.org/wcc/what/interreligious/cd36-03.html accessed September 2010.

heavily in the poor peripheries, due not just to poverty but also to virtual absence of the state and Catholic Church.

In the Chilean census of 2002, Protestants were 15.1 percent, with slow growth. There is a marked social and educational ceiling. Nicaragua, on the other hand, has had rapid growth: in the 2005 census, Protestants were 22 percent, up by seven points in a decade.

Mexico is different from all the aforementioned countries. If Chile had historically high growth that has rceently slowed down, and Nicaragua was historically weaker and recently stronger, while Brazil's growth has been rapid throughout, Mexico is one of the few Latin American countries yet to experience a Protestant "take-off." Its 2010 census revealed only 7.5 percent of Protestants (although up from 5.2 percent in 2000). Only four Mexican states have a Protestant percentage in double digits: the four southernmost. Five central states are still less than 2 percent Protestant.

Finally, Bolivia and Peru represent historically weaker Protestantisms that have expanded recently, but not on the scale of Nicaragua. The Bolivian census of 2001 put Protestants at 16 percent, while the Peruvian figure for 2007 was 12.5 percent.

In 2014, the Pew Forum produced a survey called "Religion in Latin America." Its figures do not always reflect the censuses commented on, but they do cover the whole region and ask more questions. According to the Pew, 19 percent of Latin Americans are Protestant. But this regional average hides massive variations. Four Central American republics lead the way: Honduras and Guatemala with 41 percent each, Nicaragua with 40 percent, and El Salvador with 36 percent. Puerto Rico follows with 33 percent, and then Brazil with 26 percent. At the bottom end, Paraguay is only 7 percent, preceded by Mexico with 9 percent, Colombia and Ecuador with 13 percent each, and Uruguay and Argentina with 15 percent each. Because of its size, Mexico lowers the regional average considerably, aided by Colombia and Argentina. The most Protestantized countries are small, except for Brazil. The pioneer of Latin American Protestant growth, Chile, is now below the regional average with 17 percent.

In terms of regional patterns, the Pew data and the national censuses suggest the following (if we imagine a map, colored darkest where Protestantism is strongest). First, the most heavily Protestant region is Central America, with a very dark core comprising the four neighboring countries mentioned previously, and a still fairly dark periphery consisting of Costa Rica and Panama, and even spilling into the borderlands of southern Mexico. Puerto Rico and the Dominican Republic in the nearby Caribbean are also part. (Cuba was not surveyed.) Second, another fairly dark area is Brazil, ranging from well-colored areas in the Amazon and around Rio de Janeiro, to far lighter areas in much of the North-East. Third, most of Spanish-speaking South America lags between single digits and the mid-teens. And fourth, the lightest colored area of all covers the whole of Mexico outside of its southern borderlands.

Slightly more than half of Latin American Protestants are converts from Catholicism. But this capacity to attract outsiders also varies considerably. In five contiguous countries from Colombia to Paraguay, more than 60 percent of Protestants are converts, whereas converts are 30 percent or fewer in the Central American countries of Panama, Guatemala, and Honduras, as well as in Chile. In other words, growth is now rapid in the heavily Amerindian areas of South America, all Protestant "late developers." Growth is now slow, both in the old 'lead' country of Chile and the more recent "lead" countries of Central America. Brazil, however, bucks the trend of lower growth now for earlier developers; its proportion of converts is still relatively high at 54 percent. Although growth rates vary widely, there are still no countries where Protestant expansion has totally ceased. The overall regional rate continues high, thanks largely to Brazil and the South American "late developers."

It is probable that there are both region-wide causes and country-specific ones for this unexpected growth of Protestantism in Latin America, with the latter helping to explain some of the considerable differences within the region. External factors such as well-funded American missionary initiatives and possible encouragement from American official and semi-official sources, especially during the Cold War, were once touted as fundamental and near-sufficient explanations; but over time, internal factors have come to be given more prominence. Among these, one can distinguish between those that originate in Latin American socioeconomic and political reality (such as large-scale migration from rural to urban areas, and in some countries the traumas and dislocations of civil war); those that stem from the broader religious field per se (e.g., perceived Catholic "weaknesses," such as territorialism, clericalism, and a chronic shortage of clergy [although Latin America has 42 percent of the world's Catholics, it has only 15 percent of its priests]); and those that reflect characteristics and initiatives from within the Protestant field itself (such as geographical flexibility and a style more in tune with popular culture and grassroots concerns). The 2014 Pew survey asked former Catholics who are now Protestant why they had converted, offering eight possible choices. The most popular was "seeking a personal connection with God" (cited by 81 percent of converts), followed by the attraction of "the style of worship at the new church" (69 percent), wanting a "greater emphasis on morality"

(60 percent), and the desire for "a church that helps members more" (59 percent). Two factors emphasized in many academic explanations for conversion to Protestantism ("personal problems" and "seeking a better financial future") were mentioned by only 20 percent and 14 percent of respondents respectively. Of course, actors' own explanations of their actions do not constitute a sufficient sociological account; but when the gap between the former and the latter is persistently wide, it may suggest that something else is going on.

That seems to be the case not only with explanations for conversion but also with accounts of the depth (or lack thereof) of conversion. In the Brazilian case, the hegemonic interpretation of the effects of Pentecostal conversion is hampered by an unwillingness to accept the reimagining of national culture. For a long time now, the core project of the Brazilian intelligentsia has been to create "a sense of the Brazilian nation distinct from its neighbors and from Europe," "a unified national identity ... [with] a strong emphasis on totality, integration, and permanence," which involves asserting "the permanence of the syncretism of Brazilian culture, since fluidity and multiple identities are regarded as Brazilian cultural traits."[7] In contrast to North Americans and Europeans, a key trait of Brazilians is said to be the tendency to mix races and religions. Because of all this, say Mariz and Campos, the dominant trend in Brazilian social science is to refute the idea that Pentecostalism's success implies a radical change in the nature of the Brazilian religious field. Rather, Pentecostalism itself ends up being absorbed into the traditional pattern of nonexclusivity, syncretism, loose ethical rules, and an emphasis on magical thinking, despite all the qualitative and quantitative evidence to the contrary in sociological work. Mariz and Campos' hope, however, is that the growing international literature on the anthropology of Christianity may lessen the ideological rigidity undergirding much study of Brazilian Pentecostalism.

Another region-wide tendency demonstrated by the Pew data is for Protestantism to constitute the "second force" in each country's religious field. The exception is Uruguay, where it loses heavily to the "nonreligious."

All of the aforementioned data refers to Protestants in general. But, as we know, in Latin America, Pentecostalism is the Protestant numerical mainstream. The Pew data suggest that 65 percent of Protestants are Pentecostal either by denominational affiliation or personal identity, varying from 81 percent in the Dominican Republic and 80 percent in Brazil and Panama, down

---

7 Cecilia Mariz and Robert Campos, "Pentecostalism and 'National Culture': A Dialogue between Brazilian Social Sciences and the Anthropology of Christianity," *Religion and Society: Advances in Research*, 2 (2011): 106–121.

to 49 percent in Bolivia, 52 percent in Peru, and 53 percent in Uruguay. Actual membership of a Pentecostal denomination oscillates between 72 percent in the Dominican Republic and 41 percent in Peru.

Prospects

The heavily indigenous areas of Bolivia, Peru, and Mexico are twice as Protestant as their national average. In recent decades, Protestantism (especially in Pentecostalized forms) has made considerable headway among Amerindian peoples in Mayan and Andean areas. It seems to reflect a vision of autonomy in a globalizing world, rejecting both assimilation into national society and the assumption that indigenous cultures can be sealed off.

If this trend continues, it will help Protestant growth for some time. Nevertheless, we are probably nearer the end than the beginning of the Protestant "explosion" in Latin America as a whole. In some countries, stabilization may be near. In others, it will take a few decades. The regional average will be heavily influenced by when stabilization occurs in Brazil, and whether Mexico experiences the Protestant take-off that has so far eluded all but its heavily indigenous south.

Among factors in this will be a lessening attraction of Protestantism, especially in Pentecostal forms, and a strengthening of other actors, especially Catholicism. Several factors might favor stronger Catholic resistance to Protestant advance than hitherto. One is demography. Catholic clericalism and territorial structure struggled in eras characterized by demographic mobility. But now, population growth is slowing, internal migrations are diminishing, and urban growth is stronger in medium-sized cities, all of which should favor Catholicism's capacity to react. A second factor is Catholic adaptation. Almost inevitably, Catholicism suffered heavy losses once real religious competition began. But that is only a first moment. As Froehle and Gautier say: "In countries [such as the United States] where the Church has long existed side by side with evangelical Protestants in an open, pluralist setting ... the Church has learned from the strengths characteristic of these other Christian traditions."[8] Probably not coincidentally, the most vibrant Catholic movement today, the Charismatic Renewal, began in the United States and fits well with the Latin American Church's need to reinvent itself in a more "denominational" context. (In the 2014 Pew survey, a median of 40 percent of Catholics across Latin America define themselves as "charismatic.")

---

8 Bryan Froehle and Mary Gautier, *Global Catholicism* (Maryknoll, NY: Orbis, 2003), 132.

Lessening attraction might be related to socioeconomic change and government policies such as the Brazilian *"bolsa-família,"* reducing somewhat the need for economic "crisis management" that Pentecostal churches cater for so well. Another factor in lessening attraction might be related to gender. One interpretation of religious change in Brazil cites the parallel curves of conversion and increasing female participation in the labor market.[9] Women have migrated disproportionately to other religions, especially Pentecostalism. The author attributes this to the Catholic Church's difficulty in questions of female emancipation such as contraception, divorce, and professional success. But, as Brusco clarifies, Pentecostalism effectively addresses the problems of machismo, but not of patriarchy. In consequence, I would add, Pentecostalism's advantages for women at lower social levels seem clear: it is efficacious in restoring the dignity of women and often also in domesticating men. In any case, other discourses of female empowerment are inaudible in that social context, or virtually impossible to appropriate. But at the middle-class level in Brazil, the situation is different; alternative discourses can be heard and appropriated. If Pentecostal growth is slowing now in Brazil (as recent studies suggest), it may be partly because it is less attractive to women who are moving into the lower middle class and accessing higher levels of education.

Finally, there is incipient "historicization," a process observable in Brazil, in which historical Protestant (though usually theologically conservative) thinking and practices are adopted. Some church leaders deem this necessary because they perceive Pentecostalism as insurmountably deficient in social and political dimensions, or because of exhaustion with its pragmatic attempts to maximize its share of the religious market. Historicization can imply total abandonment of Pentecostal practices, beliefs, or self-labeling, or just partial abandonment; and it can apply to individuals or to institutions.

Would widespread historicization presage a repeat of the Western trajectory toward theological liberalism? Perhaps not. The Brazilian context, far less secularized, may favor a transition to various types of more conservative theology. But an important factor in Pentecostal evolution may be the relative strength of historical Protestantism in each country. Chile and Central America are far weaker than Brazil in that respect, and thus offer fewer options to Pentecostals for personal and ecclesiastical experimentation or ecclesiastical

---

9 Neri, Marcelo, "A Ética Pentecostal e o Declínio Católico," Rio de Janeiro, Fundação Getúlio Vargas. 2005. www.fgv.br/cps/artigos/conjuntura/2005/a%20ética%20pentecostal%20e%20o%20declínio%20católico_mai2005.pdf (Accessed September 2010).

transfer. If (or when) Pentecostalism does become more numerically stabilized in Latin America, its historical trajectory will change dramatically. More birth members and fewer converts will increase demand for greater teaching and different types of leadership. There will be greater expectations regarding presence in society, and interactions with other religions will take place on a very different basis.

Although Pentecostalism does seem to have many advantages in modern Latin America, some of these may be only temporary (until rivals learn to imitate them), or until some of its limitations become more obvious. Many observers see Pentecostalism as a major wave of the future, as what David Martin styles "a natural denizen of deregulated religious markets."[10] But Martin himself also recognizes that it lives in tension with resistant forms of (Catholic, Islamic, or Buddhist) religion rooted in some sort of union of faith with polity, territory, or ethnicity; and he also speculates about an upper limit in the 10 to 20 percent range in China and Latin America, because success stimulates competition and emulation. Pentecostalism's initial comparative advantage in globalizing conditions will not last. None of this, of course, means that it will disappear. Much of it will feed into new Christian syntheses, both in new denominations and in influence on existing non-Pentecostal ones, as well as a profound reshaping of (at least portions of) existing Pentecostal denominations. But the future of Latin American Pentecostalism will be very different from its past.

Bibliography and Suggested Readings

Anderson, Allan. *Spreading Fires: The Missionary Nature of Early Pentecostalism*. London: SCM Press, 2007.
   To the Ends of the Earth: Pentecostalism and the Transformation of World Christianity. New York: Oxford University Press, 2013.
Bowen, Kurt. *Evangelism and Apostasy*. Montreal and Kingston: McGill-Queen's University Press, 1996.
Brusco, Elizabeth. "Gender and Power." In Allan Anderson, Michael Bergunder, André Droogers, and Cornelis van der Laan (eds.), *Studying Global Pentecostalism: Theories and Methods*, 74–92. Berkeley: University of California Press, 2010.
Cleary, Edward. "Shopping Around: Questions about Latin American Conversions." *International Bulletin of Missionary Research*, 28, no. 2 (2004): 50–55.
D'Epinay, Christian Lalive. *O Refúgio das Massas*. Rio de Janeiro: Paz e Terra, 1970.
Freston, Paul. "The Future of Pentecostalism in Brazil: The Limits to Growth." In R. Hefner and P. Berger (eds.), *Global Pentecostalism in the Twenty-First Century*, 63–90. Bloomfield: Indiana University Press, 2013.

---

10 David Martin, *The Future of Christianity* (Farnham: Ashgate, 2011).

"Pentecostalism in Brazil: A Brief History." *Religion*, 25 (1995): 119–133.
Froehle, B., and M. Gautier. *Global Catholicism*. Maryknoll, NY: Orbis, 2003.
Garrard-Burnett, Virginia. "Protestantism in Rural Guatemala, 1872–1954." *Latin American Research Review*, XXIV, no. 2 (1989): 127–142.
Protestantism in Guatemala: Living in the New Jerusalem. Austin: University of Texas Press, 1998.
Gaxiola-Gaxiola, Manuel. *La Serpiente y la Paloma*. South Pasadena: William Carey Library, 1970.
Gómez, Jorge. *El Crecimiento y la Deserción en la Iglesia Evangélica Costarricense*. San José: IINDEF, 1996.
Léonard, Émile-G. *O Protestantismo Brasileiro*. São Paulo: ASTE, 1963.
Mariz, Cecilia, and Robert Campos. "Pentecostalism and 'National Culture': A Dialogue between Brazilian Social Sciences and the Anthropology of Christianity." *Religion and Society: Advances in Research*, 2 (2011):106–121.
Martin, David. "Evangelical Expansion in Global Society." In Donald Lewis (ed.), *Christianity Reborn*, 273–294. Grand Rapids: Eerdmans, 2004.
The Future of Christianity. Farnham, UK: Ashgate, 2011.
Tongues of Fire, Oxford: Blackwell, 1990.
Novaes, Regina Reyes. "Os Pentecostais e a Organização dos Trabalhadores." *Religião e Sociedade*, 5 (June 1980): 65–93.
Smith, Dennis. "Coming of Age: A Reflection on Pentecostals, Politics and Popular Religion in Guatemala." *Pneuma*, 13 (Fall 1991): 131–139.
Velho, Otávio. "An Assessment of the Interreligious Situation in Brazil." World Council of Churches. 2000. www.wcc-coe.org/wcc/what/interreligious/cd36-03.html 2000 (Accessed September 2010).
Willems, Emílio. *Followers of the New Faith: Culture Change and the Rise of Protestantism in Brazil and Chile*. Nashville: Vanderbilt University Press, 1967.
Wilson, Bryan. *Religion in Sociological Perspective*, New York: Oxford University Press, 1982.
Zavala, Rubén. *Historia de las Asambleas de Dios del Perú*. Lima: Ediciones Dios es Amor, 1989.

29

The Religious Media and Visual Culture in Latin America

KARINA KOSICKI BELLOTTI

On the national holiday of Our Lady of Aparecida, patroness of Brazil, on October 12, 1995, many Brazilian Catholic viewers were appalled by the televised images of a Pentecostal bishop from the Universal Church of the Kingdom of God kicking a plaster sculpture of Aparecida. In his TV show, the bishop complained that Brazilian people devoted their faith to the lifeless image of a saint, instead of concentrating on God and Jesus. This iconoclastic outburst (which became colloquially known as the "kick to the saint") not only revived old controversies from the time of the Reformation, but it also demonstrated the strength of religious images on a national scale, amplified by the power of the electronic media. The subject of this chapter is the history and functions of the religious media and visual culture in Latin America, especially in the nineteenth and twentieth centuries.

Defining Visual Culture and Media

According to art historian David Morgan, religious visual culture is produced for several purposes including communication, education, celebration, ceremonies, and communion. It can be displayed in diverse formats: as images for the domestic realm, for public purposes or for consumption in temples; in the form of statues, sculptures, portraits, or photographs in educational books, catechisms, and so forth. A historical approach to religious visual culture aims to analyze the meanings that such images acquire in relation to their producers, their formats, and their recipients. There is no inherent and essential meaning for each religious image because the sacred meaning of visual culture is produced and learned in a cultural context, which means that sacredness is in the eye of the beholder.

For historians, any image that is considered sacred for a certain culture may be considered a subject of study, whether produced by institutions or by lay people. Other questions must be taken into account as well: What and who makes an image sacred? Who does not accept this sacredness and in what contexts? What are the possible readings for a religious image? In the case of the "kick to the saint," not only have Protestants always rejected images of Catholic saints but also in the Brazilian context of the 1990s, the "kick to the saint" was a matter of religious and media competition between the Catholic Church, which has always been supported by the largest TV network in Brazil, Rede Globo, and the Universal Church of the Kingdom of God, whose bishop Edir Macedo owns Rede Record, another large TV network. Nevertheless, not all Evangelicals approved such gestures.

The episode became well known because it was broadcast on television, the most popular means of communication in Brazil and in Latin America as a whole. For the sake of this chapter, the term media encompasses printed, electronic, and digital forms. In the age of convergence, all media may be gathered in one place, such as cell phones and computer-mediated communication, which allows multiple uses of images, texts, and sounds. According to Henry Jenkins, the convergence is in the mind of the consumers and producers of images, not so much in the means of communication per se. This is also relevant for the religious media that is produced by institutions and by

laypeople for instruction, interpersonal communication, publicity, protest, and sympathy. According to historian Colleen McDannell, "it is through the visible world that the invisible world becomes known and felt,"[1] which reinforces the importance of visual and material culture in understanding religions as dynamic social phenomena, demonstrating identities, hierarchies, and feelings.

Religious Visual Culture in Latin America

Religion is a Western concept construed in Judeo-Christian culture as a connection between human beings and God, assuming that men and women have become separated from the divine creator. However, in cultures such as those of pre-Columbian indigenous societies, what Europeans considered religion (paganism/pantheism) was a system of practices and beliefs in which all creatures were interconnected; in a way, everything could be "sacred" in many indigenous societies. Therefore, we consider religion as a set of practices and beliefs related to superhuman beings, a broader definition to understand the peculiarities of Latin American societies. However, when the Spanish invaded

---

[1] Colleen McDannell, *Material Christianity, Religion and Popular Culture in America* (New Haven, CT: Yale University Press, 1995), 272.

the Americas, the spiritual conquest of the indigenous attempted by the Catholic Church used visual elements of Catholic and Indian cultures, which resulted in a Baroque America.

Although always depicted as mystical cultures, some indigenous societies in pre-Columbian America developed rational and deductive knowledge that allowed them to survive in the face of the Spanish colonization. The visual culture of some Mexican cosmogonies – such as the image of Tlaloc, the Aztec god of rain and fertility – shows a different concept of the creation of the universe, in which indigenous people played a crucial role. The Brazilian historian Janice Theodoro points out that it is necessary to include visual and material culture in the understanding of indigenous cultures, avoiding the translation of the indigenous culture by European standards. This is a powerful reminder that religious visual culture is both a subject of study and an agent of history.

The Colonial Period

Along with the accumulation of gold and silver, another objective of the Spanish expeditions to America in the sixteenth century was the Christianization of indigenous Americans, considered pagans by the Catholic Church. For this effort, the Church drew on existing Catholic orders such as the Franciscans and the Dominicans, and the Counter-Reformation of the sixteenth century also created new groups such as the Company of Jesus (Jesuits), which headed to the New World with priests and strategies to convert peoples with different creeds. Theodoro pointed out that the spirit of the Renaissance that animated Europeans to expand to unknown territories went side by side with the spirit of destruction that followed the conquest of America. Europeans felt superior to indigenous people, and were eager to construct a new world, devoid of the vices and evils of the old, but in the image of a European utopia.

However, if the first encounters between the Spanish and the natives resulted in death and the destruction of many American cities, the Spaniards fixation in America needed new strategies to convert the natives. It was in the symbolic realm that the Jesuits, Franciscans, and Dominicans worked their catechisms. By the time of Baroque art, images were a powerful resources; the façades and the interiors of churches mixed images of saints, the Stations of the Cross, local animals and fruits, and images of natives. Often, the Franciscan charisma of poverty was rejected by the natives, as they did not show respect for anything or anyone who looked poor. Therefore, Franciscans built rich and embellished churches to attract Indians to Catholicism.

The devotion to Mary was also boosted in America in response to the rejection by the natives of the image of a suffering Christ on the Cross. Not long after the beginning of colonization, there were manifestations of the Virgin Mary in American lands. The most famous was that of Our Lady of Guadalupe, a *mestiza* Virgin who appeared to the native Juan Diego in 1531 in the region of what is now Mexico City. The Catholic cult of Mary is one of the most poignant characteristics of Latin America, and most countries have the Virgin as national patroness, for example, Our Lady of Luján (Argentina), Our Lady of Copacabana (Bolivia), Our Lady of Chiquinquirá (Colombia), Our Lady of Caacupé (Paraguay), Our Lady of Coromoto (Venezuela), and Our Lady of Aparecida (Brazil).

The manifestations of the Virgin in America served as confirmation for Catholics that God acknowledged American territories in his religious geography. Therefore, neither indigenous people nor Spanish descendants in America were disenfranchised. These episodes were used by the Catholic Church as tools of propaganda to achieve evangelization. Indeed, the term "propaganda" was born at the time of Reformation, with a derogatory meaning coined by Protestants who accused Catholics of using any means to evangelize. However, the Catholic Church used propaganda to face religious competition in Europe and to conquer the souls of distant lands. One of the most impressive cultural characteristics of colonial times, which survives to this day, was the mixture of native, Catholic and, later, African traditions to create a Catholic culture in the Americas. Each part of Latin America received the visit of the *mestiza* Virgin Maries, which helped to manage the tensions of Hispanic-American society.

The Independent Americas in the Nineteenth Century

Religion, society, and politics were closely articulated in the processes of independence of the Hispanic colonies but less so than the case of Brazil, where there was no significant rupture between the colonial past and the monarchy that succeeded it. In both cases, however, the Catholic Church remained a strong cultural and political force, while other religious and philosophical ideas also began arriving, such as Spiritism, Positivism, and Protestantism. This is not to mention the development of religious practices derived from the African diaspora, brought by the influx of slaves over 300 years. In Brazil, for instance, religions such as Candomblé, Tambor-de-Mina, Jurema (Catimbó), Xangô, Batuque, and Umbanda originated during the nineteenth and early twentieth centuries from the mixture of African, indigenous, and Catholic devotions, producing an astonishing visual culture in their rites, clothing, food, offerings, and celebrations.

Historian Andrew Chesnut affirms that the religious monopoly of the Catholic Church led to a continuous lack of communication between the Church and the majority of the population in Latin America. This favored several popular practices within Catholicism, such as devotion to unofficial local saints and martyrs (deceased infants, clergy, and even Che Guevara) to whom people attributed miracles and cures, lit candles, and offered *ex votos* (tokens of the grace received, such as plaques, sculptures of parts of the body, etc.). Processions of Corpus Christi, where the main streets of small towns are covered with images of Christ, saints, and messages of peace, are remnants of Medieval and modern Catholicism cultivated in Latin America from colonial times until the twenty-first century.

When the monopoly of Catholicism was "broken" by the separation between church and state in many independent countries during the nineteenth century, religious competitors invested in propaganda and evangelization which, in relative terms, weakened Catholic influence in those territories. With the advent of the mass media in the twentieth century, this competition became fierce.

Religious Media in Latin America from the Nineteenth to Twenty-first Centuries

What are the roles of the media in the religious field? Can the media alter the dynamics of religious competition? To understand the influences of the media in religious choices, it is worth noting that the media have been inserted in a complex network of communications and cultural relations in the Western world since the late-nineteenth century. In the Latin American continent, printed media has always had a limited reach, owing to the high rate of illiteracy. Nevertheless, the printed media were the first resources used by the newly arrived Protestants in the nineteenth century to communicate with potential converts. Editing journals, newspapers, and bulletins, Presbyterians, Methodists, Congregationalists, Lutherans, Baptists, and Seventh-Day Adventists aimed at social insertion and legitimacy. Even in Brazil, where Catholicism was the official religion until 1890, Protestants started their missionary work with the goodwill of anticlerical, liberal, and republican groups. The first Protestant newspaper was *O Puritano* (The Puritan) in 1859, edited by Ashbel Green Simonton, the first Presbyterian Missionary. Before him, there had been the representatives of the Bible Societies (of British and American origin), who had distributed Bibles among the population, sometimes with the support of sectors of the Catholic clergy and of the local authorities.

However, Protestantism was spread mainly by the spoken word of preaching and by its adaptation to the Latin American social realities and languages. In Brazil, for instance, Presbyterians managed to grow along the trails of the coffee plantations, providing schools, hospitals, and spiritual counseling where the Catholic Church did not reach. Owing to the oral culture and communication predominant in Latin America, radio was the crucial tool adopted by the Protestant churches in the mid-twentieth century. In Latin America, the first Protestant transmission was in 1931 by the World Radio Missionary Fellowship in Quito, Ecuador, with the program "The Voice of the Andes" in Spanish. By 1932, the program was also available in Quíchua and by 1942 in Portuguese. In Brazil, the first known Protestant transmissions were from the "The Evangelical Voice of Brazil" in 1938 and the Rádio Transmissora Brasileira of Rio de Janeiro. However, the "Voice of Prophecy" of the Seventh-Day Adventists is the oldest evangelical radio show in Brazil, dating back to 1943.

The National Council of the Churches of Christ in the United States also sponsored audiovisual centers in several parts of the world. In Latin America there were two called CAVE (Centro Audiovisual Evangélico) in the 1950s, one in Mexico and the other in Brazil. They both produced audiovisual material (slideshows, radio shows, flannel graphs, etc.) with interdenominational funding and national personnel.

During the first half of the twentieth century, the Catholic Church still held great influence in politics and education in Latin America, running radio stations, publishing houses, and schools. Yet, during the 1960s, the Church took a progressive turn in most of Latin America as a response to the dictatorships in various countries. At the Latin American Bishops Conference in Medellín (1968), the champions of Liberation Theology were extremely critical of the commercial use of the secular media and defended a social use that could bring social and political awareness to the poor majority. The preferential option for the poor led to a communitarian use of radio and print media in the context of Ecclesial Base Communities (comunidades eclesiales de base – CEBs) in the 1960s and the 1970s.

At the same time, Pentecostals were increasingly using radio, TV, and printed media to reach potential believers. In Central America, American preachers such as Pat Roberston, Jimmy Swaggart, and Rex Humbard purchased prime time on TV to broadcast their shows. According to sociologist Sara Diamond, these preachers were allies of the US administration in the anticommunist campaign during the Cold War, helping to raise funds for the Contras in Nicaragua and for the low-tension, antirevolutionary campaign, through the distribution of food, medicines, and literature to the poor in those areas.

Despite the US Evangelical presence in Latin America, Protestants and Pentecostals in the region also constructed national cultures, addressing everyday issues such as poverty, alcoholism, domestic violence, and familiar breakdown. Media productions served two main purposes: instruction of new converts and publicity to potential ones. It also provided social status for the communicators within the churches. On the one hand, Protestants used TV, radio, and printed media (pamphlets, bulletins, journals, tracts, and books) to achieve social legitimacy and visibility; on the other hand, the Catholic Church in the 1980s, with the end of several dictatorships and the conservative turn of the Vatican, awoke to the fierce Evangelical competition in the media.

The Catholic Church thus invested in TV and radio stations in the 1980s and 1990s in several Latin American countries. In Brazil, the Catholic Charismatic Renewal (CCR) was in the vanguard of media use, with investments in three TV networks by the mid-1990s (Rede Vida, Rede Canção Nova, and Rede Século XXI). The last of these was associated with the Associação do Nosso Senhor Jesus, of Father Edward Dougherty, the American pioneer of Charismaticism in Brazil from the late 1960s. The CCR also led to the rise of "singing priests" such as Father Marcelo Rossi (one of the best-selling singers of all time in Brazil, outstripping popular secular artists). These developments were in addition to the fact that the Catholic Church has always had a presence in Brazil's largest TV network, Rede Globo. The CCR is also heavily dependent on the cult of Mary as a distinctive visual and ritual feature in the religious field.

Catholic attention to TV in Brazil was also accelerated by the multimillion-dollar purchase of the Rede Record network in 1989 by Bishop Edir Macedo, leader of the Universal Church of the Kingdom of God, then one of the fastest growing Pentecostal churches in Latin America. The entrepreneurial vision of this church created a new paradigm for communication and marketing for other Protestant churches and even for the Catholic Church in Latin America, inciting religious and media competition, as seen in the aforementioned episode of the "kick to the saint" in 1995. One of the main concerns of many Evangelical communicators since the early-twentieth century has been to incorporate secular media formats into the biblical message. The purchase of a bankrupt network was the chance to expand this vision, which Bishop Macedo has been doing since his first radio transmissions in the late 1970s. The Universal Church has exported its churches and TV and radio shows to other Latin American countries and to Africa.

The Universal Church invests heavily in visual and symbolic elements, incorporating practices from popular Catholicism including *correntes* (periodical services to achieve a personal "grace"), blessed water, and blessed and anointed objects (e.g., roses, piece of garment, rings, etc.) and practices from Candomblé and Umbanda such as *descarregos*, in which evil spirits identified with the African religious pantheon are expelled from the lives of the believers. From time to time these so-called "campaigns" renew these symbolic elements, at the pace of the religious market, to maintain a fresh supply of religious goods available on TV and to attract people to the churches. Such strategies have been adopted by other Pentecostal churches, and a new market of material objects to be used in Evangelical churches has arisen.

Other religions were not as concerned with media investments as the Catholics and the Protestants. However, the marketing mentality has undeniably become a strong reference point in terms of the social insertion of religious traditions in modern society. On the one hand, some religious traditions partially refuse to adhere to such practices, such as most of the Spiritist centers and associations and part of traditional Protestantism that does not want to be considered "Evangelical" at the same level as the Universal Church of the Kingdom of God. On the other hand, Spiritist writers such as Zibia Gasparetto have been best-selling authors for decades in Brazil. New religious movements, commonly known as New Age movements, achieve great visibility through the use of modern and diffuse networks of communication such as workshops, bookstores, temples, Internet websites, and discussion groups.

Interestingly, other minority religions in Latin America such as Buddhism, Islam, and Judaism also maintain channels of modern communication with their flock, but from time to time they come under the public gaze in the *telenovelas*, especially in Brazil. The scriptwriters usually use these religions to add information and exoticism to the plots. But they also cause a rush to libraries, bookstores, and websites to seek more information on these traditions.

Special consideration must be given to the African diaspora religions, which have been a strong presence in Brazil and the Caribbean, where African slavery was the basis of the economy until the late nineteenth century. Their visual culture has always been rich and diverse, adapting to the realities of Catholic culture and slavery. From the colonial era until the early twentieth century, African rites were persecuted and condemned by governments, with support from the Catholic Church. During the second half of the twentieth century, these religions earned official and academic recognition of their importance for the cultural formation of Latin American identities. Their visual culture can be seen in the Portuguese-Brazilian singer Carmen Miranda, who dressed as a stylish *filha-de-santo*, and their music can be heard in the sambas of Dorival Caymmi, Clara Nunes, and Martinho da Vila. The African-Brazilian religions have been exported to Argentina, Uruguay, Spain, Italy, France, Portugal, and the United States, and they compete with Caribbean Vodou in the United States and Europe. Yet, on television, the representation of African rites often echoes old prejudices against them. The appropriation of African religions symbols is used by artists and individuals from the middle and upper classes to establish a *mestizo* identity, while the producers of such images are still in marginal positions in society.

Conclusion

One of the roles of the media is the spread of information about diverse traditions, which reinforces the religious autonomy of individuals in Latin America. The new context of religious pluralism, implanted in Latin America in the twentieth century, brings with it a valuing of ancient traditions that range from the use of indigenous rites such as *ayahuasca* (a psychotropic drink used by Amazonian shamans) to increased tourism focused on Aztec and Inca culture. It also raises the visibility of new religious movements such as Hare Krishna and Seicho-no-ie, and of Catholic and Protestant messages in a supermarket of Christian goods. African rites strive to maintain their traditions, while Pentecostals convert some of their adherents.

Through the religious visual culture and media, individuals may combine the beliefs and practices that suit them best at a certain moment. In the age of convergence, believers also become preachers or marketers of their faith, creating webpages to display their personal belief and finding people to share it. Although religious institutions sponsor means of communication, believers enjoy the opportunity to take hold of their expressions. Even Protestantism, with its historical rejection to images, is using a colorful visual culture available in the Christian market in the forms of greetings cards, apparel, school supplies, children's literature, games, and more.

For historians, the current context of religious pluralism and competition in Latin America demonstrates the power of communication in the transformation of the religious field by the incorporation of a marketing mentality. The secular media show the religious responses to social issues such as abortion, teenage pregnancy, family values, youth, and euthanasia; most of the time, Catholics and Protestants convey conservative messages, although they use modern marketing techniques to address these to their flock. On the one hand, this means that the use of modern media does not necessarily represent up-to-date attitudes toward social problems, which gives a sense of certainty and permanence in times of incertitude. On the other hand, access to religious media and marketing is a crucial element for individuals to craft their own religiosities, spread the word of God or gods/goddesses, and find new co-religionists.

Bibliography and Suggested Readings

Almeida, Ronaldo de. *A Igreja Universal e seus demônios*. São Paulo: Terceiro Nome/FAPESP, 2009.

Amaral, Leila. *Carnaval da alma*. Comunidade, essência e sincretismo na Nova Era. Petrópolis: Vozes, 2000.

Assmann, Hugo. *A Igreja Eletrônica e seu impacto na América Latina*. Petrópolis: Vozes, 1986.

Bastide, Roger. *As religiões africanas no Brasil*. São Paulo: Pioneira, 1985.

Bellotti, Karina Kosicki. *Delas é o Reino dos Céus: Mídia evangélica infantil na cultura pós-moderna do Brasil (1950–2000)*. Tese de doutoramento. Campinas-SP: IFCH/Unicamp, 2007.

Mídia Presbiteriana no Brasil – Luz para o Caminho e Editora Cultura Cristã (1976–2001). São Paulo: Annablume/FAPESP, 2005.

Uma Igreja Invisível? Protestantes históricos e meios de comunicação no Brasil (anos 50 a 80). Monografia de conclusão de graduação em História. Campinas-SP: IFCH/Unicamp, 2000.

Briggs, Asa, and Peter Burke. *A Social History of the Media: From Gutenberg to Internet*. London: Routledge, 2002.

Campos, Leonildo Silveira. *Teatro, Templo e Mercado*. Vozes/Simpósio Editora/Umesp, Petrópolis. São Paulo: São Bernardo do Campo, 1997.

Cava, Ralph Della, and Paula Montero. *...E o verbo se faz imagem – Igreja Católica e os meios de comunicação no Brasil: 1962–1989*. Petrópolis: Vozes, 1991.

Chesnut, R. Andrew. *Born again in Brazil: The Pentecostal boom and the pathogens of poverty*. New Brunswick, NJ: Rutgers University Press, 1997.

Competitive Spirits: Latin America's New Religious Economy. Oxford: Oxford University Press, 2003.

Diamond, Sara. *Spiritual Warfare: The Politics of the Christian Right*. Boston: South End Press, 1989.

Freston, Paul. *Protestantes e política no Brasil: Da Constituinte ao Impeachment*. Tese de doutoramento em Sociologia. Campinas: IFCH/Unicamp, 1993.

Guerreiro, Silas. *Novos Movimentos Religiosos: O quadro brasileiro*. São Paulo: Editora Paulinas, 2006.

Jenkins, Henry. *Convergence culture: Where old and new media collide*. New York and London: New York University Press, 2008.

Karnal, Leandro. *Teatro da Fé*. São Paulo: Hucitec, 1998.

Lewgoy, Bernardo. "Incluídos e letrados – Reflexões sobre a vitalidade do espiritismo kardecista no Brasil atual." In Faustino Teixeira and Renata Menezes (eds.), *As Religiões no Brasil: continuidades e rupturas*, 174–188. Petrópolis: Vozes, 2006.

Maggie, Yonne. *Medo de feitiço: relações entre magia e poder no Brasil*. Rio de Janeiro: Arquivo Nacional, 1992.

Mariano, Ricardo. *Neopentecostais: Sociologia do novo pentecostalismo no Brasil*. São Paulo: Loyola, 1997.

Martin, David. *Tongues of Fire: The explosion of Protestantism in Latin America*. Cambridge, MA: Blackwell, 1990.

McDannell, Colleen. *Material Christianity, Religion and Popular Culture in America*. New Haven, CT: Yale University Press, 1995.

Mendonça, Antônio Gouvêa. *O Celeste Porvir*, 2nd ed. São Paulo: Aste, 1995.

Morgan, David, and Promey, Sally, eds. *Visual Culture in American Religions*. Los Angeles: University of California Press, 2001.

Nuno, Rubén Bonifaz. *Imagem de Tláloc*. México: Universidad Autónoma de México, 1988.

Oro, Ari Pedro. *Axé Mercosul: As religiões afro-brasileiras nos países do Prata*. Petrópolis: Vozes, 1999.

Oro, Ari Pedro, André Corten, and Jean-Pierre Dozon, eds. *Igreja Universal do Reino de Deus: Os novos conquistadores da fé*. São Paulo: Paulinas, 2003.

Schultze, Quentin J. "Orality and power in Latin American Pentecostalism." In Daniel R. Miller (ed.), *Coming of Age: Protestantism in Contemporary Latin America*, 65–88. Lanham, MD: University Press of America, 1994.

Silva, Vagner G. *Candomblé e Umbanda – Caminhos da Devoção Brasileira*, 2nd ed. São Paulo: Selo Negro, 2005.

Souza, André Ricardo de. *Igreja in concert: Padres cantores, mídia e marketing*. São Paulo: FAPESP/ Annablume, 2005.

Theodoro, Janice. *América Barroca*. São Paulo/Rio de Janeiro: Edusp/Nova Fronteira, 1992.

Verger, Pierre Fatumbi. *Orixás*. Salvador: Corrupio, 1981.

Vieira, David Gueiros. *O Protestantismo, a Maçonaria e a Questão religiosa no Brasil*. Brasília: Editora da UnB, 1980.

30
The Catholic Charismatic Renewal and the Incipient Pentecostalization of Latin American Catholicism

JAKOB EGERIS THORSEN

At the beginning of the third millennium, global Christianity is undergoing enormous transformations. Whereas church membership and attendance is on the decline in Europe and North America, Christianity is spreading rapidly in the Global South, where most of the new Christians are joining Pentecostal-type Churches. Latin America has been Christian for almost five centuries, but here too an impressive awakening ties people closer to the churches. Many have left the once-absolute Catholic Church and joined Pentecostal and Evangelical communities, but a significant number are also experiencing the Pentecostal revival *within* the Catholic Church, forming part of an internal Charismatic movement.

This Charismatic revival in the Catholic Church has drawn increased academic attention over the last decade, and with good reason: Charismatic prayer groups are by far the most common form of organized lay engagement today, and this Catholic version of Pentecostalism is probably the most influential spiritual current within the vibrant and gaudy Catholicism of Latin America. The backbone of the Charismatic movement is the international organization The Catholic Charismatic Renewal (CCR), but since its arrival in Latin America forty years ago, numerous independent Charismatic groups and ministries have emerged across the continent as well. Statistics indicate that around 16 percent of all baptized Catholics in Latin America are Charismatic, and a single survey in Brazil and Guatemala has estimated the number as high as 60 percent. With such levels of participation, it comes as no surprise that the movement is leaving its mark on the Church to which it belongs. In regions where this enthusiastic new form of Catholicism has gained a strong foothold, Charismatic practices are gradually permeating Catholic Church life as a whole and are changing the face and expression of Latin American Catholicism.

This chapter argues that the increased role of the CCR in the Catholic Church reflects a broader shift in the self-understanding of the Church in Latin America. The Catholic Church today accentuates its denominational distinctiveness within an increasingly pluralist society, and it deemphasizes the, until recently, taken-for-granted relationship between the Catholic faith and popular culture. This increase in Catholic confessionalism bears the mark of the CCR by stressing the importance of experienced personal conversion, a proactive missionary attitude, and a countercultural lifestyle. The result is an incipient Pentecostalization of the Catholic Church in Latin America, visible both in daily Church life and in official Church documents.

The chapter is organized in three sections. First, it presents a brief historical introduction to the Catholic Charismatic movement in Latin America. Second, it addresses the main characteristics of Charismatic practices and beliefs and describes their spread into mainstream Church life. Third, it discusses the role of the Charismatic movement in the latest developments in the Catholic Church in Latin America, such as in the documents of the Fifth Conference of Latin American Bishops in Aparecida (Brazil, May 2007), where the initiative A Continental Mission was launched.

This chapter thus focuses on the Charismatic Renewal in its intra-Catholic context but does not address the complex relationship between the growth of Pentecostalism and the ascent of the CCR within the Catholic Church. This issue has been thoroughly explored by Andrew Chesnut.[1]

Origins and Growth of the Charismatic Movement

The CCR emerged in the enthusiastic and confused aftermath of the Second Vatican Council (1962–1965), which opened the Catholic Church to hitherto unseen new ways of religious expression and lay engagement. It formed a somewhat delayed part of what is known as the *second wave*, which brought Pentecostal beliefs and practices into the traditional denominations as intra-ecclesial but ecumenically oriented awakening movements, later known as the Charismatic Renewal. The CCR ascribes its origin to a retreat held in February 1967, where several faculty members and students from Duquesne University, a Catholic university in Pittsburgh (USA), experienced an *outpouring of the Spirit* with Spirit baptism and speaking in tongues. The movement grew quickly and Charismatic prayer groups spread rapidly to other Catholic

---

[1] R. Andrew Chesnut, *Competitive Spirits: Latin America's New Religious Economy* (New York: Oxford University Press, 2003).

universities and eventually to the Catholic parishes in the United States and across the borders to Catholics worldwide, including Latin America. Edward L. Cleary draws attention to a similar event, in which participants experienced Spirit baptism and speaking in tongues, that occurred in Bogotá, Colombia around the same time. The origin of Charismatic Catholicism thus appears to have more than one center.[2]

The spread of the CCR within the different countries in Latin America at the beginning of the 1970s followed a basic pattern. It was generally introduced by North American priests, mostly Jesuit and Dominican, who, by invitation from interested local bishops or influential priests, arranged *Life in the Spirit* retreats. Here the participants were introduced to the Charismatic signs, such as speaking in tongues, faith healing, and the experience of baptism in the Spirit. After their initiation, priests and nuns spread the movement to Catholic educational institutions and from there to the parishes.

During its first decade, the CCR attracted its adherents mainly from the urban middle class, primarily middle-aged women already engaged in regular Church life and other lay movements. This profile of the archetypical Charismatic Catholic has been quite consistent, but during the next three decades the movement increasingly managed to spread to both the lower and upper classes. Today one may consider Charismatic Catholicism to be a broad popular mass movement.

The reaction of the Church hierarchy to the new and enthusiastic, but also unfamiliar, way of expressing the Catholic faith was ambivalent. Although the CCR often entered a country with the consent of a local bishop, the national bishops' conferences approached the movement with considerable caution. Opposition came from two sides. For one thing, some conservative bishops had doubts about the movement's catholicity. As it resembled the growing Pentecostal churches in style and practice, they wondered whether they were bringing a Trojan horse within the once secure Roman Catholic walls, which would eventually function as a stepping stone to Protestantism for baptized Catholics. This fear has largely proven wrong, except in cases where groups left the Church for a Pentecostal congregation because of the fierce resistance of priests and bishops. For another, opposition came from bishops and theologians adhering to Liberation Theology, who in the CCR saw a retreat to a

---

2 Edward L. Cleary, "The Catholic Charismatic Renewal: Revitalization Movements and Conversion," in *Conversion of a Continent: Contemporary Religious Change in Latin America*, eds. Timothy J. Steigenga and Edward L. Cleary (New Brunswick, NJ: Rutgers University Press, 2007), 167.

purely spiritual understanding of Christianity that would betray the Church's recent social justice engagement in favor of the poor.

The majority of dioceses allowed the CCR to form prayer groups, and they established clergy-led supervisory boards to monitor and correct the movement. During the 1970s and 1980s, national bishops' conferences one by one officially approved the CCR, always with accompanying words of admonition about possible deviations from the Catholic faith, such as the overemphasis on personal experience and the neglect of obedience to the hierarchy of the Church. The Brazilian bishops' conference was the last to give its recognition to the movement in 1994, probably because of the particular strength of the liberationist wing in the Brazilian Church.

The CCR began as an ecumenically oriented movement, and worshippers from Protestant churches were frequent visitors and preachers at the prayer meetings. This changed at the end of the 1970s with the increasing number of Protestants in Latin America, partly as a result of door-to-door missionary campaigns, which the Catholic Church perceived as proselytizing. The CCR began to acquire a more distinct Catholic identity and integrated traditional Catholic prayers and devotions in its practice.

By invitation of Pope John Paul II, the Virgin Mary was placed at the center of the movement as its patron saint, thereby clearly distinguishing the CCR from Pentecostal groups and Charismatic Protestants. This is marked virtually by a statue of the Virgin, which is always present on the interim altars during Charismatic prayer meetings, while the crucifix seems optional. Today, Charismatic Catholics no longer worship with Protestants and have adopted the Church's official designation for them as *separated brethren* and sometimes, polemically, as *sects*.

The CCR currently represents the biggest lay movement within the Latin American Church and is widely accepted and often represented in parish councils and in the lay boards of dioceses and deaneries. Though the CCR is led by laypeople, hundreds of priests and many bishops are affiliated with the movement. Parishes led by a priest from the Renewal often acquire a Charismatic touch and tend to draw worshippers from the surrounding areas. An extreme example is the famous Brazilian priest Marcelo Rossi, whose popularity forced the diocese to rent an old factory to accommodate the up to 30,000 worshippers who gathered for daily mass.

In general, Charismatic Catholics gather in small parish-based groups of fifteen to fifty persons. Large parishes often have many such groups specialized for men, women, couples, and youths, each meeting at different times during the week. While the small groups form the heart of the movement, big events – healing rallies, concerts, and meetings with specially gifted revivalist preachers – are much coveted as peak experiences by Charismatic worshippers who periodically gather in CCR centers, gymnasiums, and sometimes even soccer stadiums. The Charismatic movement has created new para-ecclesial organizations of lay ministries who service the prayer groups with preachers, musicians, and healers. These independent ministries are linked to the official Church mostly by a priest who functions as spiritual advisor and guarantor, but in many dioceses they operate with considerable independence.

By the year 2000, more than half of the world's 120 million Charismatic Catholics lived in Latin America, and while CCR participation in the United States has been declining (except in predominantly Latino parishes), it is growing in numbers south of the border. Statistics about religious affiliation in Latin America vary considerably, and figures should therefore always be read with much caution. According to the CCR, 73.6 million Latin American Catholics have participated to some degree in Charismatic events and meetings. That is 16 percent of all Catholics in Latin America.

This figure seems to be in accord with *World Christian Trends* from 2001, where the percentages of Catholics with a Charismatic affiliation in three selected countries are estimated as follows: Brazil 22 percent, Chile 14 percent, and Guatemala 9 percent. But if one turns to a 2006 survey conducted by the Pew Forum on Religion and Public Life, the percentage of Charismatic worshippers among the Catholics surveyed is estimated strikingly higher with Brazil at 57 percent, Chile at 26 percent, and Guatemala at 62 percent, although this figure for what Pew termed "renewalists" included both Catholic Charismatics and Protestant Pentecostals.[3] It is almost impossible to explain such statistical discrepancies, but regardless of whether the first, the last, or – most probably – a figure in between the two statistical surveys is correct, it tells us something about the magnitude of the Charismatic movement.

In the same time span, the famous liberation-oriented *Christian Base Communities* have only engaged between 20 and 30 million people throughout Latin America, which is the equivalent of 2 to 5 percent of the Catholic population. Although Liberation Theology is often portrayed as the theological counterpoint to Charismatic spirituality, this is not always necessarily the case. There have been examples of fusions where Base Communities and liberationist priests adopt the Charismatic prayer style and music and combine it with their liberationist agenda.

---

3 The Pew Forum on Religion & Public Life, *Spirit and Power: A 10-Country Survey of Pentecostals* (Washington, DC: Pew Research Center, 2006), 76–79.

Another connection lies in the rapid expansion of the CCR, having been facilitated by the existing organization of the parishes in small communities and prayer groups, where the new Charismatic impulses could rapidly spread and unfold among the laity. This way of organizing lay people was undertaken during the 1970s and was heavily inspired by liberationist ideas. The Church has stuck to this organizing principle, but has changed the name to *Small Ecclesial Communities*, which today are often Charismatic or semi-Charismatic.

The Charismatic field within the Catholic Church is diverse. Some groups have integrated the Charismatic experience and practices into traditional Catholic piety and tradition. Others have a style of worship that is almost indistinguishable from that of neo-Pentecostal Churches. The description that follows is meant to give an overall account of the movement and does not encompass all variations of its expression.

The Faith and Practices of Charismatic Catholics

Using the words of Walter Hollenweger, one of the first scholars of global Pentecostalism, one can best describe Charismatic and Pentecostal Christianity as *high-voltage religion*.[4] This is due to the high level of enthusiasm and engagement experienced by its adherents and that ideally spill over into all aspects of life. Charismatic Catholicism thus differs from ordinary popular Catholicism in Latin America, which could be labeled *low tension*, where low levels of engagement are common and tolerated.

The core of Charismatic spirituality is not primarily a distinctive theology or understanding of Scripture, but the concrete and very joyful experience of the divine through different religious practices, mostly carried out in the religious community. There are five traits that characterize a Charismatic prayer meeting: (1) the vivid and rhythmic songs of praise that open the assembly and are accompanied with palm clapping and arm waving; (2) the oral character of prayers, preaching, and individual testimonies, which are carried out with great pathos in a popular language; (3) resting in the Spirit, which is a type of religious trance that worshippers receive mostly after intensive intercessory prayer and laying on of hands by the preacher and the other believers; (4) faith healing of physical and psychological distresses, which is carried out in the same way as resting in the Spirit and is often combined with it; and finally, (5) speaking in tongues during sessions of prayer, which is less prominent in

---

4 Walter Hollenweger, *Pentecostalism: Origins and Developments Worldwide* (Peabody, MA: Hendrickson Publishers, 1997), Introduction.

Catholic Charismatic groups than in classical Pentecostal Churches. The same applies for receiving and speaking words of prophecy.

Charismatic Catholic spirituality and practice is thus characterized by its focus on the experiential and ecstatic elements in Christianity that either play a minor role or are absent in traditional Catholicism and Protestantism. Similar to Pentecostalism, the essence of Charismatic spirituality is an experience of a *personal encounter with the divine*, and prayer meetings revolve around reviving this encounter, rejoicing in it, and applying it to challenges of daily life. Like Pentecostalism, Charismatic Catholicism is passionate and joyful. The ecstatic and mystical self-delivery to God lies at the heart of its spirituality and is often articulated in a quasi-erotic language. If it was not for the aforementioned statue of the Virgin Mary and the Marian devotional acts, the Catholic Charismatic prayer meeting is almost indistinguishable from its Pentecostal counterpart.

The prayer groups are also healing communities, where the wounds of broken relationships, addictions, and physical and psychological abuses are laid open; cured in the communal prayer and intercession; and testified about for the spiritual edification of group and individual. The importance of this function, which is another similarity with the Pentecostal Churches, cannot be overestimated. The elements of ecstasy and healing are probably the most direct link between Charismatic Catholicism and traditional popular religion in Latin America; Charismatic healers and prayer groups have some of the same functions as those of the wise women, the traditional healer or shaman (*curandero/a*), or even the witch (*brujo/a*) in earlier times, namely to serve as bridges to a supernatural world inhabited by angels and demons.

As in popular religion, individuals often perceive personal problems as being rooted in the supernatural world and seek help from the Charismatic healer to receive protection, healing, or liberation from *el enemigo* ("the enemy," the devil) and his cohort of evil helpers. Charismatic preachers frown upon popular religious practices as being pagan and denounce witchcraft as satanic. But unlike much contemporary Catholic theology that de facto adheres to a disenchanted modern worldview, Charismatic Catholicism acknowledges the existence of a supernatural cosmos that interferes in the everyday lives of people. And it provides its followers with the tools to handle it.

There are differences between modern Charismatic and traditional piety, however. In popular Catholic devotion, God the Father is experienced as an idle and distant figure, and people therefore seek refuge in wounds of the suffering Christ and in his mother Mary, or try to obtain a favor by making vows to the saints. In Charismatic Catholicism, the suffering Christ, the saints, and the local versions of Mary such as the Virgin of Guadalupe, Aparecida, or Suyapa disappear from the cult in favor of the attentive loving Father (sometimes even addressed with a familiar *Papito Dios* or *Diosito lindo*), the victorious Christ, and the empowering Holy Spirit. The Virgin – in a universal representation – is the only remaining holy being outside of the Trinity.

Whereas traditional Catholic piety tries to influence a distant Godhead through prayers and saintly intercession, Charismatic worship rather aims at equipping the believer to take part in a universal battle between God and Satan. The vivid and pulsating life in the public space – outside the Church, prayer group, and family – is the battlefield. There "the enemy" lies in wait, to lure with his snares in the form of alcohol, rousing rhythms and dances, gambling, and promiscuity.

The dangers of *la calle* (the street) are a recurrent theme among lay preachers. The street is traditionally the male domain, and men joining the Renewal will have to perform a more radical break with their customs and circle of acquaintances than women. But in the CCR they will be attached to a new masculine fellowship that supports them in a sober and family-friendly lifestyle. The prayers and the preaching change between the jubilant joy of having been drawn into the love of God and the worrisome anxiety of standing in the midst of the battle.

With few exceptions, the Charismatic movement is conservative, both theologically and morally. The movement is today characterized by a remarkable and highly accentuated loyalty to the Church's hierarchy as well as to the pope and the curia in Rome, and religious books and pamphlets by the CCR and Charismatic priests and leaders overflow with references to council decrees and to papal encyclicals and addresses in order deliberately to display catholicity of the movement. This is probably due to the suspicion with which the hierarchy met the CCR in the early years, and that still persists in some sectors of the Church.

On moral questions, the CCR backs the Church's teaching on same-sex relations and abortion, and the perceived horrors of both are frequent themes in Charismatic lay preaching. Family values are held in high regard, and homilies often deal with the challenges of raising children and partnership. Surprisingly, the Church's bans on divorce and artificial birth control are not as prominent themes as one could expect, bearing in mind that the proportion of women in CCR groups who are of reproductive ages and who live in relationships with a husband or cohabiter is high.

As mentioned in the introduction, the Charismatic movement is not confined to the CCR. Numerous independent Charismatic and semi-Charismatic groups have emerged, and Charismatic practices have permeated wider sectors of the Church. This may also be the reason for the uncertainty regarding the aggregate of Charismatic Catholics, as the number of Catholics occasionally adhering to Charismatic beliefs and practices is considerably higher than that of of core CCR-group participants. To comprehend the diversity of the Charismatic movement and to examine its influence on the whole of the Church, as attempted in the last section of this chapter, it is helpful to distinguish between what one might describe as *strong* and *soft* Charismatic elements.

The strong elements are the classic ecstatic Pentecostal elements such as Spirit baptism, speaking in tongues, and healing. These are practiced in prayer groups and in specific Charismatic events. Ordinary Catholics will normally not be exposed to them unless they seek out a Charismatic group or event.

The soft elements, on the other hand, are the enthusiastic elements such as vivid songs of praise with dance and shout (*alabanza*), the colloquial and fervent way of praying and preaching, and the use of personal testimonies, which now are not only found in the Charismatic groups but have also spread to large sectors of the Church. Catholics attaining an obligatory premarital or prebaptismal course, Bible study groups, a parish retreat, or even a Sunday mass will often encounter these elements and often no longer identify them as Charismatic, although they have gradually been diffusing from the CCR. Whereas the soft elements are perceived as uncontroversial by most, the strong can still cause a stir if introduced outside of Charismatic settings.

An example from my own fieldwork in Guatemala City describes that tension well. In August 2009, a parish council had arranged a one-day retreat in the parish hall. About 350 people attended. The program included songs of praise, lay preaching, prayers, group work, rosary, and what was supposed to be twenty minutes of adoration of the exposed sacrament. The style and content of praise, prayers, and preaching were soft Charismatic.

At the end of the retreat, however, the old parish priest brought the monstrance from the Church for adoration, and this situation resulted in a clash between two types of piety. The exposition of the sacrament is normally an act carried out in deep silence and solemnity where the prayers led by the parish priest are followed by long periods of silence and meditation, and so it began. But after fifteen minutes, one woman, a Charismatic, suddenly broke the silence with loud laments, and soon others followed. The lamentations were about an ongoing extortion of the parish school and about the general situation of poverty and violence. Another woman then began to prophesy with a strident voice. The parish priest was uncomfortable but paralyzed, and so the loud prayers and lamentations continued. Two of the young women in the choir fell into "rest in the Spirit," and one of them began speaking in tongues afterwards.

After an hour, in a short moment of relative calm, the priest managed to end the devotional act and get out of the assembly hall with the monstrance. After the retreat, parishioners were divided in their judgment of the incident. Some expressed great delight and told me that this was a true outpouring of the Spirit. Others were not that happy and expressed their discomfort about the lack of respect for the consecrated host. What complicated the situation was that strong Charismatic expressions were used in a traditional ritual where a special behavior is expected. For most Catholics, including many members of CCR groups, strong Charismatic expressions belong to certain occasions, namely the prayer meeting or the healing rallies, but not in the Church room or to traditional rituals such as the exposition of the sacrament.

In places with a strong Charismatic presence, Charismatic practice is permeating Catholic Church life. This does not happen because of a certain ecclesial strategy. Rather, it is due to the fact that individual Charismatic Catholics are often very active in the local parish, for example as catechists, Eucharistic ministers, and lectors, wherein they introduce soft Charismatic practices in wider circles. In the parish in Guatemala City where I conducted fieldwork, two-thirds of the volunteers in the Church belonged to a Charismatic prayer group. Catholic TV and radio stations are also most frequently operated by Charismatic Catholics, the best examples being *Rede Brasil Cristão* and *Redevida* in Brazil and – on a small scale – radio stations such as *Radio Estrella* in Guatemala.

After this description of the practices and beliefs of Charismatic Catholics, let us broaden the view and examine the influence of the movement on the whole of the Catholic Church in Latin America.

The CCR and the Continental Mission in Latin America

In May 2007 the Latin American bishops (Consejo Episcopal Latinoamericano – CELAM) held their Fifth General Conference in Aparecida, Brazil, where they launched a Great Continental Mission. The resulting final document of the conference is interesting for several reasons. First, it reveals how the bishops interpret contemporary Latin American societies and the situation of the Church. Second, it shows which pastoral landmarks the Church will steer by during the next decade. Third, it provides us with a good example of how the theological language of the Charismatic Renewal is gaining influence even at the top level of the Catholic Church in Latin America.

This chapter does not allow for a thorough analysis of the document and will thus mainly focus on the connection between the CCR and the Aparecida Document (*Documento de Aparecida* – DA). At a first glance, the DA seems somewhat inaccessible to a reader. It appears to be incomplete and lacking specific orientations, a patchwork of sometimes mutually contradictory voices, and a compromise between different factions. At the same time, it is a document characterized by a striking optimism and drive. According to CELAM president and Chilean archbishop Francisco Cardinal Errázuriz, the importance of DA lies rather in the overall direction given to the Church, which exposes a new orientation of the Church in Latin America around the concept and practice of "mission."[5]

Examining the bishops' analysis of contemporary Latin American societies and the situation of the Church, we can make some interesting observations. Earlier CELAM meetings spoke of the Catholic faith as the real substratum in Latin American culture and as "constitutive of its being and identity."[6] Aparecida is more modest and less essentialist in its description of the "gift of Catholic tradition" as a "foundation stone" and a "historical-cultural reality," which is "a reality abounding in sin – disregard for God," a gift that can be lost.[7] The analysis of reality uses the concept of globalization, which is understood primarily as having a negative influence on economy, environment, politics, and – above all – cultures in the Americas. The judgment of the increasingly pluralist, late-modern Latin American societies is ambivalent but has tendencies to cultural pessimism. This is especially the case when DA addresses the consequences of cultural change for individuals who according to the bishops fall prey of existential alienation and moral relativism:

> We are living through a change of epoch, the deepest level of which is cultural. The all-embracing conception of the human being, in relationship with the world and with God is vanishing... Today an overvaluing of individual subjectivity is very much to the fore. The freedom and dignity of the person are acknowledged, regardless of the form they take.[8]

---

5 Cardinal Francisco Javier Errázuriz Ossa, "Die Bedeutung des Dokuments von Aparecida für die zukünftige Arbeit der Kirche in Lateinamerika" *Zeitschrift für Missionswissenschaft und Religionswissenschaft*, 92, no. 1–2 (2008): 5-282008.
6 CELAM Documento Puebla, #412.
7 CELAM DA, #8; Verdugo 2008, 677–678.
8 CELAM DA, #44.

When addressing the situation of the youth, the DA resorts to sweeping generalizations with clear antimodernist traits:

> They grow up under the thrust of a pragmatic and narcissistic individualism, which arouses in them special imaginary worlds of freedom and equality... They likewise participate in the logic of life as spectacle, and regard the body as focal point of their present reality. They have a new addiction to sensations, and most of them grow up without regard for values and religious occasions.[9]

This analysis of life in partly secularized modern Latin America is shared within the CCR, and is a common position held among all conservative sectors of the Church.

To counter the cultural tendencies towards secularization and relativism, the bishops launch a "Great Continental Mission" and the DA declares the Church to be "in permanent mission." The aim is to transform all baptized Catholics into "disciples and missionaries" through a "personal encounter with Jesus Christ," which is explained as "a profound and intense religious experience ... that leads to a personal conversion and to a thorough change of life."[10] The bishops express the need of a new Pentecost and state that "with the fire of the Spirit we will inflame our Continent with love."[11] The DA urges the support of communities where the "encounter" can take place and mentions, apart from the Catholic family and the parish, especially the ecclesial movements and the small ecclesial communities.

Although the words used in the DA citations in the preceding paragraph are common in the Christian tradition, the frequency of the use of words such as "mission" (140 times), "Spirit" (149), "encounter with Jesus" (47), "conversion" (46), "experience" (44), "joy" (73), and "fire" (7) strikes a reader as uncommon within a Catholic context and as a possible sign of the influence of Pentecostal and Charismatic theology. Theological observers have made the same point. German-Brazilian liberation theologian Paulo Suess, for instance, is skeptical about what he polemically calls the document's "cheap manifestations of joy," in which he sees "a sign of the presence of the Charismatic movements in Aparecida," and he makes the ironic comment that the bishop's manifold use of the term "joy" (*alegría*) when describing the Latin American faith experience appears to be "an overheated compensation, bearing in mind that

---

9 CELAM DA, #51; Gerhard Kruip, "Neuaufbruch oder Regression? die Ergebnisse der lateinamerikanischen Bischofsversammlung in Aparecida (13.-31.5.2007) aus sozialethischer Sicht," *Zeitschrift für Missionswissenschaft und Religionswissenschaft*, 92, no. 1–2 (2008): 130.
10 CELAM DA #226.
11 CELAM DA: Final Message.

the word *cross* does not appear a single time [in the index]" as a theological category that encapsulates the harsh reality faced by most faithful. Brazilian João Libanio also wonders whether the insistence on *alegría* is a "postmodern, Charismatic touch" and a German accredited observer at the conference, Norbert Arntz, understands DA's focus on the Holy Spirit as a reaction to the growth of the Pentecostal-type Christianity in the region.[12] In the urge to form community it is striking that the DA has a strong focus on *ecclesial* community, whereas earlier CELAM conferences urged for community and collaboration in general. The question is whether the preceding observations can be taken as a sign of increased Charismatic influence in the Church.

Based on the fact that no official CCR delegate was invited to the conference, Edward Cleary argued that the CCR "is still the invisible giant" in the Latin American Church, and he claimed that none of the themes favored by the CCR were emphasized in the DA.[13] Whereas Cleary was right about the official role of the CCR during the Aparecida conference as being minimal, I think he misjudged the influence of the movement by describing it as "invisible." I believe that the influence of the CCR on the Church today is visible in language usage of the DA as exemplified previously. It might not be a direct influence, but rather a permeation of Charismatic language and theology, equivalent to the gradual spread of soft Charismatic practices portrayed in the former section. The missionary Church portrayed in DA has much in common with the Church ideal of the CCR. It is a Church that values experience and conversion in close-knit communities, prioritizes missionary activity by laymen, holds a countercultural value system, and expects high levels of engagement from parishioners.

The Continental Mission is aimed both at "the fallen away Catholics and ... those who know little or nothing about Jesus Christ," and the term itself shows that Latin America is no longer automatically perceived as the Catholic continent.[14] The DA urges every parish and community to enter "decidedly with all its might into the ongoing processes of missionary renewal and [to give up] outdated structures" and to pass from "pastoral ministry of mere conservation to a decidedly missionary pastoral ministry ..., making the

---

12 João Batista Libanio, "Conferencia de Aparecida. Documento final." *Revista Iberoamericana de Teología*, 6 (2008): 44; Norbert Arntz, "Einführung in Aufbau und Inhalt des Schlussdokuments der 5. Generalversammlung des Episkopats von Lateinamerika und der Karibik," *Zeitschrift für Missionswissenschaft und Religionswissenschaft*, 92 (2008): 56.
13 Edward L. Cleary, *How Latin America Saved the Soul of the Catholic Church* (New York: Paulist Press, 2009), 66.
14 CELAM DA, "Message."

Church visibly present as a mother who reaches out."[15] To do so, dioceses are supposed to develop detailed pastoral plans of action, and laypeople are explicitly supposed to participate in "discernment, decision making, planning and execution."[16] The expectations of the Church toward the baptized laity have thus been altered dramatically, and the practices of low-tension popular Catholicism is ... described by the DA as a

> ...faith reduced to mere baggage ..., to fragmented devotional practices, to selective and partial adherence to the truths of the faith, to occasional participation in some sacraments ..., that does not convert the life of the baptized [and] would not withstand the trials of time.[17]

The missionary zeal and engagement once only expected from priests and religious people has effectively been expanded toward all Catholics, dragging the pious, converted, and devoted into the midst of the Church and recasting the lukewarm baptized masses as objects of evangelization. What meets the pious outside the Church door, the people and popular culture, is no longer perceived as the cultural prolongation of the Catholic Church, but as a field of mission.

This role fits laity in the CCR well, and the reception of DA has been enthusiastic within the Renewal. The CCR has embraced the Continental Mission and is heavily engaged in its planning, both with an intense participation in national mission congresses called for in the DA and in the local dioceses and parishes. Representatives of the CCR from all Latin America countries met in Paraguay at the beginning of September 2010 to follow up on the Continental Mission in the different countries.

Within the CCR, there is an experience that the Church is finally following along the path long trodden by the movement. Charismatic priest and long-time accompanier of the Renewal in Guatemala F. Hugo Estrada explained to me, how the CCR had been talking about "disciples and missionaries" for decades, about the "personal encounter with Jesus, and about the necessity of organizing evangelization campaigns, e.g. dinners, retreats and door-to-door missions.[18]

Door-to-door mission, which is a characteristic of the Pentecostal churches, has been controversial within the Catholic Church, but was enthusiastically embraced by the CCR and other lay movements. Cleary describes how a

---

15 CELAM DA, #365; 370.
16 CELAM DA, #371.
17 CELAM DA, #12.
18 Interview F. Hugo Estrada, September 9, 2009.

Catholic door-to-door campaign in a parish in Guatemala City in 1989 proved successful in bringing converts to Evangelical churches back to Catholicism, but in the following years the Church was generally reluctant to use it.[19]

By the year 2009, door-to-door missions have become more frequent in Guatemalan parishes, and with the implementation of the Continental Mission it will probably be a common practice. This can create paradoxical situations because the street missionaries are often confused with Pentecostals or Jehovah's Witnesses. People inside the houses thus shout out through the window, "We are Catholics in this house; we're not interested," as two Charismatic informants laughingly told me about their experiences with door-to-door mission in Guatemala City in 2009.

Another effort is to *sanctify* popular religious traditions such as the massive processions during *Semana Santa* (Holy Week), which Charismatics both cherish for their abundance of traditional and folkloristic elements but at the same time frown upon for the supposed lack of genuine piety among the procession bearers and participants. The CCR in Guatemala takes efforts at offering Charismatic retreats to the *cucuruchos* (bearers) to ensure a "personal encounter with Jesus" and to prevent them from getting drunk in the subsequent celebrations. Elsewhere the CCR has become a vehicle in promoting pious celebrations of other popular religious traditions such as pilgrimages.

This leads to a last observation regarding, on the one hand, the relationship between Charismatic and otherwise awakened Catholics and, on the other hand, more traditional low-practicing Catholics. By promoting the renewalist language and practices, and by urging the need of personal conversion, the Church runs the risk of alienating common Church members who are reluctant to adopt the missionary expression of faith. When speaking with non-Charismatic and occasionally practicing Catholics, I was often met with statements such as: "Mucho aleluya ya en la iglesia" ("[Too] much hallelujah now in the Church").

The other side of the coin is that the missionary efforts by the Church might be dissociation by baptized Catholics who cannot identify themselves with the agenda of religious awakening. Along with secularization, it could be a contributing reason for the rise of the number of Latin Americans who identify themselves as having "no religion" or as being "a Catholic who doesn't

---

19 Edward L. Cleary, "Evangelicals and Competition in Guatemala." in *Conflict and Competition: The Latin American Church in a Changing Environment*, eds. Edward L. Cleary and Hannah W. Stewart-Gambino (Boulder, CO: Lynne Rienner Publications, 1992), 184. The reluctance to use the door-to-door method was described to me by sociologist and theologian Juan Carlos Nuñez S. J., interview March 2, 2005.

follow rules." The increased Catholic confessionalism that bears the mark of the Charismatic Renewal, and that is visible both in everyday parish practice and in Church documents such as *Aparecida*, can thus have a polarizing effect among the Latin American Catholics.

Conclusion

This chapter has aimed to give a comprehensive introduction to the phenomenon of Charismatic Catholicism in Latin America by briefly addressing its history and by investigating its main characteristics, beliefs, and practices and how they unfold within the context of the Catholic Church today. Furthermore, it has addressed the gradual spread of Charismatic language, beliefs, and practices into mainstream Catholicism. The outcome is an incipient Pentecostalization of Latin American Catholicism, which is visible both in everyday parish life and on a continental and Church-institutional level, such as in the concluding document of the Fifth General Conference of the Latin American bishops, the Aparecida Document (DA). The DA maps out the pastoral strategies of the future and priority areas of the Church and reveals a marked Charismatic influence. This is visible in the stress put on personal experience and conversion, the promotion of joyful close-knit prayer communities, a proactive missionary attitude, and a countercultural life style. In this process, Pentecostal and traditional Catholic elements are combined in varying ways while traditional, low-practicing, popular Catholicism is rejected.

The result is a reinvigorated Catholic Church and an increased Catholic confessionalism where the demarcation line between the Church and the surrounding society and popular culture is emphasized. The consequence is a stronger polarization between Church and popular culture, and between renewed, confessing, and mostly Charismatic Catholics and non-Charismatic low-tension cultural Catholics, who have become the target of intense missionary efforts by their brothers and sisters.

Bibliography and Suggested Readings

Arntz, Norbert. "Einführung in Aufbau und Inhalt des Schlussdokuments der 5. Generalversammlung des Episkopats von Lateinamerika und der Karibik." *Zeitschrift für Missionswissenschaft und Religionswissenschaft*, 92 (2008): 48–67.

Barrett, David B., and Todd M. Johnson. *World Christian Trends AD 30-AD 2200: Interpreting the Annual Christian Megacensus*. Pasadena, CA: William Carey Library, 2001.

Becka, Michelle. "'Globalisierung' im Schlussdokument von Aparecida." *Zeitschrift für Missionswissenschaft und Religionswissenschaft*, 92, no. 1–2 (2008): 195–118.

Cavendish, James C. "Christian Base Communities and the Building of Democracy: Brazil and Chile." *Sociology of Religion*, 55, no. 2 (1994): 179–195.

Chesnut, R. Andrew. *Competitive Spirits: Latin America's New Religious Economy*. New York: Oxford University Press, 2003.

Cleary, Edward L. "The Catholic Charismatic Renewal: Revitalization Movements and Conversion." In Timothy J. Steigenga and Edward L. Cleary, *Conversion of a Continent: Contemporary Religious Change in Latin America*, 153–173. New Brunswick, NJ: Rutgers University Press, 2007.

"Evangelicals and Competition in Guatemala." In Edward L. Cleary and Hannah W. Stewart-Gambino (eds.), *Conflict and Competition: The Latin American Church in a Changing Environment*, 167–196. Boulder, CO: Lynne Rienner, 1992.

How Latin America Saved the Soul of the Catholic Church. New York: Paulist Press, 2009.

Codina, Víctor. "Eclesiología de Aparecida." *Revista Iberoamericana de Teología*, 6 (2008): 69–85.

Errázuriz Ossa, Francisco Javier Cardinal. "Die Bedeutung des Dokuments von Aparecida für die zukünftige Arbeit der Kirche in Lateinamerika." *Zeitschrift für Missionswissenschaft und Religionswissenschaft*, 92, no. 1–2 (2008): 5–28.

Gooren, Henri. "The Catholic Charismatic Renewal in Latin America." Walter Sullivan Lecture given at Virginia Commonwealth University, Richmond VA. October 13, 2010.

Hagopian, Frances. "Introduction." In Frances Hagopian (ed.), *Religious Pluralism, Democracy, and the Catholic Church in Latin America*, 1–64. Notre Dame, IN: University of Notre Dame Press, 2009.

Hollenweger, Walter. *Pentecostalism: Origins and Developments Worldwide*. Peabody, MA: Hendrickson, 1997.

Kruip, Gerhard. "Neuaufbruch oder Regression? die Ergebnisse der lateinamerikanischen Bischofsversammlung in Aparecida (13.-31.5.2007) aus sozialethischer Sicht." *Zeitschrift für Missionswissenschaft und Religionswissenschaft*, 92, no. 1–2 (2008): 119–132.

Libanio, Joao Batista. "Conferencia de Aparecida. Documento final." *Revista Iberoamericana de Teología*, 6 (2008): 23–45.

Oliveira, P. et al. *Renovação Carismática Católica: Uma Analise Sociológica, Interpretações Teológicas*, Petropolis: Vozes, 1978.

O'Neill, Kevin Lewis. "I Want More of You: The Politics of Christian Eroticism in Postwar Guatemala." *Comparative Studies in Society and History*, 52, no. 131 (2010): 131–156.

Ospina Martínez, María Angélica. "Satanás se 'desregula': sobre la paradoja del fundamentalismo moderno en la renovación carismática católica." *Universitas Humanística*, 61 (2006): 135–162.

Parker Gumuchio, Cristian. "Education and Increasing Religious Pluralism." In Francis Hagopian (ed.), *Religious Pluralism, Democracy, and the Catholic Church in Latin America*, 131–181.Notre Dame, IN: University of Notre Dame Press, 2009.

The Pew Forum on Religion & Public Life. *Spirit and Power: A 10-Country Survey of Pentecostals*. Washington, DC: Pew Research Center, 2006.

Suess, P. "Die missionarische Synthese nach Aparecida." *Zeitschrift für Missionswissenschaft und Religionswissenschaft*, 92 no. 1–2 (2008): 68–83.

De Theije, Marjo. "CEBs and Catholic Charismatics in Brazil." In Christian Smith and Joshua Prokopy (eds.), *Latin American Religion in Motion*, 108–121. New York: Routledge, 1999.

De Theije Marjo, and Mariz Cecilia L. "Localizing and Globalizing Processes in Brazilian Catholicism: Comparing Inculturation in Liberationist and Charismatic Catholic Cultures." *Latin American Research Review*, 43, no. 1 (2008): 33–54.

Várgues Pasos, Luis A. "Construyendo y reconstruyendo las fronteras de la tradición y la modernidad. La iglesia Católica y el movimiento de Renovación Carismática en el Espíritu Santo." *Convergencia*, 15, no. 46 (2008): 195–224.

Verdugo, Fernando. "Aparecida: perspectiva teológico-cultural." *Teología y Vida*, 49 (2008): 673–684.

31

Contemporary Popular Catholicism in Latin America

JENNIFER SCHEPER HUGHES

In theory Roman Catholicism is an exclusive religion, its boundaries and borders carefully controlled and regulated by ecclesiastical guardians of the tradition. However, on the ground and in practice Catholicism has proven surprisingly expansive, inclusive, and adaptive. It is, in fact, stunningly pliant: in the hands of adept practitioners the religion manifests a tremendous capacity to accommodate local cultural and social realities. The resulting culturally specific practices are often encompassed by the term "popular Catholicism" although other terms have been applied. In the past, scholars have thought about these practices as "folk Catholicism." More recently, the terms "lived," "local," and "vernacular" have been preferred to describe religious belief and practice accurately and with respect.

These terms refer to a range of devotional activities and beliefs that constitute the daily religious practices of ordinary lay Catholics. The lived practice of Catholicism includes, for example, local collective celebrations of Jesus, Mary, and the saints through the observance of an annual cycle of religious festivals, public processions, and pilgrimage to shrines and other holy sites. Devotional engagement with sculpted or painted religious images in daily domestic rituals and ritual healing and intercessory prayer and petition are also common, as are innovated practices that may appear to depart significantly from "traditional" Catholic norms. One finds these practices almost worldwide, wherever Catholicism has shaped religious culture. The practice of Latin American Catholicism is distinguished by the particularity of its historical origins, by its specific votive practices, and by the way in which it intersects with the political sphere. With respect to the use of the term "popular" ("*lo popular*" in Spanish) this also has a particular valence within the Latin American context.[1]

---

[1] Nestor Canclini, "¿De qué estamos hablando cuando hablamos de lo popular?" Culturales pouplares e indígenas. Diálogos en la acción. 2004. http://correo3.perio.unlp.edu.ar/catedras/system/files/garcia_canclini_-_de_que_estamos_hablando_cuando_hablamos_de_lo_popular.pdf (Accessed November 7, 2014).

Cultural-Historical Legacies

Although popular Catholicism is a global phenomenon, it is not in fact singular or homogeneous. Rather, the term encompasses a diversity and myriad of culturally specific local practices, of "catholicisms" in the plural. The religious specificity of popular Catholicism in Latin America arises from its cultural-historical origins. It began as a colonial religion, born in the context of sixteenth-century European global expansion, the product of an imperial exercise in which European conquerors imposed their religion on subjugated indigenous, African, and eventually *"mestizo"* and *"casta"* (or "mixed raced") populations. European Catholic missionaries arrived in the New World on the heels of the military conquest. As emissaries of the Church and missionaries to the indigenous peoples, they desired to shape New World Christendom modeled after a monastic (specifically, Franciscan) version of European Catholicism. They were visionaries, idealists, and utopians who imagined their ministry to the "Indians" of the New World as a "spiritual conquest." The missionary friars employed a panoply of methods in their efforts to evangelize including extirpation (the destruction of indigenous religions), debate, catechesis, physical discipline, preaching, and exhortation. They labored intensively to communicate their love for Christ, the Virgin, and the saints to the recently converted population. The friars also sought to instill in indigenous people a confessional consciousness and penitential practice such as that which anchored and sustained their own spirituality. The local Catholic religion of ordinary Spanish colonials who arrived in the New World as laborers, craftsmen, fortune-seekers, and small business entrepreneurs also shaped Latin American practice.[2] They brought with them regional devotional practices, for example the collective, ritual celebration of specific manifestations of the Virgin Mary and a belief in the power of religious objects to protect, heal, and otherwise communicate the potency of the sacred.

For their part, indigenous communities greatly grieved the destruction of their religions – their sacred texts, their imaged gods, their public rites. They and their descendants were faced with the challenge of making an imposed religion, the religion of their invaders, authentic and meaningful. That is, they had to engage in the substantive work of making Christianity a usable religion in spite of the ways in which it had functioned as an apparatus of colonial rule. Through a process of deliberation and discernment they accepted some

---

[2] William A. Christian, *Local Religion in Sixteenth-century Spain* (Princeton, NJ: Princeton University Press, 1989).

elements of the new Christian religion, especially celebration of images; statues; and paintings of Mary, Jesus, and the saints, as holy, good, and powerful. Other elements were rejected as problematic or simply irrelevant. In particular, indigenous Christians resisted the claims of European priests to exclusive power to legislate Catholic belief and practice and, instead, cultivated and refined local structures and institutions through which they could exert some degree of control over the organization of collective religious life. These local organizations, the religious brotherhoods known as *mayordomías* or *cofradías* in Spanish, continue to structure lay religious practice across the continent today, often independently of or even in tension with parish priests and bishops.

The contemporary practice of Catholicism in Latin America still bears the marks (the wounds, or scars, one could say) of its colonial heritage. At the same time, popular Catholicism as it is practiced today is the product of a painstaking process of recovery, reinvention, appropriation, and meaning-making through which descendants of diverse racial and ethnic colonial populations preserved and maintained a sense of spiritual coherence and community integrity. That is to say, the practices that we understand as "popular Catholicism" are the outcome of this cultural labor. Sometimes this has meant that Latin American Catholicism has drawn on or preserved indigenous or African cultural traditions, incorporating them into new hybrid expressions. So, for example, in the Andes the Virgin Mary sometimes resembles the *Pachamama* the indigenous mother goddess. Andean painted works show Mary figured as a great mountain mother. Among the Maya of Guatemala Jesus is celebrated alongside the Maya god, Mam in his new post-colonial manifestation as Máximon. Today, during Holy Week effigies of each deity (one of Jesus and the other of Máximon) lie in state together, side-by-side, as brothers.[3] Among some Brazilians an African slave women known as Anastácia is revered as a saint and honored alongside more traditional Catholic icons.[4]

Latin American Votive Culture

Like many expressions of popular Catholicism globally, Latin American Catholicism as it is lived in practice across the continent is a votive religion. Votive cultures are anchored in a particular set of material practices in which

---

[3] Vincent Stanzione, *Rituals of Sacrifice: Walking the Face of the Earth on the Sacred Path of the Sun* (Albuquerque: University of New Mexico Press, 2003).

[4] John Burdick, *Blessed Anastacia: Women, Race, and Popular Christianity in Brazil* (London: Routledge, 1998).

objects and ritual actions are offered or consecrated in fulfillment of a vow, or *por promesa* or *manda* in Spanish. In Latin America, votive objects most commonly include incense (*copal*), candles, flowers, photographs of loved ones, and the small metal tokens in the shape of body parts known as *milagros* or *ex-votos*. *Milagros* are simultaneously tokens of gratitude and expressions of faith, diminutive and delicate anchors that secure and seal the relational dimension of religious devotion. Food and alcohol for feeding the spirits are offered particularly in rituals honoring the dead such as in the *Día de Muertos* and in African cultural articulations of Catholicism in Brazil and the Caribbean.[5] When the infant Jesus is the subject of devotion, offered objects may include toys, balloons, candies, and other gifts suitable for a young child. Votive objects are typically presented at shrines, churches, or on home altars. In each of these settings, the altar is the primary ritual location of votive action.

Latin American votive culture is strongly evident in contemporary devotion to the region's most famous patron: the Virgin of Guadalupe, the Mexican apparition of the Virgin Mary. Guadalupe is the *Mater Mexicana*: the point of origin for Mexican Catholic faith. Now with a worldwide following, one might rightly conceive of her as Latin America's greatest religious export. According to centuries of belief, the Virgin Mary, calling herself Guadalupe, appeared to the indigenous convert to Christianity, Juan Diego, at Tepeyac Hill, the site of a previous devotion to an Aztec Goddess, Tonantzín. By way of a miracle Guadalupe imprinted her image (her likeness) on Juan Diego's *tilma*, a piece of native clothing resembling a cloak. Today, Juan Diego's *"tilma"* is housed at the basilica in Mexico City that serves as a national shrine in Guadalupe's honor.

Every year some 20 million pilgrims visit Tepeyac to pay homage to the Virgin. Many visitors manifest their devotion by making a rigorous pilgrimage of several days by foot or bicycle. Sometimes the pilgrimage is made *por promesa*, in fulfillment of a special petition or in gratitude for an extraordinary (especially lifesaving) intervention: the safe delivery of a child after a difficult pregnancy or an exceptional recovery from a grave illness. Often, a neighborhood or pueblo organizes a collective annual pilgrimage to the Guadalupe shrine that may be attended by anywhere from several dozen to several thousand people.[6] In this instance, the votive act of pilgrimage is related less to a particular event than it is to a sustained practice through which the community itself is solidified and consecrated.

---

5 Stanley Brandes, *Skulls to the Living, Bread to the Dead: The Day of the Dead in Mexico and Beyond* (Hoboken, NJ: Wiley Blackwell, 2007).
6 Elaine Peña, *Performing Piety: Making Space Sacred with the Virgin of Guadalupe* (Berkeley: University of California Press, 2011).

On these pilgrimages, devotees sometimes carry votive objects on their backs as they make the sojourn, including statues or printed images of the Virgin herself. These can be quite large and burdensome, and are adorned with photographs, flowers, streamers, and so forth.[7] Once they arrive at the shrine, these offered objects are presented to priests who bless them with holy water: their power and potency revitalized by the blessing and through contact with the original image at the shrine. At the conclusion of the journey the images are returned to home altars where they are able to protect and watch over family members until the following year when they are again renewed. The act of pilgrimage sustains the individual and collective relationship with the sacred; builds moral, physical, and spiritual stamina; and solidifies the religious standing of the pilgrim in their community of origin.

In the votive religious imaginary, a constellation of objects are engaged within a ritual matrix that binds human beings to one another and to the sacred. That is to say, votive religion in Latin America is fundamentally relational and affective in nature. Some observers have focused on the obligatory nature of the *promesa* or have understood the offered object as propitiation, as an exchange intended to appease a distant god. In fact, the *promesa* or *manda* is not so much a sacred bargain as it is an expression of plenitude. One practitioner of indigenous (Nahua) Mexican origin explains, "The *manda* is not an obligation. It is feeling the Spirit inside you. You are thinking of someone. It fills you with the desire to weep." The devotee is moved by this emotion to a devotional practice that expresses faith. Votive culture is sensorial, affective, and aesthetic. The devotee is neither submissive nor subservient to the divine personage; rather, they are co-equal agents who engage in mutual care. Votive acts within this frame are about both tending to and keeping company with the sacred.

In the domestic sphere, daily acts of devotion maintain a relationship with particular household saints. A particular sort of doting care for images of the saints recognizes and maintains their complex status as both material objects and living entities in a way that is uniquely Latin American. That is, in Latin America the sacred image is often not just comprehended as a symbolic representation of Jesus, Mary, or the saints, but is also engaged as an agentic, animate being: a fully materialized spirit. The complex and analogical relationship between spirit and matter in Latin American Catholicism is often quite difficult for outside observers to comprehend.

---

7 Jennifer Scheper Hughes, *Biography of a Mexican Crucifix: Lived Religion and Local Faith from the Conquest to the Present* (New York: Oxford University Press, 2010).

The "Popular" in Popular Catholicism

There was a time when we thought of popular religion as autonomous from and in opposition to ecclesial religion. We now understand better how popular expressions of Catholicism function in relationship to more formal institutional structures and ecclesial authorities, how the religion of the margins relates to the religion of the center. In fact, in some contexts it is not possible to distinguish between popular religion and ecclesial religion. For example, priests may share in the local beliefs and practices of their parishioners, just as parishioners may incorporate traditional rites into their daily lives. We see this, for example, when priests lend their support to the celebration of locally significant patron saints or affirm local experiences of the miraculous. Also, community rituals and celebrations designed and organized completely by laypeople are often felt to be incomplete without the presence and benediction of clergy. From the perspective of many ordinary Catholics, theirs is a seamless experience of faith that they feel to be in strong accord with the full arc of Christian history – not separate from it.

Nonetheless, in demographic terms alone, Catholicism in Latin America became incarnate in the large, impoverished, racially complex, subject, and politically marginalized population that the Church itself helped create through the long colonial period. When we speak of "popular Catholicism" in Latin America we are most often speaking of the religion of the *classes populares*, the popular classes: the religion of the poor. The practice of popular religion is fundamentally about access to the sacred for the large masses of disenfranchised Latin Americans. Mass-produced plaster images of Mary and inexpensive color prints of Jesus for sale in every local market; the most common and inexpensive flowers; the ubiquitous roadside shrine in slum, favela, shantytown: the instruments of devotion are readily available. Mary, in particular, makes herself accessible to her faithful. Never stinting, she appears in the most common places: a kernel of corn, a tortilla, an oil spill in a subway station.

The Catholic faith and practice of the *classes populares* has, periodically in the history of Latin America, come into conflict both with state authorities and with the Church hierarchy. This was the case, for example, at the turn of the twentieth century when the Brazilian government, with the tacit consent of the Brazilian Church, launched a series of violent and ultimately deadly military campaigns against the utopian, millenarian Catholic community of impoverished, landless peasants and recently freed slaves known as Canudos.[8]

---

8 Robert Levine, *Vale of Tears: Revisiting the Canudos Massacre* (Berkeley: University of California, 1995).

The faith, devotion, and hopes of "popular" Catholics have often been perceived as unpredictable, dangerous, and even subversive by the magisterium as by the nation state. But again, at other key junctures the aims of the state appear to align neatly with popular practice, such as when Miguel Hidalgo, the hero of Mexican independence, emblazoned the Virgin of Guadalupe on his banner and (essentially) made war in her name. Miguel Hidalgo's banner has come to stand as a symbol of Mexican independence and nationhood, not least of all in the Mexican diaspora.

Particularly since the Second Vatican Council (1962–1965), theological resources have become accessible within the church that allow for a more conciliatory attitude toward the faith and practice of lay Catholics. Drawing on Vatican II's theological formulation of the "Church as the people of God," intellectual movements emerging from the Latin American context sought to ground theological reflection in the experience and realities of the *base*, the grassroots. In Brazil, liberation theologians devised a *pé-no-chão* theology: theology with its "feet on the ground."[9] More recently theological movements emerging from the Latino context have been seeking to interpret the popular religion of poor Catholics as the *sensus fidelium*, the faith of the people. Latino theologians in particular have sought to articulate the theological legitimacy of popular piety: Orlando Espín explains that popular engagement with (for example) the crucifixion of Jesus is not inconsistent with canonical theology. That is to say, in this particular example, we observe evidence of a theological rapprochement between the Church magisterium and the popular practice of the disenfranchised poor.

For the most part the term "popular Catholicism" is not meant to connect religious practice to popular culture, in the sense of relating to the mainstream of Western culture such as through the mass media. However, there are occasions when lived and local expressions of Latin American Catholicism do engage popular culture. In the Guatemalan highlands, dedicated groups of traditional Maya women don elaborate costumes of Xena, the warrior princess, and other powerful American female superheroes to participate in Holy Week processions.[10] Similarly, the worst villains of late twentieth-century Hollywood cinema play the role of devils in Holy Week pageants in Ayacucho, Peru (and elsewhere): with ritual actors dressed as Darth Vader, the Alien, and Predator.

9 Clodovis Boff, *Teologia pé-no-chão* (Petrópolis: Vozes, 1978).
10 Rhonda Taube, "Manufacturing Identities: Masking in Postwar Highland Guatemala," *Latin American Perspectives* 39:2, 2011: 61–81.

The Politics of Popular Catholicism

Popular Catholicism in Latin America frequently intersects with the political sphere, although it is neither inherently conservative nor inherently liberating in its political ethos: it can be affiliated with either agenda or with none at all. In Nicaragua in the 1970s, for example, the Liberation Theology that emerged after the gathering of bishops at Medellín, Colombia in 1968 had strong resonances with popular religion. That is, devotion to saints and a theology of sacrifice and martyrdom folded neatly into the Sandinista revolutionary sensibility.[11] In some sense, Liberation Theology itself can be regarded as a culturally and historically specific expression of popular Catholicism.

The intersection of politics and popular religion is evident in the dual canonization processes for the liberationist bishop of El Salvador, Óscar Arnulfo Romero. Romero spoke out strongly against the state-sponsored military violence of the Salvadoran government and on behalf of tens of thousands of Salvadorans who were "disappeared." He was assassinated by government-sanctioned death squads in March of 1980 while celebrating a small, private memorial mass. While the official process for canonization stalled under Popes John Paul II and Benedict XVI (and now seems to be moving forward again under Francis I), for millions of Salvadoran believers today the beloved martyred archbishop is already celebrated as San Óscar, Saint Óscar Romero.

Salvadorans have insisted on honoring the deceased archbishop's memory even in the face of considerable personal risk. An estimated 100,000 people attended the funeral mass when bombs and sniper fire interrupted the ceremony and resulted in the deaths of as many as forty people. Five years later, in 1985, thousands attended a memorial celebration, again in the face of considerable threat of by the Salvadoran army. Today Romero's body is entombed in the basement crypt in the cathedral in San Salvador. More than thirty years after his death, every Sunday morning a liberationist mass takes place in the cathedral basement. The faithful gather around the bishop's interred remains to celebrate the persistence of Romero's radical, liberationist vision. The convent where Romero resided during his episcopacy and the chapel where he was celebrating mass when he was assassinated are today pilgrimage sites, drawing visitors from throughout El Salvador and abroad who come to pay homage. These popular devotions reflect an insistence on remembering not

---

11 Rodger Nelson Lancaster, *Thanks to God and the Revolution: Popular Religion and Class Consciousness in the New Nicaragua* (New York: Columbia University Press, 1988).

only the violent death of the beloved saint but also the violence suffered by the entire country at the hands of the Salvadoran army.

Pope John Paul II was anxious precisely because of the political legacy embodied in these popular celebrations. Although he insisted that Romero was indeed a martyr, the pope expressed a strong desire to wait for a "new generation of Salvadorans" before pursuing canonization. He advised a sort of twenty-five-year cooling off period for things to settle down in El Salvador, in essence for people to forget their national trauma so that the canonization of Romero would not have explicitly political implications. The case of the popular (one could say de facto) canonization of Romero is an instance in which popular religious sensibilities cohere with and articulate a radical theological and political imaginary.

Yet, at other moments, the relationship of popular piety to politics has been more ambiguous, or has been affiliated with a conservative political agenda. In the impoverished backlands of northeast Brazil, the much beloved folk saint Frai Damião was celebrated as a mystic and magician. In the late 1980s, on the eve of Brazil's first democratic elections after decades of military dictatorship, the aged, diminutive saint wearing the rough brown robes of his Franciscan order, arrived in rural communities in the state of Pernambuco on the back of a new, very large and shiny red pickup truck. Crowds rushed to greet him and followed him into town in an impromptu welcome procession. While the liberationist Christian Base Communities mobilized behind the Worker's Party Candidate, Lula da Silva, Frai Damião appeared in regional newspapers in the embrace of his financial sponsor: Collar de Mello, the archconservative candidate. Poor Brazilians in the region found themselves simultaneously drawn to Damião's mystical spiritual power and to Lula's political charisma and vision.

Popular religion also has a historical affiliation with conservative politics in Chiapas, where the rotating practice of *costumbre*, a system of obligatory religious service organized around celebration of the saints, mired indigenous communities in a cycle of debt and dependence on *latifundistas* from which there appeared to be no escape. The liberationist indigenous deacons program spearheaded by the bishop Samuel Ruiz persuaded Maya couples to abandon the rotating practice of *costumbre* (the cargo) and to reject participation in the popular Catholic festival cycle. Instead, they were to take up reading the Bible and work as catechists.[12] In freeing communities from the cargo and from the burdensome labor of popular Catholicism the indigenous

---

12 Ruth Chojnacki, *Indigenous Apostles: Maya Catholic Catechists Working the Word in Highland Chiapas* (Amsterdam: Rodopi, 2012).

deacons program paved the way for the Zapatista rebellion. Finally, we note that today certain popular Catholic celebrations are associated with Opus Dei.

The seeming unpredictability of the political implications of popular religious practice frequently produces skepticism on the part of the left, including leftist priests and theologians, who historically worried that popular religion is the "opiate of the masses" and sought to liberate the poor from their religious observances. As explored in the preceding text on the violent repression of the Canudos movement, Latin American governments have often had a similarly anxious and apprehensive relationship to popular Catholic practice, which they regard as volatile and even dangerous to the stability of the state. The shifting political affiliations and purposes of popular Catholicism in Latin America are not always understandable to outsiders or to state authorities.

Conclusions

Contemporary popular Catholicism bears the affective and material traces of its colonial origins; among these is its sometimes ambivalent relationship to ecclesial structures and traditions. For some critics, this ambivalence marks popular practice as somehow outside the parameters of the Catholic tradition, or even outside of Christianity. It is not the task of the scholar, however, to weigh one practice as more or less authentic or authoritative to the tradition than the next. Rather, each culturally specific practice must be encountered, interpreted, and analyzed on its own terms as we seek to understand the internal coherence and referents of each religious cultural system.

Bibliography and Suggested Readings

Boff, Clodovis, *Teologia pé-no-chão*. Petrópolis: Vozes, 1978.

Brandes, Stanley. *Skulls to the Living, Bread to the Dead: The Day of the Dead in Mexico and Beyond*. Hoboken, NJ: Wiley Blackwell, 2007.

Burdick, John. *Blessed Anastacia: Women, Race, and Popular Christianity in Brazil*. London: Routledge, 1998.

Canclini, Nestor. "¿De qué estamos hablando cuando hablamos de lo popular?" Culturales pouplares e indígenas. Diálogos en la acción. 2004 http://correo3.perio.unlp.edu.ar/catedras/system/files/garcia_canclini_-_de_que_estamos_hablando_cuando_hablamos_de_lo_popular.pdf (Accessed November 7, 2014).

Chojnacki, Ruth. *Indigenous Apostles: Maya Catholic Catechists Working the Word in Highland Chiapas*. Amsterdam: Rodopi, 2012.

Christian, William A. *Local Religion in Sixteenth-century Spain*. Princeton, NJ: Princeton University Press, 1989.

Espin, Orlando. *The Faith of the People: Theological Reflections on Popular Catholicism.* Maryknoll, NY: Orbis Press, 1997.

Gebara, Ivone, and Maria Clara Bingemer. *Mary, Mother of God, Mother of the Poor.* Maryknoll, NY: Orbis Press, 1989.

Graziano, Frank. *The Millennial New World.* New York: Oxford University Press, 1999.

Hughes, Jennifer Scheper. *Biography of a Mexican Crucifix: Lived Religion and Local Faith from the Conquest to the Present.* New York: Oxford University Press, 2010.

——— "God-bearers on Pilgrimage to Tepeyac: A scholar of Religion Encounters the Material Dimension of Marian Devotion in Mexico," *Journal of Religion and the Arts,* 18 (2014): 156–183.

Lancaster, Rodger Nelson. *Thanks to God and the Revolution: Popular Religion and Class Consciousness in the New Nicaragua.* New York: Columbia University Press, 1988.

Levine, Robert. *Vale of Tears: Revisiting the Canudos Massacre.* Berkeley: University of California, 1995.

Peña, Elaine *Performing Piety: Making Space Sacred with the Virgin of Guadalupe.* Berkeley: University of California Press, 2011.

Schmidt, Jalane. *Cachita's Streets: The Virgin of Charity, Race and Revolution in Cuba.* Durham, NC: Duke University Press, 2015.

Stanzione, Vincent. *Rituals of Sacrifice: Walking the Face of the Earth on the Sacred Path of the Sun.* Albuquerque: University of New Mexico Press, 2003.

Taube, Rhonda. "Manufacturing Identities: Masking in Postwar Highland Guatemala." *Latin American Perspectives,* 39, no. 2 (2011): 61–81.

Turner, Victor, and Edith Turner. *Image and Pilgrimage in Christian Culture.* New York: Columbia University Press (reprint edition), 1995.

32

Catholicism and Political Parties in Modern Latin America

MICHAEL FLEET

Political parties have played visible and occasionally dominant roles in Latin America in the modern era. As national legislatures emerged as sources of restraint on once all-powerful executives, their members formed political blocs to coordinate legislative efforts and later to connect with social forces whose interests they presumed to represent. As they did, institutional actors such as the Catholic Church, which were previously dependent on a ruler's deference or a good word from their "friends" at court, acquired additional advocates to whom they could turn.

Parties quickly emerged as significant political actors in roughly half of Latin America's newly independent countries. They would remain significant actors in almost as many countries during most of the twentieth century as well. This changed, however, with the onset of military regimes in the 1960s and 1970s, and in the subsequent decades once the military returned to the barracks. Where parties played important roles in the political process, Church authorities developed ties with those willing to support them on certain matters. Where parties did not, or could not, play important roles, the Church sought assurances or concessions from autocratic rulers or fell back on its own, not inconsiderable, resources.

Relations between the Catholic Church and political parties in Latin America in the late twentieth century can be best understood if placed in historical context. In what follows, four phases of post-independence political life are distinguished: (1) the nineteenth century, (2) the modern era (late nineteenth to mid-twentieth century), (3) a period of military rule from the 1960s to the 1980s, and (4) the late twentieth and early twenty first centuries. In each period, emphasis will be placed on changing social and political contexts, their effect on political parties, and the response of Church authorities.

The Nineteenth Century

During the colonial period, the Latin American Church was an instrument of the Spanish and Portuguese Crowns and was an integral but dependent part of colonial government. Most bishops stood by the Crown during the wars of independence, and many clerics were expelled by the incoming governments. When Rome initially refused to recognize the new governments or to appoint new bishops, it left the Latin American Church short-handed at a critical juncture.

The remaining bishops adjusted as best they could to their new circumstances. They looked to conservative elites or emerging *caudillos* for help in resisting challenges to their privileged status and their various public functions, such as control of education; administration of cemeteries; and serving as the official registries for births, marriages, and deaths. In roughly half the newly independent countries, political forces divided into Liberal and Conservative parties. Disagreements between them resulted in violent and sustained clashes in some cases and in moderate reforms acceptable to both sides in many others. In most instances, Liberal reformers prevailed, and the Church lost some, though rarely all, of its prerogatives and public stature.

In this initial period, the Church found itself weaker socially and politically in all but two countries: Colombia and Peru, where the Church alliance with Conservatives was particularly strong. Elsewhere, its options were limited. In most cases it retreated inward, to put its own house in order and to focus on its religious mission in areas such as organizing worship and devotions, providing education, and encouraging good works and the pursuit of personal salvation.

Modern Latin America from 1880 to the 1970s

The second phase of the post-independence period was marked by the onset of industrialization, the emergence of labor movements, the modernization and export orientation of agricultural economies, the appearance of populist movements, and the creation of left and left-of-center parties. During these years, political parties in most Latin American countries were neither strong nor cohesive. Military elites intervened regularly and held power for lengthy periods, preventing parties from functioning openly or developing fully. In most instances, the Church was left to deal with the regime of the day, occasionally bringing up its excesses and squeezing from it what concessions it could in support of its own spiritual mission. In other cases, it had more options from which to choose.

In fact, one can distinguish four distinct political contexts during the period: (1) oligarchic democracies in which popular social forces were contained and/or accommodated by Conservative or Liberal elites (Uruguay before the late 1940s and Colombia before 1956); (2) enduring military or single-party regimes (Argentina, Mexico, Bolivia, the Dominican Republic, the Central American republics except Costa Rica, Panama, Paraguay, Haiti, and Cuba); (3) military regimes that began liberalizing between the 1940s and the 1960s (Brazil, Peru, Ecuador, and Venezuela); and (4) longer standing liberal democracies (Chile, Costa Rica, Uruguay beginning in the late 1940s, and Colombia after 1956).

Oligarchic Democracies

In both Colombia and Uruguay, the Church retained a close relationship with Conservative parties into the new century as Liberals sought to bring it under state control and to strip it of its privileges. They failed in their efforts in Colombia but succeeded roundly in Uruguay. In Colombia in the mid-1880s, the national government reversed anticlerical reforms introduced earlier by Liberal governments but matters were hardly resolved. Church–state issues remained contentious and served as a basis for political and military confrontations between Liberal and Conservative forces for the next seventy years, particularly in rural areas. These culminated in a thirty-year civil war known as *la violencia* that took the lives of more than 200,000 people, many of them peasant conscripts. A resolution of differences came with a military coup in 1954 and the subsequent negotiation of a power-sharing system under which Liberal and Conservative governments would alternately succeed one another. The arrangement preserved Conservatives from a decline they otherwise would have suffered, and it forestalled the emergence of a more liberal (Christian Democratic) expression of Catholicism in Colombia.

In Uruguay, liberals of the Colorado Party emerged victorious in the church–state conflict. At the outset of the twentieth century, they carried out a radical program of secularization to which the much weaker, pro-Church National Party offered only token opposition. This led the Church to launch a new Catholic party, the Civic Union, from which a Christian Democratic party would later emerge, at first on its own and then as a founding member of the left-wing Broad Front alliance that came to power in 2004. For the better part of the twentieth century, however, Uruguayan politics were dominated by the more or less liberal Colorados with occasional interludes of conservative National Party rule.

Enduring Authoritarian Regimes

In Argentina, despite the absence of a strong conservative party at the national level, church–state issues were resolved favorably for the Church by 1890, and parties moved on to questions involving the country's political structure and economic policy. One of the effects of the agro-export boom that occurred between 1880 and 1914 was that a new secular party, the Radical Civic Union, captured the presidency in 1916 and began moving the country in a more democratic direction. Economic decline and alarm at the support the party enjoyed among urban workers prevented it from completing this move and brought the military to power in 1930, a development applauded by Church leaders who viewed the military as their only defense from further attack.

However, then-army colonel Juan Domingo Perón (with the help of his glamorous wife Eva Duarte de Perón) used his post as labor minister to win over those same workers, capture the presidency in the 1946 election, and win reelection in 1951, and the Church again found its interests in peril. Some bishops thought highly of Perón, although not of his wife; and others worried about his fiery and unpredictable temperament. In the end, Perón was ousted from power in 1955 in a coup in which the bishops played an important supporting role. However, in the unsettled politics that followed, the bishops found themselves again without congenial or stable partners, and again the military stepped into the political vacuum.

In Mexico, the Church lost its status and privileges during the reforms of President Benito Juárez in the 1850s and 1860s and then unexpectedly recovered them under the "Liberal" dictator Porfirio Díaz, who came to power in 1876. However, when Díaz resigned from office at the start of the Mexican Revolution that began in 1910, the Church became a scapegoat for his regime's crimes and excesses. For the next thirty years, the Church was the object of government abuse and persecution, but during the 1940s and 1950s, hostilities between church and state abated.

After the Revolution, Mexico was governed for the rest of the twentieth century by a single party, best known by its post-1946 name, the Institutional Revolutionary Party (Partido Revolucionario Institucional – PRI). The party turned its attention to economic growth and better relations with the private sector while Church officials sought a *modus vivendi* with party leaders in the late 1930s and later adopted a posture described as "equivocal complicity." These were also years of uncertainty for the smaller and less influential

National Action Party (Partido Acción Nacional – PAN), a Catholic party founded in 1944 that was built around both a concern for the Church's social teaching and the political promise of closer ties to the business community.

Church–state and church–party relations in Bolivia, the Dominican Republic, Panama, Paraguay, the four Central American republics, and Haiti broadly resembled the patterns described for Argentina and Mexico. Cuba was the exception. With Fidel Castro's Revolution of 1959 and the country's conversion to Marxism-Leninism, dissident elements, including Catholics, emigrated in large numbers. During the 1960s, the Cuban government actively suppressed practicing Catholics; Catholic clergy, many of whom were foreign, fled the island, as did many foreign Protestant missionaries. In the early years of the regime, active Christians were sometimes confined in UMAP (Unidades Militares de Ayuda a la Producción) camps with other social and political "deviants" as perceived enemies of the state. Three decades later, the visit of Pope John Paul II to Cuba in 1998 signaled a thaw in relations between the Catholic Church and the Cuban state, as well as the beginning of an uptick in Cuban attendance at religious services among both Catholics and Protestants alike.

Late Liberalizing Authoritarian Regimes

Under authoritarian regimes that began to liberalize in the 1940s, the Church had more political options from which to choose. For most of the nineteenth century, the Brazilian Church was weak, dissolute, and in decline, but its separation from the state under the republic, launched in 1889, allowed it to break free from its dependence on regional and federal power brokers and to develop its own institutions, programs, and resources such as Catholic Action and the Centro Dom Vital. In 1930, economic instability, widespread fraud, and corruption prompted the military to remove the incumbent president and hand power over to a dissident oligarch, Getulio Vargas, who would rule unencumbered for the next fifteen years. The Church never formally endorsed Vargas, but it welcomed his attention and was not overly troubled by his high-handed methods.

Vargas was ousted by a military coup in 1945 and was succeeded by a new republic that was more democratic than its predecessor but equally burdened by fraudulence, corruption, and cynical alliances between fragmented elites. With the electorate expanding, parties sought the support of middle- and lower-class clients to whom they offered tangible benefits in exchange for commitments of political support. The three most important parties offered favors to the Church in exchange for its blessing, but it declined, preferring to rely on its own resources and the energy of its own organizations. During this period, the Brazilian Church changed dramatically. The appointment of more liberal bishops reinforced the growing tendency of priests, nuns, and lay volunteers to live and work alongside the poor, be they urban workers, landless peasants, or economic refugees settling in shantytowns on the outskirts of São Paulo and other large cities.

Similar patterns occurred in Peru, Ecuador, and Venezuela during this period. The Peruvian and Venezuelan Churches were weak and depended on state support and foreign-born clergy to sustain themselves. The Ecuadorian Church was less weak because it had conservative protectors in the military that the Peruvians and Venezuelans did not have. However, while the Ecuadorian and Venezuelan Churches faced determined liberal adversaries and ended up losing their privileged status and benefits, the Peruvians did not and kept virtually all of theirs.

The military remained a dominant political force in all three countries well into the twentieth century. There were democratic interludes, however, in which parties began to establish an institutional presence and a political following. The military intervened again in both Peru and Ecuador in the 1960s, but these parties continued to operate and thus provided the Church with additional options from which to choose in both promoting causes and defending interests. Additionally, as in Brazil, the appointment in Peru and Ecuador of more progressive bishops during the 1960s and 1970s, and the influence of foreign-born priests, especially in Peru, led to increased Church support of the efforts of socially conscious priests and nuns and to a more critical stance vis-à-vis their respective military governments.

Long-Standing Liberal Democracies

Christian Democratic parties have been important political forces in three of the four long-standing democratic countries of Latin America: Chile, Costa Rica, and Uruguay. They have also arisen in early-liberalizing countries such as Ecuador, Peru, and Venezuela and in several late-liberalizing authoritarian countries such as Mexico, Peru, El Salvador, and the Dominican Republic. In explaining why strong Christian Democratic parties emerged and endured in some countries but not in others, and why they stand for different things and play different roles in different places, scholars point to five variables: (1) the presence of a strong and enduring Catholic culture; (2) a national Catholic Church whose leadership is open to liberal values and to some aspects of modernization; (3) the continuing salience of political issues lending themselves to moral reflection and judgment; (4) appealing, if not charismatic, leadership;

and (5) a political arena in which the reformist center, between left and right, has not already been captured by a secular political forces.

It is also the case that Latin American Christian Democratic parties occupy different spaces or positions in the party systems of their respective countries. Some emerged as "third-way" alternatives to parties of the right and the left. Others, in countries without established rightist parties, appealed to constituencies fearful of the country's liberal forces. Factors that pushed a Christian Democratic party in either a conservative or progressive direction included (1) the characteristics of the country's party system; (2) the ideological convictions of its leaders; (3) leaders' social background and relationships; and (4) the relative strength of popular organizations to which a party might appeal for support.

Chile's Christian Democratic Party (Partido Demócrata Cristiano – PDC) has been the most successful party of its type in Latin America in terms of impact on national politics. Christian Democrats occupied Chile's presidency from 1964 to 1970, were a leading source of opposition to the military dictatorship of Augusto Pinochet in the 1970s and 1980s, and have headed two of the five governments since democracy was restored in 1990. Most of its leaders and active members have been, and continue to be, the products of a Catholic upbringing, educated in Catholic institutions and active in Catholic Action and other apostolic organizations when younger.

Over the years, the PDC's ties to the Chilean Church have been close, but hardly free of conflict. It took time for the bishops to accept that people who embraced the same values and principles that they did could disagree on how best to apply them in cases involving unclear technical issues or where a successful outcome required concessions to other forces. However, during the papacies of John XXIII (1958–1963) and Paul VI (1963–1978), most bishops who were appointed or promoted to new positions were liberals or progressives who blended nicely with party leaders and activists on both personal and ideological levels. Under the papacy of John Paul II (1978–2005), the composition of Chile's Episcopal Conference became more conservative, both ideologically and pastorally, and the gap between the Church and the PDC widened. Even before these changes, however, the bishops had pulled back from their initial preferential option for Christian Democracy, although not because they objected to its policies. Instead, they hoped to remain accessible and credible to other political groups.

Christian Democracy has also been a significant force in Costa Rican politics, where it operates politically as the United Social Christian Party (Partido de Unidad Socialcristiana – PUSC). This party has held the country's presidency four times since 1978, and it has been well represented in the Legislative Assembly. Its political and economic views are more conservative than many other Christian Democratic parties, which is a consequence of the strong support it enjoys among the country's business class and of the party's function as an alternative to the National Liberation Party (Partido Liberación Nacional – PLN) in what was, until recently, basically a two-party system.

Likewise, the Costa Rican Church and its bishops have been more conservative than other Latin American Churches since the 1950s. Demographic differences among dioceses and the impact of episcopal appointments have been partly responsible for this unevenness. Costa Rican bishops, though signatories to the resolutions of the 1968 Medellín Conference of the Latin American Conference of Bishops (Consejo Episcopal Latinoamericano – CELAM), went their own way on the issues raised by Vatican II on social justice, preferring instead to continue along the distinctly Costa Rican path forged a generation earlier by Jorge Volio Jiménez and Mons. Víctor Manuel Sanabria.

In Uruguay, the young Catholics who left the Civic Union Party to form that country's Christian Democratic Party (PDC) in the early 1960s won several seats in the national legislature in elections in 1962 and 1966, no small achievement in what had been a two-party system. More significantly, they later formed a Broad Front (Frente Amplio) coalition with leftist groups in the years leading up to the military's intervention and takeover of the national government in 1973. The PDC's move greatly troubled most Uruguayan bishops but not Msgr. Carlos Parteli, who was apostolic administrator of the Archdiocese of Montevideo in 1966 and who became archbishop of the same diocese in 1976. Parteli was the lone progressive among the bishops, but he was highly regarded by the Vatican. In addition to being a strong advocate of a socially engaged Church and of dialogue with other religions and non-believers, Parteli was also a mentor and protector to a generation of Uruguayan Christian Democrats.

In Ecuador, centrist Christian Democrats and center-right Social Christians headed governments between 1981 and 1996, although they have been reduced to a minor role following the upheavals of the late 1990s and early 2000s. In Peru, the center-right Popular Christian Party had a substantial following in the 1960s and again in the 1980s, but it was one of the many political casualties of the authoritarian rule of Alberto Fujimori in the 1990s. In Venezuela, the centrist Committee for Independent Political Electoral Organization (Comité de Organización Política Electoral Independiente – COPEI) shared power with the center-left Democratic Action Party from 1958 through the early 1990s when the emergence of Hugo Chávez relegated it to secondary status. In El Salvador and the Dominican Republic, Christian Democratic parties emerged once their military governments withdrew. Each group was heavily dependent on its respective leaders, José Napoleon Duarte in the case of the Salvadoran Christian Democratic Party (PDC) and the populist Joaquín Balaguer in the case of the Dominican Social Christian Reform Party (*Partido Reformista Social Cristiano* – PRSC). Once these influential leaders departed, neither group was able to maintain its political following. The PDC was also weakened by the desertion of young progressives who wanted to join with politicians on the left rather than displace them.

In Mexico, the PAN has long been divided between its pro-business elements, some of whom were Catholic, and its not-so-wealthy Catholic reformists who wanted the PAN to embrace Christian Democracy. The Mexican bishops, not wanting to jeopardize their own rapprochement with the PRI, played little or no part in the PAN's internal debates in the 1960s and 1970s, nor when they later resumed. In the 1980s and 1990s, pro-business elements again prevailed, and talk of Christian Democratic reform and social change was shelved. Ironically, however, the party later applied for, and was granted, membership in the international and Latin American regional organizations of Christian Democratic parties.

Military Rule

This section deals with the period of military rule in Latin America from the mid-1960s to the late-1980s. However, rather than focusing on the military regimes themselves, it is concerned with the impact of the regimes on people living under and through them. This analysis underscores how military rule affected political life in the region, what people learned from it about the risks and possible consequences of political engagement, and how it affected relations between the Catholic Church and its political parties in various countries.

Between the 1960s and the 1980s, most Latin American countries lived under military governments of one sort or another. Only five countries – Mexico, Costa Rica, Colombia, the Dominican Republic, and Venezuela – escaped the experience entirely, and, generally speaking, they were hardly models of stability or constitutional government. The violence of military governments was particularly acute in Central America and the Southern Cone. In South America, military governments in Chile and Brazil held power the longest while Chile, Argentina, and Uruguay were the most repressive and bloodstained. However, there were some variations among the Southern Cone countries as well. In Argentina, the military continued a long-established pattern of intervention and rule, but in Chile and Uruguay, on the other hand, military governments were notable departures from their respective electoral traditions.

The years of military rule left significant marks on the national economies of some countries, on the political institutions of many others, and on the psychology of their populations. The impacts most worthy of note were on people generally; on the political parties that were displaced; and, in particular, on the Catholic Church, which helped to mitigate the harshness of military rule and bring it to an end in some cases but in other cases remained silent.

Military rule was traumatic for countries where it was not a historical phenomenon, particularly for those such as Chile and Uruguay. In most countries, the armed forces assumed power with the intention of holding control until the "problems" that prompted them to act were corrected or resolved. Regimes varied in length, intensity of repression, and the number of lives damaged and lost. Killings of suspected militants on a large scale occurred in Argentina (22,000), Chile (3,200), Brazil (500), and Uruguay (180). Typically, elected civilian leaders were deposed and their collaborators were jailed, treated badly if not tortured, and then either killed or sent into exile. Additionally, supporters of the previous government were routinely dismissed from their jobs, taken from their homes in the middle of the night, or pulled off sidewalks in broad daylight for questioning. In virtually all cases, curfews were imposed, universities taken over, radio stations closed down, and television stations and the press either monitored or managed directly.

In the various military regimes' early stages, the official hierarchy of the Church often emerged as an ally – albeit a cautious one – of new dictators, often viewing the new authoritarians as having delivered their countries from the threat of communism. This was the case in Brazil in the 1960s, Chile in the first months of the Pinochet regime, and Argentina in the mid-1970s. Relatively quickly, however, the Church itself experienced repression, and many – though not all – Catholic leaders denounced authoritarian repression and came to the assistance of victims spiritually and materially. At a time when many families were struggling because their breadwinners were in jail, in hiding, or simply missing, priests, nuns, and lay workers at parish centers provided comfort, consolation, and material assistance. In some cases in which there were no platforms from which to complain or denounce, and in which there few people willing to do so, the Church became the voice of the voiceless, a public defender of human rights and democracy. Its often-forceful criticism dealt a powerful blow to the hopes for legitimacy of a number of these regimes.

Their experiences under military rule left many Latin Americans hostile to and fearful of the armed forces, newly appreciative of the Catholic Church, and generally disenchanted with political parties, even those they had supported in the past. Aversion to the military was intense among those who had been detained and mistreated as well as among those who knew others who had been detained. Many citizens experienced first hand how cruel, vindictive, and deadly soldiers could be in the heat of "battle" and when not accountable for their actions. They feared and resented them deeply. The Catholic Church, on the other hand, won the gratitude of some victims of repression and of the parties, generally of the left, with which they were affiliated. Both were grateful for the Church's services to victims and their families regardless of background provided by agencies like the Vicaría de Solidaridad in Chile and the Oficina de Tutela Legal in El Salvador, which provided victims' families with information and support. The Church also took a role in providing social services to people in need generally and served as a surrogate social and political force that spoke for people who could not speak for themselves. In several countries such as El Salvador and Guatemala, the Church brought together parties long hostile to one another to help broker agreements that would restore civilian rule. Contrarily, however, other victims continue to raise questions about the Church's inaction during the early stages of dictatorship.

The years of military rule were less favorable to parties as such, although the period did have a moderating effect on most leftist groups. Parties were outlawed in some cases, harassed and persecuted in most, and effectively neutralized as a political force in many Latin American countries. With their leaders jailed initially and later sent into exile, parties could do little for their members or their families. The latter frequently were left with a sense of frustration and abandonment that was compounded in some instances by the gnawing suspicion that politics was somehow to blame for the loss of their jobs, the repression to which their neighborhoods were subjected, and the disruption of families and personal relationships. More than a few of these people came to conclude, more or less reluctantly, that politics and partisan struggle generally were potentially dangerous activities that were best avoided.

The Late Twentieth and Early Twenty-first Centuries

With the restoration of civilian rule and the reemergence of more or less democratic politics, relations between the Church and political parties improved significantly in the late twentieth century. In most countries, the Church's role as a provider of refuge and a defender of human rights lifted its moral authority and credibility to new heights with political elites across the spectrum and with the public at large, as measured in the levels of confidence it enjoyed relative to other national institutions. A notable exception to this rule was Chile's right-wing Catholic party, the Independent Democratic Union (Unión Demócrata Independiente – UDI), which collaborated with Pinochet's regime and was later repudiated by the Church.

Public opinion of the Church was highly favorable and sustained initially by its support of calls by families of victims for clarification and accountability in connection with human rights violations under military rule, but the parties themselves were not doing as well even under governments in which they were leaders or coalition partners. In countries where Catholic-aligned parties had been a force to be reckoned with, their role and influence in decision making diminished; where they had been weak, they became even more peripheral and were reduced to "empty vessels," whose principal function was to help elect a government and then to get out of the way.

The diminished political significance of Catholic-aligned parties was a consequence of several factors that included changes in the nature and practice of politics in increasingly mediated societies, a sharp reduction in policy options and room for political maneuvering available to many post-military governments and their constituents, and the legacy of political trauma with which many citizens emerged from the years of military rule. In Latin America, technology-driven media have changed the political arena dramatically, often at the expense of political parties. Mediated messages and appeals give governments and their opponents new ways to define issues, set agendas, and shape debates that are then resolved at levels less accessible to the public eye and from which party officials can be excluded.

The declining political strength and fortunes of once prominent parties with seemingly stable constituencies led to the emergence of new parties, party fractions, and blocs and fronts of parties. Many of these carry vague but evocative names designed to appeal to the broadest possible number of voters in a given election such as the Victory Front in Argentina, Radical Change in Colombia, the National Unity of Hope in Guatemala, Country for Everyone in Panama, and Progressive Encounter in Uruguay. In some cases, these blocs or alliances are a response to electoral laws that encourage agglomeration, but in others they reflect the fragmentation of large, once-cohesive parties that dissident leaders abandon hoping to take their supporters with them while appealing to new ones as well.

Parties are not the only institutions whose make-up and fortunes have undergone change in the post-military period, however. The Catholic Church has as well. During the twenty-six years of his papacy, John Paul II appointed or promoted more than 90 percent of the then active Latin American bishops, most of whom were socially conscious but moral and ecclesial conservatives. Many of these bishops shared the pontiff's view that the Church ought to reaffirm its traditional moral teaching and to avoid entanglement in partisan politics, however righteous its intentions or aspirations. The appointment of these antipartisan bishops and the aging of earlier generations of priests, nuns, and lay workers changed the Church's character and appearance in relation to the 1960s and 1970s. The newer bishops have been fairly progressive on issues of poverty, inequality, and the need to extend access to health care and education to those most in need of them. However, their public statements on these issues get little, if any, consideration from either the press or the government and are overshadowed and likely diluted by their aggressive pressing of hotter button issues such as divorce, contraception, the decriminalization of abortion, gay marriage, and the use of fetal stem cells in research.

Many parties, including those whose members are largely practicing Catholics, are divided on these issues. Most of the Catholic-aligned parties accept the Church's moral positions, but many question the propriety of having state authorities enforce those position on others, Catholics or not, thereby not allowing them to make their own conscientious decisions. In this context, the bishops have turned their attention away from the parties and to other political actors. Among these new groups are decision makers in the executive branch, individual Catholic legislators, sympathetic advocacy groups that are mobilized around these issues, and public opinion generally, which the bishops address with the help of wealthy allies and the resources and techniques of the modern media.

Since the early 1990s, in a region that is both modernizing and becoming steadily more secular, the bishops have not always succeeded. They have failed to prevent the liberalization of laws concerning divorce in Chile and Colombia; contraception in Argentina and Brazil; and gay marriage or civil unions in Argentina, Brazil, Colombia, Ecuador, and Uruguay. However, bishops and their new political allies have managed to block efforts to decriminalize abortion and to extend the criteria that would make an abortion legal in arguably more modern and secular countries such as Argentina, Uruguay, and Brazil.

Bibliography and Suggested Readings

Gómez Peralta, Hector. "La Iglesia Católica en México como institución de derecha." *Revista Mexicana de Ciencias Politicas y Sociales*, 49, no. 199 (2007): 63–78.

Klaiber, Jeffrey. *The Church, Dictatorships, and Democracy in Latin America*. Eugene, OR: Wipf & Stock, 1998.

Mainwaring, Scott, and Timothy Scully, eds. *Christian Democracy in Latin America: Electoral Competition and Regime Conflicts*. Stanford, CA: Stanford University Press, 2003.

Núncio, Abraham. *El PAN: Alternativa de poder o instrumento de la oligarquía empresarial?* Ciudad de México Coyoacán: Editora Nueva Imagen, 1986.

Sawchuk, Dana. *The Costa Rican Catholic Church, Social Justice, and the Rights of Workers, 1979–1996*. Waterloo, Ontario: Wilfred Lauier University Press, 2004.

33
Human Rights: An Ongoing Concern

CHRISTINE KOVIC

Myriad groups throughout Latin America have mobilized for the defense of human rights in the contemporary period. In times of dictatorship, women have come together in search of "disappeared" loved ones and to provide food to those in need and at risk of persecution. Peasants and indigenous peoples have organized to gain access to land, education, and health care. Church leaders and lay people have formed human rights organizations, creating a permanent record of abuses and laying the groundwork for transitions to democracy. Along with denouncing cases of torture, arbitrary arrest, and assassinations, Latin Americans have fought for social justice, including structural change, racial and ethnic equality, and the defense of economic rights. Religious institutions and ideology, particularly that of progressive Catholicism, have played a key role in many of these mobilizations. In many instances, religion provided resources (from material assistance to a safe space for meetings and information); supported the formation of regional, national, and international networks; and gave moral justification and legitimacy to human rights struggles, especially at times when these struggles challenged the status quo.

Latin American contributions to the conceptualization and defense of human rights are seldom recognized. As Paolo Carozza notes, Latin America has mostly been viewed as an arena of human rights abuses, yet Latin Americans are also actors in advancing human rights thinking. Indeed, Latin American delegates to the United Nations played an important role in creating the Declaration of Human Rights. At the founding meetings of the United Nations held in San Francisco in 1945, the Latin American contingent – twenty-one of the fifty representatives and the largest regional group – worked to place human rights at the center of the UN's new agenda. Representatives of Chile, Uruguay, and Panama served as three of the eighteen-member commission that wrote the Human Rights Declaration. Latin American representatives ensured that social, economic, and cultural rights were included in the

Declaration alongside political and civil rights; they emphasized racial and gender equality; and included both individual and collective rights.

This piece explores key issues of religion and rights in Latin America from the 1960s to 2000. It begins with an overview of changes in the religious panorama, especially in the Catholic Church, and is followed by sections on dictatorship and democracy, peace building, women's movements, indigenous rights, struggles for land, and immigrant rights. The chapter is not by any means a complete overview of these topics. In highlighting key issues, it maps out the ways religion has impacted and has been impacted by Latin American struggles to defend human rights through their own visions of justice and within their own historic context.

Changes in the Catholic Church: Opening to the World

The 1960s were a time of dramatic change for the Catholic Church in Latin America. Tremendous poverty and political repression, the hope some saw in revolutionary movements such as the Cuban Revolution, the meetings of Vatican II and Medellin, and Liberation Theology came together to push significant sectors of the Church to become directly involved in the defense of human rights.

The Second Vatican Council (1962–1965) convened by Pope John XXIII challenged the Church's traditional role as a supporter of the political and economic elite. The meetings had been organized to discuss issues "internal" to the Church such as faith and style of public workshop, yet they are remembered as a time of *aggiornamiento*, an opening of the Church to the world. The Church recognized the need to be actively involved in the daily reality faced by the people, especially the poor. Following Vatican II, the mass was translated into local languages rather than being read in Latin, and priests faced their congregations from the altar. The people were recognized as the Church, and the Church was turned around in more ways than one. As Phillip Berryman notes, Vatican II did not only open windows, it "opened a floodgate of energy and creativity."[1]

Gaudium et Spes (Latin for "Joy and Hope"), one of the documents produced as a result of Vatican II, strongly promotes human dignity as underlying human rights. It notes that humans have the right to "everything necessary for

---

[1] Phillip Berryman, *Stubborn Hope: Religion, Politics, and Revolution in Central America* (Maryknoll, NY: Orbis Books, 1994), 26.

leading a life truly human" including food, clothing, education, employment, and respect. It denounces poverty and proclaims the right of all people to have what is necessary to live. This moved the Church from being an ally of the elite to working in solidarity with the poor and supports a broad understanding of rights that incorporates human needs.

In 1968 Latin American Bishops met in Medellín, Colombia to address issues of the Church within their regional context. The resulting documents demand taking a role in defense of "the rights of the poor and the oppressed, following the gospel mandate." The bishops recognized and denounced structural sin, which causes poverty and is embedded in institutions as they critically assessed the Church's own complicity in oppression in Latin America. A decade later at the meetings of Puebla, Mexico in 1979, Latin American bishops deepened their commitment to the poor and oppressed supporting the "preferential option for the poor." They committed themselves to work to "uproot poverty and create a more just and fraternal world."

Liberation Theology, one of several pastoral lines that emerged from Vatican II and Medellin and produced primarily by Latin Americans, had a dramatic impact on Catholic pastoral practice in the region. At its center, Liberation Theology is reading the Bible from the perspective of the poor, addressing the suffering and hopes of the oppressed. In *A Theology of Liberation*, Peruvian Gustavo Gutiérrez notes that this theology "does not stop with reflecting on the world, but rather tries to be part of the process through which the world is transformed."[2] As the Vatican worked to discredit Liberation Theology, especially under the papacy of Pope John Paul II, a number of priests and bishops in Latin America avoided naming it, yet the basic principles are evident in their work.

Following the model of Liberation Theology, Christian Base Communities (comunidades eclesiales de base – CEBS), were established as small prayer and reflection groups following Paulo Freire's approach of *concientización*, or building a critical reflection of one's reality. From the 1960s onward, CEBs connected people in neighborhoods and parishes as they shared stories, learned about one another's lives, and reflected on biblical readings. They were particularly important in supporting social movements that challenged repressive governments in Haiti, Nicaragua, Brazil, Chile, Guatemala, and El Salvador. In CEBs, participants began to challenge social and economic inequalities in contemporary society through discussion of biblical texts. Through participation

---

[2] Gustavo Gutiérrez, *A Theology of Liberation: History, Politics, Salvation* (Maryknoll, NY: Orbis Books, 1988), 87.

in CEBs, peasants and the urban poor (both men and women) built networks and cultivated leadership skills, which were important in social movements for the promotion of human rights.

A unique human rights perspective was developed by Latin American theologians including Gustavo Gutiérrez, Hugo Assmann, Juan Luis Segundo, and Franz Hinkelammert, who challenged limited Western-European notions of human rights. They denounced what they viewed as a discourse narrowly focused on political and civil rights, which support capitalism and liberalism without commitment to fundamental economic and social rights. Gustavo Gutiérrez, among others, used the term "rights of the poor" to emphasize economic rights and the necessity of profound structural change to achieve respect for human rights in Latin America. Gutiérrez observed that "The Church's denunciation of violations of human rights will quickly become a hollow cry if Church officials rest content with the beginnings of a 'democracy' that is only for the middle class and actually only enhances the flexibility with which the prevailing system exercises its domination over the popular masses." The concept rights of the poor allows the poor agency to define and defend rights "as utopian norms at the root of a vision of just relations and as a set of demands that mandate immediate historical action by many persons and groups working with the poor for a better society."[3] This model of human rights impacted much of the faith-based human rights work in Latin America.

In the late 1960s, significant numbers of Latin Americans began to convert to Protestantism. At present, an estimated 15 percent of Latin Americans are Protestant, with Pentecostals making up the largest group. In some regions the percentage is much higher. Protestants make up an estimated 30 to 40 percent of the population of Guatemala, El Salvador, and Chiapas, Mexico, among other locations.

Although scholars took note of religious pluralism in Latin American following Protestant conversions, the religious panorama of Latin America is and has been extremely diverse. Along with Catholics and Protestants are indigenous religious traditions and African traditions, including *vodou* and *Cadomblé*, all of which have been influenced by Christianity. Althogh some of the most visible human rights work in the region has been carried out by the Catholic Church, a Church with a strong institutional presence and international networks, other faith traditions also played a key role.

---

3   Mark Engler, "Toward the 'Rights of the Poor:' Human Rights in Liberation Theology," *Journal of Religious Ethics*, 28 (2000): 358.

Important scholarship has unearthed the political diversity among Latin American Protestants, challenging the idea that they are politically passive. Indeed, in Brazil, the progressive Workers Party has had significant numbers of Protestant supporters, including two practicing Pentecostals of the Assemblies of God: Benedita da Silva, a former governor of the state of Rio de Janeiro, and Marina Silva, a senator from the Amazonian state of Acre, both of whom were ministers in the Lula government. Marina Silva ran vigorous, if ultimately unsuccessful, campaigns for the presidency in 2010 and 2014. At times Catholics and Protestants worked together to defend human rights; at other times specific Churches took on leadership roles. Movements from the grassroots, such as indigenous mobilizations, forced institutional churches to change their practices, to incorporate diverse social and religious views, and to reconceptualize their understandings of and participation in human rights.

Dictatorship and Transitions to Democracy

The 1960s, 1970s, and 1980s were a time of military dictatorships in much of Latin American and the Caribbean, including those of General Augusto Pinochet in Chile, who ruled from 1973 to 1990; Alfredo Stroessner in Paraguay (1954–1989); and the Somoza dynasty in Nicaragua (1937–1979), among many others. Duncan Green observes that by the end of 1976 two-thirds of the population of Latin America was living under dictatorships, which were strongly supported by the United States government in the context of the Cold War.[4] Historically, the Latin American Catholic hierarchy supported and was linked to the dominant elite. Yet following the changes brought by Vatican II and Medellín, among others, significant sectors of the Catholic Church supported or even joined in popular movements that challenged repressive regimes.

A dynamic relationship existed among repression, social movements, and the defense of human rights. Social movements grew with support from religious movements, leading to state repression against such movements. This in turn led to churches' denouncing violence and demanding respect for human rights. In some cases, church leaders established human rights centers, providing funding, staff, space, transnational networks, and other resources for the dangerous work of denouncing abuses. In other cases, religious leaders allied themselves with repressive governments. While visible leaders such as Catholic bishops sometimes took strong positions for or against repressive regimes, multiple voices existed within churches, with some bishops, priests, or lay leaders supporting

---

4 Duncan Green, *Faces of Latin America* (London: Latin American Bureau, 1997).

repressive governments and others actively working to end such regimes. In isolated and dramatic instances, Catholic priests joined the ranks of guerrilla forces in what they viewed as the only way to stop state-sponsored killings. In Colombia, Camilo Torres, priest and sociologist, joined the National Liberation Army and died in combat in 1966; in Nicaragua, Spanish priest Gaspar García Laviana joined the Sandinista National Liberation Front in 1977. As churches in Latin America became increasingly vocal in their criticisms, repression against them also increased. Religious leaders including priests, nuns, lay leaders, and others were killed, imprisoned, censored, or exiled.

One powerful example of Catholic and Protestant churches denouncing human rights abuses together was Brazil. In 1973, an ecumenical group including Catholic archbishop Paulo Arns, A Coordenadoria Ecumênica de Serviço (CESE, or Ecumenical Service Agency), and the World Council of Churches (representing hundreds of Protestant, Orthodox, and Pentecostal churches internationally) published the Universal Declaration of Human Rights with quotes from Scripture or Catholic and Protestant theology following each article. In a strong challenge to the torture, disappearances, assassinations, and arbitrary arrests committed under the military regime, five million copies of the Human Rights Declaration were posted throughout the country.

In Chile, a variety of faith-based organizations joined together to challenge Augusto Pinochet. More than 3,000 people died or "were disappeared" under the Pinochet regime, many of their bodies never found. In response to the repression, religious leaders including Catholics, Lutherans, Methodists, Pentecostals, Jews, and others created the Committee of Cooperation for Peace in Chile (Comité de Cooperación para la Paz en Chile – COPACHI) under the leadership of Santiago's archbishop Cardinal Raúl Silva Henríquez and Lutheran bishop Helmut Frenz. The committee, with financial support from the World Council of Churches, began the political work of searching for those who were missing and also set up soup kitchens and other services to help people with material needs. After two years, the junta ordered the Committee to close. In response, Cardinal Henríquez defiantly opened the Vicariate of Solidarity directly under the Episcopal vicar, the Reverend Cristián Precht. The Vicariate played a critical role in documenting abuses as well as in supporting local, grassroots human rights initiatives. As Thomas Quigley notes, the act of creating such a vicariate demonstrated that the defense of human rights was "part and parcel of the Church's mission in the world."[5]

---

5 Thomas Quigley, "The Chilean Coup, the Church and the Human Rights Movement," *America*, 4 (2002): 12–14.

In Central America, particularly during the armed conflicts in Guatemala (1960–1996), El Salvador (1980–1992), and Nicaragua (1972–1979), the Catholic Church denounced human rights abuses committed by the military and government-supported groups. Well-known public figures such as Oscar Arnulfo Romero, archbishop of San Salvador from 1977 until he was assassinated while celebrating mass in 1980, condemned military violence as well as the structural violence faced by those living in poverty. Romero supported popular organizations working for change, noting in a sermon just months before he was killed, "I am simply doing what Medellín recommends: raising the conscience of my people on the need to organize so that they may not be mere passive spectators but rather protagonists of their own destiny."[6]

In 1989, Salvadoran soldiers killed six well-known Jesuits of the Central American University including rector Ignacio Ellacuría along with their housekeeper and her daughter. These are some of the well-known cases among thousands of deaths, most at the hands of the army or death squads, that took place during the civil war. Anna Peterson writes of ways that progressive Catholics in El Salvador linked the killings to Christ's passion, giving new meaning to the deaths. People viewed them as "sacrifices necessary for ultimate liberation and as a guarantee of life in abundance for succeeding generations."[7] Their religious views of the violence motivated activism, even in the face of great risk.

At the community level, the CEBs provided a space for support for personal, political, and economic difficulties, but they also provided a space for discussion of revolutionary movements. In Nicaragua, Catholic clergy began to implement CEBs in the 1960s in impoverished areas. Certainly not all CEBS were engaged in politics, but a significant number joined popular movements or engaged in civil disobedience against the Somoza regime responsible for the gross violation of human rights. In addition, a group of priests and other pastoral agents supported the insurgency in Nicaragua as a way of carrying out the option for the poor. Indeed, four Catholic priests (including Minister of Culture Ernesto Cardenal and Foreign Minister Miguel d'Escoto) served in the Sandinista government, which overthrew the Somoza regime in 1979.

Yet religion in Latin America often served to legitimize repression and the violation of human rights. The Catholic Church of Argentina was complicit with the military regime of the "Dirty War" of the 1970s to 1980s that

---

6 Scott Wright, *Promised Land: Death and Life in El Salvador* (Maryknoll, NY: Orbis Books, 1994), xxiv.
7 Anna L. Peterson, *Martyrdom and the Politics of Religion: Progressive Catholicism in El Salvador's Civil War* (Albany: State University of New York Press, 1997), 90–91.

was responsible for "disappearing" some 30,000 people. General Jorge Rafael Videla declared that the military regime was engaged in a Holy War to eliminate subversion and preserve obedience, harmony, and the nation, and tens of thousands of people were detained and "disappeared." Significant sectors of the Argentine Catholic Church, including the papal nuncio, actively supported the military regime, turned in those defined as "subversive," and held masses for members of the junta. In September 2000, decades after the fall of the military regime, Argentina's bishops formally and publically asked forgiveness for the Church's participation and complicity in the Dirty War. Current Pope Francis I (Jorge Mario Bergoglio) has been criticized for failing to firmly and publicly denounce the Argentinean junta during the years of the "Dirty War."

In Haiti, François "Papa Doc" Duvalier made use of Catholic symbols to legitimize his dictatorship (1957–1971). He revised the Lord's Prayer to reflect his total power: "Our Doc, who art in the National Palace for life, hallowed by Thy name, by present and future generations. Thy will be done in Port-au-Prince and its provinces."[8] The prayer was recited by schoolchildren and at public events. Duvalier expelled priests, including the entire Jesuit order in 1964, and staged the arrest of sixty people praying at the national Cathedral. The Vatican broke off relations with Duvalier in 1960, but five years later Pope Paul VI reconciled, signing an agreement conceding to Duvalier.

General José Efraín Ríos Montt, who ruled Guatemala from 1982 to 1983 during the worst violence of the country's civil war, justified many acts of counterinsurgency through the idiom of religion. Under Ríos Montt, an evangelical Pentecostal, thousands of Guatemalans were killed or disappeared and entire villages were destroyed in the scorched earth policy. In an analysis of Ríos Montt's public sermons of early 1982, Virginia Garrard-Burnett notes that "his objective was nothing less than to bring salvation to a country plagued by war, corruption, and poverty and raise it to its destiny as the City on the Hill, divinely blessed by God."[9]

Building Peace in Central and South America

In times of armed conflict and violence, faith-based groups supported dialogue and nonviolent movements and played a critical role in establishing

---

[8] Terry Rey, "Catholicism and Human Rights in Haiti: Past, Present, and Future," *Religion and Human Rights*, 3 (2006): 239.

[9] Virginia Garrard-Burnett, *Terror in the Land of the Holy Spirit: Guatemala under General Efraín Ríos Montt, 1982–1983* (Oxford: Oxford University Press, 2010), 64.

public memory of human rights abuses. In El Salvador in the 1980s, Lutherans, Episcopalians, and the Baptist Assembly joined in political opposition to the government or provided humanitarian aid to those who resisted. Lutheran bishop Medardo Gómez of El Salvador's Resurrection Church worked in solidarity with the poor, supporting popular movements and following the model of Archbishop Romero. Protestant leaders participated in the organization National Debate for Peace (Debate Nacional por la Paz), which worked to end El Salvador's Civil War. Although the Debate had been organized by the Catholic hierarchy in 1988, Baptist pastor Edgar Palacios became president of the organization. The Central American Peace Portfolio established by the Mennonite Central Committee in 1985 encouraged nonviolent means to social change and dialogue, collaborating with local initiatives such as that of the Moravian Church in Nicaragua. The Colombian Mennonite Church created a Justice and Peace Commission in 1990, which addressed conscientious objection to military service, constitutional reform, and education and networking for nonviolence, among other issues.

In Brazil Catholics and Protestants worked together to create the best-selling book *Brasil: Nunca Mais*, first published in Portuguese in 1985. The report documents 1,843 cases of torture, showing it to be a systematic practice of the military regime from 1964 to 1979. Cardenal Arns of the Catholic Archdiocese of Sao Paulo and Presbyterian pastor Jaime Wright secretly worked for five years to oversee the painstaking photocopying of more than a million pages of military files detailing the abuses committed under the dictatorship. The story of the creation of the report is powerfully narrated in Lawrence Weschler's *A Miracle, A Universe*. The World Council of Churches had strong links with the ecumenical community in Brazil and funded the secret project with more than $350,000.

On April 24, 1998, Guatemalan bishop Juan José Gerardi presented *Nunca Más* (Never Again), the report of the Recovery of Historical Memory Project (*Recuperación de la Memoria Histórica* – REMHI) that documented the violence of the nation's thirty-six-year civil war. Just two days later Gerardi was killed, bludgeoned to death in Guatemala City. The testimonies of more than 5,000 people included in the report document a total of 14,291 incidents of human rights violations including individual or collective killings (the largest category), arbitrary detentions, threats, and torture, among others. It concludes that the vast majority of the violations (89.65 percent) were committed by the government, including the military and paramilitary groups. Less than a year later, the United Nations Commission for Historical Clarification (Comisión para el Esclarecimiento Histórico – CEH) presented its report on the violence, documenting that more than 200,000 people were killed or "disappeared."

Noting that Mayan peoples were primary targets of violence, the UN report names the killings genocide. Susan Fitzpatrick-Behrens observes that the earlier REMHI report "represented an essential first step in the creation of an historical memory that gave voice to the silenced victims of the violence and became the foundation for the UN's CEH Report."[10]

Women's Movements, Religion, and Human Rights

As a patriarchal and hierarchal institution, the Catholic Church is an unlikely ally in the struggle for women's rights. Yet women's organizations throughout Latin America have received significant support in the form of material resources as well as moral justification from the Catholic Church and other religious institutions. Given that religion forms an important part of many Latin American women's identities, women relied on their faith in their activism. Not all who participated were Catholic or even religious. Women commonly engaged in human rights work drawing from their traditional roles, particularly that of mothers. Yet women's roles within and beyond the household were transformed as they openly challenged state authority and traditional images of Catholic femininity as obedient, self-sacrificing, and subordinate. In many cases, women's activism grew beyond the limits set by their churches.

Nine women searching for their disappeared relatives during the civil war in El Salvador founded the organization the CoMadres (Mothers and Relatives of Political Prisoners, Disappeared, and Assassinated of El Salvador "Monseñor Romero," literally, Co-Mothers) on Christmas Eve of 1977. The group grew quickly to dozens and eventually hundreds of members as women whose family suffered repression joined. The CoMadres formed with the support of the Catholic Diocese and named themselves after Archbishop Romero. Many of the women had been involved in Christian Base Communities; indeed, many family members had been targeted because of their Church-based activism. One of the founders, Alicia, remembers the blessing of Archbishop Romero just a month before his assassination and how it provided a moral basis for their work. "Ah, you women are the Marys of today. Mary spent a long time searching for her son, and you mothers are also walking along the same path that Mary walked. All of you are suffering the same loss, the same pain."[11] The

---

10 Susan Fitzpatrick-Behrens, "Angels in Guatemala: Confronting a Legacy of Official Terror," NACLA Online News (January 5, 2010), https://nacla.org/node/6337 Accessed February 19, 2014.
11 Jennifer Schirmer, "The Seeking of Truth and the Gendering of Consciousness: The CoMadres of El Salvador and the CONAVIGUA Widows of Guatemala," in 'Viva:'

women searched jails and military barracks in the country to find the "disappeared," demanded investigation of clandestine cemeteries, cared for orphans of the war, and provided food and clothing to the imprisoned. Members of CoMadres suffered significant repression from the government for their activism. Their offices were under military surveillance and bombed several times; members were threatened, detained, tortured, and raped, and several were assassinated. Through their continued efforts the women carry out a "political motherhood ... in which they believe that there can be no national security without social justice."[12]

During the Pinochet years in Chile, women's work of sewing and cooking took on powerful political meaning. Supported by the Catholic Church, in this case the Vicariate of Solidarity, women began to make *arpilleras* – tapestries, or small pieces of cloth sewn together and embroidered – which visually narrated repression under the Pinochet dictatorship. Many *arpilleras* were smuggled out of Chile, creating an international documentation of Chile's repression. In their testimonies, the Chilean *arpilleristas* recount the way that faith lends meaning and strength to their struggles. As Valentina Bonne, an artist and teacher of the workshops notes, "The most Christian workshops spoke of how to keep one's faith in the shantytowns, of the persecution today that was similar to that imposed by the Pharaohs on the Israelites. They spoke of the faith that obliges one to help the neediest, of the faith that lives asking for understanding, of the faith that is sustained by the love of one for another."[13]

Responding to the hunger and lack of basic economic rights during the military regime, Chilean women also set up *ollas comúnes* (communal kitchens) in poor neighborhoods. Again, women who had worked together in CEBs joined to search for food and cooked together to feed their families and neighborhoods. The kitchens, aside from meeting basic economic needs, were also a form of protest against the economic hardships under the regime. As one woman explains,

> In the beginning we each brought what food we could, and we asked for donations from the local shops. Then we went everywhere begging, in the community, in the markets. One day we decided to go to the army barracks. We took pots and tin cans and a letter. I explained that we were from a communal kitchen and that we had a lot of unemployed people and the children

---

Women and Popular Protest in Latin America, ed. Sarah A. Radcliffe and Sallie Westwood (London and New York: Routledge, 1993), 36.
12 Ibid., 49.
13 Marjorie Agosín, *Tapestries of Hope, Threads of Love: The Arpillera Movement in Chile* (Lanham, MD: Rowman & Littlefield Publishers, 2008), 99.

were hungry. We asked for paraffin for the fires, blankets and food and clothes for the children. We wanted to go inside to speak to them but they wouldn't let me or any of the other leaders in ... The kitchen never stopped. During all the protests and the repression we kept the kitchen open.[14]

The women describe the way working in the communal kitchen broke the isolation of working alone at home. From the planning, decision making, and administrative tasks carried out thorough the kitchens, the women gained self-confidence and also increased political awareness.

Catholic nuns in Chiapas, Mexico have worked for decades with indigenous and *mestiza* women as part of a diocesan project to support human dignity and human rights. Since 1992, women have come together through the Diocesan Coordination of Women (Coordinación Diocesana de Mujeres – CODIMUJ) a grassroots group through which they join local discussion groups, regional workshops, and meetings. Those who participate in CODIMUJ are lay Catholics; the nuns participate as "advisors" and supporters. Laywomen share their reflections on biblical readings; analyze the political, economic, and social situations in which they live; and discuss their experiences with other women. They also participate in workshops on health, literacy, and human rights, and form local cooperatives to bake bread, raise chickens, and grow vegetables. Thousands of indigenous and *mestiza* women (primarily members of impoverished communities) take part in CODIMUJ, many of whom have participated directly in political organizations. As women participate in local meetings, travel to regional meetings where they meet other women and share their concerns and hopes, and create local cooperatives, they form networks and resist structural inequalities such as racism, sexism, and poverty.

The case of the Mothers of the Plaza del Mayo in Argentina is in stark contrast to the support the Church offered to these women's groups. As women came together to search for their loved ones during the military junta, they were repeatedly denied support from priests, bishops, and others. As one member put it, "The Church didn't answer."[15] Likewise in Bolivia, Domitila Barrios, the wife of a miner, notes that religion "put itself at the service of the powerful, listening to their points of view."[16] Barrios participated in organizing miner families, strikes, marches, and other forms of protest and joined

---

14 Jo Fisher, *Out of the Shadows: Women, Resistance and Politics in South America* (London: Latin America Bureau, 1993), 31.
15 Matilde Mellibovsky, *Circle of Love Over Death: Testimonies of the Mothers of the Plaza de Mayo* (Willimantic, CT: Curbstone Press, 1997), 67.
16 Domitila Barrios de Chungara, *Let Me Speak! Testimony of Domitila, a Woman of the Bolivian Mines* (New York: Monthly Review Press, 1978), 64.

the Housewives' Committee of Siglo XX, a militant group defending miners' rights. She was arrested, and the Housewives Committee was attacked by the government of President Barrientos (1964–1969).

Indigenous Rights

In the 1980s and 1990s the struggle for indigenous rights took center stage in many regions of Latin America. Demanding political, cultural, and economic rights (especially in the form of land and other natural resources), dramatic mobilizations and protests captured public attention. In 1994 in Chiapas, Mexico, the Zapatista Army of National Liberation, composed primarily of Mayas, took over seven towns in the state and demanded democracy, social justice, and an end to the hundreds of years of exploitation of indigenous peoples and peasants.

Religion has played an important role in indigenous movements, in part because it is central to indigenous life and community. Historically, the Catholic Church has been responsible for tremendous repression of indigenous peoples. During the colonial period, Catholic hierarchy took indigenous land, controlled labor, and supported the domination of indigenous peoples. The Barbados Declaration of 1971, resulting from a conference of the International Working Group for Indigenous Affairs, harshly criticized the work of Christian missionaries as ethnocide.

In time, a significant number of clergy were transformed by their work with indigenous peoples and became allies in indigenous struggles for liberation. Such was the case of Samuel Ruiz Garcia, bishop of the Diocese of San Cristobal de Las Casas from 1960 to 2000. Arriving in the diocese as a staunch anticommunist who wished to Westernize indigenous Mayas to Christianize them, in time, he was "converted by the poor." He saw the need to walk with them, rather than in front of them, in their struggles for justice. As Bishop, Ruiz supported the formation of thousands of indigenous catechists who served as leaders in their own communities as well as agents of inculturation as they appropriated religious texts that were meaningful in their own lives. The diocese supported indigenous organizations working for social change and in 1989 established the "Fray Bartolomé de las Casas" Center for Human Rights to challenge human rights abuses committed by the state and train local rights promoters.

The Church has played an important role as an ally to indigenous rights movements in several regions of Latin America. As Alison Brysk argues, "At the broad historical level, religion has moved from opiate to liberator to increasing political independence."[17] In Ecuador, Brysk points to the role that the Catholic Church played as an external interlocutor. She notes, "The Church is not on an equal footing with other social forces; it stands *between* the state and society in Latin America" and as such has mediated in conflicts, provided resources for movements or communities, and sponsored political organizations.[18] Bishop Leonidas Proaño, influenced by Liberation Theology and the pedagogy of Paulo Freire, returned Church lands to indigenous peoples in the highlands, founded agricultural cooperatives, and formed an indigenous seminary, among other tasks. Because of his work, he became known as "Bishop of the Indians."

Land and the Struggle for Survival

Land distribution is a critical human rights issue in Latin America. It is an economic right given that those dependent on agricultural require land for subsistence as well as a political right given that government repression, corruption, and negligence have prevented small-scale farmers from gaining access to land. In the countryside of Latin America, peasants lack sufficient land to survive and commonly work as agricultural day laborers for low wages.

Anthropologist Beatriz Manz writes of the conditions on the *fincas* (plantations) of coastal Guatemala, where impoverished Mayas and *mestizos* from the highland department of El Quiché sought work.[19] The workers faced racism, crude housing, disease, and above all, difficult work, including being sprayed by pesticide along with the crops – all for extremely low pay. Given the unequal land distribution in places like Guatemala, El Salvador, and Chiapas, Mexico, CEBs commonly took up the biblical story of Exodus, drawing parallels to their own search for a promised land where they could work for themselves. In Guatemala, the Catholic Church supported peasants of the highlands in purchasing lands in the jungles of Ixcán and El Petén. The Catholic Church contributed to the success of the new settlements in the jungle through assisting in purchasing land and in supporting the formation of cooperatives.

The Catholic Church also assisted, directly or indirectly, in the formation of organizations through which peasants fought for the right to land. In Paraguay, the Christian-based peasant land cooperative called the Peasant Leagues (*ligas*

---

17 Alison Brysk, *From Tribal Village to Global Village: Indian Rights and International Relations in Latin America* (Stanford, CA: Stanford University Press, 2000), 40.
18 Ibid., 209.
19 Beatriz. Mantz, *Paradise in Ashes: A Guatemalan Journey of Courage, Terror, and Hope* (Berkeley, CA: University of California Press, 2004).

campesinas) were created to challenge inequalities in land distribution under General Alfredo Stroessner. Under his regime, the military took the most fertile lands, displacing huge numbers of peasants. By the early 1970s, an estimated 20,000 people had joined the Peasant Leagues, with significant participation by peasant women. Guatemala's Committee for Campesino Unity (Comité de Unidad Campesino – CUC) drew on ideas of Liberation Theology, and significant numbers of its members and leaders were Catholic catechists.

The Movement of Landless Rural Workers (Movimento Sem Terra – MST) of Brazil is one of the largest and most important social movements in contemporary Latin America. Formed in the mid-1980s in southern Brazil, it became a national movement through which rural dwellers pressured government officials for land redistribution and carried out land occupations. Brazil had one of the highest concentrations of land in the world following the plantation agriculture of the colonial period. A small number of people own much of the land, especially the most fertile land.

The MST received logistical support as well as moral endorsement from progressive sectors of the Catholic Church, which established the Pastoral Land Commission (Comissão Pastoral da Terra – CPT) in 1975. This commission would play an important role in the movement for land rights, including land occupations, and the foundation of the MST. The CPT criticized the "unemployment, eviction of peasants, pauperization, and the exodus from the countryside."[20] While the organizing efforts of the Catholic Church were important to the MST, it was not by any means exclusively Catholic. People of a variety of religions including Lutherans and Pentecostals participated, as did labor unions, human rights organizations, and others. "Land, agrarian reform, and a more just society" were the goals set at the first national congress, held in 1985 with more than 1,500 delegates, and remain the goals of the movement. While the Catholic Church played an important leadership role in the early stages of the movement, the MST pulled away from Church leaders in the 1990s. According to figures from the MST in 2002, the organization had acquired land for 350,000 families in 3,000 settlements in Brazil. Some 2000,000 Brazilians are affiliated with the MST and the organization can mobilize thousands of people for a land takeover or for national or regional marches that press for reform. Nonetheless, in 2001 there were still 4.5 million landless rural workers in the nation who struggle to survive as temporary agricultural workers.

---

20 Michael Lowy, "The Socio-Religious Origins of Brazil's Landless Rural Workers Movement," *Monthly Review* 53:2 (2001), 36.

Migrants and Social Justice

On World Migrant Day in 1995, Catholic bishops of the United States and Mexico affirmed their support for migrants noting, "In the Church no one is a stranger, and the Church is not foreign to anyone, anywhere." In a time when millions of Latin Americans (especially Mexicans and Central Americans) are migrating to the United States, faith communities have defended the right to human mobility and provided humanitarian and human rights support for undocumented migrants traveling toward the United States.

Regarding the Catholic hierarchy, the United States Conference of Catholic Bishops and the Mexican Conference of Bishops jointly approved a pastoral letter on migration titled "Strangers No Longer: Together on the Journey of Hope" in January 2003. The letter states, "Catholic teaching has a long and rich tradition in defending the right to migrate." It notes that people have the right to migrate "to support themselves and their families" when they cannot find work in their homeland. It demands that churches build solidarity with migrants in providing social services, advocating for them, and denouncing human rights abuses. Finally, the letter calls for significant revisions of migration laws to guarantee the dignity and rights of migrants, criticizes enforcement policies along the US–Mexican border and in southern Mexico, and calls for the legalization of undocumented immigrants in the United States.

In Mexico and Guatemala, religious organizations have opened safe houses or shelters (*albergues*) that support Central Americans passing through the region on their journey toward the United States. These shelters provide a variety of services, depending on the context, including food, shelter, a safe place to stay, moral and religious support, medical attention, and information on the migrant journey. The Congregation of Scalabrinian Missionaries has established a network of immigrant shelters called *Casas del Migrate* in Mexico and Central America. Local parishes as well as dioceses have responded to the thousands of migrants passing through their regions by providing shelters or other services.

In the town of Arriaga, Chiapas where migrants gather to wait to jump the freight train to begin their slow journey across Mexico, the shelter *Hogar de la Misericordia* (Home of Mercy) run by the Catholic Church takes in thousands of migrants a year. In some cases, Church groups have opened human rights centers alongside shelters. In the Catholic Diocese of Saltillo in Coahuila, *Frontera con Justicia* was founded in 2003 to respond to the violence and human rights abuses faced by migrants who cross the region. *Frontera con Justicia* together with the regional shelter, *Belén Posada del Migrante* (Bethlehem Migrant Shelter), publishes an annual report documenting immigrant rights and has initiated legal cases in defense of rights.

On both sides of the US–Mexico border, organizations supported by a variety of religious groups have worked to protect immigrant life and promote policy change. The Quaker organization the American Friends Service Committee established the Immigration Law Enforcement Monitoring Project (ILEMP) in 1987 when it began to work to defend human rights in the border region. Under the leadership of María Jiménez, the ILEMP was important in documenting deaths along the US–Mexico border resulting from increased border enforcement. Since 1993, more than 5,000 people have died in attempts to cross the border. The organizations No More Deaths, the Samaritan Patrol, and Humane Borders, which work to provide humanitarian aid and support immigration reform, are composed of faith-based and secular groups.

Walking toward the Future

The actions taken by members of religious groups in the later part of the twentieth century responded to the extreme political repression and poverty of the times. Significant sectors of the Latin American Catholic Church broke with the ruling elite to defend human rights. Although religious leaders are most recognized for their work, laypeople and communities of faith have been the protagonists of human rights mobilization in the region. Religious institutions were changed in the process of walking with the poor. More recently, bishops of Latin America have criticized free trade agreements and neo-liberal reforms, which negatively impact poor families, small-scale farmers, and vulnerable workers.

At the beginning of the twenty-first century, there are signs that the Catholic Church is again an ally of the powerful. It was Cardinal Joseph Ratzinger (later Pope Benedict XVI) who led the silencing of liberation theologian and then-Franciscan priest Leonardo Boff in 1985. The Catholic Church has systematically covered up sex abuse cases and protected those responsible in complicity with government officials. The powerful Mexican priest Marcial Maciel, leader of the Legionaries of Christ, was not held accountable for cases of sexual abuse beginning decades ago until quite recently. Catholic leaders have clashed with Evo Morales (President of Bolivia and an Aymara Indian) and other progressive leaders over their political and social policies.

Yet, there are also signs that the Church may continue to be an important ally in the area of human rights and one that may shift the focus from human rights defined in terms of limiting violent repression to those more broadly defined by access to economic resources and structural change. Pope Francis I is the first pope from Latin America, home to more than 40 percent of the world's Catholics. Taking the name of Francis of Assisi, a saint remembered for his commitment to peace and the poor, Pope Francis called for a Church "which is poor and for the poor," naming the need for just wages, access to education and health care, and a distribution of wealth as central to human rights.

At the local level, churches and individuals of a variety of faiths continue to work in solidarity with indigenous movements, women's organizations, and migrants in struggles to defend their human rights. In southern Mexico women such as *Las Patronas* prepare and distribute food and water to migrants crossing the region riding atop cargo trains in extreme heat. These women, often from impoverished, rural communities, are inspired by their faith to assist those in need. At Mexico's northern border, people wash the feet and clean the wounds of migrants who have crossed the desert on foot. It is in these powerful yet seldom visible acts in which people recognize the face of their God in the poor and continue pushing religious institutions in Latin America to address the multiple challenges of human rights in the region.

Bibliography and Suggested Readings

Agosín, Marjorie. *Tapestries of Hope, Threads of Love: The Arpillera Movement in Chile*. Lanham, MD: Rowman & Littlefield, 2008.

Archdiocese of Sao Paulo. *Torture in Brazil*. Trans. Jaime Wright. New York: Random House, 1986.

Barrios de Chungara, Domitila. *Let Me Speak! Testimony of Domitila, a Woman of the Bolivian Mines*. New York: Monthly Review Press, 1978.

Berryman, Phillip. *The Religious Roots of Rebellion: Christians in Central American Revolutions*. Maryknoll, NY: Orbis Books, 1984.

Stubborn Hope: Religion, Politics, and Revolution in Central America. Maryknoll, NY: Orbis Books, 1994.

Bouvard, Marguerite Guzman. *Revolutionizing Motherhood: The Mothers of the Plaza de Mayo*. Wilmington, DE: Scholarly Resources, 1994.

Brysk, Alison. "From Civil Society to Collective Action: The Politics of Religion in Ecuador." In Edward L. Cleary and Timothy J. Steigenga (eds.), *Resurgent Voices in Latin America: Indigenous Peoples, Political Mobilization, and Religious Change*, 25–42. New Brunswick, NJ: Rutgers University Press, 2004.

From Tribal Village to Global Village: Indian Rights and International Relations in Latin America. Stanford, CA: Stanford University Press, 2000.

Carozza, Paolo G. "From Conquest to constitutions: Retrieving a Latin American Tradition of the Idea of Human Rights." *Human Rights Quarterly,* 25 (2003): 281–313.

Chupp, Mark. "Creating Space for Peace: The Central American Peace Portfolio." In Cynthia Sampson and John Paul Lederach (eds.), *From the Ground Up: Mennonite Contributions to International Peacebuilding,* 104–121. Oxford: Oxford University Press, 2000.

Cleary, Edward L. *Mobilizing for Human Rights in Latin America.* Bloomfield, CT: Kumarian Press, 2007.

Engler, Mark. "Toward the 'Rights of the Poor:' Human Rights in Liberation Theology." *Journal of Religious Ethics,* 28 (2000): 339–365.

Esquivia, Ricardo, with Paul Stucky. "Building Peace from Below and Inside: The Mennonite Experience in Colombia." In Cynthia Sampson and John Paul Lederach (eds.), *From the Ground Up: Mennonite Contributions to International Peacebuilding,* 122–140. Oxford: Oxford University Press, 2000.

Fisher, Jo. *Out of the Shadows: Women, Resistance and Politics in South America.* London: Latin America Bureau, 1993.

Fitzpatrick-Behrens, Susan. "Angels in Guatemala: Confronting a Legacy of Official Terror." NACLA Online News (January 5, 2010), https://nacla.org/node/6337

Garrard-Burnett, Virginia. *Terror in the Land of the Holy Spirit: Guatemala under General Efraín Ríos Montt, 1982–1983.* Oxford: Oxford University Press, 2010.

Glendon, Mary Ann. *A World Made New: Eleanor Roosevelt and the Universal Declaration of Human Rights.* New York: Random House, 2001.

Green, Duncan. *Faces of Latin America.* London: Latin American Bureau, 1997.

Gutiérrez, Gustavo. *A Theology of Liberation: History, Politics, Salvation.* Maryknoll, NY: Orbis Books, 1988.

"Church of the Poor." In Edward L. Cleary (ed.), *Born of the Poor: The Latin American Church since Medellín,* 9–25. (Notre Dame: University of Notre Dame Press, 1990).

Hagan, Jacqueline Marie. *Migration Miracle: Faith, Hope, and Meaning on the Undocumented Journey.* Cambridge, MA: Cambridge University Press, 2008.

Hondagneu-Sotelo, Pierrette. *God's Heart Has No Borders: How Religious Activists are Working for Immigrant Rights.* Berkeley: University of California Press, 2008.

Jimenez, Maria. *Humanitarian Crisis: Migrant Deaths at the U.S.-Mexico Border.* American Civil Liberties Union of San Diego and Mexico's National Commission of Human Rights, 2009.

Kovic, Christine. "Demanding Their Dignity as Daughters of God: Catholic Women and Human Rights." In Christine Eber and Christine Kovic (eds.), *Women of Chiapas: Making History in Times of Struggle and Hope,* 131–146. New York: Routledge, 2003.

Mayan Voices for Human Rights: Displaced Catholics in Highland Chiapas. Austin: University of Texas Press, 2005.

Lernoux, Penny. *Cry of the People: The Struggle for Human Rights in Latin America-The Catholic Church in Conflict with U.S. Policy.* New York: Penguin Books, 1980.

Lowy, Michael. "The Socio-Religious Origins of Brazil's Landless Rural Workers Movement." *Monthly Review,* 53(2) (2001): 32.

Mantz, Beatriz. *Paradise in Ashes: A Guatemalan Journey of Courage, Terror, and Hope.* Berkeley, CA: University of California Press, 2004.

Mellibovsky, Matilde. *Circle of Love Over Death: Testimonies of the Mothers of the Plaza de Mayo*. Willimantic, CT: Curbstone Press, 1997.

Navarro, Zander. "Breaking New Ground in Brazil's MST." *NACLA Report on the Americas*, 33 (2000): 36–39.

Ondetti, Gabriel. *Land, Protest, and Politics: The Landless Movement and the Struggle for Agrarian Reform in Brazil*. University Park: Pennsylvania University Press, 2008.

Peterson, Anna L. *Martyrdom and the Politics of Religion: Progressive Catholicism in El Salvador's Civil War*. Albany: State University of New York Press, 1997.

Quigley, Thomas. "The Chilean Coup, the Church and the Human Rights Movement." *America*, 4 (2002): 12–14.

Recovery of Historical Memory Project (REMHI). *Guatemala, Never Again!* Maryknoll, NY: Orbis Books; London: CIIR; Latin America Bureau, 1999.

Rey, Terry. "Catholicism and Human Rights in Haiti: Past, Present, and Future." *Religion and Human Rights*, 3 (2006): 229–248.

Schirmer, Jennifer. "The Seeking of Truth and the Gendering of Consciousness: The CoMadres of El Salvador and the CONAVIGUA Widows of Guatemala." In Sarah A. Radcliffe and Sallie Westwood (eds.), *'Viva:' Women and Popular Protest in Latin America*, 30–64. London and New York: Routledge.

Stephen, Lynn. *Women and Social Movements in Latin America: Power from Below*. Austin: University of Texas Press, 1997.

Traer, Robert. *Faith in Human Rights: Support in Religious Traditions for a Global Struggle*. Washington, DC: Georgetown University Press, 1991.

Weschler, Lawrence. *A Miracle, A Universe: Settling Accounts with Torturers*. Chicago: University of Chicago Press, 1990.

Wright, Scott. *Promised Land: Death and Life in El Salvador*. Maryknoll, NY: Orbis Books, 1994.

34
Religion and Gender in Latin America

KEVIN LEWIS O'NEILL

There was a period, a long stretch of time, when writing Latin American religious history meant leaning on the gendered tropes of conquest and compliance, of domination and liberation, of salvation and submission. Gender was not so much a recognizable object of study as a quiet assumption that guided analysis. Virile, masculine prose carved out seamless narratives while the more theologically inclined wrote Latin American religious history with an eye to the other – to the Other of all others. Enrique Dussel, one might remember, narrates the Church in Latin America with great attention to the face-to-face encounter – with piqued concern for the uneven and ever erotic encounter between the *patrón* and the peasant, between the *encomendero* and the indigenous, between the slave and his freedom. "The experience of being confronted by the face of Someone as someone," he writes, "of an Other as other, a mystery that opens an incomprehensible and sacred beyond which I see not with my eyes and which sees me in my innermost being."[1] Dependency as an interpersonal, existential (even ecclesiastical) condition as well as an economic fact left unquestioned more contemporary interests in subaltern femininities, hegemonic masculinities, queer theory, and, of course, how these identities coincide and collide with religious practice, performance, and patronage throughout Latin America.

That gender remained either uninteresting or unspoken is somewhat understandable. Denominational and deeply parochial research drove historical accounts of religion in Latin America. Scholars placed great emphasis on how Roman Catholic missions and missionaries provided an empirical point of departure for the theorization of contact, conflict, and contradiction. That men drove these missions with a rather robust (even muscular) Christianity did not help the historian. That the pastoral relationships established in the

---

[1] Enrique Dussel, *A History of the Church in Latin America: Colonialism to Liberation (1492–1979)*, trans. Alan Neely (Grand Rapids, MI: Eerdmans, 1981), 6.

Americas between priest and peasant traded on a deeply theological but no less erotic sense of otherness also failed to inspire a generation of scholars. Gender was an afterthought. The subsequent rise of world systems theory and Marxist analysis appreciated power relations to a greater extent to be sure, but at scales that would not glimpse in any significant way the place of gender relations and the role of religious practice in the everyday lives of men and women. A historical commitment to base and superstructure – to the notion that religion exists as a peripheral phenomenon – kept an interest in lived religion at bay. For decades, the term "religion" served as a proxy for the Church, while scholars used "gender" and "sex" interchangeably in a flat demographic sense.

A number of intellectual developments turned the tide, bringing both religion and gender into focus as co-constituting processes. Three are worth flagging. The first is feminism as a recognizable method for doing scholarship. At its most basic, feminism as a political project seeks equal rights and legal protection for women. As an intellectual endeavor, beginning in many respects with the work of Simone de Beauvoir, feminism sought to understand how "one is not born, but rather becomes, a woman."[2] Feminist history, anthropology, geography, and cultural studies quickly became interested in the social construction of woman as other. This attention to the social and existential – as well as how these two levels of sociality relate – pushed scholars of Latin America to consider not simply female leaders but also the everyday lives of women throughout Latin America. From this vantage point the question could be asked, even if the literature did not yet answer, how religion contributed to the marginalization of women – that is, how religion contributed to the production of woman as Other.

The second development is the French tradition of the sociology of religion (*la religion vécue*), or what is known in North American circles as "lived religion."[3] This approach to the study of religion pushes against theological studies and denominational histories to concern itself with religion only insofar as it relates to the context in which religion exists. This impetus to close and careful documentation of how individuals and communities lived their religion emerged for several reasons, including a pastoral concern for Church attendance. Why, some sociologists asked, were fewer French Catholics attending Sunday mass? Regardless of its origins, the approach's popularity

---

2 Simone de Beauvoir, *The Second Sex* (New York: Vintage, 1989 [1952]), 267.
3 David D. Hall, ed., *Lived Religion in America: Toward a History of Practice* (Princeton, NJ: Princeton University Press, 1997).

allowed scholarly registers to shift scales from the macro to the micro, giving historians and anthropologists license to detail the lives of ordinary men and women. And, much like the influence of feminist scholarship, lived religion shifted the analytical focus away from world systems – with its emphasis on core and periphery – to a familiar level of knowledge in which the historian and the anthropologist could assess an interplay between lived faith and gendered identities.

The third, and arguably the most important, development is the work of Michel Foucault, especially his *History of Sexuality*, Volume I. Foucault argues that as a society we are not repressive about sex but rather quite generative about sex. We cannot stop talking about sex. And, Foucault argues, since the seventeenth century this deployment of sexuality has become one of the great social machines, one that connects sexual practices with identities and institutions by way of the body: churches, hospitals, penal codes, psychoanalysis, and so on. In this sense, sexuality has become the truth of our being, something that must be confessed to others. It is this emphasis on the confessional as powerful – as the very means by which subjects come into being – that ultimately inverts previous conceptions of power.

No longer does the historian track in classic Marxist fashion who controls the means of production, whether the church owns land, for example, or whether or not Christians boycott factories. Instead, the scholar follows the intimate but no less institutional confessional discourses that shape subjectivity. For Foucault, this is a methodological turn toward the body. "Hence, I do not envision a 'history of mentalities,'" he writes, "but a 'history of bodies' and the manner in which what is most material and most vital in them has been invested."[4] It is this analytical move, this shift away from structure toward the body – in conjunction with an emphasis on feminist analysis and lived religion – that has brought gender's relationship to religion into greater focus, raising new lines of inquiry about discourse, subjectivity, agency, and the body.

This chapter, in response, follows these three developments to say something about the study of religion and gender in Latin America. It is not an exhaustive review of this work. Although there is a thickening literature on this intersection, there is no canon, no thirty or forty books that one *must* read to understand the field. Instead, there is a style of thought, an approach, that arcs over a rather eclectic group of texts. To touch on a few of them is to

---

4 Michel Foucault, *The History of Sexuality, Volume I*, trans. Robert Hurley (New York: Doubleday, 1980), 152.

address significant methodological and theoretical interventions over the last quarter century within the fields of history, literary criticism, anthropology, religious studies, and theology. For this work is not so much about content as it is about method – about, as Michel Foucault has said, "a question of method."[5] How do scholars conceptualize, theorize, and document religion's relationship to gender in Latin America? Rarely is the answer to this question found in texts that charge at either of these variables head on; instead, the answer seems to be found on the margins and in the footnotes of some dynamic scholarship. Of particular interest here will be those studies that highlight how religion and gender constitute each other in specific historical contexts. It is an observation that moves steadily through the interrelated themes of discourse, bodies, agency, and subjectivities. For when one move through these interrelated themes, it becomes clear that the co-construction of religion and gender often extends beyond the region of Latin America itself to become a rather hemispheric process. It is, in fact, this last point about a hemispheric approach that this chapter stresses, suggesting that regional approaches must expand to include sources and subjects farther north.

Discourse

One configuration of religion and gender in Latin America is the sense that religion is a master narrative. Religion is words. It is discourse. Religion is ideology, and it is this ideology, this religion, that structures the conditions of possibility for gender itself. In Latin America, the master narrative has long been that of the Roman Catholic Church. The suffering body, the subservient woman, the unequivocally dominant male authority – these discourses subjugate women.

To put it another way, one dominant framing of religion and gender in Latin America has been the fastidiously documented idea that religion (as language) writes woman as other – as servant, as slave, as second to man. Complementing this conceptualization is the materiality and the metaphor of "voice" and a focus by historians, anthropologists, and theologians on the rather basic but ever political question: Who has a voice? Interestingly, it is not necessarily the voice itself that concerns many scholars writing in the late 1980s and early 1990s but rather the ability for Latin American women to write

---

5 Michel Foucault, "Questions of Method," in *The Foucault Effect: Studies in Governmentality*, eds. Graham Burchell, Colin Gordon, and Peter Miller (Chicago: University of Chicago Press, 1991), 73–86.

for Latin American women – to frame themselves as women. At the very center of these writings sit questions of agency and subjectivity. This struggle stretches across the fields of history, theology, and anthropology to say that Latin American religion – that is, the Church – is a master narrative that subjugates women. Examples abound.

"*Plotting Woman*," Jean Franco announces, "is about struggles for interpretative power, struggles not waged on the high plane of theory but very often on the margins of canonical genres – in letters and life stories."[6] The struggle that Franco follows is that of Mexican women during the colonial period, with Roman Catholicism as the era's master narrative. She follows, with an eye to the margins, these women's discursive positioning within both the convent and the public sphere. For Franco, all of this is a struggle over marginalization, over being plotted to the margins. Of centrality to this style of analysis is not just the idea of religion as a master narrative – of religion as discourse – but also a series of binaries: center/periphery, norm/exception, metropolitan/Third World, and so on. For Franco, discursive practices plot women at the level of the everyday. The pulpit and the confessional – the sermon and the confession – are privileged sites and genres that allow "celibate men to warn, harangue, interrogate, educate and interpolate the population ... with the 'natural' weakness of women [as] the ideological pin that rotated the [male] axis of power."[7]

Beyond the specificities of this argument, beyond Franco's deft analysis of gender and power, her study is an exemplary approach to this particular framing of religion and gender in Latin America – one that foregrounds discursive conditions of possibility for becoming a certain kind of woman. Central here is a critical awareness of interpretative power: Who has it? Who wants it? Who struggles for it? These are all questions of gender, Franco insists, with her own study highlighting women who wrote under the shadow of Roman Catholic male writers.

Feminist theologians, arguing alongside Franco, write through the language of struggle with great concern for their own discursive possibilities. Theologian María Pilar Aquino's *Nuestro Clamor por la Vida* (Our Cry for Life) challenges hackneyed notions of Latin American women as passive, or in Franco's terms too easily plotted. Aquino's theological voice works against the idea that Latin American women consent to their oppression. Her response is to cite moments of resistance, especially those silenced by the historical

---

6 Jean Franco, *Plotting Women: Gender and Representation in Mexico* (New York: Columbia University Press, 1989), xi.
7 Ibid., xiii.

record and by the shadows of recognized male writers. The examples run far and wide: from material conquest to the systematic silencing of voice, from rape to unequal distribution of domestic labor. Critical to Aquino's theological project is a prevailing sense that religion is a discourse, that theology demands a voice, and that machismo impedes theological discovery.

For Aquino, daily struggles and devotion have the power to rewrite these struggles from the margins to the center. Base Communities, for example, cultivate powerful contexts – spaces set apart from the pulpit and the confessional – for women "[to make] their own word."[8] And it is this productive turn – this idea of women making their own word – that builds atop Franco's sense of religion as a master narrative but in ways that ultimately allow women to reclaim their voice. Aquino writes, "It is not just the Church opting for the poor, including poor women, but that there is also a movement in the other direction – women are opting for this Church and making their own mark on it through their ways of living and reflecting on the faith."[9] Once plotted to the margins by religion, the theological project becomes one of Latin American women writing for Latin American women.

Latin American women writing for (?) Latin American women is a familiar project for the anthropologist. The most provocative effort at reclaiming a voice comes in the form of the *testimonio*. This is the socially and politically charged Latin American narrative of witnessing. Ruth Behar's *Translated Woman* pushes this politically charged genre by fusing religion and gender together through the very act of research. Narrating a powerful encounter between a Cuban-American anthropologist and Esperanza Hernández, a Mexican street peddler, *Translated Woman* centers on the power of testimony and giving voice to the voiceless. Although much the book revolves around religion and witchcraft, it is the actual telling of the story through the collection of data that fuses religion and gender. "Esperanza views her life as worthy of being turned into a story," Behar notes, "because of her notion of story. Certainly a key model for her is the Christian narrative as a story of suffering, and particularly of bodily suffering as a vehicle for the release of spirit and divinity." She continues, "A related story form is the Catholic confession narrative; in fact, Esperanza often compared the story she was telling me to a confession that I, her *comadre* from 'the other side,' was hearing rather than the priest."[10] A relic of the Church

---

8 María Pilar Aquino, *Our Cry for Life: Feminist Theology from Latin America* (Eugene, OR: Wipf and Stock, 2002 [Spanish 1992]), 65.
9 Ibid., 49.
10 Ruth Behar, *Translated Woman: Crossing the Border with Esperanza's Story* (Boston, MA: Beacon, 2003 [1993]), 11.

itself, a onetime technique to plot women, the testimony and the confession become the quintessential vehicles for Latin American women to gain a voice as well as an audience. The curiosity here is how the gender roles get reversed, with Behar serving as the priest and her informant as the confessor. It is a move that generates controversy.

"My name is Rigoberta Menchú," the most emblematic *testimonio* announces. "I am twenty-three years old. This is my testimony. I didn't learn it from a book and I didn't learn it alone. I'd like to stress that it's not only my life, it's also the testimony of my people ... My story is the story of all poor Guatemalans. My personal experience is the reality of a whole people."[11] Sincere, declarative, and gripping, *I, Rigoberta Menchú* follows the same rapprochement between religion and gender in Latin America that Behar produces while also narrating the life of an indigenous woman who must navigate the Catholic Church and indigenous spirituality amid the unthinkably difficult circumstance of genocide.

That the book takes the form of an extended confession; that it was transcribed by a journalist, allows the text to take the form of similar testimonies such as Augustine's *Confessions*. Yet, unlike Augustine, whom many consider to have initiated the genre, an anthropologist named David Stoll found error in this effort. Wrinkles emerged with her story, with a Latin American woman narrating the life of a Latin American woman. Stoll describes his moment of suspicion, "One of my questions had caught [Domingo] off guard. The Army had burned prisoners alive in the town plaza? Not here, [Domingo] said. Yet, this is what I read in *I, Rigoberta Menchú* ... yet the army had never burned prisoners alive in the town plaza, Domingo said, and he was the first of seven townsmen who told me the same."[12]

Stoll's charges lit a fuse, one that raised a powerful question wrought with pointedly gendered questions about authority: Who is Rigoberta Menchú? What emerged from this drama, this epistemological spectacle, was a conversation about truth, authority, and representation that continually returned not simply to the theme of gender (for this was a woman's story) but also to Christian themes of truth and confession. They proved to be challenging debates, never truly settled but that nonetheless pointed to the limitations of language – not simply in reporting events but also in communicating the felt experience of religion and gender in Latin America.

11 Rigoberta Menchú, *I, Rigoberta Menchú: An Indian Woman in Guatemala*, trans. and ed. Elisabeth Burgos-Debray (London: Verso, 1984), 1.
12 David Stoll, *Rigoberta Menchú and the Story of All Poor Guatemalans* (Boulder, CO: Westview, 2008 [1999]), 2.

Claiming narrative authority or owning the means of discursive production productively frames religion as language and language as the means by which identity and agency come into being. The problem becomes, of course, that when religion gets reduced to language, to mere words, and when even practices are discursive, then religion's materiality fades – as does gender's materiality. Emile Durkheim famously divides the elementary forms of the religious life into not just the sacred and the profane but also into rites and beliefs. He announces, "Religious phenomena are naturally arranged in two fundamental categories: beliefs and rites. The first are states of opinion, and consist in representations; the second are determined modes of action. Between these two classes of facts there is all the difference which separates thought from action."[13]

While much of the last century has witnessed a structuralist, deeply functionalist interest in the semiotics of sacrality, Durkheim's own commitment to collective effervescence hints at much more unstable but nonetheless deeply embodied actions. Durkheim's notion of collective effervescence – the perception of collective energy that people experience together – even invites the scholar to forever qualify his or her study with a concern for the corporeal. It is, Durkheim insists, "warmth, life, enthusiasm, enhancement of all mental activity, uplift of the individual above himself."[14] Collective effervescence shapes a group into a crowd, a mob into a church; it sets aside particular people or places as sacred. It also reminds the scholar of religion and gender in Latin America that such analysis cannot just be about words. It must also be about bodies.

Bodies

Gian Lorenzo Bernini's sculpture *St. Teresa in Ecstasy* (1652), located in Rome, represents one of Teresa of Ávila's (1515–1582) mystical experiences of God, which the sixteenth-century Spanish saint narrates with unblinkingly erotic imagery. In her autobiography, St. Teresa writes how "the great love of God" often left her "utterly consumed," "penetrated to [her] entrails," and made her "utter several moans" for both the "intense pain" and its "sweetness."[15] Over the years, more than one visitor has parroted Jacques Lacan's response to

---

13 Emile Durkheim, *The Elementary Forms of the Religious Life* (New York: Dover Publications, 2008 [1915]), 36.
14 Ibid., 427.
15 Edgar Allison Peers, *Studies of the Spanish Mystics* (London: The Sheldon Press, 1927), 197.

Bernini's statue. "She's coming," Lacan commented, "There's no doubt about it."[16] It is amidst intense pain and pleasure that one finds not simply a picture of divine joy in all of its excess but also a sign that the body sits at the intersection of religion and gender, even sexuality, in Latin America but also beyond.

Whether tickled or tortured, excited or exacerbated, the body produces gendered and gendering effects throughout the literature on Latin American religion – that, to quote Caroline Walker Bynum, all Christian language "opens out beyond itself to an intractable physicality."[17] The metaphor of Christ as bridegroom says as much. St. John of the Cross (1542–1591), a contemporary of St. Teresa of Ávila, describes his overwhelming yearning for a deep, spiritual connection with God. He writes: "I abandoned and forgot myself, / laying my face on my Beloved; / all things ceased; I went out from myself, / leaving my cares / forgotten among the lilies."[18] What St. John of the Cross accomplishes throughout his writings is to establish the notion that "losing oneself in the lilies" is a deeply religious, explicitly Christian concern. His poetry makes thinkable today what was obviously salient in the Medieval era – that eroticism is central to Christianity and that desire is a narrative device, if not a phenomenological tool, that contributes to the production of Christian worlds as well as bodies.

Peter Sigal's work advances this line of questioning by exploring homosexual desire in the Spanish America during the colonial era. What did it mean for indigenous and Iberian groups for men to have sexual relations with other men? For Sigal, this remains a question of marking the body, of looking at the archive in ways that reveal the body's centrality to these cultural and social processes. He writes, "Homosexual desires and acts were written onto the human body in a way that allowed for a broad social critique." Sigal suggests, "The body itself was rewritten and revised during the process of colonization.... Sodomy was presented within colonialist discourse as an act which showed a degraded, effeminate nobility."[19]

For religion to revise bodies it is important to understand religion's hold on the body and its ability to mark the body both through ritual and also everyday

---

16 Jacques Lacan, "God and Woman's Jouissance" in *On Feminine Sexuality: The Limits of Love and Knowledge, Book XX: Encore, 1972–73* (New York: Norton, 1998), 76.
17 Caroline Walker Bynum, *Fragmentation and Redemption: Essays on Gender and the Human Body in Medieval Religion* (New York: Zone Books, 1992), 20.
18 John of the Cross, *The Collected Works of Saint John of the Cross*, trans. Kieran Kavanaugh and Otilio Rodriguez (Washington, DC: Institute of Carmelite Studies, 1991), 359.
19 Pete Sigal, ed., *Infamous Desire: Male Homosexuality in Colonial Latin America* (Chicago: University of Chicago Press, 2003), 13.

practices and religious routines. The discursive dimensions of such acts begin with missionary work and writings that describe homosexual acts as effeminate. The Jesuit Blàs Valera, in the Andes, helped to set the horizon against which these colonial subjects and their bodies came to be understood. He writes that many indigenous priests "offered themselves from childhood and lasted, not only in continence until old age, but in virginity ... Many of these or others were eunuchs, what they called *corrasca*, and either they castrated themselves, in reverence to their gods, or others castrated them when they were children, so that they served in this way."[20] It is ultimately the uncolonial body that resists discipline that missionaries try most to manage. Reading third gender subjectivities across heteronormative assumptions, these missionaries ultimately make the seemingly unusual (at least to colonial sensibilities) universally abnormal.

The postcolonial body seems to fare no better even if the cultural and historical coordinates change. Elizabeth Brusco's *The Reformation of Machismo* is but one example. For Brusco, corporeal motivations drive the conversion to Protestant evangelicalism in Colombia.[21] Asceticism, for example, sits at the heart of evangelicalism. No drinking. No smoking. No philandering. While Brusco provides a somewhat functional analysis of these practices, suggesting that they redirect male income back into the household, thereby raising the living standard of women and children, she nonetheless advances a clear sense that evangelicals corral their bodies. They adorn the once aberrant subject in morally righteous products, pairing proper clothes with proper etiquette and just the right confessional practices.

This all provides, to quote Jean and John Comaroff, "an effective means of working on the self and a fitting medium for signaling its interior improvements."[22] Be punctual. Sit up straight. Tuck in your shirt. This is good Christian living, and this is what they do. They discipline themselves for God along rather gendered lines. One of Brusco's female informants, remembering a bout with illness that left her malnourished, preaches,

> We Christians have to feed ourselves, sisters, because, some time ago, I was completely malnourished ... And I thought to myself, if that's what it's like

---

20 Michael J. Horswell, "Toward an Andean Theory of Ritual Same-Sex Sexuality and Third-Gender Subjectivity," in *Infamous Desire: Male Homosexuality in Colonial Latin America*, ed. Pete Sigal (Chicago: University of Chicago Press, 2003), 44.
21 Elizabeth E. Brusco, *The Reformation of Machismo: Evangelical Conversion and Gender in Colombia* (Austin, TX: University of Texas Press, 1995).
22 Jean Comaroff and John Comaroff, *Of Revelation and Revolution*, Vol. 2: *The Dialectics of Modernity on a South African Frontier* (Chicago: University of Chicago Press, 1997), 223.

for the body to be malnourished, what must the person be like who is malnourished spiritually? We are nourished – body, soul, and spirit. And our spirit must be completely nourished, fat, but if we don't eat the word of the Lord, if we don't nourish ourselves with it, we are going to be more malnourished than I was when I was sick.[23]

Healthy or malnourished, skinny or fat, devoted or delinquent – the body becomes not simply the metaphor for spiritual cultivation but also the very material that evangelical Protestants manipulate.

Discipline and punishment go hand in hand, as Foucault notes and the literature on Latin America demonstrates. Much of this literature animates torture's passion – its pain, its pleasure, its religious overtones. One of the most powerful passion narratives to emerge in recent memory comes from the spiritual biography of Dianna Ortiz. Ortiz is an Ursuline missionary from the United States who was kidnapped in 1989 by Guatemalan security forces operating under the direction of a US official. Blindfolded, burned with cigarettes 111 times, and gang-raped, Ortiz was filmed by her torturers. Guatemalan security forces intensified Ortiz's humiliation by prompting Ortiz to consider those who might one day view her anguish. Her family? Her friends? Her sisters in Christ? "Well, you know, we have the photos of you, and the videos," Ortiz's captors told her. "Those could be embarrassing."[24] Ortiz reflects, "Jesus also was tortured, and he cried out on the cross, 'My God, my God, why have you forsaken me?' When I was first taken down into the basement of that building in Guatemala I asked myself the same question – why had God abandoned me?"[25]

For Ortiz, there is no glamour in Jesus' death. This is why Ortiz parallels her experience of torture with Jesus' crucifixion, even going so far as modeling her moments in a Guatemalan torture chamber after the Stations of the Cross, the Church's formal meditation on Jesus' final hours:

Jesus meets his mother ... I see my mother, as I saw her when José left me in the dark, before the interrogation started ... I traveled in my mind or with my spirit and found her in her bedroom, lying on her side, facing the wall. She is sobbing ... *Veronica wipes the face of Jesus* ... I remember Alejandro bringing the wet cloth near my face. *Jesus is stripped of his garments*... I am not

---

23 Elizabeth E. Brusco, *The Reformation of Machismo: Evangelical Conversion and Gender in Colombia* (Austin: University of Texas Press, 1995), 133.
24 Dianna Ortiz and Patricia Davis, *The Blindfold's Eyes: My Journey from Torture to Truth* (Maryknoll, NY: Orbis Books, 2004), 33.
25 Ibid., 132.

reflecting, but remembering when and how each piece of my clothing was removed.²⁶

Christ's passion is Ortiz's passion. The body sits at the center of both engagements, in need of healing, a need that fills the literature on Latin America. Ortiz's story serves as a proxy for so many others who have suffered. The pain, and its call for relief, demands healing.

Healing is, for many, the underside of terror. Michael Taussig tells us as much. In *Shamanism, Colonialism, and the Wild Man*, Taussig details events during the first quarter of the twentieth century when the Indians of the Putumayo River in South America suffered extreme terror and torture, all to make them dependent on the rubber companies. The result was absurd levels of violence that Taussig represents with gruesome quotes. Women raped, men quartered, children left to die, bodies lying upon bodies – all evoking a somewhat cultural explanation. Taussig reflects, "Torture and terror are ritualized art forms and ... far from being spontaneous, sui generis, and an abandonment of what are often called the values of civilization, such rites of terror have a deep history deriving power and meaning from those very values."²⁷

Woven into these rites is an interdependently complex set of cultural traditions that include the colonial and the capitalistic but also the Catholic and the shamanic. Taussig pulls his reader in, closer to the body of the abused, in the name of knowledge. For beyond the rationalized body, the one systematized by Christianity and capitalism, the one murdered by rubber extraction, sits an ability to heal that Taussig also elucidates. Taussig writes, "The road became an object of Indian image-making too ... [The events that took place on that road] became that against which one defined oneself as superior and civilized, so the Indian shaman could be a source of esoteric power, a beacon of relief in a beleaguered world."²⁸ This is how Taussig as anthropologist found himself amid the Indians of the Putumayo River, ingesting a ritualized hallucinogenic called *yage* for the sake of fieldwork, for the sake of knowledge. His own reflections, while in the midst of *yage* trips, or even following a long night with a shaman, allowed his body to serve as the principal medium through which to understand not just religion in Latin American but also the power, the potential, of healing.

---

26 Ibid., 50.
27 Michael Taussig, *Shamanism, Colonialism, and the Wild Man: A Study in Terror and Healing* (Chicago: University of Chicago Press, 1991), 133.
28 Ibid., 320.

Agency

The problem with the body, or at least with how the body has come to be theorized at the intersection of religion and gender, especially in Latin America, is that discursive analyses tend to render the body limp. Michel Foucault, for example, tends to treat the body like a big lump of clay. "Society has an immediate hold on the body," Foucault writes, "Society invests it, marks it, trains it, tortures it, forces it to carry out tasks, to perform ceremonies, to emit signs."[29] This does not satisfy everyone, if only because bodies are not always docile. They yelp. They howl. They moan. Or, in more liberal terms, they make decisions.

Pierre Bourdieu's *Outline to a Theory of Practice* productively struck this debate between the limits of structure and the power of agency. Do societal structures make the person, or can the person navigate societal structures? Which determines which? A dense vocabulary, inspired by Bourdieu, quickly provided the tools by which to navigate the phenomenological and the structural. These terms included habitus, field, heterodoxy, capital, orthodoxy, and so on, all to focus analytical interest onto the context in which one acts and lives. Bourdieu writes, "When habitus encounters a social world of which it is the product, it finds itself 'as a fish in water,' it does not feel the weight of water and takes the world about itself for granted."[30]

This interest in fish amid water, or people within their society, not only grounded much of the historical and ethnographic accounts of religion and gender in Latin America but also pushed this debate over structure and agency to some important conclusions – to argue that structure, especially superstructure, dominates but that resistance remains, even at everyday levels. It is a debate directly concerned with the question of religion and gender, as scholars throughout Latin America continue to assess the means by which religious subjects either cultivate agency amid a gendered or gendering religious context or submit to that very context in the name of religion and gender norms.

The clearest example of this debate bounces between Puerto Rico and Spanish Harlem in an ethnography of not Christianity but rather crack. Philippe Bourgois's *In Search of Respect* is a study of social marginalization in inner city America through an intimate look at street-level drug dealers in East Harlem. Driving this study is a concern for agency amid structure.

---

29 Michel Foucault, *Discipline and Punish: The Birth of the Prison*, trans. Alan Sheridan (New York: Vintage, 1995 [1977]), 23.
30 Pierre Bourdieu and Loic J.D. Wacquant, *An Invitation to Reflexive Sociology* (Chicago: University of Chicago Press, 1992), 127.

Bourgois writes, "Building on the analytic framework of cultural production theory and drawing from feminism, I hope to restore the agency of culture, the autonomy of individuals, and the centrality of gender and the domestic sphere to a political economic understanding of persistent poverty and social marginalization."[31] To be sure, religion is hardly present – minus a few references now and again to the loss of religion. Bourgois writes,

> In the late 1920s, the Italian priest of the Catholic Church two blocks down from the Game Room [or drug distribution point] told a graduate student that 'the reckless destruction of the spirit of youth is getting worse and there is less and less consideration of property rights. This is due to the want of religion and the lack of respect for authority.'[32]

However, it is ultimately Bourgois's use of ritual action that links this study to the question of religion and gender that has since propelled scholars to think about agency within society. Keying in on the question of agency, wondering aloud whether his informants were navigating society or simply sociopathic, Bourgois looks at the ritualization of gang rape among Puerto Rican males. "Learning to be a rapist was very definitely part of Primo's coming-of-age," writes Bourgois, "Tagging after the big boys on the street, he was repeatedly excluded for being too young – or for not wanting – to participate ... The alternative was for Primo to bond with his older peer group by participating in this violent male ritual. It was only later that Primo learned to become sexually aroused."[33]

As Bourgois follows this thread from life history to life history, from New York to Puerto Rico, what becomes apparent is an approach to agency that pits the individual against society at some of the most morally charged moments of a person's life. Also argued is the power of ritual, something that scholars of religion have long advocated, and its ability to shape behavior. To linger on moments of ritualization, when practice becomes rote, is to watch society forming agents.

Donald Kulick's *Travestis* explores this further. He ethnographically details the lives of transgendered prostitutes (called *travestis* in Portuguese) in the Brazilian city of Salvador. As Kulick explains, *Travestis* are males who adopt female clothing styles and hairstyles while at the same time undergoing hormone treatment and breast augmentation. Kulick writes that, in spite of

---

31 Philippe Bourgois, *In Search of Respect: Selling Crack in El Barrio* (Cambridge: Cambridge University Press, 2002), 12.
32 Ibid., 261.
33 Ibid., 206.

these efforts at transformation, "there is strong consensus among travestis in Salvador that any travesti who claims to be a woman is mentally disturbed. A travesti is not a woman and can never be a woman, they tell one another, because God created him male."[34] It is this last point, the one about God, about a person being unable to change himself into a herself, that lines the outer edges of this study, with the Catholic Church and the Afrobrazilian religion of Candomblé sharing equal footing. For *travestis* speak of agency a great deal, Kulick tells us.

> Whenever travestis talk about their relationships with their boyfriends and about the presents and money that they give them, they always stress their own agency. They all emphasize that they chose their boyfriends, not vice versa, and they maintain that they select to support them and give them things because they want to ... But is this magnanimity really entirely uncoerced?[35]

Although it is difficult to settle such debates, it is telling how theories of ritualization fortify their efforts at making gender. Predictably, at least for the scholar of religion, altars and their accoutrements remain forever present during this struggle between individual and society:

> From somewhere near the front of this altar, Banana reached up and took down a wad of newspaper filled with what looked like a pale green powder.... She sprinkled some of the powder on her head. I asked Banana what the powder was for, and she replied, as I expected she would, with her habitual gesture of pulling down the lower lid of one eye and gazing at me meaningfully for a second: the Olho Grosso. Thus protected [from the evil eye], Banana walked over to her little shelf and took a small squeeze bottle of deodorant ... Banana was clearly taking no chances that customers would pass her by.[36]

Curiously functionalist but forever empirical, Kulick's nod toward ritual proves productive for those interested in understanding how subjects not only navigate their gendered identities but also produce them actively, not in spite of religion but often through their religion.

This struggle between structure and agency, between subject and society, intersects constantly with religion and gender for those wrestling with addiction. Stanley Brandes's seminal ethnography, *Staying Sober in Mexico*, focuses on Alcoholics Anonymous, a common therapeutic response to alcoholism. Brandes notes not only its centrality to Mexican sobriety, at least in Mexico

---

34 Don Kulick, *Travesti: Sex, Gender, and Culture among Brazilian Transgendered Prostitutes* (Chicago: University of Chicago Press, 1998), 84.
35 Ibid., 112.
36 Ibid., 4–5.

City, but also the therapy's tendency to rely on rather gendered and Catholic tropes of self-reliance and self-discovery. Much of the process, much of sobriety, Brandes observes, involving redefining gender roles to maintain one's masculinity. What does it mean to be a sober man?

Of curious interest is also how this Protestant organization, or at least one with Protestant roots, has been able to flourish in Mexico's Roman Catholic context. This intersection of masculinity and Catholicism not only remakes inner worlds but also demonstrates how rituals of self-disclosure of trust and fraternity place the individual between will indiscretions and societal expectations. Brandes makes this dynamic clear at every turn. He writes, "Continuity is expressed in the social structure, the sets of relations which make for firmness of expectation, for validation of past experience in terms of similar experience in the future. Members of a society look for a reliable guide to action, and the structure of the society gives this."[37] Much of this structure emerges in the small group settings, the tremendously effective (even affective) all-men meetings that Brandes attended. "What the meetings accomplish, as much as anything, is to structure the men's lives and fill otherwise dangerously free moments with a small, tight-knit society of caring companions."[38]

The injection of Roman Catholicism into all of this strategized homosociality comes as little surprise given the context and the intent of Alcoholics Anonymous in Mexico City. How could Catholicism not form the very field upon which these men struggle for sobriety? Brandes sees sobriety and devotion conveniently coinciding alongside each other, knitting together a set of practices that structure the agency of each individual alcoholic.

> The social structure of Alcoholics Anonymous," Brandes explains, "is consonant with a key element of Mexican popular Catholicism: the *compadrazgo*, a major variant of what anthropologists call ritual or fictive kinship ... *Compadarazgo*, in George Foster's words, 'is the Spanish term denoting the reciprocal relationships resulting from the several ritual sponsorships required by the Catholic Church: baptism, confirmation, first communion, and marriage.[39]

Ritualized kinship structures, bolstering confessional communities, make agentive masculinities in Mexico City. This is the place of agency and of structure in studies of religion and gender in Latin America.

---

37 Stanley Brandes, *Staying Sober in Mexico City* (Austin: University of Texas Press, 2002), 206.
38 Ibid., 197.
39 Ibid., 45.

Subjectivity

"In Greek ethics," writes Michel Foucault, "people were concerned with their moral conduct, their ethics, their relations to themselves and to others ... what they were worried about, their theme was to constitute a kind of ethics which was an aesthetics of existence."[40] By ethics, Foucault does not mean morality. Gilles Deleuze writes, "The key thing, for Foucault, is that subjectification isn't to do with morality, with any moral code: it's ethical and aesthetic, as opposed to morality, which partakes of knowledge and power."[41] Ethics is a way of seeing the world and of living in the world.

It is this ethics, this way of seeing the world, that contributes to the constitution of subjectivity – because Foucault, following Plato, sees the practice of virtue as a skill or craft that makes a person. This includes crafts such as medicine or fitness but also religious practices. Individuals employ each of these to make their lives more: more virtuous, more pious, more fulfilling. The key to ethical subjectivity is this focus on micropractices and how these minute devotionals contribute to the construction of not just manliness or womanliness but also a human, a citizen, even a consumer.

Religion and gender, by way of subjectivity, define micropolitics throughout Latin America with a growing number of scholars exploring their intersections in new and exciting ways. They often do so by extending their analysis, at least in part, beyond Latin America because it is difficult to circumscribe subjectivity with regional coordinates. The works reviewed in this subsection, for example, traverse the globe with mega-churches, migration, pharmaceutical industries, and the largest retail store in the world. It is this boundlessness, in fact, that makes subjectivity and the processes of subjectification such a dynamic object of inquiry for scholars interested in the intersection of religion and gender not just in Latin America but across the Americas as a whole.

"There is a place in the South of Brazil called Vita," writes João Biehl. "Vita was founded in 1987 by Zé das Drogas, a former street kid and drug dealer. After having converted to Pentecostalism, Zé had a vision in which the Spirit told him to open a place where people like him could find God and regenerate."[42] Biehl tells a story of this one community and "subjectivities unmade and remade under

---

40 Michel Foucault, "On the Genealogy of Ethics: An Overview of the Work in Progress," in *The Essential Works of Foucault, 1954–1984*, Vol. 1: *Ethics, Subjectivity, and Truth*, ed. Paul Rabinow, trans. Robert Hurley et al. (New York: The New Press, 1997), 255.
41 Gilles Deleuze, *Negotiations, 1972–1990* (New York: Columbia University Press, 1995), 114.
42 João Biehl, "Vita: Life in a Zone of Social Abandonment," *Social Text*, 19, no. 3 (Fall 2001), 131. See also João Biehl, *Vita: Life in a Zone of Social Abandonment* (Berkeley: University of California Press, 2005), 43.

economic pressures, pharmaceuticals as moral technologies, a public common sense that lets the unsound and unproductive die."[43]

These are processes by which humans become animals – processes that can be observed through the subtle gestures of not just what people do to themselves but what people of authority and power allow those of less authority and less power do to themselves. "You will see what being human in this land is becoming, what men do to men," explains an AIDS worker.[44] Biehl focuses his ethnographic efforts on one informant, Catalina, and thinks about her being cast aside and the subjectivity this yields. It is an important question that again places religion at the margins of analysis but nonetheless allows room to consider the Pentecostal legacies of Vita, the religious subjectivities implied by Catalina's own struggles, and what these contribute to making this woman a woman in spite of being rendered inhuman. Biehl writes, "The truth of Catarina's condition as a 'leftover' is located in the split between her own mortified body and a social body that vanishes from her. The abandoned subject is not originally so."[45]

Of possibly most interest when considering the religious dimensions of this story and how the author constructs Catalina's own subjectivity as something representable is that Biehl himself, a scholar with a PhD in not just anthropology but also religious studies, relies methodologically on the practice of what he calls "witnessing." Catalina, Biehl argues, marks "a socially authorized death, mundane and unaccounted for, and we partook of it in our foreign and native gazing, in our blend of learned indifference, sense of intolerability, and failed witnessing."[46] The charge to witness better, to witness more, carries Christian connotations that color the study of subjectivity, that even herald back to an interest in *testimonio*.

Yet, there is also the story of what Christians do to themselves. This is the story that I tell in *City of God*. There, I assess neo-Pentecostal formations of citizenship in postwar Guatemala City with an observation and a pair of arguments. The observation is that neo-Pentecostalism provides an increasing number of postwar Guatemalans with their sense of citizenship – with a sense of belonging to Guatemala, of being responsible for Guatemala, and of having the means to act on behalf of Guatemala. The first argument is that Christian practices such as praying and fasting against electoral violence not only constitute Christians as citizens but also shift the moral responsibility for

---

43 Biehl, *Vita*, book jacket.
44 Ibid., 132.
45 Ibid., 145.
46 Ibid., 133.

postwar Guatemala from historical and structural factors onto the shoulders of believers. The second argument is that the practice of Christian citizenship provides an increasing number of Guatemalans with a deep sense of meaning while also limiting the avenues through which they can act. The more Christian citizens link themselves to the fate of the nation by praying and fasting a new Guatemala into existence the less time, energy, and interest they have to participate in more traditional modes of citizenship, what some commentators would call "real" politics, such as community organizing, public demonstrations, and voter registration campaigns.

All of this plays out rather dramatically, for example, during neo-Pentecostal formations of fatherhood, when it is seen that proper fatherhood will generate a new generation of citizens as well as the kind of change that this small, postwar country really needs. One informant explained, "It's so profound to think about. You need a father with principles to form children into people who can make decisions. The right decisions. You see!" He continued, "Guatemala needs a generation of fathers to make the next generation and then the next generation and the next generation."[47] Fatherhood thus becomes a vehicle through which neo-Pentecostals grapple with the weight of transitional times, through which they come to own and answer their responsibilities.

It is also with Guatemala and responsibilities that Bethany Moreton begins an essay on Wal-Mart. She makes clear not only that Wal-Mart fulfills a Christian mission, with its college scholarship programs for Central Americans, but also that its brand of capitalism intersects brilliantly with new forms of Christianity – that there exists an observable relationship between the post-Fordist service industry and the kind of service-driven Christianity at play today. Of particular interest is how this commitment to service, with its hemispheric reach, remodels a trope of religion and gender such that a one-time muscular Christianity now takes backstage to a much softer service-driven masculinity.

Moreton writes, "The most conservative branches of Protestantism kept the obsession with missionary manliness on display well into the new era, and the constant harping on 'softness' left little to the imagination. In 1976, the Southern Baptist Convention launched a twenty-five-year missionary campaign called, incredibly, 'Bold Mission Thrust.'" But this changed, she notes, with a need for service in the global service economy pacing alongside the kind

---

[47] Kevin Lewis O'Neill, *City of God: Christian Citizenship in Postwar Guatemala* (Berkeley: University of California Press, 2009), 121.

of Christian subjectivities that Protestants actively cultivated. At the core of all of this was an interest in the servant – the humble servant as Christianity's paragon of subjectivity but also of masculinity. Moreton continues,

> This servant would win followers by humbling himself; he would lead men by declining to command them. Of course, there is no merit in humbling yourself if you are already genuinely outranked. It is specifically the act of choosing humility that proves your superiority – choice, that key moment of Protestant conversion, that signal virtue of contracts and consumption, that irreducible constituent of freedom defined for all the world in market terms.[48]

The key here is how the simple act of buying and selling, of serving the global service economy, connects the world of religion and gender at a micropolitical level, where the individual's very lifestyle gets cultivated through the very institutions they serve.

The Future

The last quarter century moved beyond the macropolitics of Marxist thought with an attention to the micropolitical production of gender by way of religious practice and performance. The yield has been a growing number of studies that focus on otherwise ignored distinctions and devotionals. The effect has been tremendous. Yet, the future holds more complicated approaches for the future holds more complicated formations. Moreton's work on Wal-Mart suggests as much. The focus can no longer be on that one community or that one practice. It must turn toward more dynamic scales, including the close study but in a way that the archival or ethnographic focus links up to processes described as transnational or global.

The problem is that it is not yet obvious how to do this well. Historians and anthropologists now do a fine job of looking at the local – at the production of a certain kind of gendered religiosity, for example – but then tend to jump from this supposed local to a much grander global. The same can be said for those who project their local study as representative of Latin America and for those who cordon off their study to demonstrate its own mechanics. Both approaches seem inadequate for the worlds in which scholars think. Too much gets lost in such conversion.

---

48 Bethany E. Moreton, "The Soul of Neoliberalism," *Social Text*, 25, no. 3 (Fall 2007): 115. See also Bethany Moreton, *To Serve God and Wal-Mart: The Making of Christian Free Enterprise* (Cambridge, MA: Harvard University Press, 2010).

While anthropology has not yet "gotten it right" and while a range of disciplines still wrestle with questions of scale in assessing whether "the local" and "the global" provide any kind of analytical clarity, the study of religion and gender in Latin America must move beyond its own regional assumptions. As a question of method, scholars must develop their own conceptual register for religion's gendering movement and for the kinds of ambivalent interrelationships that stretch beyond oceans and borders. The field must respatialize its approach to the study of religion to better assess the transnational processes that mold and mediate belief and belonging today. A focus on gender, as it relates to religion, will help to move this process along.

Bibliography and Suggested Readings

Aquino, María Pilar. *Our Cry for Life: Feminist Theology from Latin America*. Eugene, OR: Wipf and Stock, 2002.
de Beauvoir, Simone. *The Second Sex*. New York: Vintage, 1989 [1952].
Behar, Ruth. *Translated Woman: Crossing the Border with Esperanza's Story*. Boston, MA: Beacon, 2003.
Beverley, John. *Testimonio: On the Politics of Truth*. Minneapolis: University of Minnesota Press, 2004.
Biehl, João. "Vita: Life in a Zone of Social Abandonment." *Social Text*, 19, no. 3 (Fall 2001): 131–149.
Bourdieu, Pierre. *Outline of a Theory of Practice*. trans. Richard Nice. Cambridge: Cambridge University Press, 1977.
Bourdieu, Pierre, and Loic J.D. Wacquant. *An Invitation to Reflexive Sociology*. Chicago: University of Chicago Press, 1992.
Bourgois, Philippe. *In Search of Respect: Selling Crack in El Barrio*. Cambridge: Cambridge University Press, 2002.
Brandes, Stanley. *Staying Sober in Mexico City*. Austin: University of Texas Press, 2002.
Brusco, Elizabeth E. *The Reformation of Machismo: Evangelical Conversion and Gender in Colombia*. Austin: University of Texas Press, 1995.
Comaroff, Jean, and John Comaroff. *Of Revelation and Revolution*, Vol. 2: *The Dialectics of Modernity on a South African Frontier*. Chicago: University of Chicago Press, 1997.
Deleuze, Gilles. *Negotiations, 1972–1990*. New York: Columbia University Press, 1995.
Durkheim, Emile. *The Elementary Forms of the Religious Life*. New York: Dover Publications, 2008 [1915].
Dussel, Enrique. *A History of the Church in Latin America: Colonialism to Liberation (1492–1979)*. Trans. Alan Neely. Grand Rapids, MI: Eerdmans, 1981.
Foucault, Michel. *Discipline and Punish: The Birth of the Prison*. Trans. Alan Sheridan. New York: Vintage, 1995.
  "On the Genealogy of Ethics: An Overview of the Work in Progress." In *The Essential Works of Foucault, 1954–1984*, Vol. 1: *Ethics, Subjectivity, and Truth*, edited by Paul Rabinow. Trans. Robert Hurley et al., 253–280. New York: The New Press, 1997.

The History of Sexuality, Vol. I. Trans. Robert Hurley. New York: Doubleday, 1980.

"Questions of Method." In Graham Burchell, Colin Gordon, and Peter Miller (eds.), *The Foucault Effect: Studies in Governmentality*, 73–86.Chicago: University of Chicago Press, 1991.

Franco, Jean. *Plotting Women: Gender and Representation in Mexico*. New York: Columbia University Press, 1989.

Grandin, Greg. *Who Is Rigoberta Menchú?* London: Verso, 2011.

Hall, David D. *Lived Religion in America: Toward a History of Practice*. Princeton, NJ: Princeton University Press, 1997.

Horswell, Michael J. "Toward an Andean Theory of Ritual Same-Sex Sexuality and Third-Gender Subjectivity." In Pete Sigal (ed.), *Infamous Desire: Male Homosexuality in Colonial Latin America*, 25–69. Chicago: University of Chicago Press, 2003.

Kulick, Don. *Travesti: Sex, Gender, and Culture among Brazilian Transgendered Prostitutes*. Chicago: University of Chicago Press, 1998.

Lacan, Jacques. "God and Woman's Jouissance." In *On Feminine Sexuality: The Limits of Love and Knowledge, Book XX: Encore, 1972–73*. New York: W. W. Norton, 1998.

Menchú, Rigoberta. *I, Rigoberta Menchú: An Indian Woman in Guatemala*. Trans. and ed. Elisabeth Burgos-Debray. London: Verso, 1984.

Moreton, Bethany. *To Serve God and Wal-Mart: The Making of Christian Free Enterprise*. Cambridge, MA: Harvard University Press, 2010.

"The Soul of Neoliberalism." *Social Text*, 25, no. 3 (Fall 2007): 103–123.

O'Neill, Kevin Lewis. *City of God: Christian Citizenship in Postwar Guatemala*. Berkeley: University of California Press, 2009.

Ortiz, Dianna, and Patricia Davis. *The Blindfold's Eyes: My Journey from Torture to Truth*. Maryknoll, NY: Orbis Books, 2004.

Peers, Edgar Allison. *Studies of the Spanish Mystics*. London: The Sheldon Press, 1927.

Sigal, Pete. *Infamous Desire: Male Homosexuality in Colonial Latin America*. Chicago: University of Chicago Press, 2003.

Stoll, David. *Rigoberta Menchú and the Story of All Poor Guatemalans*. Boulder, CO: Westview, 2008 [1999].

Taussig, Michael. *Shamanism, Colonialism, and the Wild Man: A Study in Terror and Healing*. Chicago: University of Chicago Press, 1991.

Walker Bynum, Caroline. *Fragmentation and Redemption: Essays on Gender and the Human Body in Medieval Religion*. New York: Zone Books, 1992.

35
Christian Churches, Reproduction, and Sexuality in Latin America

MARIA DAS DORES CAMPOS MACHADO
TRANSLATED BY RODRIGO FRESTON

Although there is great ethnic and cultural diversity in Latin America, scholars recognize that Catholicism has taken a leading role in shaping the region's mentalities and also the intricate relationships between the ecclesiastical institutions and political power in different countries. In this chapter, we wish to emphasize the contribution of religion to the patriarchal order that characterized a large part of the region's history and the interference of local churches in the formulation of laws related to family and reproductive behavior. We also explore the sexual policies of national governments in recent decades.

This patriarchal order manifested itself through an array of power relations between generations and genders, and it combined with various religious ideologies to make a profound impression on sexual and affective attachments. The core of patriarchal power can be found in the power of the father over the daughter and of the husband over the wife. However, patriarchy also characterizes the asymmetrical relations between father and son and between daughters-in-law and mothers-in-law. For centuries, this family system in Latin America found the fundamental ideological elements of its subsistence in the representations of gender in Catholicism, particularly through Marianism.

The paradigmatic function that the sentimental and mystical cult of the mother can have in the regulation of a woman's body and life is a recurrent theme in the studies on the hegemony of patriarchal relations in the region. This occurs even though there seems to be a recent tendency to identify the ambivalent consequences of this ideology, as the central role reserved to the mother in the family expresses women's moral authority in the private sphere. The key to this interpretation is that Marianism would be "the cult of women's spiritual superiority" and a "secular building of beliefs and practices relative to the position of women in society." The belief that women are morally superior to men can be identified at the base of this theoretical construction.[1]

What is interesting in this type of approach is that this spiritual appreciation of women represents, more than a threat to men's position of power, the other side of the predominant sexism in Latin America. The hegemony of this Catholic ideology allowed some countries to develop a double morality guaranteeing men the free exercise of sexuality and a strong control over women's body and sexual life for the most part of the region's history. This duplicity in moral standards postponed the development of a strictly lay culture over the region's sexuality, which became an obstacle for the recognition of sexual and reproductive rights in different nations.

It bears noting that a series of tendencies developed from the second half of the twentieth century onwards altered the ability of the ecclesiastical institution to influence local populations. To begin with, although there were other contraceptive methods that allowed a certain control over women's fertility, the development of the birth control pill brought about a great revolution in sexual and reproductive behaviors in the urban segments of the region. Governments of different countries, urged on by international agencies interested in containing poverty in the region, implemented policies of family planning and propagated new technologies in the field of birth control, opposing the pro-natalist culture of the Catholic Church. Although they had distinct impacts in shaping each nation, these policies introduced new values and spread urban standards of reproductive behavior to rural populations. The effects were quick and measureable, reducing the fertility rate in the continent, which plummeted from 5.96 lifetime births per woman in 1960 to 2.94 lifetime births per woman in 2000.

The second half of the last century was also notable for the emergence of important social movements in the public sphere (feminism, gay rights movements, etc.) that extended the range of collective subjects that the Catholic Church had to deal with. This institutional multiplicity in the continent undeniably not only contributed to the transformations in social imaginary, but also affected the sexual and reproductive behaviors of men and women of the region. During the 1980s, the issue of reproductive health care stimulated the debate between the Catholic Church, the feminist movements, and international aid agencies. In the International Conference on Population and Development in Cairo (1994), reproductive health was recognized as a

---

1 Evelyn Stevens, "Marianismo: La Outra Cara del Machismo en Latino-America," in *A Pescatelo, Hembra y Macho em Latino América- Ensaios* (México:Ed. Diana, 1977).

paradigm for the formulation of national policies concerning population and development. Opposition to the program emerging from the Cairo conference was led by the Vatican and by Muslim societies, and many Catholic countries in Latin America – notably Argentina, Ecuador, Guatemala, Honduras, Nicaragua, Paraguay, Peru, and Dominican Republic – were on their side, even though many would adopt the recommendations of the conference at later dates.

Despite declines in top-down Catholic influence in the late twentieth century, the literature suggests that the influence of local churches in institutional politics is still very significant. There is porousness to Catholic movements. One finds conservative sectors such as Opus Dei and Charismatic Renewal on the more traditional side and the Christian Base Communities (comunidades eclesiales de base – CEBs) and Catholics for the Right to Decide on the more progressive side, regarding much of the collective action that develops in the different nations of the continent (pro-life movement and feminism, respectively).

Although there is a historical tendency toward alignment between the Catholic hierarchy and the state political structure in Latin America, there still remains a multiplicity of arrangements between the political and religious actors in each nation, with the Cuban, Mexican, and Uruguayan experiences undergoing the most radical laicization in the region. Even in these cases, however, the Catholic Church continues trying to influence legislation, as can be seen in the recent history of Mexico and Uruguay. In 2007, Mexico, which has long embraced liberal birth control practices, approved a law that decriminalized abortion until twelve weeks of pregnancy. This provoked a strong reaction from the local Church official and from Pope Benedict XVI, who threatened to excommunicate lawmakers responsible for the law's revision.

In Uruguay, the threats were repeated, and even though the project of decriminalization had been approved in the General Assembly in 2008, socialist president Tabaré Vásquez, whose wife is a devout Catholic, vetoed the law that same year and legislators were not able to overturn the veto. In 2012, the Uruguayan Congress again passed a draft law on termination of pregnancy and this time, President José Alberto Mujica, who succeeded Vasquez, signed into law decriminalizing abortion up to 12 weeks of gestation. This type of pressure on the First Ladies, lawmakers, and executive leaders has been continuously denounced by the press, by social movements, and even by some evangelical churches, as was the case when evangelical leaders applied the label "fundamentalist" to Catholic leaders who opposed Chile's emergency contraception laws.

These examples demonstrate a broader trend of intervention by Catholic religious leaders in the revision of laws regarding family, sexuality, and birth control in Latin American nations. Even though some Catholic intellectuals mediate with feminism through transnational networks such as the Catholics for the Right to Decide – which connects groups in Mexico, Brazil, Chile, Argentina, and Uruguay – it is undeniable that local hierarchies have taken the inflexible position of rejecting the political agenda of the movement, creating a series of obstacles to the process of social mobilization for sexual and reproductive rights.

Analyzing the hierarchy's ability to influence public debate and Chilean policies, Marcela Soto Reys argues that the actions of the local religious leadership are clear when it comes to the debate over decriminalization of abortion, sexual education, and the campaigns for STD and AIDS prevention.[2] In addition to the traditional homilies and pastoral documents, bishops and priests have been pressuring high-ranking public servants by asking for explanations regarding public policies in health and education as well as by warning Catholic congressmen about the emblematic character of their positions in the formulation and voting of laws related to human sexuality and reproduction.

More recently, segments of the Catholic hierarchy have gone to court to block the demands of progressive social movements and even to overturn decisions and discontinue the development of reproductive health programs. Free distribution of emergency contraceptives, or the morning-after pill, has generated a series of judicial lawsuits in countries including Peru, Ecuador, Colombia, Chile, and Argentina in the past few years. The same happened in Brazil, where the difficulty in passing the most liberal proposals on abortion made the social movements entered with action in the Supreme Court (Arquição de Descumprimento de Preceito Fundamental 154) and in 2012, the judges decided that women who decide to abort anencephalic fetus and doctors who perform procedures interruption of pregnancy do not commit crimes.

Religious Multiplicity in Latin America

The decline of Catholicism relative to the expansion of other religious movements in the final decades of the twentieth century has caught the attention of

---

2 Marcela Soto Reys, "Estado Laico, Iglesia católica y sociedad civil: Debates y controversias en torno a la salud y los DSR en la Democracia chilena (1990–2005)," in *Memorias del Primer Seminario Internacional Fomentando las Libertades Laicas*, eds. Marco A. Huaco Palomino, George Liendo, and Violeta Barrientos (Lima: Universidad Nacional Mayor de San Marcos, Libertades Laicas, 2008), 336.

social scientists and individual and collective political actors interested in extending their support bases in Latin American societies. Though the multiplicity of the Christian universe follows a distinct rhythm in each nation, the literature relates the attraction of new religious movements. These movements speak to to macrosocial tendencies in the region such as poverty, growing discredit of institutions, the ideology of individualism, and changes in family arrangements.

With political strength and a bigger capacity to mobilize and organize in countries such as Brazil, Chile, Nicaragua, and Colombia, the Christian Base Communities (CEB) movement became an important place for the formation of popular women's leadership in the 1960s, 1970s, and 1980s. In a region marked by authoritarianism and political instability, the emergence of Liberation Theology generated hope that the religious sphere would create an inclination in individuals toward an engagement with progressive movements, especially women's movements. Liberation Theology opened doors for new appraisals of Mary and for the creation of cognitive bridges with the ideologies of feminist groups. Regarding poor women, it was hoped that the experience of community organization would help in enabling leaders that could articulate the theme of inequality between social classes with the asymmetry of gender. This, in turn, would introduce this segment of the population to feminist ideology.

Sociological investigations show, however, that there was little sensitivity to issues of gender among those who defined the guidelines and strategies of the CEBs. Feminist theology faced resistance among the leaders of the grassroots movement in such a way that topics relevant to feminism's political agenda, such as sexuality and birth control, were insufficiently elaborated on in the CEBs of that time. Moreover, the Catholic movement began to lose its vitality around the 1980s, affected by the policies of Pope John Paul II of appointing more conservative bishops to the dioceses of the countries where Liberation Theology was spreading.

Simultaneously, religious movements with a stronger affinity for individualist ideology, especially the Catholic Charismatic Renewal (CCR) and Pentecostalism, spread to the middle and lower classes of many countries of the continent. The weakening of the CEBs and the expansion of CCR groups occurred at different times in each nation. However, feminist protagonism still exists in the new Catholic movement, with women becoming leaders of prayer and intercessory groups as well as being responsible for social actions among the marginalized sectors.

Similar to what happened with divorce, where Catholic pressure deferred its legality for many years in many Latin American countries, a large number of clergymen and CCR leaders joined with Catholic pro-life initiatives. The conservative Opus Dei movement continues to create obstacles to the development of public policies in the area of reproductive health and HIV prevention, not to mention the attempts to intervene in the revision of laws pertaining to abortion and regulation of the use of embryos in scientific research. These actions clearly portray the difficulty of the Catholic leadership in accepting the secularization of culture and of nations. Feminist groups across the region have regularly denounced such positions.

Public opinion research suggests, however, that there is a large gap between the sexual morality of the Vatican and the opinion of the faithful in societies such as Chile, Mexico, Argentina, and Brazil. In the latter case, a large survey conducted in 2007, just before a visit from the pope, demonstrated that most Brazilian Catholics are autonomous in their conscience and decision making, deviating from Pope Benedict XVI, for example, in his condemnation of the use of condoms. Ninety-four percent of Catholics interviewed were in favor of the use of condoms – the same as the percentage of the total population who approved their use. Regarding abortion, an investigation in 2004 had already shown that 70 percent of Catholic women would be in favor of increasing the number of situations in which it would be allowed. Current attitudes approve of abortion only when there is a health risk to the mother, when it is a consequence of rape, or when the fetus itself is mortally compromised, as in the case of anencephaly.

Evangelicals and the Current Debate on Reproductive Rights

Though still a minority, evangelicals have a well-established presence in Latin America. The scholarly literature on these movements charts their development across the region, and it also attests to their political participation, both as conservatives and also in more progressive ecumenical movements, such as Liberation Theology. In light of this, it is important to explore the participation of the Pentecostal ecclesiastical structures in public debates about sexuality, reproduction, and research with human embryos.

Despite the recent surge in studies of Pentecostalism, it is not a new phenomenon in Latin America. In countries such as Chile and Brazil, Pentecostals have been present since the beginning of the twentieth century. What the literature does reveal to be the most recent changes in this field are the multiplication of transnational denominations and the increase in the ability to mobilize the lower classes in a larger number of nations. We also witness an increase in the influence of evangelical leaders in institutional politics in countries such as Guatemala, El Salvador, Nicaragua, Venezuela, Brazil, and Peru.

In contrast to what happened within Catholicism, there are relatively few studies that delve into the political conduct of Pentecostal religious leaders in the fields of reproductive health and sexual morality. The internal diversity of this religious tradition is a significant challenge to the region's experts, but studies tend to associate liberal positions on issues of contraception to the historical evangelical churches and more conservative views to the Pentecostals. However, the strong competition between Pentecostal churches and the flexibility of some denominations of this branch of Protestantism leads to such a diverse and dynamic religious field as to make it difficult to make large generalizations.

In a 1993 study on the participation of Pentecostal legislators in Brazil's Constituent Assembly, Paul Freston points out *evangélicos* more conservative positions in issues related to family and sexual morality.[3] However, one decade later, studies in the Brazilian Congress had already detected divergent positions among Pentecostal legislators regarding the use of embryos in scientific research and the extension of situations in which pregnancy could be terminated.[4]

These changes appear to have come about in large measure because of the political growth of the Universal Church of the Kingdom of God. Created in 1977, this denomination has for years criticized the natalist vision of the Catholic Church and emphasized the need to come up with an effective policy of family planning from the government as a way of fighting against poverty. In a society with strong sexist characteristics, the leaders innovated by suggesting pastors recommend vasectomy to their faithful who already had two or more children. They also included issues such as teenage pregnancy, sexual education, and abortion in their media outlets' programming. This was one of the few denominations in Brazil that publicly defended the extension of abortion access to cases of anencephalic fetuses, but its participation in public debate is a counterpoint to the inflexible positions of the Catholic Church toward the poorer sectors of the population.

Analyses of the perceptions and attitudes of the Pentecostal faithful also indicate changes in the family ethos and in the sexual morality of Pentecostals in the last four decades, bringing them closer to the standards of conjugality and reproductive behavior predominant in the populations of their

---

3 Paul Freston, "Protestantes e Política no Brasil: Da Constituinte ao Impeachment," doctoral thesis (Campinas: Unicamp, 1993).
4 Maria das Dores Campo Machado, *Política e Religião: A participacão dos evangélicos nas eleições* (Rio de Janeiro: Editora FGV, 2006).

respective nations. Studies done in Chile, Colombia, and Brazil emphasized the ambivalent dimension of the Pentecostal doctrine and its disruptive capacity in relation to the patriarchal order, as adhering to Pentecostalism promotes transformations in the behavior of men and women that deviate from the definitions of dominant genders in these societies.[5] According to this perspective, Pentecostal doctrine shows a virtual capacity of empowering women and domesticating men, reducing the distance between genders in couples in which the male partner has converted to Pentecostalism. These studies also demonstrate that among the factors of attraction of Pentecostalism among lower class women is the space reserved to family issues and to the new challenges ushered in by modernity to women such as entry into the workforce, heading households, and urban violence.

Regarding family planning, research done during the 1990s by the Institute of Religious Studies (Instituto de Estudos da Religiao – ISER) in the metropolitan region of Rio de Janeiro, where the proportion of Pentecostals among evangelicals is greater than 70 percent, demonstrated that this religious segment has followed the modernizing tendency of the reproductive behavior of the Brazilian woman. ISER researchers found that fertility rate of evangelicals (2.74) was similar to the one found in the general population (2.58). Most evangelical women (74 percent) used some type of contraceptive, and the majority resorted to fallopian tube sterilization (60 percent) and then to the birth control pill (30 percent). It demonstrated that, although members of Pentecostal denominations had more children on average than members of historical Protestant churches, there was also a downward tendency among the younger Pentecostal women toward larger families.

On the other hand, the issue of abortion is what seems to distance Pentecostals more from other social groups. A 2006 survey conducted by the Pew Forum on Religion & Public Life in ten nations worldwide, including the three Latin American countries with large evangelical populations – Guatemala, Chile, and Brazil – showed that the proportion of Pentecostals who reject abortion in all circumstances tends to be bigger (91 percent, 88 percent, and 90 percent, respectively) than in other segments of Christianity in these nations (82 percent, 72 percent, and 86 percent, respectively) or in the population at large (85 percent, 71 percent, and 79 percent, respectively). It bears noting, however, Brazilian research showed that Brazilian evangelicals overwhelmingly rejected abortion in principle (90 percent), but close to half

---

5 Elizabeth E. Brusco, *The Reformation of Machismo: Evangelical Conversion and Gender in Colombia* (Austin: University of Texas Press, 1995); Maria das Dores Campo, "Sexual Values and Family Planning among Charismatic and Pentecostal Movements," *Reproductive Health Matter*, 8, no. 4 (1996): 77–85.

(40 percent) were willing to make exceptions under special extenuating circumstances. These conditions were: health – risk to the fetus (39 percent) and to the mother (36 percent) – followed by the woman's conscientious objection as a result of rape (23 percent) or as someone responsible for her own decisions (15 percent).

That said, in countries such as Argentina, Panama, Chile, Venezuela, Guatemala, and Peru Pentecostal groups have been mobilizing to fight against proposals creating sex education and reproductive health laws in schools. They have also begun to rally against the attempts to define reproductive health and abortion as basic human rights. In Argentina, soon after the approval of the Reproductive Health and Assisted Procreation Law (2000) in the city of Buenos Aires, the Federation of Churches and Argentinean Evangelical Christian Institutions sent letters to the national and provincial authorities positioning themselves against the use of abortive methods, the genetic manipulation of human embryos, and sex education in public schools without authorization from the responsible parties. A few years later, leaders of the Christian Alliance of Evangelical Churches of the Argentinean Republic entered the public debate, with their leadership announcing to the media declarations against the inclusion of sexual education content in school curriculums for children and teenagers. In Panama in 2008, the Evangelical Alliance of Panama summoned its members to a demonstration in front of the National Assembly to protest against the bill sent by the Health Ministry.

Conclusion

Because of Catholicism's hegemony in Latin America, there is great imbalance in the literature in relation to sexual morals and the influence of religious groups in public debate and in institutional politics in the field of sexuality, contraceptives, and abortion. Most of the work focuses on the actions of conservative Catholic movements in denouncing the interference of local hierarchies in legislation regarding sex education, family planning campaigns, and STD and AIDS prevention. It also reveals a large gap between doctrinal positions and pastoral work, as well as between the orientations of the Vatican and the sexual and reproductive opinions and behaviors of lay Catholics.

The few studies that analyze evangelicals suggest more freedom of conduct in the field of reproduction, with some historical groups and even Pentecostals supporting some of governments' health initiatives. This is especially true in regard to programs related to contraceptives and AIDS prevention. In any case, one realizes that issues such as sex education in schools, emergency contraceptives, and abortion still provoke very negative reactions in evangelical leaders. In many countries, evangelicals have joined forces with the Catholic Church to avoid changes to laws.

In 2004, the Catholic Church threatened to withdraw its political support of Bolivia's then-president Carlos Mesa because of his support of a bill on sexual and reproductive rights that was scheduled for a referendum at the end of 2005. Faced with such pressure, Mesa returned the Bill of Reproductive Rights to the Bolivian congress, suggesting that public hearings should be made with the whole population. In March of 2005, the National Association of Evangelicals and the United Evangelical Churches summoned the faithful to march on the streets of La Paz, reinforcing the religious opposition to the bill. A similar alliance, known as the Parliamentary Front in Defense of Life, has also formed to lobby the Brazilian congress. It brings together Catholic and evangelical politicians in the effort to thwart revision of legislation regarding abortion in the country.

In sum, one can argue that, beyond the internal competition in the religious sphere, especially between Catholicism and Pentecostalism, we can observe an uncompromising debate over sexuality and human life between Christian and secular ideologies. This latter group, which includes feminist and sexual diversity movements, is intensifying demands for a secular state in Latin America.

The legal adjudication of social conflicts, which initially favored the ideology of human rights and social movements, has been rapidly assimilated by the Catholic Church and by evangelical groups. As a result, the religious sector has become an active player in the legal and judicial struggles over reproductive health, abortion, sex education, and gay rights. At the very least, the vitality of religious debates on sexuality and reproduction reveal the multileveled complexity of the process of secularization in the region.

Bibliography and Suggested Readings

Arraigada, Irma. "Transformações sociais e demográficas das famílias latino-americanas." In J. M. Domingues and M. Maneiro (eds.), *América Latina hoje: Conceitos e interpretações*, 197–222. Rio de Janeiro: Civilização Brasileira, 2006.

Bastian, Jean Pierre. *La mutación religiosa de America Latina*. México: Fondo de Cultura Económica, 1997.

Bingemer, Maria Clara Lucchetti, and Ivone Gebara. *Maria, mãe de Deus de Deus e mãe dos pobres*, 6th ed. Petrópolis: Vozes, 1987.

Blancarte, Roberto. "El porqué de un estado laico." In Marco A. Huaco Palomino, George Liendo, and Violeta Barrientos (eds.), *Memorias del Primer Seminario Internacional Fomentando las Libertades Laicas,* Lima: Universidad Nacional Mayor de San Marcos, Libertades Laicas, 2008.

Brusco, Elizabeth E. *The Reformation of Machismo: Evangelical Conversion and Gender in Colombia*. Austin: University of Texas Press, 1995.
Cátolicas Pelo Direito de Decidir. "Resultados de La encuesta de opinión publica de los católicos em México-2003." www.popcouncil.org/pdfs/EncuestaOpinionCatolicasSummary.pdf (November 12, 2015).
Drogus, Carol Ann, and Hannah Stewart-Gambino. *Activist Faith: Grassroots Women in Democratic Brazil and Chile*. Philadelphia: Pennsylvania State University Press, 2005.
Drogus, Carol Ann, Hannah Stewart-Gambino, Cecilia L. Mariz, and Maria das Dores Campos Machado. "Earthquake versus Erosion: Church Retreat and Social Movement Decline." In Carol Ann Drogus and Hannah Stewart-Gambino (eds.), *Activist Faith: Grassroots Women in Democratic Brazil and Chile*, 70–102. Philadelphia: Pennsylvania State University Press, 2005.
Fernandes, Rubem Cesar. *Novo Nascimento: Os evangélicos em casa, na Igreja e na política*. Rio de Janeiro: Mauad Editora, 1998.
Freston, Paul. *Protestant Political Parties: A Global Survey*. Aldershot, UK: Ashgate, 2004.
  "Protestantes e Política no Brasil: Da Constituinte ao Impeachment." Doctoral thesis. Campinas: Unicamp, 1993.
Gimenez, Verónica. "La comunidad, la Iglesia, los peregrinos. Formas de sociabilidad en dos grupos católicos emocionales de la periferia de Buenos Aires." *Religião & Sociedade*, 23, no.1 (2003): 73–106.
Lanza, Teresa. "Situación de los derechos sexuales y reproductivos en Bolivia." In Marco A. Huaco Palomino, George Liendo, and Violeta Barrientos (eds.), *Memorias del Primer Seminario Internacional Fomentando las Libertades Laicas*, Lima: Universidad Nacional Mayor de San Marcos, Libertades Laicas, 2008.
Machado, Maria das Dores Campos. *Os efeitos da adesão religiosa na esfera familiar*. São Paulo: ANPOCS, 1996.
  Política e Religião: A participacão dos evangélicos nas eleições. Rio de Janeiro: Editora FGV, 2006.
  "Sexual Values and Family Planning among Charismatic and Pentecostal Movements." *Reproductive Health Matter*, 8, no. 4 (1996): 77–85.
Machado, Maria das Dores Campos, and Silvia Regina Fernandes. "Mídia Pentecostal: Saúde feminina e planejamento familiar em perspectiva." *Cadernos de Antropologia e Imagem*, 2, no. 7 (1995): 19–40.
Machado, Maria das Dores Campos, and Cecilia Loreto Mariz. "Mujeres em três grupos religiosos em Brasil: Uma comparación entre pentecostales y católicas." Pages 203–231 in *Religión y Género*, edited by Sylvia Marcos. Madrid: Editorial Trotta, 2004.
  "Religião, mulheres e política institucional: Evangélicas e católicas na disputa pelo poder no Rio de Janeiro." In Sandra Duarte de Souza (ed.), *Gênero e religião no Brasil: Ensaios feministas*, 45–69. São Bernardo dos Campos: Editora da Universidade Metodista, 2007.
Maduro, Otto. *Religion and Social Conflicts*. Maryknoll, NY: Orbis Books, 1982.
Mannarelli, María Emma. "Comentários a las Ponencias." In Marco A. Huaco Palomino, George Liendo, and Violeta Barrientos (eds.), *Memorias del Primer Seminario Internacional Fomentando las Libertades Laicas*. Lima: Universidad Nacional Mayor de San Marcos, Libertades Laicas, 2008.
Mariz, Cecilia. *Coping with Poverty: Pentecostals and Base Communities in Brazil*. Philadelphia: Temple University Press, 1994.

Mariz, Cecilia Loreto, and Maria Das Dores Campos Machado. "Changement recents dans le champ religieux bresilien." *Social Compass*, 45 (1998): 350–378.

Mariz, Cecilia Loreto, Maria das Dores Campos Machado, Carol Ann Drogus and Hannah Stewart-Gambino. "Catholics and Pentecostals: Possibilities for Alliance." In Carol Ann Drogus and Hannah Stewart-Gambino (eds.), *Activist Faith: Grassroots Women in Democratic Brazil and Chile*, 120–160. Philadelphia: Pennsylvania State University Press, 2005.

Martin, David. *Pentecostalism: The World Their Parish*. Malden, MA: Blackwell, 2002.

Martín Ballero, Jaime. "Entre La Iglesia católica y el estado: Una mirada a la comunidad política desde el deseo." In Marco A. Huaco Palomino, George Liendo, and Violeta Barrientos (eds.), *Memorias del Primer Seminario Internacional Fomentando las Libertades Laicas*, 339–363. Lima: Universidad Nacional Mayor de San Marcos, Libertades Laicas, 2008.

Mundigo, Axel I. "Religión y salud reproductiva: Encrucijadas y conflictos." II Reunión de investigación sobre embarazo no deseado y aborto inseguro. Desafíos de salud pública en América Latina y el Caribe. Ciudad de Mexico, 2005.

Navarro, Marysa, and Maria Consuelo La Red Mejia. "Latinoamericana de catolicas por el derecho a Decidir." In Augusta Lynn Bolles, Nathalie Lebon, and Elizabeth Maier (eds.), *De lo Privado a lo Público: 30 años de lucha ciudadana de las mujeres en la América Latina*, 367–379 México: Siglo Veinteuno, 2006.

Parker, Cristían, and Attílio Brunetta. *Religião Popular e modernização capitalista: Outra lógica na América Latina*. Petrópolis: Editora Vozes, 1996.

Rosado Nunes, María José. "De mulheres, sexo e Igreja: Uma pesquisa e muitas interrogações." In Albertina de Oliveira Costa and Tina Amado (eds.), *Alternativas Escassas: Saude, Sexualidade E Reprodução Na America Latina*, 177–203. São Paulo: Fundaçao Carlos Chages, 1994.

Reys, Marcela Soto. "Estado Laico, Iglesia católica y sociedad civil: Debates y controversias en torno a la salud y los DSR en la Democracia chilena (1990–2005)." In Marco A. Huaco Palomino, George Liendo, and Violeta Barrientos (eds.), *Memorias del Primer Seminario Internacional Fomentando las Libertades Laicas*. Lima: Universidad Nacional Mayor de San Marcos, Libertades Laicas, 2008.

Ribeiro, Lúcia. *Sexualidade E Reprodução: O Que Os Padres Dizem E O Que Deixam De Dizer*. Petrópolis: Vozes, 2001.

Smilde, David. "Popular Publics: Street Protest and Plaza Preachers in Caracas." *International Review of Social History*, 49 (2004): 179–195.

Stevens, Evelyn. "Marianismo: La Outra Cara del Machismo en Latino-America." In Ann Pescatelo (ed.), *Hembra y macho en Latinoamerica: Ensaios*, 123–134. México: Editorial Diana, 1977.

Stoll, David. *Is Latin America Turning Protestant?* Berkley: University of California Press, 1990.

Therborn, Goran. *Sexo e poder: A família no mundo:1900–2000*. São Paulo: Contexto, 2006.

Villanueva Flores, Rocío. "Situación de los derechos sexuales y reproductivos en Perú." In Marco A. Huaco Palomino, George Liendo, and Violeta Barrientos (eds.), *Memorias del Primer Seminario Internacional Fomentando las Libertades Laicas*. Lima: Universidad Nacional Mayor de San Marcos, Libertades Laicas, 2008.

36

Indigenous Peoples: Religious Change and Political Awakening

TIMOTHY J. STEIGENGA AND SANDRA LAZO DE LA VEGA

In 2009, tens of thousands of indigenous people across the Americas took part in *Día de la Raza* protests to draw attention to issues of environmental damage, economic injustice, and past and present violations of indigenous rights in the region. In Bolivia, the country's first indigenous president, Evo Morales, declared October 12 to be a "day of mourning." In Venezuela, the National Assembly passed a bill for a "Day of Indigenous Resistance," which they proposed for celebration throughout Latin America. Major marches and protests also took place in Chile, Ecuador, Panama, and Guatemala.

While Columbus Day and *Día de la Raza* celebrations have long drawn criticism for downplaying the inhumane treatment of the indigenous during and after the process of colonization, the degree of local, national, and transnational participation and organization of Latin American indigenous groups in the protests began to multiply in the 1990s. In 1990, as the Americas prepared for the Columbian quincentenary, indigenous groups throughout the hemisphere met to organize protests against the celebration. From there, Latin America's indigenous peoples took part in a new wave of political mobilization and protest. Grassroots indigenous organizations, international organizations, and religious and secular nongovernmental organizations (NGOs) raised questions of indigenous land rights, cultural rights, and social and economic rights. The next ten years would witness the Zapatista rebellion in Chiapas, indigenous uprisings in Ecuador and Bolivia, and the growth of myriad national and transnational indigenous social movements and organizations. Indigenous peoples made an impact on national authorities like never before in the modern history of Latin America, toppling governments, demanding rights, and achieving significant positions in national representative assemblies.

Latin America's recent indigenous mobilization cannot be understood without a careful consideration of religious factors. Although specific political openings and social and economic processes facilitated indigenous mobilization, religious institutions, beliefs, and practices provided many of the resources, motivations, identities, and networks that have motivated and framed indigenous movements. At the same time, indigenous religious practitioners have reshaped the religious field in Latin America, struggled with issues of co-optation and identity, and negotiated new spaces for indigenous culture both within and outside of institutional religion. This chapter explores three interrelated sets of questions about the connections among religion, identity, and indigenous social movements in Latin America.

The first set of questions relates to the connections between religion and social movements. What sort of societal and religious contextual factors led to the openings for indigenous social movements in Latin America? What resources, motivations, and ideological legitimacy has religion provided indigenous social movements? How does religion impact identity and collective action? How has this process played out on the ground for different indigenous groups in different countries?

The second set of questions deals with how indigenous activism and participation has changed the practice and institutions of religion in the region. What happens when religious indigenous beliefs and practices interact with Christian institutions, theology, and practice? What do these interactions mean for relationships of power and identity among religious participants and social activists? What issues emerge in terms of agency and the potential for co-optation of indigenous movements?

A third set of questions has to do with evaluating outcomes. How effective are religiously based or identity based social movements in achieving their goals? What has been achieved and what are the obstacles facing indigenous movements in Latin America? What roles do changes at the level of personal empowerment and collective identity play in our assessment of religiously based indigenous social movements?

The Context for Indigenous Mobilization

Estimates for the total number of indigenous people living in Latin America and the Caribbean generally fall between 35 and 50 million (accounting for between 8 and 11 percent of the total population of the region). The largest concentrations of indigenous people in the Americas are in the countries whose national territories were part of two large pre-Columbian civilizations: the Inca in South America and the Maya in Central America. The countries with the largest indigenous populations are Bolivia, Guatemala, Peru, and

Ecuador, with an estimated indigenous population of 71 percent, 66 percent, 47 percent, and 43 percent of the national population respectively. Uruguay is the country with the smallest indigenous population, with an estimated total of fewer than one thousand indigenous people, making up less than 1 percent of the national population.

On almost every social indicator, indigenous people in Latin America do not fare well when compared to the nonindigenous population. Despite great changes and increased globalization, the majority of indigenous people in Latin America continue to live in rural areas, with limited access to social services and high levels of poverty. In Ecuador, for example, the rate of poverty for the indigenous population in 2001 was twenty points higher than the rate of poverty for the nonindigenous population. In Mexico, the poverty gap is even greater, with 90 percent of the indigenous and 51 percent of the nonindigenous living in poverty. The educational gap between indigenous and nonindigenous people in Latin America is also remarkable, ranging from 2.3 years in Ecuador to 3.7 years in Bolivia. Health indicators also show a dire picture for the indigenous. Infant mortality rates are almost double those of the nonindigenous population in Mexico, Bolivia, and Ecuador. There is also a considerable gap in wages, with indigenous women faring the worst. For example, in Bolivia an indigenous woman on average earns only 41.4 percent of what her nonindigenous counterpart earns for comparable work.[1]

In great part as a result of these difficulties, many indigenous people have made their way to urban centers (both in their own countries and abroad) to look for work and other means to improve their lives. Relatively large indigenous settlements have formed in the outskirts of major cities throughout Latin America. Despite their increasingly visible national presence, indigenous groups face many obstacles to organization. One of the most important obstacles is the internal diversity within the indigenous communities in these countries. Latin America's indigenous are internally divided into many different ethnicities and are regionally dispersed even within the same country. In Guatemala, for example, there are more than twenty different ethnic groups with unique forms of dress (*traje*) and language (though the languages are related, they remain distinct). In Peru, there are more than fifty-six ethnic

---

[1] Rachel Sieder, ed., *Multiculturalism in Latin America: Indigenous Rights, Diversity, and Democracy* (New York: Palgrave Macmillan, 2002); Raul Montenegro and Carolyn Stephens, "Indigenous Health in Latin America and the Caribbean" *Lancet* (2006): 1859–1869; and "Operational Policy for Indigenous Peoples and Strategy for Indigenous Development," 48–49. http://idbdocs.iadb.org/wsdocs/getdocument.aspx?docnum=2032081 (Accessed November 18, 2015).

groups and seventeen linguistic families. While Peru's Amazonian people have organized under the umbrella of the Interethnic Association for the Development of the Peruvian Rainforest (Asociación Interétnica de Desarrollo de la Selva Peruana – AIDESEP) and some regional organizations, Peru's indigenous remain divided between Andean and Amazonian peoples.

In the last few decades, increased globalization, political liberalization, a backlash against neoliberal policies in the region, and electoral reforms have combined to open new opportunities for a resurgence in indigenous movements in Latin America. Three factors have been particularly important in this process. First, administrative decentralization and devolution of power to the departmental or municipal level has created the possibility for greater ethnic and territorial autonomy for indigenous groups in the region. In particular, the cases of Bolivia, Colombia, and Ecuador suggest that a political opportunity structure that combines a severe governmental legitimacy crisis with elite-driven movements for reform may provide an opening for indigenous groups to effectively insert their agenda into national and constitutional dialogue.

In the case of Bolivia, the political crisis (created by the inability of the political system to produce effective legislation in the face of executive and legislative deadlock) opened the path for constitutional reform that recognized indigenous groups and incorporated indigenous demands. The indigenous themselves, however, were largely absent from the constitutional assembly; instead they were represented by social scientists within the Sánchez Lozada administration who saw the inclusion of all groups as a necessary move toward increased democratization.[2] The electoral reform in 1994 opened up a political space for smaller local parties by creating municipalities and calling for local elections. The Movimiento al Socialismo (MAS) party was formed soon after this electoral reform and was able to grow from a relatively small movement of coca growers in Cochabamba to win the national presidential elections with candidate Evo Morales in 2006. Massive discontent with the established parties (not just in part of the indigenous, but other ethnic groups as well) contributed to the rise of this previously unknown party to the national level.

In Colombia as well, the relatively small and geographically dispersed indigenous population made great gains in the 1991 election. This was made possible because in 1989 the Colombian government was facing a serious crisis as a result of its inability to protect the Colombian people from the rampant

---

2 Donna Lee Van Cott, "Constitutional Reform in the Andes: Redefining Indigenous-State Relations," in Rachel Sieder (ed.), *Multiculturalism in Latin America*, 45–73.

violence between drug cartels, paramilitary groups, and the military themselves. The Colombian elites supported a constitutional assembly that would increase internal security. Given the growing influence of the human rights discourse in Colombia and internationally, the indigenous were able to ally themselves with the elite, arguing that a constitution that could generate increased safety for all Colombians had to respect human rights, and by consequence, indigenous rights. Four indigenous representatives were elected to Congress as well as several dozen indigenous municipal councilors. Several indigenous mayors, hundreds of municipal councilors, and one governor had been elected by 1997 in Colombia. In spite of the geographical dispersion, small numbers, and relatively low levels of voter registration, Colombia's indigenous political parties continue to enjoy a measure of success today.

Prior to the constitutional reform in Ecuador, the existing political institutions also had lost authority and credibility. They were internally fragmented, facing increasing accusations of corruption, and it was evident that there was a lack of representativeness in the system. One of the main segments of Ecuadorian society that was lacking representation was the indigenous population. In 1997, indigenous groups organized marches to oust the unpopular president. They then traded support for politician Fabian Alarcón in exchange for a promise of a constitutional assembly. In late 1997, when the constitutional assembly met, the indigenous movement of Ecuador was well represented, with more than 10 percent of the members of the assembly. The indigenous representation in the constitutional assembly opened a political space for organized indigenous parties to begin participating, and in many cases winning, local elections.[3]

A second major factor that opened spaces for indigenous mobilization relates to economics. As state programs such as Mexico's National Indigenista Institute (Instituto Nacional Indigenista – INI) have lost funding because of government downsizing and budget shortfalls, international and local NGOs have come to play a larger role in providing resources in indigenous areas. In many cases, the NGOs have years of experience working with indigenous communities and have ideological positions that coincide with indigenous agendas. Many of these NGOs have religious missions or are affiliated with religious institutions. As we shall see, some of the programs sponsored by such NGOs correspond with the general state retreat from responsibility for social and economic welfare in the region. Simply put, as states have backed

---

3 Van Cott, "Constitutional Reform in the Andes," 48–52, 58–67; and Donna Lee VanCott, "Latin America's Indigenous Peoples," *Journal of Democracy*, 18, no. 4 (October 2007): 133.

away from major social and economic initiatives aimed at their indigenous populations, religious and other NGOs have increasingly targeted those populations with their own programs.

A final set of factors influencing indigenous mobilization has to do with globalization and transnationalism. The process of globalization has opened opportunities for NGOs and indigenous organizations to expand their networks and ties across borders. Alison Brysk, Kay Warren, and others have documented the transnational networks that increasingly link national and local movements for indigenous rights.[4] Transnational and national economic structures and policies provide both the incentives for indigenous mobilization and a context that permits it. Across Latin America, state actors have attempted to incorporate indigenous groups into national society through corporatist and populist forms of interest mediation. However, these projects lost economic, institutional, and ideological support with the onset of the debt crisis in the 1980s, eventual structural adjustment, privatization, decentralization, and other neoliberal reforms. Left without traditional sources of access to the state, indigenous groups made use of the resources available to them: religious institutions and resources, the increasing role of NGOs in previously state-led development projects, and a devolution of state power to local and municipal levels. Not surprisingly, they framed their demands in terms of the very language of political liberalization that was becoming more popular in the region, complete with reference to constitutional rights and inclusiveness.[5]

Out of these transnational connections, a transnational advocacy network developed around indigenous movements in Latin America. Transnational advocacy networks include NGOs, scholarly networks, local social movements, and some international and national governmental organizations and actors. According to Margaret E. Keck and Kathryn Sikkink, such networks tend to arise when local social movements find their access to the state or policymakers blocked. Local actors may then turn to the international realm to create and maintain pressure on their governments.

In the case of indigenous movements in Latin America, the transnational network includes the United Nations and the Organization of American

---

4 Kay B. Warren, *Indigenous Movements and Their Critics: Pan-Maya Activism in Guatemala* (Princeton, NJ: Princeton University Press, 1998), 180–191. See also Alison Brysk, *From Tribal Village to Global Village: Indian Rights and International Relations in Latin America* (Stanford, CA: Stanford University Press, 2000).
5 Deborah J. Yashar, "Contesting Citizenship: Indigenous Movements and Democracy in Latin America," *Comparative Politics*, 31(October 1998): 23–42.

States (through declaring 1993 to be the year of indigenous peoples, the International Labor Organization's Convention 169, and the United Nations and Organization of American States draft Declarations on Indigenous Rights), the Catholic Church (through regularly held bishops meetings, Catholic universities and seminaries, and the training of catechists), and scholarly networks (as evidenced in the role of the Barbados I and Barbados II meetings of the 1970s that drew international attention to violations of indigenous rights in Latin America). As Keck and Sikkink point out, social movements that involve a vulnerable population and raise issues of legal equality and opportunity have been most successful in organizing effective transnational networks. The movement for indigenous rights in Latin America meets both of these criteria.[6]

The indigenous movement has used this transnational stage to voice its concerns and promote its agenda. The core elements of what might be called the "indigenous agenda" in Latin America include the recognition and respect of communally owned lands, the preservation of certain natural areas and resources, the recognition of ethnic diversity, the preservation of indigenous cultures and languages, and a measure of political inclusion and representation. Although Latin America's indigenous groups are extremely diverse, most indigenous social movements in the region continue to devote a portion of their agenda to achieving some measure of territorial and political autonomy. This agenda is frequently combined with a strong critique of neoliberal economic policies, as those policies are seen as threats to indigenous culture, land, and resources.

The Latin American Religious Context: Openings and Challenges

As with the political and economic changes that provided an opening for indigenous mobilization in Latin America, a set of specific religious changes also facilitated indigenous social movements. A particular moment in the history of the institutional Catholic Church, the Second Vatican Council, provided the context for the growth of Liberation Theology and Inculturation Theology. Inculturation Theology emerged out of Vatican II documents such as *Gaudium et Spes*, which specified an openness of the Church and theology to the world, and *Ad Gentes*, which pointed to the "seeds of the Word" said

---

6 Margaret E. Keck and Kathryn Sikkink, *Activists Beyond Borders: Advocacy networks in International Politics* (Ithaca, NY and London: Cornell University Press, 1998), 9–12, 27.

to be contained in the world's variant cultures. These messages were reaffirmed in 1968 at the Latin American Bishops Conference (Consejo Episcopal Latinoamericano – CELAM) in Medellín, again with Redemptoris Missio in 1979, and expanded in the 1992 CELAM conference in Santo Domingo.

Beginning with the 1968 meetings, the influence of dependency theory was evident in the documents produced by the council. The inclusion of lay Catholic leaders in the conference also impacted the meetings. As many more lay leaders were indigenous themselves, they could attest to the veracity of political and economic oppression in Latin America. Some of the priests present at CELAM also had been conscienticized through interactions with the indigenous. Priests such as Nicaragua's Ernesto Cardenal had gone out to live with the poor and had been victims of government persecution. These experiences also gave personal faces to the more abstract concepts of dependency and underdevelopment introduced to the bishops at CELAM and beyond.

Another important change in the Catholic Church was the recognition of Ecclesial Base Communities (comunidades eclesiales de base – CEBs). These communities were essentially community Bible study groups, but they also served other important functions for many small indigenous communities. CEBs not only facilitated organized meetings of indigenous people, but they also cultivated local leadership within these communities that had been previously without a priest. The increased growth in the influence and leadership of local lay people provided part of the necessary structure for political mobilization. A prime example is the Comite de Unidad Campesina (CUC) in Guatemala, an important peasant organization in the 1970s and 1980s that counted many Mayan Catechists among its leadership.

These changes within the Catholic Church also corresponded with the rapid growth of Pentecostal Protestantism in the region. Pentecostalism in Latin America grew relatively quickly beginning in the 1960s, especially among the indigenous population. The Pentecostal message of millennialism found an increasingly receptive audience among indigenous people whose traditional survival strategies were quickly becoming obsolete in the face of modernization, economic change, and in some cases government-sponsored political violence.

Pentecostal churches also grew rapidly because local religious leaders (in many cases indigenous) were able to change the North American evangelical discourse and infuse it with local and regional ideas and practices. Within Pentecostalism, pastors do not necessarily have to rely on formal training to lead a congregation. Thus, indigenous Pentecostal leaders were able to make personal appeals to their co-ethnics to grow their churches. Anthony Gill and other proponents of the religious economy model point to this Pentecostal growth as one of the catalysts for the major changes within the Catholic Church in terms of treatment and understanding of the indigenous (and the poor in general) in Latin America.[7]

These major changes in the religious institutions of Latin America provided new openings for ideas and agendas that would directly impact indigenous communities and for increased indigenous participation within religious, social, and political organizations. At the same time, religious changes led to new lines of conflict and tensions within indigenous communities. The interactions between these major religious changes and the indigenous people played out differently across countries and even within countries in Latin America, depending on local contexts. A brief overview of examples from Mexico, Guatemala, El Salvador, and Ecuador illustrate some of these complex interactions.

In Mexico, the regions of Oaxaca and Chiapas provide both similarities and contrasts. In Chiapas, Bishop Samuel Ruiz played a pivotal role in promoting traditional indigenous expressions. Though on the date of his appointment in 1960, Bishop Ruiz reportedly wanted to "Westernize" the indigenous of his diocese, he became one of the most outspoken and progressive priests in Mexico. After realizing that the traditional paternalistic structure of catechist schools was not effective, Bishop Ruiz opened the diocese to implement indigenous practices and to connect the scripture to the daily struggles of the indigenous in Chiapas. Under the direction of Bishop Ruiz in the 1970s, catechesis in Chiapas began to include more elements of indigenous culture, such as symbols and myths. While during the first years of Ruiz's appointment he had wanted all indigenous catechists to learn Spanish, later he encouraged pastoral workers to learn indigenous languages instead. Furthermore, several indigenous deacons were ordained, recognizing that indigenous culture was considered an asset and not an obstacle to Catholicism in Chiapas.[8]

In Oaxaca, the growth of the *pastoral indígena*, an official policy of sensitivity toward indigenous communities, also came about as a result of the changes in the direction of the institutional Catholic Church outlined earlier.

---

7 Anthony Gill, *Rendering Unto Ceasar: The Catholic Church and the State in Latin America* (Chicago and London: University of Chicago Press, 1998), 83.
8 Christine Kovic, "Mayan Catholics in Chiapas, Mexico: Practicing Faith on Their Own Terms," in *Resurgent Voices in Latin America: Indigenous Peoples, Political Mobilization and Religious Change*, eds. Edward Cleary and Timothy Steigenga (New Brunswick, NJ and London: Rutgers University Press, 2004), 187–209; Christine Eber, *Women and Alcohol in a Highland Maya Town: Water of Hope, Water of Sorrow* (Austin: University of Texas Press, 1995), 223.

However, Kristin Norget argues that more recent ideological shifts in the Vatican combined with altered Church–state relations in Mexico have undermined the religious support for indigenous movements in Oaxaca through the appointment of more conservative local bishops and the closing of key seminaries.[9] Thus, although Bishop Ruiz was able to implement the teachings of Liberation Theology in Chiapas, the recent withdrawal of institutional Catholic support has diminished the influence and effectiveness of the *pastoral indigena* in Oaxaca.

In El Salvador, repression of religious leaders or Church representatives served as a catalyzing factor for indigenous mobilization. As John Booth has argued, religious organizations play a key role in rebellions because they generate grievances both through their ideology and through the victimization of their members.[10] In the cases of Central and South America, this process has been repeated over time. As Church leaders became the target of government repression and intimidation, local and transnational movements became energized to take up their cause. Archbishop Oscar Romero of El Salvador is an emblematic case. Following the death of a personal friend and fellow priest, Romero became an increasingly outspoken critic of the government and its right-wing paramilitary group. Romero was especially outspoken about what he saw as the systematic targeting and murdering of Church workers. During a sermon in which he appealed to the basic humanity of the members of the government squads, he was shot and killed. His martyrdom served as a rallying point for the indigenous and for the oppressed in general in El Salvador.

Local leadership also played a key role in the case of Guatemala. Bruce Calder argues that conservative Guatemalan archbishop Mario Casariego (1968–1983) severely limited the impact of Inculturation Theology during his tenure, while his successor, Próspero Penados del Barrio encouraged it. Bishop Julio Cabrera accelerated the impact of Inculturation Theology after he was ordained as bishop of El Quiché in 1987. Calder also notes the case of Jim Curtin, a Maryknoll priest who organized *pastoral indigena* workshops in Guatemala in the 1970s. With these workshops, Curtin sought to educate people about the indigenous. Eventually, he was able to create a

---

9 Kristin Norget, "*Knowing Where We Enter*: Indigenous Theology and the Popular Church in Oaxaca, Mexico," in *Resurgent Voices in Latin America: Indigenous Peoples, Political Mobilization and Religious Change*, eds. Edward Cleary and Timothy Steigenga (New Brunswick, NJ and London: Rutgers University Press, 2004), 154–186.

10 John A. Booth "Theories of Religion and Rebellion: The Central American Experience," Paper presented at the Midwestern Political Science Association Meeting, Chicago, 1991, 5.

center in Guatemala City that catered to the cultural needs of the indigenous community.[11]

The growth of Protestantism also provided some opportunities for indigenous mobilization. Though many Protestants, especially Pentecostals, remained apolitical, some Mayan pastors in Guatemala did engage politics directly. Virginia Garrard-Burnett points to the case of a Kaqchikel Presbyterian pastor, Vitalino Similox, who was a negotiator during the Oslo peace talks and ran for vice president of Guatemala in 1999. Garrard-Burnett, however, does point out that the case of the Presbyterian activist is more the exception than the rule. Generally, indigenous Protestant leadership did not encourage political involvement or participation, nor did Protestantism always encourage celebration of indigenous identity in the Guatemalan case.[12]

The influx of evangelical missionaries into indigenous areas and growth of Pentecostal Protestantism among indigenous peoples has also led to conflicts in other areas, many times over the very traditional religious practices that Inculturation Theology had reinvigorated. Alison Brysk describes how Protestant missionaries in Ecuador have undermined indigenous "social capital" because converts refused to participate in the *minga* because the communal work is done on Sundays. Brysk also notes the role of the Summer Institute of Linguistics (SIL) in Ecuador. The SIL was eventually accused of ethnocide of indigenous cultures in the regions where it had a strong presence.[13] The issues that arise from these conflicts present serious challenges for state and local authorities in terms of defining and protecting communal and individual citizenship rights.

As these examples illustrate, local conditions and actors played a key role in determining the evolution of larger institutional changes within the Catholic Church and between religious groups. In some cases, the resources, ideas, and institutions that were planted with liberation and Inculturation Theology

---

11 Calder, Bruce. "Interwoven Histories: The Catholic Church and the Maya, 1940 to the Present," in *Resurgent Voices in Latin America: Indigenous Peoples, Political Mobilization and Religious Change*, eds. Edward Cleary and Timothy Steigenga (New Brunswick, NJ: Rutgers University Press, 2004), 93–124.

12 Virginia Garrard-Burnett, "God Was Already Here When Colombus Arrived: Inculturation Theology and the Mayan Movement in Guatemala," in *Resurgent Voices in Latin America: Indigenous Peoples, Political Mobilization and Religious Change*, eds. Edward Cleary and Timothy Steigenga (New Brunswick, NJ and London: Rutgers University Press, 2004), 125–153.

13 Alison Brysk, "From Civil Society to Collective Action: The Politics of Religion in Ecuador," in *Resurgent Voices in Latin America: Indigenous Peoples, Political Mobilization and Religious Change*, eds. Edward Cleary and Timothy Steigenga (New Brunswick, NJ and London: Rutgers University Press, 2004), 25–42.

were carried through by local actors and have been embraced by indigenous practitioners. In other cases, such as Oaxaca, as the institutional Catholic Church has pulled back it has left little support for movements such as the *pastoral indigena*. At the same time, the rapid growth of Protestantism has provided both new opportunities and challenges for indigenous movements across the region. These examples lead us to an evaluation of the multiple ways that religion provides resources and frames the identities of indigenous groups in Latin America.

More than Context: Religious Frames and Resources for Indigenous Social Movements

Although the religious context is certainly important for understanding indigenous mobilization in Latin America, social movement theory points toward other critical roles of religion in "framing" ideological or motivational resources to social movements. Activists (in this case religious workers and indigenous leaders) "frame" their identity (often in opposition to other identities – Indian versus *ladino*, peasant versus *patrón*) through certain religious resources, beliefs, practices, rituals, and cultures that make adherents more prone to be engaged and mobilized for collective action.[14] In the context of Latin America, indigenous peoples and the religious workers who interacted with them became more receptive to the potential for mobilization as they developed religiously based critiques of existing structures of power and authority. These critiques emerged partly from a combination of elements of traditional indigenous beliefs and practices and elements of liberation, inculturation, and indigenous theologies.

Religious Frames

The case of southern Mexico represents a prime example of the role of religious framing for indigenous mobilization. Religious workers including Dominican priests and indigenous catechists in Ocosingo, Mexico, used the book of Exodus to frame the struggle for land, thereby bridging the gap

---

14 David A. Snow, "Frame Alignment Processes, Micromobilization, and Movement Participation," *American Sociological Review*, 51: 464–481; David A. Snow and Robert D. Benford, "Ideology, Frame Resonance, and Participant Mobilization," in *International Social Movements Research*, Vol. 1 (Greenwich, CT: JAI Press, 1988): 197–217; and Christian Smith, *The Emergence of Liberation Theology: Radical Religion and Social Movement Theory* (Chicago: University of Chicago Press, 1991).

between Catholic catechesis and the reality of indigenous life. The landless indigenous people who had migrated to the Lacandon region searching for land could easily identify themselves with the Israelites and their exodus from Egypt in search of the Promised Land. The Exodus story allowed the indigenous to frame their identity in opposition to the landowners, but most importantly, this identity was a communal one that allowed them to mobilize for political action. Furthermore, the indigenous were able to frame their struggle against large landowners in solidarity with other indigenous groups who were facing the same hardships in their struggle to colonize the Lacandon, temporarily uniting the Tzeltales, Ch'oles, Tojolabales, and Tzotziles.

Christine Kovic points to the role of religious beliefs in justifying certain ideological stances in the case of indigenous Christians in Chiapas, Mexico. Kovic recounts the story of an indigenous catechist, Juan, who returns to a critical biblical theme that crosses denominational lines in Latin America: the notion that all people are equal in the eyes of God. This powerful notion of equality within both liberationist Catholic and Pentecostal Protestant discourse has important implications for inequalities relating to gender as well as class. For Juan, this religious concept framed his struggle for social and economic equality in Chiapas.[15]

Simply put, the interactions between Christianity and indigenous religion in the past forty years gave rise to the basis for an insurgent consciousness framed within an identity as both Christian and Indian. Indigenous peoples and the religious workers who interacted with them became more receptive to the potential for mobilization as they developed religiously based critiques of existing structures of power and authority. However, these religiously based critiques and emerging identities were more than simply new ways of thinking about structural change. They emerged within a context that provided critical resources for emerging indigenous social movements.

Religious Resources

In numerous social movement studies, religious organizations have also been found to provide the networks, skills, discretionary resources (time and effort of members), free spaces (from the physical or ideological control of other powerful actors), and collective identity (shared sense of community)

---

15 Christine Kovic, "Mayan Catholics in Chiapas, Mexico: Practicing Faith on Their Own Terms," in *Resurgent Voices in Latin America: Indigenous Peoples, Political Mobilization and Religious Change*, eds. Edward Cleary and Timothy Steigenga (New Brunswick, NJ and London: Rutgers University Press, 2004), 187–209.

necessary to begin and maintain social movements. The common factors frequently linking religion and indigenous mobilization are community building, resource mobilization, education, and a role for religious institutions in fostering leadership. A few examples from South and Central American cases help to illustrate these points.

In the case of Ecuador, Alison Brysk notes that the Italy-based Salesian order worked closely with the Shuar, while Monseñor Leonidas Proaño (known as the "Bishop of the Indians") developed agricultural cooperatives in the highlands, began an Indian seminary, and lobbied to return Church lands to indigenous groups. Furthermore, the Church in Ecuador provided logistical and direct support to indigenous protestors against government programs. In 1994, indigenous leaders found sanctuary and protection from arrest warrants that had been issued by the government in the National Bishop's Headquarters in Quito. Churches also provided material goods such as blankets and presses for newsletters to support the indigenous movement in Ecuador. The Church in Ecuador lent its spiritual support as well. In 2002, priests said mass in a local park for thousands of indigenous marchers before they entered the Ministerial Summit.[16]

Edward Cleary's work on Bolivia and Peru illustrates the key role that religious education played in indigenous mobilization. Cleary notes the role of Adventist schools around Lake Titicaca in producing graduates who would go on to fill local and national leadership roles. In Ecuador, Mexico, Bolivia, and Peru, Catholic seminaries also trained indigenous and nonindigenous priests, who, in turn, trained catechists who would later go on to become community leaders and key organizers in indigenous social movements.

Cleary argues that intellectual and cultural centers and indigenous catechists were essential in the process of developing the intellectual basis for indigenous political activism in the region. As Cleary explains, indigenous catechists have become community leaders, in many cases nudging traditionally reticent indigenous communities into the more contentious public sphere. At the same time, a number of Catholic religious studies centers conducted fieldwork in the region, producing high-quality research and a network of religious scholars and practitioners who began to weave calls for cultural liberation into their perspectives on Liberation Theology. Out of this movement for consciousness-raising emerged such social movements and organizations as the Confederation of Peasant Workers and the Kataristas in Bolivia.[17]

---

16 Brysk, "From Civil Society to Collective Action," 33.
17 Edward L. Cleary, "New Voice in Religion and Politics in Bolivia and Peru," in Cleary and Steigenga, 43–64.

In Chiapas, religion played an important role in providing the indigenous with access to networks that would facilitate the assertion of a shared indigenous identity. Christine Kovic explains that Catechists who went to school to receive religious training came from different ethnic groups. In Chiapas, one of the Catechists recalls meeting Tzeltales, Tzotziles, Ch'oles, Tojolabales, Mams, and Zoques, and being able to identify with them because their people were experiencing similar struggles with poverty. Religion also provided indigenous people from Chiapas with a more concrete network and a free space to speak at the indigenous congress of 1974. The work of preparing for the congress lasted for a year, in which indigenous communities gathered to discuss issues important to them. Religion provided the necessary networks to convene more than 1,200 people from more than 300 indigenous communities to address issues of land, commerce, education, and health.[18]

As Protestantism has grown most rapidly among indigenous communities in Latin America it has also provided valuable resources for indigenous movements. Under successive repressive governments in Guatemala, Protestant churches provided alternative survival strategies for indigenous groups at a time when being Catholic may have been associated with social radicalism. Protestant churches, especially Pentecostalized groups that encourage the involved participation of a large portion of its membership, are essentially providing training for community leadership and organization. Some studies have suggested that Pentecostals in Guatemala, for example, are civically engaged in terms of volunteerism significantly more than their Catholic counterparts.[19] As Hortensia Muñoz found in Peru, the struggle to establish evangelical churches also provides people with the skills and social capital necessary to make demands from the state.[20]

Some indigenous people are also moving closer to what has been called a "neo-native" type of religious practice in Latin America. This form of religious expression also provides the indigenous with resources necessary for effective political mobilization. Indigenous spirituality is based on a discourse that calls for unity among indigenous people, which can be an invaluable resource in overcoming regional differences.

---

18 Kovic, "Mayan Catholics in Chiapas."
19 Timothy Steigenga, *The Politics of the Spirit* (Lanham, MD: Lexington Books, 2001), 85–86.
20 Hortensia Muñoz, Carmen Meyers, and Manuel A. Vásquez. "Believers and Neighbors: 'Huaycán is One and no One Shall Divide It'," *Journal of Interamerican Studies and World Affairs*, 41, no. 4 (1999): 73–92.

Also, indigenous traditions that are revived or reinterpreted to create neo-native spirituality foster a sense of pride in ethnic identity. Indigenous spirituality has also played an important educational role within the indigenous movement. The Universidad Intercultural de las Nacionalidades y Pueblos Indígenas Amawtay Wasi in Ecuador is focused on Andean spirituality and wisdom. Students must engage in community projects that are then evaluated by community elders as well as university authorities. This type of leadership training is an important resource for the indigenous movement. Indigenous people who practice neo-native spirituality are engaging in active resistance to the colonial impositions of Westernized religion; therefore, the very act of adopting a neo-native spirituality furnishes a strong frame from which a pan-indigenous movement can mobilize its base.[21]

In sum, religion in its multiple forms provides the indigenous movement with valuable resources. Christian seminaries, catechist schools, and the indigenous university in Ecuador have all provided participants in the indigenous movement with education and training. During demonstrations and marches, indigenous people have received shelter, material goods, and spiritual support from churches along the way. Religion in the multiple forms in which indigenous people choose to practice it has provided valuable resources for the larger indigenous movement in the Americas.

Power, Identity, and Religion: Who Speaks for Whom When Religions Meet?

One of the most controversial roles played by religious institutions in social movements is the role of mediator or interlocutor. After all, when religious leaders or institutions provide both ideological frames and specific resources to indigenous movements it raises questions about how much of the movement reflects indigenous goals and how much it reflects the goals of the particular religious institution. Kristin Norget's analysis of Oaxaca provides an excellent case in point. According to Norget, the notion that Catholic priests in Oaxaca serve as Gramcian "organic intellectuals" for the indigenous community is problematic because the majority of the priests are not from the community and serve the community most effectively precisely because of that fact. In other words, the very individuals who serve as leaders of the

---

21 Rachel Corr, "Conversion to Native Spirituality in the Andes: From Corpus Christi to Inti Raymi," in *Conversion of a Continent*, eds. Timothy Steigenga and Edward Cleary (New Brunswick, NJ: Rutgers University Press, 2007), 174–198.

indigenous community and who promote a powerful, identity-based critique of the existing social structure are best able to serve their adopted community because of their strong connections to powerful actors within the social structure (through the institutional Church, philanthropic organizations, and NGOs). Norget cautions us about accepting religiously based intermediaries for indigenous communities with an uncritical eye.

Norget's warning raises one of the basic challenges involved in the study of religion and politics in Latin America: Can religious actors be expected or trusted to speak *for* other groups? Norget raises the question of whether or not the larger strategic purpose of challenging powerful structures justify some "essentialization" of the indigenous community by actors who seek to represent that community. She cautions both researchers and activists to reflect carefully on whether or not their arguments and actions may deny agency to the very groups and individuals they seek to study or support.

Specifically, Norget describes an indigenous development model in Mexico with emphasis on collectives and ecological goals that contains an inherent critique of neoliberalism.[22] In other words, she outlines a powerful ideological perspective that emerges from the synthesis of religious and indigenous identities. Furthermore, church-based programs in southern Mexico were often organized around indigenous customs of communalism. The Worker–Peasant–Student coalition of the Isthmus of Tehuantepec (Coalición Obrera, Campesina, Estudiantil del Istmo – COCEI), the Truique Unified Movement for Struggle (Movimiento Unido para la Lucha Trique – MULT), and the Union for Indigenous Communities of the North Zone of the Isthmus (La Unión de Comunidades de la Zona Norte del Istmo – UCIZONI) in Oaxaca all owe some debt to the training and resources that came to the region through the *pastoral indígena*. At first blush, this appears like a straightforward example of the sort of ideological framing discussed earlier.

However, Norget goes on to point out that the construction of this sort of "authentic" indigenous identity politics allowed the Catholic Church to both justify an intermediary role and control the process of religious synthesis, a process that was previously out of its reach in the realm of "popular religion." Norget argues that, in crude terms, some liberationist Catholics in Mexico adopted indigenous identity politics because it promoted their liberationist social and political agenda. The institutional Church was tolerant of this process only insofar as it allowed a blurring of the lines between indigenous

---

22 Norget, "Knowing Where We Enter," 154–186.

culture and Catholic culture and thus provided a strategy for competing with religious challengers such as Pentecostalism.[23]

Norget's logic has been applied on a larger scale to explain the actions of the institutional Catholic Church continent-wide. According to Anthony Gill, recognizing the loss of believers to Pentecostalism, the institutional Catholic Church made a clear decision to increase its physical presence in areas that it had previously neglected. In many cases, these areas were rural, indigenous regions. Catholic Action and other missionaries were sent to rural areas, while the Church also increased the authority of local lay leaders. According to Gill, Protestantism grew in areas and within populations that had largely been ignored by the Church, so the Church started increasing its resources in these same areas to counteract Protestant growth.[24]

Protestant organizations have come under even more fire for inserting their own agendas into their missions to indigenous areas. In Ecuador, for example, the Summer Institute of Linguistics (SIL) was accused of ethnocide by the indigenous movement. The SIL is a US-based Protestant organization, and an important part of its work involves making the Bible available to indigenous populations in their own languages. SIL played an important part in the "civilization" of several indigenous groups in Ecuador in the 1950s when oil was discovered in their lands. An information campaign in Ecuador revealed the extent of the work of the SIL in the *"mestizaje"* of the indigenous people who suffered "a typical syndrome of cultural collapse, including epidemics, economic dependency, and social breakdown" as a result.[25] The expulsion of the SIL from Ecuador was one of the main demands from the Confederation of Indigenous Nationalities of Ecuador, as the institute was seen as a threat to the flourishing of an indigenous cultural identity.

However, the asymmetrical power relationships that characterize indigenous interactions with religious groups are not one-way streets. As numerous authors point out, such relationships can also be used by subaltern groups to subvert existing power structures. The interpretations, symbols, rituals, and practices of the more dominant or orthodox religion may be used in ways that go well beyond the intent of those who originally framed or defined orthodoxy. Rene Harder Horst makes this argument in the case of Paraguay, noting that the choices of indigenous groups to adopt different religious elements may have to do with social or economic advantage, or simply with the

---

23 Ibid.
24 Anthony Gill, *Rendering Unto Caesar: The Catholic Church and the State in Latin America* (Chicago and London: University of Chicago Press, 1998), 96–97.
25 Alison Brysk, "From Civil Society to Collective Action," 37.

resources necessary for survival. For example, the Enxet people of Paraguay had converted to an Anglican missionary Church when the Anglicans were in charge of the mission and controlled access to its resources. The Enxet, however, quickly abandoned Anglicanism to convert to an interdenominational Protestantism introduced by the US-based New Tribes Mission when this group was briefly in charge of the mission. When asked about the conversion, they explained that they had converted because while the Anglicans traveled by oxcart, the New Tribes missionaries had airplanes. When the Anglicans returned six years later, the indigenous group eased back into their Anglican practices. In either case, the meaning of religious symbols and practices hold the potential to be transformed into a subversive act or protest against more powerful actors that can include government authorities, Protestant missionaries, or the Catholic Church.[26]

Virginia Garrard-Burnett's recent work also provides evidence that the authors of Mayanized theology in Guatemala appropriate and invert the powerful messages and symbols of Christianity for their own purposes. This is not to say that their project is a singularly political one but rather to note that the intersection of Christian and Mayan theology provides a milieu for multiple political, social, and theological agendas. Indigenous activists and the Catholic Church may each have a stake in the elaboration of a *teología maya*, but the process and results of creating such a theology are unlikely to match perfectly with either party's agenda. Mayan theologians make use of religious resources and protection to explore, valorize, and interpret their own culture. It should come as no surprise that some Mayan activists sought to abandon Christianity all together as part of the vindication of Mayan culture. Garrard-Burnett also explains, however, that although the possibility remains for many Mayans to abandon Christianity in favor of a more "authentic" Mayan religious identity, the initial push toward that goal remained mostly among the Mayan intellectual leadership. Within the general population, it is more likely that Mayans will continue to identify themselves as Christians, though still within the Maya inculturated practice of Christianity. For many, Christianity has been a part of Maya culture for so long that it may no longer be seen strictly as a colonizing weapon or European imposition.[27]

---

26 Rene Harder Horst, "Breaking Down Religious Barriers: Indigenous People and Christian Churches in Paraguay." in *Resurgent Voices in Latin America: Indigenous Peoples, Political Mobilization and Religious Change*, eds. Edward Cleary and Timothy Steigenga (New Brunswick, NJ and London: Rutgers University Press, 2004), 65–92.

27 Virginia Garrard-Burnett, "God was Already Here When Columbus Arrives: Inculturation Theology and the Maya Movement in Guatemala," in Cleary and Steigenga, 125–153.

The fact that indigenous people have actively changed the way Christianity is practiced in Latin America means that Christianity cannot be singularly interpreted as a European imposition in the region. Since the beginning of the colonial period indigenous people have been active in changing the meaning and practice of Christianity by incorporating regional beliefs and practices. From Mexico to the Southern Cone, Christian practices and beliefs have been reinterpreted through the lens of indigenous practice.

In Paraguay, Rene Harder Horst explains that the indigenous have changed the practice of religion in several ways. A Jesuit priest working with indigenous populations in eastern Paraguay used his training as an anthropologist to encourage the acceptance of indigenous practices as true expressions of faith. Indigenous people were encouraged by the Church to worship within their own cultural framework. In 1983, a new pastoral document outlining Catholic interaction with the indigenous in Paraguay was released. This new program called for Catholic collaboration with indigenous goals while recognizing that the indigenous themselves were agents of change. This document highlighted a "conversion by the indigenous world."[28] The indigenous in this case were able to change not just Church practice, but Church policy toward the indigenous through participation.

The indigenous have not only changed official Church policy, but they have also appropriated Christian beliefs and rituals to fit the immediate needs of the individual in the community. For example, Rachel Corr explains that indigenous people use the *compadrazgo* system to solidify ties with other people, including other indigenous people, *mestizos*, and foreigners. Corr explains that "the compadrazgo system serves as an example of how indigenous people appropriated and reworked colonial Catholic practices within their own local traditions."[29] In other words, the indigenous are using a Christian practice to actively create and maintain social capital.

In simple terms, when the agendas of religious institutions and indigenous people intersect it is important to remain aware of the goals of all groups involved. When religious groups claim to speak on behalf of the indigenous, we must recognize that the message may reflect a combination of the agenda and worldview of both the religious organizations and the indigenous groups for whom they advocate. The indigenous people of Latin America are neither

---

28 Rene Harder Horst, "Breaking Down Religious Barriers: Indigenous People and Christian Churches in Paraguay," in Cleary and Steigenga, 65–92.
29 Rachel Corr, "Conversion to Native Spirituality in the Andes: From Corpus Christi to Inti Raymi," in *Conversion of a Continent*, eds. Timothy Steigenga and Edward Cleary (New Brunswick, NJ: Rutgers University Press, 2007), 175.

passive receivers of religion nor passive participants in religious organizations. Rather, they are active agents of change in the religious landscape in Latin America. Indigenous groups have changed the meaning and practice of religion in Latin America, infusing it with local customs and interpreting in ways that allow for the inclusion of elements of indigenous cosmovision. At the same time, the nature of the interactions between religious groups and the indigenous raises questions about the potential for co-optation.

Critiques of Identity Politics: Co-optation and Church–State Relations

Any time significant resources are at stake in social movements or one group seeks to speak for another, the potential for co-optation becomes greater. One perspective on the identity-based social movements that have proliferated in Latin America is that states encourage them because they are easily co-opted and represent a much less powerful challenge than class-based or popular movements.[30] Critics argue that "identity groups are about themselves, for themselves and nobody else," and that this exclusionary nature dooms them for failure when they are seeking social reform.[31] For its critics, religiously based identity politics is a threat to effective class-based social movements because they mobilize small numbers of people who articulate their concerns narrowly and cannot achieve the type of numbers or pressure on the state that class-based social movements could. In other words, indigenous movements in Latin America may hinder social reform because they take membership, resources, and focus away from the traditional reform-seeking leftist groups and they are ultimately unlikely to succeed.

An analysis of the existing evidence, however, suggests that such characterizations may be overstated. Religious institutions are driven by a complex set of motivations. State actors who actively seek alliances with religious organizations should be careful what they wish for. The Paraguayan and Ecuadorian cases demonstrate the dilemmas faced by state actors who wish to use religious organizations to pursue their own agendas. In Paraguay, the Stroessner regime was frustrated as its traditional ally, the Catholic Church, began to turn against the regime and advocate indigenous rights. In the final analysis, Pope

---

30 N. Larson, "Postmodernism and Imperialism: Theory and Politics in Latin America" in John Beverly, José Oviedo, and Michael Aronna (eds.), *The Postmodern Debate in Latin America* (Durham, NC: Duke University Press, 1995), 110–134.
31 Eric Hobsbawm, "Identity Politics and the Left," *New Left Review*, 217 (May/June 1996): 38–74.

John Paul II's 1988 meeting with indigenous leaders at the Santa Teresita mission in the Chaco played a key role in galvanizing international and internal opposition to Stroessner's regime. The Paraguayan case is not an exception.

In Ecuador, Alison Brysk raises the issue of Evangelical missionaries acting as delegated authorities of the state. Brysk outlines the roles of the SIL and World Vision, and concludes that the effect of these organizations is far from universally negative. On one hand, SIL's missions clearly aided the state in resource extraction and acculturation of indigenous groups. On the other hand, the missionaries provided their converts with social services and many of the basic skills that would later be used to promote their cause. World Vision, through contracts related to its humanitarian missions, initially fomented a series divisions and conflicts within some indigenous communities. However, the eventual results of the World Vision projects included greater indigenous input and representation in the development programs, and greater cooperation with the Catholic Church and other NGOs. Some indigenous evangelicals involved in World Vision went on to become activists in Ecuador's indigenous rights movement.[32]

Edward Cleary's analysis of Peru and Bolivia confirms the image of religious missions as a double-edged sword for states seeking social control over their indigenous populations. In these countries, the short-range radio stations used in missionary work came to serve as key elements in the movement for the vindication of indigenous culture and the eventual political mobilization of Aymara and Guaraní people. Again, religious actors relieved the state of costs by providing infrastructure (this time in terms of communications), but that infrastructure was used by indigenous groups to spread the news of their own rebellion against the state.[33]

The perception that religious movements and identity-based indigenous movements are less threatening to elite actors than traditional class alliances is increasingly being questioned in Latin America. As Amalia Pallares has recently argued in the context of Ecuador, the shift toward identity politics has strengthened indigenous movements, allowing them to effectively incorporate rather than reject many of the material concerns of earlier class-based movements.[34] Indigenous groups have made major strides in gaining official recognition and in increasing their political capacity. Religious actors, for their

---

[32] Brysk, "From Civil Society to Collective Action," 37.
[33] Edward L. Cleary, "New Voice in Religion and Politics in Bolivia and Peru."
[34] Amalia Pallares, *From Peasant Struggles to Indian Resistance: The Ecuadorian Andes in the Late 20th Century* (Norman: University of Oklahoma Press, 2002).

part, frequently act on their own agendas and impact the process of indigenous mobilization in unexpected ways.

Goals and Outcomes: Evaluating Indigenous Mobilization

The goals of the indigenous movement in Latin America are ambitious, including the recognition and respect of communally owned lands, the preservation of certain natural areas and resources, the recognition of ethnic diversity, the preservation of indigenous cultures and languages, and a measure of political inclusion and representation. Among the obstacles to achieving these goals in the context of Latin America, two stand out in particular.

First, there are a multitude of indigenous groups in Latin America; they are diverse and distinct in their cultural backgrounds, languages, geographic location, religion, and cosmovision. The success of an indigenous agenda hinges, among many other things, on the ability to express and prioritize demands in a unified manner to create enough pressure on states to respond favorably. Second, demands of cultural autonomy, the recognition of customary law, land rights, and alternative development policies represent major challenges to the neoliberal economic policies that Latin American states have recently pursued as well as the very notion of the sovereign nation state.

In essence, the indigenous movement is asking that Latin American states let go of development strategies, and of the historical pursuit of a national cultural identity to be achieved by way of *mestizaje*, in favor of policies that favor the cultural practices and cultural autonomy of populations that have historically been marginalized by the state itself. In other words, unqualified "success" for the indigenous agenda would mean a major reformulation of the meaning of citizenship and nationhood in Latin America. This is a great deal to ask of governments struggling with a wide variety of social and economic problems. The very fact that the indigenous question is on the agenda at all should be viewed as a major accomplishment.

Despite these substantial obstacles, indigenous groups in Latin America have made progress toward their goals at both the national and international levels. At the national level, the indigenous have gained significant representation in the governments of several Latin American countries, including Bolivia, where Evo Morales's ethnic appeals contributed greatly to his electoral success. In Ecuador, indigenous groups successfully lobbied to change constitutional language, recognizing Ecuador as a "plurinational" state. In Peru, the Alan García government repealed the most contentious decrees that had led to the 2009 Bagua protests. These indigenous groups have been able to achieve this success in part because of their association with international NGOs, religious organizations, and the recognition of the legitimacy of the "indigenous cause" by several international organizations.

At the international level the International Labor Organization's Convention 169 of 1989 and the United Nations Declaration of Indigenous Rights of 2007 are two particularly notable milestones for the indigenous movement. In 2009, the Supreme Court in Chile used Convention 169 to justify ruling in favor of a group of indigenous people in a lawsuit over water rights that had lasted for fourteen years. This high court decision may set a legal precedent and encourage other indigenous communities to use the courts of law as vehicles to achieve their demands.

Despite these high-profile successes, the indigenous movement of Latin America continues to run the risk of being divided or co-opted by other actors. Following neoliberal prescriptions and implementing structural adjustment programs, some states have cut social services, eliminated agricultural subsidies, privatized land markets, and ended support for the peasant federations that had previously connected indigenous groups to the state. As they lose state protection for their traditional survival strategies, indigenous groups face difficult questions about how to pursue their agenda and which political alliances are most likely to be fruitful. It is at this juncture that the danger of the sort of identity politics that characterizes much of indigenous mobilization becomes apparent. Some analysts argue that identity-based movements hold the potential to "atomize" society, diminishing the chance for success for larger class-based movements. This pessimistic view predicts that the atomization of society through cultural or religious identity politics fosters divisions that reduce the effectiveness of coalitions that might otherwise mobilize against neoliberal economic policy.[35]

Another potential threat to the advancement of an indigenous agenda in Latin America comes from the growth of ethnopopulist parties in the region. Raúl L. Madrid defines ethnopopulist parties as "inclusive, ethnically-based parties that adopt classical populist electoral strategies."[36] In Latin America, a party that is exclusively based on ethnic identity is likely to be short lived

---

35 Sonia E. Alvarez, Evelina Dagnino, and Arturo Escobar, "Introduction: The Cultural and the Political in Latin American Social Movements," in *Cultures of Politics, Politics of Cultures: Re-visioning Latin American Social Movements*, eds. Sonia E. Alvarez, Evelina Dagnino, Arturo Escobar (Boulder, CO: Westview Press, 1998), 1–32.
36 Raul L. Madrid, "The Rise of Ethnopopulism in Latin America," *World Politics*, 60, no. 3 (April 2003): 475.

or ineffective in the long term. Considering that historically many Latin American countries pushed for *mestizaje*, it comes as no surprise that some of the most electorally successful ethnic parties have adopted more inclusive strategies over time to attract the largest electoral base.

Evo Morales's success in Bolivia is due in no small part to the fact that the MAS engaged in an inclusive ethnic appeal, capitalizing on *mestizo* support to carry their national-level victories. However, Morales' success and steady popularity can also be attributed to increased revenues from oil exports that have allowed him to carry out redistributive policies. As the MAS has adopted a more inclusive stance toward whites and *mestizos* in Bolivia, some have accused it of using its indigenous base for demonstrations and marches, while often choosing candidates from different ethnic constituencies such as Antonio Peredo and Alvaro García Linera to run for office at the national level.[37] The fear is that the indigenous movement itself runs the risk of being co-opted by ethnopopulist leaders or movements that may use the mobilized indigenous base in Latin America to win elections but may not deliver on the long-term goals of the movement.

In sum, Latin America's indigenous movement has achieved a great deal, but it continues to face major hurdles to it long-term goals in the region. The indigenous movement has been able to ally itself with international organizations and religious institutions to advance its cause. The United Nations, the International Labour Organization (ILO), and several religious NGOs have supported indigenous groups in multiple ways, providing structural and organizational support as well as specific policy statements. The 2009 Chilean court case that used Convention 169 to rule in favor of an indigenous community's rights to water resources illuminates the potential that these actors have to interact and provide the indigenous movement with an avenue for future success.

Because Latin America's indigenous movement is diverse, identity-based, and interwoven with religious and secular transnational actors, we may need to evaluate its progress in ways that go beyond specific policy and structural changes in the region. Speaking of the indigenous movement in Guatemala, Kay Warren warned, "There will be no demonstrations to count because this is not a mass movement that generates protest. But there will be new generations of students, leaders, teachers, development workers, and community elders who have been touched in one way or another by the Pan-Mayan

---

37 Ibid., 488.

movement and its cultural production."[38] While Latin America's indigenous revival *has* led to protests and demonstrations, Warren was correct in predicting that the type of increased cultural awareness of the new generations of indigenous people in Latin America may be a greater measure of its success. This cultural reassertion of indigenous people is perhaps the most valuable outcome of the mixing of religious institutions and indigenous groups in Latin America.

Studies from across Latin America support the idea that training provided by religious institutions for indigenous people have borne increased "cultural production." Religious institutions have provided the schools, pastoral training, and research centers where indigenous people have acquired the skills necessary to organize their communities. The indigenous may use the type of resources and training provided by religious institutions in whatever way they see fit: in their churches, homes, social relations, as well as in organizing their communities to protest and pressure state actors to hear and respond to their demands. This is the perspective from which we can evaluate the outcome of the indigenous movement in a way that best captures the scope of its success. Individual empowerment is an important outcome of the interactions between indigenous groups and their multiple forms of religious participation that may not "fit" neatly within the traditional measures social scientists utilize to evaluate the success of social movements.

Religion has played a crucial role in providing indigenous people with the networks, training, and support to develop a discourse that includes recognition of human rights and a sense of pride about indigenous identity. Religion has also provided indigenous social movements with symbols and narratives from which they have reformulated their role as a community within the larger context of the nation state. Given the historical, social, economic, and political context of Latin America, the fact that indigenous communities have been able to maintain and build upon a sense of pride and identity in their ethnicity, and have been able to use it to formulate a set of coherent demands that has made its way onto the national and international agenda is a major accomplishment in itself.

Daniel Levine and Scott Mainwaring have argued that religion plays another important role that may not be easily measure or captured in traditional measures of political success. They posit that people learn about society from the

---

38 Kay B. Warren, "Indigenous Movements as a Challenge to the Unified Social Movement Paradigm for Guatemala," in *Cultures of Politics, Politics of Cultures: Re-Visioning Latin American Social Movements*, eds. Sonia E. Alvarez, Evelina Dagnino, Arturo Escobar (Boulder, CO: Westview Press, 1998), 165–195.

implicit messages in religious teachings. In other words, people learn about good societies and adequate behavior through everyday activities. Values and skills such as trust and community solidarity that are necessary for effective participation in civil society emerge from such activities. Shared identity, in turn, is about the way in which communities choose to live and act in the world. In Latin America, religion provides indigenous people and communities with the resources they need to maintain a shared identity and become more effective participants in a wide variety of civil and political projects.[39]

As Manuel Vásquez and David Smilde have argued, we should avoid the temptation to reduce religious movements in Latin America into specific class, ethnic, or even religious components.[40] Smilde has recently argued that speaking of "Catholicism" or "Evangelicalism" in Latin America has become increasingly meaningless because Catholicism and Evangelicalism in Latin America are each as diverse as their practitioners. When it comes to politics, Smilde believes it is time to adopt a broader understanding of many "Catholicisms" and many "Evangelicalisms."[41] We must also be careful of speaking of the indigenous as a homogeneous group. Diverse indigenous groups in Latin America may pursue different, sometimes conflicting agendas and they may practice religion and participate in politics in the way that best suits their cause. As Lois Ann Lorentzen explains, the indigenous people of Latin America are "again transforming religious traditions and indigenous beliefs, making them their own."[42]

It is also critical to avoid romanticizing or inserting external agendas into the indigenous movement in Latin America. Conserving the natural environment and preserving a sense of community may be important aspects of the indigenous agenda, but we simply cannot ask the indigenous movement to single-handedly change government policies pertaining to sustainability, responsible development, and progress in areas of equality and human

---

39 Daniel H. Levine and Scott Mainwaring, "Religion and Popular Protest," in *Power and Popular Protest: Latin American Social Movements*, ed. Susan Eckstein (Berkeley: University of California Press, 2000), 203–240; Daniel H. Levine and David Stoll, "Bridging the Gap between Empowerment and Power," in *Transnational Religion: Fading States*, eds. Susanne Hoeber Rudolph and James Piscatori (Boulder, CO: Westview Press, 1997), 63–103.
40 Manuel A. Vasquez, "Toward a New Agenda for the Study of Religion in the Americas," *Journal of Interamerica Studies and World Affairs*, 41, no.4 (Winter 1999): 1–20.
41 David Smilde, "Evangelicals and Politics in Latin America: Moving Beyond Monolithic Portraits," *History of Religions*, 42, no. 3 (2003): 245.
42 Lorentzen, "Who Is an Indian?" in *Liberation Theologies, Post-modernity, and the Americas*, eds. David Batstone, Eduardo Mendieta, Lous Ann Lorentzen, and Dwight N. Hopins (London and New York: Routledge, 1997), 99.

development indicators. We must also be prepared to take the bad with the good. Some analysts have pointed out that devolving a measure of local autonomy to indigenous population can lead to unintended negative effects. For example, issues of existing clientelist networks and gender inequality may be aggravated under a fully autonomous scenario. As Jeffrey Rubin argues, ambiguous and contradictory positions on these issues may even be a prime source of the strength of some indigenous social movements.[43]

To understand the resurgent indigenous movement in Latin America, we must first recognize that this movement was forged within a varying context at the local, national, and international levels. Religious networks, ideological framing, resource mobilization, and specific openings in the political structure are all factors that change depending on the particular context and help determine the ultimate outcome of the indigenous movements that mobilize within these contexts. The poverty, inequality, and racism that spurred indigenous mobilization remain aspects of everyday life in Latin America. The indigenous movement continues to struggle to translate its international support and political gains into concrete policy. As the indigenous movement continues to push toward concrete social and economic change, religion will continue to play an important role, providing networks, frames, and resources. The increasingly fluid forms of practice and beliefs that make up Latin America's religious geography will have their greatest impact where they always have, at the level of lived reality of Latin America's poor and indigenous populations.

Bibliography and Suggested Readings

Alvarez, Sonia E., Evelina Dagnino, and Arturo Escobar. "Introduction: The Cultural and Political in Latin American Social Movements. In Sonia E. Alvarez, Evelina Dagnino, and Arturo Escobar (eds.), *Cultures of Politics, Politics of Cultures: Re-visioning Latin American Social Movements*, 1–32.Boulder, CO: Westview Press, 1998.

Annis, Sheldon. *God and Production in a Guatemalan Town*. Austin: University of Texas Press, 1987.

Batstone, David, Eduardo Mendieta, Lous Ann Lorentzen, and Dwight N. Hopkins eds. *Liberation Theologies, Post-modernity, and the Americas*. New York: Routledge, 1997.

Berryman, Philip. *Stubborn Hope*. New York: Orbis, 1998.

---

43 Jeffrey Rubin, "Ambiguity and Contradiction in a Radical Popular Movement," in *Cultures of Politics, Politics of Cultures: Re-visioning Latin American Social Movements*, eds. Sonia E. Alvarez, Evelina Dagnino, and Arturo Escobar (Boulder, CO: Westview Press, 1998), 141–163.

Booth, John A. "Theories of Religion and Rebellion: The Central American Experience." Paper presented at the Midwestern Political Science Association Meeting, Chicago, 1991.

Brysk, Alison Brysk. "From Civil Society to Collective Action: The Politics of Religion in Ecuador." In Edward Cleary and Timothy Steigenga (eds.), *Resurgent Voices in Latin America: Indigenous Peoples, Political Mobilization and Religious Change*, 25–42. New Brunswick, NJ: Rutgers University Press, 2004.

From Tribal Village to Global Village: Indian Rights and International Relations in Latin America. Stanford, CA: Stanford University Press, 2000.

Calder, Bruce. "Interwoven Histories: The Catholic Church and the Maya, 1940 to the Present." In Edward Cleary and Timothy Steigenga (eds.), *Resurgent Voices in Latin America: Indigenous Peoples, Political Mobilization and Religious Change*, 93–124. New Brunswick, NJ: Rutgers University Press, 2004.

Cardoso, Fernando Henrique, and Enzo Faletto. *Dependencia y Desarrollo en América Latina: Ensayo de Interpretación Sociológica*. México: Siglo XXI Editores, 1969.

Cleary, Edward, and Timothy Steigenga, eds. *Resurgent Voices in Latin America: Indigenous Peoples, Political Mobilization and Religious Change*. New Brunswick, NJ: Rutgers University Press, 2004.

Corr, Rachel. "Conversion to Native Spirituality in the Andes: From Corpus Christi to Inti Raymi." In Timothy Steigenga and Edward Cleary (eds.), *Conversion of a Continent*, 174–198. New Brunswick, NJ: Rutgers University Press, 2007.

Dos Santos, Theotonio. "The Structure of Dependence." *The American Economic Review*, 60, no. 2 (1970): 231–236.

Garrard-Burnett, Virginia. "God Was Already Here When Columbus Arrived: Inculturation Theology and the Mayan Movement in Guatemala." In Edward Cleary and Timothy Steigenga (eds.), *Resurgent Voices in Latin America: Indigenous Peoples, Political Mobilization and Religious Change*, 125–153. New Brunswick, NJ: Rutgers University Press, 2004.

Gill, Anthony. *Rendering Unto Caesar: The Catholic Church and the State in Latin America*. Chicago and London: University of Chicago Press, 1998.

Gossen, Gary H. *Telling Maya Tales: Tzotzil Identities in Modern Mexico*. New York: Routledge, 1999.

Greely, Andrew. "The Other Civic America: Religion and Social Capital." *The American Prospect*, 32 (1997): 68–73.

Hale, Charles. "Cultural Politics of Identity in Latin America." *Annual Review of Anthropology*, 26, no. 6 (1997): 567–590.

Hobsbawm, Eric. "Identity Politics and the Left." *New Left Review*, 217 (1996): 38–74.

Horst, Rene Harder. "Breaking Down Religious Barriers: Indigenous People and Christian Churches in Paraguay." In Edward Cleary and Timothy Steigenga (eds.), *Resurgent Voices in Latin America: Indigenous Peoples, Political Mobilization and Religious Change*, 65–92. New Brunswick, NJ: Rutgers University Press, 2004.

Keck, Margaret E., and Kathryn Sikkink, eds. *Activists Beyond Borders: Advocacy Networks in International Politics*. Ithaca, NY: Cornell University Press, 1998.

Kovic, Christine. "Mayan Catholics in Chiapas, Mexico: Practicing Faith on Their Own Terms." In Edward Cleary and Timothy Steigenga (eds.), *Resurgent Voices in Latin America: Indigenous Peoples, Political Mobilization and Religious Change*, 187–209. New Brunswick, NJ: Rutgers University Press, 2004.

Larson, Neil. "Postmodernism and Imperialism: Theory and Politics in Latin America." In John Beverly, José Oviedo, and Michael Aronna (eds.), *The Postmodern Debate in Latin America*, 110–134. Durham, NC: Duke University Press, 1995.

Laurie, Nina, Robert Andolina, and Sarach Radcliffe. "The Excluded 'Indigenous'? The implications of Multi-Ethnic Policies for Water Reform in Bolivia." In Rachel Sieder (ed.), *Multiculturalism in Latin America: Indigenous Rights, Diversity, and Democracy*, 252–276. New York: Palgrave Macmillan, 2002.

Lehmann, David. "Fundamentalism and Globalism." *Third World Quarterly*, 12, no. 4 (1998): 607–634.

Levine, Daniel H., and Scott Mainwaring. "Religion and Popular Protest." In Susan Eckstein (eds.), *Power and Popular Protest: Latin American Social Movements*, 203–240. Berkeley: University of California Press, 2000.

Levine, Daniel H., and David Stoll, "Bridging the Gap Between Empowerment and Power." In Susanne Hoeber Rudolph and James Piscatori. *Transnational Religion: Fading States*, 63–103. Boulder, CO: Westview Press, 1997.

Leyva Solano, Xochil. "Militancia político-religiosa e identidad en Lacandona," *Estudios Sobre Estado y Sociedad*, 1 (1995): 59–88.

Lorentzen, Lois Ann. "Who Is and Indian? Religion, Globalization, and Chiapas." In Dwight N. Hopkins, Lois Ann Lorentzen, Eduardo Mendieta, and David Batstone (eds.), *Religions/Globalizations: Theories and Cases*, 84–102. Durham, NC: Duke University Press, 2001.

Madrid, Raúl L. "The Rise of Ethnopopulism in Latin America." *World Politics*, 60 (2008): 475–508.

McAdam, Doug. *Political Process and the Development of Black Insurgency: 1930–1970*. Chicago: University of Chicago Press, 1982.

McCarthy, John D., and Mayer N. Zald. "Resources Mobilization and Social Movements: A Partial Theory." *American Journal of Sociology*, 82 (1977): 1212–1239.

Mignolo, Walter. "Globalizations, Civilization Processes, and the Relocation of Languages and Cultures." In Fredric Jameson and Masao Miyoshi (eds.), *The Cultures of Globalization*, 44–51. Durham, NC: Duke University Press, 1998.

Montenegro, Raul, and Carolyn Stephens. "Indigenous Health in Latin America and the Caribbean." *Lancet*, 367, no. 9525 (2006): 1859–1869.

Muñoz, Hortensia, Carmen Meyers, and Manuel A. Vásquez. "Believers and Neighbors: 'Huaycán Is One and No One Shall Divide It'." *Journal of Interamerican Studies and World Affairs*, 41, no. 4 (1999): 73–92.

Norget, Kristin. "Knowing Where We Enter: Indigenous Theology and the Popular Church in Oaxaca, Mexico." In Edward Cleary and Timothy Steigenga (eds.), *Resurgent Voices in Latin America: Indigenous Peoples, Political Mobilization and Religious Change*, 154–186. New Brunswick, NJ: Rutgers University Press, 2004.

Pallares, Amalia. *From Peasant Struggles to Indian Resistance: The Ecuadorian Andes in the Late 20th Century*. Norman: University of Oklahoma Press, 2002.

de la Peña, Guillermo. "Social Citizenship, Ethnic Minority Demands, Human Rights and Neoliberal Paradoxes: A Case Study in Western Mexico." In Rachel Sieder (ed.), *Multiculturalism in Latin America: Indigenous Rights, Diversity, and Democracy*, 129–156. New York: Palgrave Macmillan, 2002.

Rubin, Jeffrey. "Ambiguity and Contradiction in a Radical Popular Movement." In Sonia E. Alvarez, Evelina Dagnino, and Arturo Escobar (eds.), *Cultures of Politics, Politics of Cultures: Re-visioning Latin American Social Movements*, 141–163. Boulder, CO: Westview Press, 1998.

Selka, Stephen L. "Religious Synthesis and Change in the New World: Syncretism, Revitalization and Conversion." Master's thesis. Boca Raton: Florida Atlantic University, 1997.

Sherkat, Darren E., and Christopher G. Ellison. "Recent Developments and Current Controversies in the Sociology of Religion." *Annual Review of Sociology*, 25 (1999): 363–394.

Siebers, Hans. "Globalization and Religious Creolization among the Q'eqchi'es of Guatemala." In Christian Smith and Joshua Prokopy (eds.), *Latin American Religion in Motion: Tracking Innovation, Unexpected Change, and Complexity*, 261–274. New York: Routledge, 1999.

Sieder, Rachel. *Multiculturalism in Latin America: Indigenous Rights, Diversity, and Democracy*. New York: Palgrave Macmillan, 2002.

Smilde, David. "Evangelicals and Politics in Latin America: Moving Beyond Monolithic Portraits." *History of Religions*, 42, no. 3 (2003): 245.

Smith, Christian. *Disruptive Religion: The Force of Faith in Social Movement Activism*. New York: Routledge, 1996.

The Emergence of Liberation Theology: Radical Religion and Social Movement Theory. Chicago: University of Chicago Press, 1991.

Smith, Christian, and Joshua Prokopy, eds. *Latin American Religion in Motion: Tracking Innovation, Unexpected Change, and Complexity*. New York and London: Routledge Press, 1999.

Snow, David A. "Frame Alignment Processes, Micromobilization, and Movement Participation." *American Sociological Review*, 51, no. 4 (1986): 464–481.

Snow, David A., and Robert D. Benford, "Ideology, Frame Resonance, and Participant Mobilization." In *International Social Movement Research*, Vol. 1, 197–217. Greenwich, CT: JAI Press, 1988.

Steigenga, Timothy. *The Politics of the Spirit*. Lanham, MD: Lexington Books, 2001.

Steigenga, Timothy H., and David Smilde. "Wrapped in the Holy Shawl: The Strange Case of Conservative Christians and Gender Equality in Latin America." In Christian Smith and Joshua Prokopy (eds.), *Latin American Religion in Motion: Tracking Innovation, Unexpected Change, and Complexity*, 173–186. New York: Routledge, 1999.

Stoll, David. *Is Latin America Turning Protestant? The Politics of Evangelical Growth*. Berkeley: University of California Press, 1990.

Tilly, Charles. *From Mobilization to Revolution*. Reading, MA: Addison Wesley, 1978.

Van Cott, Donna. "Constitutional Reform in the Andes: Redefining Indigenous-State Relations." In Rachel Sieder (ed.), *Multiculturalism in Latin America: Indigenous Rights, Diversity, and Democracy*, 45–73. New York: Palgrave Macmillan, 2002.

The Friendly Liquidation of the Past: The Politics of Diversity in Latin America. Pittsburgh: University of Pittsburgh Press, 2000.

"Latin America's Indigenous Peoples." *Journal of Democracy*, 18, no. 4 (2007): 127–141.

Vásquez, Manuel A. "Toward a New Agenda for the Study of Religion in the Americas." *Journal of Interamerican Studies and World Affairs*, 41, no. 4 (1999): 1–20.

Warren, Kay B. *Indigenous Movements and Their Critics: Pan-Maya Activism in Guatemala.* Princeton, NJ: Princeton University Press, 1998.
Yashar, Deborah J. *Contesting Citizenship In Latin America. The Rise of Indigenous Movements and the Postliberal Challenge.* New York: Cambridge University Press, 2005.
——— "Democracy, Indigenous Movements, and the Postliberal Challenge in Latin America." *World Politics: A Quarterly Journal of International Relations*, 52, no. 1 (1999): 76–104.
Yrigoyen, Raquel. *Pautas de coordinación entre el derecho indígena y el derecho estatal.* Guatemala: Fundanción Myrna Mack, 1999.
Zald, Mayer N. "Theological Crucibles: Social Movements in and of Religion." *Review of Religious Research*, 23, no. 4 (1982): 317–336.

37
Inculturation Theology and the "New Evangelization"

ANDREW ORTA

"Inculturation" is a new term for an old issue in Christianity concerning the translation and realization of Christian meanings and practices in different cultural contexts. Although inculturation is not limited to Latin America, the region looms large in discussions of inculturation both for the profound histories of cultural encounters deriving from the colonial evangelization of the continent and intensifying efforts, beginning during the twentieth century and continuing into the twenty-first, devoted to a "new evangelization" of the region. Moreover, inculturation promises a certain degree of localization of Christian practice. In this, it dovetails with the much-studied "openings" provided by the Second Vatican Council that have been a source of particular dynamism in Latin America.

This chapter sketches the basic premises of inculturation and reviews its emergence as an explicit missionary objective across key historical moments in Latin American Christianity. It then looks at inculturation in practice drawing on a set of contemporary case studies, including my own research with Bolivian Aymara communities. The chapter concludes with some comments on the promises and the limits of inculturation as these reflect broader developments in indigenous politics across much of Latin America. Although I focus on the Catholic Church, inculturationist approaches figure in some Protestant churches, and the influence of Protestantism and various ecumenical movements is an important part of the story of inculturation in Latin America.

Inculturation rests upon a pastoral premise that "Christian" meanings are already available in other cultural traditions. It is a modified missionary stance, less about rescuing souls from paganism than about revalorizing other cultural practices as locally specific expressions of Christianity. In his 1995 statement "Local Churches Have a Missionary Task," Pope John Paul II described evangelization as entailing an "integration of the Gospel" with a "core of truth" to be found in local cultures. "The Gospel message ..." he wrote, "should be presented to different cultures by fostering the development of the seeds, longings, expectations – it could be said, almost the presentiments of Gospel values – already present within them."[1]

Inculturation implies a missionary encounter or dialogue that is mutually, but not equally, transformative. The transformation is presented as the fulfillment of what existed before the missionary encounter. In John Paul II's words: "It stimulates [the local culture] and encourages it to yield new fruits at the highest level to which Christ's presence brings it, with the grace of the Holy Spirit and the light of the Gospel."[2]

Inculturation is deeply linked to the missionary encounter and the challenges of translating putatively universal meanings into local practices and understandings. Other scholars of Christian missions have noted the strategy of identifying functional equivalences between local practices and the rites and values of Christian ritual. Missionaries, for instance, might seek to include or reference a local custom in Christian liturgy, underscoring its meaning as an act of thanksgiving or pardon. However, such claims, like all acts of translation or commensuration, are social processes; their success is contingent upon many other factors. The extensive literature on syncretism and folk Catholicism addresses less official examples of such processes.

Students of the colonial evangelization will see in inculturation a familiar theme: identifying seeds of the divine word and laudable practices and accomplishments in some indigenous societies. Some of this involved efforts to make sense of, and calibrate the military and missiological approach to, other societies as ignorant children of nature or as fallen apostates with prior knowledge of the Christian message. Some of this involved early modern Iberian clerics engaged in an evangelization of the New World as they were also aggressively reforming Catholicism in Spain. Some of this also reflects the humanistic scholarship of a remarkable roster of missionaries working in the Americas who gained a subtle knowledge of the linguistic and cultural intricacies of indigenous societies.

Colonial efforts to identify in local mythic histories traces of the universal evangelizing labors of the apostles, or rueful reflections that the reverence shown by Andean populations at Incan holy sites might set a good example for peasant congregations in Spain, or the frank admiration for the linguistic subtleties of native languages by friars compiling the earliest grammars, all

---

[1] John Paul II, "Local Churches Have a Missionary Task," *The Vatican*, June 14, 1995, www.ewtn.com/library/papaldoc/jp950614.htm (Accessed November 12, 2015).
[2] Ibid.

share the flavor of contemporary inculturation. Similarly, the complex tension between the local expression of Catholicism and its claims to a universal grid of meaning are well reflected in the early modern translational hierarchy that sought to configure and reform local vernaculars along the grammatical lines of the sacred language of Latin.

Working in a more cosmological vein, and with different historical parameters, contemporary theologians point to the diversification of creation described in Genesis as a template for the theological embrace of cultural difference, and also note the linguistic diversity bridged in the story of Pentecost told in the book of Acts. Similarly, the very cultural complexity of the biblical setting – the Holy Land as a rich cultural crossroads – spurs some theologians to suggest that the history of Christian meaning is inseparable from acts of inculturation expressed initially through Hebrew, Greek, or Roman cultural categories.

Setting aside these historical analogs and more fundamental tensions in Christian missions, inculturation is tightly linked to the history of the Church over the late twentieth and early twenty-first centuries. The earliest uses of the term appear in the late 1950s and follow closely a then-burgeoning vocabulary of social scientific culture-talk with "inculturation" translating the term "enculturation," coined by anthropologist Melville Herskovits to denote the ways an individual becomes a socialized member of a cultural community. For a variety of reasons, including the increasingly institutionalized application of the social sciences to understanding sociocultural differences in the newly defined Third World, academic and policy talk about culture and cultural change – enculturation, acculturation, assimilation – were very much "in the air." Theologians and missionaries were paying attention.

With good reason, too, for the Catholic Church was struggling with comparable questions provoked by the challenges of the mid-century moment. The preoccupation of the Church with the "threats" of modernity, secular humanism, historical materialism, and so forth were evident from the turn of the twentieth century in such papal encyclicals as Leo XIII's *Rerum Novarum* (1891). Over the first half of the twentieth century, the Church's ambivalence regarding a rapidly changing world became an engagement, or rather a re-engagement, through a renewed missionary focus on Latin America, Africa, and other parts of the world. A telling index of the relative isolation from which the Vatican was emerging over this time is Paul VI's 1964 trip to the Holy Land, the "first foreign visit of a Roman Pontiff outside the Vatican since the beginning of the nineteenth century," followed by subsequent first-ever visits by a pope to Africa, Asia, and the Americas. This reorientation took its clearest institutional form in the work of the Second Vatican Council (1962–1965).[3]

Waves of missionaries to Latin America constituted a "new evangelization" of the region, which was premised on completing what was widely seen as a deficient colonial evangelization. The flood of foreign pastoral workers was matched by the consolidation of regional institutions such as the Latin American Bishops' Conference (Consejo Episcopal Latinoamericano – CELAM) established in 1955. Although a good deal of the early focus was on shoring up religious orthodoxy, growing pastoral experience in the region combined with the openings afforded after the Council created spaces for pastoral experimentation and innovation geared to regional specificities. Localizing innovations such as increasing reliance on local catechists or the ecclesial model of Base Communities shaped modes of pastoral work seen as based in Latin American realities. Liberation Theology is surely the best known of these developments. Although elements of inculturationist thought are certainly present in Liberation Theology, exemplified by pastoral cases such as the work of Bishops Samuel Ruiz in Chiapas, Mexico or Leonidas Proaño in Chimborazo, Ecuador, classical liberationist thought continued a strong line of reformist, modernist missionization that was heavily text based, critical of what were seen as the excesses of colonially derived forms of piety and suspicious of indigenous, syncretic, or folk religious practices as evidence of a superficial or inauthentic Christianization. Liberation Theology was a precursor of inculturation, but they should not be confused.

Inculturation appears in a more missionary-inflected sense in the late 1970s through a series of writings by the Jesuit Pedro Arrupe.[4] These more official uses of the term built upon references to "culture" in the Vatican II documents (e.g., *Gaudium et Spes* #53). Although the term does not appear in the proceedings of the CELAM meetings at Medellín (1968) or Puebla (1979), an intensifying focus on regional and local culture is certainly evident, particularly at Puebla. The term appears in the Vatican's 1985 Final Report of the Extraordinary Synod of Bishops, which introduces language that is echoed in later texts:

> Because the Church is communion, which joins diversity and unity in being present throughout the world, it takes from every culture all that it encounters of positive value. Yet inculturation is different from a simple external

---

[3] I. Linden, *Global Catholicism: Diversity and Change Since Vatican II* (New York: Columbia University Press, 2009), 95.
[4] Pedro Arrupe, "Letter to the Whole Society on Inculturation." *Studies in the International Apostolate of Jesuits* (Washington: Jesuit Missions, June, 1978).

adaptation, because it means the intimate transformation of authentic cultural values through their integration in Christianity in the various human cultures.[5]

The "intimate transformation" is signaled again by Pope John Paul II in Redemptoris Missio (1990). Building upon all of this magisterial precedent, inculturation established Latin American roots in the documents of the 1992 meeting of CELAM in Santo Domingo. The bishops at Santo Domingo, seeking explicitly to commemorate the Quincentenary of "the beginning of the evangelization of the New World," expressed a pastoral commitment to:

1. "A New Evangelization to our people"
2. "A comprehensive promotion of the Latin American and Caribbean people"
3. "An inculturated evangelization."[6]

These commitments sketch the core episodes of the pastoral reengagement over the twentieth century. The primary frame is a reintensified missionary effort: a "second evangelization." Within this arc, pastoral workers came to focus on a sociopolitical engagement with Latin American societies with the most dramatic results evident in the "option for the poor" and the activism associated with Liberation Theology. The third leg of the stool crafted at Santo Domingo both names a long-running thread in Catholic pastoral work and marks a pivot. The formal naming of "inculturation" in Latin America announces its transformation.

The Columbian quincentenary of 1992 became a potent context for a focused reflection on the cultural politics of evangelization in Latin America. However, a number of additional factors gave this moment additional salience. The official crystallization of inculturation can be seen as the outcome of sustained efforts by the Church hierarchy to rein in liberationist theologians and activists during the 1980s. These institutional efforts often compounded the effects of state repression of Church activists, such as those of the notorious "Banzer Plan," a scheme in the mid-1970s on the part of the Bolivian and other Latin American governments and the CIA to discredit Liberation Theology and its clergy. The breaking up of the Soviet Union, heralded by some as signaling the end of alternatives to Western capitalism, further muted the voices

---

5 The Final Report of the 1985 Extraordinary Synod of Bishops, Section D, no. 4.
6 CELAM, Documento de Santo Domingo, no. 292, p. 100 of a document titled Documento de Santo Domingo available on the CELEM website: www.celam.org/doc_conferencias/Documento_Conclusivo_Santo_Domingo.pdf

of those liberationist activists who drew on Marxist critiques in their critical reflections upon the signs of the times. The charismatic influence of John Paul II was another factor impelling the spread of inculturation as a dominant frame of Catholic pastoral work, which might also be read as the promotion of inculturation as a palatable moderate alternative to the more radical liberationist pastoral efforts that were so effectively checked during his papacy.

The turn toward inculturation, and the correlated dilution of Liberation Theology, was reinforced by other signs of the emerging neoliberal times, notably a broader turning away from class-based discourses of politics and development to those based more in ethnicity and identity politics. Convention 169 of the International Labour Organization (ILO), adopted in 1989 and updating the ILO's positions on the rights of indigenous peoples, has been very influential in articulating a shift from assimilationist to more multicultural approaches to indigenous cultural diversity. Finally, the relatively decentralizing thrust of inculturation was congruent with a wider ethos of decentralization evident in such developments as political reorganizations stemming from reforming neoliberal states and shifting models of multinational corporate management stressing the importance of local competence and organizational flexibility within a complexly connected global world. If the missionary reanimation of the mid-century can be read as the Vatican's efforts to assert its relevance in the developmentalist postwar context, it is striking that the 1990s were marked by a set of consultative synods hosted on five different continents. In this regard, inculturation reflects both long-standing tensions and challenges within the Church as well as the shifting position of the Church with respect to changing conditions of globalization at the turn of the twenty-first century.

The remainder of this discussion turns to inculturation in practice, drawing from cases in Bolivia, Colombia, Ecuador, Guatemala, and Mexico. In such areas, local lay pastoral workers –usually called catechists or delegates of the Word – have played crucial roles as the primary indigenous interlocutors of missionaries and as the principal agents disseminating new pastoral ideas. On the ground, inculturation often entails a radical shift in pastoral positions as practices that were regarded critically by previous cohorts of missionaries become embraced as local expressions of Christian meaning. For catechists, whose service often exceeds the tenure of any pastoral team or dominant pastoral paradigm, the evangelical whiplash can be acutely felt.

More than a historically shaped ideology, inculturation is also a pastoral practice pursued through a variety of day-to-day and year-to-year activities. In many indigenous contexts, lay catechists have long been the principal vehicles for transmitting emergent missionary messages to the grassroots level. In the Bolivian Aymara case, inculturation has shaped the latest themes for the seemingly endless series of *cursillos* that have come to mark participation in the "new evangelization." Ruth Chojnacki describes a similar process for the Tzotzil Maya of Chiapas, Mexico. In Chimborazo, Ecuador, the Centro de Formación Indígena trains indigenous lay pastoral agents who work with community catechists developing an "indigenous Church."[7]

On the *altiplano* of Bolivia, inculturation was introduced to the catechists beginning in 1989 through a combination of small, parish-level courses as well as regional courses assembling catechists from multiple parishes. The courses I witnessed challenged catechists to serve as native ethnographers, generating an inventory of ritual practices undertaken in their communities to create an "Aymara liturgical year." The discomfort in the room was palpable as pastoral workers encouraged catechists to talk about ritual activities long denounced by the Catholic Church such as offerings (*waxt'as*) to local place deities undertaken by traditional ritual specialists (*yatiris*) as well as elements of popular Catholic practices such as dancing and drinking in the contexts of saints' festivals. These were aggressively discouraged under the banners of neo-Catholic and liberationist pastoral work.

The catechists were challenged to reflect on these practices, evaluating them along two dimensions: those that were "foreign" versus those that were "ours" and those that "promoted community" versus those that did not. Between these two is the complex work of inculturation, evaluating native practices in an environment irreversibly shaped by the presence of Christianity. Although not all foreign Christian practices were judged favorably along the criteria of supporting community, the reassessment of indigenous religious practices was fundamentally conditioned by a distilled, implicitly context-free Christian message.

Alignment within this grid of Christian meaning was the condition for the inclusion of a given indigenous practice within inculturated Aymara Catholicism. One foreign pastoral worker made this all too clear as she exhorted catechists to take up the difficult task of reflecting on their own cultural traditions. "Don't be afraid that there may have been bad customs here ... All that which facilitates life, living in community ... This should be conserved and dynamized. I cannot do this [selecting] for you. The inculturation of the Gospel is for you to do. We give you the criteria."[8]

---

7 Ruth J. Chojnacki, *Indigenous Apostles: Maya Catholic Catechists Working the Word in Highland Chiapas* (Amsterdam: Rodopi, 2010).
8 Andrew Orta, *Catechizing Culture Missionaries, Aymara, and the "New Evangelization"* (New York: Columbia University Press, 2004), 122.

These sentiments reflect the localizing thrust of inculturation, which continues a line of other post-conciliar pastoral innovations aimed at empowering grassroots Christians. Native pastoral agents are key mediators in the process, and the framework of inculturation, with its insistence that even the biblical record of Jesus' life is a foundational example of inculturation, poses a profound challenge to them. Missionaries I observed suggested that just as Jesus built upon and perfected the existing religious traditions of his day, Aymara catechists must view the practices of their own communities through the eyes of Jesus, writing through their actions an Aymara New Testament. Chojnacki reports that Mayan catechists are characterized as "indigenous apostles," engaged in a similar task through worship practices focused on a newly empowered Maya exegesis of the Bible.

In such exhortations, the figure of Jesus plays a double role. On the one hand, Jesus is a man of his place and time who incarnates the universal message of Christianity in his lived context. On the other, as the bridge between context and the assumed universal message, the figure of Jesus is a point of access to an essential Christianity, distilled from any particular cultural or historical setting. Writing of the Guatemalan Mayan case, Virginia Garrard-Burnett describes inculturationist practices as an effort to "decontextualize" Christian narratives from their Western referents and recontextualize them in local Maya circumstances.[9]

For their part, catechists often struggle with the discomfort of embracing practices they once denounced and reshaping their local identities as experts of a kind of ritual authority similar to that of others they once saw as rivals and frauds. They must negotiate this carefully in their respective communities while also bringing along the members of their local faith groups who are often extremely committed to a sort of neo-orthodoxy promoted under earlier pastoral paradigms of the second evangelization. In the inculturationist courses I have observed, catechists often push back against missionary efforts to prescribe specific rites as the favored indigenous vehicles for an inculturated Christianity. I believe their reluctance stems from a strategic concern to control their own public religious reorientation in their communities as well as a broader Aymara preference to maintain some secrecy between communities in their ritual practices. These data also point to the capillary end of circulating

---

[9] Virginia Garrard-Burnett, "God Was Already Here When Columbus Arrived: Inculturation Theology and the Maya Movement in Guatemala," in *Resurgent Voices: Indigenous Peoples, Political Mobilization, and Religious Change*, eds. Edward L. Cleary and Timothy Steigenga (New Brunswick, NJ: Rutgers University Press, 2004), 125.

religious ideologies as the inculturationist message is ultimately realized in highly contingent ways in different local communities of faith practice.

For some catechists, an increased use of the native language across all parts of the liturgy or a greater willingness to participate publicly in communal events once regarded with suspicion may be the limits of their inculturationist practices. Others may emphatically embrace selected indigenous practices and seek out new ways to collaborate with traditional ritual authorities in public rites, more closely realizing the aims of the missionaries. This range of outcomes, beyond the control of missionaries, is certainly not new. However, in the context of inculturation this capillary part of the process is explicitly declared as integral to the emergence of an inculturated Christianity.

Elsewhere, inculturationist catechists and their followers seem to reject more completely elements of the fiesta-cargo or *costumbre* complex linked to saints' festivals and their sponsorship. In the Tzotzil Maya case, the financing of these expensive ritual practices has been criticized by missionaries and catechists as compelling Mayan participation in a local political economy that maintains the dominance of nonindigenous landholders. As described by Chojnacki, inculturated Tzotzil worship focuses more on acts of exegesis performed by catechists. In a rite of baptism, for instance, catechists evoke analogies between Mayan conceptualization of three creations and the Christian Trinity and also gloss the baptism as bestowing a vocational "gift," linked to a capacity to work, on the initiate. This gloss is resonant with a focus at the core of new, inculturationist Mayan communities on an entrepreneurial work ethic linked to coffee production and indigenous control of lands.

An emphasis on key traits and practices as at once representative of indigenous tradition and potential vehicles for inculturated Christian meaning is evident in other cases from Latin America. In her discussion of an emergent "teología Maya" in Guatemala, Garrard-Burnett describes the systematization of what are taken to be key elements of Maya spirituality. Cultural values such as "peace" – with the natural world, with people living and deceased, and with place deities – along with core concepts such as soul shifting, centeredness, or complementary opposition become the Mayan framework within and through which inculturationists seek to identify and express Christian meanings. Barry Lyons describes the ways an inculturationist turn in Quichua communities of Chimborazo, Ecuador, has focused on the indigenous social value of "respect" toward elders. He points out the ways this rhetoric of respect conflates contemporary elders with idealized distant ancestors as well as the uncomfortable echoes of a different language of respect deriving from the social hierarchy of *haciendas* that were dominant in the region through the mid-twentieth century.[10]

Doing theology in these ways involves complex metacultural interpretations – readings and assertions of what it means essentially to be Maya or Aymara or Quichua – that are themselves complex and historically conditioned. One challenge of course is that contemporary expressions of indigeneity are inseparable from their fraught history of entanglement with Christianity. Noting the sort of "hermeneutic puzzle" entailed by inculturationists' renderings of Mayanness, Garrard-Burnett discusses the key role of the *Popul Vuh*, a historic text that at once provides some basis for commensurability between Maya tradition and the textually encoded core of Christianity and, as it was produced as a text during the earliest moments of Maya-Spanish engagement, seems to offer a glimpse of a pre-Columbian Maya spirituality.

A related challenge of systematizing an indigenous theology involves the standardization of what are inevitably diverse and ever-changing identities within any one cultural group. Inculturationists are not alone in this regard as the broader turn toward "official multiculturalisms" across Latin America has had a paradoxically homogenizing effect, marking cultural differences in increasingly similar and comparable ways. The inculturationist elaboration of a serial set of indigenous theologies, each with key features highlighting core values and/or metonymic rituals, runs precisely these risks.

Yet these limitations do not contain localizing efforts such as inculturation, which establishes spaces for improvisation and channels for reciprocal changes. Conversion-like accounts of spiritual and political transformation are staples of contemporary missionary autobiographies in Latin America. The increasing use of indigenous languages similarly opens up new arenas of challenge, recalibrating received categories routinely expressed in dominant languages. Joanne Rappaport, writing of inculturationist-influenced work by Nasa Uwe speakers in Colombia, describes intercultural processes whereby documents in Spanish are translated into Nasa Uwe and then "back translated" into Spanish.[11] The reversal of the translational arrows creates new semantic fields for key terms and meanings in the "original" documents. The Nasa activists were focusing on the Colombian constitution; the biblical exegesis

---

10 Barry J. Lyons, *Remembering the Hacienda Religion, Authority, and Social Change in Highland Ecuador* (Austin: University of Texas Press, 2006).
11 Joanne Rappaport, *Intercultural Utopias: Public Intellectuals, Cultural Experimentation, and Ethnic Pluralism in Colombia* (Durham, NC: Duke University Press, 2005).

of the "indigenous apostles" among the Tzotzil or elsewhere does potentially similar work.

Inculturation is caught in the tension of how many directional arrows it will embrace. At the official level, it is a form of managed multiculturalism. However, the long history of Catholicism shows that this has never been under the full control of its institutional messengers. After half a millennium of evangelization, the Church is inextricably entangled with life in Latin America; elements of Catholicism are often necessary components of "indigenous" spiritual contexts. Beyond the hermeneutic puzzles for indigenous theology or identity politics, this marks a space of action for indigenous practitioners, such as the catechists, who take as their starting point a world in which Christianity is already a self-evident local reality. As we track official efforts to define inculturation as neither "enculturation" nor "Liberation Theology" we would do well to note this complex context of entanglement as a fertile and vibrant setting of religious transformation.

Bibliography and Suggested Readings

Albó, Xavier. "Jesuitas y culturas indígenas: Perú 1568–1606. Su actitud, métodos y criterios de aculturación." *América Indígena*, 26, no. 3 (1966): 249–308 and 26, no. 4 (1966):395–445.

Arrupe, Pedro. "Letter to the Whole Society on Inculturation." *Studies in the International Apostolate of Jesuits*. Washington, DC: Jesuit Missions, June, 1978.

Calder, Bruce. "Interwoven Histories: The Catholic Church and the Maya, 1940 to the Present." In Edward L. Cleary and Timothy J. Steigenga (eds.), *Resurgent Voices in Latin America: Indigenous Peoples, Political Mobilization, and Religious Change*, 93–124. New Brunswick, NJ: Rutgers University Press, 2004.

Chojnacki, Ruth J. *Indigenous Apostles Maya Catholic Catechists Working the Word in Highland Chiapas*. Amsterdam: Rodopi, 2010.

Cleary Edward L., and Timothy J. Steigenga. *Resurgent Voices in Latin America Indigenous Peoples, Political Mobilization, and Religious Change*. New Brunswick, NJ: Rutgers University Press, 2004.

Clenndinnen, Inga. *Ambivalent Conquests: Maya and Spaniard in Yucatan, 1517–1570*. New York: Cambridge University Press, 1987.

Garrard-Burnett, Virginia. "God Was Already Here when Columbus Arrived: Inculturation Theology and the Maya Movement in Guatemala. In Edward L. Cleary and Timothy J. Steigenga (eds.), *Resurgent voices in Latin America: Indigenous Peoples, Political Mobilization, and Religious Change*, 125–153. New Brunswick, NJ: Rutgers University Press, 2004.

Hale, Charles R. "Rethinking Indigenous Politics in the Era of the '*Indio Permitido*.'" *NACLA Report on the Americas*, 38, no. 2 (2004): 16–21.

Herskovits, Melville J. *Man and His Works: The Science of Cultural Anthropology*. New York: Alfred A. Knopf, 1948.

Irrarázaval, Diego. *Inculturación: Amanecer eclesial en América Latina*. Lima: CEP, 1998.
Linden, I. *Global Catholicism: Diversity and Change since Vatican II*. New York: Columbia University Press, 2009.
Lyons, Barry J. *Remembering the Hacienda Religion, Authority, and Social Change in Highland Ecuador*. Austin: University of Texas Press, 2006.
MacCormack, Sabine. *Religion in the Andes: Vision and Imagination in Early Colonial Peru*. Princeton, NJ: Princeton University Press, 1991.
Martínez Ferrer, Luis. *Inculturación: Magisterio de la Iglesia y documentos eclesiásticos*. San José, CR: Promesa, 2006.
Miller, Daniel, ed. *Worlds Apart: Modernity through the Prism of the Local*. London: Routledge, 1995.
Norget, Kristin. "Knowing where we enter": Indigenous Theology and the Popular Church in Oaxaca, Mexico. In Edward L. Cleary and Timothy J. Steigenga (eds.), *Resurgent Voices in Latin America: Indigenous Peoples, Political Mobilization, and Religious Change*, 154–186. New Brunswick, NJ: Rutgers University Press, 2004.
Orta, Andrew. *Catechizing Culture Missionaries, Aymara, and the "New Evangelization."* New York: Columbia University Press, 2004.
——— "'Living the Past in Another Way:' Reciprocal Conversions in Missionary-Aymara Interactions." *Anthropological Quarterly*, 75, no. 4 (2002): 707–743.
Pagden, Anthony. *The Fall of Natural Man: The American Indian and the Origins of Comparative Ethnology*. New York: Cambridge University Press, 1982.
Rafael, Vincente L. *Contracting Colonialism: Translation and Christian Conversion in Tagalog Society under Early Spanish Rule*. Ithaca, NY: Cornell University Press, 1988.
Ramos Gavilán, Alonso. *Historia del Celebre Santuario de Nuestra Señora de Copacabana*. Edited by Ignacio Prado Pastor. Lima: Edición Ignacio Prado P., 1988 [1621].
Rappaport, Joanne. *Intercultural Utopias: Public Intellectuals, Cultural Experimentation, and Ethnic Pluralism in Colombia*. Durham, NC: Duke University Press, 2005.
Roest-Crollius, Ary A. "What Is so New About Inculturation? A Concept and Its Implications." *Gregorianum*, 59, no. 4 (1978): 721–773.
Stewart, Charles, and Rosalind Shaw. *Syncretism/Anti-Syncretism: The Politics of Religious Synthesis*. London: Routledge, 1994.
Suess, Paulo. *La nueva evangelización: Desafíos históricos y pautas culturales*. Quito: ABYA-YALA, 1991.
Van Cott, Donna Lee. *The Friendly Liquidation of the Past: The Politics of Diversity in Latin America*. Pittsburgh: University of Pittsburgh Press, 2000.
Wilk, Richard. "Learning to Be Local in Belize: Global Systems of Common Difference. In Daniel Miller (ed.), *Worlds Apart: Modernity through the Prism of the Local*, 110–133. London: Routledge, 1995.

38

African Diaspora Religions in Latin America Today

STEPHEN SELKA

The religions of the African diaspora in Latin America illustrate the complex interplay of cultural continuity and disjunction resulting from the forcible displacement of millions of people across the Atlantic. Brought to the Americas by slaves, these religions emerged through the efforts of Africans and their descendants to maintain some semblance of their religion and culture in the context of domination. Many African diaspora religions throughout Latin America, including Santería in Cuba, Candomblé in Brazil, and Vodou in Haiti, share basic beliefs and practices, including the veneration of African deities and ancestral spirits, complex initiation ceremonies, and an emphasis on healing. At the same time, African diaspora religions are as varied as they are similar. Moreover, even when similarities are apparent, they do not necessarily indicate identical meanings. This makes it difficult to make simple generalizations about this topic.

To complicate matters further, African diaspora religions emerged in places where Christianity was dominant. This shaped the way that African religions were practiced in the Americas, although in different ways and to varying degrees. Many people "converted" to Christianity, for example – some earnestly, others for expedient purposes, and many in-between. As Andrew Apter argues:

> The Catholicism of Vodun, Candomblé, and Santería was not an ecumenical screen, hiding the worship of African deities from persecution. It was the religion of the masters, revised, transformed, and appropriated by slaves to harness its power within their universes of discourse. In this way the slaves took possession of Catholicism and thereby repossessed themselves as active spiritual subjects.[1]

---

[1] Andrew Apter, "Herskovits' Heritage: Rethinking Syncretism in the African Diaspora." In *Syncretism in Religion: A Reader*, ed. Anita Maria Leopold and Jeppe Sinding Jensen (New York: Routledge, 2005), 178.

Christianity shaped the practice of African religion in the Americas, but slaves also Africanized the Christianity they practiced. Accordingly, as I discuss in more depth in the text that follows, we can see that it makes little sense to limit the focus of the study of African diaspora religions to the search for African continuities.

This chapter addresses a number of questions and concerns related to these points in particular and to the study and practice of African diaspora religions in Latin America more generally. After providing an overview of African diaspora religions in Latin America, the first set of concerns I explore are related to issues of racialization and nationalization. To the extent that African diaspora religions originated from processes of racial domination, they have always been "racialized." Indeed, many scholars, activists, and practitioners have represented African-derived religions as black religions and emblems of racial resistance.

The racialization of African-derived religions, however, is often in tension with the incorporation of African-derived culture and religion in discourses of national identity. At the beginning of the twentieth century, for example, Brazilian elites saw Candomblé as a degenerate African cult that was inimical to modernization. By the twenty-first century, however, it was embraced as part of the Brazilian cultural heritage to be valued, preserved, and even promoted as a tourist attraction. As I discuss later, although this has apparently led to more public acceptance of Candomblé, practitioners and activists have objected to the appropriation, domestication, and folklorization of Afro-Brazilian religion in the process.

The issues I examine next are Africanization and antisyncretism. Africanization refers to a diverse set of processes and practices that aim to (re)connect Africa and the Americas in a variety of ways. Africanization usually includes an emphasis on "African purity," more often than not based in Yorùbá culture. Among other things, this discourse establishes a hierarchy of practices that marginalizes those that are mixed with Christianity. Accordingly, over the past few decades, the discourse of antisyncretism has called for the separation of African-derived religions and Catholicism. This reflects efforts to recognize African-derived religions as independent religions in their own right, but also engendered debates about authenticity and how to define it.

At the same time, however, African diaspora religions and Christianity continue to be linked in a variety of ways in popular practice. Furthermore, initiatives have recently emerged within the Catholic Church to foster interfaith dialogue with African diaspora religions. By contrast, Catholicism's chief rival – Pentecostal Christianity – has grown rapidly in Latin America partly by explicitly opposing itself to African diaspora religions. In fact, one of the most interesting topics of current research is on the ways that neo-Pentecostalism has "keyed" itself to African-derived religions through a set of parallel practices based in variations on common cosmological principles.

The final issue I explore is the movement of African diaspora religions across borders and boundaries. Although these religions have been shaped by new forms of movement and mobility in recent decades, African diaspora religions have of course been transnational from the very beginning. In the second half of the twentieth century, however, boundary crossings have intensified in a number of ways. As a result, many African diaspora religions have moved from the local and national spaces where they developed – the sites of "primary diaspora" – to other places in the Americas and beyond through "secondary diasporas." As I discuss in the text that follows, secondary diasporas are often associated with flows of immigration, but other transnational phenomena such as the Internet and tourism have also contributed to the apparently increasing de-territorialization of African diaspora religions.

African Diaspora Religions

The term "African diaspora religions" (ADRs) can be understood in at least two different but overlapping ways. The first, which is more narrow, concerns the dispersal of African religions to places other than Africa, a definition that, as we will see, is deceptively straightforward. The second is more encompassing and concerns the religions that are practiced by people of African descent in the diaspora, which may include traditions that are not African in origin. This chapter focuses primarily on religions that are derived from or indexed to Africa in discourse or practice, including explicitly African-derived religions such as Candomblé, Vodou, and Santería.

Between the sixteenth and nineteenth centuries, approximately ten to twelve million Africans were brought to the Americas as slaves. Roughly speaking, a third went to Brazil, a third to the Caribbean, and most of the rest to Central America, Peru, and the United States. Most of the Africans who came to the Americas originated in West and Central Africa; in addition, approximately 5 percent came from southeast Africa. Although these regions shared broad cultural, linguistic, and religious similarities, there was considerable ethnic diversity among the Africans who crossed the Atlantic.

The places of origin of African slaves changed from century to century, and the composition of ethnic diversity in particular destinations in the Americas shifted accordingly over time. Paul Lovejoy explains that "new slaves were constantly arriving and thereby infusing slave communities with new information and ideas which had to be assimilated in ways that we do not always understand at present."[2] In Brazil, for example, 90 percent of enslaved Africans arrived from Central Africa until 1690, but after that point, most slaves came from the region of West Africa around the Bight of Benin. The volume of the trade also varied considerably over the centuries. The lowest volume was in the sixteenth century and the greatest in the eighteenth and nineteenth centuries. Because most of the slaves who arrived in the later centuries came from West Africa, this higher volume meant that, in total, a greater number of slaves came from West Africa than from any other region.

Yorùbá religion, language, and culture became dominant in many communities in the Americas, especially in Brazil and Cuba. In Africa, the Yorùbá occupied the area of the Bight of Benin that is now Nigeria. The strong influence of the Yorùbá has been attributed to the fact that more Yorùbá slaves arrived in the Americas both more recently and in greater numbers than other ethnic groups. In addition, practitioners and scholars have argued that Yorùbá religion was more complex and integrated than the practices that other groups brought to the Americas. As I discuss in more depth later, however, this view is problematic and largely ideological, rather than simply empirical, in nature.

Other ethnic groups that were important in the formation of the African diaspora in Latin America include the Fon and the Bantu. The Fon, who had extensive interaction and conflict with the Yorùbá during the time of the slave trade, are from the area of West Africa in and around what is now Benin. The Fon influence is particularly prominent in Haiti, partly because the French took a relatively large proportion of its slaves from Dahomey (now Benin), and also because the Haitian Revolution ended the slave trade to Saint-Domingue before the nineteenth century, during which Yorùbá slaves made up the majority of the new arrivals in the Americas. Bantu-derived practices are prevalent in the diaspora, including Candomblé Angola in Brazil, Palo in Cuba, and Petro rites in Haiti, but as I discuss in depth in the text that follows, these traditions are often represented as less integrated and not as morally grounded as Yorùbá-derived ones. Partly as a result of this, Yorùbá has become somewhat of a cultural and linguistic *lingua franca* for ADRs. This is evident in Brazil, for

---

2 Paul Lovejoy, "Conditions of Slaves in the Americas," in *From Chains to Bonds: The Slave Trade Revisited* ed. Doudou Diène (New York: UNESCO and Berghagn Books), 2001, 125–138 at 130.

example, in the fact that both Fon-derived Candomblé Jeje and Bantu-derived Candomblé Angola often use the Yorùbá names for the African spirits they venerate.

This discussion does not exhaust the large number of ethnic groups that were brought to the Americas as slaves, but it highlights the distinctions that are most salient in the African diaspora in Latin America. Over time, and particularly after the abolition of slavery, these distinctions largely ceased to be indicators of actual ethnic belonging. Today these terms are more indicative of religious differences and do not necessarily correspond to the particular ancestries of their practitioners.

This cultural complexity was a central part of the story of the emergence of ADRs. Yet the vague term "traditional African religion" continues to appear as a gloss for indigenous religions of Africa, despite the fact that African religions take on different and not necessarily interchangeable forms in different settings. As Lovejoy explains, the concept of traditional African religion

> ...has been presented as an unchanging force that was all-embracing over vast parts of the continent; observations from a variety of sources are merged to fabricate a common tradition that may or may not have had legitimacy. For want of historical research, the religious histories of Africans from the Bight of Bénin, the Bight of Biafra, Kongo, and the interior of Angola are accordingly reduced to the meaningless concept of "traditional." Hence the concept "traditional" has little functional or analytical use.[3]

Along these lines, Lovejoy and others call for greater attention to the role of Africa in the formation of American societies along with greater specificity with respect to the specific African contributions to particular communities and societies in the Americas.

None of this is to deny, however, the important similarities that many of the religious practiced in Africa during the time of the slave trade shared. James Sweet points out that when "Africans were enslaved and brought together in the diaspora, they encountered other Africans who spoke different languages and who came from varying cultural and social traditions, but whose core religious beliefs were remarkably similar to their own."[4] Sweet points to similarities between divination in Central Africa and Lower Guinea as an example

---

[3] Paul Lovejoy, "The African Diaspora: Revisionist Interpretations of Ethnicity, Culture and Religion under Slavery," *Studies in the World History of Slavery, Abolition and Emancipation*, 2:1 (1997), http://ejournalofpoliticalscience.org/diaspora.html (Accessed May 14, 2013).

[4] James Sweet, *Recreating Africa: Culture, Kinship and Religion in the African-Portuguese World, 1441–1770* (Chapel Hill, NC: University of North Carolina Press, 2003), 132.

and argues that in some cases the rituals appeared to be "almost mirror images of one another."[5]

That many of the Africans who came to the Americas were also Muslims or Christians, however, complicates the situation. Islam arrived in many areas of Africa right around or shortly after the time of Mohammed in the seventh century. Although estimates vary, a significant proportion of the slaves who came to the Americas from West and Central Africa were Muslim. At least initially, however, Islam did not take root in the Americas. Sylviane Diouf, for example, argues that Muslim education was difficult to institute under slavery, and syncretism with Christianity was not an option in the same way that it was for practitioners of African religions. Nevertheless, Muslim slaves had a large impact in the early histories of many American societies. One of the most visible signs of this was the Malê Revolt of 1835 in Bahia, Brazil, which was planned and executed by Muslim slaves and was one of the more significant slave rebellions in Brazilian history. Yet, according to João José Reis, this very militancy may be one of the reasons why Islam virtually disappeared among Africans and their descendants in Brazil.

Both Coptic Christianity and the Ethiopian Orthodox Church existed in Africa before the advent of the transatlantic slave trade. Most of the Christianized Africans who came to the Americas as slaves during the eighteenth and nineteenth centuries, however, were Catholic. Some had already been exposed to Catholicism in Spain and Portugal, while others from Angola and Kongo were already Catholic before reaching the Americas because the African Catholic Church had been present there since the 1500s. African Christians often performed the role of catechists in the Americas and thus were part of the process of evangelization. At the same time, however, the Christianity that they practiced was already "Africanized."

Whether they were initially Christian or not, the religious practices of Africans in the Americas were heavily influenced by the vernacular Christianity that was practiced in the colonies. In most places in Latin America, Africans were at least required to be baptized into the Catholic Church if not to participate in other sacraments and devotional practices. Africans and indigenous Americans commonly participated in lay Catholic devotional organizations called *cofradias*, *cabildos*, or *irmandades* that were based on organizations that were central to popular Catholicism in Spain, Portugal, and France at the time of colonization. These groups were devoted to specific patron saints and often based in particular churches. They performed a number of functions,

---

5 Ibid., 131.

including organizing religious processions on feast days. They typically grouped together slaves of the same ethnic groups, a practice that colonial administrators encouraged as a divide-and-conquer strategy.

At the same time, these organizations also served the purposes of their members, many of whom were free people of color who participated voluntarily. As Kim Butler explains, Afro-Brazilian *irmandades*, much like *cabildos* throughout Spanish America, served as "cultural orientation centers, support networks, insurance funds, and provided a religious superstructure through which Afro-Brazilians could seek spiritual support from Catholic deities as well as the African deities with which they were syncretized."[6] In fact, some organizations served the purpose of pooling funds to buy others out of slavery.

Those who were elected to officer positions in these organizations held much prestige in their communities. Many slaves embraced Catholicism and its sacraments for the spiritual benefits it offered – although they did so mostly on their own terms. At the same time, *cabildos* and *irmandades*, along with communities of escaped slaves and free people of color, provided spaces for the continuation of African religion and played a central role in the re-creation of Africa in the Americas.

Contemporary ADRs such as Candomblé, Santería, and Vodou came together in something like their current form in the late nineteenth century. This does not mean, however, that African and African-derived religions were not practiced earlier. Recent scholarship on Brazil, for example, has shown that the practice of African-derived religions during the colonial period was more autonomous and coherent than scholars previously thought. Yet a number of important conditions came about at the end of the nineteenth century that transformed the practice of and crystallized these religions, including the abolition of slavery – or in the case of Haiti, revolution – and the migration of people of African descent to the cities. At the same time, other developments brought these religions under the increasing scrutiny of Latin American elites, including efforts at modernization and the development of disciplines such as anthropology, which helped to crystallize the idea of these religions as discrete traditions. It is important to note, however, that the labels used for these religions gloss over a great deal of diversity and complex interconnections. The term "Vodou," for example, is one not generally used by practitioners in Haiti.

---

6 Kim Butler, *Freedoms Given, Freedoms Won: Afro-Brazilians in Post-Abolition São Paulo and Salvador* (New Brunswick, NJ: Rutgers University Press, 1998), 147.

Although the explicitly African-derived religions that are practiced in the Americas today differ significantly, George Simpson emphasizes that many of them have the following elements in common:

> ...the names and characteristics of African deities, 'soul' concepts, ritual objects, drum rhythms, song styles, dance steps, spirit possession, the ritual use of stones, herbs, and water, seclusion and 'mourning,' animal sacrifices, belief in the immediacy of intervention of supernatural beings in human affairs, utilization of spirits of the dead, and ritual words ... blended with Christian elements – including the names of Catholic saints, Catholic and Protestant theological concepts, hymns, prayers, Bible verses, the cross and crucifixes, and with spiritualist doctrine – in diverse ways.[7]

This list provides a starting point for understanding the "family resemblances" between these religions. Indeed, the ritual logics and cosmological grammars of ADRs appear to be broadly similar. Moreover, there is wide agreement that African continuities in the Americas are particularly visible in the realm of religious practice.

It is important to stress again, however, that similarities among religions in the Americas may be but are not necessarily due to similarities among religions in Africa. Specific convergences may have been the result of the syncretism of African religions that occurred in the Americas or of more recent processes of religious legitimation, including the privileging of practices of putative Yorùbá origin. In the case of Candomblé in Brazil, for example, Yorùbá traditions came to be dominant through a confluence of discourses about purity and authenticity among practitioners, scholars and politicians.

Generally speaking, however, a key aspect that Candomblé, Vodou, and Santería share is their focus on affliction and healing. Andrew Chesnut argues that the primary reason that people practice African-derived religions (as well as their primary competitor, Pentecostalism) is to find relief from the "pathogens of poverty" in general and illness in particular. These religions also share an emphasis on reciprocal relationships between humans and the spirits (African and otherwise), a creative and animating energy or force that permeates the world (called *ashé* in Yorùbá), the importance of the dead as powerful and potentially dangerous agents in the everyday lives of the living, and the balance between harmony and discord. Nevertheless, it is important to note that practices differ widely according to social context. For example,

---

7 George Eaton Simpson, *Black Religions in the New World* (New York, NY: Columbia University Press, 1978), 61.

urban, upper-middle class practitioners may be more concerned with emotional than physical healing.

In addition, ADRs in the Americas typically bring together practices under one roof that usually constituted ritual specializations in West African contexts. For example, divination is often a ritual specialty in West Africa, but in the Americas this is one of the many practices for which most Candomblé leaders are responsible. Furthermore, whereas African temples are often devoted to a single *orisha* (deity), in the diaspora a temple is expected to accommodate the full range of gods, even if one is singled out as a favored patron.

Practice varies significantly among ADRs, but many communities host public ceremonies in which the spirits become embodied in their devotees. These ceremonies are generally dedicated to particular spirits and their timing is determined by the yearly ritual cycle, which is often partially synchronized with the Catholic ritual calendar. These public ceremonies often involve elaborate celebrations with song, dance, and food offered to the particular spirits. During these ceremonies initiates, and sometimes others, will "dance" – that is, become the bodily vessel for their deity.

Day-to-day practice generally revolves around fulfilling ritual obligations to the spirits, including offerings of food; animals; and, for some, spirits, tobacco, and liquor. These religions also focus on doing "work" for a client, including healing, love spells, and defending against offensive work or sorcery. Consultations commonly involve some form of divination to reveal the client's situation, after which the client is given instructions on how to proceed. Practitioners receive donations for these services that help to sustain his or her community and help fund whatever celebrations it may host.

The distinction between "good" and "bad" work is a common theme in ADRs. This difference is encapsulated in oppositions such as *"fazer por bem"* versus *"fazer por mal"* (to do for good versus to do for evil, in Portuguese) or as Todd Ochoa discusses in his work on sorcery in Cuba, *"trabajo cristiano"* versus *"trabajo judio"*[8] (Christian work versus Jewish work). These descriptions are often applied to different traditions that are practiced in close proximity, such as Candomblé, Macumba, Umbanda, and Quimbanda in Brazil, rite Rada and rite Petro in Haiti, or Regla de Ocha and Regla de Palo Monte in Cuba. It is common for good work to be associated with Yorùbá traditions and bad work with Bantu traditions.

---

8 Todd Ochoa. *Society of the Dead: Quite Manaquita and Palo Praise in Cuba* (Berkeley: University of California Press, 2010).

In practice, however, none of these traditions are clearly separate from one another, and in the case of Candomblé and Macumba, these are often used as alternative labels for the same practices. Furthermore, even though most practitioners claim that they do not do bad or negative work, all practitioners must work with ambiguous spirits and be able to defend against their spiritual weapons, as Kelly Hayes has stressed in her study of Umbanda in Brazil. And as Kristina Wirtz points out with respect to the Cuban context, participants in these supposedly separate traditions are interconnected through their ongoing discussions about and interpretations of practice.

Although ADRs vary in their level of institutionalization, their initiates are usually ranked into a hierarchy by degree of initiation and ceremonial function. Initiation is typically a long and complex rite of passage that prepares one to properly embody the spirits. It generally involves practices such as seclusion; bodily modifications such as to the hair and skin; and observing certain taboos, including those requiring abstinence from sex and particular foods. Some of the roles that one might perform in the temple do not require this kind of initiation, however. In Candomblé, for example, drummers and other kinds of temple helpers are chosen precisely because they are not prone to possession.

Those who are initiated or have a formal role in the community make up a small percentage of those involved with these religions. A significantly larger number of people attend or have attended ceremonies or have consulted with a practitioner for a number of possible reasons, including problems with health, money, or relationships. Nevertheless, only a small percentage of people report being involved in ADRs.

In Brazil, for example, surveys indicate that about 1.3 percent of the Brazilian population reports being involved with Candomblé. This may only reflect those who are formally initiated and/or those who feel comfortable claiming Candomblé as their religion, however; the figure certainly does not reflect the large number of people who participate in Candomblé but still identify themselves as Catholic. In the Haitian context, there is a popular saying that Haiti is 90 percent Catholic and 99 percent Vodou, but in reality as much as 40 percent of the population is Pentecostal, and Pentecostals generally eschew ADRs.

In Cuba, studies that have attempted to estimate rates of participation usually show that those who identify with African-derived religions such as Santería and Vodú number less than 10 percent of the population. Yet in Cuba, as in Brazil and Haiti, religious affiliation is notoriously difficult to quantify and define because many people participate in multiple religions at the same time. Accordingly, Kristina Wirtz argues that the religions of Cuba, including

Santería, Spiritism, Pentecostalism, and Catholicism, make up "elements of a single popular religious complex."[9]

Gender roles in ADRs tend to be well defined. Some roles, such as that of drummer, are nearly always filled by men. Most initiates are women, although there are significant numbers of men who are initiated. With respect to leadership roles, these are highly variable. Candomblé, for example, has famously been represented as a "religion of women" because women have, at least since the early twentieth century in Bahia, dominated the leadership of the most prestigious temples. By contrast, the highest levels of leadership in Santería and Vodou are generally occupied by men. Gender roles in these religions are complex, however, and generalizations about them are hotly contested, as J. Lorand Matory has explored in his work. As Matory also discusses, sexuality is a complicated issue in ADRs. Male priests and initiates in Candomblé have often been stereotyped as "passive homosexuals," and Matory argues that this reflects efforts to cast male priests as anomalous. At the same time, these religions are generally more accepting of homosexuality than their Christian competitors, which is one of the reasons that they are more appealing to some than Pentecostalism.

Issues

Racialization and Nationalization

As we have seen, there are many more issues to address in the study of ADRs than can be dealt with in a single chapter. The interrelated themes of race and nationalism, however, figure prominently in much of the recent literature on ADRs. With respect to race, for example, scholars, activists and practitioners often frame Candomblé, Santería, and Vodou as countercultural expressions of black resistance. Yet the connections between African diaspora religion and race are not always straightforward. Before the abolition of slavery, for example, although practitioners of these religions were primarily people of African descent, whites were often clients and patrons.

White patronage did not mean that white authorities accepted these religions, however. Indeed, at the turn of the twentieth century in Brazil and Cuba, scientists saw African-derived religions as evidence of African inferiority and irrationality and as barriers to modernization and progress. Later, during the US occupation of Haiti in the early twentieth century, images flourished of Vodou as a barbaric African cult. These kinds of representations not

---

9 Ibid., 30.

only tended to reinforce the relationship between religion and race but also clearly framed ADRs and their practitioners as a problem.

Throughout the history of Latin America, priests, scientists, and government officials have more often than not taken an oppositional stance toward ADRs. By the 1930s, however, Latin American intellectuals began to integrate these religions into discourses of national identity and pride. The Afro-Cubanidad movement in Cuba and the First Afro-Brazilian Congress in Brazil, for example, represented shifts away from the racism and racial determinism that had characterized earlier intellectuals' views toward an enthusiastic affirmation of African-derived culture. Nevertheless, these developments were largely driven by elites who embodied a patronizing attitude toward people of African descent and their cultures.

After the second half of the twentieth century, ADRs were gradually integrated not only into elite circles but also into national popular culture. Founded on claims that African culture was part of a shared national heritage, this integration into popular culture implied a de-racialization of African-derived religions. Indeed, embracing these religions fit neatly into imaginations of national identity that emphasized racial mixture and denied racism. The post-revolutionary Cuban state, for example, sponsored efforts to *rescatar* (to rescue, reclaim or recover, a term commonly used in relation to cultural heritage in Latin America) Afro-Cuban religion. At least initially, Cuba stressed its ties to Africa as a way to appeal to Afro-Cubans and as an affirmation of Third World solidarity. Over time, however, Santería became nationalized – critics would say "folklorized" – and transformed into a tourist attraction.

As Christine Ayorinde points out, this process of nationalization and domestication is reflected in the shift in terminology from *"brujería"* (witchcraft) to "so-called syncretic cults" to "Cuban religions of African origins."[10] Similarly, although Haitian elites at the turn of the twentieth century saw Vodou as inimical to civilization, by the middle of the century many intellectuals had embraced it, and today it is regarded as part of national heritage – even if it was subject to legal discrimination until as late as 1987. Likewise, as Paul Johnson discusses, in Brazil, the state formation project that elevated African heritage transformed Candomblé from a "tumor" that was an offense to moral hygiene to a "trophy" to the "trademark" of the state of Bahia in particular over the course of the twentieth century.[11]

---

10 Christine Ayorinde, *Afro-Cuba Religiosity, Revolution, and National Identity* (Gainesville: University Press of Florida, 2004).
11 Paul Johnson, *Secrets, Gossip and Gods: The Transformation of Brazilian Candomblé* (New York: Oxford University Press, 2005).

In addition to being integrated into imaginations of national identity, ADRs are often seen as intertwined with the operations of the state. Many *santeros*, for example, insist that Fidel Castro is involved in Santería. In Haiti, in addition to the fact that many attribute the success of the Haitian revolution to an African ritual performed at Bois Caiman in 1791, Papa Doc Duvalier's secret police, the Tonton Macoute, reputedly employed Vodou in their work. More recently, in 2003, Jean-Bertrand Aristide, a former Catholic priest and the first democratically elected president of Haiti who was rumored to have connections with Vodou despite being a priest, officially recognized Vodou as a religion. Furthermore, in Brazil, the death of Tancredo Neves, who died in 1985 before he was able to take office as the first president of a newly democratized Brazil, was rumored to be the result of African sorcery.

Beyond the nationalization of ADRs "from above" by elites, practitioners of Santería and Candomblé often emphasize the national character of their religions. Although often referred to as Afro-Cuban or Afro-Brazilian, for example, many practitioners describe Santería and Candomblé simply as Cuban or Brazilian. No doubt this resonates with dominant discourses that deny the importance or even existence of race in these national contexts, but it also reflects the racial diversity of the practitioners of these religions. Along these lines, some white Cubans resent being told that their religion is of African origin. Moreover, some Cubans and Brazilians express skepticism about looking to Africa for their identities, as they feel they carry Africa within them. This is especially true in Bahia, where some temples present themselves as more "African than Africa."

Nevertheless, the nationalization of ADRs has encountered resistance. Although ADRs have become more visible in the public sphere over the past few decades, a development that is at least partly positive, these increasing public engagements have sparked debates about appropriation. In Bahia, for example, Candomblé leaders have objected to the "folklorization" of their religion through its integration into public festivals and tourist itineraries; some have objected that turning these religions into public spectacles constitutes sacrilege. Along these lines, race-based initiatives have emerged that counter both the public appropriation and negative representations of them. Activists in Brazil's black movement, for example, have drawn upon the iconography of Candomblé in their campaigns and young people have been drawn to Candomblé as a way to embrace their black identity. In addition, activists and practitioners have equated evangelical Christians' demonization of Candomblé with racism, which further links African-derived religion and blackness.

Nevertheless, as Palmié has pointed out focusing mainly on Cuba, images of Candomblé, Santería, and Vodou as "black religions" are complicated by the number of nonblack practitioners and initiates and by the fact that temples in Latin America generally do not exclude initiates, clients, or patrons on the basis of race.[12] Half of Candomblé practitioners in Brazil identify themselves as "white," as do many Santería practitioners. It may be the case, of course, that those who are lighter skinned and more privileged are more willing to identify with a controversial religion than those who are poor and relatively powerless. Nevertheless, in practice there appears to be no contradiction in affirming that a religion is both African and open to practitioners of all colors. This is reflected in the cosmology of ADRs. In a story told in Cuba, for example, the *orisha* Ochun asked her sister Yemanja to straighten her hair and lighten her skin so that when she went to Cuba to help her suffering people she could be worshiped by everyone.

This is not to suggest that race is not a critical issue, however. Despite Santería's multiracial membership and its label as a Cuban religion, for example, debates about its racial status are becoming more noticeable. Moreover, critics rightly point out that white involvement in African diaspora religions can be problematic. The practice of Umbanda in Rio de Janeiro, for example, takes place along a spectrum of practices ranging from "White" to "Africanized." Although the "white" in White Umbanda ostensibly refers to the spiritual distinction between white and black magic and not to race, it is no coincidence that the practitioners of White Umbanda tend to be lighter skinned and have eliminated traces of "African" practices they deem savage or primitive, such as animal sacrifice. Critics point to how patterns of racial inequality are replicated with Umbanda centers, including through the ways that the spirits of old slaves are called on to help solve the problems of white patrons.

Africanization and Antisyncretism

Although discourses focusing on African purity have been important since at least the nineteenth century, they are particularly visible in Africanization – or re-Africanization – movements that have emerged since the 1960s. Among other objectives, these movements aim at the elimination of Catholic elements from the practice of ADRs and often emphasize Yorùbá language and culture. This trend is evident in Cuba, for example, in the shift of the name of

---

12 Stephan Palmié, "Against Syncretism" in *Counterworks: Managing the Diversity of Knowledge*, ed. R. Fardon (London: Routledge, 2003), 73–104.

the religion from Santería to Regla de Ocha or Ifá and of the names of practitioners from *"santero"* to *"babalocha."*

Peter Clarke identifies four groups of practitioners of *"orisha* religion" who have different levels of engagement with Africanization, namely practitioners in West Africa, practitioners in Latin America and the Caribbean, post-1960s (mostly black) *"orisha* revivalists," and post-1980s (mostly white) "modernists."[13] It is the revivalists who have been the most active proponents of Africanization, and some of the most enthusiastic and influential revivalists are African Americans concerned with orthodox practice and black consciousness.

In fact, American practitioners of *orisha* religion have played a role in the Africanization of African diaspora religion throughout the Americas, including in Trinidad. As in Cuba, the use of Yorùbá terms in Trinidad is increasing, and there has been a shift in the terminology used to refer to Afro-Trinidadian religion from "Shango Baptist" to terms such as "Orisha movement" and "Orisha religion." Although Africanization and the elimination of Christian practices is largely a local initiative in Trinidad, Americans in Trinidad have helped to encourage this transformation. This has met with resistance, however, with some locals responding that it is "just like Americans" to come to their home and tell others that they are doing it wrong.[14] As Palmié points out, the American Yorùbá religion practitioners' drive to get rid of "Cuban admixtures," such as the synchronization of ceremonies with the Catholic calendar, has led to similar tensions because many Cuban *santeros* continue to see Santería as a product of the encounter between African religion and Catholicism.[15]

The process of Africanization commonly involves eliminating "syncretic" elements such as images of saints and the use of Christian prayers during, before, or after rituals; encouraging and expanding the use of the Yorùbá language both in ritual contexts and in the everyday activities of the community; and reclaiming rituals and practices deemed authentically African. This ritual reclamation, however, can create tension between communities of practitioners. The founding of Egungun societies (ritual organizations

---

13 Peter Clarke, "Accounting for Recent Anti-Syncretist Trends in Candomblé-Catholic Relations." In *New Trends and Developments in African Religions*, edited by Peter Clarke (Westport, CT: Greenwood Press, 1998), 17–36.
14 Frances Henry, *Reclaiming African Religions in Trinidad: The Socio-Political Legitimation of the Orisha and Spiritual Baptist Faiths* (Kingston, Jamaica: University of West Indies Press, 2003), 153.
15 Stephan Palmié, "Against Syncretism: 'Africanizing' and 'Cubanizing' Discourses in North American Orisa Worship," in *Counterworks: Managing the Diversity of Knowledge*, ed. Richard Fardon (New York: Routledge, 1995), 73–104.

that focus on ancestor veneration) in the Americas provides a good example of this. Although these societies are common in West Africa, they are rare in the Americas. In fact, working with the dead is considered particularly dangerous in ADRs in Latin America. For many revivalists, however, Egungun societies represent, among other things, a way of recovering and enacting a sense of collective memory. In addition, many Egungun societies in the Americas allow women to fully participate, something that is generally not permitted either in West Africa or in those societies that exist in Latin America. This indicates a more general difference between revivalists and "traditional" practitioners in Latin America – revivalists often place a strong emphasis on gender inclusivity.

Disagreements over what is most purely "African" are nothing new, of course; questions of African purity and authenticity, for example, were central to the ongoing formation of Candomblé in the nineteenth century. Despite continual contact across the Atlantic from the time of slavery to the present, however, the Africa that is often imagined in the Americas is an idealized one. That is, Africa is often imagined as something unitary, and little of the religious heterogeneity that I discussed earlier, let alone the religious diversity and complexity of West and Central African societies today, finds its way into these imaginaries.

At the same time, the vision of pure Africa that is most common in the diaspora is very specific: that of Africa as Yorùbá. In Brazil, for example, anthropologists and sociologists have argued for the purity and integrity of Nago (Yorùbá) versus Jeje (Fon) and Angola (Bantu) traditions since the beginning of the twentieth century. Through the work of these scholars, the cultivation of Yorùbá-derived Candomblé was promoted as evidence of racial democracy in northeastern Brazil. More recently, people of African descent throughout the Americas concerned with the fight against racism and the recovery of an African identity have taken up Africanization as a kind of social movement.

As Africanization generally focuses on Yorùbá-derived traditions, however, it creates value-laden distinctions between practices considered purely Yorùbá and practices seen as having other origins. In Cuba, for example, Yorùbá-derived Regla de Ocha is viewed as moral and respectable as opposed to the amoral and instrumental Bantu-derived Palo. Yorùbá practices are often identified with the benevolent "right-hand" path and Bantu as well as other non-Yorùbá practices with the malicious "left-hand" path.

As Lorand Matory argues, the very idea of the Yorùbá nation and its associated characteristics emerged from dialogues across the black Atlantic. That is, Yorùbá identity did not precede the diaspora in its origins and roots; instead, it emerged simultaneous and in tandem with the diaspora in the Americas. As James Sweet puts it, "Becoming African was essentially an American phenomenon."[16] Accordingly, many scholars emphasize that contemporary connections between Africa and the Americas, such as between Yorùbá and Lukumi, are constructed rather than discovered.

This process of becoming African, whether Yorùbá or not, is still in operation today. In the Garifuna diaspora in the United States, for example, it is often when African-derived religions cross boundaries that their practitioners come to see their religions as "African." In fact, practitioners have been equally important in the production and deployment of discourses about African origins, which often turn on competitive claims to African purity. Along these lines, although it might seem at first glance that Africanization and racialization are identical, Africanization primarily concerns faithfulness to particular African traditions, at least as they are imagined in the Americas. Indeed, in Latin America, Africanization is often more about establishing ritual "authenticity" than racial exclusion.

A central emphasis of Africanization is the elimination of Catholic symbols and practices from Candomblé, Vodou, and Santería. Indeed, in Brazil African "purity" has been equated with resistance and mixture with integration. The issue of the relationship of Catholic saints to African spirits is a very complex one, and there appears to be wide variation in the ways in which these relationships are formed and understood. Nevertheless, practitioners commonly distinguish between saints and the spirits, for example, even if they are part of a common cosmology with overlapping sets of symbols and associations. That is, the distinction between Christianity and African-derived religion is generally salient to practitioners of the latter, even if these religions are intertwined in complicated ways.

It is this intertwining that antisyncretism movements seek to undo. In the early 1980s in Bahia, for example, a group of prominent leaders in the Candomblé community publicly objected to the appropriation of Candomblé as folklore for the consumption of tourists and asserted Candomblé's independence from the Roman Catholic Church. In a statement published in the local newspaper, the authors identified syncretic practices as major culprits in the de-legitimatization of Candomblé. In response, the authors denounced syncretism and relegated it to a thing of the past; to be a legitimate religion, they argue, Candomblé must be independent and autonomous, not derivative

---

16 James Sweet, *Recreating Africa: Culture, Kinship and Religion in the African-Portuguese World, 1441–1770* (Chapel Hill, NC: University of North Carolina Press, 2003), 115–117.

of or dependent on Catholicism. The leader of this movement, Mãe Stella of Ilé Axé Opô Afonjá, one of the oldest and most prominent *terreiros* (Umbanda centers) in Salvador, removed all of the Catholic saints' images from her temple and put them on display in a museum on the terreiro grounds. These Catholic items on display at Mãe Stella's terreiro represent a fascinating inversion of the displays of Candomblé paraphernalia at Salvador's Afro–Brazilian museum, a prime tourist destination located in the center of the city's historical district flanked by several of the most prominent Catholic churches in Salvador.

Ironically, however, antisyncretism movements may end up "Christianizing" that which they seek to Africanize. With respect to an antisyncretism that began in Haiti in 1986, for example, Laënnec Hurbon writes, "Paradoxically, the more vigorous the movement's effort to safeguard Vodou's original purity, the more it is influenced by Christian ecclesiological models."[17] That is, to assert its autonomy, Vodou needed to present itself as a "religion" – a concept that is itself thoroughly Christian. Similarly, Paul Johnson has argued that Candomblé in Brazil has become "Protestantized" in the sense that it needs to present itself in terms of a coherent set of beliefs to be considered a bone fide religion.[18]

The widespread persistence of "double participation" in popular practice, however, represents a challenge to antisyncretism. In Bahia, for example, the interlacing of Candomblé and Catholicism is alive and well outside of the major temples in the cities. The Afro-Catholic Festival of Bonfim in Bahia, one of the most important festivals in the city of Salvador outside of Carnaval, culminates with Candomblé practitioners washing the steps of the church of the city's patron saint.

Although the notion that these religions are separate and self-sufficient is widely accepted, the idea that one has to adhere exclusively to one or the other is not. This is most visible in Afro-Catholic *cofradias* and *irmandades* as well as in Marian devotions throughout the Americas. In Cuba and Miami, for example, Our Lady of Charity, the patron saint of Cuba, is very popular, including among Santería practitioners who identify her with Ochun. Similarly, in Haiti and Miami, Our Lady of Perpetual Help, the patron saint of Haiti, is identified

---

17 Laënnec Hurbon, "Globalization and the Evolution of Haitain Vodou," in *Orisa Devotion as World Religion: The Globalization of Yoruba Religious Culture*, eds. Jacob Obafẹmi Kẹhinde Olupọna and Terry Rey, translated by Terry Rey (Madison: University of Wisconsin Press, 2008), 274.
18 Paul C. Johnson, *Secret, Gossip and Gods*.

with Ezili. In Brazil, *irmandades* devoted to Our Lady of the Rosary are often linked with Afro-Brazilian communities and with Candomblé. In addition, the *irmandade* of Our Lady of Good Death in Bahia is an excellent example of an Afro-Catholic group that has been praised as a symbol of both religious mixture and black resistance.

At the same time, at least some Catholic clergy have adopted more accepting attitudes toward ADRs. The "theology of inculturation" has paved the way for fostering respect for local culture and religious practice. Inculturated masses in Brazil, Haiti, and Colombia, for example, incorporate African-style drumming into the liturgy. In some contexts in Cuba, seminarians are encouraged to be sensitive to Afro-Cuban religions and drums are allowed in church. The Catholic Church in Cuba has opposed antisyncretism because of the belief that syncretism domesticates and elevates Afro-Cuban religion.

Such efforts to create dialogue between Catholicism and ADRs provide an interesting counterpoint to antisyncretism movements. Yet not everyone in the church has embraced these trends, of course, and even the Church's engagements with Afro-Catholic practice that appear benign sometimes represent "kinder and gentler" attempts to reinstitute orthodox Catholic practice. Thomas Tweed illustrates this approach with his description of how a Catholic priest at the shrine of Our Lady of Exile in Miami engages Cuban devotees in discussions about proper Catholic practice and the true nature of Santería. A more dramatic example comes from Brazil, where in the 1980s and 1990s the archbishop of Bahia attempted to disband many of the black *irmandades* under his domain, largely due to their connections with Candomblé.

In terms of antagonism toward ADRs, however, Pentecostal Christianity, especially its more recent incarnations, defines itself in direct opposition to religions such as Candomblé, Vodou, and Santería. In Bahia, for example, where evangelical televangelists condemn Candomblé as demonic, several cases of evangelicals attacking Candomblé temples have appeared in the news. Although in some ways Pentecostalism represents a radical break from African-derived religion – as seen in the strict behavioral code required of its members, the emphasis on a cosmos in which the division between good and evil is clear and sharp, and the practice of proselytization – there are important continuities as well. The logics of possession, sacrifice, and even sorcery are taken up in a new form in the Pentecostal context. The Universal Church of the Kingdom of God in Brazil in particular has worship services that respond directly to the ritual cycle in Candomblé and Umbanda.

Transnational Crossings

Although we often speak of transnationalism as if it were something new, ADRs have been mobile from the beginning. The transatlantic slave trade was of course quintessentially transnational, involving flows of human beings not only from Africa to the Americas, but from the Americas to Africa as well. In fact, it is difficult to point to a period in the past that did not involve movement across borders, as critics of the idea that transnationalism is new have pointed out. Yet the movement of ADRs across borders has intensified over the course of the twentieth century. Migration and other flows of people throughout the Americas have led to the "secondary diaspora" of ADRs, and more recently, these religions have circulated even more widely via the Internet and other media.

Movements of people across borders have shaped the practice of ADRs particularly since the second half of the twentieth century. While primary diasporas refer to the development of ADRs in cities such as Salvador, Havana, and Port-au-Prince, secondary diasporas indicate subsequent migrations of these religions from these cities to other places. Many of these movements have been internal to the nation: in Brazil, for example, Candomblé moved from Bahia to Rio de Janeiro and other cities in the south through labor migrations and other displacements of people. Other movements cut across national borders, such as flows of immigrants from the Caribbean to the United States. Waves of Cuban immigrants, for example, arrived in the United States at different times in the twentieth century, establishing communities in places like New York and Miami. As a result, according to Gregory, as long ago as the 1990s, there were an estimated 250,000 to 1,000,000 practitioners of Santería in the United States, including approximately 5,000 to 10,000 African Americans.[19]

When Santería began to spread beyond immigrant communities in the United States, it mainly grew among African Americans and Latinos. In the 1960s, African religion became part of a search for the religious foundations of black identity as black nationalist movements in New York in particular embraced African and Afro-Caribbean cultures as part of their political agenda. The first full initiation of an American in the United States was performed in 1961; before then, initiations were performed in Cuba.

New York's Caribbean Cultural Center was an early institution that celebrated Afro-Caribbean religion and culture and brought together diverse groups from Latin America and the Caribbean. Eventually, however,

---

[19] Stephen Gregory, *Santeria in New York City: A Study in Cultural Resistance* (New York: Garland Publishing, 1999).

specifically American institutions emerged – such as the Yorùbá Temple and later the Oyotunji African Village – that emphasized that which was seen as African over that which was seen as specifically Caribbean and that refused to initiate whites. As I discussed previously, many Cuban practitioners stress the syncretic and inclusive nature of their practice, which encouraged African American revivalists to form their own communities.

Over the course of the 1960s and 1970s, however, many Santería practitioners also came to emphasize the African nature of their religious practice, leading to a convergence between Caribbean and African American understandings at least in some contexts. More broadly, some degree of convergence has also occurred between the different Afro-Caribbean religions that find themselves in overlapping spaces in the United States. In this context practitioners often borrow from each other's traditions through a process of *bricolage* that draws upon Latin American notions of cultural hybridity or *mestizaje*. In addition, African diaspora religious practices in the United States often become intertwined with local forms of devotion. Elizabeth McAlister, for example, describes how Haitian immigrants in New York participate in the festival of Our Lady of Mount Carmel, a practice that is associated with older waves of Italian immigrants.

Beyond the complex interactions that practitioners of ADRs have with one another and with other religions in new spaces, a critical issue is how these religions are received by nonpractitioners, government authorities, and the media. In 1993, for example, the case of *Church of Lukumi Babalu Aye v. City of Hialeah*, in which Santería practitioners objected to restrictions on animal sacrifice that Hialeah had imposed on them, was heard before the Supreme Court, bringing to light deeply held prejudices against ADRs. Although the Supreme Court ultimately declared Hialeah's selectively applied ordinance against the "unnecessary killing" of animals unconstitutional, ADRs continue to appear in American popular culture as primitive and nefarious cults. As a result of widespread prejudice against these religions, many practitioners elect to keep a low profile and may operate informally in connection with neighborhood *botanicas*. Although the institutionalization of African diaspora religions has been used as a strategy to counter persecution in some contexts, such as in Brazil, some in the United States believe that it might actually attract further repression.

Despite all of these movements and border crossings – or perhaps more accurately because of them – the relationship between these religions in diaspora and their "homelands" in the Americas is a major concern. Haitian immigrants, for example, who are a significant presence in New York and Florida, maintain close ties to their ritual communities in Haiti and often travel back home for ceremonial purposes. In addition, practitioners improvise ways of staying connected with their ritual communities through the use of various technologies. As Karen Richman points out, for example, Haitians in the United States often listen to ceremonies recorded in Haiti or more recently, watch them on posted on YouTube.

At the same time, ADRs anchor themselves in their new settings. There are some typical transformations that they undergo as they become localized, however. As Johnson explains, for example, the common process of "hooking" involves the reinscription of rituals onto new maps, such as the substitution of a local site or geographical formation – such as a mountain or body of water – for one back in the homeland. In addition, what Johnson calls "telescoping" involves not simply the transportation of rituals to a new site, but the transformation and sometimes reductions of those rituals. This might involve replacing the soil of the forest with a small pot of dirt in an apartment, for example. Finally, "additivity" involves the increased focus of some aspect of the religion when it disperses or the incorporation of elements of another religion, such as the Garifuna adopting elements of Vodou.[20]

Beside the United States, of course, there are significant migrations from Latin America to Europe, and ADRs have a substantial presence in Portugal, France, and Germany, among other places. These religions are also well dispersed within Latin America. Brazilian Umbanda is popular throughout South America, for example, including in neighboring Argentina, Uruguay, and Venezuela. In addition, Santería is part of an emerging "Afro-Caribbean identity" in Veracruz, Mexico – although in Veracruz Santería is more a matter of individual than community practice and is strongly based on links to Cuba.

Technological developments have facilitated the globalization and de-territorialization of ADRs. In addition to the flow of bodies – and spirits – across borders, media such as the Internet have contributed considerable to the dispersal of these religions across the globe. The numerous websites devoted to ADRs expand ways in which practitioners and seekers can interact. According to George Edward Brandon, by 2008 there were approximately 160 sites devoted to *orishas* that ranged in purpose from organizational to individual, devotional, academic, and commercial. Brandon identified several types of visitors to these sites, including "Recruiters," "Lost Souls," "Cyber Elders," and the "Web Bricoleur." These cyber-practitioners – particularly the Web

---

20 Paul Christopher Johnson, *Diaspora Conversions: Black Carib Religion and the Recovery of Africa* (Berkeley: University of California Press, 2007), 55–59.

bricoleurs who bring together strands from different traditions – are part of a larger trend of "tertiary diasporas" in which lines of dispersal have become very complex and origins are increasing difficult to trace. One example of this is the spread of Santería to the Philippines, where the *orishas* are syncretized not only with Catholic saints but also with Asian deities such as Kwan Yin through multiple paths from the Americas, including both Cuba and the United States.

As one might expect, the dispersal of ADRs into cyberspace has met with skepticism and criticism. One such objection is that the proliferation of websites has led to an anthropomorphization and pantheonization of ADRs that are at odds with local understandings of these traditions. Another criticism is that there is a clear "digital divide" in the production of information about ADRs on the Web. Along these lines, Olabiyi Babalola Yai objects that although in terms of knowledge about and authority within these religions, Africans in Africa rank highest, Africans in diaspora second highest, and non-Africans last, this ranking is reversed with respect to knowledge about and access to the Web, which means that the majority of the information on the Web is produced by white Americans. Not surprisingly, another major criticism is that the "internetization" of ADRs is at odds with the communal nature of their practice and that online engagement with these religions tends to be oriented toward concerns that are more personal and individual.

The proliferation of websites about ADRs on the Internet has helped to pave the way for movements that generally go the opposite way from immigration, including tourism. Tourism is a top industry in many Latin American and Caribbean countries, including Cuba, Haiti, and Brazil. ADRs – or at least performances based on them – have become a major attraction in these places. As Karen Richman writes about Haiti,

> Witnessing a Vodou ceremony has been the climax of North American tourists' exploration of the forbidden island. Without even leaving their hotels, they could watch staged performances of ritual dance, drumming, singing, and feigned possessions put on by professional troupes. More adventuresome tourists could venture out in the dark to a "Vodou temple–nightclub" to watch a more comprehensive staged performance of possession and animal sacrifice.... Finally, members of "the little band of (literary) Haiti addicts" could visit temples that welcomed outsiders from other classes or countries to their "secret" rites. Revelation of entrées into these ceremonies was, of course, a key source of authority for their writings.[21]

---

21 Karen Richman, "Innocent Imitations? Authenticity and Mimesis in Haitian Vodou Art, Tourism and Anthropology," *Ethnohistory*, 55, no. 2 (2008), 215.

In fact, today Vodou is promoted as Haiti's "quintessential living commodity:"[22]

Although ADRs are attractive to a wide variety of tourists, they are of particular interest to tourists seeking deeper engagements with ADRs. Visitors from North America and Europe, for example, travel to Haiti, Cuba, and Brazil to be initiated into Vodou, Santería, and Candomblé. As a result of the global expansion of interest in *orisha* religion, this has become a lucrative source of income for some local communities. Some initiations are abbreviated – including false initiations performed for unsuspecting gringos – while others may be more "orthodox," requiring the initiates to maintain their obligations to the spirits, including by returning on a regular basis.

African diaspora tourism in which African Americans seek their "roots" has grown over the past few decades and over the past few years Brazil and the state of Bahia in particular has been paying particular attention to promoting this kind of tourism. African diaspora tourism gathered momentum in the 1960s and 1970s in conjunction with the civil rights and Black Power movements in the United States. At about the same time, Bahia began attempts to develop itself as a tourism destination, and by the 2000s, it was explicitly seeking to attract African American visitors. Interestingly, although some of the African American visitors are initiated into African or African diaspora religions, the majority of the visitors are Protestant Christians. This is confusing, of course, to many Brazilians who see an inherent conflict between Protestant Christianity and African-derived religion. Yet religious difference do not prevent practitioners of Candomblé from engaging with African American visitors, as many locals see diasporic tourism as particularly lucrative for their communities.

Conclusion

The presence of African American seekers in Bahia and other destinations on the "map of Africanness" in the Americas has contributed to what Yai refers to as the "post-Atlantic globalization" of African diaspora religions. Other important developments that have contributed to this process include, as mentioned previously, the US civil rights movement and similar movements in Latin America, black nationalism, the Cuban diaspora, and the promotion of orisha religion as a world religion. All of these factors have fostered the emergence of a "modern, theologically rationalized twentieth century religion"[23]

---

22 Karen Richman, *Migration and Vodou* (Gainesville: University Press of Florida, 2007), 215.
23 David Brown, *Santería Enthroned: Art, Ritual and Innovation in an Afro-Cuban Religion* (Chicago: University of Chicago Press, 2003), 19.

and have made plausible a cosmopolitan African diasporic metareligion. This trend toward the universalization of ADRs is evident in the World Orisha Conference, the most recent meeting of which took place in Havana in 2003, a gathering that helps to make the unity of ADRs plausible.

Although the idea of having ADRs taken seriously as something more than disparate, localized traditions – an idea that underlies the fact that this chapter is included in this volume – we should be cautious. Proponents of Yorùbá or Òrìṣà as a world religion argue that the differences among ADRs are no greater than the differences within Christianity. This is arguably true. Yet the uncritical use of categories such as *"orisha religion"* runs the risk of setting up a particular vision of authentic African religion grounded in problematic notions of origins, continuity, and purity. Besides further marginalizing certain traditions, this has the potential to gloss over the ways in which ADRs are intertwined with Christianity and the central place of Christianity, for better or for worse, in the African diaspora. That is, if there is any lesson to draw from the scholarship on ADRs, it is how critically important it is to pay attention to these religions as they are practiced and not simply as they are represented by those who have privileged access to the means of representation.

Bibliography and Suggested Readings

Andrews, George Reid. *Afro-Latin America, 1800–2000*. New York: Oxford University Press, 2004.

Apter, Andrew. "Herskovits' Heritage: Rethinking Syncretism in the African Diaspora." In Anita Maria Leopold and Jeppe Sinding Jensen, *Syncretism in Religion: A Reader*, 160–184. New York: Routledge, 2005.

Asad, Talal. *Geneaologies of Religion: Discipline and Reasons of Power in Christianity and Islam*. Baltimore: The Johns Hopkins University Press, 1993.

Ayorinde, Christine. *Afro-Cuban Religiosity, Revolution, and National Identity*. Gainesville: University Press of Florida, 2004.

Bastide, Roger. *The African Religions of Brazil: Toward a Sociology of the Interpenetration of Civilizations*. Baltimore: The Johns Hopkins University Press, 1978.

O Candomblé da Bahia (Rite Nagô). São Paulo: Editora Schwarcz Ltda., 1958.

Birman, Patrícia. *Fazer Estilo, Criando Gêneros*. Rio de Janeiro: Edições UERJ/Relume Dumará, 1995.

Brandon, George Edward. "From Oral to Digital: Rethinking the Transition of Yorùbá Religion." In Jacob Obafẹmi Kẹhinde Olupọna and Terry Rey (eds.), *Òrisa Devotion as World Religion: The Globalization of Yorùbá Religious Culture*, 448–469. Madison: University of Wisconsin Press, 2008.

Brazeal, Brian. "Blood, Money and Fame: Nago Magic in the Bahian Backlands." PhD dissertation, University of Chicago, 2007.

Brown, David. *Santería Enthroned: Art, Ritual and Innovation in an Afro-Cuban Religion.* Chicago: University of Chicago Press, 2003.

Brown, Diana DeGroats. *Umbanda.* New York: Columbia University Press, 1994.

Brown, Karen McCarthy. *Mama Lola: A Vodou Priestess in Brooklyn.* Berkeley: University of California Press, 2001.

Burdick, John. *Blessed Anastacia: Women, Race and Popular Christianity in Brazil.* New York: Routledge, 1998.

Legacies of Liberation: The Progressive Catholic Church in Brazil and the Start of a New Millennium. Aldershot, UK: Ashgate, 2004.

Butler, Kim. *Freedoms Given, Freedoms Won: Afro-Brazilians in Post-Abolition São Paulo and Salvador.* New Brunswick, NJ: Rutgers University Press, 1998.

Capone, Stephania. *Searching for Africa in Brazil: Power and Tradition in Candomblé.* Durham, NC: Duke University Press, 2010.

Chesnut, R. Andrew., *Born Again in Brazil: The Pentecostal Boom and the Pathogens of Poverty.* New Brunswick, NJ: Rutgers University Press, 1997.

Competitive Spirits: Latin America's New Religious Economy. New York: Oxford University Press, 2007.

Christian, William. *Local Religions in Sixteenth-Century Spain.* Princeton, NJ: Princeton University Press, 1981.

Clark, Mary Ann. *Where Men Are Wives and Mothers Rule: Santería Ritual Practices and Their Gender Implications.* Gainesville: University Press of Florida, 2005.

Clarke, Kamari Maxine. "Ritual Change and the Changing Canon: Divinatory Legitimization of Yoruba Ancestral Roots in Oyotunji African Village." In Jacob K. Olupona and Terry Rey (eds.), *Orisa Devotion as World Religion: The Globalization of Yoruba Religious Culture*, 286–319. Madison: University of Wisconsin Press, 2008.

Clarke, Peter. "Accounting for Recent Anti-Syncretist Trends in Candomblé-Catholic Relations." In Peter Clarke (eds.), *New Trends and Developments in African Religions*, 17–36. Westport, CT: Greenwood Press, 1998.

Curry, Mary Cuthrell. *Making the Gods in New York: The Yoruba Religion in the African American Community.* New York: Routledge, 1997.

Dantas, Beatriz Gois. *Nago Grandma and White Papa: Candomblé and the Creation of Afro-Brazilian Identity.* Trans. Stephen Berg. Chapel Hill: University of North Carolina Press, 2009.

Diouf, Sylviane. *Servants of Allah: African Muslims Enslaved in the Americas.* New York: New York University Press, 1998.

Edmonds, Ennis, and Michelle Gonzalez. *Caribbean Religious History: An Introduction.* New York: New York University Press, 2010.

Flores, Maria Magarita Castro. "Religions of African Origin in Cuba: A Gender Perspective." In Patrick Taylor (ed.), *Nation Dance: Religion, Identity and Cultural Difference in the Caribbean*, 54–64. Bloomington: Indiana University Press, 2001.

Frandrich, Ina. "Yorùbá Influences on Haitian Vodou and New Orleans Voodoo." *Journal of Black Studies*, 37, no. 5 (2007): 775–791.

Frigerio, Alejandro. "Re-Africanization in Secondary Religious Diasporas: Constructing a World Religion." *Civilisations: Revue Internationale d'Anthropologie et de Sciences Humaines*, 51 (2004): 39–60.

Fuente, Alejandro de la. *A Nation for All*. Chapel Hill: University of North Carolina Press, 2000.

Gomez, Michael. *Black Crescent: The Experience and Legacy of Black Muslims in the Americas*. New York: Cambridge University Press, 2005.

Gregory, Stephen. *Santeria in New York City: A Study in Cultural Resistance*. New York: Garland, 1999.

Hale, Lindsay. *Hearing the Mermaid's Song: The Umbanda Religion of Rio de Janeiro*. Santa Fe: University of New Mexico Press, 2009.

Harding, Rachel. *A Refuge in Thunder: Candomblé and Alternative Spaces of Blackness in Brazil*. Bloomington: Indiana University Press, 2000.

Hayes, Kelly. *Holy Harlots: Femininity, Sexuality and Black Magic in Brazil*. University of California Press, 2011.

Henry, Frances. *Reclaiming African Religions in Trinidad: The Socio-Political Legitimation of the Orisha and Spiritual Baptist Faiths*. Kingston, Jamaica: University of West Indies Press, 2003.

Herskovits, Melville. "The Negro in Bahia, Brazil: A Problem in Method." *American Sociological Review*, 8, no. 4 (1943): 394–404.

Hurbon, Laënnec. "Current Evolution of Relations between Religion and Politics in Haiti." In Patrick Taylor (ed.), *Nation Dance: Religion, Identity and Cultural Difference in the Caribbean*, 118–128. Bloomington, IN: Indiana University Press, 2001.

"Globalization and the Evolution of Haitain Vodou." In Jacob K. Olupọna and Terry Rey (eds.). Trans. Terry Rey. *Orisa Devotion as World Religion: The Globalization of Yoruba Religious Culture*, 263–277. Madison: University of Wisconsin Press, 2008.

Jensen, Tina Gudrun. "Discourses on Afro-Brazilian religion: From de-Africanization to re-Africanization." s In Christian Smith and Joshua Prokopy (eds.), *Latin American Religion in Motion*, 265–283. New York: Routledge, 1999.

Johnson, Paul. *Diasporic Conversions: Black Carib Religion and the Recovery of Africa*. Berkeley: University of California Press, 2007.

Secrets, Gossip and Gods: The Transformation of Brazilian Candomblé. New York: Oxford University Press, 2002.

Kiddy, Elizabeth. *Blacks of the Rosary: Memory and History in Minas Gerais, Brazil*. University Park: Pennsylvania State University Press, 2007.

Klein, Herbert. *The Atlantic Slave Trade*. New York: Cambridge University Press, 1999.

Lopes, Nei. "African Religions in Brazil, Negotiation and Resistance: A Look from Within." *Journal of Black Studies*, 34, no. 6 (2004): 838–860.

Lovejoy, Paul. "The African Diaspora: Revisionist Interpretations of Ethnicity, Culture and Religion under Slavery." *Studies in the World History of Slavery, Abolition and Emancipation*, 2, no. 1 (1997). http://ejournalofpoliticalscience.org/diaspora.html

"Background to Rebellion: The Origins of Muslim Slaves in Bahia." *Slavery and Abolition*, 15, no. 2 (1994): 151–180.

"Conditions of Slaves in the Americas." In Doudou Diène (eds.), *From Chains to Bonds: The Slave Trade Revisited*, 125–138. New York: UNESCO/Berghagn Books, 2001.

Matory, J. Lorand. *Black Atlantic Religion: Tradition, Transnationalism and Matriarchy in the Afro-Brazilian Candomblé*. Princeton, NJ: Princeton University Press, 2005.

Mbiti, John. *Introduction to African Religion*, 2nd ed. Portsmouth, NH: Heinemann Educational Books, 1991.

McAlister, Elizabeth. "The Madonna of 115th Street Revisited: Vodou and Haitian Catholicism in the Age of Transnationalism." In R. Stephen Warner and Judith G. Wittner (eds.), *Gatherings in Diaspora: Religious Communities and the New Immigration*, 123–169.Philadelphia: Temple University Press, 1998.

Rara! Vodou, Power and Performance in Haiti and Its Diaspora. University of California Press, 2002.

Moore, Robin. *Nationalizing Blackness: Afrocubanismo and Artistic Revolution in Havana, 1920–1940*. Pittsburgh: University of Pittsburgh Press, 1997.

Mulvey, Patricia. "Black Brothers and Sisters: Membership in the Lay Black Brotherhoods of Colonial Brazil." *Luso-Brazilian Review*, 17, no. 2 (1980): 253–279.

"Slave Confraternities in Brazil: Their Role in Colonial Society." *The Americas*, 39, no. 1 (1982): 39–68.

Murphy, Joseph. "Òrìsà Traditions and the Internet Diaspora." In Jacob Obafẹmi Kẹhinde Olupọna and Terry Rey (eds.), *Òrìsà Devotion as World Religion: The Globalization of Yorùbá Religious Culture*, 470–484. Madison: University of Wisconsin Press, 2008.

O'Brien, David. *Animal Sacrifice and Religious Freedom: Church of the Lukumi Babalu v. City of Hialeah*. Lawrence: University Press of Kansas, 2004.

Ochoa, Todd. *Society of the Dead: Quita Manaquita and Palo Praise in Cuba*. Berkeley: University of California Press, 2010.

Oliveira, Marcelo Natividade, and Leandro de. "Religião e Intolerância á Homosexualidade: Tendências Contemporâneas no Brasil. In Vagner Gonçalves da Silva (ed.), *Intolerancia Religosa: Impactos do Neopentecostalismo no Campo Religioso Afro-brasileiro*, 261–302. São Paulo, Brazil: EDUSP, 2007.

Olupona, Jacob K., and Terry Rey, eds. *Òrìsà Devotion as World Religion: The Globalization of Yorùbá Religious Culture*. Madison: University of Wisconsin Press, 2008.

Oro, Ari Pedro. "A Desterritorialização das Religiões Afro-Brasileiras." *Horizonte Antropológos*, 1, no. 3 (1995).

Ortiz, Fernando. *Los Negros Brujos*. Miami: Ediciones Universal, 2005.

Palmié, Stephan. "Against Syncretism: 'Africanizing' and 'Cubanizing' Discourses in North American Orisa Worship." In Richard Fardon (ed.), *Counterworks: Managing the Diversity of Knowledge*, 73–104. New York: Routledge, 1995.

"Introduction: On Predications of Africanity." In Stephan Palmié. *Africas of the Americas: Beyond the Search for Origins in the Study of Afro-Atlantic Religions*, 1–38. Boston: Brill, 2008.

The Cooking of History: How Not to Study Afro-Cuban Religion. University of Chicago Press, 2013.

Parés, Luis Nicolau. *A Formação do Candomblé: História e Ritual da Nação Jeje na Bahia*. Campinas, Brazil: Editora Unicamp, 2006.

Parrinder, Geoffrey. *Religion in Africa*. London: Pall Mall Press, 1969.

Pinho, Patricia de Santana. "African-American Roots Tourism in Brazil." *Latin American Perspectives*, 35, no. 3 (2008): 70–86.

Prandi, Reginaldo. "Raça e Religião." *Novo Estudos*, 42 (1995): 113–129.

Reis, João. *Slave Rebellion in Brazil: The Muslim Uprising of 1835 in Bahia*. Baltimore: The Johns Hopkins University Press, 1995.

Rey, Terry. "Marian Devotion at a Catholic Parish in Miami: The Feast of Our Lady of Perpetual Help." *Journal of Contemporary Religion*, 19, no. 3 (2004): 353–374.

Richman, Karen. *Migration and Vodou*. Gainesville: University Press of Florida, 2007.
Rodriques, Raimundo Nina. *O Animismo Fetichista Dos Negros Bahianos*. Rio de Janeiro: Civilização Brasileira S.A., 1935.
Romo, Anadelia. *Brazil's Living Museum: Race, Reform and Tradition in Bahia*. Chapel Hill: University of North Carolina Press, 2010.
Rossbach de Olmos, Lioba. "Santeria Abroad: The Short History of an Afro-Cuban Religion in Germany by Means of Biographies of Some of its Priests." *Anthropos*, 104 (2009): 1–15.
Sandoval, Mercedes Cros. "Santería: Afrocuban Concepts of Disease and Its Treatment in Miami." *Journal of Operational Psychology*, 8, no. 2 (1977): 52–63.
— "Santería in the Twenty-first Century." In Jacob K. Olupona and Terry Rey (eds.), *Òrìṣà Devotion as World Religion: The Globalization of Yorùbá Religious Culture*, 355–371. Madison: University of Wisconsin Press, 2008.
— *Worldview, the Orichas, and Santeria: Africa to Cuba and Beyond*. Gainesville: University Press of Florida, 2009.
Sansi, Roger. *Fetishes and Monuments: Afro-Brazilian Art and Culture in the 20th Century*. New York: Berghahn Books, 2007.
Sansone, Livo. *Blackness without Ethnicity: Constructing Race in Brazil*. New York: Palgrave Macmillan, 2003.
Santos, Jocélio Telles dos. *O Poder da Cultura e a Cultura no Poder: Disputa Simbólica da Herança Cultural Negra no Brasil*. Salvador, Brazil: Edufba, 2005.
Saraiva, Clara. "Afro-Brazilian Religions in Portugal: Bruxos, Priest and Pais de Santo." *Ethnográfica*, 14, no. 2 (2010): 265–288.
Schmidt, Bettina. *The Caribbean Diaspora in the USA*. Brookfield, VT: Ashgate, 2008.
Selka, Stephen. "Mediated Authenticity: Tradition, Modernity and Postmodernity in Brazilian Candomblé." *Nova Religio*, 11, no. 1 (2007): 5–30.
— *Religion and the Politics of Ethnic Identity in Bahia, Brazil*. Gainesville: University Press of Florida, 2007.
Sheller, Mimi. *Consuming the Caribbean: From Arawaks to Zombies*. New York: Routledge, 2003.
Silva, Vagner Gonçalves da. *Intolerácia Religiosa: Impactos do Neopenecostalismo no Campo Religioso Afro-Brasileiro*. São Paulo, Brazil: EDUSP, 2007.
Simpson, George Eaton. *Black Religions in the New World*. New York: Columbia University Press, 1978.
Sweet, James. *Recreating Africa: Culture, Kinship and Religion in the African-Portuguese World, 1441–1770*. Chapel Hill: University of North Carolina Press, 2003.
Taylor, Patrick. *Nation Dance: Religion, Identity and Cultural Difference in the Caribbean*. Bloomington: Indiana University Press, 2001.
Thornton, John. *Africa and Africans in the Making of the Atlantic World, 1400–1800*. New York: Cambridge University Press, 1998.
Trost, Theodore Louis, ed. *The African Diaspora and the Study of Religion*. New York: Palgrave Macmillan, 2007.
Tweed, Thomas. *Our Lady of Exile: Diasporic Religion at a Cuban Catholic Shrine in Miami*. New York: Oxford University Press, 2002.
Wirtz, Kristina. "Diving the Past: The Linguistic Reconstruction of 'African' Roots in Diasporic Ritual Registers and Songs." In Stephan Palmié (ed.), *Africa of the Americas: Beyond the Search for Origins in the Study of Afro-Atlantic Religions*, 141–178. Boston: Brill, 2008.

Ritual, Discourse and Community in Cuban Santería: Speaking a Sacred Word. Gainesville, FL: University Press of Florida, 2007.

Yai, Olabiyi Babalola. "Yorùbá Religion and Globalization: Some Reflections." In Jacob K. Olupọna and Terry Rey (eds.), *Òrìṣà Devotion as World Religion: The Globalization of Yorùbá Religious Culture*, 233–246.Madison: University of Wisconsin Press, 2008.

Yelvington, Kevin. *Afro-Atlantic Dialogues: Anthropology in the Diaspora.* Santa Fe, NM: School of American Research Press, 2006.

"The Anthropology of Afro-Latin America and the Caribbean: Diasporic Dimensions." *Annual Review of Anthropology,* 30 (2001): 227–260.

39
Afro-Caribbean Religious Expressions

MIGUEL A. DE LA TORRE

The story of the presence of African-based religious expressions in the Spanish Caribbean (Cuba, the Dominican Republic, and Puerto Rico) begins centuries prior to the first African or European ever setting foot in the Antilles. This narrative begins in 711 CE, when Moorish general Tarik ibn Ziyad, under the direction of Musa ibn Nusayr, assembled seven thousand warriors, mostly North Africans – specifically Moors and Berbers – to conquer the Visigothic Christian Iberian Peninsula in the name of Islam. For almost eight centuries, what would become Spain and Portugal struggled to have the cross vanquish the crescent. On January 2, 1492, the last Muslim caliphate in Granada capitulated to a united Christian Spain, a unity brought about through the marriage of Ferdinand II of Aragon and Isabella I of Castile, also known as "the Last Crusader." Muslims and Jews remaining after the Spanish Reconquest (*Reconquista*) of the peninsula were given a choice: leave, convert to Roman Catholicism, or be killed. While the Moors were losing land, power, and influence on the Iberian Peninsula, Portuguese sailors started to explore the west coast of Africa searching for treasures, specifically gold and trade routes abandoned by the Moors. By 1448, with the blessings of the Catholic Church, these sailors brought the first African slaves to Europe.

After extirpating the Moors from Spain, the Christian monarchs were in need of establishing new trade routes to India free from hostile Islamic forces that might attack their ships; hence Christopher Columbus sailed westward in 1492. Rather than discovering a short cut to India, the lost Columbus encountered the Taíno, the indigenous people of the Caribbean. The Taíno, whose name means "good" or "noble," offered hospitality to Columbus's men. In return, they were decimated within a generation. The Reconquest of the Iberian Peninsula, with its religious fervor, continued in the new lands of what would become the Americas. Faith and empire building merged as men called conquistadores sailed west in search of riches, fame, and glory. The Greater Antilles, specifically the island of Cuba, became a stopping-off place on the way to conquer other people in new places including the Aztecs of Mexico, the Maya of Central America, the Seminoles of Florida, and the Inca of Peru.

The faith brought by the conquistadores was a premodern Catholicism (the Council of Trent would not convene until 1545). They brought a Spanish folk Catholicism that emphasized holy personages such as the Virgin Mary and the saints rather than holy sacraments, a faith steeped in the Counter-Reformation that privileged itself as the sole interpreter of spiritual reality, and a faith forged by centuries of struggle against Muslim rule. It is this manifestation of Catholicism that would eventually influence the Afro-Caribbean religions.

In the wake of the conquest, the almost complete decimation of Caribbean indigenous populations meant that there was a lack of indigenous people to cultivate the lands of those islands and to build their cities and ports. This led to the import of slaves, first Mayans from the Yucatán and eventually Africans. The need for laborers to work the land became acute as the production of sugar proved profitable, spurring the establishment of sugar plantations. Ironically, Bishop Bartolomé de las Casas, known as the defender of the Indians for his book, *A Very Short Account of the Destruction of the Indies*, which chronicled the atrocities suffered by Indians at the hands of Spaniards, was among the first to advocate the importation of Africans to replace Indians as slaves, an argument he would live to regret.

The profitability of and demand for sugar triggered a demographic shift during the late 1600s. More than half of all Africans brought as slaves to the Americas worked on sugar plantations throughout the Caribbean, especially in Cuba. Conservatively, by the abolition of slavery in the 1880s, ten million Africans were brought across the Atlantic against their will. Approximately 4.7 million came to the Caribbean where life was brutal – filled with eighteen-hour workdays, six days a week. Their life expectancy on arriving was seven years. It was more profitable to work a slave to death than to provide resources for adequate care.

Although ethnographer Fernando Ortiz identifies ninety-nine African ethnicities represented in the Caribbean, a plurality (23 percent) came from the Slave Coast in western Nigeria, Benin, and Togo, lands that represented the Yoruba kingdoms and consisted of several ethnic groups including the Egba, Ife, Ijebu, and Kentu. These Africans arrived in the Caribbean with nothing but their languages, customs, traditions, and gods; yet their spiritual traditions survived because (1) Caribbean Catholicism was more conducive to preserving their faith than North American Protestantism; (2) importation of Africans continued until 1886, bringing newer Africans to maintain the original faith; (3) a system called *cabildos*, or mutual aid societies, maintained ethnic traditions and served as a forerunner to house churches; and (4) since 1503, runaway slaves formed their own "free" societies in remote mountain areas where they could practice their faith apart from the Spanish overlords.

The Caribbean was more congenial to the preservation of enslaved peoples' religion than the southern United States for several reasons. Slave owners in the Caribbean, unlike those in the United States who bred their slaves, found it more cost-effective to replace slaves after they were worked to death. While the United States officially stopped importing slaves in 1808 and abolished the practice in the 1860s, slavery continued in the Caribbean into the late 1800s. As late as 1930, *negros de nación* (African-born slaves) could be found who remembered the religious practices of their homeland. By the time slavery was gradually abolished in Cuba (1880–1886), one-third of the population was African, of which 75 percent were negros de nación.

By contrast, at the end of the US Civil War in 1865, the existing four million US slaves were ten times the total number imported. Hence, Caribbean slaves were better able to preserve their faith because their culture and traditions were not diluted and forgotten by ensuring generations. Also, sugar plantations, unlike plantations in the United States, required numerous slaves. Smaller slave plantations denied US slaves the support systems that could have assisted in the preservation of their faith. Smaller Anglo-American plantations made the "seasoning" or "breaking in" process more available – a process that attempted to de-Africanize the slave. Through violence, slaves were taught to look down on African languages, customs, traditions, and religion as remnants of a "savage," if not satanic, past.

In the United States, the loss of African spirituality was replaced by Protestantism, which usually required a personal conversion narrative. By contrast, in Cuba, although the Catholic Church also attempted to eventually stamp out Africanism through religious assimilation, conversion was less intense, usually consisting of baptism and learning certain prayers by rote. Although this process was most pronounced in the Spanish Caribbean, where Catholicism dominated, parallel African-derived religions also emerged and thrived in non-Spanish areas such as Jamaica and Trinidad.

Within Catholic thinking, the evangelization of Africans would be more effective if slaves were initially permitted to participate in their cultural traditions within the structures of Catholicism, although the ultimate (and largely unsuccessful) goal was to eventually achieve full conversion. The Church permitted blacks to form cabildos, social clubs that served as mutual aid societies, usually under the supervision of the diocesan priest. These cabildos created a space where African religions could be preserved and passed down to future generations.

The Caribbean also provided places for runaway slaves to hide. As early as 1503, runaway slaves, known as *cimarrones* or *maroons*, established armed-camp communities in Hispañola (Dominican Republic and Haiti), joining the remaining Taíno natives in their fight against the Spaniard invaders. Free of European subjugation, they could participate in their faith unmolested, preserving their customs and traditions. These communities were usually located in the mountains of the Caribbean islands, where remnants still exists to this day, specifically in Viñales, Cuba and Adjuntas, Puerto Rico. Cimarron communities also existed in the United States, but they were not as prevalent. The best example was found in Florida, where the Seminole Wars (1816–1819, 1835–1842, and 1855–1858) were partly an attempt to eradicate them.

Afro-Caribbean religions, which originated as the faith of the oppressed, are earth-centered and lack any centralized religious hierarchy. These religions share certain common traits, despite considerable diversity among them as well. For example, there is no devil or Satan; instead there is a belief in a benevolent, transcendent, Supreme Being who is the ultimate source of human destiny. There are several intermediate gods with whom humans communicate to align their lives with their destinies. There is also a recognition that these quasi-gods or spirits animate the forces of nature and are able to take possession of humans for the benefit of devotees.

Afro-Caribbean religious practices often focus more on the everyday trials and tribulations of life that deal with issues of health, money, or love than on abstract theological concepts. The goal is to provide assistance to anyone wishing to find and live in harmony with the destiny they were assigned by ensuring that the proper rituals needed to navigate life are performed. One does not become a devotee of an Afro-Caribbean faith tradition through a profession of faith but by performing the rituals. A homogeneous belief system is not as important as conducting the correct ritual practices.

Afro-Caribbean religious expressions can best be understood as forms of hybridity. Although different historical religious strands combined to create different manifestations of Afro-Caribbean spirituality, it would be an error to relegate these faiths to the realm of the syncretic. Syncretism has historically been used as a label for faith traditions deemed to be a confused mixture of different religious expressions, thus connoting a certain impurity. These Afro-Caribbean religions are not confused religious expressions. Rather, they are their own realities with their own worldviews that stand apart from the different strands that originally contributed to their formation. To illustrate this development, this chapter examines the three major religious traditions prevalent in the Spanish Caribbean: Espiritismo, Santería, and Palo.

Espiritismo

Espiritismo, or Spiritism, should not be confused with Espiritualismo, a Mexican form of spiritualism. Espiritismo, as practiced in the Caribbean, is also known as Kardecism and has its origins in mid-nineteenth century France, eventually spreading to Latin America, where it particularly took root in the Caribbean and in Brazil. The Spiritist movement was started by an engineer named Hippolyte Léon Denizard Rivail, who wrote under the pseudonym Allan Kardec. He attempted to apply a scientific methodology of observation and experimentation to the investigation of supernatural phenomenon by merging strands of Christian morality, scientism, mysticism, and progressivist ideology. Although Kardec did not perceive the Spiritist movement to be a religion, he employed mediums to serve as the means by which he queried the spirits to codify their responses. The results became a series of books titled *Spiritist Codification*. For Kardec, Spiritism became a compilation of principles rooted in every aspect of human knowledge influencing the sciences, religion, philosophy, ethics, and life that humans could access for personal benefit.

In Kardec's Spiritism, small groups would gather around a table to conduct a séance. Once the medium entered into a trance, she or he would become a conduit between the physical and spiritual worlds. Through the medium, the spirits provided the participants sitting around the table with solutions to whatever ailed them. In their minds, speaking with the spirits of the dead was not some magical or supernatural feat, but the result of rigorous scientific observation and experimentation. For Kardec, God was the Supreme Being and primary cause of all that is, both visible (physical) and invisible (spiritual). Contact between these two worlds was possible, and humans could learn how to communicate with the dead, receiving from them spiritual energies that led to physical and spiritual health and advice on how to move closer to enlightenment.

When Spiritism moved to the Caribbean as Espiritismo, Kardec's ideas expanded to allow for speaking with ancestral spirits that reconnected the living with their pre-Christian past – practices repressed by the Catholic Church – such as Native Indian healing practices, African religious practices, Medieval Spanish folk traditions, and herbalism. Not only do the spirits of the dead help the living, but the living can also assist the dead. *Espritistas* believe that reincarnation occurs along a karma-type principle by which human happiness or sufferings are consequences of previous lives.

On death, humans ceased being material beings and transformed into spiritual entities. In this new stage, the spirit of the deceased attempts to seek advancement in the hierarchy of perfection. Moving toward this enlightenment facilitates their reincarnation in this, or other worlds. The espritista can assist the dead to move to the next higher spiritual level of existence. Christ, who is believed to have achieved the highest level of spiritual incarnation, becomes the paragon for the supreme virtue of love needing emulation. Following Christian moral teaching based on love ensures movement toward higher spiritual levels on death.

The first literature about Spiritism arrived in the Caribbean in 1856, where it was immediately banned because of the anticlerical views it expressed. Yet it was precisely this perspective that initially contributed to the movement's popularity, attracting disenfranchised Catholics suspicious of the social and political power held by the institutional Church. Almost immediately, Spiritism began to appeal to people who sought an alternative – sometimes even an oppositional – religious milieu to Catholicism, which in Cuba in particular retained a fiercely colonial and Spanish association. Members of radical organizations of the time such as women suffragists, abolitionists, and freedom fighters against Spain's colonial rule found Spiritism individualist teachings attractive. Spiritism provided a pseudo-religious ideology conducive to democracy, science, and modernity and created a political and spiritual space for progressive liberal ideas to flourish. By the 1870s, Espritismo became fashionable, especially among the middle and upper economic classes.

Eventually, Espiritismo moved beyond the Caribbean elites and made its way to the lower economic classes, rural poor, blacks, and disenfranchised urban populations. These communities turned to Espiritismo for assistance in dealing with the difficulties of their daily lives. With time, the movement moved away from its philosophical, scientific, and intellectual claims. Although many within these groups seldom visited a priest or attended mass, they still considered themselves Catholics, and as such, found no conflict with the teachings and practices of Espiritismo and the Christian worldview.

More important for our purposes, a hybrid spirituality developed between Espiritismo and Spanish-based folk religion, Native American healing practices, herbalism, and African-based religions such as Santería or Palo, which we discuss in the text that follows. Espritismo evolved into a belief system based on good and evil spirits that could influence a person's health, wealth, family, or luck. These spirits were subordinate to the particular African quasi-deity that they belonged to when they were alive. Séances came to be called *misas* (masses), incorporating Caribbean religious practices, foreign to how Kardec first envisioned the movement or how the original middle and upper economic classes of the Caribbean participated.

Espritismo became an important component in Afro-Caribbean religious traditions such as Santería and other *orisha*-based faith traditions, recovering an ancestral worship lost due to slavery. Until slavery, African religions included some form of ancestral worship; however, slavery destroyed family unity, wreaking havoc on the key practice of the veneration of ancestors. Slavery prevented family members from gathering to carry out the rituals and ancestral worship. When Espiritismo was introduced in the Caribbean, Africans were able to reincorporate ancestral worship into their religious traditions. Not only did Espiritismo impact orisha-based religious expressions, but African religious traditions also changed Espiritismo. Unlike their European counterparts, during their trances Caribbean mediums relied on spiritual guides who were African born but died during slavery. In some cases, these guides were from the original Taíno people. With time, devotees from all forms of African-based religious expressions throughout the Caribbean became espiritistas, even though not all espiritistas became devotees of the African-based faiths.

Santería

The term Santería is derived from the Spanish word *santo* and literally means "the way of the saints." It was used as a pejorative word by Catholic clerics to describe what they considered to be a syncretism of the veneration of Catholic saints with African traditional spirituality, particularly in its Yorùbán expression. In reality, Santería was the product of a survival technique employed by the enslaved African people who masked their deities, known as *orishas*, behind the "faces" of Catholic saints. This allowed them to continue worshipping their gods while under the constant supervision of their overlords. Today, some prefer the terms *lucumí* (friendship), *regla de ocha* (rule of Ocha), or *regla de ocha-Ifá* (rule of the Ocha's sacred text) rather than the Christian-inflected name, Santería.

Prior to slavery, each city-state in Yorubaland (much of sub-Saharan West Africa, including mainly what is today Nigeria, Benin, and Togo) had their own orisha, but captivity in the Caribbean forced Africans from different municipalities to live together, thus creating a new pantheon of orishas. The religious practices of different city-states began to merge in the Caribbean environment as the different orishas developed familial relationships. This reorganization of African religious beings and their followers took place secretly, under the shadow of Iberian Catholicism. Not surprisingly, a hybrid spirituality developed, blending the African orisha worship practices of West Africa with the premodern Catholicism of Iberia, with the additional influence of other elements, such as Kardecist spiritualism, as we have seen in the preceding text.

The foundational building block of the Santería is *ashé*, which is defined as a sacred energy that becomes the power, grace, blood, and life force of all reality, embracing mystery, secret power, and divinity. This transcendent world force is absolute, illimitable, pure power, nondefinite, and nondefinable. It is a neutral cosmic energy that is amoral, unable to be seen or personified, and is the underpinning of all existence. Every life and every manifestation of power has ashé. The movement of the wind, the strike of lightening, the "breathing" of plants, the crash of a wave, the flow of blood, and the streaming of water all expend ashé.

When a candle is lit to an orisha, the act releases power – the power of fire, smoke, burning wax. This ashé feeds the orisha, who is then empowered to fulfill the request of the devotee lighting the candle. Orishas and humans exist in a codependent relationship where humans need the ashé of the orishas in the form of protection and guidance, while the orishas need to be fed ashé in the form of sacrifices and rituals. If humans lacked ashé, they would live aimless lives; and if the orishas were to lack ashé, then they would cease to exist. The most potent ashé is found in the spilling of sacrificial blood. Through ashé all things came into being, and all things will eventually return to ashé.

Ashé is the very the substance of Olodumare – the Creator of all that is and all that is, is an expression of Olodumare. At the beginning of time, whenever anyone needed anything, they would have to come to Olodumare for ashé. But Olodumare grew weary of this arrangement and departed the earth. In his place he left intermediaries, called orishas, in charge and gave each reign over different aspects of nature and life. Today, no one worships or sacrifices to Olodumare, for he is too transcendent to intervene in human affairs. Humans instead approach the orishas who grant requests in Olodumare's stead. When offering a sacrifice to an orisha, the believer is making an offering to the part of Olodumare exemplified by the particular orisha for whom the sacrifice was made.

These orishas are the quasi-deities, secondary gods representing forces of nature. Santería is thus a form of nature worship, for as an orisha is worshipped, reverence is given to the force of nature the orisha signifies. Although no one knows how many orishas exist; some claim over 1,700 while others list them at 400 plus one (400 is the mystical number signifying a multitude); nevertheless, only a few made it to the Western Hemisphere. Eighteen are worshipped within Santería. They are:

- Obatalá (ruler of the gods, lord of the head and king of purity),
- Elegguá (messenger of the gods, lord of the crossroads and trickster),
- Orúnla (god of divination),
- Yemayá (goddess of the sea and mother of the fishes),
- Changó (god of thunder),
- Oggún (god of war and lord of iron),
- Oshún (goddess of love),
- Ochosi (god of the hunt),
- Babalú-Ayé (god of healings and lord over illnesses),
- Oyá (goddess of cemeteries),
- Osain (god of nature and lord of the forest),
- Olocun (queen of the ocean's depths),
- Aganyú (god of the volcano and patron of travelers),
- Oko (god of agriculture and lord of the harvest),
- Inle (god of science and the androgynous healer),
- Ósun (messenger of Obatalá),
- Obba (goddess of wifely role and patron of neglected wives), and
- Ibeyi (twins considered one Orisha).

Within the United States, special attention is given to the first seven orishas named above, referred to as *la siete potencias africanas* (the Seven African Powers). The orishas' stories and adventures are told as legends known as *patakis*. These patakis are seldom interpreted literally. They are used to provide guidance in the here-and-now for devotees asking for their assistance. When these patakis are recited, each orisha, each person, each animal, or each earth object symbolizes a meaning pointing to a truth that exists beyond the legend.

Unlike Western religions, Santería is not a corpus of doctrines; rather, it is a set of rituals. Although doctrinal purity is unimportant, proper conduct of the ritual is. As a terrestrial religion, these rituals focus and use the elements from the earth such as stones, herbs, seashell, trees, water, and so on. The earth provides all that is needed to live a full and abundant life. These rituals take place at a *casa de santos* (house of saints) also known as an *ilé*. The ilé, usually located in a room or basement within a house, becomes the center of worship as devotees come to seek consultations or perform rituals. The priest/priestess, known as either *santero/a*, *olorisha*, or *olosha*, are also called the *padrino* or *madrina* (godfather or godmother) of the flock who regularly comes to their ilé. Those initiated into the faith are called *iyawó* (bride). A male high priest who is able to perform duties (specifically within divination) beyond the ability of santero/as is called the *babalawo* (father of mystery).

There are four basic ways to enter the faith. The first is by obtaining the beaded necklaces called *elekes*. Each eleke has a color and pattern that corresponds to a particular orisha. Elekes protect the wearer for as long as they are worn. The second way is by receiving the Elegguá. An image of the orisha Elegguá's head is made and placed close to the front door of the house to protect it from evil spiritual forces. Inside the image is a stone that the devotee found in the forest that resonates with ashé.

The third way is by receiving the amulets of the orisha warriors who are called *guerreros*. There are four orishas guerreros: Elegguá, Ochosi, Oggún, and Osún. While the elekes protect from dangers, the guerreros attack enemies. The final way of entering the faith is by making saint, known as the *asiento* (seat). This is a process by which the individual learns the mystery of the faith and becomes a santera/o. The santera/o's mind and body are conditioned so that they could be possessed by supernatural powers, serving as a seat for the orisha who "mounts" them in the form of spiritual possession. These possessions usually occur during a *bembe*, a drumming festival at which participants dance, inviting the orishas to take spiritual possession of some of the participants. Once the orisha possesses his or her devotee, also known as her/his child, the orisha communicate directly with his/her followers.

Another way by which orishas communicate is through divination. At the beginning of time, every human head, known as *ori*, that was or was to be, prostrated before Olodumare to negotiate its assigned fate on earth – a fate that is preordained, but not predetermined. Through Orúnla, who was the only orisha present when the different fates were dispersed, the individual can safeguard against evil spells or spirits designed to wreak havoc. The purpose of divination is not to foretell the future, although this may happen, but to ensure harmony exists with one's fate in this life and in others via reincarnation. Santería's central philosophy is centered on the here and now, finding resolutions to the trials and tribulations faced by the devotee.

Three divination systems can be employed to ensure harmony. The first system is known as the four coconut pieces, or *obi*, the word for coconut. The dead, known as *egun*, serve as spirit guides. These guides can be one's ancestors, but need not be a deceased family member. Some of the guides are old African slaves, gypsies, or Native Americans. Communication with the egun occurs through a yes/no divination system. Depending on how the coconut pieces land (curve side up or down), five possible answers can occur. The answer to the yes/no question can be (1) tentative yes, but try again; (2) yes, but try again because of error made during the divination procedure; (3) positive yes; (4) no; and (5) no, and beware of danger.

The second form of divination is through the use of sixteen cowrie shells, also known as the *regla de ocha* or the *dilogún*. Only santero/as can cast the shells. Depending on how they land (shell opening facing up or down), they will correspond to a particular *odu*, which is a specific legend, proverb, verse, or sacrifice. There are more than 256 possible combinations, each signifying a complex odu that requires santera/o interpretation.

The third form of divination, and most elaborate, is known as the *Ifá*, and only men who are called babalawos can use this system. These Ifá priests are priests of the orisha Orúnla. Through the casting of cowrie shells on a rectangular wooden tray eight times, the babalawo creates one of a possible sixteen binary patterns. From these patterns he is referred to an *odu* that can have as many as sixteen verses. It is his job from as many as 4,096 (conservatively estimated) possible interpretations to correctly divine the solution for the problem being asked of the Ifá.

The major purpose of Santería is to find harmony for the devotee with what is visible and invisible. As a religion of oppressed groups, Santería served to bring power and answers to a brutal life filled with hardships and disharmony. It would be an error to assume that this faith, originally formed among slaves, has remained unchanged. Santería has always been in the process of change. Although it may have once been the religion of black slaves, today many followers are white and/or from middle and upper economic classes. As a result of migration from the Caribbean, many devotees can be found in the United States, where Santería has become a link for many Cuban exiles.

But followers are no longer limited to those who come from the Caribbean. The religion, interacting in a pluralistic society, has become more multicultural, multiethnic, and global. Not surprisingly, the faith is presently undergoing a process of modernization so as to become more mainstream. Hence, the emphasis on rituals such as animal sacrifices is becoming less common. For some devotees, the future of the faith will be its institutionalization as it becomes more Americanized.

Because of Santería's heterodoxy and its association with enslavement and blackness, devotees of Santería have historically been linked to criminal activities by authorities, and persecuted by them. Many *brujo* (witch doctor) crazes swept the islands, leading elite outsiders to lynch santero/as (priests/priestesses) who they believed were kidnapping white children and offering them up as sacrifices. For example, in Cuba, involvement in Santería was a punishable crime until 1940. Even after the 1959 Castro revolution, devotees during the 1960s faced arrest, imprisonment, and death. Persecution ceased by the 1980s as the faith was relegated to the folkloric for touristic benefits.

As Cuban refugees came to the United States, however, they brought Santería with them. As Santería became more transnational, it also became more transracial, as "whiter" Cubans began to embrace a religion that they positively associated with their lost homeland. Even though many did not participate in the faith on the island, they found Santería served as a way of maintaining their community and Cuban identity in exile. Mercedes Noble is credited with ordaining, in 1961, the first *santera* in New York City. Still, the faith somewhat remained underground until June 11, 1992, when the United States Supreme Court ruled that Santería devotees in Florida had a constitutional right to engage in animal sacrifices. With this ruling, a diasporan religion became, unofficially, the representational faith of an entirely different sort of diaspora.

Palo

Palo, also referred to as *Reglas de Congo* (rule of the Kongo) or *Palo Monte*, among other names, traces its roots to various secret religious practices of the Bantu-speaking peoples of the Kongo basin of central Africa. The Bantu (a general label for a widely diverse group of people) brought their highly decentralized faith traditions to Hispañola and Cuba. Although it never proselytizes, by the mid-nineteenth century, Palo had spread to African communities throughout the United States, Venezuela, Colombia, and Puerto Rico. Palo is best known for venerating *mpungus*, the spirits of ancestors who are considered to be independent and fierce and the spiritual beings of nature that dwell in rivers, oceans, and trees.

The origins of the religious practice Spanish name reveal intriguing insights. The word *palo* is Spanish for stick, a talisman used by practitioners who are called *palero/as*. These palos are believed to contain powers that are linked to the spirits of the dead or nature. *Monte* refers to the mountainous forested, rural area of the Caribbean. Palo Monte, then, refers to "spirits in the sticks of the forest."

Though often confused with Santería, Palo constitutes a distinct religious expression with a different historical origin. Santería springs from Yorùbá culture while Palo has its origins in Kongo culture. Santería centers on veneration of deities, the orishas, who differ from the *nfumbe*, or dead spirits, in Palo. Palo lacks a concept of final reckoning, or karma.

Central to the faith is human association with certain spirits of the dead. One of the objectives is to identify the restless spirit of a person, usually someone who in life was mentally ill or a criminal. Such persons are relegated to the bad heaven and forbidden reincarnation; thus they are cursed to wander the earth. Filled with anger and envy, such spirits, known as the *nfumbe*, can be easily manipulated by a palero/a to serve as guides, providing insight to both the physical and spiritual worlds. The guide can warn of upcoming dangers or reveal upcoming opportunities that the palera/o can either avoid or take advantage of. Such a spirit can even be used to harm or torment an enemy of the palero/a through illness, loss of fortune, marital discord, or even death.

The focus of Palo's magic and rituals is the *nganga*, also known as the *prenda* or *cazuela*. The nganga is not only a receptacle of a supernatural force; it is also a spirit. This receptacle can be a three-legged iron cauldron, an altar, a clay pot, or a bag. The palera/o accumulates power by depositing objects in the nganga that represent the powers of nature. These objects can include soil from a cemetery or crossroad, sticks (*palos*), stones, insects, the carcasses of birds or other animals, herbs, and most importantly, human remains – ideally a skull with parts of the brain still present. Especially prized are the remains of the insane or criminals, who are usually more willing to carry out immoral acts without reservations.

The human bone becomes the means by which the spirit of the deceased, the nfumbe, is captured, providing the palero/a with guidance and power in exchange for regular feedings of sacrificial blood. Within this nganga, all supernatural beings, known as *mpungus*, are condensed like a microcosm. These mpungus, venerated as Kongo gods, are known for the forces over which they rule. Still, they are below the supreme creator of all, who is known as *Nzambi (*or *Zambi).*

Though often perceived as involving exclusively "dark" religious practices, Palo can be used for either good or evil, for the nganga can contain good or bad spirits. Palera/os who operate with the spirits of good people are referred to as practitioners of *nganga cristiana* ("Christian" nganga), while those operating with the spirits of evil people work with *nganga judía* ("Jewish" nganga). Those working with *nganga cristiana* often work with the crucifix in an attempt to help those who are ill or in distress. *Nganga judía*, on the other hand, often use the railroad spike as they attempt to seek vengeance, to humble, and humiliate enemies.

Some argue that the usage of the term *nganga judía* refers to a purer and more traditional practice of the faith that refused to "convert," the practice of Palo before it was Christianized. One practice picked up by Hollywood movies is the so-called "voodoo doll." A palero/a wishing to harm an enemy might fashion a doll from discarded clothes of the intended victim, or dress a wax image in the scraps of a victim's clothing. The doll is named after the intended victim offered to the god of the dead, asking that the person be claimed. The doll is then buried in the cemetery with the expectation that the person it represents would soon follow.

The Cuban branch of Palo is known as *Palo Mayombe*, and it mainly deals with the spiritual energies of the dead (nfumbe). The *Palo Brillumba* branch is more common and probably the most Christianized. They deal with both the spiritual energies of nfumbe and mpungus (Kongo gods), who are syncretized with Catholic saints. For example, Nsasi, god of thunder and fire, is equated with Santa Barbara, and Kobayende (Kañeñe), god of diseases and king of the dead, is associated with San Lazaro. Brillumba is derived from the Kongolese word *"krillumba,"* which means skull. As the name indicates, there is a strong reliance on human remains. The final branch is known as Palo Kimbisa and is considered to be the first manifestation of Palo in the Caribbean. It is believed to have been established by the *kimbisa*, the high priests of the Kongo, when they were brought over as slaves.

Conclusion

As Cubans, Puerto Ricans, and Dominicans, regardless of race, migrated to the United States, their Afro-based religious practices became a means of survival. The healing components of these faith traditions became the poor person's medical and mental health plan. Many Latino/a immigrants from the Caribbean go to the priests and priestesses of these religious traditions as if they were visiting a medical doctor or psychiatrist. These African-based religious expressions are available as a vital resource for migrants, regardless of race, as they navigate the daily struggles of life, especially in the areas of health, wealth, love, and employment. They proactively deal with the immediate concerns of the Hispanic in need of help, not just Latino/as whose country of origin is the Spanish Caribbean, but Hispanics from any nations, as well as a growing number of African-Americans and Euroamericans.

Bibliography and Suggested Readings

Bettelheim, Judith, "Palo Monte Mayombe and Its Influence on Cuban Contemporary Art." *African Arts*, 34, no. 2 (Summer, 2001): 36–49, 94–96.

Brandon, George. *Santería from Africa to the New World*. Bloomington: Indiana University Press, 1997.

Cabrera, Lydia. *Reglas de Congo: Palo Monte Mayombe.* Miami: Ediciones Universal, 1986.
De La Torre, Miguel A. *Santería: The Beliefs and Rituals of a Growing Religion in America.* Grand Rapids: Eerdmans, 2004.
Fernández Olmos, Margarite, and Lizebeth Paravisini-Gebert. *Creole Religions of the Caribbean: An Introduction from Vodou to Santería to Obeah and Espiritismo.* New York: New York University Press, 2003.
Morales Dorta, Jose. *Puerto Rican Espiritismo: Religion and Psychotherapy.* New York: Vantage, 1976.
Ortiz, Fernando. *Los negros esclavos.* La Habana: Editorial de ciencias socials, 1975.
Pérez y Mena, Andrés Isidoro. *Speaking with the Dead: Development of Afro-Latin Religion among Puerto Ricans in the United States.* New York: AMS Press, 1991.

40
Spiritism in Latin America

SIDNEY M. GREENFIELD

Spiritism is a belief system that was born in North America, codified in France, and whose greatest success has been in Brazil and the Caribbean. In Brazil its mostly educated practitioners have elaborated it by incorporating elements of folk Catholicism and Amerindian and African-derived traditions. This reformulated Latin-Americanized Spiritism subsequently became interwoven into a variety of "popular" religions throughout the region.

The belief that spirits of the dead can communicate with the living is known as Spiritualism in North America and Europe and Spiritism in Brazil and the Caribbean. Its modern origins can be traced to reports of the teen-aged Fox sisters claiming that the "rappings" they heard coming from beneath the floorboards of their parents' home in Hydesville, New York, in the 1840s were messages sent by someone whose body was buried in their basement. Word of this spread rapidly, first in North America and then across the Atlantic Ocean. In England the revised interest in communication with the dead developed into a vibrant Spiritualist movement out of which psychic research and parapsychology emerged. In France, a Parisian schoolmaster from Lyons, Hippolyte Léon Denizard Rivail (1804–1869), after learning about communication with spirits of the deceased, organized séances in the 1850s at which he posed more than a thousand questions that were replied to by what he referred to as "enlightened spirits." Rivail did not present his questions, or receive the replies directly, but via the teenage daughters of a friend who served as intermediaries, or mediums. After "confirming" the information received with materials obtained from colleagues around the world asking similar questions, Rivail published the answers in a number of books and magazines that he wrote under the pseudonym Allan Kardec. He used that name so that readers would not confuse his Spiritist writings with the many academic books he had authored previously.

The first of Kardec's volumes that were the result of his communications with the enlightened spirits in the other world, *The Spirit's Book* (1857), serves as the founding text of the movement associated with his name. *The Medium's Book* in 1861, *The Gospel as Explained by Spirits* in 1864, *Heaven and Hell* in 1865, *Genesis* in 1867 and a volume of posthumous works followed it. Kardec also wrote two other short volumes, *What Is Spiritism?* and *Spiritism In Its Simplest Expression* before his death in 1869.

The child of a successful family of lawyers and magistrates, Rivail was sent in 1814, at the age of ten, to the famous Pestalozzi Institute in Yverdun, Switzerland. A decade later when he completed his studies, Rivail returned to France intending at first to devote himself to the law, but decided instead to become a teacher. He soon moved to Paris, where he published the first of many scholarly books. Rivail opened a primary school in 1828 and a year later a technical school, both based on the ideas of Pestalozzi. In 1832 he married Amélie Gabrielle Boudet, a teacher, artist, and poet nine years his senior.

Rivail's academic books were on a variety of scholarly subjects ranging from history and classical studies to science and mathematics. He authored works on Asian and other esoteric philosophies and religions and psychic phenomena. As a gifted intellectual, he was able to integrate specifics from his studies into his grand Spiritist philosophical system.

Under the name of Kardec, Rivail offered his codification of Spiritism, based on what the enlightened spirits reported to him, as a new, or third "revelation," intended to explain, elaborate, and expand the prophecies brought to humanity by Moses and Christ. His revised version of God's word differed significantly from the view of the world advanced by the Roman Catholic Church, into which he was born, that still dominated much of French thinking at the time. The new framework displayed the rational, progressive, evolutionary, and Positivist thinking then prevalent among European intellectuals. The Codifier, as Kardec's followers in Brazil and the Caribbean refer to him, eliminated the Trinity, Original Sin, the Final Judgment, hell, sacraments, and miracles from his revised theology. He retained neither demons nor angels. These changes removed those who ascribed to these altered beliefs from the theological web of sin and salvation and, equally important, from the reach of priests and popes.

Kardec accepted the Judeo-Christian postulation of an all-powerful Supreme Being who had created the cosmos and is the "First Cause" of all things. He referred to this all-powerful force as the "Supreme Intelligence." At the beginning, according to the new beliefs, The Supreme Intelligence (God) made, not one world, but two. Both were interdependent and interconnected with the inhabitants of each in potential communication and contact with those in the other.

Living human beings existed in what the Codifier called the "material world," the place where they are born, live, and eventually die. But it is the spirits, created prior to humans, who are the "intelligent principle of the universe" (Kardec n.d.: Book II, Chapter I). To emphasize the opposition of his vision to materialism, Kardec called his new revelation Spiritism or Spiritualism, a usage common in his day. In stark contrast with Hebrew and Christian teachings, Kardec contends that spirits are the vital forces that intertwine the worlds of spirit and matter. In the beginning, he maintained, the Supreme Intelligence created not humans, as we perceive them to be, but spirits who then take (incarnate in) material bodies when they come to earth from the spirit world. After spending a lifetime here (or on other planets that, although not know to science, are believed to be inhabited), they disincarnate (die), discard the disposable container of a physical body that they had occupied and used for a single lifetime, and return to the spirit world.

According to this view, spirits have an everlasting astral body that enables them to live in the ethereal, low-density world of the spirit. Attached to this body is a permanent semimaterial covering composed of a bioplasmic substance (ectoplasm), called the *perispirit*. The perispirit is fastened at birth to the somatic body that has been selected for use in an incarnation. This brings together the domains of spirit and matter. In this way Kardec unified in a single interrelated system what Descartes had previously opposed as body and mind. Descartes' metaphor was adopted as the paradigmatic imagery on which modern medicine is based. The Codifier's view, in contrast, became the basis for an alternative approach to healing and therapy that is practiced today in Brazil and the Caribbean and known as "Spiritist healing."

According to Kardecist belief, a spirit is not limited to a single birth to death experience. It travels from the spirit plane to the material world and then back again across an extended period of time. These repeated incarnations (or rebirths) are not aimless. For the Codifier and his disciples they are part of a moral dynamic that provides meaning to life and the universe.

When the world was formed, Kardec contends, each of the countless number of spirits the Supreme Intelligence created was placed on an individual course of development that was defined in moral terms. The presence of a specific spirit in the material world at a particular time is part of its transcendental project to improve and advance ethically to a point at which it no longer will be required to return to the material domain. The objective of each specific incarnation is to learn lessons that contribute to the spirit's long-term moral growth. The goal for each being is to master, after a series of rebirths in the material world, whatever is necessary so that eventually it no longer will need to return. The Codifier defined moral perfection in Judeo-Christian terms. Jesus Christ, though not believed to be the Son of God, is accepted as a prophet and the most advanced spirit ever to come into our world. His words and deeds, as interpreted by Kardec, are taken to be the standard of virtue and righteousness.

When death in our world occurs, the spirit abandons its material body and departs from here to go to the other domain. There it is counseled by enlightened beings that help to evaluate its just completed incarnation and advise the spirit in the selection of the next lesson(s) it needs to undertake in its transcendental development program. In this sense, a schoolhouse may serve as a metaphor for the material world in the sense that it offers a series of lessons each spirit must master to advance along its personal path to perfection.

But spirits, according to Kardec, have free will. They may, if they wish, choose to disregard the lesson(s) they selected for a given incarnation. If a spirit returns to acquire the value of temperance, for example, it may experience such pleasure drinking, taking drugs, or engaging in other excesses that it may choose to disregard what it has returned to accomplish. Between when it selects what it is to learn in a specific lifetime – in the spirit world prior to incarnating – and its death, a spirit also might forget the lesson(s) it had come back to earth to master. There is no punishment for not accomplishing this goal, but there are consequences that may manifest as personal problems at any time, either here or in the spirit world. The balance between good and bad (or right and wrong) choices made by a spirit over multiple incarnations on earth and in the other world is conceptualized by the Sanskrit term karma or fate. When a spirit does not learn the intent of an incarnation, or makes other bad choices, it does not fall back along its developmental trajectory. Instead, the lessons must be repeated and conquered in a future incarnation. It may take some spirits several rebirths to surmount certain obstacles. Consequently, the spirits on earth, and those in the spirit world, are highly diverse in their degree of advancement along their respective paths to perfection.

Paris in the middle years of the nineteenth century was the epicenter where the most dynamic and transformative scientific, political, and intellectual ideas in the Western world were being formulated and debated. The educator from Lyon was an active participant in these seminal activities. The foundations of modern science and medicine emanated from this dynamic city at this period of time. Of special relevance to later developments in Spiritist healing,

Kardec was a member of the Society of Magnetism. It was here that Franz Anton Mesmer's late-eighteenth century theory of animal magnetism, out of which our modern understanding of hypnotism and hypnotherapy developed, was being articulated and elaborated. Kardec participated in studies of trance and clairvoyance. Although healing did not play a major role in the new system the Codifier proposed to his at first mostly European readers, this was to change dramatically when his new revelation recrossed the Atlantic Ocean and was studied by intellectuals in Brazil, other parts of Latin America, and the Caribbean.

The nineteenth century was also a period of upheaval and transformation in the New World. The belief that enlightened spirits could direct people in creating a progressive, morally sound world served Latin American elites as a counterforce to the hegemony of Spanish colonial and Brazilian imperial rule and the controlling efforts of the Catholic Church. As Romberg writes, it created "a legitimate sphere for alternative transcendental practices."[1]

Revolutionary movements in the former Spanish colonies gave birth to the formation of a number of independent nations. Portugal's colony became independent (without violence) in 1822 as the only empire in the Western Hemisphere. In 1889 a second peaceful revolution transformed it into a republic. Only Cuba and Puerto Rico, where Spiritism provided a space for frustrated liberal ideas to flourish, remained colonies until the end of the century. Small cities that were backwaters of colonial administration were in the process of becoming dynamic modernizing national capitals. The French immigrants and Brazilian elites, who brought Kardec's writings to Brazil shortly after their initial publication, like their Hispanic counterparts elsewhere in the region, followed events in Europe and participated actively in the emergence and transformation of their nations. Prior to Kardec's codification many already were familiar with Mesmer's theory of animal magnetism and its treatments intended to restore the flow of universal magnetic fluids. They read about and applied the homeopathic treatments developed in Germany by Samuel Hahnemann (1755–1843). And they followed the work of Mesmer's disciple, the Marquis de Puysegur, who was experimenting with hypnotism in his medical practice. Table turning – popular in the Francophone and Anglo-Saxon worlds as the means to communicate with those in the spirit world – had become part of the daily activities of many of these Brazilian elites who examined and discussed Kardec's writings in their original French.

[1] Raquel Romberg, *Healing Dramas: Divination and Magic in Modern Puerto Rico* (Austin: University of Texas Press, 2009), 15.

The Codifier's post-Enlightenment, rational, anti-official Catholic Church vision of the world was interpreted in Brazil through lenses that were the product of the previous syncretism of three long-standing religious heritages. These influences modified Spiritism subtly, but significantly. One of the traditions was a mystical, folk, or popular Catholicism. Like the belief system that prevailed in Europe prior to the Reformation and Counter-Reformation popular Catholicism was infused with saints and spirits of the dead with whom the faithful interacted and to whom they often turned for help with their daily problems. The most ubiquitous of the problems Brazilians, and others in the Americas, faced were illnesses that caused pain and suffering. Another tradition contributing to the reinterpretation was Pagelança or Catimbó, a vestige of Amerindian religious practice that at an earlier period had been mixed with folk-Catholicism. The cornerstone of its basic ritual was a curing consultation in which a shaman, often dancing in a whirl of smoke, offered help to members of the community about their health, welfare, or other predicaments. The final element to influence Kardecism was the diverse beliefs and ritual practices brought to Brazil and the Spanish colonies in the Caribbean from Africa by slaves.

Kardec's Brazilian followers quickly identified around three distinct currents. The first, which Kardec emphasized in his later years, was his version of Christian evangelism. Unfortunately, this option opened the fledgling movement to criticism and repression by the Roman Catholic Church that until the establishment of the Republic in 1889 was Brazil's official religion. The second organizing theme was philosophical and enabled this segment of the French theoretician's followers to avoid confrontation with the Church. A third trend was stressed by those interested primarily in the material or physical effects resulting from the coming together of the two worlds during a séance.

Strange things were reported when Kardec's followers communicated with spirits. In addition to the exchange of words, some individuals claimed that the spirit of a departed loved one had actually appeared materially, or that items on the table, or elsewhere in the room where the séance was held, moved. Many concluded that the spirit they were in contact with had returned (to the material plane) and was the causal agent. Supporters of the Codifier concerned with these events were referred to as the "scientific group." They were to have much in common with parapsychologists and others to challenge science with data they considered to be anomalous.

The organizer or leader of a séance often communicated with a deceased loved one on behalf of a bereaved party. At some Brazilian sessions, at the time the movement was taking hold during latter years of the nineteenth century, some organizers of séances asked unspecified spirits on the other plane why a specific incarnate person was experiencing physical or emotional symptoms that were described. When a spirit replied with instructions for a therapeutic procedure or a prescription, mostly for homeopathic medications, some future séances took the form of a healing consultation in which the spirits were asked to help sick people. It is interesting to note that the ill party did not necessarily have to be physically present at the séance. The organizer wrote the instructions for therapy or prescriptions for medications, often automatically without seemingly being consciously aware of what he was doing. He then passed the directions along to the ailing party or his or her representative. The session leader was perceived to be an intermediary between the two worlds and was believed to have entered into trance so as to serve as a medium. In this way questions about health-related problems on this plane were transmitted and responded to by helpful entities on the other side.

Some in the new movement interested in physical effects built on the Codifier's adoption of Mesmer's theory of animal magnetism and performed hand passes to unblock the flow of fluids and magnetic energies. They also elaborated Kardec's examination of obsession to develop their own distinctive form of treatment for people suffering from illnesses just beginning to be diagnosed by the medical profession in the newly developing field of psychiatry.

Kardec contended that little developed and malevolent spirits in the other world were able to influence and, at times, control the bodies, and hence behaviors, of mediums and other incarnate beings by means of magnetic fluids and energies. A low-level spirit many have had a negative encounter or relationship with someone in one of its earlier lifetimes and choose to seek revenge in the present incarnation. The malevolent spirit was said to do this by emitting negative energies and influences intended to obsess, or even subjugate (to its will) the unsuspecting being in the material world. A highly evolved incarnate spirit might deflect these negative influences and not be affected by them. A less evolved spirit is said to be more subject to the negative influences and would be led to behave in ways medical science was beginning to designate as "insane." In the treatment that came to be known as "disobsession," the disturbing spirit is engaged in a conversation by one or more mediums. During what has become a ritually patterned conversation, the offending spirit is convinced through patient and persistent effort to cease what it is doing, leave the person who offended them alone, and devote itself to preparing for its own advancement in its next incarnation. When patients treated in this way improved, Kardec's followers adopted the new treatment and regularly performed disobsessions on those medical practitioners and psychiatrists designate as mentally ill.

As reports of patients "recovering" after interventions by the spirits circulated among the less educated and less affluent segments of the population large numbers of Brazilians sought the assistance of Spiritist healer mediums for help with health-related problems. In parallel with the folk Catholic practice of making and fulfilling a vow by performing ritual acts in return or exchange for the successful intervention of a saint, those who recovered through the intermediacy of a healing medium and his spirit guides felt obliged to attend Kardicest-Spiritist meetings and participate in their ritual sessions, thereby increasing the numbers involved in the new movement. What kept the several factions of the movement from splitting apart was the importance all attached to what was rapidly becoming the belief system's primary mission: performing charity.

For Kardec, whose revised view of Christianity had dispensed with heaven and hell, charity was seen as the way the wishes of the Supreme Intelligence were satisfied. It was the highest moral value the Codifier distilled from the teachings of Christ. "Without charity," he titled the widely quoted Chapter 15 of his interpretation of the Christian Gospel (1987), "there is no salvation."

As Spiritism's teachings, and the ritual practices that came to be associated with it, diffused from a small, educated elite to the Brazilian masses, the tradition came to be infused with an ethic of practical charity. Kardecist charity took two main forms: the giving of assistance to the poor and healing. Followers of the Codifier collect and distribute significant amounts of food, clothing, and other items to assist the needy. Many volunteer to work with the elderly and with children, especially in local slums. They aid in schools and participate in numerous programs designed to ease the hardships faced by those most impoverished. Their mediums provide comfort for the bereaved by enabling them to maintain contact with departed loved ones. But healing is the most sought after form of charity they provide. Since Spiritist healer mediums do not charge for the services they offer, growing numbers of those unable to pay for medical services seek out healer mediums and their spirit guides, increasing the numbers of those participating in the movement.

Another significant dimension was added to Kardecist-Spiritism, and what their healer-mediums were able to offer the sick and suffering, as a consequence of emancipation. When some freedmen and women relocated to the cities in Brazil after 1888, they established places, called *terreiros*, at which they performed rituals based on memories, reinforced at times by continuing trans-Atlantic contacts, of life and culture in Africa. These African-derived religious practices took a variety of names such as Macumba, Candomblé, Xangô, Batuque, and Tambor de Minas, depending on the provenience of the slaves brought to different parts of the nation. The centers established by the followers of Kardec's new vision of Christianity often were in close physical proximity to the religious places of those who were reimagining, adapting, and reviving religious practices brought to the New World by their ancestors from Africa.

The religions of West Africa differed from those of Europe and North America in many ways. In the latter, the faithful communicated and interacted with their conceptualization of the supernatural almost exclusively through spoken words or silent prayers. African deities, in contrast, were believed to "come down" from another plane of reality and incorporate, taking possession of the bodies of specially trained devotees so that they would be able to interact with those who venerated them. Like Spiritists elsewhere in Europe and Euro-America, followers of Kardec in Latin America and the Caribbean at first communicated in words with those in the other domain. Through mediums they asked questions and received replies. Exposure to the recently freed Afro-Brazilians (and descendants of Africans elsewhere in Latin America and the Caribbean) engaged in spirit possession led some to experiment with and eventually adopt this African-derived custom.

A significant ramification of this for healing was that eventually spirits of deceased doctors or of healers from other traditions no longer simply communicated prescriptions for medications and other therapeutic procedures. Some were said to incorporate into mediums that invoked them and interacted directly with those in need of their services. Most mediums were untrained in medicine and many had no more than an elementary school education. To the outside observer, however, they appeared to be behaving as if they were incarnate medical providers. In addition, spirits of doctors working through the bodies of incarnate mediums were believed to have at their disposal what were said to be the "more advanced" techniques known in the other realm. This enabled them, for example, to do surgeries, making incisions and removing tissue, without (visibly) sterilizing instruments or anesthetizing the patients.

Since healing is offered as charity in the Kardecist tradition, neither those to come from the other plane to provide the treatments, nor the mediums through whom they performed, charged a fee. Many of the growing number of sick Brazilians availing themselves of these services then behaved like folk Catholics who had benefited from "supernatural" intervention. They performed Kardecist rituals in repayment of the debt. The ranks of the movement consequently grew. Those availing themselves of Spiritist healing included not just the poor, who might be influenced by the lack of a fee, but also the more affluent and better educated, many of whom were dissatisfied with treatments they received from conventional medicine. Their level of satisfaction with the outcomes of what they received from the spirits is shown in the results of a small sample of patients treated by the spirit of Dr. Fritz – through the medium Mauricio Magalhães – conducted several years ago. Eighty-eight percent of the respondents claimed that they had been helped by the treatment while 81 percent said that they felt better after receiving it. Moreover, 88 percent said that they would recommend Dr. Fritz to others while 91 percent said that should they take sick again they would prefer to seek help from a healer-medium and his guide(s). Of those who previously had been prescribed treatment by a doctor for the same symptoms, most no longer were following that regimen.

But why should a spirit who had been educated as a doctor (or healer in another "advanced" tradition) in a previous life and was preparing to continue its transcendental trajectory in pursuit of perfection by reincarnating be expected to take the time to apply its training and skills temporarily through the body of a medium? The answer is to be found in Kardec's view of the concept of karma.

As each spirit travels across its numerous lifetimes it makes countless choices. Decisions made in both the material and spirit worlds are evaluated morally as good or bad. The positive or negative balance (of these choices) at any point in time was conceptualized in Kardecist thought as its karma. Spirits with negative karmic balances generally have the opportunity to correct them during succeeding incarnations. Syncretism with African-derived spirit possession made it possible to improve a negative karmic balance much faster than would be required by reincarnating by doing the valued charitable act of healing. While still in the other world a spirit with valued learning gained in previous incarnations can "come back" temporarily and, by performing charitable acts such as treating the sick through a medium, make up for previous bad choices.

Dr. Adolph Fritz is a fabled example whose spectacular surgeries, through several different mediums over a period of more than half a century, have been reported by both the Brazilian and international media. Fritz was reputed to have last lived on earth during World War I, when he served as a doctor in the German army. It was rumored that his lavish lifestyle prior to joining the Kaiser's forces was made possible by the ill-gotten gains of his maternal grandparents and his father. After the doctor was killed in the war and was being assisted in preparing for his next incarnation by several enlightened beings in the other world, the spirit of Alijadinho, the famous eighteenth-century Brazilian sculptor, informed Fritz of the great need for medical services in that country.

In the 1950s the German doctor, believed to be attempting to rebalance his karmic deficit, incorporated in a poor, unsuspecting Roman Catholic man from the state of Minas Gerais commonly known by his nickname, "Zé Arigó." Records indicate that Arigó performed dramatic surgeries and treated tens of thousands of sick and needy patients, all without charging a fee. After Arigó was killed in an automobile accident, Dr. Fritz reappeared in several other mediums over the course of the next six decades. Spirits of other doctors and healers selected their own mediums to do similar work. Believers maintain that the many spirits of healers returning temporarily to treat patients through the bodies of mediums have provided the living with a valuable form of alternative healing. Some claim it to be more advanced than conventional medicine because it is based on what they believe to be a superior form of science not yet known or appreciated in this world.

If spirits could return to the material world temporarily to do the good work of healing, why, some followers of Kardec asked, could it not work the other way? Could the sick go temporarily, without disincarnating, to the "other world" to obtain the more advanced forms of treatment available there?

Applying innovative forms of modern physics, one group of Brazilian followers of Kardec claims to be able to do just that. By concentrating intense forms of energy, they contend that they are able to separate the astral body from the somatic one a spirit uses while in the material world and then transport (or teleport) it to the astral plane. There, through an arrangement with a hospital run by spirit doctors, they "transmit" patients, accompanied by mediums. On a large television-like screen, past lives of the patient, both on earth and on the spirit plane, are divulged and shared with ritual participants on earth. The action is stopped to emphasize an incident in which the spirit of the suffering patient committed an offense, considered immoral, against another who has chosen to take revenge rather than reincarnate and pursue its own moral advancement.

Often the spirit of the offended party is reported to have enlisted the aid of a practitioner of black magic who placed an electrical charge or other device in his incarnate victim's body and that is the immediate cause of its suffering. Treatment is a variation of the disobsession. The leader of the group on earth challenges the spirit responsible for the pain, reminding it that revenge is immoral and inappropriate. Instead it is implored to move on by reincarnating and pursuing its own development. When its deed is placed in the context of Kardec's vision of morality the offending party eventually is convinced by reason and logic to admit that seeking vengeance is wrong. It apologizes and asks the spirit whose pain it has caused for forgiveness. The practitioner of black magic is ordered to remove all devices. The spirit of the suffering patient apologizes for what it did that precipitated the desire for reprisal. Both reaffirm the moral principles of the belief system and agree on the importance of reincarnation and development. The high incidence of positive results obtained from disobsessions, done both here and on the spirit plane, have convinced believers, and those who have availed themselves of this form of charity, that Spiritism offers a number of viable forms of alternative healing. Moreover, it spares the recipient from the expectations of conventional medicine for payments they often can little afford.

As Spiritism was influenced and changed as the result of its contacts with folk Catholicism, Amerindian ritual practices, and West African spirit possession, so too did a syncretized Spiritism in turn influence the African-derived traditions. By the end of the nineteenth century, as practitioners of Macumba, Candomblé, Xangô, and other religions practiced by the emancipated slaves in the *terreiros* of Rio de Janeiro, Salvador, and other Brazilian cities adapted to their new conditions, they incorporated the model of the healing consultation and made it central to their reinterpreted rituals. In what sometimes is referred to as "low Spiritism" or *mesa branca* (white table – because of the freshly washed cloth on the table around which participants sit), deities who had protected and performed services in African tribal societies across the Atlantic were offering healing consultations for their New World devotees. Given the pervasive poverty faced by the freedmen and freedwomen and their descendants in urban centers, the transaction between deity and worshipper was broadened to include supernatural help with a variety of issues, of which healing was often only the primary one. The African *orixás* (deities) also advised devotees about their domestic affairs, precarious love lives, employment possibilities, and economic arrangements. Kardec's framework, as modified by his followers, became so much a part of the constantly mixing popular religious scene that many of the diverse religions practiced by the African-derived poor are referred to as Spiritist.

Kardec's vision of a dual universe gained a cadre of staunch followers in Cuba, where the syncretism with West African spirit possession and folk Catholicism was called Santería. In Venezuela a similar mixture emerged into the María Lionza cult, while in Brazil the mixing of beliefs and worldviews spun off into a distinctive syncretized religious form called Umbanda. This new religion is claimed by its followers to have an estimated 40 million believers – in Brazil, North America, and Europe – more than the recorded number of practitioners of all of the other purportedly more authentic African-derived and Karecist groups combined.

Umbanda, according to its origin myth, came into being at a Kardecist-Spiritist meeting early in the second decade of the twentieth century. At a session held in the city of Niterói, across Guanabara Bay from Rio de Janeiro, a tall, young, blond man of European descent named Zélio de Morais received a spirit who identified itself as the *Cabolco das Sete Encruzilhadas* (the Mixed-blood Spirit of the Seven Crossroad). The spirit brought instructions for establishing a new religion. The following day Morais received a second spirit, a *Preto Velho* (a former African slave) who completed the instructions. Until that time Brazilian Kardecists, consistent with racist beliefs then prevalent, did not believe that the enlightenment they sought in their communication with beings from the other plane could be obtained from spirits who had not been European in previous lifetimes. They did not communicate with or receive messages from "less enlightened" beings.

Intellectual and spiritual ferment meanwhile continued in Brazil as the twentieth century began. An educated elite was struggling to provide the new republican regime with symbols and images of national unity and identity. Racist thinking presented them with a dilemma. The nation's nonwhite majority was considered incapable of contributing to the development of the modern, advanced society Brazil aspired to be. To counter this, some intellectuals invented the myth that their country was a racial democracy that had been formed by the blending, both physically and culturally – because biology and culture were fused in racist thinking – of its founding populations of Amerindians, Europeans, and Africans. Furthermore, they contended that the nonwhite population would combine with the Europeans, descendants of early settlers and new immigrants, to "whiten" the future citizenry.

Morais, a Catholic who became a Kardecist, initially attended Macumba and sessions of other African-derived groups. The *Caboclo das Sete Encrizilhadas* is reported to have proclaimed through him that none of the other religions practiced in the country were right or proper. He dictated "a brand new set of rules, regulations, chants, drumbeats, herbal cures, curses, dance steps, etc." His novice religion explicitly combined representations and symbolic imageries of the three founding populations and their cultures. Umbanda was intended to resolve the dilemma of Brazil's complicated racial mixture. It was to be a religion for the new multiracial and multicultural nation the mythmakers were attempting to create.

The cosmology of the incipient religion was taken, in part, from the supernatural pantheons of its contributors. God, the Supreme Intelligence, is viewed in the Positivist, scientific vision of Kardec. The creator no longer is involved in the day-to-day operations of the universe. He is assumed to have left running the world, not in the hands of humans as European Enlightenment thinkers proposed, but with lesser supernatural beings such as the already syncretized Christian saints and African orixás. Four new categories of uniquely Brazilian beings were added: (1) the *caboclos*, or spirits of cooperative and helpful Amerindians; (2) the *pretos velhos*, subservient spirits of former slaves devoted to their masters; (3) *exus*, street people who represented spirits that had incarnated previously in the many diverse types of ordinary Brazilians; and (4) *crianças*, the children who were the racially mixed and unified Brazilians of the future. One or more of these entities are received by and incorporate in Umbanda mediums when they enter trance states while singing and dancing in ritualized ways. It is through the mediums that the supernatural beings do, as in Kardecist-Spiritism, the charity of helping those in need. This charity and the belief in reincarnation provide the basis for Umbanda's view of spiritual evolution.

The new religion is organized in centers large and small. Some are big enough to accommodate several hundred or more adherents and visitors at a time, although many are so small that they can accommodate no more than a dozen or so individuals. Each group is autonomous. The only relationship that occurs between one center and another is when its head, called a *pae* (father) or a *mãe* (mother) *de santo* (in sainthood), has been initiated ritually by the leader of another center.

Rituals begin with a cleansing ceremony after which devotees dance in a characteristic circle (*gira*) to music provided by drums. They sing special chants to invoke a variety of African deities whose characteristics have been syncretized with Catholic saints. A second ritual segment follows during which the head of the center and his *filhos* (children he is teaching the tradition) receive the uniquely Umbanda spirits. It is through these spirits that healing and other forms of charity are provided. During individual consultations caboclos, pretos velhos, exus, and crianças assist members and visitors with their personal problems. In return (or exchange) for the aid received, those who are informed by the spirits that they have the ability to serve as mediums are urged to return to the center at another time to develop this ability. When their training is completed and their ritual initiation over, the new mediums may open their own center at which they and the spirits they receive increase the good works and charity of the religion.

As participation in Umbanda expanded in the midyears of the twentieth century and new centers appeared all over Brazil, the product of the syncretism of Kardecist-Spiritism with West African religions itself was modified. In many parts of the country people practice both Umbanda and more traditional African-derived religions such as Candomblé in adjoining facilities. The result has been a continuing mixing of beliefs and rituals with a blurring of how the practices of any single group are to be classified or to which specific religion a devotee belongs. Followers of these numerous faiths, except for Evangelical Protestants, still self-identify as Christians and permit those collecting census data or taking other formal counts to list them as Catholic. Hence Kardecist-Spiritists and the leadership of the African-derived religions have long considered themselves to be underrepresented in the official figures. In the last five decades the number of Brazilians to participate in Spiritism, the African-derived religions, and non-Catholic Christian churches has increased significantly. As the nation's population became steadily more urban, these "popular" religious groups – to differentiate them from official Catholicism – entered into a competition for members, especially in the fast-growing poverty-stricken slums of the rapidly expanding urban centers.

In 1940, for example, only 26 percent, or slightly less than 11 of the 41 million Brazilians, lived in cities. Three decades later the total population swelled to more than 119 million; 69 percent of them, or 82 million people, were urban dwellers. By the turn of the twenty-first century the national population was 180 million, ten times what it had been at the beginning of the century. There were more than 100 million more people living in cities than there had been at mid-century.

The vast majority of these new city dwellers were either internal emigrants from the rural areas or their descendants. Brazil's cities were unprepared for this influx. In spite of industrializing and modernizing, the economy was unable to provide employment for vast segments of the newcomers. Without resources, large numbers of people squatted forming shantytowns, called *favelas*, where they continue to suffer from high rates of un- or underemployment, the absence of water and sewage facilities, and inadequate transportation and electricity. Endemic diseases such as cholera, dengue fever, meningitis, and viral and bacterial infections abound. Alcoholism, drugs, prostitution, gambling, gangs, and gang warfare further complicate their plight.

When the authorities did not act to remediate the situation, the formerly small and marginal religious groups filled the void by offering assistance. In the still omnipresent image of patron–client exchange, the conversion of those helped was to be expected. Unable to obtain assistance from anyone else, slum-dwellers often accepted the bargain. Given the pervasiveness of the folk-Catholic vow, or bargain with a saint, according to which the recipient of a petitioned gift is obligated to fulfill a promise made to obtain it, Spiritists, leaders of Umbanda, Candomblé, and other African-derived groups and even pastors of the mostly evangelical Protestant denominations have offered healing and other help in exchange for conversion. The membership rolls of the once small groups have expanded, with much of their increase composed of those who formerly nominally affiliated with the Roman Catholic Church.

Spiritists entered into what has developed into a competition for followers between the numerous popular religious groups. In addition to providing food and clothing, followers of Kardec founded hospitals that they staffed with conventional doctors and medical personnel. They also added some of their own forms of alternative medical treatments. Mediums brought curing energy from the other world; they wrote prescriptions for allopathic, homeopathic, and herbal medications dictated by doctors and healers on the other plane; and they performed disobsessions. In what has become one of their major means of proselytizing practiced outside the hospitals, they established centers where doctors and healers from the spirit world, incorporated temporarily in the bodies of mediums, do inexplicable surgeries with a rusty knife or an electric saw and without anesthesia or antisepsis. As the spirit of Dr. Fritz once declared through the medium Edson Querioz, the surgeries are not really necessary because, according to the belief system, they are actually performed spiritually. Dr. Fritz went on to say that he only cut to force those operated on, and friends and relatives accompanying them, plus observers, including the media, to explain what they have experienced or witnessed.

Our conventional frames of comprehension, which provide commonsense understanding of the world and what is experienced, he maintained, do not work. The surgeries are an inexplicable anomaly. Only Kardec's framework and Spiritism, Dr. Fritz argued, can account for it. When forced by the experience to seek an explanation, following on Kardec's belief in rationalism, he affirmed that people would have no choice but to adopt the new beliefs and become followers of the Codifier's vision. And in the tradition of folk-Catholicism and its imagery of patron–client exchange, those of the patients and their loved ones who are told that they have the ability to become mediums will be obligated to develop it. To complete their cure they are advised to attend sessions at a Kardecist (or Umbanda) Center where mediumship training is offered. When the instruction is completed, the new mediums will be hosts to their own spirits, who through them will provide help to others. This will expand the numbers receiving charitable assistance and increase the body of adherents to the belief system. The challenge to explain the unexplainable also is extended, implicitly if not explicitly, through the many mediums who receive artists, poets, and writers who through them replicate the styles of Picasso, Van Gogh, Machado de Assis, Humberto de Campos, and other luminaries of the past. In these various ways Spiritism is attracting not just the poor, but also Brazilians and other Latin Americans from all classes and segments of society.

Umbanda and other popular religions offer their own forms of healing and means of resolving the problems of the needy. Evangelical churches provide healing by the Holy Spirit, popular Catholicism enjoins the intermediacy of the saints to a God who solves all problems and the African-derived traditions petition the aid of the deities from their distant homelands. As they vie with each other for followers in the religious marketplace that has emerged in Brazil's overpopulated and underserved urban centers and elsewhere in Latin America and the Caribbean, faith groups are attempting to fill a void that is the result of undirected urbanization and modernity. The spread and growth of Kardec's vision, as it was reformulated in the Americas with aspects of folk-Catholicism, Amerindian traditions, and African-derived practices and then re-mixed into these and yet other faiths across the continent may be seen as a response to the multitude of human problems created, but not solved, by a politico-economic system that has swept the earth. Some scholars and Spiritist intellectuals interpret the Codifier's revelation as a response to the early manifestation of problems faced in North American and Europe. Their reformulation, they believe, makes Spiritism more relevant for satisfying the needs of humanity in today's world.

Bibliography and Suggested Readings

Brown, Diana DeGroats. *Umbanda: Religion and Politics in Urban Brazil*. New York: Columbia University Press, 1994.

Damazio, S.F. *Da elite ao pove: Advento e espansão do Espiritismo no Rio de Janeiro*. Rio de Janeiro: Editora Bertrand, 1994.

Greenfield, Sidney M. "Our Science Is Better than Yours: Two Decades of Data on Patients Treated by a Kardecist-Spiritist Healing Group in Rio Grande do Sul." *Anthropology of Consciousness*, 20, no. 2 (2009): 101–110.

"The Patients of Dr. Fritz: Assessment of Treatment by a Brazilian Spiritist Healer." *British Journal of Psychical Research*, 61, no. 847 (1997): 372–387.

Spirits with Scalpels: The Culturalbiology of Spirit Healing in Brazil. Walnut Creek, CA: Left Coast Press, 2008.

"Treating the Sick with a Morality Play: The Kardecist-Spiritist Disobsession in Brazil." *Social Analysis*, 48, no. 2 (2006): 174–194.

Kardec, Allan. *The Gospel According to Spiritism*. Trans. J. Duncan. London: Headquarters Publishing, 1987 [1864].

The Mediums' Book. Trans. Anna Blackwell. São Paulo: Lake – Livraria Allan Kardec Editora., 1975 [1861].

The Spirits' Book. Trans. Anna Blackwell. São Paulo: Lake – Livraria Allan Kardec Editora., [1857] n.d.

Maggie, Yvonne. "Aqueles a Quem foi Negado a Cor do Dia: As Categories Cor e Raça na Cultura Brasileira." In Marcos C. Maio and Ricardo V. Santos (eds.), *Raça, Ciência e Sociedade*, 225–234. Rio de Janeiro: Editora FIOCRUZ/CCBB, 1996.

Maio, Marcos C., and Ricardo V. Santos. *Raça Ciência e Sociedade*. Rio de Janeiro: Editora FIOCRUZ/CCBB, 1996.

Romberg, Raquel. *Healing Dramas: Divination and Magic in Modern Puerto Rico*. Austin: University of Texas Press, 2009.

St. Clair, David. *Drum and Candle*. Garden City, NY: Doubleday, 1971.

Trinidade, Diamantino Fernandes. *Iniciação à Umbanda*, 2nd ed. São Paulo: Triade Editora, 1989.

Weisberg, Barbara. *Talking to the Dead: Kate and Maggie Fox and the Rise of Spiritism*. San Francisco: Harper San Francisco, 2004.

41
Transnationalism, Globalization, and Latin American Religions

TODD HARTCH

Latin America has a long tradition of participating in religious transnationalism as a recipient of religious ideas and personnel. However, in the past century, Latin Americans have reshaped this process by actively asserting their roles as exporters of theology, missionaries, and institutions rather than merely being importers. Three examples from across the region illustrate the recent changes in Latin American religious transnationalism and how the traditional model of global religion has merged with a newer one.

First, when Catholics in Mexico were being persecuted in the 1920s and 1930s Pope Pius XI issued two encyclicals that denounced the actions of the Mexican government. While Vatican diplomats negotiated with the Mexican government, in the United States the Knights of Columbus, an organization of Catholic laymen, put pressure on the Coolidge, Hoover, and Roosevelt administrations to intervene on behalf of Mexican Catholics. An emissary of the American bishops, Father John Burke, played a central role in negotiating the *modus vivendi* between Church and state in 1929.

Second is the case of Luis Bush, who was born in Argentina in 1946, went to college in the United States, and in the late 1970s became pastor of a church in El Salvador affiliated with the Central American Mission, a fundamentalist Protestant missionary organization headquartered in Texas. In seven years, he led the church in a massive numerical expansion, "forged its entire ethos around missionary activity," and inspired thirty-five congregants to go as missionaries to other countries.[1] He put together a missions conference in 1987 in Brazil to mobilize Latin Americans for missionary service around the world and then led Partners International (1986–1992) and AD 2000 (1992–2002), organizations based in the United States and dedicated to strategic planning for world evangelization.

---

1 Stephen Offutt, *The Changing Face of Evangelicalism in the Gobal South: Moral Entrepreneurship in El Salvador and South Africa* (PhD dissertation, Boston University, 2009), 147.

Third, in 2013 Costa Rican pastor Rony Cháves traveled to ten European countries for what he called his "European Campaign." Cháves and his "prophetic and apostolic team" met with local leaders, prayed at strategic locations, and led meetings at Pentecostal churches. While visiting Debrecen, Hungary, once a center of the Protestant Reformation, Cháves preached that God was going to start a new movement of the Holy Spirit there. In another meeting, Cháves delivered a "prophetic word" that Hungary was about to experience a "year of jubilee" in which God would pour out special blessings. When he returned to Costa Rica, he featured videos from the trip prominently on his website.[2]

The religious transnationalism in these three examples involves the movement of people and ideas between nations, the religious organizations that foster those movements, and the formation of religious identities that transcend individual nation-states. In the first example, a European-based religion and its adherents in the United States played important roles in Mexican religious affairs; in the second, an Argentine developed a successful and influential career in religious organizations based in the United States; in the third example, a Costa Rican brought his religious message to Europe and then used that trip in his construction of an identity as a latter-day prophet.

In a broad sense, these three examples represent two main versions of Latin American religious transnationalism: the traditional version that emphasizes the agency of Europeans and North Americans and a newer version that emphasizes the agency of Latin Americans. This is not to say that the newer version replaced the traditional version; rather, both continue to operate, as do various hybrid configurations.

The other crucial element in these examples is the rise of Pentecostalism as the most dynamic contemporary transnational religion. For most of Latin American history, it went without saying that Catholicism was the dominant transnational religion, but Protestantism and especially its Pentecostal version emerged after 1950 as more vigorous competitors. Of course, Catholicism continues to be the numerically dominant religion and one that, headquartered as it is in Rome, cannot help but carry out transnational actions and foster transnational identities. However, in terms of sheer dynamism, the transnational religious force of the late twentieth and early twenty-first centuries has been Pentecostalism.

---

2 Rony Cháves, Avance Misionero Mundial, "Activa Europa 2013," *Avance Misionero Mundial*, http://www.ronychaves.org/tvweb.aspx?a=5 (Accessed October 6, 2014); Frédéric Dejean, "L'évangélisme et le Pentecôtisme," *Géographie et Cultures*, 68 (2009): 50.

"Transnational" is an anachronistic term when applied before the flowering of European nationalism in the Napoleonic age, but it applies in the sense that since the early days of conquest and colonization, Latin American Catholicism had strong personal, institutional, and cultural connections to Europe. The spread of Catholicism to the Caribbean islands, Mexico, Central America, and South America meant that by 1600, millions of people whose ancestors had no idea that Asia and Europe even existed came to practice a religion centered on a Palestinian Jew and administered from Rome. Of course, the most consciously "transnational" religious agents were Catholic priests and friars, who maintained allegiances to their home countries while they adapted themselves to colonial or indigenous culture. Yet even practitioners of folk Catholicism, who tended to emphasize local saints and customs more than Roman doctrines, were aware that Catholicism claimed to be a universal religion. The Latin of the Mass, the mother tongue of neither the colonizers nor the colonized, made clear that this was a religion that transcended local and regional boundaries.

Throughout the colonial period and the early national period of the nineteenth century, Catholicism maintained its international connections and orientations more in the cities than in the countryside, where folk religion could at times become almost entirely oriented toward the local pantheon and the local sacred geography. However, even in remote areas, the visit of a priest signaled the religion's connection to the larger Church and to the wider world, and when missionaries from European religious orders arrived, the universal nature of the religion could not be avoided. Similarly, the African-derived religions that prospered in Brazil, Cuba, and other areas with large African populations could not help but be transnational. Their beliefs and practices claimed African roots and thus fostered African practices and African-Latin American transnational identities.

In the twentieth century, the increasing process of globalization, concerted efforts by the Vatican, and the arrival of Protestant missionaries intensified the connections between Latin America, Europe, and later the United States. In the second half of the twentieth century, a new form of transnationalism occurred as Latin American migrants, missionaries, and evangelists brought versions of Christianity and Afro-American religions to Europe, Asia, Africa, and the United States. It is with this new religious transnationalism that this chapter is primarily concerned, but that is not to say that the traditional religious transnationalism – driven by religious agents from Europe and the United States operating in Latin America – ended or stopped having a prominent role in the region. Both versions have continued to the present day. This chapter first examines traditional religious transnationalism in the years since 1950 and then looks at the new religious transnationalism, with special attention to Pentecostalism.

Traditional Religious Transnationalism

By the late 1950s many members of the Catholic hierarchy, both inside and outside of Latin America, and many educated members of the Catholic laity were worried about the state of Catholicism in Latin America. A shortage of priests and religious meant that the Church could not respond adequately to significant challenges that were coming from several directions. On the religious front, Protestant missionaries from the United States and various independent Latin American churches (mostly Pentecostal) were experiencing great success in converting Catholics. Meanwhile, especially after Fidel Castro's revolution in Cuba, other portions of the citizenry were leaving the Church to embrace Marxism and other atheistic political philosophies.

Most importantly, industrialization and urbanization were drawing millions of migrants to urban peripheries in which Catholicism had little institutional presence. Many recent urban migrants did not reject Catholicism outright, but rather slowly lost their traditions and beliefs in a new and confusing environment. Others turned to religions such as Pentecostalism, whose flexibility and agility seemed better suited to the new urban zones.

A call by Pope John XXIII in 1961 for a massive infusion of Catholic missionaries from the United States led to a flurry of activity in the early part of the decade, but opposition by Ivan Illich and other critics of Western cultural imperialism quickly undermined the missionary initiative. European nations continued to send large numbers of priests and religious to the region, but their role changed in the 1970s.

Influenced by the Second Vatican Council (1962–1965) and Latin America's emerging Liberation Theology movement and responding to oppressive military governments, many European priests and religious and many Latin American clergy struck an adversarial pose toward the region's governments and elites. Catholic transnationalism of the 1970s and 1980s thus often functioned as a defense of human rights. Where purely national organizations and groups could be co-opted, intimidated, or destroyed, Catholicism's international networks provided it with resources and encouragement that others lacked. The Latin American Church received financial support, personnel, and moral encouragement from the Vatican and from European Catholics throughout the region's darkest hours. Latin American governments that did not think twice about striking out at other domestic opponents were reluctant to move against Catholic figures because they knew that the imprisonment or murder of bishops, priests, and nuns inevitably attracted negative attention from both the Vatican and the international press corps. Attacks on missionaries also added the intense criticism of the missionaries' home countries. For example, the murder in 1989 of six Jesuits (five of them from Spain) at El Salvador's Central American University made the country an international pariah. Catholicism's transnational nature transformed local and national issues into international ones.

On the other hand, traditional Catholic missionary work also continued. Jesuits, Franciscans, Dominicans, and other orders played vital roles in education, parish ministry, and medical work. Opus Dei, based in Spain, and the new ecclesial movements, such as Italy's Focolare, and Communion and Liberation, fostered new forms of lay spirituality. Largely eschewing direct political involvement, such groups produced large cohorts of educated and committed lay Catholics.

Meanwhile, Protestants from the United States were playing a major role in the region. Evangelists such as Jimmy Swaggart spoke to large audiences in several countries in the 1970s and 1980s. Parachurch organizations such as Youth With A Mission, Campus Crusade for Christ, and World Vision worked with students and the poor in many areas. Denominational missionaries, such as those of the Southern Baptist Convention and the Assemblies of God, were joined by representatives of nondenominational mission organizations such as the New Tribes Mission, the Central American Mission, and the Wycliffe Bible Translators. Short-term missionaries (with stays as short as one week) came from churches across the United States and put Latin Americans in contact with lay Protestants, in many places on an annual basis.

In more recent years, mega-church pastors such as Rick Warren of Saddleback Church of California and Bill Hybels of Willow Creek Church of Illinois not only visited the region but also had significant influence there through media and networking. Warren, for instance, inspired Latin American pastors through his "Purpose Driven Church" materials and planted a satellite church in Argentina. Christian leadership guru John Maxwell also enjoyed a large following in the region.

Consequently, for many Latin American Catholics and Protestants in the late twentieth and early twenty-first centuries, contact with religious leaders and organizations from the United States and Europe served as clear evidence that their faith had transnational dimensions. The impact of transnational religious media has also been profound. Their contact with religious personnel and ideas from the United States and Europe and their association with or participation in religious organizations based in other parts of the world encouraged them to form transnational religious identities.

The New Religious Transnationalism

However, this sort of religious transnationalism was not qualitatively different from what occurred during the colonial period: outside religious organizations brought Latin Americans into the experience of religious transnationalism in Latin America. Even as this traditional version continued, a new form of Latin American religious transnationalism emerged as Latin Americans formed their own organizations, traveled to other parts of the world, shared their religious messages and experiences with non-Latin Americans, and brought non-Latin Americans into a transnational religious experience.

Massive migration to the United States and Europe from Latin America was only part of the picture. In many cases, Latin Americans developed specific religious ideas and practices that they disseminated around the world; in many other cases Latin Americans consciously chose to go to the United States, Europe, Asia, and Africa as missionaries, evangelists, and teachers. In other words, since 1950 the major new form of Latin American religious transnationalism involved Latin American agency and innovation.

While the traditional version consisted of Latin American participation in religious networks centered in Europe and the United States, the new version featured Latin Americans creating their own networks and expanding them around the world. The novelty was not that the United States had stopped sending missionaries – in fact, the almost 43,000 American Protestant missionaries serving overseas in 2008 was a higher number than ever – but that Latin Americans were now dynamic agents in an increasingly complex global religious environment. The great exemplars of this new Latin American religious agency were the Pentecostals and the similar Catholic Charismatics, but it is also worth looking at similar religious agency among the practitioners of African-derived religions and in the rise of Catholic Liberation Theology.

Candomblé and Batuque are Afro-Brazilian religions, while Santería is Afro-Cuban. All three, and several other similar religions, have spread to other nations, and not just to the Afro-Brazilian and Afro-Cuban diasporas. In fact, the Batuque that came to Montevideo in the 1950s and the Candomblé that arrived in Buenos Aires in the 1960s were brought more often by white, lower middle-class Brazilians than by blacks; their converts included many white Uruguayans and Argentines. The most numerically successful of such religions was Umbanda, which developed in the 1920s in Rio de Janeiro as a blend of the earlier and more African Candomblé with popular Catholicism and with a form of European spiritualism known as Kardecism. Brazilians brought Umbanda to Uruguay and Argentina, and then migrants from those countries took it to Venezuela, Spain, and Italy. It can now be found in Los Angeles, San Francisco, Miami, New York, and Portugal.

Alejandro Frigerio notes a sort of spiritual migration in which practitioners of Umbanda, even in Europe and North America, move to Candomblé or Batuque in a search for a deeper and more authentic African religious experiences; similarly, practitioners of Candomblé and Batuque seek out Yorùbá religious knowledge and experience from contemporary Africa, especially Nigeria and Benin, sometimes going so far as to travel to Nigeria to pursue honorary religious titles from Yorùbá priests. Thus, African-derived religions are transnational not only in the sense that their practitioners now have networks that include Europe and North America but also in the sense that they consciously seek out African knowledge and identity.

Another successful Latin American religious export was Liberation Theology. A group of progressive theologians including Gustavo Gutiérrez and Juan Luis Segundo began meeting in the mid-1960s to develop a distinctively Latin American theology. They were worried not just about doctrinal issues but also about Latin America's economic dependency and unjust social systems. They came to believe that "liberation" – economic and political as much as spiritual – was at the heart of the Christian Gospel and that it was the great necessity for Latin America. In 1971, Gutiérrez published his ground-breaking *A Theology of Liberation*, in which he employed Marxist class analysis to argue that the church should join the class struggle on the side of the oppressed. Other writers such as Segundo and Leonardo Boff soon produced their own liberationist works; by the mid-1970s there were dozens of books and articles in the field. Ecclesial Base Communities, local Christian communities in which believers studied, worshiped, and worked together for social justice, often embraced the new theology. As these communities multiplied in the 1970s – in Brazil alone there were 80,000 communities with as many as four million members at the height of the movement – they brought Liberation Theology out of the classrooms and into the streets.

Also receptive to the theology were academics, priests, religious sisters, and Protestant pastors in the developed world. Starting with the Theology in the Americas conference in Detroit in 1975, Liberation Theology swept through North American and European universities and seminaries, Catholic and Protestant alike. For example, Presbyterian scholar Robert McAfee Brown was so impressed by Liberation Theology that he devoted much of his scholarly career to explaining it to North American audiences. Although the theology lost some of its luster in the 1990s because of resistance in the Vatican and a neoliberal turn in Latin American politics, it continued to be one of Latin America's most influential intellectual exports. In 2001, Gutiérrez joined the faculty of the most prestigious Catholic university in the United States, the University of Notre Dame. It was no small matter to have a region once considered an intellectual backwater now setting the agenda for some of the world's leading scholars and institutions of higher learning.

In contrast to the sort of intellectual transnationalism Liberation Theology fostered, Pentecostalism developed numerous networks, circuits, and organizations of mostly poor and lower class Latin Americans. Where liberation theologians convened international conferences; published articles and books; and developed networks of scholars, priests, bishops, and religious sisters, Pentecostals built their networks through migration and more intentional missionary and evangelistic activities. Migration itself was part of the Pentecostal transnational religious experience, largely because the stress, adversity, and real danger of travel across borders (especially in the case of undocumented migrants to the United States) pushed migrants to the limits of their own resources. "For Pentecostals," explains Leah Sarat, "the border is a space of divine encounter where the hardship of crossing sometimes serves as a catalyst for conversion."[3]

In fact, for Pentecostals the migratory experience was utterly infused with religion. Deciding whether to leave involved prayer and prophecy, as did preparation for the trip. Once in the new country, the local Pentecostal church provided various emotional, spiritual, and practical services. When migrants returned to their home communities, they brought back new religious practices and new financial resources, which were often used to improve home churches.

For example, Mayan immigrants from three Pentecostal churches in a small village in the department of Totonicapán, Guatemala, established three sister churches in Houston, Texas, that served as nodes of a complex network of prayer, prophecy, religious ideas, and financial aid circulating between the two communities. Mexican and Central American pastors traveled back and

---

3 Leah Sarat, *The God without Borders and the Mexican Dream: Religion, Space, and Migration in El Alberto, Hidalgo* (PhD dissertation, University of Florida, 2010), 9.

forth across the border, ministering to flocks on both sides, and often preached specifically about migration. A pastor preaching to a congregation in Arizona of mostly Otomí migrants from Mexico, for instance, changed the words of Psalm 121 from "I lift my eyes up to the mountains, from whence cometh my help" to "I lift my eyes to *el norte*" to show how many of them were trusting in the United States rather than God. Similarly, in a San Francisco storefront church with members from Mexico, Central America, Argentina, and Peru, the pastor preached, "God brought you miles away because you could not accept God in your country. You could not leave the life that you were living."[4] The border and migration itself became infused with religious meaning.

In addition to propagating the faith and building transnational identities through migration, Latin American Pentecostals also did so in a more intentional way as missionaries and evangelists. Typically, evangelists started in their home countries, and then, after successfully producing conversions and healings, visited neighboring Latin American countries, and perhaps Europe and the United States. Carlos Annacondia, an influential Argentine evangelist and the catalyst of the Argentine Pentecostal revival of the 1990s, started his evangelistic work in Buenos Aires province in 1981, began preaching in other parts of Argentina in 1987, and then conducted campaigns in El Salvador, Peru, the United States, Finland, Japan, and several other countries over the following years.

Annacondia's friend and protégé, Claudio Friedzón, experienced a spiritual anointing in 1992 that he shared with his Rey de Reyes church in Buenos Aires, making it a pilgrimage site, first for Argentine pastors and then for Pentecostals from around the world. The two most influential proponents of the Toronto Blessing, a Charismatic Revival movement that spread through North America in the 1990s, first experienced the anointing at Friedzón's church. Later, Friedzón and his wife Betty developed The Ministry to the Nations, which was designed to bring "the fire, the revival, and the devotion to God" from Argentina to the whole world by means of crusades, conferences, books, and television shows. By 2014, they were leading campaigns and conferences in Argentina, New Jersey, Sicily, Peru, Texas, and Florida. Their annual Breakthrough conference attracted people from all over Latin America and the rest of the world.

Argentine pastors Edgardo Silvoso and Sergio Scataglini, although not as influential as Annacondia and Friedzón, played important transnational roles

4 Lois Ann Lorentzen and Rosalina Mira, "El milagro está en casa: Gender and Private/Public Empowerment in a Migrant Pentecostal Church," *Latin American Perspectives*, 32, no. 1 (January 2005): 59.

by connecting visitors from other parts of the world to the Argentine revival. When Australian Baptist pastor Rod Denton visited Scataglini's church in La Plata in 1994, he experienced the "anointing" and then brought the same sort of spiritual experience back to Australia. Similarly, Japanese pastor Paul Ariga came to Argentina in 1993 through Silvoso's Harvest Evangelism International Institute and met Annacondia, Friedzón and other prominent Argentine Pentecostal leaders. Although unsure at the time if he had received the "anointing," Ariga nevertheless applied the Argentine approach to evangelism in Japan and saw thousands of conversions for his All Japan Revival Mission in 1994. Both Scataglini and Silvoso moved to the United States to lead ministries (Harvest Evangelism and Scataglini Ministries, respectively) that used their Argentine connections and experiences as bridges to status and influence in the global Pentecostal community.

Latin American Pentecostals also have sent long-term missionaries to North America, Africa, Asia, and Europe. For example, in 2006 one Assemblies of God church in El Salvador devoted $165,000 of its yearly budget to Salvadoran church planters in India, the Philippines, Africa, and other Latin American countries, as well as short-term trips to Kosovo, Equatorial Guinea, Niger, and Vietnam. Europe, the former colonial power and for centuries the global center of Christianity, has a strong appeal to many Latin Americans. The depth of this attraction was evident in Porto Alegre, Brazil, where two large churches were sponsoring a total of ninety-five missionaries to Europe in 2014. Josué Dilermando, the head pastor of Igreja Maanaim in the same city, had neither an especially large church nor a national reputation. Nevertheless, he had a strong desire to evangelize Europe, going so far as to send one of his church's three pastors to serve as a missionary in Rome in 2011. "My concern," Dilermando said, "is not with evangelizing Brazil; today my concern lies in evangelizing Europe."[5]

Brazil's controversial Universal Church of the Kingdom of God made world mission a central activity from its early years. Founded in 1977 by Edir Macedo, an employee of Brazil's national lottery, the church planted churches in Paraguay and the United States in its first decade and by 1993 had spread to most of Latin America, six nations in Africa, and four in Europe; by 2004 its churches were present in more than seventy countries around the world. Two of its most successful mission fields were Portugal, where it had sixty-two churches by 1997, and South Africa, where it had 115 churches in 1998 and 165 in 2005. Brazil and Brazilianness featured strongly in the church's style and

---

5 Oro, "South American Evangelicals' Re-conquest," 226.

appeal, with Portuguese adherents, for example, adopting Brazilian accents and longing for the chance to travel to Brazil to see the home country of the denomination.

The Universal Church was not alone. Another Brazilian denomination, God Is Love Pentecostal Church, founded by David Miranda in 1962 in São Paulo, by 2014 had established churches in more than 100 countries, including Greece, Ireland, Italy, and Switzerland.

Less prolific but still quite important in the spread of Latin American Pentecostalism were the Central American megachurches. By 2014 each nation from Guatemala to Panama hosted at least one, and often several, enormous Pentecostal churches with branches in the United States and sometimes other countries. El Salvador, the smallest of the Central American nations and only slightly larger than New Jersey, had several large churches with branches in the United States. The largest of these, Elim, had a congregation of 130,000 people in El Salvador in 2009 and had daughter churches in Los Angeles and several other American cities.

Elim traces its roots to a church in Guatemala City started in the 1960s by Otoniel Rios Paredes, who sent a young Guatemalan pastor, Sergio Solórzano, to plant a church in Ilopango, just outside of San Salvador. The new church grew quickly and, after separating from its Guatemalan mother church in 1983 in a doctrinal dispute, soon became one of the largest Pentecostal churches in El Salvador, in large part through adopting the cell group strategy of Korean megachurch pastor David Yonggi Cho. By 2006, the church was boasting more than 120,000 members, making Elim the second largest individual congregation in the world.

Salvadoran migrants brought Elim to the United States in the 1980s, and then to Honduras, Costa Rica, Canada, and Australia. By 2014, Elim had branches also in Belgium, Spain, and Italy. The Los Angeles affiliate of Elim has become a megachurch itself, with 5,000 members in 2007; its pastor, Salvadoran immigrant Rene Molina, now travels to Cuba, Australia, Peru, Spain, and Argentina on his own mission trips, speaks at political rallies, and works with African American pastors on racial issues in Los Angeles.

Guatemala, which in terms of overall percentages became the most Protestant of all the Latin American nations, with Protestants making up about 40 percent of its population in 2014, had several prominent megachurches, including Ebenezer, Casa de Dios, Fraternidad Cristiana, and El Calvario. Among the most influential, however, was El Shaddai (Hebrew for "God Almighty"), with about 12,000 members participating in 500 cell groups in Guatemala City in 2007. The central church building seats 6,000 and has a café and a bookstore. The church also sponsored thirty-one satellite churches, seventeen radio stations, a television show, ten schools, and a university. Started by lawyer Harold Caballeros in 1982 in a rented room, El Shaddai quickly became one of the leading churches in Guatemala City and then followed the Guatemalan diaspora to the United States and Europe. One of the secrets to the church's rapid growth was a 1990 campaign in which its members gave out thousands of stickers, banners, and t-shirts with the words *"Jesus es Señor de Guatemala"* (Jesus is Lord of Guatemala) all over the country; the corresponding belief that Guatemala was specially chosen by God had a catalytic relationship with the church's growing international presence.

Even as El Shaddai was working for more national pride and better citizenship among Guatemalans it was also participating in international Pentecostal networks and fostering transnational identities in its members. The church distributed books, compact disks, DVDs, and radio and Internet broadcasts; it sent out migrants to many countries; Caballeros preached and taught at various churches and conferences in the United States and Europe.

Meanwhile, the church attracted, especially in its biennial international conferences, famous prophets and other visitors from the United States, Latin America, and Europe. These visitors often saw Guatemala as especially favored by God because of its rapid Protestant growth and they prophesied its special role in world evangelization. Just as in the 1990s Argentine Pentecostals celebrated their country's becoming a place of Pentecostal pilgrimage, El Shaddai used Guatemala's widely accepted central role in God's plan to attract international visitors and to inspire the Guatemalan faithful. For example, the 2000 conference was called "The World Will Come to Guatemala and the Revival Will Go Out to the World" and the 2006 conference, with representatives from twenty-four nations, featured a speaker from New Zealand who revered Guatemala as the center of a worldwide Pentecostal revival.

The Catholic Charismatic Renewal, a manifestation of Pentecostal-type phenomena inside the Catholic Church, came to Latin America shortly after its beginning in the United States in 1967. The Latin American movement soon surpassed the one in the United States in terms of both numbers and dynamism, and eventually surpassed Latin American Pentecostalism, at least in a numerical sense. Of all the streams of Latin American Catholicism, the Charismatic Renewal seems the most dynamic and the most resistant to Pentecostal inroads, in large part because it provides many of the same spiritual experiences without requiring its adherents to leave behind the mass, the saints, or Catholic family members.

It is interesting, therefore, that Charismatic Catholics have not been as committed to mission and international networking as Pentecostals, perhaps because the Catholic Church is, in and of itself, one of the world's first and largest transnational organizations. Still, Charismatics constitute by far the largest group of lay Catholics involved in intentional missionary activity. Two Charismatic organizations begun in Mexico, Father Alfonso Navarro's Systemic Integral New Evangelization and layman José "Pepe" Prado's San Andrés Schools of Evangelization, took the lead in training Catholics in Latin American and the United States in evangelization. Wherever they ran their programs Catholics proved more resistant than before to Protestant charms.

The Charismatic community, a distinctive form of religious organization in which lay Catholics sometimes lived together and typically carried out various ministries without taking vows, seemed almost to be genetically programmed for missionary activity. Typically, a community began in one city, then established new communities in other cities in the same country, and finally sent teams to foreign countries, often in Europe. For instance, Obra de Maria, founded in Recife in 1990, spread to seventeen Brazilian cities and sixteen foreign countries, including Israel, Angola, and Italy, by 2013. Like Pentecostals, Catholic Charismatics were masters of popular culture and popular media, especially music and television, and used them to attract attention and win converts at home and overseas.

The shift of Christianity to the Global South was one of the most dramatic large-scale changes of the late twentieth century. Latin America plays a special role in this new era of southern Christianity because, unlike Asia and Africa, it has a long and deep Christian history of five centuries. While, with some obvious exceptions such as the Philippines, Asia and Africa are experiencing Christians and Christianity as new phenomena, Latin America is entering a different stage in its history, a stage of global religious leadership, innovation, export, and mission.

Bibliography and Suggested Readings

Anderson, Allan. *To the Ends of the Earth: Pentecostalism and the Transformation of World Christianity*. New York: Oxford University Press, 2013.

Bush, Luis. *Catalysts of World Evangelization*. PhD dissertation, Fuller Theological Seminary, 2002.

Chaves, Rony. Avance Misionero Mundial. "Activa Europa 2013," www.ronychaves.org/tvweb.aspx?a=5 (June 14, 2014).

Cleary, Edward. *The Catholic Charismatic Renewal in Latin America*. Tallahassee: University Press of Florida, 2011.

Coleman, William. *Latin American Catholicism: A Self-evaluation*. Maryknoll, NY: Maryknoll Publications, 1958.

Costello, Gerald. *Mission to Latin America: Successes and Failures of a Twentieth-Century Crusade*. Maryknoll, NY: Orbis, 1979.

Dejean, Frédéric. "L'évangélisme et le Pentecôtisme." *Géographie et Cultures*, 68 (2009): 43–61.

Gutiérrez, Gustavo. *A Theology of Liberation: History, Politics, and Salvation*. Maryknoll, NY: Orbis, 1971.

Hagan, Jacqueline, and Helen Rose Ebaugh. "Calling upon the Sacred: Migrants' Use of Religion in the Migration Process." *International Migration Review*, 37, no. 4 (Winter 2003): 1145–1162.

Hartch, Todd. *The Rebirth of Latin American Christianity*. New York: Oxford University Press, 2014.

Hewitt, W. E. *Base Christian Communities and Social Change in Brazil*. Lincoln: University of Nebraska Press, 1991.

Jenkins, Philip. *The Next Christendom: The Coming of Global Christianity*. New York: Oxford University Press, 2011.

Lorentzen, Lois Ann, and Rosalina Mira. "El milagro está en casa: Gender and Private/Public Empowerment in a Migrant Pentecostal Church." *Latin American Perspectives*, 32, no. 1 (January 2005): 57–71.

Marostica, Matthew "Learning from the Master: Carlos Annacondia and the Standardization of Pentecostal Practices in and beyond Argentina." In Candy Gunther Brown (ed.), *Global Pentecostal and Charismatic Healing*, 207–230. New York: Oxford University Press, 2011.

McAfee Brown, Robert. *Gustavo Gutiérrez: An Introduction to Liberation Theology*. Maryknoll, NY: Orbis, 1990.

Liberation Theology: An Introductory Guide. Louisville: Westminster/John Knox, 1993.

O'Neill, Kevin. *City of God: Neo-Pentecostal Formations of Christian Citizenship in Postwar Guatemala City*. PhD dissertation, Stanford University, 2007.

Redinger, Matthew. *American Catholics and the Mexican Revolution, 1924–1936*. Notre Dame, IN: University of Notre Dame Press, 2005.

Sarat, Leah. *The God without Borders and the Mexican Dream: Religion, Space, and Migration in El Alberto, Hidalgo*. PhD dissertation, University of Florida, 2010.

Steffen, Tom, and Lois McKinney Douglas. *Encountering Missionary Life and Work: Preparing for Intercultural Ministry*. Grand Rapids: Baker Academic, 2008.

Stoll, David. *Is Latin America Turning Protestant? The Politics of Evangelical Growth*. Berkeley: University of California Press, 1990.

Winter, Roberta. "Luis Bush, Latin America, and the End of History." *Mission Frontiers*, 8, no. 3 (March 1986), 3–5.

Wuthnow, Robert, and Stephen Offutt. "Transnational Religious Connections." *Sociology of Religion*, 69, no. 2 (Summer, 2008): 209–232.

42
Religious Identity and Emigration from Latin America

THOMAS A. TWEED

"The Mexicans are great movers, here today and gone tomorrow," one US Catholic bishop observed in 1927, and he predicted that their migratory inclinations would persist.[1] That ecclesiastical leader was thinking of the Mexican Catholics who had come to the US. Midwest during the 1920s, but other Latin Americans also were on the move before and after the first decades of the twentieth century. The religious practice and collective identity of those who emigrated changed in some ways as they moved. Some emigrants headed toward Asia, like the Mexicans who settled in the Philippines, where a somewhat familiar form of Catholicism predominated, and like the ethnic Japanese in Brazil who returned as Portuguese-speaking Catholics and Protestants to their ancestral home in Buddhist East Asia during the last quarter of the twentieth century.

Latin American migrants also traveled to other parts of the world, including Europe, such as those who settled in Protestant Britain or Catholic Spain. However, many migrants from the southern portion of the Western Hemisphere journeyed north. They went to Canada, which by the twenty-first century reported a foreign-born population of 18.4 percent and hosted hundreds of thousands of Latin American emigrants, and they moved to the United States, where "Hispanics" (the federal census's term) numbered almost 36 million and constituted 12.5 percent of the population by the start of the new century – and made up even greater proportions of the native-born and foreign-born residents after 2000 (Table 42.1). Focusing on Latin American emigration to the United States, this entry offers an overview of emigrants' religious practice, which varied according to the individual's place of birth, motive for relocation, and area of settlement but also displayed

---

[1] David Badillo, *Latinos and the New Immigrant Church* (Baltimore: Johns Hopkins University Press, 2006), 120.

TABLE 42.1. *US Foreign Born by Region of Birth and Date of Arrival*

Region	Before 1990	1990–1999	2000 and later	Total (2008)
Mexico	4,192,979	3,668,343	3,589,977	11,451,299
Caribbean	1,740,413	906,016	782,993	3,429,422
Central America	1,088,422	784,136	876,513	2,749,071
South America	934,382	715,142	906,196	2,555,720
Total	7,956,196	6,073,637	6,155,679	20,185,512

Source: Pew Hispanic Center tabulations of 2008 American Community Survey.

some important commonalities that distinguished Latinos from other US residents and connected them to their Latin American homelands.

Divergent Migration Flows and Varying Religious Practices

The flow of migrants from Latin America was not a steady stream – notice the increase during the 1990s shown in Table 42.1 – and the boundaries of "Latin America" changed over time: for example, Mexico's national borders in 1830 extended northward toward territory that is now the southwestern states and California. Further, different factors led residents in Latin American nations to make the journey. Not only concerned to practice their faith and care for their family, they also were pushed and pulled by economic, social, and political forces. Migration from Mexico, the birthplace of the majority of Latin American emigrants, accelerated during political crises and religious controversies of the 1910s and 1920s but slowed in the 1930s, when the Great Depression limited opportunities.

It was the same with the other Latin American homelands that have provided the highest proportion of Latino residents in the United States – Cuba, Puerto Rico, Dominican Republic, El Salvador, and Guatemala. Those emigrants sometimes left when they felt forced or coerced into exile, such as when wars, revolutions, and persecutions made life at home unbearable, or when the promise of new opportunities abroad drew them. Sometimes laws made the trek more dangerous and difficult, even impossible. When the more restrictive legal guidelines of the United States were eased after President Lyndon B. Johnson signed the Immigration and Nationality Act of 1965, the flow of emigrants out of Latin America became a roaring stream, though it slowed somewhat by 2010, when counter-immigration campaigns had reemerged and an economic recession had hit (Table 42.2).

TABLE 42.2. US Immigration by Country from Major Latin American Sending Nations, 1901–2000

Country	1901–1910	1911–1920	1921–1930	1931–1940	1941–1950	1951–1960	1961–1970	1971–1980	1981–1990	1991–2000
Cuba	Not reported	Not reported	15,901	9,571	26,313	78,948	208,536	264,863	144,578	169,332
Dominican Republic	Not reported	Not reported	Not reported	1,150	5,627	9,897	93,292	148,135	252,035	335,251
Mexico	49,642	219,004	459,287	22,319	60,589	299,811	453,937	640,294	1,655,843	2,249,421

Source: US Immigration and Naturalization Service, Statistical Yearbook of the Immigration and Naturalization Service, 2001 (US Government Printing Office: Washington, D.C., 2003), table 2.

It was not only the shifts in historical context or the varying motives for moving that affected emigrants and shaped their sense of identity and practice of religion. The length of displacement mattered too; so the children of emigrants felt the loosening of some links with their parents' natal place, while circular migrants, who traveled seasonally to work in fields or factories, maintained persistent connections with their extended family and home church. The religious practice of those who did settle more permanently – whether or not they had intended to stay – also varied because of other factors: their homeland's historic religious practices and their new destinations' cultural landscape.

On the first factor – the sending nations' religious situation – not all countries in Latin America have the same spiritual history or show the same contemporary patterns. From the Paleolithic peopling of the Americas to the modern relocation of laborers, the influx of migrants of Asian descent brought religious diversity to Latin America, such as with the Chinese who settled in Cuba and the Japanese Buddhists who lived in Brazil. Some Jews, who had to hide their religious identity, arrived with the first colonial expeditions and in the later centuries many more followed, including those who settled in Argentina.

European and North American occult traditions, including Spiritism, circulated in the Caribbean and South America and marked ritual practice that traced its origins to Africa. Some of the African slaves who arrived between the seventeenth and nineteenth centuries had been raised as Muslims, and most nations in the region also had a religious past that included contact and exchange among indigenous traditions, African religions, and European Christianities.

Because the first colonizers came from the Iberian Peninsula, where forms of Roman Catholicism predominated, that faith marked the region's religious history. That pattern began to change in the nineteenth century as Protestant missionaries from the Global North arrived to spread the Gospel, and by the end of the twentieth century the spiritual descendants of the Reformation, especially but not only evangelicals and Pentecostals, had transformed the religious life of many nations in Latin America, just as outreach by Mormons and Jehovah's Witnesses also had its effects. According to recent surveys of religion in Latin America, Catholicism remains the dominant faith in the region, though Protestantism has gained a significant following. About 80 percent of Mexicans still describe themselves as Catholic, for example, and South Americans are more likely to maintain their allegiance to the Roman Catholic Church, though Protestants claim increasing proportions of the religious.

Protestantism has a significant presence in Puerto Rico and in Central American nations such as El Salvador, Guatemala, Honduras, and Nicaragua.

According to the Pew Research Center, those regional patterns are evident among immigrants to the United States, too. A higher proportion of Latinos identify themselves as religious and as Christian than other adults in the US population, with fewer than 8 percent reporting they are secular and fewer than 1 percent identifying with a non-Christian religion. About two-thirds (68 percent) are Catholic and one-fifth identify as Protestant. Of those Protestants, 15 percent say they are "evangelicals," a term that in Spanish (*evangélico*) generally refers to any Protestant, regardless of denomination or theological tendency.

However, slight differences emerge among immigrants. Cubans are most likely to be unchurched (14 percent). South American newcomers (71 percent) are slightly more likely to say they are Catholic than Central American emigrants (60 percent). Mexicans, who constitute about one-third of all US Catholics, remain the most loyal to their homeland's historic faith (74 percent) and are the least likely to convert to evangelical or Pentecostal churches.

On the second factor that produced variations – emigrants' US destinations – the cultural environment of the place they settled influenced how their neighbors viewed them. It also affected how they practiced their faith. It mattered whether they went to historic settlements, gateway cities, or new destinations.

Many US residents who claim Latin American heritage live in the broad sweep of terrain that arcs from southeastern Texas to northern California. Faiths from Latin America, especially Catholicism, have long roots there. Claiming Latino Catholic allegiance in Texas, New Mexico, or California is not unusual. Many residents share that identity and enjoy cultural resources to support their spiritual practice, including both historic mission churches that serve as monuments to that heritage and newer ecclesiastical centers that sponsor Spanish-language worship.

In these historic settlements that once were part of New Spain, other ethnic groups and religious traditions have competed for public power and popular approval, but Latin American immigrants during and after the twentieth century found much that was familiar there. For example, San Antonio's San Fernando Cathedral, established by migrants from the Canary Islands, has welcomed immigrants, mostly from Mexico, since its completion in 1755. Indigenous peoples settled the area long before the Europeans came and continued to be part of the cultural landscape when that parish was founded.

Over the next century the borderland town would be part of New Spain, Mexico, the Republic of Texas, and the United States. That church in San Antonio's central plaza, however, had been dedicated to the Virgin of Guadalupe, the patroness of both the municipality and the Mexican homeland, and it continued to attract predominantly ethnic Mexican devotees. In 1901, Texas-born Mexicans formed more than two-thirds of the parishioners and more than one-quarter were born in Mexico. A century later, the city's ethnically diverse Catholic population had a presence, but that historic parish continued to appeal to Spanish-speaking devotees and honor its Latin American connections. So immigrants who arrived in San Antonio in the twentieth century found a cultural landscape that had been transformed by earlier transregional migrations and enduring ethnic traditions.

Latin Americans who entered the United States through "gateway cities" such as New York, Los Angeles, and Miami had a slightly different experience, although the urban environment attracted large numbers of others from their natal country and that allowed inherited traditions to be kept alive in their adopted land. In Miami, for example, massive migrations after 1959, when Fidel Castro assumed political control in Cuba, changed the cityscape. By 1990, more than a half-million Cuban exiles constituted almost one-third of the metropolitan population, and those immigrants changed the social profile of local parishes.

In 1973, the displaced consecrated a new shrine to their homeland's national patroness, Our Lady of Charity. Many exiles who had relocated to that Florida gateway city with a large Spanish-speaking population found they could conduct most daily activities without speaking English, and at the worship space led by Cuban-born clergy and dedicated to their beloved Virgin, who had been named the island's patroness in 1916, the pilgrims primarily encountered other Cubans. Although Miami proved to be an especially hospitable social environment for exiles from Cuba, a similar pattern repeated itself with other migrant groups who entered America's gateway cities, where recently established ethnic institutions appealed to religious symbols and practices the Latin American migrants recognized.

Immigrants also settled in new destinations, including rural areas, small towns, and suburbs. Especially since the 1990s, Latin American newcomers made their way to places in the South that were not historically home to Latino populations, including sprawling suburbs in Georgia and small towns in North Carolina. Consider two North Carolina towns with little history of immigration and long-standing mainline Protestant predominance. Clinton, a small town in eastern North Carolina, began to see some immigrants during the 1990s. The newcomers who were counted in the federal census made up only about 5 percent of the almost 9,000 local residents in 2000, and many of those immigrants, most of them from Mexico and Central America, attended the local Roman Catholic parish, Immaculate Conception, or the Latino Pentecostal church, Templo De Dios Pentecostés.

As in some other small towns and rural areas, Latinos remained a visible minority. In some "new destinations" the transnational flows produced larger ethnic enclaves, however, though newcomers still struggled to find their place in towns that had little experience with immigrants, especially those who spoke Spanish and came from Latin America. During the 1990s, for example, immigrants transformed Siler City, North Carolina. Most of that small town's residents had been native-born European Americans and African Americans who worshiped in Baptist and Methodist congregations. During that decade, however, migrants who worked in the nearby poultry plants swelled the Latino population. By the turn of the twenty-first century they constituted at least 40 percent of the local residents, and their children formed a majority in the public school classrooms.

In these new destinations, where there were fewer Latino migrants and fewer historic connections to Latin America, hostility from the native-born population often was greater than in historic settlements and gateway cities, as in 2000, when the racist Ku Klux Klan held a well-publicized rally to protest Siler City's new residents. In that town, and other new destinations, the pressures to acculturate could be intense. Some responded by reaffirming their natal piety and attending the local Catholic church, St. Julia's, yet other migrants adapted more fully to local practice by worshipping in Spanish-speaking congregations associated with Siler City's traditional mainline Protestant churches, such as the Baptist congregation Iglesia Hispana Ebenezer.

Commonalities in Emigration Patterns and Religious Practice

Despite emigrants' multiple destinations, varying motives, and distinct histories, Latino religious practice also has shown some commonalities. Public opinion surveys identify two major patterns. First, Latinos' religious practice is distinctively ethnic. Whether they are recent migrants or not, two-thirds of Latino worshippers attend Spanish-speaking churches with Latino clerical leaders and predominantly Latino congregations. Second, they are more likely to emphasize the "spirit-filled" piety of Charismatic and Pentecostal movements: more than half of Latino Catholics identify themselves as

Charismatics, a much higher proportion than among US Catholics in general, and half of Latino Protestants identify with worship practices that encourage personal religious experience and highlight the Holy Spirit's miraculous intervention. Yet Catholicism shapes Protestant practice just as Protestantism shapes Catholic practice. Latino piety often shows the lingering traces of Roman Catholic heritage. A large proportion of those with Latin American connections report that religious statues adorn their home, for example, and three quarters of Latinos – including 35 percent of evangelicals and 43 percent of mainline Protestants – believe that the Virgin Mary watches over believers, a much higher proportion than among non-Latino Protestants in the United States. Immigrants and their descendants carried some common doctrines and shared practices with them from their homelands.

Latino evangelicals often emphasized US patriotism and prized American acculturation, but much of Latino material culture and ritual practice – among both Protestants and Catholics in all three destination sites – established links with the homeland's history and geography. Their piety, in other words, was *transtemporal* and *translocative*, propelling devotees back and forth between their ancestors' home and their adopted land.

Worship services at Templo de Dios Pentecostés, the North Carolina Pentecostal congregation, included live music that recalls the instruments and rhythms of the Mexican migrants' rural hometowns, and on Our Lady of Guadalupe's feast day, Clinton's Latino Catholics processed through the heart of that southern Protestant town, striding slowing behind a pick-up truck carrying a large of statue of their familiar national patroness who has been linked with Mexican collective identity for centuries. Devotees in the ethnic parish in San Antonio, a historic settlement for immigrants from Latin America, also celebrated Our Lady of Guadalupe's feast day in public processions, as they have since the founding of that congregation. Processions sponsored by Siler City's Catholic congregation, St. Julia's, recalled other times and places – and other devotional practices – by replicating Good Friday celebrations in the migrants' distant hometowns. In some years, before the event drew too much media attention and sparked too much anti-immigrant sentiment, those ceremonies claimed Clinton's main streets and included a male parishioner reenacting Jesus's carrying of the cross and shedding of blood, a familiar sight for many of the migrants in the procession or lining the route.

In the gateway city of Miami, Latino devotees also bridged distance and duration with familiar symbols and practices. They celebrated their national patroness' feast day, when thousands of exiles gathered in large arenas and stadiums, far from the gaze of most Anglo residents in that multiethnic urban center. The Virgin of Charity, who traditionally was associated with water, usually arrived by boat to the festivities.

At the feast day rosary and mass, the Cuban community used artifacts, narratives, and ritual to transport themselves back in time and across the miles that separate them from their natal land. They flew the Cuban flag, sang the Cuban national anthem, and recounted the history of the Virgin, whose image soldiers had sewn on their uniforms during the nineteenth-century battles for independence. The feast day rosary usually was interrupted by shouts from the large crowd, which expressed the shared hope that the patroness might return them to homeland and restore democracy on the island.

Like other emigrants who settled in gateway cities, historic territories, and new destinations, those Cuban Catholics drew on transtemporal and translocative practices that transported them in time and space. The global flows that carried them to South Florida did not stop after they arrived, however, and during the twenty-first century people, artifacts, and practices continued to circulate between Latin America and the United States. As in earlier decades, the flows have surged and receded, as varying forces have had their effects. The piety of the displaced also continued to retain the distinctive marks of emigrants' varied homelands. At the same time, many emigrants and their descendants continued to gather in ethnic congregations, prefer spirit-filled worship, and affirm some elements of their shared Catholic heritage – whether or not they converted to Protestantism. In all these ways, their religious practice not only connected them to their Latin American homelands but also continued to distinguish them from other worshipers in the United States.

Bibliography and Suggested Readings

Badillo, David. *Latinos and the New Immigrant Church*. Baltimore: Johns Hopkins University Press, 2006.
Consejo Nacional de Población, available at www.conapo.gob.mx (Accessed January 8, 2016).
Latinobarómetro: Opinion Pública Latinomericana, available at www.latinobarometro.org (Accessed January 8, 2016).
Matovina, Timothy. *Guadalupe and Her Faithful: Latino Catholics in San Antonio, from Colonial Origins to the Present*. Baltimore: Johns Hopkins University Press, 2005.
  Latino Catholicism: Transformation in America's Largest Church. Princeton: Princeton University, 2011.
Pew Research Center. 2007. *Changing Faiths: Latinos and the Transformation of American Religion*. Washington, DC: Pew Forum on Religion and Public Life and the Pew Hispanic Center, http://pewhispanic.org.

Pew Research Center: Hispanic Trends. 2008. *Statistical Portrait of Hispanics in the United States, 2008.* Washington, DC: Pew Hispanic Center, http://pewhispanic.org/.

Seales, Chad E. *The Secular Spectacle: Performing Religion in a Southern Town.* New York: Oxford University Press, 2013.

Statistics Canada/Statisque Canada. 2007. *Immigration in Canada: A Portrait of the Foreign-Born Population, 2006 Census.* Catalogue no. 97-557-XIE. Ottawa, Canada: Statistics Canada.

Tweed, Thomas A. *Our Lady of the Exile: Diasporic Religion at a Cuban Catholic Shrine in Miami.* New York and Oxford: Oxford University Press, 1997.

——— "Our Lady of Guadalupe Visits the Confederate Memorial." *Southern Cultures,* 2002 (Summer): 72–93.

US Immigration and Naturalization Service. 2001. *Statistical Yearbook of the Immigration and Naturalization Service.* Washington, DC: US Government Printing Office.

Vásquez, Manuel A., and Marie Friedmann Marquardt. *Globalizing the Sacred: Religion Across the Americas.* New Brunswick, NJ: Rutgers University Press, 2003.

Williams, Philip, Timothy Steigenga, and Manuel A. Vásquez. *A Place to Be: Brazilian, Guatemalan, and Mexican Immigrants in Florida's New Destinations.* New Brunswick, NJ: Rutgers University Press, 2009.

43

Neither Catholics nor Protestants: Mormons, Jehovah's Witnesses, Adventists, and La Luz del Mundo

PATRICIA FORTUNY AND HENRI GOOREN

Mormonism, Adventism, and Jehovah's Witnesses are the three great North American religions of the nineteenth century. Their missionary zeal led to extensive proselytizing efforts, first in the United States and soon abroad. Adventist and Witness missionaries arrived in Latin American countries in the late 1890s, and Mormon missionaries began efforts in the mid-twentieth century. Hence, these religions currently have a greater proportion of their total world membership living in the region than Mormonism. All three churches have experienced strong membership growth in Latin America, which we analyze here together with two case studies: Guatemala and Mexico. As yet, no literature exists that explicitly compares the three religions in the region.

Latter-day Saints (LDS), Seventh-day Adventists (SDA), and Jehovah's Witnesses (JW) consider themselves Christians, although most Christian churches would disagree. At best, they are described by conventional Christians as "Christian cults" or "marginal Christians," although the Adventists consider themselves Protestants and are increasingly accepted as such in Latin America and elsewhere. Their shared origin in the nineteenth-century United States, their bold theological innovations, and their strong growth in Latin America justify their inclusion in one chapter. We use case studies from Guatemala and Mexico to illustrate the impact of these groups.

Iglesia La Luz del Mundo (The Light of the World Church) is a religious movement that was founded in Mexico but is rapidly becoming a global church. Just like Mormonism, Adventism, and Jehovah's Witnesses, La Luz del Mundo claims to be the restoration of the primitive Christian church of Jesus Christ in modern times and is experiencing strong growth in the United States and Latin America.

Latter-day Saints (Mormons)

The Church of Jesus Christ of Latter-day Saints – usually called LDS or the Mormon Church – was formally founded in 1830 by young prophet Joseph Smith in Fayette, New York. Following his "First Vision," Smith claimed to receive plates of gold from an angel, which he subsequently translated with divine help into the Book of Mormon.

Essential LDS doctrines are the inevitability of Adam's fall in the development of humanity and God's plan of salvation for people through Christ's atonement. To achieve salvation, human beings must have faith in Christ, show repentance for their sins, be baptized by full immersion in water by an elder, and be active in the LDS Church. This means going to church on Sunday, obeying the biblical Commandments and the "Word of Wisdom," paying their tithes, and leading a righteous life.

Several Mormon doctrines and practices are controversial. Other Christian churches reject the prophetic claims of Joseph Smith, the additions to the Scriptures, the "Work for the Dead," and especially the belief (called *exaltation*) that the ultimate purpose of humans is to become like God. Until 1890, when it was outlawed by the church, the practice of polygamy made the Mormon Church extremely controversial. Since the 1950s, LDS leaders have made a deliberate effort to move the LDS Church closer to US mainstream society, but without compromising its unique doctrines and organization.

The LDS Church boasts a strongly hierarchical organization. At the apex stands the church president with his two counselors. They comprise the First Presidency, which is chosen from the Quorum of the Twelve Apostles. This body is "equal in authority and power" to the First Presidency. Together, these fifteen men are called "prophets, seers, and revelators," capable of receiving direct prophecies from God. They delegate part of their responsibilities to the Quorum of the Seventy and the Area Representatives. The LDS geographical "areas" are divided administratively into *stakes* (provinces), *wards* (congregations), *missions* (mission provinces), and *branches* (mission congregations).

A ward is directed by a *bishop* and his two counselors. They supervise the functioning and organization of the age quorums, oversee the assignment of *callings*, and take care of the membership administration. The bishop makes frequent house calls, which he coordinates with the adult priesthood quorum. All LDS men are involved in the priesthood, which consists of two groups. The lower, Aaronic priesthood (males aged twelve to seventeen years) prepares and distributes the sacrament. The Melchizedek priesthood, organized in the Quorum of Elders, consists of men older than eighteen and holds "the keys of all spiritual blessings of the church." There are also quorums for women (the Relief Society) and children. All groups work together with the LDS missionaries, who are men between nineteen and twenty-one years old or women between twenty-one and twenty-three years old. The missionaries work full time on bringing new members into the LDS Church. One area where they have been extremely successful is Latin America, home to 38 percent of the LDS's total worldwide membership.

Between 1960 and 2007, the total contribution of all nineteen countries in Latin America to the worldwide LDS membership increased from 2 percent to 38 percent, while the US proportion declined from 90 percent in 1960 to 45 percent by 2007. If current growth rates continue, the majority of Mormons will be Latin Americans by 2020.

The LDS membership explosion in the region happened only in the last twenty to forty years. Although there were early missions to Mexico (1876), Argentina (1925), and Brazil (1928), the Mormon Church arrived in five countries in the 1940s, four countries in the 1950s, and five more countries in the 1960s. The most recent LDS mission opened in the Dominican Republic in 1978.

A basic indicator of Mormon growth is the officially registered LDS membership as a percentage of the total population for each country. By this standard, Chile (3.3 percent), Uruguay (2.7 percent), and Honduras (1.77 percent) are the most heavily Mormon countries of Latin America, while Venezuela (0.53 percent), Puerto Rico (0.5 percent), and Colombia (0.36 percent) are the *least* Mormon ones.

In 2006–2007, LDS membership growth stagnated at 1 to 3 percent annually – comparable to population growth – in thirteen countries. LDS growth in most Latin American countries started to slow down after 2000 for three main reasons. First, most people who might be interested in joining the church had probably heard the Mormon message by now. Second, the number of missionaries declined in some countries. Third and most important, "missionaries began to concentrate on reactivation and retention, and the number of baptisms fell."[1]

However, LDS membership growth in 2006 and 2007 was still strong in a second group of Latin American countries: the Dominican Republic, Honduras, Brazil, Paraguay, and especially Nicaragua. The average annual growth rates

---

1 Mark L. Grover, "The Maturing of the Oak: The Dynamics of LDS Growth in Latin America," *Dialogue: A Journal of Mormon Thought*, 38, no. 2 (2005): 88.

for these five countries ranged from 4 percent in the Dominican Republic to more than 8 percent in Nicaragua. To explain why growth persists there would require a country-by-country analysis.

The typical LDS convert in Latin America is a young (fifteen to twenty-five years), urban woman of upper lower class or lower middle-class origins. She is attracted to Mormonism because of its smooth organization radiating success and middle-class values, its strict code of conduct, its practical teachings, its doctrines and spirituality, its style of worship and hymns, and its lay priesthood for men. Some new members explicitly reported being dissatisfied with Catholicism. Most people are recruited through their own social networks (LDS friends and relatives) or through the huge missionary force. When asked about main attraction factors, Guatemalan Mormons mentioned its strict code of conduct, learning new things in church, feeling the joy of God's love, being blessed with miracles, and receiving support from fellow members.

However, LDS retention rates are low, 20 to 30 percent, all over Latin America. The typical LDS dropout in Latin America is an urban man of upper-lower class or lower-middle class origins. Studies by the LDS Church showed that 80 percent of all inactivity had its origin in the first two months after baptism. For some new converts, receiving a "calling" helped them become integrated in the ward organization. But for others, performing in a calling was a pressure they were unable to deal with, and so they dropped out. Other important factors influencing retention were the time and money demands the church made and backsliding into alcohol problems. Inactivity was often related to bad experiences with leaders and members who would rarely devote time to them and often ignored them entirely. All in all, at least half of all new Mormon members in Latin America became inactive within a year.

Statistics from Guatemala offer a detailed example of these changes in conversion and recidivism over time. According to the membership on record, more than 1.5 percent of the Guatemalan population has been baptized into the Mormon Church. We can distinguish five main LDS growth periods in Guatemala's Average Annual Growth Rate (AAGR) of 12.6 percent between 1949 and 2007.

The first period, running from 1949 to 1956 was characterized by high growth rates averaging 27 percent per year. In 1949, the LDS Church had been in Guatemala for one year, and there were exactly forty-eight baptized members. Seven years later, the number of members was 250. The LDS Church had a foreign origin and a doctrine and ethic that were very different from those of the majority religion of Roman Catholicism. The LDS Central American

Mission was not officially founded until 1952. In that year, there were only twelve full-time missionaries, who were mainly working in Guatemala City and other major cities.

The second period, from 1956 to 1966, was a booming era in which growth averaged 42 percent per year as the number of registered members increased sharply from 250 to almost 10,000. Dissatisfaction with Catholicism led many to desert to Protestantism and Mormonism. The number of LDS missionaries steadily increased, and after 1955 they were much better prepared for their proselytizing. The LDS Church thoroughly revised its worldwide missionary program and required missionaries to use six standardized lessons (nowadays called "discussions") to teach people all over the world the same basic principles of Mormonism. Meanwhile, the urbanization process was in full swing. Guatemala City grew by an average annual rate of about 7 percent from 1950 to 1964. For the Mormons (and the Pentecostals), these new city dwellers formed an easily accessible reservoir for recruitment.

From 1966 to 1978, Mormonism entered its third period, which was characterized by stagnation. In May 1967, Guatemala City became the first Central American stake. Yet the average annual growth rate for 1967 to 1978 was only 1 percent. Essentially, LDS Church growth was stagnating and even turned negative in 1972, 1974, and 1976. Pentecostal churches boomed during this time, in part because their leaders were almost all Guatemalans whereas in the LDS Church all important leadership positions were occupied by North Americans. An economic boom might have decreased the demand for religion, the urban growth rate slowed, and LDS missionaries were withdrawn for security reasons during the country's internal armed conflict between the army and the guerrillas – also affecting growth negatively.

The fourth period, from 1978 to 1990, was again characterized by high growth. From 1978 to 1982, the average annual growth rate was 12 percent, but from 1982 to 1990 it was an amazing 24 percent. The real LDS boom years in Guatemala were 1984 (44 percent) and 1988 (36 percent). Guatemalans were facing a severe economic crisis, rising poverty, an intensification of the war and political violence, political instability, and general turmoil. Meanwhile, more Guatemalans than ever before came into contact with the LDS Church. The full-time LDS missionary force had increased enormously to about 320 in 1985. A great many converts were baptized within two to six weeks after their first meeting with the missionaries. Competition for members with Catholicism and Pentecostalism remained intense in the 1980s, but Pentecostal growth went down after the bloody dictatorship of General Efraín Ríos Montt (1982–1983).

The LDS Church experienced its recent boom exactly in 1988–1990, when Pentecostal growth was already waning.

From 1990 until 2007, Mormonism experienced a fifth period, this one marked by low growth. After the 1980s boom, growth rates decreased sharply and rapidly. The average annual growth rate for the entire 1990 to 2007 period was 3 percent: comparable to population growth, but not representing any net expansion in membership. What happened? The LDS missionary effort had only expanded more, with 590 missionaries present in late 1993, 25 percent Latin Americans and 75 percent North Americans. However, the reservoir of dissatisfied Catholics was probably running low by this point; the Guatemalan economy slowly began to recover; and the 1996 Peace Accords ended the war and significantly reduced political violence. Democracy in Guatemala was strengthened, although crime rates remained very high and political stability elusive.

As in Guatemala, growth was typically high in the early years of Mormonism across the region, but this growth was soon followed by periods of stagnation and low growth. The 1980s also saw high growth in Guatemala from 1982 to 1990, but low growth (3 percent) after 1990. After 2000, the average annual growth rates decreased even more as a result of the new mission policy stressing retention and reactivation of members over recruitment (see earlier). The average annual growth rate after 2000 in Guatemala was 2.7 percent.

The main factors to explain the 1960s boom periods were the novelty of the religious innovation of Mormonism appealing to people dissatisfied with Catholicism, which coincided with the takeoff of the urbanization process and the reorganization of the LDS mission guidelines for the full-time missionary force. The 1980s boom is more difficult to account for. The first main factor was the intensification of political violence in Guatemala from 1980 to 1983. LDS growth rates went up a few years later. This delay was probably related to the waning of the earlier Pentecostal boom. Other main factors were the well-documented expansion of the size of the LDS missionary force in the 1980s and the global economic crisis, starting in the early 1980s. It seems we follow a crude form of deprivation theory here, which assumes that people will turn more to religion when they face stress and political persecution or when coping with poverty and economic uncertainty.

But how do we explain why people in Guatemala turned specifically to Mormonism instead of Pentecostalism – or Catholicism? I mentioned earlier that Guatemalans were attracted to Mormonism for six main factors connected to its organization and lay priesthood, its style of worship, being blessed with miracles, its strict code of conduct, its practical teachings, and receiving support from fellow members. The last three factors are not unique to Mormonism; Pentecostalism and Adventism also stress a strict code of conduct, practical teachings, and support from members.

We need to study in-depth, through ethnographic methods, how and why the three uniquely Mormon attraction factors work for people in Latin America. What are the unique features of the LDS organization and its lay priesthood? What specific miracles and blessings do active Mormons report? How do Mormons receive concrete support from their fellow Mormons? When they *don't* receive the support they need, they seem quick to drop out of Mormonism altogether. That may be the main explanation for the low LDS retention rates all over Latin America.

Seventh-day Adventists

The Seventh-day Adventist Church, organized in 1863, traces its origin to the "Great Disappointment" of 1844, when Jesus Christ did not return to Earth as was predicted by William Miller, a popular Baptist revival preacher of the period. Adventists were one of a number of groups who emerged from this "disappointment" and reinterpreted Miller's date as a heavenly event that marked the beginning of a new era rather than the return of Christ to Earth. This new era required believers to follow biblical regulations long neglected by Christians including the observation of the Jewish Sabbath, a practice that gave the new church its name. Sociologist Ronald Lawson argues that until the mid-twentieth century, Adventism was a religion that existed in tension with mainstream culture in the United States because of its restrictions on everything from drinking coffee to reading fiction, its expectation of the imminent return of Christ, and its belief that other groups were apostate. Lawson argued that this tension decreased after World War II because of Adventists' successful medical and educational institutions as well as their intentional improvement of relations with both governmental authorities and other Christian groups.

By 2008, the Adventist *Yearbook* highlighted twenty-eight key doctrines, but only five of these could be considered remotely controversial. The Seventh-Day Adventist Church is described as "the body of Christ, a community of faith of which Christ Himself is the Head." The Sabbath is declared as a fundamental commandment, but not explicitly defined as being on Saturday (although that is still the understanding). Under "Christian Behavior," it states: "While recognizing cultural differences, our dress is to be simple, modest, and neat." Adventists are to abstain from "alcoholic beverages, tobacco, and the irresponsible use of drugs and narcotics." Finally, divorce is prohibited implicitly but not explicitly.[2]

This transition occurred because Adventist leaders consciously sought to decrease tension with mainstream society, eventually leading to a "marked relaxation of tension with governments, other churches, and societies in general" all over the world – including Latin America.[3] Lawson concluded, "Seventh-day Adventists have shown considerable willingness to compromise their positions whenever external threat or opportunities to gain acceptance have made this auspicious. Their expediency is correlated with their greater ideological diversity and organizational openness and their diminishing concern for indoctrinating converts. These flowed from their experience of upward social mobility, which led them to relax the urgency of their apocalyptic[ism] and to claim an increasing stake in society."[4]

Together with Africa, Latin America is the main membership growth area for Adventism. The contribution of Latin American countries to the worldwide membership increased from 20.3 percent in 1960 to 34.7 percent in 2008, while the US membership proportion declined from 26.7 percent in 1960 to 6.4 percent by 2007.

The Seven-Day Adventist Church has been present in most Latin American countries for at least a century, as the earliest independent SDA missionaries in ten countries arrived between 1887 and 1898. The first official SDA mission in Latin America opened in Argentina in 1894. In the early twentieth century, Adventist missionaries arrived in six countries before 1910 and another three countries in the 1920s.

The result of this early, gradual SDA missionary expansion into Latin America was a highly uneven growth distribution. The simplest indicator is to look again at the officially registered SDA membership as a percentage of the total population for each country. By this standard, Peru (2.76 percent), Honduras (2.67 percent), the Dominican Republic (2.58 percent), El Salvador (2.46 percent), and Panama (2.44 percent) are the most heavily Adventist countries of Latin America, while Argentina (0.25 percent), Paraguay (0.22 percent), and especially Uruguay (0.21 percent) are the *least* Adventist ones.

---

2 General Conference of Seventh-day Adventists, *Seventh-Day Adventist Yearbook 2008* (Hagerstown, MD: Review and Herald Publishing Association, 2008), 5–8.
3 Ronald Lawson, "Sect-State Relations: Accounting for the Differing Trajectories of Seventh-Day Adventists and Jehovah's Witnesses," *Sociology of Religion*, 56, no. 4 (1995): 362. Thanks to Ron Lawson for collecting and sharing Seventh-day Adventist data and for commenting extensively on the entire article.
4 Lawson, "Sect-State Relations," 375.

Another way to analyze the SDA presence in Latin America is by looking at the most recent SDA annual membership growth rate for each country. After four decades of high growth, SDA growth in Latin America seems to be slowing down in only a few countries. As a result of cleaning the rosters, an actual SDA membership decrease occurred in four countries in 2006–2007: Peru (–0.21 percent), Uruguay (–0.96 percent), Chile (–2.68 percent), and Brazil (–3.66 percent). SDA membership growth stagnated at 1 to 3 percent annually – comparable to population growth – in two countries: Costa Rica (1.74 percent) and Puerto Rico (2.57 percent).

However, SDA membership growth in 2006–2007 was still going strong in the third and largest group of Latin American countries: Mexico, Colombia, Argentina, the Dominican Republic, Paraguay, Panama, Guatemala, Bolivia, Honduras, Ecuador, Venezuela, Nicaragua, and especially El Salvador. The average annual growth rates for these thirteen countries ranged from almost 4 percent in Mexico to almost 14 percent in El Salvador. All six Central American countries are represented in this group.

For 2006, the SDA Church reported a general worldwide retention rate of 76 percent in the first year of membership. In the United States, 73 percent of people raised as Adventists remained in that church as adults in 2001; by 2008 this percentage had decreased to 60 percent. No information is available for SDA retention rates in Latin America as a whole or on specific Latin America countries.

Guatemala again provides a specific case for examining Adventist growth rates. Adventism in Guatemala has had considerable success in membership growth, reaching a population percentage of almost 1.5 percent in 2007. Based on the data in Seventh-day Adventist Statistics (2008), we can distinguish eight main SDA growth periods in Guatemala since the middle of the twentieth century, although it should be noted that Adventist missionaries first arrived in the country in 1908 and opened a formal mission in 1913.

SDA membership growth in Guatemala has been relatively remarkably constant, possibly because there is no fluctuating missionary force as in the LDS Church, registering an average annual growth rate for the entire 1948 to 2007 period of 9.1 percent. In the first period from 1948 to 1960, SDA growth was low, averaging 7.7 percent per year. A second period from 1960 to 1965, however, saw a boom as the number of registered members increased from 2,893 to 5,285, reflecting an average annual growth rate of almost 13 percent. As with Mormonism, this was driven in part by urbanization.

In the third period, from 1966 to 1973, and the fourth period, from 1974 to 1978, growth was around 8 percent and 12 percent per year, respectively.

This was due, in part, to the fact that Adventists in Guatemala followed the church's regional trend of seeking religious protections and favors such as permits to open schools by recognizing military regimes. This recognition of military regimes seemed to encourage growth in the 1970s and 1980s, although it may have become a factor in the slowing down of SDA membership growth after 1990. The peak years of growth in the 1970s coincide with the demographic boom of Pentecostalism in the country following Guatemala's 1976 earthquake.

The fifth period from 1979 to 1981 saw a negative growth rate, –2 percent, during a period of increased economic crisis and rising poverty, but in the sixth period from 1981 to 1985, growth returned to a near-average 9.3 percent per year. Growth again peaked in the seventh period from 1986 to 1989, when it averaged 14 percent, and in the final period after 1990, growth rates decreased sharply and rapidly, although they still remained relatively high compared to other religions at 8.7 percent. By 2003, there were 343 SDA churches in Guatemala, and in 2007, Adventist membership in Guatemala stood at 123,412.

The similarities in growth patterns for both Mormons and Adventists in Guatemala until 1990 perhaps evince a partial confirmation of deprivation theory and even modernization theory. In the period of early industrialization and high urbanization, the 1950s and 1960s, both Mormons and Adventists grew strongly all over Latin America. After the 1973 oil crisis, Mormon growth went down, whereas Adventist growth remained high until 1979. SDA growth remained average afterwards, while Mormon growth peaked. The main factor here seemed to be the growth of the fulltime LDS missionary force, which proved to be an important factor to explain LDS expansion in Latin America – although not necessarily the main factor.

Mormon growth periods generally follow Pentecostal growth periods chronologically, but Adventist growth often coincided with Pentecostal membership expansion. LDS missionaries after 2000 focused more on retention than on recruitment, which explained the lower Mormon growth rates all over Latin America in recent years. Mormonism has retention rates of 20 to 30 percent in Latin America, whereas Adventism has a global retention rate of 76 percent and US retention rates of 60 to 71 percent. Further study of these and other differences is necessary to better analyze and understand both the differences and the similarities between LDS and SDA growth patterns – whether in Latin America or elsewhere.

Jehovah's Witnesses

The Jehovah's Witnesses (JW) religious organization was founded in 1879 by Charles Taze Russell, who was born in Pittsburgh, Pennsylvania in 1852 and raised as a Presbyterian by his profoundly religious parents. Russell began to gather followers around his beliefs that everyone who obeyed Jehovah would be saved and that the principal aim of all creation is to defend the name and word of Jehovah. This group was named "Jehovah's Witnesses" in 1930 under the presidency of Joseph Franklin Rutherford. JW were controversial from the beginning because of their heterodoxy relative to traditional Christian beliefs. They deny the Trinity, the divinity of Christ, the immortality of the soul, and the torments of hell. Moreover, they are pacifists and antinationalists who condemn both states and ecclesiastical organizations. Especially influenced by Adventism, Russell renovated ideas on millenarianism and reinterpreted the *Book of Revelation* within a more radical view.

Until 1950, the majority of Witnesses were found in English-speaking countries and in the majority Protestant countries of northern Europe. After 1950, this tendency changed, and the growth of Witnesses became greater in the Catholic countries of Europe, Latin America and Africa, and in the Philippines. The figures reflected this change. While in 1950, 75 percent of all members lived in Protestant countries, that figure had dropped to 50 percent by 1981. In the 1980s, more than 40 percent of the global number of Witnesses members lived in countries with Catholic majorities. In 2007, the JW organization counted almost 18 million attending members in 236 countries.

The JW are a religious group that offers matter-of-fact answers to life without demanding any political commitment from its faithful. In countries such as Mexico, where social and political uncertainties prevail, a religion like this is especially attractive to many people. The JW offer concrete answers to solve immediate, practical problems including dress, childbearing, marital relations, determining appropriate secular activities, and selecting sanctioned attitudes in a society with ambivalent values toward women. Indeed, it regulates precisely what position believers should take with respect to the economic domain. That is, the JW provide members with a total set of ethical and aesthetic codes, a system of order. Bryan Wilson emphasized the pragmatic and rational side of the JW by commenting, "The teachings are clear and unequivocal, and uniformly understood among all informed participants."[5] The JW

---

[5] Bryan Wilson, "Aspects of Kinship and the Rise of Jehovah's Witnesses in Japan," *Social Compass*, 24, no. 1 (1977): 104.

organization is authoritarian and patriarchal par excellence, but these characteristics translate into positive features for the members because they find protection and certainty in the church, factors absent from society at large. In the JW organization there is no tithing; resources are acquired through the sale of literature bought by the faithful and the public in general. The JW have succeeded in developing a sophisticated publishing empire with headquarters in Brooklyn, New York, and also established publishing houses in many other countries.

JW missionaries arrived in nine Latin American countries in the 1920s, and seven more in the 1930s, and encountered varying levels of success in terms of membership growth. The simplest indicator is to look at the officially reported JW memorial service attendance for 2007 as a percentage of the total population for each country. By this measure, Mexico (1.81 percent), Ecuador (1.62 percent), El Salvador (1.52 percent), Puerto Rico (1.51 percent), and Nicaragua (1.44 percent) are the countries of Latin America where the JW have had most success. On the other hand, Honduras (0.7 percent), Bolivia (0.63 percent), Guatemala (0.55 percent), and Paraguay (0.27 percent) are the countries where the JW have encountered least success. Based on memorial attendance, Latin America is home to 34 percent of the total worldwide JW membership of 6 million members.

Mexico offers a detailed look at the expansion of JW during the past century. The JW began evangelizing in Mexico in 1893. However, religious minorities did not increase rapidly in the country relative to the Catholic Church until the 1950s. It was during the subsequent decades that the country experienced important economic and social changes that not only created a certain degree of modernity but also brought with them some of the consequences of modern life such as secularization, which provided social space for the expansion of religious pluralism. Since the 1970s, large sectors of the population have abandoned Catholicism and converted to new forms of religion. In 1986, Mexico was the country with the second largest population of JW in the world after the United States. During the 1980s, membership continued to increase at an annual growth rate of 16 percent. This growth rate decreased in the 1990s, although the JW in Mexico remained the second largest national JW population in the world. Memorial attendance in Mexico was 619,564 in 1983, and by 2007 it was 1,931,041.

In contrast to the 1990s growth rates, the JW in Mexico are currently experiencing a severe stagnation in numbers. The available figures for 2003 give an annual increase of only 1 percent. Despite their slow growth, the JW have been able to expand into 90 percent of the municipalities of the country.

Around 15 percent of the total membership is concentrated in cities such as Mexico City, Tijuana, Ciudad Juárez, Puebla, Mérida, Culiacán, Monterrey, Tuxtla Gutiérrez, and Guadalajara, but the JW in Mexico are not predominantly urban. Most members can be found in small towns with indigenous populations, particularly in the south of the country.

La Luz del Mundo

Not all Christian churches that lay outside of both Protestant and Catholic orthodoxy are an imported faith. Iglesia La Luz del Mundo (The Light of the World Church) is a religious movement that began in Mexico and has become a global church that claims to be "the restoration of the primitive Christian church of Jesus Christ" in modern times. Its international headquarters are located in Guadalajara, Jalisco, at the very heart of the most traditional Catholic region of Mexico. Though Catholics are still the largest contingent of believers, with 89 percent of the total population nationally, they are not distributed evenly across the country. In the southern states, around 30 percent of the people claim to belong to a Christian religion other than Catholicism, while in the western and central region of the country, including around Jalisco, non-Catholics account for fewer than 2 percent of the population.

At present, Iglesia La Luz del Mundo is the second largest religious body in Mexico after the Roman Catholic Church, with approximately 1.5 million adherents claimed nationally. According to the official data of the church, it has grown worldwide to at least 5 million believers. Its international headquarters are situated in the far east of the city of Guadalajara in an area called *Hermosa Provincia* (Beautiful Province). Members from other Latin American countries and the United States return every August to attend the *Santa Cena* (Holy Supper) at *Hermosa Provincia*, in the same way that thousands of Catholics return to their towns to attend their rituals of the *Santo Patrón*.

Aaron Joaquín González, a man of peasant origins, founded the church in the late 1920s. After the Mexican Revolution (1910–1920) and during the Great Depression, many poor Mexican migrants left the United States and then returned to Mexico. Aaron recruited his first followers from among such poor, displaced people. The rise of the Luz del Mundo movement also coincided with a expansion of Pentecostalism in the United States, which in turn was exported to Mexico via returning migrants. Aaron died in 1964 and his son, Samuel Joaquín Flores, succeeded him as head of the church.

Luz del Mundo draws on Pentecostal theology – especially through an emphasis on prophecy – and also on local culture in defining its belief system.

Luz del Mundo followers consider themselves Christians who follow the Bible and believe that Jesus Christ is the savior of humanity. However, for them Jesus is only a prophet, not a god. The church has also appropriated some symbols from the Jewish tradition. For example, members see themselves as the "chosen people" and call outsiders "gentiles." According to Luz del Mundo beliefs, God elected the apostles Aaron and Samuel to keep His church alive in the modern world. The highest authority of the religious community is embedded in the dual nature of Samuel Joaquín Flores; within the sacred sphere he is considered "the Apostle," and in the profane sphere, he is the international president of Iglesia Luz del Mundo.

Women are excluded from priesthood, which is composed of bishops, pastors, deacons, and *encargados* (persons in charge of congregations), all of whom are anointed in a special ceremony. Although the subordination of women in the church does not differ greatly from the position that the system of male domination has assigned them in Latin American societies as a whole, its doctrine provides a religious framework that legitimizes subordination. However, many educated women in the Luz del Mundo have become the main cultural brokers between their church and the world. Despite the fact that they cannot achieve official posts within the church, because of their high level of education, many female members represent the religious community and dialogue with the outside world as journalists, academics, and professionals.

Luz del Mundo also adopted a missionary outlook early in its history. Founder Aaron Joaquín González initiated missionary work beyond Mexico's borders in the mid-1950s when he visited Los Angeles. In the early 1960s, he also traveled to San Antonio, Texas to evangelize. Geographical proximity between Jalisco and Texas can only partly explain this choice; migration of Mexicans from the western states to the United States had been a traditional pattern since the nineteenth century. To spread its doctrine into foreign countries, the church takes advantage of members living outside of Mexico, and automatically those believers become missionaries wherever they are, as has happened not only in the United States, but also in such countries as Great Britain, Spain, France, Italy, Australia and many others.

Today, La Luz del Mundo has opened congregations and missions in at least nineteen US states and in Washington, DC. California and Texas not only have the highest rate of Mexican immigrants but also the highest numbers of Luz del Mundo believers. California has at least thirty congregations plus its missions, while Texas has nineteen congregations plus their corresponding missions. According to official sources there are around seventy-five established congregations plus some 150 missions. Altogether, these numbers give us a conservative estimate of almost 50,000 believers in the United States.

In the United States context, Luz del Mundo functions as an "ethnic church" because it is composed of mainly Mexican immigrants and a very small percentage of Central American people, mostly from El Salvador. It plays the role of an ethnic enclave as it encourages the believers to speak, read, and sing in their native language, Spanish, therefore reinforcing national cultural ties amongst its members, much as Spanish-language masses do for immigrant Catholics. Through its multiple activities such as the everyday religious services and gatherings, but above all the annual *Santa Cena* (Holy Supper) at Hermosa Provincia, the church provides the ideal social space for second-generation migrants to both maintain and improve their native language. This is possible to some extent thanks to the ministers or spiritual leaders, all of whom are of Latin American – and normally Mexican – origin. In this respect, outside of Mexico Luz del Mundo functions not so much as a missionary church as a diasporic one.

James Clifford has described the discourse of diaspora as the voice of "displaced peoples who feel (maintain, revive, invent) a connection with a prior home."[6] Luz del Mundo migrant believers participate in this diasporic discourse by claiming the right to return to a "mythical homeland," represented by Hermosa Provincia. They share a history of dispersal and are often alienated from social and economic systems in the receiving country. The church gives them the opportunity to construct an identity that transcends national or regional identities; it provides its followers with a discourse of a shared history, memory, longing, dreams, meaningful narratives, and a place to return – a place where everybody can feel at home.

The US congregations are connected at multiple levels and also with other congregations located in Mexico, El Salvador, Costa Rica, Colombia, Spain, and other countries. Luz del Mundo migrant believers are loyal to and identify with not only members in their sending country, but also with co-members living in these other countries. With its utopian discourse, Iglesia Luz del Mundo succeeds in unifying dispersed populations and social minorities from diverse parts of the world into one religious community whose members see themselves as the "chosen people" who have been redeemed in modern times through their two apostles.

Although La Luz del Mundo functions in Mexico as a religious minority, its growth and organizational development in the last decades, both within and

---

6 James Clifford, "Diasporas," *Cultural Anthropology*, 9 (1994): 310.

outside of Mexico, have allowed it to achieve an extraordinary success among urban and rural people of middle and lower social classes, which distinguishes it from other Mexican Pentecostal movements. Success here can be explained mostly as the result of its solid and authoritarian doctrine and hierarchy, in which the central figure, Samuel the Apostle, keeps the whole community united despite its dispersion throughout the world. The church is traditional and modern at the same time, so old and young people (female and male) can meet their respective spiritual and social needs. Doctrine and practices are adjusted to the surrounding contemporary world and life, therefore offering its members not only spiritual satisfaction but also social fulfillment and certainties.

Conclusion

Although Mormons, Jehovah's Witnesses, Adventists, and Luz del Mundo are distinct religious movements, it is clear that both their restorationist theologies and their demographic trajectories in the twentieth century bind them together. Further, these four religious groups share with one another an ambiguous place in the Latin American religious landscape, clearly not Catholic but neither a definite part of the Protestant–Pentecostal nexus that defines the most dominant alternative religious affiliation in the region. Instead, these four movements operate in the spaces on the edges of or in the gaps between these more dominant religions. In these spaces, they have built statistically small but nonetheless substantial membership bases with clear local identities across the region. Although each group struggles with high rates of desertion and a certain level of ostracism from mainstream culture, the distinctive identity shared by those that remain in each religion appears to create lasting social bonds and strong core population of believers. Coupled with an emphasis on local leadership – whether a relatively recent development as in Mormonism or a core tenet as in Luz del Mundo – these factors indicate that these groups have staked a lasting claim to their unique corners of Latin American religion and they will remain fixtures in the region.

Bibliography and Suggested Readings

Adherents.com. *Jehovah's Witnesses Memorial Attendance* (Mexico). www.adherents.com/Na/Na_383.html (Accessed February 12, 2010).

Albrecht, Stan L. "The Consequential Dimension of Mormon Religiosity." In James T. Duke (ed.), *Latter-day Saint Social Life: Social Research on the LDS Church and Its Members*, 253–292. Proto, UT: Brigham Young University Press, 1998.

Barrett, David B., George T. Kurian, and Todd M. Johnson. *World Christian Encyclopedia*, 2nd ed. Oxford: Oxford University Press, 2001.

Bloom, Harold. *The American Religion: The Emergence of the Post-Christian Nation*. New York: Simon and Schuster, 1992.

Bryant, Seth, Henri Gooren, Rick Phillips, and David Stewart Jr. "Conversion and Retention in Mormonism." In Lewis R. Rambo and Charles E. Farhadian (eds.), *The Oxford Handbook of Religious Conversion*, 756–785. New York: Oxford University Press, 2014.

Bushman, Richard L. *Joseph Smith: Rough Stone Rolling – A Cultural Biography of Mormonism's Founder*. New York: Albert A. Knopf, 2005.

Clifford, James. "Diasporas." *Cultural Anthropology*, 9 (1994): 302–338.

Condie, Spencer J. "Missionary, Missionary Life." In Daniel H. Ludlow (ed.), *Encyclopedia of Mormonism*, 910–913. New York: Macmillan, 1992.

Cragun, Ryan, and Ronald Lawson. "The Secular Transition: The Worldwide Growth of Mormons, Jehovah's Witnesses, and Seventh-day Adventists." *Sociology of Religion*, 71, no. 3 (2010): 349–373.

de la Torre, Renée. "Testigos de Jehová." In Renée de la Torre and Cristina Gutiérrez Zúñiga (eds.), *Atlas de la diversidad religiosa en México*, 73–79. Guadalajara, Mexico: CIESAS/El Colegio de Jalisco/SEGOB, 2007.

Deseret News. *Church Almanac*. Salt Lake City: Deseret News, 2006–2009.

Fortuny, Patricia. "A Bridge between Nations: Religion and Transnationalism." Paper presented as a Public Lecture at the University of Santa Barbara, California, 2004.

——— ed. *Los "Otros Hermanos": Minorías Religiosas Protestantes en Jalisco*. Guadalajara, Mexico: Secretaría de Cultura del Estado de Jalisco, Colección Culturas Populares de Jalisco, 2005.

——— On the Road to Damascus: Pentecostals, Mormons, and Jehovah's Witnesses in Mexico. Doctoral dissertation, University College London, 1995.

——— Origins, Development and Perspectives of La Luz del Mundo Church. *Religion: An International Journal*, 25, no. 2 (1995): 147–162.

——— "The Santa Cena of The Luz del Mundo Church: A Case of Contemporary Transnationalism." In by H. R. Ebaugh and J. Chafetz (eds.), *Religion across Borders: Transnational Religious Networks*, 15–50. Walnut Creek, CA: Altamira Press, 2002.

Gellert, Gisela, and J. C. Pinto. *Ciudad de Guatemala: Dos estudios sobre su evolución urbana (1524–1950)*. Guatemala City: Universidad de San Carlos, 1992.

General Conference of Seventh-day Adventists. *Seventh-day Adventist Yearbook 2008*. Hagerstown, MD: Review and Herald Publishing Association, 2008. www.adventistarchives.org/docs/YB/YB2008.pdf (Accessed July 29, 2009).

Gooren, Henri. "Comparing Mormons and Adventists in Latin America." Paper presented at the Annual Meeting of the Society for the Scientific Study of Religion (SSSR) in Denver, CO (October 23, 2009).

——— "Conversion Careers in Latin America: Entering and Leaving Church among Pentecostals, Catholics, and Mormons." In Timothy J. Steigenga and Edward L. Cleary (eds.), *Conversion of a Continent: Contemporary Religious Change in Latin America*, 52–71. New Brunswick, NJ: Rutgers University Press, 2007.

——— "The Dynamics of LDS Growth in Guatemala, 1948–1998." *Dialogue: A Journal of Mormon Thought*, 34 (2001): 55–75.

"Latter-day Saints under Siege: The Unique Experience of Nicaraguan Mormons." *Dialogue: A Journal of Mormon Thought*, 40, no. 3 (2007): 134–155.

"The Mormons of the World: The Meaning of LDS Membership in Central America." In Cardell K. Jacobson, John P. Hoffman, and Tim B. Heaton (eds.), *Revisiting Thomas F. O'Dea's "The Mormons": Contemporary Perspectives*, 362–388. Salt Lake City, UT: University of Utah Press, 2008.

"Reconsidering Protestant Growth in Guatemala, 1900–1995.". In James W. Dow and Alan R. Sandstrom (eds.), *Holy Saints and Fiery Preachers: The Anthropology of Protestantism in Mexico and Central America*, 169–203. Westport, CT: Praeger, 2001.

Religious Disaffiliation and Conversion: Tracing Patterns of Change in Faith Practices. New York: Palgrave Macmillan, 2010.

Review of *Pioneer in Guatemala: The Personal History of John Forres O'Donnal, Including the History of the Church of Jesus-Christ of Latter-day Saints in Guatemala* (1997), by John Forres O'Donnal. *Journal of Mormon History*, 27, no. 2 (2003): 277–280.

Rich among the Poor: Church, Firm, and Household among Small-scale Entrepreneurs in Guatemala City. Amsterdam: Thela, 1999.

Greenleaf, Floyd. *The Seventh-day Adventist Church in Latin America and the Caribbean*. 2 vols. Berrien Springs, MI: Andrews University Press, 1992.

Grover, Mark L. *A Land of Promise and Prophecy: Elder A. Theodore Tuttle in South America, 1960–1965*. Provo, UT: Brigham Young University, Religious Studies Center, 2008.

"The Maturing of the Oak: The Dynamics of LDS Growth in Latin America." *Dialogue: A Journal of Mormon Thought*, 38, no. 2 (2005): 79–104.

Mormonism in Brazil: Religion and Dependency in Latin America. PhD dissertation, Indiana University, 1985.

Hansen, Terrence L. "The Church in Central America." *Ensign*, 2 (September 1972): 40–42.

Heaton, Tim. "Vital Statistics." In Daniel H. Ludlow (ed.), *Encyclopedia of Mormonism*, 1518–1537. New York: Macmillan, 1992.

Higuera, Antonio. "La Asamblea Internacional 2003–2004 de los Testigos de Jehová. ¿Una nueva oportunidad en México?" In *Revista Liminar: Estudios Sociales y Humanísticos*, 2, no. 2 (2004): 35–47. San Cristóbal de las Casas, Mexico: UNICACH.

Instituto Nacional de Estadística, Geografía e Informática (INEGI). *La diversidad religiosa en México*. Mexico City: INEGI, 2005.

Kellner, Mark A. "Study: Adventists Score High in Membership Retention." *Adventist Review* (Upper Columbia Conference). March 5, 2008. www.uccsda.org/News/Membership-Retention (Accessed September 13, 2009).

Knowlton, David C. "How Many Members Are There Really? Two Censuses and the Meaning of LDS Membership in Chile and Mexico." *Dialogue: A Journal of Mormon Thought*, 38, no. 2 (2005): 53–78.

"Mormonism in Chile." In Douglas J. Davies. *Mormon Identities in Transition*, 68–79. London and New York: Cassell, 1996.

"Mormonism in Latin America: Towards the Twenty-first Century." *Dialogue: A Journal of Mormon Thought*, 29, no. 1 (1996): 159–176.

Land, Gary. *Historical Dictionary of Seventh-day Adventists*. Lanham, MD: Scarecrow Press, 2005.

Latter-day Saints Church. *The Book of Mormon*. Salt Lake City, UT: The Church of Jesus Christ of Latter-day Saints, 1989 [1830].

Doctrine and Covenants; Pearl of Great Price. Salt Lake City, UT: the Church of Jesus Christ of Latter-day Saints, 1989 [1835; 1880].

Gospel Principles. Salt Lake City, UT: the Church of Jesus Christ of Latter-day Saints, 1988.

"Sect-State Relations: Accounting for the Differing Trajectories of Seventh-day Adventists and Jehovah's Witnesses." *Sociology of Religion,* 56, no. 4 (1995): 351–377.

Lawson, Ronald. "Broadening the Boundaries of Church-Sect Theory: Insights from the Evolution of the Nonschismatic Mission Churches of Seventh-day Adventism." *Journal for the Scientific Study of Religion,* 37, no. 4 (1998): 652–672.

"Comparing the Global Growth Rates and Distributions of Adventists, Mormons, and Witnesses." Paper presented at the annual meeting of the Society for the Scientific Study of Religion (SSSR) in Rochester, NY, 2005.

"Onward Christian Soldiers? Seventh-day Adventists and the Issue of Military Service." *Review of Religious Research,* 37, no. 3 (1996): 193–218.

Mauss, Armand L. *The Angel and the Beehive: The Mormon Struggle with Assimilation.* Champaign: University of Illinois Press, 1994.

Mormonism in the Twenty-first Century: Marketing for Miracles. *Dialogue: A Journal of Mormon Thought,* 29, no. 1 (1996): 236–249.

Molina, José Luís. *Los Testigos de Jehová y la transformación escolar de sus hijos.* Mexicali: Universidad de Baja California, 2000.

O'Donnal, John Forres. *Pioneer in Guatemala: The Personal History of John Forres O'Donnal, Including the History of the Church of Jesus-Christ of Latter-day Saints in Guatemala.* Yorba Linda, CA: Shumway Family History Services, 1997.

Osorio, Oscar. *¿Quién llama a tu puerta? Identidad y religión en la Iglesia de los testigos de Jehová en México* PhD dissertation, Univerdidad Autónoma de México Iztapalapa, 2009.

Penton, James. *Apocalypse Delayed: The Story of the Jehovah's Witnesses.* Toronto: University of Toronto Press, 1985.

Phillips, Rick. "Rethinking the International Expansion of Mormonism." *Nova Religio: The Journal of Alternative and Emergent Religions,* 10, no. 1 (2006): 52–68.

Richards, LeGrand. *A Marvelous Work and a Wonder.* Salt Lake City, UT: Deseret Book Company, 1979.

Roberts, Bryan R. Protestant Groups and Coping with Urban Life in Guatemala. *American Journal of Sociology,* 73, no. 6 (1968): 753–767.

"Statistics." Seventh-day Adventist Archives 1960. www.adventistarchives.org/docs/ASR/ASR1960.pdf (Accessed September 9, 2009).

2007. www.adventistarchives.org/docs/ASR/ASR2007.pdf (Accessed July 21, 2009).

2008. www.adventistarchives.org/docs/Stats/ACRep2008.pdf (Accessed September 9, 2009).

Seventh-day Adventist Yearbook 2008. 2008. www.adventistarchives.org/docs/YB/YB2008.pdf (Accessed July 29, 2009).

Shepherd, Gordon, and Gary Shepherd. "Membership Growth, Church Activity, and Missionary Recruitment." *Dialogue: A Journal of Mormon Thought,* 29, no. 1 (1996): 33–57.

Mormon Passage: A Missionary Chronicle. Urbana and Chicago: University of Illinois Press, 1998.

44
Jews and Judaism in Latin America

JEFFREY LESSER

Jewish practices arrived in Latin America with the early European colonizers in the fifteenth and sixteenth centuries and included both public and secret rituals. The Inquisition had forced much Jewish practice underground and many of those characterized as "Jews" by Iberian political and religious leaders were actually the descendants of converted "New Christians" (Iberian Jews who converted, often involuntarily, to Catholicism). Variously called *judaizantes, marranos, conversos*, and New Christians, they went to Latin America in small numbers to escape economic, social, and religious persecution.

Although there was an important sixteenth century Jewish presence in Brazil as a result of Portuguese colonial expansion, it would be inappropriate to characterize these Jews as a "community" in the contemporary academic sense of the word. The one exception came in 1630 when the Dutch invaded northern Brazil and allowed the open practice of Judaism. In 1654, following the expulsion of the Dutch by the Portuguese, some practicing Jews became crypto-Jews, others moved to Holland, and still others migrated to other cities in the Americas, notably to Curaçao and New Amsterdam. In the Caribbean and in northern Brazil, then, there are small, old, and continuing Sephardic communities.

More contemporary forms of Jewish practice came to Latin America in the nineteenth century, linked to independence from Spain and Portugal. Jewish ritual practice in nineteenth-century Latin America might be termed "traditional" among Sephardim and Ashkenazim. This meant that those few Jews in the region tended to focus their practice on private spaces via food rituals, daily and/or weekly religious practice as part of the Sabbath, and attempts to enforce endogamy. *Ashkenazim* are descended from the medieval Jewish communities of the Rhineland who would later form communities in both Central and Eastern Europe. *Sephardim* are those descended from Jews in the Iberian Peninsula and include the descendants of those expelled from Spain and Portugal. The term also applies to those who immigrated to Latin America from the Ottoman Empire and Arab countries. In contemporary Israel, Jews from Latin America, even if Ashkenazi, are often called "Sefardim."

The general trends changed markedly in the second half of the nineteenth century when large numbers of Central and Eastern European Jews migrated to Latin America. These new arrivals created Jewish ethnic institutions such as schools, newspapers and magazines, artistic venues, and social service organization that helped to provide a sense of community and to attract still more Jewish migrations. In terms of religious practice, Central European tended toward "Liberal Judaism," a movement that suggested that religion was a private, individual matter different from the public practice of national identity. It was these Jews, first in Argentina but later in other countries in Latin America, who created the institutions that would become critical for the expansion of Jewish communities, including synagogues, burial societies, and social service institutions, over the course of the late nineteenth and twentieth centuries.

In the late nineteenth century, Jews in Eastern Europe – especially those from the Pale of Settlement, an area containing a high proportion of Jews that encompassed part of what is today Poland and Russia – felt a growing pressure to leave Europe. Physical harassment, social pressures, and economic hardship all contributed to the sense that emigration was a priority. Around the same time, the Ottoman Empire was in crisis, and this was accompanied by the persecution of religious minorities, growing Arab nationalism, and forced military service. Economic changes in the regions that are today's Syria and Lebanon made life difficult for a growing number of craftsmen and small merchants – Christian, Jewish, and Muslim alike. The America seemed to promise prosperity and a better future, and many Latin American countries received large numbers from the regions, with Middle Eastern Jews going in significant numbers to Argentina, Brazil, and Mexico.

Among the first sponsored Jewish immigrants to Latin America were those sent by the Jewish Colonization Association (JCA), one of numerous relief organizations set up by wealthy European Jewish communities to aid poverty-stricken and oppressed East European and Balkan Jewry. In 1893, the JCA founded its first colony, Moisesville, in Santa Fé province north of Buenos Aires to provide for those Russian Jews already in Argentina. By 1889, the colonies in Argentina appeared a success, and boatloads of JCA-sponsored Jews were arriving in the country. Between l900 and l909, the ICA transported more than 770 new colonists annually to Argentina and in the decade following the annual average jumped to almost 1,500. Soon, the JCA set up other colonies in Brazil and Eastern European Jews began to migrate independently to the region.

Eastern European Jews engaged in very different rituals than central Europeans. Most Eastern European Jews had been denied citizenship rights in their countries of birth and as a result lived in relatively segregated communities in which Yiddish was the main language and many aspects of daily life were linked to ritual practices. Not surprisingly, there was often awkward contact between Eastern and Central European Jews in Latin America (as was the case in Europe and North America, and later Israel). Ashkenazi Jews were also separated from Sephardic Jews, themselves divided along the lines of place of origin, language, and ritual. In other words, long before the establishment of the contemporary major streams of Jewish ritual practice (Reform, Orthodox, and Conservative), other kinds of separations led many Jews to see themselves not as one community but as many.

The study of religious practices among Jewish-Latin Americans is modest. Most scholarship focuses on Jewish ethnicity, using communal institutions and thus strong Jewish affiliation, as research sites. In a study done in 2005, the Latin American nations with the largest Jewish populations were Argentina (185,000), Brazil (96,700), Mexico (39,800), Chile (20,800), Uruguay (19,500), and Venezuela (15,500). These numbers should not imply that it is possible to make a broad regional statement about Jewish practice to Latin America. Argentina received primarily Ashkenazim while significant numbers of Sephardim (although still a minority of the total) went to Brazil in the nineteenth century from Morocco to the Amazon, in the early twentieth century from what today is Lebanon and Syria to southern Brazil, and in the 1950s from Egypt. Mexico, with Latin America's third largest Jewish population, in majority comprises Sephardic Jews, in large part descended from immigrants from Aleppo and Damascus. The one constant is that, as in much of the world, most Jews are not affiliated with religious institutions and thus would describe themselves as having a Jewish ethnic identity rather than a religious one.

Given the range of origin, Jewish ritual practice varies widely. For example, in Mexico City, Sephardic Jews of Syrian descent have separate schools, synagogues, and community centers based on their cities of origin. In Argentina, a Reform-movement-affiliated seminary created by the late Rabbi Marshall Meyer, a United States citizen who took the lead in fighting for human rights against Argentina's military dictators, has produced clerics who now lead congregations throughout the Americas, including non-Reform congregations.

In the past decades, some notable developments have taken place with regards to Latin American Jewry. The first is what we might term the "Sephardization" of both Jews and non-Jews who in 1992 used the 500th anniversary of the Inquisitional edict expelling Jew from Iberia as a means to claim a primordial place within national identity discourse. Thus, significant numbers of Latin Americans, especially among the elite, propose that they are descended from early Spanish and Portuguese colonists who, so the argument goes, were actually "crypto-Jews."

This is a more contemporary version of early twentieth century identity-creation myths among Jews in Latin America that suggested that indigenous peoples – whether Mexica in Mesoamerica, Inca in the Andes, or Tupi in the Amazon – were the Jewish lost tribes and that the population of Latin America was "Jewish" prior to European colonization. These kinds of discourses are widely accepted, or at least discursively projected, by both Jews and non-Jews in Latin America and to a certain extent in the United States, especially in the Southwest and in New Mexico in particular. Other ethnic groups, notably Latin Americans of Asian and Middle Eastern descent, have developed similar myths that appear to be equally widely accepted.

The second major movement, linked to the first, is the growing numbers of those who are born Christian but believe they have Jewish ancestors and thus engage in conversion processes. This has caused tensions among those traditional defined as (and who define themselves as) Jewish because many believe the converts are pretenders seeking the right to make *aliyah* ("return to Israel") and thus garner the Israeli citizenship that is available to all Jews. The interest in conversion is not a strictly Latin American phenomenon and can be found in both Africa and India in significant numbers.

The question of conversion is intertwined with the growth of evangelical and Pentecostal Christianity in Latin America, as members of those faiths often have strongly Zionistic discourses and see Judaism as an important component of their own millenarian beliefs. Latin America is also part of the broader *baal teshuva* phenomenon in which Jews brought up in secular circumstances "return" to Judaism via various forms of Orthodox practice. This movement has become highly visible in Latin America in the last three decades and is usually propagated via the Chabad Lubavitch organization, a Hasidic Orthodox movement founded in Eastern Europe in the eighteenth century and that moved to the United States in 1940. Unlike the conversionary movement discussed earlier, Chabad Lubavitch seeks only those whom they consider Jews, via a strict interpretation of traditional Jewish law that links Judaism to one's mother's Judaism, for "return."

The Chabad Lubavitch organization has brought a number of significant changes to Latin American life. Perhaps most important, it has asked its members to be Jewish publicly via the use of ritual clothing, refusal to work during the Sabbath, the insistence on food rituals, and public expression through religious ritual objects, notably the placing of Jewish lamps (*menorahs*) in central urban locations. This has challenged the presumed secular nature of the Latin American street and the idea that certain Christian aspects of Latin American culture, for example, crosses in legislative buildings, have no religious meaning. Chabad Lubavitch has also expanded Judaism to smaller cities and towns in Latin America, in some cases recuperating synagogues in areas where practice had almost disappeared. Today, the Chabad Lubavitch movement claims centers in twelve countries. In Argentina alone the movement has centers in twelve different cities and has thirty "Chabad Houses" just in Buenos Aires. In Brazil the movement has twelve city bases and fifteen houses in São Paulo. The movement also is active in countries with tiny Jewish populations including Guatemala, Bolivia, and Paraguay.

A final important contemporary phenomenon is the immigration of Latin American Jews to Israel where they have created new forms of both ethnicity and religious practice. In Israel, there is a fairly steep divide between secular and religious Jews, and Latin American Jews have been important in creating a middle path of ritually committed Jews who are neither Orthodox nor "traditional" (the term used in Israel for non-Orthodox religious Jews) nor secular. Since 1948, about 92,000 Jews have made *aliyah* from Latin America, and of this group well over half have come from Argentina. Many fled during the Argentine military dictatorship of 1976 to 1983, when the armed forces made Jews a particular target because of long-held anti-Semitic beliefs. Another significant moment was during the economic crisis of 1999 to 2002 when some 10,000 Argentines migrated to Israel.

Bibliography and Suggested Readings

American Jewish Year Book, 2005, Vol. 105, New York: American Jewish Committee and Jewish Publication Society.

Elkin, Judith Laikin. *The Jews of Latin America*. New York: Holmes & Meier, 1998.

Lesser, Jeffrey. *Welcoming the Undesirables: Brazil and the Jewish Question*. Berkeley: University of California Press, 1994.

Lesser, Jeffrey, and Raanan Rein. *Rethinking Jewish-Latin Americans*. Albuquerque: University of New Mexico Press, 2008.

Meyer, Marshall T., and Jane Isay. *You Are My Witness: The Living Words of Rabbi Marshall T. Meyer*. New York: St. Martin's Press, 2004.

45
Islam in Latin America

CECÍLIA L. MARIZ

TRANSLATED BY RODRIGO FRESTON

Latin America, that is, the group of American countries that are former Spanish and Portuguese colonies, stands out in the global scene for being the region with the lowest rates of Muslims in the world. National statistical institutes and also the Muslim media recognize this fact. However, these sources disagree considerably on the number of Muslims in each country and in the region as a whole. It is common to observe a difference between the data from surveys or national statistics and those from leaders of a certain religion or church regarding estimates of the number of followers. This phenomenon can be observed in relation to different Christian churches, including the Catholic Church and other religions. However, as a number of scholars have noted, what catches one's attention is the magnitude of the discrepancy on membership data between Muslim and secular sources in Latin America.

In Brazil, the national censuses for 2000 and 2010 counted, respectively, only 27,239 and 35,675 people of the Islam affiliation, but Muslim sources such as the website where Maria Moreira claims more than a million Muslims, as much as one and a half million.[1] The same is true for other countries. Maria Lograño shows that in the case of Argentina some sources claim there are 900,000 Muslims in the country, while others reveal that in Buenos Aires, which accounts for by far the largest proportion of this population, only 4,000 inhabitants identify as Muslims. According to Isaac Caro, the 2002 census in Chile found only 3,000 Muslims.[2]

This problem highlights what would appear to be a lack of surveys and censuses with trustworthy data on religious identity in many regions of Latin

---

1 www.islamawareness.net/LatinAmerica/brazil.html (Accessed January 8, 2016).
2 Maria Lograño, *Islam and Muslims in Latin America* (Findings Report, product of a working group, entitled, "Islam in Latin America," held at Florida International University, Miami on March 24, 2010). The papers presented at this event cited below are available at https://lacc.fiu.edu/research/islam-in-latin-america/ CE: Accessed November 5, 2015.

America. Some researchers question the data by suggesting that Muslims may feel constrained by prejudice and therefore would not identify themselves as such in surveys or censuses. However, neither of these criticisms seems to apply to the census in Brazil. There has not been any record in the country of a level of rejection or prejudice that would lead Muslims to hide their religious identity, at least not in the years of the most recent censuses (2000 and 2010). In general, Muslims in Latin America enjoy high social status, despite the criticisms they suffer from the international media. The Brazilian national census has been a trustworthy source in the collection of data on the religious identities of groups that require religious exclusivity (like Islam). Therefore, there are no reasonable motives for doubting the data collected by the well-trained experts in the Brazilian Institute of Geography and Statistics (Instituto Brasileiro de Geografiae Estatística – IBGE).

But, unlike Brazil, in many countries of Latin America there is no "religion" section in national censuses. To make up for this lack of data on Muslims, Logroño suggests counting the number of Islamic religious centers, charity organizations, and mosques.[3] Although this is interesting data to collect and account for, it is also important to remember that these sorts of figures may say more about the amount of Islamic financial resources in the country than about the number of people who adhere to this faith. However, the number of such organizations and mosques, their geographical location and the record of the years in which they were built and inaugurated, offers information that can certainly reveal many important elements in understanding what has happened to Islam in global terms and in each country. Thus, we can observe that from the 1990s onwards many mosques were inaugurated in many Latin American countries. The Muslim population also grew, as one can see, for example, in a comparison of the Brazilian censuses of 2000 and 2010. But one cannot deduce that the number of the faithful has grown in proportion to the multiplication of Islamic centers and institutions.

Besides being small, the Muslim population in Latin America has a relatively recent history. Unlike the former English and Dutch colonies in the Caribbean and in South America, which imported Indo-Asian Muslim workers in the colonial period, the countries colonized by Spain and Portugal, with a few exceptions, brought scarcely anyone from this religious tradition to their colonies. One of these exceptions was in Brazil, which received Muslim Africans as slaves. Brazilian historian João Reis describes the presence of these enslaved black Muslims and the revolt they organized in the city of Salvador in Bahia in

[3] Ibid.

1835, when Brazil was already independent from Portugal. Well-organized and educated (knowing how to read and write in Arabic), these African Muslims, known at the time as *"Malês,"* led an armed revolt against their masters, the government, and slavery. The revolt was quashed, but with difficulty; and from that point forward, the importing of Muslim slaves was suspended. There is no Islamic grouping left over from this population in present-day Brazil.

Although the first immigrants from the Middle East, especially the Syrian-Lebanese (known colloquially in Spanish as *"turcos"*), arrived at the end of the nineteenth century in Argentina and other regions of Latin America, these were almost exclusively Christian. The history of Muslims in this sub-continent begins effectively after World War II, when Muslim Syrian-Lebanese and some Palestinians immigrated to places such as Brazil, Mexico, Colombia, Chile, Paraguay, Cuba, Honduras, and Argentina. Therefore, most Latin American Muslim communities are formed from this period onwards. In Brazil, Muslims arrived mostly between 1945 and 1985. The first mosque in Brazil was built in São Paulo and inaugurated in 1956.

Research has shown that initially, the newcomers did not intend to settle in Latin America, but only to earn money and return to their countries. Over time, however, they decided to bring their relatives and try their luck definitively in the region. There was no missionary project among these immigrants. They led their religious lives discreetly and restricted it to the immigrant communities and their descendants. That is why sociologist Procópio Camargo, who researched religion in São Paulo in the 1960s and 1970s, considered Islam to be an "almost ethnic" religion there.[4] Despite being a world religion, it was identified at that time with an ethnicity and with a small group of immigrants. In turn, the immigrants' children demonstrated less attachment to the faith of their parents and searched for more integration to society at large. Therefore, in the beginning Islam in Latin America was restricted to the regions where there were immigrants of Arab origin. In Brazil, these regions were in the state of São Paulo, in Paraná – especially Foz do Iguaçu – and in Rio de Janeiro.

This pattern in Brazil was repeated in other countries of Latin America, although there were some differences within each national context. Muslims arrived earlier and in relatively larger numbers in Argentina, a little later and in relatively smaller numbers in Mexico. Analyzing the Muslim presence in the region known as the "Triple Frontier" of Brazil, Argentina, and Paraguay,

---

4 Cândido Propócio F. Carmago, *Católicos, protestantes, espíritas* (Petrópolis: Editora Vozes, 1973).

Karam describes a similar history. From the end of the nineteenth century there were Arab merchants in the area, but the establishment of families and of a Muslim community did not take place until around 1950. Today, the media has identified this region as a center for "radical Islamism." Karam takes the opposite view, arguing that media accusations over the relationship between this community and the terrorist attack of 1994 on the Jewish community of Buenos Aires have not been proven. In fact, with the exception of Caro, most scholars of Islam in Latin America tend to reject the idea that there is radical Islamism in the countries that they research.

Sunni Islam predominates in Latin America, as most of the immigrants came from this branch. The Triple Frontier region stands out for having the same amount of Shia and Sunni. In the rest of the continent – Brazil, Chile, Argentina, Colombia, and Mexico – the Shia are always a minority. In some countries there is a bigger diversity of Islamic branches than in others. Silvia Montenegro highlights the pluralism of Argentine Islam when she comments on a Shia mosque, founded in 1983, that has links to the Union of Argentine Muslim Women (Unión de Mujeres Musulmanas Argentinas – UMMA), created in 1995.[5] In Brazil, Pinto notes the presence of Shia in Curitiba. He observes that this community is "led by a Shia *shaykh* born in Lebanon," who has also led a Muslim community in Santiago, Chile.[6]

Various researchers have shown that many mosques in Latin America are relatively recent constructions. Until the late 1980s, many communities did not have mosques, but only charity organizations. Until 1990, throughout the Islamic communities of Latin America, the sheikhs (Islamic teachers/clerics) used to come from abroad, staying in each country for only a relatively short time (about two years). Most of them could speak only Arabic, and sometimes were not able to learn the local language. According to reports from Muslim leaders in a São Paulo mosque, these sheikhs would come at the request of the local communities, usually from countries such as Egypt and Saudi Arabia, often with their salaries paid by the Muslim communities in the sending countries.

At the end of the 1980s, Saudi Arabia began to grant scholarships to young Latin American descendants of Muslim immigrants to study in that country and go back to their native countries as sheikhs. The first sheikhs born in Latin America, in Brazil and in Argentina, graduated, and then returned to their countries in the 1990s. However, they were not many. From a first wave of

---

5   Montenegro, op cit.
6   Paulo Hilu Rocha Pinto, "Ritual etnicidade e identidade religiosa comunidades mulçumanas no Brasil," *Revista USP*, 67 (2005): 236.

around ten youngsters between fifteen and seventeen years of age that left São Paulo (Brazil) to Saudi Arabia, only two managed to conclude the course and return to Brazil. The two first Brazilian-born successful explained that other youngsters had returned to Brazil before finishing their studies because they had found their experience in Saudi Arabia very different and much tougher than their previous lives as Brazilian-born descendants of successful and well-integrated immigrants. Since then, Saudi Arabia has continued to receive young men from all over Latin America, and the number of sheikhs born in the region has continued to grow. Nevertheless, by the first decade of the twenty-first century most sheikhs were still from outside of Latin America.

From the 1990s onwards, mosques were built in areas with less of a tradition of Arab immigration. During this period, a project of disseminating Islam started and led to the adherence of individuals of a different social and ethnic origin than that of the immigrants. The number of Muslims who were neither Arabs nor descendants of immigrants slowly started to grow. These new developments seem to be due not only to a movement to promote Islam but also to a renewal among those who were already part of the religion. The proceeds from the oil wealth of the Arab world helped to support many initiatives to internationalize these movements.

The Center for Dissemination of Islam to Latin America (Centro de Divulgacao do Islam – CDIAL), headquartered in São Bernardo do Campo in Greater São Paulo, was created to support the "dissemination" and "promotion" of Islam – terms adopted by Islamic leaders, who have opted not to use the word "mission." CDIAL has at its disposal a large number of diverse publications (magazines, books, and brochures) which, besides listing the addresses of Islamic centers and websites, has information on the religion's doctrine, creed, and code of conduct. The World Assembly of Muslim Youth (WAMY) was also installed in this same city in 1999. Founded in 1973 with the goal of supporting young Muslims throughout the world through events and backing for journeys to Mecca (the *hajj*, one of Islam's "five pillars"). WAMY is an international nongovernmental organization headquartered in Saudi Arabia. Because of the many Muslim activities and organizations located in São Bernardo do Campo, Muslims themselves call the city the "capital of Muslims in Brazil."

This dissemination work has occurred in all of Latin America and has resulted in the appearance, already mentioned, of a new type of Muslim. This type is constituted by people without an Islamic background who "converted" to Islam, or "reverted," "returning" to Islam, as those surveyed and Ferreira like to say. This author defends the use of an Islamic, non-Christian, terminology for the study of Islam: in this religion all are born Muslims and the new member has "reverted" or "returned," not "converted." The number of new followers in some contexts is very small, even using the numbers given by Islamic sources, as Oliveira shows for Brazil.

Montenegro (2010) observes, however, that in Argentina these new followers can constitute up to half of the communities. Indeed, she also notes that there is already a generation of sheikhs born in the country, and that not all of them are of Arab descent. These new sheikhs perform functions that were until recently off-limits to them, both in Argentina and in Brazil. Senna observed in a study of the mosque in Belo Horizonte – the capital of the state of Minas Gerais in Brazil – that the new followers were 40 percent of its members and, on average, much younger than the other Muslims. With a mosque inaugurated in 1992, this region received far fewer Muslim immigrants than other regions of Brazil, such as São Paulo, Foz do Iguaçu or Rio de Janeiro.

Various reasons are given for this type of religious adhesion among Latin Americans with no Arab descent. Paulo Hilu Pinto observes that conversions in Brazil occur "through personal relationships (through work, friendship or marriage) or missionary work done by Muslim institutions organized in mosques or Sufi brotherhoods."[7] This author identifies, among Brazilian Muslims, the members of Sufi associations such as the Naqshbandi. Likewise, Silvia Montenegro counts the Sufi members of the Naqshbandi Haqqani association and of the Yerrahi al Halveti Sufi order among the converts to Islam. In contrast, studies by Oliveira and Oliveira and Mariz in Brazil note that members of the Naqshbandi order do not consider themselves Muslims. According to the research above, members of this Sufi order consider their spirituality sometimes described as an "expansion of awareness," as having spiritual affinities with the mystic traditions of all religions, Islam being just one of them. Nevertheless, they found reports of some of these Sufi people who abandoned the order to become Muslims.[8]

Among the new converts in Brazil there are also reports of Islam's struggle for racial equality. More than one person interviewed mentions having seen the movie depicting Malcolm X's life, thus coming to an understanding of Islam as a religion of blacks and the oppressed. There are also those who came closer to Islam to learn Arabic or because of curiosity sparked by the disseminated material and courses. Generally, new followers have become important

---

7   Pinto, 230.
8   Oliveira, *O caminho do silêncio*; Oliveira and Mariz, "Conversion to Islam."

disseminators of the faith and are more active in seeking more members for the new religion they have embraced. Since the movement promoting Islam is linked to the Sunni tradition, most of the new converts tend to be Sunnis, according to research done in Rio de Janeiro and São Paulo.

Maria Lograño draws attention to the rise of the Murabitun community among the indigenous population (Tzotzils and Tzeltals) in Chiapas, southern Mexico. Neither of Arab nor indigenous descent, the founder of the community is a Spaniard who claims he was a Marxist before adhering to Islam. According to Gavin and Zeraoui, many of these converts used to be Protestants who had been expelled from their villages. In Gavin's estimation, however, this community had only 200 indigenous people in 2005.

In Latin America, the economic and social status of Arabs and their descendants is much higher than the national average. Thus, on average Muslims tend to have more education and higher incomes than the rest of the population. In Argentina, there has been one president, Carlos Saul Menem (1989–1999), from a Muslim family. Since the immigrants to Latin America generally worked in commerce, Islam has been a predominantly urban religion. In Brazil it is found almost exclusively in urban areas; according to the 2010 census, 99.3 percent of Muslims live in cities. Another characteristic that distinguishes them from Christian traditions is that there is a higher percentage of men among their followers, relative to the total population. The same census estimates that of the 35,675 Muslims in Brazil, 21,042 are men, that is, 59 percent.

Not all new converts, however, enjoy the same social and economic status as the population of immigrant Muslim descent. This may be one factor that generates tension, but in general these pressure relates more to cultural issues, as shown by some studies in Brazil that discuss the relationship between the Muslims of Arab descent and the newly converted who had no Islamic past.[9] According to Castro, another problem recent converts face, especially women, is the difficulty that others have in understanding why they would opt for a religion that is seen as preaching women's submission.

Despite these cultural tensions and differences, one can predict a stronger growth for Islam in the region in the near future. For example, the census data in Brazil show that while the Brazilian population grew 12.3 percent from 2000 to 2010, Muslims grew more than 29 percent. The demand in contemporary

---

9   Cristina M. de Castro, *The Construction of Muslim Identities in Contemporary Brazil* (Lanham, MD: Lexington Books, 2013); Oliveira and Mariz, "Muslims in Contemporary Brazil."

Latin American society for new religious experiences and beliefs distinct from those they were brought up in, combined with the intensified dissemination of Islam – which has been embraced especially by the new followers – will certainly result in a revival and more members.

Bibliography and Suggested Readings

Carmago, Cândido Procópio F. *Católicos, protestantes, espíritas.* Petrópolis: Editora Vozes, 1973.
Caro, Isaac. "Identidades Islámicas Contemporáneas." *América Latina Revista Universum*, 22, no. 2(2007): 27–39.
Castellanos, Diego. "Islam en Colombia: Entre la Asimilación y la Exclusión," Florida International University Project, *Islam in Latin America, March*, 2010. This and all papers associated with this project can be found at https://lacc.fiu.edu/research/islam-in-latin-america/
Castro, Cristina M. de. *The Construction of Muslim Identities in Contemporary Brazil.* Lanham, MD: Lexington Books, 2013.
  "O papel da religião islâmica na integração de imigrantes no Brasil." Paper presented at *Fazendo Gênero 9: Diásporas, Diversidades, Deslocamentos*, Santa Catarina. 2010.
Ferreira, Francirosy Campos Barbosa. "Redes Islâmicas em São Paulo: 'Nascidos muçulmanos' e 'revertidos'." *Revista Litteri*, 3 (November), Dossiê Estudos Árabes & Islâmicos, 2009.
Gavin, Natasha. *Conversion and Conflict: Muslims in Mexico.* Spring 2005 issue of the ISIM Review, International Institute for the Study of Islam in the Modern World, 2005.
Karam, John Tofik. "(Un)covering Islam and Its Fifty-Year History in a South American Frontier Region." Florida International University Project *Islam in Latin America*, 2010.
Logroño, Maria. *Islam and Muslims in Latin America.* Florida International University, *Islam in Latin America* project, 2010.
Montenegro, Silvia. *Musulmanes en Argentina: instituciones, identidades y membresía*, Florida International University Project *Islam in Latin America*, 2010.
Oliveira, Vitória Peres de. *O caminho do silêncio (uma busca do auto-conhecimento): Um estudo de um grupo sufi*, M. A. in Anthropology. Universidade Estadual de Campinas, Brazil, 1991.
  "Islam in Brazil or the Islam of Brazil?" *Religião e Sociedade* 2 (2006).
Oliveira, Peres de, and Cecília Mariz. "Brasileiros e árabes: Conversão ao islã no Brasil." Paper presented at the XIII Jornadas sobre Alternativas Religiosas na América Latina, Porto Alegre, 2005.
  "Conversion to Islam in Contemporary Brazil." *Exchange*, 35, no. 1 (2006):102–115.
  "Muslims in Contemporary Brazil – A Preliminary Study." Paper presented at the XXXVIII Conference of the Société Internationale de Sociologie des Religions, Zagreb, 2005.
Pinto, Paulo Hilu Rocha. "Ritual etnicidade e identidade religiosa comunidades mulçumanas no Brasil." *Revista USP*, 67 (2005): 228–250.
Reis, João José. *Rebelião escrava no Brasil: A história do levante dos Malês em 1835.* São Paulo: Companhia das Letras, 2003.

Senna, Edmar Avelar de. *Islã e Modernidade: Um estudo sobre a comunidade islâmica de Belo Horizonte* Masters in Religion studies. Universidade Federal de Juiz de Fora, 2007.

Truzzi, Oswaldo. *De mascates a doutores: Sírios e libaneses em São Paulo*, Vol. 2. São Paulo: Sumaré. Série imigração, 1991.

Zeraoui, Zidane. *"Islam in Mexico: Defining a National Islam."* Florida International University *Islam in Latin America* project, 2010.

46
Asian Religions in Latin America

JEFFREY LESSER

Asian-derived religions in Latin America are linked to the nineteenth-century arrival of Asian migrants, historically from South Asia (to the Caribbean), China (to Peru and Mexico), Japan (to Brazil, Peru, and Bolivia), and more recently from Korea (to Brazil and Paraguay) and China (to Brazil, Argentina, and Mexico). Each national group and subgroup brought a variety of religious practices that were transformed in the new Latin American context. Practitioners of Hindu-based religions in the Caribbean continue to be primarily of South Asian descent. Most contemporary members of East Asian religions (notably Buddhism) are not of Asian descent, a pattern replicated among the growing sects of the so-called "New Japanese religions" such as Seichō-no-ie, the Church of World Messianity, and Sōka Gakkai.

New scholarly ideas about transnationalism have underscored that "Asian religions" and "religious practices among Latin Americans of Asian descent" must be put into conversation. Thus, it is important to note the rise of evangelical and Pentecostal Protestant worship among many Latin Americans of Asian descent as part of a broader trend in the region. In addition, the continuing migration of Koreans to Latin America has made the practice of adult baptism and other Protestant faith rituals among immigrants and their children an important part of Latin American religious practice. Finally, some 300,000 Latin Americans (250,000 Brazilians, 40,000 Peruvians, and 10,000 Bolivians) currently live and work in Japan, where they have created new forms of syncretic Japanese and Latin American religious practices. As these migrants return to their homelands, the growth of new religious practices will certainly take place.

The scholarship on Asian-based religions in Latin America is modest. Few scholars from Asia work on the region, and scholars of Latin America from the Americas and Europe, have tended to focus more on syncretism and new religions than on traditional Asian religions. Furthermore, the discursive exclusion of Latin Americans of Asian descent from national identity categories (for example, a Mexican whose great-great grandparents immigrated in the nineteenth century is termed a *"chino,"* not a *"mexicano"*) has made the study of Asian-based religions in Latin America a foreign rather than national project.

The scholarship on Asian religions in Latin America is heavily oriented toward Japanese-based religions in Brazil. This should come as no surprise, as there are more people of Japanese descent in Brazil than in the rest of Latin America combined. Furthermore, the size of Brazil and its tradition of syncretism have historically meant that country's population engages openly with multiple religious ideas. Finally, because of Brazil's large urban centers and long-term desire to be considered "modern," members of the Brazilian middle and upper classes have been attracted to Japanese-based religions (both traditional and new) as representing a form of personal first-worldism and a means to situate individuals in the capitalist world.

Japanese-based Religions

Prior to World War II, some 245,000 Japanese immigrated to Latin America, mainly to Brazil (about 188,000), Peru (about 33,070), Mexico (about 14,000), and Argentina (about 5,000). Whereas scholars of religion have for the most part ignored religious practice among Japanese in Latin America prior to World War II, recent scholarship has taken a new path. Although there were some Buddhist adherents among the new immigrants, most practiced what might be termed collective emperor-worship–based Shinto. However, one finds very few Shinto shrines in Latin America. For example, the state of São Paulo, Brazil, with the largest community of Japanese immigrants and descendants in the world, has only two shrines. The state-oriented nature of Shinto had the dual effect of encouraging immigrants to be loyal to their new countries (Brazil, Peru, and Bolivia) and led to the emperor-worship–based Shindo Renmei movement that emerged in Brazil in the mid-1940s and that proposed that Japan had won World War II.

The Catholic Church was able to make major inroads among the generation born in Latin America (*nisei*), and the same Church was active in the anti–Shindo Renmei campaigns, often using Latin American Japanese Catholic symbols and rituals as conversionary tools. Thus, Japanese Catholic movements in the 1950s and 1960s were composed heavily of young Brazilians of immigrant parents. One of the most important movements, the Estrela da Manhã, was active in politicizing the *nisei* to combat the Brazilian dictatorship that began in 1964.

After World War II, a little fewer than 100,000 more Japanese immigrated to Latin America. These new immigrants brought with them the *Sôtô Zenshu* school of Zen Buddhism, which focuses on meditation as the primary path to enlightenment. In Latin America, even Sôtô Zen moved from the individualistic approach practiced in Japan to a more mass-based approached based on group devotional practices and funeral rituals that many scholars argue shows the influence of dominant Catholic society. These patterns are clear not only in Brazil's urban centers, which witnessed the arrival of Japanese immigrants in the early twentieth century, but also in new Japanese colonies in southern Bolivia that were funded by the United States as it expelled Okinawans from their land to build army bases in the post–World War II era. A study of 262 family heads in the San Juan Yapacani agricultural settlement (a department of Santa Cruz in eastern Bolivia) conducted by Stephen I. Thompson in 1965 about a decade after formation is a microcosm of how Japanese immigrants and their descendants engaged with religion more broadly in Latin America. In the community, there were eighty-four Buddhists, six Shinto, thirty-four who were Catholic before immigrating, fifty who converted to Catholicism in Bolivia, thirty-five who were Soka Gakkai before immigrating, eleven who converted to Soka Gakkai in Bolivia, six who practiced other religions, thirty with no affiliation, and six for whom there was no data.[1]

As Zen Buddhism became part of worldwide religious practice, rituals functioned among Japanese Latin Americans as an ethnicity building experience and among non-Japanese as a way to participate in a "modern" and "first-world" experience. Today, Zen Buddhism practitioners in Latin America are in the majority urban dwellers who are not ethnically Japanese and who are seeking new religious forms to deal with the stresses of metropolitan life and aggressive capitalism. Indeed, even the Zen Buddhist monasteries based in rural areas of Latin America tend to function as retreat spaces for urban dwellers. Following the visit to Latin America of the president of the Sōka Gakkai lay organization Ikeda Daisaku in 1960, "Sōka Gakkai [became] the only group in the Buddhist spectrum with a considerable growth rate in terms of members. It is estimated that there are some 120,000 Sōka Gakkai adherents in (Brazil), more than fifty percent of all Brazilian Buddhists counted in the last national census in 2000."[2]

---

[1] Stephen I. Thompson, "Religious Conversion and Religious Zeal in an Overseas Enclave: The Case of the Japanese in Bolivia," *Anthropological Quarterly*, 41, no. 4 (October 1968): 201–208.

[2] Rafael Shoji and Frank Usarski, "Japanese Religions in Brazil," *Japanese Journal of Religious Studies*, 35, no. 1 (2008): 1–12, at 2.

In the postwar period there were two important trends in Japanese-based worship. The first was related to the large numbers of Okinawans among immigrants to Latin America, a percentage much larger than in the Japanese population as a whole. Many Okinawans sought to create a distinct ethnicity in Latin America (in other words, to separate themselves from mainland Japanese) by focusing on premigratory based regional forms ancestor worship, often led by female shamans. In the 1960s, a number of syncretic Afro-Okinawan sects emerged that included, for example, possession by both African and Okinawan spirits. Such sects have increasingly become part of global networks of Okinawan ethnicity, and many Latin Americans of Okinawan descent are committed to bringing the remains of ancestors from Japan to Latin America, in effect creating Okinawa abroad.

The second important trend stems from the growth of "New Religions" that emerged in Japan and spread rapidly to Latin America. Among these new religions, only Tenrikyō and Seichō-no-ie had any presence in Latin America before World War II, and it was a small one at that. In the post-war period, the largest of the new religions is Seichō-no-ie, which claims more than one million adherents and uses all forms of media in spreading its doctrine. The next largest group is the Church of World Messianity, which was founded in 1935 but began its activities in Latin America in 1955; it has at least one hundred thousand adherents jut in Brazil. These are followed by Perfect Liberty, Tenrikyō, and Mahikari. Most practitioners to these religions are not of Asian descent but rather members of the middle and upper classes engaged in what Cristina Rocha terms "the quest for cosmopolitan modernity."[3]

Hinduism

Hinduism in Latin America and the Caribbean takes two very different forms. In Suriname, Guyana, and Trinidad, more traditionally based Hinduism is practiced among the descendants of indentured servants from South Asia. In the rest of Latin America, newer forms such as Hare Krishna are practiced almost exclusively among those of non–South Asian descent. In Suriname, Guyana, and Trinidad, the numbers of Hindus are declining because of out-migration and conversion to other religions in the face of intense Christian proselytizing, especially from Pentecostal groups.

---

3 Cristina Rocha, *Zen in Brazil: The Quest for Cosmopolitan Modernity* (Honolulu: University of Hawaii Press, 2006).

There are aspects of Hinduism among South Asians that have clearly diverged from practices and beliefs in the pre-immigration period. For example, there is not a rigid caste system among descendants, and thus the readings of certain texts, such as the Gita and Ramayan, are much more widespread than in South Asia. These changes are related in part to community size but also to a long-term sense (that continues) that South Asians are a minority in Latin America and the Caribbean that faces particular discrimination.

Chinese-based Religions

In 1848, the Peruvian government decided to import Chinese contract laborers who they hoped would help them duplicate the success of the sugar export trade in the West Indies and Cuba. Between 1848 and 1874, some 91,000 Chinese entered Peru with contracts, almost all males, with some 42,000 arriving in the half decade after 1870. Other significant numbers of Chinese immigrants went to Cuba and Mexico. More recently, Chinese immigrants have arrived in Latin America as part of China's expanded trade in the region. Today, unreliable statistics suggests that 1.3 million people of Chinese descent including immigrants and descendants live in Latin America, with the largest numbers in Peru, Brazil, Panama, Cuba, and Jamaica.

Chinese who came to Latin America and the Caribbean in the nineteenth century had little opportunity for religious practice and were often under intense pressure to convert to Christianity. More recent immigrants from the People's Republic of China often do not consider themselves traditionally religious. Even so, Latin American cities with large populations of Chinese descent often have temples that are used primarily for ethnicity-building experiences (for example, food and martial arts) and for rituals related to ancestor worship.

Korean Christianity

Korean immigration to South America began on a small scale in the mid-1950s and was formalized in 1962 when the South Korean government passed its "Overseas Emigration Law" to control population, reduce unemployment, and garner foreign exchange via immigrant remittances. Korean Ministry of Foreign Affairs statistics suggest that about 100,000 Koreans live in Latin America, overwhelmingly in Brazil but also with strong presences in Argentina, Mexico, and Paraguay. Many scholars believe the numbers are at least three times larger.

While Korean-based new religions such as the Family Federation for World Peace and Unification (formerly the Unification Church) are small, Protestant and Catholic Christian worship among Korean immigrants and their descendants is large and growing. As is the case among other immigrant groups, religious affiliation functions both as a faith orientation and as a community building exercise, as rituals are conducted in both Korean (as a maintenance effort) and Spanish and Portuguese (as an acculturation effort). One aspect of Korean Christianity in Latin America that is noticeable is its transnationality. This stems from the patterns of Korean migration that often send family members to several countries simultaneously and then move young adults among the family to establish various work and educational experiences, multiple citizenships, and permanent residence spaces. As a result, Korean churches in Latin America often have a segment of worshippers who are transitory in a national sense.

Bibliography and Suggested Readings

Alves, Ronan, and Hideaki Matsuoka. *Japanese Religions in and Beyond the Japanese Diaspora*. Berkeley: Institute of East Asian Studies, 2007.

Lesser, Jeffrey. *Negotiating National Identity: Immigrants, Minorities and the Struggle for Ethnicity in Brazil*. Durham, NC: Duke University Press, 1999.

Matsuoka, Hideaki. *Japanese Prayer Below the Equator: How Brazilians Believe in the Church of World Messianity*. Lanham, MD: Lexington Books, 2007.

Rocha, Cristina. *Zen in Brazil: The Quest for Cosmopolitan Modernity*. Honolulu: University of Hawaii Press, 2006.

Shoji, Rafael, and Frank Usarski. "Japanese Religions in Brazil." *Japanese Journal of Religious Studies*, 35, no. 1 (2008): 1–12.

Siu, Lok. *Memories of a Future Home: Diasporic Citizenship of Chinese in Panama*. Stanford, CA: Stanford University Press, 2005.

Thompson, Stephen I. "Religious Conversion and Religious Zeal in an Overseas Enclave: The Case of the Japanese in Bolivia." *Anthropological Quarterly*, 41, no. 4 (October 1968): 201–208.

47
Ecumenism in Latin America: Between the Marketplace and the Desert

EDIN SUED ABUMANSSUR
TRANSLATED BY RODRIGO FRESTON

The term "ecumenism" refers to the general concept of convivial agreement and relationship between Christian churches, but in the diverse religious marketplace of Latin America, the term has several varied meanings. One result of the countless divisions within Christianity and the existence of an incalculable number of Christian churches is the growth of movements toward convergence. These convergence movements emphasize the theological unity that underlies these diverse ecclesiastical organizations. However, these ecumenical unity movements are also diverse in their forms, in their exercise of authority, in their self-understanding, and in their respective theologies, so that any search for unity that goes beyond these differences without compromising their diversity is to be admired. Only recently in the history of ecumenism has *diversity* ceased to be a synonym for division. Instead, there is an increasing tendency to see diversity as an asset in faith and culture.

The various forms and manifestations of ecumenism fall into three broad models. The first, and most pragmatic, focuses not on the unity of churches but rather on the interest of the collectivity regarding any particular problem that affects a larger community than the confessional one. In this case, the combined actions of the churches in favor of some common civil cause such as advocating for public transport in a poor neighborhood, combating racism, or organizing in favor of some environmental question, are considered ecumenical.

This ecumenism does not involve any theological discussion or any special ecclesiastical approach. It is an ecumenism that leaves each church organization safeguarded against the need to give up its own particular interests. Ecumenical actions of this nature often involve several Christian churches and even other religions because the struggle for the draining of a river, for example, does not demand any particular religious attitude or faith manifestation from those involved. This type of ecumenism, which is necessary when standing up to extreme poverty or organizing the community, has not produced theological reflections of any great consequence.

The second model of ecumenism is more official and occurs when churches or individuals of different confessions go in search of mutual recognition and a more peaceful existence side by side. All confessions may well feel at ease to participate in the pragmatic model of popular struggle. However, in this more official form involving the ecclesiastical bureaucracy of the different confessions, not all churches are willing to take part. In fact, this type of ecumenism often causes more resistance than empathy among the faithful.

Finally, the third model is daily ecumenism, in which members of different confessions meet one another in a religious environment created by circumstance. Chief examples of this in Latin America are weddings where the bride or groom are from different Christian churches, festive celebrations in support of some popular demand, liturgical memorial services for a famous person, or protests marking the assassination of a popular leader. These ecumenical celebrations typically are never the object of theological reflection, nor do they produce any consequences other than the beauty of the meetings themselves.

In Latin America, ecumenism has had a unique history. The organizations that raised the banner of the unity of the churches were not representative of them. Their main commitment was to the grassroots revolutionary process of the 1950s, 1960s, and 1970s, and again at the end of the twentieth century, in favor of democratic rights.

Ecumenism and the Field of Politics in Latin America

In the recent history of ecumenism in Latin America, theological and religious questions of unity were intertwined with the struggles against military dictatorships and in support of popular social revolutions. More than just proposing the unity of the churches, ecumenical movements in Latin America during the last four decades of the twentieth century asserted that for churches to be unified they had to undergo a social transformation. The unity of the churches was not limited to mere interdenominational cooperation. Rather, the essence of the question was ecclesial unity as the supporting force for a political-strategic vision of social action. Because of this, the ecumenical movement was capable of developing a theology of ecumenism in which the unity of the churches was seen as a sacramental sign of a sociopolitical utopia. As Julio Barreiro writes,

Our opinion is that we Latin Americans will accomplish the definitive liberation of our people through more integrated, more united and more organized social agreements, which allow us to overcome the injustices of the capitalist society. Because of this our proposal also envisages the need for the unity of the Church. (...). The problem of the unity of the Church in Latin America is also a political problem.[1]

This was the basis of the theology of ecumenism put forward by the ecumenical movement in Latin America. Although observers might expect this movement to unify various churches to emerge from the churches themselves, in many cases ecumenism attempted to replace existing ecclesial structures and emerged despite of, rather than because of, these existing structures. For the ecumenical movement, the discussion on the unity of the churches went beyond ecclesiastical and even religious boundaries. Thus, ecumenism became an expression that, by its mere mention, was capable of bringing together Christians with a political proposal for social transformation. Because of this, in the case of Latin America it is important not to confuse the idea of interchurch ecumenism, which tended by be local and ad hoc, with the ecumenical movement, which sought to be more inclusive and enduring. This movement was the more visible, more active, and more organized face of a proposal for religious unity. This unity, however, to a great extent, dispensed with the churches. The focus, target, and destiny of these ecumenical activities were a social revolution.

The maintenance of the ecumenical movement outside the ecclesiastical institutions would not have been possible had it not found efficient forms of organization, resistance, and expression. The type of organization that best suited these Christian groups searching for alternative institutional spaces to meet and work together was the nonprofit organization: easily formed and presenting few fiscal or bureaucratic problems. These societies made it possible for the ecumenical movement to work autonomously from the churches and, more important still, gave them the minimal juridical structure for receiving national and foreign donations. They also made it possible to hire employees and to maintain offices. Some of these societies even developed into companies of notable size such as Latin American Evangelical Social Action (Accion Social Ecuménica Latinoamericana – ASEL) in Cuba, the Universal Federation of Christian Student Movements (Federación Universal de Movimientos Estudiantiles Cristianos – FUMEC) in Argentina, and the Union

---

[1] Julio Barreiro, "Nuevas dimensiones para la misión de la Iglesia en América Latina," *El futuro del ecumenismo en América Latina*, eds. Julio Barreiro, Oscar Bolioli, and Jorge E. Monterroso (Buenos Aires: Tierra Nueva, 1977).

of Latin American Evangelical Youth (Unión Latinoamericana de Juventud Evangélica – ULAJE).

The ecumenical movement, therefore, consisted of the joint action of several non-governmental organizations set up by Latin American Protestants who did not find room in their churches to exercise their recently discovered faith in a God that forced them to break with the established socioeconomic order. For these Christians, the ecumenical movement was a refuge and also a platform from which they could witness to their faith. It served as an alternative, or complementary, space to the Protestant churches. Strategically, by organizing itself through the action of a group of nongovernmental organizations, the ecumenical movement obtained functional and operational courage for the accomplishment of proposals rejected by the churches. At the same time that these organizations guaranteed full autonomy from their historical Protestant churches, they also made it possible to maintain a referential connection with them.

For the organizations of the ecumenical movement, the referent that gave them their identity was their attitude of denial of the conservative theology normally associated with the Protestant churches. They wanted to be what the churches were not and to do what the churches could not. Even during the 1980s, when there was a more positive appraisal of the churches because of the action of the progressive sectors of the Catholic Church in the political arena, a critical tone in relation to the Protestant churches still remained.

It was this tradition of denial of the ecclesiastical structures that justified the existence of the ecumenical movement. However, at the same time that the movement denied the Protestant tradition in Latin America, it also reaffirmed it: although the churches might not have been capable of doing what the ecumenical movement did, the movement's need of Protestant churches was obvious. However conservative the churches were, they continued to serve as the referent around which, and for which, these organizations directed their action, at first to guarantee an alternative ecclesial space and then later, in the mid-1970s, to give the churches a more modern discourse.

According to the ecumenical movement thinking of the 1970s from a Catholic perspective, the existing Protestant churches could not serve as the basis for ecumenism because they did not represent the true Church of Christ owing to their separation from, and resistance to playing a role in, the grassroots struggles in Latin America. This criticism of the churches was, nevertheless, a focused and limited one. More than being a criticism of the churches, it was a criticism for the churches. Oscar Bolioli, the Uruguayan Methodist theologian, commented on this tense relationship and described this period as the emergence of the ecumenical movement and of its radicalization stamped by its separation from the institutional churches. The ecumenical movement, for him, was a prophetic voice calling the churches to return to their origins.

> The institution has a rich, immense deposit to be shared. It is the movement that injects life and challenge into the institutional stability. Just as there has never been a history of the people of God without prophets, neither are prophets possible without the people of God.[2]

This attitude on the part of the ecumenical movement did not mean, purely and simply, a return to the churches. Yes, it was a return, but with the intention of changing the churches and getting them more involved in ecumenical-political projects.

From the end of the 1960s through the beginning of the 1980s, the ecumenical movement saw no hope in (or need for) working with the ecclesiastical institutions, as the field of action seemed more promising with other groups and organizations that were more committed to social change. However, in the 1980s, a process of trying to give a new discourse to the churches started. One is no longer dealing with an alternative discourse to the churches but instead an alternative of and for the churches.

The last decades of the twentieth century saw the end of authoritarian regimes and dictatorships in Latin America. It also saw the end of a world characterized by a political bipolarity. Up to that point, late-twentieth century global politics was divided between the two major *oikoumenes:* one was capitalist, a defender of the free market, and politically and militarily led by the United States. The other was socialist and under the hegemony of the Soviet Union. With the exception of the so-called "nonaligned" countries, the world was divided between the areas of influence of one or other of these powers. Peoples and nations that remained outside these areas were transformed into territories to be conquered, areas of dispute, and objects to be coveted.

With the end of this bipolarity, the theology of ecumenism, which was forged amidst the fights for freedom and resistance against Latin American dictatorships strongly identified with the Western *oikoumene* and saw itself in need of finding another legitimating basis for the actions of the ecumenical bodies such as ASEL in Cuba, FUMEC in Argentina, and ULAJE.

With the rebuilding of the democracies, the churches themselves got involved in political and social issues, and the organizations of the ecumenical

---

2 Oscar Bolioli, "Una historia de unidad," in *El futuro del ecumenismo en América Latina*, eds. Julio Barreiro, Oscar Bolioli, and Jorge E. Monterroso (Buenos Aires: Tierra Nueva, 1977).

movement began to see ecclesiastical institutions as partners in projects of a social nature. In other words, the churches began to take on the role of protagonists of the ecumenical causes, and a change in emphasis and discourse about the struggle for the unity of the Churches ensued. It is in this context of the re-democratization of Latin America that organizations such as the Latin American Council of Churches (Consejo Latinoamericano de Iglesias – CLAI) and other national bodies such as the National Council of Christian Churches of Brazil (Conselho Nacional de Igrejas Cristãs do Brasil – CONIC) gained importance. These groups, different from the organizations during the previous decades, were formed by churches themselves, especially the historical Protestant churches that grasped the need for strengthening bonds of cooperation and mutual recognition.

These changes created a tension between churches searching for a new, institutionalized definition of ecumenism and the organizations of the ecumenical movement that tried to answer that search for ecumenism with their closeness to the Catholic Church and their commitments to social and political change in Latin America. From this tension there emerged a new profile for ecumenism at the end of the century: a space in which both churches and nongovernmental organizations took part, molded by a theology that understood ecumenism as being a sign of the "unity of the people in their struggle for freedom." In Latin America, the commitment to engaging social reality and the level of theological penetration that marked Protestants' lived ecumenism from the 1950s onward continues to set a high standard for modern ecumenical efforts.

Ecumenism and the Religious Field in Latin America

To the casual observer, ecumenism may appear to be experiencing an ebb tide in which churches either cannot succeed in, or do not want to work on, the implementation of processes of deeper dialogue and working together. On the surface, it seems that the influence of religious fundamentalism has created a law of institutional survival built on the philosophy of "each one for himself." In part this is true, but it is also true that for many churches cooperation is the best, if not the only, way to survive in an extremely competitive religious field in which the weaker bodies have little or no chance of survival.

The high degree of competition in the religious field is the most distinctive characteristic of contemporary Protestantism in contrast with the milieu of the ecumenical movement during the last forty years of the twentieth century in Latin America. Today, more so than in the past, the banner of ecumenism serves as the distinctive characteristic certain churches that are looking for the cutting edge in the religious marketplace. Ecumenism serves to distinguish between churches that offer religious goods of a more erudite nature and those that offer religious products for popular consumption. The erudite religious goods connected to ecumenism include, among other things, sophisticated theological reflection, a consistent code of ethics, and music of a melodic tradition and structure that refer back to the historical classics. At the other end of the spectrum are the religious goods for popular consumption such as immediate solutions for problems, the magical relationship with sacred beings, ephemeral music for immediate consumption, and the emphasis on the emotions. It is in this sense that ecumenism stops being a proposal for inclusion or a search for unity and starts to function as the operative element in identity formation of certain churches in the competition for a better position in the religious marketplace.

Ecumenism has become one of the key pieces of data used to analyze the religious marketplace in Latin America. It provides insight into the changes in power and prestige among different religious organizations and into the alliances that determine the relative positions of each group. This is true not only of the internal dynamics and relationships in the religious market but also in the contacts and wider negotiations of these bodies with the secular powers.

From a historic perspective, the development of ecumenism resulted from a long process of negotiation between various churches starting with the break-up of the monopoly supplier of religious goods. The type of denominationalism implanted in Latin America by North American missionaries beginning in the second half of the nineteenth century may not have attracted large numbers of converts, but it did draw enough followers to call the monopolistic position of the Catholic Church into question. For many decades, antagonism inside the religious field took place, on the one hand, because of the astonishment caused by the situation of pluralism on the part of the Catholic hierarchy and, on the other hand, by the thirst for the conquering of bigger and bigger slices of the market of religious goods shown by the Protestant churches. Religious pluralism is, necessarily, a situation in which the agencies and the agents that operate in the field feel themselves in need of disputing, conquering, maintaining, and guaranteeing the loyalty of those who accept their proposals. It is a market situation.

Those churches that felt they were qualified to contest for a greater share of the religious market were, and are, the most likely to reject ecumenism. The proselytizing impulse lay at the origin of the rejection of the ecumenical causes because in the calculation of the relative advantages for the more aggressive churches, any moderation in their discourse in relation to the other ecclesiastical bodies meant a smaller rate of expansion. In a situation of great competitiveness, where the survival of each group depends on its capacity to show its cutting edge in the offer of religious goods, ecumenism was of interest only to the ecclesiastical organizations less qualified to aggressively contest the market.

The proselytizing impulse that maintained the significant growth rates in some of Protestant churches has diminished in the early twenty-first century with the exception of a few, rare cases that found in charismatic discourse and behavior an alternative route for evangelization. In the case of Brazil, mainline Protestants and Pentecostals represented a mere 2.6 percent of the population in the 1940s. By the end of the 1990s they amounted to 15.4 percent of the population. However, according to the 2000 census, the Pentecostals jumped during the last decade of the twentieth century from 5.6 percent to 10.4 percent of the population while mainline Protestants moved only from 3 percent of the population to 4.1 percent.

In other words, mainline Protestants have lost their initial appeal in the search for new followers. The bad performance in the conquest and occupation of new territories, both geographical and cultural, of both Protestants and Catholics alike, is a stark contrast to the Pentecostals. More specifically still, it lies in contrast to the new Christian churches – the neo-Pentecostals – who have shown great vigor and adaptive capacity to the new times of provocative competition in the religious marketplace.

The churches most likely to participate in ecumenical bodies in Latin America in the twenty-first century are precisely the ones that are satisfied with an almost vegetative growth rate. For these churches, the sharing of forces and of resources, clergy exchanges, and a search for a consensus on some theological themes has proven to be the way forward. This is not to say that this attitude of mutual respect and coming closer is something merely utilitarian and, consequently, of doubtful moral value. Very much to the contrary, this attitude, dictated by reason and the need for survival, can provide the motivation for the maintenance of these agencies in the religious market.

This maintenance motivation has made ecumenism into an identity banner for some churches. These churches fly this banner in a context in which religious goods are reduced to a single, general exchange value. To be seen as an ecumenical church is a form of protection, while at the same time it is a proclamation of the type of theological affiliation of that church. Ecumenism is also merchandise on offer in the market of symbolic goods.

For highly competitive churches on the other hand, ecumenism is of no interest because they have more to lose with mutual recognition and collaboration than they do in continuing with the militant attitudes that have already proven effective in increasing membership numbers. Among charismatic Protestants in areas like Brazil, where they movement has taken over many traditional Protestant churches and replaced traditional theological rationality with collective behavior centered on emotions, ecumenism is seen as being a proposal for spurious and undesirable alliances and a sign of the cooling off of the evangelizing impulse. Adding to this the fact that ecumenism also has a historical association with the political liberation struggles that went hand in hand with revolutionary movements in Latin America, it is not surprising that some Protestant churches, under the direction of a leadership influenced by the charismatic movement, have opted to abandon ecumenical bodies on the national and regional level.

The main characteristic of the Latin American religious field in the early twenty-first century is the enormous segmentation of the public. This has led to the emergence of specialized churches that look after the specific needs of certain subgroups of the faithful. These are churches with specific discourses and practices to meet the needs of stigmatized social groups or those who do not find space in the other churches for them to exist the way they are. Athletes, artists, gays, police officers, and many other special interest groups have all looked for a personal church and have all found someone willing to tailor a religious product to suit them. These new churches that do not fit into existing classifications or typologies often are not worried about or interested in the type of theological discussions that have historically accompanied ecumenism. They came into existence in an atmosphere of plurality and competition and do not see in this a problem to be overcome. Ecumenism, its struggles, its proposals, and its raison d'être, do not relate to the types of concerns and demands that fill these new churches with enthusiasm.

The question that remains to be answered is this: Is there a future for ecumenism in Latin America? From the theological point of view, the challenge facing the ecumenical cause today is greater than that experienced before by the churches and other bodies committed to the question. It is hard to know if the churches and ecumenical bodies will have the capacity or desire to answer the challenge presented by the explosion of new churches and by the high level of competitiveness in the religious field. The Latin American ecumenical movement is moving very slowly and is not able to keep up with the rapid changes surrounding it. Because of this, members of the movement appear to be more comfortable remaining confined to the churches that traditionally answer the call of Christian unity. A further problem is that many of the new emerging churches do not enjoy a good reputation with the theological and ecumenical intelligentsia. In the early twenty-first century, many theologians, pastors, and religious leaders refuse to see in these new churches anything more than commercial enterprises that exploit public good faith.

However, from a sociological point of view, ecumenism can also be a channel and a source for the legitimating of those new churches that look for recognition and legitimacy in the religious field. Eventually, in the uncertain future, perhaps these new churches may see that it would be beneficial for them to sit in assembly with the churches that enjoy greater prestige with the media and other areas of power. One way or the other, perhaps it may be more fitting for the ecumenical movement in Latin America to continue as a voice calling out in the desert. That is the place of the prophets.

Bibliography and Suggested Readings

Barreiro, Julio. "Nuevas dimensiones para la misión de la Iglesia en América Latina." In Julio Barreiro, Oscar Bolioli, and Jorge E. Monterroso (eds.), *El futuro del ecumenismo en América Latina*. Buenos Aires: Tierra Nueva, 1977.

Berger, Peter L. *The Sacred Canopy: Elements of a Sociological Theory of Religion*. Garden City, NY: Doubleday, 1967.

Bolioli, Oscar. "Una historia de unidad." In Julio Barreiro, Oscar Bolioli, and Jorge E. Monterroso (eds.), *El futuro del ecumenismo en América Latina*. Buenos Aires: Tierra Nueva, 1977.

Dias, Zwinglio Mota. "Evaluación Crítica de la Pratica Ecuménica Latinoamericana." *Cristianismo y Sociedad*, 60 (1979): 3–29.

Mariano, Ricardo. "Expansão pentecostal no Brasil: O caso da Igreja Universal." *Estudos Avançados*, 18, no. 52 (2004): 121–138.

Mendonça, Antônio Gouvêa. *Protestantes, pentecostais & ecumênicos: O campo religioso e seus personagens*. São Bernardo do Campo: UMESP, 1997.

Santa Ana, Julio H. *Ecumenismo e libertação*. Petrópolis: Vozes, 1987.

Shaull, Richard. "Entre Jesus e Marx." *Religião e Sociedade*, 9 (1983): 47–58.

48

The Religious Field in Latin America: Autonomy and Fragmentation

DAVID LEHMANN

Writing on Latin American religion must take as one of its building blocks the classic distinction between erudite or institutionalized religion and popular religion, which are also distinctive features of Catholicism throughout the Latin world. They are not watertight compartments, but rather different spheres that nevertheless are engaged in a constant dialectic, mutually influencing each other's rituals and symbolism, their heroes and monsters, saints and sinners. The distinctively Catholic character of the popular-erudite dialectic derives from the Church's millennial development of a worldwide hierarchical and institutional apparatus including Holy Orders; educational and charitable institutions; and an omnipresent musical, architectural, and monumental presence, coexisting with an infinity of local saints, festivals, confraternities, shrines, pilgrimages, and superstitions, of which a small number blossom, for probably quite contingent reasons, into regional, national, and even global cults (compare, e.g., Lourdes and Guadalupe). In the words of Daniel Levine, writing in the 1980s

> ...the institutional and the popular cannot be separated. Popular religion is not an autonomous, somehow "natural" product. Indeed much of the stock of symbol and metaphor, as well as the organizational forms and practices often considered "popular," are historical products, born of the relation of subordinate groups to dominant institutions, among them the churches. The link is constant, for the churches provide legitimacy, support, continuity and a sense of meaning and moral authority to popular religious expression.[1]

Now turn to the following remark by the late Olivia Harris: "To write about practical Christianity [in the Andes in this case] is always to face a

---

[1] Daniel Levine, "Colombia: The Institutional Church and the Popular," in *Religion and Political Conflict in Latin America*, ed. Daniel Levine (Chapel Hill: University of North Carolina Press, 1986), 188.

conundrum: what to include and what to exclude?"[2] That is, what counts as Christianity and what does not? As her paper develops, Harris describes the continuing interaction between official and nonofficial practices within Andean Christianity and on its edges – but as she says, there is no consistent line. Five hundred years after the first campaigns of Christian conversion, the relationship between official and unofficial practices, even under the same church roof, continues, especially in regions with a prominent indigenous presence.

In accordance with Pierre Bourdieu, the relationship between the official and the indigenous is one of permanent negotiation. Peasants (Harris avoids calling them '*indios*') attend Mass but do not take communion, which has no interest for them, let alone confession; instead, they rush to be sprinkled with holy water. Attendance at life cycle rituals is for the purpose of ensuring health, of "satisfying God's hunger" with no regard for the idea of a sacrament or of eternal life. For the peasants, payment for a mass is essential because it ensures that an exchange has taken place and thus guarantees the benefit that otherwise would be just a promise. In Harris's account, Spanish priests schooled in post-conciliar (i.e., post–Vatican II) modernism and social commitment are utterly disconcerted; one of them is described driving away in his overloaded jeep after unwillingly accepting the payments and enduring an interminable mass – interminable no doubt because of the votive offerings, promises, and exchanges that had to be dealt with individually. These payments are not gifts because for those who make them exchange is the essence of their relationship with the supernatural, whether the supernatural being is one of "their" divinities or a Catholic one.

The bemused priest might have recalled the difficulties faced by his colonial predecessors in explaining to the ancestors of those peasants – or at least of their Mexican counterparts – that the effigies of a Virgin or of Jesus were only representations and were not themselves possessed of supernatural powers. In 1525, the Franciscans unleashed a campaign of terror in New Spain, being forced, in Serge Gruzinski's words, to remove Christian images because "images of Christ and the Virgin had been mingled with the idols and irresistibly absorbed into the autochthonous paganism."[3] His point is that in Europe itself, no less than in Latin America, images served and continue to serve

2 Olivia Harris, "The Eternal Return of Conversion: Christianity as Contested Domain in Highland Bolivia," *The Anthropology of Christianity*, ed. Fenella Cannell (Durham, NC: Duke University Press, 2006), 52.
3 Serge Gruzinski, *Images at War: Mexico from Columbus to Blade Runner (1492–2019)*, trans. Heather MacLean (Durham, NC: Duke University Press, 2001), 61.

many purposes and could not be immunized against magical manipulation any more than the people could be immunized against their own inclinations to imbue certain sorts of venerated objects with magical, supernatural, or indeed contagious qualities, or with powers of pollution. The first generation who conquered Mexico with Cortés thought that they were destroying the indigenous belief system by destroying idols, but they did not understand that supernatural forces were, and maybe still are, ubiquitous, for the indigenous saw the presence of the deities in all sorts of objects. Anthropomorphic representation was not part of their way of grasping the supernatural forces on whose appeasement – with food and human blood – their lives depended. A few years later, Franciscan missionaries – undertaking a campaign similar to those being conducted in Europe at the same time – could not understand how the monotheism they preached, or thought they were preaching, led Indians to attach the names of God and the Virgin Mary to almost any image that crossed their sight.

Popular religion focuses on individuals' life cycles and on the lives of their immediate circle, their locality, or community; it mixes the sacred and the profane, if not in the same ceremony, certainly in the same event – for example, the Saint's Day is also a market day during which the official celebrations are followed by dancing and revelry, a bullfight, a cockfight, and so on. The phrase "and so on" conveys very well the unguarded or unbounded character of popular celebrations and the proliferations of rituals and roles that they can encompass while the idea of exchange conveys the multiple social relationships that are cemented, or ruptured, by popular religious practices. The notion of exchange is derived from Bourdieu as well, and – probably unwittingly Carlos Brandão, like me, describes what I have called the dialectic of the erudite and the popular, that is, the forever frustrated efforts of the Church to "purify" or subordinate popular celebrations whose protagonists are for their part fulfilling their function as vehicles for the preservation of heritage. The public character of the celebration is not frivolous; in Brandão's words it exhibits a belief that the locality has been cleansed of the dust of sinfulness because it has recognized the majesty of divine judgment.

Despite its departure from the detail of approved ritual, popular Catholicism has remained subordinate to the official Church and has not developed any kind of dissidence, nor has it produced a distinctive theology. The traditional popular religion that survives, in the context of contemporary massive urbanization and globalization, may now show symptoms of detachment, occasionally reaching the edges of the surreal, as witness the cult of Santísima Muerte, which deploys quasi-Catholic imagery and seems little different from innumerable other saintly cults, were it not for the macabre skull of its object. In Chesnut's description, the Santa Muerte has the mission of "bestowing blessings of prosperity and abundance" among her adepts and those who, like an "Archbishop" of the cult in Mexico City who had his recognition as an association with religious purposes withdrawn as a result of pressure from the Church, "traffic in her image." From one point of view, this makes her resemble any other saint, but the scandalous character of her representation, reproduced in niches around Mexico and present also in Argentina, is a symptom of the changing religious field, as we shall see later.

The cult of Santísima Muerte, incorporating motifs from traditional popular religiosity (notably the effigies associated with Mexico's famous and colorful Day of the Dead) illustrates in a small way the need to think about hegemonic change in two ways. One focuses on the now standard observations about evangelical growth as a religious strand that is cut off from Catholicism: the classical Pentecostal churches, dispersed in innumerable small chapels and churches and with at most a skeleton central organization, do not encroach on the Church's symbolic and ritual territory. Neo-Pentecostals, which are congregations with Pentecostal practices that formed new denominations in the late twentieth century, have very occasionally engaged in skirmishes, as in the famous case of the Universal Church of the Kingdom of God (Igreja Universal do Reino de Deus – IURD) and the incident known as the *"chute na Virgem"* ("the kick against the Virgin") in 1995. But this is also one Pentecostal church whose rituals bear explicit Catholic references such as anointing the faithful with oil and adapting the idea of holy water by inviting people to sprinkle "water from the River Jordan" to cleanse their homes of diabolic influences. Surely, this is one of many signs beyond the bald ambition implicit in its name that this organization seeks to supplant Catholic hegemony.

The remainder of this chapter describes and interprets the way in which this relationship was unexpectedly transformed in the late twentieth century, how the popular became independent of the erudite, how Liberation Theology or *"basista"* Catholicism could be seen as yet another – maybe the last – strategy to capture and channel popular religion; how evangelical Christianity became a far more autonomous version of popular religion, cut off from the erudite and shorn of hegemonic potential; and finally (this is the second focus) how devotional movements within Catholicism itself represent perhaps a new stage in the gradual evolution of Catholicism from its centuries-old status as a hegemonic culture toward the conformation of a mere denomination that can, finally, live with modernity, demonstrating that it is not necessary to be liberal to achieve that, and indeed that in the religious sphere at least the reverse may be the case.

Toward Institutionalization: Popular Religion before and after Vatican II

In Latin America, the Church hierarchy in the twentieth century undertook various campaigns to make popular religion more orthodox and also to encourage commitment and religious education among more nominal Catholics. The first wave, known as Romanization, occurred in the 1930s and reflected a concerted effort at centralization of power in the Vatican especially power of appointment of bishops without government involvement (after reaching Concordats with various states), as well as involvement in education and some political alliances. In Brazil, it inspired the "neo-Christendom" strategy of Cardinal Leme da Silveira Cintra, who cultivated a cordial relationship with Brazil's reforming and authoritarian president, Getulio Vargas. The Social Doctrine of the Church as first elaborated by Leo X in *Rerum Novarum* (1891) fed into corporatist ideas of the state and of state regulation of class conflict and industrial relations that inspired labor legislation in Chile in the 1920s (under Arturo Alessandri) and in Vargas' Estado Novo.

During this period, the Church hierarchy also showed itself adept at mobilizing popular religion in the interests of its own positions. This is graphically described by Alan Knight and also by Mary Kay Vaughan in her account of fierce struggles over education in post-*Cristiada* Mexico under Cárdenas. In the different regions Vaughan studied (Sonora and Puebla), we find the clergy uniting with the more conservative post-revolutionary politicians against the more radically anticlerical and socialist educational initiatives, brandishing the threat that the new teachers would undermine traditional morals and place the virtue of their daughters at risk. In Argentina, reformist elements in the Church established influential Catholic Worker Circles to advance the interests of labor under the aegis of the Church. At the same time, the bishops took tighter control of lay organizations such as the Acción Católica. But also during this period, the French Catholic public intellectual Jacques Maritain was heralding a change in the religious field in his widely read *Humanisme Intégral* (1936) and elsewhere. Maritain was an advocate of a corporatist arrangement of society in the image of medieval guilds as a way of overcoming the contradictions of capitalism. However, he was also very unpopular in clerical circles on account of his hostility to

Franco during the Spanish Civil War, and he remains a major figure as an advocate of a nonsectarian Catholic politics in the shape of what became Christian Democracy.

While the worldwide Church hierarchy was engaged in its project of Romanization and modernization, the first half of the twentieth century also saw some instances of loss of control or emergence of popular religion onto a more political stage, as in the Brazilian conflicts of Canudos, the Contestado, and Juazeiro (where Padre Cicero established a more or less independent politico-ecclesiastical fiefdom from 1911 until his death in 1934). But these were ephemeral episodes, two of which were put down by military force, with various disconnected millenarian, messianic, or simply socio-religious movements. Being popular movements, they were more concerned with tradition than with doctrine. To some extent, Mexico's Cristero War was also such an instance, though in that case a sector of the clergy took an active part in military action, against the judgment, and even the fury, of many bishops and of the Vatican itself. Jean Meyer in his passionate account insists again and again on the betrayal of the Cristero peasants prepared to fight and die for Christ by a hierarchy who looked to the long term, did not believe the Church in Mexico was in mortal danger, and wanted peaceful coexistence with the state. Meyer exalts the popular religion of the Cristeros who accepted implicitly the message that God sent his mother the Virgin of Guadalupe specifically to Mexico and who now took the chance to reach heaven by dying in defense of their faith.

Whereas in Europe the Church was baffled and embattled politically – by socialism in Spain, France, Germany, and Italy, and by fascism in Italy and Germany (though Spanish fascism was in close alliance with the Church) – in Latin America Church leaders were less threatened, even if they were uncomfortable in some cases, notably with Peronism in mid-century Argentina. The Church gained both independence and influence vis-à-vis the state and was under little external pressure to adapt to the permissiveness that had always troubled Church leaders and to the socialist influences that were far more attenuated in Latin America than in Europe. So, the moderately modernizing changes initiated with Romanization continued unperturbed until pressures for change that had built up in Europe (not much in Latin America) eventually came to a head at Vatican II.

A group of Latin American theologians and bishops (Gustavo Gutiérrez of Peru, Msgr. Manuel Larraín of Chile, and Msgr. Hélder Câmara of Brazil) had been very active at Vatican II and brought the Council's message back to the continent. The translation of Vatican II into Spanish and Portuguese took several forms. The most intellectual was Liberation Theology, which took the project of the social doctrine much further by denouncing the Church's posture as an ally of the ruling classes and by questioning the whole idea of a salvation restricted to the next world. Liberation Theology also sought to play down the emphasis of traditional religiosity on an individual's personal relationship with the divine, drawing on the Gospel's teachings to emphasize the relationship with neighbors and with the community, and also shifting the idea of charity – with its connotations of short-term alleviation – toward structural change as a more enduring way of caring for one's neighbor. Liberation Theology was vulnerable to the charge that it represented a version of Marxism, and some followers did indeed eventually "convert" to Marxist parties or movements.

For the most part, however, the defense was that Marxism was a method, and the leading theologian of liberation, Gustavo Gutiérrez, gradually ceased to make any reference to Marxism after the controversy following publication of his first book *Teología de la Liberación: Perspectivas* in 1971. Over time, he came to pay more attention to indigenous and women's issues and looked to the sixteenth-century bishop Bartolomé de las Casas (the "Defender of the Indians") rather than to modern theology and philosophy as his inspiration. Las Casas, nonetheless, has himself even after five centuries never ceased to attract controversy, and the question of his canonization apparently arose only in the year 2000. Whatever Gutiérrez' own intentions, it was in some ways a challenge to the transcendent in religion because it inspired so much social and political activism in the name of Christianity.

Liberation Theology had broad international appeal and also broad intellectual appeal beyond the frontiers of the Church, of theology, of Catholicism, and even of religion. The range of influence of Liberation Theology, or rather of ideas derived more or less directly and more or less faithfully from Liberation Theology, has been vast: from the Brazilian Landless People's Movement (Movimento dos Sem Terra – MST) to some guerrilla ventures in Bolivia, Colombia, and Guatemala (though in this last case, the term "Liberation Theology" was rarely used, per se); it also helped to bring the themes of participation and popular education onto the international development agenda, notably because among the Ecclesial Base Communities (comunidades eclesiales de base – CEBs), which Liberation Theology inspired, the method of the Brazilian educator Paulo Freire gained much acceptance. Liberation Theology made a major contribution to the autonomy of the nongovernmental organization (NGO) field in the sphere of development policy and practice and to social movements through the work of inspired priests and nuns, which gained support from the Bishops' Conferences, at least in Brazil.

These Bishops' Conferences had not existed as decision-making bodies before Vatican II, but once formally established, they provided a bureaucratic instance and also a channel for external funding for the Pastorals, which now tended to replace what were previously known as Missions. Brazilian examples include the Pastoral da Juventude, CIMI (Conselho Indigenista Missionário), and the Pastoral da Terra, and there are similar institutions in other countries. These institutions were staffed mostly by lay activists with a sprinkling of ex-priests. A small amount of Liberation Theology in a depoliticized form was also co-opted into official Vatican doctrine. Under Pope John Paul II, the preferential option for the poor became a focus of the Church, an emphasis that Pope Francis I seems strongly inclined to revive. The CEBs, for their part, have tended to rely on the logistical, educational, and intellectual support of priests and nuns and some bishops for their organization – an observation supported by my own fieldwork and that of others. The influence of Liberation Theology on Catholic schools and universities, whose intake is mostly upper middle class, seems to have been limited, and it has remained a minority phenomenon when compared with devotional movements such as Focolari, Neocatecumenes, and above all, the Catholic Charismatic Renewal.

At first, Liberation Theology had an ambivalent relationship with popular religion, divided between a disdain for superstition – seen as a distraction from the structural problems of society – and a certain reverence for the true, unblemished religiosity of the oppressed. Under the influence of Liberation Theology's ideas – which I term *basismo* – samba drums might be brought into church, for example, or a pilgrimage that once had celebrated a fiesta would be turned into a celebration of the migrant worker as an emblem of suffering (as in the *Romaria do Migrante*, or Migrant's Pilgrimage, near Campina Grande in the northeast of Brazil).

On the whole, though, Liberation Theology and basismo had little effect on the rituals and celebrations that punctuate the calendar of many parishes, or on the routine activities of *benzedeiras* and *curandeiras* who make up the fabric of religious life in the Brazilian hinterland. Indeed, some accounts emphasize the middle, or lower-middle, class character of CEB participants and the somewhat academic character of their meetings. In my own studies in Salvador, Bahia, in the early 1990s, the striking feature was that the meetings and discussion groups – known as Educação Popular – attracted a core group of faithful participants, but did not treat evangelizing as a priority. The contrast with the expansionary energy of their Pentecostal neighbors was overwhelming, as was that between the self-financing Pentecostals and the reliance of Educação Popular on international NGO support.

Vatican II, by "opening the windows" for a spring-cleaning (as Pope John XXIII said), did shake the structure of the Catholic Church because of its demographic as well as ideological sequel. A collapse of recruitment to the clergy and religious orders in Latin America, and also in the European countries that supplied so many of them, compounded a wave of departures among the clergy of people who mostly wanted to remain good Catholics but not priests. Pope John Paul II redrew the lines of the religious field for the Church when he decreed a withdrawal from political controversy and party alignment, and undertook a campaign of marginalization against Liberation Theology and basismo. In a campaign of surveillance and personnel shifts during the 1980s, his emissaries went around Latin America removing liberationist theologians from teaching posts and positions of influence and dispatching them to obscure parishes and positions. Like Lenin, his motto could have been "better fewer, but better," with a focus on personal morality and a tightening of discipline within the structures of the Church. John Paul II also signaled a desire to encourage popular religion, with its focus on local traditions, by promoting and approving record numbers of new beatifications and sanctifications, reversing the traditionally skeptical response of the Vatican to popular beatification campaigns.

Catholic Devotional and Charismatic Movements at the Turn of the Century

The Pope was also encouraging, more or less discreetly, new types of religious renewal that Liberation Theology had simply not dreamed of and that caught its protagonists off guard. These renewal movements have been visible only since about 1980, but in that short period they have taken part in a multifaceted reshaping of Latin American Catholicism – a reshaping yet to be registered in an academic literature which, *grosso modo*, turned from enthusiasm for Liberation Theology to a fascination for Pentecostalism – and has produced changes that would have seemed inconceivable in the wake of Vatican II.

From one point of view, these changes represent a strategy to resist the pressures to democratize the Church's hierarchy, to resist the permissive society, and to resist involvement with social movements identified largely with the left by espousing conservative moral values and the religiosity of instant satisfaction and by raising, rather than lowering, the price to pay for religious recognition in terms of personal carnal and financial sacrifice.

However, that point of view is too simplistic and represents little more than an expression of distaste. The movements are too diverse in structure and ethos to be interpreted as a response to a single strategy, and they are far too wealthy, often, for their existence to be explained by Vatican or even episcopal support. This is evident from a list only of a few of them: Opus Dei, the Legionarios de Cristo, the Cursillos de Cristiandad, Focolari, Comunione e Liberazione (mostly Italian), Sodalitium and Schoenstatt, and the biggest of them all, the worldwide quasi-Pentecostal but Catholic movement known as the Charismatic Renewal. They all enjoy some kind of papal recognition, expressed in the numerous titles the pope has at his disposal. Opus is a "personal prelature," Legionarios a "religious congregation," and so on. However, none originates in a papal or episcopal initiative, and many are lay-founded and lay-driven. Some of them are quite secretive (especially Opus Dei). Opus's website says it has 88,000 *"fieles"* (followers) of whom fewer than 2,000 are priests and 77 percent are married men and women. The remainder have taken vows of chastity and of these many live in Opus houses. Opus operates schools and universities in several countries (Universidad de los Andes in Chile; Universidad del Pacífico in Mexico, and the original Universidad de Navarra in Spain) and as of 2010 included several Chilean and Peruvian bishops among its members – notably the Archbishop of Lima.

The Legionarios are more of a mass organization; they too operate a network of universities in Chile, and in Mexico under the Anahuac name, as well as schools. According to their website, the Legion has 800 priests and 2,500 seminarians being trained plus a large but unspecified number of followers in its affiliated Regnum Christi movement. In Chile at least, the Legion and Opus run schools that attract the children of the economic elite and have an explicit evangelizing agenda, notably to bring parents to religion through their children. Of Focolari, Schoenstatt, and the Neocatecumene, little is published save on Wikipedia. Comunione e Liberazione had great success setting up student residences in Italian university towns; its ethos is devotional and also encourages students to engage in social work, and until the collapse of Christian Democracy it had a prominent role in Italian politics. Its presence in Latin America seems sketchy. It does run the Universidad Sede Sapientiae in Peru – though to what extent this is intended to spread the Comunione e Liberazione ideology is unclear.

This list does not include the many Jesuit schools and universities, such as the Universidad Iberoamericana in Mexico that is at the heart of a network of Jesuit institutions of higher education. But the ethos of these institutions is different from those mentioned. Jesuit institutions are not established with a missionary or evangelizing purpose and tend to encourage a liberal atmosphere.

They are expensive, though, and so their students tend to come from the upper middle classes, like those of the institutions operated by Opus and the Legionarios, with the exception of the Jesuits' Ayuuk Intercultural University located in an indigenous community in Oaxaca, Mexico. Another example of such openness is the Catholic University of Rio de Janeiro (Pontifícia Universidade Católica do Rio de Janeiro – PUC-Rio), whose affirmative action program run in cooperation with EDUCAFRO, a network of courses led by the well-known Franciscan friar Frei David helping black and low-income applicants prepare for university entrance exams, has brought a noticeable change in the racial profile of its student body. Frei David has become a very prominent and even radical figure, devoted to the advancement of black people in the Brazilian education system

Of these movements, Catholic Charismatic Renewal (Renovación Carismática Católica – CCR) is the one that most resembles a mass movement, at least in Latin America (less so in North America, where it operates more like the "small groups" found in Protestant congregations). In the early 1990s, intellectuals linked to or identified with Liberation Theology and the Igreja Popular were contemptuous of what they saw as its conservative focus on personal religiosity and its middle class following, but the fact is that the CCR has grown rapidly and in diverse ways. Unlike Opus or the Legionarios, it is not a tight organization with clear boundaries but rather a movement animated by activists within the clergy and among the laity. It runs, or maybe just inspires, meetings of all sizes, from very small parish-based gatherings to mass meetings in football stadia and spectacles featuring celebrity preachers – like the so-called Singing Priest of São Paulo, Marcelo Rossi. Beyond events carrying the Charismatic label, one also observes Charismatic habits, such as singing with arms outstretched and speaking in tongues, infiltrating services in parish churches. The concern for the Church hierarchy, of course, is to maintain control of the CCR. So, often bishops will name a priest to oversee it, and priests require that meetings must take place in a church, not in other premises.

These movements may or may not reflect a Church institution that has come to terms, finally, with modernity, but they surely reflect the penetration of Catholicism's culture by modernity. Although some find this surprising because they seem so conservative, it is by now widely agreed that many movements whose ethos is deeply conservative with respect to religiosity and personal morality are also modern in their forms of organization and in their independence from inherited structures of religious power. This is recognized by grand theorists like Shmuel Eisenstadt and David Martin with respect to Pentecostals and fundamentalists, but it has yet to be applied to renewal movements in Catholicism and Anglicanism. The Charismatic Renewal uses phrases such as "being in the world but not of the world, 'in the media but not of the media' – in short, 'to be modern without modernity,'"[4] and this includes a prominent, even equal, role for men and women and the admission of couples in religious communities.

One feature of their modernity is the this-worldly focus on managing one's well-being, sometimes described as refashioning the self – making the individual responsible for self-transformation as opposed to waiting for supernatural intervention in response to prayer or offerings. They also seem to signify a profound change in the vast and varied institutional apparatus of Catholicism. Although recognized in their different statuses by the papacy or by local bishops, these are mostly movements in which the laity plays a prominent role, deploying substantial resources that are not under the control of bishops and priests. The flexibility of such arrangements stands in contrast to the rigidity and complex procedures of the hierarchy. The larger movements bring quite a different sort of lay involvement from the intimacy of popular religion for these are transnational organizations operating on a different scale, with elaborate formal structures, while the smaller communities seem to be made up of people who are fleeing their social networks rather than embedded within them in the classic location-based style of popular religion. In addition, Opus and the Legionarios are also concerned to gain influence among political and economic elites and in the professions. Opus is the nearest thing to a religious order. Although its members are mostly drawn from the laity, they agree to subject themselves to certain disciplines and adhere to one or more of a range of vows, and the dividing lines between clergy and laity and between men and women are very clearly drawn.

To be sure, St. Ignatius taught the fashioning of the self in the sixteenth century, but the autonomy of the organizations, their focus on gaining influence in and refashioning society, and their inclusion of clergy and laity together are all signs of innovation, of a will to distance themselves from models of the past. The question is how it has happened that out of the laity or from the periphery of the priesthood such powerful movements should grow and should be of the kind that fit well with the posture of the late John Paul II.

The redrawing of the religious field can be seen in these projects to create large-scale, global lay organizations. Previously, lay and popular religion had tended to be a local affair and often incorporated rituals, which, though not

---

4 Brenda Carranza, Cecília Mariz, and Marcelo Ayres Camurça, eds., *Novas comunidades católicas: Em busca de um espaço pós-moderno* (Aparecida, Ideias e Letras, 2009), 52.

strictly approved, were nonetheless tolerated by priests and bishops, as we saw in the Brazilian and Bolivian examples. The hierarchical mind no doubt regarded popular religion as religion for simple folk, which had no theological or structural repercussions. However, the modern organizations mentioned here seem to herald a new departure – albeit one that has been developing gradually over many decades, since Opus was founded before World War II and the Legionarios in 1941. Some (Opus and Legionarios) constitute spaces for parallel or even slightly unorthodox religiosity but always under the watchful eye of priests or bishops. They have elaborate systems of recruitment and training, and presumably also for fund-raising because they do not receive funding from bishops. Indeed, it may well be that these apparently well-endowed organizations can gain influence because they can contribute funds – a subject that is probably impossible to research. All this remains more a research agenda than a set of findings. Just as academic social science ignored the Pentecostals for a decade, paying more attention to the more ideologically and even socially congenial basista Catholicism, so maybe now it is ignoring the devotional movements in Catholicism.

Organizational features apart, it is the religiosity promoted by these different movements that has countered the claim that evangelicals have, so to speak, seized the modernity banner and left Catholicism standing. The Charismatic Renewal promotes the religiosity of instant emotional gratification that is also the trademark of evangelical churches, and although it may not, so far as I know, have adopted the ethos of prosperity theology, parts of the movement must be open to that influence, given the powerful influence already exercised on the CCR by Pentecostalism. Opus and Legionarios are clearly distinct from any charismatic movement on account of their insistence on prolonged and thorough training, education (indoctrination perhaps), and socialization. This is at the antipodes of the quantity-driven dynamic of the CCR.

Churches and Politics

The re-democratization of the late twentieth century also seems to have helped the Church hierarchy to achieve a degree of political influence that may exceed anything it has enjoyed since the high tide of Romanization. The wave of constitution making has also opened up spaces for non-Catholics to various degrees and enabled evangelical churches to gain access to resources and positions in the state. In Brazil, the opening is probably greatest because to open a church (with accompanying tax exemptions) it is not necessary to be recognized as a religious body. In Argentina, semiformal mechanisms and registration requirements remain an obstacle to the achievement of their full recognition and special status has been retained by the Catholic Church, which is exempt from the requirement of registration and receives subsidies to the salaries of some higher clergy. In Mexico, a religious body must be recognized by the state's register of associations with religious purposes. In Peru, in accordance with the 1980 Concordat, the Catholic Church has a special status as an institution of public benefit and receives exemptions and benefits including personal financial benefits for some bishops that are not counted as salaries and so are not taxed. Pentecostal churches are not subject to legal discrimination, and some of them, especially the wealthy and fastest growing neo-Pentecostals, may operate in a shady fiscal niche.

The pattern and purpose of evangelical involvement in politics, which should certainly be seen as a shift in the boundaries of the religious field, differs markedly from that of the Catholic Church. Catholic bishops do not put up candidates nor do they any longer support particular parties or create parties of their own, but as in the past they do regard intervention on issues of policy and principle as a legitimate activity. Evangelical custom, in stark contrast, is to respect the ruler, and they take up principled positions on only a very restricted range of issues (e.g., against the death penalty, against privileges for the Catholic Church, and against same-sex marriage); but in many cases they have drifted away from political invisibility to follow strategies to gain representation and influence.

Evangelical churches need channels to the state because, for example, they want to operate TV and radio stations, they want to obtain subsidies for social projects such as sometimes controversial drug rehabilitation, and they want access to potential converts in prison. They also want to place their own people in parliaments, though they are often little interested in ideology or big-picture politics. Felipe Vázquez Palacios describes Mexican evangelical churches as having "not yet created a widespread social impact" and quotes Patricia Fortuny as saying that Mexican evangelical churches "lack a clear political project, oscillating according to the space the political system permits them."[5] The churches I have studied in Brazil support their own members who stand as candidates for various parties, which are presumably pleased to receive blocks of votes guaranteed by the pastors' prestige, although elected evangelicals (like other regional politicians) are apt to switch party affiliations

---

5 Felipe Vázquez Palacios, "Democratic Activity and Religious Practices of Evangelicals," in *Mexico. Evangelical Christianity and Democracy in Latin America*, ed. Paul Freston (New York: Oxford University Press, 2008), 59–60.

for strategic reasons. The Universal Church, as always the exception, has created a party of its own: the Partido Republicano Brasileiro.

Brazilian Pentecostalism seems to be projecting itself effectively and in an institutionalized manner beyond its own boundaries, in contrast with the more common tendency of evangelical churches to keep to their own flock and draw thick boundaries around them. There are organized evangelical groups for athletes, entrepreneurs, students, police officers, and the military, and Pentecostal churches have also offered platforms for black activism and for a range of political ideas. However, it may be a tendency peculiar to Brazil where Pentecostalism seems to have acquired the epidemiological characteristics of a social movement, penetrating into unfamiliar groups and institutional niches.

Pentecostal churches until quite recently were mostly creating institutions for their own growth and their own followers, what Robert Putnam has called "bonding social capital," but there are signs that this might be changing. The Catholic Church has played a major historical role in creating and contributing to the social capital that makes Western societies function through the modern state, medical care, social welfare, schools, universities, and numerous other institutions. This is what Putnam calls bridging social capital. Maybe Pentecostal churches are beginning to look beyond their own, but it will take a long time. The IURD's charitable arm, the Associação Beneficente Cristã (ABC), seems to have a patchy record and social scientists familiar with it say it tends to be active in places where the Church itself has a political or evangelistic interest; it also tends to move its head office from place to place. Indications that Pentecostals remain entrenched in the clientelist habits of Brazilian politics are not hard to find. For example, during the tenure of the evangelical Garotinho couple as governors of the state of Rio de Janeiro (Anthony Garotinho was succeeded as governor by his wife Rosângela Matheus in 2002), an income-support program for the elderly called *"cheque-cidadão"* was distributed largely through evangelical church networks.

From Popular Religion to Mass Culture: Restructuring the Field

The institutional and political changes do signal a redrawing of the religious field, but the underlying changes in the locus of popular religion and its replacement by another form of mass religiosity take us deeper into the culture and imaginary of societies that are going through massive changes. The change that is particularly worthy of note in the context of the development of Pentecostalism is the expansion of the middle and lower middle classes – those located in the second to the fifth deciles of income strata – which has grown at an unprecedented rate in the early 2000s. According to Marcelo Neri the "middle class," generously defined in income terms rather than in decile terms, increased by 30 million people in Brazil between 2003 and 2009 – from 38 percent to 50 percent of the population, and in absolute numbers by 34.3 percent. Separate research by Neri also shows that the "Classe C" (lower middle) increased its share of Brazilian Pentecostals from 12.27 percent to 12.84 percent between 2003 and 2009, which appears to be a marginal increase but is seen to be less so when the vertiginous growth of the C class itself is taken into account. The relationship between social mobility, income growth, and religious affiliation invites more detailed research, but it is worth juxtaposing these numbers.

Within the religious field the scandalous character of the Pentecostals (above all of the neo-Pentecostals), the uncertainties surrounding what counts as a religion (would it include the *ayahuasca*-consuming cult known as Santo Daime?) and who counts as an authority in deciding that question, the shift in protagonism and initiative within Catholicism from the hierarchy to devotional movements, and the Pentecostalization of some of Catholicism's most dynamic sectors are all symptoms of a field which is undergoing deep structural change and perhaps spawning new fields. One can think of the emerging pattern in terms of two dividing lines: on one hand, the Pentecostalization that encompasses the classical Pentecostalism of small chapels and the Catholic Charismatic Renewal and on the other hand neo-Pentecostalism as an apparently dominant trend setter in global Pentecostalism. Whether neo-Pentecostal methods of organization, ritual practices, and followings are quantitatively dominant is less relevant to this claim than its high profile in politics, in the media, and in the urban landscape. Furthermore, one observes the infiltration of neo-Pentecostal habits in previous classical Pentecostal churches such as the Assemblies of God.

In explaining how he came upon the usage of "habitus" (drawn from the art historian Erwin Panofsky as he readily tells us), Pierre Bourdieu says he was inspired by the world of haute couture, which led him to the realization that one of the most fundamental features of all fields of production was "the truly magical logic of the production of the producer and the product as fetishes."[6] Earlier on, in his account of the creation of the literary field in nineteenth-century France, he had explained that a field could not be said to have achieved autonomy unless it contained a social universe that "is instituted

---

6 Pierre Bourdieu, *Les Règles de l'Art: Genèse et structure du champ littéraire* (Paris: Seuil, 1992), 257.

at once in the objective structures of a universe governed by social rules and in the mental structures of those living within it, who thus take for granted the imperatives inscribed in the immanent logic of its operation."[7]

In other words, the autonomous field imbues those who operate within it with a sense that its procedures and mental structures (or perhaps modes of thought) are self-evident and require no discussion or explanation. Note here how logic and magic seem almost indistinguishable. It is not entirely surprising that he invokes the fashion industry in this oxymoron. Haute couture has a magical way of creating itself and its ways of doing things. An autonomous field is one in which the deeply rooted logic of its operation has penetrated the unconscious assumptions that govern everyday life. The "logic" is not really logical at all; it is magical because it is so hard to understand what it is that bring and holds a subculture together, and it has a logic only in the sense that it has a dynamic of its own, determined by rules of its own.

Evangelical Christianity has today gradually created a world with its own magical logic. It presents us with an array of habits and rituals that have come together with, broadly speaking, two structures, namely the Pentecostal and the neo-Pentecostal. The culture of the classical Pentecostals spread from place to place and country to country, born mostly by local preachers and pastors with only limited initial input from foreign missionaries and without a controlling center, and yet it has reproduced a similar ethos, rituals, dress codes, techniques of organization, and public speaking from Africa to Latin America to Asia. The neo-Pentecostals are more managerial, having much larger organizations and training systems, but their style also seems to spread by mimesis or osmosis with little visible communication or transmission. Like the "magic" of Bourdieu's internal logic, the common features of Pentecostalism and neo-Pentecostalism spread across the globe yet are very hard to explain in terms of a power struggle or an organizational strategy. Nonetheless, they reflect the creation of an autonomous field, marking a radical departure not just in religious style and creed but also in what it means to adhere to a religion, in modes of religious socialization, in ideas about religious authority, and the legitimate administration of the supernatural.

Classical Pentecostalism, which still accounts for the majority of Pentecostals in Latin America and worldwide, has been exhaustively described by a distinguished sequence of monographs in Latin America, Africa, and Europe following in the wake of David Martin's *Tongues of Fire*. That wave, which in Latin America started in the first years of the twentieth century but took off

---

7 Ibid., 93–94.

spectacularly until mid-century, already brought profound changes in the relationship between popular and erudite religion, essentially by transcending the mutual dependence between them and fashioning a this-worldly religiosity of self-discipline, family values, and an acute awareness of the threat of evil in a person's life. This was radically different from a Catholic culture of exchange in which good fortune could be sought through exchanges with saints and bad behavior could be redeemed by offerings and confessions while annual celebrations would exalt the collective faith and purge the community of past wrongdoings. Pentecostals are held personally to account and have no magical way out.

The term neo-Pentecosalism was coined in the 1990s when observers noticed some important changes including the global reach of the churches, centralized management, and the open and unashamed promise of riches joined with appeals for donations. In Brazil, there was also an inordinate insistence on the threat of the diabolic and possession in people's lives. Although classical Pentecostalism also contains these themes, the point is that it contains them and handles them discreetly, not least because the diabolic is dangerous. However, neo-Pentecostalism put them at the forefront and made much of the drama of possession and healing and of enrichment. This is evident in the contrast between the participatory bands and choirs of classical Pentecostalism and the interminable backup music of neo-Pentecostal music that is used to manipulate emotions as volunteers patrol the aisles watching out for those in need of succor or a quick mini-exorcism.

Pentecostal churches do not have a liturgy in the sense of a fixed ritual sequence repeated at fixed times of the day, the week, or the year. They consist of addresses from preachers interspersed with songs or hymns that congregations often sing from memory. Some odds and ends of Catholic ritual have been incorporated, such as a version of the Holy Communion in which small beakers of grape juice are distributed with a wafer, although this is certainly not meant to be a ritual of transubstantiation and participation may be conditional on payment of monthly dues. But where the small chapels with their choirs and bands are extremely spare with any kind of ritual, neo-Pentecostal churches have engaged in what I have come to call "ritual promiscuity." They adopt ritual procedures and later drop them and move on to something else. These procedures have to be recognized as ritual, however, so they cannot be totally new. They have to strike a chord in the collective memory. Thus, in Brazil, the Universal Church of the Kingdom of God places an imitation Ark of the Covenant and a seven-branched candelabra in many of its churches and anoints followers with oil. The exorcisms in a simulacrum of the procedures of the possession cults (Umbanda and Candomblé), once widely cherished feature of Brazilian cultural heritage have now been replaced by a pastiche of Jewish ritual. These ideas are also exported by the Universal Church to its branches in Mozambique, Angola, and South Africa. Recently, the introduction of Jewish ritual paraphernalia including shofars, matzo bread, and prayer shawls has been prevalent in Pentecostal churches around Latin America.

In Pentecostalism, and especially neo-Pentecostalism, religious life is detached from heritage and a sense of continuity with ancestral practices rooted to locality. In neo-Pentecostal churches, religion becomes a path to prosperity and, for church leaders, to political power. The personal link between followers and preachers is often absent, and the place of worship or prayer can acquire the characteristics of a service center that provides counseling, legal advice, and, in the case of large-scale structures, leisure areas. The rituals of neo-Pentecostalism sometimes have the appearance of pastiche. Their exorcisms are summary procedures in contrast to the elaborate procedures of the possession cults; their version of the communion is artless. The Universal Church's temples often have a uniform neoclassical porch with the same plastic columns as if produced by the church's own factory, and finally the ultimate example of pastiche is the construction of the grandiose "Third Temple of Solomon" in the Braz district of São Paulo, fifty-three meters high, faced with stone brought from Israel, and designed in accordance with the proportions foreseen in the vision of the prophet Ezekiel.

The pastiche is to some extent replicated in the ritual promiscuity where ancient practices of donation have been surrounded by the ritual of the religious service or the celebrations of annual fiestas. In these churches they are the subject of prolonged and insistent preaching but also form part of a personal bargain with divine power that giving will lead to receiving. Attendees are expected to give 10 percent of their pretax monthly income plus extra donations as contributions to the church, but also as contributions to their own wellbeing. Sometimes a verse from St. Paul is invoked to justify asking people to give even what they do not have and cannot afford. Simon Coleman, observing these practices in a Swedish Church, reported stories of fantastic, unexpected windfalls received by people who had given freely and who interpreted free giving as a way of transmitting charismatic force from person to person, or "investing according to the laws of spiritual increase."[8]

Neo-Pentecostal exchange requires the faithful to make sacrifices and also to take control of their lives. If someone asks for help in overcoming life's

---

8 Simon Coleman, *The Globalisation of Charismatic Christianity: Spreading the Gospel of Prosperity* (New York: Cambridge University Press, 2000), 203.

problems – drink, drugs, depression, and so forth – the preacher will help but also will expect that person also to make an effort. The preacher will not endlessly offer prayers in vain. In another register, when the preacher exhorts followers to aim high and have big ambitions to achieve self-realization, they also are expected to make the effort. I am therefore not trying to contrast this modern, materialistic and individualistic ethos with a purportedly idealized former pattern of exchange in Catholic popular religion. Catholics also petition for all sorts of very concrete favors in which *votos* and *ex votos* play a prominent role. Rather, it is the unrehearsed character of Pentecostal exchange that needs emphasis, its detachment from time-honored procedure and the decorum that accompanies the rituals of popular religion. Much as this religiosity is still popular in the sense that it belongs to the *pueblo/povo*, its gestures mark a completely new configuration of religious practice, because the erudite counterpart is no longer recognized. Indeed, the leader of the Universal Church regards theology as the work of the devil, invented to lead the untutored astray and distract them from the real business of warding off or extracting diabolic forces and pursuing prosperity and health.

There is also a strong streak of mimesis, bordering on kitsch. The Universal Church builds vast cathedrals purposefully, sometimes in high-profile locations, to mimic and compete with the Catholic Church. Like all Pentecostal Churches it uses the same Bible, although many Pentecostals tend to eschew the modern translations that are now standard in Catholic and Anglican churches in favor of older versions with their archaic vocabulary. The Universal Church also has half-borrowed its logo – the white dove against the background of a red heart – from the Catholic image of the Sacred Heart, combining it with the classic symbol of the Holy Spirit. And of course, in radical contrast to classical Pentecostals, it has created a hierarchy of authority, with three hundred bishops and the founder-leader Edir Macedo at the summit. Similar remarks apply to other neo-Pentecostal churches.

The Pentecostal field recombines elements from the established field of Latin American religion, dominated by the power of the Catholic Church as well as by Catholic understandings of what religion is. The "mainstream" of religion was moving in a liberal, quasi-secular direction and had long discarded explicit references to the action of the supernatural in daily life, to ideas about evil and possession, while at the same time retaining the apparatus of power that had evolved to administer the supernatural over centuries. Now the neo-Pentecostals challenge those definitions and assumptions by restoring the action of the supernatural in daily life while adopting a completely different model of organization, revolving around the cult of personality of their leaders and dispensing with extended periods of theological education and priestly formation.

In this perspective, classical Pentecostalism, despite its massive quantitative presence, can be thought of as not achieving the autonomy necessary to command great influence. Although neo-Pentecostals have obviously drawn on their older cousins for basic ideas about conversion, about mission, about the uses of the Bible, they have gone much further by engaging in open competition with Catholicism for prestige, for the conquest of public space, the conquest of the media, for the conquest of political power, and for the capacity to legitimately define what counts as religion in the public sphere. Within the Catholic Church, by comparison, we have seen the beginnings of a reshaping of the field after several decades of attempts first to achieve a liberal modernization (Vatican II and Liberation Theology), then to roll the liberalization backwards, all the while preserving the structures of power. Now, however, we observe new structures of religious activism that also share some features with Pentecostalism.

So, the field of religion is being reshaped. The power to define what is religion is passing into new hands. The relationship between religion and politics is also changing, as is the relationship between the apparatuses of power and the administration of the supernatural. The one thing that is clear is that even ten, let alone twenty, years ago few would have predicted the developments described here.

Bibliography and Suggested Readings

Ames, Barry. *The Deadlock of Democracy in Brazil*. Ann Arbor: University of Michigan Press, 2001.

Birman, Patricia. "Feminine mediation and Pentecostal identities." *Cambridge Anthropology*, 20, no. 3 (1998): 66–83.

"Males e maleficios no Discurso Neopentecostal." In P. Birman, R. Novães, and P. Crespo (eds.), *O Mal, a cultura e as religiões populares*, 62–80. Rio de Janeiro: EdUERJ, 1997.

"A Mirror to the Future: The Media, Evangelicals, and Politics in Brazil." In B. Meyer and A. Moors (eds.), *Religion, Media and the Public Sphere*, 91–111. Bloomington: Indiana University Press, 2006.

Birman, Patricia, and David. Lehmann. "Religion and the media in a battle for ideological hegemony." *Bulletin of Latin American Research*, 18, no. 2 (1999): 145–164.

Bourdieu, Pierre. *Les Règles de l'Art: Genèse et structure du champ littéraire*. Paris: Seuil, 1992.

Brandão, Carlos Rodrigues. *A cultura na rua*. Campinas: Papirus, 1989.

Os Deuses do Povo: um estudo sobre a religião popular. Uberlândia: Editora da Universidade Federal de Uberlândia, 2007.

Burdick, John. "Collective Identity and Racial Thought in São Paulo's Black Gospel Music Scene." *Music and Arts in Action*, 1, no. 2 (2009): 16–29.
  Looking for God in Brazil. Berkeley: University of California Press, 1994.
  "Why Is the Black Evangelical Movement Growing in Brazil?" *Journal of Latin American Studies*, 37, no. 2 (2005): 311–332.
Carranza, Brenda, Cecília Mariz, and Marcelo Ayres Camurça, eds. *Novas comunidades católicas: Em busca de um espaço pós-moderno*. Aparecida: Ideias e Letras, 2009.
Chesnut, R. Andrew. *Born Again in Brazil: The Pentecostal Boom and the Pathogens of Poverty*. New Brunswick, NJ: Rutgers University Press, 1997.
  Competitive Spirits: Latin America's New Religious Economy. New York: Oxford University Press, 2003.
  Devoted to Death: Santa Muerte, the Skeleton Saint. New York: Oxford University Press, 2012.
Clarke, Peter. "Top-star Priests and the Catholic Response to the 'Explosion' of Evangelical Protestantism in Brazil: The Beginning of the End of the 'Walkout'?" *Journal of Contemporary Religion*, 14, no. 2 (1999): 203–216.
Coleman, Simon. *The Globalisation of Charismatic Christianity: Spreading the Gospel of Prosperity*. New York: Cambridge University Press, 2000.
Comaroff, Jean. "The Politics of Conviction: Faith on the Neo-liberal Frontier." *Social Analysis*, 53, no. 1 (2009): 17–38.
Corten, André. *Pentecostalism in Brazil*. Basingstoke, UK: Macmillan, 1999.
Corten, André, and Ruth Marshall-Fratani, eds. *Between Babel and Pentecost: transnational Pentecostalism in Africa and Latin America*. London: Hurst & Company, 2001.
Csordas, Thomas J. *Language, Charisma and Creativity*. Berkeley: University of California Press, 1997.
Da Cunha, Euclides. *Os sertões*. São Paulo: Brasiliense, 1985 [1902].
Della Cava, Ralph. *Miracle at Joaseiro*. New York: Columbia University Press, 1970.
Diacon, Todd A. *Millenarian Vision, Capitalist Reality: Brazil's Contestado Rebellion, 1912–1916*. Durham, NC: Duke University Press, 1991.
Eisenstadt, Shmuel N. "Fundamentalism, Phenomenology, and Comparative Dimensions." In Martin Marty and R. Scott Appleby (eds.), *Fundamentalisms Comprehended*, 259–276. Chicago: Chicago University Press, 1995.
  "Multiple modernities." *Daedalus*, 129, no. 1 (2000): 1–29.
Fernandes, Rubem Cesar. *Novo nascimento: Os Evangelicos em Casa, na Igreja e na Política*. Rio de Janeiro: MAUAD, 1998.
Fonseca, Alexandre Brasil. "Religion and Democracy in Brazil: A Study of the Leading Evangelical Politicians." In Paul Freston (ed.), *Evangelical Christianity and Democracy in Latin America*, 163–206. New York: Oxford University Press, 2008.
Frigerio, Alejandro. "Repensando el monopolio religioso del catolicismo en la Argentina." In Ronan Alves Pereira et al. (eds.), *Ciencias sociales y religión en América Latina: Perspectivas en debate*, 87–118. Buenos Aires: Editorial Biblos, 2007.
Galvão, Walnice Nogueira. *No calor da hora: A guerra de Canudos nos jornais, 4a expedição*. São Paulo: Ática, 1974.
Gifford, Paul. *Christianity and the State in Doe's Liberia*. New York: Cambridge University Press, 1993.
  Christianity, Politics, and Public Life in Kenya. London: Hurst & Co., 2009.

    Ghana's New Christianity: Pentecostalism in a Globalizing African Economy. London: Hurst and Co., 2004.

Gross, Toomas. "Protestantism and Modernity: The Implications of Religious Change in Contemporary Rural Oaxaca." *Sociology of Religion*, 64, no. 4 (2003): 479–498.

Gruzinski, Serge. *Images at War: Mexico from Columbus to Blade Runner (1492–2019).* Trans. Heather MacLean. Durham, NC: Duke University Press, 2001.

Gutiérrez, Gustavo. *Las Casas: In search of the Poor of Jesus Christ.* Maryknoll, NY: Orbis Books, 1993.

Haar, Gerrie ter. *Halfway to Paradise: African Christians in Europe.* Fairwater, Cardiff: Cardiff Academic Press, 1998.

Hagopian, Frances. "Social Justice, Moral Values, or Institutional Interests? Church Responses to the Democratic Challenge in Latin America." In Francis Hagopian (ed.), *Religious Pluralism, Democracy and the Catholic Church in Latin America*, 257–331. Notre Dame, IN: University of Notre Dame Press, 2009.

Harris, Olivia. "The Eternal Return of Conversion: Christianity as Contested Domain in Highland Bolivia." In Fenella Cannell (ed.), *The Anthropology of Christianity*, 51–78. Durham, NC: Duke University Press, 2006.

Hewitt, W. E. *Base Christian Communities and Social Change in Brazil.* Lincoln: University of Nebraska Press, 1991.

Howe, Cymene, Susan Zaraysky, and Lois Ann Lorentzen. "Devotional Crossings: Transgender Sex Workers, Santisima Muerte, and Spiritual Solidarity in Guadalajara and San Francisco." In Lois Ann Lorentzen (ed.), *Religion at the Corner of Bliss and Nirvana: Politics, Identity, and Faith in New Migrant Communities*, 3–38. Durham, NC: Duke University Press, 2009.

Htun, Mala. "Life, Liberty, and Family Values: Church and State in the Struggle over Latin America's Social Agenda." In Frances Hagopian (ed.), *Religious Pluralism, Democracy and the Catholic Church in Latin America*, 335–364. Notre Dame, IN: University of Notre Dame Press, 2009.

Hunt, Stephen, and Nicola Lightly. "The British Black Pentecostal 'Revival': Identity and Belief in the 'New' Nigerian Churches." *Ethnic and Racial Studies*, 24, no. 1 (2001): 104–124.

Iannacone, Lawrence. "Introduction to the Economics of Religion." *Journal of Economic Literature*, 36, no. 3 (1997): 1465–1495.

Kao, Chen-Yang. "The Cultural Revolution and the Emergence of Pentecostal-style Protestantism in China." *Journal of Contemporary Religion*, 24, no. 2 (2009): 171–188.

Knight, Alan. "Popular Culture and the Revolutionary State in Mexico, 1910–1940." *Hispanic American Historical Review*, 74, no. 3 (1994): 393–444.

Lehmann, David. "Dissidence and Conformism in Religious Movements: What Difference – if Any – Separates the Catholic Charismatic Renewal and Pentecostal Churches?" *Concilium*, 3 (2003): 122–138.

   "Religion and Globalization: A Comparative and Historical Perspective." In Linda Woodhead, Hiroko Kawanami, and Christopher Partridge (eds.), *Religions in the Modern World: Traditions and Transformations*, 345–364. Abingdon, UK: Routledge, 2009.

   Struggle for the Spirit: Religious Transformation and Popular Culture in Brazil and Latin America. Cambridge, MA: Polity Press, 1996.

Levine, Daniel, ed. *Churches and Politics in Latin America.* Beverly Hills: SAGE, 1980.

Levine, Daniel. "Colombia: The Institutional Church and the Popular." In Daniel Levine (eds.), *Religion and Political Conflict in Latin America*, 187–217. Chapel Hill: University of North Carolina Press, 1986.

Levine, Robert M. *Vale of Tears: Revisiting the Canudos Massacre in Northeastern Brazil, 1893–1897*. Berkeley: University of California Press, 1992.

Machado, Maria das Dores Campos. *Política e Religião: A participação dos Evangélicos nas eleições*. Rio de Janeiro: Editora FGV, 2006.

Marin, Richard. *Dom Helder Camara, les puissants et les pauvres: Pour une histoire de l'Eglise des pauvres dans le Nordeste bresilien, 1955–1985*. Paris: Editions de l'Atelier, 1995.

Mariz, Celia L. *Coping with Poverty: Pentecostals and Christian Base Communities in Brazil*. Philadelphia: Temple University Press, 1993.

Marshall, Ruth. *Political Spiritualities: the Pentecostal Revolution in Nigeria*. Chicago: University of Chicago Press, 2009.

——— "The Sovereignty of Miracles: Pentecostal Political Theology in Nigeria." *Constellations*, 17, no. 2 (2010): 197–223.

Martin, Daivd. *Tongues of Fire: The Pentecostal Revolution in Latin America*. Oxford: Blackwell, 1990.

Meyer, Brigit. "The Power of Money: Politics, Occult Forces, and Pentecostalism in Ghana." *African Studies Review*, 41, no. 3 (1998): 15–37.

Meyer, Jean. *La Cristiada*. 3 vols. Mexico, D.F.: Siglo XXI, 1973–1974.

Míguez, Daniel. *Spiritual Bonfire in Argentina: Confronting Current Theories with an Ethnographic Account of Pentecostal Growth in a Buenos Aires Suburb*. Amsterdam: CEDLA, 1998.

Neitz, Mary Jo. *Charisma and Community: A Study of Religious Commitment within the Charismatic Renewal*. New Brunswick, NJ: Transaction Books, 1987.

Neri, Marcelo. "The New Middle Class in Brazil: The Bright Side of the Poor." *Centro de Políticas Sociais*. 2010. www.fgv.br/cps (Accessed August 8, 2011).

——— "Novo mapa das religiões." *Centro de Políticas Sociais*. 2011. http://www.fgv.br/cps/religiao (Accessed August 8, 2011).

Oro, Ari Pedro, and Pablo Séman. "Brazilian Pentecostalism Crosses National Borders." In André Corten and Ruth Marshall-Fratani (eds.), *Between Babel and Pentecost: Transnational Pentecostalism in Africa and Latin America*, 181–195. London: Hurst & Company, 2001.

Parker Gumucio, Cristian. "Education and Increasing Religious Pluralism in Latin America: The case of Chile." In Frances Hagopian (eds.), *Religious Pluralism, Democracy, and the Catholic Church in Latin America*, 131–184. Notre Dame, IN: University of Notre Dame Press, 2009.

Putnam, Robert. *Bowling Alone: The Collapse and Revival of American Community*. New York: Simon and Schuster, 2000.

Romero, Catalina. "Religion and Public Spaces: Catholicism and Civil Society in Peru." In Francis Hagopian (ed.), *Religious Pluralism, Democracy and the Catholic Church in Latin America*, 365–404. Notre Dame, IN: University of Notre Dame Press, 2009.

Teixeira Monteiro, Duglas. *Os Errantes do Novo Século: Um Estudo sobre o Surto Milenarista do Contestado*. São Paulo: Livraria Duas Cidades, 1974.

Thrall, Margaret E. *The First and Second Letters of Paul to the Corinthians*. New York: Cambridge University Press, 1965.

Thumala Olave, María Angélica. *Riqueza y piedad: El catolicismo de la elite económica chilena*. Santiago: Debate, 2007

Van Wyck, Ilana. *The Case of the Universal Church of the Kingdom of God in South Africa: A Church of Strangers*. New York: Cambridge University Press, 2014.

Vásquez Palacios, Felipe. "Democratic Activity and Religious Practices of Evangelicals in Mexico." In Paul Freston (eds.), *Evangelical Christianity and Democracy in Latin America*, 37–61. New York: Oxford University Press, 2008.

Vaughan, Mary Kay. *Cultural Politics in Revolution*. Tucson: University of Arizona Press, 1997.

Vinhas de Queiroz, Maurício. *Messianismo e conflito social: A guerra sertaneja do Contestado: 1912–1916*. Rio de Janeiro: Civilzacao Brasileira, 1966 [1981].

49

Pathways to the Future

DANIEL H. LEVINE

A photograph I took more than forty years ago provides elements for reflection about likely pathways to the future of religion in Latin America. The photograph (Figure 49.1) records my first encounter with an evangelical street preacher in Latin America. This occurred in the Guatemalan town of Solalá in late 1968, where the market was in full swing. In the midst of people buying, selling, and bargaining, a Protestant preacher was working the crowd. The majority of Guatemalans are indigenous, and the audience was made up entirely of Maya men and women. Holding a Bible in his hands, the preacher illustrated his sermon by pointing to a hand-painted canvas that depicted heaven, hell, the judgment of the nations, the temptations of this world, and the ways of the righteous and of the sinner.

I found the scene stirring enough to save the slide for more than four decades, but at the time it seemed little more than an interesting sideshow. The religious experience was new, as was the leadership: ordinary, often nonwhite and barely lettered men using a popular language, who recall the circuit-riding preachers of nineteenth-century North America. The signs were there, but they slipped by most observers. None of it fitted into the accepted scheme of things at the time.

Half a century later, it is easy to see this preacher as a precursor of the wave of Protestant, especially Pentecostal, religious growth that swept Guatemala and all of Central America in subsequent years. He and others like him have since then gone on to transform the religious landscape, the public presence, and the private life of religion throughout Latin America. The 500-year monopoly of Catholicism has been replaced by religious pluralism. The religious scene is now a blooming confusion of churches, chapels, street preachers, and television and radio evangelists competing for attention and vying for members and a share of public goods and public space.

Public spaces throughout the region are now occupied by many religious actors competing for attention, members, and resources. It is now

FIGURE 49.1. Street preacher in Sololá, Guatemala, 1968.

just about impossible to walk through a public square, exit a train or bus station, transit a city street, or tune into mass media without encountering preachers and religious rallies. There is also considerable variety within religions: multiple sources of leadership, new arenas, and a myriad of voices claiming to speak in the name of religion. Simply put, there is a lot of competition out there.

The continent remains overwhelmingly Christian, but this is not the Christianity of a hundred or even fifty years ago. The available supply of religion – churches, chapels, radio and television programming, music, evangelization campaigns, associations, publications, schools, Internet platforms, and more – has increased and diversified as never before, giving ordinary people a wide range of choices. All denominations, including the Catholic Church, are also much better organized than was the case fifty years ago. New kinds of structures have been developed and new kinds of paraclerical roles – including deacons and lay preachers – have emerged, bringing a different kind of leadership and energy to the scene. A new generation of homegrown leaders has begun replacing imports from the North. A series of typically Pentecostal practices – stress on personal conversion, direct experience of the Holy Spirit, belief in divine cures for illness, ecstatic behavior, and *glossalalia* (speaking in tongues) – have spread across denominational frontiers to characterize many Christian groups, Protestant or Catholic.

This is not a case of diffusion from one center, but rather of multiple and simultaneous creation – another sign of creative cultural energy. At the same time, all the churches have learned new ways to communicate and to reach potential members, using radio, television, film, music, and public campaigns and crusades. The sheer growth of Pentecostal and Protestant churches and their diffusion in social space has meant that many Latin Americans now have friends, relatives, and neighbors who belong to different churches. This reduces the sense of distance and lays a foundation for moving beyond plurality to pluralism understood as a code of coexistence.

Of course, pluralism has always been present, with a variety of organizations and positions present within churches and with alternate voices competing for resources, members, and legitimate access to public space. It is important to acknowledge that the realities of religious pluralism extend beyond the formal boundaries of Christian churches. Devotions of African origin are increasingly recognized in Brazil and around the Caribbean, pre-Columbian rituals and beliefs are notable in the Andes and Mesoamerica. The visible presence of non-Christian religion, often tied to immigrant groups, includes Muslim, Jewish, Hindu, Buddhist, and Shinto communities. Finally, national censuses and survey research have revealed a small but growing numbers of persons who expressly declare they practice no religion at all.

The elements sketched out here point to continued vitality of religion and religious expression. This belies the expectations of generations of social scientists, according to whom religion as public phenomenon and private belief and devotion would inexorably decline and disappear as education, well-being, and modernization took hold. The experience of Latin America reveals something quite different and of great practical and theoretical interest. In the context of increasingly open civil societies and growing urbanization, literacy, and media access, churches and religious groups of all kinds have created new forms of belonging and new ways of reaching and incorporating believers. Values of individual and group autonomy and freedom of choice, on issues ranging from sexuality and family life to public morality and the conditions of group membership have worked their way into personal and community life. This is not secularization as irrelevance, decline, and disappearance. It is secularization with sustained religious vitality and innovation.

Although the Catholic Church retains legal privileges in many countries that set it apart from others (including subsidies and de facto exemption from the need to register as a church), its status as the unquestioned and unchallenged image and voice of religion is firmly in the past, despite the hopes of many of its leaders. But more is at issue here than the legal and effective separation of religion from states and public institutions. The kind of secularization that is under way in Latin America, with sustained religious vitality and multiple sources of innovation, brings with it demands for personal and group autonomy. Among others things, this means that patterns of belonging have also changed. Long-standing expectation of obedience and the habit of seeing church-affiliated groups as "resources on the ground" are no longer valid, if they ever were. If the churches wish to retain influence, they need to recruit and persuade, not attempt to manage by order and decree.

This suggests that efforts at the "reconquest" of public space, a prominent goal in much Catholic discourse since the 1990s, are unlikely to meet with success. The whole idea of "reconquering civil society" rests on fears of moral decay, and the presumed negative effects of global cultural influence. Religious leaders in Latin America, as in the United States, often conflate secularization with antireligious secularism and a generalized decline of moral standards with particular concern for norms around gender and sexuality. But secularization and secularism do not mean the same thing at all. The latter, grounded for example in French *laicite*, in the anticlerical laws that emerged from the Mexican Revolution, or for example in Uruguay, can be seen as a militant commitment to containing religion and above all limiting its place in the public sphere. Hence, the attacks on religious place names, public recognition of religious holidays, or religious displays in public places.

Secularization is a much broader concept, which also has to do with plurality of options and plurality of belongings, with the idea of plurality and choice as the new normal. Plurality of this kind carries with it a growing capacity (and growing demand) for autonomy on the part of individuals and groups, autonomy in making choices, and making connections among the plurality of options out there. This autonomy means loss of control for church leaders, many of whom equate loss of control with an inevitable decline of morals and secularization with elimination of standards of good behavior. But the idea that secularization brings moral decay is valid only if one assumes that moral norms can only come from one "authoritative" source. There is no particular reason to believe this. The Gospels offer important norms, but one would not want to say that Buddhists or Muslims or Hindus or Jews or members of any other faith, or non-believers for that matter, are devoid of a moral compass.

Despite their continuing social presence, historic churches are losing their capacity to discipline the religious thinking of large sections of the population, especially among the young. This is part of a more general turn for religion from obligation to consumption. Religious values and ideas are more likely to be served by persuasion in a competitive marketplace. For those wedded to the ideal of the Church as a unique source of norms and values, there are ironies in this situation. As Tocqueville recognized in the 1840s, it is precisely where religions have been separated from other institutions (where no official faith exists) that religious practice has flourished and diversified the most. He recognized that the very effort to prolong the existence of Christendom did grave damage to institutional religion in Europe. "So long as a religion derives its strength from sentiments, instincts, and passions which are reborn in like fashion in all periods of history," he wrote, "it can brave the assaults of time or at least can only be destroyed by another religion. But when a religion chooses to rely on the interest of the world, it becomes as fragile as all earthly powers. Alone it may hope for immortality; linked to ephemeral powers, it follows their fortunes and often falls together with the passions of the day sustaining them."[1]

General debates about secularization (in terms of rates of belief, practice, and so on) are suggestive and the findings often powerful, but they do not exhaust the questions of interest. It is also important to know how people relate to the institutions of religion, and how these institutions, and the collection of groups and movements associated in some way with them, position themselves in public life – what issues they stress, what coalitions they may form. The most interesting question about secularization have less to do with the separation of religion from other spheres of life, than with the creative syntheses continuously being invented and put into play around the world. These are further enhanced by changes that place religion outside the state, so that it no longer exercises power directly, but instead competes to wield influence in society. This is not properly understood simply a story of decline. Rather, it is a story of adjusting to a world where plurality is normal.

In more general terms, stress on boundaries and distinctions (the secular and the religious, the sacred and the profane) may reify analytical distinctions in ways that are not helpful when we come to address real behavior. These distinctions have meaning, of course, and are often enshrined in laws and institutions, but in daily practice ordinary people blur these boundaries and join one element with another, without much difficulty or complex cogitation. Churches and church groups deal with states; religious individuals belong to trade unions or political parties and churches, mosques, temples, or synagogues. People hear social and political messages all the time in churches, and

---

[1] Alexis de Tocqueville, *Democracy in America*, trans. George Lawrence, ed. J. P. Mayer (New York: Harper Perennial Classics, 2000), 297–298.

they regularly put church networks to work addressing secular problems from food to housing to transport to safety.

Pathways and Foundations

The preceding considerations provide a basis for thinking about pathways to the future for religion in Latin America. Pathways are combinations of belief, action and organization, groups, and individuals that create possibilities for future rearrangements of religion in public space and for its characteristic expressions in private life. Pathways can be understood from several different angles. From the angle of large structures and institutions, the erosion of Catholic monopoly is particularly visible in the public sphere. Although the Catholic Church retains privileged legal status and access to public resources in many countries, its long standing status as *the Church* – the presumptive exclusive voice of religion and morality in society and privileged interlocutor with the state – can no longer be taken for granted.

To be sure, official Catholic monopoly historically masked considerable variety including syncretic practices of all kinds. However, the power of institutional and legal monopoly should not therefore be discounted, and it is this monopoly that has eroded and is in all likelihood gone forever. Assuming continued openness in civil society, growth in access to media, and demographic trends that make large numbers of people readily available to campaigns of all kinds, for individuals and communities the pathway to the future of religious life presents itself in variety, richness of choice, and greater ease of access and openness to global currents of culture and practice.

One way to get a sense these pathways is to ask what new and permanent elements have been added to the landscape in which religion and churches find themselves in Latin America and what difference they make. The most obvious and prominent of these are demographic change and the multiplication and diversification of churches. The seemingly sudden flowering of Pentecostal Protestantism throughout the region beginning in the 1970s drew strength from a newly emerging audience that was available to the evangelizing message in new ways. This more literate, urban, media-soaked, and mobile population is the audience that sustains and nurtures the religious innovation so notable in recent decades. The pace of change is likely to slow, but the changes already in place have permanently altered the ground on which any possible or likely futures may be built. The next frontier, which is already a presence in some countries, will bring to center stage issues of gender and sexuality (including most prominently gay marriage) and the incorporation of women and minorities on a more equal basis in the churches, as in society at large.

These demographic changes emerged and consolidated in the context of a half-century of profound and often violent social and political transformation. By the close of the twentieth century, democracy and civilian politics had replaced authoritarian and military rule in most countries of the region. The violence of civil war and massive state repression had also passed from center stage, although violence of other kinds – with a higher toll of victims – continues to be the daily bread of many Latin Americans. The political changes and continued violence of the period had an enduring impact on religion. The return to democracy was accompanied by the development of a more open civil society with lower barriers to organization. These changes eased the path for new churches to organize and get their message out.

A further new and seemingly permanent element is the accelerated and intense presence of global cultural and organizational influences. To be sure, globalization itself is nothing new in Latin America, a region whose historical identity is the outgrowth of global ambitions of the Spanish Crown and the Catholic Church. What is new is the pace and scale of global transfers. The transformational impact of these flows of ideas and models of church has been reinforced in Latin America by the emergence of a new generation of homegrown religious leaders. The expansion of Protestant and Pentecostal churches has been accompanied by reduction of long-standing dependence on imported clergy and models of organization. Latin America has changed from being a net importer to a being a net exporter of cultural and specifically religious influences, with outreach to the global south and also to the north.

Part of the power of religion is how it spans and combines public and private life. Two areas of change that will reshape pathways to religion's future in Latin America, and that combine public and private life, are norms and practices around sexuality and the growing presence of charismatic and Pentecostal practices in the region's churches. Gender and sexuality have long been flash points for the role of religion in public and private life. The new element here is that the contest has moved beyond divorce, birth control, and abortion (although these remain) to include same-sex relations including marriage. The enormous presence of charismatic and Pentecostal beliefs and practices, and of organizations that promote them, is something that cuts across denominational barriers. The well-known expansion of Pentecostal churches in the region has its counterpart in the surge of the Catholic Charismatic renewal across the region. Both are instances of creative religious energy bubbling up from below, energizing new practices that impact personal and family lives.

Finally, politics and violence offer two fields that are central to thinking about the likely future of religion and the churches. Starting in the 1980s, democracies were restored and civil society opened and strengthened all across the region in a wave of change that has endured and consolidated. Open political systems and open civil societies create a new environment for all the churches, facilitating communications, recruitment of new leaders and members, and open competition. This alters the internal dynamics of many churches, bringing new leadership generations and new kinds of members to the fore. The meaning of violence for religion and the church has changed because the nature of the prevailing violence has itself been transformed. Although what we might call "the old violence" of civil war (e.g., in Central America and Peru) and massive state repression (e.g., in Argentina, Chile, Brazil, and Uruguay) has passed from the scene, violence of other kinds remains. In contrast to the old violence, the new violence is decentralized, with multiple actors, and manifests itself in ordinary criminality (assault, rape, robbery, vendettas, domestic abuse, and murder) that has surged in the region's cities; violence associated with migration (attacks on migrants passing through an area, extortion rape, and abuse); violence associated with gangs and with the drug trade; continued official impunity and abuse, for example in police raids of poor areas, often targeting young men; violence in prisons; and continuing violence associated with struggles over land and land use.

The toll exacted by such violence often outstrips the worst levels of the old violence of war and state repression. Churches, religious groups, and individuals of religious inspiration have been deeply engaged with violence in all these forms, but the nature of that engagement has changed because religion itself has been transformed. Facing the old violence, leading elements in the churches took up the cause of human rights, defended victims, and played a key role in facilitating national organizations linked to rights. But with the passing of Catholic monopoly, there is no comparable single spokesman now. The response of churches and religious actors to the new violence reflects the diverse and decentralized character of religion in Latin America today.

Evangelical and Pentecostal churches have been prominent in efforts to engage gang violence in Central America, seeking out and evangelizing victims and perpetrators alike. The churches provide shelter, healing, and access to networks in which those ready leave drugs, alcohol, promiscuity, and violence behind can take the first step. This is not a one-time event; conversion is accompanied by sustained efforts to facilitate incorporation into ordinary social life. A striking example is the case of gang tattoos, which are a common marker of gang membership. The very visibility of tattoos, which often cover the whole body, presents a barrier to a new life. Potential employers and neighbors are understandably wary of people with prominent tattoos. Pentecostal churches in Central America facilitate access to tattoo removal clinics as one step on the road to a different life. Efforts of this kind are linked to campaigns for disarmament and are folded into a general rhetoric of conversion as an essential foundation of a new life The effort to engage directly with violent individuals and social contexts extends to the region's notoriously overcrowded and dangerous prisons. The office of prison chaplain (almost always Catholic) has existed for a long time, but the new religion has brought a different and much more active role for the churches, a permanent presence with sustained efforts at conversion and reform of life. Entire cellblocks are marked off as "believer" territory, and inmate pastors take a leading role. The result has been cellblocks with lower violence and less chaotic conditions.

A final example of how the new religion and the new violence interact comes from the experience of migration. Rural to urban migration has long been a motor of accelerated urbanization in Latin America. Fleeing bad living conditions, limited opportunities, and pervasive violence, individuals and families have sought better lives in the cities, often to meet violence of different kinds. This is well documented. What is only now starting to be explored on a systematic basis is the violence associated with international migration. Central American migrants to the United States often make the trip riding through Mexico on top of long-distance trains, which are known colloquially as "the beast" (*la bestia*). The inherent dangers of this kind of transport (storms, low lying branches, low bridges and tunnels, and inevitable accidents) are exacerbated by robbery, extortion, kidnapping for ransom, beatings, rape, and murder. In the teeth of widespread local hostility to migrants, official responses are at best indifferent to migrants and often add to the harassment. Often, the only shelter, protection, and help provided to those making these journeys comes from scattered initiatives sponsored by individual priests and parishes, sometimes with support from transnational religious sources.

The transformations and dynamic innovations of the late twentieth century were all the more startling coming from Latin America, where for so long the monopoly of the Catholic Church seemed secure, if not wholly unchallenged. Indeed, change arising from within religion (any religion) was a surprise to most social scientists who remained wedded to theories of secularization (and related ideas about of modernization) according to which the spread of science, education, industrialization, and urban life would cut the ground out from under religion. Religion would simply fade away, disengaging from state institutions, fading from public life and becoming a matter of scattered, and declining, personal devotions or ritualized markers of the passage of life stages.

But as we have seen, religion has not withered and does not appear likely to disappear in the face of modernization in Latin America. Religion has flourished, multiplied, and diversified, with new churches, new forms of organization, and new ways of delivering the message crowding the scene. The demographic and political transformations of the region have created a different kind of audience for religion and introduced new generations of leaders. There is no sign of the force of this change letting up. Efforts to construct the future are themselves the subject of continuing, often intense conflict between and within religious groups. How these struggles will turn out and what they will lead to depends on configurations of elements as yet unknown. All we can be sure of is continued change, a continued public presence for religion, and the continued overwhelming dominance of Christianity in the culture and public life of the region.

The pathways to the future outlined here bring us squarely up against the question of what that future may look like. The multiple legacies of the past are not well understood as mere collections of events, once and done, left in the past. Together they leave an imprint on institutions and expectations, make some outcomes more possible than others, and weigh the scales for the evolution of religion's place in public life and for its impact on personal and family life, on belief, and on practice. Latin America is one of the great reservoirs of Christianity in the world and a major source of innovation and growth. But as I suggested at the outset, this is not the Christianity of a hundred or even fifty years ago. The meteoric growth of Pentecostal churches is likely to slow down; hardly anything in nature grows at that pace over a sustained period. But this does not mean a return to Catholic monopoly. The more probable future in the short and medium term is continued plurality and efforts by challengers to the status quo to consolidate their position in public space.

Simple extrapolation from the past is a risky way to think about the future. The recent history of religion in Latin America is full of surprises and the plural, decentralized, and competitive reality that emerged in the late twentieth century makes any specific prediction uncertain. The particular institutional form that religions assume (parishes or local churches, religious orders, groups like Ecclesial Base Communities, crusades, and media campaigns to name a few) is less significant for the future than the general pattern of innovation that continues to bubble up and the ongoing capacity of churches that makes it possible for scattered initiatives to "scale up" and consolidate on larger levels and to broker connections with transnational groups and ideas. Projections of religion on a large scale (in traditional media or on the Internet) will be more than matched by multiple and simultaneous creations at the local level. Long a net importer of religious ideas, practices, and organizational models, Latin America has become a source of change, with vigorous outreach across the Global South and to the north as well.

The experience of living and working in a plural and open civil society has an impact on the internal life of churches, bringing ideas about participation and equality into the daily life of the institution. Urbanized people with access to media and experience of mobility are no mere sheep to be led. They face a wide range of options and are used to making decisions on their own. The pluralism and competition that mark the contemporary scene make their impact in the multiple ways in which churches and religious groups reach out to and hold new audiences. There are no institutions without members, no leaders without followers, at least not for very long, and this new kind of population is the source of those who will build pathways to the future. The continued ability of churches to reach and motivate this new population is what will ultimately shape the future for religion in Latin America.

Index

Note: A t following a page number indicates a table on that page.

Abad y Queipo, Manuel, 235
ABC (Associação Beneficente Cristã), 753
abogados, 143
   See also saints
abortion
   Catholics on, 503, 552
   Charismatic Catholics on, 469
   decriminalization of, 343, 503, 549
   evangelicals on, 554–555
   fetus risk cases, 550, 552, 553, 555
   maternal health risk cases, 552, 555
   Pentecostals on, 553, 554–555
   rape cases, 552, 555
   See also reproduction and sexuality
A Coordenadoria Ecumênica de Serviço (CESE), 510
Acosta, José de, 75, 80–81
Acre, Mariano José de, 241
Acuña, Clodomiro Siller, 329
Ad Gentes, 565–566
Adriano of Utrecht, 134
Adrian VI (pope), 134
AEMINPU (Peruvian Asociación Evangélica de la Misión Israelita del Nuevo Pacto Universal), 214–216
affirmative action programs, 749
Africa
   Pentecostalism in, 422–423, 430
   Protestant missionaries in, 287, 288
   Seventh-Day Adventists in, 697
   television ownership in, 426
   See also Africa, religion in pre-contact; African diaspora religions (ADRs); Afro-Caribbean religions
Africa, religion in pre-contact, 47–59
   African cosmovisions, 49–50
      human world, 49
      natural world, 49–50
      spiritual world, 50
   Benin Kingdom, 47
   healing function of religion, 55–59
      primary causes of illness, 58
      secondary causes of illness, 58
   influence on Baroque, 166–167
   overview of, 47–49
   universe of gods, 50–55
      ancestors, 53–55
      concept of "time," 51
      deities, 52–53
      deities, number of, 53
      sacrifices, 57
      Supreme Being, 50–52
   See also Akan people; Igbo people; Yoruba
African diaspora religions (ADRs), 603–627
   Africanization of, 604–605, 616–621
   and anti-syncretism, 617, 619–620
   disagreements over African purity/authenticity, 618–619
   and double participation, 620–621
   and gender inclusivity, 618
   orisha revivalists role in, 617
   process of, 617–618
   by reclaiming authentic African rituals, 617–618
   in Trinidad, 617
   by use of Yoruba language, 617
   Africans Christianized before coming to Americas, 608
   antagonism toward, 621
   Bantu-derived practices, 606–607
      Angola in Brazil, 606–607, 618
      bad work as associated with, 611
      Palo in Cuba, 606–607
      Petro rites in Haiti, 606–607

Index

African diaspora religions (ADRs) *(cont.)*
  Candomblé in Brazil (*see* Candomblé (Brazil))
  Catholic acceptance of, 621
  defining, 605
  devotional organizations, 608–609
  differences among, 603
  and divination, 611
  and healing, 664
  Macumba in Brazil, 611
  Muslim slaves, 608
  and nationalization, 604, 613–616
  overview of, 605–613
  Pentecostal attitude toward, 604–605, 621
  Petro rite in Haiti, 611
  Quimbanda in Brazil, 611
  race issues, 613–614, 616
  Rada rite in Haiti, 611
  Santería in Cuba (*see* Santería (Cuba))
  similarities among, 603, 607–608, 610–613
    affliction/healing focus, 610
    gender roles, 613
    good/bad work distinction, 611–612, 618
    initiates, 612
    participation rates, 612–613
    reciprocal relationships between humans/spirits, 610–611
    rituals, 611
    sexuality, 613
  "traditional" African religion concept, 607
  Umbanda in Brazil (*see* Umbanda (Brazil))
  Vodou in Haiti (*see* Vodou (Haiti))
  Vodú in Cuba, participation rates, 612–613
  Yoruba-derived practices, 606, 618–619
    good work as associated with, 611
    Nago, 618
    Regla de Ocha in Cuba, 616–617
    Regla de Palo Monte in Cuba, 611, 618
  See also slave religions; slavery; transnationalism
Afro-Caribbean religions, 633–646
  and Catholicism, 635–636
  common traits of, 636–637
  Espiritismo (Spiritism), 637–639
    and ancestor worship, 639
    beginnings among elites, 638
    as hybrid spirituality, 638–639
    and Kardecism, 637–638
    spread beyond elites, 638
  in Jamaica, 635
  overview of, 633
  Palo *see* Palo (Cuba)
  reasons for survival of spiritual traditions of Africans, 634–635
  and run-away slaves, 636
  Santería (*see* Santería (Cuba))
  and slavery, 634
  in Trinidad, 635
Afro-Okinawan sects, 726
agency and gender, 537–540
  Outline to a Theory of Practice, 537
  and ritualization, 538–539
  In Search of Respect, 537–538
  Staying Sober in Mexico City, 539–540
  structure-agency struggle, 537–538, 539–540
  subject-society struggle, 538–539
  Travestis, 538–539
AIDSEP *(Asociación Interétnica de Desarrollo de la Selva Peruana)*, 562
Akan people, 51, 52
Alarcón, Ferndando Ruiz de, 84
Alberro, Solange, 138
Alcalá y Mendiola, Miguel de, 151
Alcoholics Anonymous, in Mexico, 539–540
Aldama, Juan de, 237
Alexander VI (pope), 90
Allende, Ignacio, 237, 238
Allende, Salvador, 308, 404
Alliance for Progress, 361
Almedida, Rondaldo de, 421
Alta California
  Jesuit missions in, 184
  See also missions, Franciscan in Alta California
Altamirano, Ignacio Manuel, 327–328
altar screens, 121–122
alternativa, 231, 235
Althaus-Reid, Marcella, 369
Alvarado, Juan Velasco, 403
Alves, J. E. D., 15
American Seaman's Friend Society (Brazil), 288
Amezaga, Mariano, 262
amulets, 139, 203
Anastácia (Brazilian saint), 482
ancestor worship
  Egungun societies, 617–618
  and Espiritismo, 639
  by Incas, 28
  by Palo followers, 644, 645
Anderson, Allan, 431
Andes
  Baroque era artwork in, 165
  communal piety in, 168

776

indigenous representation of Virgin Mary in, 482
messianic/revitalization movements in, 212–216
    indigenous cosmological background, 212–213
    indigenous millenarian movements, 213–216
    pachakuti concept, 213
    Spanish influences, 213
popular-erudite dialectic in, 739–740
progressive Catholicism in, 385–386
witchcraft in, 103–104
See also Incas; Peru
Andreas, Rafael, 243
Ángeles, Francisca de los, 124–125
Anglicans, 299–300, 576–577
Angola (Brazil), 606–607, 618
Angulo, Mariano, 241
animal magnetism, 651–652, 654–655
animal sacrifice, and Santería practitioners in US, 623
Ann (Saint), 153
Annacondia, Carlos, 674
Annals of Cuauhtinchan, 82–83
Anthony (Saint), 166
anthropophagy, 77–79
    European debate on, 77–78
    human sacrifice as reinforcing notion of, 79
    and Protestant view on Eucharist, 80
    ritual cannibalism, 79
anticlericalism
    background to, 251–255
    beyond churches phase, 1880–1900s, 255, 264–267
        Argentina, 266
        González Prada, writings of, 264–265
        Guatemala, 265
        Mexico, 266–267
        and Social Darwinism, 264
    church-nation phase, 1750–1850, 255–260
        Argentina, 258–259
        Gran Colombia, 257
        Guatemala, 259–260
        Mexico, 258
        Paraguay, 257–258
        practical focus, 256
        Río de la Plata, 257
    and conservatives, 251, 252, 258–260
    defining, 252–254
    historical typology of, 254
    independence influence on, 252
    influence of Positivism on, 251–255, 264

    and liberals, 252, 261–263, 266
    nations with churches phase, 1850–1880, 255, 260–264
        Church wealth, 263
        Colombia, 263
        Mexico, 261, 262–263
        Peru, 262
        privatizing *vs.* eradicating religion, 261
        Venezuela, 264
    and regalism, 251, 252
    and statism, 251–252
Aora, Juan de, 91
Aparicio, Sebastián de, 163–164
apocalyptic vision of friars, 89–90
Apologética Historia (Las Casas), 69–70, 77, 80–81
Apostolic Church (Pentecostal; Mexico), 433
Apter, Andrew, 603
Aquino, María Pilar, 529–530
Araucanians (Mapuches), 234
Araújo, Maria de, 211
Arbenz, Jacobo, 435
Arce, Mariano José de
architecture
    atrios, 98–100
    fortress-monasteries, 89–90
    See also Baroque era
Argentina
    abortion in, 343, 503
    anticlericalism in, 258–259, 266, 347
    Catholicism in
        Church-state relationship, 352, 494
        dictatorships, 409–411
        human rights violations, 409–411, 511–512
        lay Catholic organizations, 354, 355
        moral concordat, 339
        number of followers, 342
        Our Lady of Lujan shrine, 278–279
        popular, 274, 278–279
        progressive, 385
        reforms, 743
    Chinese immigrants in, 723
    clerical support for independence, 399
    decline in institutional religious practices in, 340
    Dirty War in, 511–512
    ecumenical movement in, 731, 733
    expulsion of Jesuits from, 259
    independence of, 243
    Japanese immigrants in, 724
    Jews in, 683, 710, 711, 713
    Korean immigrants in, 727
    Latter-Day Saints in, 692

Argentina (cont.)
    Lutheranism in, 305–306, 307–308
    military coup in, 378
    military rule in, 499–500
    Mothers of the Plaza del Mayo in
        Argentina, 516
    Muslims in, 714, 716–717, 719
    patron saint of, 278–279, 454
    Pentecostalism in, 422
        beginnings, 432
        denomination composition/
            nationalization process, 434–435
        revival of 1990s, 674
        sex education, 555
    Protestantism in
        growth rate, 444
        missionary efforts, 288, 291
    religious/non-religious pluralism in, 13
    reproduction/sexuality in
        abortion, 343, 503
        contraception, 503
        difference of opinion from sexual
            morality of Vatican, 552
        emergency contraception, 550
        gay marriage/civil unions, 503
        sex education, 555
    Seventh-Day Adventists in, 698–699
    Umbanda in, 624
    See also Southern Cone
Ariga, Paul, 675
Aristide, Jean-Bertrand, 615
Ariztía, Santiago Fernando, 405
Arns, Paulo Evaristo, 386, 510, 513
Arntz, Norbert, 474
Arocha, Guillermo González, 247
Arrupe, Pedro, 594
Arteaga, Ignacio de, 225
ASEL (Latin American Evangelical Social
    Action, Cuba), 731, 733
Ashkenazi Jews, 709–710, 711
Asia
    early Protestant missionary work in,
        287, 288
    emigration to Latin America from, 683
    Pentecostalism in, 430
    television ownership in, 426
    See also Asian religions; China; Japan;
        Korea; South Korea
Asian religions, 723–728
    Chinese-based religions, 727
    Hinduism, 723, 726–727
        Hare Krishna, 726
    Japanese-based religions, 723, 724–726

Afro-Okinawan sects, 726
    in Brazil, 724, 725, 726
    Japanese-Catholic movements, 724
    New Religions, 726
    Okinawan, 726
    Shindo Renmei movement, 724
    Shintoism, 724
    Zen Buddhism, 725
Korean Christianity, 727–728
overview of, 723–724
Asociación Interétnica de Desarrollo de
    la Selva Peruana (AIDESEP,
    Inerethnic Association for the
    Development of the Peruvian
    Rainforest), 562
Aspiazu, Mariano, 241
Assemblies of God (AG), 670
    in Brazil, 415, 433, 435–436, 437–438
    in El Salvador, 434
    General Convention, 438
    and Madureira Convention, 438
    organization of, 438
    origins of, 433
    in Peru, 434
    schisms within, 438
    and Swedish Pentecostals, 437–438
    in United States, 433
Assmann, Hugo, 362–363, 369, 508
Associação Beneficente Cristã (ABC), 753
Associação do Nosso Senhor Jesus, 457
Association of Evangelical Congregations of
    Santa Catarina and Paraná, 313
Association of Free Lutheran Congregations
    (Brazil), 308
Asunción, Paraguay, 186, 187, 304–305
    See also Guaraní people
Atahuallpa (Inkan emperor), 214
atheists in Latin America, 12
atrios, 98–100
Augustinian Order, 175
    and expulsion of Jesuits, 227
    and holy theft of Cristo Renovado, 170
    in New Spain, 92–94
    promotion of cult of Virgin of
        Copacabana by, 113
    views on Indians in Peru, 75
Auh-Ho-Oh, CheeQweesh, 194
autos-da-fé, 141
Ávila, Francisco de, 29, 30
Aymara people
    and inculturation theology, 597
    Marian patroness of, 319
    political mobilization of, 580

Index

Aztecs
  Cortés and Christianization of, 175
  human sacrifice by, 66
  military conquest of, 173–174
  Spanish conquistador view on religiosity of, 45
Azusa Street Revival (1906), 300, 415, 431

Bahia, Brazil
  confraternities in, 167
  Malê Revolt in, 608
  millenarianism in, 212
  Reconçavo movement of, 209
  See also Candomblé
Baja California, Jesuit missions in, 184
Bantu-derived practices, 606–607
  Angola in Brazil, 606–607, 618
  Palo in Cuba, 606–607
  Petro rites in Haiti, 606–607
Banzer Plan, 595
baptism
  and Charismatic Catholicism, 463, 464
  and inculturation theology, 599
Baptists
  early missionaries in Mexico, 293
  and human rights, 513
  use of print media in conversions, 455
Barbados Declaration (1971), 517
Barbados I, 565
Barbados II, 565
Barbara (Saint), 204
Baroque era, 160–172
  artwork in, 164–167
    altar screens, 121–122
    in Andes, 165
    in Bogota, 165
    as element of Tridentine Catholicism, 121–122
    emotionality of, 165–166
    in Europe, 164–165
    in New Spain, 165
    role in Indian conversion, 165
  communal piety in, 167–169
    African and Indian women, 168
    confraternities, 167–168
    group performances as instruction, 168
    Maya of Yucatán, 168–169
  as cultural logic, 169–172
  Franciscan use of Baroque style, 453
  holy people outside official male hierarchy, 162–163
  images in, 164
  legitimation of relics, 163–164

  overview of, 160–161
  pre-contact Indian culture / African religions, 166–167
  regulation of beatification / canonization, 162
  saintly mediation in, 161–164
Barreda, Gabino, 266–267
Barreiro, Julio, 730–731
Barrios, Domitila, 516–517
Barrios, Rufino, 265
Barros, L. F. W., 15
Base Ecclesial Communities (CEBs)
  difference from Catholic Charismatic Renewal, 391–392
  diversity among, 380
  education programs, 379–380
  female leadership, 551
  and gender, 530
  human rights support by, 511
  and indigenous mobilization, 566
  land distribution issues, 518
  and Liberation Theology, 672, 745
  political mobilization efforts, 381
  as result of CELAM, Medellín, 378–381, 386
  revolutionary movement involvement, 380
Basel Mission Society, 313
basismo, 746–747
Batista, Cícero Romão, 211–212
Batista Báez, Juan, 299
Batllori, Miquel, 234
Batuque (religion), 454–455
beatification, 144
  Baroque era regulation of, 162
  Council of Trent on criteria for, 110–111
  of Serra, 194–195
Beauvior, Simone de, 526
Bedford, Nancy, 369
Behar, Ruth, 530–531
Béjar, José Gabriel, 241
Belén Posada del Migrante (Bethlehem Migrant Shelter), 520–521
Belgrano, Manuel, 274
Beltrán, Nuño, 68
Benavente, Toribio de, 93
Benedict XV (pope), 323
Benedict XVI (pope)
  and canonization of Óscar Romero, 487
  condemnation of condom use, 552
  continuities with Pope Francis I, 395–396
  and culture of secrecy, 392
  and decriminalization of abortion in Mexico, 549

Benedict XVI (pope) (*cont.*)
   and Liberation Theology, 372
   Lumen Fidei, 395
   on unity and purity, 389
   See also Ratzinger, Joseph
Benin Kingdom, 47
Berg, Daniel, 433
Bergoglio, Jorge
   and human rights violations in Argentina, 410, 512
   See also Francis (pope)
Berlin Wall, 368
Bermúdez, Francisco Morales, 403
Bernini, Gian Lorenzo, 532–533
Berryman, Phillip, 506
Betanzos, Domingo de, 67, 69
Bethlehem Migrant Shelter (Belén Posada del Migrante), 520–521
Biehl, João, 541–542
bigamy, and Inquisition, 140
Bingemer, Maria Clara, 328
birth control pill
   effect on fertility rates, 548
   See also contraception
birth registers, civil, 334
Bishop, Albert, 295
black ventriloquists, 139
bodies, gendered and religion, 532–536
   Christ as bridegroom metaphor, 533
   colonial-era body, 533–534
   discipline and punishment, 535–536
   homosexual desire, 533
   power of healing, 536
   and Protestant evangelism, 534–535
   The Reformation of Machismo, 534–535
   Shamanism, Colonialism, and the Wild Man, 536
Boff, Clodovis, 363
Boff, Leonardo
   on ecclesiology, 384–385
   education of, 362
   investigated for deviations from orthodoxy, 388
   leaves priesthood, 368
   on Liberation Theology-Vatican collaboration, 393–394
   publications of, 362
   and silencing of Liberation Theology, 521
Bogotá, Colombia
   Baroque artwork in, 166
   effect of expulsion of Jesuits on education in, 228
   independence movement in, 239, 240
   See also Colombia

"Bold Mission Thrust" campaign, 543–544
Bolioli, Oscar, 732–733
Bolívar, Simon, 238, 242, 246, 257
Bolivia
   AEMINPU in, 215
   Banzer Plan, 595
   Catholicism in
      Church-state relationship, 495, 580
      eroding dominance, 13
      gender issues, 341
      popular, 274
      survey on what Church should devote attention to, 341
      Tridentine, and rural Indians, 127
   clerical support for independence movements in, 399
   Día de la Raza in, 559
   ethnopopulist parties, 583
   and inculturation theology, 597
   indigenous in
      electoral success, 581
      and identity politics, 580
      number of, 560–561
      and political reform, 562
      religious resources for mobilization in, 572
      uprisings by, 559
      and wage gap, 561
   Japanese immigrants in, 723, 725
   Jehovah's Witnesses in, 701
   and Liberation Theology, 595, 745
   Lutheranism in
      merchant/craftsmen congregations, 305
      missions, 307
   patron saint of, 274, 319, 454
   Pentecostal percentage of Protestants in, 446–447
   Protestantism in, 444, 447
   reproduction/sexuality in, 556
   Seventh-Day Adventists in, 698
   unaffiliated in, 12
   women's movements and human rights in, 516–517
bolsa de mandinga (Afro-Brazilian amulet), 139
bonding social capital, 753
Bonino, José Míguez, 362, 365–366
Bonne, Valentina, 515
books, forbidden by Inquisition, 236
Booth, John, 568
Borah, Woodrow, 192
Borgia Group codices, 26
Boukman, Dutty, 205, 269

Index

Bourbon reforms in Latin America
  need for, 231
  religious Creole clergy objections to, 231–232
  secular Creole clergy objections to, 232–233
Bourdieu, Pierre, 426, 537, 740, 741, 754–755
Bourgois, Philippe, 537–538
BPC (Brazil for Christ, Pentecostal), 433, 436
Brading, David A., 274–275, 278
Brandão, Carlos, 741
Brandes, Stanley, 539–540
Brandon, George Edward, 624–625
Brasil: Nunca Mais, 513
Brazil
  African-derived religions during colonial period, 609
  Afro-Catholic beliefs/practices in, 349, 458–459
  American Seaman's Friend Society in, 288
  anticlericalism in, 347
  Assemblies of God in, 415, 433, 435–436, 437–438
  Baroque-era art in, 166
  bolsa-família in, 448
  Catholicism in
    acceptance of ADRs, 621
    Charismatic, 457, 465, 466, 678, 749
    Church-state relationship, 352–353, 495–496, 743
    dictatorship opposition/support, 404
    media use, 457
    member numbers, 7, 15, 342
    number of followers, 7, 15, 342
    popular, 482, 486, 488
    post-independence popular, 280–282
    progressive, 385–386, 390
  CEBs in, 379, 507, 551, 672
  Chinese immigrants in, 723, 727
  Christian Base Communities in, 404
  Contestado Rebellion in, 210–211, 744
  decline in institutional religious practices in, 340
  diaspora tourism in, 626
  early travel narratives on, 78–79
  evangelicals in
    gender equity, 553–554
    political involvement, 752–753
  gay marriage/civil unions in, 503
  human rights in, 510, 513
  independence of, 652
  Inquisition in, 136, 138
    number of proceedings, 140
    public *autos-da-fé* ceremonies, 141
    types of offenses specific to, 139

Japanese-based religions in, 724, 725, 726
Japanese Buddhist immigration to, 683
Japanese immigrants in, 723, 724, 725
Jesuits and messianic movements, 208
Jews in, 709, 710, 711
Korean immigrants in, 723, 727
laicicism in, 343
land distribution in, 519
Latter-Day Saints in, 692–693
and Liberation Theology, 486, 745, 746–747
Lutheranism in (*See also* Evangelical Church of the Lutheran Confession in Brazil (IECLB))
  ethnic background of missionaries, 306
  first congregations, 304–305, 308, 311–312
  merchant/craftsmen congregations, 305
Macumba in, 611
Malê Revolt in, 608
media use by religions in
  Catholic Charismatic Renewal, 457
  Igreja Universal do Reino de Deus, 457–458
  print media, 455–456
  telenovelas, 458
  televangelism, 426
messianic movement of Conselheiro in, 269
military rule in, 499–500
millenarianism in, 212
Muslims in (*see* Muslims, in Brazil)
non-religious in, 15
other religions in, 15
overthrow of Goulart, 378
Pastorals in, 746
patron saint of, 319, 451, 454
Pentecostalism in (*see* Brazil, Pentecostalism in)
Pentecostal percentage of Protestants in, 446–447
pluri-confessionalism in, 343
Pope Francis's trip to, 395–396
Protestantism in
  converts from Catholicism, 445
  early missionaries, 288, 292–293
  growth, 15, 443–444, 736
  number of followers, 12, 15
  Pentecostal percentage of Protestants, 446–447
  progressive party of, 509
  use of radio transmission for conversions in, 456
racism in, 660
re-democratization in, 751

Brazil (cont.)
  religious diversity in, 15
    Christian pluralism zone, 12–13
    religious/non-religious pluralism zone, 13
  reproduction/sexuality
    abortion, 503, 550, 552, 554–555, 556
    contraception, 503, 554
    difference of opinion from sexual morality of Vatican, 552
    gay marriage/civil unions, 503
  saints, hybrid representations of, 482
  secularization of public institutions in, 339
  Seventh-Day Adventists in, 698
  slave religions in, 204–205
  slaves in
    places of origin, 606
    religions of, 4, 204–205
    revolts by, 205, 608
  Spiritism in (see Spiritism (Espiritismo))
  sponsorship of audiovisual centers in, 456
  visual culture of religions in, 454–455
    Xangô in, 454–455
    See also Candomblé (Brazil); Umbanda (Brazil); Igreja Universal do Reino de Deus (IURD, Brazil)
Brazil, Pentecostalism in
  attendance rates, 442
  beginnings, 432, 552
  and competitive pluralism, 443
  denomination composition/nationalization process in, 435–442
    Assemblies of God, 435–436, 437–438
    Brazil for Christ, 436, 439–440
    Christian Congregation, 435–436, 438
    Church of the Four-Square Gospel, 436, 438–439
    first wave, 436
    God is Love, 436, 440
    International Church of the Grace of God, 436
    second wave, 436
    third wave, 436
    Universal Church of the Kingdom of God (see Igreja Universal do Reino de Deus (IURD, Brazil))
    wave thesis of, 435–437
  divine healing, 439
  ethnicity of founders of, 433
  exorcism and liberation sessions, 423
  forerunners, 432
  founders, 433

  gender equity, 554
  growth, 433, 736, 753–754
  institutional politics, 552–553
  internationalization of, 420
  political involvement, 753
  reasons for Catholics convert, 446
  reproduction/sexuality, 553, 554–555
  Swedish Pentecostals, 437–438
  See also Igreja Universal do Reino de Deus (IURD, Brazil)
Brazil for Christ (BPC, Pentecostal), 433, 436, 439–440
Brazil Never Again, 386
Bricker, Victoria R., 216
bridging social capital, 753
Broad Front (Frente Amplio) coalition (Uruguay), 493, 498
Brown, Diana, 616
Brown, Michael F., 209
Brown, Peter, 271–272
Brown, Robert McAfee, 673
Brusco, Elizabeth, 534–535
Brysk, Alison, 517–518, 564, 569, 572–573, 580
Bucareli, Francisco de, 222
Buddhism, 458, 723
  Japanese immigration to Brazil, 683
  Zen Buddhism, 725
Buenos Aires, Argentina
  early Protestant missionary enterprise in, 288
  effect of expulsion of Jesuits on education in, 228
  immigrant Lutheranism in, 304–305
  independence of, 243
  Muslims in, 714
  See also Argentina
Bulnes, Francisco, 267
Bundles (iconography), 83–84
Burke, John, 666
Bush, Luis, 666
Bustamante, Francisco de, 322–323
Butler, Kim, 609

Caballeros, Harold, 677
Cabot, Sebastian, 185–186
Cabrera, Miguel, 323
caciques, 179
Cádiz Cortes (Spain's first "national" assembly), 252
Caicedo, José María Torres, 13
Calancha, Antonio de la, 75, 165
Calder, Bruce, 568–569
Caldera, Luis, 97–98

Index

California
  Franciscans in, 93
  See also missions, Franciscan in Alta California
Calles, Plutarco Elías, 270
Callistus III (pope), 44
Calvin, John, 44–45, 110
Câmara, Hélder, 386, 388, 744
Camargo, Procópio, 716
Campo, Gonzalo de, 96
Campomanes, Count of, 224, 225, 226–227
Campos, Robert, 446
Campus Crusade for Christ, 670
Candomblé (Brazil), 4, 204, 454–455, 508
  and anti-syncretism, 619–620
  and double participation, 620–621
  gender roles, 613
  good/bad work distinction, 611
  nationalization of, 614, 615–616
  participation rates, 612
  Pentecostal attitude toward, 621
  Pentecostal use of elements of, 458
  public acceptance of, 604
  race issues, 613–614
  ritual specialists, 611
  sexuality, 613
  similarities to African diaspora religions, 603
  spread through secondary diaspora, 622
  Yoruba influences on, 610, 618
cannibalism. *See* anthropophagy
canonization
  Council of Trent on criteria for, 110–111
  regulation during Baroque era, 162
Canudos (Império do Belo Monte) movement, 210–211, 281–282, 489, 744
Capuchins, expulsion from Guatemala, 400
Caracas, Venezuela
  independence movement in, 239
  Lutheran merchant/craftsmen congregations in, 305
  Muslims in, 718
  patron saint of, 153
  See also Venezuela
Cardenal, Ernesto, 387, 406, 511, 566
Cárdenas, Lázaro, 296
Cárdenas, Nabor, 217
Cardijn, Joseph, 375–376
Cardim, Fernão, 78
Caribbean
  abolishment of slavery in, 635
  blending of beliefs/practices in, 349
  diversification of Christianity in, 12
  emigration to US form, 681t42.1

  expulsion of Jesuits from, 227
  Inquisition in, 136
  Jews in, 709
  Lutheran missions in, 305, 306
  origin areas of slaves in, 634
  slave religions in, 204–205
  South Asian immigrants in, 723
  See also Afro-Caribbean religions; New Granada; Santo Domingo
Caribbean Synod of the American Lutheran Church, 306
Carnival, in late medieval Europe, 40
Caro, Isaac, 714, 717
Carozza, Paolo, 505
Carrascón, Francisco, 242
Carrera, José María, 244
Carrera, Rafael, 251, 259–260, 276, 400
Carroll, John, 245
Carta a los españoles americanos (Letter Addressed to the Spanish Americans; Viscardo), 234
Cartegena, Colombia, independence movement in, 239
Cartegena de Indias tribunal, 136, 140
Casa, Cristóbal Choque, 29
Casáldaliga, Pedro, 386
Casanova, José, 17–18
Casanova Estrada, Ricardo, 351
Casariego, Mario, 408
Casas del Migrate in Mexico and Central America, 520
Castillo, Bernal Díaz del, 79, 81, 90, 175
Castillo Morales, Juan (Juan Solado), 349
Castillo Velasco, José María, 262
Castro, Fidel, 495, 615, 669
Catharina de San Juan, 148, 162
Catholic Action
  in Chile, 497
  influence of, 376, 495
  methods used by, 379
  overview of, 355, 375–376
  and reaction to growth of Protestantism, 576
  see-act-judge model of, 379, 394
  and shift from exclusive clerical power, 400
Catholic Charismatic Renewal (CCR, Renovación Carismática Católica), 462–477
  Aparecida Document, 471–475, 477
  on cultural change, 472
  importance of, 472
  polarizing effect of, 473
  on youth, 473

Catholic Charismatic Renewal (CCR,
    Renovación Carismática Católica)
    (cont.)
  Church hierarchy reaction to, 464–465
  denominational model as basis of, 16
  and door-to-door missions, 475–476
  and feminism, 551–552
  Great Continental Mission, 471–477
  growth of, 462, 770
  history of, 463–467
  and Liberation Theology, 464–465
  main characteristics of practices/beliefs,
      467–471, 751
    conservatism, 469
    difference from traditional piety, 468–469
    faith healing, 467, 468
    masculine fellowship, 469
    morality, 469
    oral character of prayers/preaching/
        testimony, 467
    resting in the Spirit, 467
    similarities to Pentecostalism, 468
    soft/strong elements, 469–471, 474
    speaking in tongues, 415, 463, 464,
        467–468
    Spirit baptism, 463, 464
    vivid/rhythmic songs of praise, 467
  on modernity, 750
  organization of, 465–466, 467
  overview of, 391–392, 749
  on Protestants, 465
  and reproduction/sexuality, 551–552
  and sanctification of popular traditions, 476
  self-identification as Charismatic, 447, 466
  in Southern Cone countries, 13
  and transnationalism, 677–678
  use of media by, 457, 471, 678
  Virgin Mary as patron saint of, 465
Catholic Church
  colonial
    control over education/intellectual
        endeavors, 5
    effect of Liberal reforms on, 5–7
    as key benefactor of honor and status, 5
    as pervasive economic institution, 5
    power/influence of, compared with
        Crown, 4
  on communism, 337–338
  erosion of monopoly in Latin America, 769
  and globalization
    human rights movement, 18–19
    as one of most globalized religions, 18
    transnational nature of, 18

Hieronymites, 64–65, 66
  as indigenous advocate, 564–565
  membership Latin America, 12
Mendicants, 177, 181
and nationalization of ecclesiastic
    property, 334
and Pentecostalism, 415
sex abuse cover-up by, 521
shortage of priests, 102, 346, 349, 669
support of women's movements, 514–517
See also Augustinian Order; Catholic
    Action; Catholic Charismatic
    Renewal (CCR); dictatorship, and
    Catholic Church; diversification in
    Latin America; Dominican Order;
    Franciscan Order; independence,
    and Catholic Church; Jesuits
Catholic Counter Reformation, 143
Catholic Enlightenment tradition, 251, 256
Catholic Foreign Mission Society of America
    (Maryknoll), 354, 402
Catholicism
  folk, 6–7, 210, 349–350, 634
  Japanese-Catholic movements, 724
  member numbers in Latin America, 12
  moral concordats, 335–339
  response to Protestant media
      productions, 457
  on transubstantiation, 108
  use of media in context of CEBs, 456
  See also Catholicism, progressive;
      diversification in Latin America;
      folk Catholicism; Marianism in
      Latin America; Pentecostalism;
      political parties, and Catholicism;
      popular Catholicism,
      contemporary; popular
      Catholicism, nineteenth century;
      Tridentine Catholicism; *individual
      countries*
Catholicism, institutional/political
    resurgence, 1900–1960s, 346–356
  emergence of Church-state
      rapprochement, 350–353
    in liberal dictatorships, 350–351
    origins of, 350
    in populist regimes, 351–353
  on eve of twentieth century, 347–348
    anticlericalism, 347–348
    liberals vs. conservatives, 347
  institutional resurgence, 353–355
    and proliferation of lay organizations,
        354–355

Index

and recruitment of foreign religious personnel, 354
and training/education of Latin American clerics, 354
overview of, 346–347
popular religiosity, 348–350
    blending of beliefs and practices, 349
    faith healers, 348
    syncretic practices, 349–350
    women's role in, 348–349
and shortage of priests, 346, 349
Catholicism, popular-erudite dialectic, 739–759
    churches and politics, 751–753
        Catholic Church, 752
        evangelical churches, 752
    devotional/charismatic movements at turn of century, 764–766
        Catholic Charismatic Renewal, 749, 750
        Catholic University of Rio de Janeiro, 749
        Comunione e Liberazione, 748
        Focolari, 748
        Jesuit schools and universities, 748–749
        Legionarios, 748, 750, 751
        Neocatecumene, 748
        Opus Dei, 748, 750, 751
        organizational features of, 749–751
        and refashioning of self, 750
        religiosity of, 751
        Schoenstatt, 748
    overview of, 739–743
    popular religion
        after Vatican II, 744–747
        and cult of Santísima Muerte, 741–742
        description of, 741
        detachment from official Church, 741–742
        Liberation Theology as strategy to capture/channel, 745–747
        political movements, 744
        Romanization/modernization before Vatican II, 743–744
        subordination to official Church, 741
    restructuring of religious field, 753–759
        growth of Pentecostalism, 753–754
        Pentecostalism/Catholicism vs. neo-Pentecostalism, 754
        traditional vs. neo-Pentecostalism, 755–759
Catholicism, progressive, 372–396
    CELAM in Medellín, 377–382
    CELAM in Puebla, 387–388
    and John Paul II, 385–389

opening address at Puebla conference, 387–388
legacy of, 390–392
    New Evangelization crusade, 390–391
Liberation Theology influence on, 382–385
    Gustavo Gutiérrez, 382–384
    Jon Sobriono, 384
    Leonardo Boff, 384–385
and Pope Francis, 392–396
    diversity of permanent advisory council of, 392–393
    ideology of, 392–393, 395
    influence on US bishops, 394
    and Liberation Theology, 393–394
    re-articulation of progressive themes, 394–396
pre-origins of, 373–376
    Antonio de Montesinos, 373
    Bartolomé de las Casas, 373–374
    Catholic lay movements, 375–376
    Church-Crown relationship in Latin America, 374
    Rerum Novarum, 7, 352, 375, 400, 593, 743
    Vatican I, 374
and Vatican II, 375, 376–377
    aggiornamento process, 376
    Gaudium et Spes, 376–377, 506–507, 565, 594
    on liturgical change, 377
    on social justice, 377
Catholic transition, 15
Catholic Union (Argentina), 266
Catholic University of Rio de Janeiro (PUC-Rio), 749
Catholic Workers Circles (Argentina), 743
Catimbó (Jurema) (religion), 454–455, 653
caudillo (strong man), 332
Cava, Ralph Della, 281
Cavenaghi, S. M., 15
Caymmi, Dorival, 459
CDIAL (Center for Dissemination of Islam to Latin America), 718
CEBs. *See* Base Ecclesial Communities (CEBs)
Cédula Grande (1743), 226
CEH (UN Commission for Historical Clarification), 513–514
Celestial Church of Christ, 416
cemeteries
    secularization of, 334
    separate Catholic/Protestant, 312
Center for Dissemination of Islam to Latin America (CDIAL), 718

Central America
　Church-state relationship in, 495
　emigration to US from, 686
　　foreign born by birth region/date of arrival, 681t42.1
　Lutheran missions in, 306
　migrants and social justice in, 520
　number of Catholics in, 342
　Pentecostalism in
　　beginnings of, 432–433
　　growth, 764
　　media use, 456–457
　Protestantism in, 684
　　converts from Catholicism, 445
　　growth, 444
　religious diversification in, 12
　religious self-identification, 684
　violence of military regimes in, 499
　See also individual countries
Central American Mission (CAM), 295–296, 298, 670
Central Brazil Synod, 313
Central Mexican codices, 26
Centro de Formación Indígena (Ecuador), 597
Centro Dom Vital (Brazil), 495
CEPAD, 301
CESE (A Coordenadoria Ecumênica de Serviço), 510
Céspedes, Roque Antonio, 257–258
Chabad Lubavitch movement, 712–713
Chadwick, Owen, 252–253
Chamorro, Pedro Joaquín, 406
chancas worship in Peru, 103, 104–105
charity, Liberation Theology on, 745
Charles I (Spain), 304
Charles II (Spain), 149
Charles III (Spain), on expulsion of Jesuits, 223–224
Charles IV (Spain), 233
Charles V (Spain), 66, 91, 304
Cháves, Rony, 667
Chávez, Hugo, 498–499
Chávez, Juan de, 75
Chesnut, Andrew, 391, 455, 610, 742
Chiapanec Maya, nativist movement among, 216
Chiapas, Mexico
　indigenous in
　　contextual interaction and mobilization, 567
　　inculturation theology, 597, 599
　　movements in, 517
　　religious framing for mobilization, 571

religious resources for mobilization, 573
land distribution issues, 518
and Liberation Theology, 594
migrants and social justice in, 520
Murabitun community in, 720
popular Catholicism in, 488–489
Protestants in, number of followers, 508
Sufi Muslims in, 718
women's movements and human rights in, 516
Zapatista rebellion in, 488–489, 517, 559
See also Mexico
Chichén Itzá, Postclassic, 25–26
Chichimecatecotl, Carlos, 83, 135
Chile
　Catholicism in
　　Charismatic, 466
　　Church-state relationship, 353, 502, 743
　　dictatorship opposition/support, 404–405
　　difference of opinion from sexual morality of Vatican, 552
　　lay organizations, 355
　　Legionarios de Cristo, 748
　　moral concordat, 339
　　Opus Dei, 748
　　progressive, 386
　CEBs in, 507, 551
　Christian Democratic parties in, 496, 497
　Día de la Raza in, 559
　divorce in, 503
　evangelicals in, 553–554
　expulsion of Jesuits from, 222
　gender equity in, 553–554
　human rights in, 510
　immigrant Lutheranism in, 305, 308
　importance of religion in life in, 10
　independence of, 243–245
　indigenous movement success in, 582, 583
　Jews in, 711
　Latter-Day Saints in, 692
　military coup in, 378
　military rule in, 499–500, 501
　and moral concordat, 339
　Muslims in, 714, 716, 717
　Pentecostalism in
　　abortion, 554
　　beginnings, 432, 552
　　founders, 433
　　gender equity, 554
　　growth, 433
　　as homegrown, 433
　　lack of regular attendance, 442

786

Index

as national in origin, 434
  sex education, 555
pluri-confessionalism in, 343
Protestantism in, 300
  converts from Catholicism, 445
  early missionaries, 292
  growth, 444
religious/non-religious pluralism in, 13
reproduction/sexuality, 550
  abortion, 554
  emergency contraception, 549, 550
Seventh-Day Adventists in, 698
women's movements and human rights in, 515–516
See also Southern Cone
Chimborazo, Ecuador, and inculturation theology, 594, 597, 599–600
China
  early Protestant missions in, 288
  emigration to Cuba from, 683
  Pentecostalism in, 430
China Poblana. *See* Catharina de San Juan
Chinese-based religions in Latin America, 727
Chiribí Indians, 66–67
Chiriguana, Paraguay, messianic movements in, 209
Cho, David Yonggi, 423, 676
Chojnacki, Ruth, 597, 598, 599
Ch'ol people, mobilization by, 571, 573
cholera epidemic, 276
Cholula, Postclassic, 26
Christ. *See* Jesus Christ
Christian, William, 152
Christian Base Communities
  in Brazil, 404
  in El Salvador, 407
  and human rights, 507–508
  in Nicaragua, 406–407
  percentage of Catholics affiliated with, 466
Christian Congregation (Brazil), 433, 435–436, 438
Christian Democracy, 744, 748
Christian Democratic parties, 355, 493
Christian Democratic Party (PDC, Chile), 496, 497
Christian Democratic Party (PDC, El Salvador), 496, 499
Christian Democratic Party (PDC, Uruguay), 493, 498
Christ of Chalma, 127
Christ of Totolapan, 170
Christos of Santa Teresa (Ixmiquilpán), 112

church, as sacred space in late medieval Europe, 38, 39
Church and State in Latin America (Mecham), 270–271
Church of Jesus Christ of Latter-day Saints. *See* Latter-Day Saints (LDS)
Church of Lukumi Babalu Aye v. City of Hialeah, 623
Church of the Foursquare Gospel (Brazil), 433, 436, 438–439
Church of the Word (Verbo) (Guatemala), 435
Church of World Messianity, 726
Churruca, Agustín, 232–233
Cienfuegos, José Ignacio, 243, 244–245, 246
Cisneros, Sandra, 328
Ciudad Juárez, Jehovah's Witnesses in, 702
Ciudad Rodrigo, Antonio de, 67–68
Civic Union (Uruguay), 493
civilized *vs.* barbaric peoples, Iberian view on, 3
civil marriage, 334, 352–353
CLAI (Latin American Council of Churches, Brazil), 734
Clarke, Peter, 617
Classic Zapotec architecture, 24–25
Clavijero, Francisco, 234
Cleary, Edward, 442, 464, 474, 572, 580
Clement IX (pope), 162
Clement XIV (pope), 233–234
clerical immunity, 232
Clifford, James, 704
CNBB (National Conference of Brazilian Bishops), 385, 404
Cocama people, messianism among, 209–210
COCEI (Worker-Peasant-Student coalition of the Isthmus of Tehuantepec), 575
Codices
  Central Mexican, 26
    Borgia Group, 26
    Mexica tradition, 26
    Mixtec tradition, 26
  Mesoamerican, 26
  Precolumbian Maya texts, 26
Codifier. *See* Kardec, Allan (Hoppolyte Léon Denizard Rivail)
CODIMUJ (Coordinación Diocesana de Mujeres), 516
Cold War
  and growth of Protestantism, 445
  lay Catholic movements during, 355
  and TV evangelism, 456–457

Colima, Mexico, Franciscans in, 93
collective effervescence, 532
Coll y Prat, Narciso, 240
Colombia
  anticlericalism in, 347
  Base Ecclesial Communities movement in, 551
  Catholicism in
    acceptance of ADRs, 621
    Charismatic, 464
    Church-state relationship, 493
    eroding dominance, 13
    number of followers, 12, 342
    progressive, 385
    survey on what Church should devote attention to, 341
    views on gender issues, 341
  dictatorship in, 510
  divorce in, 503
  emergency contraception, 550
  gay marriage/civil unions in, 503
  human rights in, 513
  independence, 240, 492
  indigenous and political reform in, 562–563
  La Luz del Mundo in, 704
  Latter-Day Saints in, 692
  Liberation Theology in, 745
  Lutheran missions in, 307
  Muslims in, 716, 717
  patron saint of, 454
  Pentecostalism in
    exorcism and liberation sessions, 423
    gender equity, 554
  Protestantism in
    converts from Catholicism, 445
    growth, 444
    number of followers, 12
    restraint in secularization of public institutions, 336–337
  Seventh-Day Adventists in, 698
Colón, Diego, 87
Columbus, Christopher, 173, 174, 633
CoMadres (Mothers and Relatives of Political Prisoners, Disappeared, and Assassinated of El Salvador), 514–515
Comblin, José, 367
Comissão Pastoral da Terra (CPT, Brazil), 386, 390, 519
Comité de Cooperación para la Paz en Chile (COPACHI), 405, 510
Comité de Unidad Campesino (CUC, Guatemala), 519, 566

Committee for Independent Political Electoral Organization (COPEI, Venezuela), 498–499
communism, 8, 337–338
  See also Cold War
compadrazgo system, 578
Compañón, Baltasar Jaime Martínez de, 235
competitive pluralism, 443
Comte, Auguste, 264, 313
comunidades eclesiales de base. *See* Base Ecclesial Communities (CEBs)
Comunione e Liberazione (Italy), 748
Conceição, José Manoel da, 432
Confederación Latinoamericana y Caribeña de Religiosos, 356
Confederation of Peasant Workers (Bolivia), 572
confraternities
  of Afro-Latin Americans, 202–203
  in Bahia, Brazil, 167
  in Baroque era, 167–168
  black, in Mexico City, 202–203, 205
  established by Cortés, 123
  and identity, 202
  in late medieval Europe, 41–42
  in New Spain
    decline at end of colonial period, 130
    as means of community formation, 127–128
    patron saint as unifying symbol of, 153–154
    role in Corpus Christi processions, 116, 153
  overview of, 123–124
  in Quito, Ecuador, 149
  and resurgence of Catholicism, 354
  and women, 168
Congar, Yves, 382
congregaciones, 179
Congregationalists
  missionaries in Chile, 292
  Scottish, missionaries in Brazil, 292–293
  use of print media in conversions, 455
Congregation for the Doctrine of the Faith, 367, 387, 388
Congregation of Relics and Indulgences, 163
Congregation of Rites, 163
Congregation of Sacred Rites, 194
Congregation of Scalabrinian Missionaries, 520
CONIC (National Council of Christian Churches of Brazil), 734

conopas worship, 103, 104–105
conquest/colonization, 87–105
   and apocalyptic vision of friars, 89–90
   art and architecture role in, 98–100
      churches/convents with *atrios,* 98–100
      tequitqui (Indian-Christian) art, 98
   Christian/indigenous liturgical practice linkages, 88–89
   Crown/Church cooperation, 90–91
   evangelization strategies, 96–98
      education, 97–98
      mission/Indian towns, 97
      syncretism examples in modern Mexico, 88
      syncretism examples in New Spain, 96–97
   indigenous reactions to Christianity, 100–105
      resistance and adaptation in Peru, 100–101
      resistance in New Spain, 100–101
   overview of, 87–90
   religious orders in New Spain, 90–95
      Augustinians, 92–94
      Crown/Church cooperation, 90–91
      Dominicans, 93
      Franciscans, 91–93
      Jesuits, 94–95
   religious orders in Peru, 74–75, 95–96
      Dominicans, 95
      Jesuits, 96
   role of natives in salvation, 89
Consejo Episcopal Latinoamericano (CELAM). *See* Latin American Bishops' Conference (CELAM)
Conselheiro, Antônio (Antônio Vicente Mendes Maciel), 211, 269, 281–282
Conselho Missionário Indigenistas (CIMI), 386
Conservatives, 6
Contestado Rebellion (1912–1916), 210–211, 744
contraception, 503
   Catholics on, 341, 469, 503
   Charismatic Catholicism on, 469
   condemnation of condom use by Vatican, 552
   effect of birth control pill on, 548
   emergency contraception, 549, 550
   and evangelicals, 554
   opposition to emergency, in Chile, 549
   Pentecostals on, 448, 554
   See also reproduction and sexuality
Contras, fund raising for, 456–457

Cook, Sherburne F., 192
COPACHI (Comité de Cooperación para la Paz en Chile), 405, 510
COPEI (Committee for Independent Political Electoral Organization, Venezuela), 498–499
Copeland, Kenneth, 423
Córdoba, Francisco Hernández de, 90
Coronado, Francisco Vásquez de, 182
Corpus Christi processions, 116–117, 455
   in Cuzco, 117, 126, 127
   in late medieval Europe, 38
   in Mexico City, 116
   participation by confraternities, 116, 153
Corr, Rachel, 578
Cortés, Hernán
   and Christianization of Aztecs, 175
   devotion to Virgin Mary, 174
   establishment of confraternity, 123
   expedition to Veracruz, 90
   and indigenous religion, 81–82, 90, 92
   on replacing idols with Christian images, 145
   support of monastic Inquisition, 134
   symbolism actions to impress indigenous, 92
   and tribute demands from Aztecs, 173
Coruña, Martin de La, 85
Costa Rica
   Christian Democratic parties in, 496, 497–498
   La Luz del Mundo in, 704
   Lutheran missions in, 306
   Seventh-Day Adventists in, 698
Costo, Jeannette Henry, 194–195
Costo, Rupert, 194–195
costumbre, 349–350, 488–489, 599
Council of the Indies, 66–68, 70–71
Council of Trent (1545-1563), 108–109
   on Baroque, 160–161
   on Corpus Christi, 170–171
   on images, 79
   on Tridentine Catholicism, 110–111, 120
Council of Valladolid, 360, 373
Counter Reformation, 143
CPT (Comissão Pastoral da Terra, Brazil), 386, 390, 519
creoles
   clerical objection to Bourbon reforms, 231–233
   and cult of the saints in New Spain, 146
   pro-Americanism of elites, 13–14
   role of clergy in independence movements, 235–238, 242

Index

creolized religions, 2
Cristero War (1926-1929), 271, 337, 353, 744
Cristos of Chalma, 112
Crowe, Frederick, 290
Crucified Christ of Esquipulas (Black Christ), 275, 276–277
Cruz, Francisco de la, 93
crypto Jews, 141, 210, 709, 711–712
Cuba
  abolishment of slavery in, 635
  Afro-Cubanidad movement in, 614
  Catholicism in
    and Africanism, 635
    Church-state relationship, 495
    opposition to anti-syncretism, 621
    popular, 274
  challenges to laicicism in, 343
  Chinese immigrants in, 683, 727
  ecumenical movement in, 731, 733
  emigration to US from, 681t42.2, 682, 685
  faith healers in, 348
  independence of, 246–247, 321
  Lutheran missions in, 306
  Marianism in, 320–321
  migration to Miami from, 685
  Muslims in, 716
  patron saint of, 274, 320–321, 620, 685
  Protestantism in, 299–300
  Regla de Ocha in, 611, 616–617, 618
  Regla de Palo Monte in, 611, 618
  religious self-identification, 684
  slave religions in, 204
  Spiritism in, 652
  See also Afro-Caribbean religions; Palo (Cuba); Santería (Cuba)
Cuban Revolution (1959), 337, 361, 378, 401, 669
CUC (Comité de Unidad Campesino, Guatemala), 519
Cuero y Caicedo, José, 239–240
Cuevas, Mariano, 232, 238
Culiacán, Mexico, Jehovah's Witnesses in, 702
The Cult of the Saints (Brown), 271–272
Cunha, Euclides da, 281
Curitiba Document, 316–317
Cursillos de Cristiandad, 376
Curtin, Jim, 568–569
Cuscat's War (1867-1869), 216
Cuzco
  Corpus Christi festival in, 117, 126, 127, 170–172
  independence movement in, 241–242
  See also Incas

Danzantes, 24
Davie, Grace, 14–15
Davis, Mike, 414
Davis, Natalie Z., 271–272
Debate Nacional por la Paz (National Debate for Peace, El Salvador), 513
de la Torre, Manuel Antonio, 223
Deleuze, Gilles, 541
Democratic Action Party (Venezuela), 498–499
demographic change, as pathway to the future, 769–770
Denton, Rod, 675
dependency theory, 364, 382, 566
deprivation theory, 695
descarrego (release) concept of Pentecostalism, 423, 458
Descartes, René, 650
D'Escoto, Miguel, 406, 511
de Theije, Marjo, 391–392
Deutsche Evangelische Kirchenbund, 314
development theory, 364
Día de la Raza, 559
Diamond, Sarah, 456–457
Diaspora seminar, 313
diaspora tourism, 625–626
Díaz, Porfirio, 294, 350–351, 400, 494
Díaz Covarrubias, Juan, 261, 267
dictatorship, and Catholic Church, 398–411
  in Argentina, 409–411
  in Brazil, 404
  in Chile, 404–405
  in colonial era, 398
  in El Salvador, 407–408, 409
  in Guatemala, 408–409
  in independence era, 399
  in Nicaragua, 405–407, 409
  in Panama, 402–403
  in Peru, 403
  in post-independence era, 399–400
  in twentieth century, 400–401
    early reforms, 400
    late century dictatorships, 401
    mid-century reforms, 400–401
Dilermando, Josué, 675
Diocesan Coordination of Women (Coordinación Diocesana de Mujeres, CODIMUJ), 516
Dirty War (Argentina), 511–512
Discalced Carmelite nuns, 202
discourse, gendered, 528–532
  "collective effervescence" concept, 532

struggles for interpretive power, 529–530
  Nuestro Clamor por la Vida (Our Cry for Life), 529–530
  Plotting Woman, 529
  "voice" concept, 528–529, 530
  women as other, 528
diversification in Latin America
  Christian near-parity zone, 12
  Christian pluralism zone, 12–13
  eroding Catholic dominance zone, 13
  religious/non-religious pluralism zone, 13
  resistant Catholic dominance zone, 13
divination
  and African diaspora religions, 611
  and Santería, 642–643
divine healing. *See* healing
divine presence. *See* sacred immanence, as element of Tridentine Catholicism
divorce, 352–353, 448, 469, 503, 697
  Charismatic Catholicism on, 469
doctrine of national security, 337–338
Doing Theology in a Revolutionary Situation (Bonino), 362
domestic violence, Catholic denunciation of, 341
Dominican Order, 65–66
  and expulsion of Jesuits, 227
  and independence of Chile, 244
  and indigenous mobilization, 570–571
  inquisitorial powers of, 134, 135
  in New Spain, 93
  numbers in Americas, 175
  See also las Casas, Bartolomé de
Dominican Republic
  Christian Democratic parties in, 496, 499
  Church-state relationship, 495
  emigration to US, 681
  and emigration to US, 682t42.2
  faith healers in, 349
  Latter-Day Saints in, 692–693
  military rule in, 378
  patron saint of, 319
  Pentecostal percentage of Protestants in, 446–447
  religious diversification in, 12
  Seventh-Day Adventists in, 698–699
  statistics on unaffiliated in, 12
  See also Afro-Caribbean religions
Dominican Social Christian Reform Party (PURS), 499
Dougherty, Edward, 457

Duarte, José Napoleon, 499
Dunn, Henry, 289–290
Durán, Diego, 73, 85
Durango (New Spain), Franciscans in, 93
Durán Martel, Marcos, 241
Durkheim, Émile, 23, 532
Dussel, Enrique, 359, 360, 362, 364, 525
Duvalier, François "Papa Doc," 512, 615

Eastern European Jews, 710–711
Ecclesial Base Communities. *See* Base Ecclesial Communities (CEBs) (comunidades eclesiales de base)
ecclesiastic property, nationalization of, 334
Echeverría, Mariano Fernández de, 151
Ecuador
  Catholicism in
    Church-state relationship, 496, 580
    eroding dominance, 13
    number of followers, 12
  Christian Democratic parties in, 496, 498
  Día de la Raza in, 559
  emergency contraception in, 550
  gay marriage/civil unions in, 503
  and inculturation theology, 597, 599–600
  independence movement in, 239–240
  indigenous in
    charges of ethnocide, 576
    identity politics, 580
    movements, 517–518
    numbers of indigenous, 560–561
    political reform, 563
    poverty rate, 561
    religious context of mobilization, 569
    religious resources for mobilization in, 572, 574
    success of mobilization, 581
    uprisings, 559
  Jehovah's Witnesses in, 701
  and Liberation Theology, 594
  Lutheran missions in, 307
  Pentecostalism, beginnings of, 433
  Protestantism in
    growth, 444
    use of radio for conversions in, 456
  Sacred Heart of Jesus as symbol of nationalism in, 6
  Seventh-Day Adventists in, 698
Ecumenical Department of Investigations (DEI; Departamento Ecuménico de Investigaciones, Costa Rica), 369

791

ecumenism, 729–738
  and churches motivated toward maintenance, 736
  and competition in religious marketplace, 734–737
  criticism of Protestant churches, 732–733
  daily model of, 730
  defining, 729–730
  and end of political bipolarity, 733
  future of, 737–738
  and highly competitive churches, 737
  historic perspective on, 735
  nonprofit as organizational form of, 731–732
  official model of, 730
  partnerships with ecclesiastical institutions, 733–734
  and political field, 730–734
  pragmatic model of, 729–730
  as provider of religious goods, 735, 736
  and religious field, 734–738
  and specialized churches, 737
Educação Popular (Bahia), 746–747
education
  colonial Catholic Church control over, 5
  controversy in Mexico, 743
  efforts by colporteurs, 289
  as evangelization strategy, 97–98
  indigenous/non-indigenous gap in, 561
  influence of Liberation Theology on, 745, 746
  and Jesuits, 94–95, 227–228, 748
  Lancasterian system, 289
  mission schools, 297–298
  public, in new republics, 334
Egungun societies (ancestor worship), 617–618
Eisenstadt, Shmuel, 749–750
Elim church (Pentecostal, El Salvador), 676
Elizondo, Virgilio, 329
Ellacuría, Ignacio, 368, 511
El Salvador
  Catholicism in
    dictatorships, 407–408, 409
    moral concordat, 339
    number of followers, 12
    popular, 487–488
    progressive, 384, 385, 390
  CEBs in, 379, 380, 507
  Christian Democratic parties in, 496, 499
  CoMadres in, 514–515
  emigration to US, 681
  human rights in, 511, 513
  indigenous mobilization in, 568
  Jehovah's Witnesses in, 701
  La Luz del Mundo in, 704
  land distribution issues, 518
  Lutheran missions in, 306
  military rule in, 378, 501
  murder of Jesuits in, 368, 511, 670
  Pentecostalism in
    denomination composition/nationalization process, 434
    institutional politics, 552–553
    megachurches, 676–677
  Protestantism in, 12, 444, 508, 684
  Seventh-Day Adventists in, 698–699
El Shaddai megachurch (Guatemala), 435
El Silencio (Verbitsky), 410
embryo research, and Pentecostals, 553
emigration from Latin America and religious identity, 680–688
  to Asia, 680
  to Canada, 680
  commonalities in patterns and religious practice, 686–688
    ethnicity, 686
    spirit-filled piety, 686–687
    transtemporal/translocative culture, 687–688
  to Europe, 680
  factors shaping identity/religious practice, 681–686
    destination in US, 684–686
      former New Spain settlements, 684–685
      gateway cities, 685
      rural areas/small towns/suburbs, 685–686
    length of displacement, 683
    push/pull factors, 681
    religious self-identification, 684
    religious situation in sending nation, 683–684
  to United States, 680–681
    foreign born by birth region/date of arrival, 681t42.1
    by major Latin American sending nations, 1901–2000, 682t42.2
encomenderos, 64–66, 67, 69, 92, 177
encomienda mitaya, 187
encomienda originaria, 187
encomienda system, 177–178
  justification of, 200
England, Spiritualist movement in, 648
Enlightenment, 128, 141, 229

Enríquez, Raúl Silva, 386
Enxet people, 576
epidemics
　effect on African slave trade, 200
　in New Spain, 100
Episcopalians, in El Salvador, 513
Epistolary Narrative of a Voyage and Jesuit Mission (Cardim), 78
Erasmus of Rotterdam, 44, 161, 164
Errázuriz, Francisco Cardinal, 472
escolas radiofônicas (radio schools), 379
Espín, Orlando, 319–320, 486
Espiritismo. *See* Spiritism (Espiritismo)
Esquivel, Adolfo Perez, 410
estancias, 177
Estrada, Hugo F., 475
Estrada, Juan Manuel de, 266
Estrada Cabrera, Manuel, 351
Estrela da Manhã, 724
ethics, 43, 541
ethnocide
　charges by Ecuadorean indigenous, 576
　during colonial period, 517
ethnopopulist parties, 582–583
Etsi Iam Diu, 258
Eucharist
　as element of Tridentine Catholicism, 110, 114–115
　in late medieval Europe, 37
　Protestant criticism of Catholic belief, 108
Evangelical Church of the Lutheran Confession in Brazil (IECLB), 304, 308
　beginnings of in, 311–312
　colonist-pastors, 312
　and Curitiba Document, 316–317
　and demographic transition, 317
　diversity of piety of, 310
　effect of World Wars on, 314–315
　and evangelical pietistic movement, 317
　initial church structures, 313–314
　　pastors from Germany, 313
　　pastors from United States, 313
　　regional churches, 313
　issues in formation of
　　Brazilian economics, 311
　　economics/politics in homeland, 309–310
　　race issues, 310–311
　and Liberation Theology, 317
　post-World War II, 315–316
　role of women in, 315
　theological training, 315

Evangelical Church of the River Plate (Argentina), 308
Evangelical Lutheran Church in Chile, 308
Evangelical Lutheran Church of Argentina, 308
Evangelical Lutheran Church of Brazil (Igreja Evangélica Luterana do Brasil, IELB), 308
Evangelical Lutheran Synod of Santa Catarina, Paraná and other States of South America, 313
evangelicals
　affect on Church-state relations, 339
　as factor in restraint in secularization of public institutions, 339
　and gang violence, 756
　and healing, 664
　and reproduction/sexuality, 556
　and reproductive rights, 552–556
　See also Pentecostalism
Evangelical Society for Protestant Germans in America (Barmen), 313
Evangelical Synod of Chile, 305
Evangelical Synod of the River Plate, 305
Evangelical Women's Association (Frauenhilfe), 315
evangelization. *See* conquest/colonization
exorcism
　in late medieval Europe, 43
　and Pentecostalism, 441
Ezequiel (Ezequiel Ataucusi Gamonal), 214–215

Fabián y Fuero, Francisco, 221, 222
Fabri, Friedrich, 314
Fabro, Fernando, 221–222
faith healing. *See* healing
faith missions, 294–298
　Central American Mission, 295–296
　and denominationalism, 296–298
　differences, 294–295
　frictions, 295–296
　mission hospitals, 297
　mission schools, 297–298
　funding of, 294, 296
　spiritual entrepreneurs, 296
　traits of, 294–295
Family Federation for World Peace and Unification (Korea), 728
Farabundo Martí National Liberation Front (FMLN), 407
　See also El Salvador
Farmer, Paul, 370

fasting, in late medieval Europe, 40
Fejérváry-Mayer codice, 26
feminism
   and Base Ecclesial Communities movement, 551
   on gender and religion, 526
   and Liberation Theology, 369–370
   on Virgin of Guadalupe, 328
Ferdinand II (Spain), 360
Ferdinand III (Saint), 149
Ferdinand VI (Spain), 149
Ferdinand VII (Spain), 142, 233, 238–239, 241, 245
Ferreira, Francirosy Campos Barbosa, 718–719
Ferreti, Mastai, 279
fertility rates, effect of birth control pill on, 548
Figueroa, Luis de, 64
Final Report of the Extraordinary Synod of Bishops (1985), 594–595
Fiore, Joachim de, 89, 161
First Afro-Brazilian Congress, 614
First Mexican Provincial Council
   and Baroque, 160–161
   on orthodoxy of image makers, 112
First Vatican Council. *See* Vatican I
Fitzpatrick-Behrens, Susan, 514
Florencia, Francisco de, 113
Florentine Codex (Sahagún), 71–72, 93
Flores, Samuel Joaquín, 702, 703
Flores Magón, Ricardo, 265
FMLN (Farabundo Martí National Liberation Front), 407
Focolari movement, 748
folk Catholicism, 6–7, 210, 349–350, 634
   See also popular Catholicism, contemporary; popular Catholicism, nineteenth century
Fon-derived practices, 606–607, 618
Fon people, deities of, 204
Foucault, Michel, 527, 535, 537, 541
Fourth Lateran Council, 110
Fourth Mexican Provincial Council, on self-flagellation, 119
Frai Damião (Brazilian folk saint), 488
France
   and origin of concept of Latin America, 13
   origins of Spiritism in, 648
Franceschi, Gustavo, 352
Francescon, Luigi, 432, 433
Francia, José de Gaspar, 257–258
Franciscan Order
   and Baroque art, 453
   belief in role of natives in salvation, 89

   and education in Brazil, 749
   and expulsion of Jesuits, 227
   and independence movement in Peru, 242
   inquisitorial powers of, 134–135
   linguistic limitations of, 181–182
   mystics, 124–125
   in New Spain, 68, 70–72, 91–93
      effectiveness of missionary work, 92–93
      establishment of convents, 92
      images, 740–741
      Twelve Apostles, 91–92
   numbers in Americas, 175
   reaction to Bourbon reformism, 231
   recruitment to Latin America during Catholic resurgence, 354
   views on Indians in Peru, 75
   See also missions, Franciscan in Alta California; missions, Franciscan in New Mexico
Francis I (pope), 9, 372, 392–396
   and canonization of Óscar Romero, 487
   diversity of permanent advisory council of, 392–393
   and human rights, 522
   ideology of, 392–393, 395
   influence on US bishops, 394
   and Liberation Theology, 393–394, 746
   re-articulation of progressive themes, 394–396
   See also Bergoglio, Jorge
Francis Javier (Saint), 149
Francis of Assisi (Saint), 99, 392, 395
Franco, Jean, 529
Frank, Andre Gunder, 364
free will, and Spiritism, 651
Freire, Paulo, 379, 507, 745
Freitas, José Pedro de (Zé Arigó), 658
French Revolution, 245
Frenz, Helmut, 405, 510
Freston, Paul, 416, 553
Friedzón, Betty, 674
Friedzón, Claudio, 674
Fritz, Dr. Adolph, 657–658, 663
Froehle, Bryan, 16, 447
Frontera con Justicia (Mexico), 520–521
FSLN (Sandinista Front for National Liberation), 380, 406–407
   See also Nicaragua
fuero eclesiástico (legal forum), 256, 347
Fujimori, Alberto, 498
FUMEC (Universal Federation of Christian Student Movements, Argentina), 731, 733

Index

FUNAI (National Foundation for the Indians, Brazil), 317
funerals, reform of, 129–130
Funes, Gregorio, 243
Funes, Mauricio, 390

Gallegos, Hector, 402
Gálvez, José de, 221
Gamboy, Pedro, 103–104
Gamonal, Ezequiel Ataucusi, 214–215
gang violence, 756
Gante, Pedro de, 91, 99
Garcés, Julián, 68–69, 154–155
García, Gaspar, 510
García, Gregorio, 64
García Granados, Miguel, 265
García Linera, Alvaro, 583
García Peláez, Francisco de Paul, 259–260
Garifuna diaspora, 619, 624
Garma, Carlos, 14
Garotinho, Anthony, 753
Garrard-Burnett, Virginia, 512, 569, 577, 598, 599, 600
Gasparetto, Zibia, 458
Gaudium et Spes (Pastoral Constitution on the Church in the Modern World), 376–377, 506–507, 565, 594
Gautier, Mary, 16, 447
Gavin, Natasha, 720
gay marriage. *See* same-sex marriage
Gebara, Ivone, 328
gender, changing norms of, 770
  See also gender and religion; reproduction and sexuality; women
gender and religion, 525–545
  African diaspora religions, 613, 618
  agency, 537–540
    Outline to a Theory of Practice, 537
    and ritualization, 538–539
    In Search of Respect, 537–538
    Staying Sober in Mexico City, 539–540
    structure-agency struggle, 537–538, 539–540
    subject-society struggle, 538–539
    Travestis, 538–539
  bodies, 532–536
    Christ as bridegroom metaphor, 533
    colonial-era body, 533–534
    discipline and punishment, 535–536
    homosexual desire, 533
    post-colonial body and Protestant evangelism, 534–535
    power of healing, 536
    The Reformation of Machismo, 534–535
    Shamanism, Colonialism, and the Wild Man, 536
  discourse, 528–532
    "collective effervescence" concept, 532
    struggles for interpretive power, 529–530
    Nuestro Clamor por la Vida (Our Cry for Life), 529–530
    Plotting Woman, 529
    testimonio, 530–531
    I, Rigoberta Menchú, 531
    Translated Woman, 530–531
    "voice" concept, 528–529, 530
    women as other, 528
  Durkheim on, 532
  feminist approach to, 526
  Foucault on, 527, 535, 537, 541
  future research areas, 544–545
  Islam, 720
  lack of research on, 525–526
  lived religion approach to, 526–527
  Pentecostalism, 448
    gender equity, 553–554
    subjectivity, 541–544
  subjectivity, 541–544
    focus on micro-politics, 541–544
    and missionary manliness, 543–544
    and neo-Pentecostalism, 541–544
    and pharmaceutical industries, 541–542
    and retail business, 543–544
    witnessing, 542
  See also reproduction and sexuality; women
genocide, in Guatemala, 408
George Jorge (Saint), 153
Gerardi, Juan José, 408–409, 513
Geremoabo, Baron of, 281–282
Ghana
  and internationalization of Pentecostalism, 420
  See also Akan people
Gill, Anthony, 566–567, 576
Gillow, Eulogio, 351
globalization
  importance of Latin America in, 17–19
  and indigenous mobilization, 564
  most globalized religions, 18
  and Pentecostalism
    conversionism, 17
    decentralization, 18
    human rights, 19
  scale and pace of global transfers, 770
  as undermining territorially national religions, 17–18

glossolalia (speaking in tongues)
  and Charismatic Catholicism, 415, 463, 464, 467–468
  and Pentecostalism, 415–417
God, statistics on belief in Christian, 10
God is Love Pentecostal Church (IPDA, Brazil), 433, 436, 440, 676
Godoy, Juan José, 234
Gómez, Medardo, 513
Gómez Farías, Valentin, 255, 260
González, Aaron Joaquín, 702, 703
González Prada, Manuel, 251, 264–265, 267
González Vigil, Francisco de Paula, 256, 262
Gotteskasten (God's Chest), 313
Goulart, João, 378
Graham, Billy, 424–425, 426
Gramsci, Antonio, 427
Granada, Spain, 2–3, 633
Gran Chaco, 185
Gran Colombia Patronage Law (1824), 257
Grasselli, Emilio Teodoro, 410
Graziano, Frank, 214, 215
Great Pueblo Revolt, 180
Green, Duncan, 509
Gregory VIII (pope), 148
Grela, Ignacio, 399
Grijalva, Juan de, 90
Gruzinski, Serge, 145, 216, 740
Guadalajara, Mexico
  Creole clergy in, 235–236
  Jehovah's Witnesses in, 702
  La Luz del Mundo in, 702
  Marian shrines surrounding, 151–152
Guanajuato, Mexico
  Augustinians in, 94
  expulsion of Jesuits from, 221
  faith healers in, 348
  Franciscans in, 93
  "spiritual exercises" practiced in, 88
Guaraní people
  and expulsion of Jesuits, 228–229
  and expulsion of Jesuits, 222, 224–226
  messianic movements, 209
  motivation for migration of, 208
  political mobilization of, 580
  See also missions, Jesuit in Paraguay
Guatemala
  anticlericalism in, 347, 400
  belief in God in, 10
  Catholicism in
    Catholic resurgence, 354
    Church-state relationship, 351
    costumbre, 349–350

    dictatorships, opposition/support, 400, 408–409
    number of followers, 12
    post-independence popular Catholicism in, 275–278
    progressive Catholicism in, 385–386
    rural Catholic Action groups among Maya, 355
  CEBs in, 507, 566
  challenges to laicicism in, 343
  Charismatic Catholicism in, 475–476
    number of followers, 466
    strong/soft elements, 470–471
  Crucified Christ of Esquipulas, 275, 276–277, 278
  Día de la Raza in, 559
  emigration to US, 681
  expulsion of Jesuits from, 260, 265, 400
  Franciscans in, 93
  genocide in, 408
  human rights in, 511, 512, 513–514
  inculturation theology and Maya, 598, 599
  indigenous in
    and cultural awareness, 583–584
    diversity among, 561
    Mayan identity, 577
    numbers of, 560–561
    religious resources for mobilization in, 572
  influence of Liberation Theology in, 745
  Jehovah's Witnesses in, 701
  land distribution in, 518, 519
  Latter-Day Saints in, 693–696
  Lutheran merchant/craftsmen congregations in, 305
  Lutheran missions in, 306
  migrants and social justice in, 520
  military rule in, 378, 501
  millenarianism among Highland Maya, 216
  neo-Pentecostal formations of citizenship in, 542–543
  Pentecostalism in
    abortion, 554
    denomination composition/ nationalization process, 435
    growth, 699, 764
    institutional politics, 552–553
    megachurches, 676
    sex education, 555
  popular religion in, 486
  Protestantism in, 684
    colporteurs, 289–290
    converts from Catholicism, 445

796

early missionaries, 293
faith missions, 295
growth, 444
native contributions to missionary work, 298
number of followers, 12, 508
Seventh-Day Adventists in, 698–699
torture of Ursuline nun in, 535–536
Guerra, García, 169–170
Guevara, Silvestre, 264
guilds, patron saint as unifying symbol of, 153–154
Gutiérrez, Gustavo
collaboration with Vatican on Liberation Theology, 393–394
and development of Liberation Theology, 672, 745
education of, 362
and human rights, 507, 508
influence on Medellín Conference, 382–384
investigated for deviations from orthodoxy, 388
joins faculty at Notre Dame, 673
on las Casas, 360
on non-person/non-human, 364
publications of, 362
on traditional theology, 363
and Vatican II, 367, 744
Vatican reception of, 372
Gutwirth, Jacque, 425
Guyana, Hinduism in, 726
Guzmán, Nuño Beltrán de, 68
Guzmán Blanco, Antonio, 264

habitus, 754–755
Hagin, Kenneth, 423
Haiti
Catholic acceptance of ADRs in, 621
CEBs in, 507
Church-state relationship in, 495
emigrant connections to ritual communities in, 623–624
expulsion of Jesuits from, 512
good/bad work distinction in, 611
human rights in, 512
independence of, 246, 269
patron saint of, 620
Pentecostal offshoot in, 416
Pentecostals in, 612
slave revolt in, 205
See also Vodou (Haiti)
Haitian emigrants, and diaspora religious practices, 623

Hakluyt, Richard, 78
Hall, Linda, 319
Hare Krishna, 726
Harris, Olivia, 739–740
Haya de la Torre, Victor Raúl, 297
healing
and African diaspora religions, 610, 664
and Catholicism, 348
and Charismatic Catholicism, 464, 468
female healers, 349
and Pentecostalism, 417–418, 439
and popular Catholicism, 664
and pre-contact African religions, 55–59
and slave religions, 203–204
and Spiritism, 655–659, 663–664
and Umbanda, 664
as witchcraft, 203
health indictors, indigenous/non-indigenous gap, 561
Henríquez, Camilo, 244
Henríquez, Raúl Silva, 404–405, 510
Herskovits, Melville, 593
Hidalgo, Mexico, Augustinians in, 94
Hidalgo, Miguel, 236–237, 247, 248, 327, 399, 486
Hidalgo y Costilla, Miguel, 374
hierarchical syncretism, 443
Hieronymite Order, 64–65, 66
Hill, John, 293
Hinkelammert, Franz, 369, 508
Historia de las Indias (Las Casas), 69
Historia de las Indias de la Nueva España (Durán), 73
Historia eclesiástica indiana (Mendieta), 74
Historia general de las cosas de Nueva España (Florentine Codex; Sahagún), 71–72, 93
Historia natural y moral de las Indias (Acosta), 75
Historical Commission for the Serra Cause, 194
Hollenweger, Walter, 467
Home of Mercy (Hogar de la Misericordia, Chiapas), 520
homeopathy, 652
homosexuality
and African diaspora religions, 613
and Catholicism, 341
in colonial era, 533
Honduras
Catholics in, 12
importance of religion in life in, 10
Jehovah's Witnesses in, 701

Honduras (*cont.*)
　Latter-Day Saints in, 692–693
　Lutheran missions in Tegucigalpa, 306
　Muslims in, 716
　Protestantism in, 684
　　converts from Catholicism, 445
　　growth rate of, 444
　　number of followers, 12
　Seventh-Day Adventists in, 698–699
Hoover, Willis C., 300, 432, 433
Horst, Rene Harder, 576–577, 578
hospitals, mission, 297
Housewives' Committee of Siglo XX (Bolivia), 516–517
huacas worship, 102–103, 104–105
　similarities/differences to saints, 145
Huarochirí Manuscript, 29–30, 103
Huei tlamahuiçoltica (By a Great Miracle; Laso de la Vega), 325
Huejotzingo (New Spain), 92
Huerta, Victoriano, 335
human rights, 505–522
　and Catholic Church
　　in Argentina, 409–411, 511–512
　　in Brazil, 509–510
　　and CEBs, 511
　　in Chile, 510
　　defense of violations, 509–511
　　effect of changes in Church, 506–509
　　in El Salvador, 511
　　globalization, 18–19
　　in Guatemala, 512
　　in Haiti, 512
　　historical repression of indigenous rights, 517
　　land distribution, 518–519
　　legitimation of violations, 511–512
　　Marianism, 328
　　support of indigenous rights, 517–518
　　transnationalism, 669–670
　　Vatican II, 506
　　women's movements, 514–517
　Catholic/Protestant cooperation for peace building, 512–514
　　in Brazil, 513
　　in Colombia, 513
　　in El Salvador, 513
　　in Guatemala, 513–514
　　in Nicaragua, 513
　and Christian Base Communities, 507–508
　dictatorship and transitions to democracy, 509–512
　future of, 521–522

indigenous rights, 517–518
　in Chiapas, 517
　in Ecuador, 517–518
　and Liberation Theology, 507–508
　and Medellín Conference, 507
　migrants and social justice, 520–521
　overview of, 505–506
　and Pentecostalism, 19
　and Pope Francis I, 522
　and Protestantism, 508–509, 512–514
　and Puebla Conference, 507
　and reactivation of laicity of public institutions, 342
　and social movements, 509–510
human sacrifice
　European interpretation/misinterpretation of, 82–83
　las Casas on, 66
　practiced by Yucatán Maya, 79
　as reinforcing notion of anthropophagy, 79
Humbard, Rex, 456–457
hunters/gatherers, 176–177
Hurbon, Laënnec, 620
Hurtado, Albert, 346
Hurtado, Manuel, 241
Hybels, Bill, 670
hypnotism, 652

I, Rigoberta Menchú, 531
Ibañez de Echavarri, Bernardo, 224–225
Iberian Union, 136
iconoclastism, Pentecostalism on, 451, 452
identity
　Marianism link with, 327–328
　Mayan, 577
　saints as symbols of, 153–156
　through confraternity membership, 202
　traditional Catholic in Latin America, 11
　transnationalism effect on, 667
　See also emigration from Latin America and religious identity
identity politics, 580
idolatry
　European interpretation/misinterpretation of, 83–85
　Protestant/Catholic debate in New World, 79–80
　Protestant/Catholic debate in Old World, 79
Idowu, Bolaji, 51, 52, 53
IECLB. *See* Evangelical Church of the Lutheran Confession in Brazil (IECLB)

Index

IELB (Evangelical Lutheran Church of Brazil), 308
Ifá (Cuba), 616–617
Igbo people, 48
    ancestor worship by, 54, 55
    deities of, 50, 52, 56
    healers, 59
    Supreme Being of, 51, 52
Iglesia La Luz del Mundo (The Light of the World Church). *See* La Luz del Mundo
Igreja Presbiteriana Renovada (Brazil), 301
Igreja Universal do Reino de Deus (IURD, Brazil)
    architectural pastiche of, 757
    attitude toward Candomblé, 621
    charitable arm of, 753
    and demonic possession, 421–423
    and dramatization of struggle against evil, 421–423
    emphasis on exorcisms, 441
    ethical teachings of, 441
    "kick to the saint" episode of, 451, 457, 742
    and mimesis, 758
    origins of, 433, 436, 440–442
    and prosperity gospel, 424
    and prosperity theology, 441
    and reproduction/sexuality, 553
    ritual in, 756–757
    and televangelism, 426
    television network of, 442
    television station of, 452, 457–458
    and transnationalism, 420, 675–676
    use of visual/symbolic elements, 458
    See also Pentecostalism
Ikenga-Metuh, Emefie, 57
ILEMP (Immigration Law Enforcement Monitoring Project), 521
Imagen de la Virgen María (Sánchez), 325
images
    in Baroque era, 164
    as *ixiptla*, 145
    and Tridentine Catholicism
        Christ, 112
        Mary (mother of Jesus), 112–114
        saints, 110, 112–115, 117
Immaculate Conception, 279, 319
Immigration Act of 1965 (US), 681
Immigration Law Enforcement Monitoring Project (ILEMP), 521
Império do Belo Monte (Canudos) movement, 210–211, 281–282, 489, 744

Incas (Inkas)
    and ancestor worship, 28
    conquering of, 173–174
    creation story of Huanacauri, 27–28
    Huarochirí manuscript, 29–30
    and idolatry debate, 80
    Kechwa cosmology of, 212–213
    and messianism, 212–213
    Pizarro and Christianization of, 175
    regional cosmologies, 28–30
    ritual specialists, 29, 31
    role of disease in conquest of, 174
    social/kinship unit as basis of society, 28
    state religion, 27–30
inculturation, defining, 591, 593
inculturation theology, 591–601
    and ADRs, 621
    basic premises of, 591–593
    and CELAM, Santo Domingo, 566, 595
    contemporary case studies on, 596–600
        Bolivian Aymara, 597–599
        Chimborazo, Ecuador, 597, 599–600
        Guatemalan Maya, 598, 599
        Tzotzil Maya, Chiapas, Mexico, 597, 599
    emergence as explicit missionary objective, 593–596
    and indigenous mobilization, 565–566
    and Liberation Theology, 594, 595–596
    limitations of, 600–601
    and neoliberalism, 596
    and "new" evangelization, 594
    and use of indigenous languages, 600–601
    and Vatican II, 565–566, 594–595
independence, and Catholic Church, 231–248
    in Argentina, 399
    background to, 231–233
    in Bolivia, 274, 399
    in Chile, 243–245
    clerical support/opposition, 232–233
    Creole clergy, 235–238
    in Cuba, 246–247
    dictatorships, 399
    enlightened bishops and clergy, 235–236
    influence of expelled Jesuits on, 233–234
    in Mexico, 235, 399
    in New Granada, 239–240
    papal response to, 245–246
    in Peru, 240–242
    and popular Catholicism, 270, 274
    in Río de la Plata, 243
    roots of, 233

Independent Democratic Union (UDI, Chile), 502
Indians, Iberian friar/missionary understanding of, 62–76
　and *encomenderos,* 64–66, 67, 69
　ethnic origins, 62–63, 64
　idolatrous practices, 63
　intellectual capacity, 63, 64–66
　opposing images of nature by, 66–75
　　Alonso de la Vera Cruz, 72
　　Antonio de la Calancha, 75
　　Bartolomé de las Casas, 66, 69–70
　　Bernardino de Sahagún, 71–72
　　Diego de Landa, 73–74
　　Diego Durán, 73
　　Domingo de Santo Tomás, 75
　　Gaspar de Vera, 75
　　Jacobo de Tastera, 67–68, 70–71
　　Jerónimo de Mendieta, 74
　　José de Acosta, 75
　　Juan de Chávez, 75
　　New Spain and *Sublimis Deus,* 68–69
　　in Peru, 74–75
　　Tomás de San Martín, 75
　　Toribio de Benavente Motolinía, 70
　overview of Iberian friars, 62–63
indigenous. *See* conquest/colonization; indigenous mobilization
indigenous mobilization, 559–586
　context of, 560–565
　　advocacy networks, 564–565
　　decentralization/devolution of power, 562–563
　　economics, 563–564
　　globalization, 564
　　and indigenous agenda, 565
　　internal diversity, 561–562
　　number of indigenous, 560–561
　　social indicators, 561
　　transnationalism, 564–565
　critique of identity politics, 579–581
　evaluation of, 581–586
　　alliances, 583
　　cultural awareness, 583–584
　　diversity among indigenous, 585
　　external agendas, 585–586
　　goals of movements, 581–582
　　role of religion, 584–585
　　threats to movements, 582–583
　and identity politics, 574–579
　　Catholic *vs.* indigenous goals, 574–576, 578
　　Protestant *vs.* indigenous goals, 576–577
　nongovernmental organizations, 563–564
　religious context of, 565–570
　　dependency theory, 566
　　Ecclesial Base Communities, 566
　　in Ecuador, 569
　　in El Salvador, 568
　　in Guatemala, 568–569
　　inculturation theology, 565–566
　　in Mexico, 567–568
　　Pentecostal growth, 566–567
　　Protestant growth, 569
　　reaction of local conditions/actors to changes, 567–569
　religious frames/resources for, 570–574
　　Adventist, 572
　　Catholic, 572–573
　　for mobilization in southern Mexico, 570–571
　　neo-native spirituality, 573–574
　　Protestant, 573
　　religious resources for, 571–574
　surge in, 559
In Face of Mystery (Kaufman), 363
infant mortality, indigenous/non-indigenous gap, 561
Inglehart, Ronald, 10
Inka. *See* Incas
Inkarrí myth cycle, 214
Inquisition, New World, 133–142
　decline/abolishment of, 141–142
　foundation of tribunals, 135–138
　Inquisition before "Inquisition," 133–135
　　Dominicans, 134, 135
　　early tribunes, 133–134
　　Franciscans, 134–135
　　Monastic Inquisition, 134–135
　inquisitorial action, 138–142
　　main objective of, 138
　　number of proceedings, Portuguese, 140
　　number of proceedings, Spanish, 140
　　public *autos-da-fé* ceremonies, 141
　　punishment for heresy, 139
　　and secular court cases, 139–140
　　sentencing/punishments, 139
　　trials, 139
　　types of offenses, 138–139
　investigations into unofficial local saints, 148
　Ometochtzin trial and murder by, 71
　Portuguese dominions, 136, 138
　　exemption of Indians from jurisdiction, 138
　　lack of autonomy of inquisitors, 137
　　types of offenses specific to, 138, 139
　proceedings against false mystics, 125–126

Index

Spanish dominions, 135–137
    autonomy of inquisitors, 136–137
    Cartegena de Indias tribunal, 136
    exemption of Indians from jurisdiction, 137
    lay officials, 137
    Lima tribunal, 136, 140
    Mexican tribunal, 136
    types of offenses specific to, 139, 140
    See also Inquisition, Old World
Inquisition, Old World
    in Portugal, 133
    in Spain, 5, 133
    See also Inquisition, New World
In Search of Respect (Bourgois), 537–538
Institute of Religious Studies (ISER, Brazil), 554
Institutional Revolutionary Party (PRI, Mexico), 494
Instruction on Christian Freedom, 389
"Instruction on Christian Freedom and Liberation," 367
Instructions on Certain Aspects of the "Theology of Liberation," 367, 388–389
Inter-American Commission on Human Rights, 410
Interethnic Association for the Development of the Peruvian Rainforest (AIDESEP), 561
International Church of the Foursquare Gospel (US), 418
International Church of the Grace of God (Pentecostal; Brazil), 436
International Labor Organization's Convention 169, 564–565, 582, 583, 596
Isabella (Spain), 5
ISER (Institute of Religious Studies, Brazil), 554
Isidore (Saint), 149
Islam, 714–721
    dissemination of, 718–720
    as ethnic religion, 716
    globalization of, 18
    and media, 458
    membership data discrepancies, 714–715
    radical, 717
    training of sheikhs in Latin America, 717–718
    women as converts, 720
    See also Muslims
Israel, immigration of Latin American Jews to, 713
Iturbide, Agustín de, 238, 239

IURD. *See* Igreja Universal do Reino de Deus (IURD, Brazil)
Ivereigh, Austen, 272–273, 279
ixiptla, images of saints as, 145

Jalics, Francisco, 410
Jalisco, Mexico, Franciscans in, 93
Jamaica
    Afro-Caribbean religions in, 635
    Chinese immigrants in, 727
James (Saint), 147
Japan
    Japanese Buddhist immigration to Brazil, 683
    Latin Americans in, 723
    Pentecostalism in, 675
Japanese-based religions, 723, 724–726
    Afro-Okinawan sects, 726
    in Brazil, 724, 725, 726
    Japanese-Catholic movements, 724
    New Religions, 726
    Okinawan, 726
    Shindo Renmei movement, 724
    Shintoism, 724
    Zen Buddhism, 725
Jara, José de la, 406
JCA (Jewish Colonization Association), 710
Jehovah's Witnesses (JW), 690, 700–702
    controversy over doctrines/practices of, 700
    Latin American membership, 701
    in Mexico, 700, 701–702
    organization of, 700–701
    origins of, 700
    teachings of, 700
    worldwide membership, 700
Jeje, 606–607, 618
Jenkins, Henry, 452
Jesuits, 175
    and Brazilian messianic indigenous movements, 208
    and canonization of Catharina de San Juan, 162
    contemporary schools/universities, 748–749
    expulsion from Americas, 220–229
        from Argentina by Rosas, 259
        Charles III on, 223–224
        detrimental effects of, 227–229
        enemies among clerical and lay public in Spain, 224
        from Guatemala, 260, 265, 400

Jesuits (*cont.*)
  from Haiti by Duvalier, 512
  influence on independence movements, 233–234
  justification for, 222–227
    in Americas, 224–227
    in Spain, 224
  process of, 220
  as prototype of progressive Catholicism, 374
  reactions to, 221–222, 227, 232
  reasons for, 220–221
  support for Mexican nationalism, 399
  and Treaty of Madrid (1750), 226
  and inculturation theology, 594
  mastery of Indian languages by, 181, 182
  murder of, in El Salvador, 511, 670
  in New Spain, 94–95
    educational efforts, 94–95
    festivities honoring relics of European saints, 148
    martyrs, 95
  numbers/resources of, 1766, 220
  and Portuguese millenarianism, 210
  and tithing, 225
  See also Francis I (pope); missions, Jesuit in Paraguay
Jesús, Juan Bautista de, 150
Jesus Christ
  inculturation theology on, 598
  metaphor of Christ as bridegroom, 533
  sacred immanence of images of, 112
  Spiritism on, 651
Jesus Christ, Liberator (Boff), 362
Jesus the Nazarene (image), 155
Jewish Colonization Association (JCA), 710
Jews, 709–713
  Ashkenazi, 709–710, 711
  Central European, 710, 711
  Chabad Lubavitch movement, 712–713
  claim of indigenous as descendants of, 64, 712
  conversions to Judaism, 712
  countries of origin, 711
  crypto Jews, 141, 210, 709, 711–712
  Eastern European, 710–711
  emigration of Latin American Jews to Israel, 713
  forced conversions of, 133
  immigration to Latin America, 683
    in colonial period, 709
    in nineteenth century, 709–711
    sending countries, 711
  Judaizing heresy, 133

Liberal Judaism, 710
  and media, 458
  number of followers, 711
  Sephardic, 709–710, 711
  traditional practices among, 709–710
  variation in ritual practices, 711
Jimena Villanueva, Gaspar de, 149
Jímenez, Francisco, 161
Jiménez, María, 521
Joan of Arc, 44
João Reis, José, 715–716
Joaseiro do Norte movement, 210–212
John of the Cross (Saint), 533
John Paul II (pope)
  and beatification of Junípero Serra, 194, 195
  and canonization of Juan Diego, 322
  and canonization of Óscar Romero, 487, 488
  and Christian Democratic Party in Chile, 497
  continuities with Pope Francis I, 395–396
  and El Salvador, 408
  on evangelization, 591–592
  and Guatemala, 409
  and inculturation theology, 596
  and Liberation Theology, 9, 507, 551, 746, 747
  new evangelization crusade of, 390–391
  opening address at Puebla conference by, 387–388
  on Our Lady of Guadalupe, 328
  and Paraguay, 579–580
  on political involvement, 503
  on popular religion, 747
  and progressive Catholicism, 385–389
  Redemptoris Missio, 566, 595
  and Vicariate of Solidarity, 405
  visit to Cuba, 495
Johnson, Lyndon B., 681
Johnson, Maxwell, 329–330
Johnson, Paul, 620, 624
John the Baptist (Saint), 152
John XXIII (pope), 8, 375, 497
  See also Vatican II
José Manuel, 280
Joseph (Saint), 116, 147, 156
Joyos (Hoyos), Juan, 320
Joyos (Hoyos), Rodrigo, 320
Juan Diego, 150, 322, 323, 326, 329, 454, 483
Juárez, Benito, 260
Juazeiro, 744
Judaizing heresy, 133, 140–141
Junta de Valladolid (rationality debates), 69
Jurema (Catimbó), 454–455
jurisdictionalism, 332, 333, 343–344

Index

"just war" doctrine, 199
Juventud Obrera Católica, 355
JW. *See* Jehovah's Witnesses (JW)

Kalley, Robert, 292–293
Kalley, Sarah, 292–293
Karam, John Tofik, 716–717
Kardec, Allan (Hoppolyte Léon Denizard Rivail), 637–638
Kardecism, 637–638
Karlstadt, Andreas, 79
Kataristas (Bolivia), 572
Kaufman, Gordon, 363
Kechwa (Inka) cosmology, 212–213
Keck, Margaret E., 564, 565
Kennedy, John F., 361
"kick to the saint," 451, 457, 742
King, Rufus, 234
Kingdom of Kongo
  Christianization in, 199, 201
  ritual specialists in, 203
Kino, Francisco Eusebio, 95
Klaiber, Jeffrey, 254
Knight, Alan, 743
Kongo. *See* Kingdom of Kongo
Korea
  Pentecostal megachurch in, 676
  See also South Korea
Korean immigrants
  in Argentina, 727
  in Brazil, 723, 727
  Christianity of, 727–728
  in Mexico, 727
  in Paraguay, 723, 727
  and Protestant rituals, 723
Kovic, Christine, 571, 573
Kubitschek, Juscelino, 439
Ku Klux Klan, 686
Kulick, Donald, 538–539
Küng, Hans, 382

Lacan, Jacques, 532–533
Lacrimabili Statu, 400
laicization. *See* secularism and secularization
Lalive d'Epinay, Christian, 419, 442
La Luz del Mundo, 702–705
  female members, 703
  founder of, 702
  membership, 702
  in Mexico, 702–703, 704–705
  missionary outlook in, 703
  theology of, 702–703
  in United States, 703–704

La Navas, Francisco de, 85
Lancasterian educational system, 289
Landa, Diego de, 73–74, 134–135
Landázuri, Juan, 386
land distribution, 518–519
  in Brazil, 519
  in Guatemala, 518, 519
  in Paraguay, 518–519
La Paz, Bolivia, Lutherans in, 305, 307
  See also Bolivia
la religion vécue (sociology of religion), 526–527
Larraín, Joaquín, 244
Larraín, Manuel Vicuña, 244–245, 744
Larraín, Vincente, 244
La Santa, Remigio, 242
las Casas, Bartolomé de Casas, 66, 68–70
  canonization of, 745
  as champion of Indians, 93, 177
  comparison of indigenous to ancients, 77
  and Council of Valladolid, 360, 373
  on enslavement of Africans, 200, 634
  on evangelization, 14
  on human sacrifice, 80–81
  on idolatry, 80
  on Indian enslavement, 199
  influence on Dominicans, 74–75
  influence on progressive Catholicism, 373–375
  joins Dominican order, 66
  request for inquisitorial tribunal, 133–134
  theology of liberation of, 360
Las Heras, Bartolomé, 242
Laso de la Vega, Luis, 325
Las Patronas, 522
late medieval Europe, 34–45
  Corpus Christi feast in, 38
  fasting in, 40
  Latin as language of Church in, 38
  Mass in, 37
  piety in, 36–44
  practical focus of religion in, 35
  Protestant criticism of piety in, 108
  Protestant view on religion in, 44–45
  religion as integral to life in, 34–35
  sacred behavior, 42–43
    ethics/morality, 43
    private devotion, 42
  sacred bonds, 40–42
    confraternities, 41–42
    cult of saints, 41
    godparent relationship, 41

803

late medieval Europe (cont.)
  sacred contention, truth vs. error, 43–44
  sacred rites, 36–38
    Eucharist, 37
    list of sacraments, 37
    Masses for the dead, 37
    Protestant criticism of, 108
  sacred space, 38–39
    churches, 38, 39
    graves and relics of saints, 38–39
    outdoor processions, 39
    pilgrimages, 39
    sacred images/relics, 39
  sacred time, 39–40
    Carnival, 40
    Easter/Christmas seasons, 40
    feast days, 39–40
    Sundays, 39
  social structures in, 35–36
  votive masses in, 37
Latin America
  contemporary centrality of religion in, 10
  continued vitality of religion/religious expression in, 766
  difference from other Old/New World regions, 11
  diversity between countries within, 12–13
  double origin of concept of, 13
  future of, 15–17, 764–774
    adaptability of Catholic Church, 16
    charismatic practices, 770
    continued vitality of religion/religious expression, 766
    demographic change, 769–770
    demographic superiority of Catholic Church, 16
    gender and sexuality, 770
    globalization, 770
    new violence, 771–772
    political change, 770, 771
    religious pluralism, 764–766
    secularization, 766–769
    social change, 770
    strong Catholic resistance to Protestantism, 16
  historical centrality of religion in, 1–9
  implications of changes in, 13–16
  life expectancy in, 417
  rapid change in religious field in, 10–17
  social organization at Conquest, 176–177
  statistics
    belief in God, 10
    importance of religion in life, 10
    number of Catholics, 12, 341–342
    number of "other religions," 12
    number of Protestants, 12, 342
    unaffiliated persons, 12
  television ownership in, 426
  and traditional Catholic identity, 11
Latin American Bishops' Conference (CELAM)
  creation of, 355–356, 377
  See also individual conference
Latin American Bishops' Conference (CELAM), Aparecida
  Aparecida Document (DA), 471–475, 477
    on cultural change, 472
    importance of, 472
    polarizing effect of, 473
    on youth, 473
  Great Continental Mission, 471–477
    and door-to-door missions, 475–476
    and sanctification of popular traditions, 476
Latin American Bishops' Conference (CELAM), Medellín, 8, 377–382, 400, 594
  bishops' support for progressive reforms after, 386
  CEBs as result of, 378–381
  grassroots pastoral projects as result of, 386–387
  and human rights, 507
  and inculturation theology, 566
  on institutionalized violence of poverty, 381–382
  use of radio and print media in context of CEBs, 456
Latin American Bishops' Conference (CELAM), Puebla, 387–388
  conclusions of, 388
  and human rights, 507
  and Liberation Theology, 383–384, 388–389
  opening address by John Paul II, 387–388
Latin American Bishops' Conference (CELAM), Santo Domingo, 9, 566, 595
Latin American Council of Churches (CLAI, Brazil), 734
Latin American Evangelical Social Action (ASEL, Cuba), 731, 733
Latin American Mission, 295
Latter-Day Saints (LDS, Mormons), 690, 691–696
  Central American Mission of, 693–694
  church hierarchy, 691–692
  controversy over doctrines/practices of, 691

Index

essential doctrines of, 691
founding of, 691
growth in Latin America, 692–693
in Guatemala, 693–696
retention rates, 693, 699
revision of worldwide missionary program, 694, 695
typical convert, 693
urbanization effect on membership, 694, 695, 699
la Virgen Mambisa (Revolutionary Virgin), 321
Law, Bernard, 393
Law 1420 (Argentina), 266
Laws of Burgos (1512), 360
LDS. *See* Latter-Day Saints
Legionarios de Cristo, 390–391, 748, 750, 751
Leguía, Augusto, 351
Leo XII (pope), 245–246
Leo XIII (pope), 7, 273, 283, 375, 400
Lerdo Law (1856), 263
Lettre aux Espagnols-Américains (Viscardo), 228
Levine, Daniel, 380, 401, 584–585, 739
Ley de reforma del clero (1822, Río de la Plata), 257
Libanio, João, 474
liberal Judaism, 710
The Liberation of Theology (Segundo), 362
Liberation Theology, 8–9, 317
  and Banzer Plan, 595
  and Catholic Charismatic Renewal, 464–465
  and CEBs, 551
  critique after Puebla CELAM meeting, 388–389
  effect of collapse of socialism on, 368
  and human rights, 507–508
  and inculturation theology, 594, 595–596
  influence of, 745–746
  influence on NGOs, 745–746
  influence on progressive Catholicism, 382–385
  and Lutheranism, 317
  and Marxism, 367, 388–389, 745
  and Pope Francis I, 393–394
  and popular religion, 746–747
  and prosperity gospel, 424
  and secularization, 338, 340
  See also Christian Base Communities; Liberation Theology, intellectual roots of
Liberation Theology, intellectual roots of, 359–370

and Antonio de Montesinos, 359–360, 373
and Bartolomé de las Casas, 360, 373–374
consolidation of, 366–368
  changes in intellectual/political context of 1989, 368
  political influence of, 366
  Vatican reaction to, 366–368
foundational texts, 362–366
  epistemological break as element of, 362–364
  practical/moral imperative as element of, 365–366
  presuppositions of, 362
growth of, 362–366
history of, 359–362
  political/economic trends, 361
  religious trends, 361
renewal of, 368–370
  expansion into other disciplines, 370
  lay people as producers of, 368–370
  new disciplinary tools, approaches, topics, 369–370
Libro de los Guardianes, 82–83
life expectancy, in Latin America, 417
ligas campesinas (Peasant Leagues), 518–519
The Light of the World Church. *See* La Luz del Mundo
Lima, Peru
  Baroque church in, 122
  canonization campaign of Francisco Solano, 136
  Creole clergy in, 235–236
  Inquisition in, 136, 140
  Lutheran merchant/craftsmen congregations in, 305
  patron saint of, 162
  pilgrimages, 152
  succor outside official male hierarchy, 162–163
  See also Peru; Rose of Lima (Saint)
Lisboa, Antonio Francisco, 166
Lisson, Emilio, 351
Lobo Guerrero, Bartolomé, 96
Logroño, Maria, 714, 715, 720
Lombardi, Federico, 410
López, José Hilario, 261–263
López Trujillo, Alfonso, 387
Lorentzen, Lois Ann, 585
Lorenzana, Francisco Antonio de, 111–112, 221, 222–223
Lovejoy, Paul, 606, 607
low Spiritism *(mesa branca)*, 659

Loyola, Ignacio de
  death of, 94
  founding of Society of Jesus, 175
  influence on mysticism, 124
  sainthood of, 149
Lozano, Jorge Tadeo, 240
Lubac, Henri de, 382
Lué, Benito de, 243
Lugo Albarracin, Pedro de, 166
Lula da Silva, Luiz Inácio, 390, 488
Lumen Fidei, 395
Luther, Martin, 110
Lutheran Church – Missouri Synod, 306, 307, 308, 313
Lutheranism, 304–317
  beginnings of in, 311–312
  colonist-pastors, 312
  and Curitiba Document, 316–317
  and demographic transition, 317
  diversity of piety of, 310
  effect of World Wars on, 314–315
  establishment of immigrant, 304–305
  and evangelical pietistic movement, 317
  faith missions, 306, 307
  historical development/legal status of, 304
  and human rights, 513
  immigrant churches, 307–309
    in Argentina, 307–308
    in Brazil, 308
    in Chile, 308
  incorporation of Marianism, 329–330
  initial church structures, 313–314
  and land reform, 519
  and Liberation Theology, 317
  marriage restrictions, 312
  merchant/craftsmen congregations, 305
  origins of missions in, 305–307
  overall characteristics of, 309
  post-World War II, 315–316
  role of women in, 315
  on Roman Catholics as Christians, 305
  theological training, 315
  use of print media in conversions, 455
  See also Evangelical Church of the Lutheran Confession in Brazil (IECLB)
"Lutheranism," and Spanish American Inquisition, 140
Lutheran World Federation (LWF), 306, 308, 316
Lyons, Barry, 599–600

Macedo, Edir, 433, 441, 452, 457, 675. *See also* Igreja Universal do Reino de Deus (IURD, Brazil)
Maciel, António Mendes (Conselheiro), 211
Maciel, Marcial, 521
Macumba, good/bad work distinction in, 611
Madrid, Raúl L., 582
Mãe Stella, 620
Magesa, Laurenti, 54
magic, healing as, 203
Mahikari, 726
Mahon, Leo, 379, 402–403
Mainwaring, Scott, 584–585
Maldonado, Martín, 94
Malês revolt, 716
malquis, 104–105
Mam (Mayan god), 482, 573
Manco Capac, 215
Manso, Alonso, 134
Manso y Zúñiga, Francisco, 324–325
Manz, Beatrice, 518
Mapuches (Araucanians), 234
Maradiaga, Oscar Rodríguez, 393
María Lionza cult, 659
Marianism in Latin America, 319–330
  adaptability of, 320
  African influence on, 320, 321
  ambiguity of, 320–321, 547–548
  and Catholic Charismatic Renewal, 391
  commonalities, 322, 324, 325, 326, 327, 329
  and contemporary popular religion, 485
  and double participation, 620–621
  and Immaculate Conception, 319
  origins of, 319–320
  and Our Lady of Guadalupe in Mexico (*See* Our Lady of Guadalupe (Mexico))
  plethora of patronesses, 319, 454
  Protestant incorporation of, 329–330
  Santería incorporation of, 620
Marian Zodiac (Florencia), 113
Mariátegui, José Carlos, 265
Maritain Jacques, 743–744
Mariz, Cecilia, 446, 719
Marquis de Pombal, 141
Marquis de Puysegur, 652
marriage
  bigamy, 140
  civil, 334, 352–353
  polygamy, 691
  racialization in Paraguay, 257–258
  restrictions on mixed, 312
  restrictions on Protestant, 312
  same-sex, 343, 503, 769–770

Index

Martí, José, 247
Martin, David, 14–15, 430, 449, 749–750, 755
Martínez, Teodoro Hampe, 146
Martínez-Fernández, Luis, 299
Marxism
 and Cuban Revolution, 669
 and Liberation Theology, 367, 388–389, 745
Mary (mother of Jesus). *See* Virgin Mary
Maryknoll (Catholic Foreign Mission Society of America), 354, 402, 406
MAS (Movimiento al Socialismo, Bolivia), 562, 583
Mass, Catholic
 in late medieval Europe, 37
 Tridentine Catholicism on, 117–118
Mateo, Olivorio (Dios Oliverio), 349
Mater et Magistra (1961), 361, 375
Matheus, Rosângela, 753
matlazahuatl (typhus/typhoid fever) epidemic
Matory, Lorand, 618–619
Maxwell, John, 670
Maya
 ceremonial centers of, 24
 Chiapanec, nativist movement among, 216
 communal piety of, 168–169
 and *costumbre*, 349–350, 488–489
 Guatemalan
  contemporary case studies on, 598, 599
  millenarianism among, 216
  religious identity of, 577
  rural Catholic Action groups among, 355
  transnationalism of, 673
 land distribution issues, 518
 Maya Long Count cycle, 23
 movements by, 517
 participation in Holy Week processions, 486
 and *Popul Vuh*, 600
 Precolumbian texts, 26
 representation of Jesus by, 482
 Tzotzil Maya
  contemporary case studies on, 597, 599
  converts to Islam, 597, 599, 718
  mobilization by, 571, 573
 violence against, 514
 Yucatán
  assessemnt by Diego de Landa, 73–74
  communal piety of, 168–169
  destruction of sacred texts of, 134–135
  human sacrifice practiced by, 79
Mbiti, John, 47
McAlister, Elizabeth, 623
McDannell, Colleen, 452

McPherson, Aimee Semple, 418
McWilliams, Carey, 194
Mecham, J. Lloyd, 270–271
media
 Charismatic Catholicism use of, 471, 678
 See also religious media and visual culture
Medina, José Toribio, 243
Mello, Manoel de, 433, 439–440
Mendicant Orders, 177, 181
Mendieta, Gerónimo de, 74, 94, 181
Mendoza, Antonio de, 92
Mendoza, Pedro de, 185–186
Menem, Carlos Saul, 720
Mennonites, 513
Mercedarians, 175
Mérida, Mexico, Jehovah's Witnesses in, 702
Mesa, Carlos, 556
mesa branca (low Spiritism), 659
Mesmer, Franz Anton, 652
Mesoamerica, religion in from Formative to Postclassic, 22–27
 ceremonial centers, 23–26
  Classic Maya architecture, 24
  Classic Zapotec architecture, 24–25
  cross-regional influences, 25–26
  Postclassic Chichén Itzá, 25–26
  Postclassic Cholula, 26
  Postclassic Tula, 25
  Teotihuacan, 25
 codices, 26
  Borgia Group, 26
  Central Mexican codices, 26
  Mexica tradition, 26
  Mixtec tradition, 26
  Precolumbian Maya texts, 26
 contrasts with Christianity, 30
 major periods correlating with shifts in religious practices, 22
 Maya Long Count cycle, 23
 Mexica society, 26–27
  teixiptla notion in, 27
  Templo Mayor structure, 26
  teotl notion in, 27
 parallel calendrical cycles, 22–23
 as rooted in autonomous territorial/social units, 30–31
 sacrificial offerings
  animal, 24
  complexity of, 23–24
  human, 24
 temporal structure for collective religious observances, 22–23

messianic/revitalization movements, 207–217
  Andean religious movements, 212–216
    indigenous cosmological background, 212–213
    indigenous millenarian movements, 213–216
    pachakuti concept, 213
    Spanish influences, 213
  Brazilian millenarianism, 208–212
    folk-Catholic movements, 210
    Império do Belo Monte ("Canudos") movement, 210–211
    indigenous movements, 208–210
    Joaseiro do Norte movement, 210–212
    messianic movement of Conselheiro in, 269
    in northeast, 210–212
    in northwest/upper Amazon, 209
    Portuguese influences, 210
    reasons precipitating, 212
    santidade movements, 209
    sources of, 210
    terra-sem-mal concept, 208
  characterizations of millenarianism, 207
  and Incas, 212–213
  Mexican millenarian movements, 216–217
  in Paraguay, 209
mestizaje, 581, 583
Methodist Chile Conference, 300
Methodist Episcopal Church (Brazil), 288
Methodist Pentecostal Church (Chile), 433
Methodists
  in Brazil, 288, 292–293
  in Chile, 300, 433
  schools in Peru, 297–298
  use of print media in conversions, 455
Metz, Johan Baptist, 365–366
Mexica codice, 26
Mexican-American War, Protestant missionary efforts during, 291
Mexican Conference of Bishops, 520
Mexican Revolution, 353, 374
Mexica society, 26–27
  human sacrifice in, 79
  teixiptla notion in, 27
  Templo Mayor structure, 26
  teotl notion in, 27
Mexico
  abortion in, 549
  Alcoholics Anonymous in, 539–540
  anticlericism in, 347
  apparitions of Virgin Mary in, 350
  Catholicism in

Charismatic, 678
Church-state relationship, 350–351, 494–495
dictatorship opposition/support, 400
difference of opinion from sexual morality of Vatican, 552
eroding dominance, 13
images, 740–741
Legionarios de Cristo, 748
number of followers, 12, 342
Opus Dei, 748
popular, 270, 488–489
post-independence, 400
progressive, 385–386
survey on what Church should devote attention to, 341
Vatican response to persecution of Catholics, 666
views on gender issues, 341
wealth of Church, 260
Central Mexican codices, 26
  Borgia Group, 26
  Mexica tradition, 26
  Mixtec tradition, 26
challenges to laicicism in, 343
Chinese immigrants in, 723, 727
Christian Democratic parties in, 496, 499
controversy over education in, 743
Creole clergy in, 235–236
Cristero War in, 271, 744
cult of Santísima Muerte in, 741–742
decline in institutional religious practice in, 340
early Protestant missionaries in, 293–294
emigration from, 681
emigration to US from, 684–685, 686
  1901–2000, 682t42.2
  foreign born by birth region/date of arrival, 681t42.1
evangelical involvement in politics, 752
expulsion of Jesuits from, 221, 222–223
faith and politics in, 302
faith healers in, 348, 349
and inculturation theology, 597, 599
independence, 235, 237–239, 270, 399
indigenous mobilization in
  Dominican role in, 570–571
  indigenous vs. religious institutional goals, 578
  interaction between religious/local context, 567
  religious framing, 570–571
  religious resources for, 572, 573

808

Inquisition in, 136
Japanese immigrants in, 724
Jehovah's Witnesses in, 700, 701–702
Jesuits
  expulsion from, 221, 222–223
  higher education institutions in, contemporary, 748
Jews in, 709, 710, 711
Korean immigrants in, 727
La Luz del Mundo in, 702–703, 704–705
Latter-Day Saints in, 692
Lutheran merchant/craftsmen congregations in, 305
migrants in, 520–521, 522
millenarian movements, 216–217
Muslims in, 716, 717, 718
Pentecostalism in
  beginnings of, 432–433
  founders of, 433
  internationalization of, 420
popularity of Santería in, 624
poverty rate of indigenous in, 561
Precolumbian Maya texts, 26
Protestantism in, 447
  early missionaries, 293–294
  faith missions, 296
  growth, 444
  during Mexican-American War, 291
  number of followers, 12
Reform Wars (1858-1860), 262
religious orders in, 90–95
religious self-identification, 684
secularization of public institutions in, 335–339
Seventh-Day Adventists in, 698
sponsorship of audiovisual centers in, 456
state recognition of religious bodies in, 752
syncretism examples, 88
  manifestations of Virgin Mary, 88
  Sanctuary of Jesus the Nazarene, 88
television ownership in, 426
and tithing, 260
Zapatista rebellion in, 488–489, 517, 559
See also Mexico (New Spain); Our Lady of Guadalupe (Mexico)
Mexico (New Spain)
epidemics in, 100
indigenous reactions to Christianity in, 100–101
Inquisition in
  number of proceedings, 140
  types of offenses specific to, 139
and popular-erudite dialectic, 740–741
religious art in, 89
religious orders in, 90–95
  Augustinians, 92–94
  cooperation with Crown in colonization/conversion, 90–91
  Dominicans, 68–69, 73, 93
  Franciscans, 68, 70–72, 73–74, 91–93, 740–741
  Jesuits, 94–95
  and *Sublimis Deus*, 68–69
syncretism in, 96–97
Tlacatecolotl as substitution devil in, 97
Mexico City
  black confraternities in, 202–203, 205
  Corpus Christi processions in, 116
  Creole clergy in, 235–236
  Jehovah's Witnesses in, 702
  Jews in, 709
  Marian shrines surrounding, 151
  pilgrimage to Virgin of Guadalupe, 152
  relics of European saints donated to, 148
  See also Mexico
Meyer, Albert, 402
Meyer, Jean, 254, 271, 744
Meyer, Marshall, 711
Miami, Florida, Cuban immigrants in, 685, 687–688
Michael (Saint), 147, 151, 154–155
Michoacán, Mexico
  Augustinians in, 94
  effect of expulsion of Jesuits on education in, 227–228
  Franciscans in, 93
  Nueva Jerusalén colony in, 216–217
  reform-minded clergy in, 235
Mier, Servando Teresa de, 232, 239, 258
Mignone, Emilio, 409
milagros, 483
millenarianism. *See* messianic/revitalization movements
Miller, William, 696
Mills, Kenneth, 105
Minaya, Bernardino de, 68–69
Ministry of the Nations, 674
Miranda, Carmen, 459
Miranda, David, 416, 440, 676
  See also God is Love Pentecostal Church (IPDA, Brazil)
Miranda, Francisco, 234
Miskito Coast, 291
Mission Purísima Concepción, 191

missions, Franciscan in Alta California,
  190–195
 coerced labor in, 193
 corporal punishment in, 193–194
 Crown impetus for, 190–191
 disease in, 192–193
 Franciscan impetus for, 191
 Indian labor issues, 191
 restoration of, 192
 role of Serra in, 190
 sexual abstinence/regulation in, 193
missions, Franciscan in New Mexico,
  178–185
 approach to Natives as *caciques*, 179
 concentration patterns, 179
 conversion model, 179–180
 conversion strategies, 180–182
  explication/understanding of
   sacraments, 181–182
  intensive instruction at doctrinas, 181
  linguistic limitations of, 181–182
  purging of lust, 180
  substitution of Christian rites for native,
   180, 182, 183
  success of, 182–183
  use of young Indian boys, 180–181
 and Pueblo Revolt, 184
 types of missions, 178–179
missions, Jesuit in Paraguay, 185–190
 concubinage, 186–187
 conversion methods, 189–190
 demise of, 190
 disease as threat to, 188
 establishment of *reduccións/doctrinas*,
  188–189
 first Jesuits, 187–188
 formation of encomiendas, 187
 geography and establishment of
  missions, 185
  change in geographical location, 188
 Indian labor issues, 189
 mineral wealth as impetus for, 185–186
 slave raiders as threat to, 188–189
 social organization of Guaraní, 186
 Spanish colonists as threat to, 189
 success of, 190
 use of native boys to assist in conversions,
  189–190
missions, Protestant
 historical, 6
 Protestant mission hospitals, 297
missions, Spanish, 173–196
 background to, 173–178
 conclusions about, 195–196

Mission San Buenaventura, 191
Mission San Diego de Alcalá, 190
Mission San Francisco de Solano, 190
Mission Santa Barbara, 191
Mixtec
 bundles in iconography of, 83–84
 codice of, 26
modernization theory, 364
Mogrovejo, Toribio Alfonso de, 96
Moixó, Benet María, 242
Molina, Alonso de, 165
Molina, Juan Ignacio de, 234
Molina, Rene, 676
Moltmann, Jürgen, 365–366
Monroe Doctrine, 305
Montaigne, Michel de, 81
Monte Albán site, 24–25
Montenegro, Silvia, 719
Monterrey, Mexico, Jehovah's Witnesses
 in, 702
Montesinos, Antonio de, 160.130, 66, 87,
 359–360, 373
Montevideo, Uruguay, immigrant
 Lutheranism in, 304–305
Montúfar, Alonso de, 135
Montúfar, Lorenzo, 290
Moody, Dwight L., 295
Moors, 2–3, 633
Mora, José María, 260, 399
Mora, Victor, 433
Morais, Zélio de, 660
Morales, Evo, 521, 559, 562, 583
morality
 and Catholic Charismatic
  Renewal, 469
 of Catholics *vs.* morality of Vatican, 552
 in late medieval Europe, 43
Moravians, 291
Morazán, Francisco, 255, 275–276
Moreira, Maria, 714
Morell de Santa Cruz, Pedro
 Agustín, 321
Morelos, José María, 237–238, 247, 248, 273
Morelos, Mexico
 Augustinians in, 94
 Franciscans in, 93
Moreno, Juan, 320–321
Moreton, Bethany E., 543–544
Morgan, David, 451
Morgan, Ronald, 147
Mormons. *See* Latter-Day Saints (LDS)
Moscoso y Peralta, Juan Manuel de, 399
Mosquera, Tomás Cipriano de, 255, 263
Mota Padilla, Matias de la, 151

Index

Mothers and Relatives of Political Prisoners, Disappeared, and Assassinated of El Salvador (CoMadres), 514–515
Mothers of the Plaza del Mayo in Argentina, 516
Mother Teresa, 395
Movement of Landless Rural Workers (Movimento dos Sem Terra, MST, Brazil), 390, 519, 745
Movimiento al Socialismo (MAS, Bolivia), 562, 583
Movimento dos Sem Terra (MST, Brazil), 519, 745
Mukti Revival (1905), 300
Müller, Gerhard, 393–394
MULT (Truique Unified Movement for Struggle), 575
Muñecas, Ildefonso de las, 241
Muñoz, Hortensia, 573
Muñoz, Miguel, 277, 278
Murabitun community in Chiapas, 720
Muslims
  in Brazil, 280
    census data on, 714, 715
    dissemination of Islam, 718
    early immigrants, 716
    enslaved Africans, 715–716
    gender of followers, 720
    growth of population, 715, 720
    mosques, 718
    settlement patterns, 716–717
    Sunnis / Shias in, 717
    uprising of 1835, 281, 716
    urbanites, 720
  early immigrants, 716
  economic / social status of, 720
  mosque building, 717, 718
  of non-Arab descent, 719
  and racial equality, 719
  in Senegal, 203
  settlement patterns, 716–717
  Shias, 717
  slaves and religion, 608, 683
  and Sufis, 719
  Sunnis, 717, 720
  See also Islam
Mustelier Garzón, Hilario (San Hilarón), 348
Muzi, Giovanni, 245–246
mysticism
  false mystics, 125–126
  and Teresa of Ávila, 532–533
  and Tridentine Catholicism, 124–126, 128

Nagô religion, 618
Nahua people
  bundles in iconography of, 83–84
  European interpretations of idolatry of, 85
  incorporation of Christian images by, 127
  social organization of, 31
  traditional elements used in conversion of, 81–82, 91
Napoleon, 233, 238
National Action Party (PAN, Mexico), 494–495, 499
National Association of Evangelicals (Bolivia), 556
National Catholic Party (Mexico), 335
National Conference of Brazilian Bishops (CNBB), 385, 404
National Council of Christian Churches of Brazil (CONIC), 734
National Council of the Churches of Christ (US), 456
National Debate for Peace (Debate Nacional por la Paz), 513
National Foundation for the Indians (FUNAI, Brazil), 317
National Methodist Church (Chile), 300
National Office for Social Information (ONIS, Peru), 386
National Party (Uruguay), 493–494
National Security Doctrine, 337–338
National Wesleyan Church (Chile), 433
Navarro, Alfonso, 678
Nebel, Richard, 329
Neocatecumene, 390–391, 748
neoliberalism, and inculturation theology, 596
neo-native spirituality, 573–574
neo-Pentecostalism
  coining of term, 756
  diabolic in, 756
  exchange concept in, 757–758
  formations of citizenship, 542–543
  and mimesis, 758
  ritual promiscuity in, 756–757
  similarity to Catholicism, 742
  and subjectivity, 541–544
  and tithing, 757
  transmission of, 755
  See also Pentecostalism
Never Again (Nunca Más), 513–514
Neves, Tancredo, 615
New Age movements, 458
New Evangelization crusade, 390–391
New Granada
  expulsion of Jesuits from, 227
  independence of, 239–240

Index

New Granada (cont.)
  Inquisition in, 136
  See also Caribbean
New Laws (1542), 177, 187, 360
New Mexico. See missions, Franciscan in New Mexico
New Spain. See Mexico (New Spain)
New Tribes Mission, 577, 670
Nican mopohua, 325, 329
Nican motecpana, 322, 323, 324, 325
Nicaragua
  belief in God in, 10
  Catholicism in
    number of followers, 12
    opposition to/support of dictatorship, 405–407, 409
    popular, 487
    progressive, 385
  CEBs in, 379, 380, 507, 511, 551
  dictatorship in, 405–407, 409, 510
  fund raising for Contras through TV evangelism in, 456–457
  human rights in, 511, 513
  Jehovah's Witnesses in, 701
  Latter-Day Saints in, 692–693
  Liberation Theology in, 424, 487
  Lutheran missions in Managua, 306
  military rule in, 378
  patron saint of, 319
  Pentecostalism in, 444, 552–553
  Protestantism in, 12, 444, 684
  Sandinista Revolution in, 301, 366
  Seventh-Day Adventists in, 698
  See also Sandinista Front for National Liberation (FSLN)
Nigeria
  and internationalization of Pentecostalism, 420
  See also Igbo people; Yoruba
Noble, Mercedes, 644
nongovernmental organizations (NGOs)
  and indigenous mobilization, 563–564, 583
  influence of Liberation Theology on, 745–746
Norget, Kristin, 568, 574–576
North American Evangelical movement, 305
"Notes for a Theology of Liberation" (Gutiérrez), 382
Nova Friburgo, Brazil, first Lutheran congregation at, 304–305, 311–312
Noya, Emilio, 280
Nuestra Señora de la Defensa, 150–151
Nuestra Señora del Carmen, 274

Nuestro Clamor por la Vida (Our Cry for Life, Aquino), 529–530
Nueva Jerusalén, 216–217
Nunca Más (Never Again), 513–514
Nunes, Clara, 459
Nunis, Doyce, Jr., 195

Oaxaca, Mexico
  Church-state relationship in, 350–351
  Classic Zapotec ceremonial centers in, 24–25
  indigenous mobilization in
    indigenous vs. religious institutional goals, 578
    interaction between religious/local context, 567–568
  inquisition in, 135
  See also Mexico; Mexico (New Spain)
Obando y Bravo, Miguel, 406
Oberkirchenrat Berlin, 313, 314
Ocampo, Melchor, 261, 262
Ocosingo, Mexico, indigenous mobilization in, 570–571
O'Higgins, Bernardo, 244
Okinawan religions, 726
Oliva, Isabel Flores de. See Rose of Lima (Saint)
Oliveira, Vitória Peres de, 718, 719
Olmedo, Bartolomé de, 90, 175
Olmos, Andrés de, 85
Olodumare (Creator deity), 640, 642
ololiuhqui, 139
O'Malley, Sean Patrick, 393
Ometochtli-Chichimecatecuhtli, Carlos, 100–101
Ometochtzin, Carlos, 71
Oñate, Juan de, 182
ONIS (National Office for Social Information, Peru), 386
On Religion: Speeches to its Cultured Despisers (Schleiermacher), 363
On the Origin of the Indians of Brazil (Cardim), 78
O Paraíso Terrestre, 210–211
Opus Dei, 390–391, 489, 552, 670, 748, 750, 751
Order of Preachers. See Dominican Order
Ordinances of Discovery (1573), 177–178, 188
O Reino Encantado, 210–211
Organization of American States, as indigenous advocate, 564–565
Orishas. See Santería

812

Index

Ortiz, Dianna, 535–536
Ortiz, Fernando, 634
Ortiz, Tomás, 66–67, 93
Osborn, T. L., 423
Oshún (goddess), 321
Ossio, Juan, 215
"other religions" in Latin America, statistics on, 12
Our Cry for Life (*Nuestro Clamor por la Vida*, Aquino), 529–530
Our Lady of Altagracia (Dominican Republic), 319
Our Lady of Aparecida (Brazil), 319, 451, 454, 468–469
Our Lady of Charity of El Cobre (Cuba), 320–321, 620, 685
Our Lady of Chiquinquirá (Colombia), 454
Our Lady of Copacabana (Bolivia), 319, 454
Our Lady of Coromoto (Venezuela), 454
Our Lady of Exile (Miami), 621
Our Lady of Good Death (Brazil), 620–621
Our Lady of Grace (New Spain), 149
Our Lady of Guadalupe (Mexico), 322–329
 appearance to Juan Diego, 114, 150
 and Charismatic Catholicism, 468–469
 as counternarrative to complete defeat of native peoples, 329
 foundational text of apparitions, 322, 323, 324, 325
 healing powers of, 116
 historical origins of, 322–324
 and human rights, 328
 and immigrant ritual practices, 687
 indigenous forerunners of, 97
 and Mexican independence, 237–238, 273–274, 399, 486
 as model for evangelization, 328
 origin of *tilma* of Juan Diego, 323–324
 as patroness of San Antonio, 685
 pilgrimage in Mexico City, 152
 and popular Catholicism, 273–274
 popularity of, 145–146, 322–329, 454
 popularity of name Guadalupe among non-Indians, 274
 reasons for prominence of, 322, 324–325
  celebrations/building projects/art, 326–327
  codification of worship, 325
  link to national pride and identity, 327–328
  location of Tepeyac, 327
  spread of devotion through preaching, 325–326

 as symbol of Mexican nationalism, 6
 tetralogy of, 88, 151
 and Zumárraga, 322–323
Our Lady of Lujan (Argentina), 278–279, 454
Our Lady of Mercy (Ecuador), 153, 319
Our Lady of Perpetual Help (Haiti), 620
Our Lady of Piety (Mexico), 151
Our Lady of Remedies (Latin America), 116, 319
Our Lady of Sorrows (Latin America), 319
Our Lady of the Bullet (Mexico), 151
Our Lady of the Defense (Mexico), 150–151
Our Lady of the Immaculate Conception of El Viejo (Nicaragua), 319
Our Lady of the Miracles of Caacupé (Paraguay), 319, 454
Our Lady of the Rosary (Brazil), 620–621
Outline to a Theory of Practice (Bourdieu), 537

Pacem in Terris (1963), 361, 375
Pachamama (Earth Mother), 97, 165, 482
Pagden, Anthony, 77
Pagelança, and Spiritism, 653
Palacios, Edgar, 513
Palacios, Felipe Vázquez, 752
Palacios, Vicente Riva, 95
Palafox y Mendoza, Juan de, 147, 148, 150, 151, 152
Pallares, Amalia, 580
Palma, Joaquín de, 299
Palo (Cuba), 606–607, 644–646
 and ancestor worship, 644, 645
 nganga as focus of magic/rituals, 645–646
 origins of, 644
 origins of Spanish name of, 644
 Palo Brillumba branch of, 646
 Palo Kimbisa branch of, 646
 Palo Mayombe branch of, 646
 "voodoo dolls," 645–646
Palo Monte. *See* Palo (Cuba)
PAN (National Action Party, Mexico), 266, 494–495, 499
PAN (National Autonomy Party, Argentina), 266
Panama
 Catholicism in
  Church-state relationship in, 495
  dictatorship opposition/support, 402–403
 Chinese immigrants in, 727
 Día de la Raza in, 559
 grassroots organizations in, 379
 Lutheran missions in, 306

Panama (cont.)
  Pentecostalism in
    megachurches, 676
    sex education, 555
  Protestantism in
    converts from Catholicism, 445
    Pentecostal percentage, 446–447
    Seventh-Day Adventists in, 698–699
Panama City, grassroots organizations in, 379
papal infallibility, 279, 374
Paraguay
  Catholicism in
    Church-state relationship, 495, 579–580
    dictatorship opposition/support, 400
    erosion of dominance, 13
    number of followers, 12, 342
    expulsion of Jesuits from, 222, 224–226
  indigenous in
    identity politics, 576, 578, 579–580
    messianic movements, 209
  Jehovah's Witnesses in, 701
  Korean immigrants in, 723, 727
  land distribution issues, 518–519
  Latter-Day Saints in, 692–693
  messianic movements in, 209
  military rule in, 378
  Muslims in, 716–717
  oath of clerical loyalty, 257
  patron saint of, 319, 454
  Protestantism in
    Catholic converts, 445
    growth, 444
    number of followers, 12
  Seventh-Day Adventists in, 698–699
  unaffiliated in, 12
  See also Guaraní people; missions, Jesuit in Paraguay
Paredes, Otoniel Ríos, 676
Parliamentary Front in the Defense of Life, 556
Parra, Porfirio, 267
Parrinder, Geoffrey, 54
Parteli, Carlos, 498
Partido Autonomista Nacional (PAN, Argentina), 266
pastoral indígena, 567, 568–569, 575
Pastoral Land Commission (CPT, Comissão Pastoral da Terra), 519
Pastorals, 746
Patagonia Missionary Society, 291
patriarchy, 547
Patria Vieja (1811-1814), 244
Patronage Law (1824; Gran Colombia), 257

patronato real (padroado), 4, 135–136, 226, 332–333, 334
374, 400, 410
Pauccar, Hernando, 96
Paul III (pope), 68–69, 91
Paul VI (pope), 497, 512
Paz Solórzano, Juan, 278
PCP-SL (Shining Path), 403
PDC (Christian Democratic Party, Chile), 496, 497
PDC (Christian Democratic Party, El Salvador), 496, 499
PDC (Christian Democratic Party, Uruguay), 493, 498
Peasant Leagues (ligas campesinas), 518–519
Pedro II (Portugal), 211
Pedro of Cordoba, 134
Peel, J.D.Y., 47–48
Pentecostal Deus é amor, 416
Pentecostalism, 430–449
  attack on Umbanda, 440
  attitude toward Candomblé, 621
  and Azusa Street Revival, 300, 415, 431
  and Catholic Church, 415
  Charismatic Catholicism similarity to, 468
  and current era (see Protestantism, in current era)
  denomination composition/ nationalization process, 433–442
    in Argentina, 434–435
    in Brazil, 435–442
    in Chile, 434
    in El Salvador, 434
    in Guatemala, 435, 699
    in Peru, 434
  descarrego (release) concept of, 423
  features of
    African churches, 422–423
    divine healing, 417–418, 439
    dramatization of struggle against evil, 421–423
    migration/immigration, 420
    nationalization/transnationalization, 419–423, 552
    poverty discourse, 423–424
    radiophonic culture, 418–419
    speaking in tongues, 415–417
    televangelism, 424–426
  forerunners of, 432
  founding of, 433
    abroad vs. homegrown denominations, 433
    social composition of founders, 433

Index

and gang violence, 756
and gender equity, 553–554
and globalization
    as conversionist, 17
    as decentralized religion, 18
    and human rights movement, 19
    as one of most globalized religions, 18
growth of, 430–431, 552–553, 764, 765, 766, 770
historical churches, 432–433
historical research on, difficulty in, 431
and iconoclastism, 451, 452
and indigenous mobilization, 566–567
    religious resources for, 573
influence on popular/erudite religion relationship, 755–756
and institutional politics, 552–553
international expansion of, 431–432
and land reform, 519
and Latin Americans of Asian descent, 723
media use
    purpose of media productions, 457
    use of media, 456–458
    use of visual/symbolic elements, 458
mission work in Chile, 300
as new form of popular religion, 414–427
origins in US, 431
prospects for, 447–449
    gender issues, 448
    historical Protestantism, 448–449
    socio-economic change/government policy, 448
    stronger Catholic resistance to Protestant advance, 447
and reproduction/sexuality, 553
    abortion, 553, 554–555
    contraception, 554
    on sex education, 553, 555
ritual in, 756
and Satan, 414–415, 421
and secularization of public institutions in Brazil, 339
and subjectivity, 541–544
in United States
    megachurches, 676
    origins of, 431
    prosperity gospel, 423
and urbanization, 419, 436, 669, 694
use of elements of Umbanda, 441, 458
See also Assemblies of God (AG); Brazil, Pentecostalism in; neo-Pentecostalism
Peredo, Antonio, 583

Pérez Armendáriz, José de, 241
Perfect Liberty, 726
Perón, Eva Duarte de, 494
Perón, Juan Domingo, 352, 494
Peru
    abortion in, 343
    Catholicism in
        Church-state relationship, 351, 400, 496, 580
        dictatorship opposition/support, 403
        eroding dominance, 13
        lay organizations, 355
        number of followers, 342
        Opus Dei, 748
        popular, 279–280
        progressive, 386
        status of Church, 752
    Chinese immigrants in, 723, 727
    Christian Democratic parties in, 496, 498
    Comunione e Liberazione in, 748
    Creole clergy in, 235–236
    emergency contraception in, 550
    idolatry in, 80, 103, 104–105
    independence in Upper Peru, 241–242
    independence movements in, 240–242, 399
    independence of, 240–242, 492
    indigenous in
        chancas worship, 103
        conopas worship, 103
        diversity among, 561
        huacas worship, 102–103
        numbers of, 560–561
        religious resources for mobilization, 572, 573
        resistance/adaptation to Christianity, 100–101
        success of mobilization, 581–582
    introduction of concept of the devil in, 104
    Japanese immigrants in, 723, 724
    Lutheran merchant/craftsmen congregations in, 305
    Lutheran missions in, 307
    Methodist schools in, 297–298
    military coup in, 378
    missionary views on Indians in, 74–75
    opposing images of nature of Indians in, 74–75
    participation in Holy Week processions, 486
    patron saint of, 162
    Pentecostalism in
        beginnings, 433

815

Peru (*cont.*)
   denomination composition/
      nationalization process, 434
   and institutional politics, 552–553
   Pentecostal percentage of Protestants
      in, 446–447
   sex education, 555
   status of church, 752
   pluri-confessionalism in, 343
   Protestantism in, growth of, 444, 447
   reform-minded clergy in, 235
   religious orders in, 74–75, 95–96
      Dominicans, 95
      Jesuits, 96
   resistance to evangelization in, 100–101
   rural Indians and Tridentine Catholicism
      in, 127
   Seventh-Day Adventists in, 698–699
   Tupac Amaru II, 234, 240, 399
   unaffiliated in, 12
   See also Incas; Lima, Peru
Pessar, Patrica R., 208
Peterson, Anna, 384, 511
peyote, 139, 166–167, 203
pharmaceutical industries, and subjectivity,
   541–542
Philip II (Spain), 135–136, 360
Philip III (Portugal), 136
Philip IV (Portugal), 136
Philippines, spread of Santería to, 625
Philips, Miles, 324
piety, as element of Tridentine Catholicism,
   109–126
   collective nature of devotion, 122–124
   mysticism, 124–126
   ornate decoration of sacred space, 120–122
   ritual and performance, 115–120
   sacred immanence, 110–115
Pigafeta, Francesco A., 78
pilgrimages
   in late medieval Europe, 39
   to Lima, 152
   to Mexico City, 152
   and Tridentine Catholicism, 115–116
Pimería Alta, Jesuit missions in, 184
Pinochet, Augusto, 308, 386, 404–405, 497, 509,
   510, 515–516
Piñol y Aycinena, José Bernardo, 265
Pinto, Paulo Hilu Rocha, 717, 719
Pittini, Ricardo, 353
Pius IX (pope), 263, 273, 279, 374
Pius VII (pope), 245
Pius X (pope), 355, 400

Pius XI (pope), 7, 353–354, 400, 666
Pius XII (pope), 353–354
Pizarro, Francisco
   and Christianization of Incas, 175
   and conquest of Inca Empire, 173–174
Pizarro, Luna, 242
Plan of Iguala (1821), 238, 239
PLN (National Liberation Party, Costa
   Rica), 498
Plotting Women (Franco), 529
pluralism
   competitive, 443
   in Latin America, 508, 764–766
   and reactivation of laicity of public
      institutions, 341–342
pluri-confessionalism, 343–344
Poewe, Karla, 420–421
political change, as pathway to the future, 770, 771
political parties, and Catholicism, 491–503
   from 1880 to 1970s, 492–496
      in Argentina, 494
      in Brazil, 495–496
      in Colombia, 493
      in Cuba, 495
      in Ecuador, 496
      enduring authoritarian regimes, 494–495
      liberalizing authoritarian regimes, 495–496
      in Mexico, 494–495
      oligarchic democracies, 493–494
      in Peru, 496
      in Uruguay, 493–494
      in Venezuela, 496
   Christian Democratic parties, 496–499
      in Chile, 496, 497
      conservative *vs.* progressive, 497
      in Costa Rica, 497–498
      in Dominican Republic, 496, 499
      in Ecuador, 496, 498
      in El Salvador, 496, 499
      in Mexico, 496, 499
      in Peru, 496, 498
      in Uruguay, 496, 498
      variables in emergence/roles among,
         496–499
      in Venezuela, 496, 498–499
   military rule, impact of, 499–501
      on Church, 500–501
      on people in general, 500, 501
      on political parties, 501
   nineteenth century, 492
      colonial period, 492
      independence era, 492
   overview of, 491

Index

political secularization, defining, 331–332
The Politics of Religion in an Age of Revival (Ivereigh), 272–273
polygamy, 691
Popé, 180
popular Catholicism, contemporary, 480–489
  and Church hierarchy, 486
  conflict with state authorities, 485–486
  cultural-historical legacies, 481–482
    colonial, 481
    indigenous, 481–482
    influence on contemporary practice, 482
  and healing, 664
  overview of, 480
  politics of, 487–489
    in El Salvador, 487–488
  relationship to ecclesial religion, 485
  as religion of the poor, 485
  and Spiritism, 653
  as votive culture, 482–484
    and devotion to Virgin of Guadalupe, 483–484
    in domestic sphere, 484
    pilgrimage as votive act, 483–484
    por promesa / manda concept, 482–483, 484
    relationality / affectivity of, 484
    votive objects, 483, 484
  See also popular Catholicism, nineteenth century
popular Catholicism, nineteenth century
  and Catholic revival, 272–273
  eighteenth century influences on, 269, 272–273
  elite-popular dynamic on, 270–271
  historical context of, 270–271, 272
  and independence movements and shrines, 273–275
    Argentina, 274
    Bolivia, 274
    Cuba, 274
    Virgin of Guadalupe in Mexico, 273–274
  multifaceted views of, 271–272
  plebian expressions of faith, 271
  post-independence
    Argentina, 278–279
    Brazil, 280–282
    Guatemala, 275–278
    messianism, 281–282
    Peru, 279–280
    shrines, 275–283
  and response to independence movements, 270
  See also popular Catholicism, contemporary
Popular Christian Party (Peru), 498

Popularum Progressio, 361
Popul Vuh, 600
Porras, Martín de, 145
Portugal, Inquisition in, 133
Positivism, influence on anticlericism, 251–255, 264, 265, 266
Potosí, Bolivia, silver discovered at, 186
poverty
  indigenous / non-indigenous gap in, 561
  Latin American Bishops' Conference on, 381–382
  and Pentecostalism, 423–424
  Pope Francis I on, 392–393, 395
Prado, José "Pepe," 678
Precht, Cristián, 510
pre-Contact New World. *See* Incas; Mesoamerica, religion in from Formative to Postclassic
pre-Contact Old World. *See* Africa, religion in pre-contact; late medieval Europe
predestination, 438
Presbyterians
  early missionaries in Guatemala, 293
  early missionaries in Mexico, 293
  missionaries in Chile, 292
  use of print media in conversions, 455
PRI (Institutional Revolutionary Party, Mexico), 494
priests, shortage of Catholic, 102, 346, 349, 669
Prieto, Guillermo, 261
Proaño, Leonidas, 518, 594
processions
  Corpus Christi, 116–117, 455
    in Cuzco, 117, 126, 127
  in late medieval Europe, 38
  in Mexico City, 116
  participation by confraternities, 116, 153
  Maya participation, 486
  as performative piety, 116–117
  in Puebla, 155
  as ritual and performance, 116–117
  as sacred space, 39
prosperity gospel, and Pentecostalism, 423–424
Protestantism
  and African spirituality, 635
  on Catholic Eucharistic beliefs, 108
  on Charismatic Catholicism, 465
  in current era, 442–447
    apostasy, 442
    competitive pluralism, 443
    external factors in growth of, 445
    flattening growth curves, 442
    growth rate, 443–444

Protestantism (cont.)
    internal factors in growth of, 445–446
    lack of regular attendance, 442
    leveling off of growth, 442–443
    percentage as Pentecostals, 446–447
    proportion of converts from
        Catholicism, 445
    reasons to convert from Catholicism,
        445–446
    regional patterns of, 444–445
    faith missions (see faith missions)
    growth in Latin America, 683–684, 766
    and human rights, 508–509, 512–514
    incorporation of Marianism, 329–330
    and inculturation theology, 591
    and indigenous mobilization, 573
    and Korean immigrants, 723
    number in Latin America, 12, 342, 508
    and post-colonial body, 534–535
    purpose of media productions, 457
    on transubstantiation, 108
    on Tridentine Catholicism, 108–109, 110,
        118, 121
    use of print media, 455–456
    See also diversification in Latin America;
        ecumenism; Lutheranism;
        Pentecostalism; Protestantism,
        historical; individual countries
Protestantism, historical, 286–303
    denominationalism, 291–294
    in Brazil, 292–293
    in Chile, 292
    educational efforts, 292–294
    faith missions as challenge to, 294–298
    in Guatemala, 293
    liberal politics as impetus for, 292–294
    in Mexico, 293–294
    early nineteenth century, 286–291
    colporteurs, 288–290
        educational efforts of, 289
        in Guatemala, 289–290
    Miskito Coast, 291
    political impediments to entry of
        Protestantism, 287
    Moravians, 291
    Society for the Propagation of the
        Gospel, 290–291
    theological impediments to entry of
        Protestantism, 287–288
    US vs. European missionary efforts, 288
    at end of twentieth century, 300–302
    faith-politics relationship, 301
    rise of Pentecostalism, 301

    missionaries under Liberal rule, 6
    numbers of native constituents, beginning
        20th century, 294
    shifts to local leadership, 298–300
        in Chile, 300
        in Cuba, 299–300
    underreporting of native
        contributions to missionary
        work, 298
    variations in church nationalization
        movements, 298–300
Protestant transition, 15–16
Prussian Moravians, 291
public education. See education
Puebla, Mexico
    apparitions in, 150–151
    Baroque artwork in, 165
    enslaved woman as nun in, 202
    feast day celebrations in, 155, 156
    Franciscans in, 93
    Jehovah's Witnesses in, 702
    religious processions in, 155
Pueblo Indians
    fusion of Christian calendar with lunar
        calendar of, 182
    population decline, 182
    See also missions, Franciscan in
        New Mexico
Pueblo Revolt, 184
Puerto Rico
    emigration to US from, 681
    female role in local religious practices in,
        348–349
    internationalization of Pentecostal
        churches in, 420
    Jehovah's Witnesses in, 701
    Latter-Day Saints in, 692
    Lutheran missions in, 305, 306
    Protestantism in, 684
        growth, 444
        number of followers, 12
    religious diversification in, 12
    Seventh-Day Adventists in, 698
    Spiritism in, 652
    See also Afro-Caribbean religions
Pumachua, Mateo, 241
PURS (Dominican Social Christian Reform
    Party), 499
PUSC (United Social Christian Party, Costa
    Rica), 497–498
Putnam, Robert, 753
Putumayo River Indians, 536
puyomate, 139

Index

Quadragesimo Anno (1931), 7, 352, 375
Quakers, and migrant justice, 521
Quechua
　language of, 75
　patron saint of, 319
Queen of the Incas, 319
Queiroz, Maria Isaura Pereira de, 212, 281
Querétaro, New Spain, Franciscans in, 93
Quetzalcoatl, 25, 26
Quichua (Ecuador), and inculturation theology, 597, 599–600
Quigley, Thomas, 510
Quiroga, Vasco de, 94
Quito, Ecuador
　independence movement in, 239
　patron saint of, 153
　as site of first Protestant radio transmission, 456
　and St. Isidore confraternity, 149
　See also Ecuador

racial equality, and Muslims, 719
Radical Civic Union (Argentina), 494
radio, use by Charismatic Catholicism, 471
Radio Estrella, 471
radio schools *(escolas radiofônicas)*, 379
Rahner, Karl, 363, 382
Ramírez, Ignacio, 261, 262
Ramírez de Fuenleal, Sebastián, 68
Ramos, Juan, 289
rancherías, 176
Rankin, Melinda, 293
rationality debates (Junta de Valladolid), 69
Ratzinger, Joseph, 366–367, 387, 389, 393, 521
　See also Benedict XVI (pope)
real patronato de las Indias, 398
Reconçavo movement of Bahia, 209
Reconquista, 2–3, 633
Recovery of Historical Memory Project (REMHI), 409, 513–514
Rede Brasil Cristão, 471
Rede Canção Nova, 457
Rede Global, 452, 457
Redemptoris Missio, 566, 595
Rede Record, 452, 457–458
Rede Século XXI, 457
Rede Vida, 457, 471
reducciones, 179
The Reformation of Machismo (Brusco), 534–535
regalism, and secularism/secularization, 343–344
Regla de Ocha (Cuba), 611, 616–617, 618
Regla de Palo Monte (Cuba), 611, 618

Reglas de Congo (Rule of the Kongo). *See* Palo
Regnum Christi movement, 748
reincarnation, 650–651
Relación de las cosas de Yucatán (Landa), 73–74
relativism *vs.* fundamentalism model, 17
"Religion in Latin America" survey (Pew Forum), 444–447
religious, percentage of people identifying as, 340
religious media and visual culture, 448
　African religions, 458–459
　audiovisual materials, 456
　Catholics
　　media in context of CBCs, 456
　　response to Protestant productions, 457
　　in colonial period, 453–454
　　Franciscan use of Baroque style, 453
　　Marian images, 454
　definitions, 451–452
　in independence era, 454–455
　and marketing mentality, 459–460
　minority religions, 458
　from nineteenth to twenty-first centuries, 455–459
　Pentecostals
　　media, 456–458
　　purpose of productions, 457
　　visual/symbolic elements, 458
　pre-Colombian societies, 452–453
　Protestants
　　print media, 455–456
　　purpose of productions, 457
　　radio transmission, 456
　role of media, 459
　See also Baroque era
religious pluralism, in Latin America, 764–766
REMHI (Recovery of Historical Memory Project), 409, 513–514
Rémond, René, 253
reproduction and sexuality, 541–542
　abortion *(see* abortion)
　birth control pill effect on, 548
　and Catholic Charismatic Renewal, 551–552
　and CEBs, 551
　contraceptives *(see* contraceptives)
　duplicity in moral standards effect on, 548
　and evangelicals, 552–556
　Marianism effect on, 547–548
　patriarchy effect on, 547
　sex education, 553, 555
　social movements effect on, 548, 551
Reproductive Health and Assisted Procreation Law (2000; Argentina), 555

republicanism, 331
requerimiento, 174
Rerum Novarum (1891), 7, 352, 375, 400, 593, 743
retablo (wooden cabinet to house statues), 163, 165
Rethorica Christiana (Valadés), 89
Revillagigedo (Viceroy of Mexico), 228
Revolutionary Virgin (la Virgen Mambisa), 321
Ricard, Robert, 1
Richman, Karen, 625–626
Riego, Rafael de, 238
Right to Decide, 550
Río, Vial del, 245
Rio de Janeiro, Brazil
   Catholic University at, 749
   CEBs in, 379
   Church-state relationship in, 352–353
   first Lutheran congregation in, 311–312
   Institute of Religious Studies in, 554
   Lutheran merchant/craftsmen congregations in, 305
   Muslims in, 716
   Pentecostalism in, 436, 439–440
   Protestant use of radio for conversions in, 456
   religious diversity in, 15
   See also Brazil
Río de la Plata
   expulsion of Jesuits from, 221–222, 223
   independence of, 243
   Ley de reforma del clero (1822), 257
Rio Grande Synod, 313
Ríos Montt, José Efraín, 286, 435, 512, 694–695
Ripalda, Gerónimo de, 119
rite Petro (Haiti), 611
rite Rada (Haiti), 611
Rivadavia, Bernardo, 246, 252, 259, 279
Rivera Damas, Arturo, 408
Roberts, Oral, 423
Robertson, Pat, 425, 426, 456–457
Rocha, Cristina, 726
Rodríguez, José Santiago, 244
Rodríguez de Mendoza, Toribio, 236
Romberg, Raquel, 652
Romero, Óscar, 384, 407–408, 487–488, 511, 514, 568
Rosa, Pedro José Chávez de la, 235
Rosa Figueroa, Francisco Antonio de la, 148
Rosas, Juan Manuel de, 251, 252, 258–259, 279
Rose of Lima (Saint)
   becomes first official saint of America, 162
   as member of Dominican third order, 124
   mysticism of, 110, 124
   overview of life of, 107, 279–280
   as patron saint, 274
   piety of, 109, 118–119
   relics of, 111, 115
   representation in artwork, 165
   as symbol, 146
Rossi, Marcelo, 457, 465, 749
Rousseau, Jean Jacques, 236, 262
royal patronage *(atronato real)*, 332–333, 334
Rubial, Antonio, 147
Rubin, Jeffrey, 586
Ruether, Rosemary Radford, 369
Ruiz, Samuel, 386, 488, 567
Ruiz García, Samuel, 517, 594
Russell, Charles Taze, 700
Rutherford, Joseph Franklin, 700

sacraments
   decline in practice of, 340–341
   Eucharist, 37, 110, 114–115
   in late medieval Europe, 36–38
   list of, 37
   and Masses for the dead, 37
   use by Franciscans in conversions, 181–182
Sacred Congregation of Holy Rites (Vatican), 162
Sacred Heart missionaries, recruitment during Catholic resurgence, 354
Sacred Heart of Jesus (Ecuador), 6
sacred immanence, as element of Tridentine Catholicism, 110–115
   Council of Trent on, 110–111
   Eucharist, 110, 114–115
   images of Christ, 112
   images of Mary (mother of Jesus), 112–114
   images of saints, 110, 112–115
   Protestant criticism of, 110
   relics of saints, 110, 111–112
sacred space, and Tridentine Catholicism, 120–122, 128
sacred time, in late medieval Europe, 39–40
Sáenz, Moisés, 296, 297
Sahagún, Bernardino de, 71–72, 85, 93
Saint Michael of the Miracles, 151, 152
saints
   in Baroque era, 160–161, 163–164
   beati status, 144
   changes in canonization rules, 144
   in colonial Spanish America, 143–157
   Council of Trent on, 143–144, 160–161
   images as *ixiptla*, 145
   in late medieval Europe, 38–39, 41

Index

patron saints, 152–156
   election by *cabildos*, 152–153
   feast day celebrations, 154–156
   as symbols of identity, 153–156
promotion of shrines and images, 147–152
   apparitions, 150–151
   engravings of European saints, 148
   images as *ixiptla*, 145
   pilgrimages, 148–149, 152
   relics of European saints, 148
   shrines, 151–152
Protestant challenges to belief in, 143
   Counter Reformation response, 143
reasons to appeal to saints, 144
relics of Rose of Lima, 111, 115
role in evangelization, 145
as symbol of local patriotism, 146–147
and Tridentine Catholicism, 110, 111–115, 117
unifying potential of, 145–146
Sales, Eugenio, 379
Salesians, recruitment during Catholic resurgence, 354
Salomon, Frank, 30
Salvador de Bahia, Brazil
   Educação Popular in, 746–747
   slave religions in, 4, 204
   slave revolt in, 205
Salvatierra, Juan Manuel, 95
salvation, belief in role of natives in, 89
sambenito/sanbenito (penitential garment), 139
same-sex marriage, 343, 503, 769–770
Sanabria, Victor, 498
San Alberto, Juana Esperanza de, 202
San Buenaventura Mission, 191
Sánchez, Miguel, 114, 325, 326
Sanctuary of Jesus the Nazarene (Mexico), 88
San Diego de Alcalá Mission, 190
Sandinista Front for National Liberation (FSLN), 380, 406–407, 511
   See also Nicaragua
Sandinista Revolution, 301, 366, 380
Sandoval, Alonso de, 200
Sandoval, Francisco Tello de, 135
San Francisco de Solano Mission, 190
San Isidro Labrador, 96–97
San José Betancur, Pedro de, 150
San Luis Potosí, Mexico
   Franciscans in, 93
   Marian devotion at, 326
San Martín, José de, 240, 242, 244, 274
San Martín, Tomás de, 75
San Miguelito, Panama, 402–403

San Salvador, El Salvador, progressive Catholicism in, 385
Santa Barbara Mission, 191
Santa Brígida movement (Brazil), 212
Santa Catarina, Guatemala, first Lutheran congregation at, 311–312
Santería (Cuba), 4, 204, 603, 639–644
   Africanization of, 616–617
   animal sacrifice, 623
   ashé as foundation of, 640
   divination, 642–643
      cowrie shells (regla de ocha/dilogún) system, 643
      four coconut pieces (obi) system, 642–643
      Ifá system, 643
   double participation, 620
   gender roles, 613
   heterodoxy of followers, 643
   as hybrid spirituality, 639–640
   influence on Catholicism, 321
   nationalization of, 614, 615
   Olodumare (Creator deity), 640, 642
   origins of, 639
   orishas (quasi-deities), 640–641
      guerreros (warriors), 642
      la siete potencias africanas, 641
      patakis of (legends), 641
   participation rates, 612–613
   pathways to membership, 642
   persecution of followers, 643–644
   popularity in Mexico, 624
   purpose of, 643
   race issues, 616
   ritual in, 641–642
   similarities to African diaspora religions, 603
   Spiritism influence on, 659
   as transnational, 671–672
   in US, 622, 623, 644
Santiago, Chile
   independence of, 243–245
   Muslims in, 717
   See also Chile
Santiago de Costa Rica, patron saint of, 153
santidade movements, 209
Santísima Muerte, 741–742
Santo Domingo
   Church-state relationship in, 353
   independence of, 246
   religious orders in
      Dominicans, 65–66
      Hieronymites, 64–65, 66
   Spanish views of Indians on, 64–66
Santo Tomás, Domingo de, 75

Index

San Vicente, Juan Manuel de, 164
São Leopoldo, Brazil, first Lutheran congregation at, 304–305, 311–312
São Paulo, Brazil
 Lutheran merchant/craftsmen congregations in, 305
 Muslims in, 716, 718
 Pentecostalism in, 436, 438, 440
 See also Brazil
Sarat, Leah, 673
Sarmiento, Domingo Faustino, 3, 252, 259
Scataglini, Sergio, 674–675
Schillebeck, Edward, 382
Schleiermacher, Friedrich, 363
Schmiedl, Ulrich, 304
Schoenstatt, 748
scholarly networks, as indigenous advocates, 565
Schwartz, Stuart, 281
Scofield, C. I., 295
Scottish Congregationalists, in Brazil, 292–293
SDA. *See* Seventh-Day Adventists (SDA)
séances, 653–654
Sebastian (Saint), 153
Sebastianismo (*Quinto* Império, Fifth Empire), 210
Sebastião (mythical king), 210, 211
Second General Conference of Latin American Bishops, 361–362
Second Mexican Provincial Council
 and Baroque, 160–161
 promotion of Saint Joseph by, 147
Second Vatican Council. *See* Vatican II
secularism and secularization, 331–344
 and future of religion in Latin America, 766–769
 and jurisdictionalism, 332, 333, 343–344
 laicization, defining, 331
 and liberal-conservative dichotomy, 331–332
 in new republics, 334
 and political liberalism, 333–334
 and public education, 334
 and religious intolerance, 333
 use of *patronato real*, 332–333, 334
 political secularization, defining, 331–332
 reactivation of laicity of public institutions, factors in, 339–344
  democratization, 342–343
  gestation of effective/significant religious plurality, 341–342
  greater consciousness of human rights, 342
  growing secularization of society, 340–341

 and regalism, 343–344
 restraint in secularization of public institutions, 335–339
  Catholic nationalism effect on, 335–339
  Cold War effect on, 337–338
  in Colombia, 336–337
  internal reaction within Catholic Church, 338
  in Mexico, 335–339
  and rise of Evangelical churches, 339
  in Southern Cone, 338–339
 secularism, defining, 331
Segundo, Juan Luis, 362, 508, 672
Seichō-no-ie, 726
self-flagellation, 119, 126
self-mortification, 118–119
Semán, Pablo, 422
Seminário Regional do Nordeste II (SERENE II), 386, 388
Seminole Wars, 636
Senna, Edmar Avelar de, 719
separation of church and state, 334
Sephardic Jews, 709–710, 711
Sepulveda, Juan, 69
Sepúlveda, Juan Ginés de, 360, 373
Serbin, Kenneth, 337–338, 404
Serra, Junípero
 beatification of, 194–195
 on corporal punishment, 193–194
 See also missions, Franciscan, in Alta California
Serrano, Jorge, 435
Seventh-Day Adventists (SDA), 690, 696–699
 and AEMINPU, 214–216
 controversy over doctrines/practices of, 696–697
 and divorce, 697
 growth in Latin America, 697–698
 in Guatemala, 698–699
 and indigenous mobilization, 572
 origins of, 696
 retention rates, 698, 699
 urbanization effect on membership, 698, 699
 use of print media in conversions, 455
 use of radio transmission for conversions in, 456
sex education, 553, 555
sexuality
 and Candomblé, 613
 changing norms of, 770
 See also gender; reproduction and sexuality

Index

Shamanism, Colonialism, and the Wild Man (Taussig), 536
Shango, 204
Shia Muslims, 717
Shindo Renmei movement, 724
Shining Path (PCP-SL), 403
Shintoism, 724
A Short Account of the Destruction of the Indies (las Casas), 360, 634
Shubsda, Thaddeus, 195
Sickness of the Dance (Taki Onqoy), 95, 213–214
Sieber, Hans, 2
Sierra, Justo, 267
Sigal, Peter, 533
Sikkink, Kathryn, 564, 565
SIL (Summer Institute of Linguistics, Ecuador), 296, 569, 576
Silva, Benedita da, 509
Silva, Francisco Maldonado de, 140
Silva, Marina, 509
Silveira Cintra, Leme da, 743
silver deposits, 178
Silvoso, Edgardo, 674–675
Similox, Vitalino, 569
Simonton, Ashbel Green, 455
Simpson, George, 610
Sinodal Federation in 1949
Sintora Constantino, José Fidencio (El Niño Fidencio), 348
slave religions, 198–206
    control issues, 205
    fusion of religious ideas/imagery by slave converts, 3–4
    outside Catholic Church, 203–205
        in Brazil, 204–205, 280
        healing practices, 203–204
    participation in Catholic life, 202–203
        confraternities, 202–203
        non-European lay brothers, 202
        non-European lay nuns, 202
    routes to Christianization of Africans, 201–203
        after arrival in Americas, 201–202
        prior to enslavement, 199, 201
        at slaving posts in Africa, 201
    See also Africans; Candomblé (Brazil); slavery
slavery
    abolishment of, 360, 635
    amulets used by slaves, 203
    António Vieira on, 374
    brought to Caribbean, 634

    Catholicism on theory of, 198–201
    legality of enslavement methods, 200
    Muslims in Brazil, 715–716
        uprisings, 281, 716
    places of origin, 605–606, 634
    revolts, 608
    run-away slaves, 636
Small Ecclesial Communities, 467
Smilde, David, 585
Smith, Joseph, 691
Sobrinho, José Cardoso, 388
Sobrino, Jon, 368, 384, 388
social change, as pathway to the future, 770
Social Christians (Ecuador), 498
Social Darwinism, 264
Social Gospel movement, 295
socialism, effect of collapse on Liberation Theology, 368
social movement theory, 570
Society and Culture in Early Modern France (Davis), 271–272
Society for the Propagation of the Gospel, 290–291
Society of Jesus, 175
sociology of religion *(la religion vécue)*, 526–527
sodomy in Portuguese America, 138
Sogolo, Godwin, 57
Sōka Gakkai lay organization, 725
Solano, Francisco, 136, 163
Solís, Díaz de, 185–186
Somoza Debayle, Anastacio, 406, 509, 511
Soto Reyes, Marcela, 550
Sôtô Zenshu school of Zen Buddhism, 725
South America
    eroding Catholic dominance in, 13
    religious self-identification, 684
    See also individual country
South American Mission Prayer League (renamed World Mission Prayer League), 307
Southern Baptist Convention, 543–544, 670
Southern Baptists, mission work in Cuba, 299
Southern Cone
    Lutheran missions in, 305–306
    religious commitment in, 13
    religious/non-religious pluralism in, 13
    restraint in secularization of public institutions in, 338–339
    violence of military regimes in, 499
    See also Argentina; Chile; Uruguay

South Korea
    Pentecostalism in, 430
    prosperity gospel in, 423
    See also Korea
Souza, Pero Lopes de, 78
Spain
    La Luz del Mundo in, 704
    Opus Dei in, 748
Spanish Inquisition, 5, 133
speaking in tongues (glossolalia)
    and Charismatic Catholicism, 415, 463, 464, 467–468
    and Pentecostalism, 415–417
Spirit baptism, and Charismatic Catholicism, 463, 464
Spiritism, 637–639, 648–664
    African origins of, 683
    and ancestor worship, 639
    beginnings among elites, 638
    in Brazil, 648, 652–655
        and African-derived religions, 655–656, 659–660, 661–662
        and animal magnetism, 654–655
        and assistance to the poor, 655
        Catholic repression of, 653
        charity as primary mission of, 655
        and Christian evangelism, 653
        and Dr. Adolph Fritz, 657–658, 663
        and healing, 655–659, 663–664
        and Karma, 657
        number of followers, 655, 656
        organizing themes of, 653
        séances, 653–654
        and syncretism, 653, 657
        by teleporting to astral plane, 658–659
        and Umbanda, 659–661
        and urbanization, 662–663
    as hybrid spirituality, 638–639
    low Spiritism *(mesa branca)*, 659
    and marketing mentality, 458
    modern origins of, 648
    and Rivail (Allan Kardec), 637–638, 648–652
        and animal magnetism, 651–652
        on charity, 655
        early life of, 649
        on incarnations, 650–651
        on spirits, 650–651
        theology as different/similar to Judeo-Christian tradition, 649–650
        writings of, 649
    spread beyond elites, 638
    and syncretism, 653
spiritual conquest, notion of, 1

Staden, Hans, 78
Staying Sober in Mexico City (Brandes), 539–540
stem cell research, 503
Stoll, David, 531
Stradanus, Samuel, 324
Stroessner, Alfredo, 509, 518–519, 579–580
St. Teresa in Ecstasy (sculpture), 532–533
St. Thomas, as site of first Lutheran congregation, 304
Suárez, Francisco, 232–233
subjectivity, gendered, 541–544
    focus on micro-politics, 541–544
    and missionary manliness, 543–544
    and neo-Pentecostalism, 541–544
    and pharmaceutical industries, 541–542
    and retail business, 543–544
    witnessing, 542
Sublimis Deus (papal bull), 68–69, 91
sub-Saharan Africa, Pentecostalism in, 430
Sucre, José Antonio de, 242
Suess, Paulo, 473–474
Sufi Muslims, 719
Summer Institute of Linguistics (SIL, Ecuador), 296, 569, 576, 580
Sung, Jung Mo, 369
Sunni Muslims, 717, 720
Suriname
    Hinduism in, 726
    as site of second Lutheran congregation, 304
Swaggart, Jimmy, 456–457, 670
Swedish Pentecostals, 437–438
Sweet, James, 607–608, 619
Swenson, Gustav Sigfrid, 306
Syllabus of Errors, 279, 374
symbolism, and Tridentine Catholicism, 119–120
syncretism
    anti-syncretism and ADRs, 617, 619–620
    hierarchical, 443

Taíno people, 633, 636
Taki Onqoy (Sickness of the Dance), 95, 213–214
Tambor-de-Mina, 454–455
Tamez, Elsa, 369
Tarasco people, European interpretations of idolatry of, 85
Tastera, Jacobo de, 67–68, 70–71
Taussig, Michael, 536
Taylor, William, 146, 235–236, 273–274
Tecto, Juan de, 91
telenovelas, 458

Index

televangelism, 424–426
television
    use by Catholic Charismatics, 457, 471
    use by Protestants, 456–457
    See also religious media and visual culture
Templo Mayor structure, 26
Tenochtitlán, 25, 26–27, 79, 90, 92, 173, 175
Tenrikyō, 726
Ten Years War (1868–1878), 247, 321
Teotihuacan, 25
Tepeyac, 327
tequitqui (Indian-Christian) art, 98
Teresa (Saint; image), 166
Teresa of Ávila (Saint), 149, 532–533
terra-sem-mal (land without evil) movements, 208
Terrazas, Matías, 242
terreiros (Umbanda centers), 620, 655
testimonio, 530–531
    I, Rigoberta Menchú, 531
    Translated Woman, 530–531
Testino, Luis Miguel Glave, 146
Texas, Franciscan missions in, 93, 184
Texcoco (New Spain), 83, 92, 135
Theodoro, Janice, 453
Theological Institute of Recife, 386
Theology for a Nomad Church (Assmann), 362
A Theology of Liberation (Gutiérrez), 362, 507, 672
Third Mexican Provincial Council, on self-flagellation, 119
Thompson, Damien, 215
Thomson, James, 289
Tibesar, Antonine, 235–236
Tijuana, Mexico, Jehovah's Witnesses in, 702
tithing
    abolishment of, 256, 334
    and Jehovah's Witnesses, 701
    and Jesuits, 225
    and Latter-Day Saints, 691
    and neo-Pentecostalism, 757
    and reforms in Mexico, 260
Tito, Diego Quispe, 165
Tito Yupanqui, Francisco, 113
Tlacatecolotl, 97
Tlaloc (Aztec god), 96–97, 453
Tlaxcala (New Spain), 68, 90, 92, 93, 150, 151, 154–155
Tocqueville, Alexis de, 768
Todorov, Tzvetan, 81
Tojolabale people, mobilization by, 571, 573
Toledo, Francisco de, 95–96
Tonal, Tomás, 84
Tonantzin (Aztec goddess), 97

Toronto Blessing, 674
Toro y Zambrano, Mateo de, 244
Torres, Camilo, 361, 510
Torres Bollo, Diego de, 188
Torrijos, Omar, 402–403
Tortolo, Adolfo Servando, 410
tourism, diaspora, 625–626
Tovar, Juan de, 85
Townsend, Cameron, 296
Townsend, Elvira, 296
tranquilly religious, 10
Translated Woman (Behar), 530–531
transnationalism
    and African-derived religions, 668, 671–672
        Batuque, 671–672
        Candomblé, 671–672
        Santería, 671–672
        Umbanda, 672
    and African diaspora religions, 605, 622–626
        connection to homelands, 623–624
        diaspora tourism, 625–626
        within Latin America, 624
        localization of, 624
        primary diasporas, 622
        reactions from nonpractictioners/state, 623
        secondary diasporas, 622
        and United States, 622–624
        use of technology to connect to homeland, 624–626
    and Catholicism, 667
        Charismatic, 677–678
        colonial Catholic Church, 668
        human rights, 669–670
        traditional, 669–670
    and indigenous mobilization, 564–565
    and Liberation Theology, 672–673
    new version of, 667, 668, 671–678
    and new violence, 772
    and Pentecostalism, 667, 673–677
        evangelization, 674–675
        God Is Love Pentecostal Church, 676
        Igreja Universal do Reino de Deus, 675–676
        megachurches, 676–677
        migration, 673–674
    and Protestantism, 670
    recent changes in Latin American, 666–667
        fostering movement of peoples/ideas, 666, 667
        identity issues, 667
        movement of people/ideas, 666, 667
    traditional version of, 655, 667

transubstantiation, 108, 110
Tratado acerca del dominio de los infieles y de la guerra fusta (Treatise on the Subjugation of the Infidels and Just War; Vera Cruz), 72
Travestis (Kulick), 538–539
Treatise on Heathen Superstitions (Alarcón), 84
Treaty of Madrid (1750), 226
Treaty of Tordesillas (1494), 199
treche Marists, 354
Trento, Jean-Batiste, 80
Três Forquilhas, Brazil, first Lutheran congregation at, 311–312
Tridentine Catholicism
  late-eighteenth-century reforms, 128–130
    collective forms of piety, 128, 130
    funerals, 129–130
    mysticism, 128
    simplification of church interiors, 128
    undermining of piety, 128
  overview of, 107–108
  piety elements in, 109–126
    collective nature of devotion, 122–124
    mysticism, 124–126
    ornate decoration of sacred space, 120–122
      alter screens, 121–122
      Baroque influences, 121–122
      Protestant criticism of, 121
    ritual and performance, 115–120
      bestowal of gifts on images and relics, 117
      Council of Trent on, 120
      mass, 117–118
      numeric and temporal symbolism, 119–120
      pilgrimages, 115–116
      processions, 116–117
      Protestant criticism of, 118
      self-mortification, 118–119
      sign of the cross, 119
    sacred immanence (divine presence), 110–115
      Council of Trent on, 110–111
      Eucharist, 110, 114–115
      images of Christ, 112
      images of Mary, 112–114
      images of saints, 110, 112–115
      Protestant criticism of, 110
      relics of saints, 110, 111–112
  Protestant criticism of, 108–109
  social characteristics of, 126–128
    in cities/towns dominated by Spanish authority, 126–127
    in Indian villages, 127
Trinidad
  African diaspora religions in, 617
  Afro-Caribbean religions in, 635
  Hinduism in, 726
True History (Staden), 78
Truique Unified Movement for Struggle (MULT), 575
Truman Doctrine, 337
Trumbell, David, 292
tuberculosis, 370
Tula, Postclassic, 25
Tupac Amaru, 95, 214
Tupac Amaru II, 234, 240
Tupác Amarú rebellion, 399
Tupi-Guaraní Indians
  and expulsion of Jesuits, 374
  motivation for migration of, 208
Tuxtla Gutiérrez, Mexico, Jehovah's Witnesses in, 702
TV evangelism, during Cold War, 456–457
TV Record (Brazil), 426, 436, 442
Tweed, Thomas A., 621
Twelve Apostles, 91–92, 175
Tzotzil Maya
  contemporary case studies on, 597, 599
  converts to Islam, 597, 599, 718
  mobilization by, 571, 573

Ubico, Jorge, 354
UCIZONI (Union for Indigenous Communities of the North Zone of the Isthmus), 575
UDI (Independent Democratic Union, Chile), 502
Ugarte, Hernando Arias de, 103
Ugarte, Juan, 95
Uillacapitz, Tomás, 82
ULAJE (Union of Latin American Evangelical Youth), 731–732, 733
UMAP (Unidades Militares de Ayuda a la Producción) camps, 495
Umbanda (Brazil)
  cosmology, 660–661
  deities, 349
  good/bad work distinction in, 611
  and healing, 664
  multiracial/multicultural claim of, 660
  number of followers, 659–660
  organization of, 661
  origins of, 454–455, 660

Pentecostal attack on, 440
Pentecostal use of elements of, 441, 458
popularity in South America, 624
race issues, 616
rituals, 661
and Spiritism, 659–661
as transnational, 672
See also Brazil
"unaffiliated" persons, number in Latin America, 12
UN Commission for Historical Clarification (CEH), 513–514
UN Declaration of Human Rights, 505–506
UN Declaration of Indigenous Rights, 582
Unidades Militares de Ayuda a la Producción (UMAP) camps, 495
Union for Indigenous Communities of the North Zone of the Isthmus (UCIZONI), 575
Union of Latin American Evangelical Youth (ULAJE), 731–732, 733
United Evangelical Churches (Bolivia), 556
United Evangelical Lutheran Church (Argentina), 308
United Nations, as indigenous advocate, 564–565, 583
United Nations Historical Clarification Commission, 408
United Social Christian Party (PUSC, Costa Rica), 497–498
United States (US)
 abolishment of slavery in, 635
 Assemblies of God in, 433
 La Luz del Mundo in, 703–704
 Pentecostalism in
  megachurches, 676
  origins of, 431
  prosperity gospel, 423
  use of media, 418
 Santería in, 622, 623, 644
 Spiritualism in, origins of, 648
 sponsorship of audiovisual centers in Mexico/Brazil, 456
 statistics on importance of religion in life, 10
 televangelism in, 425–426
United States Conference of Catholic Bishops, 520
Universal Church of the Kingdom of God. *See* Igreja Universal do Reino de Deus (IURD, Brazil)
Universal Declaration of Human Rights, 510
Universal Federation of Christian Student Movements (FUMEC, Argentina), 731, 733
urbanization
 of Latin America, 419
 and Latter-day Saints, 694, 695, 699
 and Muslims in Brazil, 720
 and Pentecostalism, 419, 436, 669, 694
 and Seventh Day Adventists, 698, 699
 and Spiritism, 662–663
Urban VIII (pope), 144, 162, 164–165
Urioste, George, 30
Ursula de Jesus, 202
Uruguay
 abortion in
 anticlericalism in, 347
 atheists in, 342
 belief in God in, 10
 Broad Front coalition, 493, 498
 Catholics in, 12, 342
 Christian Democratic parties in, 496, 498
 Church-state relationship in, 493–494
 Civic Union, 493
 decline in institutional religious practice in, 340
 immigrant Lutheran churches in, 307–308
 importance of religion in life in, 10
 indigenous in, 560–561
 Jews in, 711
 Latter-Day Saints in, 692
 military coup in, 378
 military rule in, 499–500
 National Party, 493–494
 non-religious in, 446
 Pentecostal percentage of Protestants in, 446–447
 Protestantism in, 444
 religious/non-religious pluralism in, 13
 reproduction/sexuality
  abortion, 503, 549
  gay marriage/civil unions, 503
 Seventh-Day Adventists in, 698–699
 Umbanda in, 624
 unaffiliated in, 12
 See also Southern Cone

Valadés, Diego de, 89, 99–100
Valdivieso, Antonio de, 374
Valencia, Martín de, 67–68, 91, 92, 99, 175
Valladolid Council, 360, 373
Valley of the Dawn (Brazil), 212
Valparaíso, Chile, Pentecostalism in, 432

Valverde, Vicente, 95, 175
Varela, Felix, 247
Vargas, Getúlio, 352–353, 495, 743
Vargas Laguna, Antonio, 245
Vásquez, Julia (La Samaritana), 348–349
Vásquez, Manuel, 585
Vásquez, Marcos, 244
Vásquez, Tabaré, 549
Vatican I, 374
Vatican II, 375, 376–377
  aggorniamento process, 376
  Gaudium et Spes, 376–377, 506–507, 565, 594
  and human rights, 506
  and inculturation theology, 565–566, 594–595
  influence on Catholic Charismatic Renewal, 463
  and liberation theology, 361
  on liturgical change, 377
  overview of, 8
  and popular Catholicism, 486
  on social justice, 377
Vaughn, Mary Kay, 743–744
Vega, Garcilaso de la, 27–28
Velarde, Ramón López, 255
Velasco, Luis de, 92, 176
Velho, Octavio, 443
Velho, Pedro, 212
Venancio Christu movement, 209
Venezuela
  anticlericalism in, 347
  Christian Democratic parties in, 496, 498–499
  Church-state relationship in, 496
  "Day for Indigenous Resistance" in, 559
  eroding Catholic dominance in, 13
  independence movement in, 240
  Jews in, 711
  Latter-Day Saints in, 692
  Lutheran merchant/craftsmen congregations in, 305
  Lutheran missions in, 307
  María Lionza cult in, 659
  Muslims in, 718
  patron saint of, 454
  Pentecostalism in
    beginnings of, 433
    exorcism and liberation sessions, 423
    institutional politics, 552–553
    sex education, 555
  Seventh-Day Adventists in, 698
  Umbanda in, 624
  See also Chiribí Indians
Vera, Gaspar de, 75
Veracruz, Alonso de la, 93–94

Vera Cruz, Alonso de la, 72
Veracruz, Mexico, Santería in, 624
Vera Cruz, patron saint of, 153
Verbitsky, Horacio, 410
Vicaría de la Solidaridad (Vicariate of Solidarity, Chile), 386, 405, 510, 515
Victoria, Guadalupe, 238
Victoria, Romeo Luna, 403
Vidaurre, Manuel Lorenzo de, 256, 257
Videla, Jorge Rafael, 511–512
Videla del Pino, Nicolás, 243
Vieira, António, 210, 374
Vierra Ferreira, Miguel, 432
Vila, Martinho da, 459
Villagómez, Pedro de, 103–104
Villavicencio, Ignacio, 241
violence, new, 771–772
Virgin Mary
  apparitions of, 150–151
  as patron saint of Catholic Charismatic Renewal, 465
  and popular Catholicism, 485
  promotion by Cortés, 174
  promotion by friars, 147
  sacred immanence of images of, 112–114
  shrines to, 151–152
  syncretism example in modern Mexico, 88
  syncretism example in New Spain, 97
  as universal saint, 41
  use of engravings to promote cult of, 148
  See also Our Lady of Guadalupe (Mexico)
Virgin of Aparecida. *See* Our Lady of Aparecida (Brazil)
Virgin of Charity (Miami), 688
Virgin of Copacabana (Bolivia), 113
Virgin of Guadalupe. *See* Our Lady of Guadalupe (Mexico)
Virgin of Ixpantepec (Mexico), 350
Virgin of San Juan de los Lagos (Mexico), 88
Virgin of Sorrows (Mexico), 116
Virgin of Suyapa (Honduras), 468–469
Virgin of Talpa (Mexico), 88
Virgin of the Immaculate Conception (Spain/Mexico), 155, 156
Virgin of the Remedies (Mexico), 151
Virgin of the Rosary (Mexico), 217
Virgin of Zapopan (Mexico), 88
Viscardo y Guzmán, Juan Pablo, 228, 234, 248
visions, in late medieval Europe, 43–44
visual culture. *See* religious media and visual culture
vocation, in colonial Catholic Church, 5
Vodou (Haiti), 508

and anti-syncretism, 620
gender roles, 613
influences on, 204
nationalization of, 614, 615
participation rates, 612
race issues, 613
similarities to African diaspora religions, 603
and tourism, 625–626
"voodoo dolls," 645–646
Vodú in Cuba, participation rates, 612–613
Volio, Jorge, 498
votive culture, 482–484
and devotion to Virgin of Guadalupe, 483–484
in domestic sphere, 484
masses in late medieval Europe, 37
pilgrimage as votive act, 483–484
por promesa/manda concept, 482–483, 484
relationality/affectivity of, 484
votive objects, 483, 484

wages, indigenous/non-indigenous gap, 561
Walker Bynum, Caroline, 533
Wal-Mart, 543
WAMY (World Assembly of Muslim Youth), 718
War of Paraguay (1754-1756), 223
War of the Pacific (1879-1884)
War of the Triple Alliance (1865-1869), 280
Warren, Kay, 564, 583–584
Warren, Rick, 670
Weber, Max, 425
Welser, Bartholomeus V., 304
Weschler, Lawrence, 513
West Africa
early Protestant missions in, 288
See also Africa; Africa, religion in pre-contact; African diaspora religions (ADRs)
Westerlund, David, 58
Willems, Emilio, 419
Wilson, Bryan, 700
Wirtz, Kristina, 612–613
witchcraft
amulets/charms against, 203
and Andean beliefs, 103–104
and Aztecs, 97
as cause of illness, 58
and Charismatic Catholicism, 468
in early modern Europe, 44
healing as, 203
and Inquisition, 138, 140
witch doctors, in Cuba, 643

Witness to the Truth (Mignone), 409
Wojtyła, Karol Józef. *See* John Paul II (pope)
Wolf, Eric, 382
women
Catholic support of movements by, 514–517
in Chile, 515–516
CODIMUJ in Chiapas, 516
CoMadres in El Salvador, 514–515
Housewives' Committee of Siglo XX in Bolivia, 516–517
Mothers of the Plaza del Mayo in Argentina, 516
and confraternities, 168
as healers, 349
and La Luz del Mundo, 703
as leaders of CEBs, 551
and Lutheranism, 315
role in local religion in Puerto Rico, 348–349
Wood, Leonard, 247
Worker-Peasant-Student coalition of the Isthmus of Tehuantepec (COCEI), 575
Workers Party (Brazil), 509
World Assembly of Muslim Youth (WAMY), 718
World Council of Churches, 405, 440, 510
World Missionary Conference (1910), 288
World Mission Prayer League, 317
World Orisha Conference, 627
World Vision, 580, 670
Wright, Jaime, 386, 513
Wright, Stuart, 207
Wycliffe Bible Translators, 295, 296, 301, 670

Xangô (religion), 454–455

Yage (hallucinogenic), 536
Yai, Olabiyi Babalola, 625, 626
yerba maté, 189
Yorio, Orlando, 410
Yoruba
Alafia concept of, 55–56
deities, 52–53, 204, 321
healers, 59
influence on African diaspora religions, 606, 610, 611, 616–617, 618–619
Nago, 618
notion of religion, 48
Supreme Being of, 51, 52
See also Candomblé (Brazil); Santería (Cuba)
Young, Eric Van, 273–274
Youth With A Mission, 670

Zacatecas, Mexico, Franciscans in, 93
Zapatista rebellion, 488–489, 517, 559
Zapotec Classic architecture, 24–25
Zé Arigó (José Pedro de Freitas), 658
Zen Buddhism, 725
Zeraoui, Zidane, 720
Zodiaco mariano (Florencia), 113

Zoques (Chiapas), 573
Zumárraga, Juan de
   denunciation of Nuño Beltrán, 68
   inquisitorial powers of, 83, 101, 134, 135
   and Virgin of Guadalupe, 322–323
Zúñiga, Olga Portuondo, 321
Zwingli, Huldrych, 79